Flash MX

Creative Web Animation and Interactivity

Derek Franklin

Flash MX Creative Web Animation and Interactivity

Derek Franklin

Published by Macromedia Press, in association with Peachpit Press,
a division of Pearson Education

Macromedia Press
1249 Eighth Street
Berkeley, CA 94710
(510) 524-2178
(800) 283-9444
(510) 524-2221 (fax)

http://www.peachpit.com or http://www.macromedia.com

Copyright © 2003 by Macromedia Press Inc., Derek Franklin

Editor	Jill Simonsen
Copyeditor	Douglas Clark
Production Coordinator	David Van Ness
Compositors	Rick Gordon, Emerald Valley Graphics
	Myrna Vladic, Bad Dog Graphics
Cover Design	Mimi Heft
Interior Design Modifications	Owen Wolfson, Rick Gordon
Indexer	Emily Glossbrenner
Macromedia Tech Reader	Bentley Wolfe

Notice of Rights

All rights reserved. No part of this book or CD-ROM may be reproduced or transmitted in any form by any means, electronic, mechanical, photocopying, recording, or otherwise, without the prior written permission of the publisher. For information on getting permission for reprints and excerpts, contact Macromedia Press..

Trademark Notice

Flash, FreeHand, Director, Generator, Macromedia, and the Macromedia logo are trademarks of Macromedia Inc. Apple, QuickTime, and Macintosh are registered trademarks of Apple Computer Inc. The Peachpit logo is a registered trademark of Peachpit Press. Throughout this book, trademark names are used. Rather than put a trademark symbol in each occurrence of a trademarked name, we state we are using the names only in an editorial fashion and to the benefit of the trademark owner with no intention of infringement of the trademark.

Notice of Liability

The information in this book and CD-ROM is distributed on an "As Is" basis, without warranty. While every precaution has been taken in the preparation of the book and CD-ROM, neither the authors nor Macromedia Press shall have any liability to any person or entity with respect to any loss or damage caused or alleged to be caused directly or indirectly by the instructions contained in this book or by the computer software and hardware products described in it.

ISBN 0-321-11785-9

9 8 7 6 5 4 3 2 1

Printed and bound in the United States of America.

Dedication

Andy Rooney once said that death is just a distant rumor to the young. Unfortunately, this is not always true. During the week I wrote this dedication, a beautiful, young 18-year-old lady, Krystal Coleman, lost her life in a tragic automobile accident. Those of us who knew her will never forget her cheerfulness and unbelievable smile. While we didn't talk to each other regularly, she always showed an interest in my books, asking about them and about how my writing was going. When I would jokingly tell her that I was going insane trying to hit my deadlines, she would always laugh in such a way that suggested she thought I had already achieved that state! While I wish I could do more, I dedicate this book to her, in honor of her memory.

Acknowledgments

Thanks is not a big enough word to convey my appreciation to all the folks that made this book a reality.

First, I'd like to acknowledge the hard work of Jill Simonsen, the editor of this book. What a privilege and pleasure it has been to work with someone of her caliber. Her input and direction over this very ambitious revision have helped shape it into an incredibly useful learning resource. Despite the pace and quantity of material, her pleasantness and dedication made the process much easier. Her editorial partner, Doug Clark, did an equally fantastic job of copyediting the book, offering numerous insightful suggestions. Thanks, Doug! This book's updated look and graphical features are due in large part to the efforts of David Van Ness and Rick Gordon. The book looks more polished than ever! Big, big thanks go out to Marjorie Baer and Nancy Ruenszel, for all they've done for me the past few years. And to all those at Peachpit in production, promotion, and distribution, thanks for your hard work as well!

There are a number of friends who have either been understanding of my absence in social situations (due to my writing schedule) or have helped me forget my writing schedule altogether! They include: Jack Stailey, Matt Stailey, Mark Stailey (those Staileys are animals), Dennis Demaree (little drummer boy), Martin Boling (Mac Maniac), Charlie Schulze (flash54.com), Ali Esfandiar (the man from Iran), and Clint Dunbar (guitar guru).

And of course my family has always been a great support. Thanks, Kathy, Ashlie, my Moms (Edeltraud and Sue), Petra, George (George, you talk way too much), Eddie, and Marliese. I love all of you very much!

Contents

Introduction   xi

Part 1: Welcome to Flash MX

Chapter 1   Flash MX: The Rich-Client Revolution   3
- User Benefits   5
- Developer Benefits   11

Chapter 2   Getting Started   21
- How Flash Works   21
- What's New in Flash MX   24
- Interface   30
- Options and Settings   50
- Setting Movie Properties   61
- Setting up Accessibility   63
- Templates   65
- Getting Help   68
- About the Video Tutorials   72

Part 2: Movie Elements

Chapter 3   Graphics   75
- Tools and Options   76
- Drawing Tasks   85
- Using the Pen Tool   93
- Pen and Drawing Preferences   99
- Editing Simple Shapes   100
- Strokes and Fills   106
- Importing Vector Graphics   119
- Optimizing Vector Graphics   122
- Using Color   126
- Video Tutorial   134

Chapter 4   Text   135
- Creating Text Elements   136
- Editing and Configuring Text Elements   142
- Using Font Symbols for Dynamic Type Styling   161
- Breaking Text Apart   164
- Animation Considerations   165
- Video Tutorial   166

Chapter 5 Sound _____ **167**
    Understanding Sound   168
    Importing Sounds   169
    Adding Sounds to the Timeline   171
    Configuring and Editing Sound Instances   174
    Sound Properties   183
    Video Tutorials   192

Chapter 6 Bitmaps _____ **193**
    Importing Bitmaps   194
    Adding Bitmaps to Your Movie   197
    Working with Bitmaps   198
    Adjusting Bitmap Properties   206
    Optimizing Your Images   207
    Updating Bitmaps   211
    Using Bitmaps in Shared Libraries   212
    Using Animated GIFs   212
    Using PNGs   215
    Making Creative Use of Bitmaps   217
    Video Tutorial   222

Chapter 7 Symbols _____ **223**
    Understanding Symbols and Instances   223
    Creating Symbols   228
    Editing Symbols   239
    Working with Instances   242
    Video Tutorials   254

Chapter 8 Working with Elements on the Stage ___ **255**
    Selecting   255
    Groups   261
    Positioning Elements on the Stage   262
    Transforming Elements   273
    Duplicating Elements   280
    Cutting, Copying, Deleting, and Pasting   280
    Video Tutorial   282

Part 3: Movie Production, Visual

Chapter 9 Using Layers to Separate Content and Functionality — 285

- Understanding Layers — 286
- Working with Layers — 288
- Identifying Graphical Elements on Different Layers — 298
- Using Guide Layers — 300
- Special-Purpose Layers — 302
- Layer Folders — 309
- Layer Properties — 311
- Video Tutorial — 312

Chapter 10 Using Animation to Build Movement — 313

- How Animation Works — 314
- Understanding the Timeline — 316
- Working with Scenes — 324
- Frames — 326
- Creating Animation — 341
- Putting It All Together — 358
- Video Tutorials — 362

Chapter 11 Video — 363

- Importing Video — 364
- Working with Video in Your Projects — 370
- Making Your Video Clips Interactive — 375
- Using Video Creatively — 380
- Video Tutorial — 382

Part 4: Movie Production, Interactive

Chapter 12 Getting Started with ActionScript — 385

- What Is ActionScript? — 386
- How ActionScript Creates Interactivity — 386
- Using the Actions Panel — 402
- Fundamental Interactivity — 414
- Video Tutorials — 442

Chapter 13 Understanding ActionScript _____ **443**

    Getting Familiar with ActionScript   444
    Variables   451
    Operators   459
    Expressions   468
    Statements   471
    Functions   479
    Using Event Handler Methods   487
    Listeners   500
    Working with Multiple Timelines   502
    Advanced Actions Panel Features   519
    Video Tutorials   533

Chapter 14 ActionScript Objects _____ **535**

    Object Primer   535
    Object Sampler   543
    Video Tutorial   581

Chapter 15 Components _____ **583**

    Working with and Configuring Components   585
    Using Flash MX's Built-In Components   596
    Customizing Flash's Built-In Components   622
    Downloading and Installing Additional
        Components   635
    Video Tutorial   640

Chapter 16 Using ActionScript in Your Projects ___ **641**

    Chaining the Loading and Playback of
        External Movies   641
    Chaining the Loading and Playback of
        External MP3s   646
    Creating Keyboard Shortcuts   647
    Dynamically Disabling Flash Movies   649
    Integrating Flash with HTML   655
    Class-Wide Functionality via the
        Prototype Object   659

Preloaders	662
Detecting Collisions	668
Printing Movies	670
Dynamic Drawing	677
Dynamic Masking	681
Fast-Forwarding/Rewinding	684
Dynamic Names	686

Part 5: Movie Management

Chapter 17 Using the Library to Manage Your Assets — 693

Introducing the Library Panel	694
Managing Library Assets	697
Working with Symbols in the Library Panel	700
Working with Sounds, Bitmaps, and Videos in the Library Panel	702
Viewing and Organizing Library Items	703
Special Libraries	706
Updating Symbols from External Libraries	713
Video Tutorials	716

Chapter 18 Using Movie Explorer to Manage Structure — 717

Understanding the Display List	717
Movie Explorer Tasks	726
Video Tutorial	730

Part 6: Movie Distribution

Chapter 19 Testing — 733

Testing Within the Flash Authoring Environment	734
The Test Movie and Test Scene Commands	736
The Testing Environment	736
Testing Functionality	738
Debugging	744
Testing Download Performance	760

Chapter 20 Publishing Your Work _____ **769**
    Delivery Methods   769
    Flash and HTML   801
    Player Issues   812
    Understanding Templates   815
    Video Tutorial   823

Part 7: Putting It All Together

Chapter 21 Projects _____ **827**
    Hawaii Travel Application (Beginner)   828
    Flash Folio Media Browser (Intermediate)   854

Appendix A _____ **897**

Index _____ **899**

Introduction

Eighteen months ago, when Flash 5 was introduced, most developers had a hard time containing their excitement over its slew of new features—capabilities that transformed the program into a true Web development tool. While it's a given that innovation will never cease, back then, many of us wondered how Macromedia could even come close to matching the number of revolutionary enhancements added in that single release, in any new version of the program.

But then came Flash MX, and we were dazzled all over again. Macromedia continues to overdeliver, and for proof of that, one need look no further than this version's embarrassingly long list of enhancements and new features—all of which make Flash MX a mature platform for creating sophisticated interactive applications for the Web and CDs. If, as a Web developer, you only have time to learn one program, Flash MX is your ticket: As a drawing, animation, and interactivity powerhouse, Flash can take care of all your needs, and then some.

Of course, as is usually the case, new capabilities mean a heightened learning curve. Although the user's manual is adequate, at just 300 pages, it lacks the depth to really get the most out of Flash MX. That's where this book can help. In it, you'll find complete coverage of all aspects of the program, including hundreds of tips, tricks, notes, and sample scripts, as well as myriad custom graphics (not just interface screenshots) to illustrate difficult concepts. You'll also be exposed to material that's more hands-on in nature: source files, step-by-step projects, and of course the video tutorials for which this book has become known. Best of all, we'll show you all sorts of useful and creative ways to put Flash to use in your own projects. Add it all together, and you've got a complete tool for learning and using Flash MX!

What you'll learn…

What's new in this edition

About this book's organization and contents

How to use this book

What's New in This Edition

Not only has this book been revised substantially to cover all of MX's new features, it's changed in other ways as well. The first thing readers familiar with the previous edition will notice is the name: The word *interactivity* has been added to the title, denoting an increased focus on ways you can use ActionScript—Flash's scripting language—to make your projects more lively and interactive. In fact, three of this edition's five new chapters focus on ActionScript. The other new chapters cover two of Flash MX's most important new features: video and components.

 { *ActionScript* } You'll also notice the use of two new icons: MX and ActionScript alerts (like those in the left margin here). The MX alert indicates a discussion of MX features or enhancements, or MX-specific methods of accomplishing a task. An MX alert can refer to an entire chapter (in which case the icon will appear beside the chapter introduction, as in Chapter 11, "Video"), or to a discussion of just a sentence or two. The ActionScript alert indicates that there's an ActionScript-based method of performing or enhancing the functionality of the task under discussion.

The Parts

Before you begin, we should explain some terminology. First, the terms *movie, presentation, content,* and *project* all refer to basically the same thing: the Flash file you create to show to the world. *Animation* in this context means any kind of onscreen movement you intentionally create. *Interactivity* refers to anything you create in Flash that reacts to viewer input—via keyboard or mouse. Finally, *multimedia* is where all of these things, including sound, come together.

Now take a look at the following list of chapters to see what's in store:

Part 1: Welcome to Flash MX

Chapter 1—Flash MX—The Rich Client Revolution. Flash MX's many new features could change the way we look at and use the Web for years to come. For those interested in how, this chapter explains it all.

Chapter 2—Getting Started. If you want to find out what's new in Flash MX as well as familiarize yourself with the redesigned authoring environment and its enhancements, this is the place to go.

Part 2: Movie Elements

Chapter 3—Graphics. Although some people find Flash's drawing tools limited, we believe just the opposite to be true. Here we'll show you why as well as provide an in-depth discussion of the program's powerful tool set, including the new Free Transform tool. If you work with FreeHand and Fireworks, this is where you can learn how to import files created with those programs directly into Flash.

Chapter 4—Text. Although text is far from the most exciting part of a movie, it doesn't have to be boring. In this chapter, we'll show you how to use text to receive user input and liven up your presentation.

Chapter 5—Sound. Visual effects are wonderful, but their impact is even greater if you use them in conjunction with sound. Here, we show you how to harness the power of audio.

Chapter 6—Bitmaps. When you add bitmap elements (or photos) to your Flash presentations, there's no limit to the visual effects you can achieve. Here, we'll show you how, and then detail some of their great uses.

Chapter 7—Symbols. These "do all" elements represent the heart of Flash's Web multimedia capabilities. If you can master the use of symbols, you're halfway to handling most of what you'll encounter in Flash.

Chapter 8—Working with Elements on the Stage. Learn how to move, align, flip, skew, and transform your movie elements in almost every way imaginable. In this chapter, you'll find out how to create new movie elements and edit existing ones on Flash's stage.

Part 3: Movie Production, Visual

Chapter 9—Using Layers to Separate Content and Functionality. Learning how to use layers is the first step in creating an interactive presentation. Here, we'll show you how to use them to separate the content and functionality within your movie, as well as how layers can help give your project dimension and depth.

Chapter 10—Using Animation to Build Movement. Bring your movie to life with frame-by-frame and tweened animation. In this chapter, we'll describe both techniques as well as teach you how to create flowing transitions and deal with processor issues that may hinder your movie's playback.

Chapter 11—Video. The ability to embed video clips within Flash movies is one of the most exciting new features in Flash MX. Here, you'll learn how to import and work with video, as well as how to use ActionScript to manipulate video clips. We'll also introduce you to some creative ways of incorporating video into your projects.

Part 4: Movie Production, Interactive

Chapter 12—Getting Started with ActionScript. In this chapter we'll introduce you to the powerful ways you can use ActionScript to add interactive features to your movies. We'll take you through a series of step-by-step projects, where you'll learn how to navigate a movie using buttons, how to load and unload external SWF files, and more.

Chapter 13—Understanding ActionScript. This chapter builds on the last, providing an in-depth look at what makes ActionScript tick. Dozens of sample scripts and accompanying explanations are provided.

Chapter 14—ActionScript Objects. In Flash, interactivity is largely accomplished via ActionScript objects, which allow you to control and manipulate timelines, text, color, sound, and more. In this chapter, we'll introduce you to many of ActionScript's objects as well as explain how you can change their characteristics or instruct them to perform actions.

Chapter 15—Components. These sophisticated yet easy-to-use movie elements allow you to quickly add advanced interactivity to your projects. In this chapter, you'll learn how to place, configure, and customize the components that come with Flash MX. Plus, we'll show you how to download and install additional components available through Macromedia and third-party developers.

Chapter 16—Using ActionScript in Your Projects. This chapter provides numerous mini-tutorials demonstrating how to use ActionScript for everything from creating keyboard shortcuts to drawing shapes dynamically.

Part 5: Movie Management

Chapter 17—Using the Library to Manage Your Assets. A movie contains many elements; Flash's library is where you keep track of them all. In this chapter we'll show you how to organize your movie assets in the library as well as describe shared libraries—the answer to easy updates to your content, as well as revision control issues that can arise from working on group authoring projects on multiple machines.

Chapter 18—Using Movie Explorer to Manage Structure. If you want a blueprint of your movie project, this is your tool. In this chapter we'll show you how to use Movie Explorer to analyze and manage your projects.

Part 6: Movie Distribution

Chapter 19—Testing. With so many things to consider when creating a Flash movie, things can sometimes slip through the cracks. Here, we'll show you how to use Flash's testing tools to create compact, smooth-running, error-free movies.

Chapter 20—Publishing. All your hard work is for naught if you're unable to share the final product. Here, we'll familiarize you with the many formats in which Flash allows you to present your work, and describe the potential and appropriate uses of each. You'll also learn about how to place a Flash movie on an HTML page and how to deal with plug-ins.

Part 7: Putting It All Together

Chapter 21—Projects. If you've made it this far, you're probably eager to put your knowledge to test—to create a full-fledged Flash project. In this chapter you'll have two chances to do just that. In the projects we build and script here, you'll do everything from creating animation and a scrollable map, to validating user input and loading external MP3 files using XML.

How to Use This Book

We've tried to organize this book so that it echoes a Flash project's stages of development—first discussing the elements that make up a movie, then taking you through the ins and outs of movie production (both visual and interactive), management, and distribution. Although we recommend that you go through this book from front to back, sections are organized so that you can easily reference them in the future. The book also includes plenty of tips, tricks, warnings, and other learning aids to keep you on track.

The CD-ROM contains the QuickTime video tutorials that accompany most chapters (plus a QuickTime installer so that you can view the movies). It also contains project source files, which you'll want to copy to your hard drive and work with from there—a necessity for testing. Also on the CD are several of this book's appendixes: "Appendix B: Keyboard Shortcuts," "Appendix C: Resource Sites," and "Appendix D: Third-Party Software."

With this revision, I've worked hard to make this book as easy, enjoyable, and informative as possible. Now it's up to you to take the information and run with it. I'd love to hear of your successes as well as view what you've created. Contact me at derek@derekfranklin.com. Although I may not be able to respond to all of your emails, I'll certainly do my best. Tell me what you think of the book, and what you'd like to see in future editions. I'll be listening.

1

Welcome to Flash MX

Flash MX: The Rich-Client Revolution   3
Getting Started 21

IF YOU'RE NEW TO FLASH, or even just accustomed to a previous version, you may find Flash MX overwhelming at first. There's a lot to discover. What's now possible with Flash MX? What features have been added? What do you need to know to begin your Flash MX journey? You'll find the answers to these questions and more in this first section.

Flash MX: The Rich-Client Revolution

CHAPTER 1

What you'll learn...

What a rich client is

How Flash benefits users

How Flash benefits developers

When you think of the word *rich*, many things are likely to come to mind: that scrumptious slice of chocolate cake you had (or maybe shouldn't have had) last night; someone you know who seems to have it all; or perhaps even your favorite painting, which is full of rich colors. Whatever the case, one thing is certain: The term *rich* connotes abundance. And in terms of the rich-client revolution, this translates into an abundantly richer, faster, more productive, and ultimately more enjoyable Web experience.

So what exactly is this *rich client* everyone's talking about? Until now, the transfer and display of information via the Internet has been based largely on what's called the *client/server relationship*. As its name implies, the server does the bulk of the work, while the client benefits from those labors. Whenever you visit a Web site, there is a server at the other end sending data (usually HTML and graphics) to multiple connections. The same server might also process monetary transactions, validate data, dynamically generate pages (based on information in a database), and more. Extend this equation to encompass thousands of simultaneously connected users, and you begin to understand how *hard* servers work.

By contrast, a client is simply software that displays or otherwise uses the data churned out by the server. The most popular form of client software—a Web browser—simply displays whatever the server sends to it. But as the Internet continues to expand its reach, more and more is being demanded of servers, and companies are being forced to spend truckloads of money on additional servers and administrators to manage them. What's more, users are beginning to demand from their Web experience the same sophisticated interactive content they've grown accustomed to in video games, on TV, and in movies—on demand and with no waiting (**Figure 1.1**).

Figure 1.1
Users expect more from their Web experience in the year 2002. The plain, unimaginative sites of the early '90's no longer cut it.

Enter the rich client. With Flash MX and the Flash player (which you use to play Flash content), the folks at Macromedia have come up with what the company has dubbed the "rich-client experience." Although the client—in this case, the Flash player—still interacts with a server when necessary, it's also able to handle tasks that were once the exclusive purview of servers, as well as some that not even servers would allow. As you will soon see, the benefits to users are myriad, promising to revolutionize the way people use and experience the Web: They'll be able to interact with Web applications in new ways, in less time, in more engaging environments.

User Benefits

As any developer worth his or her salt knows, the user experience is paramount: If users find your site difficult to navigate, slow, or just plain boring, they're unlikely to return—and in the end, they're the ones paying your bill (whether directly or indirectly)! In the sections that follow, we'll look at ways you can use a rich client (in this case, the Flash player) to enhance the user's experience—going well beyond anything you could accomplish in a non-Flash environment using a typical Web browser.

NOTE *In this volume we typically use the Web browser/HTML experience as a point of comparison—that is, to demonstrate how much more you can accomplish via Flash MX and the rich client. Keep in mind, however, that while browser/HTML design tools have distinct limitations, we aren't implying that they're never useful. We simply believe that being aware of those limitations will help you make informed decisions when it comes to developing your own Web projects. Remember that even though Flash is a great design tool, it's not necessarily the right choice for every project.*

True Interactivity

The most exciting and interactive elements you'll find on a typical HTML-based interface are the ever-popular image-rollover and those lovely alert boxes that appear when you enter or exit certain pages. Beyond that, they consist of mostly static text and images—makes you sleepy just to think about it! You may even have had the ironic experience of viewing a site whose Flash banner ad was more engaging than the site itself—sort of like watching a TV commercial that's funnier than the sitcom it's sponsoring.

Luckily for us, rich clients like the Flash player are capable of much more. With Flash MX, you can create applications that users interact with in all kinds of sophisticated ways—via menus, knobs, sliders, and drag and drop (not to mention your everyday buttons) (**Figure 1.2**). Your Flash movie can display data in a database, print information, play and control both audio and video, take users to different points in your movie, and react to various mouse events. In addition, users can drag around and manipulate elements of your movie. You can also create unique games and complete Web applications with built-in logic, and your movie can move along at a predefined pace or follow a path defined by viewer input. In short, you can provide the user with a more intuitive and enjoyable experience.

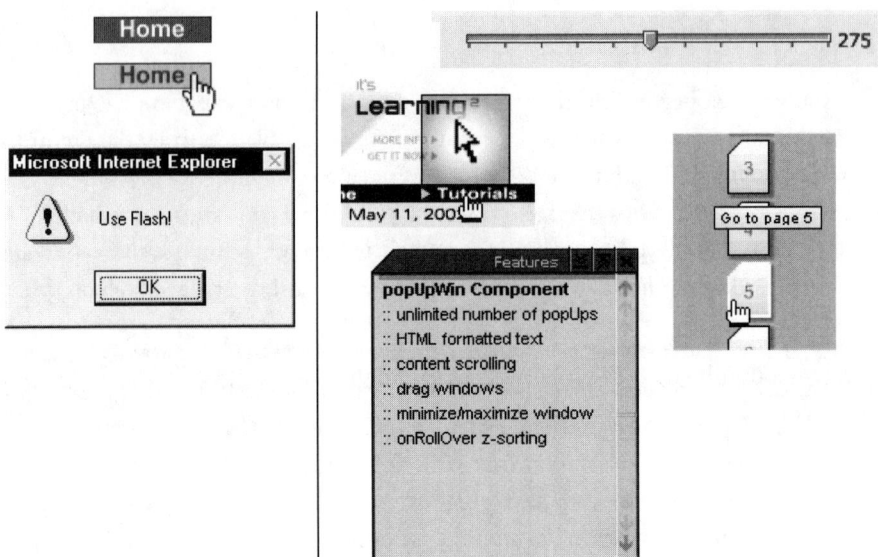

Figure 1.2
The old, generic interactive experience afforded by HTML vs. the engaging visuals enabled by Flash!

To give you an idea of what a rich client like Flash can do, consider a car company site: While many such sites let you build custom vehicles by pressing buttons to add or remove various options—press a red color-swatch button to load a new page displaying your dream car in red—a more intuitive and fun approach would be to let you drag and drop colors directly onto the body of a car. Or how about providing a gearshift knob to select engine size (to the accompaniment of engine-revving audio!), or a volume knob to select the sound system. All of these ideas—which are difficult or impossible to implement using HTML and JavaScript—are easily accomplished via Flash MX.

Less Waiting

Imagine what kind of shape you'd be in if every time you encountered some type of danger, you had to wait several seconds for your brain to update its information before you could react: Chances are, you wouldn't be walking around today! Fortunately, in most cases our brains and reflexes react in milliseconds, allowing us to respond in the blink of an eye. Which is what we've come to expect from our Web interactions as well. Our brains' hard-wiring, combined with our desire for instant gratification, has led us to feel that waiting for *anything*—even for a few seconds—is unacceptable.

In fact, *unacceptable* is the perfect term to describe the time it takes to perform even the simplest tasks on most Web sites. Just updating personal information typically requires you to jump through more hoops than a circus animal. It's all about click-and-wait, click-and-wait, click-and-wait. And if you make a mistake? *More* click-and-wait! And we're not talking processor-intensive stuff here like applying a Gaussian blur to a five-hour video clip. No, this is about exchanging maybe ten characters of text for another ten characters. Putting your users through this kind of torture in the year 2002 is ludicrous—especially when a rich-client application like Flash can solve such problems in several ways.

First, a dumb client (Web browser) can only hold one page of information at a time. This means that if changing a user's personal information is a five-page/step process, the Web browser has to make five requests to the server to complete the task. In contrast, a single Flash movie can take care of the entire process, communicating just *twice* with the server: once to retrieve the movie itself and another time to send and process the final data submitted by the user. Everything in between, such as the display of various input elements and instructions, can be updated or changed, on the fly, within that single Flash movie. In other words, no more click-and-wait (**Figure 1.3**).

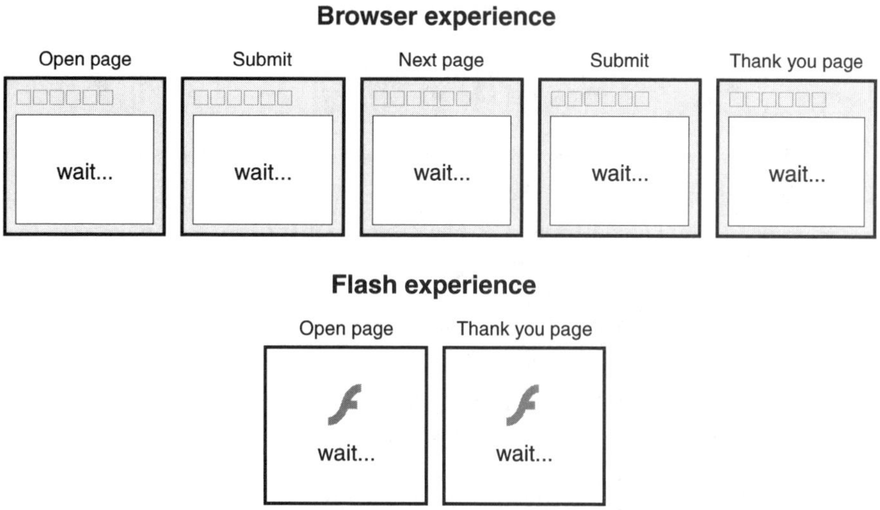

Figure 1.3
Flash content requires less interaction with the server, so that tasks like updating personal information can be performed much more quickly.

And if the user makes a mistake during the process? The dumb client—being totally reliant on a server—will require an additional two to three excruciating click-and-wait periods: first, when the client submits the data and the server detects the error and sends back an error page, and then after the user corrects the error and waits for either the next step in the process or another error page. You can almost see your customers exiting your site.

With a rich client like the Flash player, however, user data can be validated within the movie itself—*before* it's sent to the server, and in real time. This means that you can program visual cues (like a big red *X* or a flashing warning sign) to instantly appear onscreen when the user enters incorrect data (for example, inputting too many or too few characters) (**Figure 1.4**).

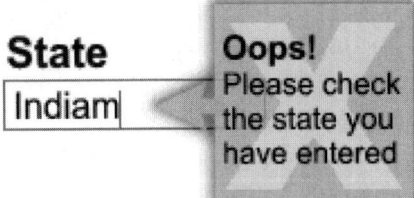

Figure 1.4
Data entered into a Flash movie can be validated in real time—that is, as the user types. In addition, error indicators can look like something other than ugly alert boxes.

Interfaces That React in Real Time

Let's consider the typical online shopping experience: You place an order (by pressing a button), then after a good click-and-wait period, the screen updates your shopping cart (a simple text box) so that it displays the number of items you've selected to purchase—overall, a less-than-thrilling experience.

Now consider a typical *Flash-based* online shopping experience: You drag and drop items into an onscreen shopping cart, which appears to fill up as you do so. At the same time, a sales receipt appears, displaying the items selected thus far as well as a running total. As you drop specific items into the cart, an animated window showing add-ons and/or complementary items appears (**Figure 1.5**). You can zoom in on items to get a closer look, and you may even be able to "sample" the product through online simulations (for example, by pushing buttons, adding an entry, or playing a game on a simulated PDA).

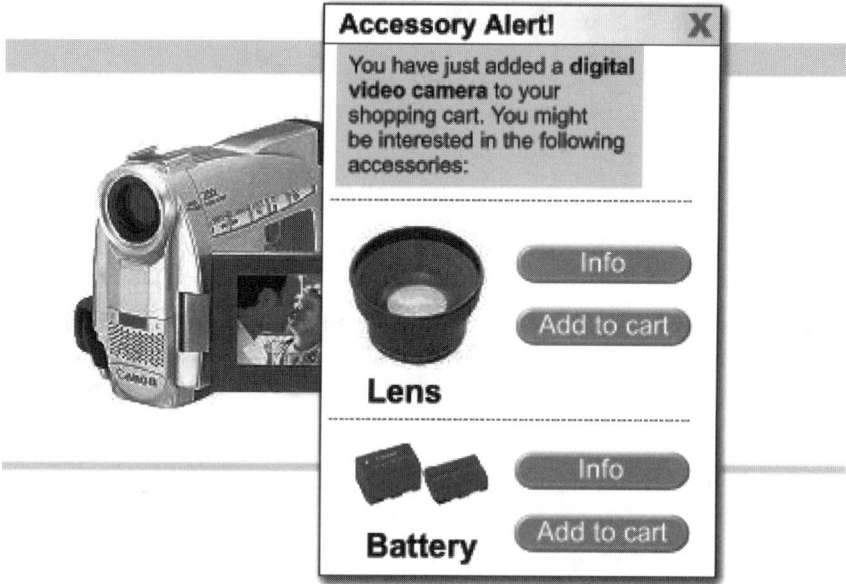

Figure 1.5
A Flash shopping cart application is much more interactive than your typical HTML shopping cart application: This graphic demonstrates how a small window could show add-on items in response to the user adding a digital camera to his or her shopping cart

Flash MX also lets you reposition, enable/disable, and even hide or show Flash movie elements on the fly, depending on user input or interaction. Take, for example, giving users an online form to fill out: Should be simple, right? Not with a dumb client. Typically, HTML-based forms are designed to accommodate a broad range of users—which may mean skipping questions or whole sections, depending on how you answer certain questions. Soon it starts to feel a lot like filling out your tax return—a sure way to lose users. In contrast, a rich client like Flash enables forms that reposition their elements or even hide/disable others dynamically, as the user progresses through the form. You can also tailor your forms to reconfigure based on users' responses.

Invisible Server Interaction

In designing Web content, you can make users happier by creating applications that anticipate their needs, by interacting with the server in the background *without* requiring user input. In this way, you can provide information and content tailored to your users' needs—without making them specifically ask for it.

Say you own a company that sells its products nationwide, but those products vary according to geographic location. If the Request Information form on your Web site requires an address, Flash can automatically communicate with the server as soon as the user selects a state—even as the user continues to fill out the form—and request information about the products available in that state. Flash can then immediately display this information in a sidebar that users view as they continue to fill in the form.

You can also leave Flash applications running, and their content will update automatically—without user interaction. The days of having the user press the Refresh button on their browser just to update the page are over!

Multimedia Integration

Ever go to a Web site that immediately warns you that you need a laundry list of plug-ins and mini-apps (Flash, QuickTime, Windows Media Player, RealPlayer, and so on) to enjoy the site's content? It's a bit like inviting customers into your store, then telling them they need a special ID card to enter certain departments. While customers may wait through a couple such delays, if they encounter too many roadblocks they'll be heading for the door faster than Michael Johnson running the 200 meters!

As the ultimate media player/rich client, Flash provides an all-in-one solution for viewing graphics, text, and video, as well as for listening to MP3s. This integration means that with just one download (to get the Flash Player), users will be able to fully experience all of your site's offerings. Not only do users save time by downloading just one plug-in, but their experience is enhanced by Flash's tight integration of video, MP3s, graphics, and text. By combining all of these elements in a single environment—a Flash movie—that communicates efficiently with a server (to transfer data), you gain almost limitless possibilities for providing rich, dynamic content.

 NOTE *Video integration is a feature new to Flash MX. For more information, see Chapter 11, "Video."*

Developer Benefits

It isn't just users who benefit from the rich-client experience provided by Flash content. In the following sections, we'll show you some of the reasons Flash MX provides such a rewarding environment for developers—and why nothing else compares when it comes to creating interactive, high-impact content.

Bandwidth-Friendly Content

One reason Flash makes such an incredible Web development tool is its use of vector graphics as the default graphics mode. Vector graphics are objects defined by mathematical equations, or *vectors*, that include information about the object's size, shape, color, outline, and position. This mode of handling graphics keeps files relatively small—even when you're dealing with complex drawings. What's more, because vector graphics are resolution-independent, a vector graphic the size of a pinhead will retain the same file size—with no degradation in quality—even when enlarged to fit your entire screen (**Figure 1.6**).

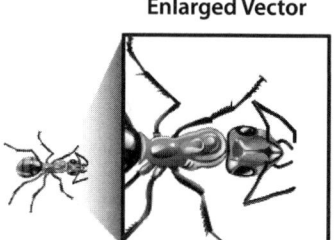 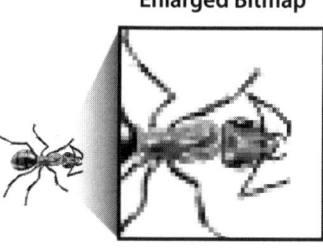

Figure 1.6 An enlarged vector graphic vs. an enlarged bitmap graphic.

Traditionally (and particularly on the Web), graphics have been delivered primarily in the form of *bitmaps*. Although effective and often quite artistic, bitmaps are bandwidth-intensive and share none of the benefits of vector graphics. Bitmap graphic files, for example, are almost always larger than their vector counterparts (even when visually similar)—a fact that becomes more apparent as the displayed dimensions of the graphic increase. The construction of bitmaps accounts for this difference.

Unlike vector images, which are encoded as mathematical equations, bitmaps comprise collections of dots, or *pixels*, lined up in a grid pattern. These pixels are usually so small that, viewed from a distance, they blend seamlessly to form a picture onscreen. But if you were to zoom in on this picture, the tiny square pixels would become apparent. Each pixel in a bitmap has associated coding that relates to its color. Most images incorporate thousands, hundreds of thousands, or even millions of pixels: Obviously, the larger the graphic, the more pixels it contains. Even a small bitmap 100 pixels tall by 100 pixels wide contains information for 10,000 pixels. Thus, you can begin to see the benefits of vector graphics, in terms of reducing the download time for end users.

Although vector graphics offer file size advantages, some graphic effects can only be achieved with bitmaps. Fortunately, Flash supports bitmap graphics; in fact, it can even directly import Macromedia Fireworks 3 or later files. And by utilizing the compression technologies, Flash helps you keep file sizes to a minimum even when you're using bitmaps.

Flash's development approach also facilitates the creation of complex multimedia presentations while still keeping files relatively small. Because elements like vectors, bitmaps, and sounds are typically employed more than once in a given movie, Flash allows you to create a single version of an object, which you can then reuse elsewhere without having to re-create it each time—a capability that is particularly useful in minimizing file size.

For example, if you wanted to use a 10K bitmap graphic in ten **different** locations in your Flash presentation, it would *appear* to require 100K (10K used ten times) of file space. However, Flash stores only one actual copy of the 10K graphic; the other nine instances are simply references to the main file. Although these "references" look just like the actual file, they require less than 100 bytes per instance to reference the actual file (**Figure 1.7**). Thus, you save nearly 90K —a considerable benefit when you're designing for the Web. You can use this powerful capability—incorporating vectors, bitmaps, sounds, and more—to create compelling yet compact multimedia productions.

10K   10K

Figure 1.7
Flash lets you re-use a single graphic without increasing your movie's overall file size.

A final—and perhaps defining—factor in Flash's capacity to quickly deliver multimedia over the Web is its ability to stream content. Streaming content is another example of a technology born out of necessity on the Web. Before streaming, bandwidth issues prevented users from viewing or listening to files until all of their contents had been downloaded. Engineers, however, realized that users don't see or hear every byte in a file simultaneously: They could still enjoy the full impact of the content even if they received it incrementally. As with reading a book, viewers only need to see one page at a time. If that book was being delivered to you over the Web, you'd probably appreciate being able to read the first few pages while the rest was downloading in the background. It might even keep you from giving up and going elsewhere (**Figure 1.8**).

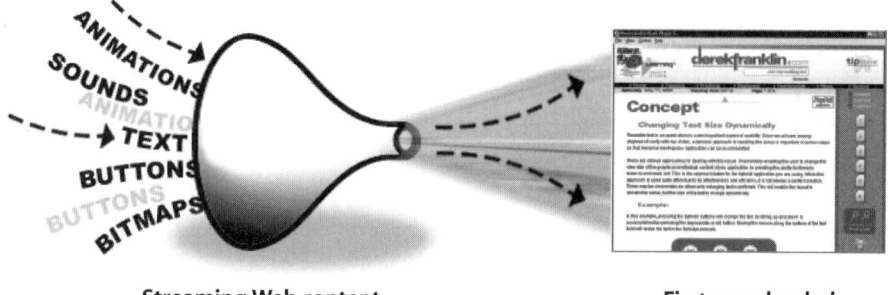

Streaming Web content   First page loaded

Figure 1.8
Flash allows content to be streamed, so that users can view downloaded portions while other content continues to load.

Flash's streaming capabilities mean that even large files with sound, animation, and bitmaps can begin playing almost instantaneously. If you plan your project precisely, your audience can view a 10- to 15-minute presentation over the Web without noticing that content is being downloaded in the background.

Integrated Graphics

Although the tools for creating Web content have become much more advanced in recent years, creating a complex site layout usually still involves producing graphics in some sort of paint or illustration program and then sending them through a chopping, slicing, and dicing process, which includes placing chopped-up pieces of images in table cells. If you want to make even minor design changes, you have to change the original graphic file and put it through the HTML blender all over again—a real drag on your creative flow.

In contrast, Flash allows you to work with graphic elements just as you would in any illustration program. This means you can place graphics precisely where you want on the page, using grids, guides, and rulers. You can also stack graphic elements on layers. In addition, Flash's transparency capabilities give your layouts depth and greater visual appeal. You can even use a background that doesn't tile across the screen. When you're ready to create a Flash movie from your efforts, just press the Publish button, and—voila!—in a matter of seconds you have a new movie file. If you want to edit your movie, just open the authoring file, make your changes, and hit Publish again. Even if you ignore its multimedia capabilities altogether, you'll still find Flash to be the most precise Web page layout tool available today.

Creating content in Flash gives designers complete control over how *everything* looks—from buttons and scroll bars to pop-up windows and video controls (**Figure 1.9**). Although newer versions of both Windows and Mac OS have greatly improved their visual appeal, Flash's capabilities still outshine the general OS look that comes from using HTML buttons, pop-up windows, alert boxes, and so on.

Figure 1.9
This scroll bar is just one example of how Flash lets you control the look of traditional interface elements.

A Multiplatform Standard

Today, more than 98 percent of the people using the Web have the ability to view Flash content—a fact that attests to the program's enormous popularity. However, Flash has become more than just a standard for creating rich content on the Web.

Unless you've been living in a cave for the last few years, you know that people are now connecting to the Internet through all sorts of devices besides home or office computers. PDAs, cell phones, video game consoles, even kitchen appliances can come equipped with some sort of Web capability. And each of these devices has its own unique programming language, which developers creating applications for it must use. Thanks to Macromedia's focus on these markets, however, the Flash player is now being incorporated into many of these devices—which means that the game you created for your Web site can now be viewed just as easily on a Flash-enabled cell phone or PDA. Thus, you can create content that can be used by many types of devices.

The icing on the cake is Macromedia's decision to make the SWF (Flash movie) format available to the public, allowing any software developer to create products that export content in Flash's file format. In response to this action—and in tacit acknowledgement of Flash's popularity—Adobe has included support for the Flash format in its own Web content development product, LiveMotion. This means that content created in LiveMotion can be exported to the Flash format—great news for developers, who now have a choice of authoring tools (though LiveMotion's interactive capabilities don't compare to Flash MX's). What's more, a number of other third-party developers have also begun creating all sorts of animation, 3-D, and other production tools that export content to the SWF file format. In addition, many popular graphics applications (including Adobe Illustrator and CorelDraw) can now export directly to the SWF format as well.

The bottom line is that Flash developers can create content once—and include all the design and interactive wizardry they want—using any Flash development tool they choose (preferably Flash MX), and know that it will look and act the same, regardless of the platform, browser, or Web-enabled electronic appliance used to access it.

Online/Offline Capabilities

Although the Internet represents the future of communications, not everyone has an Internet connection, and even if they do, it may not always be available to them.

Although Flash was designed to create compact, fast-loading multimedia—making it an ideal technology for the Web—you're not restricted to delivering your Flash content online. You can export any Flash-created content not only as a multimedia movie for the Web, but also as video that can be displayed on both Windows and Macintosh computers.

You can even distribute your Flash-created content as a stand-alone program on floppy disks or CDs. You can use these stand-alone versions of Flash movies to download data and content from a Web server; however, they will also work without a Web connection.

Rich-Client Workhorse

As the Web has extended its reach, servers are being asked to do more—and to do it more quickly. This demand for increased stability, security, and processing power has resulted in extremely high costs to companies with a Web presence. Flash can help alleviate this problem by allowing the client to perform many tasks traditionally carried out by the server. These include validating data, refreshing the interface (without having to load a new page from the server), displaying the current date, and much more. In this manner, Flash allows you to shift some of your site's processing functions to your users' computers, thereby reducing the server's workload—as well as your own computing costs (**Figure 1.10**).

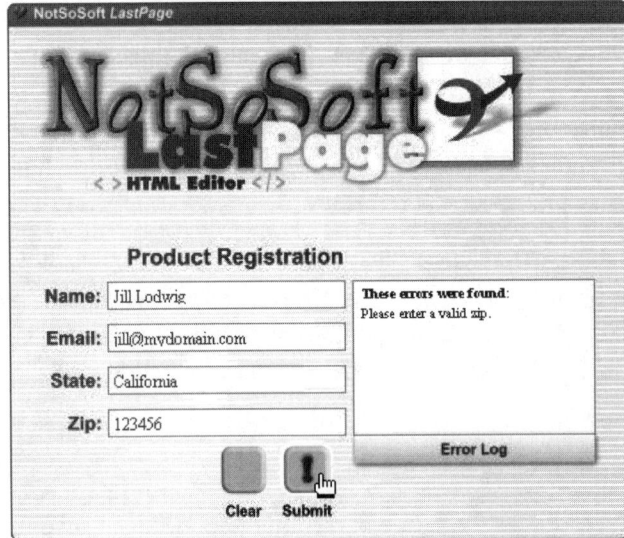

Figure 1.10
With Flash, you can shift a number of traditional server tasks, such as data validation, to the client side, thus easing the load on the server.

Versatile Project Applications

Flash can handle projects of all shapes and sizes. You can use it to create a full multimedia Web site with lots of cool graphics, form elements, and interaction, or simply to create a navigation bar or banner. Here are just a few of the kinds of projects Flash can help you create:

- Games
- Cartoons
- Interactive maps
- Single Web pages

- Full-blown multimedia-enhanced Web sites
- Web database front ends
- Promotional and marketing tools
- Vacation presentations
- Web jukeboxes
- Shopping cart systems
- Ebooks
- Interactive training
- Newsletters
- Screen savers

Perfect Complement to HTML

As great as Flash is, it's not necessarily the perfect solution for every project. For example, text within a Flash movie isn't indexed by search engines in the same manner as text appearing on typical HTML pages. Consequently, search engines may not be able to locate Flash content as easily as HTML-based Web pages. There are several ways to deal with this issue, but if accurate indexing is a key aspect of a given Web page or site, you may choose to stick with tried-and-true HTML. Even then, however, Flash may still be worth using in conjunction with HTML to create interactive, rich content. Some targeted, specific uses for Flash elements in an HTML page include:

- Displaying the current date (**Figure 1.11**)

Figure 1.11
By using small Flash movies in conjunction with HTML, you can add interactive features to otherwise static pages. Here, we've used a small Flash movie to display the current date.

- Playing a music track
- Displaying random banner ads

- Displaying random graphics
- Creating an embedded video window
- Creating highly interactive forms

Although you could produce many of these elements without using Flash, the process wouldn't be nearly as easy or elegant. By incorporating Flash content on HTML pages, you can get the best of both worlds.

Ease of Use

As cool as Flash MX's capabilities are, the icing on the cake is that all of these elements are easy to work with: You can produce a full-blown multimedia extravaganza, complete with interactive controls and buttons, without opening another graphics program or scripting anything in an HTML editor. And your creation will look and function the same in any Flash-enabled device.

Flash's development metaphor—incorporating timelines, frames, and scenes—makes it easy to conceptualize animations and interactive content. Flash offers additional tools for organizing content and assets, streamlining workflow, and analyzing and testing your project before distribution. Together, these features allow you to be more creative and ambitious with your productions.

In those rare cases where Flash's own drawing tools are insufficient (for example, when you need to use a bitmap graphic), you can take advantage of the program's extensive import capabilities, creating artwork in your favorite illustration or photo editing program and then importing it into Flash for use in your movie. In addition, Flash can import FreeHand and Fireworks files directly—giving you the flexibility you need to create great-looking movies.

To top it off, with Flash MX, Macromedia has introduced Components—special movie elements that make adding advanced interactivity (form elements, dynamic charts, draggable windows, and so on) a breeze—even if you know little about scripting or programming. Advanced users will even be able to create their own components, which they can then customize for use in multiple projects. With Flash MX's components, reusing code becomes as easy as dragging and dropping.

Components replace and extend Smart Clips, which were introduced in the previous version of Flash. To learn more about them, see Chapter 15, "Components."

MX Product-Family Integration

In April 2002, Macromedia announced its MX family of products: the new version of Flash itself, Dreamweaver (an HTML editor), Fireworks (a graphics editor), and ColdFusion (a Web application server). Designed as a fully integrated group of products, the MX family allows users to work seamlessly within the MX development environment to create rich Web applications. Macromedia has approached this integration concept from several angles:

First, the MX applications—with the exception of ColdFusion, which is a server—share a common interface, and thus a similar workflow (**Figure 1.12**). This means that you can perform tasks common to all of the applications (drawing, coding, interface configuration, and more) in similar fashion. What's more, even tasks that are unique to a single application are easier to learn, because you can usually apply principles that are common to all three. With the MX family of products providing all of the tools required to create rich content, you no longer have to spend extra time learning to use different vendors' products, and adapting to different workflows and styles.

Figure 1.12
The MX-family products share similar interfaces and workflows, enabling you to quickly and efficiently create complex applications.

In addition to sharing a common workflow/development environment, MX products are designed to work seamlessly with one another—in effect, functioning as a single super-app! For example, you can create a graphic in Fireworks, bring it into Flash, animate it, create a Flash movie, place that movie in an HTML page using Dreamweaver, and then connect your Flash movie to a database using ColdFusion. Need to use Fireworks to edit the graphic you animated in Flash? No problem! Just open Flash, select the graphic to edit it in Fireworks, then when you've finished editing it in Fireworks, the changes you've made can be saved and automatically reflected in Flash—without exporting from Fireworks, then re-importing back into Flash. Not only that, but both Fireworks and Dreamweaver can create simple Flash content on their own—meaning you don't even need to open Flash!

TIP *Macromedia has created the Macromedia MX Designer & Development Center, an online resource to help users learn to work with the MX products as a suite. Be sure to check out this useful resource: www.macromedia.com/desdev/*

Getting Started

CHAPTER 2

What you'll learn...

How Flash works

What's new in Flash MX

About the various interface elements

How to configure Flash's options and settings

How to set movie properties

How to make your movie accessible to the visually impaired

How to work with templates

Where and how to get help

About this book's video tutorials

One of the great things about using Macromedia Flash is that it's not rocket science. With a little practice, you can soon be on your way to creating fun, interactive movies. In the first part of this chapter, we'll help you gain a basic understanding of how Flash works, focusing on a few simple but essential concepts. Then we'll look at some of Flash MX's many enhancements from previous versions. Lastly, you can get your feet wet with a video tutorial that helps you create your first Flash movie.

By the time you finish this chapter, we'll have covered the basics you need to work through the rest of this book. Keep in mind that you'll be building momentum as you go. And don't be discouraged if you get hung up working with a new feature somewhere down the line. It's impossible to become a Flash master overnight—especially with all the new features Macromedia has crammed into this update.

How Flash Works

Flash uses two different types of files to produce and then distribute content: an authoring file, where you create content, animation, and interactivity, and a compressed and optimized version of this file, better known as a Flash movie.

The authoring file, which has an **.fla** extension, is your production file. It's where you store your work while you're assembling your movie—that is, the file you actually work on when Flash MX is open. The authoring file contains all the sounds, bitmaps, drawings, text, and interactivity featured in your final movie, and represents that movie in its *preoptimized* state—meaning its size can balloon to many megabytes.

When you've gotten your authoring file to look and work the way you want, you're then able to distribute it by converting it into a Flash movie. This is known as *exporting* (publishing). When you export your authoring file to a movie, (which will have a .swf file extension), Flash compresses and optimizes the exported data, so that the movie (.swf) file is dramatically smaller than the original authoring (.fla) file (**Figure 2.1**). You can then place this smaller file on your Web page, or distribute it on disk or CD. While an exported movie can be imported back into the authoring environment, where some of the graphics are editable, most editing functionality is lost (layers, scripts, and symbols are not editable). If you wish to edit your movie's content, you must reopen the original authoring file, make your changes, and then re-export the authoring file to a Flash movie.

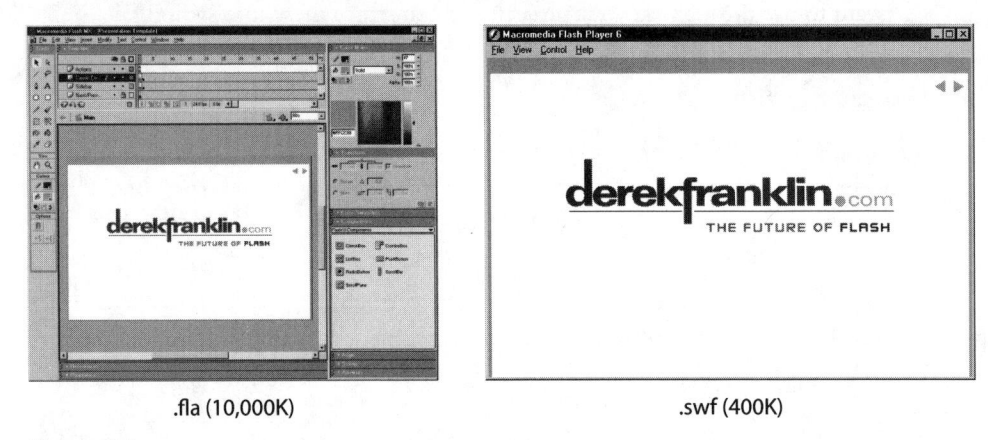

.fla (10,000K)   .swf (400K)

Figure 2.1
Exporting your authoring file (.fla) to a Flash movie (.swf) creates an optimized version that looks and acts like the authoring file, but is much smaller in size.

The size of your Flash movie is affected by many factors; fortunately, you can exercise at least some control over most of them. Attaining the smallest file size for your final movie usually involves balancing the quality of your movie's elements (bitmaps, audio, and so on) against its overall file size. Sometimes you'll need to compromise, sacrificing some aspects of quality—such as sound clarity or picture sharpness—in order to get a smaller exported movie. We'll discuss how you can use Flash's tools to produce the best-quality movie possible, while still retaining a reasonable file size.

With your movie's authoring file, you can not only create Flash movies but also export your work as QuickTime movies, animated GIFs, and even static or nonanimated graphics—all of which Flash can generate simultaneously! This means you can create content once (in the authoring file) and then distribute it in multiple formats.

Content Creation

Flash projects can take many forms, including presentations, tutorials, product demos, slide shows, and even games. Some Flash projects use interactivity but little or no animation, while others employ motion graphics but include little interactivity.

Regardless of your project's scope, your work will typically proceed as follows:

1. Create graphics in Flash or import them from another program.

2. Identify graphics, independent animations, and any other elements that you'll want to use throughout your project, and transform these into symbols.

3. Place your movie elements (including vector graphics, bitmaps, and symbols) on the stage.

4. Attach actions (via ActionScript, Flash's scripting language) to buttons, movie clips, or frames on the timeline to make them interactive.

5. Select a frame, symbol, stroke, fill, or text block on the stage to adjust its properties via the Property inspector or other panels.

Of course, the creative process takes many forms, and your project doesn't have to proceed exactly as described above. However, these steps represent what is generally the most practical work sequence.

Content Distribution

After you've created content in your authoring file, you must export it as a Flash movie and then decide how you want to distribute the finished, optimized SWF. One option is to embed your movie in a Web page, where it will be displayed as a regular graphic—but one that's animated and interactive. You can, in fact, create an entire Web site out of a single Flash movie—but be aware that visitors must have the Flash Player installed to experience the site.

If you choose this option, your Flash movie will be streamed over the Web, allowing viewers to begin playing it almost immediately while the rest of the movie is being downloaded in the background. You can instruct Flash to open and close browser windows, accept user information (which can then be processed by a Web server), play sounds, interact with the user, and more—all while the movie is playing.

Another popular way to deliver your Flash movies is as *projectors*, or stand-alone players, which transform your movies into self-running applications. This enables you to store your movie on a disk or CD, which anyone can view immediately just by opening it—without having the Flash Player on his or her system. Using this projector mode, and Flash's powerful scripting engine and capacity to communicate with Web servers, you can create full-blown, powerful Flash applications and distribute them via projector file. In fact, you can create your Web site entirely in Flash, then put it on the Web *and* offer it to your customers on disk or CD.

You can also turn your Flash project into a QuickTime movie or Windows AVI file.

What's New in Flash MX

MX ALERT The fact that Macromedia named this update Flash MX—rather than Flash 6—is your first clue that this version is special. The *MX* moniker signifies that Flash is now part of an integrated set of Macromedia Web development tools (including Dreamweaver MX, Fireworks MX, and ColdFusion MX) designed to facilitate the next-generation Internet experience—an experience Macromedia believes is evolving from surfing to *doing*. Now rather than simply jumping from site to site, reading information, and downloading files, Web users are visiting interactive, dynamic sites that let them build, test, play, experience, and learn—all from within their Web browsers. And with the new MX suite of products, creating these types of dynamic experiences is easier than ever. Fireworks MX, for example, allows you to create stunning graphics; Flash MX is the ticket for producing interactive content with sound and animation; Coldfusion MX provides the server-based functionality required to talk to databases; and Dreamweaver MX is the tool that brings it all together. The tightly integrated MX product line makes moving between applications seamless—which means that you're more productive and your Web applications can be even more mind-blowing than ever before! To that end, Flash MX includes numerous enhancements that enable you to create some very sophisticated applications.

The following is a summary of the enhancements and additions incorporated in Flash MX; we'll look more closely at all of these in subsequent chapters:

Accessibility features (new). For visually impaired users, Flash MX includes accessibility features that allow text as well as special accessibility information attached to movie clip instances (in essence, information describing the object) to be read by screen readers (see "What Is a Screen Reader?" later in this chapter").

Actions panel (enhanced). The Actions panel—which now has its own toolbar for quick access to associated commands—includes several enhancements that make it easy to create complex yet readable scripts. For more information about these enhancements, see Chapter 13, "Understanding ActionScript."

- Code hints are "tooltips" that provide clues about syntax, as well as available parameter settings for actions as you add code to a script.

- The auto-formatting feature reformats manually entered code, by automatically indenting, color-coding and intelligently inserting spaces where needed, so that the code is easier to read.

- Advanced, customizable options for color-coding script elements and an automatic line-renumbering function also make ActionScripts easier to read (**Figure 2.2**).

Code hints

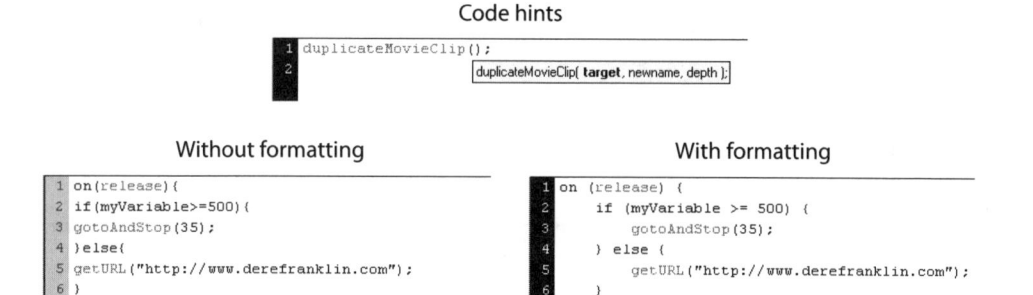

```
1 duplicateMovieClip();
2
   duplicateMovieClip( target, newname, depth );
```

Without formatting

```
1 on(release){
2 if(myVariable>=500){
3 gotoAndStop(35);
4 }else{
5 getURL("http://www.derefranklin.com");
6 }
7 }
```

With formatting

```
1 on (release) {
2     if (myVariable >= 500) {
3         gotoAndStop(35);
4     } else {
5         getURL("http://www.derefranklin.com");
6     }
7 }
8
```

Figure 2.2
New Actions panel features, such as code hints and auto-formatting, make it easier to create and read scripts.

Button objects (enhanced). Button instances can now be given instance names, so that they can be controlled in various ways via ActionScript.

Components (enhanced). Components—an enhanced version of what were formally known in Flash as Smart Clips—let you add advanced functionality and interactivity (such as scrollbars, radio buttons, drop-down menus, and so forth) with minimal scripting. Most components also have their own properties and methods, which means they can be changed, controlled, and updated dynamically via ActionScript. For more information about Components, see Chapter 15, "Components."

Debugger (enhanced). Flash MX adds a slew of advanced features to the Debugger, including breakpoint control (which lets you pause your script's execution during the debugging process), a code window for viewing scripts as they're executed, a new Locals tab for viewing local variables that are created as a function executes, and a Call Stack window for viewing a script's flow as it executes. Each of these improvements makes it easier to find bugs within complex applications. For more information about the Debugger, see Chapter 19, "Testing."

Distort (new). As an option associated with the new Free Transform tool (see below), the Distort feature allows you to drag control points on a vector shape, changing the viewer's apparent perspective on the shape. For more information about the Distort tool, see Chapter 3, "Graphics."

Distribute to Layers command (new). This function allows you to select numerous elements on the stage, then quickly distribute each element to its own layer, ready for tweening or other editing. For more information about this command, see Chapter 9, "Using Layers to Separate Content and Functionality."

Dynamic drawing (new). You can now use ActionScript to create lines and filled shapes *as* a movie plays. Line size, color, and transparency, as well as fill color and type (solid, linear gradient, or radial gradient) can also be controlled dynamically. For more information about this new functionality, see Chapter 16, "Using ActionScript in Your Projects."

Dynamic masks (new). Using ActionScript, you can now dynamically mask one movie clip instance using the shape of another. For more information about this new functionality, see Chapter 16, "Using ActionScript in Your Projects."

Dynamic movie layout (new). New ActionScript allows your movie to execute a script upon being resized. This makes it possible for you to modify your movie's layout dynamically in response to the resizing. For more information about this new functionality, see Chapter 16, "Using ActionScript in Your Projects."

Envelope (new). The new Free Transform tool's Envelope feature allows you to place an *envelope* (that is, an invisible grid) over a vector shape, then transform the shape by moving anchor points and dragging tangent handles on the envelope. For more information about this tool, see Chapter 3, "Graphics."

Event model (enhanced). Flash now allows you to execute scripts in response to various new events in your movie, such as a text field being clicked, a sound completing its playback, and more. In addition, you can assign events to scriptable elements (such as movie clip instances) on the fly—which means you can dynamically attach scripts or alter a script's functionality while your movie plays. For more information about these new events, see Chapter 13, "Understanding ActionScript."

Font mapping (new). With Flash MX, when users try to open Flash files on computers that don't contain all of a project's original fonts, they'll be presented with a dialog box that lets them quickly and easily select substitute fonts. When the file is reopened on the computer on which it was created, the original fonts will remain intact.

Free Transform tool (new). This new tool brings together the rotation and scaling functionality that used to be a function of the Arrow tool, and adds new distort and envelope capabilities to create a powerful tool for transforming shapes. For more information about this tool, see Chapter 8, "Working with Elements on the Stage."

Library drag and drop (new). Graphics can now be clicked and dragged directly onto the Library panel, which will automatically open the Convert to Symbol dialog box, allowing for more automated creation of symbols. For more information about this new functionality, see Chapter 17, "Using the Library to Manage Your Assets."

Library conflict resolution (new). If a symbol you drag from an external library has the same name as a symbol already stored in the current library, an alert box opens in Flash MX, asking whether you wish to overwrite the existing symbol with the new one. For more information about this new functionality, see Chapter 17, "Using the Library to Manage Your Assets."

Loading of external JPGs (new). JPG images can now be loaded from an external source, as your movie plays. Once loaded, they are treated as movie clip instances and can be controlled via ActionScript. For more information about this new functionality, see Chapter 12, "Getting Started with ActionScript."

Loading of external MP3s (new). MP3s can also be loaded from an external source, and controlled via ActionScript (**Figure 2.3**). For more information about this new functionality, see Chapter 14, "ActionScript Objects."

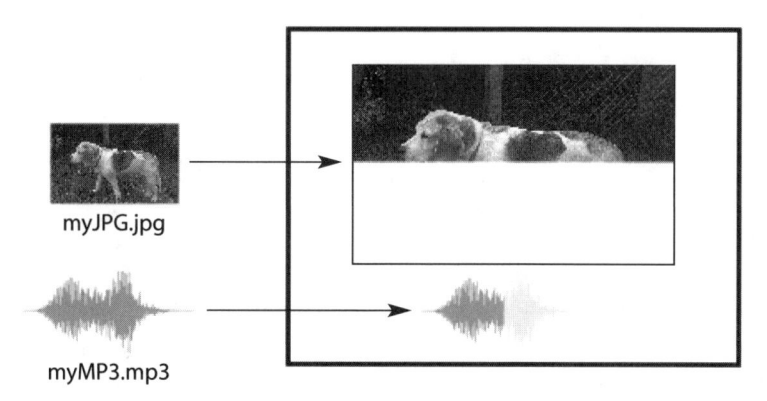

Figure 2.3
The ability to load external JPGs and MP3s was one of the most requested additions to Flash MX.

Movie clips as buttons (enhanced). Movie clip instances can now be scripted to react to mouse events (press, release, rollOver, and so on)—just the way buttons always have. For more information about this new functionality, see Chapter 7, "Symbols."

Named anchors (new). These special frame labels allow users to navigate through your movie using the Back and Forward buttons on their Web browsers. You can also insert bookmarks in your movie at these anchor positions—similar to bookmarking individual pages within a Web site. For more information about named anchors, see Chapter 10, "Using Layers to Separate Content and Functionality."

Object/Embed variables (new). Using the new Vars parameter, you can specify a number of variables within the OBJECT and EMBED tags, and they will be automatically loaded into the movie when it plays in a Web browser. For more information about this new parameter, see Chapter 20, "Publishing."

Property inspector (new). This new *context-sensitive* panel (meaning its controls and settings change depending on what's currently selected) replaces the functionality of numerous Flash 5 panels (see "Property Inspector" section later in this chapter for more details).

Reference panel (new). This panel provides a dictionary-type reference manual of the ActionScript language used in the Flash authoring environment. For more information about this new panel, see Chapter 12, "Getting Started with ActionScript."

Save as Flash 5 (new). This feature allows you to author a file using Flash MX, then save it as a Flash 5 file—which means it can be opened and edited in Flash 5.

setInterval() (new). This ActionScript action allows you to continually call a function at a specified interval. For more information about this new functionality, see Chapter 13, "Understanding ActionScript."

Shared objects (new). This ActionScript object allows you to easily store data on a user's hard drive, for later retrieval.

Snap to pixel (new). This feature splits the stage up into a pixel-sized grid, which allows you to draw and move shapes and other movie elements, so that movement snaps to the nearest pixel (**Figure 2.4**). For more information about this new functionality, see Chapter 8, "Working with Elements on the Stage."

Sound object (enhanced). Sound objects can now be scripted to react to various events; for instance, when they finish loading (if the sound object is loading an external MP3) or playing. In addition, Sound objects now incorporate position and duration properties, allowing you to determine their playback length and current playback position. For more information about this new functionality, see Chapter 14, "ActionScript Objects."

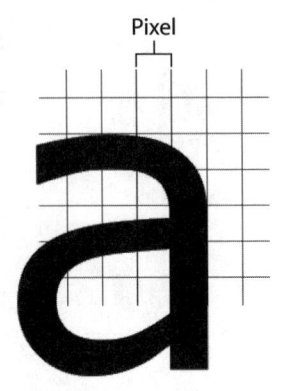

Figure 2.4
The Snap to Pixel feature allows you to place items on the stage with pixel-based accuracy.

switch() statement (new). The `switch()` statement allows you to use a conditional structure (similar to `if/else if`) common to several other programming languages, providing another means of creating conditional statements. For more information about this new statement, see Chapter 13, "Understanding ActionScript."

SWF compression (new). You can now even further compress SWF files that contain lots of ActionScript. For more information about this new functionality, see Chapter 20, "Publishing."

Templates (new). Templates allow you to begin a new project using a Flash file (template) that already contains a number of generic elements, which you can then configure and optimize as you see fit. You can even create templates that others can use. For more information about templates, see "Templates" later in this chapter.

Text Field object (new). This new object allows you to control text fields dynamically (changing their border/background colors, size, the text they contain, and more). For more information about this new object, see Chapter 14, "ActionScript Objects."

TextFormat object (new). This new ActionScript object allows you to create objects that contain text formatting. You can then "apply" these objects to text field objects, so that the text they contain reflects that formatting. For more information about this new object, see Chapter 14, "ActionScript Objects."

Vertical text (new). Text within text blocks can now be vertically aligned—that is, with text flowing from top to bottom (or bottom to top) rather than side to side. For more information about vertical text, see Chapter 4, "Text."

Video objects (new). You can now import video clips into Flash and play them back *within* the Flash player (rather than in a separate window). You can even convert video clips into movie clip instances, allowing you to control them as such. For more information about using video, see Chapter 11, "Video."

In addition to the enhancements described here, Flash MX includes other minor enhancements and additions that we'll point out throughout the book. (Our discussions of these enhancements will be indicated by the MX Alert icon described in the Introduction.)

Interface

Now let's get acquainted with, and learn how to customize, Flash MX's interface—including the toolbars, menu bar, drop-down menus, panels, and so on (**Figure 2.5**). We'll take a broad look at the interface before we go on to examine each area in more detail. Some areas, such as the timeline and the layer interface, are covered in more depth in Chapters 9 and 10.

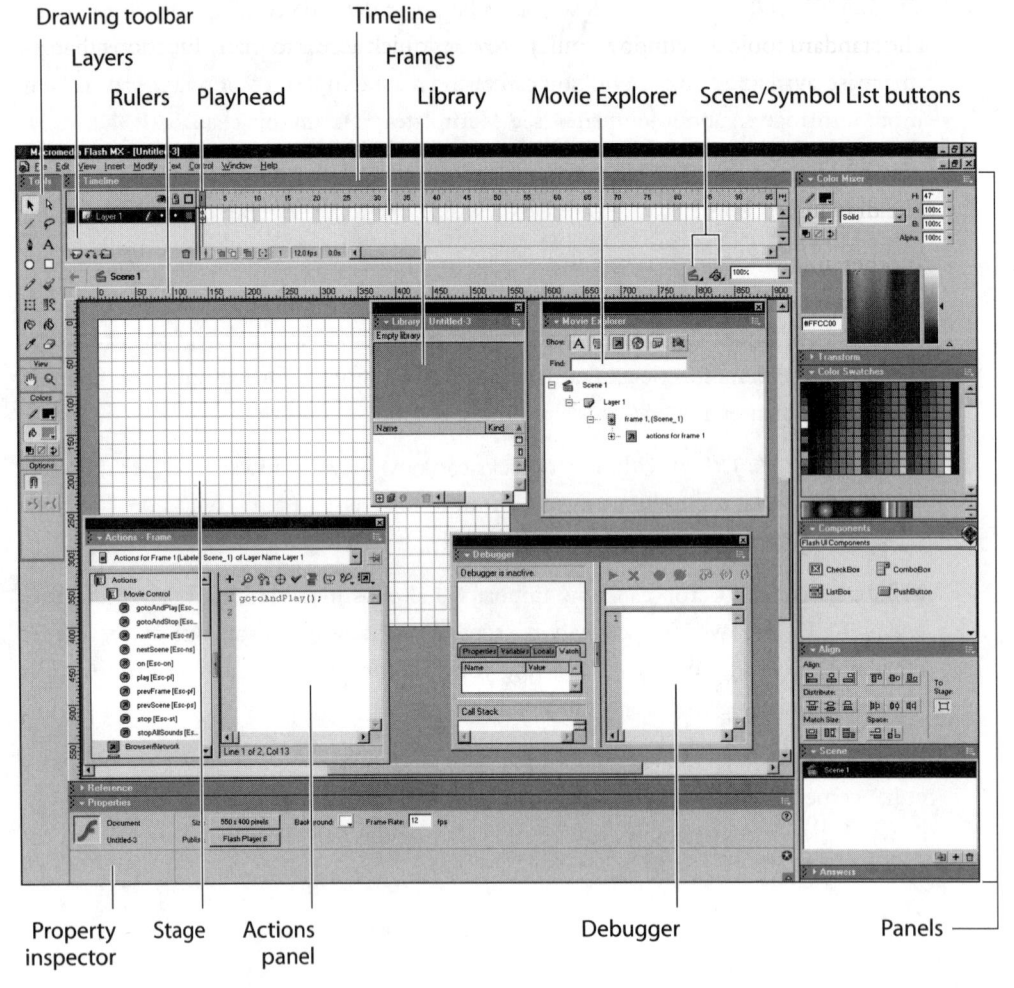

Figure 2.5
The various parts of the Flash interface.

Toolbars

The Windows version of Flash has two primary toolbars (standard and drawing), while the Macintosh version has just one, a drawing toolbar. This is one of the relatively few ways the Flash interface varies between operating systems.

NOTE *The Windows version also has a Status toolbar— a simple toolbar that appears at the bottom of the screen to indicate when the Number and Caps Lock keys are active.*

The standard toolbar (Windows only) provides quick access to many functions that are otherwise available from the menus. This toolbar includes buttons for creating new projects and for common commands such as opening, saving, printing, cutting, copying, and pasting.

The drawing toolbar includes a complete set of Flash's graphic tools.

Another important toolbar, the controller, provides VCR-like controls for playing, stopping, rewinding, and fast-forwarding your movie within the authoring environment (**Figure 2.6**). In Windows, the standard, drawing, and controller toolbars can be docked to a screen edge or float above it. On Macintosh computers, the toolbars cannot dock to the interface—they must always remain floating.

Figure 2.6
The controller lets you play, stop, rewind, and fast-forward your movie within the Flash authoring environment.

To dock a toolbar on another edge of the screen (Windows only):

1. Click and hold on an area on the toolbar with no buttons.

2. Drag the toolbar to an edge of the screen, then release.

TIP *To make a toolbar float separately on the screen, place the cursor over an area on the toolbar with no buttons. Then click while holding down the Control key. The docked toolbar will become a floating toolbar (**Figure 2.7**).*

NOTE *The drawing toolbar in Windows can only be docked on either the left or right of the screen.*

You can also turn toolbars on or off, to include them in or remove them from the interface.

To configure which toolbars are visible (Windows):

- From the menu bar, choose Window > Toolbars > then one of the following options to make a toolbar visible (indicated by a check) or invisible (unchecked).

    Main. Check this option to display the standard toolbar.

    Status. Check this option to display the status toolbar.

    Controller. Check this option to display the controller.

- From the menu bar, choose Window > Tools to make the drawing toolbar visible (indicated by a check) or invisible (unchecked).

To configure which toolbars are visible (Macintosh):

- From the menu bar, choose Window > Tools to make the drawing toolbar visible (indicated by a check) or invisible (unchecked), or Window > Controller to make the controller visible or invisible.

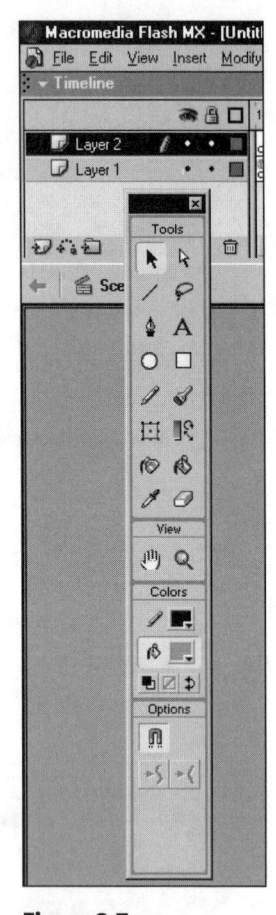

Figure 2.7
The Drawing toolbar can float over the Flash interface, allowing you to arrange your Flash desktop in whatever way works best for you.

Menu Bar

Flash's menus provide access to many of the program's commands. An arrow to the far right of a selection in the menu bar indicates a submenu, and keyboard shortcuts for menu commands are shown to the right of some commands. Most of these menu choices (and their uses) are discussed in various places throughout the book.

Context Menus

Flash includes several additional menus that are not available from the main menu bar. Known as *context menus*, they provide commands determined by the cursor's position. If, for example, you access a context menu while your cursor is over a frame, you'll be able to access commands pertaining to that frame (**Figure 2.8**). These menus are useful for quickly accessing appropriate commands without moving the mouse too much.

To access a context menu:

- Right-click (Windows) or Control-click (Macintosh) any of the following screen objects: toolbar, timeline frame, layer, stage (or an element placed on the stage), panel name, any Flash area that can accept or display text, Library panel preview window, library item, or any item in the Action panel or Movie Explorer windows.

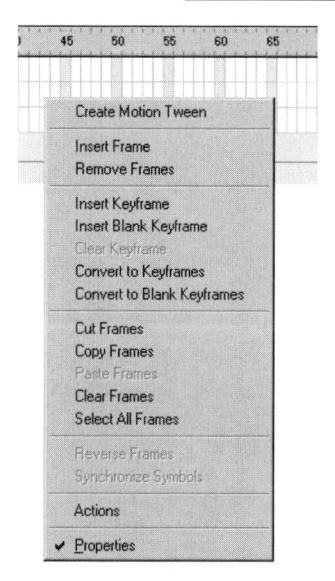

Figure 2.8
Placing your mouse over an item and then right-clicking (Windows) or Control-clicking (Macintosh) opens a context-sensitive drop-down menu relating to the item clicked.

Timeline

The timeline is where you'll work with the layers and frames that make up your project's content and animation. Layers represent the visual "stacking order" of elements in your animation, and the row of frames associated with each layer represents the way in which that layer's elements transform over time (**Figure 2.9**).

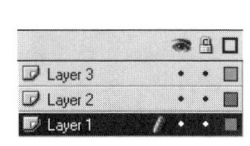

Figure 2.9
The order in which layers are "stacked" on the timeline relates directly to how their contents are displayed on the stage.

When you select a layer and then draw on the stage or import content there, that content becomes part of the selected layer. You move, add, change, and delete content from layers on various frames to create movement and animation. Using multiple layers, you can stack content layers over one another on the timeline to create a sense of depth in your animation—for example, making objects appear as if they're in front of a background. For more information about the timeline, see Chapter 10, "Building Movement Using Animation."

You can resize the timeline to display as few or as many layers as you wish, by increasing or decreasing the screen space allocated to the stage and work areas. You can also move the timeline from its default position at the top of the authoring environment, to any edge of the screen. Relocating the timeline this way lets you display either more frames or more layers of the timeline—whichever works best for your current task (**Figure 2.10**).

Figure 2.10
Moving the timeline to a different edge of the screen lets you view either more frames or more layers of the timeline—whichever is most efficient for what you're doing.

To resize the timeline:

1. Place your mouse over the line that separates the timeline from the stage. The onscreen cursor will turn into a double-sided arrow.

2. Click and drag the separating bar to a new location, then release.

To move the timeline to another edge of the screen:

1. Place the cursor over the area above the time ruler, then click and drag. An outline of the timeline will appear as you drag.

2. Once you've reached the edge of the screen, release the cursor. The timeline will dock there.

> **TIPS** *If you hold down the Control key as you drag, the timeline will not dock, even to areas where it normally would. This allows you to position it at any location on the interface.*
>
> *You can turn the timeline docking feature off altogether, if you find it interferes with the way you work. From the Edit menu choose Preferences, and check the Disable Timeline Docking option located on the General Preferences tab.*

Stage

The stage is the rectangular area of the Flash interface where you draw and place the content that will go into your movie. Content must be placed within this area to be exported as part of your final movie. The items displayed on the stage at any given time represent the contents of the current frame.

The stage—which Flash assigns a default color of white—also serves as the background for your movie, and will be visible in any screen areas of your final movie that are not covered by a movie element. The background color remains the same throughout the length of your movie. By importing a bitmap and placing it on the bottommost layer of a scene, so that it completely covers the stage, you can make the bitmap your stage background.

To change the background color of the stage:

1. From the Modify menu, choose Document to open the Document Properties dialog box.

2. Click the Background Color control button.

3. Using the Eyedropper tool, click a color on the palette or click anywhere within the Flash authoring environment, then click OK (**Figure 2.11**).

The stage color will change to the color you selected.

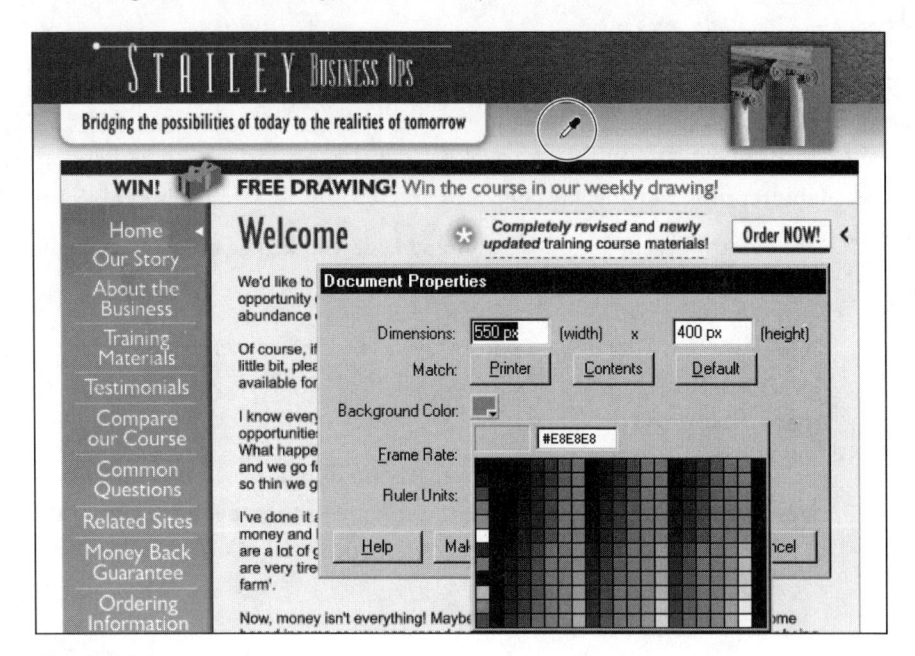

Figure 2.11
The Eyedropper tool lets you select colors from anywhere within the authoring environment.

Work Area

The work area is the gray area surrounding the rectangle that represents the stage. You can draw and place experimental elements in this area, and they will not be seen in your final movie. The work area is also commonly used as a starting or ending point of an animation where an object appears to slide in or out of a movie.

TIP *If you don't want to be distracted by elements in the work area, from the View menu choose Work Area. This will hide all elements except the stage and the empty work area. Repeating this step will "unhide" the elements, making them viewable again within the work area.*

Property Inspector

MX ALERT There's no doubt that software has become smarter. These days, lots of applications are able to anticipate what you need, and quickly display the appropriate tools. One of the more common ways of accomplishing this is with context-sensitive interface elements, such as toolbars that change and present different options depending on the currently selected element. This means the settings you need are never more than a click or drag away.

With Flash MX, Macromedia has introduced the Property inspector, a context-sensitive panel that replaces the functionality of numerous panels that existed in Flash 5, including the following:

- Stroke Panel
- Fill Panel
- Instance Panel
- Effect Panel
- Sound Panel
- Frame Panel
- Character Panel
- Paragraph Options Panel
- Text Options Panel

Tasks that previously could only be accomplished via several panels placed at different areas of the interface can now be carried out in a central location by means of this new "super" panel. All you have to do is select editable and configurable elements within the authoring environment, and the Property inspector will present you with the available options for working with them (**Figure 2.12**).

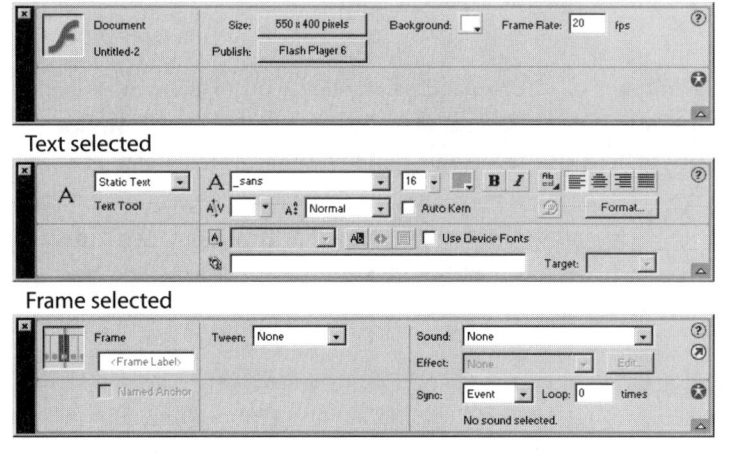

Figure 2.12 The options displayed on the Property inspector will change depending on the type of item currently selected in the authoring environment.

The following summarizes what the Property inspector allows you to do when you select a particular type of element. A more detailed discussion of each can be found in the appropriate sections of the book:

- **Strokes and fills.** Allows you to set stroke style, color, and size as well as fill color. In addition, since strokes and fills are shapes, text boxes are provided in order for you to move or resize them. For more information, see Chapter 3, "Graphics."

- **Text.** Allows you to set various text attributes like font color, style, and size, as well as paragraph settings such as justification, margins, and line spacing. For more information, see Chapter 4, "Text."

- **Symbol instances.** Allows you to set an instance's behavior, name, size, and position, and also add color and transparency effects. For more information, see Chapter 7, "Symbols."

- **Frame.** Allows you to set a frame label, adjust tweening properties, or adjust sound settings. For more information, see Chapter 10, "Building Movement with Animation."

- **Bitmaps, groups, videos.** Allows you to set position and size properties.

- **Drawing tools.** Depending on which drawing tool is selected, the Property inspector will usually display a set of options for configuring the tool. For more information, see Chapter 3, "Drawing."

- **Nothing.** When nothing is currently selected, the Property inspector displays options for configuring the overall settings of the current project, including its size, background color, and playback speed.

Panels

MX ALERT Flash now provides a number of screen panels that allow you to perform tasks for which you formerly had to use dialog boxes. These can streamline your workflow by providing a quick means of accessing—and adjusting—settings and parameters as you develop your project. You can use them to create colors and gradients; align movie elements; precisely move, rotate, and skew movie elements; and more. We'll discuss panels in greater depth later in this chapter, but first let's take a look at the individual panels Flash gives you to work with.

Info panel

The Info panel (**Figure 2.13**) shows the size, both vertical and horizontal, and the position, from the top and left sides of the stage, of the currently selected object. You can enter new values in the setting boxes and press Enter/Return to resize or reposition selected objects.

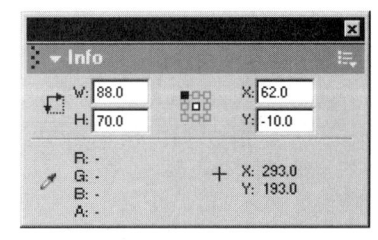

Figure 2.13
The Info panel contains information about the currently selected element, including its width and height as well as its X and Y coordinates

If you place the cursor over a stroke or fill that's not part of a group or symbol on the stage, its color and alpha values will be displayed.

The Info panel always displays the current position of the mouse in relation to the top-left corner of the stage.

Transform panel

The Transform panel (**Figure 2.14**) allows you to scale, rotate, and skew selected elements, with the degree of change determined by the value you enter into the appropriate setting boxes. When you select an element on the stage, the values that initially appear in the Transform panel reflect how much the element has been transformed from its original state. (For more information on how to use this panel, see Chapter 8, "Working with Elements on the Stage.")

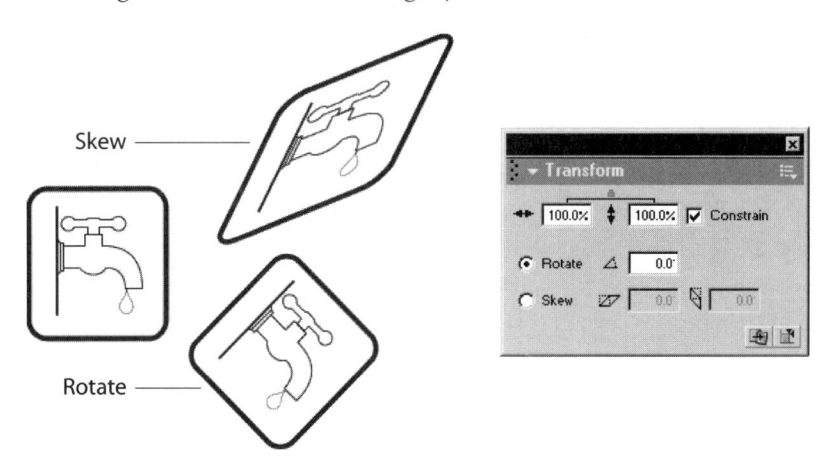

Figure 2.14
The Transform panel lets you rotate or skew selected elements on the stage.

Align panel

The Align panel (**Figure 2.15**) provides options for aligning, distributing, sizing, and spacing several selected elements in relation to each other. (For more information on how to use this panel, see Chapter 8, "Working with Elements on the Stage.")

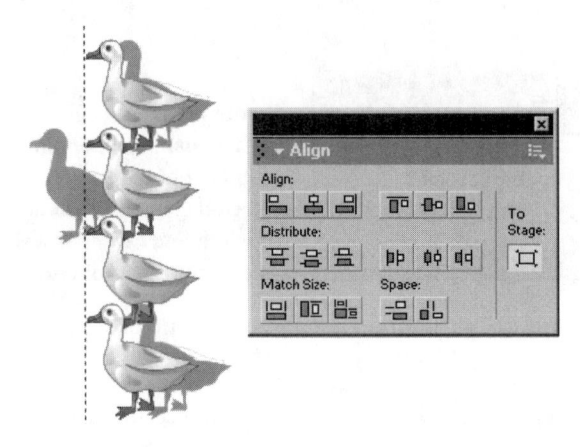

Figure 2.15
You can use Align panel settings to precisely align selected elements on the stage.

Color Mixer panel

The Color Mixer panel (**Figure 2.16**) allows you to create new colors or edit existing ones, using any of three modes: RGB, HSB, or Hexadecimal. In addition, this panel allows you to create and edit gradient fills. (For more information on how to use this panel, see Chapter 3, "Graphics.")

Figure 2.16
The Color Mixer panel is where you edit and create new colors and gradient fills.

Color Swatches panel

The Color Swatches panel (**Figure 2.17**) allows you to choose colors from predefined or custom palettes that you've created or imported. (For more information on how to use this panel, see Chapter 3, "Graphics.")

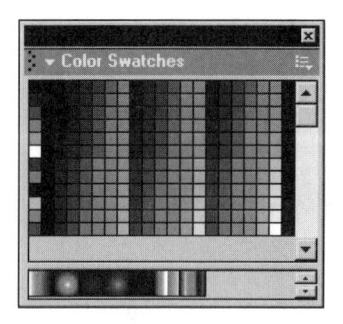

Figure 2.17
The Color Swatches panel displays all the colors and gradients available on the current palette.

Scene panel

The Scene panel (**Figure 2.18**) allows you to create, delete, reorganize, and switch between scenes in your project. (For more information on how to use this panel, see Chapter 10, "Building Movement with Animation.")

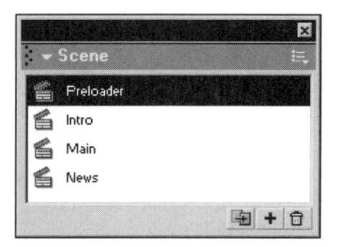

Figure 2.18
The Scene panel is where you create, delete, and organize scenes.

Components panel

The Components panel (**Figure 2.19**) contains a palette of components (interactive movie elements) that can be added to your projects. (For more information on how to use this panel, see Chapter 15, "Components.")

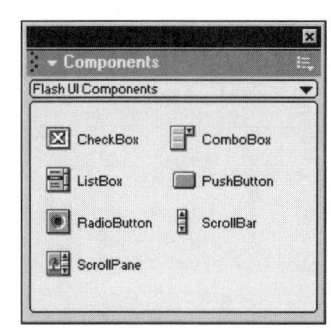

Figure 2.19
The Components panel contains interactive movie elements that can be used in your projects.

Component Parameters panel

The Component Parameters panel (**Figure 2.20**) allows you to set parameters for a component that's been selected on the stage. (For more information on how to use this panel, see Chapter 15, "Components.")

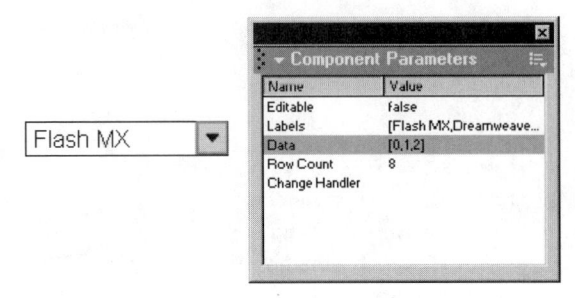

Figure 2.20
The Component Parameters panel lets you set various parameters for selected components, such as the ComboBox component shown here.

Accessibility panel

The Accessibility panel (**Figure 2.21**) allows you to add accessibility features to various movie elements, including names and descriptions that can be read aloud by a screen reader when an element is interacted with. (For more information on how to use this panel, see "Setting up Accessibility" later in this chapter.)

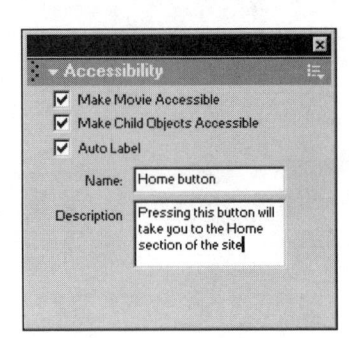

Figure 2.21
The Accessibility panel provides options for making elements in your movie accessible to people with visual disabilities.

Library panel

The Library panel (also known simply as the library) (**Figure 2.22**) is where you manage Flash project assets such as graphics, sounds, and video. For more information about the library, see Chapter 17, "Using the Library to Manage Your Assets."

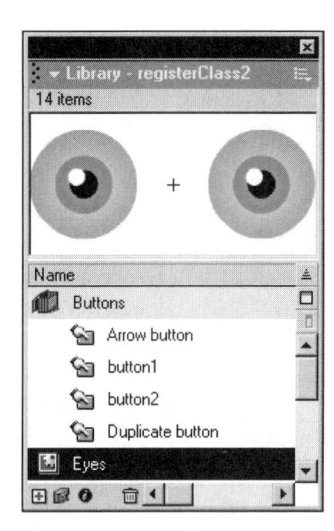

Figure 2.22
The Library panel is used to organize the various assets used in your project.

Movie Explorer panel

The Movie Explorer panel, or just Movie Explorer (**Figure 2.23**), offers a snapshot of your entire Flash project, including its construction (hierarchical structure) and the elements it contains. You can use this panel to quickly locate and navigate to specific elements within even the most complex projects. (For more information about Movie Explorer, see Chapter 18, "Using Movie Explorer to Manage Structure.")

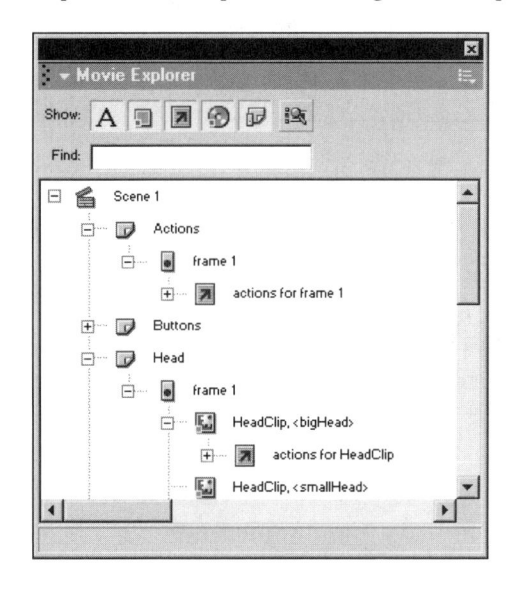

Figure 2.23
The Movie Explorer panel provides a snapshot view of your movie's elements and overall structure.

Actions panel

The Actions panel (**Figure 2.24**) is used for adding scripts to various elements in your movie. Clicking a frame, button, or movie clip makes the options on the Actions panel available. The panel provides quick access to ActionScript code elements, as well as tools to make the scripting process easier. You can work with it in normal mode or expert mode: Normal mode provides beginning scripters with more visual cues and automated features, while expert mode is for more advanced scripters, who want total control over how their scripts are created. (For more information on how to use this panel, see Chapter 12, "Getting Started with ActionScript.")

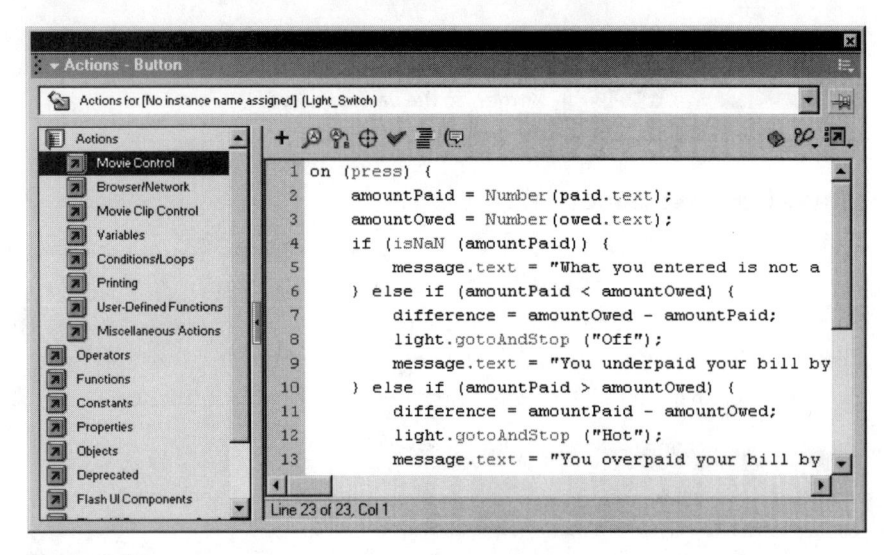

Figure 2.24
The Actions panel is where you work with ActionScript in order to add interactivity to your movie.

Debugger panel

The Debugger panel, or simply the Debugger (**Figure 2.25**), allows you to detect problems (or *bugs*, usually the result of ActionScript syntax errors) in your movie *before* you make it available to the world at large. Using the Debugger, you can test your movie far more thoroughly than would be possible by simply viewing it and interacting with it. Although the debugger may constitute overkill for simple projects, it can be a real time-saver (not to mention reputation-saver) for complex projects, or any time there's a lot on the line.

Chapter 2 Getting Started

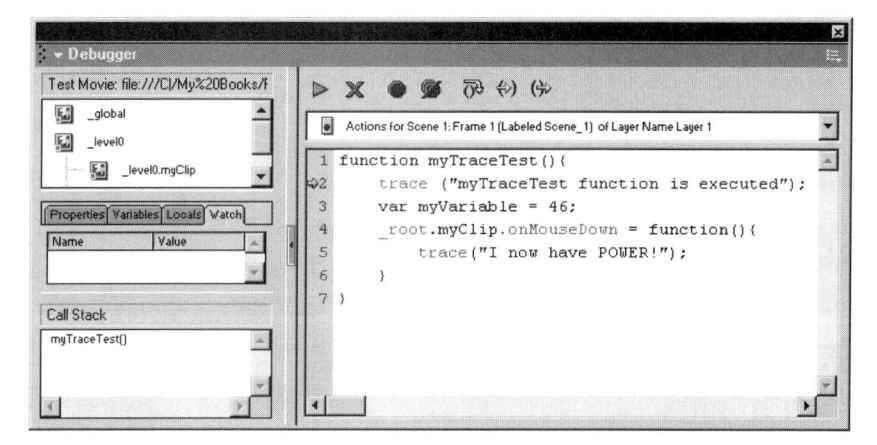

Figure 2.25
The Debugger panel enables you to test your project's interactive features.

Working with panels

MX ALERT

Let's first look at a few of the interface elements common to all panels (Figure 2.26):

- **Gripper.** The Gripper is an area of the panel that allows it to be clicked and dragged, or docked to other panels.

- **Title bar.** This contains the panel's name/function. Clicking here will either maximize (expand) or minimize (collapse) the panel—whichever state it's not currently in.

- **Options button.** Every expanded panel contains an Options button, which if pressed reveals a menu of commands. A given panel's Options menu may include a list of commands unique to that panel's function, as well as common commands found on every panel—including Help, Maximize Panel, and Close Panel

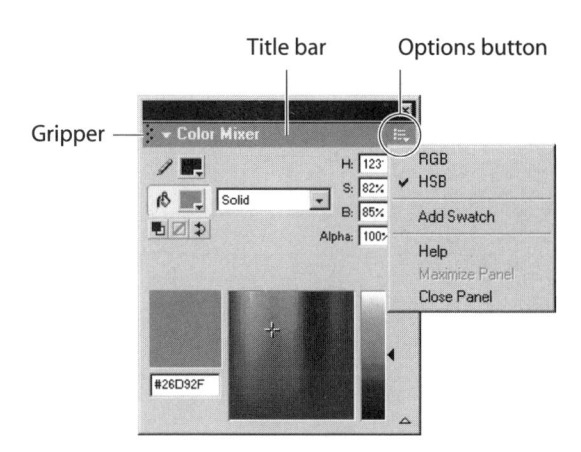

Figure 2.26
All panels in Flash have these interface elements in common.

Depending on your work style or available work space, customizing the various panels can greatly boost your productivity.

To display or hide individual panels:

- From the Window menu, select the panel you wish to display. Note that if a panel is already visible, a checkmark is displayed next to it, and performing this step will actually hide it.

Or

- Click the Panel Options button and choose Close Panel from the menu that appears.

To display, hide, or close all panels:

- Press the Tab key. This is a toggle-style command that either hides or displays all currently active panels, depending on their current state. This command is also available by choosing View > Hide Panels.

Or

- Choose Window > Close All Panels. This action closes all currently open panels.

Panels can be docked to sides of the interface, or to other panels in order to group panels with similar functions, so that less mouse movement is required to perform various edits on movie elements.

To dock panels:

1. Click the panel's gripper, and drag it to a side of the interface or on top of another panel.

   As you drag, a transparent gray outline of the panel will turn into a solid-black outline to indicate a dockable area (**Figure 2.27**).

Chapter 2 *Getting Started*

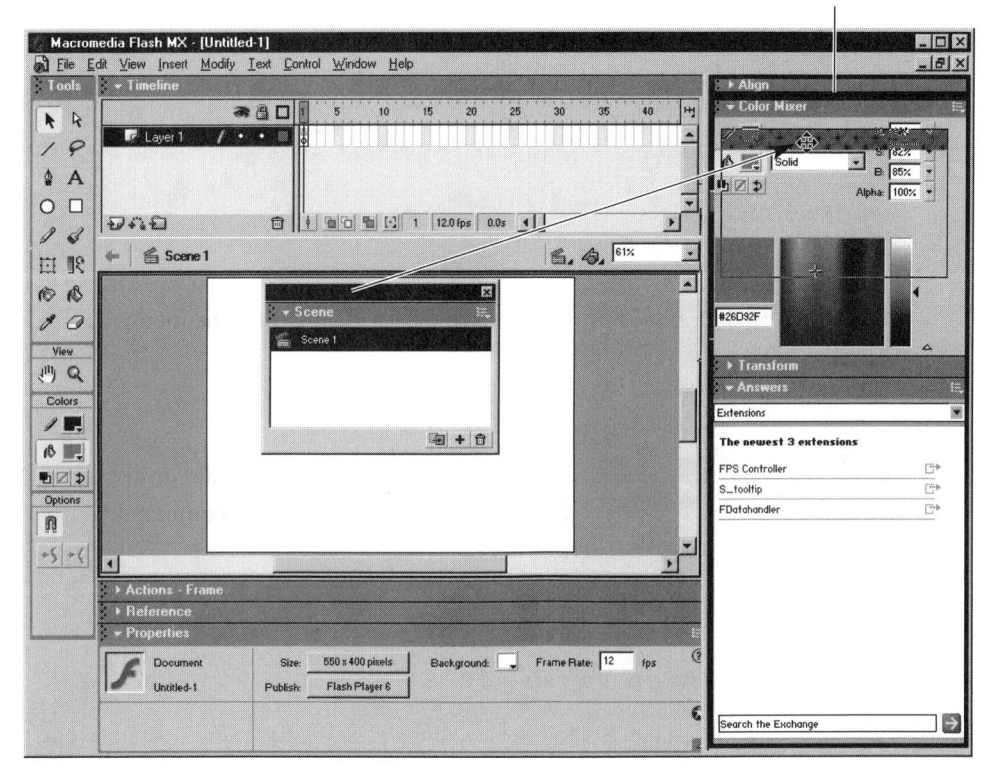

Black outline indicates dockable area

Figure 2.27
Dragging a panel onto a dockable area will cause a solid black outline to appear, indicating the location the panel will be docked to if the mouse is released.

    2. When the panel is over an area where you want to dock it, release the mouse.

        The panel you dragged will dock to the area where it was dropped.

        TIP *If you wish to disable the docking feature of panels (so that you can drag them around more freely), choose Edit > Preferences... and on the General tab select the Disable Panel Docking option.*

To undock panels:

- Click the gripper of the panel you wish to undock, drag it away from its current location, and then release the mouse.

    The panel you just dragged is now undocked.

47

Panel sets

If you've arranged panels in a manner you may want to use again in the future, you can save that panel layout with just a simple click of the mouse. These custom panel layouts, called *panel sets*, are great for reconfiguring the authoring environment to facilitate specific tasks.

To save a panel set:

1. Arrange panels as needed.

2. Choose Window > Save Panel Layout to open the Save Panel Layout dialog box (**Figure 2.28**).

3. Give your panel set a name and click OK.

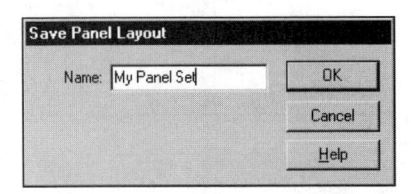

Figure 2.28
The Save Panel Layout dialog box.

To use a previously saved panel set:

◆ Choose Window > Panel Set to open a submenu listing the default panel layout, along with any custom layouts you have created.

NOTE *Flash comes preinstalled with several panel sets designed to maximize your work space, depending on your screen resolution.*

To delete a previously saved panel set:

◆ To delete a panel set, locate it in the Flash MX\First Run\Panel Sets folder, and delete it. Flash will remove the panel set from its list of choices the next time the folder is opened.

Grid, Rulers, and Guides

Flash offers several alignment tools that help you precisely place items on the stage as you develop your project. These include a grid overlay (the digital world's answer to graph paper), rulers, and guides (**Figure 2.29**). By learning how to make effective use of these tools, you can save numerous steps in laying out your design. (For more information on how to use these alignment tools, see Chapter 8, "Working with Elements on the Stage.")

Chapter 2 *Getting Started*

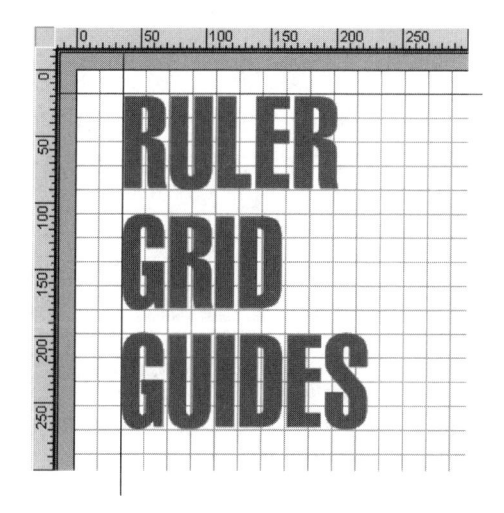

Figure 2.29
Flash's grid, guides, and rulers can help you place graphics accurately on the stage.

Scene and Symbol Buttons

The Scene and Symbol buttons (**Figure 2.30**) provide pop-up menus that allow you to quickly navigate to and edit scenes (sections of a timeline) or symbols (interactive elements) in your project.

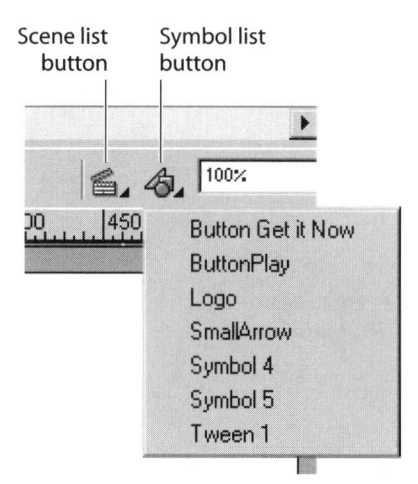

Figure 2.30
Clicking an item in the Scene or Symbol list takes you to the Editing window for that scene or symbol.

49

Options and Settings

No two people's work styles are identical—and thus the logic behind user-definable settings. You may feel that working within Flash is too slow under its current settings, or that you liked the features of an older version better, or that the "help" you're being offered just gets in the way. Whatever the case, Flash MX is easy to configure so that it works best for *you*.

Preferences

MX ALERT By choosing Edit > Preferences, you bring up the Preferences settings dialog box (**Figure 2.31**), which contains three tabs where you can set General, Editing, and Clipboard preferences. Let's take a look at each group of settings.

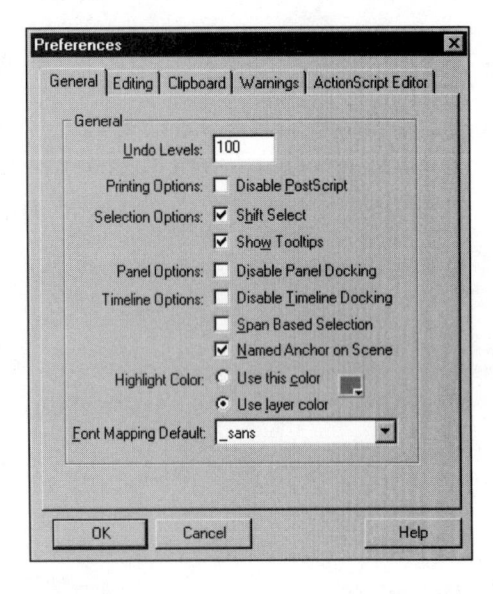

Figure 2.31
The Preferences dialog box.

General

The following settings are available on the General tab of the Preferences dialog box.

- **Undo Levels.** This setting allows you to set the levels of undo/redo available in Flash. The higher the setting, the more memory is required—and thus the more your computer's speed and performance may suffer. The maximum setting is 200. The default setting of 100 is usually more than adequate unless your system has memory to spare—in which case you may want to raise the setting to provide more breathing room for experimentation.

- **Printing Options—Disable Postscript (Windows only).** This option enables or disables PostScript output when printing to a PostScript printer.

- **Selection Options—Shift Select.** This option affects how elements are selected on the stage and work area. If it is checked, selecting an element will deselect other elements, and requires you to hold down the Shift key to select multiple objects. If this option is not checked, you need only click once on any element to add it to the current selection.

- **Selection Options—Show Tooltips.** Selecting this option will cause tooltips to appear when the mouse pauses on various parts of the interface. These tooltips contain information pertaining to the particular element that the mouse is paused over. If you find them annoying, you can deselect this option.

- **Panel Options—Disable Panel Docking.** Selecting this option will undock any currently docked panels, and also prevent panels from docking to the interface or other panels when you drag them around.

- **Timeline Options—Disable Timeline Docking.** When you disable Timeline Docking, the timeline visually detaches from the Flash interface and will remain free-floating (as is already the case with the Macintosh version)—similar to the effect of disabling panel docking.

- **Timeline Options—Span Based Selection.** This option will allow you to select entire spans of frames (such as those that make up a tween) simply by clicking on a single frame in the span (Flash 5 behavior). Disabling this option means you'll have to *double-click* a frame within a span in order to perform the same task.

- **Timeline Options—Named Anchor on Scene.** When this option is enabled, Flash will automatically place a named anchor (containing the scene's name) on Frame 1 of every new scene you create. For more information about named anchors, see Chapter 10, "Using Animation to Build Movement."

- **Highlight Color.** When you select on-stage elements such as groups, text, and symbols, a colored box is displayed around them to indicate that they have been selected. If you choose "Use this color" as the highlight color, the color you select from the accompanying color box will be used to identify selected elements on *all* layers. If you choose "Use layer color," the color of an element's selection box will reflect the color used to identify the layer on which it resides (**Figure 2.32**). Selecting the latter option allows you to quickly identify the layer on which a selected element resides. For more information, see Chapter 9, "Using Layers to Separate Content and Functionality."

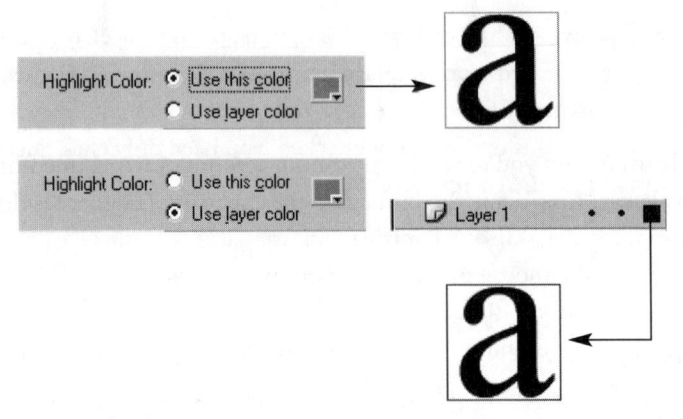

Figure 2.32
Selecting the "Use this color" option will cause the bounding boxes of selected objects to be displayed in the color shown. Selecting the "Use layer color" option will cause the bounding boxes of selected objects to match the color of the layer on which they reside.

- **Font Mapping Default.** This menu lets you choose the *default* font style that Flash will use to replace font styles it can't find on a user's computer—helpful if you're opening a FLA (Flash authoring file) on a computer other than the one on which it was created, and the font styles stored on that computer don't match the originals.

Editing

See Chapter 3, "Graphics," for a complete discussion of these options.

Clipboard

In Windows, when you cut or copy a graphic from Flash, two versions of the graphic are placed on the clipboard: one based on Windows metafile information (useful for pasting vector-based graphics into other vector programs), and a bitmap version for pasting into a bitmap program.

Windows settings for bitmaps on the clipboard include the following:

- **Color Depth.** Sets the color depth. The higher the value, the larger the graphic file will be when placed on the clipboard. Choose 32-bit color w/alpha to maintain any transparency settings in elements when they are placed on the clipboard.

- **Resolution.** Sets the resolution of the bitmap in pixels. Once again, higher resolution equals larger files.

- **Size Limit.** Allows you to set the maximum amount of RAM (memory) you wish to allocate for placing the bitmap on the clipboard. (Higher resolutions require more RAM.) Choose None if your computer has limited memory, as this option will set aside the specified amount of memory regardless of whether it's used.

- **Smooth.** Antialiases, or smoothes, the bitmap when it's placed on the clipboard.

- **Gradients.** This option sets the quality of the gradients in files created by copying Flash graphics (containing gradients) to the clipboard. Choose None for this setting if you will only be copying and pasting content within Flash itself. This will reduce the time it takes to copy complex drawings with color gradients.

- **FreeHand Text.** If you're pasting text blocks from a Macromedia Freehand document, select this option to keep them editable within Flash.

Macintosh settings for bitmaps on the clipboard include the following:

- **Type.** Lets you choose—when you're placing content on the clipboard—whether to convert objects cut or copied from Flash into bitmaps, or leave them as vector shapes.

- **Resolution.** Sets the resolution of the bitmap. A higher resolution means a larger file.

- **Including PostScript.** If you are exporting a PICT file as object- or vector-based, including PostScript information will optimize the graphic for PostScript printing.

- **Gradients.** Sets the quality of the gradients in PICT files created by copying objects to the clipboard. You should choose None for this setting if you will only be copying and pasting content within Flash itself. This will speed the time it takes to copy complex drawings with color gradients.

Warnings

Flash incorporates various warning messages to help prevent you from performing a task that could have a potentially undesirable outcome. These messages are usually displayed with OK/Continue and Cancel buttons, allowing you to confirm or cancel the task. Although such messages can be helpful to those still learning how Flash functions in certain situations, they can get annoying once you've got the hang of things. The Warnings tab of the Preferences dialog box lets you enable and disable the following warning messages, as you see fit.

- **Warn on Save for Macromedia Flash 5 compatibility.** Flash MX lets you save an MX-created authoring file as a Flash 5 authoring file, so that you can open and edit it in Flash 5. However, problems may arise if you have included MX-specific features that can't be read in Flash 5. To prevent this, the Save as Macromedia Flash 5 command removes all MX-specific functionality from the file in order to make the file compatible with Flash 5. If you enable this warning message, you'll be asked for confirmation any time you choose to delete MX-only functionality.

- **Warn on missing fonts.** If you attempt to open an authoring file that uses fonts not installed on your computer, this warning (when enabled) will alert you to this when you attempt to open the file. You'll also be presented with a dialog box for selecting substitute fonts.

- **Warn on loss of Expert Mode formatting.** The Actions panel allows you to enter code via two modes: Expert and Normal. Expert mode allows you to create and format scripts with great flexibility. Normal mode requires a rigid formatting structure. If you attempt to switch from Expert to Normal modes, Flash may reformat your code to fit Normal mode requirements. Enabling this option will ensure that you'll be asked to confirm before this occurs.

- **Warn on reading Generator content.** Since Generator is not supported in Flash MX, enabling this option will cause Flash to place an X over any Generator objects found when opening an older-version authoring file. Disable this feature, and you're left to figure it out on your own.

- **Warn on inserting frames when importing content.** When you import certain content (such as video clips and animated GIFs) Flash requires a certain number of frames to exist on the timeline in order for the import process to function correctly. If you enable this option, Flash will warn you whenever there aren't enough frames on the timeline, and will also offer to automatically insert frames.

ActionScript Editor

For a detailed discussion of these options, see Chapter 13, "Understanding ActionScript."

Display Options

Not all of us work on dual-processor Macintosh G4s. If we did, the tips in this section would be largely unnecessary. However, since so many of us remain "processor challenged," working on projects with numerous vector graphics can often get in the way of productivity—especially when you're constantly waiting for the screen to redraw after you edit a graphic.

Flash deals with processor constraints by providing different options for displaying elements within the authoring environment. These are available by choosing View > and then selecting from the following options (**Figure 2.33**):

- **Outlines.** If you choose this option, fills will not be displayed, and elements will only be displayed by their outlines (vector graphics) or bounding boxes (bitmaps). This will help speed the display of complex layouts.

- **Fast.** If you choose this option, all of a graphic's characteristics will be displayed, but smoothing (antialiasing) will be turned off.

- **Antialiasing.** This option smoothes graphics, but not text—the reason being that very small text can be harder to read if it's antialiased.

- **Antialias Text.** This option smoothes everything, including text. Although this is the most processor-intensive option, it's also the one most developers prefer.

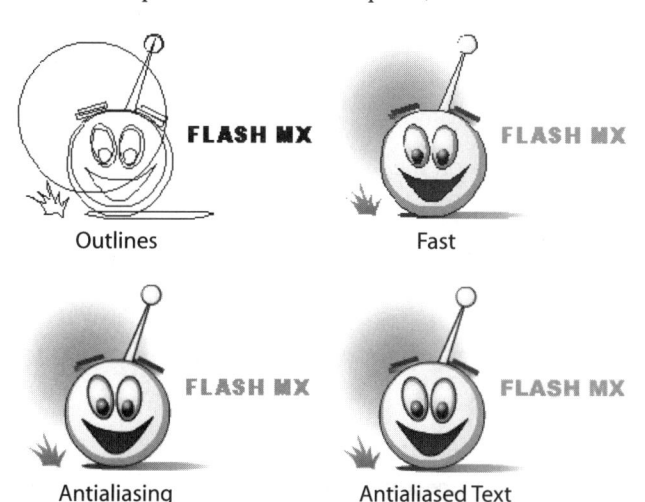

Figure 2.33 Samples of the various display options.

Viewing Options

In Flash, you can zoom in on the stage and work area for more detailed work, or zoom out for an overall look at your layout. These functions are available on the View pop-up menu, located just below the timeline (**Figure 2.34**). You can choose from a range of percentages to enlarge or shrink the stage. You can also choose the Show Frame option to make the entire stage visible, or the Show All option to make all objects on the stage and work area visible.

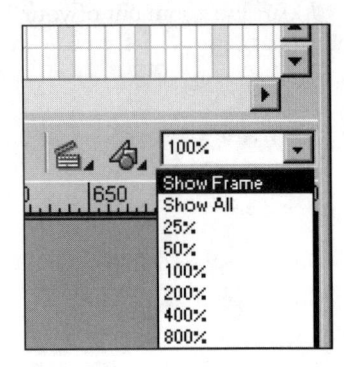

Figure 2.34
The View pop-up menu lets you choose a magnification percentage for viewing content on the stage.

TIP *These same options are available from the menu bar by choosing View > Magnification, then selecting a setting from the submenu that appears.*

Hand tool

The Hand tool serves only one purpose: to help you easily navigate the stage/work area, when you're zoomed in to your layout and want to move the display to an area not currently in view. (You can use scroll bars to accomplish the same thing, though they're not as efficient.)

To use the Hand tool:

1. Click the Hand tool button on the toolbar or press *H* on the keyboard. The cursor will turn into a small hand.

2. Place the cursor over any area on the stage or work area, then click and drag to navigate around your layout.

   TIPS *For this tool to work, you must make the work area viewable by selecting View > Work Area.*

   Any time you're drawing with another tool, you can hold down the spacebar to activate the Hand tool. Releasing the spacebar returns you to the tool you were previously using.

Magnifier tool

The Magnifier tool allows you to zoom in or out of your drawing, so you can work on fine details or back up to get a good overall look.

The Magnifier tool has two options, or modifiers:

- **Enlarge.** Allows you to click on the stage or work area to zoom in on your drawing, magnifying it by 200 percent.

- **Reduce.** Allows you to click on the stage or work area to zoom out of your drawing, reducing its current magnification by 50 percent.

TIP *To enlarge an area of the stage, select the Magnifier tool and then click and drag on the stage. The area you're defining will be identified by a thin, black outline. Release the mouse to complete your selection. Flash will automatically zoom in on the area you defined (**Figure 2.35**). (The maximum zoom amount is 2000 percent.)*

Figure 2.35
The Zoom tool lets you magnify portions of the stage so you can edit elements more precisely.

Keyboard Shortcuts

While menus, toolbars, and buttons all make working in Flash easier, sometimes there's no quicker or more efficient way to perform a task than with a keystroke or two. With Flash, you can use keyboard shortcuts for all sorts of actions, including cutting, copying, deleting, adding and removing scenes, adding and removing frames, hiding and displaying panels, and more.

Flash has also taken keyboard shortcuts to a new level, by giving users the ability to create or assign their own: You can set up a number of custom shortcuts, and save them together in a custom keyboard shortcut set. In fact, Flash comes with several sets of shortcuts already installed, including its default set and sets used in other graphics programs such as Photoshop, Fireworks, Freehand 9, and Illustrator.

You create and edit keyboard shortcuts using the Keyboard Shortcuts dialog box.

To open the Keyboard Shortcuts dialog box:

◆ Choose Edit > Keyboard Shortcuts.

First let's examine the interface (**Figure 2.36**), then look at the actual process of creating a keyboard shortcut set. The following options are available from the Keyboard Shortcuts dialog box:

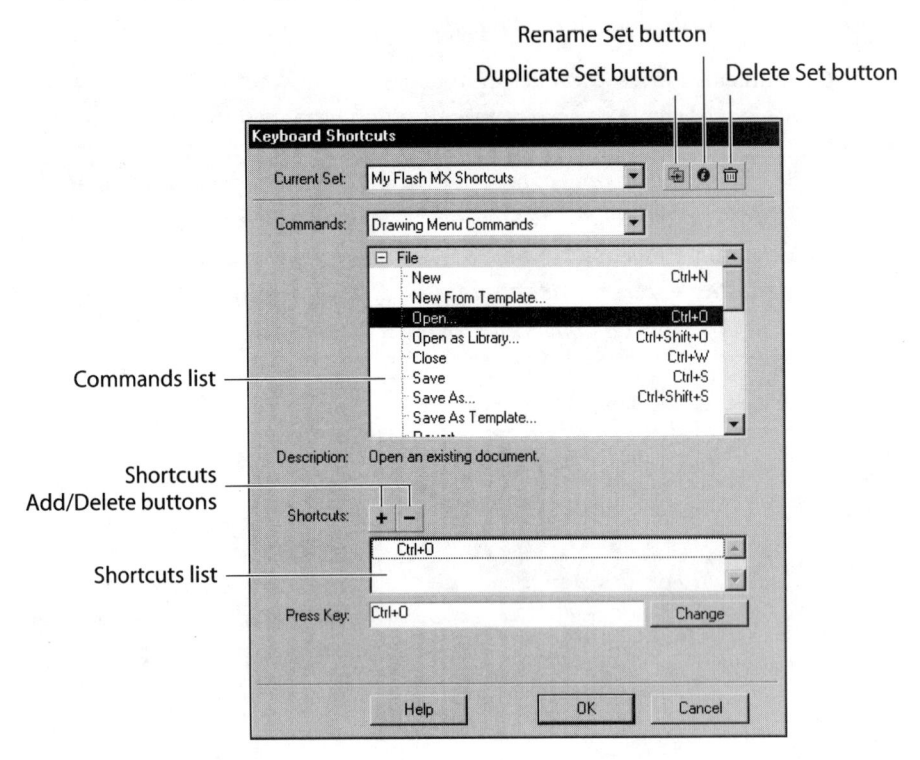

Figure 2.36
The Keyboard Shortcuts dialog box.

- **Current Set.** When you open the Keyboard Shortcuts dialog box, this drop-down box shows the set of keyboard shortcuts currently in use. You also use this box to select other shortcut sets.

- **Duplicate Set button.** Creates a duplicate set of shortcuts based on the currently selected set, which you can start with to create a new custom set.

- **Rename Set button.** Opens the Rename dialog box, where you can rename the currently selected set of shortcuts. You cannot perform this action on the default set of shortcuts.

- **Delete Set button.** Deletes the currently selected keyboard shortcuts. You cannot perform this action on the default set of shortcuts.

- **Commands.** There are four categories of shortcut commands: Drawing Menu Commands, Drawing Tools, Test Movie Menu Commands, and Actions Panel Commands (**Figure 2.37**). Selecting a category from the drop-down box will display all the commands that can be set for that category. The Commands list window, below the Commands drop-down box, will display a hierarchical list of commands for the selected category.

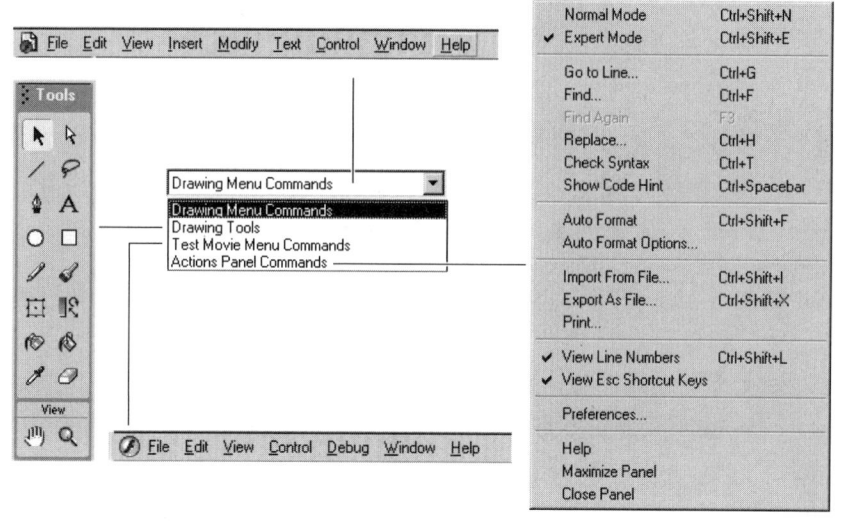

Figure 2.37
The Commands drop-down list lets you select a category of commands to work with.

- **Commands list.** This hierarchical list, which is available when a Command category is selected (see above), displays all available commands that can have associated keyboard shortcuts.

- **Description.** When a menu command is selected from the Commands list window, this area will provide a short description of the selected command.

- **Shortcuts Add/Delete buttons.** The "+" and "–" buttons let you add or remove shortcuts associated with specific commands. The Shortcuts window provides a list of shortcuts associated with the command currently selected in the Commands list window.

- **Shortcuts list.** Displays all keyboard shortcuts associated with the currently selected command in the Commands list window.

- **Press Key.** Displays either the key combination for the currently selected shortcut (as shown in the Shortcuts window), or any new key combination you have entered for the particular shortcut.
- **Change button.** Associates the key combination displayed in the Press Key box with the shortcut currently selected in the Shortcut window.

Now that you're familiar with the interface, let's look at how to create a custom keyboard shortcut set.

To create a custom keyboard shortcut set:

1. With the Keyboard Shortcuts dialog box open, select an existing set from the Current Set drop-down box.
2. Press the Duplicate Set button. From the Duplicate dialog box that appears, give this duplicate set a name and press OK.
3. From the Commands drop-down menu, select a command category.

   A hierarchical list of available commands for that category will appear in the Commands list.
4. Select a command from the Commands list.

   A description of the command appears in the Description area of the dialog box.
5. To associate a new key combination with the currently selected command, press the Add ("+") button. To change the key combination, select it from the Shortcuts list.

   TIP *You can also remove a keyboard shortcut, by selecting it in the Shortcut list and pressing the Remove Shortcut button (**Figure 2.38**).*

Figure 2.38
Selecting a shortcut from the Shortcut list, then pressing the Remove Shortcut button, removes the selected shortcut.

6. Select the Press Key text box, and then the key combination you want to associate with the currently selected command.
7. Click the Change button.
8. Repeat these steps to add or edit shortcuts associated with commands.
9. Click the OK button to close the dialog box and activate your new shortcut(s).

   TIP *Several shortcuts can be associated with a single command.*

To remove a custom keyboard shortcut set:

1. With the Keyboard Shortcuts dialog box open, click the Delete Set button.

2. From the Delete Set dialog box that appears, select the set you wish to delete and click OK.

To rename a custom keyboard shortcut set:

1. With the Keyboard Shortcuts dialog box open, click the Rename Set button.

2. Enter a new name in the Rename dialog box that appears, and click OK.

Setting Movie Properties

To begin a Flash project, you must specify the number of frames you want it to play per second (the frame rate), as well as its vertical and horizontal size. You should have a clear idea of what you want these settings to be right from the start, because changing them halfway into your project can adversely affect everything you've already created. For example, animated movie elements that look just right when viewed at 12 frames per second (fps) probably won't look so good at another frame rate. You can re-edit to compensate, but that can take a considerable amount of time. Better to plan ahead and get it right the first time.

To set your movie's properties:

1. Choose Modify > Document to bring up the Document Properties dialog box (**Figure 2.39**).

2. In the Frame Rate box, type the number of frames per second you would like your movie to play.

The default setting of 12 is sufficient for most projects. However, you can choose a higher or lower number if you wish. The higher the frame rate, the more difficult it will be for slower computers to play back your movie.

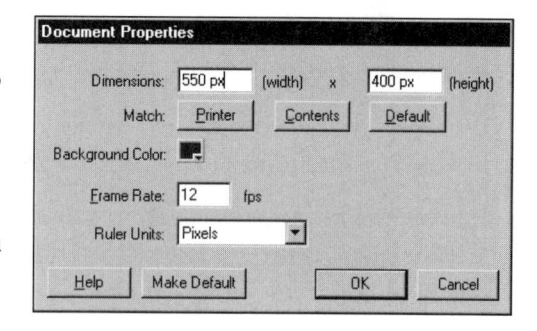

Figure 2.39
The Document Properties dialog box.

3. In the Dimensions boxes, enter values for the width and height of your movie's display.

The minimum width or height is 1 pixel; the maximum is 2880 pixels.

4. Choose a background color using the Background Color control.

The background color is also known as the *stage color*.

5. From the drop-down menu, choose a ruler unit.

The ruler unit you choose (inches, points, pixels, and so on) will affect all areas of the program where incremental values are used (for example, grid settings and Info panel settings).

> **MX ALERT — TIP** *Several of these settings can be adjusted directly from the Property inspector when nothing is selected on the stage*

Several other settings are available when you finally export your project to a movie. We'll look at those in more detail in Chapter 20, "Publishing."

Planning Your Project

Size Considerations

When you set your movie's dimensions, it's important to realize that a larger movie usually means viewers' computer processors will have to work harder. While your movie won't blow up their machines, the animated content you worked so hard to create may play back much more slowly than you intended.

You can balance the thrill of super-dazzling presentations with the limitations posed by processors, by making your movie smaller: All you need to do is change its dimensions. A full-screen animated movie will typically play much more slowly than the same movie displayed at half the size.

Once again, this isn't to say you can't ever consider creating full-screen presentations. Sometimes it's more important to use a lot of screen space than it is to employ a lot of animation.

If, for example, you're trying to showcase the beauty and craftsmanship of a product, you may want to adopt the full-screen approach and cut back on animation effects. However, if you're trying to evoke a sense of excitement through movement, you should probably employ smaller dimensions for your movie so that you can use animation without overburdening your viewers' processors.

Another option is to create a full-screen presentation with colorful, imaginative, and effective static (or nonmoving) content, and then just animate a portion of the screen at a time. If, for example, you wanted to display a large picture of your products that changed occasionally, you could still animate some content placed next to each product picture, providing a workable compromise.

Setting up Accessibility

MX ALERT If you're interested in learning Flash, chances are you want your message to reach as many people as possible—a bit of a challenge since the Web user population embodies a staggering array of cultures, operating systems, software, and skill levels. Fortunately, technology has been able to bridge some of the gaps that once limited information exchange. Among the users who have benefited are those with visual disabilities. Technological advancements have made it possible for visually impaired users to have their computers provide "spoken" information about what is on their computer screens (see "What Is a Screen Reader?" sidebar). Using what's known as *accessibility* technology, Flash MX enables you to make your Flash content more appealing to people with visual disabilities.

Making a Flash movie accessible simply means exposing elements within it—such as text fields and buttons—to any running screen reader. The screen reader will then read aloud information about the element, so that the user can interact with your movie without having to "read" it. For example, you might make a Home navigation button accessible by setting it up so that when the user places his or her mouse over it, the screen reader will say, "Home button. Click this button to return to the home page of this site."

There are a couple of stages involved in making a movie and its elements accessible to people with visual disabilities. The first thing you need to do is set up your movie so that it's accessible to this audience—which basically involves turning on or off accessibility for the movie and all its elements. After you've done this, you need to make individual

What Is a Screen Reader?

A screen reader is a software application that makes the Web (and many other resources) easier for blind and visually impaired people to use. It does this via computer-generated speech that reads out information about the elements on screen. On a typical HTML page, the screen reader will read back the information in the ALT tags of various screen elements, whenever the mouse is positioned over these elements. Screen readers can also read any text on the page. In a Flash movie, screen readers can read back both text in dynamic text fields, and any information about symbol instances that you've set up to be accessible.

Currently, users can only "view" Flash MX accessible content via Internet Explorer on Windows (with the Window Eyes screen reader installed). However, you can create accessible content with both the Windows and Mac versions of Flash MX.

You can download a demo version of Window Eyes from www.gwmicro.com.

elements, such as buttons and movie clips (if universal accessibility is enabled for the movie), accessible. This enables you to decide which elements will be made available to the screen reader.

We'll look now at the process of setting up your entire movie for accessibility. For information on setting up individual elements, see Chapter 7, "Symbols."

To make your movie accessible:

1. Deselect everything (click on an empty portion of the stage.)

2. Choose Window > Accessibility to open the Accessibility panel (**Figure 2.40**).

3. Check the Make Movie Accessible option to expose elements of your movie to a screen reader. If you deselect this option, screen readers will not function with your movie.

4. Check the Make Child Objects Accessible option to allow the screen reader to make child objects (movie elements inside of movie elements) accessible.

   Flash allows you to place movie elements, such as buttons, inside other movie elements, such as movie clips—thus converting the buttons into child objects of the movie clip (which is called the *parent*). This option allows such child objects to be accessible, which means they can convey information to a screen reader.

5. Check the Auto Label option to automatically associate text with a symbol that it is placed close to, or actually in contact with.

   For example, if a button is close to or touching the text "Home page," Flash will detect this and read that text aloud when a user's mouse interacts with the button (**Figure 2.41**).

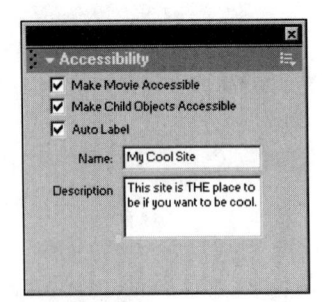

Figure 2.40
The Accessibility panel.

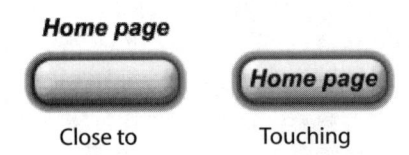

Figure 2.41
When you select the Auto Label option on the Accessibility panel, any text close to or touching a symbol, such as a button, will be read aloud when that symbol is interacted with.

6. In the Name and Description boxes, give your movie a name (such as My Cool Site and description.

7. Close the panel when finished.

Your movie is now accessible to visually impaired users. To find the accessibility settings for individual elements (such as text, buttons, and movie clips), simply select them and make adjustments from the Accessibility panel. For more information, see Chapter 7, Symbols."

MX ALERT { *ActionScript* } *You can use ActionScript to check whether the person viewing your movie has a screen reader running on his or her computer. For example,* `myVariable = Accessibility.isActive` *will set the value of* `myVariable` *to* `true` *if a screen reader is detected, or* `false` *if it is not. This will enable you to provide the user with a version of your movie that is customized for the visually impaired (fewer to no moving elements, little sound content in order to minimize conflict with the screen reader's "voice," and so on).*

Templates

MX ALERT While creating multisensory interactive experiences from scratch is something to be proud of, there's also something to be said for saving lots of time. You can accomplish the latter by using templates. These partly developed Flash authoring files allow you to start a project with most of its elements in place—so that all *you* need to do is tweak the file a bit to create a unique movie of your own. Templates can be either complex (containing layers, graphics, sounds, and even scripts) or simple (containing nothing more than several layers and stage dimensions set to a specific size).

Flash MX comes with a number of pre-installed templates, ready for you to tweak and configure to your heart's content. There are templates for creating banners, presentations, PocketPC content, and more; most include instructions for using and configuring them. You can also create your own templates, which we'll discuss shortly.

To start a new project from a template:

1. Choose File > New From Template…

   The New Document dialog box will appear (**Figure 2.42**). This dialog box includes four sections: Category, Category Items, Preview, and Description. The Category section contains a list of the types of templates that are available for the job at hand. You can choose from categories such as Ads, Mobile Devices, Presentations, and others.

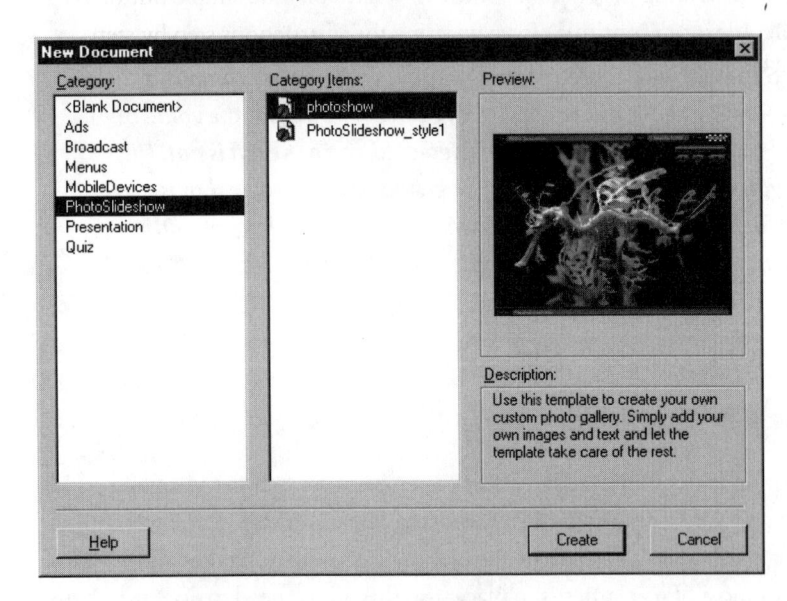

Figure 2.42
The New Document dialog box.

2. Click to select one of the categories.

   A sublist of items will appear in the Category Items section of the dialog box, with the first item on the list automatically selected. This is a list of actual template files. When you select an item from this list, the Preview window will display a thumbnail of Frame 1 of the template, and the Description box will display a brief description of the template's use.

3. Click to select a choice from the Category list, then press the Create button.

   After a few seconds of processing, Flash will open the template you selected, in the authoring environment.

4. Follow the instructions provided to configure the template for your own use.

   The instructions are placed on a special layer of the timeline, called a *guide* layer. Although you can see the content of these special layers within the Flash authoring environment, this content is not exported in the Flash movie you create (and thus not visible within the movie). Guide layers contain content that is only saved with the authoring file, not exported when the project is turned into a SWF file. For more information about guide layers, see Chapter 10, "Building Movement with Animation."

NOTE *If you don't see instructions, make sure the Guide layer is not hidden (indicated by a red X in the "eye" column of the layer).*

In addition to providing instructions, most templates include simple buttons (for example, Next or Continue) for navigating the instructions step by step (**Figure 2.43**).

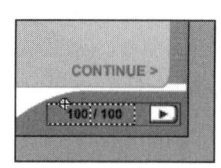

Figure 2.43
Most templates provided with Flash MX contain navigation buttons to help you through the instructions for customizing them.

If you really want to save time, creating your own templates may be the answer. Say you typically use particular dimensions, playback speed, and initial layer structure (for sounds, scripts, buttons, and so forth) to begin all of your Flash projects. By creating a template that contains these settings, you can begin your project with all these elements already in place—a true time-saver. Templates are especially convenient when you need to create a series of Flash movies that employ common structures and content. And if you're really enterprising, you can even create custom templates and sell them to other Flash producers.

To create your own template:

1. Create the file you wish to use as a template.

2. Choose File > Save As Template...

This will open the Save As Template dialog box (**Figure 2.44**).

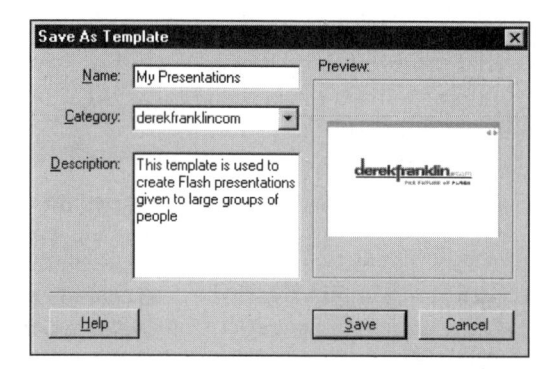

Figure 2.44
The Save As Template dialog box.

3. In the Name box, give this template a short but descriptive name.

4. In the Category box, either select a category from the drop-down menu, or manually enter a name to create a new category.

   A category name cannot contain more than 31 characters and must not contain any special characters (such as question marks, asterisks, equal signs, and so on).

5. In the Description box, type a summary of the template's use.

6. Press Save.

   If you chose to place your template in an existing category, it will be available from that category when you select the New From Template… command on the File menu. If you've created a new category, that new category will appear in the same dialog box, with the template appearing when you select your new category from the list.

Getting Help

Given all that Flash MX can do, it's not surprising that working with it can sometimes be daunting, even with Macromedia's best efforts to keep the work process as intuitive as possible. Luckily, there are an abundance of Flash references and help files—both within the application and on the Web—to help us get the most out of our favorite application.

Help Menu

The Help menu (**Figure 2.45**) is the first place to go for information about Flash MX. From here you can access not only help files, but information about what's new, lessons, Macromedia's site, and more. Let's take a look at these options.

- **Welcome.** This opens a Flash MX–created panel that provides a general starting point for getting up and running with Flash MX. It provides links to content geared toward users who are updating to Flash MX from older version (What's New), as well as new users (Take a Lesson, Take a Tutorial, and Read the online Help).

- **What's New.** This opens another Flash-based panel with information about new features in Flash MX. The content is designed to assist both designers

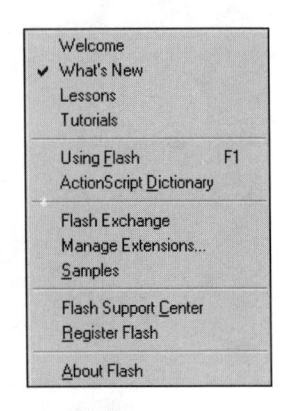

Figure 2.45
The Help menu offers a wide range of resources to help you become proficient with Flash MX.

(looking for design-specific enhancements) and developers (looking for interactive enhancements). You can navigate within this panel (as well as within some of the others) via the buttons at the bottom of the panel (**Figure 2.46**).

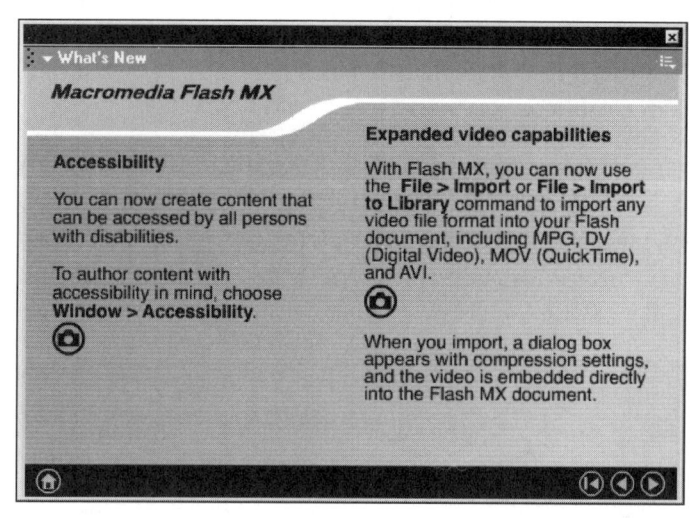

Figure 2.46
Navigation controls for Flash's help panels are located at the bottom of the panel.

- **Lessons.** This opens another panel with a list of short lessons focusing on how to perform various tasks using Flash MX.

- **Tutorials.** This opens a panel offering a series of tutorials that will help you not only learn Flash MX, but also familiarize yourself with the workflow involved in creating a project. Tutorials are more extensive than lessons, and involve actually creating a project rather than simply learning how to perform various tasks.

- **Using Flash.** This opens Flash's browser-based users manual/documentation, where you can find information about Flash MX via a table of contents, index, or search utility.

- **ActionScript Dictionary.** This opens Flash's browser-based ActionScript dictionary, where you can find information about ActionScript via a table of contents, index, or search utility.

- **Flash Exchange.** This opens the Macromedia Flash Exchange in your default browser. This Web site contains extensions (additions and enhancements) that can be installed to extend Flash MX's capabilities. For more information about extensions, see Chapter 15, "Components."

- **Manage Extensions.** Opens the Macromedia Extensions Manager. For more information about the Extensions Manager, see Chapter 15, "Components."

- **Samples.** Opens an HTML page containing links to sample Flash MX movies that demonstrate some of the program's capabilities. These movies were automatically installed on your hard drive when Flash MX was installed; thus, you can view them offline.

- **Flash Support Center.** Opens the Flash Support Center Web site (**Figure 2.47**), which includes a wealth of information about Flash MX: answers to technical questions, unique ways of using Flash MX, projects, lessons, tutorials, articles, downloads, documentation (beyond what's provided with the installed program), and a lot more. Once you discover this site, chances are you'll be back often.

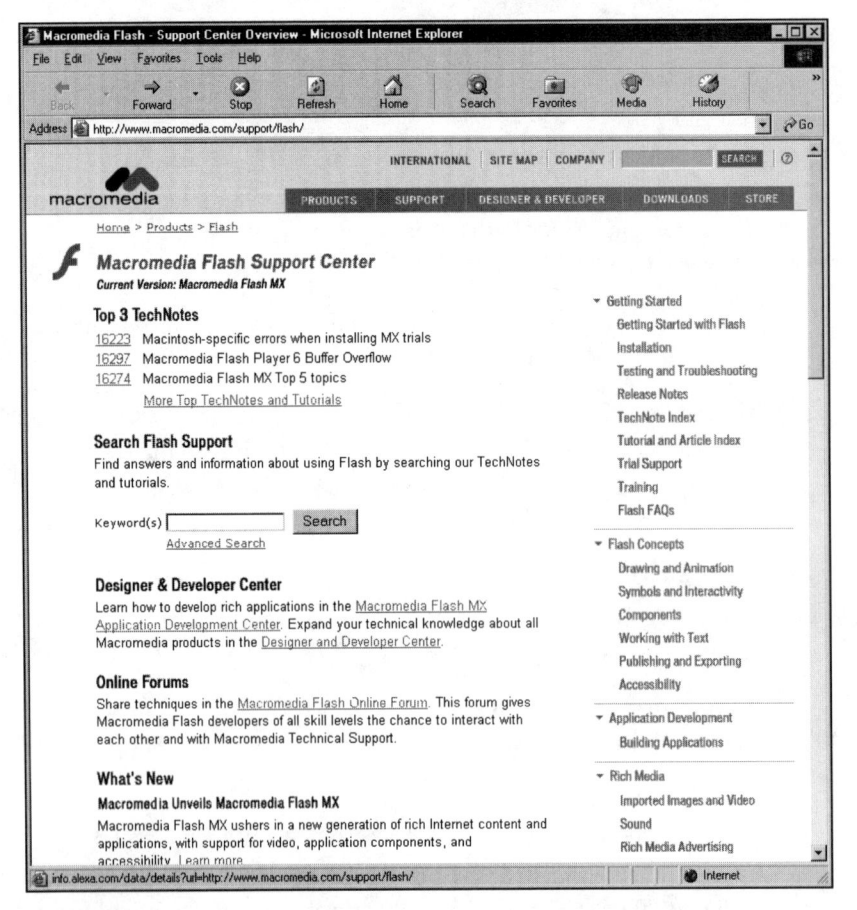

Figure 2.47
The Flash Support Center Web site contains a wealth of searchable content dealing with issues that may arise while you're working with Flash MX.

TIP When you visit Macromedia's site, be sure to visit the Flash MX Developers Center (www.macromedia.com/desdev/mx/flash/), which provides information, projects, and movies demonstrating how to use Flash MX and supporting technologies (including XML, ColdFusion, Flash Remoting, and Flash Communication Server).

- **Register Flash.** Opens the Macromedia Software Registration Center, where you can register your Flash software online.

- **About Flash.** If you ever wanted to know whom to thank for creating Flash MX, this is the place: It opens a window with scrolling credits, naming the people who had a hand in creating Flash MX.

Reference Panel

The Reference panel is an authoring environment resource that provides quick access to information about ActionScript. For more information about this panel, see Chapter 12, "Getting Started with ActionScript."

Answers Panel

The Answers panel (Window > Answers), which itself is a Flash movie, provides concise, up-to-date information as well as links to Macromedia's Web site. You can go to this panel to quickly determine whether there's any new content that you might want to view—without having to first open your browser, navigate to Macromedia's site, and manually check for updates. You can thus make sure you get timely information on the latest tech notes, application extensions, and more (**Figure 2.48**).

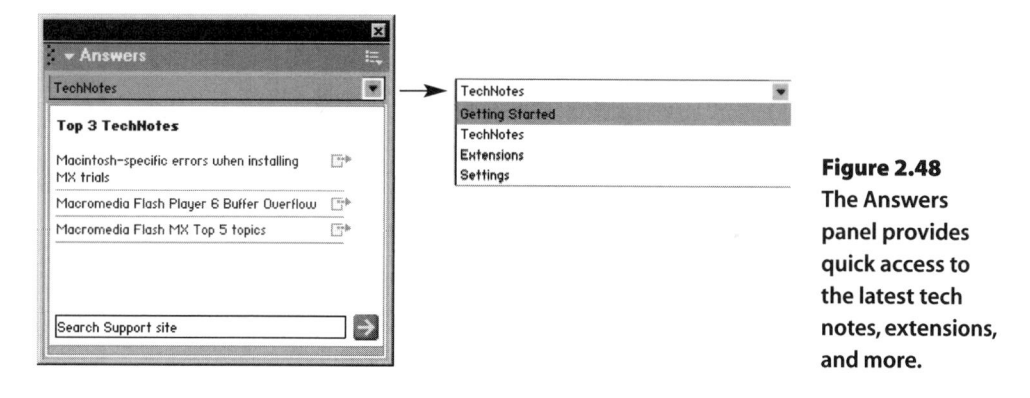

Figure 2.48
The Answers panel provides quick access to the latest tech notes, extensions, and more.

About the Video Tutorials

And now, it's initiation time: Time to get acquainted with the video tutorials. These video tutorials—included on the CD-ROM that accompanies this book—demonstrate how to perform various tasks within Flash MX. They're the best way to apply what you've learned in each chapter. You can go through each tutorial with Flash open on your computer, then pause the tutorial to perform the tasks it describes yourself. Naturally, you can replay sections as many times as you need to grasp a given concept before moving on.

For information about the accompanying CD, how to use the tutorials, and the demo software included, see Appendix A at the back of this book.

The CD includes the following tutorials for this chapter, along with a source file for the first one:

- ***Introducing Flash.*** This tutorial will introduce you to the Flash workflow process, and guide you through the steps of creating your first interactive Flash movie. You'll be able to see how drawing tools work, create movement, assign variable names for interactive effects, and test your project. This tutorial will give you an overall feel for authoring in the Flash environment.

- ***Creating a Custom Keyboard Shortcut Set.*** This tutorial guides you through the process of creating a custom keyboard shortcut set for use in our project.

2

Movie Elements

Graphics	75
Text	135
Sound	167
Bitmaps	193
Symbols	223
Working with Elements on the Stage	255

A **FLASH MOVIE IS MADE** by combining a number of disparate items to create a coherent, interactive experience. These elements can include vector graphics, sound clips, bitmap images, and special movie elements, called symbols, which are indigenous to Flash. In the pages that follow, we'll focus on creating and importing these various elements, how they work in the context of a Flash movie, how you can use them creatively, and how you can optimize them to create engaging interactive content without burdening your audience with long downloads.

Graphics

CHAPTER 3

Ready to play the role of production designer? The person charged with creating a project's look and feel plays an essential role in a movie's development. After all, without their spectacular visual effects, even such wildly successful films as *Spiderman* and *Star Wars* would be little more than exciting soundtracks.

In this chapter we'll show you how to use Flash's powerful drawing tools to create stunning animated, interactive works of art. With these tools, you can draw perfect squares and rectangles, paint with myriad colors, and erase your mistakes—in short, everything you can do with real-world drawing tools, and more. If you can point and click a mouse, you can create graphic elements in Flash. Nor does its ease of use come at the expense of graphic sophistication. The artwork you create with Macromedia Flash can be as complex as anything you could produce using the leading vector art tools on the market.

You may notice, however, that Flash handles some aspects of graphics creation differently than other drawing programs. Although this may seem awkward at first, once you've grown accustomed to the tool set, you may just decide that the Flash way is the only way.

As mentioned earlier, Flash drawing tools create vector graphics—mathematical equations that your computer translates and displays as drawn objects. This equation contains all the information your computer needs to display the object accurately, including its size, shape, and position; whether it has a fill (and if so, what color); and whether it has an outline (and if so, what type). The best part of this process is that you never see the mathematical equation; all you see is the computer representation of the equation. If only all math were so easy.

Let's take a look at how Flash's tool set works.

What you'll learn...

How to work with Flash's drawing tools

About pen and drawing preferences

How to work with strokes and fills

How to import vector graphics

Ways to optimize graphics

About working with color

Tools and Options

The Flash drawing toolbar is what you use to create graphic elements within Flash (bitmaps and graphics from other programs are imported). The toolbar consists of two areas: the individual tool buttons, and the various options associated with them (**Figure 3.1**). When you click a tool, it becomes active, displaying a set of options you can use to adjust its settings: Select the Eraser tool, for example, and only those options that apply to it will appear in the Options section of the toolbar.

This type of context-sensitive interface makes numerous settings readily accessible, without requiring you to access the menu bar—a visually efficient, timesaving feature that surprisingly few other programs incorporate. In addition, when you select a tool or an object on the stage, the Property inspector display changes to indicate settings that you can adjust for the currently selected item (such as fill and stroke colors); more on this later.

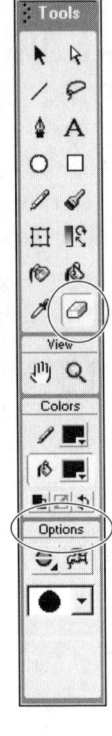

Figure 3.1
Many drawing tools have associated options, which appear at the bottom of the toolbar when you click a tool's button.

We'll look now at Flash's graphic tools and options, in the order they appear on the toolbar. Later we'll explore drawing tasks in depth. Because one of the toolbar features—the Text tool—has so many unique settings and uses, we'll discuss it separately in the next chapter.

Before getting started, we should clarify some of the terms we'll be using: *Simple shapes* refers to the initial state of the graphic elements (lines and fills) you create with the drawing tools. Groups, text, symbols, and bitmaps are considered *graphic objects* (more on this later). Both simple shapes and objects make up what are known as *movie elements*, or simply elements (**Figure 3.2**). Also, note that the terms *lines* and *strokes* are used interchangeably, as are the terms *fill*, *filled shape*, and *outline*.

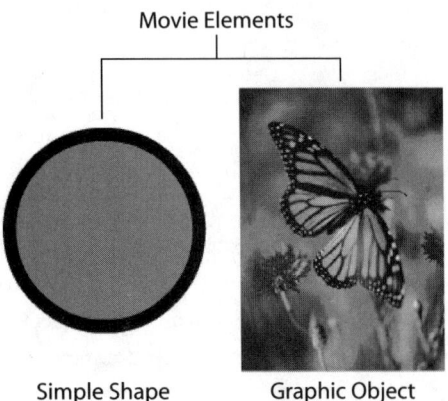

Figure 3.2
All graphical movie elements are made up of simple shapes and graphic objects.

The letter in parentheses following each tool name below represents a keyboard shortcut: Simply press that letter on the keyboard to quickly switch between tools.

Arrow Tool (V)

There's a reason this is the first tool in the toolbar: It's the one you'll use the most. The Arrow tool acts as your "hands" in the Flash environment, letting you grab, select, and move your graphics (**Figure 3.3**). However, you must select an object before you can do anything with it—and you usually do so by mouse-clicking it.

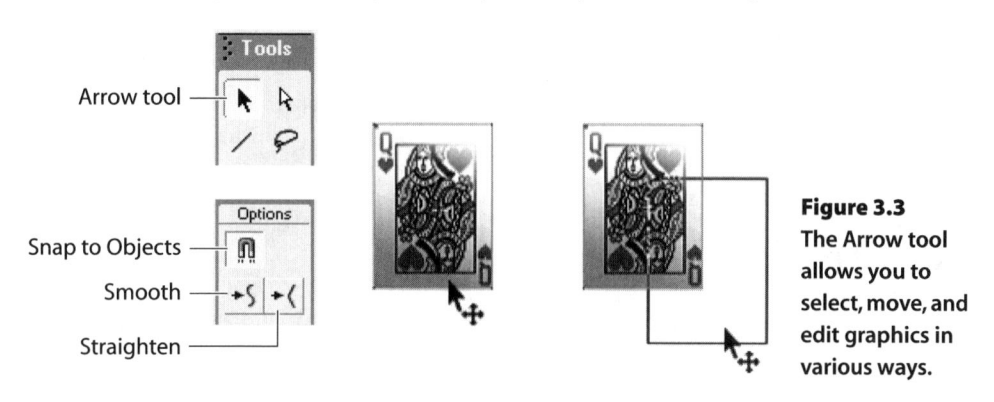

Figure 3.3
The Arrow tool allows you to select, move, and edit graphics in various ways.

The Arrow tool includes the following options:

- **Snap to Objects.** If you choose this option, objects that you draw, move, rotate, or resize will "snap" into place next to other lines or shapes on the stage, making it easy to place your movie elements precisely. For more on this feature, see Chapter 8, "Working with Elements on the Stage."

- **Smooth.** Allows you to smooth lines or simple shapes on the stage.

- **Straighten.** Allows you to straighten lines or simple shapes on the stage.

TIP *All of the Arrow tool option displays, except Snap to Objects, will be grayed out until you select an object.*

MX ALERT **NOTE** *In Flash 5, the Arrow tool was used to rotate and scale objects. In Flash MX, you use the new Free Transform tool to accomplish these tasks (see discussion later in chapter).*

Subselect Tool (A)

The Subselect tool (**Figure 3.4**) is similar to the Arrow tool except that instead of selecting an entire object, the Subselect tool allows you to select and work with anchor points that exist along the shape's *path*, or outline. We'll take a closer look at this later in the chapter.

Subselect tool

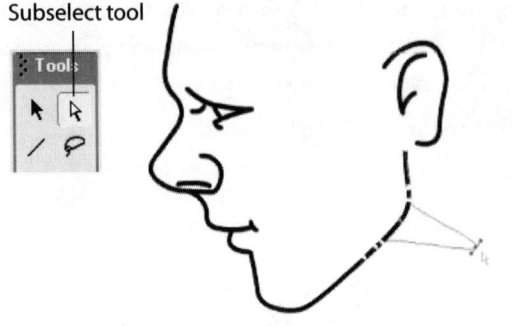

Figure 3.4
The Subselect tool is used for working with anchor points on a path.

Line Tool (N)

The Line tool is as straightforward as its name suggests: You use it to draw straight lines (which are initially simple shapes), employing the current settings on the Property inspector (**Figure 3.5**).

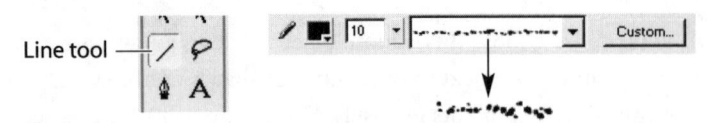

Line tool

Figure 3.5
The Line tool and Property inspector work in tandem when you draw lines: The Line tool creates the line, but the Property inspector allows you to configure its attributes.

TIP *To color a line with a gradient or even a bitmap fill, you must first convert it into a fillable area by selecting the line with the Arrow tool, then choosing Modify > Shape > Convert Lines to Fills.*

Lasso Tool (L)

The Lasso tool is similar to the Arrow tool, in that you use it to select simple shapes on the stage. Its function is a bit more specialized, however. With the Lasso tool, you define odd-shaped areas inside simple shapes to select them for editing. You also use this tool to select colors in bitmaps—if the bitmaps have been broken apart first (**Figure 3.6**).

Figure 3.6
The Lasso tool lets you select odd-shaped areas in simple shapes.

The Lasso tool includes the following options:

- **Magic Wand.** This is the default setting; it allows you to select odd-shaped areas inside simple shapes.

- **Magic Wand Properties.** Allows you to adjust Magic Wand tool settings.

- **Polygon Mode.** Allows you to select polygon-shaped areas in simple shapes.

Pen Tool (P)

This versatile tool allows you to precisely create a wide variety of open or closed shapes, using straight or curved line segments, based on the current settings on the Property inspector. If you draw a closed shape (that is, you connect the starting and ending points of a line segment), it will automatically be filled with the current default fill color (**Figure 3.7**).

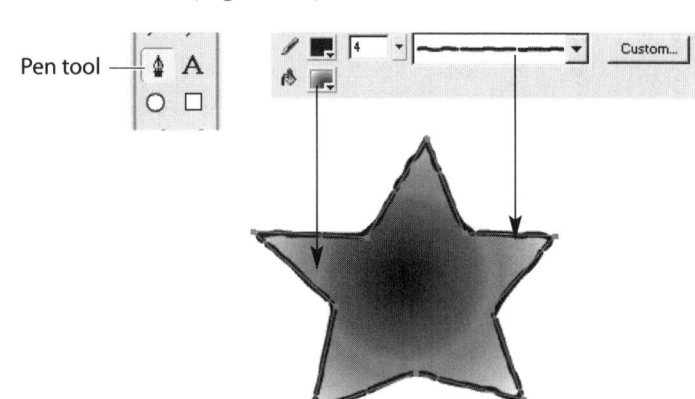

Figure 3.7
The Pen tool works in tandem with the Property inspector when you create shapes. The Pen tool creates the line, but the Property inspector allows you to configure its attributes.

Text Tool (T)

We look at the Text tool in detail in Chapter 4, "Text."

Oval Tool (O)

You use the Oval tool to create ovals (circles)—which are initially simple shapes—employing the current settings on the Property inspector (**Figure 3.8**).

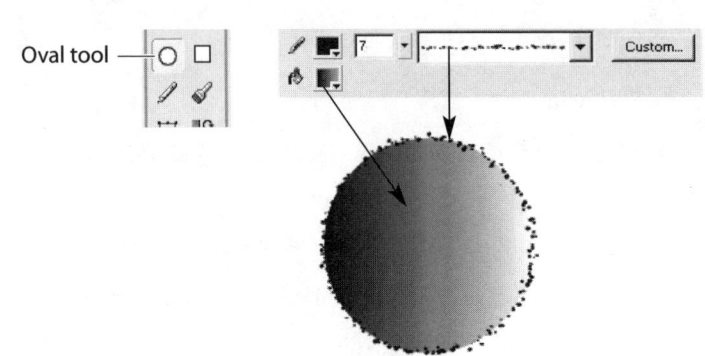

Oval tool

Figure 3.8
The Oval tool works in tandem with the Property inspector when creating ovals. The Oval tool creates the shape, but the Property inspector allows you to configure its attributes.

Rectangle Tool (R)

You use the Rectangle tool to create rectangles (squares)—which are initially simple shapes—employing the current settings on the Property inspector.

The Rectangle tool includes the following option:

- **Round Rectangle Radius.** Allows you to create rectangles with rounded corners. Clicking this button opens the Rectangle Settings dialog box, where you can set the radius of the rounded corners on newly created rectangles (**Figure 3.9**).

Rectangle tool

Round Rectangle Radius

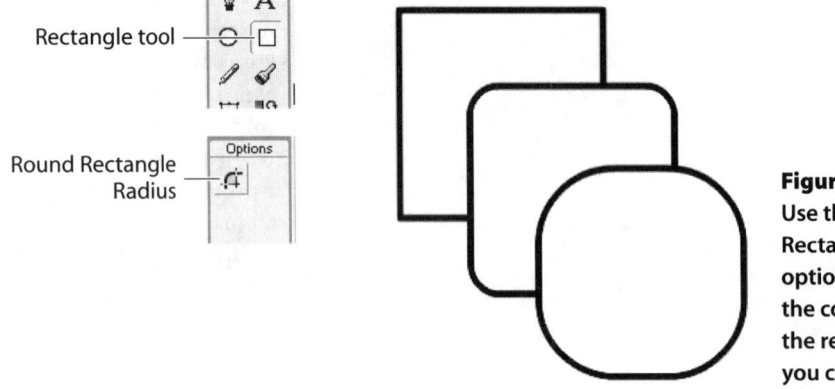

Figure 3.9
Use the Round Rectangle Radius option to round the corners of the rectangles you create.

Pencil Tool (Y)

Using the current settings on the Stroke panel, the Pencil tool lets you draw freehand straight or curved lines, which begin as simple shapes. The Pencil tool includes three pencil-mode options (**Figure 3.10**), which allow you to designate how you want Flash to modify drawn lines:

- **Straighten.** Performs shape recognition, which means that if you draw a rough square, circle, straight line, or curve, Flash will perfect the shape based on what it thinks you're trying to draw.

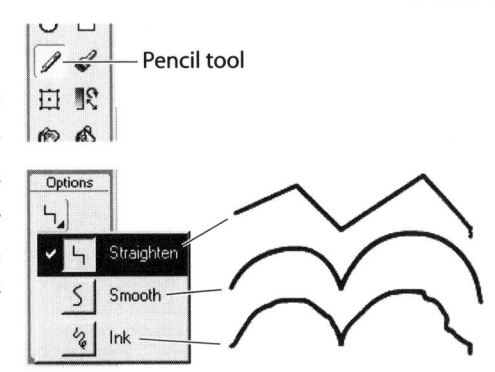

Figure 3.10
The effect produced using each of the three Pencil modes.

- **Smooth.** Does just what its name implies: It smoothes jagged lines, giving them a smoother, curvier look.

- **Ink.** This option does *nothing* to your line—which means you can draw a line and be assured that Flash won't modify it.

Brush Tool (B)

Use the Brush tool to fill, or *brush*, areas with a solid color, bitmap, or gradient fill. When creating brush strokes—which begin as simple shapes—you employ the current settings on the Property inspector.

The Brush tool includes the following five options:

- **Brush Mode.** This setting determines how brush strokes are applied to your drawing (**Figure 3.11**):

  Paint Fills paints filled areas, but not lines.

  Paint Normal paints over any area on the stage.

  Paint Behind paints around simple shapes on the stage but not over them, giving the appearance of painting behind a shape.

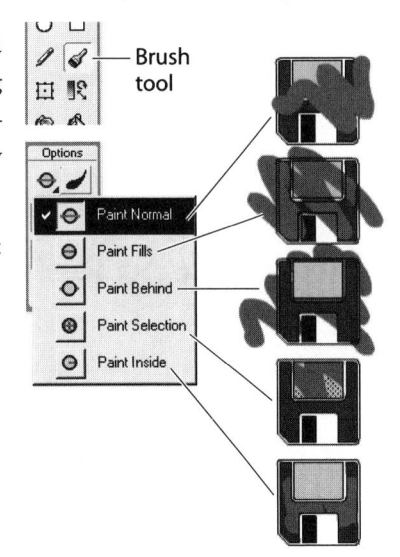

Figure 3.11
The effect of the different Brush modes.

Paint Selection paints only inside filled areas that are selected.

Paint Inside allows you to begin a brush stroke inside a filled area, and thereafter paint only within that area, without affecting any lines. If the point where you begin does not have a fill, your brush stroke will not affect previously filled areas.

- **Use Pressure.** Available only for pressure-sensitive graphics tablets, this option lets you create pressure-sensitive brush strokes. (A mouse can't make use of this feature.)
- **Brush Size.** Lets you set the size of the brush stroke. Employed with the Use Pressure option, it defines the maximum size of the pressure-sensitive stroke.
- **Brush Shape.** Lets you set the shape of your brush, which enables all sorts of interesting effects.
- **Lock Fill.** Allows you to control how Flash paints areas with gradients. When the option is turned off, each brush stroke will be distinct and display the entire gradient range. When Lock Fill is turned on, all brush strokes that use the same gradient will appear to be part of one large gradient stretching across the stage (**Figure 3.12**).

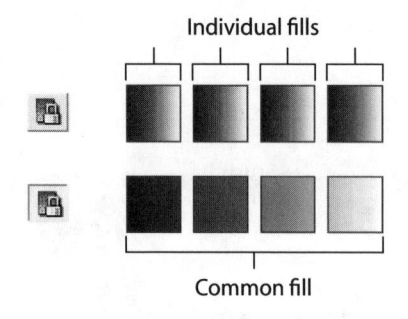

Individual fills

Common fill

Figure 3.12
The Lock Fill option determines how fills are painted on the stage. When the button is *not* depressed, each brush stroke has an individual fill. When the button is pressed, all brush strokes share a common fill.

Free Transform Tool (Q)

MX ALERT You can use the Free Transform tool to alter the size and rotation of all types of movie elements, as well as the shape of simple shapes.

The Free Transform tool includes the following four options (**Figure 3.13**):

- **Rotate.** Allows you to rotate elements on the stage in any direction. In addition, shapes can be skewed when this option is selected.
- **Scale.** Allows you to resize elements on the stage.

- **Distort.** Allows you to add a perspective to a simple shape, giving the effect of a different viewing angle. This option only works on simple shapes.

- **Envelope.** Allows you to dramatically alter a simple shape using an envelope, which is a series of points around the shape which can be moved and rotated, essentially making the shape malleable like a piece of clay.

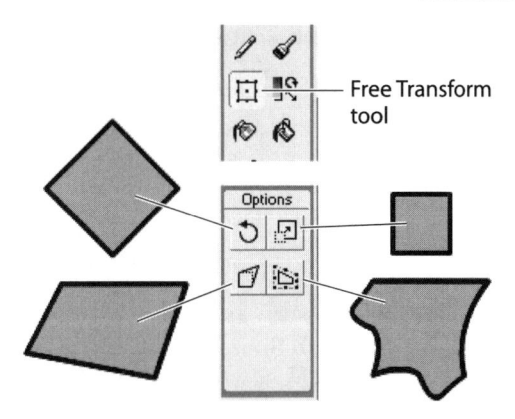

Figure 3.13
The Free Transform tool and its options, which allow you to alter shapes in a number of ways.

Fill Transform Tool (F)

MX ALERT The Fill Transform tool allows you to resize, rotate, and skew gradient or bitmap fills. We discuss this in more detail in the "Strokes and Fills" section later in this chapter.

Ink Bottle Tool (S)

The Ink Bottle tool allows you create and modify the color, size, and style of the stroke that outlines a shape, employing the current settings on the Property inspector (**Figure 3.14**).

Paint Bucket Tool (K)

You use the Paint Bucket tool (**Figure 3.15**) to add a fill to a shape made up only of a stroke, or to change a shape's existing fill, employing the current settings on the Property inspector.

Figure 3.14
You can use the Ink Bottle tool to quickly change the stroke attributes of multiple shapes.

Figure 3.15
The Paint Bucket tool can quickly change the fill attributes of multiple shapes.

The Paint Bucket tool includes the following options:

- **Gap Size.** Allows you to adjust the way the Paint Bucket tool handles outlines that are not completely filled.
- **Lock Fill.** Allows you to adjust the way Flash fills areas with gradients. This has the same effect as the Lock Fill option for the previously described Brush tool.

Dropper Tool (I)

The Dropper tool lets you *sample*, or pick up, the fill or line style of a simple shape that's already on the stage, and apply it to another simple shape on the stage.

Eraser Tool (E)

The Eraser tool does just what its name implies: It erases. You can use it to completely or partially erase lines and fills, as well as to erase simple shapes.

The Eraser tool includes the following three options:

- ◆ **Eraser Mode.** This mode provides several ways to control how Flash erases areas of your drawing (**Figure 3.16**):

    Erase Normal erases lines and fills.

    Erase Fills erases only fills, leaving lines untouched.

    Erase Lines erases only lines, leaving fills untouched.

    Erase Selected Fills erases only currently selected fills, leaving lines unchanged.

    Erase Inside lets you begin erasing inside a filled area and thereafter erase only within that filled area, without affecting any lines.

- **Faucet.** Allows you to erase a line or fill by just clicking somewhere on the line or fill itself. (The function is the same as if you had selected a line or fill, then pressed the Delete key.)

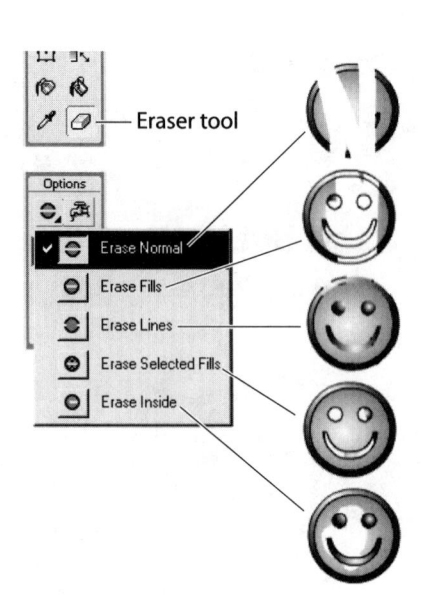

Figure 3.16
The effects of the different eraser modes.

- **Eraser Shape.** Configures the shape of your eraser, allowing you to use the tool with greater precision.

Drawing Tasks

Now that we've introduced you to the drawing tools, it's time to learn how to put them to work to create graphics and lay out pages. So put on your beret, and get ready to create your first masterpiece!

Simple Shapes vs. Graphic Objects

Flash uses two types of visual movie elements: simple shapes and graphic objects.

Simple shapes consist of the following:

- **Any stroke, fill, or shape created using a Flash drawing tool in its initial state.** An oval, square, line, or brush stroke that you draw on the stage will always begin as a simple shape. You can reshape elements that are in this state, and you can edit their strokes and fills.

- **Any graphic element on the stage whose parts can be edited individually.** This includes blocks of text or bitmaps that have been broken apart. For example, a block of text is initially considered a graphic object because you can rotate, move, or otherwise edit it as a whole, but you can't edit individual characters until the text block has been broken apart, thus turning individual characters into simple shapes (**Figure 3.17**). For more information on breaking text apart, see Chapter 4, "Text" and "Breaking Up is Not Hard to Do" later in this chapter.

Figure 3.17
Normally a text object can only be edited as whole (top). Breaking an object apart lets you edit individual parts of it (bottom).

Graphic objects consist of the following:

- **Groups.** Groups consist of several simple shapes (or even other objects) that have been *grouped* together in Flash as a single object. In this state, individual elements within the group cannot be edited. You can, however, convert the elements in a group into simple shapes simply by ungrouping it, or breaking it apart (for more information about groups see Chapter 8, "Working with Elements on the Stage").

- **Text.** Similar to groups, text blocks are actually just sections of editable text—and the only element created with one of Flash's drawing tools that's initially considered an graphic object. Again, this is because a text block is moved and edited as a whole. Breaking a text block apart can turn individual characters into simple shapes, so that you can edit them in ways not otherwise possible (for example, reshaping them or adding gradient fills). It's important to note that once you break apart characters in this manner, you will no longer be able to edit them as text (that is, changing fonts, font style, tracking, margins, line spacing, and so on).

- **Symbols.** These are special movie elements that can contain all other types of objects as well as sound and animation. For more information, see Chapter 7, "Symbols."

- **Imported graphics.** Flash imports all graphics, including bitmaps, as graphic objects. Only after it has been broken apart can an imported graphic become an editable simple shape.

Simple shapes will always appear below objects if they are all on the same layer.

Breaking Up Is Not Hard to Do

Although it may sound harsh, breaking apart graphics is actually a gentle process. It's how you turn graphic objects—including bitmaps, text, and symbols—into simple shapes, reducing them to their most basic elements so that you can edit and control them.

To break apart a graphic object:

- Select it on the stage and then choose Modify > Break Apart.

You will need to repeat this step for some graphic objects, including text and some groups and symbols, depending on how they're constructed.

Chapter 3 *Graphics*

Creating Simple Shapes

As already mentioned, simple shapes can include (among other things) lines, fills, rectangles, ovals, and brush strokes. It's important to note that fills and strokes—which in other vector drawing programs are part of a single vector element—are separate in Flash, which means you can move them around independently of one another. For example, after you've created a graphic on the stage that includes both a stroke and a fill, you can select the fill with the Arrow tool and move it to another location—without altering the stroke you also drew (**Figure 3.18**). Although this may seem awkward at first, it actually represents a very efficient way of drawing and is particularly useful for animation (as you'll shortly discover).

Figure 3.18
In Flash, strokes and fills are mapped separately from one another, and can be moved independently.

Creating lines

Although simple lines may not represent the height of your design ambitions, they are still an essential part of almost any graphic layout, animated or otherwise.

To create straight lines:

1. From the toolbar select the Line tool, or press the *N* key.

2. With the Property inspector open, choose a line color, size, and style.

3. Move the cursor to the stage, and you'll notice it changes to a crosshair.

4. Click and drag, and you'll see a basic representation of your line. Release when your line is the desired angle and length (**Figure 3.19**).

   TIPS *If you've turned on Snapping, the beginning and end points of the line, along with the angle, will "snap" to the grid of the stage. For more information about snapping, see Chapter 8, "Working with Elements on the Stage."*

   Pressing the Shift key while creating a line will constrain the angle of the line in increments of 45 degrees.

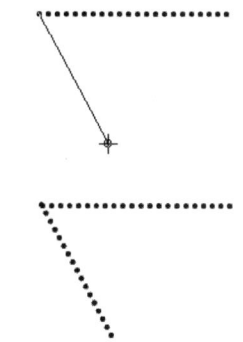

Figure 3.19
A preview of your line appears as you create it, making it easier to set its length and angle.

87

To create regular lines:

1. From the toolbar select the Pencil tool, or press the Y key.
2. From the options that appear, choose a pencil mode.
3. With the Property inspector open, choose a line color, size, and style.
4. Move the cursor to the stage area, where you'll notice it changes to a pencil.
5. Click and drag around the stage to create a line, then release to finish drawing. Depending on which pencil mode you choose, Flash may straighten or smooth the line.

Creating shapes using shape recognition

Few of us were born with surgeons' hands. And even if we were, we *still* probably wouldn't be able to draw perfect circles, squares, triangles, and straight lines. However, we know you have the *brains* of a surgeon because you purchased Flash MX—which can draw precise shapes for you.

With shape recognition, you draw a rough idea of what you want, and Flash cleans it up, perfecting the shape and smoothing any roughness. Shape recognition does have its limits, however. You must give it a legitimate rough shape to work with—that is, you can't just close your eyes, draw a shape, and expect Flash to turn it into a square. You need to draw something *approximating* a square for shape recognition to work properly.

To use shape recognition to draw shapes:

1. From the toolbar select the Pencil tool, or press the Y key.
2. Choose Straighten from the pencil-mode option that appears.
3. With the Property inspector open, choose a line color, size, and style.
4. Move the cursor onto the stage and draw a rough shape (for example, a square, triangle, or circle). When you release the mouse, Flash will try to perfect it (**Figure 3.20**).

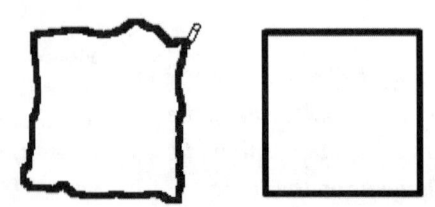

Figure 3.20
By taking advantage of Flash's shape recognition capability, you can draw "freehand" and still create precise shapes.

TIP *For information on how to adjust the settings that determine how intuitively Flash recognizes shapes, see "Pen and Drawing Preferences" later in this chapter.*

Planning Your Project

Using Metaphors to Make Your Projects Clearer

Have you ever thought about the way you work with your computer? You may have noticed how the use of metaphors helps us understand various tasks and tools. Consider a typical graphics program such as Adobe PhotoShop or Macromedia Fireworks: The interface includes a bunch of palettes and brushes, as well as a clean, white canvas—all of which are metaphors for traditional artists' tools. In reality, the interface is made up of intangible functions; however, because the images onscreen look and act like common tools, we're able to work more efficiently. Imagine having to create an image by entering the appropriate computer code!

Interface designers understand the importance of such metaphors: They also know that's it's not enough to just make them easy; they need to be obvious. That said, you too can put the power of metaphors to work in creating Flash content. Let's say you're creating the interface for a building-supply Web site: You could design a blueprint for the initial page that shows hammers "nailing" interface elements onto the appropriate places on the blueprint. Your navigation buttons could be images of power switches, which users turn off and on to move to various "rooms" on the site.

So think about using metaphors for your design, and let your imagination run wild. Be aware, however, that metaphors are not always necessary or even appropriate. Sometimes it's best to make user interaction as straightforward as possible—that is, letting users enter information via the keyboard, without all the allusions to real-life tools. Even graphics programs such as Photoshop or Fireworks sometimes require users to enter information this way.

In addition, when using metaphors, it's best to simulate things that move or change—that is, things that can be clicked, moved, picked up, selected, felt, or heard. You can use buttons and levers (and even have them make clicking sounds when pressed), flashing lights, gauges, doors, animals, staplers, speakers, knobs, and all kinds of other effects. The trick is to make the viewer forget that he or she is actually staring at a computer monitor.

Creating ovals

You can create ovals in Flash that are either strokes or fills. You can even create an oval using both strokes and fills, in one fell swoop!

To create ovals:

1. From the toolbar select the Oval tool, or press the O key.

2. To set the stroke and fill attributes, do one of the following:

   - With the Property inspector open, choose a line color, size, and style, as well as a fill color.

   - Click the stroke and/or fill color control on the drawing toolbar to select a line and/or fill color. If you want your oval to include a fill but not an outline, or vice versa, select the appropriate color control, and then click the No Color button (**Figure 3.21**).

   - If you want to give the oval a gradient or bitmap fill, open the Color Mixer panel and choose a fill type from the Fill Style drop-down menu.

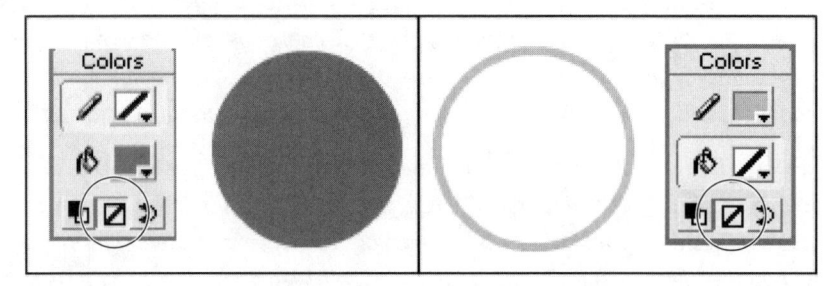

Figure 3.21
Pressing the No Color button when selecting the stroke and fill color of shapes lets you create closed shapes (like ovals or rectangles) without strokes or fills.

3. Move the cursor to the stage area, where you'll notice it changes to a crosshair.

4. Click and drag, and you'll see a basic representation of your oval. Release when your oval is the size and shape you desire.

   TIP *To draw perfect circles, turn on snapping or hold down the Shift key when dragging.*

Creating rectangles

Rectangles are probably the shape you'll most commonly use in your project. Flash allows you to easily create rectangles of all sizes and shapes, including ones with rounded corners.

To create rectangles:

1. From the toolbar select the Rectangle tool, or press the *M* key.

2. To set the stroke and fill attributes, do one of the following:

   - With the Property inspector open, choose a line color, size, and style, as well as a fill color.

   - Click the stroke and/or fill color control on the drawing toolbar to select a line and/or fill color. If you want your rectangle to include a fill but not an outline, or vice versa, select the appropriate color control and then click the No Color button.

   - If you wish to give the rectangle a gradient or bitmap fill, open the Color Mixer panel and choose a fill type from the Fill Style drop-down menu.

3. If you want your rectangle to have rounded corners, click the Round Rectangle Radius button on the Options part of the Drawing toolbar and set a radius for the rounded corner.

4. Move the cursor to the stage area, where you'll notice it changes to a crosshair.

5. Click and drag, and you'll see a basic representation of your rectangle. Release when your rectangle is the size and shape you desire.

   TIPS *To create perfect squares, turn on snapping or hold down the Shift key when dragging.*

   An easier way to create a rectangle with rounded corners is to drag while pressing the down-arrow key (for corners with a larger radius) or the up-arrow key (for sharper corners).

   MX ALERT { *ActionScript* } *Strokes and fills can be created dynamically using drawing methods available in ActionScript. These methods allow you to control the size, shape, line size, style, and color, as well as the fill (solid or gradient) of dynamically created shapes. For more information, see Chapter 16, "Using ActionScript in Your Projects".*

Creating shapes using the Brush tool

Using the Brush tool, you can create shapes that look like they've been painted or drawn with a marking pen—great for simulating calligraphy effects, or to achieve a painterly look.

The Brush tool provides a number of options for configuring your brush strokes. If you've got an electronic drawing tablet hooked up to your computer, the Use Pressure option automatically becomes available, allowing you to create pressure-sensitive brush strokes (**Figure 3.22**).

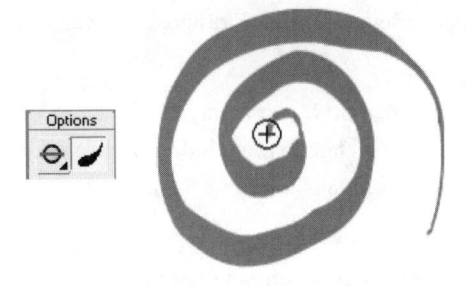

Figure 3.22
If you have a drawing tablet installed on your system, press the Use Pressure option to give your brush strokes a more realistic look.

The shapes you create with the Brush tool are really nothing more than brush-shaped fills. Although lines are not added to them initially (even though the stroke color control is available on the drawing toolbar), you can add lines or strokes later using the Ink Bottle tool. For more information on the Ink Bottle tool, see "Working with Strokes" later in this chapter.

To create shapes using the Brush tool:

1. From the toolbar select the Brush tool, or press the *B* key.

2. To set the fill attributes, do one of the following:

- With the Property inspector open, choose a fill type.

- Click the fill color control on the drawing toolbar to select a fill color.

- If you wish to give the brush stroke a gradient or bitmap fill, open the Color Mixer panel and choose a fill type from the Fill style drop down menu.

3. Using the Lock Fill option (at the bottom of the Options section on the Drawing toolbar), specify how you want the Brush to apply strokes and handle gradients.

4. If you use a pressure-sensitive drawing tablet, you can select the Use Pressure option to create brush strokes of varying widths, based on how much pressure you apply to your tablet. This option is not available if such a tablet is not connected to your computer.

5. Move the cursor to the stage, where it will become a representation of what your brush looks like based on the size and shape you selected. If you selected the Use Pressure modifier, the cursor will look like a circle with a crosshair inside.

6. Click and drag, and you'll see a basic representation of your brush stroke. Release when your brush stroke looks the way you want it to.

Using the Pen Tool

The Pen tool is one of the most versatile tools in the Flash toolbox; it can also be one of the most challenging to master. Other vector graphics programs such as Adobe Illustrator and Macromedia FreeHand employ a similar tool, as do many drawing programs. Fortunately, Flash's Pen tool works in much the same way as these.

What makes the Pen tool so special? Once mastered, it provides the quickest and most precise way to create lines and shapes. To use it effectively, however, you need to know a bit about how it operates.

Understanding Paths, Path Segments, Anchor Points, and Tangent Handles

A path that you create with the Pen tool is nothing more than a line or shape made up of three elements: path segments, anchor points, and tangent handles. *Path segments* are small portions of an overall path (line) that have an anchor point at each end. Several path segments make up a path. *Anchor points* connect various path segments and define where the path changes. The length and angle of *tangent handles*—which extend out from an anchor point—determine the shape and size of a curved path segment (**Figure 3.23**).

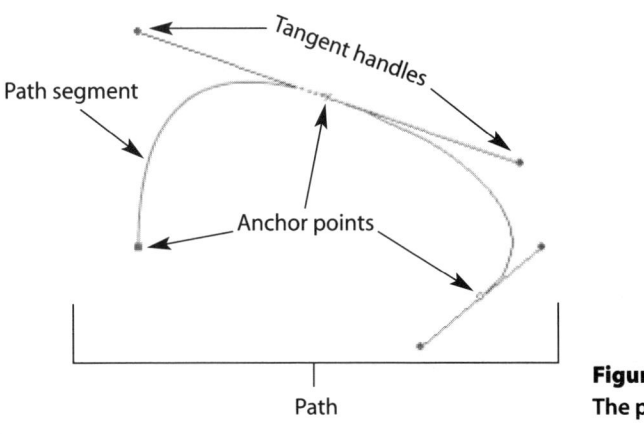

Figure 3.23
The parts of a path.

You can use the Pen tool to create two kinds of paths: open and closed. In an open path, the shape remains partly open (for example, as in the letter *U*); in a closed path, the shape has no openings (for example, as in the letter *O*) (**Figure 3.24**). Flash will automatically fill a closed path, with the current fill displayed on the Fill panel.

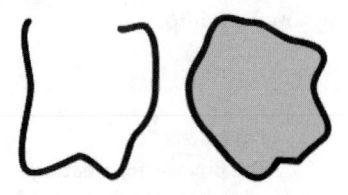

Figure 3.24
An open (left) and closed path (right).

The best way to understand how the Pen tool works is to use it—which is what we'll cover now.

Creating Paths

Creating straight and curved paths are the main tasks you'll use the Pen tool for. The process for creating straight paths is straightforward. However, creating curved lines may take some practice.

To create straight paths with the Pen tool:

1. From the toolbar select the Pen tool, or press the *P* key.

2. To set attributes for the line, do one of the following:
- With the Property inspector open, choose a line color, size, and style.
- Click the stroke color control on the drawing toolbar to select a line color.

3. Move the cursor to the stage, where you'll see it change to a pen.

4. Click the point on the stage where you want the line to begin.

5. Continue clicking on various spots on the stage. Each time you click, you're creating a new anchor point and adding a straight path segment. Pressing the Shift key when clicking from one point to the next will constrain the angle of the next path segment created by 45-degree increments from the current path segment.

6. To finish drawing, do one of the following:
- If you want to create a closed path, place your cursor on top of the first anchor point you created. A small circle will appear next to the pen tip indicating that if you click, you'll create a closed path.

- If you want to create an open path, either double-click the last point you created, select the Pen tool again, or Control-click (Windows) or Command-click (Macintosh) anywhere on the stage (**Figure 3.25**).

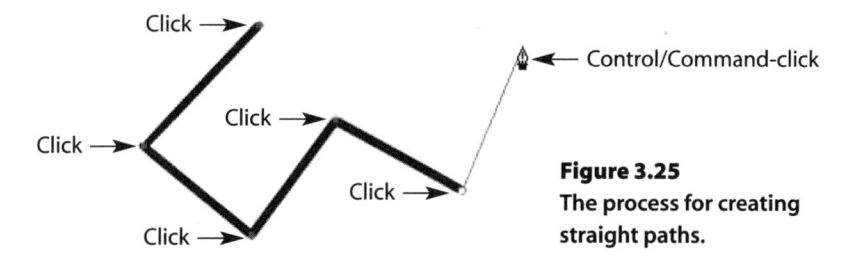

Figure 3.25
The process for creating straight paths.

To create curved paths with the Pen tool:

1. From the toolbar select the Pen tool, or press the *P* key.

2. To set attributes for the line, do one of the following:

- With the Property inspector open, choose a line color, size, and style.
- Click the stroke color control on the drawing toolbar to select a line color.

3. Move the cursor to the stage, where you'll notice it changes to a pen.

4. Click and drag on the stage to create an anchor point with tangent handles. Pressing the Shift key while dragging constrains the movement of a tangent handle's angle by 45-degree increments.

5. Release the mouse button. The length, direction (dragging left or right), and angle of the handle determines the shape, size, and direction of the curve.

6. Move the cursor to where you want to place the path's next anchor point.

7. Click and drag to finish creating a curved segment between the two anchor points.

8. Continue to create curved segments by repeating Steps 4 and 5.

9. To finish drawing, do one of the following:

- For a closed path, place your cursor on top of the first anchor point you created. A small circle will appear next to the pen tip indicating that if you click, you'll create a closed path.

- For an open path, either double-click the last point you created, select the Pen tool again, or Control-click (Windows) or Command-click (Macintosh) anywhere on the stage (**Figure 3.26**).

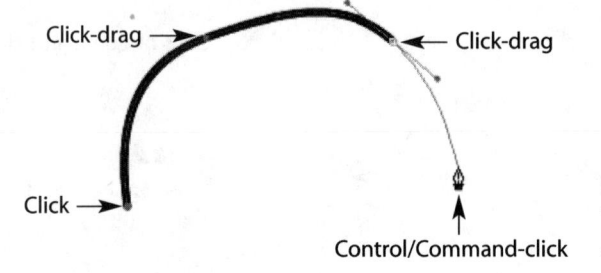

Figure 3.26
The process for creating curved paths.

Working with Path Segments

By adjusting the length or shape of path segments, you can change the shape of the overall path they are part of.

To reshape a path segment using the Arrow tool:

1. From the toolbar select the Arrow tool, or press the *V* key.

2. Click and drag the path segment to reshape it. For additional information on reshaping path segments, see "Editing Simple Shapes" later in this chapter.

To reshape a curved path segment using tangent handles:

1. From the toolbar select the Subselection tool, or press the *A* key.

2. Click on the path with the segment you wish to reshape to make its anchor points visible.

3. Click on an anchor point that's part of a curved path segment. Tangent handles will appear.

4. Click and drag the end of one of the tangent handles to adjust the curved path segment (**Figure 3.27**).

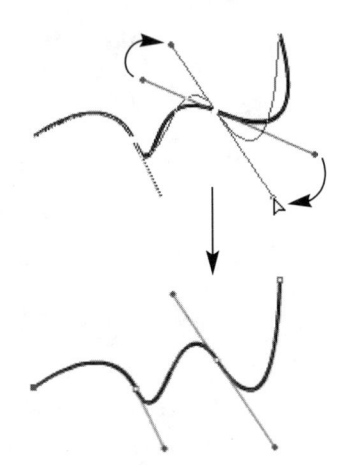

Figure 3.27
To change the shape of a path segment, adjust the angle of its tangent handles.

Working with Anchor Points

Every time you use the Pen tool to click or click-drag on the stage, you're laying down anchor points that determine where your path changes. Regardless of how masterful you become with the Pen tool, you'll still need to edit, move, add, or delete anchor points. Fortunately, anchor points are easy to work with, once you understand what you can do with them. By manipulating anchor points, you can change the shape and length of path segments, and thus the overall path.

You can manipulate anchors in the following ways:

- Convert a corner point to a curve point, or vice versa, to change the way path segments connect.

- Using the Subselect tool, move anchor points alone or together to change sections of your shape.

- Add an anchor point to transform a single path segment into two path segments, or remove anchor points to merge two path segments into one.

- Stretch and rotate the tangent handle on an anchor point to change the way two path segments connect.

The Subselect tool is the main tool for editing anchor points and paths created with the Pen tool; it has no other function. Clicking a path with the Subselect tool makes its path segments, anchor points, and tangent handles visible onscreen, where you can manipulate and edit them any way you desire.

To convert a corner point to a curve point:

1. From the toolbar select the Subselect tool, or press the *A* key.

2. Click on the path containing the anchor point you wish to convert. Its anchor points will become visible.

3. Alt-drag (Windows) or Option-drag (Macintosh) on the corner point you wish to convert.

To convert a curve point to a corner point:

1. From the toolbar select the Pen tool, or press the *P* key.

2. Click on the path containing the anchor point you wish to convert. Its anchor points will become visible.

3. Click once on the curve point you wish to convert.

TIP *Clicking the same point again will delete it.*

To move an anchor point:

1. From the toolbar select the Subselect tool, or press the *A* key.
2. Click on the path containing the anchor point(s) you wish to move. Its anchor points will become visible.
3. To move an anchor point, do one of the following:
   - Click-drag it.
   - Click once to select it (it will turn black), and then use the arrow keys on your keyboard to move it in any direction. Holding the Shift key down while pressing an arrow key accelerates the movement of the selected anchor point.

TIP *You can select and move more than one anchor point at once. Repeat Steps 1 and 2 from above, and then in Step 3 either marquee-select anchor points, or hold down the Shift key and click on all anchor points you wish to move. Once anchor points are selected, use the arrow keys to move them* (**Figure 3.28**).

To remove an anchor point from a path:

1. From the toolbar select the Subselect tool, or press the *A* key.
2. Click on the path containing the anchor point(s) you wish to remove. Its anchor points will become visible.
3. Click once to select the anchor point you wish to remove, then choose Edit > Clear or simply press the Delete key.

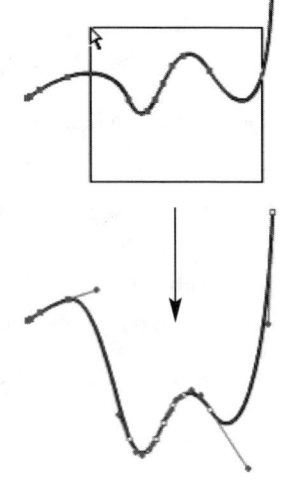

Figure 3.28 Selecting multiple anchor points allows you to move them simultaneously.

TIP *You can also remove an anchor point by double-clicking it with the Pen tool.*

To add an anchor point to a path:

1. From the toolbar select the Pen tool, or press the *P* key.
2. Click on the path where you wish to add an anchor point.

Chapter 3 **Graphics**

Pen and Drawing Preferences

We all have our own styles when it comes to drawing and creating graphics. Being forced to work in one particular mode could slow down the creative process. Fortunately, Flash offers you a range of pen and drawing preferences, giving you the freedom to do what you do best—create stunning Flash movies. To configure these preferences, from the File menu choose Preferences, then select the Editing tab.

Let's take a look at the available options (**Figure 3.29**):

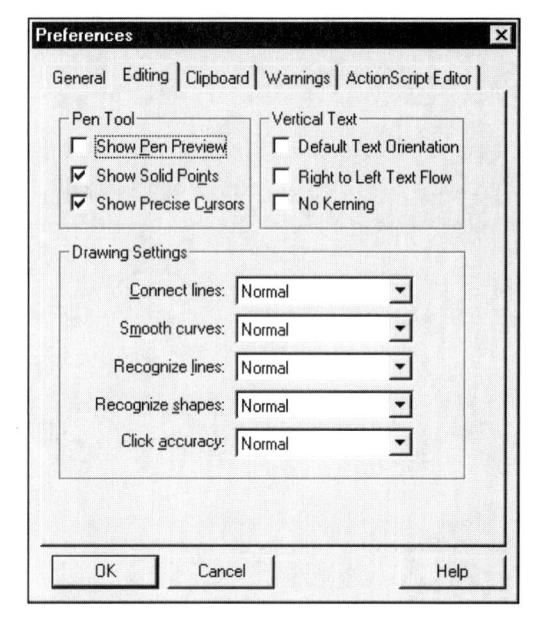

Figure 3.29
Pen and drawing preferences are set on the Editing tab of the Preferences dialog box.

- **Show Pen Preview.** Determines how the lines you are drawing will appear. Select this option to preview a line as you draw it. You may find that enabling this option allows you to work more accurately with the Pen tool.

- **Show Solid Points.** Determines the way a selected path's anchor points will appear on the stage. If you select this option, anchor points will appear hollow when selected, but solid when unselected. (Deselecting this option does the reverse.)

- **Show Precise Cursors.** Displays a crosshair cursor for the Pen tool, allowing greater precision in placing anchor points. Deselecting this option will cause the standard Pen tool icon to appear.

- **Connect lines.** Determines how close two end points must be on the stage before Flash automatically connects them.

- **Smooth curves.** Sets the degree of smoothing Flash will apply to lines drawn with the Pencil tool, when you select the Straighten or Smooth modifiers.

- **Recognize lines.** Determines how straight a line drawn with the Pencil tool must be for Flash to recognize and straighten it.

- **Recognize shapes.** Sets how close you must come to a pencil-drawn shape—such as an oval or a square—for Flash to recognize and perfect the shape.

- **Click accuracy.** Determines how close you must click to an element to select it.

Editing Simple Shapes

Occasionally you'll need to tweak a shape to get it looking just right. Thankfully, Flash makes editing simple shapes nearly as easy as creating them. When you edit a shape, you can change its shape, its smoothness, or its line angles. You can even delete parts of it by erasing.

Transforming Lines

The only way you can transform lines is to change their length and angle. Fortunately, you can perform both tasks simultaneously.

To change a line's length and angle:

1. From the toolbar select the Arrow tool, or press the *V* key.

2. Place your cursor over the end of a nonselected line. A small angle will appear next to the arrow.

3. Click and drag the endpoint of the line to change its length and angle.

Straightening and Smoothing Lines and Shapes with Fills

Flash lets you refine a shape or line to your heart's content, so that you can remove bumps and smooth rough edges.

To straighten or smooth a line or shape with a fill:

1. From the toolbar select the Arrow tool, or press the *V* key.

2. Select the shape or line you want to modify.

3. With your shape selected, press either the Straighten or Smooth button on the Options section of the Drawing toolbar, depending on which effect you want applied.

   TIPS *If one click of the Straighten or Smooth button doesn't perfect your shape, keep pressing it. Eventually you'll have a perfect square or circle, or a line that's perfectly straight.*

   You can also apply these effects by selecting the shape or line and then choosing Modify > Smooth/Straighten. However, using the Straighten and Smooth options on the toolbar is much quicker and more efficient.

Reshaping Lines and Shapes with Fills

Just as a sculptor transforms a lump of clay, digital artists working in Flash can form lines, squares, circles, and brush strokes in all sorts of ways—without even getting their hands dirty.

To reshape a line or shape with a fill:

1. From the toolbar, select the Arrow tool, or press the *V* key.

   Move your cursor over a line or along the edge of a filled shape; it will change appearance to indicate which type of reshaping you can perform at that point (**Figure 3.30**).

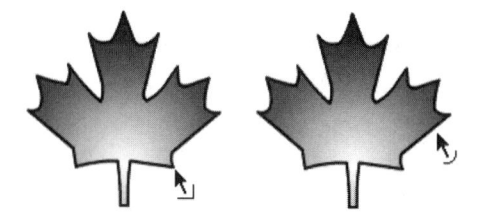

Figure 3.30
When you're reshaping, an angle appears next to the cursor indicating you can reshape a corner point, or a curve appears indicating you can reshape a line.

2. Choose the area you want to reshape: You can select sides of filled shapes and lengths of lines, or corners of shapes.

3. When you've reached the place you wish to reshape, click and drag the cursor until the point is where you want it, then release.

TIPS *If you hold down the Control key (Windows) or Command key (Macintosh) when dragging a side, you can add a new corner point to the shape.*

If a shape you want to work with has too many corner points, select it and press the Arrow tool's Smooth modifier to eliminate one or more of them.

You can also reshape a line or shape by using the Subselect tool to modify anchor points along the path. For more information, see "Using the Pen Tool," earlier in this chapter.

Distorting Shapes

MX ALERT *Distorting* a shape means pulling its corner points so that the shape is displayed as if viewed from other than a head-on perspective. This is a useful effect for creating interesting shape tweens. (For more on shape tweening, see Chapter 10, "Using Animation to Create Movement.")

To distort a shape:

1. From the toolbar select the Free Transform tool, or press the Q key.

2. Click on the shape or line you want to distort. Double-click on the fill to select both the fill and outline of a shape (if it has both).

At this point a bounding box with eight handles will appear around the shape.

3. Press the Distort button on the Options section of the Drawing toolbar.

4. Click-drag one of the corner handles on the shape, then release. Hold down the Shift key while click-dragging in order to drag two corners on the same side in opposite directions (**Figure 3.31**).

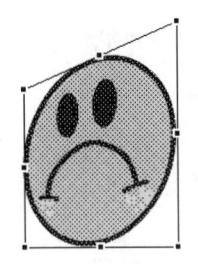

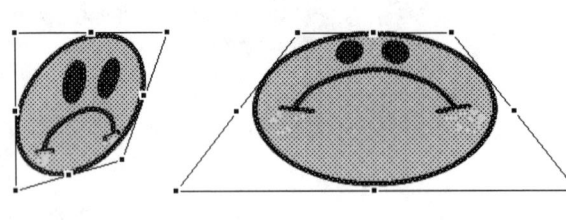

Figure 3.31 Some of the many ways shapes can be distorted.

TIP *Graphic objects such as text, bitmaps, symbols, and so forth cannot be distorted in this manner. However, breaking them apart will convert them to simple shapes, which you can then distort to your heart's desire.*

Reshaping Using an Envelope

MX ALERT

In Flash, what's known as an "envelope" is a special display grid that you place over a shape on the stage. When you reshape this grid, or envelope, by click-dragging anchor points and tangents, these movements change the underlying shape as well. This allows you to warp shapes as if they were made of Silly Putty.

To reshape using an envelope:

1. From the toolbar select the Freeform Transform tool, or press the Q key.

2. Click on the shape or line you want to distort. Double-click on the fill to select both the fill and outline of a shape (if it has both).

   A bounding box with eight handles will appear around the shape.

3. Press the Envelope button on the Options section of the Drawing toolbar.

   The shape now has eight anchor points and 16 tangent handles (similar to those created by the Pen tool discussed earlier in this chapter) (**Figure 3.32**).

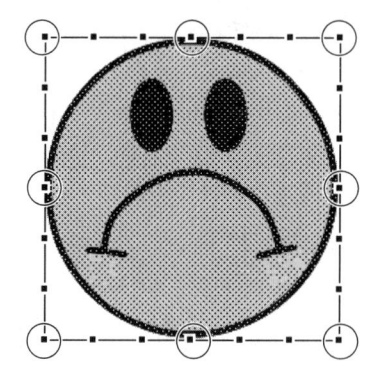

Figure 3.32
The anchor points (circled) and tangent handles (all other points) that appear when reshaping with an envelope.

4. Click and move an anchor point, or twist a tangent handle in order to reshape. Alt-dragging (Windows) or Option-dragging a side tangent handle will temporarily convert that tangent's anchor point to a corner anchor point (**Figure 3.33**).

Figure 3.33
One result of reshaping using an envelope.

TIPS *Control-dragging (Windows) or Command-dragging (Macintosh) a side anchor point will cause all of the anchor points on that side to move in unison.*

Control-dragging (Windows) or Command-dragging (Macintosh) a corner anchor point will lock that corner's tangent handles to their current position as you drag.

Double-clicking an anchor point or tangent handle on the envelope will reset the envelope.

Once you've clicked off of a shape that is being edited with an envelope, the envelope disappears and will be reset to its default rectangular shape the next time you use it. In other words, you can't pick up editing an envelope where you left off. So make sure you're really finished before you click off of the shape.

Segmenting and Connecting

You don't really segment and connect shapes in Flash; those actions occur automatically when shapes come into contact with one another on the stage—a process that enables you to create fairly complex shapes that would not otherwise be possible using Flash's drawing tools. For example, with segmenting, one shape acts as a "cookie-cutter" in relation to other shapes, allowing you to create unique holes in shapes or to partially cut away parts of a shape. With connecting, individual shapes (circles, squares, triangles, etc.) are fused into one super-shape. You can segment and connect any type of shape, including ovals, rectangles, lines, and brush strokes, as long as they haven't been grouped or turned into symbols.

Let's first take a look at segmenting, which allows you to cut away and slice shapes in unique ways. Segmenting occurs when one shape or line is placed over another line or filled shape on the same layer. Lines and shapes on the stage can be segmented in the following ways (**Figure 3.34**):

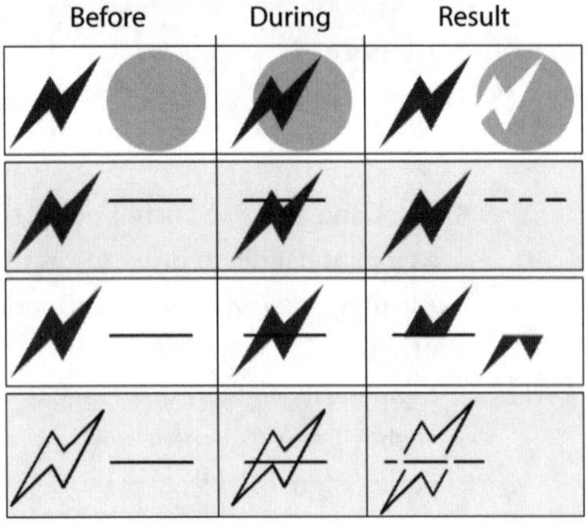

Figure 3.34
The four kinds of segmenting that Flash performs.

- Placing one filled shape on top of another of a different color, then deselecting the top shape will cause the bottom shape to be cut out in the same way a cookie-cutter cuts out cookie dough.

- Placing a filled shape on top of a line, then deselecting the filled shape will erase the portion of the line that the shape overlapped.

- Placing a line on top of a filled shape so that it traverses its entire width or height, then deselecting the line will slice in half the filled shape along the path of the line.

- Placing a line on top of another of a different color will cause both lines to become "broken apart" at the point where they intersect.

TIP *You can segment a bitmap if you break it apart first.*

Connecting (combining) shapes is the visual opposite of segmenting them: By combining shapes, you can create new ones that would be difficult to make using Flash's other drawing tools by themselves. It's important to note, however, that you can only connect simple shapes of the same color on the same layer (gradient-filled shapes will not work). In addition, shapes that you want to connect cannot be surrounded by an outline.

To connect two shapes:

1. Select one shape and drag it on top of another.

2. Deselect the shape that you dragged.

The two shapes automatically connect and transform into a single shape (**Figure 3.35**).

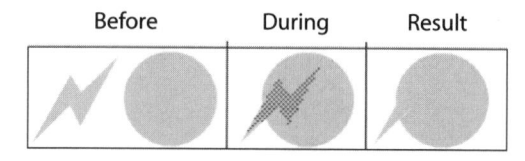

Figure 3.35
Connecting two (or more) shapes so that they become one.

Erasing

Erasing allows you to remove portions of shapes or lines with precision. You can change the size and shape of the eraser, as well as the portions of any shape you want to erase, by adjusting the associated options.

To erase with the Eraser tool:

1. From the toolbar select the Eraser tool, or press the *E* key.

2. From the options that appear, select an eraser mode.

3. Choose an eraser size and shape.

   Move the cursor to the stage area, where it will change into a representation of your eraser settings. (Make sure at this point that you don't have the Faucet modifier on; size and shape settings won't work with it on.)

4. Click and drag on a shape or line.

5. Release when you've erased the portions you want removed.

   TIPS *The Eraser tool normally erases only a portion of a shape at a time. However, by selecting the Faucet option, you can delete entire lines and fills just by clicking them. (This is similar to selecting a line or fill, then pressing the Delete key.)*

   To delete everything on the stage, simply double-click the Eraser tool.

Strokes and Fills

Every simple shape you create using Flash's drawing tools is made up of a stroke, a fill, or both. Each stroke or fill has a set of attributes that determines how it looks. For strokes, this includes things such as color, style, and thickness. For fills, this includes fill types such as solid color, gradient, and bitmap.

The Flash drawing toolbar has two color controls that you can use to easily choose a stroke or fill color you want applied to shapes that you're creating or editing (**Figure 3.36**). However, you'll probably need to adjust more than just these two attributes, which is where the Property inspector and Color Mixer panel can help.

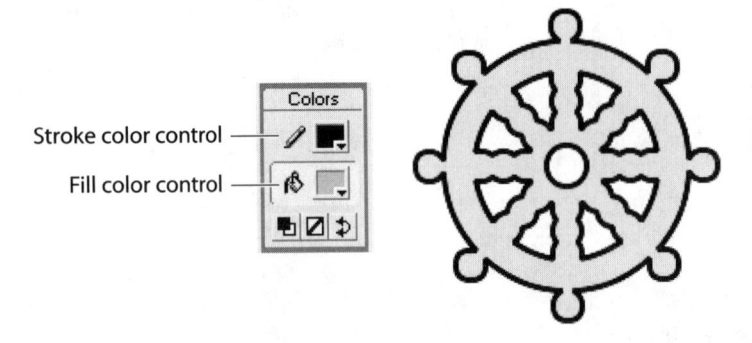

Figure 3.36
The stroke and fill color controls on the Drawing toolbar let you quickly choose colors for the shapes you're creating or editing.

Next we'll look at various interface controls you can use to adjust the attributes of a stroke or fill. We'll also discuss how to customize attributes to fit your needs.

Working with Strokes

MX ALERT Although you might not think there's much you can accomplish with strokes (also known as lines), they actually offer a wealth of possibilities once you learn how to change their attributes.

In Flash, strokes come in two varieties: regular lines and outlines. A regular line has a beginning and end point. An outline, on the other hand, has no beginning or end (think of the line defining an oval or rectangle). By using the Property inspector and the Ink Bottle tool, you can add to or alter strokes on existing shapes on the stage.

Stroke settings on the Property inspector

The Property inspector is where you configure all of a stroke's attributes, including style, color, and thickness. You can apply these settings in one of two ways: If no stroke is selected on the stage, any attributes you adjust on the Property inspector will become the default attributes for all new strokes created. If a stroke *is* selected on the stage, the current attributes for that stroke will appear on the Property inspector, and any adjustments made in the panel will be reflected immediately on the selected stroke. Let's take a look at the attributes that are available from the Property inspector (**Figure 3.37**).

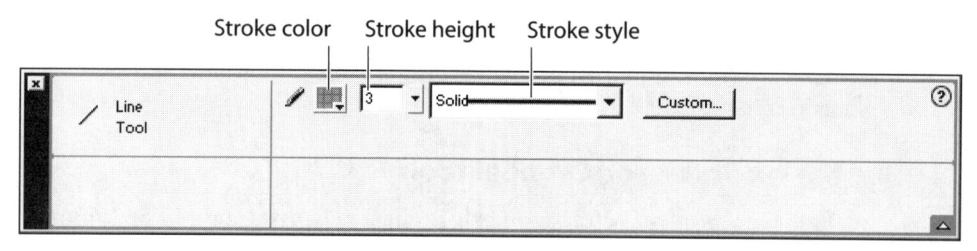

Figure 3.37
The stroke settings on the Property inspector.

- **Stroke color.** Allows you to select any color from the current palette. If you don't like the colors on the palette, you can always create your own by opening the Color Mixer panel (Window > Color Mixer) and creating a custom color (for more on this, see the "Color" section later in this chapter). If you're creating ovals or rectangles, you can also press the No Color button on the drawing toolbar or the Color Mixer panel to create an object without a fill.

- **Stroke height.** The slider control to the right of the stroke color box allows you to select a line size of up to 10 points. You can also enter a number directly into the size text box.

- **Stroke style.** This drop-down box offers a handful of line/stroke styles. If you don't see one you want, you can create a custom style by pressing the Custom... button (to the right of the menu). The Stroke Style dialog box appears, allowing you to create your own custom styles. For a detailed view of your custom settings' effect, check the Zoom 4x box.

To set the default attributes for new strokes and outlines:

1. Choose Edit > Deselect All to make sure nothing on the stage is selected.
2. With the Property inspector open, adjust the various stroke attributes. To set custom color or transparency settings, open the Color Mixer panel, press the Stroke Color control, and make any needed color and transparency adjustments.
3. All strokes created from this point on will reflect your adjustments.

To change a stroke's attributes:

1. Select a stroke on the stage.
2. With the Property inspector open, you'll see the selected stroke's current attributes. Adjust them as you see fit, and the selected stroke will be updated automatically. To set custom color or transparency settings, open the Color Mixer panel, press the Stroke Color control, and make any color and transparency adjustments you require.

Using the Ink Bottle and Dropper tools

The Ink Bottle tool is most useful for quickly adding or changing a stroke on a number of shapes. Using it gives you the Midas touch: Just clicking on any filled shape will add a stroke where none existed, and clicking on an existing stroke will change it to reflect the current default stroke settings on the Property inspector.

The Dropper tool works in conjunction with the Ink Bottle tool, allowing you to *sample*, or copy, a line's color, thickness, and style (metaphorically, pulling them into the dropper) and then apply those visual characteristics to another line (squeezing them out of the dropper).

To add or change a line or outline using the Ink Bottle tool:

1. From the toolbar select the Ink Bottle tool, or press the *S* key.
2. With the Property inspector open, adjust the various stroke attributes. To set custom color or transparency settings, open the Color Mixer panel, press the Stroke Color control, and make any color and transparency adjustments you require.

3. Move the cursor to the stage, where it will change to an ink bottle.

4. Use the tip of the bottle (where it looks like ink is pouring out) to click a line in order to change its attributes. Click the edge of a filled shape with the bottle tip to add an outline.

To apply one line's attributes to another:

1. From the toolbar select the Dropper tool, or press the *I* key.

2. Move the cursor over the stage, where it will change to a dropper.

3. When you position the dropper over the line that has the attributes you wish to copy, a Pencil icon will appear next to the dropper. Click once to activate the Ink Bottle tool.

4. Click an existing line to change it, or click the edge of a fill to create a line with the same attributes as those you picked up with the Dropper tool (**Figure 3.38**).

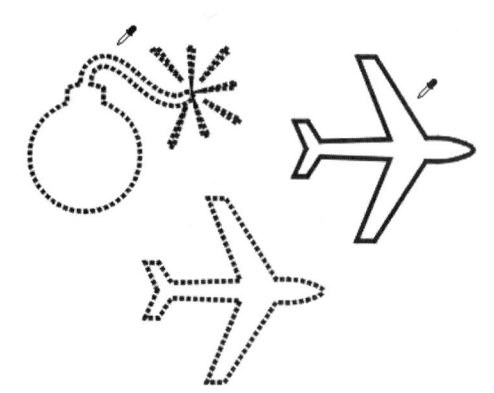

Figure 3.38
It's easy to copy stroke attributes from one image to another. Clicking on the bomb image here using the Dropper tool copies its stroke attributes. Clicking on the plane on the right applies those attributes to the current stroke, so that the plane in the center displays the same stroke as the bomb.

Working with Fills

MX ALERT Although lines and outlines go a long way toward sprucing up designs, to come up with something really special, you need to give them some substance. Adding fills to closed shapes is a great way to start. By combining several filled objects with the right colors and gradients, you can create surprisingly lifelike graphics.

Use the Property inspector, Color Mixer panel, and the Paint Bucket tool on the drawing toolbar to add to or alter a fill on an existing shape on the stage.

Setting fills from the Property inspector

The Property inspector offers the most direct means of setting a fill for a shape; however, it's also quite limited, as you can only select a fill from the palette that appears when you click the Fill Color box (**Figure 3.39**). To apply a custom fill (one that doesn't appear on the palette), you will need to use the Color Mixer panel (see "Using the Color Mixer Panel" later in this chapter).

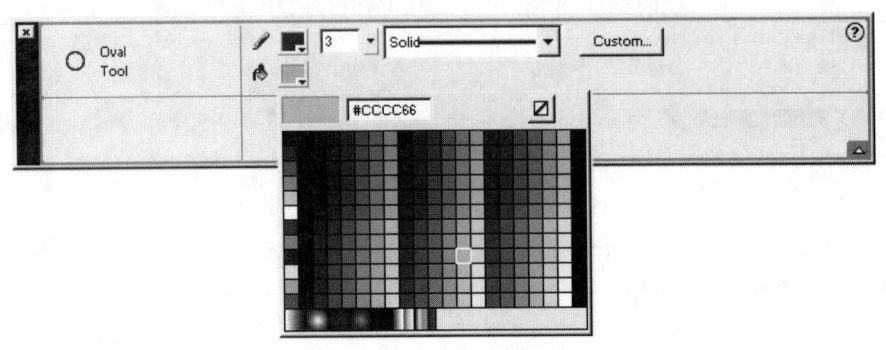

Figure 3.39
If you're using the Property inspector to set a fill color, you can only use those available on the palette that appears when you click the Fill Color box.

To set the default fill used for newly created shapes using the Property inspector:

1. Choose Edit > Deselect All to make sure nothing on the stage is selected.
2. With the Property inspector open, click on the Fill Color box and choose a color or gradient from the palette that appears.
3. All newly created filled shapes will reflect your adjustments.

To change a shape's fill using the Property inspector:

1. Select a filled shape on the stage.
2. With the Property inspector open, click on the Fill Color box and choose a color or gradient from the palette that appears, and the selected filled shape will be updated automatically.

Setting fills from the Color Mixer panel

For choosing and editing fills, the Color Mixer panel gives you more options than the Property inspector. You work with the Color Mixer in one of two ways: If no filled shape is selected on the stage, the fill you select/create on the Color Mixer panel will become the default fill for all newly created filled shapes. If a fill *is* selected on the stage, any adjustments made in the panel will be reflected immediately on the selected fill. Let's take a look at the fill types available from the Fill drop-down menu on the Color Mixer panel (**Figure 3.40**).

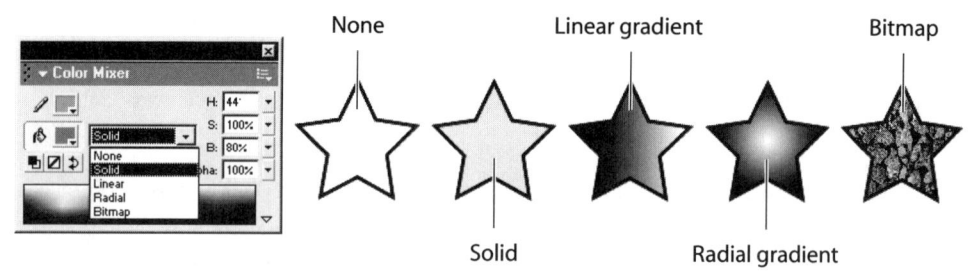

Figure 3.40
The various fill types available on the Color Mixer panel.

- **None.** No fill.

- **Solid.** Color fills such as red, green, and blue.

- **Linear (gradient).** Special fills where one color fades into another from top to bottom or horizontally.

- **Radial (gradient).** Similar to linear gradients except that they fade from the shape's center out.

- **Bitmap.** Fills created from an imported bitmap. You can make a bitmap fill look however you want; you can even tile it inside a shape. For more about creating and editing bitmap fills, see Chapter 6, "Bitmaps."

To set the default fill used for newly created shapes using the Color Mixer panel:

1. Choose Edit > Deselect All to make sure nothing on the stage is selected.

2. With the Color Mixer panel open, choose a fill type from the drop-down menu, and then edit that fill as needed using the tools on the mixer panel (see "Transforming fills on the stage" below for how to edit fills. If the Color Swatches panel is open, you can also choose a gradient from the set of available gradient swatches.

3. All newly created filled shapes will reflect your adjustments.

To change a shape's fill using the Color Mixer panel:

1. Select a filled shape on the stage.

2. With the Color Mixer panel open, choose a fill type from the drop-down menu, edit it as you wish, and the selected filled shape will be updated automatically.

NOTE *For more information about editing colors with the Color Mixer panel, see "Using the Color Mixer Panel" later in this chapter.*

To create a gradient fill using the Color Mixer panel:

1. With the Color Mixer panel open, select either Linear or Gradient from the Fill type drop-down menu. The Color Mixer panel will change to accommodate editing the gradient (**Figure 3.41**).

2. To change a color in the gradient, click one of the pointers below the gradient definition bar to activate it. Choose a color by clicking the color box that appears above the gradient definition bar, or adjust the color and alpha sliders on the right side of the Color Mixer panel.

3. To add a pointer (color) to the gradient, click just below the gradient definition bar, then select a color for the pointer as described in Step 2.

4. To remove a pointer from the gradient, click and drag it away from the gradient definition bar.

5. To add the gradient to the current palette, click the Options button at the top-right corner of the panel, and from the menu that appears, choose Add Swatch. The gradient is now available on the Color Swatches panel.

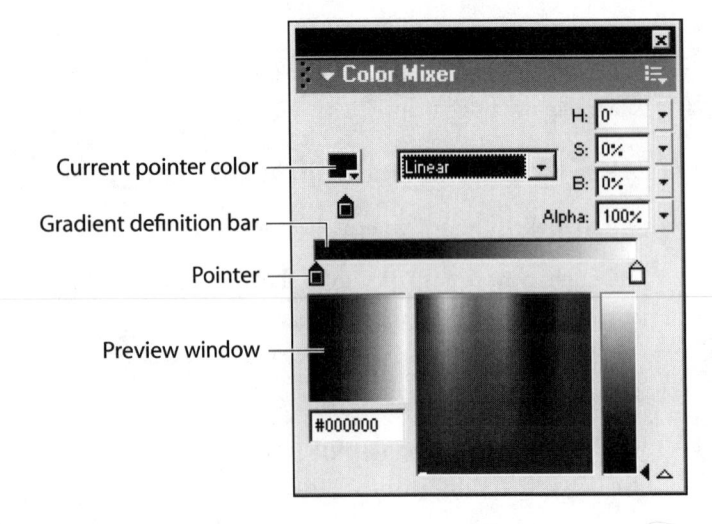

Figure 3.41
The areas of the Color Mixer panel available when creating or editing a fill.

To edit a shape's gradient fill using the Color Mixer panel:

1. Select a filled shape on the stage.

2. With the Property inspector open, click the Fill Color box and then click on the current color Preview window (**Figure 3.42**).

3. The gradient can now be edited from the Color Mixer panel as described on the preceding page.

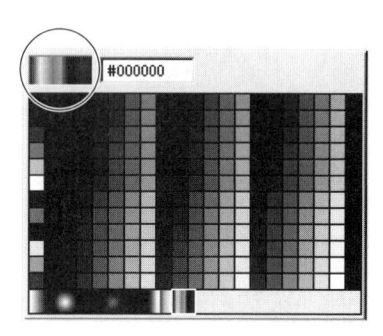

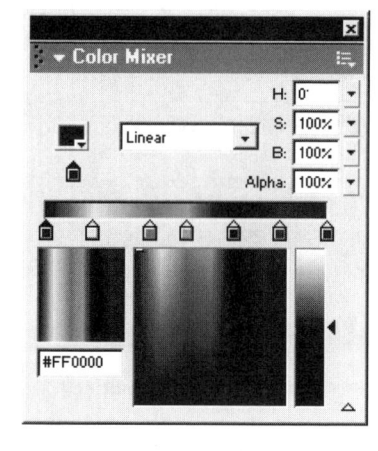

Figure 3.42 Selecting a gradient fill, then pressing the current color Preview window will make the gradient available for editing on the Color Mixer panel.

Using the Paint Bucket and Dropper tools

The Paint Bucket tool is used for fills in much the same way the Ink Bottle tool is used for strokes: Clicking on any empty closed shape will add a fill to it, while clicking on an existing fill will replace it with the Color Mixer panel's current Fill settings. Used in conjunction with the Dropper tool, the Paint Bucket is useful for quickly adding or changing fills on a number of closed shapes. You first use the Dropper tool to sample (copy) a fill from one shape (pulling it into the dropper), then switch to the Paint Bucket tool to apply the copied fill to another shape (squeezing it out of the dropper).

The following options are available when you're working with the Paint Bucket tool:

- **Gap Size.** Allows you to adjust how the Paint Bucket tool handles unclosed outlines. There are four modes to choose from: Don't Close Gaps, Close Small Gaps, Close Medium Gaps, and Close Large Gaps

    TIP *Although it can close many gaps, the Close Large Gaps mode has practical limits. If you find that it won't close a particular gap, you may need to perform the task manually—or at least make the gap smaller to allow this mode to work.*

- **Lock Fill.** Allows you to adjust how Flash fills areas with gradients. When you turn on this option, all fills that use the same gradient will appear to be part of one large gradient stretching across the stage. When it's turned off, each fill will be distinct and display the entire gradient.

To add or change a fill using the Paint Bucket tool:

1. From the toolbar select the Paint Bucket tool, or press the *K* key.

2. With the Color Mixer panel open, choose a fill.

3. Move the cursor over the stage, where you'll notice it changes to a paint bucket.

4. Use the tip of the bucket (where it looks like paint is pouring out) to click on a filled shape to change its fill, or to click on an outline to add a fill.

To apply one shape's fill to another:

1. From the toolbar select the Dropper tool, or press the *I* key.

2. Move the cursor over the stage, where you'll see that it changes to a dropper.

3. When you position the dropper over a fill that you wish to copy, a paint brush icon appears next to the dropper. Click once to activate the Paint Bucket tool.

4. Click a filled shape to change it, or click the outline of a closed shape to add a fill with the same attributes as those you picked up with the Dropper tool.

Transforming a fill on the stage

Using the Fill Transform tool on the Drawing toolbar, you can move, rotate, reshape, or scale a fill within a shape, providing an amazing number of ways to use fills in your layout.

Chapter 3 **Graphics**

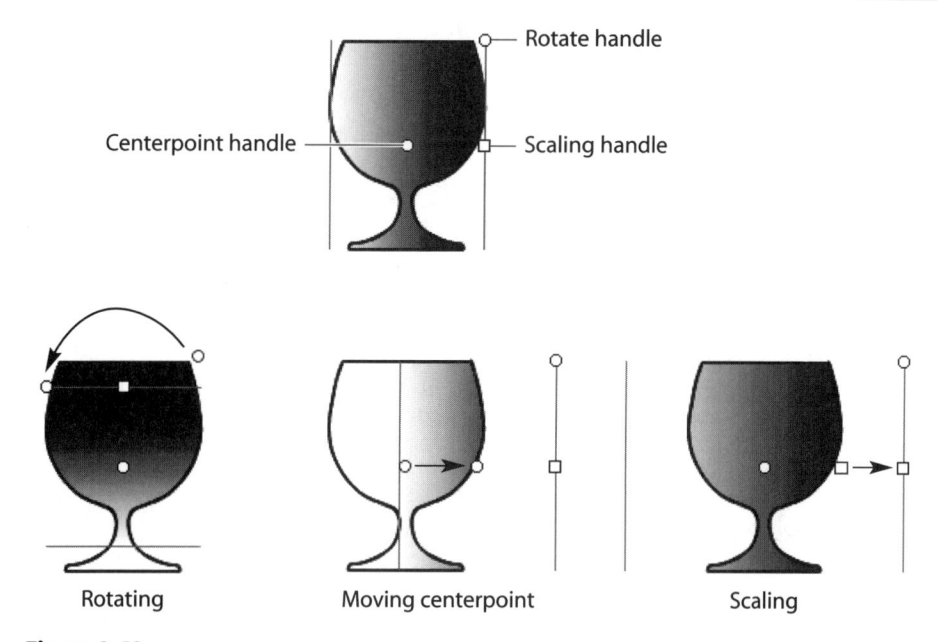

Figure 3.43
The handles associated with the Fill Transform tool that let you manipulate a linear gradient fill.

To transform a linear gradient fill:

1. From the toolbar select the Fill Transform tool, or press the *F* key.

2. Click anywhere on a linear gradient to make it editable.

Editing handles appear (**Figure 3.43**), which allow you to move, rotate, and resize a gradient's center point. If you move your cursor over one of the handles, the cursor changes to reflect the handle's function.

3. Edit the linear gradient by doing any of the following:

- To move the gradient's center point, click and drag the center handle with the four-headed arrow.

- To rotate the gradient, click and drag the handle with the circling arrow.

- To resize the gradient, click and drag the handle with the two-headed arrow.

To transform a radial gradient fill:

1. From the toolbar select the Fill Transform tool, or press the *F* key.

2. Click on a radial gradient fill. The gradient becomes editable, displaying editing handles that allow you to move, rotate, resize, and reshape a gradient. If you move your cursor over one of the handles, it changes to reflect that handle's function.

3. Edit the gradient by doing any of the following (**Figure 3.44**):

   - To move the gradient's center point, click and drag the center handle with the four-headed arrow.

   - To rotate the gradient, click and drag the small circle handle with the circling arrow.

   - To resize the gradient, click and drag the small circle handle with the circle with an arrow inside.

   - To reshape the gradient, click and drag the small square handle with the two-headed arrow.

TIP *For information about working with and transforming bitmap fills, see Chapter 6, "Bitmaps."*

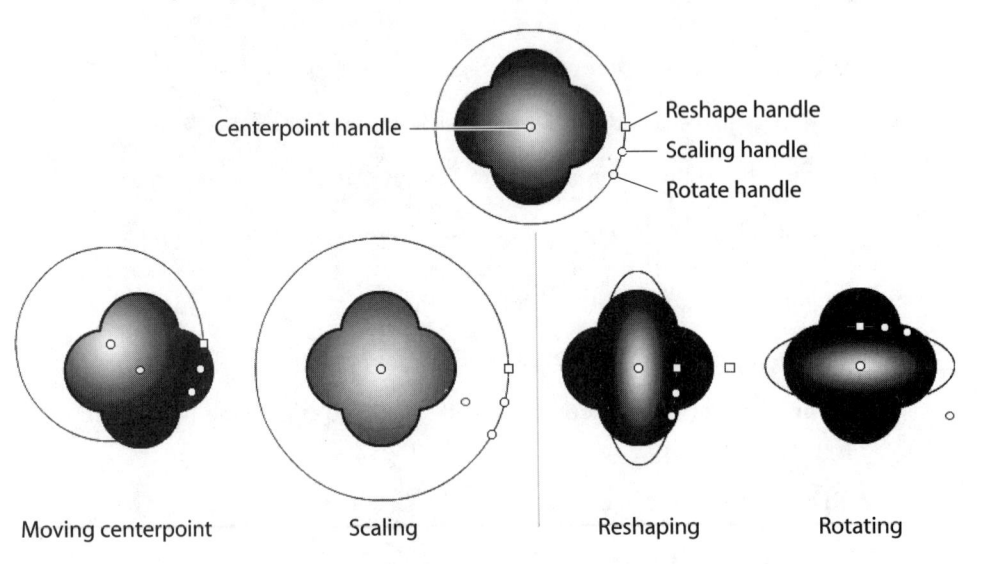

Figure 3.44
The various handles that allow you to manipulate a radial gradient fill.

Line and Fill Effects

Flash provides a few simple but useful effects to aid in the design process (**Figure 3.45**). For example, although you can't usually fill lines with a gradient, Flash lets you turn a line into a shape that can have a fill of any kind, including a gradient or bitmap. This allows you to spice up those boring one-color lines.

You can also quickly create a larger or smaller version of a shape—a process known as contouring in some illustration programs. Referred to in Flash as *expanding* (or insetting) a shape, this process is a bit different than scaling or resizing. Whereas scaling makes a shape proportionally larger or smaller, expanding a shape makes it appear swollen—that is, it looks bigger and fatter and loses some of its detail and crispness, which can be useful in creating a morphing transition where the outline of the shape becomes more defined over time (for more information, see Chapter 10, "Using Animation to Build Movement.").

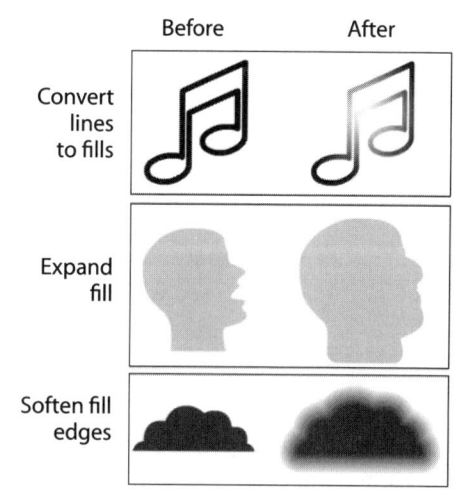

Figure 3.45
Line and fill effects give you more flexibility when you're working with vector shapes.

A third Flash effect allows you to soften a shape's edges. Flash does this by automatically creating a series of incrementally larger versions of the shape, each a little more transparent than the last. This makes the edge of the shape blend more easily with shapes or graphics behind it, and makes vector shapes more realistic looking.

To turn a line or outline into a fill:

1. Select one or more lines on the stage that aren't part of a group or symbol.

2. Choose Modify > Shape > Convert Lines to Fills to convert the line into a fillable shape.

To expand or inset a shape:

1. Select one or more shapes on the stage that aren't part of a group or symbol.

2. Choose Modify > Shape > Expand Shape.

3. In the dialog box that appears, choose your settings (**Figure 3.46**).

   - **Distance.** Allows you to set the distance, in pixels, from the boundary of the expanded (or inset) edge to the original boundary of the shape.

   - **Direction.** Allows you to choose whether you want the shape to expand or shrink. (Expand will make the shape appear fatter; Inset will make it look skinnier.)

4. Click OK.

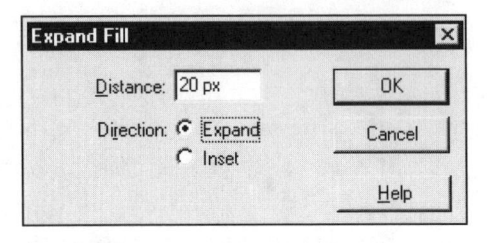

Figure 3.46
The settings on the Expand Fill dialog box.

To soften the edges of a shape:

1. Select one or more shapes on the stage that aren't part of a group or symbol.

2. Choose Modify > Shape > Soften Fill Edges.

3. In the dialog box that appears, choose your settings (**Figure 3.47**):

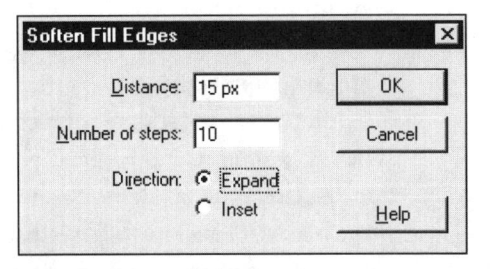

Figure 3.47
The settings on the Soften Fill Edges dialog box.

   - **Distance.** Allows you to set the distance, in pixels, from the boundary of the softened edge to the original boundary of the shape.

   - **Number of steps.** Lets you set the number of incremental "softening" steps that Flash maps from the original boundary of the shape to the boundary of the softened edge. You gain a smoother edge with a greater number of steps; however, this also results in a larger file size. Using too many steps can adversely affect your movie's playback, since Flash has to calculate an individual shape for each step. If you set 20 to 30 steps, you're using a lot of processing power.

   - **Direction.** Allows you to choose whether you want the soft edge effect to be applied inside or outside a shape's defined boundary. Selecting Expand will soften from the current edge of the shape outward; Inset will soften inward from the same boundary.

4. Click OK.

TIP *Use the Soften Edges option to give your shapes a drop-shadow effect.*

Importing Vector Graphics

Even with all of Flash's powerful capabilities, there are still a few tasks that require you to look beyond the Flash tool set.

For example, you could be trying to create polygons, spirals, or 3D objects. Or maybe you've created a bunch of artwork in FreeHand that you now want to use in a Flash presentation. Or you may have just invested in one of the many fabulous clip-art collections available today, and you want to put it to work.

Importing files is the solution for each of these scenarios—allowing you to bring outside graphics into Flash, then edit and animate them just as you do with Flash-created content.

Most vector graphics programs on the market today—including Macromedia FreeHand, Adobe Illustrator, CorelDraw, Deneba Canvas, and even Macromedia Flash—can import and export vector graphics, so you can easily create a graphic in one program and use it in another. And when you import and export files, the vector format provides the most accurate reproduction of artwork.

SWF—It's Everywhere!

It used to be that creating Flash content in another program was a limited, painful, and sometimes frustrating experience. But as Flash has become more popular, a number of companies have designed new software or enhanced existing programs so that they can export their content directly to the SWF file format (Flash's optimized file format). From there the file can be easily be imported into Flash, and used just as if it had been created in Flash.

A number of third-party developers are creating programs that can quickly create 3D content, cool text effects (some that would take hours to produce in Flash), and other animations, all of it exportable to the SWF format—so they can easily be brought in and used in your Flash project. Even some of the major illustration packages, such as Adobe Illustrator and CorelDraw, let you create content in the SWF format. You can download and install a free plug-in to add this functionality to either of these programs—and Adobe Illustrator 9 can generate SWF files right out of the box. For information about either of the plug-ins, visit www.adobe.com or www.corel.com.

For more information about the software available for creating SWF-based content, see Appendix D on the accompanying CD-ROM.

Although Adobe Illustrator may be the most popular format for sharing graphics among programs, it's not the only way. Table 3.1 lists the vector graphic formats that Flash can import.

Table 3.1
Vector Formats Supported by Flash MX

Type	Windows	Macintosh
Macromedia FreeHand (.fh7, .fh8, .fh9, fh10)	X	X
Enhanced Metafile (.emf)	X	
Windows Metafile (.wmf)	X	
Adobe Illustrator - version 7 or earlier (.ai, .eps)	X	X
Flash Player (.swf, .spl)	X	X
AutoCAD DXF (.dxf)	X	X

To import vector graphics into Flash:

1. From the File menu choose Import.

    The Import dialog box appears.

2. Locate the file you wish to use, and click Open.

    If the imported file's name ends with a number—for example, Ball1.ai—Flash will look for a related sequence of files, such as Ball2.ai and Ball3.ai. If it finds a sequence, you'll be asked whether you want to import just the file you first specified or the whole sequence of files.

    TIP When you import a .swf file (which is actually a Flash movie), it will not include individual layers, actions, or tweening effects.

Importing FreeHand Files

Since FreeHand (the vector illustration tool) comes from the same company that makes Flash (Macromedia), it should be no surprise that Flash works more harmoniously with it than any other program or file format.

Although Flash can create any number of vector shapes, FreeHand, a professional vector illustration program, provides a number of powerful shape and layout tools that Flash does not. Using FreeHand, you can easily create storyboards and other graphics and import them directly into your Flash project, with layers, pages, gradients, blends, and more all intact.

Flash can import files from FreeHand 7 or later. There are several things to be aware of when importing FreeHand files into Flash:

- Overlapping objects in the FreeHand file that belong to the same layer are segmented or connected when imported into Flash. If you don't want such objects to be segmented or connected, place them on separate layers within FreeHand and choose Layers on the FreeHand Import dialog box.

- Steps of a blend created in FreeHand are converted to individual shapes when imported into Flash. Thus, a blend with numerous steps can substantially increase your movie's file size.

- FreeHand supports gradients of numerous colors, whereas Flash only supports gradients with a maximum of eight colors. If you're using FreeHand to create Flash content, be aware of this limitation and don't use more than eight colors in your gradients.

- Flash does not support strokes with square caps (squared-off ends). Thus, any strokes in your FreeHand file that contain square caps will be converted to round caps when imported.

To import a FreeHand file into Flash:

1. From the File menu choose Import; the Import dialog box will appear.

2. Locate the file you wish to use and click Open. Flash will display a progress bar for the import process, and the FreeHand Import dialog box will appear.

3. Choose from the following settings on the FreeHand Import dialog box (**Figure 3.48**):

- **Mapping Pages.** Determines how FreeHand document pages are imported into Flash: If you choose Scenes, each page is converted into a scene in Flash. If you choose Key Frames, each page is converted into a keyframe.

- **Mapping Layers.** Determines how individual layers within your FreeHand document are imported into Flash: If you choose Layers, the layers in your FreeHand document are retained as

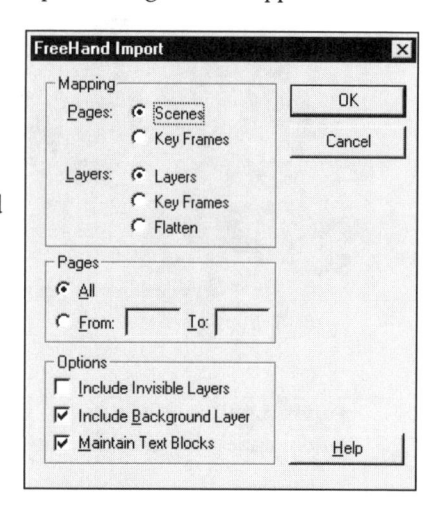

Figure 3.48
The FreeHand Import dialog box.

layers in Flash. If you choose Key Frames, the layers are converted into keyframes. If you choose Flatten, all of the content on individual layers in your FreeHand document will be placed on a single layer in Flash.

- **Pages.** Lets you specify a range of pages in your FreeHand Document that you want to import.

- **Options.** Provides a miscellaneous set of options: **Include Invisible Layers** applies to any layers that were not visible in FreeHand when the file was saved; checking this option includes them in the import process. **Include Background Layer** retains the FreeHand background layer in the imported file. **Maintain Text Blocks** allows editable text blocks in the FreeHand file to remain editable when they're imported into Flash.

Optimizing Vector Graphics

When you create or import a vector graphic, you may need to optimize it to remove some of the unnecessary vector curves. The process is a bit like removing "vector splinters"—things you can't see from a distance but are noticeable up close (**Figure 3.49**). This task is important because fewer curves mean smaller files, and small files usually indicate well-executed Flash projects. In addition, graphics with lots of vector curves require a lot of processing power, and can thus slow down your presentation's animation effects.

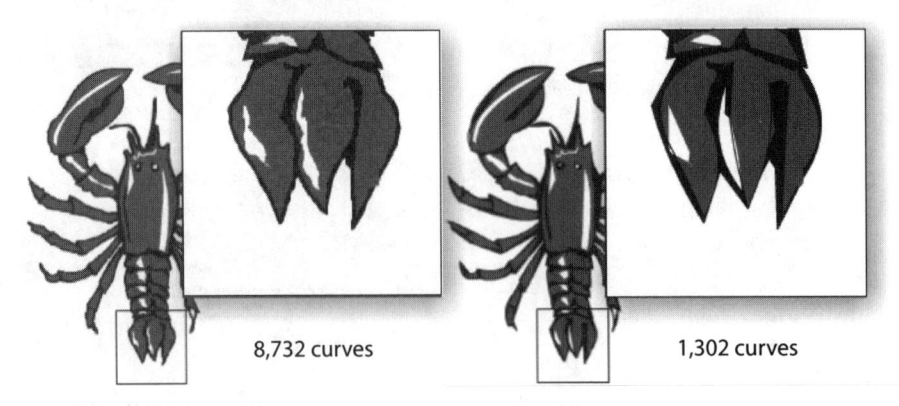

Figure 3.49
Before optimizing graphics, and after.

Imported graphics, such as those from a clip-art gallery, are good candidates for optimization. (We've seen it reduce file sizes by as much as 70 percent.) However, imported files aren't the only graphics that can benefit from being optimized. Believe it or not, even shapes you create with Flash's own drawing tools can be optimized. For example, hand-drawn lines that appear smooth from a distance may look crooked when you zoom in on them; optimizing helps here too.

Because optimization actually edits the vectors that make up a shape, it can potentially change a graphic's appearance—especially pieces of clip art. Usually, though, such changes aren't too noticeable. And fortunately, Flash lets you control the degree of optimization, so you can keep distortion to a minimum.

To optimize a graphic:

1. On the stage, select the line or fill you wish to modify.

   If you want to optimize an imported graphic that is normally imported as a group, make sure you ungroup it first.

2. Choose Modify > Optimize. The Optimize Curves dialog box will appear.

3. Select your settings from the following dialog box options:

   - **Smoothing.** Use this option to set the degree to which Flash will smooth, or optimize, the item.

   - **Use Multiple Passes.** Select this option to have Flash automatically optimize, scan, and then re-optimize a vector graphic until it can't be optimized any further.

   - **Show Totals Message.** Employ this option if you want to see just how much optimization Flash applied to your graphic.

4. Click OK.

   Flash will optimize the shape based on your settings. If you don't like the results, simply click Undo, and pick new settings.

Planning Your Project

Defining Your Audience

If you're thinking about how to put together effective presentations, one of the best things—if not *the* best thing—you can do is watch TV commercials! One thing you'll notice is that certain types of commercials play only at specific times. If you watch a male-oriented program (say, a football game), most of the ads will likely involve trucks, scantily clad women, and beer—sometimes all three. Meanwhile, programs with a predominantly female audience (like something on the Lifetime Network) will tend to feature commercials full of flowers, families, and love. Watch the Cartoon Network (our personal favorite), and you'll see commercials touting super-sweetened corn meal, high-octane sodas, and the latest in action figures—and chances are you won't see an ad about investing your retirement funds.

It's also worth paying attention to commercials' use of imagery. You won't find an older gentleman in a three-piece suit promoting the benefits of marshmallow-laced cereal; more than likely it'll be a cartoon character making the pitch. And a mud-soaked pickup making its way through the Grand Canyon can convey just the image of rugged durability that makes truck buyers swoon. On the other hand, tracking a sports car down the highway at breakneck speed is probably a better approach for selling *that* product.

To maximize the response to your project, do what TV advertisers do: Define your audience. Figure out whom you're trying to reach, and then refine your message accordingly. Use adjectives to describe your audience, then ask yourself some of the following questions:

- Do you want to promote, entertain, inform, or convince? Or are you striving for a combination of all four?
- What do you want your audience to be thinking as they come away from your presentation?
- Is it more important to give a visual presentation or a textual one?
- Do you want to build a new image or reuse an existing one?
- Do you have persuasive facts to back up your message?

These questions are just a starting point. The most important thing is to clarify your goals and what you're trying to promote. Once you've digested this information, you should write a statement that describes your goal in one sentence. Something like, "We want to get kids addicted to our sugar-coated product based on the fact that it's the 'in' thing to do."

Once you've defined your audience and refined your message, you need to establish some project guidelines. Say you've been commissioned to create a Flash-based Web site, for a company that wants to promote the benefits of its new vitamin, Perfectium2002. After discussing the project

Planning Your Project continued

with company staff, you've determined that your audience consists of men and women, ages 20 to 50, who are healthy but concerned about maintaining *optimal health.*

The company wants to get out the message that by taking Perfectium2002 and eating well, you can sustain the high energy levels required for an active lifestyle. The company also wants to demonstrate how easy this is to do. The product already has a large base of faithful users, but your client wants to attract new customers. If you're using such adjectives as healthy, active, athletic, *and* informed *to describe your audience, what kind of imagery comes to mind? Sports, healthy-looking people, an organized home life, smiles, facts and figures, the great outdoors, successful people? Any of these images are appropriate for your site, because they are all things to which your target audience will relate.*

Your client also wants new customers to realize that its vitamin regimen is easy to start and maintain. Thus, you could contrast a busy lifestyle with a vitamin routine that takes only minutes a day. Put a small timer on the page with a quickly rotating second hand. To show that the product is safe, present some data along with your images of happy people. To show that it's effective, provide testimonials or show before-and-after pictures. Use morphing to turn fat letters (which may be part of a header) into skinny ones, thereby planting the subliminal message that big turns to small with the help of this product.

The effective use of color is equally important in your movie. Because colors evoke moods and promote responses, choose your color scheme carefully. For example, bright, sunny, and earthy colors would be perfect for our vitamin product. Fluorescent colors, on the other hand, may prompt the audience to think the product glows in the dark or is radioactive—obviously, not the impression we're after. Get a color wheel at an art store to help select complementary colors, and be careful not to overuse black, which can send a negative message.

Finally, to help make your message memorable, try to incorporate humor and movement whenever appropriate.

Using Color

Who can forget the moment in *The Wizard of Oz* when the dull, lifeless, black-and-white world of reality is replaced by the beautiful, full-color world of Oz? Sixty years ago, those filmmakers understood something we still know to be true: Color evokes an emotional response. By using color effectively, you can grab your audience's attention and guide the way they react to your presentation.

Great artists have used all sorts of tools to create and mix the colors in their masterpieces. Digital artists are no different: They need effective tools as well, and Flash comes through with eyedroppers, palettes, and Color Mixer and Color Swatches panels.

Selecting Colors Using Color Boxes

Color boxes (**Figure 3.50**) are used throughout Flash to quickly select colors for various tasks. They can be found on the Document Properties dialog box, the Layer Properties dialog box, the Property inspector, the drawing toolbar, and the Color Mixer panel.

Clicking a color box initiates two actions: The current palette of swatches appears, and an Eyedropper tool becomes active. Use the Eyedropper tool to select a color from the swatches shown, or move it around the interface, and the color that's beneath the tip of the eyedropper when you click it will be selected. Clicking the top of the swatch palette allows you to close the palette and remove the eyedropper, essentially canceling the color selection process.

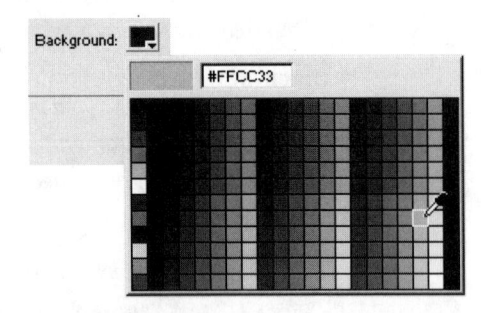

Figure 3.50
When clicked, color boxes display the current palette and an Eyedropper tool for quickly choosing colors.

Using the Color Mixer Panel

The Color Mixer panel is where you create, edit, and choose the solid colors and gradients used on shapes in your project. Once you've created or edited a color or gradient in the Color Mixer panel, you can add it to the list of available color swatches that appear on the Color Swatches panel.

The Color Mixer panel is made up of the following areas (**Figure 3.51**):

- **Stroke Color control.** Clicking this control will set the stroke color as the *focus* for any adjustments made in the Color Mixer panel (to indicate this, the control button will appear to be pressed). For example, if both a stroke and a fill are selected on the stage, clicking this control will apply whatever adjustments you've made in the Color Mixer panel to the selected stroke. Flash will not automatically set the focus of the Color Mixer to the stroke color just because you select a stroke on the stage. You may need to select this option manually.

- **Fill Color control.** Clicking this control will set the fill color as the focus for any adjustments made in the Color Mixer panel (the control button will appear pressed in to indicate this). For example, if both a stroke and a fill are selected on the stage, clicking this control will apply whatever adjustments you've made in the Color Mixer panel to the selected fill. As with the Stroke Color control, Flash will not automatically set the focus to the fill color just because you select a fill on the stage. (See Stroke Color control above.)

- **Black-and-White button.** Regardless of the current colors displayed, clicking this button will set the stroke color to black and the fill color to white (the default colors).

- **No Color button.** Choosing the Oval or Rectangle tools on the drawing toolbar, then the Stroke or Fill Color control and then this button, will set the stroke or fill color to no color—so that the shape created by either tool will not contain a stroke or fill (depending on the adjustments you make). This option does not affect selected strokes or fills, only newly created strokes or fills.

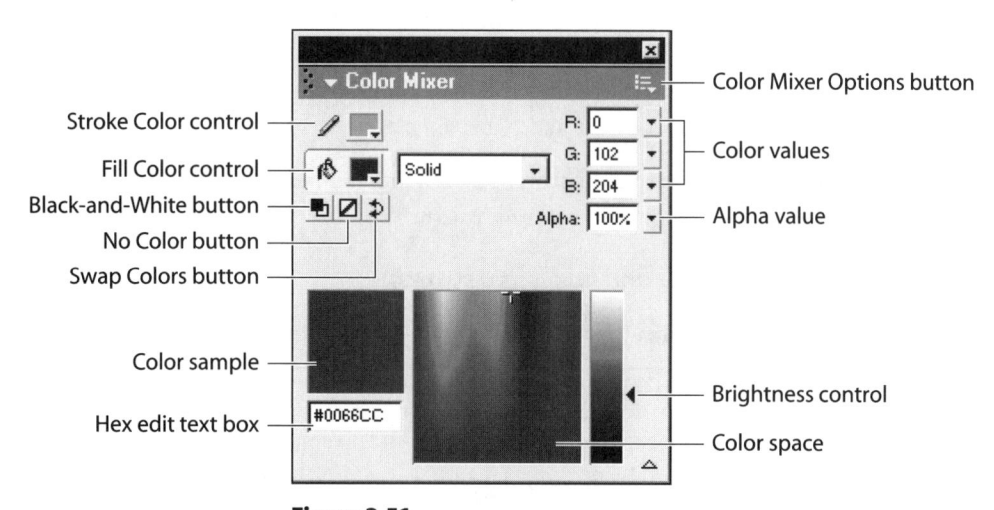

Figure 3.51
Areas of the Color Mixer panel.

- **Swap Colors button.** Clicking this button swaps the color in the Stroke Color control with the color in the Fill Color control, and vice versa. If the Fill Color control contains a gradient fill when you swap colors, the first color in the gradient (the leftmost color of the gradient, as shown on the Gradient Definition bar) will be used instead—since strokes cannot contain gradients.

- **Color space.** This box contains various colors that you can quickly select, by simply clicking an area with the mouse.

- **Brightness control.** This slider tool allows you to quickly adjust the brightness of the current color.

- **Color sample.** This box displays a large preview of the current color.

- **Hex edit text box.** This text box displays the hex value of the currently selected color. In addition, entering a different hex value here will update the current color accordingly. For more information about hex values, see "Understanding Color Modes" later in this chapter.

- **Color values.** Using this area you can create or edit colors by entering values based on the selected color mode. You can enter values by typing them directly into the text boxes, or by clicking the Arrow button next to the text box, then adjusting the slider that appears. Depending on which color control has focus (stroke or fill), these boxes will display the values for the currently active or selected color.

- **Alpha value.** This text box/slider is used to set the alpha (transparency) level for the currently active color in the Color Mixer panel. This can be either a stroke or fill color, based on which color control is currently selected. You can enter a value by typing it into the text box, or by clicking the arrow button next to the text box then adjusting the slider that appears.

- **Color Mixer Options button.** Opens a menu that lets you choose a color mode or add a color to the current palette.

To create a new color and add it as a swatch:

1. With the Color Mixer panel open, do one of the following:

    - Type values into the color value boxes.

    - Enter values by clicking the color value slider controls.

    - Click at any point on the color bar.

2. Adjust the Alpha value of the color if you want to adjust its transparency.

3. Click the Color Mixer panel Options button, and choose Add Swatch from the menu that appears.

Your color will be added to the bottom of the palette of currently available swatches.

To edit the stroke or fill color of the currently selected shape:

1. On the stage, select a stroke, a fill, or both.

2. With the Color Mixer panel open, click either the Stroke or Fill Color control to set the focus of adjustments made on the Color Mixer panel. If you click the Stroke Color control, any color adjustments you make will be reflected on the selected stroke. If you choose the Fill Color control, any color adjustments you make will be reflected on the selected fill.

Understanding Color Modes

When using the Color Mixer panel to create or choose colors, you can enter color values in one of three mapping standards, or modes: RGB, HSB, or Hex. Each of these modes simply represents a different way of describing colors. The mode you choose is usually a matter of preference, though sometimes your task will determine your mode (as we'll describe shortly). You can create the same basic colors with all three modes.

To choose a color mode:

1. Click the Color Mixer panel Options button. A menu of color modes will appear.

2. Select a color mode. The Color Value boxes on the Color Mixer panel will change accordingly (**Figure 3.52**).

   NOTE *You work with Hex color values via the Hex edit text box, which is always visible on the Color Mixer panel.*

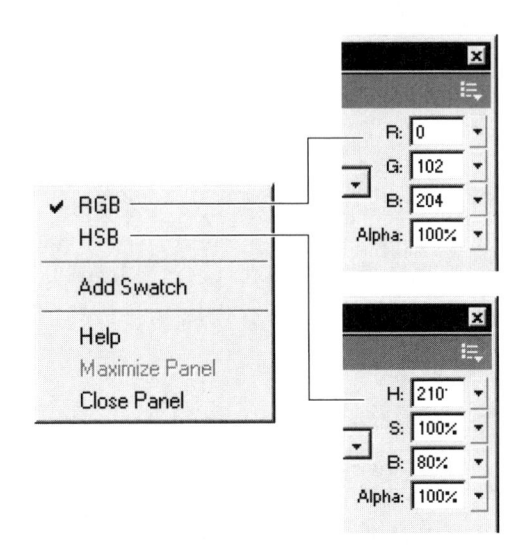

Figure 3.52
The Color Value boxes change depending on the current color mode.

RGB

RGB stands for *red, green, blue*. Your computer monitor mixes these three colors to display every color you see. The amount of each color used is expressed as a value between 0 and 255. Mixing colors on a monitor is quite different from working with watercolors on paper. Using watercolors, the darker or blacker we want something, the more color we apply. The whiter we want something, the less color we use. It works just the opposite way with your monitor and RGB values. If *R*, *G*, and *B* each have a value of 0 (represented as 0-0-0), your screen will be black. If they each have a value of 255 (or 255-255-255), your screen will be white. The first number value in the sequence represents red; thus the value 255-0-0 displays as pure red. Likewise, 0-255-0 displays as pure green, and 0-0-255 as pure blue.

Although in art class you created orange by mixing the two primary colors red and yellow, with RGB you create orange using the value 255-177-0—the maximum value of red, half the value of green, and no blue. If this seems confusing, just experiment a bit and you'll soon get the hang of it.

HSB

This mapping mode is probably the most widely used for describing color. *HSB* stands for *hue, saturation*, and *brightness*.

- **Hue.** Specifies colors by their names (for example, red, yellow, and blue). Every color falls into a hue category in the *spectrum*, or range, of colors.
- **Saturation.** Specifies the intensity of hue. Saturated colors are intense and deep; less saturated colors are washed-out or dull.
- **Brightness.** Specifies a color's illumination intensity, and expresses that value as a point along a scale of grays going from black to white.

If a color is too dark, you can just adjust its brightness. If it's too rich or intense, adjust its saturation. If the saturation and brightness are fine, but you want to use a different color entirely, adjust the hue.

Hex

The third mode Flash can use to define colors is hex values. *Hex*, short for *hexadecimal*, is a six-digit value that describes a color. Most HTML documents and Web pages use hexadecimal values to describe colors. Being able to enter the same color value on a Web page as you do in your Flash movie makes it easy to maintain color consistency.

With hex, instead of assigning a value from 0 to 255 to *R*, *G*, and *B* as described earlier, you assign a value of 00 to ff. Let us explain.

We're used to the base ten system, where the numerals run 0 to 9 and then repeat with a *1* attached to them—10 to 19—and repeat again with a 2 attached—20 to 29—and so on. Hex values are a little different. Instead of going from 0 to 9 and then repeating, hex values run 0 to 9 but continue on with *a* to *f*—…8, 9, A, B, C, D, E, and F—before repeating. The hex system is base 16, so *15* in base 10 is equivalent to *F* in base 16. When you've run through the first sixteen 0 to F hex values, they repeat with a *1* attached: 10, 11, 12, 13, 14, 15, 16, 17, 18, 19, 1a, 1b, 1c, 1d, 1e, 1f. The value 1f is equal to 31 in our more usual base ten system, and ff is equal to 255. **Table 3.2** shows the complete hex values for 0 to 255.

Table 3.2
Hex-to-Decimal Conversion Table

	0	1	2	3	4	5	6	7	8	9	a	b	c	d	e	f
0	0	1	2	3	4	5	6	7	8	9	10	11	12	13	14	15
1	16	17	18	19	20	21	22	23	24	25	26	27	28	29	30	31
2	32	33	34	35	36	37	38	39	40	41	42	43	44	45	46	47
3	48	49	50	51	52	53	54	55	56	57	58	59	60	61	62	63
4	64	65	66	67	68	69	70	71	72	73	74	75	76	77	78	79
5	80	81	82	83	84	85	86	87	88	89	90	91	92	93	94	95
6	96	97	98	99	100	101	102	103	104	105	106	107	108	109	110	111
7	112	113	114	115	116	117	118	119	120	121	122	123	124	125	126	127
8	128	129	130	131	132	133	134	135	136	137	138	139	140	141	142	143
9	144	145	146	147	148	149	150	151	152	153	154	155	156	157	158	159
a	160	161	162	163	164	165	166	167	168	169	170	171	172	173	174	175
b	176	177	178	179	180	181	182	183	184	185	186	187	188	189	190	191
c	192	193	194	195	196	197	198	199	200	201	202	203	204	205	206	207
d	208	209	210	211	212	213	214	215	216	217	218	219	220	221	222	223
e	224	225	226	227	228	229	230	231	232	233	234	235	236	237	238	239
f	240	241	242	243	244	245	246	247	248	249	250	251	252	253	254	255

Swatches and Palettes

If you've ever shopped for an item that comes in various colors, you may be familiar with the term *swatches*. These small squares, or samples, of color allow us to see some or all of the available color choices. A set of swatches is known as a *palette* in Flash.

Flash's Color Swatches panel (**Figure 3.53**) uses the concepts of swatches and palettes to help you work with and organize colors in your movie. The Color Swatches panel displays all of the available solid colors and gradients for the current palette. Change the current palette (see below), and the colors and gradients on the Color Swatches panel will change as well.

The Color Swatches panel is where you select colors and fills for the strokes or shapes that are selected on the stage. For example, choosing a solid color or gradient from the Color Swatches panel will update the fill of the selected shape on stage. The Color Swatches panel also allows you to remove or duplicate swatches, so that you have a "starting point" for creating a new color or gradient.

To delete a swatch from the current palette:

1. With the Color Swatches panel open (Window > Color Swatches), select the swatch you wish to delete by clicking it. It will appear highlighted.

2. Click the Color Swatches panel Options button, and choose Delete Swatch from the menu that appears.

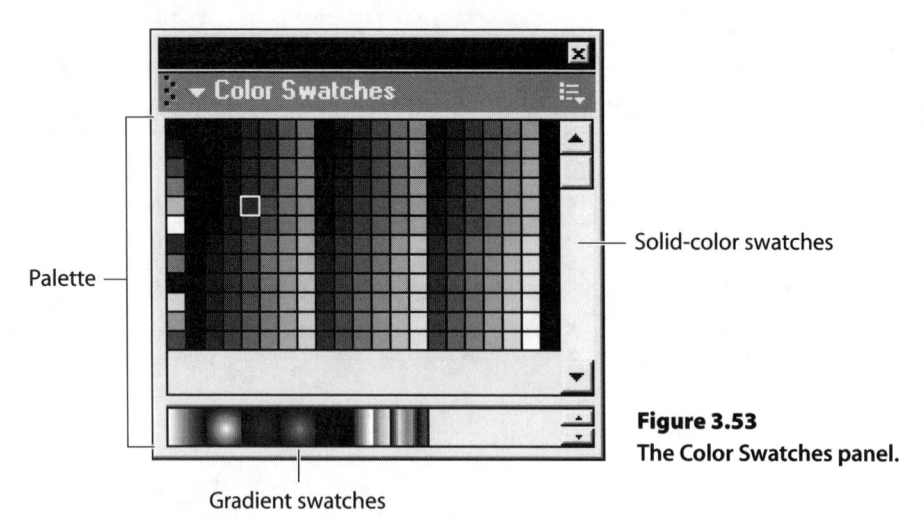

Figure 3.53
The Color Swatches panel.

Palette

Solid-color swatches

Gradient swatches

To duplicate a swatch from the current palette:

1. With the Color Swatch panel open, select the swatch you wish to duplicate by clicking it. It will appear highlighted.

2. Click the Color Swatches panel Options button, and choose Duplicate Swatch from the menu that appears. A duplicate of the selected swatch will be added to the bottom of the Swatches panel.

Importing and exporting palettes

Flash makes it easy to import color palettes from other Flash projects, as well as different programs such as Macromedia Fireworks. This means you don't need to waste time re-creating a custom palette from another project. You can also export your current color palette from Flash for use elsewhere.

Flash can export palettes in two formats: .CLR (or .FCLR for Macintosh) and Adobe color tables, known as .ACT files. While CLR files include both solid-color and gradient information, only Flash can use this type of palette. ACT files cannot store gradient information, but they *can* be used in such programs as Flash, Macromedia Fireworks, and Adobe Photoshop. Your particular needs will determine which format is the better choice.

You can import both .CLR and .ACT palettes, and also import the color palette belonging to a .GIF graphic file. This means all of the colors in a .GIF file will import as a palette.

You use the following options on the Color Swatches Options menu (**Figure 3.54**) to import and export palettes:

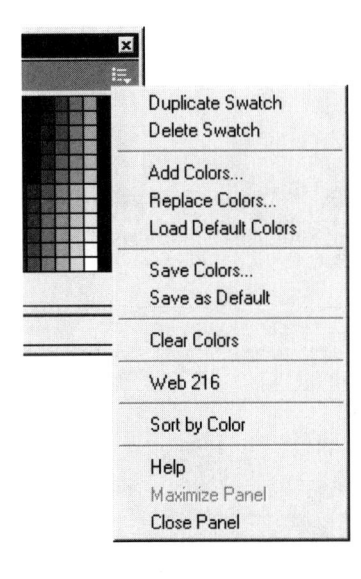

Figure 3.54
The Color Swatches Options menu.

- **Add Colors.** This allows you to import a palette from a .CLR, ACT, or .GIF file, and add it to the current palette. Selecting this option opens the Import Color Swatch dialog box, where you can locate the palette you want.

- **Replace Colors.** This lets you replace the current palette with an imported one. Selecting this option opens the Import Color Swatch dialog box, where you can locate the palette you want.

- **Load Default Colors.** This loads Flash's default color palette, or one that you defined with the Save as Default option (see below). Selecting this option automatically updates the current palette with the palette set as the default.

- **Save Colors.** This allows you to save the current palette as a .CLR or .ACT file, for use either in other Flash projects or in other programs. Selecting this option opens up the Export Color Swatch dialog box, where you can name your palette and choose a format (.CLR or .ACT).

- **Save as Default.** This lets you specify the current palette as the one Flash automatically uses when you start a new Flash project. Selecting this option will open an alert box asking you to confirm your decision. Choose Yes or No.

- **Clear Colors.** This clears all colors from the current palette except black and white and one gradient.

- **Web 216.** This option loads the Web-safe palette of 216 colors that is shipped with Flash.

- **Sort by Color.** This sorts the colors on the current palette by their luminosity (brightness) values.

Video Tutorial

Creating Graphic Elements. This tutorial reviews most of the concepts covered in this chapter: using the graphic tools, working with strokes and fills, applying color, and more.

Text

CHAPTER 4

Despite their versatility, graphics alone can't always convey our message—at least not quickly and clearly. We often need to add text to eliminate ambiguity. For example, a picture of the sun can represent any number of things—heat, nuclear energy, the solar system—but place the word *summer* next to it, and your message is instantly clearer. In Macromedia Flash, text can not only inform, it can slide in, fade in or out, grow, or shrink. You can even make it "explode" if that's the effect you want. Although Flash isn't designed to be a full-featured word processor, it does let you format text in a number of ways: setting margins, kerning, line spacing, and many other attributes.

You can also use text elements (that is, *blocks* of text) to display text that doesn't change onscreen (called *static* text) or to accept user input. You can even display HTML-formatted text that's been loaded from an external file. And if you're really feeling adventurous, you can create animation effects specifically for text, a topic we'll discuss at the end of the chapter.

What you'll learn...

About different types of text elements

How to create and work with text elements

How to edit and configure text elements

How to use font symbols to make movies more dynamic

How to break apart text

About animation considerations for text

Creating Text Elements

Because Flash functions primarily as a graphics program rather than a word processor, it handles text in a unique way. Any group of characters that you type in Flash (such as a paragraph) is initially a self-contained entity on the stage that you can resize, rotate, and move as a single object (**Figure 4.1**). As long as text elements remain in their original state, you can re-edit them using any of the available text tools. However, once you break apart a text element (that is, separate a block of text into its individual characters), you can no longer edit it as text. Instead, the individual characters are converted into shapes, which you can alter and dress up in ways you couldn't with normal text.

Figure 4.1
Text blocks are groups of characters that you work with as a single unit.

Later in this chapter we'll discuss how to break up text objects, as well as some of the ways you can improve the look of your text by doing so.

Flash can create four types of text elements: static text labels, static text blocks, input text blocks, and dynamic text blocks (**Figure 4.2**). We'll discuss input and dynamic text blocks later in the chapter. Right now we'll look at static text elements and how they work.

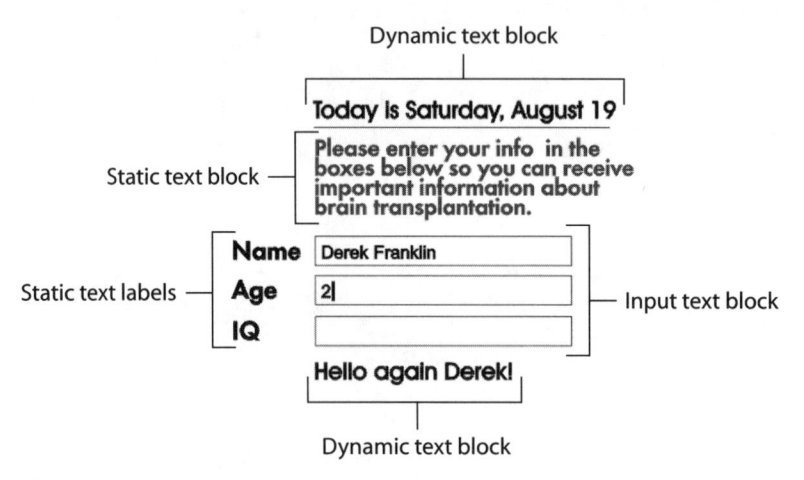

Figure 4.2
The four types of text elements that Flash creates: Static text labels and static text blocks for displaying static information, input text blocks for accepting user input, and dynamic text blocks for displaying up-to-date info that Flash can generate automatically.

Static Text Elements

In contrast to input text blocks and dynamic text blocks—whose contents can change while your movie is playing—the contents of static text elements cannot be changed outside of the authoring environment. Thus, to create a static text label or static text block, you enter text just as you want it to appear in your movie, where it will remain static.

A text *label* is simply text that continues on a single line until you manually insert a line break by pressing either the Enter key or the Return key. This type of text object does not wrap text automatically, as do most of today's word-processing applications. Instead, text labels allow you to determine where each line ends (**Figure 4.3**). Text labels are useful mainly for placing just one or two words of text.

Static text *blocks* have a fixed width, which you designate when you create the text block. Any text you type into it will "wrap" to the next line, based on the width you defined (**Figure 4.4**). Text blocks are useful for displaying any more than a few words of text.

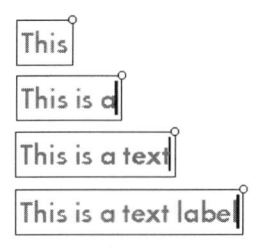

Figure 4.3
Text labels expand as you type text into them, and are best suited for short text phrases.

Figure 4.4
Text in a text block automatically wraps to the next line.

To create a static text label:

1. On the toolbar, choose the Text tool, or press the *T* key.

2. With the Property inspector open, select Static Text from the menu of choices.

3. Set the text attributes—font, font size, and color—that you want to use for this label.

Move the cursor to the stage area, where it will turn into a crosshair with a small *A* in its bottom-right corner. The center of the crosshair indicates the bottom-left corner of any new text labels created.

4. Click on the stage where you want to place your text label.

A small box with a circle in its top-right corner and a blinking insertion point appears. This is an empty text label.

5. Enter the text you desire, and the text label will automatically expand to accommodate it.

TIPS *If you click elsewhere before entering text, your empty text label will disappear.*

Be careful in choosing a font for text elements. Due primarily to antialiasing effects, some fonts are hard to read at small sizes—especially when viewed in the final presentation. If you can't enlarge your text, you can select one of three special fonts from the font pop-up list: _sans, _serif, or _typewriter. These fonts are always displayed with antialiasing turned off.

To create a static text block:

1. On the toolbar select the Text tool, or press the *T* key.
2. With the Property inspector open, select Static Text from the menu of choices.
3. Set your text attributes for the block, including font, font size, and color.

   Move the cursor to the stage, where it will turn into a crosshair with a small *A* in its bottom-right corner. The center of the crosshair indicates the bottom-right corner of any new text blocks you create.
4. Click and drag from left to right to define the width of your text block, then release to complete the action.

   A rectangle defining your text block appears, with a small square in its top-right corner and a blinking insertion point.
5. Enter the text you want, and the text block will automatically wrap text to the width you defined.

   TIPS *Once you set any options on the Property inspector for both static text blocks and static text labels, these settings will be used for all new text elements (until you change them).*

   Any text you type may initially appear rough. To obtain smoother-looking text, from the View menu choose Antialias Text.

To change the width of a text block:

1. On the toolbar select the Arrow tool, or press the *V* key.
2. Click and drag the text block's resize handle. Any text in the block will be automatically reformatted to fit the new size (**Figure 4.5**).

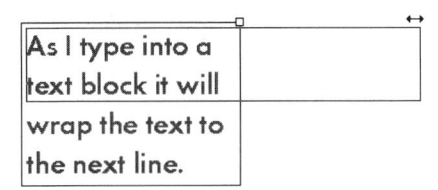

Figure 4.5 Resizing a text block automatically reformats the text displayed in it.

To change a text block to a label, or vice versa:

- Double-click the resize handle of the text element.

Input and Dynamic Text Elements

Since input and dynamic text elements serve a different function than static text elements, it's not surprising that you create them differently than you do their static counterparts. Because input and dynamic text fields need to accommodate an unknown amount of text, you can drag their size vertically as well as horizontally when creating them—in essence, creating a text "window" in which any amount of text can be displayed (you simply define how much you want the window to display at once). You create input and dynamic text elements in the same way. However, as we'll discuss in the next section, you must configure them to work differently in your movie.

To create an input or dynamic text element:

1. On the toolbar select the Text tool, or press the *T* key.

2. With the Property inspector open, select either Input or Dynamic Text from the menu of choices.

3. Set the text attributes you want to use for this element, including font, font size, and color.

   Move the cursor to the stage area, where it will turn into a crosshair with a small *A* in its bottom-right corner. The center of the crosshair indicates the bottom-right corner of any new text blocks you create.

4. Click and drag from left to right and from top to bottom to define the width and height of your text element, then release to complete the action.

   A rectangle defining your text block appears, with a small square in its top-right corner and a blinking insertion point.

5. Enter the text you want, and the text element will automatically wrap to the width you defined.

6. Return to the Property inspector and give the text field an instance name.

This name cannot contain spaces; it is used to identify the text field for ActionScripting purposes.

> **MX ALERT** **NOTE** *In Flash 5, text fields were given variable names. They are now given* **instance** *names because they are treated as scriptable objects (similar to movie clips)— which means they have properties and methods that allow you to control them dynamically. Text fields are now instances of the Text Field object. Although you can still assign a text field a variable name, we don't encourage you to do so because much of the new ActionScript pertaining to text fields only works properly when a field is given an instance name. For more information, see Chapter 14, "ActionScript Objects."*

If the text elements you're creating are going to change, why bother to set text attributes or enter initial text (as described in Step 5 above)? First, typing in text allows you to define what appears onscreen initially (for example, instructions for a user input box). That text can subsequently be erased and replaced by the user (an input text element), or replaced dynamically (**Figure 4.6**). Second, setting text attributes lets you define the default attributes that will be used for user- or dynamically-entered text. For more information, see "Powering Input and Dynamic Text Elements with Rich-Text Formatting" later in this chapter.

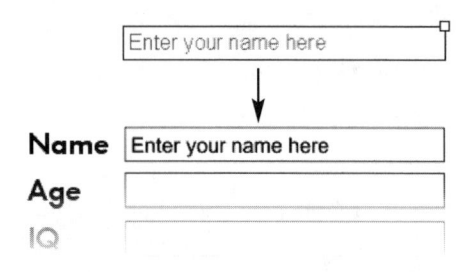

Figure 4.6
Any text you type into an input text block—for example, user instructions—will be displayed in that text element until it's replaced by user-entered text.

> **MX ALERT** **{ ActionScript }** *You can leave an input or dynamic text element empty, then use ActionScript to dynamically fill it. For example, if you've given a text field an instance name of* **myField***, then* `myField.text = "Hello"` *will display* **Hello** *in that field. (Look for more on this in Chapter 14, "ActionScript Objects," Jand Chapter 16, "Using ActionScript in Your Projects").*
>
> *You can create input and dynamic text fields via ActionScript by employing the* `createTextField()` *method. This allows you to dynamically create lists, forms, and more, as your movie plays.*

To change the width or height of an input or dynamic text element:

1. On the toolbar select the Arrow tool, or press the *V* key.

2. Click and drag the text element's resize handle horizontally or vertically to resize its width or height, respectively. Any text will be automatically reformatted to fit the new size.

TIPS *You can turn a dynamic text element into a static element by simply selecting it on the stage with the Arrow tool, then changing its definition on the Property inspector.*

MX ALERT { **ActionScript** } *You can set a text field's height and width dynamically via ActionScript. For example, to set the height of a text field instance named* **myField***, you would enter something like:* `myField._height = 20`*. Input and dynamic text fields have a number of additional properties that can be set dynamically via ActionScript. For more information, see Chapter 14, "ActionScript Objects").*

Scrolling Dynamic Text Fields

MX ALERT

One of the great things you can do with dynamic text fields is use them as "windows" for long blocks of text—that is, more lines of text than can be displayed in the field at one time. Users can scroll through in order to view all of the text the field contains. As an example, a dynamic text field may contain 50 or more lines of text but only be tall enough to display 10 of them at a time.

When you manually enter text into a newly created text field (rather than choose to have it entered dynamically), normally that field will expand to accommodate the text entered. If you type in ten lines of text, the field will, by default, expand to display all ten lines. But say you only want to display five lines of text at a time. To do so, you must resize the "window" that represents the boundaries of the text field itself. When you make this window shorter, you reduce the amount of text that will be visible within the window, but you don't change the amount of text the field can contain.

To resize the dynamic text field window within the authoring environment:

1. *Select the Text tool on the toolbar.*

2. *Select the dynamic text field that you wish to resize.*

3. *While holding down the Shift key, double-click the text field's resize handle. The resize handle will turn solid black, indicating a change in its functionality. Double-clicking the handle again will switch it back to its original functionality.*

(continued on next page)

Scrolling Dynamic Text Fields *continued*

4. Click and drag the resize handle to resize the text window. The text contained in the field will not change, even if the portion you can see displayed changes (**Figure 4.7**).

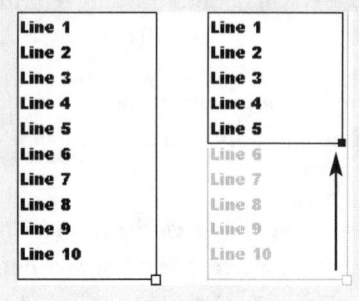

Figure 4.7
You can resize a dynamic text field and make the text within it scrollable.

Now that you've resized your text field so that only a portion of the text it contains is visible, you need a mechanism to scroll the field within the authoring environment, as well as in the exported movie. Scrolling the text within the authoring file simply involves selecting the text field and then using the arrow keys on the keyboard—a fine solution for developers within the authoring environment, but not really practical for users when your project is exported to a SWF. This is where the ScrollBar component comes in handy.

To make text within a dynamic field scrollable:

1. Open the Component panel by choosing Window > Components.

2. Click and drag a ScrollBar component onto the text field. It should automatically snap into place on the side of the field.

Now, when your movie is exported as a SWF, the text within the field can be scrolled using the component you just dragged onto it—talk about simple! For more information on components, see Chapter 15, "Components."

Editing and Configuring Text Elements

MX ALERT Once you've created a text element, you'll usually want to edit its appearance. Flash lets you change character and paragraph attributes such as font, font color, margins, line spacing, and more. You may also want to alter the way a text element is defined (static, input, or dynamic) or change some of its core attributes (which determine how it works within your movie)—especially if it's a dynamic text element. You make all text adjustments via the Property inspector. First, however, you need to know how to link your edits to a particular block or section of text.

Selecting and Editing Text Blocks

You can edit text as blocks (meaning the entire text element) or as individual text within a block (for example, correcting spelling or changing words, setting character options for individual characters, and so on). The latter function is known as working in text-edit mode.

When you select a text block, you can restyle the text as a block; you can also move, rotate, and scale that text. Once it's selected, a colored selection box surrounds the block. Any adjustments you make in the Property inspector will be applied to all of the text in the block.

When you select text *within* a block, that text will be highlighted (**Figure 4.8**). When individual text is selected, adjustments you make in the Property inspector will affect only the selected text, rather than the entire text block (**Figure 4.9**).

TIP *Character or paragraph edits to individual text will be reflected in the exported movie only if the text is within a static text block. If the text is in an input or dynamic text element, you must check the HTML option on the Property inspector for the edits to be reflected.*

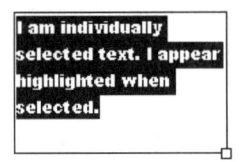

Figure 4.8
When you select a text block, a colored selection box surrounds it (left). By contrast, individually selected text appears highlighted (right).

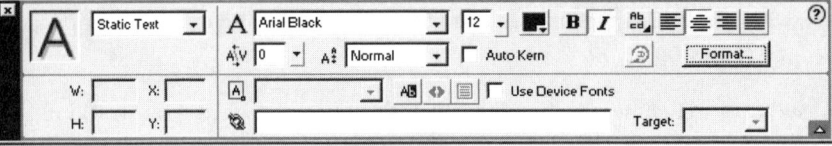

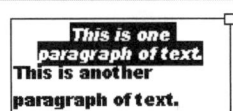

Figure 4.9
When you select individual text, editing adjustments you make on the Property Inspector will affect only the selected text, not the entire text block.

To select and edit a text block:

1. On the toolbar, choose the Arrow tool, or press the *V* key.

2. Move your cursor onto the stage and click on any text block.

   The text block will be surrounded by a colored selection box.

3. Resize, move, rotate, or align the text element on the stage, or format text within the text block by making adjustments in the Property inspector as described above.

To select and edit individual text inside a text block:

1. Do any of the following:

   - On the toolbar, select the Arrow tool, or press the *V* key

   - Double-click any text to place it in text-edit mode. You can then edit individual letters, words, or paragraphs in the text block.

   - On the toolbar, select the Text tool.

   On the stage, the cursor will change to an I-beam shape when you pass it over a text element.

2. Click between characters to place the insertion point for entering more text.

3. In text-edit mode, do any of the following:

   - Select a letter, word, or paragraph for editing by click-dragging from the first letter you wish to edit to the last; then release. This highlights and selects the text, which you can then edit in all sorts of ways (changing font, font size, color, and so on).

   - Delete text by click-dragging to select it, and then pressing the Delete or Backspace key.

   - Copy text by click-dragging the text you wish to copy and choosing Copy from the Edit menu.

   - Paste text by clicking once to place the insertion point where you would like the text to be added. Then from the Edit menu, choose Paste.

Character-Level Formatting

Although Flash cannot match the text editing capabilities of a dedicated word processor, it can handle some of the more common formatting tasks, like setting font size, line spacing, and kerning. You make these types of edits—known as character-level formatting—by means of the Property inspector.

Any character-level formatting attributes you set on the Property inspector will become the default attributes for all new text blocks, if no text block or individual text is selected on the stage. If a text block or individual text is selected on the stage, the current character attributes will appear on the Property inspector, and any adjustments made there will be reflected immediately in the selected text.

TIP *When you select a text block or individual text that contains more than one set of formatted text (for example, part of the text is green and bold, while the rest is red and italic), the Property inspector will display the attributes of the first character of the selected text.*

The Property inspector includes most of the usual options for character-level formatting, including font and font size, and the Bold and Italic buttons, as well as some other settings with which you may be less familiar (**Figure 4.10**):

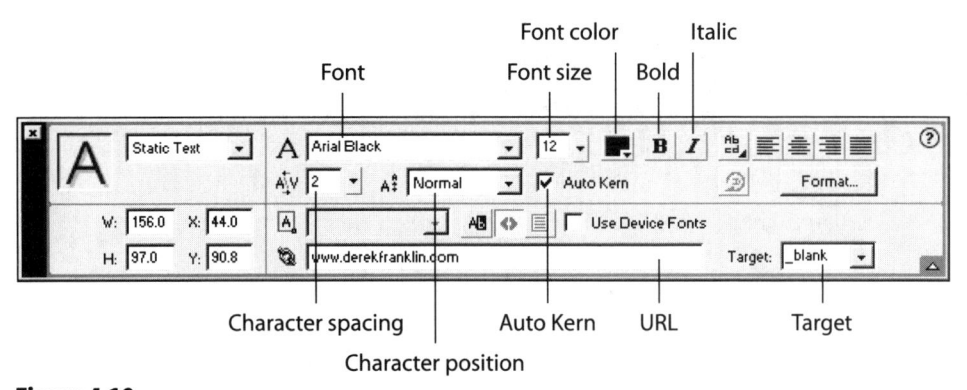

Figure 4.10
Character settings on the Property inspector.

NOTE *Unless noted below, these settings are available for all types of text fields (static, dynamic, and input).*

- **Font color.** Allows you to choose a font color. Clicking this color box will display a list of available solid colors. You'll notice that gradients are not available for text objects; we discuss a way around this constraint in "Breaking Text Apart" later in the chapter.

- **Character spacing.** Defines the amount of space between characters. You can set a new amount by typing it into the text box, or adjusting the slider next to the text box.

- **Auto Kern.** Most fonts contain information that describes how to handle the space between characters (for example, the letters *AB* require more space (kerning) in between them than *II* or *AV*. Check this box to utilize the font's built-in kerning information.

- **Character position.** Controls how text appears in relation to its baseline (**Figure 4.11**).

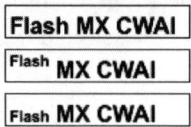

Figure 4.11
The "Character position" setting is used to set the text's relation to the baseline.

- **URL.** Allows you to associate a URL with currently selected text—similar to creating hyperlinked text in HTML documents. You can associate sections of text within the same text block with different URLs. Text with an associated URL is indicated by a dotted underline in the authoring environment. While hyperlinks in an HTML page are normally identified by colored-underlined text, the hyperlinks you create using this Flash feature will not be visually identified in your exported movie as a hyperlink (except by a hand cursor)—unless you format it differently. This option is not available for input text fields.

- **Target.** When a URL has been set up for a text block or selected text within a text block, this option becomes available. It allows you to define the target window that the specified URL should open in. If you want the specified URL to open in a particular frame of an HTML page, enter the name of that frame here.

To set default character formatting for new text elements:

◆ With the Property inspector open (and no text selected), adjust the various character attributes to your liking.

Afterward, all new text elements will have those attributes.

To change character formatting for selected text:

1. Select a text block or any individual text you wish to edit.

2. With the Property inspector open, make any desired adjustments. The text on the stage will be automatically updated to reflect your edits.

> **TIP** *Most character formatting options are also available from the Text menu.*

Paragraph-Level Formatting

Paragraphs are sections of text separated by a hard return (that is, by pressing Return or Enter on your keyboard). Paragraph-level formatting allows you to set alignment, margin, line spacing, and indentation. These type of edits are also accomplished via the Property inspector.

When you set paragraph-level formatting options, if no text block or individual text is selected on the stage, any attributes you set on the Property inspector become the default attributes for all new text blocks. If a text block or individual text is selected on the stage, the current paragraph attributes will appear on the Property inspector, and any adjustments made in the panel will be reflected immediately in the selected text.

The Property inspector lets you align text to the left, right, center, or justify it to both right and left; you can also set the right and left margins, indentation, and line spacing. Several of these options are available by pressing the Format button on the Property inspector once you've selected some text (**Figure 4.12**).

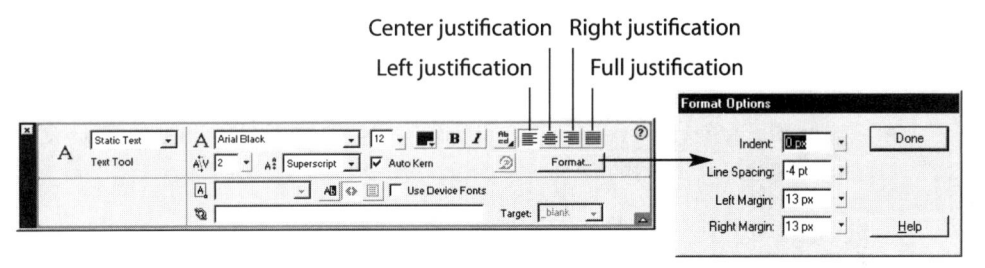

Figure 4.12
Paragraph settings on the Property inspector. Pressing the Format button reveals several of these.

TIPS With the exception of line spacing (which always defaults to points), the measurement units for paragraph settings default to the measurement units used in your onscreen rulers.

You can apply different attributes to individual paragraphs within the same text block.

Alignment options are also available from the Text menu.

To set default paragraph formatting for new text elements:

◆ With the Property inspector open but no text selected, adjust the paragraph attributes. All new text elements will have those attributes.

To change paragraph formatting for selected text:

1. Select a text block or any individual text you wish to edit.

2. With the Property inspector open, make any necessary adjustments. The text on the stage will be automatically updated to reflect your edits.

Static Text Options

Static text elements—which contain text that doesn't change while your movie is playing—are best for form element labels, navigation labels, button labels, animated chunks of text, and any sections of text that will not be dynamically loaded from a text file or server. There are two settings on the Property inspector specific to static text fields (**Figure 4.13**):

- **Use Device Fonts.** Leaving this option unchecked tells Flash to embed font information for any fonts used in the text block, so that the font will appear antialiased (smoothed) in the exported movie. Checking this option will keep font information for this text block from being embedded (see "Understanding Device Fonts" for more information).

- **Selectable.** Allows users to select text within the block to cut or copy into the system's clipboard, so that it can be pasted into another program.

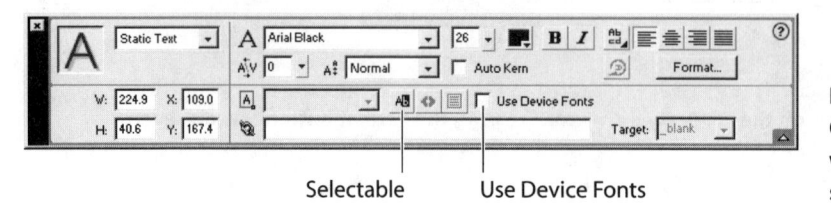

Figure 4.13 Options available when creating static text fields.

Understanding Device Fonts

Most fonts includes a built-in description that contains information about how characters look, which characters will appear in response to specific key-presses, kerning, and more. This font description also includes info that allows the text you see while working in Flash to appear smoothed (antialiased) (that is, if the View > Antialiased Text option is checked). This information is also embedded in your exported Flash movie, so that text there will appear smoothed as well. Although the results are graphically pleasing, there are drawbacks to embedding this information in your exported movie. For one, smoothing makes small fonts almost impossible to read.

Understanding Device Fonts continued

In addition, this embedded font information can add to your exported movie's file size. The solution to both of these problems is to use device fonts.

Let's say you create a static text block that uses a font called MyFavoriteFont. If you then select the Use Device Font option on the Text Options panel, when you export your movie, everyone who has MyFavoriteFont installed on their machines will see the text exactly as you intended—though it will not appear antialiased. Machines that don't have MyFavoriteFont will use the font that most closely resembles it—a process called font mapping. Be advised, however, that this is a far from perfect solution, because machines sometimes pick fonts that look nothing like the originally specified font (**Figure 4.14**).

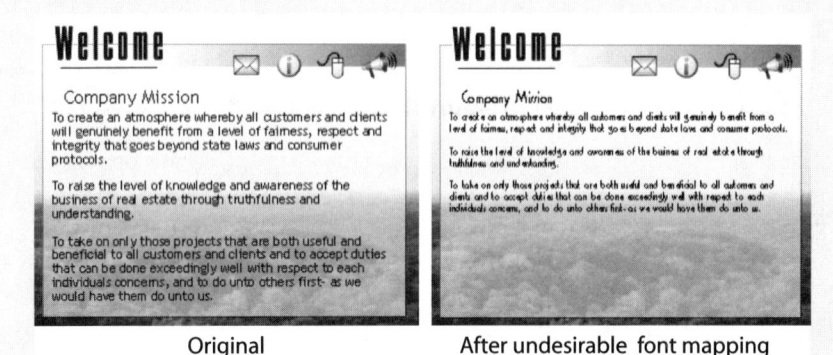

Original   After undesirable font mapping

Figure 4.14
Using device fonts can sometimes produce unexpected and unwanted results.

Because font mapping can sometimes produce unexpected results, Flash includes the following three built-in device fonts to make font mapping more predictable:

- _sans
- _serif
- _typewriter

The Flash player knows to map these fonts—which can be found at the top of the font list on the Character panel—to specific fonts available on most platforms. For example, the _sans font in Flash looks almost exactly like the Arial font in Windows and Helvetica on a Macintosh. The following describes how Flash's device fonts are mapped.

- **_sans.** Maps to Arial on Windows and Helvetica on a Macintosh
- **_serif.** Maps to Times New Roman on Windows and Times on a Macintosh
- **_typewriter.** Maps to Courier New on Windows and Courier on a Macintosh

Creating vertical text

MX ALERT Using a static text field, you can elect to display text vertically, rather than the normal horizontal mode. This option is useful for Flash content that may be viewed in some Asian countries, where text is read vertically; it can also serve other creative uses.

To create vertical text:

1. Select a static text field.
2. Press the Change Direction of Text button to reveal a list of choices.
3. Make a choice from the menu that appears.

   The text field will reflect your choice.
4. If you wish to change the rotation of individual characters, press the Rotation button, which becomes active when you choose a vertical text option from the menu mentioned in Step 3 (**Figure 4.15**).

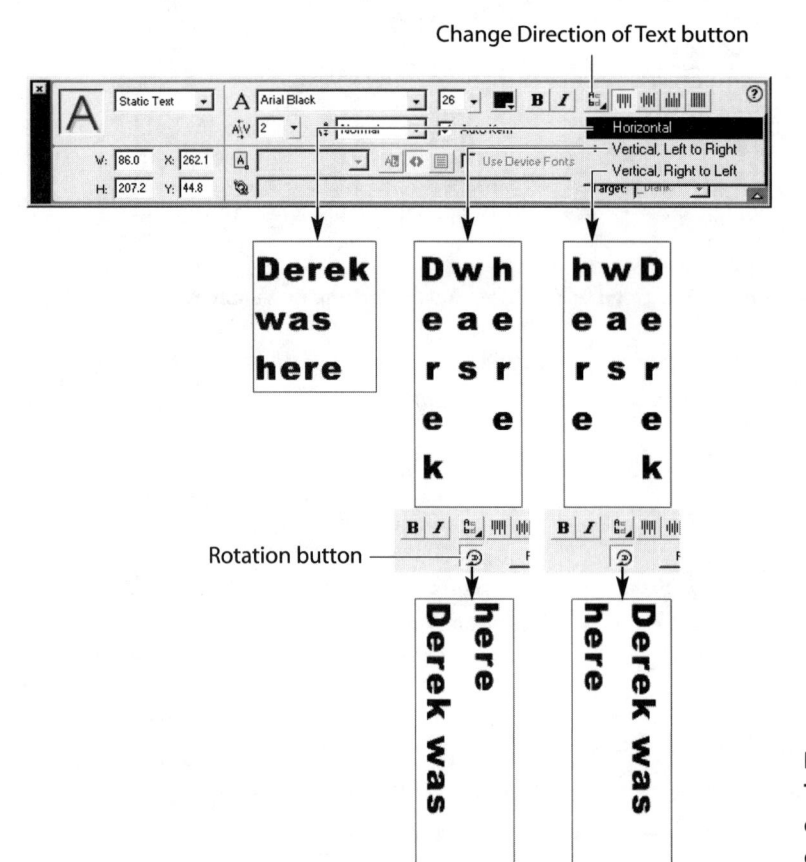

Figure 4.15
The effects of the different text direction options.

TIP *If you want to make vertical text the default orientation for all static text elements you create, go to the Editing tab on the Preferences dialog box (Edit > Preferences) and select the Default text orientation option. There are additional Vertical Text options here that you can set as default behaviors, by checking the appropriate box (**Figure 4.16**).*

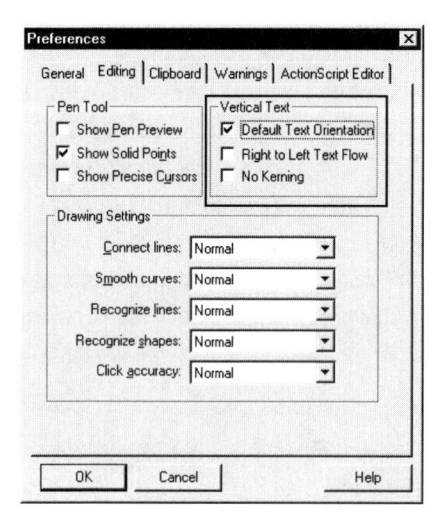

Figure 4.16
Vertical Text options on the Editing tab of the Preferences dialog box.

Dynamic Text Options

Dynamic text blocks let you do things like display text that's been dynamically generated by ActionScript or a Web server, or loaded from an external text file (**Figure 4.17**). This means that the text within a dynamic text block can change as your movie is playing, allowing you to display personalized messages, update information by changing an external file, and even display HTML-formatted text (see "Powering Input and Dynamic Text Elements with Rich-Text Formatting").

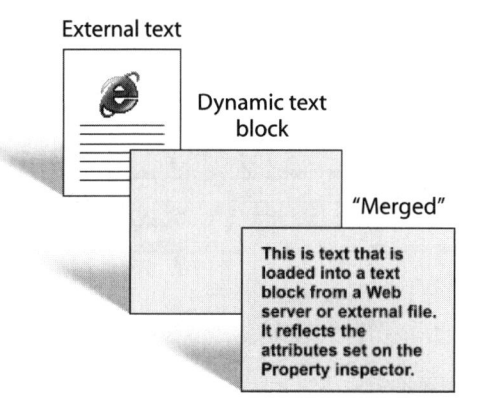

Figure 4.17
Dynamic text blocks can display text that is loaded from a source external to your movie, such as a Web server or text file.

When you create a dynamic text block, you assign it an instance name, which allows you to control it in various ways via ActionScript. For example, if you create a dynamic text block and name it **myTextBlock**, the following ActionScript code will display the message "Hello, did you know it was the year 2002?" inside the text block:

```
currentDate = new Date();
myTextBlock.text = "Hello, did you know it was the year " +
currentDate.getFullYear() + "?";
```

MX ALERT **NOTE** *To dynamically display text in Flash 5, all that was required was the associated variable name of the text field, followed by the value you wanted to display. With Flash MX dynamic text fields are now instances of the Text Field object; thus they have a* text *property that defines what text will be displayed in the field. If you attempt to dynamically fill a text field instance without using this* text *property, the display will be blank. For more information, see Chapter 14, "ActionScript Objects."*

It's not critical to understand the ActionScript code right now. You just need to know why you assign instance names to dynamic text blocks, and how those instance names are used in ActionScript to evoke interactivity.

The settings for dynamic text boxes include the following (**Figure 4.18**):

- **Instance name.** This is where you assign an instance name to the text field, so that you can communicate with it via ActionScript. The instance name must begin with a character, and cannot contain any spaces.

- **Line type.** This pop-up menu lets you specify how lines of text are displayed. Choose Single Line to display just one line; choose Multiline to allow text to wrap to the next line automatically; choose "Multiline no wrap" to begin a new line only after you enter a hard return.

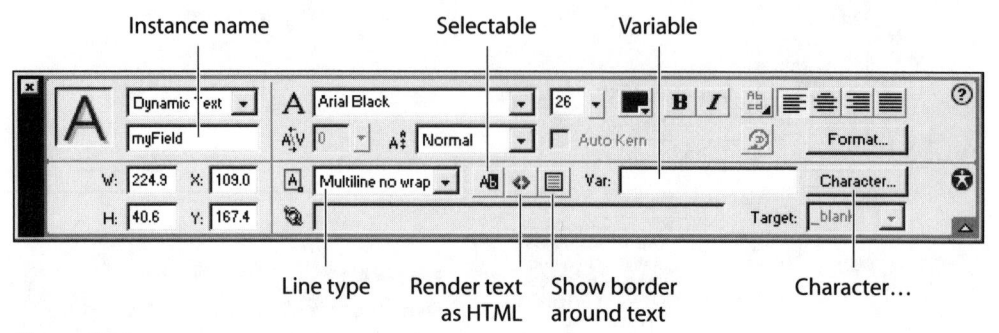

Figure 4.18
The options available when creating dynamic text blocks.

- **Selectable.** Allows users to select text within the text block, and cut or copy it to their system's clipboard for pasting into another program.

- **Render text as HTML.** This option sets the text block to interpret HTML code that's been loaded dynamically. Checking this box also allows you to use different styles of formatted text within a single input text block. For more information on this feature, see "Powering Input and Dynamic Text Elements with Rich-Text Formatting" later in this chapter.

- **Show border around text.** Allows your text box to be displayed (in Flash as well as in your final movie) with a solid thin outline and a white background. If you leave this option unchecked, your text field will still be identified within Flash by a dotted outline. However, in your exported movie the text block will no longer show a border.

- **Variable.** This is where you assign a variable name to your dynamic text block. The name must begin with a letter, not a number or space (though you may use a number after the first character). This option facilitates backward-compatibility with Flash 5. Assigning variable names to text fields is highly discouraged because most of the new ActionScript pertaining to text fields requires that they have instance names rather than variable names.

- **Character....** This button opens the Character Options dialog box (**Figure 4.19**), where you'll find options for embedding fonts in your movie. These options determine not only how text appears within the block, but also how it affects your movie's overall size. Embedding fonts allows characters within the field to appear smooth, but also adds information used to describe the font to the exported movie file, thus increasing its size. If you don't embed fonts, the aliased text within the field will appear more jagged. However, text displayed in a small font may actually be easier to read aliased. Experimentation is the key here. Font embedding options include the following:

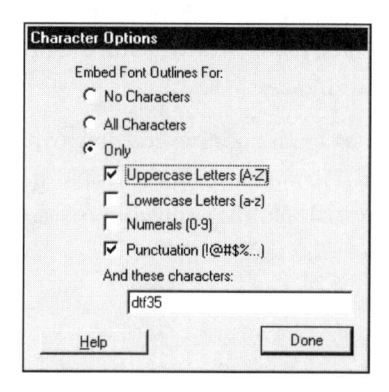

Figure 4.19
The Character Options dialog box.

No Characters. This is the default setting. This option will prevent font styles used in the field from being embedded in the movie. The result is a smaller file but more jagged text within the field.

All Characters. Embeds all of a font's characters in your exported movie. If you select this option, text within the block will appear smooth, but your file size could increase by as much as 35KB to 60KB (on average).

Only. Selecting this option makes the following options active:

Uppercase letters. Embeds uppercase characters *A* through *Z*.

Lowercase letters. Embeds lowercase characters *a* through *z*.

Numerals. Embeds numbers zero through nine.

Punctuation. Embeds special characters such as question marks, exclamation points, and more.

And these characters. Use this box to specify particular characters you want embedded. For example, if you only wanted to embed *d, t, f, 3*, and *4*, you would type those characters into this box (without commas or spaces—unless you wanted those to be embedded as well).

> **MX ALERT** { **ActionScript** } *All of these settings are actually properties of a text field instance, and can be set dynamically using ActionScript. For example, if you have a text field named myField,* `myField.border = false` *would remove the border from around the text field, even if you had previously applied one using the Property inspector. For more information, see Chapter 14, "ActionScript Objects."*

Input Text Options

Input text blocks are used as form fields, password fields, and so on. They allow users to enter text that your movie can use internally by way of ActionScript, or that can be sent to a Web server for processing. With a little bit of creativity, you can produce Flash forms that are as engaging as the rest of your movie.

When you create an input text block, you assign it an instance name, which lets you control the text box any number of ways via ActionScript. For example, if you created an input text block and named it **myInputBlock**, the following ActionScript code would convert any text entered into all lowercase text:

```
myInputBlock.text = myInputBlock.text.toLowerCase()
```

In another example, the following code tells your movie to perform an action based on whether the **myInputBlock** input text block contains text—basically stating that if **myInputBlock** is empty (equals ""), go to and stop at Scene 2, Frame 1; otherwise, go to and stop at Scene 3, Frame 1:

```
if (myInputBlock.text == "") {
    gotoAndStop ("Scene 2", 1);
} else {
    gotoAndStop ("Scene 3", 1);
}
```

The settings for input text boxes include the following:

- **Instance name.** See the Instance name setting for dynamic text elements in the previous section.

- **Line type.** With one exception, this is the same setting as that used with dynamic text: Choose Password to have asterisks (*) replace characters that have been entered into the text field.

- **Render text as HTML.** See the "Render text as HTML" setting for dynamic text elements in the previous section.

- **Show border around text.** See the "Show border around text" setting for dynamic text elements in the previous section.

- **Variable.** See the Variable setting for dynamic text elements in the previous section.

- **Maximum Chars.** Allows you to set the maximum number of characters that can be entered in the text field. If you enter zero, an unlimited number of characters can be entered.

- **Character…** Same as the corresponding button for dynamic text; allows user-entered text to be antialiased.

    NOTES *Neither input nor dynamic text blocks support kerning or character spacing.*

    Neither input nor dynamic text blocks support full justification—just left, right, and center alignment.

    If you wish to perform rotation, alpha-color transformations, or masking (with Mask layers) with dynamic or input text blocks, you need to embed fonts.

Powering Input and Dynamic Text Elements with Rich-Text Formatting

Rich-text formatting allows your input and dynamic text blocks to display text of various font styles, sizes, colors, and even hyperlinks (**Figure 4.20**). When you select the "Render text as HTML" option for either input or dynamic text blocks, they become HTML-sensitive—that is, any text displayed in the text field that contains the supported HTML tags (see below) will be displayed in rich-text format based on the tags used. For example, if you create a dynamic text block named **myDynamicText** and then select the HTML option for the text block, the following ActionScript would cause "Hello there! You are our **favorite** reader" to be displayed in the text block

```
myDynamicText.htmlText = "Hello there! You are our
<b><u>favorite</b></u>reader."
```

If, however, you had left the "Render text as HTML" option unchecked, the following text would instead be displayed:

Hello there! You are our <u>favorite</u>reader.

(For information on how to do this with a loaded text file, see below.)

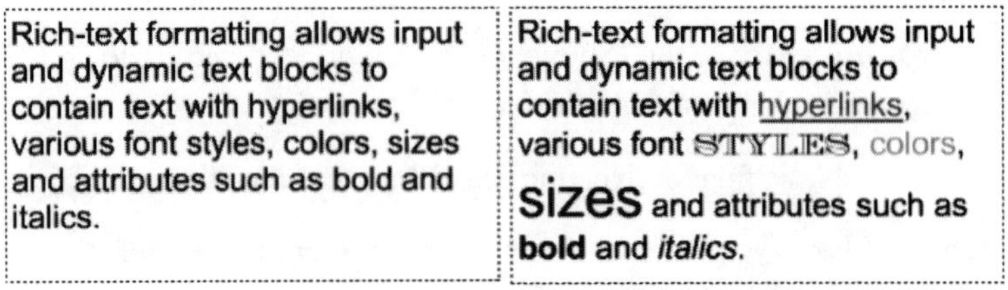

| Rich-text formatting allows input and dynamic text blocks to contain text with hyperlinks, various font styles, colors, sizes and attributes such as bold and italics. | Rich-text formatting allows input and dynamic text blocks to contain text with hyperlinks, various font STYLES, colors, sizes and attributes such as **bold** and *italics*. |

Figure 4.20
A text block without rich-text formatting (left), and one with (right).

Mixing and matching HTML tags allows you to create more sophisticated-looking text.

Flash supports the following HTML tags:

```
<A>
<B>
<FONT COLOR>
<FONT FACE>
<FONT SIZE>
<I>
<P>
<U>
```

When you combine Flash's support for HTML tags with its capability to load text from an external source such as a text file or Web server, you've got a powerful means of displaying dynamic, rich text in your movie. You can also easily update the text displayed in your movie simply by updating the external source. To use dynamic text in your movie, you must set up your movie to load a file into a dynamic text block, and then create the file that is loaded (or use one you previously created).

To load an HTML-based text file into a dynamic text block:

1. In Flash, create a dynamic text block, give it an instance name of **myField**, and then select the "Render text as HTML" option on the Property inspector. In addition, choose Multiline from the "Line type" drop-down menu.

2. Right-click (Windows) or Control-click (Macintosh) Frame 1 on the timeline, then select Actions from the menu that appears. The Actions panel will appear.

3. In the left pane, navigate to Actions > Browser/Network.

4. Double-click the `loadVariables()` action, which will make an unconfigured ActionScript statement appear in the right pane. Parameter settings are at the top of the Actions panel.

5. In the URL parameter box, type the name and directory path to the text file. (Because our text file will reside in the same directory as our exported .swf file, all we need to enter here is the name of our file, MyMovieText.txt.) Leave the other parameter settings as is.

6. Select the empty frame on Frame 10, and press F6 on your keyboard.

This will insert a keyframe at Frame 10. This is necessary in order to add a couple of additional actions to this frame on our timeline.

7. With Frame 10 still selected, open the Actions panel and in the left pane, navigate to Objects > Movie > Text Field > Properties.

8. Double-click the `htmlText` property to make an unconfigured ActionScript statement appear in the right pane.

9. In the Expression box at the top of the Actions panel, type the following: `myField.htmlText = intro.`

When this action is executed, it will display the value of `intro` (which is a text value loaded in from our external file) in the **myField** text field instance we set up in Step 1. The `htmlText` property is used to tell the **myField** text field to render the value of `intro` as HTML.

10. In the left pane of the Actions panel, Navigate to Actions > Movie Control.

11. Double-click the `stop` action to add it to the current script.

    This action is added to prevent the timeline from moving beyond Frame 10.

    NOTE *You may be wondering why we didn't just place all of our actions on Frame 1. Here's the explanation: The data is loaded into the movie by the action on Frame 1, but Flash needs a bit of time to register that it has been loaded before it can be used. Here we've designated a nine-frame interval between the loading of the data (Frame 1) and its use (Frame 10).*

12. Export this authoring file to a SWF movie.

To create the HTML-based text file that will be loaded into your movie:

1. Open either SimpleText for the Macintosh or Notepad for Windows, and type the following:

    ```
    &intro=<p align="center"><b><font size="12">Hello!!</font></b></_p><p>My <font color="#FFCC66">name</font> is <a href="http://_www.mydomain.com "><u><font color="#0066FF">Matt Stailey</font></u></a>. What is your <i>name?</i></p>
    ```

    Here you can see we've created a variable in our text file named `intro` and assigned it a value that contains HTML-formatted text. Once this text file has been loaded into Flash, the program contains the `intro` variable (same name as in the text file) as well as the variable's associated value (the HTML-formatted text)—just as if the variable were created in Flash itself. You'll remember that in Step 9 of the previous exercise we set our movie up to display this value in the **myField** text field.

2. Name this text file MyMovieText.txt (the same file name we identified in our ActionScript a moment ago), and save it to the same directory as your exported SWF.

    If you double-click and play the SWF, this text will load into the movie (per the `loadVariables()` action we set up in Steps 4 and 5 in the previous exercise) and be displayed in the **myField** text field. This field will display the text with rich-text formatting, based on the HTML tags we used (**Figure 4.21**).

Figure 4.21
The onscreen result of our external text file loading into our SWF movie.

That's all there is to it. If you re-edit and save this text file using a text editor, the SWF will reflect your edits when played again, including any changes made to formatting tags.

NOTE *You will find completed versions of these files on the accompanying CD in the Chapter 4/Assets folder.*

A couple of things to notice about this text file:

- The standard <HTML> and <BODY> tags are missing: Because they have no effect, they aren't used.
- If this page were wide enough, you'd see that the code resides on a single line. Using returns anywhere in your code will cause Flash to insert a hard return, which is not always a desirable result.

The Rich-Text Tip Sheet

There are a number of issues you should be aware of when using rich-text formatting in your movie:

- *Some HTML tags in ActionScript require the use of quotation marks to define certain values (for example, a hyperlink, font face, or font color). However, using quotes in this manner causes conflicts in ActionScript, so you need to employ what's known as an escape character (\") to make everything work properly. Instead of defining a hyperlink this way: <a href="http://www.mydomain.com">, you would define it as follows: <a href=\"http://www.mydomain.com\">. (This only pertains to HTML-based text defined internally in a script using ActionScript; it does not apply to quotes used in an externally loaded text file.)*
- *If you define a font style by using the HTML <font face> tag, your user will only see that particular font if it's installed on his or her machine; otherwise, their system will choose the closest device font (see 'Understanding Device Fonts" earlier in this chapter). To ensure that the defined font appears as intended, you should embed that font in your movie.*
- *If you embed a font for use in conjunction with the HTML <font face> tag, be aware that variations of the font face (Bold, Italic) are not embedded. Thus, text using these variations may not display.*
- *Opening the Property inspector and then selecting a text block on the stage will display that text block's default font settings. Any text with characteristics (color, face, size) not defined in the HTML <font> tag will reflect the text block's default attributes as set in the Property inspector.*
- *Using one of Flash's built-in device fonts will give you the most predictable results when displaying rich text.*

(continued on next page)

The Rich-Text Tip Sheet *continued*

- When defining a font's color using the HTML <font color> tag, use Hex-based values (see the "Color" section in the previous chapter for more information on Hex values).
- The font size value defined using the HTML <font size> tag is set in relation to the default size you defined for the text block using the Property inspector.
- Hyperlinks defined in HTML-based text are not automatically shown in a different color or with an underline, as you normally see on an HTML page. If you want to identify a section of text as a hyperlink, you need to set these attributes manually using the <font color> and <u> underline tags.
- When the "Render text as HTML" option is selected for an input or dynamic text block, rich-text formatting is only applied to text loaded into the text block, either from an external file or a script. Entering tag-based text directly into a selected text block within the authoring environment means that the tags will be included in the text block when your movie is exported (**Figure 4.22**).
- Users cannot input information with rich-text formatting (different fonts, colors, sizes, and so on) into input text blocks: Text entered into input text blocks always reflects the text block's default attributes, as defined on the Property inspector.

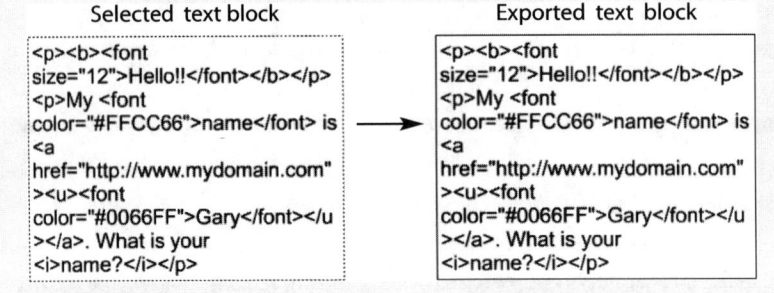

Selected text block

```
<p><b><font size="12">Hello!!</font></b></p>
<p>My <font color="#FFCC66">name</font> is <a href="http://www.mydomain.com"><u><font color="#0066FF">Gary</font></u></a>. What is your <i>name?</i></p>
```

Exported text block

```
<p><b><font size="12">Hello!!</font></b></p>
<p>My <font color="#FFCC66">name</font> is <a href="http://www.mydomain.com"><u><font color="#0066FF">Gary</font></u></a>. What is your <i>name?</i></p>
```

Figure 4.22
Entering tag-based text directly into a selected text block will export both the tags and the text block with your movie.

Using Font Symbols for Dynamic Type Styling

By using font symbols—which allow you to separate characters from their font styles—you can make your Flash movies even more dynamic. Let's say, for example, that your movie uses the text "Hello" throughout. This word contains the characters *H-e-l-l-o* but has no inherent font style—you must assign it one. To do so, you create a font symbol based on the Arial font and assign it a name, such as My Favorite Font. As you'll learn more about soon, My Favorite Font★ will now appear on the font menu of the Property inspector (**Figure 4.23**). (The asterisk indicates My Favorite Font is a font symbol.)

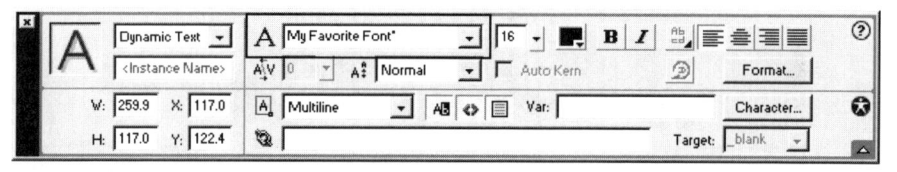

Figure 4.23
Font symbols appear on the font menu of the Property inspector with an asterisk next to them.

You can now apply My Favorite Font (which is actually the Arial font style) to the text in your movie that reads "Hello." When you export your movie, any text that says "Hello" will appear in the Arial font because that's the style on which it's based. The best thing about this feature is that if you ever change the font style associated with My Favorite Font, all the "Hello" text in your exported movie will be converted to the new style (which could be a time-consuming task to perform manually). This is similar to the way HTML uses cascading style sheets to separate content from design.

To create a font symbol:

1. Choose Window > Library to open the Library panel.

2. Press the Options button in the top-right corner of the Library panel and choose "New Font…" from the menu that appears.

3. In the Font Symbol Properties dialog box that appears, give your font a name such as My Favorite Font.

4. From the Font pop-up menu, choose the font that you want to use as a basis for this font symbol (for example, Arial).

5. Check the style options (Bold, Italic) if you want the font to apply those styles as well.

6. Click OK.

The font symbol now appears in the Library panel with the name you gave it. It will also appear in the list of available fonts on the Property inspector (**Figure 4.24**).

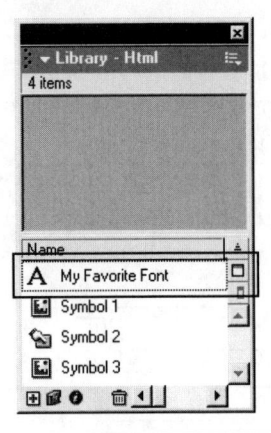

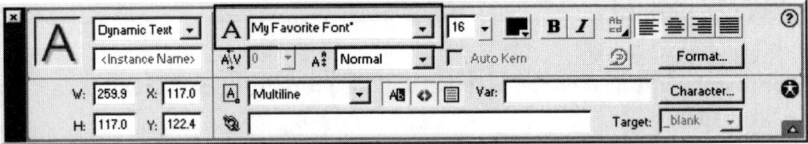

Figure 4.24
When you create a font symbol, it's automatically added to the library and to the Font menu of the Property inspector.

To use a font symbol to format text:

1. Select the text you wish to format.

2. With the Property inspector open, the name of your font symbol (My Favorite Font) will appear on the Font menu with an asterisk next to it. Select this font, which applies the Arial font style to the selected text (since that is the style associated with the My Favorite Font font symbol).

If you were now to export your movie, all of the text associated with My Favorite Font would appear in Arial. However, if you wanted your text to be displayed in Times New Roman instead, all you would need to do is open the library and edit the My Favorite Font symbol to reflect that font style.

To update the style associated with a font symbol:

1. With your authoring file open, choose Window > Library to open the Library panel.

2. Right-click (Windows) or Control-click (Macintosh) the font symbol (My Favorite Font) and choose Properties from the menu that appears. The Font Symbol Properties dialog box will appear.

3. From the Font pop-up menu, choose a different font style (Times New Roman) to associate with this font symbol.

4. Click OK.

Export the movie again, and the text formerly associated with My Favorite Font will now appear in Times New Roman (**Figure 4.25**).

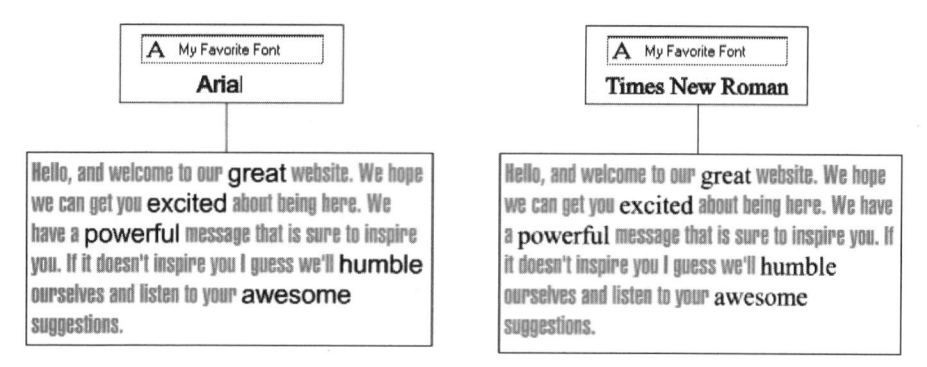

Figure 4.25
Changing the font style associated with a font symbol will update every instance in your movie where the font symbol was applied to text.

Using Font Symbols in Shared Libraries

Once you've created a font symbol, you can make it into what's known as a *shared library asset*. This entails a few more steps than we outlined above, but it also opens up new possibilities for using fonts in your movies. By turning a font symbol into a shared library asset, you can use it across multiple SWFs. The benefits of this are twofold: First, because font information is stored in a central location (the shared library), users only have to download it once rather than embed font information in every movie, thereby minimizing download time. Second, when you update the font style associated with the font symbol in the shared library, all text "linked" to that font symbol will be updated automatically to reflect the updated font style.

For more information about shared libraries, see Chapter 17, "Using the Library to Manage Your Assets."

Breaking Text Apart

MX ALERT

By breaking text apart, you accomplish one of two things (depending on the extent to which you break it up): Initially, breaking text apart will convert a block of text into the individual characters within the block. The resulting characters are still editable as text; they've just been ungrouped from the text block they were a part of.

If, at this point, you break the text apart again, you convert the individual characters into their most basic form—vector shapes (**Figure 4.26**). Once text has been broken apart twice like this, you can give it a gradient or bitmap fill, provide an outline for it, or even reshape it—none of which was possible in its previous state. Conversely, once text has been converted to vector shapes, font changes, paragraph settings, and other normal text edits can no longer be applied to it. In other words, there's no going back—make sure your text reads and looks just the way you want before you break it apart entirely.

INDIVIDUAL — Before

INDIVIDUAL — Broken apart once

INDIVIDUAL — Broken apart twice

Figure 4.26
Breaking text apart once separates a block of text into the individual characters that make it up. Breaking it apart a second time will convert those characters to vector shapes.

To break apart text:

1. Select any text element on the stage.

   A selection box will surround it.

2. From the Modify menu, choose Break Apart.

   This will convert the selected text block into its individual characters.

   TIP *Once a text block has been converted to its individual characters, you can choose Modify > Distribute to Layers to place each character on its own layer for animating purposes. For more information about the Distribute to Layers command, see Chapter 9, "Using Layers to Separate Content and Functionality."*

3. To convert the text to vector shapes, choose Modify > Break Apart again.

Once text has been broken apart twice, you can give your text a gradient fill and outline. You can even perform previously impossible graphical edits, such as reshaping your text (**Figure 4.27**).

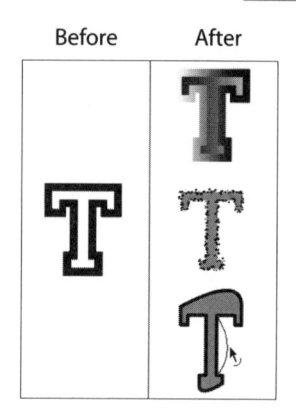

Figure 4.27
By breaking text apart, you can edit it using tools that would not be available otherwise.

Animation Considerations

Now that you've learned to control your text and its appearance, there's only one thing left to do—animate it! By bringing your text to life, you can create visual effects such as stock tickers, scrolling text, and other animations. However, you still need to find a balance between creative text animation and processor limitations.

Since each of the 100 or so letters in your text object represents an individual vector shape, animating this text block essentially entails animating 100 shapes simultaneously. Although Flash can handle this type of visual effect, it's extremely processor intensive—so don't be surprised to see your upbeat, fast-moving presentation transformed into a lesson in patience on a slower machine.

Because each project is different, there are no hard and fast rules about when to animate blocks of text; however, the following guidelines should help:

- **Avoid animating large blocks of text.** There are few visual advantages to animating a large block of text. Even if processor speed were not an issue, reading a large block of moving text can be difficult, and you don't want to frustrate your audience.

- **For visual effects, animate only a few words or letters (or just a single letter) at a time.** This type of text animation can liven up your presentation in ways no other graphic element can. This also means that if you want to bring a large block of text to life, you should bring it into the scene a sentence at a time.

- **The smaller the text element, the less processor-intensive animation will be.** This means that if you want a full-screen scrolling text effect, you had better provide your audience with plenty of caffeine—to keep them awake while they wait for the text to scroll. If you really want to animate blocks of text, make them as small as you can without rendering them unreadable.

- **When animating text, avoid animating other elements.** If you choose to animate text, avoid animating other elements at the same time, so that users' computers can focus as much processing power as possible on the text animation.

Text Animation to the Max!

Just because you need to be aware of some issues when animating text, there's no reason you can't have fun with it. In fact, quite the opposite is true. There are a number of Flash sites that make use of text in fascinating ways. And they do it not by meticulously animating each letter, as you might expect, but by using one of two animation tools: Swish (www.swishzone.com) or Wildswfx (www.wildform.com).

Both of these tools let you create interesting text effects for your Flash movies. You enter a string of text, choose an effect, adjust the setting, and—bam!—instant text utopia. What at one time would have taken hours or even days to construct within Flash can now be accomplished in just minutes (**Figure 4.28**). Both of these tools create SWF animations that you can import into your main Flash movie—forever depriving you of an excuse for sticking to dry, boring, lifeless text. Use these programs to take your text animations to the max!

Figure 4-28
Sophisticated text effects that would once have required hours of work can now be produced in minutes, using available third-party tools.

Video Tutorial

Creating and Working with Text Elements. This tutorial reviews most of the concepts we've covered here: creating text elements, creating and using dynamic text elements, font symbols, and more.

Sound

CHAPTER 5

What you'll learn...

How to import sounds

How to add sounds to the timeline

Ways to configure and edit sound instances

How to optimize and update sounds

You may have noticed in recent years that producers are no longer content to simply sit back and watch moviegoers shell out $5 for a 20-cent bag of popcorn to munch on while watching an $8 movie on the silver screen. Instead, the money men are turning their attention to a new type of revenue: *soundtracks*. These days, great effort goes into creating soundtracks that not only enhance the impact of movies, but also have commercial appeal as stand-alone products.

Music has the power to trigger all sorts of emotions and memories in people. It's not uncommon to relive scenes from a favorite movie when you hear a song from its soundtrack. Whether it excites you, provokes you, or even reduces you to tears, music can be uniquely engaging. Making intelligent use of music and other audio material can greatly enhance the impact of your movie on viewers.

Unfortunately, using sound—via HTML—on a regular Web page can be a nightmare for developers and audiences alike. Because audio is even more download-intensive than bitmaps, small sounds (and especially music soundtracks) are rarely used on the Web.

Macromedia's Flash MX provides a bit more latitude. You can add small sound effects for things like button clicks, or you can import a soundtrack to play in the background of your movie. You can even synchronize a sound or vocal track with the visual component of your movie, enabling a flowing, synchronized presentation.

Before you add any audio materials to your project, however, it's worth looking briefly at the way sound works in the digital world. Having even a basic grasp of these concepts will greatly help you in learning to use Flash's sound tools.

Understanding Sound

Although sound is invisible, we've developed tools to interpret it in mathematical terms. Those terms assert that sound is made up of *waves* that travel through the atmosphere, and that vary in length (to denote time) and size (to denote volume). These sound waves create vibrations in our eardrums, which are translated into what we "hear." We're able to distinguish among sounds because each one causes distinct vibrations in our eardrums.

Analog sounds are signals produced by sound waves that our ears are designed to detect and process. Digital sampling—which transforms analog sound waves into mathematical equations—was invented to record, edit, and reproduce analog sounds in a digital environment. Close examination of a digitally sampled sound reveals a bunch of vertical lines of varying length stacked closely together. Each of these lines represents a *sample*.

The quality of a given digital sound is determined by the number of samples used to represent each *second* of sound (the *sampling rate*) as well as the number of values each sample can contain (*sample size*) (**Figure 5.1**). For example, a 16-bit, 44.1-kHz sound contains 44,100 (44.1 kHz) lines, or samples, per second, each of which can have a value between 0 and 65,536 (16 bits). The result? A highly accurate digital sound, but also a large file. On the other hand, an 8-bit, 11.025-kHz sound contains only 11,025 samples per second, each of which can have a value between 0 and 255. The result is a duller, less precise representation of the original sound—but also a much smaller file.

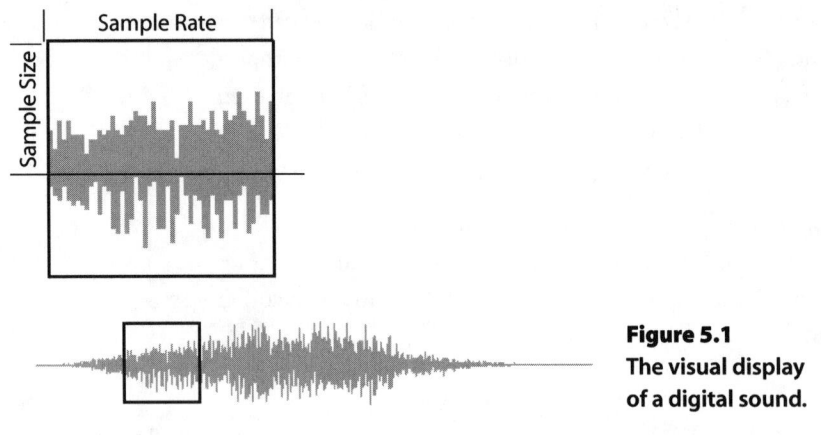

Figure 5.1
The visual display of a digital sound.

To employ sound effects and soundtracks effectively, you need to strike the right balance between audio quality and file size—which may require some experimentation. Flash provides tools to maximize audio efficiency, and the leading technologies for file compression.

The first thing you need to do, however, is bring sounds *into* Flash—which is what we'll discuss next.

Importing Sounds

You cannot record sounds in Flash MX; instead, you must import them. This means you need to record your sound files using some other application, download them from the Internet, or purchase a sound collection (see "Creative Audio," later in the chapter). Flash can import .wav (Windows), .aiff (Macintosh), and MP3 (Windows and Macintosh) sound files. If you have QuickTime 4 (or later), you can import both .wav and .aiff sound files for use with either operating system. Because any sound you import into Flash becomes part of the authoring file, you can keep your authoring file's size reasonable by importing MP3 files.

TIP *You cannot use MIDI files within Flash. The only way to control a MIDI file using Flash is via JavaScript.*

To import a sound file into Flash:

1. From the File menu, choose Import to bring up the Import dialog box.

2. Select the sound file you wish to import, and click Open.

    The sound is imported and automatically placed in your authoring file's library (**Figure 5.2**), although it doesn't initially show up on the timeline.

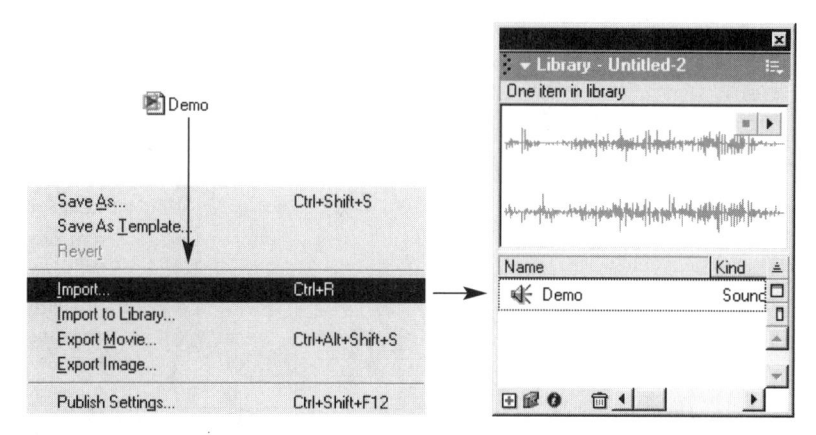

Figure 5.2
When you import a sound, Flash automatically places it in the library. To use the sound in your project, you need to manually add the sound to the timeline.

Once you've imported a sound into your authoring file, you can use all or any parts of it repeatedly in different places in your movie—without significantly increasing file size. (Later in this chapter we'll discuss how to use a single sound for different effects.)

Creative Audio

Most Web developers are expected to wear a lot of hats these days: designer, programmer, videographer—and now musician? You'll be relieved to know that while it does make you cooler (like computer geeks care, right?), you don't have to be a musician to create original music tracks these days. A number of ingenious new software applications have put that capability within the reach of just about anyone. Some of these programs allow even the rhythmically challenged to begin making music in minutes.

*Some of the most popular such tools allow you to use looped audio clips to create music: You simply place various loops (drum, bass, guitar, and so on) onto tracks, where you can then change their tempo and pitch (key) in real time (**Figure 5.3**). Many of these programs also provide digital effects that you can apply to all or part of a song. To find out for yourself what's possible, get on the Web and start downloading some demos: You'll be amazed at the audio masterpieces you'll soon be creating!*

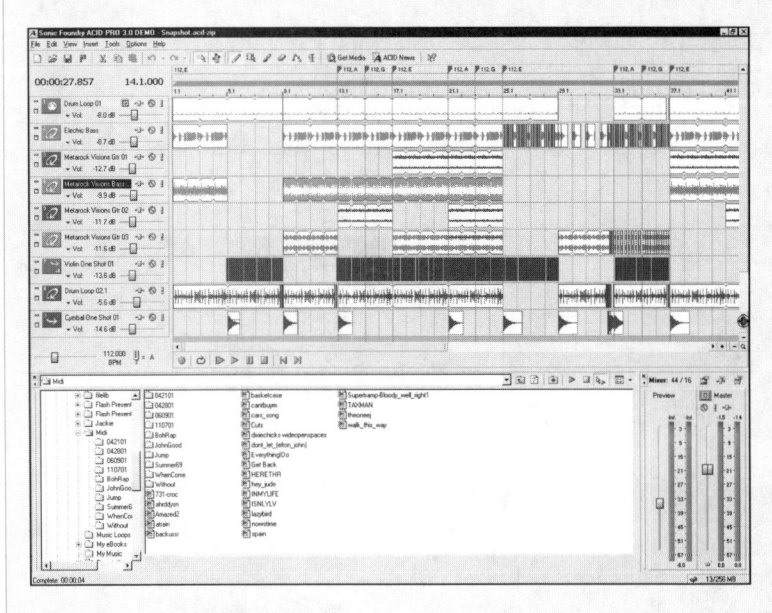

Figure 5.3
The interface of Sonic Foundry's Acid Pro 3.0, a popular Windows music-loop composition tool.

Windows-Only Applications

- **Acid.** www.acidplanet.com
- **Sonar and Plasma.** www.cakewalk.com
- **Fruityloops.** www.fruityloops.com

Macintosh-Only Applications

- **Phrazer.** www.bitheadz.com

Windows and Macintosh Applications

- **ReCycle.** www.propellerheads.se/
- **Live.** www.ableton.com

Adding Sounds to the Timeline

A sound that you have imported and placed in the library is considered the *master* version of that sound. Copies of that sound—which you will use at various points in your movie—are considered *instances* of that sound (**Figure 5.4**). Whenever you update the master version of a sound, all instances of it will reflect that change.

Master sound

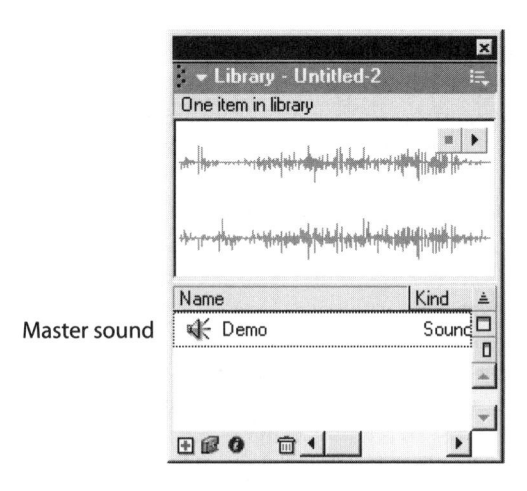

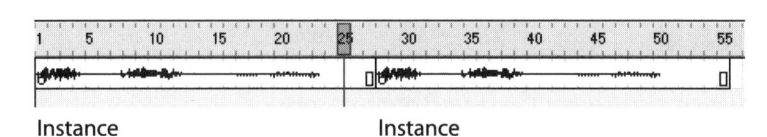

Instance   Instance

Figure 5.4
Copies of a master sound are called *instances*. A movie can contain many instances of a single sound.

Regardless of what you plan to do with a sound, you work with *instances* of it—rather than the master—which you place on a keyframe within a timeline (**Figure 5.5**). You can only adjust and work with a sound instance *after* you've placed it on the timeline—which you can do in a couple of ways.

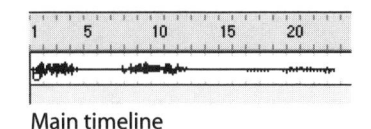

Main timeline

Button timeline

Figure 5.5
Other than when using ActionScript to dynamically add sound, any time you use a sound in your project—whether it's a sound on the main timeline or a button sound—*instances* of the sound are used, and they are always placed on a keyframe of a timeline.

To place an instance of a sound onto a timeline:

1. Create a new layer on the timeline by choosing Insert > Layer, or by pressing the Add Layer button.

2. Double-click the layer name, and rename it Sound.

   Although you don't have to create a separate layer for sound, doing so will make your project more manageable.

3. Right-click (Windows) or Control-click (Macintosh) the point on the timeline where you wish your sound to begin playing, then choose Insert Keyframe from the menu that appears.

4. With the Property inspector open, choose a sound from the menu of available sounds you've imported (**Figure 5.6**).

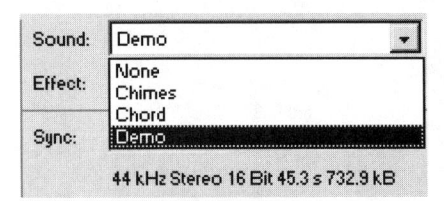

Figure 5.6
When a keyframe on the timeline is selected, a drop-down list of imported sounds appears on the Property inspector. Selecting a sound from this list will place an instance of the sound at the currently selected keyframe.

The timeline will show that you've added a sound, which should begin playing when the timeline reaches that keyframe.

Another way to place an instance of a sound onto a timeline:

1. Create a new layer on the timeline by pressing the Add Layer button, or choose Insert > Layer.

2. Double-click the layer name, and rename it Sound.

3. Right-click (Windows) or Control-click (Macintosh) the point on the timeline where you would like the sound to begin, then choose Insert Keyframe from the menu that appears.

4. From the Window menu, choose Library to open the Library panel.

5. In the library, locate the sound you wish to use.

6. Click the sound's name and drag it onto the stage (**Figure 5.7**).

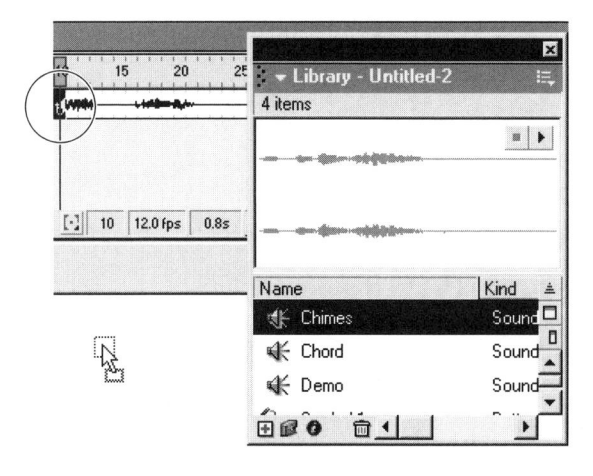

Figure 5.7
Dragging a sound from the library onto the stage places an instance of the sound at the current keyframe.

An instance of the sound will be added to the frame you previously selected. Dragging a sound from the library to the stage will cause an outline to appear that makes it look as if you're dragging an object onto it—this is not the case. The outline simply indicates that you're dragging something from the library to the stage or timeline.

Once you've placed an instance of a sound on the timeline, you may need to adjust its location to make it play earlier or later.

To relocate a sound instance on the timeline:

◆ Click and drag the sound instance on the timeline.

> **TIP** You can include as many layers with sound as you wish. If you use multiple sounds on the timeline, placing them on different layers makes it easier to identify particular sounds for editing purposes. All of the layers will be combined in your final file.

{ *ActionScript* } A sound that has been imported into the library can be inserted into a movie dynamically using the `attachSound()` method of the Sound object. This allows you to use sound instances in your project without having to actually place them on the timeline—allowing you to choose what to play and when rather than hardwiring a specific sound to the timeline.

MP3 files can be dynamically loaded into a movie as it plays using the `loadSound()` method of the Sound object. This allows you to load larger audio clips (song samples and such) into your movie on an as-needed basis. Long download times are eliminated because clips are only loaded when requested.

For more information on both of these capabilities, see Chapter 16, "Using ActionScript in your Projects."

Configuring and Editing Sound Instances

Once you've added a sound to the timeline, there are several things you need to consider:

- Will the sound instance *loop* (play repeatedly), and if so, how many times?
- Does it need to be synchronized to the animation?
- How loud should the sound be?
- Do you want the sound to play through the left speaker, right speaker, or both? Or do you want it to fade from left to right, to give a sense of motion?

Because you can uniquely configure different instances of the same master sound, you could have one instance play fairly softly and loop ten times, while another instance of the same sound plays loudly and only once.

Once you place an instance of a sound on the timeline, you configure it using the Property inspector.

To open the Property inspector:

♦ From the Window menu, choose Properties.

With the Property inspector open, selecting a sound instance on the timeline will reveal the following settings (**Figure 5.8**):

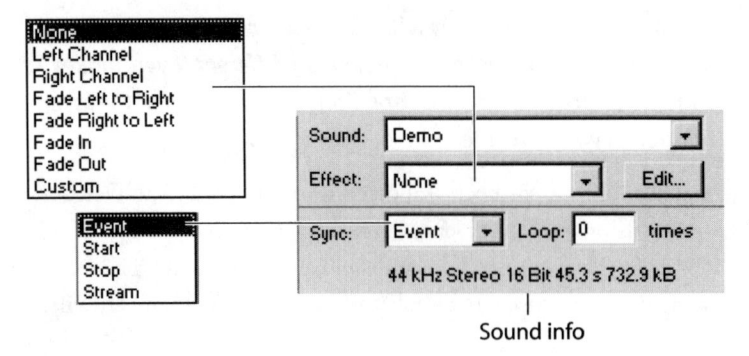

Figure 5.8
These settings appear on the Property inspector when a keyframe containing a sound instance is selected on the timeline.

- **Sound.** This is the name of the master sound on which the currently selected sound instance is based. You can use the pop-up menu to select a different master sound. Any adjustments you make on the Properties inspector will only affect that instance of the sound.
- **Effect pop-up menu.** Choose from the following effect presets (also called sound-envelope presets) to quickly adjust the volume of your sound's left and right channels (for more information, see "Making Creative Use of Sound Instances" later in this chapter).

    None. Use this option if you don't wish to apply a volume, or envelope, effect to your sound, or if you wish to remove a previously configured envelope effect. If you choose this option, the sound will play in its original form.

    Left/Right Channel. Use this option to make a sound instance play in the left or right channel (left or right speaker).

    Fade Left to Right/Fade Right to Left. Use this option to make a sound instance fade from one channel to the other.

    Fade In/Out. Use this option to make the sound instance fade in or out.

    Custom. Use this option—which is automatically displayed if you edit the sound envelope in the sound-editing window—to create your own effects.

- **Edit.** This option opens the Edit Envelope dialog box where you can adjust your sound's volume, panning (stereo) effects, and play length (see next section).
- **Sync.** This is where you set how Flash synchronizes the selected sound instance (for more information, see "Understanding the Event and Stream Sync Options" a bit later in the chapter). The options are as follows:

    Event. An event-driven sound instance will play from beginning to end the moment the timeline reaches the keyframe in which it is placed. This option works best for short sounds and background music tracks you wish to loop.

    Start. Normally, multiple instances of the same master sound can play on top of one another. If another instance of the selected master sound is already playing from beginning to end elsewhere on the timeline, this option will halt the first instance and begin a new one.

    Stop. When sound instances based on different master sounds are playing simultaneously, you may want to silence one—which is what this option allows you to do.

Stream. This option ensures that animated elements remain synchronized with the sound instance as it plays—even if some animated frames must be skipped to do so. Streamed sound instances stop any time your movie does, and they only play for the duration of the frames they occupy (**Figure 5.9**).

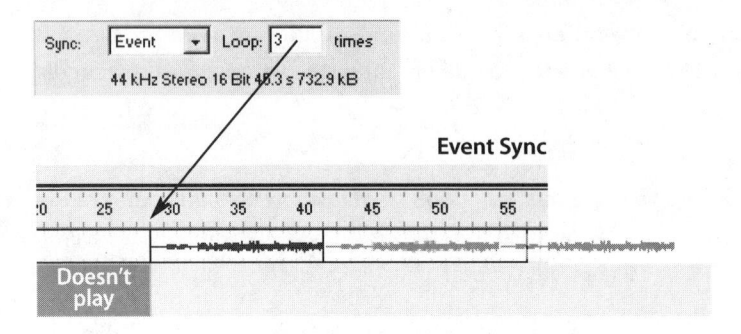

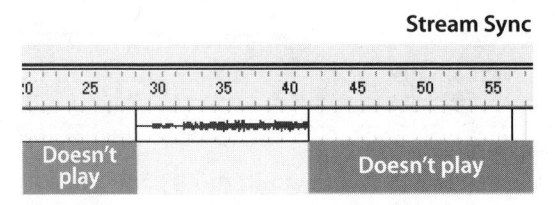

Figure 5.9
Event-synchronized sounds can play independently of their frames on the timeline, while streamed sound instances play only within the frames they occupy.

- **Loops.** Use this option to specify how many times you want the sound instance to play. You can loop a sound as many times as you wish, and it will not affect file size. This option is often used to create looping soundtracks for background music.

- **Sound Info.** Provides information about the instance's master sound, including its sample rate, playing time, and file size.

NOTE *A looped event-driven sound will continue to play for as many times as you've set it to loop—even if the movie comes to a halt.*

Understanding the Event and Stream Sync Options

Once you've placed a sound on the timeline, you need to figure out exactly how you want to use it in your presentation. Is it a short sound best suited for an action, like a button-click? Is it a section of music that you want to use in the background? Or is it a soundtrack you need to synchronize with an on-screen animation? Flash deals with each instance of a sound differently, depending on its use. This, as you're about to learn, helps minimize file size and download time.

When you place an instance of a sound on the timeline, you use the Sync options on the Property inspector to configure it. There are two categories of Sync options: **event-driven** and **streamed**. Event-driven sound instances are triggered by an action in your movie—the pressing of a button, for example, or the timeline reaching the keyframe where a sound instance is placed. Streamed sound instances, in contrast, are used strictly for synchronizing a soundtrack with animated elements.

Event-Driven Sound Instances

You can use event-driven sounds for button-click sounds and looped music clips, as well as anywhere you want a sound to play from beginning to end without interruption. When working with event-driven sounds, you need to be aware of the following:

- An event-driven sound instance must be downloaded completely before it can play. Larger sound files may significantly increase your movie's download time.
- Once a master sound has been downloaded and used in an event-driven instance, it does not need to be downloaded again. All other event-driven instances based on the sound use this information to generate the sound.
- Event-driven sounds can play from beginning to end, regardless of what's happening around them—even if your movie's timeline stops.
- An event-driven sound only needs to be inserted into a single frame—regardless of the sound's length.

Streamed Sounds

You can use streamed sounds for vocal or soundtracks that you want synchronized with visual elements of your movie. You can also use this method for sounds you only plan to use once. When working with streaming sounds, you should be aware of the following:

- You can synchronize streaming sounds with the visual elements of your movie.
- Only a small portion of the sound file needs to be downloaded before it begins to play—even with large sound files.
- A streaming sound will only play within the frames on the timeline where it is placed.

Different instances of a single master sound can be event-driven or streamed.

NOTE *For more information about event-driven and streamed sounds, see the video tutorials on the accompanying CD (which are described at the end of this chapter).*

The Edit Envelope Dialog Box

When a sound file is imported into Flash, it includes information that describes its volume, length, and panning (stereo) settings. When you place a sound instance on the timeline, you can fine-tune these settings for that particular instance—which means you can use a single master sound any number of ways (see "Making Creative Use of Sound Instances," later in this chapter).

You use the Edit Envelope dialog box to fine-tune individual sound instances placed on the timeline.

To open the Edit Envelope dialog box:

- With the Property inspector open and a sound selected on the timeline, click the Edit button on the Property inspector. The Edit Envelope dialog box will appear.

The Edit Envelope dialog box includes the following areas (**Figure 5.10**):

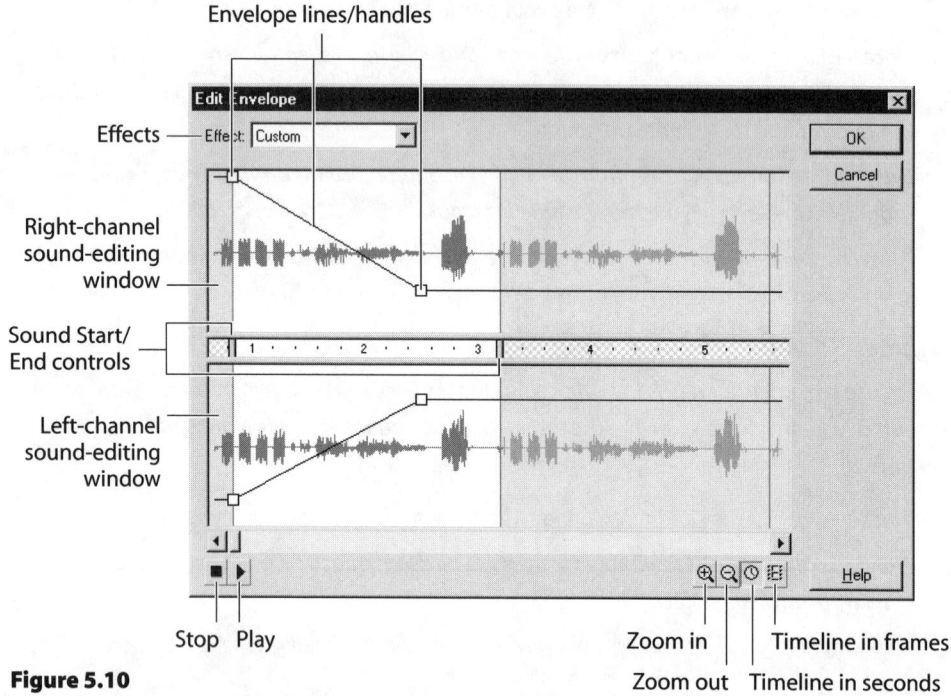

Figure 5.10
The Edit Envelope dialog box.

- **Sound-editing windows.** These display a digital representation of the master sound on which the current instance is based, plus the controls for editing this instance of it. The top window represents the left channel of the stereo, and the bottom window the right channel. If you are using mono (nonstereo) sound, both windows represent the same mono channel.

  TIP *The left and right channels in a stereo sound file usually contain unique information: This is what enables our ears to distinguish spatiality in music. In contrast, the two channels in a mono sound file contain identical data. Keep in mind, though, that even if you're using mono sound, you can still create some interesting left-to-right and right-to-left fades as well as a few other effects.*

- **Sound timeline.** Used for precise sound editing, this timeline initially displays a sound instance's duration in seconds; however, you can change the unit to frames (see below).

- **Sound Start/End controls.** Also known as Time In/Time Out controls, these allow you to specify what portion of the master sound you wish to use in a particular instance.

- **Envelope lines and handles.** Use these to adjust a sound's volume at specific points in its playing time. The lines represent the transition from one volume to another in relation to the sound instance's timeline. You may add up to eight more handles by clicking on the Envelope line where you want to place them. To remove a handle, click and drag it out of the sound-editing window.

- **Stop/Play buttons.** Use these to test adjustments you made to the sound in the Edit Envelope dialog box.

- **Zoom In/Out buttons.** Use these to fine-tune your sound. You can zoom in (enlarge the visual display of the sound in the sound-editing window) to more finely place Time In/Out controls and Envelope handles, allowing you to achieve greater precision in your sound editing.

- **Timeline in seconds/frames.** This lets you choose which units are used on the sound-editing timeline. Using seconds is good for "seeing" the duration of your sound, whereas frames are useful for synchronizing sound with visual elements, because they show the actual frame numbers in which the sound will play in your movie's timeline.

- **Effects pop-up menu.** You can use this menu to quickly adjust the volume of your sound's left and right channels. The settings are the same as those found on the Property inspector itself.

Making Creative Use of Sound Instances

Because you can configure and edit each instance of a master sound, it's relatively easy to create a number of interesting effects using sound instances while still keeping your movie's file size to a minimum—it just takes some resourcefulness and creativity! You could, for example, use the same sound you employed as a music track to provide a plethora of simple effects, by simply adjusting controls in the Edit Envelope dialog box.

Volume

You can change the volume of individual sound instances by click-dragging an envelope handle in the Edit Envelope dialog box. The higher you locate the handle, the louder the sound instance will play at that point (**Figure 5.11**). You can adjust the volume of the sound at multiple points on its timeline by adding additional envelope handles.

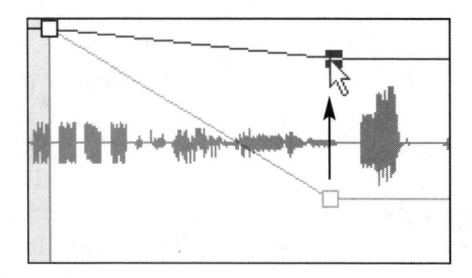

Figure 5.11
Adjust a sound's volume by moving envelope handles.

Panning

Panning involves editing a sound instance so that it moves from one speaker to another during its playback. This effect—which you can apply to both stereo and mono sounds—provides a sense of motion. You access panning from the Effect drop-down menu as Fade Left to Right, or Fade Right to Left. These settings automatically place the editing lines and handles for each channel window in inverse sloping positions (**Figure 5.12**). You can further adjust these to your liking.

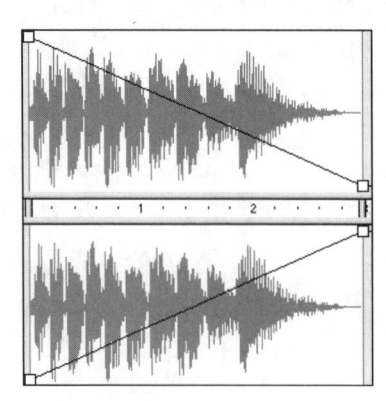

Figure 5.12
Panning a sound from one channel to the other is achieved by tracking the volume down in one channel as it tracks up in the other.

Swoosh

This variation on the panning effect involves doing a slight pan back to the starting channel. For example, if you've set an instance to pan from right to left, before its playback is complete, you would pan back to the right channel (**Figure 5.13**). You can use this effect to achieve some simple yet interesting results (such as providing an audio sound effect to accompany a object moving quickly in and out of a scene) that don't increase your movie's overall file size.

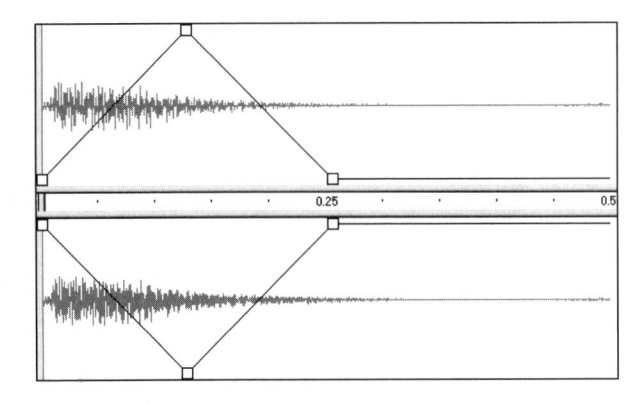

Figure 5.13
A "swooshing" effect can be achieved by arranging the envelope lines/handles as shown in this graphic.

Chopping

Chopping involves using just a section of the master sound. For example, if you had a three-second master sound, you could chop it up in various ways to create instances that would incorporate only a section of the overall sound. By isolating sections of longer sounds in this way, you have access to a number of smaller, unique sounds (especially when chopping is used in combination with some of the other ideas discussed here).

The Time In/Time Out controls are used for chopping: Click-dragging the Time In control to the right will cause the sound to start playing at the point where you dragged it (rather than its original starting point). Likewise, click-dragging the Time Out control to the left will cause the sound to stop playing at the point where you dragged it (**Figure 5.14**).

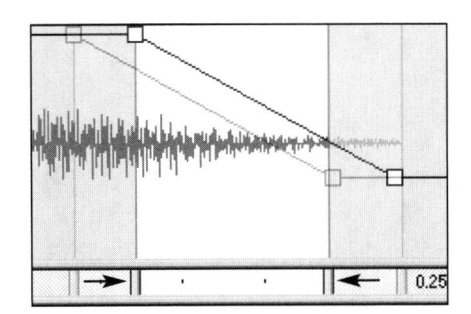

Figure 5.14
You adjust a sound's play length by moving the Time In and Time Out controls.

TIP *Some sounds you import may include blank (silent) intervals at their beginning or end. Use the Sound Start/End controls to delete these silences—another way to substantially reduce the file size of your final movie.*

Pulsing

Pulsing involves either quickly increasing a sound's volume while slowly decreasing it (repeatedly) or increasing it slowly while decreasing it quickly (repeatedly), which basically gives a sound a "womp-womp-womp" feel. It is achieved by creating what is known as a sawtooth envelope as shown in **Figure 5.15**.

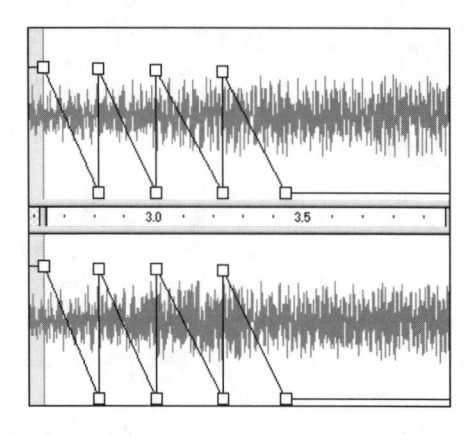

Figure 5.15
A "pulsing" effect can be achieved by arranging the envelope lines/handles as shown in this graphic.

Echoing

Echoing describes the effect of a sound moving back and forth between channels as it diminishes in volume. While you're limited to how many echoes you can produce (due to the limitation of only being able to add eight envelope handles), you can still achieve some useful results. You achieve this effect by creating what's known as a square envelope (**Figure 5.16**).

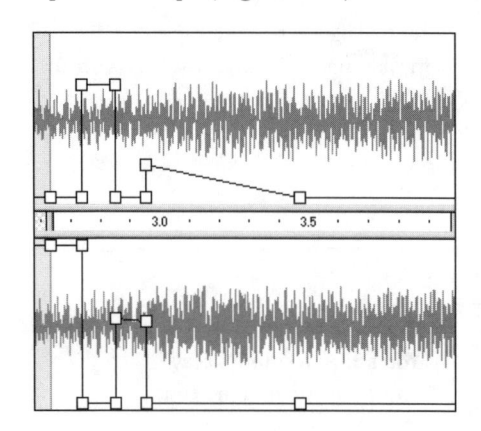

Figure 5.16
An "echo" effect can be achieved by arranging the envelope lines/handles as shown in this graphic.

Mixing

Mixing involves placing two or more sound instances at the same frame number but on different layers of the timeline, so that they are played at exactly the same time. This causes the two sound instances to be mixed together—a way to create unique sounds without importing new ones (which would increase your movie's overall file size). If you combine this effect with some of those already discussed, you'll begin to see the wide range of effects that are possible using a single master sound.

Cross-fading

An extension of the mixing effect we just discussed, cross-fading simply involves placing sound instances at the same frame number but on different layers, and configuring one instance to fade out as the other instance fades in.

{ **ActionScript** } You can control the volume, panning, and playback of sounds using the setVolume(), setPan(), and start() methods of the Sound object. This gives you the ability to perform many of the effects described here dynamically—that is, as your movie plays. For more information, see Chapter 16, "Using ActionScript in Your Projects."

NOTE *A file containing examples of these effects can be found on the accompanying CD: It's located in the Chapter 5 folder and named soundEffects.fla. Keep in mind that the samples are intended to be instructive, not inspirational!*

Sound Properties

Each sound you import into Flash has its own properties. We've described how *individual instances* of the same sound can be set to play at different volumes, loop differently, and play at varying lengths. In contrast, any adjustments you make to a sound's *properties* are incorporated in the master sound—meaning they affect *all instances* of that sound placed in your movie. Most of the adjustments you make to a master sound will have to do with how it's optimized and compressed in the exported SWF file.

You use the Sound Properties dialog box to adjust a sound's properties.

To open the Sound Properties dialog box:

1. From the Window menu, choose Library to open the Library panel.

2. Locate the sound you wish to optimize, and double-click the sound icon to the left of its name to open the Sound Properties dialog box.

> **TIP** *You can also right-click (Windows) or Control-click (Macintosh) a sound's name in the library, then choose Properties from the menu that appears.*

The Sound Properties dialog box consists of the following areas, settings, and buttons (**Figure 5.17**):

- **Preview window.** Displays a digital representation of the master sound. If the file is a stereo sound, a representation of the left and right channels will appear in the preview window. If it's a mono (non-stereo) sound, a single representation will appear.

- **File name.** Flash assigns a default name to the master sound, based on the name of the original imported file. This is what's used in the library to identify the sound. You can change the name at any time.

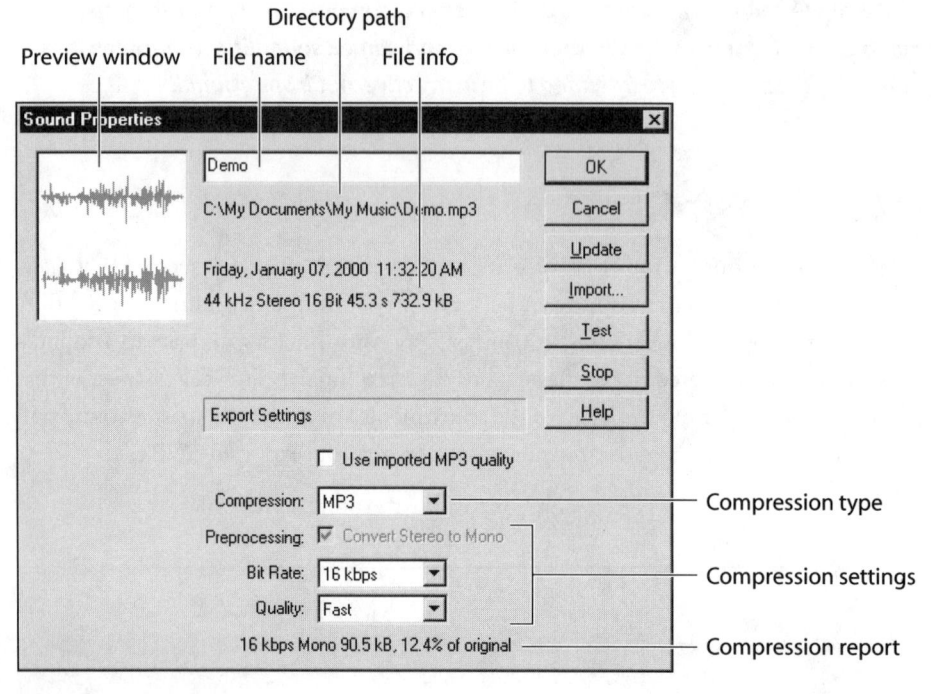

Figure 5.17
The Sound Properties dialog box.

- **Directory path.** The directory path from which the sound was imported.

- **File info.** Provides file data including date last modified, sample rate, sample size, duration (in seconds), and original size.

- **Compression type.** This pop-up menu allows you to determine how you want to compress the sound (affecting all instances of that sound) when you export your project to create a Flash movie. Each *master* sound can have its own unique settings (which we'll discuss shortly).

- **Update button.** If, using another sound-editing program, you changed or edited the file (specified at the directory path location) that you'd previously imported into Flash, this button allows you to update Flash's copy of the sound to reflect your changes.

- **Import button.** Use this button to change the sound file referenced by the directory path information. When you import a sound this way, all references to the current master sound switch to the one you are importing.

- **Test button.** Click to see how different compression settings will affect the sound.

- **Stop button.** Use this button in conjunction with the Test button to halt the audio preview's playback.

- **Compression settings.** See next section.

- **Compression report.** See next section.

Compressing a Master Sound

Creating a Flash movie is all about getting the most from the least. Part of that means figuring out how to get the best-quality sound and still maintain a reasonable file size—a process known as *compression*. To accomplish this, you use the Export settings on the bottom half of the Sound Properties dialog box.

By default, Flash uses general compression settings for all sounds you don't compress individually. To access these settings, go to File > Publish Settings and click the Flash tab of the Publish Settings dialog box (**Figure 5.18**). Although you can save time by using these settings (since you don't need to set the compression settings for each master sound individually), we don't recommend this course of action: To produce the best product, you'll want to control every aspect of your movie, including individual sound compression settings.

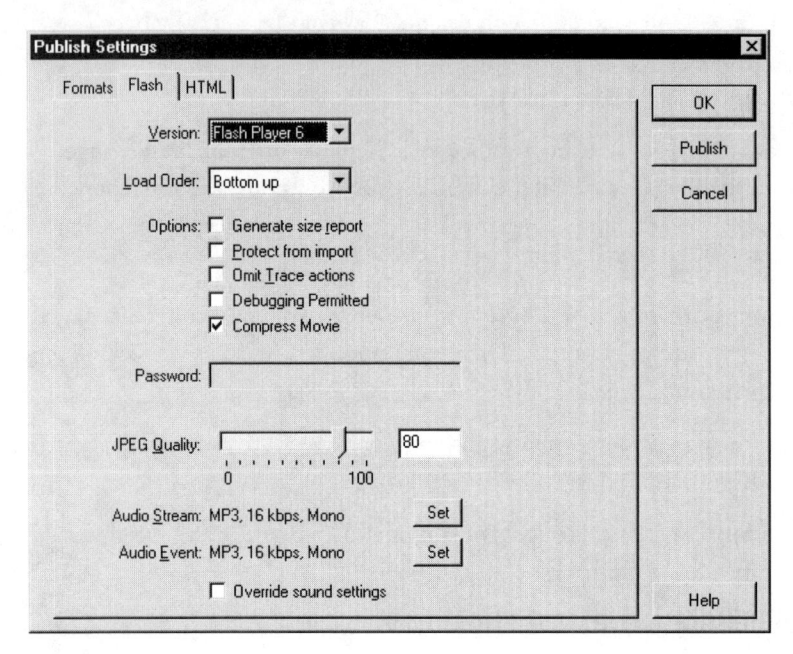

Figure 5.18
Sound compression settings can be found on the Flash tab of the Publish Settings dialog box.

Because different master sounds serve different purposes in a movie, you'll probably want to adjust compression settings according to the nature of the sound. For example, you might choose to apply minimal compression to a musical track so as to maintain its audio fidelity, but substantially compress the sound of an explosion because the degradation in quality is less noticeable. There's no set formula for getting the perfect balance—it will vary from project to project.

To make the sound editing process easier, Flash provides a Test button that lets you hear the effect of your current settings. Flash also displays a *Compression report* at the bottom of the dialog box: This tells you how large the master sound file will be when it's exported *after* being compressed. Since the master sound (as shown in the library) is only downloaded once, the figure shown here represents the sound's overall effect on your movie's file size—regardless of how many instances you use.

There are five main compression options available for sound—Default, ADPCM, MP3, Raw, and Speech—all of which are available from the Compression pop-up menu. An explanation of each follows.

Default

This option selects the default sound compression setting on the Flash tab of the Publish Settings dialog box.

ADPCM

This compression type is best for short sounds such as those used for button-clicks and sound effects, or for sounds that you plan to use primarily as events (see "Understanding the Event and Stream Sync Options," earlier in this chapter). You'll find this option also works well for looped soundtracks because it's quicker to decompress than MP3 files, which may generate *lags* (unwanted intervals of silence) between loops.

To compress a sound using the ADPCM compression option:

◆ From the Compression pop-up menu, select ADPCM compression, then choose from the following options (**Figure 5.19**):

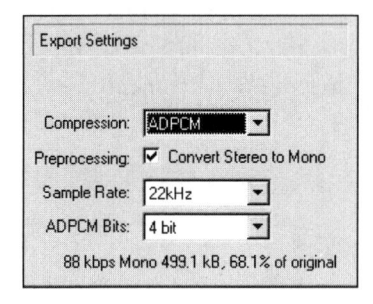

Figure 5.19
Various settings become available on the Sound Properties dialog box when you select a compression type.

Preprocessing. This option transforms a stereo sound into a mono sound, reducing by half the amount of audio data in your movie file. For example, if a stereo sound file adds 100 KB to your overall file size, checking this option reduces that increment to 50 KB. The trade-off is losing the "spatial" quality of a given stereo sound.

TIP *Flash provides immediate feedback on how the options you have selected will affect file size, displaying it in the compression report at the bottom of the Sound Properties box.*

Sample Rate. This option allows you to set the sample rate for the exported file of your final movie. Even if the sound file was originally sampled at 22 kHz, you can have Flash resample it (for export) at 5 kHz. A lower sample rate reduces the amount of sound data in your movie file, and thus the file's overall size; the trade-off is in sound quality. Be sure to press the Test button to preview your selection. Generally, you can get away with a lower sample rate when the sound content is primarily vocal, whereas music tracks typically sound much better with a higher sample rate.

ADPCM Bits. This setting allows you to specify the sample size of a given sound when it is exported in your movie. A lower bit rate will cause the sound to distort, but also helps minimize overall file size. Again, it's a matter of content and balance.

MP3

Short for MPEG-1 Layer 3, MP3 is a *lossy* type of audio compression, which means that applying it may sacrifice nuances in the original file, depending on the amount of compression used. On the other hand, compressing an audio (.wav) file using MP3 can reduce the file size by 90 percent, without any significant loss in quality. This means that a 50 MB WAV file can be compressed into a 5 MB MP3 file, with little discernible loss in sound quality. You can choose an even lower bit rate and compress the file even further—though sound quality will continue to degrade. MP3 is best suited for long nonlooped soundtracks (see the Looping option under "Configuring and Editing Sound Instances" earlier in this chapter).

To compress a sound using the MP3 compression option:

- Choose the MP3 compression type from the drop-down box, then choose from the following options:

MX ALERT **Use Imported MP3 Quality.** MP3 files are compressed prior to being brought into Flash. Selecting this option tells Flash to maintain the file's existing compression level—which means Flash won't recompress the sound and further degrade its quality.

Preprocessing. This option transforms a stereo sound into a mono sound, reducing by half the amount of audio data in your movie file. Again, the trade-off is that you lose the spatial quality of a stereo sound. If the bit rate chosen is too low to support stereo, this option will be grayed out.

Bit Rate. This setting specifies the number of bits the encoder can use to describe one second of sound. A high bit rate provides better sound quality; a lower bit rate decreases file size.

Quality. This option lets you set the quality of the sound in the exported version of your movie. The appropriate setting depends largely on how you plan to deliver your movie. Use Fast for any movie distributed over the Web, and Medium or Best for playback on a CD.

Raw

This option does not apply true compression, but allows you to resample a sound to a new sample rate for export. For example, a sound file that had a 22 kHz sample rate at import can be reset to 11 kHz or 5 kHz on export. This setting does not compress the sound, though it will still reduce the sound's size within your movie (while sacrificing quality).

Speech

MX ALERT As the name implies, this compression type is best suited for sound clips containing mainly speech (no music, background noise, and so on). This compression setting first automatically converts the sound from stereo to mono, reducing by half the amount of sound data in your movie file. Next, a speech compression algorithm is applied to reduce the clip's size even further.

To compress a sound using the Speech compression option:

- Choose the Speech compression type from the drop-down box, then adjust the following setting:

    Sample Rate. This lets you set the sample rate (quality) of the exported sound. In many cases you can use the lowest setting (5 kHz) and still get acceptable results.

Updating Master Sounds

Consider this scenario: You've completed your movie, and everything looks and acts just the way it should. The soundtrack and all the sound effects are perfect—or so you think. But after reviewing the movie, your client decides that one sound needs to be changed. You're horrified, knowing you've placed more than 50 instances of that sound in your movie. Opening the authoring file and manually fixing the problem would take all day. Luckily, Flash has engineered a way around this problem. All you need to do is update the master sound, and every instance of it will reflect that change. You can do so in any of the following ways:

- Use an external sound editor to edit the original sound file (the file you used to import the sound on which the master sound is based), then have Flash "refresh" the master sound in the authoring file.
- Import a new sound to replace your original master sound.
- Open the master sound directly, using a digital audio program from within Flash. After you edit and save it, the master sound will be automatically updated in Flash.

All three approaches accomplish the same goal. The steps for each are described below.

To update a sound and refresh the authoring file's version automatically:

1. Open the external sound file (the one you originally imported) in your favorite sound editing software, then edit and save the sound.

2. With the Library panel open in Flash, select the originally imported sound as it appears in the library window.

3. Click the Options button on the top-right corner of the library window, and choose Properties from the menu that appears. The Sound Properties dialog box will appear.

4. Press the Update button on the dialog box. The master sound used in Flash and all instances of it will be updated to reflect your edits.

   TIP *If you've edited several external sounds and want Flash to update them all at once, shift-select the sounds in the library, then right-click (Windows) or Control-click (Macintosh) on a sound in the library and choose Update from the menu that appears. This opens the Update Library Items dialog box. Place a check mark next to each of the files you want to update, then click Update (**Figure 5.20**).*

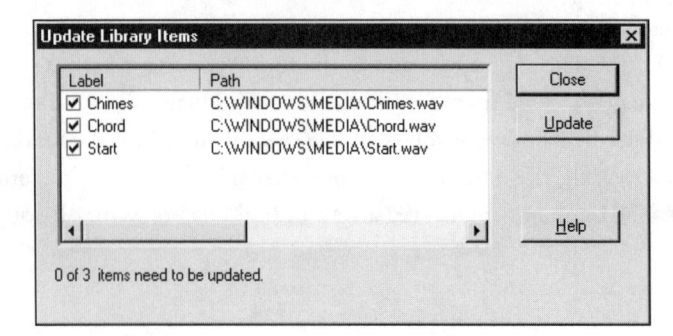

Figure 5.20
The Update Library Items dialog box lets you update multiple sounds simultaneously.

To import a new sound to replace a master sound:

1. With the Library panel open, select the sound you wish to replace.

2. Click the Options button on the top-right corner of the library window, and choose Properties from the menu that appears. The Sound Properties dialog box will appear.

3. Press the Import button on the dialog box to open the Import Sound dialog box.

4. Select a new sound and click Open. The sound that you originally imported is replaced with the sound you just selected. All instances of the old sound will be updated to reflect the new sound.

To open and edit a master sound using a sound editor from within Flash:

1. With the Library panel open, select the sound you wish to edit.

2. Click the Options button on the top-right corner of the library window, and choose one of the following (**Figure 5.21**):

   - **"Edit with [the name of a program]."** This opens the sound in whatever program is the default sound editor in your particular system. You can then use that program to edit the sound.

   Or

   - **"Edit with…."** This opens a dialog box that allows you to choose the sound-editing program you wish to use. Select a program and press Open. You can then use the program to edit the sound.

3. Using the sound-editing program you selected, edit the sound, and save the file.

4. When you return to Flash, the sound will have been automatically updated in the authoring file.

   TIP *Be careful when you're saving a file from your sound editor (as mentioned in Step 3 above): This action not only updates the file in Flash, but in the external file as well.*

   Figure 5.21
   Commands for editing sounds with an external program can be found on the Library panel Options menu.

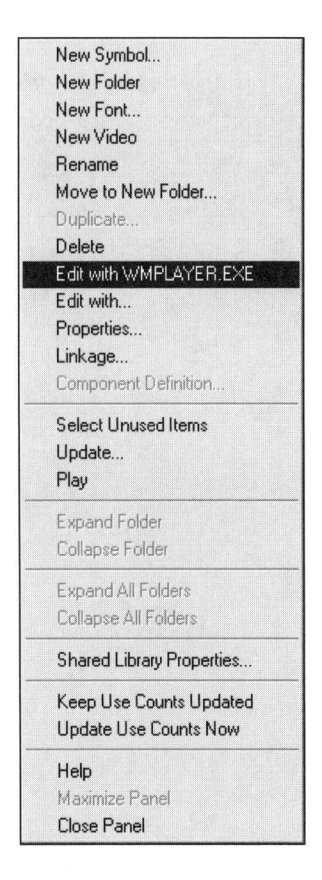

Most of the commands available on the Library Options menu can also be accessed by right-clicking (Windows) or Control-clicking (Mac) on a sound in the Library panel.

Using Sounds in Shared Libraries

Once you've imported a sound into your project's library, you can turn it into a shared library asset, which allows you to use it across multiple SWF files. The benefits of this are twofold: First, because the sound is stored in a central location, you only need to download it once, thereby minimizing download time for your movie. Second, whenever you update the sound in the shared library, any movie to which it's linked will subsequently reflect the updated sound.

For information about shared libraries, see Chapter 17, "Using the Library to Manage Movie Assets."

Video Tutorials

Importing and Working with Sound Elements. This tutorial addresses most of the concepts you've learned in this chapter, including importing sounds, working with them on the timeline, editing and optimizing them, and more.

Adding Sound to a Button. This tutorial covers the steps entailed in adding sound to a button, so that it interacts with your audience's cursor in lively ways.

Editing a Sound. This tutorial shows you how to get the most from sound materials using Flash's own sound-editing capabilities.

Syncing Sound to Animation. This tutorial demonstrates how to synchronize a simple vocal track with animated text.

Bitmaps

CHAPTER 6

What you'll learn…

How to import bitmaps

How to add bitmaps to your movies

How to work with bitmaps

Ways you can adjust bitmap properties

How to optimize your images

How to update bitmaps

How to use bitmaps in shared libraries

How to use animated GIFs with Flash

How to use PNGs with Flash

Ways you can use bitmaps creatively

In designing your presentations, you may find your visual concepts limited by Macromedia Flash's drawing tools. If you require more than vector shapes—meaning simple ovals, rectangles, and lines won't cut it—you'll need to turn to bitmaps. These allow you to add more complex images to your project such as photos, scanned images, and other sophisticated graphics.

Unlike vector graphics, which are based on mathematical equations, bitmaps are comprised of a field of small dots, or *pixels*, which are perceived as photographic images when viewed from a distance. While bitmaps are a valuable graphic tool, they can also dramatically increase your movie's file size, which in turn adds to its download time. However, there are ways to minimize this problem. In this chapter, we'll look at several Flash options for optimizing bitmaps so that you can keep file size down—though it's still prudent to use bitmaps sparingly.

You can also use bitmaps for more than just photographs in your movie. They can be employed as backgrounds and fills, for special effects, or even as buttons. In addition, you can convert a bitmap into a vector graphic, which may help minimize the bitmap's effect on your movie's file size. But before you do any of this, you have to get the bitmap into Flash—which is where importing enters the picture (excuse the pun). Because it's the first step in using bitmaps in your Flash movie, we'll look next at the import process.

Importing Bitmaps

Bringing bitmaps into Flash is a straightforward process: You simply move the graphic onto your computer's hard drive by scanning it, creating it in a photo-editing program, or obtaining it via some other electronic medium. Then you import it into Flash.

Table 6.1 lists the bitmap file types that can be imported into Flash. An asterisk (★) indicates that you can only import that file type if QuickTime 4 or a later version is installed on your machine.

To import a bitmap into Flash:

1. From the File menu, choose Import to make the Import dialog box appear.

2. On your hard drive, find the bitmap file you wish to import.

3. Select the file you wish to import, and click Open.

The image will be imported into the current frame and layer, and will appear on the stage.

Some bitmap files that you import into Flash, such as GIFs or Portable Network Graphics (PNGs), retain their transparency settings. As you'll learn later, this is a powerful feature (**Figure 6.1**).

Figure 6.1 Imported bitmaps are automatically placed in the library; files with an alpha channel, such as this gecko, retain their transparency.

Any bitmap you import into Flash is automatically added to the library. As we explain in greater detail in the following chapter ("Symbols"), you can reuse a library object (including bitmaps) as many times in a movie as you wish (and with varying dimensions)—without significantly affecting its overall file size.

Table 6.1
Bitmap File Types Supported by Flash

	Windows	Macintosh
Bitmap	X	X
PICT	X	X
JPEG Image	X	X
GIF	X	X
PNG	X	X
Photoshop*	X	X
TIF, TIFF*	X	X
QuickTime Image*	X	X
TGA*	X	X
Silicon Graphics*	X	X
MacPaint*	X	X

Importing from Fireworks

Because Macromedia makes both Flash and Fireworks (an image-editing program), importing PNG files produced in Fireworks gives you some options that aren't available with other bitmap file formats.

Fireworks files can contain vector graphics, text blocks, individual bitmap images, and other distinct elements—all of which are typically "flattened," or uneditable, on import. However, although such elements can be flattened in files imported from Fireworks, Flash gives you the option of importing such a file with these elements intact and editable. Thus, once imported, text blocks can be rewritten, vectors can be reshaped, and so on (**Figure 6.2**).

Flattened

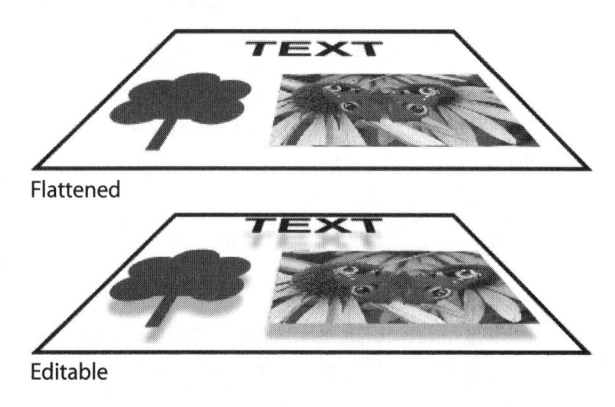

Editable

Figure 6.2
A flattened image is imported into Flash as a single element; however, Fireworks images can be imported so that distinct elements in the file remain separate and editable.

MX ALERT   *To import a Fireworks PNG into Flash:*

1. From the File menu, choose Import to make the Import dialog box appear.

2. On your hard drive, find the Fireworks file you wish to import.

3. Select the file you wish to import, and click Open.

   The Fireworks PNG Import Settings dialog box will appear (**Figure 6.3**).

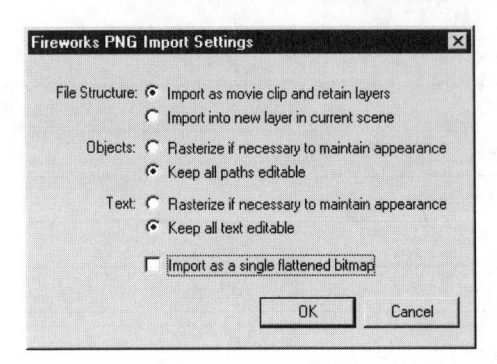

   Figure 6.3
   The Fireworks PNG Import Settings dialog box.

4. Select/deselect the "Import as a single flattened bitmap" option at the bottom of the dialog box.

   Selecting this option instructs Flash to import the image as a flattened image with uneditable elements. Deselecting this option (the default setting) will display three groups of radio buttons, which allow you to specify how various elements of the image should be imported. They include:

   - **File Structure.** Use this group to specify the overall manner in which content from the file is imported. The "Import as movie clip and retain layers option" converts the entire contents of the image to a movie clip, while retaining the layer structure of the file as it was created in Fireworks. The "Import into new layer in current scene" option imports all of the file's content into a single file in the current scene—in the process deleting the file structure defined in Fireworks.

   - **Objects.** Use this group to specify how objects in the file, such as vector shapes, are imported. The "Rasterize if necessary to maintain appearance" option converts vector objects to bitmaps, whenever this is needed to retain bitmap effects (bevels, drop shadows, and so on) applied to the vector objects in Fireworks. The "Keep all paths editable" option imports all objects as vector shapes, ignoring any bitmap effects applied to them in Fireworks.

   - **Text.** Use this group to specify how text in the file is imported. The "Rasterize if necessary to maintain appearance" option converts text objects to bitmaps, when needed, to retain bitmap effects (bevels, drop shadows, and so on) applied to

Chapter 6 **Bitmaps**

them in Fireworks. The "Keep all text editable" option ignores any bitmap effects applied to text, and simply imports text so that it remains editable.

In the end, the image (and any editable elements) will be imported into the current frame and layer, and appear on the stage.

TIP *For information about updating an imported Fireworks image, see "Updating an Imported Fireworks Image" later in this chapter.*

{ ActionScript } JPG files can be dynamically loaded into a movie as it plays, using the `loadMovie()` method—eliminating long download times since images are only loaded when requested (that is, on an as-needed basis). This comes in handy when you want to display a portfolio of images—since it's obviously impractical to place dozens of images in a single SWF. Keep in mind, however, that only standard JPGs can be loaded dynamically via this method; you cannot dynamically load progressive JPGs (that is, ones that begin displaying before completely loading), nor GIFs or PNGs. For more information, see Chapter 16, "Using ActionScript in Your Projects."

Adding Bitmaps to Your Movie

When you import a bitmap into Flash, a copy of it is placed on the current layer of the current frame in your movie. If you wish to use the same bitmap elsewhere in your movie, you simply drag a copy from the library onto the stage. You can use a bitmap many times in your movie without increasing the overall file size (**Figure 6.4**).

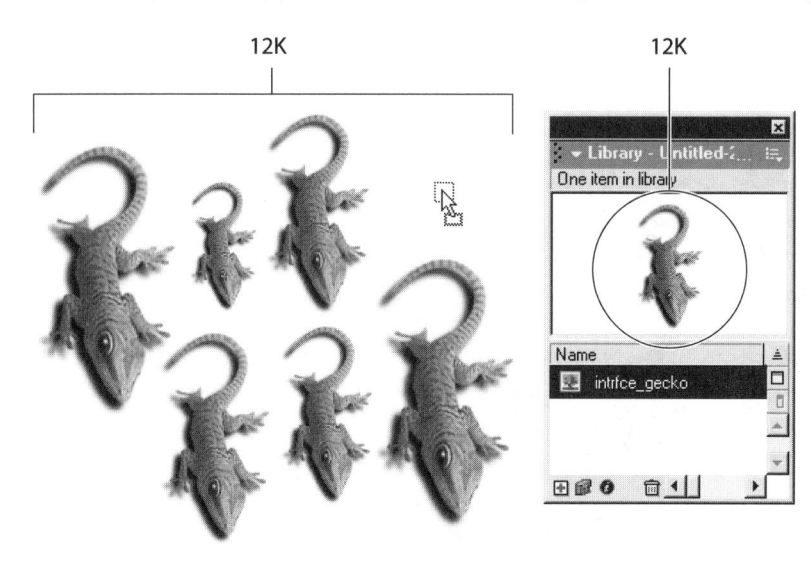

Figure 6.4
You can use an imported bitmap as many times as you want without noticeably increasing your movie's file size.

To drag a copy of a bitmap from the library:

1. From the Window menu, choose Library to open the Library panel.

2. Locate the bitmap in the library.

3. Click and drag it from the list or from the preview window onto the stage.

{ *ActionScript* } An image that has been imported into the library can be inserted into a movie dynamically using the `attachMovie()` method. This allows you to use a script to insert images in your project, rather than manually place them on the stage. For more information, see Chapter 16, "Using ActionScript in Your Projects."

Working with Bitmaps

Flash is not an image editor like Fireworks or Adobe PhotoShop—which means that you're limited in what you can do with bitmaps after importing them into the program. With little a effort, though, you can perform some simple tasks, such as using a bitmap as a fill, selecting and editing colors in a bitmap, erasing part of a bitmap, or even converting a bitmap into a vector graphic.

Using Bitmaps as Fills

You can use any image you import as a fill for a simple shape. The process is similar to applying a gradient or solid fill to a filled shape. A bitmapped fill can be scaled, rotated, or skewed inside the shape itself to create some interesting effects (**Figure 6.5**).

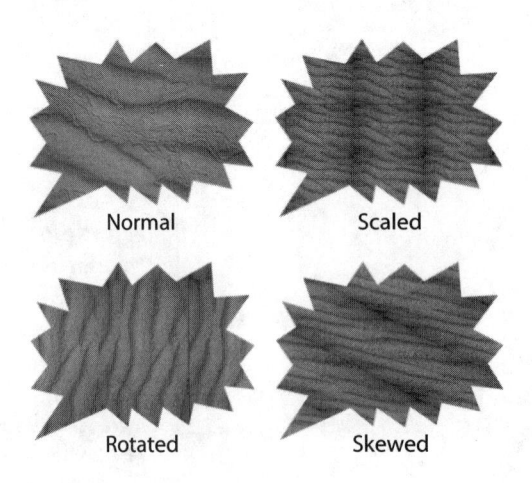

Figure 6.5
A single bitmap can be used as a fill in a number of ways.

To use a bitmap as a fill:

1. Select a shape on the stage (the shape cannot be grouped or part of a symbol).

2. With the Color Mixer panel open, choose Bitmap from the list of fill types.

   The bottom half of the Color Mixer panel will display thumbnails of all the bitmaps that have been imported.

3. Click a thumbnail to apply the bitmap fill to the selected shape (**Figure 6.6**).

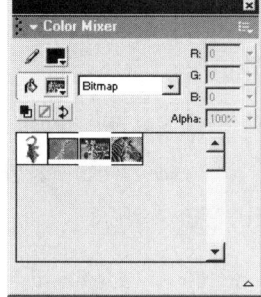

Figure 6.6 Clicking a thumbnail on the Color Mixer panel will apply the bitmap as a fill to the selected shape on the stage.

TIP *You can also use a bitmap fill when creating shapes or painting with the Brush tool by selecting the Bitmap Fill option on the Color Mixer panel, then clicking on a thumbnail of any of the imported bitmaps prior to actually drawing on the stage.*

Transforming a bitmap fill

Although your fill effect may not look exactly the way you want right off the bat, Flash allows you to transform it in the following ways (**Figure 6.7**):

- **Centerpoint.** This handle changes the centerpoint of the bitmap fill.

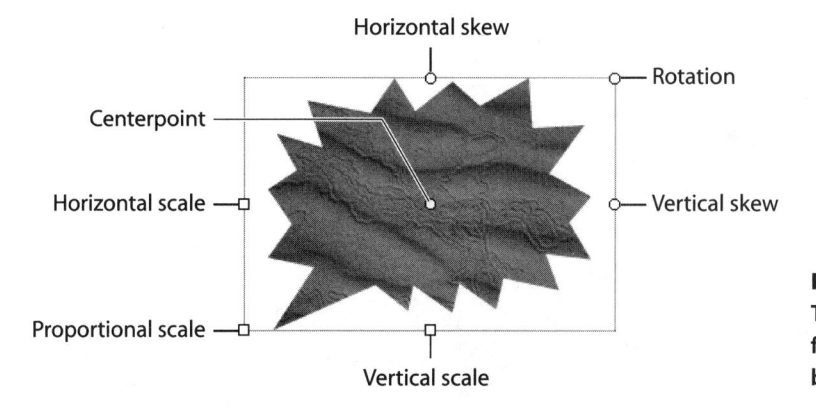

Figure 6.7 The different handles for transforming a bitmap fill.

- **Proportional scale.** This handle resizes the bitmap fill to adjust the number of tiles that display inside a shape.
- **Vertical scale.** This handle resizes the bitmap fill vertically.
- **Horizontal scale.** This handle resizes the bitmap fill horizontally.
- **Vertical skew.** This handle skews the bitmap fill vertically.
- **Horizontal skew.** This handle skews the bitmap fill horizontally.
- **Rotation.** This handle rotates the bitmap clockwise or counterclockwise.

To transform a bitmap fill:

1. From the toolbar, select the Fill Transform tool.
2. Bring the cursor onto the stage and click once on any shape with a bitmap fill.

    The transform handles will appear.
3. Click and drag a handle to transform the fill as you wish.

    TIP *Different shapes that use the same bitmap fill can each be transformed in a different manner.*

Breaking Apart a Bitmap

Although you'll usually work with bitmaps as a whole in Flash, you do have other options. By breaking apart a bitmap, you essentially convert it into a simple shape that you can work with and edit just as you would any other simple shape on the stage (for more information on simple shapes, see Chapter 3, "Graphics"). This means you can use Flash's drawing tools to change individual colors in the bitmap, erase portions of it, or even segment it using lines and shapes (**Figure 6.8**).

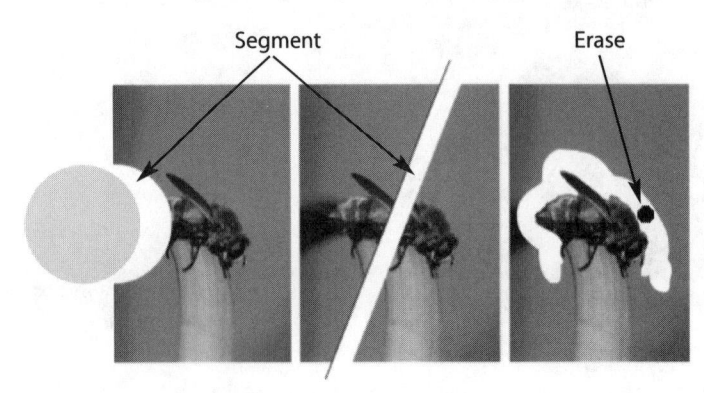

Figure 6.8
Some of the edits you can perform on a bitmap once you've broken it apart.

To break apart a bitmap:

1. Select an instance of the bitmap on the stage.

2. Choose Modify > Break Apart.

TIPS *Breaking apart a bitmap will only affect the selected instance on the stage. The bitmap copy that resides in the library will retain its original form and can still be used elsewhere if you desire.*

Bitmaps used as fills are considered broken apart, and can be edited as such.

Selecting and Modifying Colors in a Bitmap

Once you've broken apart a bitmap, you can move, delete, copy, or swap regions of color (**Figure 6.9**).

Figure 6.9
Breaking apart a bitmap lets you select distinct areas of color for editing.

To select colors in a bitmap:

1. First make sure the bitmap has been broken apart.

2. From the toolbar, choose the Lasso tool.

3. From the options that appear, press the Magic Wand Properties button.

A dialog box will appear that allows you to set two properties for the Magic Wand:

- **Threshold.** Use this to set a range for how close the color of an adjoining pixel needs to be to the original color you highlighted. A setting of "0" selects only pixels that are the exact color of the one you click; a setting of "100" selects all pixels.

- **Smoothing.** Use this to specify how Flash deals with the edge of the selected color area. The settings for this property range from Pixel, which means that the selected area will have an edge defined exactly by the selected pixels, to Smooth, which creates a much smoother selection boundary.

4. Adjust the properties according to your preferences, and click OK.

5. Select the Magic Wand option from the toolbar.

   Move the cursor onto the stage; doing this changes it into a Magic Wand icon.

6. Place the cursor over the colored area in the bitmap that you want to select, then click and release.

   All pixels whose color values fall within the Threshold range you set earlier will be selected, and you can move or delete them.

   TIP *Once you've selected colors in a bitmap, you can change them any way you wish using the Color Mixer panel (**Figure 6.10**).*

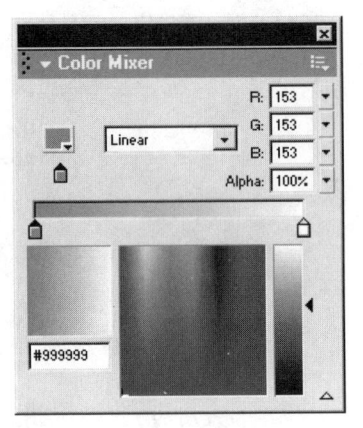

Figure 6.10
Using the Color Mixer panel, you can apply a fill to selected areas of a bitmap.

Tracing Bitmaps

Flash's tracing feature is a useful way to reduce a bitmap's impact on your project's overall file size. Tracing allows you to easily convert a bitmap graphic into a vector graphic (**Figure 6.11**). The tracing tool analyzes the pixels that make up the bitmap, locates areas with similarly colored pixels, then creates vector graphics based on the like-colored shapes it has identified.

TIPS *Tracing can only be performed on bitmaps that have not been broken apart first.*

Tracing a bitmap only affects the selected instance of the bitmap on the stage. The copy of it in the library is still a bitmap, and can be used as such elsewhere in your movie.

Tracing works best on bitmaps with few colors and no gradated areas—meaning you should steer clear of photographs. Attempting to trace a full-color photo will not only tax your computer's resources, it's likely to result in a vector graphic that's larger than the original bitmap—hardly a desirable outcome!

Figure 6.11
Tracing a bitmap turns it into a number of distinct vector shapes that approximate the look of the actual bitmap.

To trace a bitmap:

1. On the stage, select the bitmap you wish to convert into a vector graphic.

2. From the Modify menu, choose Trace Bitmap to bring up the Trace Bitmap dialog box.

   You may adjust the following settings:

   - **Color Threshold.** This option lets you set how much the color of each pixel of the bitmap can vary from adjacent pixels before it is considered a different color. The larger this number is, the fewer vector shapes will be created.

   - **Minimum Area.** This option sets the minimum size of any vector shape created by the trace. You can enter a value between 1 and 1,000.

   - **Curve Fit.** This option allows you to set how closely the trace-created shapes follow the original bitmap colors.

   - **Corner Threshold.** This option lets you set how sharply a curve can bend before the tracing tool turns it into a corner.

3. Once you've adjusted these settings, click OK.

TIPS *Tracing a bitmap usually requires some experimentation: Feel free to test your settings; if you're unhappy with the results, click the Undo button and start over.*

Remember that turning a bitmap into a vector graphic doesn't always reduce file size. You can use a before-and-after comparison to test the conversion's effect on file size. Before tracing a bitmap, choose Test Scene from the Control menu. When the Bandwidth Profiler appears, note the scene's overall file size, then close the window. Now trace your bitmap, and once again choose Test Scene from the Control menu, to see how tracing affected file size. To learn more about the Bandwidth Profiler, see Chapter 19, "Testing."

Tracing Interface Screen Shots

One of the most popular uses of Flash is for creating online demos of products, including software—and interface screen shots are an indispensable element. Clear, crisp images are essential—though not always easy to achieve via bitmaps, which can sometimes appear blurry or jagged. The best way to create interface screen shots is to take advantage of Flash's powerful tracing abilities. By so doing, you can employ graphics in your movie that are every bit as clear and sharp as the original application screens (**Figure 6.12**).

To trace interface screen shots:

1. Capture the screen shot as you normally would. Note that it's best to capture just the interface itself at this point. Other items visible onscreen (such as graphics, if your product is an illustration program) should be captured separately. Tracing any of these other elements will likely have an adverse effect on your movie's file size. You can simply place these nontraced graphics on top of the traced images in the final product.

Original enlarged   Traced enlarged

Figure 6.12
By tracing interface screen shots, you can dramatically improve their clarity, as this graphic demonstrates.

2. Import the captured image into Flash, and place an instance of it on the stage.
3. With the image selected, choose Modify > Trace Bitmap to open the Trace Bitmap dialog box.

Chapter 6 Bitmaps

Tracing Interface Screen Shots continued

4. Enter the following settings (which are ideal for tracing screen shot images):
- Color Threshold: 100
- Minimum Area: 1
- Curve Fit: Pixels
- Corner Threshold: Many Corners

5. Press OK. Flash will begin tracing the image, and after several seconds the image on stage that was once a bitmap will be converted to a vector graphic. If you zoom in on the image, you'll see that it's just as crisp up close.

The following are a few tips and notes to keep in mind when using traced screen shot graphics:

TIPS After the conversion, you may want to turn the traced graphic into a symbol so that you can use it easily throughout your demo movie.

If you've traced a graphic in Flash, such as a dialog box, and a value displayed in it (for example, a number) changes during the course of the demo, you can simply capture the element that changed, trace it, then place it on top of the original dialog box graphic; you don't need to retrace the entire dialog box (**Figure 6.13**) This will prevent you from duplicating content needlessly, which helps reduce the size of your movie.

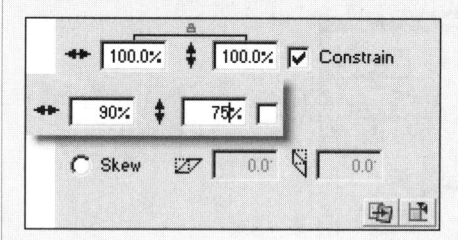

Figure 6.13
If you need to change selected portions of a traced graphic, it's best to capture the content that's changed, trace it, then place it on top of your original tracing.

Adjusting Bitmap Properties

Each bitmap you import into Flash has its own set of properties, including its assigned name, how the image appears in the authoring environment, how it's compressed, and more. Adjustments to a bitmap's properties are made to the master image, which means they affect every instance of that image. The main adjustments you'll make to a bitmap's properties are in how it's optimized and compressed in the exported .swf file.

To open the Bitmap Properties dialog box:

1. From the Window menu, choose Library to open the Library panel.

2. Locate a bitmap in the Library, and click to select it.

3. From the library Options menu, choose Properties to open the Bitmap Properties dialog box.

   TIP *You can also right-click (Windows) or Control-click (Macintosh) the bitmap's name in the library, and choose Properties from the menu that appears.*

The Bitmap Properties box includes the following areas, settings, and buttons (**Figure 6.14**):

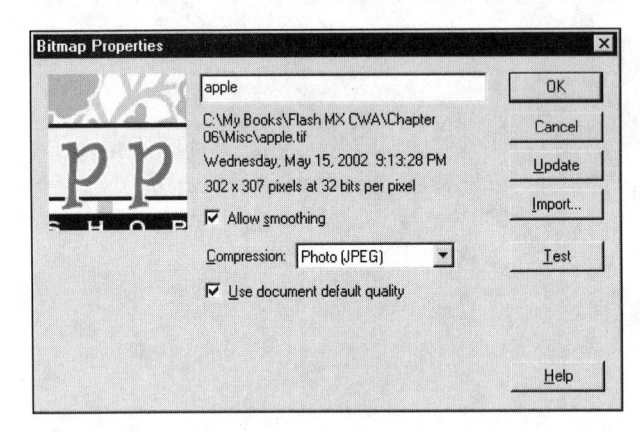

Figure 6.14
The Bitmap Properties dialog box.

- **Preview window.** This window lets you preview the effect of any changes you've made to the available settings. Clicking the Test button refreshes the image in the Preview window. You can also click and drag the image in the preview window to change the image area you wish to preview.

- **Name.** Based on the name of the external file that was imported, this is the default name given to the bitmap that the library uses to identify the image. You can change this name at any time.

- **Directory path.** This is the path from which the image was imported.

- **File info.** This provides information such as dimensions, color depth, and the date the file was last modified.

- **Allow smoothing.** This option affects the way the image appears inside the Flash authoring environment. Checking it will cause the image to be anti-aliased, or smoothed.

- **Compression type drop-down box.** This drop-down box allows you to choose the type of compression used on an image when you export your project to create a Flash movie. Each bitmap can have its own unique settings. (A more detailed discussion of this dialog box follows later in the chapter.)

- **Use document default quality.** See "Compressing Your Images in Flash" later in this chapter.

- **Update button.** If you've used an image-editing program to edit the file you imported into Flash (the one found at the directory-path location), pressing this button updates the Flash image to reflect those changes.

- **Import button.** This button allows you to change the bitmap file referenced in the directory-path information (described above). Importing an image in this manner changes all references in the movie from the current graphic to the one you're importing.

- **Test button.** Use this button in conjunction with the Preview window to see how different compression settings affect the bitmap image.

Optimizing Your Images

Although bitmaps can greatly improve your movie's overall look, this benefit comes at a price—adding to the file size of your exported movie. Thus, it's important to strike a balance between image quality and overall file size.

There are several things you can do, both within and outside of Flash (before the bitmap is actually imported), to ensure that you get the most from the bitmaps used in your project.

Before You Import

The first thing you need to be aware is a bitmap's resolution: This refers to the number of pixels (dots) displayed in each inch of a graphic, both horizontally and vertically. For example, a 1-inch-by-1-inch graphic with 10 dots per inch (dpi) would comprise 100 pixels (10 pixels vertically by 10 pixels horizontally). If you bump up the dpi setting for this graphic to 20, the number of pixels increases to 400 (20 pixels by 20 pixels). A higher dpi setting gives you clearer, sharper graphics—but it also means a larger movie file (**Figure 6.15**).

As a rule, you shouldn't import bitmaps with resolutions higher than 72 dpi into your Flash project: The benefits of the higher resolution won't be visible on your computer monitor, and it unnecessarily increases the file size. You can usually set an image's dpi when scanning or exporting it from another program—you cannot do so once it's in Flash.

Before you import a bitmap into Flash, you should also make sure the image's dimensions match the largest iteration of it in your movie. In other words, if you're using more than one copy, differently sized, of the imported bitmap, the image you import should be based on its largest display in your project. Reducing the size of a graphic has less effect on image quality than enlarging it.

Using the fewest number of colors possible in a bitmap is another way to minimize file size. Thus, whenever you're creating graphics such as GIFs, you should export them from your image-editing program with as few colors as you can without sacrificing image integrity.

150 dpi, 45K

100 dpi, 25K

25 dpi, 15K

Figure 6.15 Examples of the trade-off between resolution and file size.

Compressing Your Images in Flash

As mentioned earlier, you'll want to compress your bitmap image in Flash to minimize its effect on your project's overall size. Compressing, or *optimizing*, an image gets rid of redundant or unnecessary file information.

By default, Flash uses *general* compression settings for any bitmaps that you don't optimize individually. These settings can be accessed by going to File > Publish Settings, then clicking the Flash tab of the Publish Settings dialog box (**Figure 6.16**). Although you can save time by using these settings (since it frees you from compressing each bitmap individually), we don't recommend doing so: First, it's generally worth it to maintain control over every aspect of your movie, including individual bitmap compression settings. Second, because each bitmap in the library has a unique look and function, you'll probably want to optimize at least some of them differently. For example, you may want to apply very little compression to a full-color photograph, but use more compression with an image that contains just a few colors. There's no set formula for getting the perfect balance—it varies from project to project.

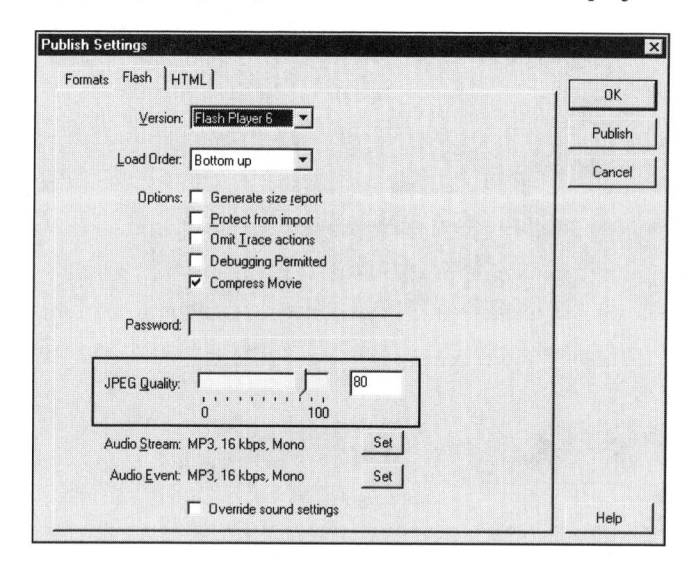

Figure 6.16
Default settings for compressing bitmaps can be found on the Flash tab of the Publish Settings dialog box.

The Bitmap Properties box is where you choose a compression setting for each bitmap in your movie. Any optimization you select here will affect each instance of the bitmap in your movie. To make it easier, Flash lets you preview the settings' effect on image quality and movie file size. When you press the Test button, the image in the preview window is updated, as is the Compression report at the bottom of the dialog box.

You can perform two types of compression on bitmap graphics, *photo* and *lossless*—both of which are available from the compression drop-down box. The trick is to find the setting that least affects overall file size while still maintaining acceptable image quality.

Photo (JPEG)

Photo compression is described as a "lossy" compression method, and is best-suited for photos or for graphics that contain numerous colors, and subtle blends between the colors. Depending on what settings you choose, the JPEG image should closely resemble the original, though it won't be identical.

NOTE *In lossy compression, minute bits of data (image quality) are sacrificed to gain a smaller image file. Unless you apply a great deal of compression to an image, the effect is often unnoticeable.*

To compress an image using the Photo Compression option:

1. Choose the photo compression type from the drop-down box.

A checkbox will appear asking if you want to use the document default quality (as described earlier). If this box is unchecked, a new option becomes available, allowing you to set the compression amount, or quality, for your image. The lower the number you enter in this box, the more the file is compressed—and the more image degradation occurs.

2. Enter a compression amount in this box, then click Test.

The Preview window shows you how the selected settings will affect the image. In addition, a compression results comparison appears at the bottom of the Bitmap Properties box, showing each setting's effect on the bitmap's file size (**Figure 6.17**).

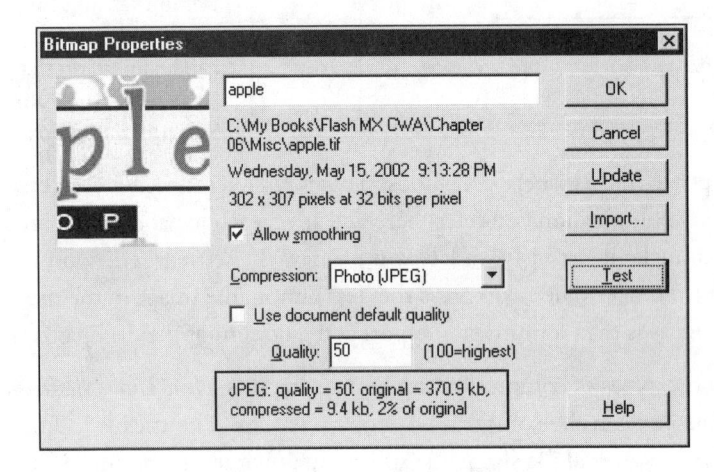

Figure 6.17 Clicking the Test button after adjusting compression settings lets you see how your settings affect the bitmap's file size.

3. If you're satisfied with your adjustments, click OK.

Lossless (PNG/GIF)

Lossless compression is best suited for images with limited numbers of colors—such as logos, line art, and nonphotographic images. If you select this option, there are no additional settings to adjust. However, you can preview the option's effect on a selected image by clicking the Test button.

TIP *Do not compress a bitmap using a lossy compression method (such as JPEG) prior to importing it. Flash will simply re-optimize it, resulting in what we call the "copier effect," which seriously degrades image quality.*

Updating Bitmaps

Updating bitmaps is much like updating sounds (which we described in the previous chapter). In fact, the steps are almost identical. Thus, to avoid redundancy, review the section on updating sounds with the following guidelines in mind.

Updating an Imported Fireworks Image

When you import a flattened PNG file created in Fireworks 3 (or later), you have some additional options for updating the image in Flash. Because these programs are so tightly integrated, Flash can automatically open the original, editable Fireworks source file, which allows you to edit it with layers, text, and vectors intact. After you've finished editing the source file in Fireworks, simply save it to update the image in Flash (**Figure 6.18**).

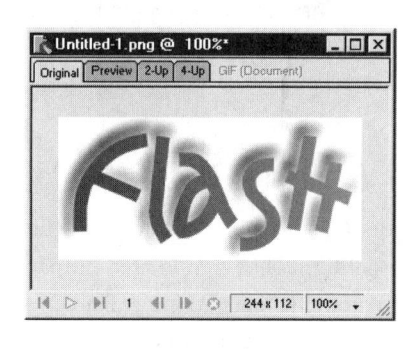

Before   Edit in Fireworks   After

Figure 6.18
A bitmap imported from a Fireworks 3 (or later) file can be opened up and edited in Fireworks, and is then automatically updated in Flash to reflect the edits.

To edit and update an image created in Fireworks 3 (or later):

1. With the Library panel open, select an image that was imported from a Fireworks 3 (or later) file.

2. Click the Options button on the top-right corner of the Library panel, and choose Edit with Fireworks x (x represents the version number of Fireworks installed on your computer).

Fireworks will open, and the editable file will appear in the Fireworks document window.

3. Edit the file as you normally would, using any of Fireworks' functions.

4. When you've finished editing the file, use the Fireworks File menu to Save the file. This updates the image in Flash.

Using Bitmaps in Shared Libraries

Once you've imported a bitmap into the library, you can turn it into a shared library asset, which enables you to use it in multiple SWF files without having to actually import it and embed it directly into each movie. The benefits of this are twofold: First, because bitmaps reside in a central location (the shared library), users only need to download them once (rather than into every movie that uses them)—which translates to substantially reduced download times. Second, whenever you update an image in the shared library, any movie that's "linked" to it will reflect those changes.

For information about shared libraries, see Chapter 17, "Using the Library to Manage Your Assets."

Using Animated GIFs

When the animated vectors that Flash creates aren't sufficient for your project, animated GIFs can provide a solution. These animated bitmaps abound on the Web, and there are tons of cool animated GIF collections available for download and purchase. GIFs facilitate such visual effects as explosions, fires, people in motion, and more. They can have transparent backgrounds (just as they would on a regular Web page), allowing you to blend them seamlessly into the rest of your layout.

To use an animated GIF in Flash, you must first import it. Animated GIFs consist of several bitmaps, or *frames*, which when played in succession appear animated. The time between frames determines the speed at which the animated GIF plays. When you import an animated GIF into Flash, each of its frames are placed in individual frames on Flash's timeline. Flash also spaces the animated GIF frames so that the speed at which the GIF plays in Flash is as close to its original speed as possible. For example, if you were to import a four-frame, 1-second animated GIF into a 12-fps Flash movie, Flash would place the individual GIF frames three frames apart on the Flash timeline (4 frames x 3 frames apart = 1 second in a 12-fps movie) (**Figure 6.19**).

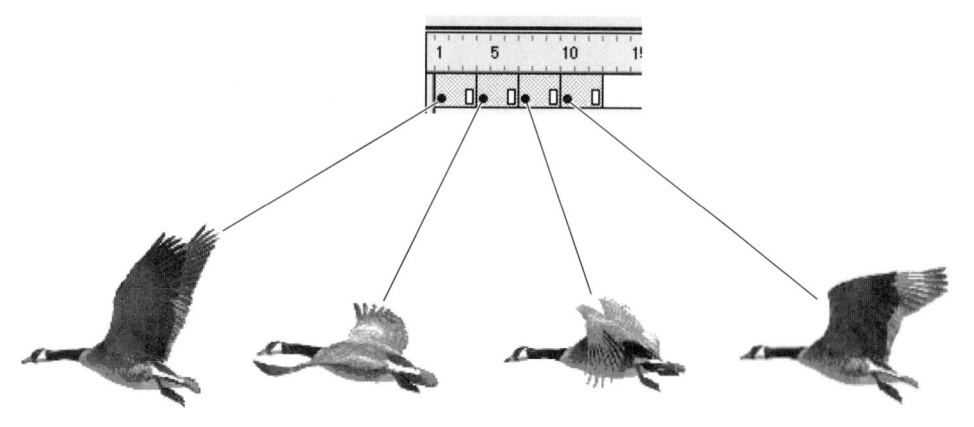

Figure 6.19
When importing an animated GIF, Flash spaces individual frames so that the GIF will appear and play back at the same speed within Flash.

We recommend importing animated GIFs directly into a movie clip, then using the movie clip on stage. Because each movie clip is a self-contained animation (see Chapter 7, "Symbols"), you can reuse a movie clip created from an animated GIF repeatedly throughout your presentation without affecting overall file size. In addition, converting an imported animated GIF to a movie clip allows you to resize, move, or even rotate its display within Flash.

To create a movie clip using an animated GIF:

1. From the Insert menu, choose New Symbol to bring up the Symbol Properties dialog box.

2. From the behavior options, choose Movie Clip, and give your movie clip a name.

3. Click OK.

The movie clip editing window will display. The timeline that appears is your movie clip's timeline, which plays independently of the main timeline. This is where the individual frames of the imported animated GIF will go.

4. From the File menu, choose Import to bring up the Import dialog box.

5. Select an animated GIF, and click Open.

Each frame of the animated GIF will be imported and placed in a frame on the movie clip's timeline.

6. Return to the main timeline.

TIP *When importing an animated GIF into a movie clip's timeline, Flash places the bitmaps that make up its individual frames into the library. Be sure not to delete any of these bitmaps if you want your movie clip to play properly. You may want to place these clips in a folder inside the library (**Figure 6.20**).*

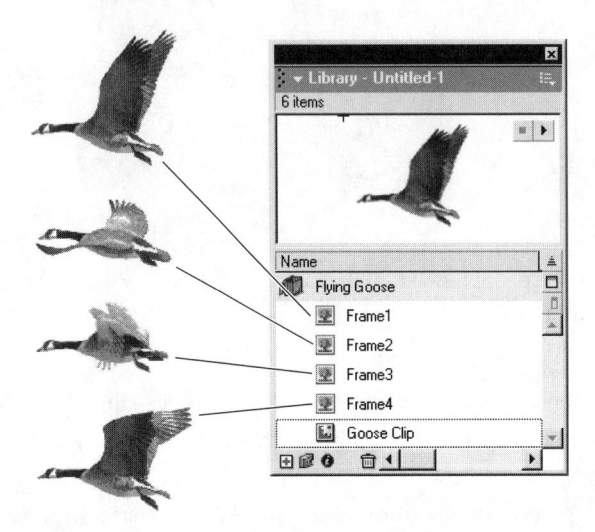

Figure 6.20
When importing an animated GIF, Flash stores each of the bitmaps that comprise individual GIF frames in the library.

Now that you've created a movie clip from an animated GIF, it's time to use it in your presentation.

To use an animated GIF/movie clip in your project:

1. From the Window menu, choose Library to open the Library panel.
2. Find the movie clip you created.
3. Click and drag it from the list or preview window onto the stage.

TIP *Only the first frame of the imported animated GIF/movie clip will be visible when it is placed on the stage. To see how the newly created movie clip will appear in your Flash movie, select Test Scene from the Control menu. Once you've finished viewing, close the test window.*

Before moving on to the next topic, we should note that Flash allows two types of bitmap animations. One, as just discussed, involves importing an animated GIF, then converting it into a movie clip. The other technique involves manipulating the entire imported bitmap (either static or animated), and creating transitions in its size, rotation, or position (**Figure 6.21**)—for example, making a photo slide from one side of the screen to the other, or causing it to grow or shrink. We discuss these effects in greater detail in the chapter on animation. Just be aware of the distinction.

Frame-sequence animation

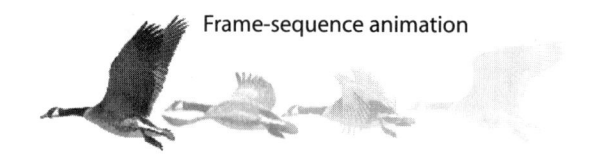

Transitional animation

Figure 6.21
Bitmaps can be used in Flash for two types of animation: In *frame-sequence animation* (like an animated GIF), a group of static bitmaps are "flipped" through, giving the effect of animation. In *transitional animation* a bitmap's size, rotation, or position is changed over time.

Using PNGs

PNG, or Portable Network Graphic, is a graphics standard that offers numerous advantages over GIFs—especially in compression, color capabilities, and transparency.

Like GIFs, PNGs use a lossless compression algorithm. This means that a PNG file is compressed at the time it is created so that when viewed, there appears to be no quality degradation from the original. Thus, you can bring or create a 1-MB bitmap in your favorite image-editing program, export it as a PNG, and end up with a file that is every bit as clear and beautiful as the original—but at a fraction of its size. In fact, PNG compression typically surpasses GIF compression by 5 percent to 25 percent (though on tiny images, it can be as much as 40 percent or 50 percent). Many programs on the market today can export to the PNG format, including Adobe Photoshop, Macromedia Fireworks, and Corel Photo-Paint.

Even more impressive than the PNG format's compression ratios is its support for 24- and 48-bit color (in contrast to GIFs, which only support 8-bit color). This means your images aren't limited to a 256-color palette, as are GIFs; instead, you can use the full range of colors—millions, if you wish.

Best of all, PNG images support full alpha transparency, which means each pixel's transparency value can range between 0 and 255. (GIFs, in contrast, only offer on/off transparency, which means that a pixel is either transparent or not.)

PNG's transparency capabilities allow you to create some impressive effects with bitmaps, including:

- Images with gradated transparencies, which can be used as masks.
- Objects with transparent backgrounds (**Figure 6.22**).

Figure 6.22
PNG images imported into Flash can have gradated transparencies or transparent backgrounds, which lets you position and animate them independently of their backgrounds within Flash. This graphic shows a composite design as well as some of the independent PNG images that comprise it.

Creating a PNG with gradated transparency in a bitmap editing program usually only involves masking off image areas that you wish to be transparent, then—with the mask still active—exporting your image to PNG.

Given these advantages, you should use PNG graphics wherever possible when you import bitmaps into Flash—both for photographic images and images with few colors. No other bitmap format allows you to do as much with graphics.

GIFs do offer one advantage over PNGs: While you can import animated GIFs, you can't import animated PNG images. Thus, if you need to use animated bitmaps in your project, don't bother looking for the animated PNG option—it's not there.

Making Creative Use of Bitmaps

Displaying images isn't the only thing you can do with bitmaps in your projects. In this section, we'll show you some other ways you can use bitmaps to create a range of effects.

NOTE *Many of these effects use animation techniques that are discussed in greater detail in Chapter 10, "Animation."*

Motion Blurs

Although Flash allows you to animate elements so that they enter a scene very quickly (sliding or fading in, and so on), it can be difficult to produce an accurate sense of motion using only vector shapes. This is because objects in motion produce what's known as *motion blur*. To picture this, think of those snapshots you've taken of moving objects—and the blurry images that resulted. In fact, that blurring effect actually plays an essential role in our visual perception of motion (hence the term *motion blur*). To accurately produce a sense of motion in your Flash projects, you can incorporate motion blurs. However, Flash's tools don't really provide a means to do so: This is where bitmaps can help.

The three primary types of motion blurs are focus, spin, and slide (**Figure 6.23**). In most image-editing programs, you apply these types of blurs by bringing an image into the editor and selecting one of those three effects. You can then export the image for use in Flash.

To create a motion blur in Flash, you need the original graphic and the version to which the blur has been applied. The trick is to animate the blur image so that its motion mimics that of the blur (thus, a spinning blur needs to be rotated), then quickly fade out the blurred image as the nonblurred image

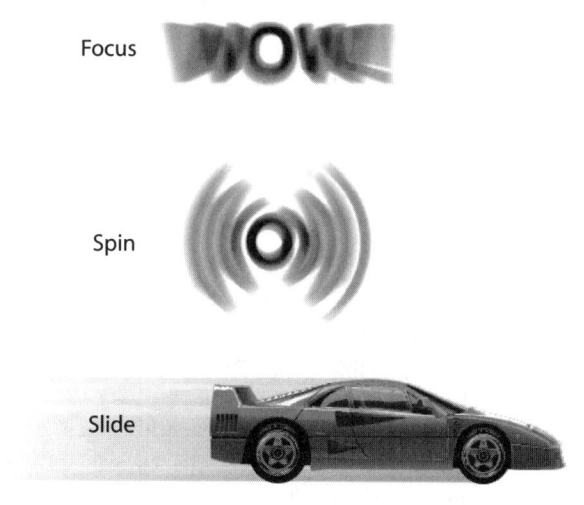

Figure 6.23
The three main types of motion blurs.

fades in (**Figure 6.24**). You can use Flash to alter the overall feel of the motion by applying different levels of motion blur, or by varying the speed of the transition from blur to clear. Experimentation is the key. You'll find several examples of motion blurs on the accompanying CD, in a file named motionBlurs.fla in the Chapter 6/Assets folder.

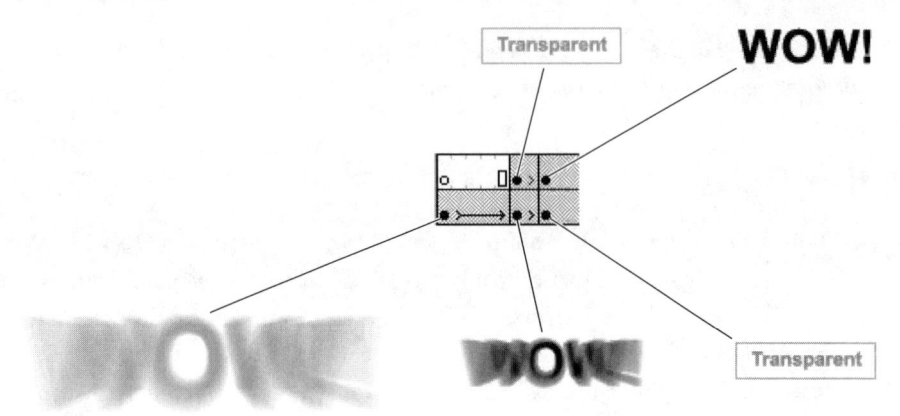

Figure 6.24
The frame/animation structure needed to create a realistic motion blur.

TIP *A number of interesting morphing effects can also be achieved by fading out one bitmap with an effect applied to it, while fading in another one with no effect applied. Have fun experimenting!*

Panoramic Views

Panoramic views are used to display an area as it would appear if you were standing on a pivot point that rotated you a full 360 degrees. As you circle back around from 359 degrees to 0, the image begins repeating itself, providing the illusion that the picture never ends. Although most of the panoramic displays you see on Web pages are created in programs like QuickTime and IPIX, you can easily create your own using Flash.

Although you can create fully controllable panoramic views in Flash (allowing viewers to use the mouse to move the view left, right, up, or down), the following exercise focuses on the *mechanics* of creating a panoramic view in Flash. Once you've learned ActionScript, you can add user controls to your panoramic view if you wish.

To begin, you must have a panoramic image that is set up so that if you placed two copies side by side, the right edge of one would match seamlessly with the left edge of the other (**Figure 6.25**). Be sure to note the width of the graphic; for this exercise, our graphic is 623 pixels wide. We'll explain the importance of this shortly.

Figure 6.25
When creating a panoramic view, you must begin with an image whose right edge matches up with its left edge when two copies are placed side-by-side.

To create a panoramic view in Flash:

1. From the File menu, choose New to start a new Flash project.

2. With the Property inspector open, give your movie a frame rate of 24.

3. From the Insert menu, choose New Symbol.

    The Create New Symbol dialog box will appear.

4. Enter the name *panoClip*, choose the Movie Clip behavior, then click OK.

    This immediately takes you to the timeline of your newly created clip, which will contain most of the functionality that makes up our panoramic view.

5. From the File menu, choose Import. Navigate to your panoramic image, then click Open.

    This will import the image and automatically place its top-left corner at a 0, 0 (*X, Y*) position on the stage.

6. Select the image, then choose Edit > Copy to copy it to the clipboard.

7. Choose Edit > Paste in Place to paste the copy directly over the original.

8. With the copy selected, position it so that its left side bumps up against the right side of the original.

    Since the graphic we're using for this exercise is 623 pixels wide, we can open the Property inspector and position it precisely by giving it *X, Y* coordinates of 623 and 0, respectively. The two images should appear to blend seamlessly.

9. Select both the original and the copy, then choose Modify > Group to group the images together.

    The reason for setting up two images in this manner will become clearer shortly.

10. On the timeline, select Frame 400, then choose Insert Keyframe.

    This keyframe is a necessary ingredient of the animation we're about to create. We chose the number of frames (400) arbitrarily. The number of frames you use will determine the speed at which the panoramic view will move. The fewer the frames, the faster it will move.

11. With the playhead still at Frame 400, select the group of images and move them to the left.

    How much? Well, there's a simple formula. First, we determine the size of the original image, which for this exercise is 623 pixels. Next, we divide that number by the total frames we're using—that is, 623 by 400—which gives us a result of roughly 1.5. Next, we subtract 1.5 from 623, which gives us 621.5. Thus, you move the group of images to an X position of *negative* 621.5 (**Figure 6.26**). Open the Property inspector to accurately move the group to that position. This will all become clearer shortly.

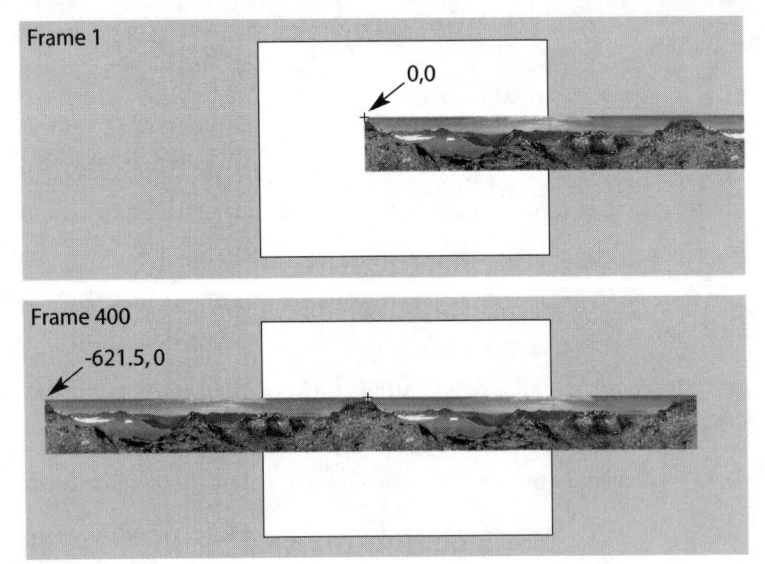

Figure 6.26
On Frame 1, the X, Y position of the group of panoramic images should be 0, 0, respectively. At Frame 400, it should be -621.5, 0, respectively.

12. Select Frame 1 of the timeline, and from the Tween drop-down box on the Property inspector, choose Motion.

    This creates a motion tween. You can move the playhead on the timeline to see that this tween sets our group of images in motion, moving them to the left.

13. On the timeline, press the Insert Layer button to insert a new layer above the current one.

    This will add a layer to the timeline named Layer 2. This layer will soon contain a mask that will act as window for displaying these panoramic images a portion at time.

14. Select Frame 1 of Layer 2 (the layer you created in the previous step). Select the Rectangle tool on the drawing toolbar and create a square with no outline and a solid fill. The width you draw the square will determine the width of the window that the panoramic view appears in.

15. Select the square you drew, and with the Property inspector open, position it so that it its *X* and *Y* positions are 0 and 0, respectively.

    The top-left corner of the square should be aligned with the top-left corner of the image group (**Figure 6.27**).

Figure 6.27
Place the square on the stage so that its top-left corner is aligned with the top-left corner of the image group.

16. Right-click (Windows) or Control-click (Mac) on Layer 2's name, and choose Mask from the menu that appears.

    This converts that layer to a Mask layer, which means that the content underneath it (the layer that contains the moving panoramic graphic) will only be seen within the area defined by the square you drew.

17. Return to the main timeline. With the Library panel open, drag an instance of the **panoClip** onto the stage.

    Position it as desired.

18. Choose Control > Test Movie to view the results.

    As soon as the movie begins to play, the panoramic view you created will appear. Notice how it moves, and how it achieves the illusion of being endless. The effect is created by a visual loop: When our tween reaches Frame 400, it automatically returns to Frame 1—a seamless transition we made possible by adding the copied panoramic graphic (as described in Step 7) and precisely placing the group of panoramic images (as described in Step 11). These are the two most crucial steps in this process.

NOTE *A completed version of this exercise (panoramic.fla) can be found in the Chapter 6/Assets folder on the CD that accompanies this book.*

360-Degree Views

Another popular feature in Flash-created online demos is the 360-degree view of a product. This effect enables you to study an object from different angles as it rotates before you—pretty cool in and of itself. However, you can make it even more interesting by adding some invisible buttons that let the user control the image's rotation.

To make this work, you need a group of several images representing different views of the item. (You can include as many different views as you want.) These images are placed on a movie clip's timeline; to provide user control, a series of invisible buttons are placed on top of the images, which when rolled over by a mouse cursor will send the movie clip to a corresponding frame (**Figure 6.28**). You'll find an example of a 360-degree view on the accompanying CD, in a file named 360DegreeView.fla in the Chapter 6/Assets folder.

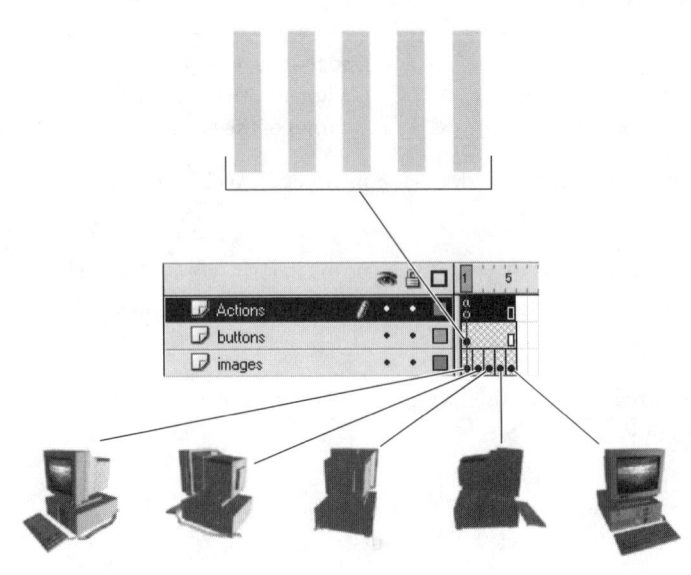

Figure 6.28
To make a 360-degree view work, a series of invisible buttons (gray rectangles) is first placed over a series of images. The buttons are then scripted so that when rolled over, a corresponding image is displayed. This graphic shows the timeline structure needed to make this work.

Video Tutorial

Importing and Working with Bitmap Elements. This tutorial demonstrates most of the concepts you've learned about in this chapter, including importing bitmaps, using bitmaps as fills, tracing, optimizing, and more.

Symbols

CHAPTER 7

What you'll learn...

About symbol types and instances

How to create symbols

How to edit symbols

Ways to work with instances

A number of today's Web technologies are built around the idea of creating content that you can use in multiple applications—not surprising, since no one wants to create the same thing again and again. Say, for example, you needed to create a logo graphic for a 50-page Web site: It would be ridiculous to painstakingly produce a copy for each page when you could instead simply reference the original in each subsequent iteration (making it easier to update your content, too).

This concept of *one object, many uses* is the guiding principle behind symbols, which are key elements supporting Flash's ability to deliver compact multimedia. Because they can help you create dynamic yet compact movies, symbols are an important piece of any Flash project. If you want to deliver interactive, compact Flash movies with the smallest file sizes possible, you need to understand symbols.

Understanding Symbols and Instances

Simply put, a symbol is a *master element*, such as a button, that you create once in Flash. *Instances* are *copies* of this master element that you can use throughout your movie. The content of symbols can range from a graphic you've drawn to an animation of, for example, a bird in flight. Any symbol you create automatically becomes part of your project's library—which is where your movie's various elements are organized (see Chapter 17, "Using the Library to Manage Your Assets").

To place instances of a symbol in your Flash project, simply drag the symbol name from the library window. If, for example, you wished to depict a flock of flying birds, you could create a symbol of a single flying bird, then drag additional instances of the symbol from the library onto the stage (**Figure 7.1**). You'll learn more about this in Chapter 17.

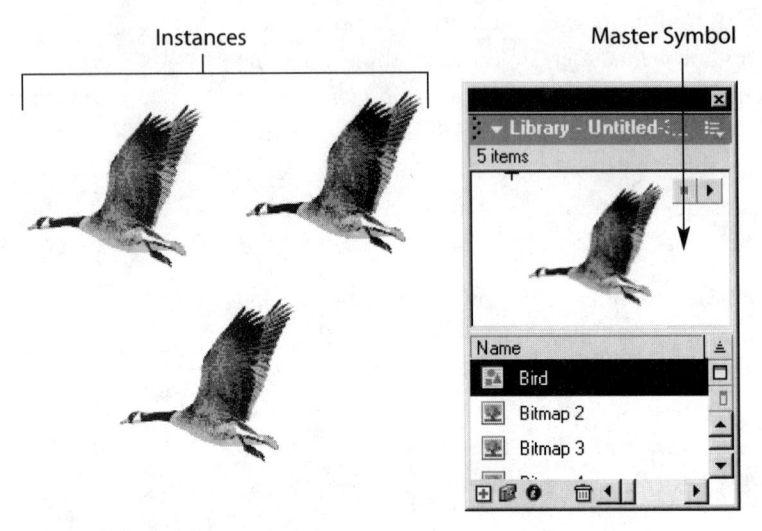

Figure 7.1
Instances on the stage are all references to the master symbol in the library.

Flash lets you place as many instances of your flying bird as you want. Each instance is only a reference to, rather than a full copy of, your original symbol—which is stored just once in your final Flash file. Referencing a symbol has very little impact on file size—regardless of how many instances of it you use. Even if creating a particular symbol initially added 25 KB (25,000 bytes) to your movie's overall file size, placing 10, 20, or even more instances of that symbol would add less than 100 bytes to the movie file—regardless of the symbol's size.

The real magic of symbols stems from the fact that individual instances don't have to look and act exactly like the master symbol. Each symbol instance can have its own tint, transparency, rotation, size, or interactive function (**Figure 7.2**). Likewise, each symbol has its own unique timeline and stage, complete with layers. Thus, placing a symbol instance in a scene is a bit like placing a small movie (the symbol instance) inside a bigger movie (your Flash project).

Figure 7.2
Separate instances of a symbol can look and function quite differently from one another.

You can also animate a symbol instance as a whole. For example, if you had a symbol of a bird flapping its wings, you could animate an instance of that symbol (the whole bird) so that it appeared to be moving across the sky in whatever direction you chose. Another thing to be aware of, at least from a graphical standpoint, is that once you've edited a master symbol's appearance, each instance of that symbol will reflect those changes. However, individual symbol instances can still have their own colors, sizes, and functionality (**Figure 7.3**).

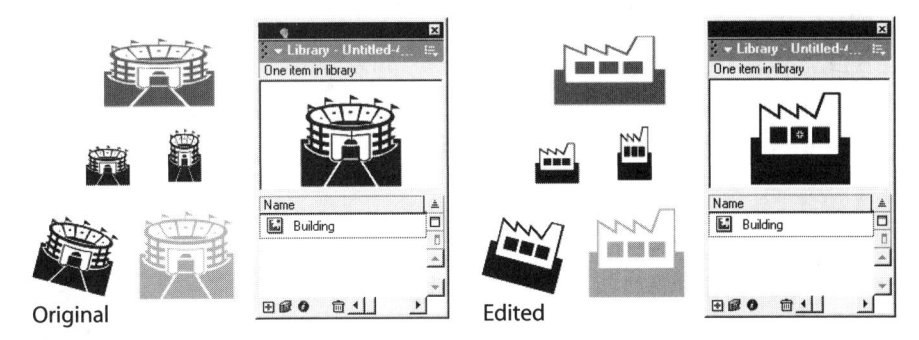

Original   Edited

Figure 7.3
Editing a master symbol in the library updates any instances of that symbol on the stage.

When creating Flash movies, it's important to understand where and when you can use symbols. First of all, not every graphic in your movie needs to be converted into a symbol. Generally, you should create symbols out of any graphic element you want to animate, or plan to use more than once in your project (with the exception of sounds, bitmaps, and video—see the "Special and Pseudo-Symbols" sidebar later in this chapter for more on this topic).

Symbol Types

You can create three master symbol types, or *behaviors*, in Flash (**Figure 7.4**).

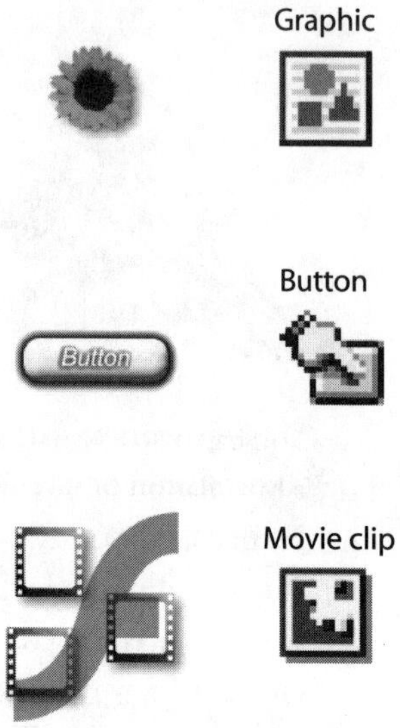

Graphics

Graphic symbols usually consist of static, or nonanimated, graphics that are used a number of times in your movie. For example, you could create a field of flowers by placing many *instances* of a flower symbol in your scene—that single, nonanimated flower is a good example of a graphic symbol. (This is not to say that graphic symbols cannot be animated. We'll discuss this in more detail in "Working with Instances" later in this chapter.)

Buttons

Button symbols react to cursor input, allowing your audience to control and interact with your movie. An onscreen button can be set to perform all kinds of actions.

Movie clips

These are the most interactive, versatile, and powerful elements in Flash. Movie clip symbols can include all of the elements used in your main movie, including sound, animation, and buttons. Movie clip symbols have their own timelines, which can run independently of your project's main timeline (meaning that even if the main movie's timeline stops, the movie clip's timeline can continue).

You can use movie clip symbols for all sorts of interactive elements, including the following:

- Independent animations that can be started and stopped independently of the main timeline
- Custom cursors
- Items you want the user to be able to drag around
- Items that can be duplicated while the movie is playing
- Slider controls

Figure 7.4
Use graphic symbols for nonanimated graphics, buttons to enable user interaction, and movie clips to place complete, self-contained movies inside your main movie.

- Items whose visibility, transparency, position, size, and other properties you want the user to be able to control
- A central location for storing information that your movie may need to track

To make a movie clip interactive, you simply "attach" ActionScript code to instances of it (we'll demonstrate how to do this later in the chapter). For more information on movie clips and ActionScript, see Chapter 16, "Using ActionScript in your Projects."

Once you've created a symbol with an associated behavior, you can easily assign different behaviors to various instances of it—for example, making a graphic symbol behave like a button or vice versa (see "Defining an Instance" later in this chapter). This means you can use a single symbol for multiple purposes in your project—another reason Flash is able to create such compact files.

Symbols are made even more powerful by the fact that you can place one within another—for example, putting buttons and graphic symbols inside movie clip symbols or movie clip symbols inside button symbols. You can even place movie clips within movie clips.

NOTE *Button symbols and frame actions don't work when placed inside graphic symbols.*

Special and Pseudo-Symbols

MX ALERT

In addition to graphics, buttons, and movie clips, Flash offers several special types of symbols:

- **Components.** *You can think of components as "enhanced" movie clips. Normally, to make a movie clip interactive, you must manually adjust ActionScript code. With components, however, the clip's interactivity is "built in," meaning that you set attributes and options using the Property inspector or Components Parameters panel. That in turn means you don't actually have to view or work with any ActionScript code. This built-in interactive functionality is the main difference between a component and a regular movie clip. For more on components, see Chapter 15, "Components."*

- **Font symbols.** *This type of symbol pertains to text displays; you'll find more information on font symbols in Chapter 4, "Text."*

- **Pseudo-Symbols.** *Though not defined as symbols, bitmaps, video and sounds are handled similarly in Flash. Like symbols, imported bitmaps, video and sounds are added to the library automatically, and can be used multiple times without significantly increasing your Flash movie's overall file size.*

Creating Symbols

When you begin creating symbols, keep in mind that you're essentially producing a movie element with its own timeline. A graphic symbol's timeline runs in conjunction with the main timeline (that is, its playback is stopped or paused when the main timeline stops or pauses), whereas a movie clip's timeline can run independently of it (that is, it continues to play after the main timeline has stopped). You work with a symbol's timeline—which has its own set of layers—much the same way you work with the main movie timeline. Later in this chapter we'll examine timelines for each type of symbol. First, however, we'll look at how to create symbols.

General Symbol Creation

Flash offers a couple of ways to create symbols: You can convert stage (or main timeline) content into symbols, or you can create a blank, or empty, symbol, which you later fill with content. Each approach offers different advantages, which we'll compare shortly.

To create a symbol using content on the stage:

1. Select the element(s) on the stage you wish to convert.

   These can include shapes, text, groups, and even other symbols.

2. From the Insert menu, choose Convert to Symbol to bring up the Convert to Symbol dialog box.

3. In the dialog box, assign a name and behavior (graphic, button, or movie clip) to your new symbol, then click OK.

4. From the Window menu, choose Library to verify that your newly created symbol has been added (**Figure 7.5**).

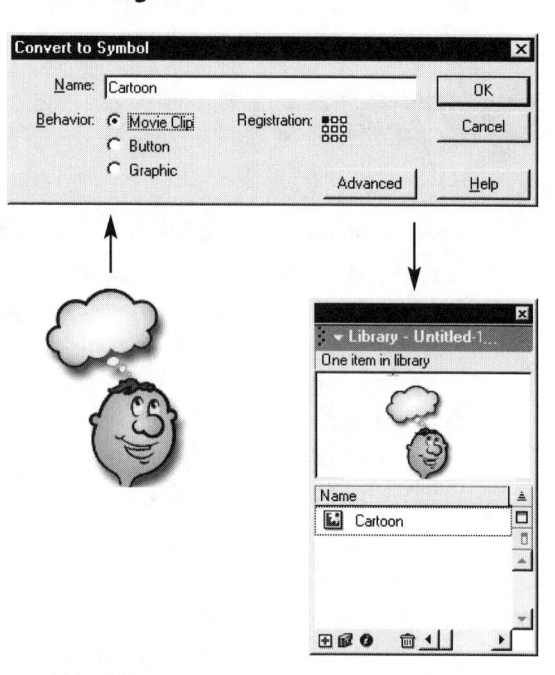

Figure 7.5
All newly created symbols are added to the library.

Chapter 7 **Symbols**

You can now drag instances of this symbol from the library to the stage. We'll look further at this process in "Working with Instances," later in this chapter.

> **MX ALERT** *Another way to create a symbol from content on the stage is by selecting the content and dragging it onto the Library panel. This opens the Convert to Symbol dialog box—at which point you can simply continue with Steps 3 and 4 above to complete the process.*

Additional Features of the Convert to Symbol Dialog Box

> **MX ALERT** *The Convert to Symbol dialog box contains a couple of features you may be wondering about. Let's take a quick look at both:*
>
> - **Registration.** *By clicking any of the nine boxes visible in this graphic, you can set the registration point of the symbol you're about to create. This represents the point at which the symbol's X and Y coordinates meet (**Figure 7.6**). The default setting is at the top-left corner of the graphic that makes up this symbol. This setting helps determine how you can work with the instance—especially in terms of positioning and rotating it. For more information, see Chapter 8, "Working with Elements on the Stage."*
>
> **Figure 7.6**
> The registration graphic on the Convert to Symbol dialog box lets you set the *X* and *Y* coordinates of the symbol you're about to create.
>
> - **Advanced button.** *Pressing this button reveals a number of additional settings for the symbol being created. Many of these settings pertain to using the clip in a dynamic fashion (either via ActionScript or Shared Libraries); you can leave them alone completely and still have a fully functioning symbol. For more information about Shared Libraries, see Chapter 17, "Using the Library to Manage Your Assets."*

Although the method outlined above provides a quick way to create any of the three symbol types, it's also a less versatile approach. By creating symbols in this manner, you're placing all of the content you selected from the main stage into the first frame of the newly created symbol's timeline (**Figure 7.7**). To create animation within your new symbol, you must edit its timeline and stage (see "Editing Symbols" later in this chapter). Most of the time it's better to start from scratch by creating a blank (or empty) symbol, which you can then later add content to or animate. Converting existing content on the main timeline into a symbol is usually the result of constructing a graphic that grows to require functionality beyond that originally intended.

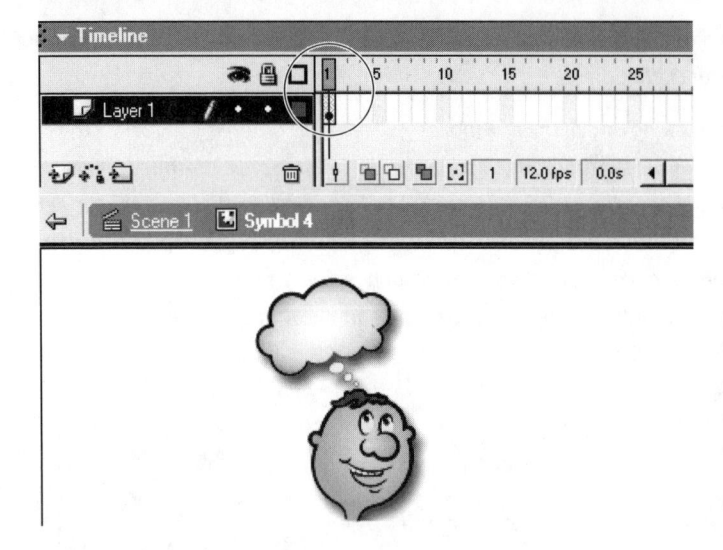

Figure 7.7
When using the Convert to Symbol command, all content of the new symbol is initially placed on its timeline's first frame.

To create an empty symbol:

1. From the Insert menu, choose New Symbol to make the Symbol Properties dialog box appear.

2. Assign a name and behavior (graphic, button, or movie clip) to your new symbol, then click OK.

The Flash authoring environment automatically converts to symbol-editing mode, which consists of a blank timeline and stage for your newly created symbol.

3. Use the steps you've already learned to draw or import and add content to your symbol's timeline. (See "Symbol-Specific Creation" for more on this topic.)

4. When you've finished creating your symbol content, from the Edit menu choose Edit Document.

   This will take you out of symbol-editing mode and return you to the main movie's timeline and stage.

   TIPS *When you re-enter your main movie's timeline and stage, your newly created symbol will not initially appear. To place an instance of it, open the library (Window > Library) and drag it to the stage.*

   Instances of movie clips will not appear animated in the authoring environment. Only the first frame will be visible. Use Control > Test Movie to view your movie clip in all its animated, interactive glory.

   MX ALERT *{ ActionScript } You can create an empty movie clip dynamically using the* `createEmptyMovieClip()` *method. This allows you to create movie clips on the fly.*

Symbol-Specific Creation

When you create a blank symbol as outlined above, the behavior (graphic, button, or movie clip) you assign to it will affect the way you construct or add content to your symbol, how you use your symbol, and how its timeline works in relation to the main timeline. The following information builds on Step 3 above. For a demonstration of how to create these types of symbols, see "Interactive Tutorials" at the end of this chapter.

Graphic symbols

When creating graphic symbols, you're presented with a stage and timeline that look just like the main stage and timeline. Not surprisingly, you also create content on them much as you do in your main movie: The drawing tools work the same; layers work the same; and creating animation across a graphic symbol's timeline is also pretty much the same. The only difference is that sounds and interactivity don't function on the graphic symbol's timeline—which means this type of symbol is best suited for movie elements that need to be reused, but don't require movement or sound. For elements that require movement, movie clip symbols are usually a better choice.

This doesn't mean, however, that you can't animate a graphic symbol's timeline. You just need to be aware of a few details. For starters, a graphic symbol's timeline is closely linked to the main timeline. This means that although you can make a graphic symbol's timeline as long (in frames) as you wish, it will only play while the main timeline is playing (**Figure 7.8**).

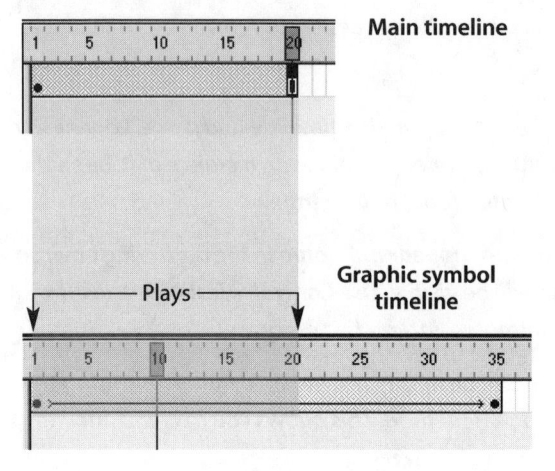

Figure 7.8
If you place an instance of a 35-frame graphic symbol on Frame 1 of the 20-frame main timeline, that instance will only play for 20 frames.

If you want your symbol's timeline to function independently of the main timeline, you should use a movie clip symbol instead.

Button symbols

When creating button symbols, you're presented with a unique timeline, whose four frames—Up, Over, Down, and Hit—represent different button symbol *states* (**Figure 7.9**):

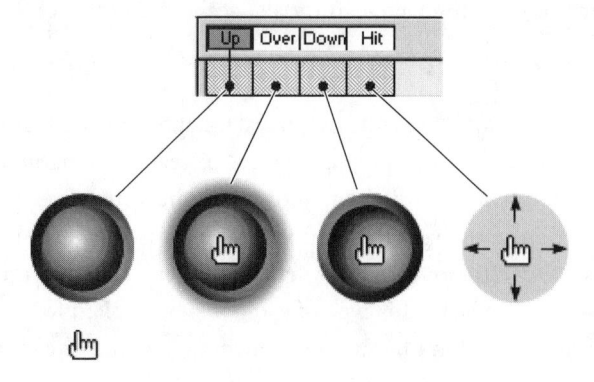

Figure 7.9
The button symbol frames (states).

- **Up.** This frame (or state) represents the button's appearance when the mouse cursor is *not* over it.

- **Over.** This frame represents the button's appearance when the cursor is over it.

- **Down.** This frame represents the button's appearance if the user clicks on it.

- **Hit.** This frame lets you define the area in which the button responds to a cursor's movement. A solid object—which can be a different size and shape than the button—usually goes here. The graphic shape on the Hit frame simply defines the "hot spot" for your button (that is, the area that will react to cursor movement); it will not be visible in the exported movie (though the cursor will still react to it).

A button symbol's timeline doesn't actually play. Instead, it simply reacts to cursor movement and actions by jumping to the appropriate frame based on the position and actions of the cursor.

Each state can have a unique appearance, though it's common to highlight buttons in their Over state and to make them smaller (or appear pressed) in their Down state—these graphic representations effectively mimic the way buttons typically work in the real world. To create dynamic-looking buttons, make full use of your drawing tools as well as the layers on the button's timeline. If you want a particular sound to play when your button is in a particular state, place the desired sound on a layer in that state (**Figure 7.10**). (See "Video Tutorials" at the end of this chapter.) You can also create animated buttons by placing instances of movie clip symbols into your button symbol's different states. However, you cannot place buttons inside buttons.

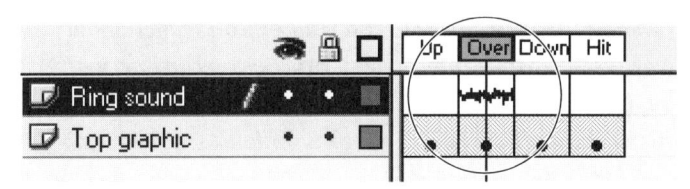

Figure 7.10
If you want a particular sound to play whenever a button is in a certain state—for example, when the cursor passes over it—place the sound at that state on the button's timeline.

To graphically define a button's states:

1. With the button's timeline visible, select the Over, Down, and Hit frames by clicking the Over frame, then dragging to the Hit frame and releasing.

The frames will appear selected.

2. Choose Modify > Frames > Convert to Keyframes.

This converts the selected frames to keyframes. Keyframes on the timeline are necessary for any type of animation since they define where changes (graphical or otherwise) occur in the animation. In the case of buttons, changes occur each time the state changes. There is no need to select the Up state when adding keyframes, since it is a keyframe already.

3. Click one of the state names on the timeline, and add content to the stage to define how the button will look when it's in that state.

4. When you've defined all four states, click the Scene button below the timeline or choose Edit > Edit Document.

This returns you to the main timeline.

> **TIPS** *If you leave the Hit state blank, the shape or element in the last defined keyframe will be used instead as the hit area for the button.*
>
> *For information about adding actions to buttons (so that the button will respond when clicked), see "Adding Actions to Buttons" under "Working with Instances" later in this chapter.*
>
> *To see how your button will look and react to cursor movement, once you've returned to the main timeline, from the Control menu choose Enable Simple Buttons. You can now use your cursor to test your button's functionality. You cannot, however, test a button's interactive features; you can only verify its visual response (Up, Down, Over, and Hit states) to cursor movement. After testing your button, turn off the Enable Buttons option so that you can select the button for further editing.*

> **MX ALERT** *Movie clip instances can now act as buttons as well. All you have to do is script them to react to mouse events such as* `on(press)`*,* `on(release)`*, and so on. There are pluses and minuses, however, in using movie clip instances as buttons. Since movie clip instances can be self-contained entities/timelines with sophisticated functionality, you can use them to create more advanced buttons. However, for simple buttons (that is, those that contain graphical Up, Over, and Down states), it's easier just to create button instances. For more information, see "Using Movie Clip Instances as Buttons" later in this chapter.*

Movie clip symbols

As mentioned earlier, a movie clip symbol is really just a small Flash movie—with all of the interactivity, sound, and functionality of your main movie. You can add any type of element to your movie clip's timeline, including buttons, sounds, and even other movie clips.

A movie clip's timeline runs independently of the main timeline, which means that the clip's timeline can continue to play after the main timeline has paused (**Figure 7.11**).

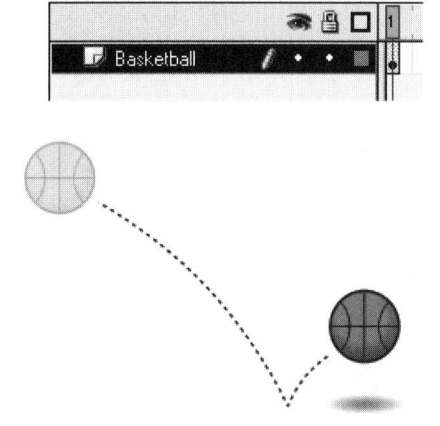

Figure 7.11
A movie clip can function independently of the main timeline, meaning its content will play even if it occupies a single frame on the main timeline. For example, this basketball is a movie clip animated to appear to bounce. It can continue to bounce although it exists in a single frame on the main timeline and that timeline is paused.

You create content for your movie clip in the same way you would create content for your main movie. In fact, you can convert any or all of the content on your main timeline into a movie clip—say, if you wanted to reuse an animation created on the main timeline in various places within your project. For more information on animation, see Chapter 10, "Using Animation to Build Movement."

To convert animation on the main timeline to a movie clip symbol, you must select the frames and layers on the main timeline that make up the section of animation you wish to use.

To create a movie clip symbol from an animation on the main timeline:

1. On the main timeline, click and drag from the first frame of the top layer to the last frame of the bottom layer to select the timeline frames you wish to use in a movie clip.

The frames will appear selected (**Figure 7.12**).

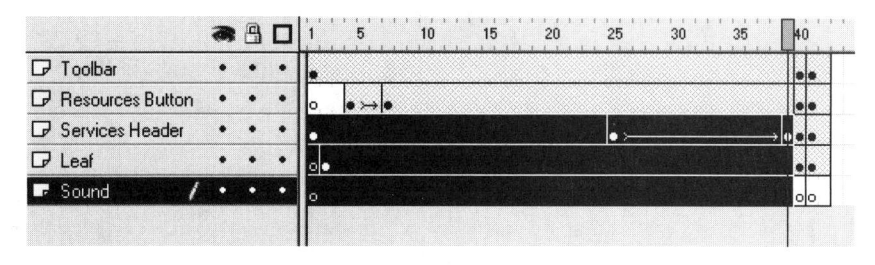

Figure 7.12
The layers and frames of an animation selected in preparation for copying.

2. Right-click (Windows) or Control-click (Macintosh) any one of the selected frames, and from the menu that appears choose Copy Frames.

   3. From the Insert menu, choose New Symbol.

   The Symbol Properties dialog box will appear.

   4. Give your new symbol a name and movie clip behavior.

   5. Click OK.

   Flash automatically converts to symbol-editing mode, where the stage is empty and the timeline has just one layer and one frame. This is your newly created symbol's timeline.

   6. On the timeline, right-click (Windows) or Control-click (Macintosh) Frame 1 on Layer 1, and from the contextual menu that appears choose Paste Frames.

   This pastes the frames that you copied earlier from the main timeline to the timeline of this movie clip symbol. Any animation, buttons, or interactivity included in the frames you copied are now part of an independent animation (a movie clip symbol) that you can reuse throughout your movie.

Duplicating Symbols

If you spend a long time creating a symbol, then decide you want to create a similar symbol with different features, duplicating it may be your answer.

Duplicating a symbol allows you to use an existing symbol as a starting point for designing a new symbol. Once duplicated, the new symbol is added to the library, and you can change it as you wish.

To duplicate a symbol:

   1. On the stage, right-click (Windows) or Control-click (Macintosh) an instance of the symbol you wish to duplicate.

   2. On the menu that appears, select the Duplicate Symbol command (**Figure 7.13**).

   The Symbol Name dialog box will appear.

   3. Give your new symbol a name, and click OK.

   You've now created a new symbol based on the existing symbol you specified. The duplicated symbol will appear in the library.

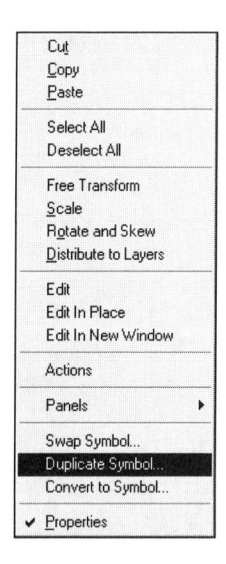

Figure 7.13
The Duplicate Symbol command can be accessed by right-clicking (Windows) or Control-clicking (Macintosh) an instance of the symbol you would like to duplicate.

TIPS When duplicating a symbol, the original instance you click in Step 1 above automatically becomes an instance of your duplicated symbol. Edits made to the duplicate will be reflected in that instance

{ *ActionScript* } Movie clips can be duplicated dynamically using the `duplicateMovieClip()` method. For more information, see Chapter 16, "Using ActionScript in your Projects."

Symbols from Other Movies

With Flash, there's no reason to reinvent the wheel: You can import symbols from previous Flash projects in your current movie. Once you bring the symbol into your current project, you can work with it just as you would any other symbol. There is no link between the symbols in the separate movie files; editing the symbol in one movie will not affect its appearance in the other. You can incorporate as many symbols from as many Flash projects as you wish.

To use a symbol from another movie:

1. From the File menu, choose Open as Library.

The Open as Library dialog box will appear.

2. Find the Flash authoring file (.fla) that contains the symbol you wish to use, and click Open.

A library window will appear that includes all of the symbols used in the Flash authoring file you just opened.

3. Drag the symbol you wish to use from the library onto the stage of your current movie.

The symbol will be automatically added (under its original name) to the library of your current project. An instance of it will also appear on your current project's stage.

4. Drag as many additional symbols as you wish from the open library onto the stage of your current project. When finished, close the library window.

> **MX ALERT** **TIPS** *If the symbol you wish to drag from a Flash library has the same name as a symbol in your current library, Flash will display an alert box asking if you wish to replace the existing symbol with the one you're bringing in.*
>
> *If your current project library is visible, you can move a symbol from another Flash library directly into it by simply dragging between windows (***Figure 7.14***). For more information about working with the library, see Chapter 17, "Using the Library to Manage your Assets."*

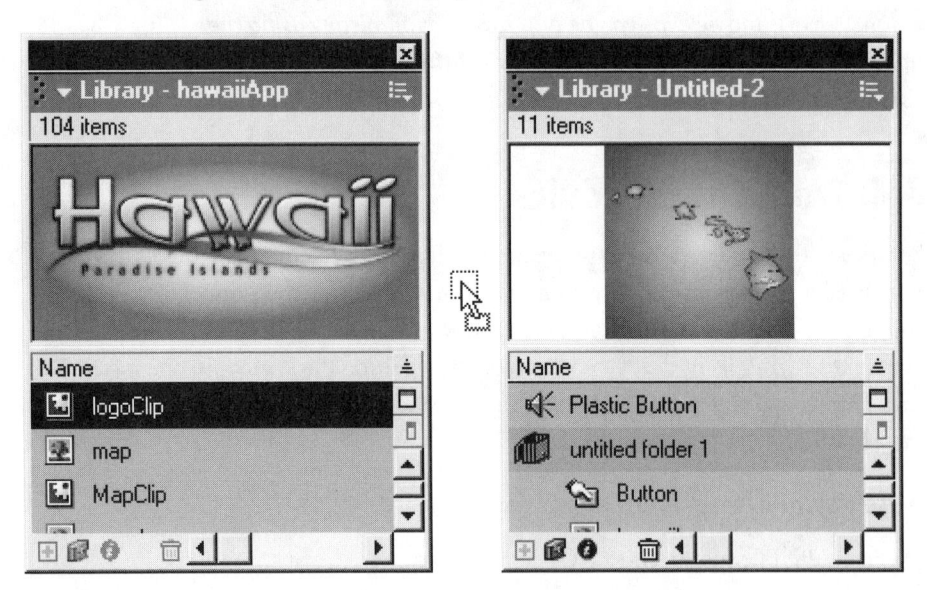

Figure 7.14
Flash lets you drag symbols from one library window directly into another.

Using Symbols in Shared Libraries

Once a symbol exists in your project library, you can turn it into a shared library asset, which means you can use it across multiple SWF files. The benefits of this are twofold: First, since the symbol is stored in a central location (the shared library), the user will only need to download it once (rather than each time it's used in a movie), which will minimize download time. Second, whenever you update the symbol in the shared library, any movie that's linked to it will automatically reflect the updated symbol.

For information about shared libraries, see Chapter 17, "Using the Library to Manage Your Assets."

Editing Symbols

Now that you've figured out how to create symbols, it's time to learn how to edit and work with them. Editing a symbol means altering its content and/or timeline. When you apply these edits, all instances of the symbol—regardless of where they exist in your movie—reflect your changes. Symbol instances *will*, however, retain instance-specific edits—such as their size, tint, and any interactivity they're set to perform.

Symbol-Editing Mode

To edit a symbol's content and timeline, you must open it in symbol-editing mode. This means that instead of working with and editing your entire movie, you're now making changes that will only affect the content and timeline of a particular symbol.

To open a symbol so that you can edit it in symbol-editing mode (Figure 7.15):

1. Click the Edit Symbol button below the timeline.

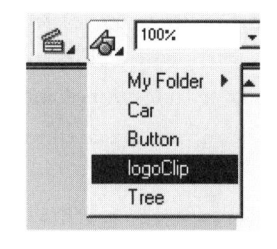

Figure 7.15
Two ways you can open a symbol from within symbol-editing mode.

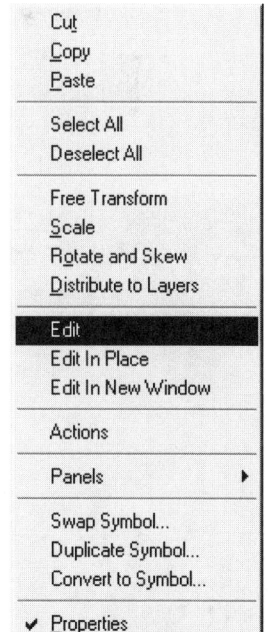

2. From the list of symbols that appears, choose the one you wish to edit.

Or

1. Right-click (Windows) or Control-click (Macintosh) a symbol instance.

2. Choose Edit from the menu that appears.

When you've finished editing your symbol, you can return to editing your entire movie by choosing Edit > Edit Document.

Edit in Place and Edit in New Window

There are a couple more ways to access a symbol in symbol-editing mode: One method is called Edit in Place; the other is Edit in New Window. Edit in Place allows you to edit a symbol in the context of the scene in which it resides. Edit in New Window allows you to enter a symbol's editing mode in a new window: Your movie's main timeline and stage will remain open, but a new window for editing the symbol's timeline and stage will appear on top of it.

To edit in place:

1. Double-click an instance of the symbol you'd like to edit.

   All of the elements on the stage (except for the symbol itself) will be lightened to indicate they cannot be edited (**Figure 7.16**). You can, however, edit the elements that make up the symbol and its timeline.

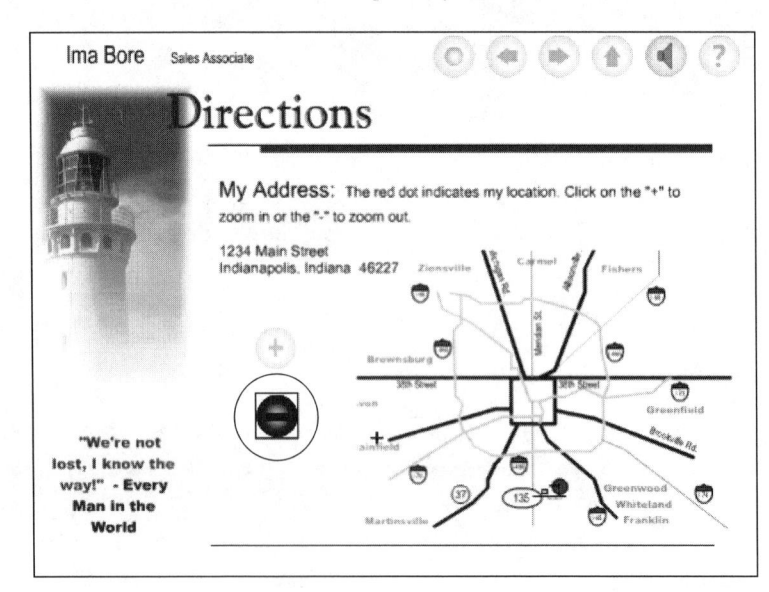

Figure 7.16 When you edit a symbol in place (such as the Zoom Out button shown here), you edit it in the context of the other content on the stage.

2. Edit the symbol's content or timeline, then double-click an empty area on the stage to return to the main timeline.

> **TIP** *If you've placed symbols within symbols, you can continue double-clicking on them as described in Step 1 to edit elements in deeper levels. Double-clicking an empty area on the stage always takes you back to the previous, or parent, level (in relation to the current element)—until eventually you're back to editing the main timeline. See "The Breadcrumb Navigation Bar" a little later in this chapter.*

To edit in a new window:

1. On the stage, right-click (Windows) or Control-click (Macintosh) an instance of the symbol you'd like to edit.

2. From the menu that appears, choose Edit in New Window.

A new window opens with the symbol in symbol-editing mode.

3. Edit the symbol's content or timeline, then click the Edit Scene button next to the Edit Symbol button.

> **TIP** *In the Flash authoring environment, you can see only the first frame of any on-stage symbol. This means that only the edits you make to Frame 1 of the symbol's timeline will be visible on the main movie's stage. To view the effect of your edits to other frames, from the Control menu choose Test Movie. This opens the Test Movie window, which allows you to preview your changes. For more information on this, see Chapter 19, "Testing."*

The Breadcrumb Navigator Bar

Since Flash allows you to place (and edit) elements within elements, it also provides a simple but handy visual indicator to help you navigate this hierarchy when you're editing. Known as the *breadcrumb navigator bar*, it's located just above the stage.

Here's how it works: If you're working on the main timeline, the breadcrumb navigator bar displays the name of the current scene. However, if you're editing an instance of a symbol that resides in Scene 1, the breadcrumb navigator bar displays the name of the scene followed by the name of the symbol (for example, Scene 1_|_MySymbol). As you edit elements within elements, this navigation trail continues to expand

(**Figure 7.17**). To return to any level of editing, you can click that level's name on the breadcrumb bar.

Figure 7.17
The breadcrumb navigator bar sits above the stage.

> **MX ALERT** *In addition to clicking names on the breadcrumb navigation trail, you can use the Back button: Pressing this button will take you to the parent timeline of the current timeline.*

Working with Instances

Symbol instances can be configured, transformed, and worked with independently of any other instance on the stage—even those based on the same master symbol. In this section, we'll look at how to maximize the effectiveness of these versatile elements.

Adding Instances to Your Movie

As mentioned earlier, you never use symbols directly in your movie; instead, you place instances of them, which you usually drag from the library to the stage.

To add a symbol instance to the stage:

1. From the Window menu choose Library.

   This opens the Library panel.

2. From the Library window, locate the symbol you wish to use.

3. Click the symbol's name and drag it onto the stage. An instance of the symbol will appear on the stage (**Figure 7.18**).

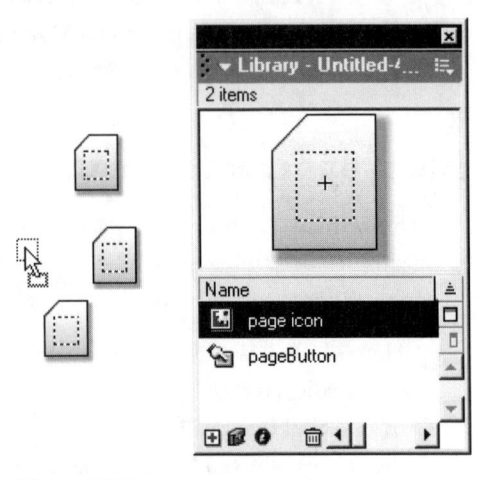

Figure 7.18
Add instances of a symbol to your movie by dragging them from the library.

TIPS *You can quickly create a number of instances of the same symbol: On the stage, simply select the instance you wish to duplicate, and press Control-D (Windows) or Command-D (Macintosh).*

{ **ActionScript** } *Instances of movie clip symbols can be dynamically added to your movie using the* `attachMovie()` *method. For more information, see Chapter 16, "Using ActionScript in your Projects."*

Changing an Instance's Tint and Transparency

By changing the tint and/or transparency of an instance, you can display a single symbol in many ways (**Figure 7.19**).

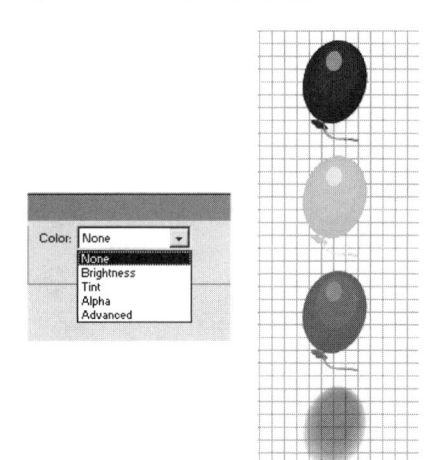

Figure 7.19
You can apply various tints and transparencies to different instances to avoid graphical redundancy.

To change an instance's tint or transparency:

1. Select an instance of a symbol on the stage.

2. On the Property inspector choose from the following options on the Color drop-down menu:

   - **None.** Causes the instance to appear as it did originally, without affecting its color or transparency.

   - **Brightness.** Allows you to adjust the overall brightness of the instance. A setting of 100 will turn the instance completely white; a setting of –100 will turn the instance completely black; and a setting of 0 represents its original brightness.

   - **Tint.** Allows you to apply a color tint of your choosing to the instance. The Tint amount lets you set the tint percentage.

- **Alpha.** Allows you to adjust an instance's transparency. A setting of 0 percent makes the instance completely transparent; a setting of 100 percent makes the instance completely opaque.

- **Advanced.** Allows you to simultaneously adjust an instance's tint and transparency. The controls on the left are for adjusting settings based on a percentage value, while the controls on the right are for adjusting settings based on a constant value.

Adjusting any of these parameters on the Property inspector updates the instance immediately.

TIPS *You can only edit color effects on symbol instances. To make these edits on other movie elements (such as text, groups, or imported bitmaps), you must first turn them into symbols, then drag an instance onto the stage for editing.*

You can create variously tinted and transparent bitmaps, by turning a bitmap into a symbol and then adjusting the colors and transparency of individual instances.

{ **ActionScript** } *Every movie clip instance has an alpha (_alpha) property that allows you to dynamically adjust the clip's transparency. An instance's color can also be changed dynamically, via ActionScript Color objects. For more information, see Chapter 14, "ActionScript Objects."*

Defining an Instance

When you create a symbol and define its behavior—making it, say, a button—any instance of that symbol that you place on the stage will initially share the original's behavior. However, Flash also allows you to define individual instances, either fine-tuning their current behavior or changing the behavior altogether (say, from a button to a movie clip). When you define an instance, it does not affect the master symbol or any other instances based on that master symbol.

To define an instance:

1. On the stage, select an instance of the symbol you wish to define.

The Property inspector reflects the current attributes and behavior (graphic, button, or movie clip) of the instance selected on the stage (**Figure 7.20**). To fine-tune this instance's behavior, adjust any of the available settings (described below). If you want to completely transform this instance's behavior, select a new behavior from the pop-up menu on the Property inspector.

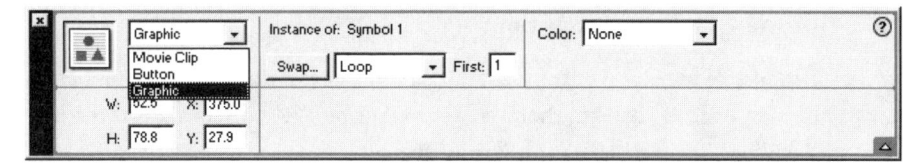

Figure 7.20
When an instance of a symbol is selected, the Property inspector shows how the current instance is defined. Here, the currently selected instance has a Graphic behavior and is set to loop on Frame 1 of its timeline.

- **Graphic behavior options:**

    Loop. Causes the instance to loop repeatedly. Because you're defining this instance as a graphic, its timeline will be linked directly to the main timeline—that is, the instance will loop as long as the main timeline is playing. When that timeline stops, so will the instance.

    Play Once. Causes the instance to play once and then stop.

    Single Frame. Allows you to display just a single frame of the graphic symbol.

    First Frame. Allows you to choose which frame on the instance's timeline will appear first.

- **Button behavior options:**

    MX ALERT ***Instance Name.*** You can make any button instance into what's known as a *target*. By doing so, you can tell it to do all kinds of things within Flash. To make a button instance a target, you select it and assign a name to it from inside the Instance Name box (for example, **myButton**). Then, using ActionScript, you can instruct the target to rotate, move, resize, and so on while the Flash movie is playing. We'll discuss this in greater detail in Chapter 14, "ActionScript Objects." For now, just be aware that once you assign names to button instances, they become interactive elements that you can control via ActionScript.

    Track as Button or Track as Menu Item. Under normal circumstances—and when the Track as Button option is selected—only one button at a time can react to cursor/mouse movement or actions. However, when Track as Menu Item is selected, multiple instances of buttons can react to the cursor—even when it's pressed down. Basically, this involves stacking buttons and assigning an action to each—used primarily for creating menu bars in Flash (see "Video Tutorials").

- **Movie Clip behavior option:**

  Instance Name. Like button instances, you can assign an instance name to movie clips in order to control them via ActionScript. We'll discuss this topic in greater detail in Chapter 14, "ActionScript Objects."

  TIP *Names for button and movie clip instances cannot contain spaces, and they must begin with a character (a-z or A-Z).*

Adding Actions to Buttons

Each button instance on the stage can be set up to perform a different action or set of actions. This means you can use the same button design for many purposes. Remember, though, not to place actions (instructing your button what to do) in the button timeline—a common mistake. Instead, you add them to individual button instances on the stage.

To add an action to a button instance:

1. On the stage, select any instance of a button symbol.

2. Open the Actions panel.

3. Click the Add an Action button (+) on the top-left corner of the Actions panel.

4. From the menu that appears, choose an action. For this exercise, choose Actions > Browser/Network > getURL.

5. Type the URL name in the URL box at the top-right section of the panel (**Figure 7.21**).

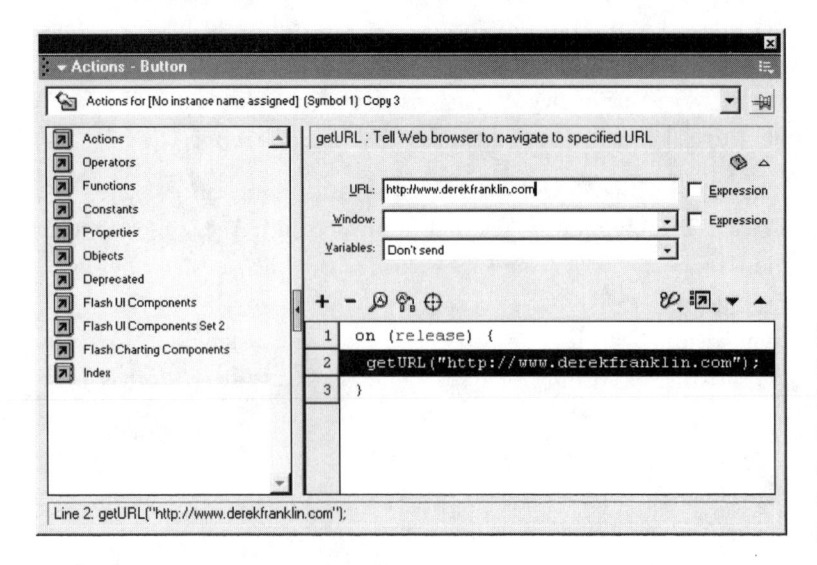

Figure 7.21
By selecting a button instance, then opening the Actions panel, you can add actions to your buttons.

6. Close the Action panel.

You have now assigned an action to your button. If you choose Control > Test Movie, you'll see that when the button is clicked, it opens a browser window and displays the URL you specified. For more information on adding an action to a button, see Chapter 12, "Getting Started with ActionScript."

> **MX ALERT** { **ActionScript** } *You can use ActionScript to enable or disable a button instance dynamically. In essence, this allows you to turn the button on and off while the movie is playing. In addition, you can choose whether the hand-cursor should appear when the mouse is over a button (a typical display option). When the hand cursor is turned off, the button remains active, but the arrow cursor appears instead. For more information on how to set this functionality, see Chapter 16, "Using ActionScript in Your Projects."*

Adding Actions to Movie Clips

By adding actions to movie clip instances you can make them perform actions (execute scripts)—when they appear in a scene, when they are removed from a scene, when the mouse is moved, and more. We'll explore this powerful capability in greater detail in Chapter 12, "Getting Started with ActionScript," and Chapter 13, "Understanding ActionScript."

To add an action to a movie clip instance:

1. On the stage, select any instance of a movie clip symbol.

2. Open the Actions panel.

3. Click the Add an Action button on the top-left corner of the Actions panel.

4. From the menu that appears, choose an action. For this exercise, choose Properties > _rotation.

The following will be automatically inserted into the code window:

```
onClipEvent (load) {
  _rotation;
}
```

This is the beginning of a script that will rotate the selected instance when it is first loaded (appears in the current scene.)

NOTE *Movie clip instances can be scripted to react to certain events (known as clip events) that occur in typical movies. These events include loading (as just described), unloading (when something disappears from the scene), mouse movements, key presses, and other actions. Any script contained in a movie clip must be triggered by a clip event. In the script we added in this step, the* `load` *event was automatically added to the script as the default event (that is, the one that's used when no other event is specifically defined). For more information, see Chapter 13, "Understanding ActionScript."*

5. In the Expression text box at the top-right section of the panel, enter `_rotation = 45`.

This action will rotate the movie clip clockwise by 45 degrees the first time it's loaded into the scene.

6. Close the Action panel.

If you choose Control > Test Movie, you'll see that when the movie clip first appears, it is rotated by 45 degrees. For more details on movie clip properties, see Chapter 14, "ActionScript Objects."

TIP *The discussion above pertains only to adding actions to an entire instance (**Figure 7.22**). However, a movie clip's timeline can also contain frame actions that are performed when the movie clip reaches a particular frame in its playback. For more information about adding frame actions to a timeline, see Chapter 12, "Getting Started with ActionScript."*

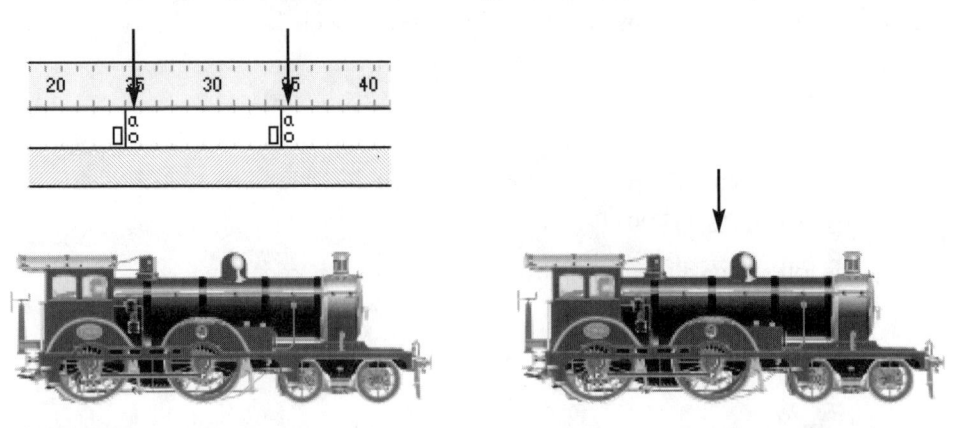

Figure 7.22
Actions can be placed on frames of a movie clip's timeline (left) so that they are triggered when the timeline reaches that frame. Or you can attach actions to the movie clip instance as a whole (right), so that they're triggered when different events occur in relation to the instance, such as it appearing or disappearing from a scene.

Using movie clip instances as buttons

MX ALERT

Flash MX now allows you to use movie clips as buttons—yes, *buttons*. This means you can set them up to react to mouse events such as on(press), on(release), on(rollOver), and so on. But why use movie clips as buttons when you already have button symbols? Because—as Flash's most versatile symbol type—movie clips can contain their own data, be created or duplicated dynamically, and perform all sorts of other actions that graphic or button symbols cannot. Thus, movie clips give you more choices in working with the interactive elements in your project.

For example, in Flash 5 (and earlier versions), you needed a button to control a movie clip instance's timeline via a mouse event (press, release, rollover, and so on). With Flash MX, you can script a movie clip to react *directly* to mouse events—enabling it to perform a dynamic task (such as load external data or become draggable) when pressed or rolled over. There are no other settings to change or adjustments to be made.

To set up a movie clip instance to react to a mouse event:

1. On the stage, select an instance of a movie clip symbol.

2. Open the Actions panel.

3. Click the Add an Action button on the top-left corner of the Actions panel.

4. From the menu that appears, choose an action. For this exercise, choose Actions > Movie Control > on.

   The following will be automatically inserted into the code window:

   ```
   on(release) {
   }
   ```

   This is the beginning of a script that will cause the selected movie clip instance to react to being pressed, then released.

5. Click the Add Action button again and choose Properties > _rotation.

6. In the Expression text box at the top of the panel, enter: _rotation = 45.

   This action will rotate the movie clip clockwise by 45 degrees.

7. Close the Actions panel.

   If you choose Control > Test Movie, you'll see that when the movie clip is pressed and released, it rotates by 45 degrees.

NOTE *You cannot script a movie clip instance to react to both clip events and mouse events; you must use either all clip events or all mouse events. To get around this limitation, you can use what are known as event handler methods. For more information about event handler methods, see Chapter 13, "Understanding ActionScript."*

One of the great things about buttons is that you can make their appearance change as a user interacts with them via the mouse. (You'll recall that you do this by editing the Up, Over, and Down frames on a button's timeline.) When using a movie clip instance as a button, you *may* (it's optional) define similar states on its timeline by using special frame labels (for more information about frame labels, see Chapter 10, "Animation"). This allows you to quickly add the functionality that allows buttons to appear differently depending on how the user is interacting with them. These special frame labels are _up, _over, and _down. When a movie clip instance has been scripted to react to mouse events, its timeline is automatically sent to one of these labels (and stopped), depending on how the user is interacting with the clip (for example, rolling over it with the mouse or pressing down on it) (**Figure 7.23**).

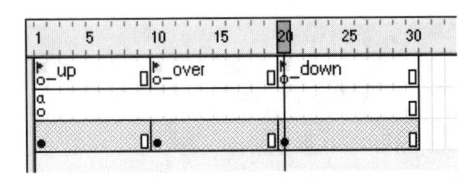

Figure 7.23
Special frame labels can be placed on a movie clip's timeline when it is set up to react to mouse events, so that the appropriate label is displayed following each user interaction with the movie clip/button.

NOTE *If you choose to use frame labels as described above, you'll still need to place a* `stop()` *action on Frame 1 of your movie clip button's timeline to prevent the timeline from playing through all the labels when it first loads.*

In case you're wondering, when a movie clip acts like a button, its hit state is defined by the size and shape of the content on the first frame of the clip, though you can change this via ActionScript (see following tip).

MX ALERT { *ActionScript* } *The hitArea of a movie clip button can be dynamically defined by setting its hitArea() property. This property lets you define the graphical content of another movie clip instance on the stage as the hit area for a movie clip button. For example,* `myButtonClip.hitArea = myHitAreaClip`*. A clip that is used as the hit area does not need to be seen (it may be on the stage, but invisible) in order for it to function as a hit-area clip.*

Swapping Symbols

Say you've carefully placed a symbol instance on the stage, and gotten all of its associated actions working perfectly, but then find yourself dissatisfied with the symbol's basic appearance. Flash lets you simply swap the master symbol on which that instance is based with a different master symbol, while preserving its other features. Say you have two master symbols in your project: a dog and a cat. You place an instance of the dog on the stage and spend a great deal of time setting it up—but then decide the cat would look better there instead. Rather than redoing all your hard work, you can simply replace the dog symbol with the cat symbol—and it will retain all of the edits, animations, and ActionScripts you earlier applied to the dog.

To swap the symbol on which an instance is based:

1. On the stage, select an instance of a symbol.

2. In the Property inspector click the Swap Symbols button.

The Swap Symbols dialog box that appears will contain a list of your project's symbols.

3. Select a symbol from the list, and click OK.

The instance you selected in Step 1 will immediately reflect the fact that it's now based on the symbol that you selected in Step 3. However, the instance will still retain any edits you made to it before swapping symbols (**Figure 7.24**).

Figure 7.24
Using the Swap Symbol button in the Property inspector lets you change the master symbol on which a particular instance is based.

Breaking Apart Instances

Breaking apart a symbol instance isn't much different from breaking apart text or bitmaps (as we discussed in earlier chapters). Since a symbol instance is a complete entity with its own timeline and stage, breaking it apart reduces the instance to its most basic graphic elements: text blocks, lines, shapes, and so on. When you break apart a symbol instance, only the content in its first frame is broken apart; all other frames are deleted.

To break apart an instance:

1. On the stage, select an instance of a symbol.

2. Choose Modify > Break Apart.

Accessibility Options

MX ALERT To make Flash content more accessible to those with visual disabilities, button and movie clip symbol instances in Flash MX can be set up so that if the user has a screen reader (such as the Windows-only Window Eyes), on mouse-over that reader will read back the information embedded in the symbol instance. To enable this, you select a symbol instance, then define what information will be displayed via the Accessibility panel.

To make a button or movie clip instance accessible:

1. On the stage, select a symbol instance.

2. Open the Accessibility panel by choosing Window > Accessibility, or by pressing the "Edit accessibility settings" button in the Property inspector.

This will open the Accessibility panel.

3. Check the Make Object Accessible option.

This will expose the object to a screen reader program, as well as enable you to adjust other settings on the panel. Only elements that are critical to the user should be made accessible—anything more is confusing.

4. If the selected instance is a movie clip, check the Make Child Objects Accessible option.

This option will make any movie clip instances inside the selected instance accessible. When choosing this option, don't enter any accessible information for the selected instance; instead, simply set up the individual child objects to be accessible.

5. In the Name field, enter a name to identify the object to the reader.

6. In the Description field, enter a short description of the selected object.

7. In the Shortcut field, enter a keyboard shortcut related to the selected instance.

In the case of buttons, this field is optional, because most buttons simply allow the user to press, roll over, or similarly interact with them via the mouse. However, if you choose to set a button instance to react to key presses (such as the user pressing the Enter key), you may want to indicate the key name (Enter, in our example) in this field (**Figure 7.25**).

Figure 7.25
One example of accessibility settings for a button instance.

Using clip events, movie clip instances can be scripted to react to a variety of key presses. If the selected instance is set up to do so, you would indicate the associated key-press combination (keyboard shortcut) in this field (otherwise, it's fine to leave it blank).

{ **ActionScript** } *For more information about mouse and clip events, see Chapter 13, "Understanding ActionScript."*

To make Flash MX's accessibility features work for symbols, you must set up your movie to be globally accessible, via a master setting that enables or disables accessibility features for the entire movie. For more information on this setting and accessibility options in general, see "Setting Up Your Movie" in Chapter 2. Also, be sure to visit Macromedia's Accessibility site: www.macromedia.com/macromedia/accessibility/features/flash/.

{ **ActionScript** } *You can use ActionScript to determine whether a user has a screen reader installed. For more information, see Chapter 16, "Using ActionScript in Your Projects."*

Video Tutorials

Creating a Movie Clip. This tutorial walks you through the process of creating a movie clip symbol, and using instances of it in your project. It also shows you how to assign instance names to each instance in your clip.

Creating a Button. This tutorial walks you through the process of creating a button symbol with Up, Over, and Down states. It also shows you how to assign actions to button instances.

Creating a Menu Bar. In this tutorial, we'll show you how to create a menu bar from a movie clip. You'll see how it "opens" and "closes," and also learn how to assign actions to buttons on the menu bar.

Working with Elements on the Stage

CHAPTER 8

What you'll learn...

How to select elements

Ways to work with groups

How to position elements on the stage

How to transform elements

All accomplished artists—be they painters, sculptors, or musicians—share one vital trait: an extraordinary command of their work environment and tools. Possessing these skills gives artists the confidence and fluency they need to produce works of greatness.

For Flash artists and developers, the stage and its elements represent the digital canvas. The stage is where you make the visual elements of your project come to life. Thus, if you want to become a proficient animator and interactive designer, you'll need to learn how to work with elements on the stage.

In this chapter we'll show you how to manipulate and transform the graphical elements on the stage that you've learned to import and create.

Selecting

Before you move, resize, rotate, or transform an element, you must *select* it. You'll most often use the Arrow tool for this function; however, you can also use the Lasso tool for a few special selection tasks. For now, though, we'll concentrate on the Arrow tool.

Selecting Individual Elements

Before trying any of the following tasks, click the Arrow tool on the toolbar or press *V* on the keyboard to activate the tool.

- To select a line, fill, or other element (for example, a group or symbol), click it once.
- To select a simple shape's line and fill simultaneously, double-click the fill.
- To select same-colored lines that touch each other, double-click one of the lines.

When you select an element, Flash provides onscreen cues to help you identify the element, its attributes, and its location on the timeline:

- Selected simple shapes such as lines and fills take on a textured look to indicate their state.
- Selected elements such as text, symbols, and groups, are surrounded by a bounding box—a thin outline of the same color as the layer on which the element resides (**Figure 8.1**).

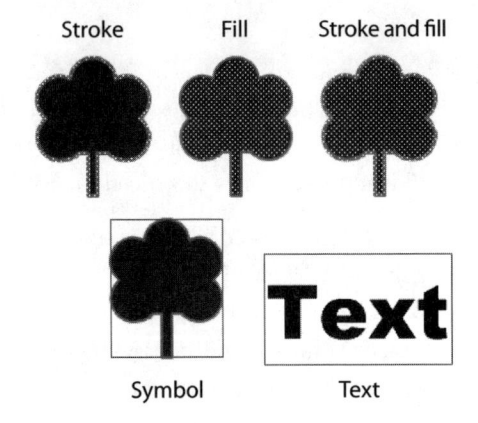

Figure 8.1
How different elements appear when they are selected.

TIP *If you want to hide the bounding box while you work with elements on the stage, choose View > Hide Edges. To make the bounding box visible, simply choose this command again.*

MX ALERT
- When you select a stroke and/or fill, its current attributes are displayed in the Property inspector. Any adjustments you make in the Property inspector will be reflected in the selected element.

- The Property inspector also displays information about the size and position of the currently selected element(s). Any adjustments you make in the Property inspector will be reflected in the selected element.

- If you select a group, symbol, or text element that you previously scaled, skewed, or rotated (which you'll learn to do shortly), the Transform panel (Window > Transform) will display the type and degree of these transformations.

- When you select a text element, the Property inspector will reflect its current attributes. Any adjustments made on the Property inspector will be reflected in the selected element.

- When you select an instance of a symbol, the Property inspector will reflect the current attributes of the instance, which you can then adjust. Any adjustments made in the Property inspector will be reflected in the selected element.

- The layer and frame span that the selected element is part of will be reflected on the timeline (**Figure 8.2**).

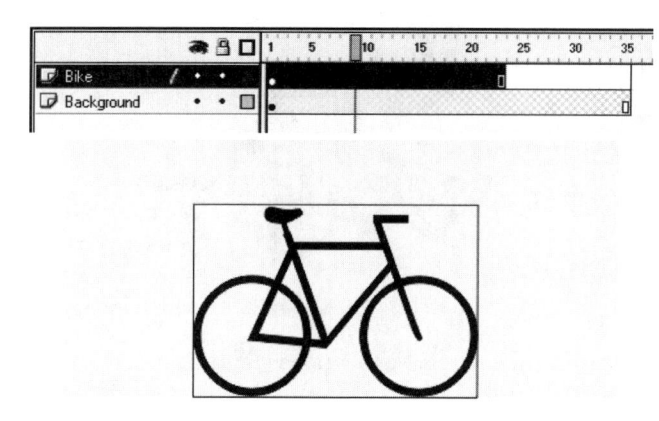

Figure 8.2
When you select an element on the stage, the layer and span of frames the element is part of are reflected on the stage.

Selecting Multiple Elements

By selecting multiple elements that you want to move, rotate, skew, or scale to the same degree, you don't have to waste time editing each one individually. There are several ways to do this:

Shift-selecting

Shift-selecting involves holding down the Shift key while clicking elements using the Arrow tool. With each click, the selected element is added to the overall selection. Using this method, you can select as many additional elements as you wish. To remove an element from the overall selection, Shift-click that element again.

TIP *If you prefer to add elements to a selection simply by clicking them (without pressing the Shift key as well), on the Edit menu choose Preferences, and then on the General tab uncheck the Shift select option.*

Marquee-selecting

Marquee-, or drag-, selecting allows you to select entire areas or parts of strokes and fills.

To marquee-select an area:

1. From the toolbar, select the Arrow key, or press the *V* key.

2. Click and drag in any direction on the stage. As you drag, you will see the outline of the selection box (**Figure 8.3**).

Figure 8.3
Marquee-selecting lets you select multiple elements on the stage simultaneously.

3. Once you've made your selection, release the mouse button.

You must completely enclose text, groups, and symbols with the selection box to select them. Strokes and fills, however, are a bit different: You select the portion of a stroke or fill that's inside the selection box, not what's outside. This allows you to select parts of a simple shape.

TIP *Once you've made a selection using this method, you can select additional areas by holding down the Shift key and marquee-selecting them in the same manner.*

Selecting All Elements

You can select every element on the stage that's not on a locked or hidden layer by choosing Edit > Select All. Using this command in conjunction with the Edit Multiple Frames command (see Chapter 10, "Animation") allows you to select and move, or otherwise edit, the entire content of an animated movie, not just a single frame.

Selecting with the Lasso Tool

Certain selection tasks can't be handled simply by clicking or by dragging a selection box. The Lasso tool enables you to select nonuniform areas of filled shapes, as well as colors in bitmaps. The Lasso basically functions as a specialized Arrow tool; its sole purpose is to select areas that you can't select using the Arrow tool. (You can only select areas consisting of simple shapes with the Lasso tool.)

To select an area with the Lasso tool's Magic Wand modifier:

1. From the toolbar, select the Lasso tool, or press the *L* key.

2. From the options that appear, select the Magic Wand tool.

Move the cursor to the stage area, where you'll notice it changes to a Lasso icon.

3. Click and drag inside or around a shape (or shapes) on the stage, and you'll see a basic representation of your selection area (**Figure 8.4**).

4. Release at the same point where you started to drag. The area you have outlined will be selected.

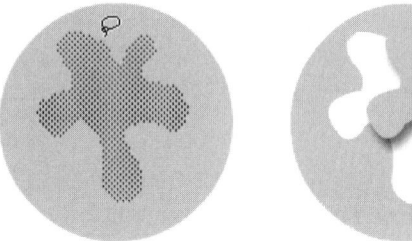

Figure 8.4
The Lasso tool lets you select irregularly shaped areas inside fills for editing.

To select a polygon-shaped area with the Lasso tool's Polygon modifier:

1. From the toolbar, select the Lasso tool, or press the *L* key.

2. From the options that appear, select the Polygon mode.

3. Click, release, and drag, and you'll see a basic representation of one side of your selection area. To add another side to your selection, click, release, and drag again. You can add as many sides as you wish by continuing to click, release, and drag.

4. Make sure you end up at the point where you started in Step 3. Double-click, and the area you have outlined will be selected.

TIP *For information on how to select colors in a bitmap using the Lasso tool, see Chapter 6, "Bitmaps."*

Selecting Using the Timeline

By clicking on a section of frames on the timeline that begins with a keyframe (that is, by clicking on a *keyframe sequence*), you automatically select everything on the stage that's part of that sequence. This is useful for quickly editing all of the elements in a particular sequence (**Figure 8.5**).

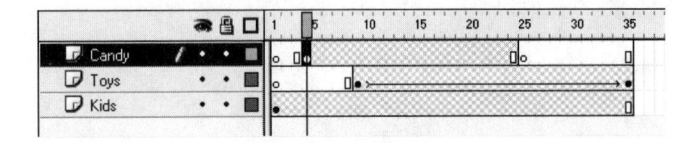

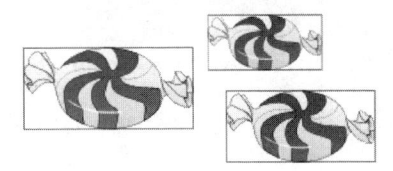

Figure 8.5
Selecting a keyframe sequence on the timeline selects any elements on the stage that are part of that sequence.

Deleting

Once they're selected, you can delete any elements or sections of shapes by pressing the Delete key, or by choosing Edit > Clear.

Deselecting

To *deselect* a selection, click an empty space on the stage, or choose Edit > Deselect All. To deselect an individual element, such as a part of a multiple selection, Shift-click on the element, or select something else.

Locking Elements

You may sometimes want to work with elements on the stage without having to worry about accidentally selecting the wrong one. You can eliminate this risk by simply locking elements on the stage. A locked element can't be selected, moved, or edited until you've unlocked it: You can, however, still see it onscreen. Flash lets you lock groups, text elements, bitmaps, and symbols—but not simple shapes.

To lock an element:

1. Select the element(s) you wish to lock.

2. Choose Modify > Arrange > Lock.

To unlock all locked elements:

◆ Choose Modify > Arrange > Unlock All.

TIPS *You can't unlock individual elements.*

Another way of keeping elements from being accidentally selected is to lock the layer on which they reside. For more information, see Chapter 9, "Using Layers to Separate Content and Functionality."

Groups

By creating groups, you can work on multiple elements as a single unit—for example, applying the same changes (such as moving or resizing) to several elements at once.

Each element in the group retains its individual properties as well as its relation to the other elements within the group. For example, if you move a group, all of its elements move as a unit, retaining their relative positions. Likewise, if you resize or rotate a group, all of its elements are resized or rotated by the same percentage or degree (**Figure 8.6**).

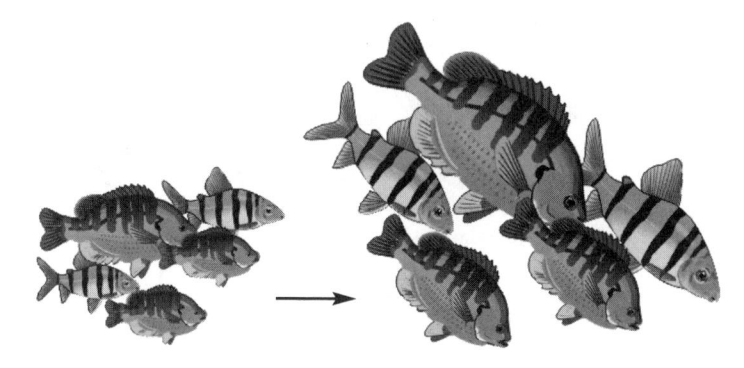

Figure 8.6
By creating groups, you can work with multiple elements as a single entity when resizing, rotating, or otherwise editing them.

To create a group:

1. Select the elements you wish to be part of your group (these can include anything on the stage).
2. Choose Modify > Group.

TIPS *Any time you want to transform a group back into its individual elements, select the group and choose Modify > Ungroup.*

You can only create groups out of elements that reside on the same layer of the timeline.

Editing Groups

Some drawing applications require that a group be ungrouped before individual elements within the group can be edited. Not so with Flash, which allows you to easily edit elements in a group in real time—without having to ungroup them first.

To edit a group:

1. Select the group and do one of the following:

    - Double-click the group.

    Or

    - Click the group, and from the Edit menu, choose Edit Selected.

2. Make your changes with the Flash drawing tools.

    Anything on the stage that is not part of the group will be dimmed to indicate you cannot edit it (**Figure 8.7**).

3. Once you're finished making edits, double-click an empty place on the stage, or from the Edit menu choose Edit All.

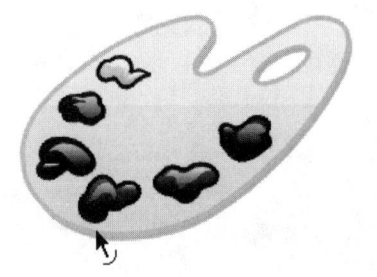

Figure 8.7
When you're editing a group, like the group of colors on this palette, other parts of the stage—in this case, the palette itself—dim to indicate that they're currently uneditable.

Positioning Elements on the Stage

Details, details! They're often tedious, but remember that just one out-of-place element can disrupt your movie's design. In fact, precise placement of a scene's elements within its frames is what good animation is all about—which is why Flash provides a number of powerful tools to help you in this task.

Moving

Consider yourself lucky any time you create a perfectly positioned element—it won't happen often! Fortunately, Flash lets you move elements around easily and with great precision.

To move a filled shape, group, text element, symbol, or bitmap, simply click and drag it to a new location. To move a line, select it, then click and drag it to a new location.

You can also select an element and press your keyboard's arrow keys to move it up, down, left, or right a pixel at a time. If you hold down the Shift key while pressing an arrow key, the element will move 8 pixels at a time (**Figure 8.8**).

If you need to place an element more precisely than these methods allow, you can use the Info panel instead.

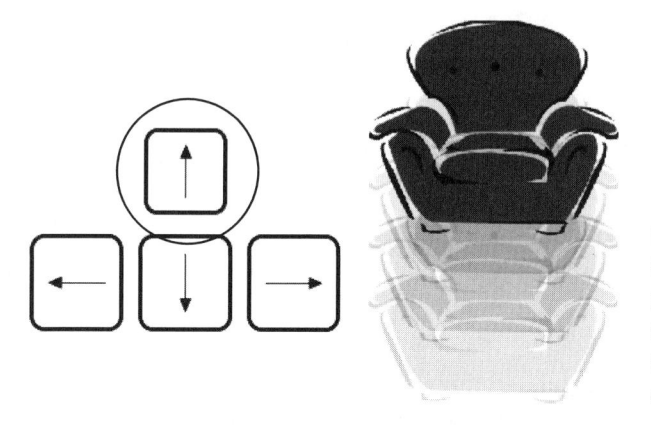

Figure 8.8
Using the arrow keys on your keyboard, you can quickly and precisely move selected elements on the stage.

To precisely place an element using the Info panel:

1. Select an element on the stage.

2. Choose Window > Info.

The Info panel will appear, offering four adjustable properties: *x, y, w,* and *h*. The *x* field sets how many pixels separate the element from the left side of the stage; *y* sets the pixel distance between the element and the top of the stage. The *w* and *h* settings define the element's *width* and *height*, respectively.

3. In the *x* and *y* fields, enter the values you want, then press Enter.

TIPS *Just to the left of the x-value and y-value boxes, you will see a graphic that includes nine small boxes—one of which is black and the rest of which are white. This is the Registration Selection tool, which lets you choose reference points for determining your x and y values: The single black box indicates the current registration point. For example, if you click the small box on the top left of this graphic, x and y values displayed or entered will reflect the distance from the left and top edges of the stage, respectively, to the left and top edges of the element's bounding box. If you click the center box in this graphic, x and y values will reflect the distance from the top and left sides of the stage to the **center** of the element (**Figure 8.9**).*

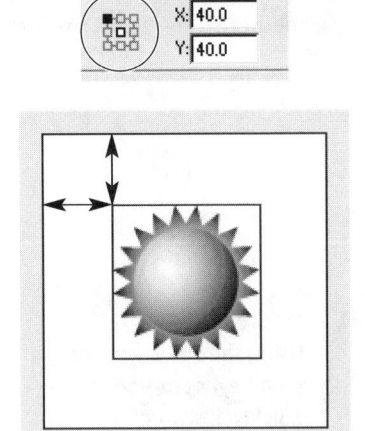

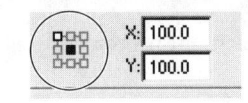

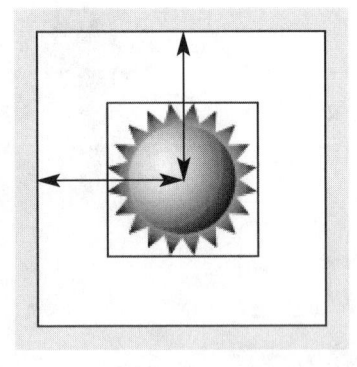

Figure 8.9
The Registration Selection tool lets you select how the *x* and *y* values used to position elements are measured on the Info panel.

You can also select multiple elements (see the "Selecting" section earlier in this chapter) and move them by setting the x and y values on the Info panel.

{ **ActionScript** } Button and movie clip instances have x and y properties whose values can be dynamically changed while a movie plays. For example, myMovieClip._x = 250 will move the movie clip instance named **myMovieClip** to an x position of 250 in relation to the left side of the stage. For more information see Chapter 14, "ActionScript Objects."

Alignment and Spacing

To be effective, most designs require perfectly aligned and spaced graphics—which would be tedious to achieve manually. Fortunately, using Flash's automated capabilities you can line up any number of elements in a perfectly straight row or column. You can also align elements to the left, right, top, bottom, or center of one another, as well as specify equal spacing between your elements.

Chapter 8 *Working with Elements on the Stage*

Flash also allows you to scale selected elements to match the size—horizontally, vertically, or both—of the largest selected element.

Alignment and spacing tasks are performed using the Align panel.

To open the Align panel:

- Choose Window > Align.

The Align panel (**Figure 8.10**) has four sets of buttons that address the following functions: Align, Distribute, Match Size, and Space. There's also a bonus button, labeled To Stage, which we'll discuss in a moment.

The Align panel button icons help you determine your alignment options. The boxes on the buttons represent elements on the stage, and the lines in the buttons represent the point at which the elements will be aligned, spaced, or distributed. Clicking a button will have an immediate effect on any currently selected elements.

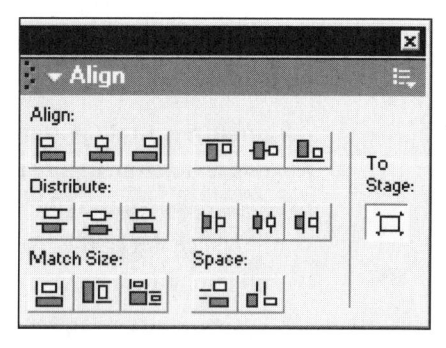

Figure 8.10
The Align panel.

You can choose one of two reference points to align or space elements: the bounding box of an overall selection, or the stage.

Bounding-box reference

Each selected element has either a visible bounding box (groups, text, symbols, bitmaps) or an invisible bounding box (lines and fills). This bounding box defines the total area (width and height) that an element occupies on the stage. When you select multiple elements for alignment purposes, the bounding box (which for multiple selections is invisible) expands to represent the total width and height of the overall selection (**Figure 8.11**). As long as the To Stage button on the Align panel is *not* pressed, this invisible bounding box serves as the reference for tasks performed on the Align panel.

When you use the bounding box as a reference, two or more elements on the stage must be selected for any buttons on the Align panel to have an effect.

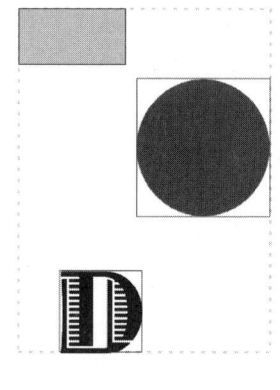

Figure 8.11
When you select multiple elements on the stage, the bounding box—which is not actually visible onscreen—defines the area of the overall selection.

The following describes the different effects you can achieve using the bounding box as a reference (**Figure 8.12**):

- **Align Left.** Aligns the left edges of selected elements to the left side of the overall bounding box.

- **Align Horizontal Center.** Aligns the horizontal center of selected elements to the horizontal center of the overall bounding box.

- **Align Right.** Aligns the right edges of selected elements to the right side of the overall bounding box.

- **Align Top.** Aligns the top edges of selected elements to the top side of the overall bounding box.

- **Align Vertical Center.** Aligns the vertical center of selected elements to the vertical center of the overall bounding box.

- **Align Bottom.** Aligns the bottom edges of selected elements to the bottom side of the overall bounding box.

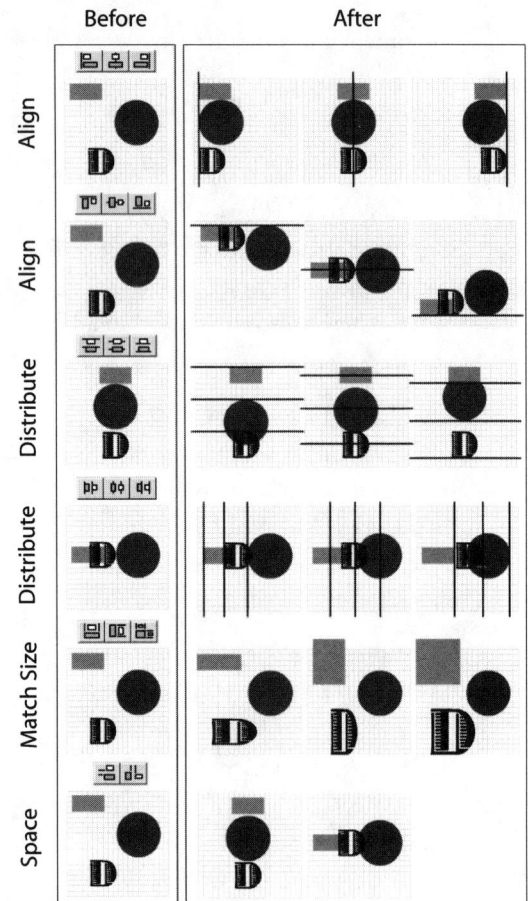

Figure 8.12
The results of using the various commands on the Align panel.

- **Distribute Top Edges.** Positions the top edges of selected elements so that they are equally spaced within the overall bounding box. Three or more elements need to be selected for this to have an effect. The positions of the top- and bottom-most elements selected do not change when this option is used.

- **Distribute Vertical Centers.** Positions the vertical centers of selected elements so that they are equally spaced within the overall bounding box. Three or more elements need to be selected for this to have an effect. The positions of the top- and bottom-most elements selected do not change when this option is used.

- **Distribute Bottom Edges.** Positions the bottom edges of selected elements so that they are equally spaced within the overall bounding box. Three or more elements need to be selected for this to have an effect. The positions of the top- and bottom-most elements selected do not change when this option is used.

- **Distribute Left Edges.** Positions the left edges of selected elements so that they are equally spaced within the overall bounding box. Three or more elements need to be selected for this to have an effect. The positions of the left- and right-most elements selected do not change when this option is used.

- **Distribute Horizontal Centers.** Positions the horizontal centers of selected elements so that they are equally spaced within the overall bounding box. Three or more elements need to be selected for this to have an effect. The positions of the top- and bottom-most elements selected do not change when this option is used.

- **Distribute Right Edges.** Positions the right edges of selected elements so they are equally spaced within the overall bounding box. Three or more elements need to be selected for this to have an effect. The positions of the right- and left-most elements selected do not change when this option is used.

- **Match Size Width.** Makes all of the selected elements the same width as the widest selected element.

- **Match Size Height.** Makes all of the selected elements the same height as the tallest selected element.

- **Space Vertically.** Positions selected elements so that the spaces between their bottom and top edges are equal within the overall bounding box. Three or more elements need to be selected for this to have an effect. The positions of the top- and bottom-most elements selected do not change when this option is used.

- **Space Horizontally.** Positions selected elements so that the spaces between their right and left edges are all equal within the overall bounding box. Three or more elements need to be selected for this to have an effect. The positions of the left- and right-most elements selected do not change when this option is used.

Stage reference

When you press the To Stage button on the Align panel, the top, right, bottom, and left boundaries of the stage (as opposed to the overall bounding box of selected elements) will be used as the reference points for tasks performed on the Align panel. There are a couple of things to be aware of when using the stage as your reference:

- You can align a single element to the stage by selecting it and pressing one of the alignment options.

- Choosing a Match Size option makes the selected element as wide or as tall as the stage.

TIP *To make alignment tasks easier, you can enable snapping, rulers, and the grid (all of which we'll discuss in a moment). By enabling any of these, you can align elements in real time, as you drag them around on the stage.*

Rulers

Rulers provide a visual cue to the placement of elements on the stage. When you move, scale, or rotate an element on the stage, lines indicating the current width and height of the element appear on the top and left rulers, respectively. You can customize the unit of measurement used by the rulers (say from pixels to inches) to suit the requirements of your project.

To set ruler units:

1. From the Modify menu, choose Document to make the Document Properties box appear.

2. From the Ruler Units pop-up box, select the measurement unit you wish to use, and click OK.

   If the rulers are visible, they will reflect your new selection (**Figure 8.13**).

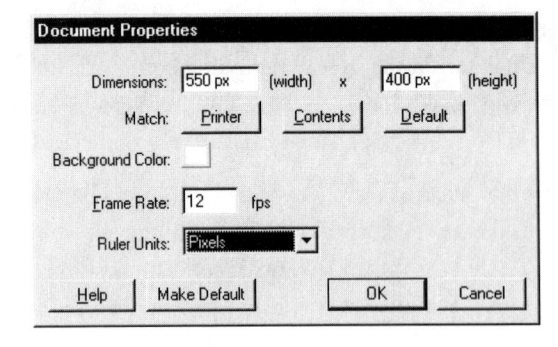

Figure 8.13
Use the Document Properties dialog box to set ruler units.

TIP *Whatever measurement unit you choose becomes the default unit used by Flash in any dialog boxes that include size values.*

To view or hide rulers:

- From the View menu, choose Rulers.

   NOTE *This command toggles between showing and hiding the rulers.*

Grid

Applying a grid in Flash places a set of intersecting horizontal and vertical lines over the stage and work area. The grid overlay can make it easier to align, scale, and place elements precisely (**Figure 8.14**). This grid will not be exported in your final movie; it's only visible in the Flash authoring environment.

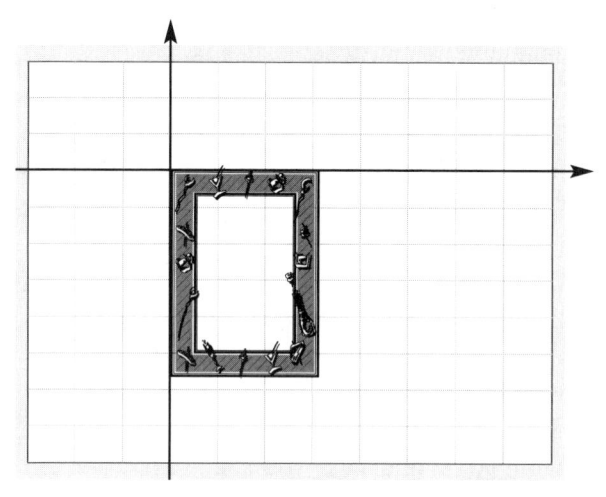

Figure 8.14
The grid makes it easy to align elements on the stage by hand, because elements are automatically snapped into position (to grid lines and intersecting points on the grid) as they're dragged.

There are several options you can set to specify how the grid display looks and works.

To set up and view the grid:

1. From the View menu, choose Grid > Edit Grid.

The Grid dialog box will appear, offering different display options:

- **Color.** Lets you choose the color of the grid display by clicking the color box, which brings up a color palette.

- **Show Grid.** Lets you choose whether you want the grid overlay to show onscreen.

- **Snap to Grid.** Lets you choose whether you want elements to "snap" to the grid (see "Snapping" later in this section).

- **Horizontal spacing.** Sets the amount of space between horizontal lines in the grid.

- **Vertical spacing.** Sets the amount of space between vertical lines in the grid.

- **Snap accuracy.** Lets you choose how close the mouse needs to be to a point on the grid before it snaps elements to the grid.

2. When you have adjusted the settings to your satisfaction, click OK. Your grid adjustments will now be reflected onscreen if the grid is visible.

TIP *You can access a couple of these options directly from the menu bar (that is, without having to open the Grid dialog box) by choosing View > Grid, then the option*

Guides

Guides are special lines that you can display horizontally or vertically across the length of the stage to help you align elements. As with the grid display, guides are only visible within the authoring environment.

To create a guide:

1. With rulers visible and the Arrow tool selected, click either the horizontal or vertical ruler, and drag toward the stage.

   As you drag the ruler, a guide will appear and move in conjunction with the mouse.

2. When the guide is positioned correctly, release the mouse.

TIP *Turning on the Snap to Grid option allows you to place guides accurately in relation to grid points.*

To move a guide:

1. With the Arrow tool selected, place the cursor over a guide. The cursor icon will change to a small black arrow to indicate that the guide can be moved.

2. Click and drag the guide to a new position (**Figure 8.15**). To delete the guide, drag it off the stage.

There are several options you can set to specify how your guides look and work.

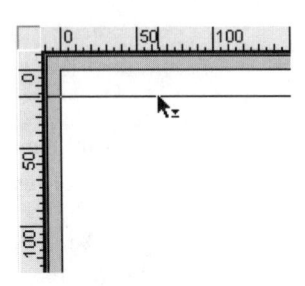

Figure 8.15
To move a guide, click and drag it to the desired position.

To set guide options:

1. From the View menu, choose Guides > Edit Guides.

   The Guide dialog box will appear, offering the following options:

   - **Color.** Lets you choose the color of your guides; click the color box to bring up a color palette.

- **Show Guides.** Lets you choose whether you want the guides to appear.
- **Snap to Guides.** Lets you choose whether you want elements to snap to guides (see "Snapping," later in this section).
- **Lock Guides.** Prevents guides from being selected and moved so that you don't accidentally drag a guide that's already perfectly positioned.
- **Snap Accuracy.** Lets you choose how close the mouse needs to be to a guide before it snaps elements to the guide.

2. When you've adjusted your settings, click OK. Your guide adjustments will now be reflected onscreen (if you've opted to make them visible).

TIP *You can access a couple of these options directly from the menu bar (that is, you don't have to open the Guide dialog box) by choosing View > Grid, and then the option.*

Snapping

When you enable Flash's snapping function, any element that you drag with the mouse to move, create, or scale will "snap" to align itself to specific points on the stage or to other elements, allowing you to quickly align or resize elements.

You can enable snapping in several ways: On the Standard toolbar (Windows) you can click the button with the magnet icon; you can choose the Arrow tool's Snap option; or from the View menu you can choose Snap to Objects.

Snapping points include the following (**Figure 8.16**):

- Lines and intersecting points on the grid (the grid must be showing onscreen)
- Guides
- Edges and corners of filled lines and filled shapes
- The edges and end points of lines
- The center of straight lines and edges
- An invisible line that follows the horizontal and vertical center of a group, text element, symbol, or bitmap

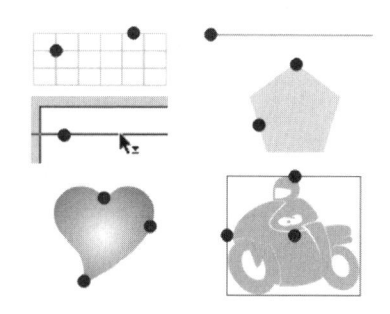

Figure 8.16
Some of the snapping points on various elements.

- The center and corner points of a group, text element, symbol, or bitmap's bounding box
- 90-degree angles
- Pixels (see next page)

When you turn on snapping, you will notice a small ring underneath the cursor when you drag to create, edit, or scale an element. When you reach a point where snapping can occur, the ring grows larger.

To snap a point on one element to a snapping point:

1. With the Arrow tool, click an element at any point where you know it can snap (as detailed above).

   For example, click the center of a group or the end of a line.

2. Drag the element onto the stage.

   The small circle underneath the cursor will get bigger as you drag it over another snapping point on the stage.

3. When your cursor is over the snapping point you wish to use, release the mouse.

To snap to a point when scaling an element:

1. With the Free Transform tool, select an element on the stage.

   The scale handles will appear around the element.

2. Click and drag one of the handles to scale your element.

   The small ring underneath the cursor will get bigger as you drag it over any snapping point on the stage (**Figure 8.17**).

3. When your cursor is over the snapping point you wish to use, release the mouse.

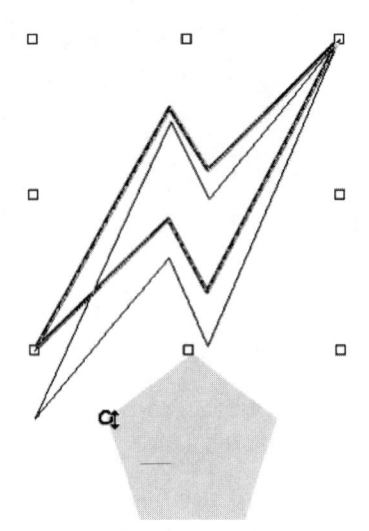

Figure 8.17
When you're scaling an element, a ring appears under the cursor when it is over a snapping point.

Snapping to pixels

MX ALERT To facilitate the most accurate snapping, Flash allows you to designate the smallest point possible: individual pixels. When you snap to pixels, elements will be moved or resized in whole pixel amounts.

To enable snapping to pixels:

1. Set the view scale to at least 400 percent to enable the Snap to Pixel function.

2. From the View menu, choose Snap to Pixels.

A grid will appear on the stage indicating individual pixel points. Elements can now be moved or resized (snapped) to these points.

TIP *The following keyboard shortcuts may come in handy when working with the Snap to Pixels feature.*

X key: Temporarily turns off pixel snapping (if it has been turned on in the menu), or temporarily turns on pixel snapping (if it has been turned off in the menu). In either case, pixel snapping will return to the state indicated in the menu when you stop pressing the key.

C key: Temporarily toggles the state of pixel snapping without changing the state of the pixel grid. Thus, if the pixel grid is not currently visible (indicating that pixel snapping is disabled), pressing the C key will temporarily enable pixel snapping without making the pixel grid visible. Conversely, if the grid is currently visible (indicating that pixel snapping is enabled), pressing the C key will temporarily disable pixel snapping without hiding the pixel grid. The effect lasts only as long as the key is pressed down.

Transforming Elements

Your Flash movie wouldn't be very appealing if all of its elements were the same size, or were all placed perpendicular to the stage. Transforming elements by scaling, rotating, skewing, and flipping them can add variety to your design. Such transformations are a key ingredient in many of the animated effects you can create with Flash (see Chapter 10, "Animation").

Scaling

When you resize or scale elements, you make them proportionately or disproportionately bigger or smaller by adjusting their width or height. Scaling changes an element's dimensions without changing its basic graphical structure.

Just as with moving, you can resize or scale an element freehand (basically by eyeballing it), or you can resize a shape with more precision by using the Info or Transform panel.

MX ALERT

To freely resize or scale an element:

1. Select the element on the stage.

2. From the Drawing toolbar, select the Free Transform tool.

   Eight small boxes—known as *scaling handles*—will surround the element.

3. Place your cursor over one of these handles (it will change into a two-headed arrow), and then click and drag.

   Dragging a corner handle scales the element's width and height proportionately; dragging a side handle adjusts only the element's width or height (depending on which side handle you choose); Command or Control-dragging a corner handle skews that corner (**Figure 8.18**).

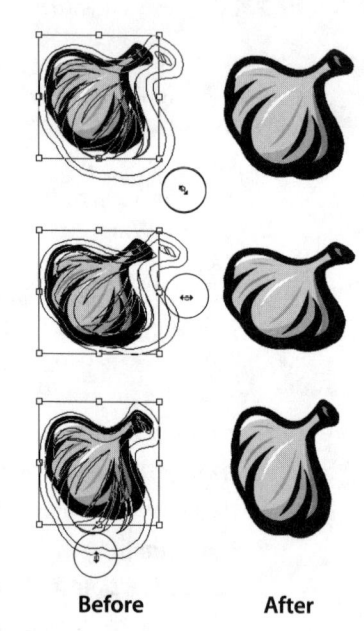

Before　　　After

Figure 8.18
Different ways a shape can be scaled using the scale handles.

To precisely scale or resize an element using the Info panel:

1. Select an element on the stage.

2. Choose Window > Info.

   The Info panel will appear on the stage with four adjustable properties: *x, y, w,* and *h*. We discussed the *x* and *y* properties in the section on moving elements. The *w* field sets the width of the element; the *h* field sets its height.

3. Enter your new values in the *w* and *h* fields, and then press Enter.

   Depending on which option you selected with the Registration Selection tool, the element will be scaled from its center or from its top-left corner (**Figure 8.19**).

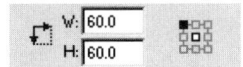

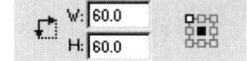

Figure 8.19
The Registration Selection setting determines the point from which elements are scaled.

To precisely scale or resize an element using the Transform panel:

1. Select an element on the stage.

2. Choose Window > Transform.

   The Transform panel will appear on the stage; at the top of the panel you'll see two boxes for entering percentage values (width and height), and the Constrain setting. If you enter a percentage greater than 100 in either box, the element's height or width will increase; if you enter a percentage less than 100, the element's height or width will decrease. Check the Constrain option if you want the amount entered in either percentage field to match the other, thus scaling your element proportionately. Conversely, leaving this option unchecked lets you enter separate percentage values in each box.

3. Enter your new values, and then click Enter.

   TIPS *Flash offers another way to transform an element using a percentage value: Select the element, then choose Modify > Transform > Scale and Rotate. A dialog box will appear. Enter a number in the Scale field, then click OK.*

   By selecting multiple elements, you can resize and scale them simultaneously.

   { **ActionScript** } *Button and movie clip instances have xscale and yscale properties that can be set dynamically so that objects are scaled as a movie plays. For example,* `myMovieClip._xscale = 75` *will horizontally scale the movie clip instance named* **myMovieClip** *to 75 percent of its original size. For more information, see Chapter 14, "ActionScript Objects."*

Rotating and Skewing

MX ALERT Rotating, as you may have guessed, allows you to spin an element based on a center point. Skewing, on the other hand, allows you to distort, or bend, an element at a vertical or horizontal angle.

By default, the point that defines each element's center of rotation is the actual center of the element—what's known as the *registration point*. With elements such as groups and symbols, you can move this center point anywhere on the stage (**Figure 8.20**).

To change an element's registration point:

1. On the stage, select a group, text element, symbol, or bitmap.

2. From the Drawing toolbar, select the Free Transform tool.

   A small circle will appear in the middle of the element. This represents the element's registration point.

3. Click and drag the registration point anywhere on the stage, and then release.

   Whenever this element is rotated, the center of rotation will be wherever you placed it.

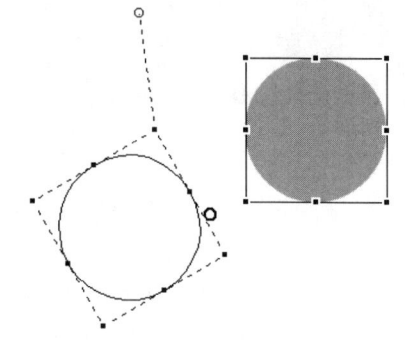

Figure 8.20
By moving an element's registration point, you change the axis around which it is rotated.

> **TIPS** *Although Flash doesn't let you change a simple shape's registration point, there is a way to rotate a shape around a point other than its true center: Simply turn it into a group, move its registration point, rotate it, and then ungroup it. You've just cheated the system—doesn't it feel great?*
>
> *With snapping turned on, you can easily move the registration point on top of a snap point, allowing you to precisely rotate elements in relation to other elements on the stage.*

To freely rotate or skew an element:

1. Select the element on the stage.

2. From the Drawing toolbar, select the Free Transform tool.

   Eight small boxes will surround the element.

3. Rotate or skew the element in one of the following ways:

- Place your cursor close to one of the corner squares (where it will change into a circling arrow), and then click and drag. By clicking and dragging one of the corner circles, or handles, you can rotate the element clockwise or counterclockwise around its registration point.

Or

- Place your cursor close to the element's bounding box (where it will change to a double-sided arrow, and then click and drag. You can skew the element vertically or horizontally, depending on which side handles you move: top and bottom, or left and right (**Figure 8.21**).

Figure 8.21
When you're rotating and skewing elements, the cursor image will change to indicate when you can perform the transformation.

TIP *By holding down the Shift key while rotating, you can make the rotation proceed in 45-degree increments.*

To precisely rotate and skew an element using the Transform panel:

1. Select an element on the stage.

2. Choose Window > Transform.

The Transform panel will appear, offering two choices:

- **Rotation.** By entering a positive rotation angle (0 to 360), you rotate the element clockwise by that amount. By entering a negative rotation angle (–1 to –360), you rotate the element counterclockwise by that amount.

- **Skew.** When you choose the Skew option, you will see two fields where you can enter a horizontal skewing angle and a vertical skewing angle.

3. Enter your values, and then press Enter.

To quickly rotate an element at a 90-degree angle:

1. Select an element on the stage.

2. Choose Modify > Transform > Rotate 90 CW or Rotate 90 CCW.

Rotate Left rotates the selected element 90 degrees clockwise; Rotate Right rotates it 90 degrees counterclockwise. You can choose this option multiple times to quickly rotate the element 180 or 270 degrees.

TIPS *You can also rotate an element in Flash by entering a rotation angle. Select the element, and then choose Modify > Transform > Scale and Rotate. In the dialog box that appears, enter a rotation angle in the Rotate field, and then click OK.*

By selecting multiple elements, you can rotate and skew them simultaneously using the steps outlined above. The registration point of the overall selection will be the center of rotation; and cannot be changed.

{ *ActionScript* } *Button and movie clip instances have a rotation property that can be set dynamically, allowing them to be rotated as a movie plays. For example,* `myMovieClip._rotation = 45` *will rotate the movie clip instance named* **myMovieClip** *by 45 degrees. For more information, see Chapter 14, "ActionScript Objects."*

Flipping

Flipping an element creates a reflection effect, similar to holding the element up to a mirror. Flash allows you to easily flip elements both horizontally and vertically.

To flip an element:

1. Select the element on the stage.

2. Choose Modify > Transform > Flip Vertically or Flip Horizontally (**Figure 8.22**).

Figure 8.22 An element can be flipped vertically or horizontally.

TIPS *The way an element is flipped is based largely on its registration point. By moving the registration point, you can change the point around which you flip it.*

{ **ActionScript** } *You can flip a button or movie clip instance dynamically by setting its xscale or yscale values to negative numbers. For example,* myMovieClip._xscale = -100 *will horizontally flip the movie clip instance named* **myMovieClip**. *For more information, see Chapter 14, "ActionScript Objects."*

Removing Transformations

Everybody knows about 20/20 hindsight. If we could just rewrite history, life would be so much better. Well, if you've ever resized, skewed, and rotated an element endlessly, only to find that it's *still* not right, you'll be pleased to learn that Flash lets you return a group or symbol to its original size and shape. Which means you can start again—*from scratch*. Keep in mind, however, that you can only remove transformations from groups, text elements, symbols, and bitmaps—not simple shapes.

To remove transformations from an element:

1. Select the group, text element, symbol, or bitmap on the stage.

2. Choose Modify > Transform > Remove Transform.

The element will revert to its original state (**Figure 8.23**).

TIP *You can accomplish the same effect from the Transform panel, by selecting the element and then clicking the Reset button.*

Figure 8.23
Removing transformations from an element restores its original form (right).

Duplicating Elements

Because of Flash's built-in copy machine, there's never a need to create a graphic more than once. Take, for example, columns on a building or stars in the sky: Since they all look pretty much the same, you can draw just one and then make duplicates, then alter the position, rotation, or size of the duplicates as your project may require. Same thing with symbols: Once you've placed a symbol instance on the stage, you don't need to continue dragging instances from the Library window. You can create as many duplicates of an element as you wish; you can even make duplicates of duplicates.

To duplicate elements:

1. Select the element(s) on the stage that you wish to duplicate.

2. Choose Edit > Duplicate, or press Control-D (Windows) or Command-D (Macintosh).

A duplicate of your element will appear on stage, offset slightly from the original.

> **TIPS** *A quicker way to duplicate an element is to hold down the Control key (Windows) or Option key (Macintosh), then place your cursor over the element, and click and drag a duplicate to any point on the stage.*
>
> *{ **ActionScript** } Movie clips can be duplicated dynamically using the* `duplicateMovieClip()` *method. For more information, see Chapter 16, "Using ActionScript in Your Projects."*

Cutting, Copying, Deleting, and Pasting

If you've ever cut, copied, and pasted information using another program, you'll find that Flash works pretty much the same way.

You can employ these functions to do any of the following:

- Move elements on the stage to a different frame, layer, scene, or movie

- Place a copy of an element in a different frame, layer, scene, or movie
- Delete an element
- Import text or graphics from other programs

Cutting, copying, and deleting are pretty straightforward. Pasting, on the other hand, can produce different results, depending on what you're pasting and where you're pasting it. The following should give you an idea of what to expect:

- Anything you cut or copy from Flash will remain the same type of element when you paste it back into Flash—regardless of where you're pasting it.

- Text that you copy from an application such as a word processing program will be pasted in Flash as editable text if you place it within an existing text block. Otherwise, it will be pasted as a group, and you will need to ungroup it before you can edit it.

- Vector graphics copied from other vector-based drawing programs (such as Macromedia FreeHand or Adobe Illustrator) are pasted as groups. If you ungroup the graphics, you can edit them just as you would any other shape in Flash. You may need to ungroup imported vectors several times to turn them into editable shapes.

- Bitmaps copied from another program cannot be pasted directly into Flash. They must be imported (see Chapter 6, "Bitmaps").

To cut or copy an element in Flash:

1. Select the element.

2. From the Edit menu, choose Cut or Copy.

To delete an element:

1. Select the element.

2. From the Edit menu, choose Clear or press the Delete key on the keyboard.

To paste an element, do one of the following:

- From the Edit menu, choose Paste to paste the element in the center of the stage of the current scene.

  Or

- From the Edit menu, choose Paste in Place to paste the element in the same relative position from the top-left corner of the stage as you cut or copied it from (**Figure 8.24**).

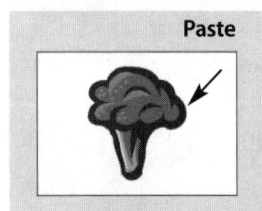

Figure 8.24
When you cut or copy an element on the stage, pasting it will place it in the center of the stage, whereas pasting in place will place it in the same relative position that you cut or copied it from.

Video Tutorial

Working with Elements on the Stage. This tutorial guides you through most of the concepts we've discussed in this chapter, including selecting elements, working with groups, and placing and transforming movie elements.

3

Movie Production, Visual

> **Using Layers to Separate Content and Functionality** 285
> **Using Animation to Build Movement** 313
> **Video** 363

SCENES, FRAMES, ANIMATION, VIDEO, and other time-based features are what make a Flash movie a movie. In this section you'll learn how to create animation using frames, keyframes, tweening, and shape hints, as well as how to use layers and scenes to organize the visual aspects of your movie. We'll also show you how to import video clips; place them on the timeline; play, pause, and rewind them; and use them creatively within your Flash projects.

Using Layers to Separate Content and Functionality

CHAPTER 9

What you'll learn...

Uses for layers

How to work with layers

How to identify graphical elements on different layers

How to use guide layers

About special-purpose layers

How to work with layer folders

How to configure layers

If you've ever seen how a movie is produced, you know that many people have a hand in the finished product: actors, writers, musicians, camera operators, Foley artists (the people who create sound effects), special-effects teams—the list goes on and on. In the end, the director and editor must transform the disparate elements created by all these people into a coherent whole—a task made easier by the fact that each element in the final production (music, sound effects, computer-generated graphics, live action, and so on) can be manipulated separately.

Flash movies are assembled in similar fashion. As a Flash artist, you import sounds and bitmaps, create and animate graphics, and place ActionScripts on layers, or tracks, that you can edit individually. By placing content on individual layers, you're able to determine its position relative to the other elements in your movie, specifying when it will be seen or heard and how long it will play. Because you can place, edit, and animate elements on their own layers, you can work with them individually—without affecting the other elements that make up your movie. In this chapter we'll show you how to use layers to get the most out of each element.

Understanding Layers

Layers—which Flash provides as receptacles for symbols, groups, sounds, scripts, and other elements—are useful for separating your movie's content from its functionality. These are just some of the movie elements you can place on individual layers:

- A looping soundtrack
- Navigation buttons
- A background image
- Animation tasks for specific elements
- ActionScript
- Timeline comments
- Timeline labels
- Sound effects

Every scene or symbol (for example, graphic, button, or movie clip) contains its own set of layers, which you work with and manage in the same way, regardless of location.

Although you can place several movie elements—say a soundtrack, some Action-Scripts, and a background image—on a single layer, we recommend that you use a separate layer for each: Your movie's content will be much easier to work with and edit (**Figure 9.1**). However, this doesn't mean you must create a different layer for every graphic and sound in your movie. Instead, you'll want to split your content into logical "chunks." For example, say your movie's background includes a bitmap and some text elements: It makes sense to place this *set* of elements on one layer, since together they represent a single entity in your movie—the background.

If, on the other hand, you're including a looping soundtrack *and* a vocal track, it makes more sense to place them on separate layers. For certain animation tasks, you don't have a choice: Flash requires you place elements on individual layers (you'll learn more about this in the next chapter).

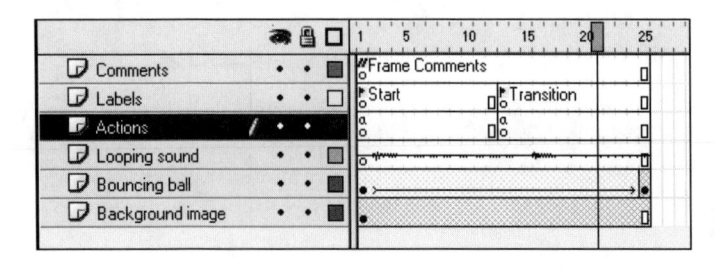

Figure 9.1
You can use layers on the timeline to separate elements and their different functions in your project.

By separating static content (that is, elements that don't change over successive frames) from animated content, you can also improve your movie's download time and performance. For example, if you have a scene that includes a plane flying across a background, you should place the background on its own layer. That way, Flash doesn't have to redraw the entire scene (background *and* plane) on each frame of the timeline, when the only element that's changing is the plane. If you did place the background on the same layer as the plane, you would need a copy of it in each frame in which the plane's movement changed—dramatically increasing file size. The lesson here? Always use different layers for static elements and animated ones (**Figure 9.2**).

Figure 9.2
The background is placed on its own layer, so that only the plane is redrawn in each frame of the animation.

Layers and the Stage

The stage is where you display and edit the graphical content of the various layers on your timeline. Layers are displayed one on top of another on the timeline in what is called the *stacking order* (**Figure 9.3**). Elements that reside in the top layer will always appear on the stage above elements contained in the layers below. When multiple elements are placed on a single layer, they have their own *internal* stacking order, which determines the depth of elements on that particular layer. What you see on the stage at any one time represents a composite rendering of all the graphical content on all visible layers, in their assigned stacking order. For more detail on this, see Chapter 10, "Using Animation to Build Movement."

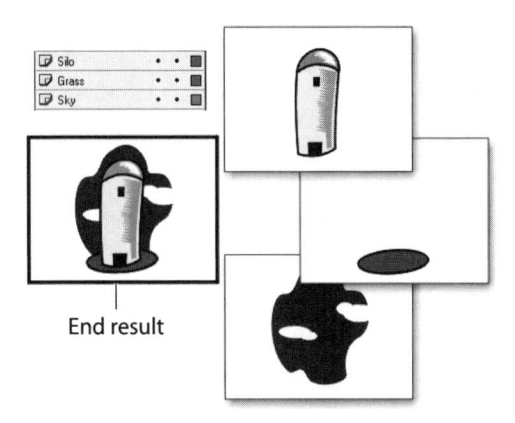

End result

Figure 9.3
The stacking order of this composition is silo, grass, and sky. The silo is the top layer, and the sky is the bottom layer.

The relationship between layers and frames

Each layer contains a span of frames that determines when and how your movie will use that layer's content. For example, if a graphic of a ball appears in a layer that spans Frames 1 to 10, once the timeline reaches Frame 11, the ball will no longer appear in your composite movie (**Figure 9.4**). Although each layer has its own assigned span of frames, these correspond directly to frames on other layers. Thus, when the movie timeline reaches Frame 9 in one layer of a scene, it reaches Frame 9 in every other layer as well. For more detail on this, see Chapter 10, "Using Animation to Build Movement."

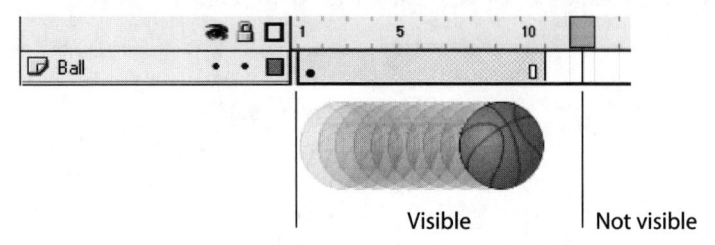

Figure 9.4
The frames included in a layer determine how and when content placed on that layer appears in the composite movie.

Working with Layers

In Flash, layers serve largely as organizational tools. You may work with them in any number of ways (depending on the needs of your project), and using them effectively is the key to creating sophisticated projects with minimal frustration. In general, you'll find that creating and working with layers is pretty straightforward. However, Flash contains some special layers, such as guide, motion guide, and mask layers that require different techniques for creating and managing them. We'll deal with these individually, later in the chapter.

Creating Layers

When you create a new scene, graphic, movie clip, or button in Flash, the process always begins with a single layer. Initially called Layer 1, this layer includes one frame with an empty keyframe (**Figure 9.5**). From here, you can create a new layer anywhere in the stacking order—and because the number of layers you create and use does not affect the file size, you can use as many layers as you need. If the number of layers exceeds the viewable area of the timeline, a scroll bar will appear to the right of the timeline.

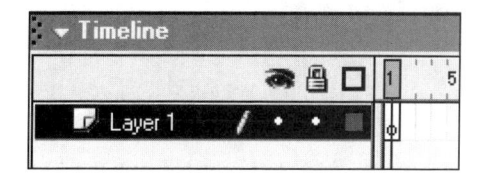

Chapter 9 *Using Layers to Separate Content and Functionality*

Figure 9.5
By default, the timeline of every new scene or symbol begins with a single layer, initially named Layer 1, which contains a single frame.

To create a layer:

1. Click the layer you wish to place the new layer above; it will become highlighted.

2. On the Layer control panel, click the Insert Layer button (**Figure 9.6**). Alternatively, you can right-click (Windows) or Control-click (Macintosh) on an existing layer's name bar, then choose Insert Layer from the menu that appears in order to place a new layer on the timeline.

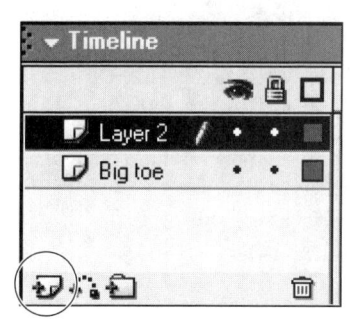

Figure 9.6
The Insert Layer button.

Whenever you add a layer to the timeline, Flash automatically assigns it the same number of frames as the longest sequence on the timeline. Thus, if a 20-frame layer is the longest sequence on a particular timeline, Flash will automatically assign 20 frames to any newly created layers (**Figure 9.7**). This is a convenience feature; you can still add or delete frames from a given layer as you see fit.

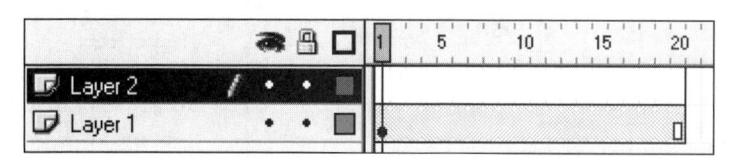

Figure 9.7
When Layer 2 was created, 20 frames were automatically added to it to match the number of frames in Layer 1.

Current Layer Mode

To work efficiently with layers, you need to understand layer modes. The appearance of the stage and the way you edit the authoring file are determined—at least in part—by the layer modes you employ. When a timeline contains two or more layers, one of them is the *current* layer. Anything drawn, cut, copied, pasted, imported, or dragged onto the stage from the library will affect that layer (**Figure 9.8**). You can make a layer current in a couple of ways (and only one layer can be current):

- By clicking its name

- By selecting a stage element that resides in a layer (thus making that layer the current one)

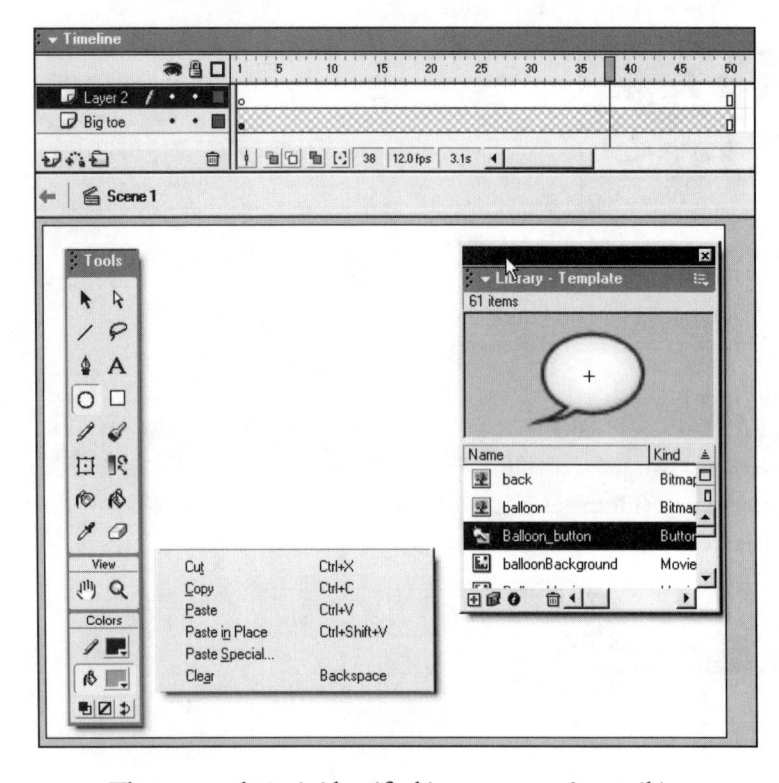

Figure 9.8
The current layer appears highlighted: Any content drawn, imported, cut, copied, pasted, or dragged from the library is reflected on that layer.

The current layer is identified in two ways: A pencil icon appears next to its name, and it is highlighted in the layer stack.

TIP *You cannot remove or place graphical content on the current layer if that layer is locked or hidden (indicated by a red slash through the pencil icon next to the current layer).*

Additional Layer Modes

In addition to the current layer mode, layers can be placed in three other modes, or *states*. These modes determine—at least in part—what type of edits you can make to the overall scene, as well as what content is visible on the stage. You place a layer in one of the following modes by clicking the appropriate icon on the layer's name bar (**Figure 9.9**).

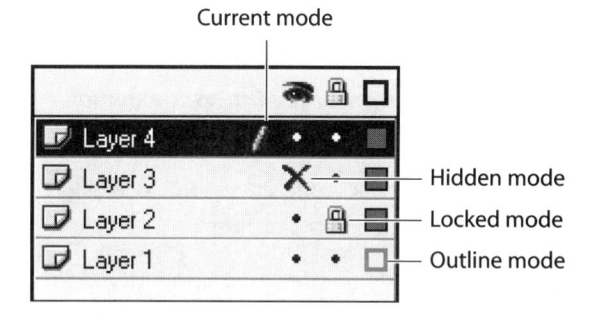

Figure 9.9
Clicking an icon on the right side of the layer name bar puts that layer in the mode indicated by that icon.

- **Hidden mode.** You may occasionally find it useful to hide the contents of one or more layers, when you're working on a particular part of your scene. A red *X* on a layer's name bar indicates that it is in hidden mode. A dot appears instead when this mode is not active.

- **Locked mode.** When a layer is locked, you can see its contents but you can't edit them. Typically, you would use this mode when you're satisfied with a layer's contents and don't want to accidentally edit or delete them. A lock on the layer's name bar indicates this mode; a dot appears instead when this mode is not active.

- **Outline mode.** When a layer is in outline mode, its contents appear only as outlines. Outline mode makes the edges of elements readily distinguishable, so they are easier to reshape and edit. A colored outline of a box on the layer's name bar indicates this mode. A solid-colored box appears instead when this mode is not active.

Placing multiple layers in a specific mode

Flash provides several commands that let you place multiple layers in a specific mode: You access these commands by right-clicking (Windows) or Control-clicking (Macintosh) the layer's name bar, and choosing the appropriate command from the menu that appears:

- **Show All.** Use this command to unlock previously locked layers, or to make previously hidden layers visible. You would typically employ this command after editing or viewing a single layer using one of the other commands listed here.

- **Lock Others.** Use this command to lock all but the layer whose pop-up menu you are using to initiate this command. That layer becomes the current layer (if it isn't already), and you cannot edit any of the other layers.

- **Hide Others.** Use this command to hide all but the layer whose pop-up menu you are using to initiate this command. That layer becomes the current layer (if it wasn't already), and you cannot see or edit any of the other layers.

TIPS *By clicking one of the three icons located above the layer stack—which represent the Show All, Lock Others, and Hide Others commands—you place all of a scene's layers in that mode (**Figure 9.10**).*

Alt-clicking (Windows) or Option-clicking (Macintosh) a mode icon will place all layers except the one being clicked in that mode.

You can place multiple layers in a particular mode by clicking that mode's icon on one layer, then dragging up or down through the mode icons on several layers. Doing this again will place the layers in the previous mode.

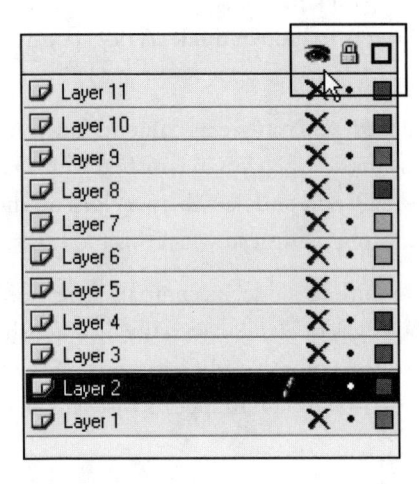

Figure 9.10
Clicking one of the mode icons displayed above the layer name bars (such as the eye icon, as shown here) will place all layers in that mode (in this case, hidden).

Deleting Layers

If you decide you no longer need a layer's contents, it's easy to delete that layer and all of its associated frames.

To delete a layer:

1. Select the layer you want to delete by clicking its name.

Chapter 9 *Using Layers to Separate Content and Functionality*

2. From the Layer control panel, click the Delete Layer button (**Figure 9.11**). You can also right-click (Windows) or Control-click (Macintosh) on the layer's name, and then from the pop-up menu, choose Delete.

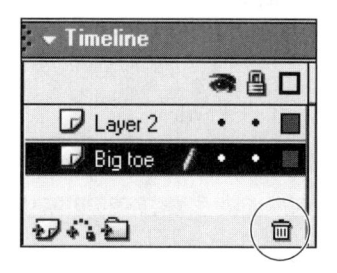

Figure 9.11
The Delete Layer button.

TIP *If you delete the wrong layer, you can choose Edit > Undo to undo the deletion.*

Renaming Layers

Flash assigns a default name (Layer 1, Layer 2, and so on) to each layer you create. Although you don't have to assign new names to your layers, they're easier to work with if their names describe their contents. For example, if you were to place a background image on a layer, it might be wise to make it the only element on that layer and to give that layer a descriptive name (using up to 65 characters), such as Background.

To rename a layer:

1. Right-click (Windows) or Control-click (Macintosh) the layer you want to rename.

2. From the pop-up menu that appears, choose Properties.

   The Layer Properties dialog box will appear.

3. Type in your own name for this layer, and then click OK.

   The new layer name will be displayed.

   TIP *A faster way to complete the same task is to double-click the layer's name to select it, then type in a new name. Once you've entered it, click elsewhere on the screen to set the new name.*

Reordering Layers

When you change your layers' stacking order, you also change the depth in which their contents appear on the stage (in relation to the contents on other layers).

To reorder a layer:

1. Click and hold the name of the layer you wish to reorder.

   A dark-gray line will appear along the bottom indicating that layer's position relative to the other layers in the stack.

2. Drag the layer up or down to where you want it in the stack order, then release the mouse button (**Figure 9.12**).

   The layer and all its contents will appear in its new position in the stacking order.

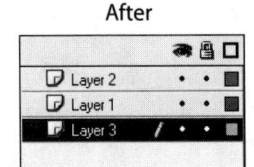

Figure 9.12
Click and drag a layer's name to reposition it in the layer stack. As you do so, a gray line will appear indicating the layer's new position.

Standardizing Your Movie's Layer Structure

Many Flash developers employ a standard naming and stacking structure for the layers in their projects. Although you don't need to follow this structure for your project to function properly, it can make things easier: For starters, elements are easier to locate if they've been placed in a pre-defined order—especially if you have to pass off your project to another developer.

The following is the layer structure we recommend for your projects. The order in which items appear here is representative of how they should appear on Flash's timeline (**Figure 9.13**):

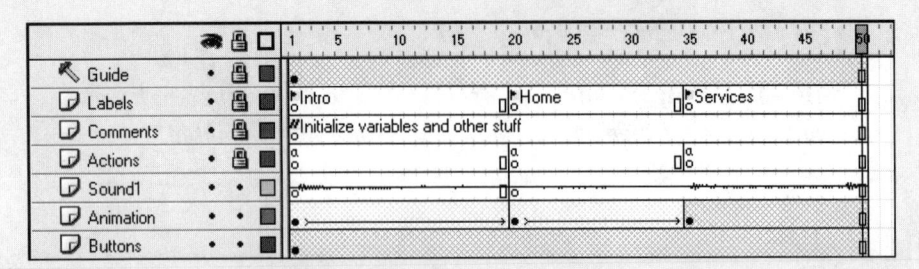

Figure 9.13
The standard layer structure for a Flash project.

Standardizing Your Movie's Layer Structure continued

- **Guides.** Place a guide layer (see "Using Guide Layers," later in this chapter) at the top of your layer stack for any graphic content you plan to use to help you lay out your design.
- **Labels.** It's a good idea to create a layer for any frame labels your project requires. You can lock this layer so that you don't unintentionally place content on it (see "Labels and Comments" in Chapter 10).
- **Comments.** You can use the comment layer to place short notes on the timeline, to help you keep track of what's happening in your Flash movie at that particular moment (see "Labels and Comments" in Chapter 10). You can lock this layer to avoid accidentally placing content on it.
- **Actions.** Add all frame actions to this layer. You can lock this layer to avoid accidentally placing content on it (see Chapter 12, "Getting Started with ActionScript).
- **Sounds.** It's most efficient to place sounds on their own layers, above any layers containing graphical content. This makes them easier to find and edit. If your project requires multiple layers containing sound, place them all immediately below the actions layer but above the content layers.
- **Content.** All of the layers below the ones discussed thus far are for placing graphical content (buttons, animations, and so on). A timeline can contain numerous content layers, each with a specific element or set of elements.

Copying Layers

You may sometimes want to copy a layer's contents and frame sequences in order to create a new layer—useful for transferring layers between scenes or movies. You can even simultaneously select all of a scene's layers, and paste them elsewhere to duplicate an entire scene. Alternatively, you can copy sections of a layer's frames to create a new layer.

To copy a section of a layer:

1. If you have not already done so, create an empty layer that can receive the copied layer's contents.

2. On the layer that contains the content you wish to copy, click and drag from the first frame through the final frame you wish to copy, and then release. To select all of the frames in a layer, click the layer's name.

   The contents should appear highlighted to show they've been selected.

3. Right-click (Windows) or Control-click (Macintosh) one of the selected frames, and from the Frame pop-up menu choose Copy Frames.

4. In the empty layer you created earlier, right-click (Windows) or Control-click (Macintosh) Frame 1, and from the Frame pop-up menu choose Paste Frames (**Figure 9.14**).

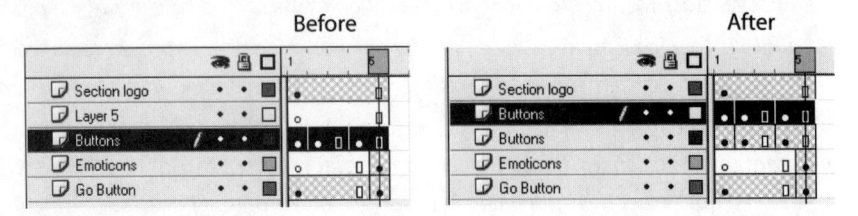

Figure 9.14
To reuse the elements of the Buttons layer, the layer is copied and pasted into Layer 5.

To copy multiple layers:

1. Create at least one empty layer, which can receive the copied layers' contents.

   Even if you're pasting multiple layers, you only need one empty layer, which occupies the top position of the multiple layers that will be pasted in.

2. On the layers whose contents you wish to copy, click and drag from Frame 1 in the top layer to the last frame on the bottom layer, and then release.

   The contents should appear highlighted to show they have been selected. You can only perform this type of edit with contiguous layers in the stacking order.

3. Right-click (Windows) or Control-click (Macintosh) one of the selected frames, and from the Frame pop-up menu choose Copy Frames.

4. In the empty layer you created, right-click (Windows) or Control-click (Macintosh) Frame 1, and from the Frame pop-up menu choose Paste Frames.

   You now have duplicate copies of the layers. Note that the pasted layers retain their relative positions.

Distribute to Layers

MX ALERT As you've learned, layers are ideal for organizing and separating the elements that make up your project. While you can create layers and place content on them manually, this is not always the most efficient method. Most imported artwork, for example, is imported onto a single layer: Thus, if you wanted to place pieces of that artwork on separate layers so that you could animate them, you would have to manually create several layers, then do a lot of cutting and pasting.

Chapter 9 Using Layers to Separate Content and Functionality

The same would hold true for a block of text you had broken apart in order to animate the characters individually. Fortunately, Flash MX provides a much more automated way of handling such tasks: The Distribute to Layers command lets you place each of the currently selected objects (shapes, text blocks, symbol instances, and so on) on its own layer automatically. You can also select objects from multiple, noncontiguous layers.

All new layers will be placed below the bottom layer in which content has been selected, and named according to their own content (**Figure 9.15**):

- A layer containing an instance will be given the name of the instance.

- A layer containing a library asset (for example, a bitmap or video) will be given the name of the asset as it appears in the library.

- A layer containing a text block will be given a name representative of the text in the block—that is, one that includes *all* of the text in the text field (which can make for a pretty long name).

- A layer containing a single character will be given that character as a name.

- A layer containing a simple shape or group will be given a default name such as Layer 5 or Layer 6, and so on.

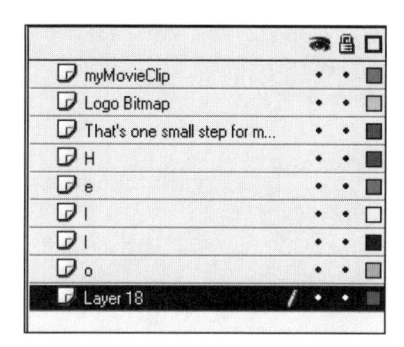

Figure 9.15
Some of the layer names created when using the Distribute to Layers command.

All layers created with this command are arranged, top to bottom, in the order in which the elements they contain were created within the realm of your overall project. When distributing individual characters of text that has been broken apart, layers are arranged based on the order of the characters as they're read. Thus, if you were to distribute the characters *J-A-C-K*, the resulting layers would be named J, A, C, and K, from top to bottom.

To distribute selected elements to layers:

1. On the stage, select all of the elements you wish to place on their own layers.

2. From the Modify menu, choose Distribute to Layers.

New layers will be created as described above; you may need to scroll to see all of them.

Identifying Graphical Elements on Different Layers

When you're working with complex scenes, it can be difficult to keep track of which layers contain what elements. Don't despair: Flash offers several features that make this task easier.

When you select an element on the stage, two visual cues appear: The name of the layer that contains it is highlighted, and the bounding box of the selected element is displayed in the same color as the layer on which it resides (as long as you're using the proper preference setting) (**Figure 9.16**).

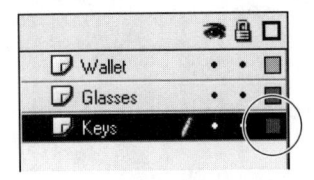

Figure 9.16
When you select an element on the stage, its layer becomes highlighted and its bounding box takes on the color of the layer, which is the color displayed in the small box to the right of the layer name (which is also the Outline mode button).

TIP To find this preference setting, choose Edit > Preferences, then the General tab. On the Highlight color option, select the Use Layer Color setting.

You can also keep track of elements and their corresponding layers by turning on layer outlines, which display all elements as color-coded outlines that correspond to the

Chapter 9 *Using Layers to Separate Content and Functionality*

layer on which they reside. Though less dynamic, this is also an effective way of keeping everything straight.

To identify elements on layers using colored outlines:

1. Select the layer whose contents you want to view as outlines; it will be highlighted.

2. From the Modify menu choose Layer, or right-click (Windows) or Control-click (Macintosh) and choose Properties from the contextual pop-up menu.

   The Layer Properties box will appear.

3. Under Outline options, select the color you wish to use for outlines and check the "View layer as outlines" option.

4. Click OK.

   The layer will now display its objects as outlines.

   TIPS *You can also accomplish this task by simply clicking the Outline On/Off toggle on the right side of the layer's name bar (**Figure 9.17**).*

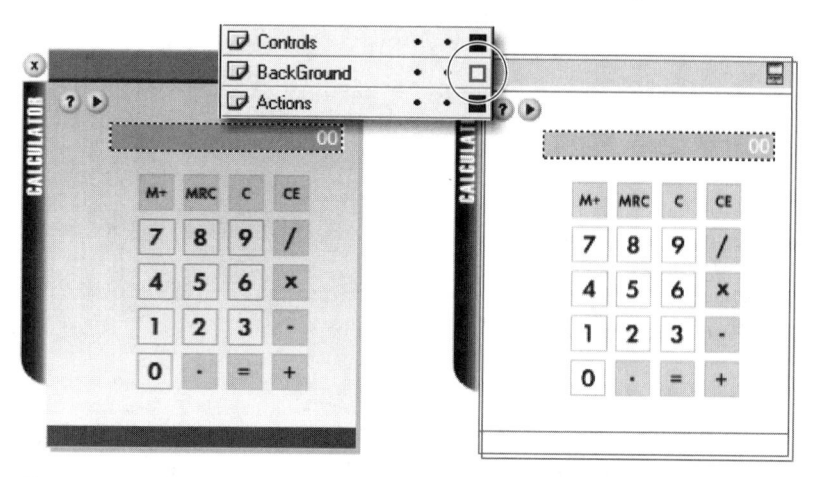

Figure 9.17
Displaying a layer's contents as outlines makes them easier to identify. Here, the Background layer's content is more clearly identifiable in outline mode.

TIP *When using outline colors to identify movie elements on a layer, the elements temporarily lose their fill. However, you can still edit them as you normally would; the only difference is that fills and fill changes will not appear until you turn the Outline feature off.*

Using Guide Layers

Guide layers can make laying out your Flash movie a breeze: Say you've used Flash (or your favorite graphics program) to create a killer layout—with menu bars and graphics placed just so—and you want to use it as the basis for your Flash movie. If you place your layout on a guide layer in Flash, you can use it as a backdrop for your movie's layout (**Figure 9.18**). Although you could accomplish the same thing by placing the graphic as a background on a normal layer, its contents would be included in the exported movie. Guide layers, in contrast, are not exported, which means their contents will not appear in the final product. You can use multiple guide layers in a given scene, and as many guide layers in your movie as you see fit.

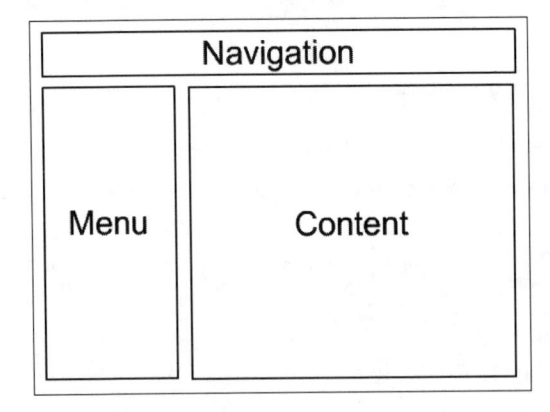

Figure 9.18
A guide layer can contain a basic layout (as shown), which you can emulate in determining how your Flash project will look.

To create a guide layer:

1. Once you've placed the graphics on a layer, right-click (Windows) or Control-click (Macintosh) that layer's name bar.

2. From the contextual menu that appears, choose Guide.

   A new T-square icon will appear next to the layer's name, indicating that the layer is a guide (**Figure 9.19**).

   TIP *A guide layer can be set to any mode a normal layer can, meaning that you can hide or lock a guide layer when you want to check your layout.*

Figure 9.19
The T-square icon on a layer's name bar indicates that it is a guide layer.

Creative Uses for Guide Layers

The fact that none of the content (including scripts on frames) placed on guide layers is included in your exported SWF means you can use them for more than just providing a graphic of your movie's layout. Let's look at some of the possibilities.

Visual experimentation

You can turn a layer into a guide if you want to see how a movie will look without that layer's contents. If you don't like the results, just go back to the layer and uncheck the Guide option on the Layer pop-up menu, so that you can once again see that layer's contents when the movie is exported. This allows you to easily create different looks for your projects using a single authoring file.

Interactive experimentation

You can place frame scripts, or movie clip instances with scripts attached to them, on a guide layer in order to turn sets of scripts on or off in an exported movie. Make the layer a normal layer to include the scripts' functionality; make it a guide layer to remove the functionality of the scripts from the exported movie. This gives you the freedom to experiment without having to keep track of numerous edits made to scripts in different places.

Debugging

Although Flash comes with an excellent debugging tool (see Chapter 19, "Testing"), it's not necessarily the best solution for every debugging situation. However, guide layers can help. Many developers place dynamic text fields or dummy clips on layers (which are eventually converted to guide layers) in order to view a script's effect on a movie. These text fields display variable values and other dynamic data you would not normally be able to see, so that you can easily track values as they change. Dummy clips are used to test a script's effect on a test clip before creating a more elaborate final clip. When testing is complete, turn the layer that contains the debugging elements into a guide layer, so that those elements are available for future use but won't be exported in the final movie.

Special-Purpose Layers

Most layers you'll create can be used for nearly any content or purpose; these are known as normal layers. However, there are other types of layers—specifically mask layers and motion guide layers—that are reserved for special uses. These differ from normal layers in that they don't contain just any content (as do normal layers), and they always work in conjunction with at least one normal layer to which they are linked. In other words, by themselves these special layers have no function; however, once linked to one or more normal layers, they affect the content of that linked normal layer in unique ways.

Mask Layers

Mask layers add even more possibilities to the vast array of effects you can apply with Flash. Think of a mask layer as a stencil: When you place a stencil over a surface and spray paint over that stencil, the paint covers all the areas that were *not* covered by the stencil; the rest of the surface is blocked off, or *masked*, from the paint.

In similar fashion, mask layers are used to mask content on linked layers. For example, if you were to draw a solid circle on a mask layer and then link a normal graphic layer to it, only the normal-layer content within that circular area would be visible (**Figure 9.20**). In other words, the circle on the mask layer becomes a "window" through which the content on the normal layer shows. You can use any solid shape—groups, text, and even symbols—as a mask. Lines cannot be used as masks.

Figure 9.20
The effect of linking a normal layer to a mask layer.

Chapter 9 *Using Layers to Separate Content and Functionality*

MX ALERT **TIP** *Movie clips containing multiple animated elements can be used as masks. You are no longer restricted to using single, solid shapes as masks (**Figure 9.21**).*

Figure 9.21
Movie clips containing multiple solid shapes can be used as masks. The shapes within the clip can be animated as well, allowing you to create sophisticated and complex masking effects.

When a normal layer is linked to a mask layer, it becomes a masked layer. Because the masked layer retains all of the functionality of a normal layer, its content can be animated and contain many graphical elements. In addition, more than one normal layer can be linked to a single mask layer—which means the content of each of the normal layers would only be visible through a single mask.

The content of any layer(s) *below* a mask layer and any normal layer(s) linked to it remain unaffected by the masking process (**Figure 9.22**).

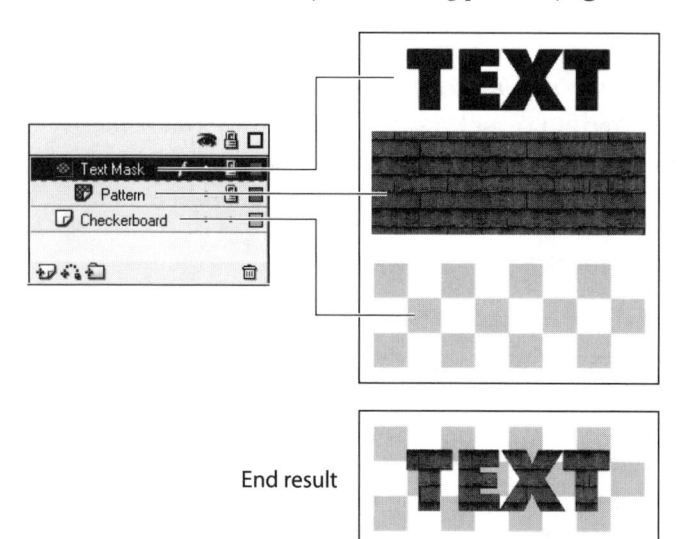

Figure 9.22
Unlinked layers below the mask are unaffected by the mask. In this example, the Checkerboard layer is not linked to the layer stack, so although it falls below the mask layer, it is not affected by it.

End result

303

To create a mask layer:

1. Once you've decided which layer's content you want to mask, place a shape, text element, or symbol on the layer above it.

This object will act as the mask.

2. Right-click (Windows) or Control-click (Macintosh) the name bar of the layer on which you placed the solid object.

3. From the Layer pop-up menu that appears, choose Mask.

The content in the bottom layer will be masked by the outline of the object you chose in Step 1. An icon will appear next to the mask layer's name and the layer directly below it, indicating that they are linked by a mask (**Figure 9.23**). By default, these layers are automatically locked.

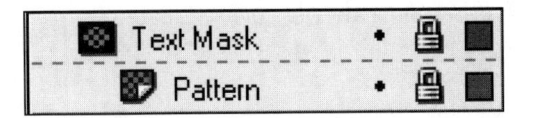

Figure 9.23
A mask layer and the layers linked to it are identified by special icons.

TIP *You can also convert a normal layer to a mask layer by changing its type through the Layer Properties box, which you access by double-clicking the Layer icon, or by selecting the layer and then choosing Modify > Layer.*

As already mentioned, only the layer directly below the mask layer will be linked to it initially. However, you can link as many additional layers to a single mask layer as you want.

MX ALERT { *ActionScript* } *One movie clip instance (its shape) can be dynamically set to mask the content of another movie clip instance using the* `setMask()` *method. For example,* `myMovieClip.setMask(myMaskClip)` *will mask the content of* **myMovieClip** *with the shape of the content in* **myMaskClip**. *For more information, see Chapter 16, "Using ActionScript in your Projects."*

To link additional layers to a mask layer:

1. Click and drag the normal layer's name bar to link it to the mask layer.

A dark-gray line will appear along the bottom, indicating that layer's position relative to the other layers in the stack.

2. Drag the layer until the gray line denoting the dragged layer's position appears just below the name bar of the mask layer itself; then release.

The layer is now linked to the mask layer (**Figure 9.24**).

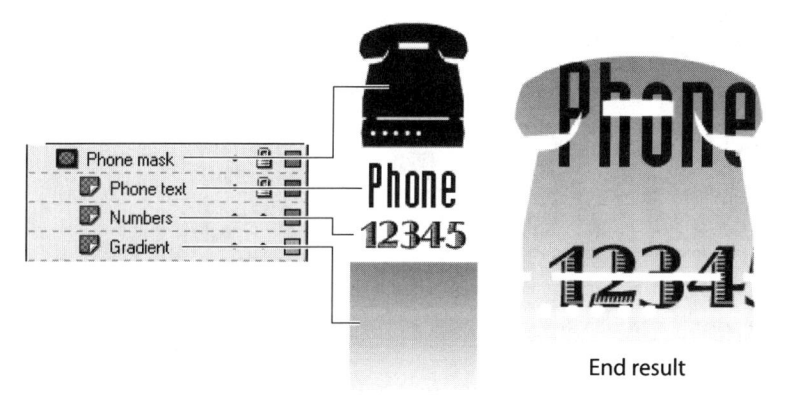

Chapter 9 *Using Layers to Separate Content and Functionality*

Figure 9.24
All of the content on the Phone text, Numbers, and Gradient layers is linked to the Phone mask layer; thus, they all are bounded by the same mask.

End result

To unlink a layer from a mask layer:

1. Click and drag the linked layer's name bar.

A dark-gray line will appear along the bottom, indicating that layer's position relative to the other layers in the stack.

2. Drag the layer until the gray line denoting its position appears either above the name bar of the mask layer itself, or below any other normal layer; then release.

The layer is now unlinked from the mask layer.

TIPS *You can also unlink a normal layer from a mask layer, by changing it from a masked layer back to a normal layer using the Layer Properties box. You can access this box by double-clicking the masked layer icon or by choosing Modify > Layer.*

*Once you've linked several layers to a mask layer, you can reorder them within the linked stack just as you would normal layers (**Figure 9.25**).*

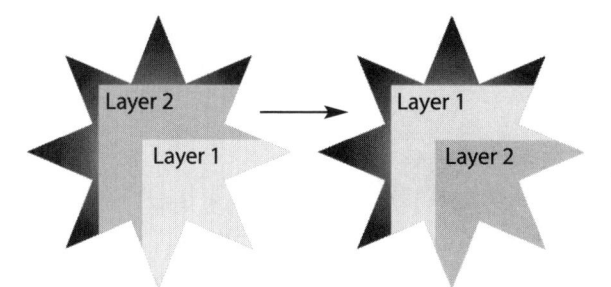

Figure 9.25
When you reorder layers linked to a mask layer, the content within the masked area will appear in a different stacking order.

Because both the layers associated with a mask are initially locked, you must unlock them before you can edit their contents. Once you've completed your edits, you can restore the mask by locking the layers again.

To edit content on masked layers:

1. Click the masked layer you wish to edit; it will appear highlighted.

2. Click the Lock/Unlock toggle button.

You can now edit the layer's contents.

3. When you've completed your edits, right-click (Windows) or Control-click (Macintosh) the layer's name bar, and from the menu that appears choose Show Masking to restore the mask effect.

TIP When editing the contents of masked layers, the mask itself may sometimes get in your way. To get around this problem, hide the mask layer using the hidden mode on the layer's name bar. To re-establish the mask effect after you've completed your edits, right-click (Windows) or Control-click (Macintosh) the name bar of one of the mask's associated layers, and choose Show Masking from the contextual pop-up menu that appears.

Creative Uses for Masks

You can achieve some interesting effects by using multiple masks, tweening or animating the element on the mask layer, or tweening or animating elements on any of the masked layers. This allows you to create visual effects, such as kaleidoscopes, spotlights, and movement inside a window.

You'll find examples of the following masking effects on the accompanying CD in the Chapter 9/Assets folder:

- **Magnifying glass and focus.** You can use a magnifying-glass effect to bring an image into focus, make it larger, or both. If you add a magnifying glass graphic and animate it to mimic the movement of the mask object, you can make it appear as if the magnifying glass is actually responsible for the magnification or focus effect (**Figure 9.26**).

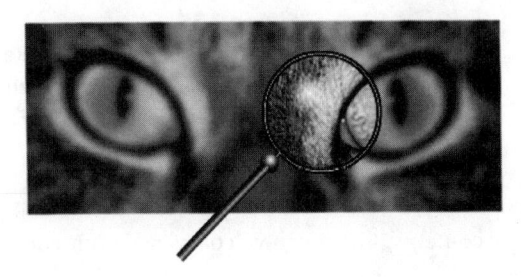

Figure 9.26
Masks let you create "focus" effects.

- **X-rays and cutouts.** In this interesting effect, a "beam" passes over a normal object to reveal an X-ray or cutout view of the object (**Figure 9.27**).

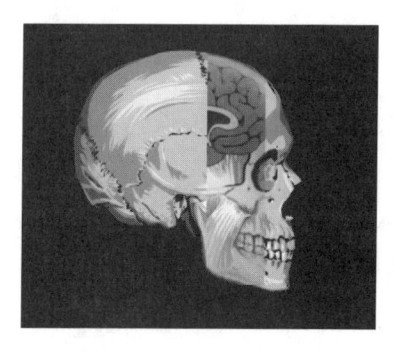

Figure 9.27
Masks can give viewers the illusion of "seeing through" an object's layers.

- **Spotlight.** You can see this effect put to use in Flash's own help files. We take it a step further here by adding a gradient transparency to make it more lifelike (**Figure 9.28**).

Figure 9.28
By placing a circle with a gradient transparency above the masked area, you can provide the illusion of diffused lighting.

- **Holes and windows.** This effect is best suited for creating animation or movement inside a window of some sort (**Figure 9.29**).

Figure 9.29
Animating masked content can create a feeling of depth. The airplane in this graphic is masked so that it appears to be flying outside the window.

- **Shattered reflections and waves** (two separate files on the CD). These effects emulate scattered reflections—like those seen through a shattered mirror or waves on water (**Figure 9.30**).

Figure 9.30
Masks can be used to create the look of scattered light reflections, like an image seen through broken glass.

MX ALERT { *ActionScript* } *Movie clip instances used as masks are still movie clip instances—which means you can set them up to react dynamically to various events in your movie. This enables you to create masks that are draggable, as well as ones that can be positioned and scaled dynamically. For more information, see Chapter 16, "Using ActionScript in Your Projects."*

Motion Guide Layers

Motion guide layers serve a simple but important function in the animation process: They contain the lines or paths that animations on linked (normal) layers must follow. For example, if you were to place a curved line on a motion guide layer and then link a normal layer to it, the animation on that normal layer would follow the curved line (**Figure 9.31**). Thus, the sole purpose of the motion guide layer is to provide you with the means to animate elements in other than a straight line.

Since you need to know something about the way Flash's animation features work to understand motion guide layers, we discuss them in greater detail in Chapter 10, "Animation."

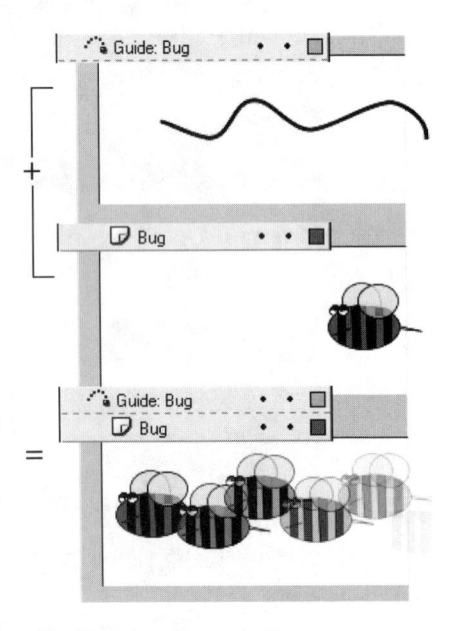

Figure 9.31
Linking a normal layer to a motion guide layer causes the animation on the normal layer to follow a line drawn on the motion guide layer.

Chapter 9 *Using Layers to Separate Content and Functionality*

Layer Folders

MX ALERT

A large project can contain dozens, even hundreds, of layers, including normal, masked, and guide layers. However, as you work with layers on the timeline, you'll probably only want to view a few of them at a time. In fact, trying to work with too many layers usually requires a great deal of scrolling up and down the timeline—a definite time-waster.

This is where layer folders can help. You can usually organize the content of various layers into categories, such as buttons, sounds, background content, and so on. By using layer folders, you can group layers with similar or related content so that you can view (or hide) them all simultaneously, depending on the task at hand. Layer folders can contain all types of layers (normal, masked, guide, and so on) as well as other layer folders, allowing you to create a hierarchical structure similar to that used by the hard drive of your computer.

When layers are placed inside a folder, any actions taken in relation to that folder will affect any layers it contains. For example, if you hide or lock a layer folder, any layers it contains will automatically become hidden and locked as well.

To create a layer folder:

1. Select a layer on the timeline.

2. Press the Insert Layer Folder button (**Figure 9.32**).

This will insert a layer folder on the timeline, above the layer selected in Step 1. Since a layer folder is simply used to hold other layers, frames will not appear on the timeline in relation to a layer folder.

Figure 9.32
The Insert Layer Folder button.

To delete a layer folder:

1. Select the layer folder you wish to delete.

2. Press the Delete Layer button.

An alert box will appear, indicating that by deleting the layer folder you will also delete any layers it currently contains. Press Yes to confirm the deletion, or No to cancel.

To place a layer inside a layer folder:

1. Click and drag the layer's name.

A dark-gray line will appear along the bottom, indicating that layer's position relative to the other layers in the stack.

2. Drag the layer on top of the folder icon of the layer folder you wish to place it in; then release.

The layer is now inside the layer folder.

To remove a layer from a layer folder:

1. Click and drag the layer's name bar.

A dark-gray line will appear along the bottom, indicating that layer's position relative to the other layers in the stack.

2. Drag the layer until the gray line denoting its position appears either above the name bar of the layer folder itself, or below any other normal layer; then release.

TIP *The dark-gray line that appears when you drag a layer contains a "notch" that provides a visual indicator of the hierarchical position in which the dragged layer will be placed if released (**Figure 9.33**).*

Figure 9.33
When you drag a layer to reposition it, a small "notch" appears to help you determine the hierarchical position of the dragged layer before releasing.

To expand or collapse a folder:

◆ Click the small triangle to the left of the folder name.

TIP *You can expand or collapse all folders simultaneously by right-clicking (Windows) or Control-clicking (Macintosh) any layer's name, then choosing Expand All Folders or Collapse All Folders from the menu that appears.*

Layer Properties

Now that you've learned how layers can be used in your project, it's time to look at the Layer Properties box, which allows you to configure layers in a number of ways—changing their names, behavior, and appearance in one centralized location. Each layer has a unique set of properties, which can include the following (**Figure 9.34**):

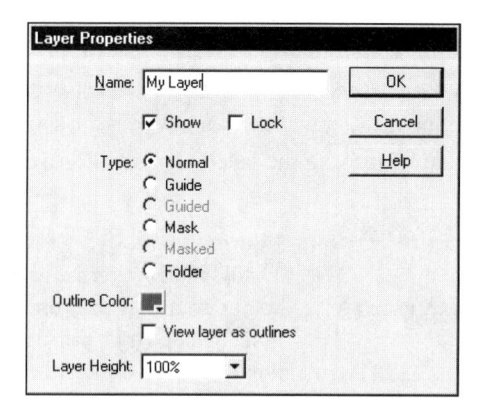

Figure 9.34
The Layer Properties dialog box.

- **Name.** Use this text box to assign a name to a layer. (See "Renaming Layers" earlier in the chapter.)

- **Show.** Determines whether a layer's graphical contents will be visible on the stage.

- **Lock.** Determines whether the layer's graphical contents can be edited on the stage.

- **Normal.** Sets the layer type to Normal.

- **Guide.** Allows you to set your layer as a motion guide (for creating animations that follow a path onscreen).

- **Guided.** Sets your layer type as Guided, which means it will be linked to a motion-guide layer. This option is only available if the layer whose properties you're adjusting is directly below a motion-guide layer or another linked, guided layer.

- **Mask.** Allows you to set your layer as a mask (see "Mask Layers" earlier in this chapter). This type of layer masks the content of any layers linked to it.

- **Masked.** Lets you set your layer as masked, which means it's linked to a mask layer. This option is only available if the layer whose properties you're adjusting is directly below a mask layer or another linked, masked layer.

- **Folder.** Lets you set a layer as a layer folder. Any content the layer contains will be deleted when you convert it to a layer folder.

- **Outline Color.** Sets the color used for outlining graphical elements on this layer as they appear on the stage (see "Identifying Graphical Elements on Different Layers" earlier in this chapter).

- **View layer as outlines.** Allows you to determine whether the graphical contents of the layer are visible as outlines on the stage.

- **Layer Height.** Allows you to set your layer's display height—100 percent, 200 percent, or 300 percent. This setting is helpful if you're working with waveforms (sounds) in the layer, because the graphical representation of the waveform—which helps you detect specific points in the waveform that need to be synchronized with an animation—changes in relation to the layer's height (**Figure 9.35**).

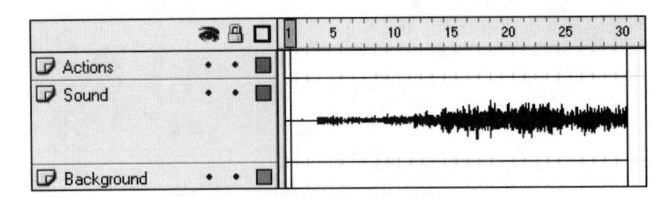

Figure 9.35
By adjusting a layer's display height, sounds placed on the timeline appear larger, making them easier to work with.

To change layer properties:

1. Select the layer whose properties you wish to change.

2. From the Modify menu choose Layer, or right-click (Windows) or Control-click (Macintosh) and choose Properties from the pop-up menu.

   The Layer Properties box will appear.

3. Make your setting adjustments, then click OK.

   The layer will reflect your changes.

   TIP *The quickest way to access a layer's Property box is to double-click the layer icon just to the left of the layer's name.*

Video Tutorial

Working with Layers. This tutorial demonstrates how layers work, and how to use them effectively.

Using Animation to Build Movement

CHAPTER 10

What you'll learn...

How animation works

About the timeline

How to work with scenes and frames

How to create animation

If all you want to do is create Web sites with cool graphics and a few text descriptions, you could easily stick with plain old HTML. However, even though HTML can effectively convey a message, its design limitations make it about as exciting as watching your hair grow. Once you've acquired even a little visual savvy, you'll to want to move beyond HTML. In fact, your interest in Macromedia Flash likely stems from your desire to not only bring your message to a large audience, but to *bring it to life* as well. That, after all, is what animation is all about.

From the early Disney cartoons to the spectacular computer-generated effects seen in today's movies, audiences have long been fascinated by the skillful combination of graphics and motion. Although in live-action films much movement is left to chance, as an animator you determine not only what action occurs in a scene, but exactly *when* it occurs as well. You can make birds fly and cartoon characters talk, or vice versa. You can even determine what your characters say, and whether they get their lights punched out for saying it.

All you've learned about Flash thus far means little without this chapter's ingredients. This is where the real excitement begins. By animating your message, you make it much more powerful. And if you do it right, you'll find that you can control your audience's emotions in ways they'll not soon forget. Sound appealing? Read on.

How Animation Works

At one time or another you've probably seen the actual film that's used to project a movie. Basically, it looks like a bunch of pictures strung together on a long strip of plastic. A Flash animation is no different. Just like a motion picture, it consists of individual frames, each slightly different from the preceding one. Special frames known as *keyframes* define where changes occur in your animation—for example, when movie elements are moved, rotated, resized, added or removed, and so on. Each frame can contain any number of symbols or graphics placed on different layers.

Like a strip of movie film, Flash's timeline includes all of your animation's layers and frames. When your movie plays, or when the playhead on the timeline is moved manually, the graphic content of each succeeding frame makes up what you see on stage. When the frames are played back at a fast enough rate, the illusion of movement occurs. And just as in a real movie, the timeline in Flash uses scenes to shift from one area of the story to another, so that you can break your movie's overall timeline into main sections.

The timeline can be as long as you wish and play at whatever speed (frames per second, or fps) you designate—within reason.

At the same time, Flash technology differs from regular movies in two important ways: First, frame actions can be placed at particular frames on the timeline to perform specific interactive tasks (for example, jumping to other frames in your movie or opening URLs in a browser). Also, Flash movies can contain mini-movies (movie clips) and buttons.

Animation Methods

Flash offers two methods of animation: *Frame-by-frame animation* provides more control over the way graphical content is animated but is more time-consuming to create. T*weened animation* provides less control but is much faster to implement. Let's take a look at both.

Frame-by-frame animation

As the most recognizable and widely used form of animation, the frame-by-frame method is employed for everything from creating animated cartoons to bringing clay figures to life. This type of animation involves taking a snapshot of a frame's content, changing the content slightly, taking another snapshot, changing the content again, and so on. When these snapshots are displayed in quick succession, movement appears and animation is accomplished. In Flash, creating this type of animation involves moving the timeline to a given frame, adjusting the content on the stage, then moving the

Chapter 10 Using Animation to Build Movement

timeline to the next frame and adjusting the content again—and so on, for each frame of the animation.

With frame-by-frame animation, you must manually edit each element's movement on the stage (**Figure 10.1**). In addition to being time-consuming, using this mode of animation can substantially increase your movie's overall file size. Thus, you should only use frame-by-frame animation when it's absolutely necessary—for quick or subtle movements, such as a mouth moving or hands playing a piano.

For a more detailed discussion of frame-by-frame animation, see "Creating Animation" later in this chapter.

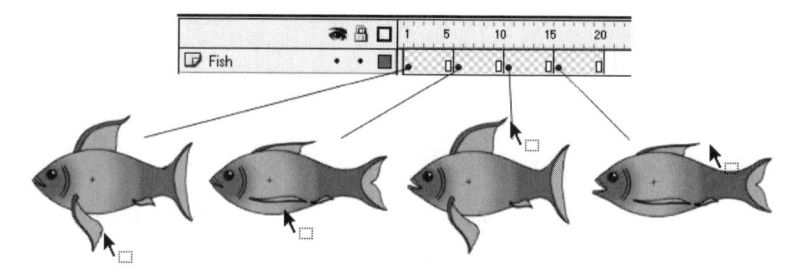

Figure 10.1
In a frame-by-frame animation, each movement is edited manually.

Tweened animation

Since we now have computers to make our lives easier, there's no reason to manually create an animation when Flash can do so automatically—especially when it requires smooth transitions in movement, size, rotation, shape, or color.

With a tweened animation, you use keyframes to specify two images of a given movie element: its appearance at the beginning of the animation, and at the end. You also specify how long the transition should take from the beginning to end (measured in frames). Flash then generates the graphic content for each of the frames in between (**Figure 10.2**).

Figure 10.2
In a tweened animation, you define the graphic images at the beginning and ending keyframes, and Flash calculates how each of the intermediate frames should look.

Obviously, it's much faster to produce animations using tweening than the frame-by-frame method. Tweened animations are also much easier to edit, because there are only two editable frames—the beginning and ending keyframes. If you change either of these, Flash will automatically recalculate the content of all of the intervening frames. In contrast, you must manually edit each frame of a frame-by-frame animation.

As you work more with animated content, you'll find that tweening works for most animation tasks that involve fluid and smooth movements as well as transitions, *or morphing*, of shapes. Frame-by-frame animation works best for delicate, complex, and quick movements. Flash's layering functions also make it possible to use both types of animation on different graphic elements in the same scene.

Understanding the Timeline

The timeline is where the bulk of the animation process takes place. This is where you control the speed at which a movie element moves, when it enters and exits the scene, and its depth, or stacking order, in relation to other elements in the scene (**Figure 10.3**). Most of what you'll learn in this chapter will also apply to animating symbols' timelines (especially graphic and movie clip symbols).

TIP *If the timeline is consuming too much screen space, click its name to collapse it as you would any other panel.*

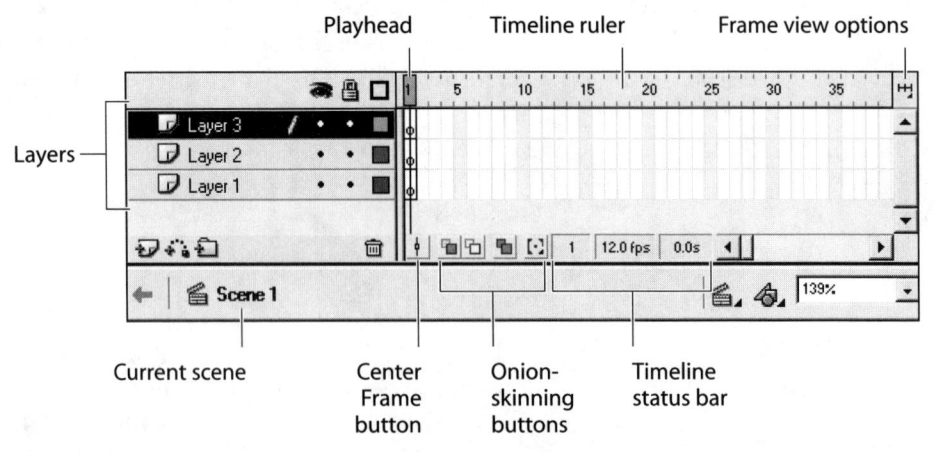

Figure 10.3
The various parts of the timeline.

Layers

Although we discussed layers in detail in Chapter 9, you'll probably find it helpful to review a couple of points here—especially those that have to do with the relationship between layers, frames, and the stage.

A single frame on the timeline can have multiple layers, whose combined content you can view on the stage (**Figure 10.4**). (For more information about how content on various layers represents the composite animation on the stage, see "Putting It All Together" later in this chapter.) This means you can split the various animated elements of each frame's content into individual layers. Just remember that a single frame can comprise hundreds of layers. Layers are useful for creating complex animations in which a number of movie elements are used simultaneously but in different ways.

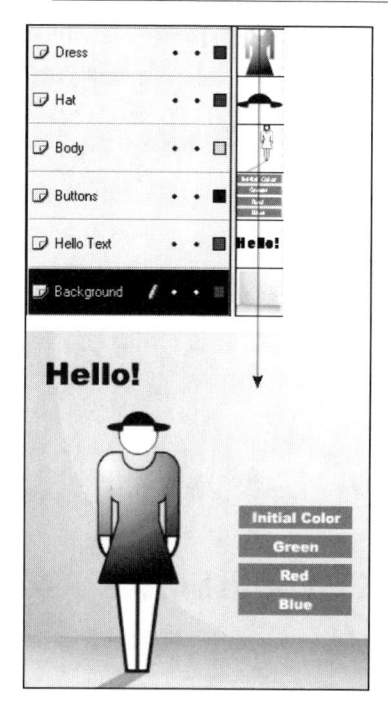

Figure 10.4
The graphical content of all visible layers is displayed on the stage.

Playhead

The playhead is to the timeline what the Arrow tool is to the stage. It allows you to identify the frame being edited, select a frame to work on, and *scrub* the movie—that is, watch it play by dragging the playhead. The red vertical line of the playhead stretches across multiple layers to help you identify all of a frame's content.

To move the playhead to a particular frame:

◆ Click a frame on any available layer, or select a frame on the timeline ruler.

  The playhead will jump to the frame you selected.

To scrub the playhead:

◆ Click and drag the playhead left or right.

  As you move the playhead, your movie will play forward or backward, depending on which direction you drag the playhead.

TIP *To perform either of these actions, your timeline must include at least one blank frame. The white and gray rectangular boxes that appear initially on the timeline are placeholder frames. With the exception of the first frame, you must add frames manually to the timeline. For more on this, see "Inserting Frames" later in this chapter.*

Timeline Ruler

The timeline ruler provides a sequential display of frames along the timeline. Frame increments are marked in two ways: frame *ticks*, which are small vertical lines on the ruler, and frame numbers, which are displayed for every fifth frame. Normally, frame numbers are centered between the two ticks that define the frame. Three-digit frame numbers are left-aligned to the frame they represent.

Timeline Status Bar

The status bar of the timeline provides the following information (**Figure 10.5**):

- **Current frame.** Indicates the frame number whose contents are currently visible on the stage. Also indicates the current position of the playhead.

- **Frame rate.** When your movie is not playing, this box displays the current frames-per-second (fps) setting for your movie. When your movie is playing in the authoring environment, this box (which is dynamically updated) reflects the *actual* playback speed. Actual playback speed can differ from the frames-per-second setting you selected in the Document Properties dialog box—often as the result of processor-intensive animation, which can cause your movie to slow in some segments.

  TIP *Double-clicking the frame-rate area of the timeline status bar will open the Document Properties dialog box.*

- **Elapsed time.** Indicates the amount of time (in seconds) between the first frame of your movie and the current frame. The number is dynamically updated as you play your movie in the authoring environment.

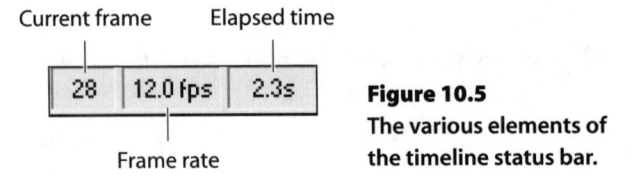

Figure 10.5
The various elements of the timeline status bar.

Chapter 10 **Using Animation to Build Movement**

Planning Your Project

Choosing the Proper Frame Rate

In one of the old I Love Lucy episodes, Lucy and Ethel get jobs packing chocolates into boxes as they come off an assembly line. In this classic TV scene, a malfunctioning conveyor belt begins spitting out chocolates faster then Lucy and Ethel can process them—so the gals resort to stuffing candies in their mouths to keep pace. A huge mess—and much hilarity—ensue.

The timeless lesson here is that faster is not always better. Although it would be nice if you could increase your movie's frame rate to create video-like transitions that never skipped, jumped, or appeared choppy, Flash's reliance on processor speed means this is not always possible. In fact, a higher frame rate can potentially harm your presentation.

Regardless of what frame rate you choose, the different processors used to play your movie can handle information only so quickly. And because there's such a great range of processor speeds out there, you can't possibly know just how fast that is. If a particular computer can render your movie properly at a maximum rate of 20 fps, setting Flash's fps to 100 won't improve matters. That computer will still show your movie at 20 fps—max. Although a faster computer may be able to play the same movie at 100 fps, few of us own the supermachines capable of this.

So increasing a movie's speed doesn't help; in fact, it could even slow things down. Here's how: Let's say your presentation is 10 seconds long. At 12 fps, there are 120 frames (10 seconds × 12 fps) that need to be played through from beginning to end. If you increase your fps rate to 20, you will have 200 frames from start to finish—or an additional 80 frames to draw over the course of your presentation. While slower computers can handle 120 frames over 10 seconds fairly easily, those additional 80 frames could slow your movie to a crawl because they create more than 60 percent more work for the computer to perform in the same 10 seconds (or over the course of your presentation). As a result, you could end up with precisely the opposite effect you were trying to achieve!

So, what's a reasonable frame rate? The default setting of 12 fps is usually a good compromise, with 20 fps at the high end and 24 fps the absolute maximum you should consider, in our opinion. The only exception might be if you were to export your Flash presentation as a video file such as QuickTime or Windows AVI. Because these formats are not as processor intensive, you can pump up the frame rate without too many problems.

Flash still allows you to produce impressive results within these parameters. There are many examples of beautiful and exciting Flash content on the Web that have been created using these same fps guidelines. All it takes is some planning.

Center Frame Button

If you click the Center Frame button in the lower left of the timeline, Flash centers the playhead's current frame position on the timeline. This means that if you scroll to Frame 900 of a 1,000-frame movie while the playhead remains on Frame 200, clicking this button will cause the timeline to quickly scroll back to Frame 200, with the playhead centered on the timeline display (**Figure 10.6**).

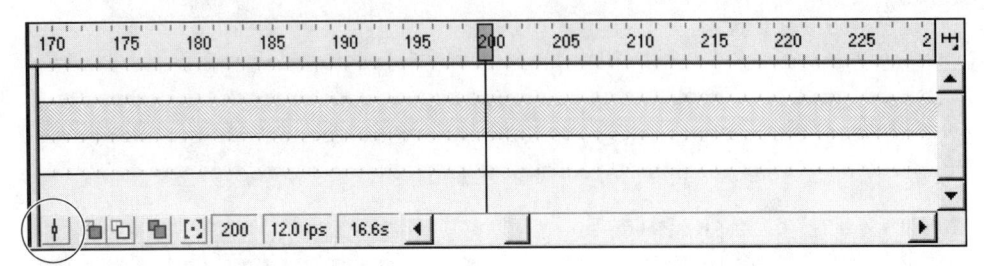

Figure 10.6
Clicking the Center Frame button positions the playhead on the center of the timeline display.

Frame View Options

The Frame View button, which is located in the upper right of the timeline window, allows you to set different modes for viewing frames on the timeline. By clicking this button, you are presented with the following options:

- **Frame Width.** Options include Tiny, Small, Normal, Medium, and Large (**Figure 10.7**).

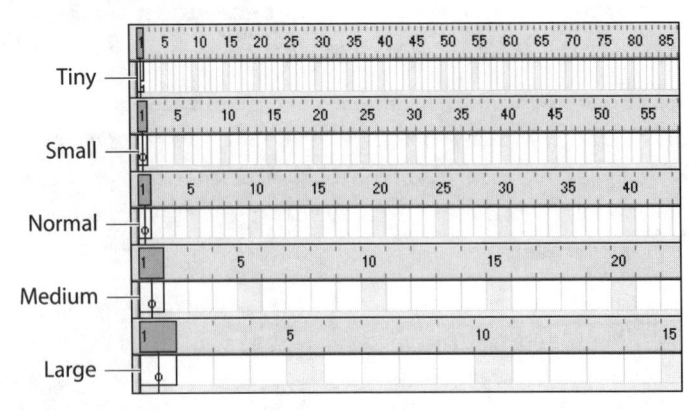

Figure 10.7
The effect of the Frame Width setting on the timeline.

- **Frame Height.** This option reduces the display height of frames on the timeline by 20 percent. If your movie contains a number of layers, choosing this option shrinks the entire stack of layers in a scene, so that more layers are displayed—and you can spend less time scrolling the timeline to access frames on a particular layer.

- **Tinted Frames.** By default, sections of frames are tinted different colors to help you distinguish them. You can turn this option on or off (see the next section for more details).

- **Preview.** This option causes the graphics on each frame in every layer to be displayed within the boxes on the timeline that represent frames. Flash automatically scales the graphics to fit within the frame boxes (**Figure 10.8**).

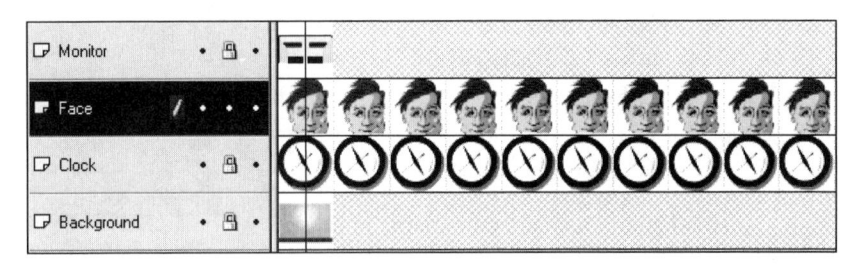

Figure 10.8
The graphics in each frame are scaled to fill the boxes representing frames on the timeline.

- **Preview in Context.** This option is similar to Preview, except that graphics are scaled to reflect their size as they will appear in the overall movie (**Figure 10.9**).

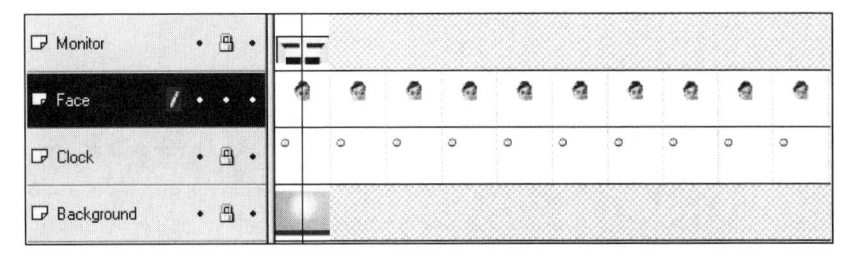

Figure 10.9
The graphics in each frame, shown at their designated size within the overall movie, appear in boxes representing frames on the timeline.

Timeline Menu

The context-sensitive Timeline menu provides quick access to several timeline-related commands, including adding and deleting frames, defining frame properties, creating motion tweens, and more (**Figure 10.10**).

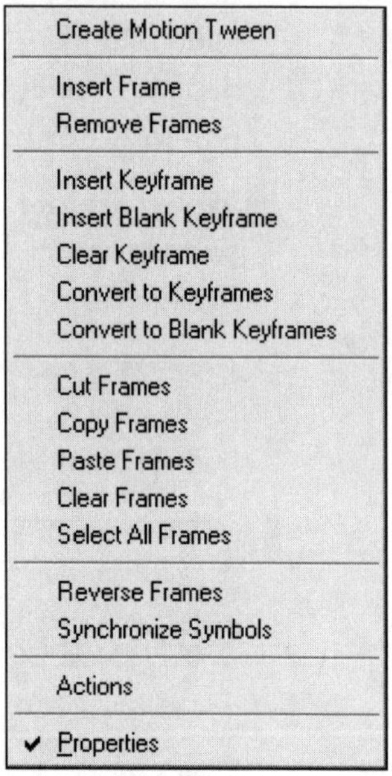

To display the Timeline menu:

- Right-click (Windows) or Control-click (Macintosh) any frame on the timeline to make the Timeline pop-up menu appear, with the following options:

    Create Motion Tween. Uses the current frame's content to automatically create a motion tween. To do so, it converts all content into graphic symbols. We discuss this option in more detail later in the chapter.

    Insert Frame. Adds a regular frame after the currently selected one. If you select a range of regular frames, Flash will add that number of frames to the timeline. If you select a placeholder frame, Flash will add regular frames up to the point of the selected placeholder frame.

Figure 10.10
The Timeline menu.

    Remove Frames. Deletes the currently selected frame. If you select a range of frames, this command deletes all of them.

    Insert Keyframe. Inserts a keyframe on the timeline, at the point where the cursor was located when you activated the menu. If a regular frame was at this position, the keyframe replaces it; if a placeholder frame was at this position, a keyframe is inserted and regular frames are added so that there are no placeholder frames prior to the newly inserted keyframe. A newly inserted keyframe starts out with the same content as the previous keyframe.

    Insert Blank Keyframe. Inserts a blank keyframe on the timeline at the position where the cursor was located when the menu was activated. This command executes in the same fashion as the Insert Keyframe command above.

Clear Keyframe. Converts the selected keyframe to a regular frame. If a range of keyframes is selected, this command converts all of them.

Convert to Keyframes. Converts the selected frame to a keyframe. If a range of frames is selected, this command converts all of them.

Convert to Blank Keyframes. Converts the selected frame to a blank keyframe. If a range of frames is selected, this command converts all of them.

Cut Frames. Cuts a frame or range of frames for pasting elsewhere.

Copy Frames. Copies a frame or range of frames for pasting elsewhere.

Paste Frames. Pastes any frames on the clipboard onto the timeline after the currently selected frame. If the clipboard contains a range of frames across multiple layers, these frames and layers will be pasted onto the timeline in their same relative positions.

Clear Frames. Removes the graphical content of any selected frames.

Select All Frames. Selects all frames on all unlocked and visible layers of the current scene. This is useful for duplicating entire scenes.

Reverse Frames. Flips, or reverses, the positions of the currently selected range of frames. The result is reversing their playback order.

Synchronize Symbols. Displays looped graphic symbols properly, even if the loop occupies an odd number of frames on the main timeline. For example, if you placed an instance of a graphic symbol with a timeline that looped every 10 frames on the main timeline to play over a stretch of 20 frames, it would loop twice without a hitch. If, however, you placed an instance of this same symbol on the main timeline to play over a stretch of 17 frames, it would loop once and then be abruptly cut off at Frame 17 during the second loop. By synchronizing symbols, you ensure that the graphic symbol will loop properly within the allotted frames on the main timeline.

Actions. Opens the Actions panel so that you can add frame actions.

Properties. Displays or hides the Property inspector.

TIP *Most of these commands are also available on the Insert and Modify > Frames menus on the menu bar. When selected, they affect the currently selected frame or range of frames.*

Working with Scenes

Scenes provide an easy way to break your movie's timeline into sections of frames. You can also think of scenes as animated "pages," each of which can be unique, though they all belong to the same timeline (**Figure 10.11**). A single movie can consist of any number of scenes, played in the order you place them. Each movie automatically starts with one scene; you manually add (or delete) the rest. Although individual scenes are all part of a single timeline (the main timeline), each new scene is made up of an independent frame number sequence, beginning with Frame 1.

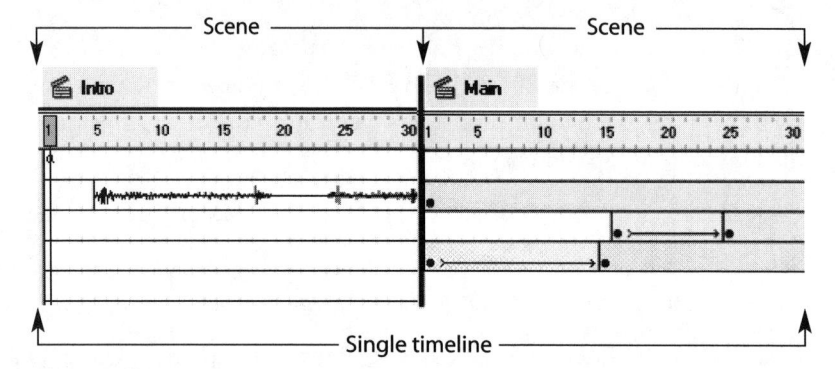

Figure 10.11
Scenes allow you to break up a single timeline into manageable sections.

Let's say you have a movie that consists of three scenes: Intro, Body, and Conclusion.

Your movie will first play the Intro scene from beginning to end, then the Body, and finally the Conclusion (at which point the movie will stop). Keep in mind, however, that you can also reorder these scenes to change their flow.

The only function of scenes is to help you organize content. A timeline that spans multiple scenes is still considered a single unit: This is especially important to remember if you're working with and updating variables in a timeline (for more on this, see Chapter 12, "Understanding ActionScript"). Scenes cannot be used inside the timeline of a symbol.

Scene Management

Scene management can encompass (among other things) adding and deleting scenes, renaming scenes, and changing the order in which scenes appear in the movie—most of which you can accomplish via the Scene panel.

To display the Scene panel:

◆ From the Window menu, choose Scene. The Scene panel will appear (**Figure 10.12**), and the movie's scenes will be listed.

To add a scene, do one of the following:

◆ On the Scene panel, click the Add Scene button.

Or

• From the Insert menu, choose Scene.

Either of these actions will generate a new scene, with the default name Scene appended by a number. The authoring environment will also automatically jump to your newly created scene.

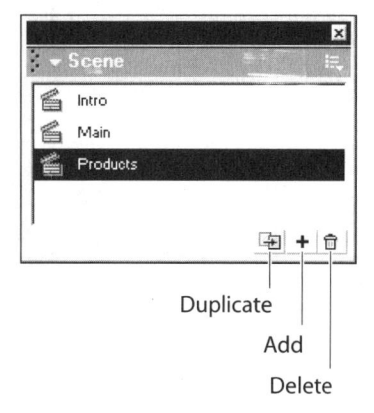

Figure 10.12
The Scene panel.

To delete a scene:

1. On the Scene panel, select the scene you wish to delete from the scene list.

2. Click the Delete Scene button on the Scene panel.

An alert box will ask you to confirm the deletion.

3. Click OK.

Or

1. Go to the scene you wish to delete.

2. From the Insert menu, choose Remove Scene.

An alert box will ask you to confirm the deletion.

3. Click OK.

To rename a scene:

1. From the scene list in the Scene panel, double-click the scene whose name you wish to change.

2. Enter a new name for the scene, then press Return/Enter.

To reorder scenes:

1. From the scene list in the Scene panel, click and hold the name of the scene you'd like to reposition.

2. Drag the scene to a new position in the list, and release (**Figure 10.13**).

   The scenes will now play sequentially in the order they appear in the list.

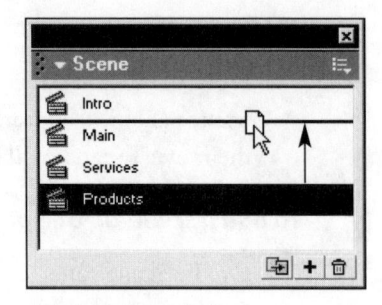

Figure 10.13
Repositioning a scene in the Scene panel changes its play order in the overall movie sequence.

To navigate between scenes, do one of the following:

- From the scene list in the Scene panel, click the name of the scene you wish to navigate to.

  Or

- From the View menu, choose Go To and then specify one of the available scenes from the list.

  The timeline will automatically jump to that scene.

Duplicating scenes

Duplicating a scene allows you to make an exact copy of it—including all frames, layers, animations, and sounds. This enables you to use an existing scene as the starting point for a new one.

To duplicate a scene:

1. From the scene list in the Scene panel, click the name of the scene you wish to duplicate.

2. Press the Duplicate Scene button on the Scene panel.

   The new scene is given a default name and appears on the scene list.

Frames

Frames are at the core of any animation, dictating each segment of time and movement. The total number of frames in your movie, and the speed at which they're played back, together determine your movie's overall length.

Frame Types

Not all frames are created equal; different frame types are designed for different animation tasks. Let's take a look at the various frame types that can exist on the timeline.

Placeholder frames

Placeholder frames are not really frames, but rather rectangular boxes where frames can be placed. They are indicated by the grid on the timeline. Devoid of content, these frames, generated automatically by Flash, make up the majority of the timeline when you begin your Flash project. Although you cannot manually create placeholder frames, they will remain present until you convert them to actual frames. Because your movie needs real frames on at least one layer of the timeline in order to play, it will cease playing once it reaches a point where all layers contain only placeholder frames (**Figure 10.14**).

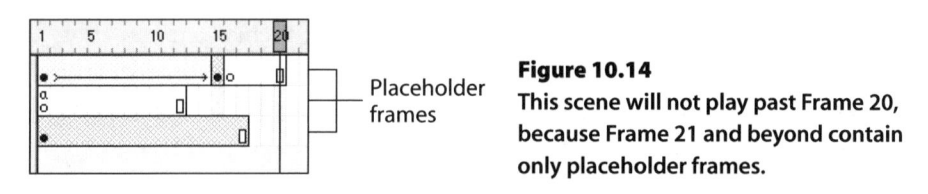

Figure 10.14
This scene will not play past Frame 20, because Frame 21 and beyond contain only placeholder frames.

Keyframes

Any time your wish your animation to undergo a visual change or you want an action to occur, you must use a keyframe at that point on the timeline (**Figure 10.15**). Obviously, frame-by-frame animations require numerous keyframes because you must edit each frame individually. A tweened animation, on the other hand, requires only two keyframes—one to begin the tween and one to end it. Changes that occur between the beginning and ending keyframes are mapped by Flash and thus do not require additional keyframes.

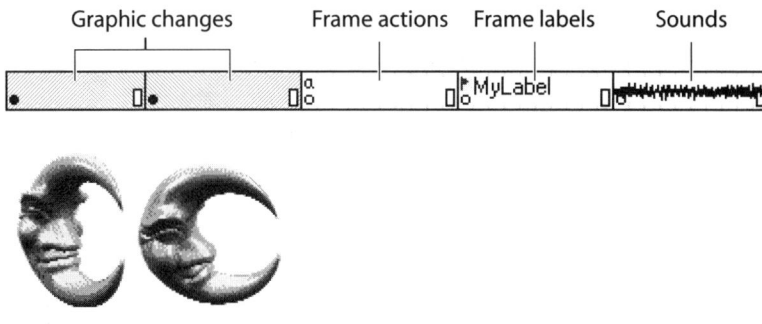

Figure 10.15
Keyframes, identified by a vertical line on the left edge of the frame and a small dot, define where changes occur on the timeline.

Although most keyframes contain content that is visible on the stage, they can also be blank—usually the result of removing a movie element from an animation. Every new project you begin in Flash starts with a blank keyframe on Frame 1 of Layer 1. A keyframe with content visible on the stage is identified by a solid black dot; a blank keyframe is identified by a hollow dot; and a keyframe with an attached action is identified with a small *a*.

Regular frames

Regular frames always follow keyframes and contain the same content as the last keyframe on the same layer. Confused? Let us explain.

A keyframe on the timeline denotes a change; the regular frames that follow a keyframe determine the duration of that change. Let's say you have a movie element that you want to appear in the middle of the stage at the beginning of your movie: You would need to place that element on a keyframe at Frame 1. If you also want it to remain in the middle of the stage until it jumps to the top-left corner at Frame 11, you would make Frames 2 through 10 regular frames (since the element does not move or change as these frames play), and then add a keyframe at Frame 11 to specify a change in the element's position on the stage (**Figure 10.16**).

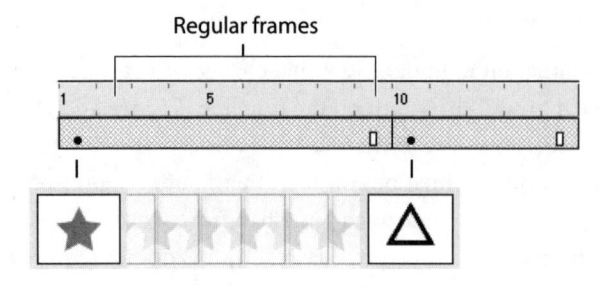

Figure 10.16
Regular frames always follow keyframes, and contain the same content as the last keyframe on the same layer.

A keyframe and the span of regular frames that follow it are known as a *keyframe sequence*. The timeline can contain any number of keyframe sequences. If the keyframe in a sequence contains graphical content that is visible on the stage, the regular frames that follow it will appear gray. If the keyframe in a sequence contains no graphical content, the regular frames that follow it appear white (**Figure 10.17**).

Contains content visible on the stage

Does not contain graphical content

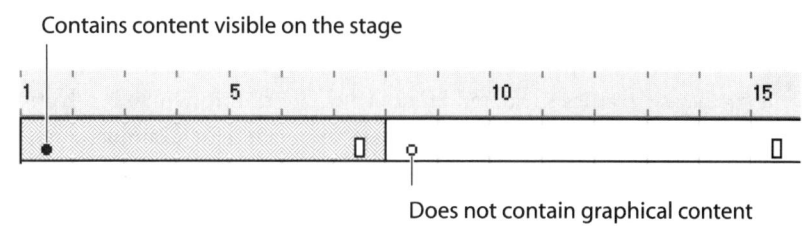

Figure 10.17
If the keyframe in a sequence contains content visible on the stage, the regular frames that follow in the sequence are shaded gray. If the keyframe contains no content visible on the stage, the regular frames that follow are white.

Tweened frames

Tweened frames are always part of a tween sequence consisting of two keyframes and any number of frames in between. The frames between the two keyframes represent computer-calculated graphics.

You can perform two types of tweening with Flash: *motion tweening* and *shape tweening*. You use motion tweening to alter the size, position, rotation, and other aspects of symbols, groups, or text blocks in your animation. You use shape tweening to morph one simple shape into another—for example, smoothly transforming a red circle into a blue square or the letter *T* into the letter *I* (**Figure 10.18**). Shape tweening only works with simple shapes such as lines and vector shapes, not with symbols or groups. If text is to be used in a shape tween, you must first break it apart, then place each letter you plan to tween on a separate layer.

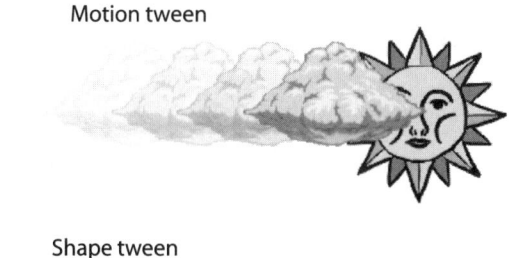

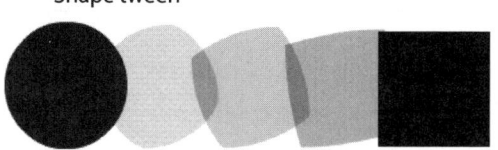

Motion tween

Shape tween

Figure 10.18
Motion tweening controls an element's size, position, rotation, and so on. Shape tweening morphs one simple shape into another.

If you plan to simultaneously tween multiple elements in a scene, each tween must be placed on its own layer. In other words, you can't tween separate movie elements on the same layer at the same time.

A motion-tweened sequence is identified by two keyframes separated by intermediate frames with a black arrow and light-blue background. A shape-tweened sequence is identified by two keyframes separated by intermediate frames with a black arrow and light-green background. A problem in a tween sequence—for example, a tween that lacks a starting or ending keyframe—is indicated by a dashed line (**Figure 10.19**).

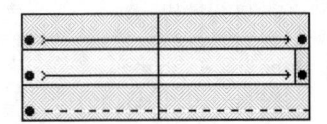

Figure 10.19
A motion tween (top layer), a shape tween (middle), and a problem tween (bottom).

Working with Frames

Now that you're familiar with the various frame types and how to use them in creating animations, let's look at the ways you can work with them on the timeline. For more information about using frames, see "Creating Animation" later in this chapter.

Selecting frames

MX ALERT
Before you can move, duplicate, or change a frame, you must first select it. When a frame is selected, the playhead automatically moves to that frame and the contents of its layers appear on the stage.

To select an individual frame:

- Click a frame once to select it.

    The frame will appear highlighted. The selected frame becomes the current frame, and any commands you enter pertaining to frames will affect it.

To select a range of frames:

- Click the first frame you want to be part of the range, drag to the last frame you want included, and then release.

    All selected frames will appear highlighted. You can now move, delete, and duplicate them as a whole.

To select a keyframe or tween sequence:

- Double-click once on any frame that is part of the sequence.

    The sequence will appear highlighted (**Figure 10.20**). You can now move, delete, and duplicate the sequence.

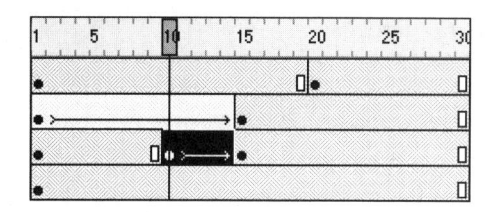

Figure 10.20
A frame sequence is highlighted to indicate that it is currently selected.

Moving and duplicating frames

By moving frames, you can edit the points where changes occur along the timeline, such as the starting and ending points of frame sequences or when frame actions occur.

By duplicating frames, you can use their content elsewhere on the timeline without having to re-create that content.

To move or duplicate frames:

1. Select a frame, range of frames, or frame sequence.

2. Click and drag the selected frames to a new location on the timeline, then release (**Figure 10.21**).

3. To duplicate the frame or range of frames at a new location, hold down the Alt key (Windows) or the Option key (Macintosh) while you drag. As you drag, a plus sign (+) will appear next to the cursor indicating that you are in the process of duplicating the selected frames.

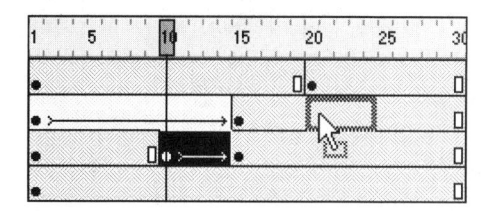

Figure 10.21
Drag selected frames to their new location, and release.

Extending or shortening a frame sequence

Selecting while holding down the Ctrl key (Windows) or the Command key (Windows), then moving the beginning or end frame of a keyframe sequence, alters the length of the sequence on the timeline and thus the duration of its content in the overall animation. As you drag, a double-headed arrow will appear next to the cursor indicating that you are in the process of shortening or lengthening a frame sequence.

Selecting, then moving the beginning or end frame of a tween sequence, determines not only its length on the timeline and its duration in the overall animation, but also how many regular frames the tweening process generates between the beginning and ending keyframes.

Adding and inserting regular frames

Adding or inserting frames at any point along a layer changes the timeline position of all frames on that layer located to the right of the added or inserted frame(s).

To add regular frames to the timeline:

1. Select a placeholder frame on the timeline.

2. Choose Insert > Frame.

Regular frames are added until the selected placeholder frame is reached.

To insert regular frames within an existing range of frames:

1. Select a single frame, range of frames, or frame sequence within an existing range of frames.

2. Choose Insert > Frame.

The same number of frames you selected will be inserted onto the timeline; the previously selected frames will be moved to the right of the newly inserted ones.

Adding keyframes

As mentioned earlier, you use keyframes on the timeline to define when changes occur in your animation. Thus, your animation is likely to contain numerous keyframes. When you add a keyframe to a layer, you have the choice of adding a normal or blank keyframe. When adding a normal keyframe, any graphical content (instances of symbols, text elements, and so on) included in the last keyframe on the same layer is automatically duplicated in the new keyframe. Adding a blank keyframe places a point on the timeline where that layer's contents are no longer visible Normal keyframes are used to signify a change in an animation while keeping the content of the animation visible. With a blank keyframe, the change is the actual removal of content (**Figure 10.22**).

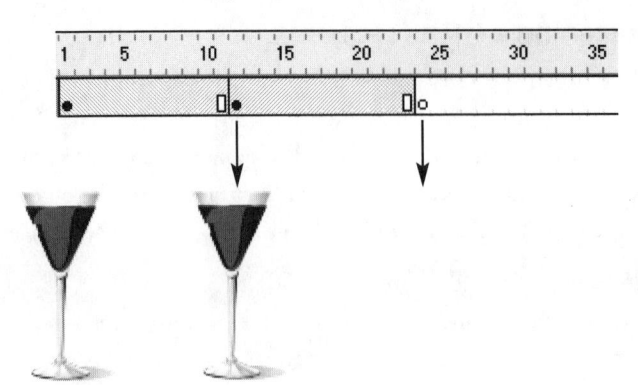

Figure 10.22
The difference between adding a normal keyframe and a blank keyframe.

To add a keyframe to the timeline:

1. Select a placeholder or regular frame on the timeline.

2. Choose Insert > Keyframe or Insert > Blank Keyframe to add a keyframe.

   If the frame you selected is a placeholder frame, regular frames will be added up to the point of the newly created keyframe. If the selected frame is a regular frame, Flash simply converts it to a regular or blank keyframe—as you specify.

To add a range of keyframes to the timeline:

1. Select a range of frames or a frame sequence.

2. Choose Modify > Frames > Convert to Keyframes or Convert to Blank Keyframes.

   A range of keyframes will be added.

Removing frames

Removing frames at any point on a layer changes the timeline position of all frames on that layer located to the right of the frame(s) you remove.

To remove frames:

1. Select a single frame, range of frames, or frame sequence.

2. Choose Insert > Remove Frame.

Reversing frames

Reversing frames will invert the timeline order of a selected span of frames, causing the graphical content of the selected frames to play in reverse.

To reverse frames:

1. Select a sequence of at least two frames.

2. Choose Modify > Frames > Reverse.

Adding frame actions

Frame actions enable your movie to perform a specified action when the timeline reaches a particular frame during playback. For more information, see Chapter 12, "Getting Started with ActionScript."

To add a frame action:

1. Right-click (Windows) or Control-click (Macintosh) on the keyframe to which you would like to add an action, and select Actions from the menu that appears.

   The Actions panel will appear next.

2. Click the Add Action button to add any actions to this frame, then close the Action panel.

   The keyframe display now includes a small *a* to indicate that an action has been assigned to it.

Labels and comments

You use frame labels in Flash to identify a particular keyframe in your movie. This is especially useful when assigning frame or button actions to certain frames in your movie (see Chapter 12, "Getting Started with ActionScript").

Say you've set up your movie so that several buttons, when clicked, begin playing your movie at Frame 35. However, you later decide that you want to delete five frames from the beginning of your movie. Unfortunately, this means that the content which once began at Frame 35 will now begin at Frame 30—but the buttons you set up earlier will still go to Frame 35 when the viewer clicks them—not the result you were looking for. Using frame labels allows you to get around this problem.

By assigning a label—for example, MyLabel—to Frame 35 and setting all of those button-clicks to begin playing your movie from that label, you can add and delete frames as needed: Regardless of how many scenes are in your movie, those button clicks will always point to MyLabel.

Frame comments allow you to write notes, or *comments*, in frames of your movie—a good way to remind yourself of the thought process that informed some portion of your movie's timeline.

Because frame labels are exported with your final movie, they can affect its overall file size (albeit minimally). For this reason, you should use short, descriptive labels. Frame comments, in contrast, are not exported, so you can include as much information in them as you want.

Wherever display room on the timeline permits, frame labels are identified by a small red flag followed by the label name, and frame comments are identified by two green forward slashes followed by the comment text (**Figure 10.23**). Where room on the timeline does not permit, only icons appear, with no accompanying text.

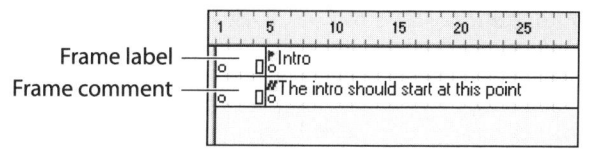

Figure 10.23
A frame label and a frame comment.

To add a label or comment to a keyframe:

1. Click the keyframe once to select it.

2. Choose Window > Properties.

The Property inspector will appear.

3. In the Frame Label box (**Figure 10.24**), enter the text you would like to use as a label for this keyframe. Entering two forward slashes (//) prior to entering any text creates a frame comment instead.

4. Press Return/Enter.

The label or comment will appear on the timeline.

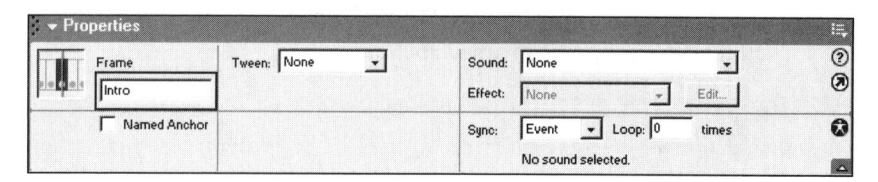

Figure 10.24
The Frame Label box on the Property inspector.

TIP *If you pause your cursor over a frame on the timeline, a "tooltip" appears with a description of the frame type. If the frame you pause the cursor over contains a label or comment, the label name or comment text is displayed.*

Named Anchors

MX ALERT By identifying a keyframe on the main timeline as a *named anchor* (in essence, an enhanced frame label), you make it possible for Web browsers to recognize those points as regular HTML pages. This means that viewers can navigate Flash movies using the Back/Forward buttons of their Web browsers—just as they would a typical Web page. As the viewer interacts with your movie, Flash records his or her navigation path—so that the user can then employ the browser's Back/Forward buttons to move backward or forward in the movie.

In addition, named anchors make it possible to bookmark keyframes—which means users can quickly return to a given point in a Flash movie simply by clicking that bookmark (again, just like a typical HTML page). Both of these capabilities address issues that had caused some companies to limit the use of Flash on their sites.

NOTE *Due to issues beyond Macromedia's control, Named anchors do not work on Macintosh-based browsers.*

As you'll soon see, once you've assigned a frame label to a keyframe, it's easy to create a named anchor.

To create a named anchor:

1. Assign a label to a keyframe, as described in the previous section.

    This will cause the Named Anchor checkbox underneath the frame label box to become selectable.

2. Check this box to create an anchor (**Figure 10.25**).

    The frame label icon on the keyframe changes to a neat little anchor icon, indicating the existence of a named anchor.

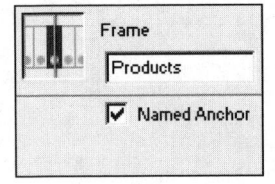

    Figure 10.25
    The Named Anchor checkbox only becomes selectable if a keyframe has been given a frame label.

3. Choose File > Publish Settings to open the Publish Settings dialog box.

4. Select the HTML tab and choose the Flash with Named Anchors template (**Figure 10.26**).

    Although your movie doesn't need to be published (exported) immediately, when it is, it must be published using this template in order for named anchors within your movie to function. For more information about publishing a movie, see Chapter 20, "Publishing."

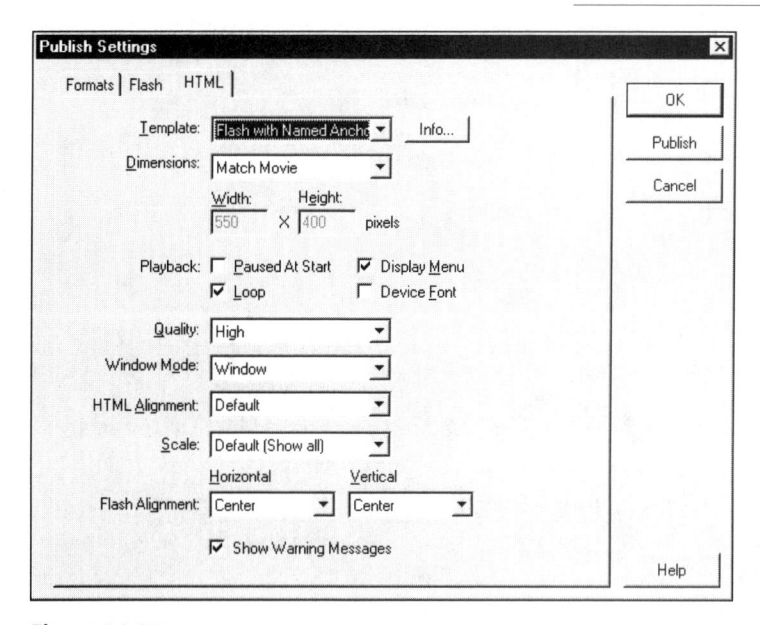

Figure 10.26
The Flash with Named Anchors template must be used for named anchors to work in your published movie.

NOTE *When a user navigates to a keyframe containing an anchor, the name of that frame label/anchor will appear in the address bar of the viewer's browser—so choose your frame label names wisely.*

TIP *Since many developers use scenes to separate content within a movie, you can enable Flash to automatically insert a named anchor at the beginning of each new scene. To do this, open the Preferences dialog box (Edit > Preferences…), select the General tab, and then check the Named Anchor on Scene option.*

Onion-Skinning

If you've ever watched a pencil-and-paper animator, you've probably noticed that he or she customarily works with a pencil in one hand and a couple of pages, or eventual frames, of the animation in the other. While drawing on the current frame, the animator will flip among frames that precede and follow it to get an idea how the drawing sequence will emulate movement when it's eventually played. Flash provides similar functionality in the form of *onion-skinning*, which allows you to view and edit multiple frames simultaneously.

To view multiple frames using onion-skinning:

- Click the Onion Skin button (**Figure 10.27**).

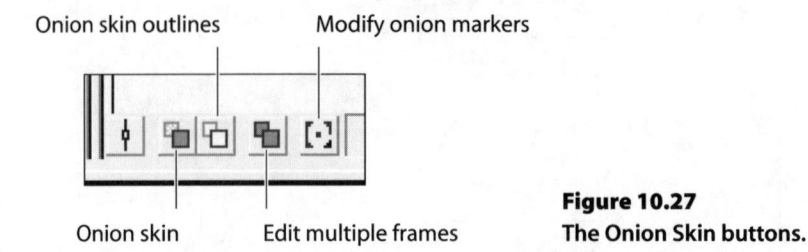

Onion skin outlines · Modify onion markers · Onion skin · Edit multiple frames

Figure 10.27
The Onion Skin buttons.

This brings up a set of onion-skinning markers, which appear next to the playhead on the timeline (for more information about onion-skinning markers see "Onion-Skinning Markers" a little later in the chapter). The content of the frames between these two markers now appears on the stage, some before the current frame and some after (**Figure 10.28**). The current frame is the one over which the playhead is positioned—and in this mode, it is the only one whose contents are editable. Content on uneditable frames appears dimmed in color. Dragging the playhead allows you to apply onion-skinning to other frames.

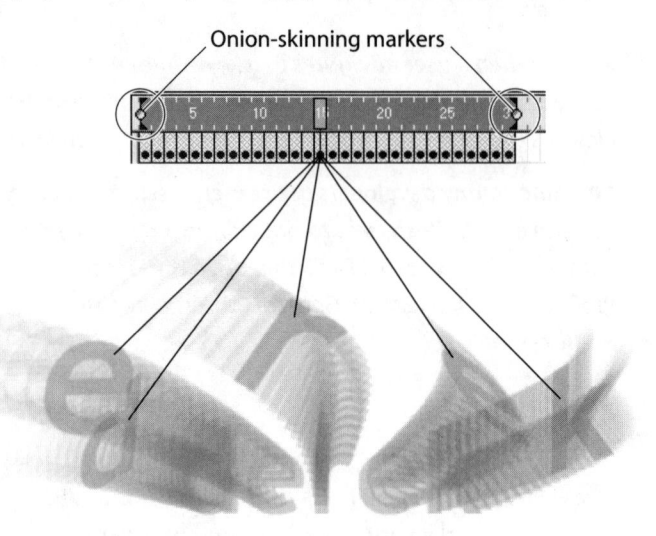

Onion-skinning markers

Figure 10.28
When onion-skinning is turned on, the stage reflects the content of multiple frames, with the current frame's content the most boldly defined.

> **TIP** You will not be able to see content on currently locked or hidden layers when using onion-skinning. Thus, you can lock or hide layers to specify which content is visible and editable when onion-skinning.

To view onion-skinned frames as outlines:

- Click the Onion Skin Outlines button.

    This option works much like the Onion Skin button, except that content on all but the current frame appears as outlines. You can assign a different outline color to each frame to help identify which layer's content needs to be edited.

Editing multiple frames

Normally, you can only edit content on the current frame when using onion-skinning; however, by making multiple frames editable during onion-skinning, you can select, move, rotate, resize, and otherwise alter the content of multiple frames simultaneously. This is a great feature for moving entire sections of content on the stage (**Figure 10.29**). For example, if you wanted to move a layer's content by 50 pixels, you could manually place the playhead at a frame, move the layer's contents, move the playhead forward a frame, move the layer's contents, and so forth. However, this is a tedious process as well as a waste of time. By editing multiple frames simultaneously, you can move everything on the layer across multiple frames simultaneously.

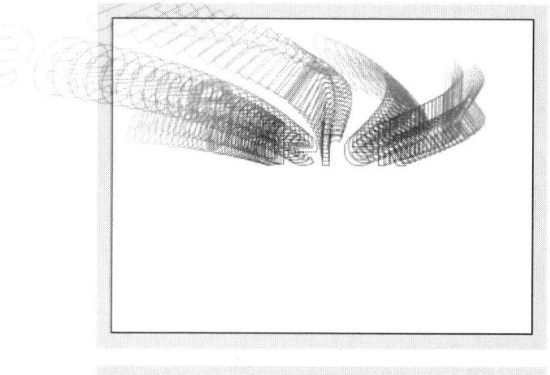

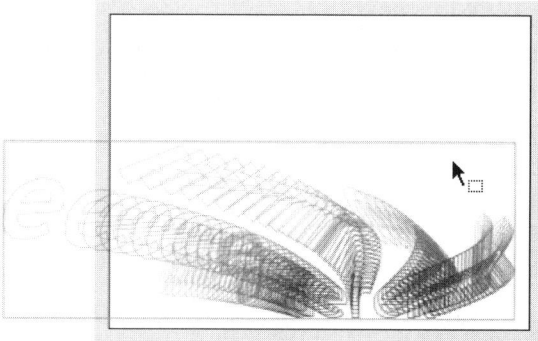

Figure 10.29
The Edit Multiple Frames feature lets you edit the content of multiple frames simultaneously—for example, moving the content on several at once, as shown here.

To make multiple frames editable:

1. Unlock and make visible all layers whose content you wish to move.

2. Click the Edit Multiple Frames button.

   All content on unlocked and visible frames between the onion-skinning markers becomes editable, meaning you can move, rotate, and otherwise edit it as a whole.

Onion-skinning markers

You use the onion-skinning markers to determine the range of frames that are onion-skinned. Usually, the markers maintain their positions relative to the playhead; however, you can also anchor them while the playhead moves. You can adjust onion-skinning markers manually or via the Modify Onion Markers pop-up menu.

To move the onion-skinning markers manually:

- Click a marker and drag it to its new position, then release.

  You can't move either marker past the position of the playhead.

To modify the onion-skinning markers:

- Click the Modify Onion Markers button.

  This brings up the Modify Onion Markers pop-up menu, which includes the following options:

  Always Show Markers. Normally, onion-skinning markers only appear when onion-skinning is turned on. This option causes them to be displayed even when it's not.

  Anchor Onion. This option anchors, or locks, the onion-skinning markers to their current position—that is, they remain stationary rather than retain their positions relative to the playhead.

  Onion 2. This option lets you quickly set onion-skinning markers two frames before and two frames after the current frame (playhead position).

  Onion 5. This option lets you quickly set onion-skinning markers five frames before and five frames after the current frame.

  Onion All. This option onion-skins all the frames in the current scene. Obviously, this works best if you're viewing a limited number of layers; lock or hide certain layers to make them invisible.

Creating Animation

In this section, we'll look at the processes for creating three simple types of animations: frame by frame, motion tweened, and shape tweened. The techniques you'll learn here can be used to create animations on a graphic or movie clip symbol's timeline, as well as your movie's main timeline.

Planning Your Project

Processor Considerations

Hollywood has a way of distorting reality. Just as teenage girls drooled at the thought of being trapped on a sinking Titanic *with Leonardo DiCaprio, anyone who regularly uses a computer has surely salivated over the speed at which they run in the movies. In Hollywood's vision of the world, every home computer is connected to the Net; you never have to boot your machine; and that desktop box contains enough power to coordinate a shuttle mission, find a cure for cancer, and crunch out the graphics for* Jurassic Park—*all at the same time!*

*Well, here's the cruel reality: Processor speed—which today can range from 400 MHz to faster than 2 GHz—is a major factor in computer performance: What takes 1 second to show up using a 2-GHz processor could take 10 seconds or longer with a slower processor (**Figure 10.30**). As you can imagine, this is a major factor in animation. On slow computers, your animated movie will probably end up looking fairly choppy. And you can forget about those cool motion effects. All is not lost, however: Even though you can't anticipate every possibility in creating your movie, you can take some steps to minimize the effect slower machines will have on your movie's playback. For starters, you can pay attention to the following guidelines:*

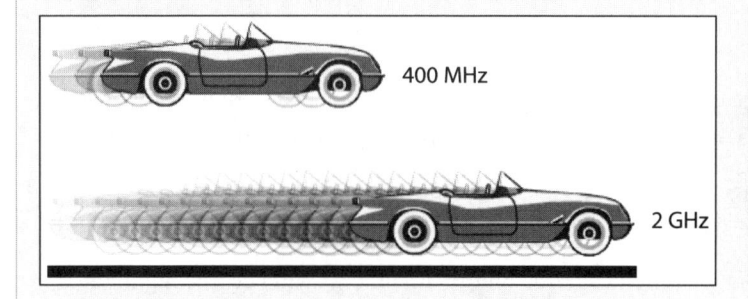

Figure 10.30
The speed at which your presentation plays will vary, depending on the processor speed of a viewer's computer.

- **Avoid animating too many things at once.** *By too many, we mean primarily large objects that require a lot of screen space to move. Although it's tempting to animate everything at once, all you need to do is play your movie on a slow computer to realize that a little self-control is worth it—that is, if you can stay awake long enough to watch your movie play!*

(continued on next page)

> **Planning Your Project** *continued*
>
> - **Animate in the smallest area possible.** Not surprisingly, it takes less processing power to animate a small image than it does to animate a large one. You can usually animate several small elements simultaneously without too much display trouble. So, instead of making that monster movie element rotate, you might make it smaller and do something else creative with it. And if you do decide to animate a large movie element, avoid animating any other elements on the screen at the same time. This will maximize the system resources available to handle the large object.
> - **Avoid tweening too many objects at once.** Although tweening can be a real time-saver in developing your Flash project, it eats up substantial system resources. Use tweening all you can; just be sure not to use too much of it at once.
>
> By following these guidelines, you can avoid overtaxing a slow processor.

Creating a Frame-by-Frame Animation

Creating frame-by-frame animations usually entails numerous keyframes, each with different content. You can use frame-by-frame animation in conjunction with other types of animation; you just need to place each on a separate layer.

To create a simple frame-by-frame animation:

1. Create a new Flash document by choosing File > New.

   Your new Flash document will initially include a single layer with one keyframe.

2. Click the Text tool on the Drawing toolbar.

3. With the Property inspector open, choose the Static Text option, then select any available font, choose 48 as the size, and specify whatever color you wish.

4. Click the stage to start a text label, and type an uppercase *H* in the lower left corner of the stage.

5. Select the next placeholder frame on the timeline (it will become highlighted), then choose Insert > Keyframe.

   A keyframe will be inserted on Frame 2 that initially contains the same content as Frame 1 (an uppercase *H*).

6. Click the Arrow tool on the Drawing toolbar, then select the text label (if it's not already selected).

7. With the *H* selected, hold down the Shift key and press the up-arrow key three times to move the text element upward.

8. Select the Text tool again, place its insertion point just after the *H* you just moved, and type an uppercase *E*.

9. Repeat Steps 5 through 8, selecting and moving all the letters in the new keyframe, until you have completed the word *HELLO* (**Figure 10.31**).

You can then move the playhead on the timeline to see your animation spring to life.

Figure 10.31
The entire sequence of our frame-by-frame text animation.

Obviously, this is a simple animation that merely demonstrates the frame-by-frame process. Some frame-by-frame animations consist of many layers with numerous elements requiring movement at each keyframe. The frame-by-frame video tutorial on the CD covers this same animation, with a few additional techniques thrown in.

TIP *If you want your animation to loop, place a Go To action at the end of the animation that tells it to Go To and Play Frame 1 of the same scene. For more on this action, see Chapter 12 "Getting Started with ActionScript."*

Creating a Shape-Tweened Animation

Shape tweening, or *morphing*, describes the process of transforming one simple shape into another over a specified time interval. Flash lets you tween the shape, color, transparency, size, and location of vector graphic elements.

Flash normally attempts to tween two shapes in the most logical manner without any additional input from you. However, because each shape has unique curves and corners, Flash's calculations will not always produce the results you were looking for. When you need more control over a shape tween transformation, you can use *shape hints* to select common points on the beginning and ending shapes, which will correspond to each other in the shape tween.

You cannot shape-tween symbols, groups, or bitmaps—only simple shapes and text (and the latter only if you've broken it apart first; see Chapter 4, "Text"). You can, however, *motion*-tween symbols, groups, and text. Although you can tween more than one shape at a time on a layer, you'll get better results by using separate layers for individual tweens.

Next we'll show you how to create a simple animation of a box that tweens into the letter *V*. You'll learn how to tween not only shapes, but color and location as well. A little later, we'll look at how to use shape hints to gain more control over the actual tween. A video tutorial on the CD demonstrates how we put together this animation.

To create a shape-tweened animation:

1. Create a new Flash document by choosing File > New.

   Your new Flash document initially includes a single layer with one keyframe.

2. Click the Rectangle tool on the Drawing toolbar.

3. Draw a square with no outline and a red fill color in the middle of the stage.

4. Select the placeholder frame on Frame 25 of the same layer on the timeline (it appears highlighted), and then choose Insert > Blank Keyframe.

   A blank keyframe is inserted at Frame 25.

5. With the playhead on Frame 25, select the Text tool on the Drawing toolbar.

6. With the Property inspector open, choose a bold font (we chose Arial Black), enter *150* as the size, and choose "blue" as the color.

7. Click somewhere on the upper right corner of the stage to create a text label, and type a capital *V*.

8. Select the Arrow tool; the text you just typed will be automatically selected.

9. Choose Modify > Break Apart (perform this action *twice*) to turn the text into a shape (**Figure 10.32**).

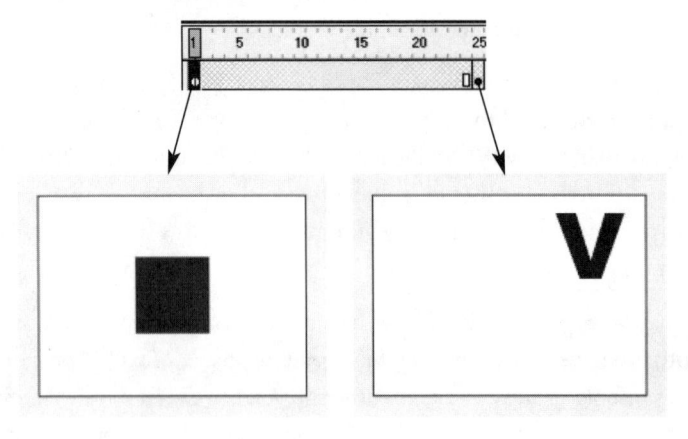

Figure 10.32 The beginning and ending keyframes of our example shape-tween sequence.

10. Click on Frame 1 to automatically move the playhead back to that frame.

11. With the timeline at Frame 1, open the Property inspector if it isn't already open.

12. Choose Shape from the Tween drop-down menu, then choose from two additional options:

    - **Blend Type.** This lets you set the way the shapes' curves and corners are blended: Distributive works best for blending smooth and curvy shapes; angular works best for shapes with sharp corners and straight sides.

    - **Easing.** Easing is all about acceleration and deceleration. In real life, motion rarely occurs at a constant speed. Using Flash's easing feature, you can make a tweened animation move faster or slower at its beginning than at its end. Easing In causes the animation to move slower at the beginning of the tween, and Easing Out causes it to move faster at the beginning of the tween. If you place the Easing slider in the middle, motion speed will be constant for the duration of the tween (**Figure 10.33**).

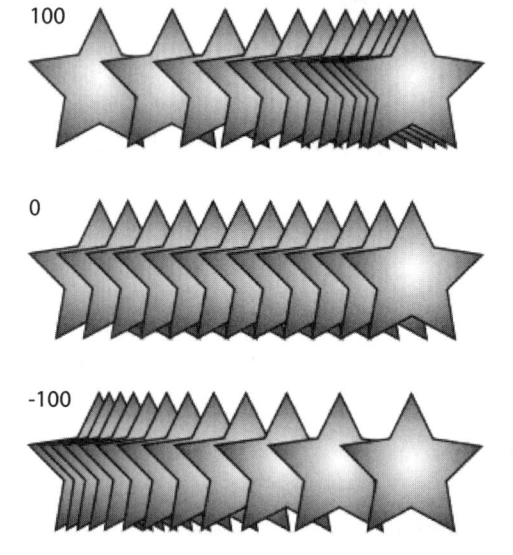

Figure 10.33
The effect that different Easing settings have on a tweened animation.

13. Set Blend Type to Angular, and leave the Easing slider at its initial setting.

    The timeline will now reflect your shape tween. By moving the playhead back and forth, you can see the tweened animation you just created. Note that the actual shape, and its color and position, are all tweened.

TIPS *After creating a tweened animation sequence, you can move the beginning or ending keyframe to lengthen or shorten the sequence, and Flash will automatically recalculate the tween sequence.*

*If you add a keyframe to the middle of the current tween sequence, and place a shape on the newly created keyframe, the result will be two distinct tween sequences (**Figure 10.34**).*

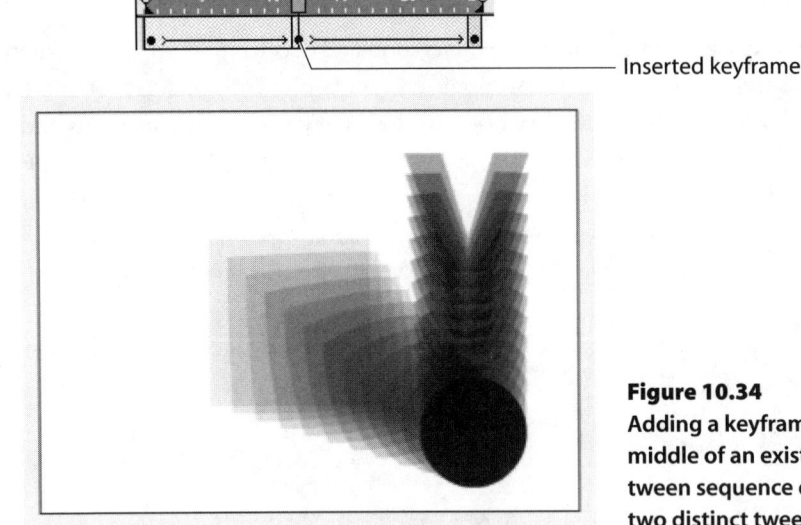

— Inserted keyframe

Figure 10.34
Adding a keyframe in the middle of an existing tween sequence creates two distinct tweens.

Shape hints

Even though our example shape tween appears to work adequately, Flash's *shape hints* settings give you even more control over the way your shapes blend onscreen.

Shape hints are small dots that are placed on beginning and ending shapes in a shape tween in order to specify that a particular point in the beginning shape should morph into a corresponding point in the end shape. For example, if you want the top-left corner of the beginning shape to morph/tween into the *bottom-left* corner of the ending shape, you would need to use a shape hint because Flash will otherwise automatically attempt to morph the top-left of the beginning shape to the top-left of the ending shape.

You can add as many as 26 shape hints, which Flash labels *a–z*, per tween. Although it's not absolutely necessary, it works best to position them in counterclockwise sequence, starting from the upper-left corner of the shapes. Flash is designed to understand this order with greater accuracy.

Chapter 10 Using Animation to Build Movement

To add shape hints to a shape tween:

1. Place the playhead on Frame 1.

This is where the first keyframe of our tween is located; shape hints are always added on the first keyframe of a tween.

2. Choose Modify > Shape > Add Shape Hint.

This places a shape hint labeled *a* on your initial shape (our red square).

3. Click and drag the shape hint to the side or corner of the shape you wish to use as a reference.

For our demonstration, move the shape hint to the upper left corner of the square.

4. Place the playhead on Frame 25.

This is where the last keyframe of our tween is located. The shape hint labeled *a* appears on the shape.

5. Click and drag the shape hint to the side or corner of the shape you wish to correspond with the point you marked on the first shape. For our demonstration, move the shape hint to the upper left corner of the *V*.

You can move the playhead any time you wish to test a shape hint's effect on a tween.

6. Repeat Steps 1 through 5 until shape hints appear on the beginning and ending shapes, as shown in **Figure 10.35**.

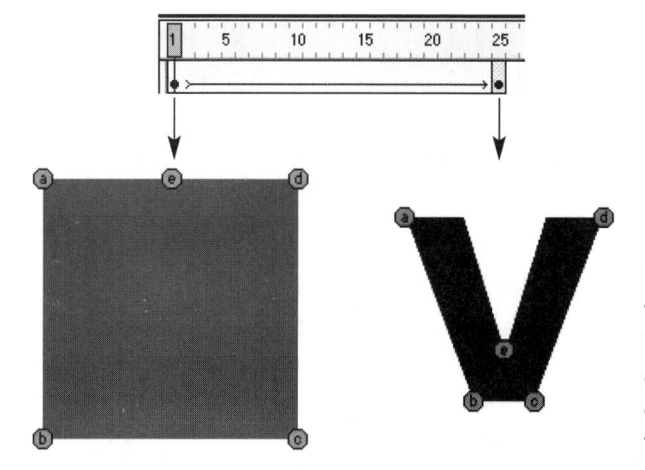

Figure 10.35
This graphic shows the location of shape hints on the beginning and ending keyframes of the tween sequence.

347

TIPS *Even though it may seem like more work, you should add a shape hint to the beginning shape, set its corresponding point on the end shape, go back to the beginning shape and add another shape hint, set its corresponding point on the end shape, and so on. You'll get unpredictable results if you add several hints to the beginning shape before setting corresponding points on the ending shape.*

Place your shape hints in a logical order—that is, with each new shape hint positioned as close as possible, in a clockwise position, to the one that precedes it. Careless placement can produce unpredictable results (defeating their purpose).

To remove a shape hint:

- Click and drag it off the stage.

    The labels of any other shape hints used for this tween will be updated to reflect the deletion.

To remove all shape hints:

- Place the playhead at the beginning keyframe of a tween sequence, and choose Modify > Shape > Remove All Hints.

    Only the shape hints applied to that tween will be removed.

To display or hide shape hints:

- Place the playhead at the beginning or ending keyframe of a tween sequence, and choose View > Show Shape Hints.

    This option toggles the onscreen display of shape hints in a tween.

Creating a Motion-Tweened Animation

Whereas shape tweening allows you to morph simple shapes, motion tweening lets you tween symbols, groups, and text blocks. With the exception of morphing, you can accomplish pretty much the same things with motion tweening as you can with shape tweening. With motion tweening, you can tween size, skew, location, rotation, color, and transparency of symbols and groups—all of which allow you to create many of the great Flash transitions you see on the Web these days. You can also use a motion tween in conjunction with a path (line) to create an object that is not only tweened but follows the shape of the line as well (see "Motion Tweening Along a Path" later in this chapter for more information).

In the following demonstration, we'll create a simple animation of a ball whose size, location, rotation, and transparency all change. A bit later, you'll learn how to add a motion path so that the ball can appear to bounce down a street in a nonlinear fashion. The accompanying CD includes a video tutorial that demonstrates how this animation was put together.

To create a motion-tweened animation:

1. Create a new Flash document by choosing File > New.

   Your new Flash document will initially include a single layer with one keyframe.

2. Click the Oval tool on the Drawing toolbar.

3. Draw a medium-size red circle, with no outline, in the lower left corner of the stage.

4. Click the Rectangle tool on the Drawing toolbar.

5. Within the red circle you just drew, draw a wide white rectangle with no outline (**Figure 10.36**).

   Figure 10.36
   Draw a wide white rectangle within the circle.

   This will help you to later see how rotation works within a motion tween.

6. Select the placeholder frame on Frame 25 of the timeline, and choose Insert > Frame.

   This inserts 24 regular frames after the keyframe on Frame 1, all of which initially have the same content as that keyframe.

7. Right-click (Windows) or Control-click (Macintosh) the keyframe on Frame 1 to bring up the Timeline menu.

8. From the menu that appears, choose Create Motion Tween.

   Because a motion tween only works with symbol instances, groups, and text blocks, this command automatically converts content of any other type (such as simple shapes) into a symbol instance and adds a new master symbol to the library with the name Tween appended by a number. Because our red ball and white rectangle are simple shapes, Flash converted them to a symbol called Tween 1, and then placed that symbol in the library. Flash then converted what was on the stage into an instance of that symbol. The timeline now shows that a motion-tween sequence exists, but the dotted line indicates that there's a problem with the tween: The reason for this is that so far, we've only defined the *beginning* of the tween. Let's now define the end of it.

9. Move the playhead to Frame 25, which is where we want the tween to end.

10. With the playhead at Frame 25, click the Arrow tool on the Drawing toolbar, then select the red circle on the stage and drag it to the middle right portion of the stage.

This action automatically adds a keyframe to Frame 25, which completes the motion tween.

11. Move the playhead back and forth to view your animation.

Because we want our animation to spin, shrink, disappear, and speed up as it moves from left to right, we'll need to make visual edits first (size and transparency) and then edit the movement of the tween (rotation and easing).

> { **ActionScript** } **TIP** *Movement similar to that produced by tweening can be achieved via ActionScript by repeatedly updating the x and/or y property values of movie clip and button instances. For more information, see Chapter 16, "Using ActionScript in Your Projects."*

To customize a motion tween:

1. Place the playhead at Frame 25.

Let's say that we want our red ball to be smaller in size and completely transparent at this point in the tween sequence.

2. Click the Arrow tool on the Drawing toolbar, and select the red ball on the stage.

3. Choose Modify > Transform > Scale and Rotate to bring up the Scale and Rotate dialog box (**Figure 10.37**).

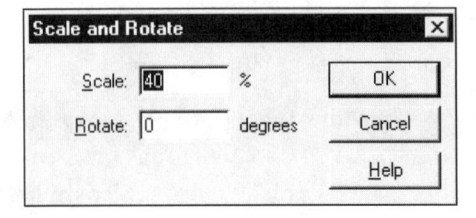

Figure 10.37
Enter *40* as the scale percentage of our red ball, to make it 40 percent of its original size.

4. Enter *40* in the Scale box, then click OK.

   The red ball on Frame 25 will be scaled to 40 percent of its original size. To make it bigger, we could have entered a percentage greater than 100. By moving the playhead back and forth, you can see the effect of this edit. Now let's make our ball transparent on this keyframe.

5. Choose Window > Properties to open the Property inspector if it isn't already open.

6. Choose Alpha from the drop-down menu that appears.

7. Enter *0* in the percentage box and press Enter/Return on the keyboard, or move the slider control all the way to the bottom.

   Though the ball seems to disappear from the stage, it's actually still there—but simply transparent. If you move the playhead back and forth, you can see the effect of this edit.

8. Click the first keyframe of the tween sequence (which in our case is on Frame 1) and enter the following settings into the Property inspector:

   - **Scale.** Checked
   - **Ease.** Push the slider all the way to the bottom, or enter *-100* in the amount box next to the slider control
   - **Rotate.** CW (clockwise)
   - **Times.** 2
   - **Orient to path.** Unchecked
   - **Sync.** Unchecked
   - **Snap.** Checked

   Because these edits only affect the tween's movement properties, you have to move the playhead back and forth to see them. Two things to notice about the red ball in the tween sequence: It rotates clockwise twice between the beginning and ending keyframe, and it moves more slowly at the beginning of the tween than it does at its end. These effects are the result of the Rotate and Ease settings we selected.

Motion-tweening properties

Motion tweens have several adjustable properties, which you can access from the Property inspector (**Figure 10.38**):

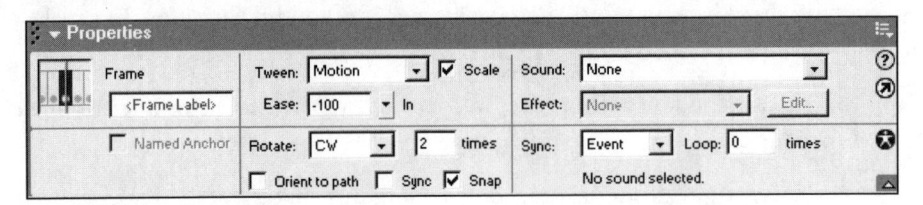

Figure 10.38
The Property inspector, where you can set motion-tweening properties.

- **Tween.** Allows you to choose the type of tweening used.

- **Scale.** If the symbols or groups at the beginning and ending keyframes differ in size, checking this option will tween that size difference. Leaving this option unchecked will cause the group or symbol to remain the same size throughout the tween sequence.

- **Ease.** See the "Creating a Shape-Tweened Animation" section above for an explanation of easing.

- **Rotate.** The options on this drop-down menu let you tween a rotation of the group or symbol between the beginning and ending keyframes:

  None. The group or symbol will not rotate.

  Auto. If you have already manually rotated the group or symbol in one of the keyframes, this option would tween that rotation in the direction that requires the least amount of motion. For example, if the group or symbol has not been rotated in the starting frame of the tween (0-degree rotation) but by the ending frame is rotated to an angle of 270 degrees, Flash will automatically rotate it at angles (degrees) of 359, 358, 357, and so on rather than 1, 2, 3, and so on because the former require less motion to reach 270 degrees.

  CW/CCW (clockwise/counterclockwise). These options let you specify whether to rotate the group or symbol instance in a clockwise or counterclockwise direction. The adjacent box indicates the number of full rotations that will be completed over the duration of the tween.

Chapter 10 Using Animation to Build Movement

- **Orient to path.** This option is only relevant if you are setting a motion tween along a path (see "Motion Tweening Along a Path" later in this section). It allows you to determine whether the baseline of a motion-tweened group or symbol instance remains at the same angle, relative to its path of movement, throughout the tween (**Figure 10.39**).

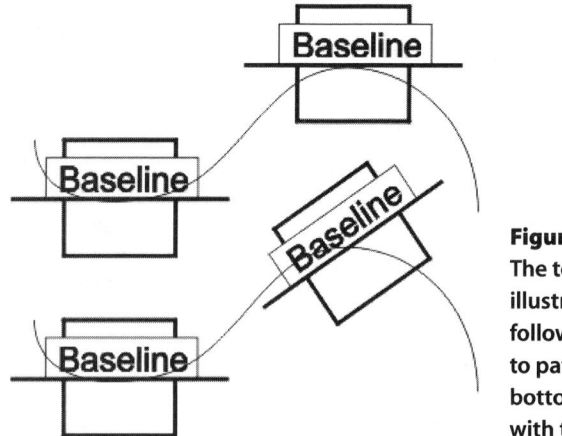

Figure 10.39
The top portion of this graphic illustrates how a motion tween follows a path with the "Orient to path" option turned off; the bottom illustrates how it moves with the option selected.

- **Sync.** See the "Timeline Menu" section earlier in the chapter for an explanation of this option.

- **Snap.** If you're using a motion guide with a tween sequence, you can choose whether objects on the keyframes of the tween 'snap' to the path designated on the motion-guide layer. We'll look more at this feature right now.

Motion tweening along a path

Given a choice, you probably won't want to have every motion-tweened animation move in a straight line from Point A to Point B. Happily, with Flash's *motion-guide layer* feature you can make a motion-tweened animation track along any line you draw or import. You simply link the layer containing your motion-tweened animation to the motion-guide layer—which can contain a line of any length, shape, or twist you desire—and the motion-tweened animation will follow the plot of the line you drew.

Using the motion-tweened ball animation we already created, we'll now add a motion path to it to make it appear as if it's bouncing.

To motion tween along a path:

1. Select the layer that contains our motion-tweened animation, and press the Add Motion Guide button.

Flash will insert a motion-guide layer above the tweened animation layer (**Figure 10.40**). The name of the layer that includes our tweened animation is indented under the name of the motion-guide layer above it, to signify that it is linked to the motion-guide layer. You can link any number of layers to a motion-guide layer.

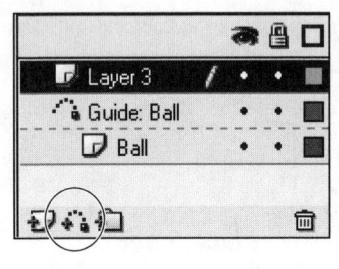

Figure 10.40
Pressing the Add Motion Guide button adds a motion-guide layer directly above the current layer, and automatically links the layers.

2. Click the name of the motion-guide layer to make it the current layer (if it isn't already).

3. On the toolbar, click the Pencil tool.

4. From the Pencil tool options, choose Smooth as the pencil mode.

5. Draw a curvy line on the stage like the one shown in **Figure 10.41**.

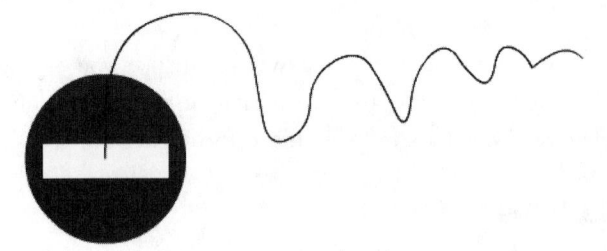

Figure 10.41
Draw a curvy line similar to the one shown here, to create the motion path the tween will follow.

If the "Snap to guide" option is checked for the tween sequence (which it should be by default), the symbol instances on the beginning and ending keyframes will snap to the closest point along the path you just drew.

6. Move the playhead back and forth to see the effect of adding a motion guide.

TIPS *The line drawn on the motion-guide layer can be edited and reshaped like any other line on the stage. Flash will simply recalculate the tween sequence to follow the edited path.*

You can redefine the beginning and ending points of a motion path, so that the tweened image only moves along a portion of the path you originally supplied.

To change the beginning and ending points of a motion tween along a path:

1. Click the Lock Layer column to lock the motion-guide layer.

   This makes it uneditable.

2. Place the playhead at Frame 1, the beginning keyframe of our tween sequence.

3. Click the Arrow tool on the toolbar, then select the center of the instance of the red ball on the stage and drag it to another section of the path.

   The ball instance will snap into place as you drag (**Figure 10.42**). You can place the symbol instance anywhere along the path—if you drag the Arrow tool away from the path, the group or symbol will still snap back onto the path.

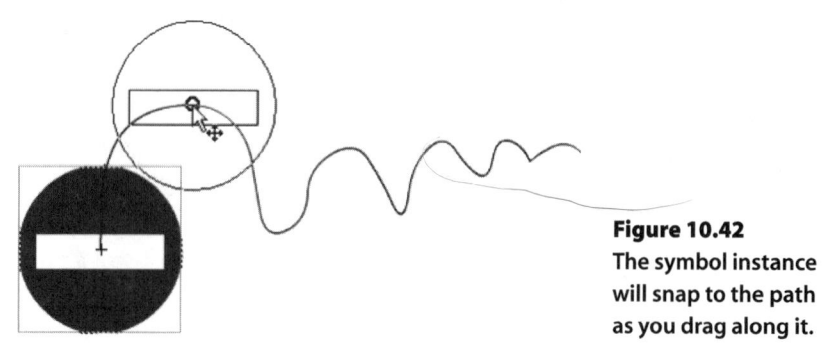

   Figure 10.42
   The symbol instance will snap to the path as you drag along it.

4. Move the playhead to the end keyframe of our tween, then perform the same actions that you did in Step 3.

A motion path is never visible when the movie is exported; if you wish, you can also make it invisible within the authoring environment.

To make a motion path invisible in the authoring environment:

◆ On the motion-guide layer, click the Hide Layer icon.

   Although the motion path is no longer visible onscreen, the linked animations will still follow it.

You can link any number of normal layers containing motion tweens to a single motion-guide layer, if you want all of the motion-tweened elements on the linked layers to share a common path.

To link additional layers to a motion-guide layer:

1. Click and drag the name bar of the layer you wish to link to the motion-guide layer.

A dark-gray line will appear along the bottom, indicating that layer's position relative to the other layers in the stack.

2. Drag the name bar until the gray line showing its position appears just below the name bar of the motion-guide layer itself, then release (**Figure 10.43**).

The layer is now linked to the motion guide

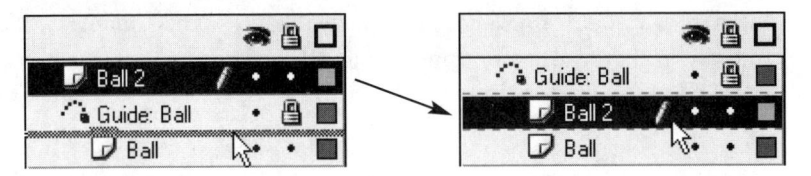

Figure 10.43
Dragging a layer underneath a motion-guide layer links it to the motion-guide layer. Thus, if the layer named Ball 2 has a motion tween on it, it will follow the same path as the layer named Ball.

3. Click and drag the linked layer's name bar to unlink it from the motion-guide layer.

A dark-gray line will appear along the bottom, indicating that layer's position relative to the other layers in the stack.

4. Drag the name bar until the gray line showing its position appears either above the name bar of the motion-guide layer itself or below any other normal layer, then release.

The layer is now unlinked from the motion-guide layer.

Creative Uses for Motion Guides

Motion guides can consist of more than just squiggly lines. In fact, depending on the effect you're trying to achieve, they can be quite complex. We'll look next at some examples of motion paths you may want to use in your projects (**Figure 10.44**). Although Flash's drawing tools are sufficient for creating some of them, others may require the use of an external vector program (such as Macromedia FreeHand or Adobe Illustrator) that allows you to create more sophisticated shapes—which you can then import into a motion-guide layer.

Figure 10.44
Examples of creative motion paths.

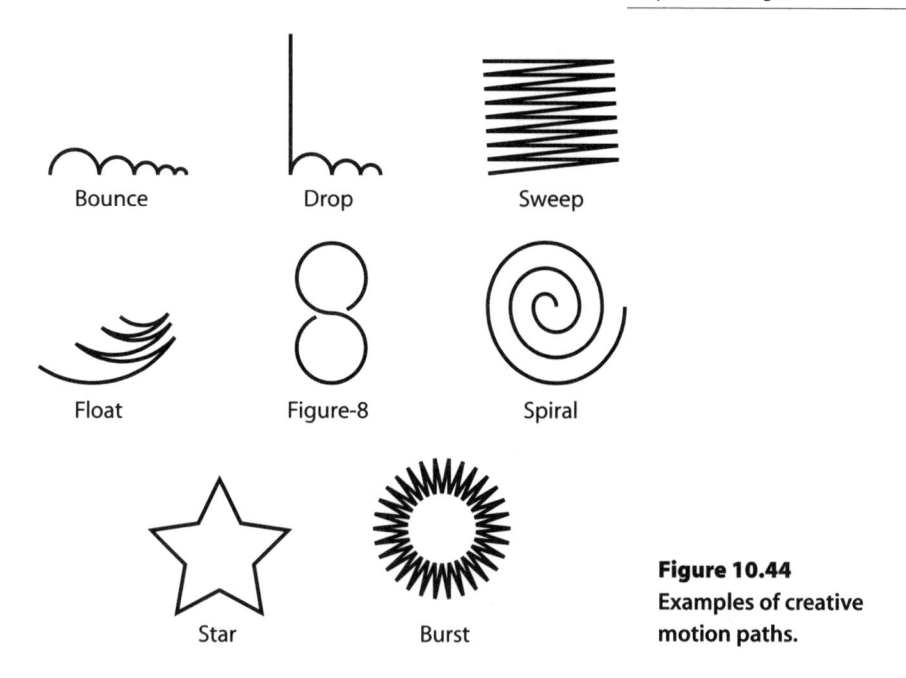

NOTE: *Samples of these motion-guide paths can be found on the accompanying CD in the Chapter 10/Assets folder.*

- **Bounce.** This motion-guide path is useful for emulating the effect of a bouncing ball: The bounce motion is higher at its beginning and then slowly tapers off.
- **Drop.** This is a variation of the Bounce motion-guide path just discussed. It begins with a free-fall drop, which is followed by a few minor bounces to indicate forceful contact.
- **Sweep.** This motion-guide path is useful for animating an object so that it appears to sweep, or zigzag, across an area.
- **Float.** This motion-Guide path emulates the motion of a very light object (like a feather or leaf) floating to the ground.
- **Spiral.** This motion-guide path can be used to emulate the motion of an object emerging from or disappearing into a vortex of some sort.
- **Figure-8.** This motion-guide path is useful for emulating the path of a racecar or figure-skater, or any other object that you usually find following a figure-8 path.
- **Star** or **Burst.** These motion-guide paths can be used to create the effect of elements moving towards and away from a central point.

Putting It All Together

Imagine trying to put together a 5,000-piece puzzle without any kind of visual reference aid. Chances are, that puzzle will soon be put together in the nearest fireplace. Since Flash animations also consist of many pieces, you're likely to get confused without practical references to help you see how it's all supposed to come together.

To that end, we've constructed an example scene that demonstrates most of the tools and principles we've covered thus far; it should also give you a better idea of how to construct your own animation (**Figure 10.45**).

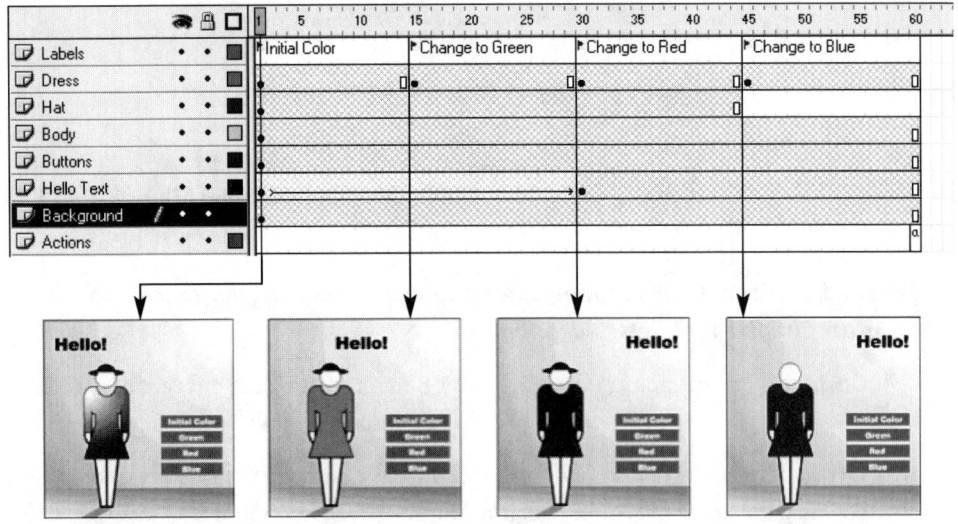

Figure 10.45
Composite animation showing how a typical scene in a project is constructed using layers, keyframes, tweens, frame labels, and actions.

We've included the source files for this animation on the accompanying CD-ROM, so that you can follow along using identical data. Here's what you need to know about our scene:

- This scene is made up of eight layers and 60 frames. The four composite pictures shown in **Figure 10.45** represent the way the animation appears on that frame of the timeline. Each layer has a name that corresponds with its content.

- The stacking order of the layers determines which elements appear above others. For example, the Background layer is meant to appear behind everything else, so it's beneath the other layers (with the exception of the Action layer, which contains no graphic content).

- The Label layer contains four labels, indicated by flags, which highlight portions of the timeline we wished to emphasize. We have assigned Go To actions to the Initial Color, Green, Red, and Blue buttons in the lower right corner of the scene, so that the timeline will jump to the appropriate label when a button is clicked.

- Labels can only be assigned to keyframes. Because the labeled keyframes have no graphic content that appears on the stage, they are represented simply by small red flags on the timeline. Likewise, the regular frames that follow the keyframes on this layer have no content and thus appear white.

- The Dress layer includes four keyframes, each of which represents a place along the timeline where the color of the dress changes. Because these keyframes contain content that appears on the stage (the dress with different colors), they are represented by solid black dots on the timeline. Likewise, the regular frames that follow these keyframes appear light gray to indicate that their content is the same as that contained in the last keyframe on the layer. Thus, regular Frames 2 through 14 of this layer contain the same content as the keyframe on Frame 1; regular Frames 16 to 29 contain the same content as the keyframe on Frame 15; and so on.

- The Hat layer holds the hat graphic. Frame 1 of this layer is where the hat graphic was initially placed. The light-gray regular frames that follow this keyframe indicate that the hat does not change in appearance on the stage until Frame 45, which is a keyframe defining where the hat graphic is removed from the scene. Since this keyframe, on Frame 45, no longer holds any graphic content, the regular frames that follow it on this layer also have no content, and thus appear white.

- The Body layer contains the legs, head, and hands of our model, which are initially placed on the keyframe on Frame 1. This keyframe appears as a solid black dot, indicating that it contains content. These graphic elements remain static throughout the sequence, hence the lack of additional keyframes on this layer. The light-gray regular frames on this layer contain the same content as the initial keyframe on Frame 1.

- The Buttons layer contains the four buttons used in the scene (which we initially placed on Frame 1's keyframe). A solid black dot denotes that this keyframe contains content (our four buttons). These graphic elements do not change during the sequence; thus, no additional keyframes are needed on this layer. The light-gray regular frames on this layer contain the same content as the initial keyframe on Frame 1.

- The Hello Text layer contains the text *Hello*, which is motion tweened between Frames 1 and 30 to move from the left to the right. On the keyframe on Frame 1, the text is positioned where it should be at the beginning of the tween, while the keyframe on Frame 30 is where the text will be at the end of the tween. Because the text does not move or change from that point forward, no additional keyframes are needed on this layer. The light-gray regular frames that appear after the last keyframe on this layer indicate that the content remains the same from Frame 30 (the position of the last keyframe) to Frame 60.

- The Background layer contains our background, which was initially placed on the keyframe on Frame 1. A solid black dot denotes that this keyframe contains content (our background). The background remains unchanged throughout the sequence; thus, no additional keyframes are needed on this layer. The light-gray regular frames on this layer contain the same content as the initial keyframe on Frame 1.

- The Action Layer contains two blank keyframes, one at Frame 1, the other at Frame 60. The keyframe on Frame 1 is there because every layer must start with a keyframe, which can't be deleted. The keyframe on Frame 60 has a frame action that causes the timeline to go back to the first frame of the animation and begin playing it again. Because the keyframes on the Action layer contain no graphic content that is visible on the stage, the regular frames that follow them have no content and thus appear white.

Planning Your Project

Creative Transitions

Generally, people don't do well with instantaneous or immediate change—we usually like to ease our way into situations. For most of us, just getting out of bed is a major transition that requires time and determination to pull off—and still we sometimes fail! The point is, we use transitions constantly to deal with change. Your Flash project should be no different.

Using transitions to transform objects—or even whole scenes—in your movie creates a smooth-flowing presentation. While you may sometimes want to create a shock effect or give the feeling of "popping" into the scene, you don't want your presentation to turn into a simple slide show—especially when you can do so much more.

Using the many tools and techniques we've discussed thus far, you can apply any of the following effects as transitions in Flash (a file containing completed versions of these effects can be found on the CD in the Chapter 10/ Assets folder):

Planning Your Project   continued

- **Fade in/fade out.** You achieve this transition by making the beginning element in a tween more transparent than the ending element (fade-in), or vice versa (fade-out).
- **Enlarge/shrink.** You achieve this transition by making the beginning element in a tween smaller or larger than the ending element.
- **Slide in/slide out.** You achieve this transition by making the beginning or ending element in a tween appear or disappear from the stage.
- **Rotate/spin.** You achieve this transition by adding a rotation to your tween from the Property inspector.
- **Flip.** You achieve this transition by selecting the beginning or ending element in a tween, and flipping it horizontally or vertically using the Modify > Transform > Flip Horizontally or Flip Vertically command.
- **Blink.** You achieve this transition by placing a graphic element on the stage, then creating a number of successive keyframes that contain the same element. You then remove the element from every other one of those keyframes.
- **Bounce.** You achieve this transition by placing a graphic element on the stage, then creating a number of successive keyframes that contain the same element. Once you have done this, you reposition the element slightly (up, down, left, right, or a combination of all four) in each successive keyframe.
- **Morph.** You achieve this transition by creating shape tweens on mask layers.
- **Color change.** You achieve this transition by applying different colors to the beginning and ending elements in a tween.
- **Add.** You achieve this transition by adding elements quickly, so that they appear to "pop" into a scene.
- **Subtract.** You achieve this transition by removing elements quickly from a scene.
- **Gradient blind.** You achieve this transition by using an alpha-gradated element to slowly reveal another element underneath it.
- **Focus.** In this transition, several copies of the same element—each of which begins as transparent and offset from the other copies—are tweened on different layers, so that by the end of the tween they are all opaque, and all at the same position on the stage.
- **Swipe.** In this transition, a graphic appears as the result of what appears to be something being swiped across the page.
- **Shine.** In this transition, a gradient is tweened behind a graphic, causing the graphic to appear to shine.

(continued on next page)

> **Planning Your Project continued**
>
> You can combine any number of these transitions to create even more sophisticated effects.
>
> Many of these transitions (as well as many others) can be created easily with third-party programs like Swish (www.swishzone.com) and Swfx (www.wildform.com/swfx). You can download fully functional demos of either at the links provided.

Video Tutorials

Creating a Frame-by-Frame Animation. This tutorial demonstrates the principles behind frame-by-frame animation.

Creating a Shape-Tweened Animation. This simple tutorial shows you how to morph one shape into another, and how to use shape hints to specify how a morphed transition should appear.

Creating a Motion-Tweened Animation. In this tutorial, we create a motion-tweened animation similar to the sample in this chapter, so that you can see how size and transparency are tweened. We also place this tween along a path to help demonstrate the concept of motion guides.

Video

CHAPTER 11

What you'll learn...

How to import video

How to work with video in your projects

How to make your video clips interactive

Creative uses of video

MX ALERT

While designers have long used Flash's animation capabilities to create visually stunning motion graphics employing vector shapes and bitmaps, there are times when nothing can compare to full-motion video. So much of our everyday experience is based on subtle movements—trees rustling in the breeze, the way our faces change as we talk, clouds rolling across the sky. And nothing can capture those defining details like video, making it the perfect medium for telling a story, teaching, entertaining, and more.

Although Flash has been able to import video for a while now, a limitation existed in that you had to then *export* the project as a QuickTime movie file. You could use Flash to add vector shapes, animations, and interactivity to the imported video, but you couldn't export it as a SWF because the Flash Player wasn't able to play back files containing video—which meant you had to use a plug-in to play and view the video in a separate browser window. With Flash MX, however, all of this has changed. Although you can still use Flash to author QuickTime content, the Flash Player itself can now play video clips—which means you can seamlessly incorporate video into your SWF files. Imagine watching a video of a news story while at the same time viewing interactive maps, timelines, and facts—all within a single window! What's more, in Flash MX, you can control and interact with video elements in pretty much the same manner as any movie clip instance, opening the door for a whole new realm of engaging Flash content in which you can not only view video elements but drag, drop, press, load, unload, reposition, and flip them as well. Combine this with Flash MX's other animation and interactive capabilities, and the possibilities are limitless!

Importing Video

Importing a video clip into Flash is the first step toward putting it to use in your project. Although the process is fairly simple, it's not as straightforward as importing other types of project elements (such as bitmaps or sounds). Among the things you need to be aware of are the types of video files that Flash allows you to import.

NOTE *Although Flash can be used for authoring QuickTime content, this chapter focuses primarily on using video to create Flash content—that is, content that can be viewed with the Flash Player.*

FLV Format

The FLV (FL-ash V-ideo) file format was designed specifically for Flash-optimized video, and video clips saved in this format have an .flv file extension. Currently, you can use two tools to create video clips in this format: Flash itself, and Sorenson Squeeze (see "Sorenson Squeeze and FLV Video" sidebar). Using the FLV format offers an important advantage: When you import a video in a format other than FLV, Flash requires that you set various parameters to optimize the clip for playback within Flash—and you must do this *prior* to actually importing the video. But with FLV files, Flash recognizes that this type of clip has already been optimized and lets you import the video directly into your project. We'll discuss other aspects of this functionality later in this chapter; for now, just be aware that this special format exists.

NOTE *The FLV video format is simply a way of saving video clips that have been preoptimized for import into a Flash project (using File > Import). You cannot directly load video clips saved in this format using the* `loadMovie()` *action.*

Other Formats

The other types of video that you can import into Flash vary, depending on which version of QuickTime or DirectX is installed on your computer.

- **With QuickTime 4 or later (Windows and Mac):** .mov, .avi, .dv, .mpg, .mpeg
- **With Direct X or later (Windows only):** .avi, .mpg, mpeg, .wmv, .asf

Sorenson Squeeze and FLV Video

Flash MX uses the Sorenson Spark video codec to compress imported video clips—an effective way of delivering quality video at very small file sizes. Flash MX uses the standard edition of the Spark codec during the import process. However, Sorenson also sells a separate stand-alone application, Sorenson Squeeze (a proprietary version of the Spark codec), which allows you to get even better visual quality—while still minimizing file size. You can also use Squeeze to create FLV files (video files designed specifically for use with Flash).

Sorenson Squeeze's many powerful features include batch processing, better video quality, finer control over compression and audio settings, minor video-editing tools (brightness, contrast, saturation, and so on), and much more (**Figure 11.1**). In addition, Squeeze can automatically generate a SWF file that contains nothing but a compressed video clip—useful for loading the clip into a project dynamically using the `loadMovie()` action.

All of these features add up to make Sorenson Squeeze a Flash MX tool worthy of serious consideration, even with a retail price of $299.

For more information, visit Sorenson on the Web at www.sorenson.com

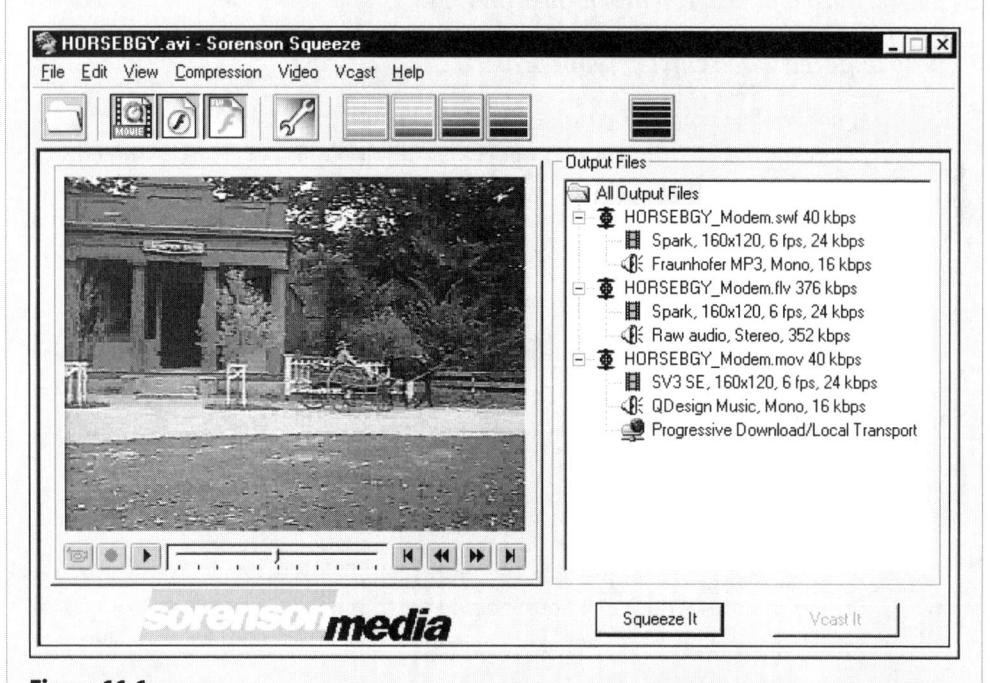

Figure 11.1
Sorenson Squeeze provides an easy-to-use interface for creating FLV files (Flash video).

The Import Process

As mentioned, if you're importing a video in something other than the FLV format, you must optimize the file first so that Flash can use it efficiently. As you will see in a moment, optimizing a video actually occurs *during* the importing process (as one of the steps). After the video has been optimized, Flash begins the actual task of bringing it into your project. You can either import the video so that it is placed directly on the current layer of the timeline, or you can import it directly into the library. When you import a video clip using either method, it becomes a movie element similar to bitmaps, sounds, and symbols: The master video clip exists in the library, and instances of it are placed in the project whenever and wherever the clip is used. This also means that you can use a single clip multiple times in your project without increasing its overall file size.

In the following, we'll step you through the process of importing a video file onto the timeline. Importing a clip directly into the library is accomplished in similar fashion; the clip is just not placed on the timeline.

NOTE *In Chapter 21, "Projects," you'll have a chance to import, use, and interact with video clips in one of the included projects.*

To import a video clip into your project:

1. From the File menu, choose Import to make the Import dialog box appear. Alternatively, you can choose Import into Library to import the clip directly into the library.

2. On your hard drive, navigate to the location of the clip you wish to import.

3. Select the file you wish to import, and click Open.

   The Import Video Settings dialog box will appear (**Figure 11.2**). The top half of this dialog box includes a Preview window for the video to be imported, as well as information about the clip being imported (hard drive location, dimensions, file size, and length).

4. Use the Quality slider to adjust the image quality of the clip you are importing.

   This setting determines the amount of file compression applied to the clip. The lower the setting, the more compression that's applied. Using more compression results in a smaller file—but also a degradation in visual integrity.

   TIP *A good rule of thumb is to always import video clips at the highest quality setting possible. Importing a video clip that has already been compressed means the clip's visual integrity has already been degraded; compressing it again will further degrade the available quality.*

Chapter 11 *Video*

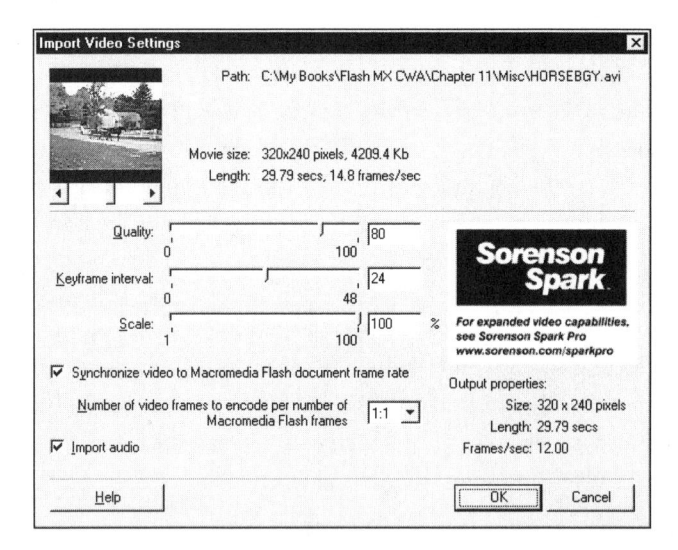

Figure 11.2
The Import Video Settings dialog box contains settings that must be adjusted prior to importing video into your project.

5. Use the "Keyframe interval" slider to adjust the frequency of keyframes in the imported clip.

   As described in the previous chapter, a keyframe in Flash represents a point in an animation when a major visual change occurs. Using keyframes in the context of importing video is very similar. A video keyframe is a frame in the video that contains all of the data used to visually create that frame. The frames *between* keyframes only contain data representative of the changes from one frame to the next. Thus, if you set "Keyframe interval" to a value of 10, Frame 1 would contain all of the data required to represent Frame 1; Frame 2 would only contain the data that changed from Frame 1; and so on—until Frame 10, the next keyframe that would include all of the data in that particular frame and restart the process (**Figure 11.3**). By using keyframes in this manner, you can greatly reduce the file size of the imported clip.

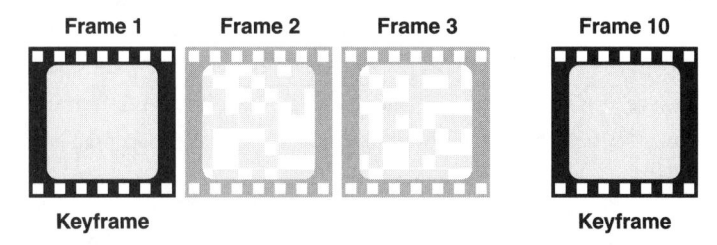

Figure 11.3
Keyframes (Frame 1 and Frame 10, as shown here) represent frames containing complete data defining the content of that frame. The frames in between each keyframe contain only the data needed to define changes in that frame in relation to the previous frame. This graphic demonstrates a "Keyframe interval" setting of 10.

If an imported video contains numerous visual transitions (as in music videos or movie trailers that cut to many different scenes), the keyframe setting should be lower (between 1 and 10). If the imported video is visually consistent throughout (as in a speech or a static nature scene), the keyframe setting can be higher (20 or more). The more keyframes you specify in the imported clip, the larger the file will be—thus, whenever possible you'll want to limit the number of transitions you use in your movie.

6. Use the Scale slider to adjust the width and height of the imported clip.

Scaling—or resizing—a clip can be helpful in several ways. For starters, the smaller the clip's dimensions, the smaller its file size and the smoother its playback (because it requires less processing power). Although you can scale the clip within Flash, you will get better results if you adjust this setting during the import process.

7. Select "Synchronize video to Macromedia Flash movie frame rate" to match the playback speed of the imported video with the playback speed of the main Flash movie timeline.

This option is important when your Flash project's frame rate differs from the frame rate of the imported clip. For example, assume your Flash movie is set to play at 12 frames per second (fps), but your imported clip is set to play at 15 fps. At 15 fps, the imported clip has a playback time of 30 seconds and is thus 450 frames long (15 fps × 30 seconds). However, a 30-second clip in your Flash movie would only require 360 frames (12 fps × 30 seconds). If you want the original clip's playback time to remain 30 seconds once it is imported into Flash, frames must be dropped from the imported file so that its 450-frame/30-second playback will fit into the 360-frame/30-second playback of your Flash movie. The end result can be glitches in the movie's playback.

If you deselect this option, the imported clip will remain 450 frames long, but its playback time will change from 30 seconds to 37.5 seconds, making it appear to play back slower than originally intended. This is what happens when you play back a 450-frame video in a Flash project set to play just 12 frames per second. To get the best results, your imported video should have the same frame rate as your Flash project. When that's not possible, this setting makes acceptable adjustments.

> **TIP** As this setting is selected and deselected, the overall effect on the movie's playback speed will be reflected in the Output properties area of the Import Video Settings dialog box. This area can be seen just above the OK and Cancel buttons on the dialog box window (**Figure 11.4**).

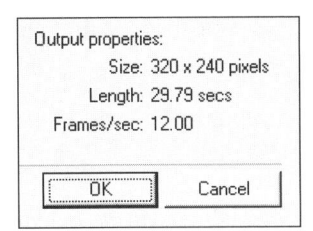

Figure 11.4
The "Output properties" portion of the Import Video Settings dialog box provides information about the video once it has been imported into Flash.

8. Select the number of video frames to encode per number of Macromedia Flash frames.

   If you want one video frame to appear for every Flash frame, choose a value of 1:1. If you want one video frame to appear for every *four* Flash frames, choose a value of 1:4, and so on. If you chose a ratio different than 1:1, the video's playback speed (length in seconds) will remain the same; it will simply appear more like a slide show as that ratio gets higher, since frames are dropped from the video clip. You can use this setting to reduce a clip's file size; just remember that it will also make the clip appear choppier during playback.

9. Select the "Import audio" option to import any audio data the clip may contain. Deselect the option if you don't want to import the clip's audio.

   NOTE *Any audio that's imported from a clip will be compressed in the exported SWF using the audio compression settings in the Publish Settings dialog box. This dialog box is discussed in detail in Chapter 20, "Publishing."*

10. Click OK.

    Flash will begin importing the clip, using the settings you chose—a process that may take several minutes, depending on the speed of your computer and the size of the clip. If you chose to import the clip directly onto the timeline (File > Import), Flash will determine whether the timeline contains sufficient frames to display the entire video. If it doesn't, Flash will display an alert, asking whether the necessary frames should be automatically added (**Figure 11.5**). You may choose Yes or No. For example, if you were to try

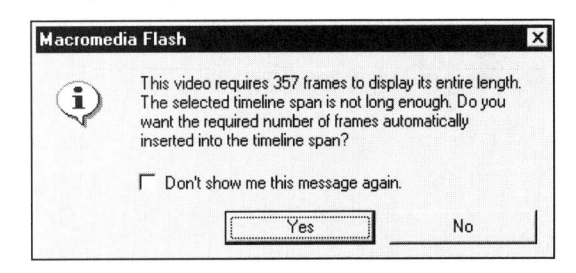

Figure 11.5
When you try to place a video clip on a timeline that does not contain enough frames to play the entire clip, Flash responds with an alert box asking you if it should automatically add the necessary frames.

importing a 357-frame video into a layer that only contained 100 frames, you would need an additional 257 frames to display the entire video.

At the end of this process, the first frame of the imported clip will appear on the stage, and the clip will appear as an asset in the library.

NOTE *The video's playback may be cut off (that is, video will disappear) if the layer it exists on does not contain sufficient frames.*

Embedding or Linking .mov Files

In most cases, when you import a video clip, Flash automatically **embeds** the imported video clip directly into the Flash file, which means:

- The video clip becomes part of the FLA authoring file.
- The clip can be played back when viewing the resulting SWF in the Flash player.

However, when you import a QuickTime video (.mov) into Flash, you can choose whether to embed the clip directly into your project or have it remain external, while linking to it. Linking to a video in this manner is useful when your final output will be a QuickTime movie; however, a linked video file cannot be viewed in the Flash player. Thus, unless you're authoring QuickTime content, when importing a .mov file you should select the option to embed the clip.

Working with Video in Your Projects

Once you've imported a video into your project, you can work with it much as you would any other graphical element.

Placing Instances

To use a video in your project, you need to place an instance of the clip on the timeline. This could be the main timeline, or the timeline of a movie clip. By placing it on a movie clip's timeline, you enable the clip to be treated as a movie clip instance, opening the door for all sorts of interaction with the clip, as we'll discuss shortly.

To place an instance of a video clip on a timeline:

1. Navigate to the timeline where you wish to place the clip (main or movie clip).
2. Select the layer and frame where the clip should be placed.

3. Choose Window > Library to open the Library panel.

4. Locate the video clip you wish to use. Click its name and drag it onto the stage (**Figure 11.6**).

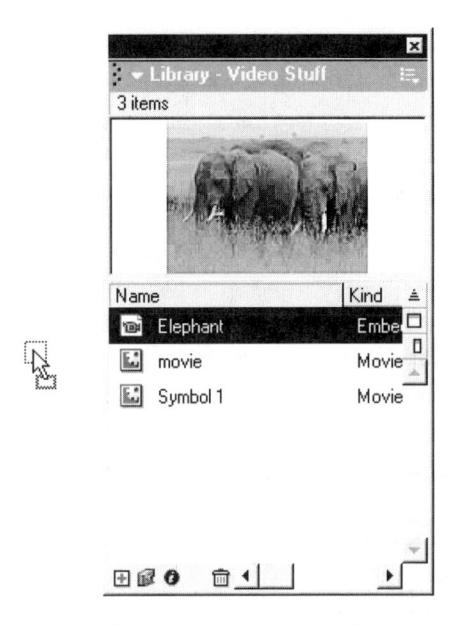

Figure 11.6
Once a video clip has been imported, you can use it wherever you like in your project by simply dragging its name from the Library onto the timeline of your choice.

Flash will determine whether the timeline contains a sufficient number of frames to display the entire clip. If it does not, an alert will appear asking whether the necessary frames should be automatically added. You may choose Yes or No.

As mentioned, when a video clip is placed in your movie, the clip that appears is an instance of the master clip that exists in the Library. Once a video has been imported into your project, using several instances of the same clip will not increase the overall file size of your movie.

Selecting the instance will display its current size and position in the Property inspector.

Previewing a Clip on the Timeline

Dragging the timeline's playhead to the point where the video clip resides allows you to preview its playback within the authoring environment. If the clip contains audio, you will not hear it during the preview.

TIP *Choosing Control > Test Movie will allow you to both watch the video's playback and hear the audio.*

By previewing clips in the authoring environment, you can synchronize the movement of other Flash content with the video clip. You can place Flash content beside, behind, or on top of the video clip.

Positioning and Scaling

A video clip is a single entity that occupies a span of frames—making it similar in functionality to a graphic symbol. Thus, if you reposition a video clip on the stage, all of the frames it contains will move to that new position.

Although you can scale a video clip on the stage using the Free Transform tool, we recommend instead that you import it at the exact size you need. Scaling a clip *larger* than the size at which it was imported will degrade its quality during playback. Scaling it *smaller* won't necessarily affect the clip visually, but it's inefficient. Here's why: If you import a 640 × 480 clip, then scale it down to half that size (320 × 240) within Flash, it will still be exported with enough data to display it at 640 × 480. By re-importing the clip at 320 × 240, you can considerably reduce the file's size (**Figure 11.7**).

Imported at 640 x 480 but scaled to 320 x 240   Imported at 320 x 240

Figure 11.7
You should always import a video clip at the exact dimensions you will need. Scaling the clip once it has been imported will result in either a degradation of its playback quality or the addition of unnecessary data, as this graphic demonstrates.

NOTE *Video clips can be rotated, if your project requires it.*

Swapping Instances

Swapping an instance allows you to replace the content of the currently selected video clip instance with the content of a different clip in the library. This is useful if you want to create several sections that look and function similarly, but include different content.

To swap the content of the currently selected clip:

1. With the Property inspector open, select the instance with the content you wish to replace.

2. On the Property inspector, Press the "Swap…" button.

The Swap Embedded Video dialog box will appear.

3. From the list that appears, select the alternative video clip that you would like to use.

4. Click OK.

The content of the selected video clip instance will be replaced with the new content you selected.

Video Clip Properties

While most of the settings that affect a clip's appearance are selected during the import process, there are several additional settings pertaining to video clips in the Embedded Video Properties dialog box.

To open the Embedded Video Properties dialog box:

♦ With the Library panel open, select a video clip, then select Properties from the Library panel Options menu (**Figure 11.8**).

The Embedded Video Properties dialog box will appear. At the top you will find a text box containing

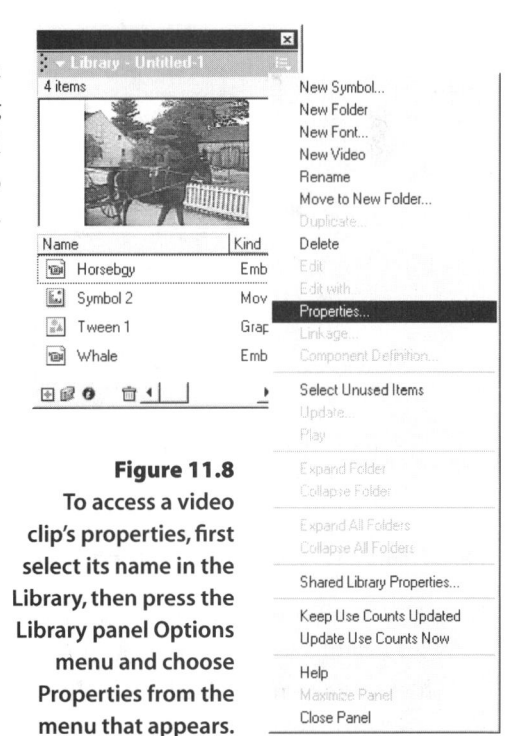

Figure 11.8
To access a video clip's properties, first select its name in the Library, then press the Library panel Options menu and choose Properties from the menu that appears.

the current name of the clip. You can enter a new name here if you wish. Below this text box you will see the directory path from which the clip was imported. Below that you will see information pertaining to the clip, including creation date, size, and more. To the right of this dialog box, you'll find a series of buttons. Read on to discover what each of these allows you to do.

Updating a video

If you use a video-editing program to change or edit a video file that you have already imported into Flash (that is, the one at the directory-path location), you can use the Update button on the Embedded Video Properties dialog box to quickly and easily update the Flash version of that clip to reflect your changes. Pressing the Update button will repeat the import process—thus importing the updated clip with the original compression settings.

Replacing a clip's content

You can replace the content of one clip (and thus any instances of it in your project) with the content of another clip by using the Import button on the dialog box.

To replace the content of a clip:

1. Press the Import button on the Embedded Video Properties dialog box.

This will open a dialog box that lets you navigate to find the new clip you want to use.

2. Locate the clip you want, and press Open.

The Import Video Settings dialog box will appear, allowing you to adjust various compression settings (as described earlier in this chapter).

3. When you have adjusted these settings to your liking, press OK.

The new clip will be imported, replacing the content of the original clip. Any other instances of the original clip will be automatically updated to reflect the updated content.

Exporting a video clip as an FLV file

If you wish to package your video clip as an FLV (so that you can send it to someone for use in another project), you can do so via the Export button on the Embedded Video Properties dialog box.

To export a clip as an FLV file:

1. Press the Export button on the Embedded Video Properties dialog box.

   This will open a Save As dialog box that lets you navigate to the directory where the file should be saved.

2. Give the file a name, and press Save.

   Flash will export the clip to the directory you selected.

Making Your Video Clips Interactive

Placing a video clip on a movie clip's timeline is pretty much like placing any other type of animation on that timeline (**Figure 11.9**). By encapsulating the video clip in this manner, you can control playback, transparency, volume, panning, and more—just as you would any other type of movie clip instance. We'll briefly discuss some of these controls in this section; for more detailed coverage, see Chapter 16, "Using Action-Script in Your Projects."

Figure 11.9
Placing a video clip on a movie clip's timeline encapsulates the video within the movie clip. Once that's done, the video can be interacted with in the same way as any other movie clip instance.

The first step in creating an interactive video clip is to encapsulate it within a movie clip.

To encapsulate a video clip within a movie clip:

1. Create a movie clip instance, then place the authoring environment in symbol-editing mode, in order to edit this clip's timeline.

2. Select Frame 1 in the layer on which the clip is to be placed.

3. Choose File > Import.

4. From the Import dialog box, locate the video clip you want to import, then press OK.

5. Adjust the settings in the Import Video Settings dialog box as described earlier.

6. Press OK.

The clip is placed on the movie clip's timeline. Dragging an instance of this movie clip onto the stage is essentially the same as dragging an instance of the video clip onto the stage—except that now you can interact with the video clip in the same way you can with a movie clip.

NOTE *For the discussion that follows, we'll assume that an instance of the just-created clip has been placed on the stage and given an instance name of myVideo.*

Controlling Playback

Once a video clip has been encapsulated into a movie clip, you can control its playback just as you would any other movie clip instance.

To play the video, you would use the following code:

```
_root.myVideo.play();
```

To stop the video you would use the following code:

```
_root.myVideo.stop();
```

To rewind the script back to the beginning, you would use the code

```
_root.myVideo.gotoAndStop(1);
```

While buttons are typically used to control a video's playback, you don't need to limit yourself to them. Remember, this is Flash: You can use just about any type of interaction you wish to control playback. You could, for example, set up your project so that when a user presses the mouse button over the video, it will play, and when the user releases the button, it will stop. Rewinding could be accomplished by double-clicking.

To control a clip's playback in the manner just described, you would select the movie clip instance that contains the video you want to control, then attach this script to it:

```
on (press) {
   this.play();
}
on (release) {
   this.stop();
   if (getTimer() - lastClick < 1000) {
     this.gotoAndStop(1);
   }
   lastClick = getTimer();
}
```

The first part of the script says that when pressed, the video should play. The next part is a bit trickier: It states that when the mouse button is released, playback should halt. In addition, an `if` statement is used to determine whether the amount of time between the current click (`getTimer()`) and the last click is less than 1,000 milliseconds. If it is, the video is rewound. After the `if` statement is evaluated, the value of `lastClick` is updated to the current time. This updated value is then again used in the `if` statement the next time the `release` event occurs. While we won't go into an in-depth discussion right now of the logic of how this works, it does provide double-click functionality—that is, it allows the computer to distinguish between "Play" (single click) and "Rewind" (double click).

TIP *If you do decide to use a custom playback-control mechanism, be sure to provide your users with clear instructions on how it works.*

In addition to this basic playback functionality, frame labels can be used as cue points that allow users to navigate to specific points in the video. For example, if a video clip contains images of different animals and their habitats, these sections could be identified in the clip using frame labels, making it easy to send the video clip to that label in the following manner (**Figure 11.10**):

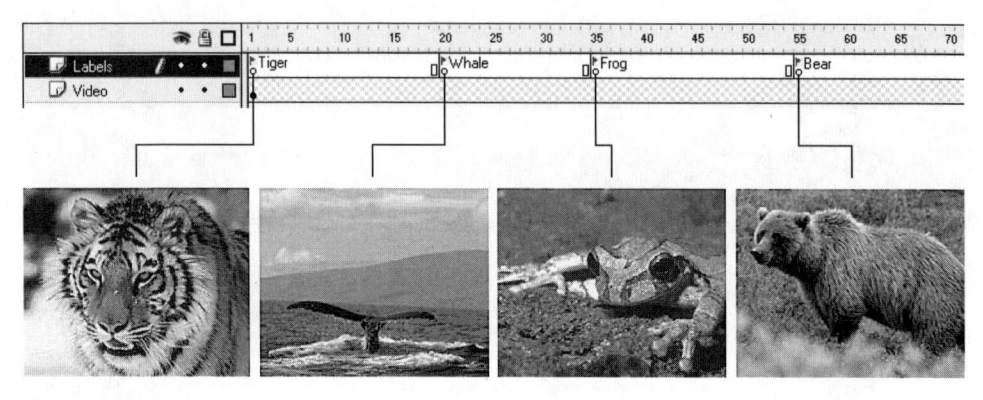

Figure 11.10
Frame labels can emulate the usefulness of cue points for identifying specific portions of a video clip.

```
_root.myVideo.gotoAndPlay("Whale");
```

Volume and Panning

When a video clip is encapsulated inside a movie clip, you can control the volume and panning of any audio it contains in the same manner (using ActionScript) as you would any other audio within the clip. For example, you would use the following ActionScript to set the volume of the video clip to 50 percent:

```
videoSound = new Sound (_root.myVideo);
videoSound.setVolume(50);
```

The first line creates a Sound object, named **videoSound**, and associates it with the **myVideo** instance (which you'll remember contains the video clip). The next line adjusts the volume of the videoSound Sound object—and thus the **myVideo** instance.

Panning can be set as follows:

```
videoSound.setPan(75);
```

This will cause the audio to be 75 percent louder in the right speaker than the left—which you may welcome if your right ear is 75 percent smaller than your left ear!

NOTE *For more information about Sound objects, see Chapter 14, "ActionScript Objects."*

Transparency, Visibility, and Position

The transparency, visibility, and position (as well as any other properties used in conjunction with movie clip instances) of a video clip can be dynamically set once it has been encapsulated in a movie clip.

The following ActionScript would change the transparency of the clip to 50 percent:

```
_root.myVideo._alpha = 50;
```

The following would make it invisible:

```
_root.myVideo._visible = false;
```

The following would position the clip at X = 100 by Y = 250:

```
_root.myVideo._x = 100;
_root.myVideo._y = 250;
```

NOTE *For more information about working with movie clip properties, see Chapter 14, "ActionScript Objects."*

External Loading of Video Clips

If your project calls for the use of several video clips, you should consider placing each clip in its own SWF file, then loading each SWF/video into the main SWF on an as-needed basis using a `loadMovie()` action. By doing this, you allow the user to download clips in piecemeal fashion rather than all at once, sparing them the time and frustration of downloading a very large SWF (containing multiple video clips), and instead allowing them to view a particular clip by just pressing a button. We'll explain this functionality in detail, as well as how to set it up, in Chapter 16, "Using ActionScript in Your Projects."

Streaming

There's no getting around it: If you use video in your projects, users will have to wait while it downloads (if your project is being delivered over the Web). Normally, a video clip will begin playing as soon as enough data has been downloaded to begin the playback process. When loading a video clip that has been placed inside a SWF (as just described), it's possible—using ActionScript—to control the amount of data that must download before the video begins to play. In addition, you can provide your users with visual or textual information about the download (for example, a progress bar)—or not. We'll explain this functionality and how to set it up in Chapter 16, "Using ActionScript in Your Projects."

Using Video Creatively

Although adding video to your project can go a long way toward making it more informative or entertaining, all you're really talking about is placing a moving picture within a rectangular area. Sound boring? Think again: By incorporating Flash's graphical abilities, you can turn those plain, rectangular picture boxes into something far more creative and compelling.

NOTE *Some of the effects outlined below can be processor-intensive when used with video clips. Always test your results; if you get acceptable results on a slower machine (that is, the video clip still plays smoothly), it's probably safe to incorporate the effect into your project.*

Masks

Masks provide a great way of "changing" the shape of the video window (**Figure 11.11**). By masking a video clip with a shape of your choosing (as discussed in Chapter 9), you can make it appear as if the video is being displayed through different viewing apparatuses—periscope, binoculars, even a keyhole (though be careful how you use this last one!).

Chapter 11 *Video*

Figure 11.11
The mask feature can be used with a video clip to provide viewing frames other than the standard (that is, rectangular) video window.

Vector, Text, and Overlays

You can easily use Flash's vector graphic and text capabilities to add visual finesse to a video clip. You can place arrows above the clip and animate them to point to a specific object in the clip. You can also use animated text and graphics can on top of a clip to enhance the presentation. You can choose fast-paced motion (using blurs and slides) or more subdued motion and transitions (using text fades and moderate tweening). Although you can include such transitions in the actual video clip, it's sometimes better to produce these effects in Flash, since these kinds of motion effects can appear choppy when included in a compressed video file.

Other Flash content, like movie clip instances and buttons (for example, Play, Stop, and Rewind), can be placed directly on top of the video clip itself. This allows you to give your video clips or interfaces a more unique look (**Figure 11.12**).

Figure 11.12
You can easily mix Flash elements (such as text, vector graphics, or even buttons and other symbols) with your video clips.

Text overlay   Playback controls

Flash Transitions

There are several simple Flash transitions that can be performed on a video clip once it has been encapsulated in a movie clip, most of which involve tweening. Using tweening, a clip can be faded in or out, moved around the screen, enlarged into view, or shrunk out of view. These effects can also be combined.

Video Tutorial

Importing and Working with Video. This tutorial will step you through the process of importing a video clip into your project, encapsulating it in a movie clip, and trying some of the cool things you can do with it once there.

4

Movie Production, Interactive

Getting Started with ActionScript	385
Understanding ActionScript	443
ActionScript Objects	535
Components	583
Using ActionScript in Your projects	641

IT'S NOT ENOUGH FOR A FLASH MOVIE to simply look good; it must be interactive as well—allowing users to navigate it, open URLs, input information, control sound, and more. All capabilities that are made possible by ActionScript, Flash's own scripting language. In this section, you'll learn how to use ActionScript to create everything from simple scripts that pause a timeline's playback to sophisticated scripts that use functions, loops, variables, expressions, and conditional logic. We'll also look at how to use and customize Components, Flash MX's highly interactive movie elements.

Getting Started with ActionScript

CHAPTER 12

What you'll learn…

About ActionScript

How you can use ActionScript to create interactivity

How to use the Actions panel

How to use basic ActionScript to control your movies

Humans thrive on interaction. We're more than willing to make fools of ourselves just to bring a smile to a baby's face. And we love pushing buttons to make things work. But a mute audience, a remote control with dead batteries, a frozen computer—these things drive us nuts. If we can't provoke a response, we usually move on to something else.

Which is precisely what you *don't* want your Flash movie audience to do. The surest way to hold your viewers' attention is to interact with them, which is what ActionScript is all about. While sound and animation may capture your viewers' attention, interactivity can *captivate* them. By enabling feedback between your movie and its viewers, interactive functions can be extremely useful. With interactivity, you can let viewers control the playback and appearance of your movie. You can also use it to create games, customizable interfaces, forms, and more.

First, however, you need to understand some of the logic behind ActionScript. But don't panic: You don't need to be a computer programmer to add simple interactivity to your project. In this chapter, we'll look at some of the basic ActionScript building blocks, which will enable you to bring your creations to life almost immediately. For more detail about ActionScript, see Chapter 13, "Understanding ActionScript."

What Is ActionScript?

ActionScript is a basic programming language—one that gives you the ability to control timelines, sounds, colors, cursors, graphics, and data—but unlike some programming languages, ActionScript commands are structured much like regular sentences. As an example, take a look at the following:

```
if (savings == 50000) {
   vehicleToBuy = "Porsche";
}else if (savings == 200) {
   vehicleToBuy = "Bicycle";
}
```

Even if you aren't familiar with ActionScript, chances are you were able to make sense of the above. The formula basically states, "If I have $50,000 in savings, I'm going to buy a Porsche; if I have $200 in savings, I'll have to settle for a bicycle."

A Flash movie can contain any number of ActionScripts, attached to frames, button instances, and movie clip instances. The execution of an ActionScript is determined by the frame or instance to which it's attached. That is, an ActionScript attached to a particular button will execute when the user, through his or her mouse, interacts with that button in some way (for example, rolling over or pressing it, depending on how the script is set up).

ActionScript uses events, variables, operators, expressions, statements, functions, and objects to do what you want it to—all of which we'll explain in this chapter and the next, "Understanding ActionScript." Since ActionScript syntax is based on the same standards as JavaScript, those familiar with that scripting language should find learning ActionScript especially easy.

How ActionScript Creates Interactivity

In terms of scripting, Flash requires three primary ingredients to create interactivity: an *event* that triggers a script to execute, *actions* within the script that tell it what to execute, and *targets* (or objects), which are controlled by the actions.

To understand this, think about setting a thermostat to keep a room cool: When you set the thermostat, you're programming it to perform an interactive function—the underlying logic of which might look something like this:

Event: The temperature of the room exceeds the amount set on the thermostat (which triggers the action that follows).

Action: Power is turned on (the action performed).

Target: Air conditioner (the object affected by the action).

If you can successfully set your thermostat, you've got what it takes to become an ActionScripting guru.

To see how this logic translates into an actual script, take a look at the following (which we'll assume is attached to a button):

```
on (press) {
  myMovieClip.gotoAndPlay (36);
}
```

In this simple script, the *event* is on(press), which instructs the script to execute when a user presses the button it's attached to. The *action* is gotoAndPlay(36), which tells a timeline to go to Frame 36. But which timeline? The *target* for the action is **myMovieClip**. Thus, when the button is pressed, **myMovieClip** will go to and play beginning at Frame 36 of its timeline.

These are the simple ingredients of most scripts that you'll create using ActionScript. Let's take a closer look at each of them.

NOTES *Scripts can contain other "ingredients" as well, including logic functions, which enable them to evaluate specific conditions before allowing an action to be executed. We'll cover these more advanced aspects of scripting, including logic, in the next chapter, "Understanding ActionScript."*

In ActionScript, a **target** *is sometimes referred to as an* **object** *and an* **action** *is often referred to as a* **method.** *You'll learn more about these programming terms in the next chapter.*

Events

The first element of any script is the event that triggers its execution. This can be any of the following:

- Mouse event
- Keyboard event
- Frame event
- Clip event

Mouse events (button actions)

Mouse events occur when your audience interacts with a button or movie clip instance using the cursor/pointer. Such events are also known as *button actions* because they're usually attached to buttons. A user can employ the pointer in any of the following ways to trigger a mouse event (**Figure 12.1**):

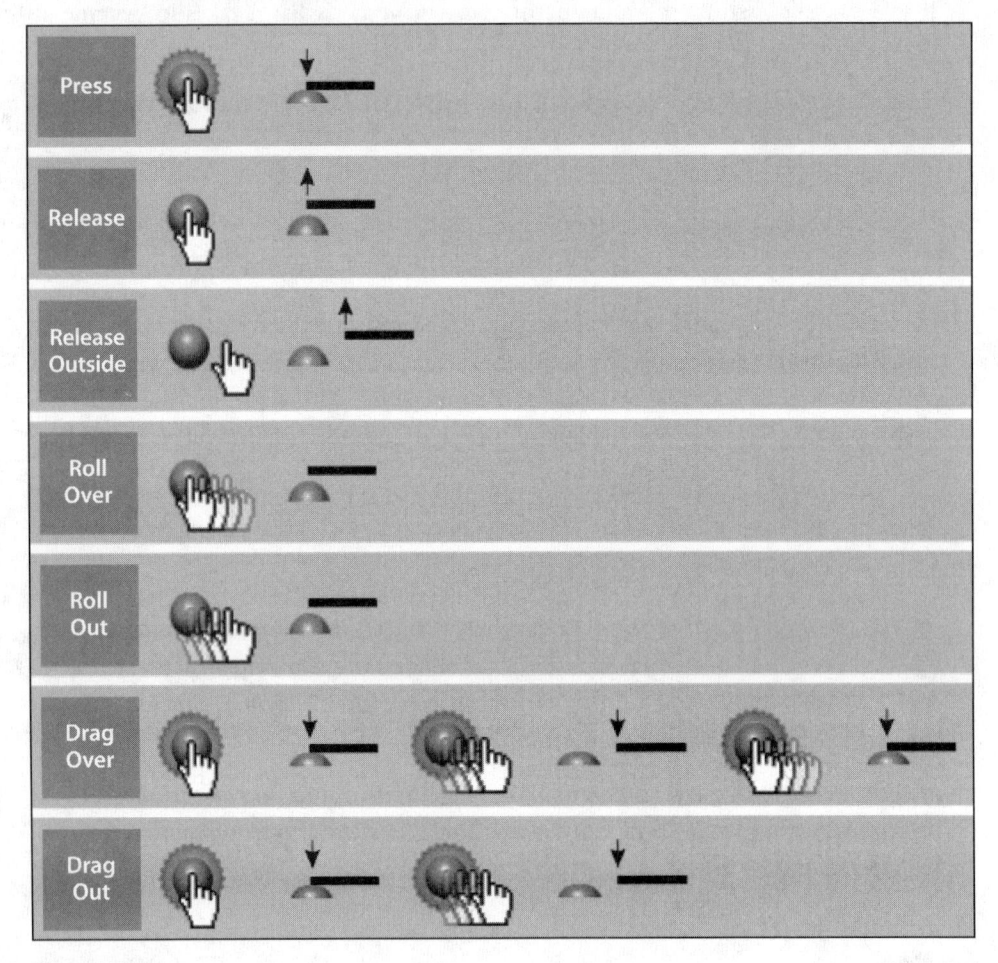

Figure 12.1
The down arrows in this graphic represent the mouse button being pressed down; the up arrows represent the button being released. The absence of an arrow means the mouse event doesn't require the mouse button to be pressed or released.

MX ALERT **NOTE** *As explained in Chapter 7, "Symbols," mouse events can now be attached to movie clip instances as well as button instances. Although the following discusses mouse events in the context of buttons, the same functionality exists when mouse events are used with movie clip instances.*

- on(press)

    The press event occurs when the user moves the pointer over a movie button and presses the mouse button.

- on(release)

    The release event occurs when the user moves the pointer over a movie button, then clicks and releases the mouse button. (This is the default event for most scripts when you don't specifically define one.)

- on(releaseOutside)

    The releaseOutside event occurs when the user mouse-clicks over a movie button, but moves the pointer away from it before releasing the mouse button.

- on(rollOver)

    The rollOver event occurs when the user moves the pointer over a movie button.

- on(rollOut)

    The rollOut event occurs when the user moves the pointer away from a button.

- on(dragOver)

    The dragOver event occurs when the user moves the pointer over a movie button while he or she is already pressing the mouse button, then drags the pointer away from the movie button (still pressing the mouse button), and then moves it back over the movie button.

- on(dragOut)

    The dragOut event occurs when the user places the pointer over a movie button, presses the mouse button, and drags the pointer away from the movie button (while still pressing the mouse button).

To attach a mouse event to a button or movie clip instance:

1. Select a button or movie clip instance on the stage.

2. Choose Window > Actions to open the Actions panel, or press F9.

3. Click the plus sign (+) to assign the action or actions that you want triggered by the mouse event.

4. For this example, choose Actions > Movie Control > stop, which will insert a stop() action to halt the playback of your movie (**Figure 12.2**).

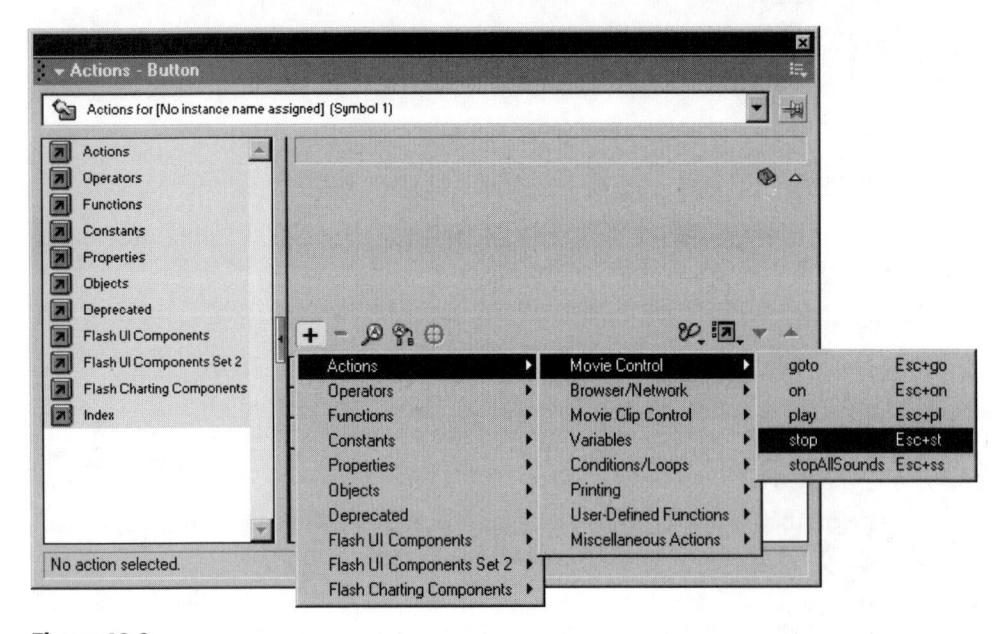

Figure 12.2
Adding a stop() **action to our script.**

The Actions List window (on the right side of the Actions panel) will display your completed ActionScript, indicating that the action will occur when the button is released (on(release)). This is the default mouse event that Flash assigns to an action. Now, let's configure the mouse event more to our liking.

5. In the Actions List window, select the on(release) statement.

The statement will be highlighted, and mouse event parameters will become available on the top of the Actions panel (**Figure 12.3**).

Chapter 12 *Getting Started with ActionScript*

Figure 12.3
If you select a statement in the Actions List window, its parameters will be displayed at the top of the Actions panel.

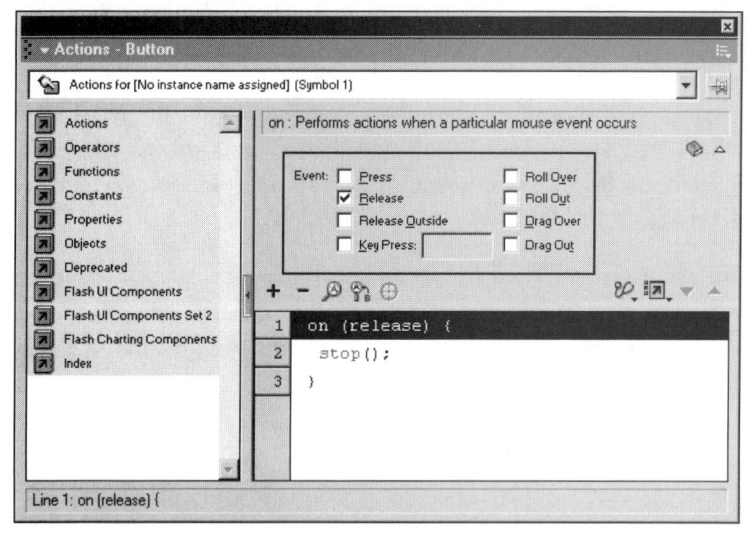

6. Check any and all mouse events that you want to trigger this script.

As you check various events, the on() statement is updated in the Actions List window. When the movie is played, the action you assigned this button will be performed when any of the mouse events you checked are triggered.

> **TIPS** *Mouse events assigned to one instance of a button or movie clip have no effect on other instances of the same button or movie clip—even if the buttons are on the stage simultaneously. Each can be assigned different events and actions.*
>
> *To assign the mouse event before assigning an action to it, perform Steps 1 and 2 above, but in Step 3, select Actions > Movie Control > on to define the mouse event. Then from the same menu, select an action.*
>
> *Many button actions cannot be tested in the authoring environment. To test buttons more thoroughly, choose Control > Test Movie.*

MX ALERT { *ActionScript* } *Using event handler methods, scripts triggered by mouse events can now be attached to button and movie clip instances dynamically, allowing you to define a button or movie clip instance's functionality on-the-fly, as your movie plays (as opposed to selecting them in the authoring environment and attaching a script directly to them). For more information about event handler methods, see Chapter 13, "Understanding ActionScript."*

Keyboard events

Flash allows you to assign keyboard events, which occur when the user presses a particular letter, number, punctuation mark, symbol, arrow, or the Backspace, Insert, Home, End, Page Up, or Page Down keys. Note that keyboard events are case-sensitive, which means that *A* is not the same as *a*. (Thus, if you assign *A* to trigger an action, *a* will not trigger it.)

Keyboard events are attached to button or movie clip instances. Although the user doesn't need to interact directly with the button or movie clip instance, the instance must be present in a scene for the keyboard event to work (though it doesn't need it to be visible or even present on the stage). The button or movie clip instance can even reside in the work area of the frame, so that it's not visible when the movie is exported (**Figure 12.4**).

Figure 12.4
You can hide buttons that contain keyboard events in areas that will not be seen when the final movie is exported—for example, outside the stage area.

To define a keyboard event that triggers an action:

1. Perform Steps 1 through 5 above (for adding a mouse event).

2. On the Parameter pane of the Actions panel, check the Key Press event.

3. In the small text box next to the Key Press option, type the key that will be used to trigger the action (**Figure 12.5**).

   When the movie is played, the actions you assigned to this button instance will be performed when the user types the key you assigned.

Figure 12.5
To assign a particular key to the event triggering an action on a button, from Event options select Key Press, then press the key you want to use.

Frame events

Whereas user interaction triggers mouse and keyboard events, the timeline triggers frame events (which are also known as frame *actions*, because they are attached to frames and always trigger an action).

Frame events—which are always placed at keyframes—are useful for making actions occur at specific points in time during your movie's playback (**Figure 12.6**).

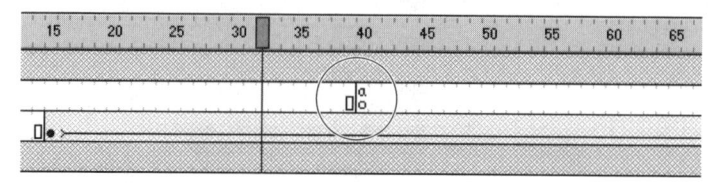

Figure 12.6
Frame events are placed on the timeline, and execute when the playhead reaches the keyframe where they reside.

To create a frame event that triggers an action:

1. Select a keyframe on the timeline where you would like the frame event to occur.

2. Choose Window > Actions to open the Actions panel.

3. Click the plus sign (+) to assign an action or actions that you want triggered when the timeline reaches this keyframe.

4. For this example, choose Actions > Movie Control > stop, which will add a stop() action that causes your movie to cease playing.

    The Actions List window will display your completed ActionScript. You will notice that even though this is the same action that was assigned to the mouse event we configured earlier, the script here is different: It lacks the on(release) statement, which is only used to define mouse or keyboard events (because both can take so many forms, such as press, release, rollOver, and so on). A frame event can only be triggered one way—by the timeline reaching that frame.

When the movie is played, it will perform the action you assigned when the timeline reaches this keyframe.

Clip events

The following clip events can be attached to movie clip instances, and are triggered when specific interactions occur in relation to the movie clip (**Figure 12.7**):

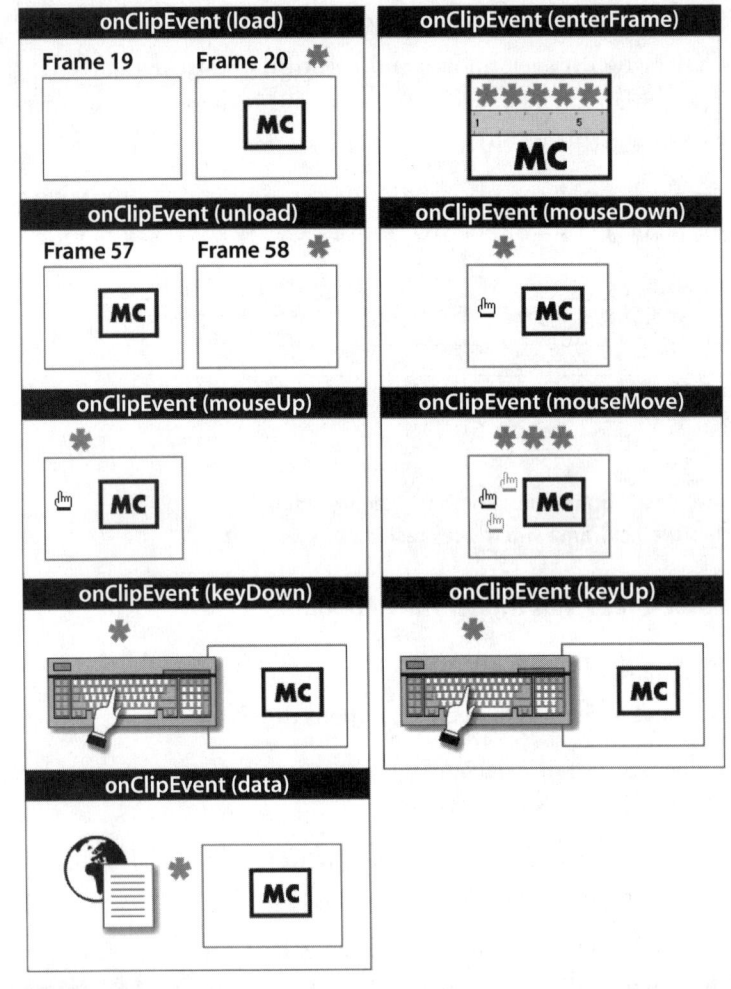

Figure 12.7
The down arrows represent the mouse button being pressed down; the up arrows represent it being released. The asterisks each represent an occurrence of the event.

- onClipEvent (load)

    The load event is triggered by the first appearance of the movie clip instance in your movie. For example, if you place the load event on a movie clip instance that doesn't appear until Frame 20 of your timeline, the associated script will be triggered when the playhead reaches Frame 20 and the movie clip loads (appears). You can use this event to execute a script that initiates the movie clip's variables or properties when it first appears.

- onClipEvent (enterFrame)

    An enterFrame event is triggered each time the movie clip's timeline reaches a new frame. Thus, if your movie plays at 12 frames per second, this event is triggered 12 times a second. If the movie clip is only one frame long, the event will continue to occur after the clip has ceased playing (that is, the event is not dependent on the clip itself playing)—useful for any script that you want continually triggered (for example, one that moves a movie clip instance each time it is executed, thereby creating a scripted animation). If you attach this event to a movie clip instance, the only way to stop it from continually triggering is to remove the instance from your movie.

- onClipEvent (unload)

    The unload event is triggered when the timeline reaches the first frame in which the movie clip instance is no longer used. Thus, if you were to place this event on a movie clip instance that appears on Frame 57, but is removed from the scene on Frame 58, the script will be triggered when the playhead reaches Frame 58 and the movie clip is unloaded. You can use this event to execute a script that will update your movie in various ways once the movie clip instance is removed.

- onClipEvent (mouseDown)

    The mouseDown event occurs when the user presses the left mouse button anywhere in the Flash movie window while the movie clip instance to which this event is attached is also present in the movie window. Thus, this event is a catch-all for any mouse-downs that occur within the movie window, not just those that occur with the cursor directly over button and movie clip instances.

- onClipEvent (mouseUp)

    The mouseUp event occurs when the user releases the mouse button anywhere in the Flash movie window while the movie clip instance to which this event is attached is also in the movie window. This event is a catch-all for any mouse-ups that occur.

- onClipEvent (mouseMove)

    The mouseMove event occurs once for each pixel that the mouse is moved anywhere in the movie window, while the attached movie clip is also in the movie window. For example, if the user moves his mouse 5 pixels, this event is triggered five times. You can use this event in conjunction with the _xmouse and _ymouse properties (which represent the current X and Y positions of the mouse) to constantly track the position of the mouse so your movie can take a specific action based on that position. You can also use this event simply to keep track of when the mouse is in motion.

- onClipEvent (keyDown)

    The keyDown event is triggered when the user presses any key while the attached movie clip is in the movie window. You can use additional ActionScript to determine which key was pressed, and then base an action in your movie on that particular key—thus letting users control the movie (and its elements) via their keyboards.

- onClipEvent (keyUp)

    This keyUp event occurs when the user releases a key while the movie clip to which this event is attached is in the movie window.

- onClipEvent (data)

    The data event occurs when the movie clip receives external data (or movies) via the loadVariables() and loadMovie() actions. When used in conjunction with a loadVariables() action, the data event occurs only once (when the last variable is loaded). When used in conjunction with a loadMovie() action, the onClipEvent(data) event occurs repeatedly, as each section of the external movie is loaded. This event allows you to execute a script in response to the completion of externally loaded data.

To define a clip event that triggers an action:

1. Select a movie clip instance on the stage.

2. Choose Window > Actions to open the actions panel.

3. Click the plus sign (+) to assign an action or actions you want triggered by the clip event.

4. For our demonstration, choose Actions > Movie Control > stop to insert a `stop()` action that will halt your movie's playback.

   The Actions List window will show your completed ActionScript, which indicates that the action will occur when the movie clip instance is loaded for the first time. The `load` event is the default clip event Flash assigns to an action whenever you don't specifically define one. Let's configure it more to our liking.

5. In the Actions List window, select the `onClipEvent(load)` statement.

   The statement will become highlighted, and the clip event parameters will become available on the top of the Actions panel.

6. Choose the clip event you want to trigger this action.

   When the movie is played, the action you assigned to this movie clip will be performed when your chosen clip event is triggered.

   TIP *Unless you specify a target (see below), actions attached to a movie clip instance affect the movie clip instance itself. For example, the `stop()` action we added in Step 4 causes the movie clip instance itself to immediately stop upon being loaded. However, you could also set up the action to halt a different timeline.*

Targets

Now that you know how to use events to trigger actions, the next step is learning how to specify which object, or *target*, will be affected by the actions that are executed when the event occurs. There are three primary kinds of targets: the current movie and its timeline, other movies and their timelines (such as movie clip instances), and external applications (such as Web browsers). The following sample ActionScripts demonstrate how each of these targets can be used to create interactivity. We'll follow those with more in-depth explanations of each target type.

In the following script, a `rollOver` (event) on a button in the current movie (target) causes that same movie's timeline to stop playing (action):

```
on(rollOver) {
   stop ();
}
```

In the next example, a rollOver (event) on a button in the current movie causes a different movie's timeline—the movie clip instance **myMovieClip** (target)—to stop playing (action).

```
on(rollOver){
   myMovieClip.stop();
}
```

The following ActionScript opens the user's default browser (target)—if it's not already open—and loads the specified URL (action) when the rollOver (event) is triggered:

```
on (rollOver) {
   getURL("http://www.derekfranklin.com");
}
```

For more information on ActionScripting syntax, see Chapter 13, "Understanding ActionScript."

Current movie

When defining a target in an ActionScript, the term "current movie" means that the same movie both contains the button, movie clip, or frame that triggers an action, *and* is itself the target of the action. Thus, if you assign a mouse event to a button, and that event executes an action that affects the movie or timeline containing the button, the target of the action is considered to be the current movie (**Figure 12.8**). If, however, you assign a mouse event to a button, and the action executed affects a movie *other* than the one it's part of, your target becomes another movie (not the current movie). The same principle applies to frame actions.

Figure 12.08 When an action (on a button, for example) causes its *own* timeline to do something (for example, stop), the target for the action is called the current movie.

Unless you specifically define another movie as your target, ActionScript will make your current movie the target, by default, for most actions. For an example, take a look at the following ActionScript:

```
on (rollOver) {
  stop();
}
```

This ActionScript indicates that a mouse event triggers the action. When the button in your movie is rolled over (event), the current movie's timeline (target) stops playing (action). We know the current movie is the target of the stop() since no other target is specifically defined.

With ActionScript, the current movie is a relative target based on the timeline on which the script is placed. For example, if you attached the above ActionScript to a button in the main movie, the main movie would be considered the current movie, or target, of the stop() action. If, however, you attached the same ActionScript to a button inside a movie clip instance, *that* movie clip's timeline would be the current movie, or target, of the action (**Figure 12.9**).

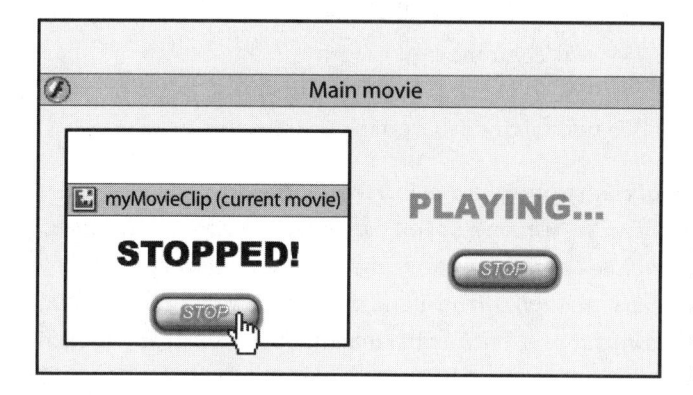

Figure 12.9
A script's placement determines what is considered the current movie in relation to that script.

Other movies

If you wish to target another movie with an action, you must specify that target in your ActionScript. Thus, if you assign an action to a button on the main timeline that targets a movie clip instance named **myMovieClip**, you would use a script similar to the one shown below. Compare the following ActionScript for controlling another movie with the ActionScript used to control the current movie in the previous example:

```
on(rollOver)
  myMovieClip.stop();
}
```

This ActionScript indicates that a mouse event triggers the action. When the button in your movie is rolled over (event), the movie clip instance named **myMovieClip** (target) will stop playing (action) (**Figure 12.10**).

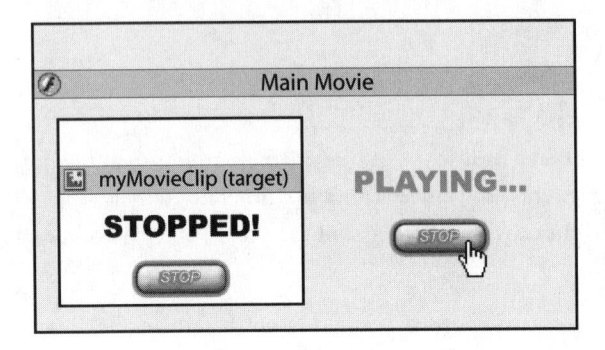

Figure 12.10
Specifically targeting another movie with an action allows you to control one movie from another.

TIP *In the ActionScript, notice the dot (.) that separates the name of the movie clip instance from the action you want it to perform. This is known as* dot syntax, *which you'll use extensively in working with ActionScript. We'll look at this topic in greater depth in the next chapter, "Understanding ActionScript."*

If you're confused by the concept of controlling one movie with instructions placed in another, hang in there—we'll continue exploring this topic throughout the chapter. For more information, see "Working with Multiple Timelines" in the next chapter, or review some of the video tutorials available on the accompanying CD.

MX ALERT **TIP** *Our discussion of controlling one movie from another involves multiple movies within a single movie window, not movies in separate movie windows, which is possible using the LocalConnection object. Documentation for this object (undocumented in Users manual) can be found on Macromedia's Web site at: /www.macromedia.com/support/flash/ts/documents/localconnection.htm.*

External targets

An external target is an application outside your movie that's required in order for an action to execute. The getURL() action, for example, uses a Web browser (the external target) to open the specified URL. Several Flash actions can target external applications, including getURL(), fscommand(), loadMovie(), loadVariables(), and some XML and LoadVars actions. The bottom line here is that all of these actions require the help of an outside application—a Web browser or Web server, or some other type of application. The following ActionScript targets a Web browser to open the specified URL:

```
on (rollOver) {
    getURL("http://www.flash.com");
}
```

This ActionScript indicates that a mouse event triggers the action. When the button in your movie is rolled over (event), a browser (target) opens the specified URL (action).

Actions

Actions represent the final piece of the interactivity puzzle. They allow you to instruct your movies (or external applications) to perform specific tasks. A single event can trigger multiple actions, which can be executed simultaneously on a single target or on different targets.

Flash can perform many actions; this chapter deals with the most basic ones. Table 12.1 indicates what these are and includes a brief description of their use. You can find these actions under Actions > Movie Control and Actions > Browser/Network, in the Toolbox List window of the Actions panel (**Figure 12.11**):

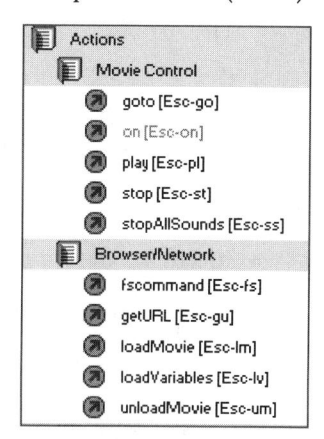

Figure 12.11
The actions in the Toolbox List window that we will be focusing on in the following sections.

Table 12.1
Basic Actions

Action	Description
gotoAndPlay()	Causes a movie to jump to the specified frame or scene on the timeline, and begin playing from that point forward.
gotoAndStop()	Causes a movie to jump to the specified frame or scene on the timeline, and stop.
on()	Allows you set a mouse event for a script (see "Mouse Events" earlier in this chapter).
play()	Causes a movie to begin playing from its current position on the timeline.
stop()	Causes a movie to stop playing.
stopAllSounds()	Stops all currently playing audio tracks.
fscommand()	Sends data to the application hosting your Flash movie (browser, projector, Director movie, and so on).
getURL()	Opens a browser window with the specified URL loaded, or sends variables to the specified URL.
loadMovie()	Loads a Flash movie, at the specified URL, within another Flash movie.
loadVariables()	Loads external variable data into a timeline.
unloadMovie()	Unloads a previously loaded movie.

Using the Actions Panel

MX ALERT The Actions panel is where interactivity is born in Flash. It's what you use to add or edit actions attached to objects, including button and movie clip instances, as well as frames (keyframes). In this section we'll look at how to use the Actions panel to create scripts—a primer for the next section, where we'll be using this panel extensively.

There are a number of ways to open the Actions panel.

To open the Actions panel, do one of the following:

- Choose Window > Actions.
- Right-click (Windows) or Control-click (Macintosh) a button or movie clip instance, or a frame on the timeline; then choose Actions from the menu that appears.
- Press F9.

  NOTE *For additional information about some of the more advanced features of the Actions panel, see Chapter 13, "Understanding ActionScript."*

Normal/Expert Modes

So you're not an ActionScript expert? Need help configuring actions and setting up your scripts? No problem. You can work with the Actions panel in one of two modes, depending on your scripting expertise and desire for control.

Normal mode

In Normal mode, you use the Toolbox List window and the Add button to add actions, the Delete button to remove actions, the Up/Down buttons to change the sequence of actions, and the Parameters panel to configure the parameters of actions.

In Normal mode, the interface is made up of the following areas (**Figure 12.12**):

- **Toolbox List window.** Contains a hierarchical list of ActionScript actions, operators, functions, constants (words with special meanings in ActionScript, such as true, false, undefined, and so on), properties, and objects. Double-clicking an icon (a book with an arrow) opens or closes a category in the Toolbox List window.
- **Actions List window.** Contains the code of the ActionScript attached to the currently selected button, movie clip, or frame. Each line represents a

Chapter 12 *Getting Started with ActionScript*

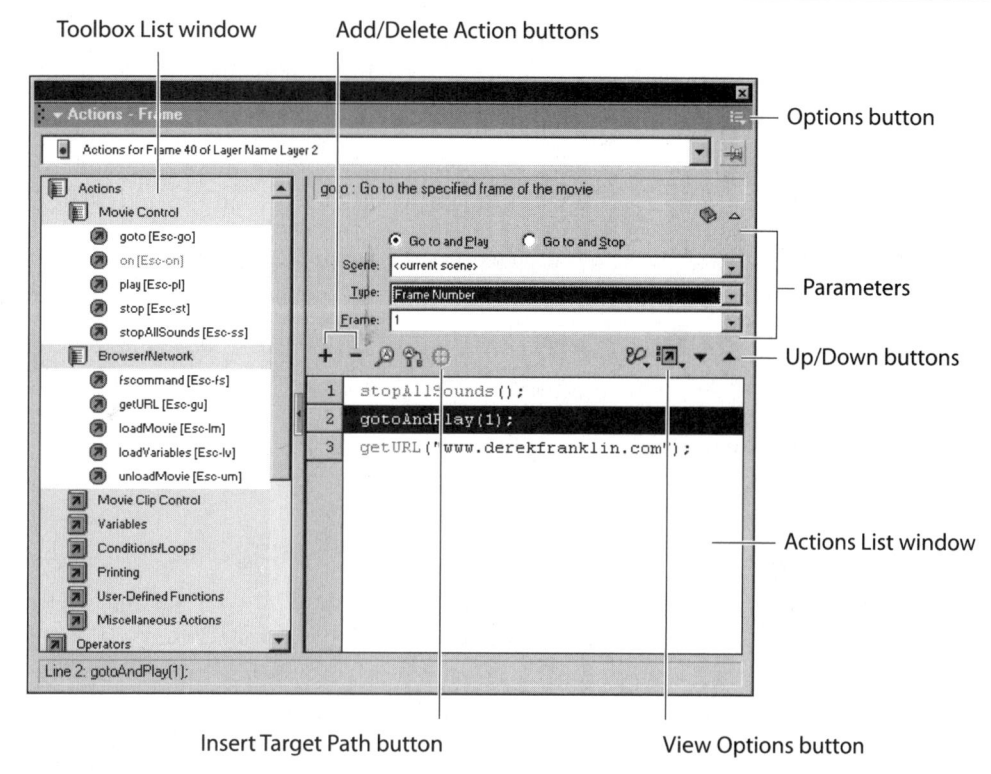

Figure 12.12
The Actions panel interface in Normal mode.

Labels (clockwise from top-left): Toolbox List window; Add/Delete Action buttons; Options button; Parameters; Up/Down buttons; Actions List window; View Options button; Insert Target Path button.

statement/action in the overall ActionScript code. Selecting a statement by clicking it causes the Parameters section of the panel to change, so that relevant parameters can be entered or edited.

- **Parameters.** This is where you can enter or edit information pertaining to the currently selected statement. This section of the Actions panel is context sensitive, and changes according to the type of statement selected in the Actions List window.

- **Insert Target Path button.** Pressing this button opens the Insert Target Path dialog box, where you can quickly choose a target for an action. This button is only activated if the parameter you're setting requires a target path. For more information on this feature, see "Working with Multiple Timelines" in the next chapter.

- **Add/Delete Action buttons.** You use these buttons to add or delete actions from the Actions List window. Pressing the Add button will reveal a hierarchical menu of ActionScript elements, similar to those found in the Toolbox List window.

- **Up/Down buttons.** These buttons enable you to move a selected statement/action up or down in the overall ActionScript. This changes the sequence of actions in the ActionScript, which can in turn change the way it works.

- **View Options button.** Provides options for displaying line numbers in the Actions List window, as well as switching between Normal and Expert modes.

- **Options button.** Press this button to display a menu that contains commands pertaining to the Actions panel.

Unless otherwise noted, the instructions in this chapter relate to using the Actions panel in Normal mode.

NOTE *We'll look at some of the more advanced features of the Actions panel in the next chapter.*

Expert mode

In Expert mode, the Actions List window acts like a text editor. You can type and edit the script directly within the window. You can still use the Toolbox List window or the Add button to add actions, but you cannot delete actions, change their sequence, or configure their parameters as you would in Normal mode. The areas where you would make these edits will be either grayed out or not displayed (**Figure 12.13**). In Expert mode, you can only perform such edits by directly editing the text in the Actions List window.

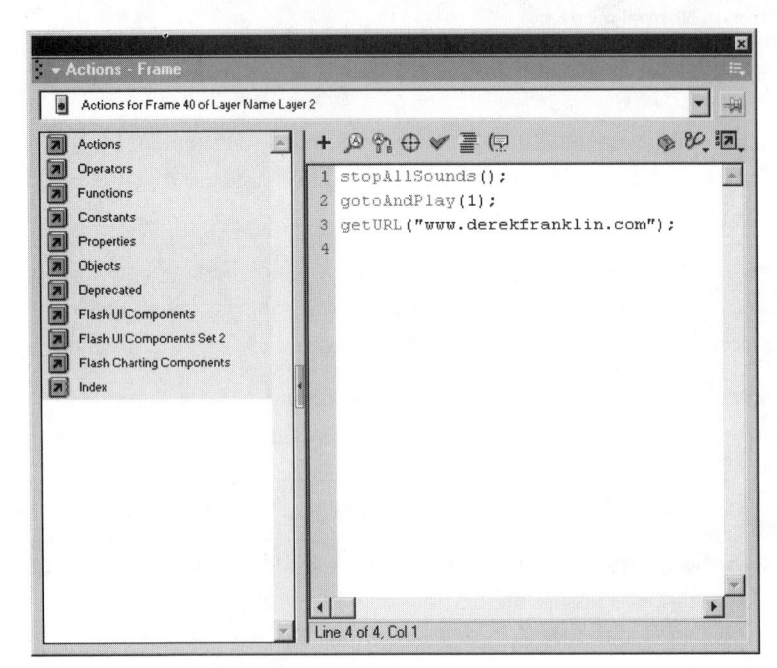

Figure 12.13
In Expert mode, you can type and edit script directly inside the Actions List window. Other editing tools, available in Normal mode, are either grayed out or unavailable.

Chapter 12 Getting Started with ActionScript

By default, the Actions panel opens in Normal mode. If you want it to open in Expert mode instead, you can set this preference.

To set the default Actions panel mode:

◆ With the Actions panel open, press the View Options button, then select Normal Mode or Expert Mode from the menu that appears.

Attaching Scripts

Attaching actions to a button or movie clip instance, or to a frame, is a simple process: You simply select the instance, then open the Actions panel. Because the Actions panel is context sensitive, it always displays the script attached to the currently selected object, as indicated by the script navigator (more on this shortly) (**Figure 12.14**).

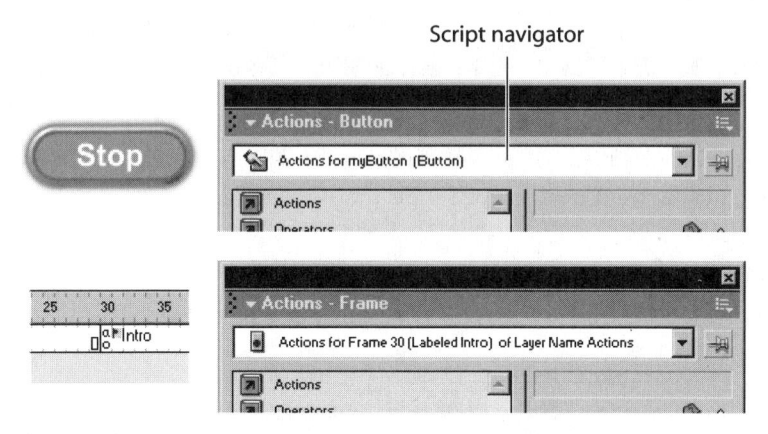

Figure 12.14
The Actions panel is context sensitive—which means that when you select an object, the Actions panel displays information relating to that object.

If you've selected a keyframe that already has an attached ActionScript, that script will appear. If the keyframe doesn't already have an attached ActionScript, any actions you enter in the Actions panel will be attached to that keyframe. The Actions panel is deactivated when the selected object can't have an attached action, as with a simple shape, bitmap, or graphic symbol instance.

While the Actions panel automatically displays any script attached to the currently selected object, you can also use the script navigator to manually choose a script to edit. The script navigator contains a drop-down list of all scriptable objects in the current frame, including the current keyframe, buttons, and movie clip instances. At any time, you can select an object from this list in order to add or edit a script on the object.

Conversely, by pressing the Pin button (**Figure 12.15**), you can "pin" a particular script to the Actions panel, so that even if you select different objects, the script displayed on the panel will not be updated. This allows you to select any number of objects while displaying a single script—eliminating some of the dizziness that can result from watching a constantly updating Action panel (as you select different objects).

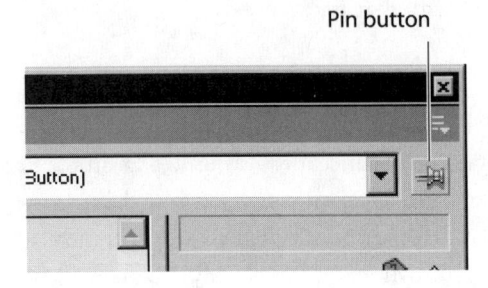

Figure 12.15
Pressing the Pin button will freeze the currently displayed script, so that it continues to be visible and editable regardless of which objects you select.

Working with Scripts in the Actions Panel

Actions can perform many powerful tasks in your movie. Once you understand some of the basic principles of working with them in the Actions panel, you'll be well on your way to making your own ActionScripts more powerful.

Adding actions

You build ActionScripts (which you attach to objects) by adding actions, one at a time, from the Toolbox List window to the Actions List window.

To add actions from the Toolbox List window to the Actions List window:

- Click the Add Action button.

  Or

- Double-click an action in the Toolbox List window.

Adding multiple actions

Flash can link multiple actions to any single event in your movie. For example, if you want a single mouse event to send the current timeline to Frame 15, while also setting the transparency property of the **myMovieClip** instance to 50 percent, you would follow the steps outlined on the next page.

The following example is based on the assumptions that the main timeline is at least 15 frames long, and that it contains a button instance and a movie clip instance named **myMovieClip**.

To add multiple actions to a single event:

1. Select the button instance on the stage.

2. Open the Actions panel.

3. Click the Add (+) button to display the action menu.

4. Because we want a rollOver mouse event to trigger our action, choose Actions > Movie Control > on.

   The mouse event will be added to the ActionScript, and parameters for the event will appear on the top of the Actions panel.

5. In the Parameters section, uncheck the Release checkbox and check the Roll Over checkbox.

   Our mouse event is now set. The Actions List window will display our mouse event, which appears highlighted.

6. Click the Add (+) button again, and select Actions > Movie Control > goto.

   The action will be placed below the mouse event in the Actions List window, and parameters for it will appear on the top of the Actions panel.

7. In the Parameters section, select Frame Number from the Type drop-down box and enter 15 in the Frame box.

8. Click the Add (+) button to display the list of actions, and select Actions > Movie Clip Control > Set Property.

   The action will be placed below the goto action in the Actions List window, and parameters for it will appear on the top of the Actions panel.

9. From the Property drop-down menu at the top of the Parameters section, choose _alpha.

10. In the Target box, enter the target whose property you want to change.

    For our demonstration, enter myMovieClip, which is our target's name and path. (For more information about target names and paths, see "Working with Multiple Timelines" in Chapter 13.)

11. In the Value box, enter the number 50.

12. Click OK.

    The button instance is now configured to perform multiple actions simultaneously when the mouse rolls over it.

You can also set up a single button instance so that one type of mouse event triggers a given action, and another type of mouse event triggers a different action. The following example script borrows from the one we just demonstrated; however, instead of using a rollOver event to trigger two different actions, in this script a rollOver event triggers one action, while a rollOut event triggers another.

```
on (rollOver) {
   gotoAndStop (15);
}
on (rollOut) {
   setProperty ("myMovieClip", _alpha, 40);
}
```

Nested actions

Nesting is an important concept—and one that is easy to grasp. By themselves, some lines of script don't do much. A with statement, for example, allows you to specify an object in order to perform a series of actions affecting that object. Take a look at the following example:

```
with (myMovieClip){
}
```

By itself, this ActionScript won't do anything. In order for it to have any effect in Flash, as well as perform any task, actions must be *nested* within it. Take a look at the following update:

```
with(myMovieClip){
   gotoAndPlay(20):
}
```

Here, the gotoAndPlay() action is nested within the with statement, as indicated by its indentation (**Figure 12.16**). This indicates that the action is tied to the with statement in some manner. In this case, since the gotoAndPlay() action is nested within the with statement that identifies **myMovieClip**, the script will cause **myMovieClip** to go to and play Frame 20.

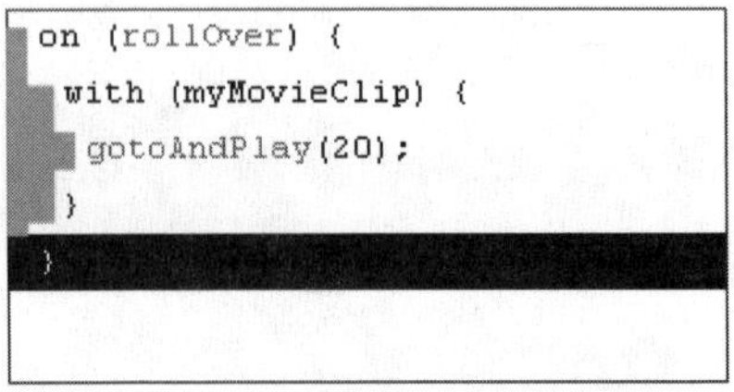

```
on (rollOver) {
   with (myMovieClip) {
      gotoAndPlay(20);
   }
}
```

Figure 12.16
Nested actions are indented in the Actions List window, making them easier to locate.

The way in which actions are nested can affect the way your ActionScript performs. Compare the following script with the preceding one:

```
on (release) {
  gotoAndPlay(20);
  with(myMovieClip) {
  }
}
```

Although this script contains the same ingredients as the previous one, it works differently because the `gotoAndPlay()` action is not nested within the `with` statement. This script causes the *current* timeline (not the **myMovieClip** timeline) to go to and play Frame 20. The `with` statement in this script has no effect because no action is nested inside it.

There are several other ActionScript elements (similar to the `with` statement) that require nested actions in order to be of use. We'll look at more of these in the next chapter.

NOTE *See the "Sequence of actions" discussion below to learn about moving actions up or down in the script, for nesting purposes.*

Deleting actions

If you've put an action somewhere it doesn't belong, you can easily remove it from the Actions list.

To delete an action:

- Select the action in the Actions list, and click the Minus (–) button at the top of it.

   TIP *If you delete a part of a script that includes nested actions (such as an `on`, `with`, or `if` statement), all nested actions will be removed as well.*

Sequence of actions

In Flash—just as in life—actions within a script need to be arranged in a certain order for the script to function in a logical and coherent manner. Flash executes actions from top to bottom, in the order they appear in the Actions list. If the sequence of actions isn't quite right, your script may not work the way you intended.

For example, look at the following scripts. The first is in the proper order:

```
on (release) {
  dynamicFrame = 20;
  gotoAndStop (dynamicFrame);
}
```

This script specifies a mouse event that creates a variable named `dynamicFrame`, with a value of 20. Once that variable is created, a `gotoAndStop()` action is set up to go to a frame number based on the value of `dynamicFrame`. Because `dynamicFrame` has been assigned a value of 20, the `gotoAndStop()` action will go to Frame 20—the desired sequence of actions.

Now take a look at the following script, which switches things around a bit:

```
on (release) {
    gotoAndStop(dynamicFrame);
    dynamicFrame = 20;
}
```

The preceding script specifies a mouse event that triggers a `gotoAndStop()` action, which is set to go to a frame number based on the value of `dynamicFrame`. The problem is, with the way the script actions are now sequenced, `dynamicFrame` has not yet been created when the `gotoAndStop()` action is executed. In fact, it will not be created until *after* the action; thus, the `gotoAndStop()` action has no effect.

The moral here is to pay attention to the order in which actions are performed in your script. These details can make or break your script.

To reorder actions:

1. In the Actions List window, click once to select the action you want to reorder.
2. Click the Up/Down arrow buttons at the top of the Actions panel to move the action up or down in the overall sequence (**Figure 12.17**).

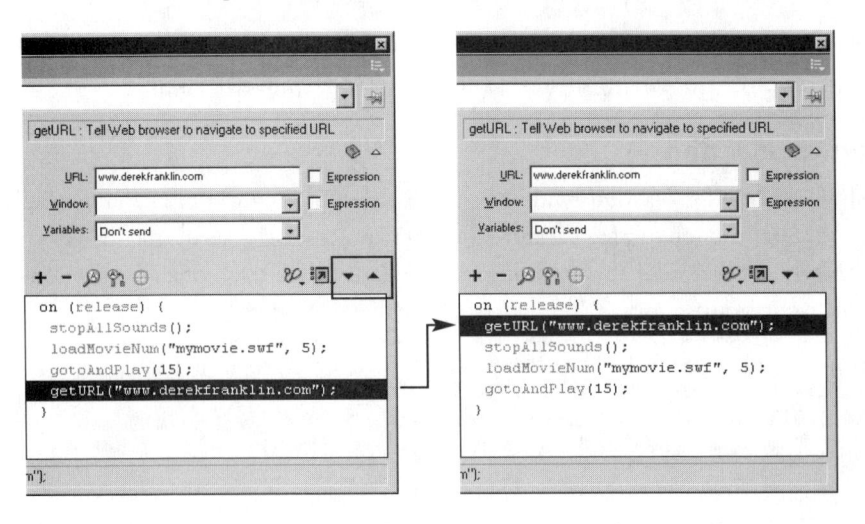

Figure 12.17 Press the Up/Down buttons above the Actions List window to reorder actions.

Cutting, copying, and pasting actions

If you've created the perfect sequence of actions on a keyframe or button and you wish to use it elsewhere, you don't need to repeat your efforts. Instead, you can simply copy and paste.

To cut (or copy) and paste actions:

1. In the Actions List window, select the actions you wish to cut or copy:

    - To select a single action, click it once.

    - To select multiple actions, hold down the Control key (Windows) or Option key (Macintosh) while clicking multiple actions.

    - To select a range of actions, click the first action in the range once, then hold down the Shift key and click the last action in the range.

2. Right-click (Windows) or Control-click (Macintosh) a selected action, and from the menu that appears, choose Cut or Copy to place the selected action or actions on the system clipboard.

3. Select the button instance, movie clip instance, or keyframe where you would like to paste these actions.

4. In the Actions List window, right-click (Windows) or Control-click (Macintosh), and from the menu that appears, choose Paste.

    The actions you placed on the clipboard now appear in the Actions List window.

    TIP *The Actions panel has its own set of undo/redo commands, available on a menu by right-clicking (Windows) or Control-clicking (Macintosh) in the Actions List window. This means that if you accidentally cut or paste something in the Actions panel, you must use the undo/redo commands available from this menu. The undo/redo commands available from the Edit menu in the authoring environment have no effect on tasks performed in the Actions panel.*

The Reference Panel

MX ALERT

The days of Flash providing just 10 actions for any kind of interactivity you wished to program are long gone. ActionScript now includes hundreds of syntactical elements, each used for a different purpose and in a different manner. For some this is a blessing, but for others it can be overwhelming. Unless you use ActionScript every day (and sometimes even then), it can be a real challenge to remember how to use a specific action, or how to configure it properly. This is where the Reference panel can help. Providing a thorough reference to all of ActionScript's syntactical elements, the panel is easily accessible within the Flash authoring environment—so that the info you need to get going is just a click away.

For each ActionScript element, the Reference panel includes information about which version of the Flash Player you can use it with; proper syntax, parameter settings, and descriptions; a description of the element and its use; and an example script showing its use (**Figure 12.18**).

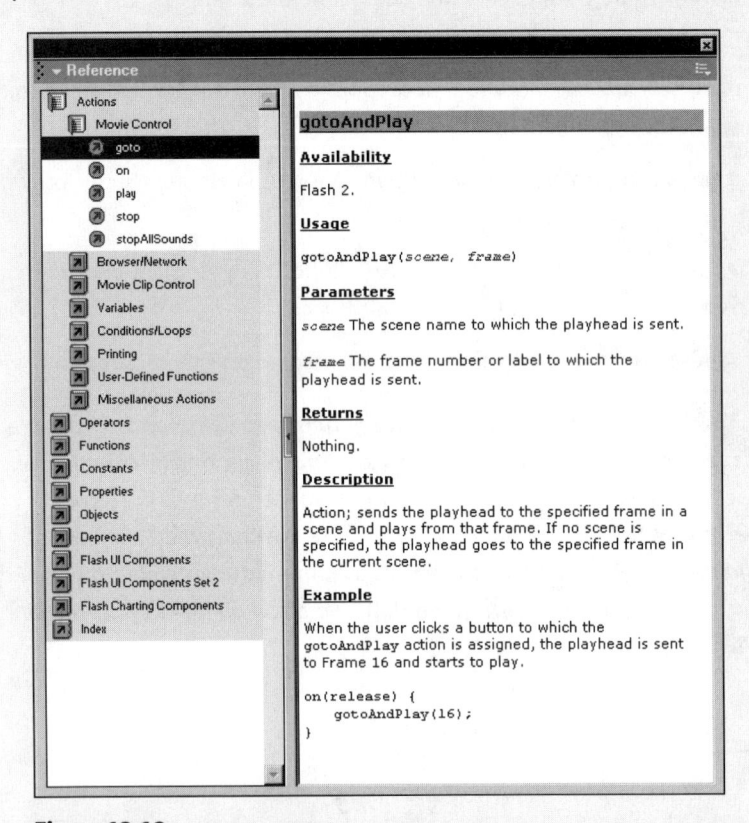

Figure 12.18
The Reference panel provides detailed information about each scripting element available in Flash MX.

Chapter 12 **Getting Started with ActionScript**

The Reference Panel *continued*

To open the Reference panel, do one of the following:

- Choose Window > Reference.
- Select a line of script in the Actions List window, then press the Reference button on the Actions panel.
- Right-click (Windows) or Control-click (Macintosh) an action in the Toolbox List window of the Actions panel, then choose View Reference from the menu that appears (**Figure 12.19**).
- Press Shift+F1.

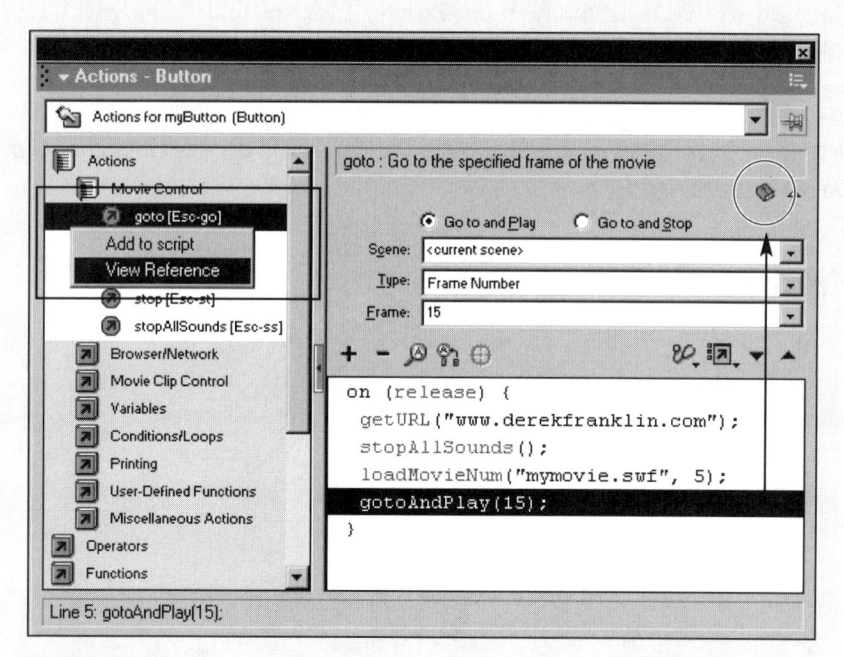

Figure 12.19
The Reference panel can be accessed by either right-clicking (Windows) or Control-clicking (Macintosh) on an action in the Actions panel, or by selecting an action in the Actions list window, then pressing the Reference button.

References to ActionScript elements are organized in two ways within the Reference panel: In the same hierarchical structure as shown in the Toolbox List window of the Actions panel, or in an alphabetical index, allowing you to find information in a way that fits your current needs.

The Reference panel can be an enormous time-saver for Flash users—and one that many developers will find more than justifies the cost of the MX upgrade.

Fundamental Interactivity

When you're learning something new, the general rule is to crawl before you try to walk. Learning to add interactivity via ActionScript is no exception. In this section, we'll introduce you to the basics of adding interactivity, by using what you've learned about ActionScript thus far. Even though these are baby steps, they're essential to understanding what follows.

In order to help you better understand the information covered here, we've created a sample Flash project, which you will be scripting as we go along. This file, named funInteractivity.fla, can be found in the Chapter 12/Assets folder (along with supporting files) on the accompanying CD. Be sure to save these files to your hard drive for testing purposes.

TIP *The terms* timeline, target, movie, *and* movie clip *are used interchangeably in the sections that follow.*

Navigating Timelines

While some Flash movies are designed to play from beginning to end without input from the user, it's more typical to provide navigational controls to the user, so he or she can move to various sections of a timeline. This type of interactivity is accomplished via the gotoAndPlay() and gotoAndStop() actions, which cause a timeline to jump to a specific frame number, frame label, or scene, where it can stop or play from that point forward (depending on how you set it up).

gotoAndPlay() and gotoAndStop() parameters

The following parameters are available for these actions (**Figure 12.20**):

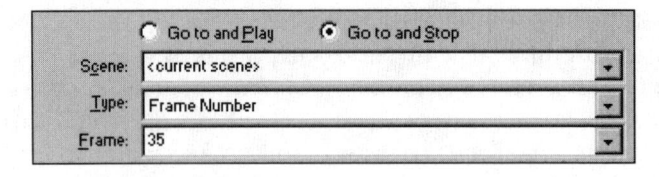

Figure 12.20
Parameter settings for the gotoAndStop() and gotoAndPlay() actions.

- **Go to and Play, Go to and Stop.** Once the timeline has jumped to a specific frame, these options allow you to specify whether the movie will stop playing at that frame, or continue playing from that frame. You can only select one of these options at a time.

- **Scene.** Allows you to choose a scene as a starting point for the goto action. Once you've defined a scene, you can then define a frame number or label within that scene. When using this action within symbols, the scene parameter is not available. The available options include the following:

    <current scene>. Allows you to choose a frame number or label (see "Frame" below) in the current scene as the point on the timeline to go to.

    <next scene>. Causes the action to go to Frame 1 of the next scene. You cannot use this option to go to a *specific* frame number or label in the scene; for this, you would use *Scene_Name*.

    <previous scene>. Causes the action to go to Frame 1 of the previous scene. You cannot use this option to go to a *specific* frame number or label in the scene; for this, you would use *Scene_Name*.

    Scene_Name. Select a scene name from the list that appears.

- **Type.** Based on the scene option you selected, this allows you to choose a specific frame in the scene to go to. The available options include the following:

    Frame Number. Select a frame number to go to (which is entered in the Frame box).

    Frame Label. Select a frame label to go to (which is entered in the Frame box).

    Expression. Allows you to dynamically set the destination frame, based on the value an expression evaluates to (which is entered in the Frame box). For more information on expressions, see Chapter 13.

    Next Frame. Causes the timeline to jump to the frame following the frame in which the action was triggered. This option is only available when selecting *<current scene>* for the scene parameter.

    Previous Frame. Causes the timeline to jump to the frame preceding the frame in which the action was triggered. This option is only available when selecting *<current scene>* for the scene parameter.

- **Frame.** If you chose Frame Number from the Type drop-down box, you would enter the frame number here. If you chose Frame Label, you would enter the name of the label here (applicable frame labels are displayed in this drop-down menu). If you chose Expression, you would enter the expression here.

Exercise

In this exercise we will add scripts to several buttons, allowing a user to navigate our project's timeline using these buttons.

1. Choose File > Open, navigate to the directory that contains funInteractivity.fla, and open it.

   Since we'll use and build on this file in the exercises that follow, let's go over its structure: The project contains six layers, named according to their content. We'll work primarily with the elements in the Content, Nav Buttons, and Actions layers. The timeline contains 60 frames. At Frames 1, 10, 20, 30, 40, and 50 there are frame labels, named according to the content that appears on the stage when the playhead is at that frame label. (You can drag the playhead to see this.) As we progress through the exercises in this chapter, we will be scripting various elements that exist on the stage at these labels (**Figure 12.21**).

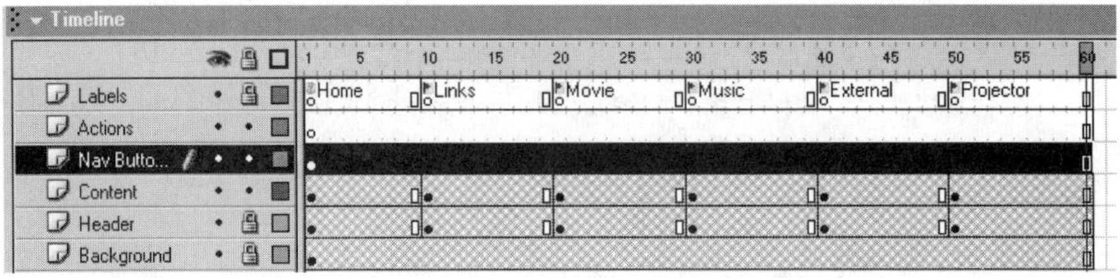

Figure 12.21
Our project's timeline.

   This exercise focuses on scripting our navigation buttons at the top of the stage to move to the appropriate frame label when pressed. Before doing that, however, let's test the movie to see how it plays.

2. Choose Control > Test Movie.

   Notice that the movie begins to play through all of the frames on the timeline as soon as it appears. The first thing we need to do is script it to pause at Frame 1, using a stop() action (which we'll learn more about shortly). Once we do this, users will have to navigate our movie via the navigation buttons we're about to script.

3. Close the test movie (File > Close), which will return you to the authoring environment, and select Frame 1 on the Actions layer. Open the Actions panel and add a stop() action.

   The movie will now pause at Frame 1 when it initially plays. Now let's begin scripting our buttons.

Chapter 12 Getting Started with ActionScript

4. On the stage, select the Home button. With the Actions panel open, locate the goto action in the Toolbox List window, and double-click it to add the action to the script.

The action will initially appear within a release event, which you'll remember is the default event used to trigger a script attached to a button (that is, when another event has not been specifically defined). So far, the script is saying that when the button is pressed and released, this goto action will be executed. However, we need to customize the action to make it go to a specific point on the timeline.

5. If the action isn't already selected in the Actions List window, select it now.

This will cause the parameters for the action to appear at the top of the Actions panel. Let's adjust these parameters.

6. Select the Go to and Stop option.

This will cause this action to move to a point on the timeline that we're about to define, then pause the playback.

7. On the Scene drop-down list, choose <current scene> (the default setting).

This indicates that the portion of the timeline we want to affect with this action is within this scene.

8. From the Type drop-down box, choose Frame Label.

This sets this action to go to a frame label. So far, the action is set up to go to a frame label within the current scene. Now we need to define *which* frame label.

9. From the Frame drop-down menu, select Home.

Since in the previous step, we choose Frame Label for the Type, this drop-down box will list every frame label in the current timeline, allowing us to quickly choose one to navigate to (**Figure 12.22**).

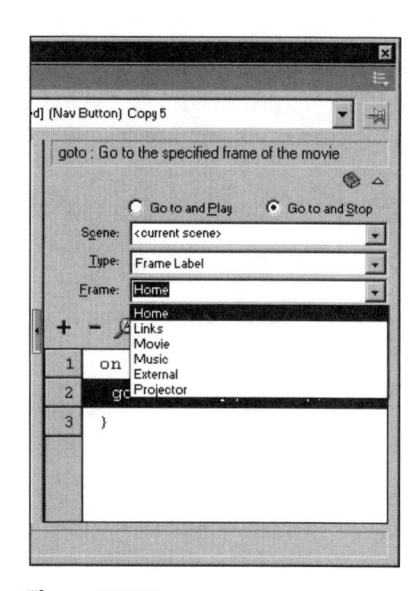

Figure 12.22
When you're setting the goto action to navigate to a frame label, the Actions panel will provide a list of frame labels, so you can quickly select the one you want.

417

We're now finished scripting our Home button. Let's move next to the Links button, which we *could* set up in similar fashion to how we set up the Home button (via a frame label); however, we're going to take a slightly different approach so that we can show you other ways to use the goto action.

10. Select the Links button. With the Actions panel open, add a goto action as already described. Use the following parameter settings for this action:

    Action: Go to and Stop

    Scene: <current scene>

    Type: Number

    Frame: 10

    Here, we've set up our action to go to a frame number (in this case, Frame 10), as opposed to a frame label as previously described. You'll notice that Frame 10 on the timeline contains the Links frame label. Thus, setting this action to move to Frame 10 has the same effect as setting it to jump to the Links label. We chose the former approach to show you the flexibility Flash offers for setting up this action. Now let's look at still another way you can set up this action.

11. Select the Movie button. With the Actions panel open, add a goto action as described. Use the following parameter settings for this action:

    Action: Go to and Stop

    Scene: <current scene>

    Type: Expression

    Frame: 15 + 5

    We've set up this goto action much like the other two, but here we're using an *expression* to tell the action which frame to go to. A what, you ask? Simply put, an expression is nothing more than an equation that is evaluated to a value, which is then used to define how the action should work. In this case, 15 + 5 will be evaluated to equal 20 (simple enough!), and thus the goto action will go to Frame 20 (which contains the Movie frame label).

    This may seem like a lot of work when you *could* just enter 20. But as we look at Flash's various features in the following chapters, you'll begin to see the power that expressions can provide when you're creating dynamic movies (**Figure 12.23**). For more about expressions, see Chapter 13, "Understanding ActionScript."

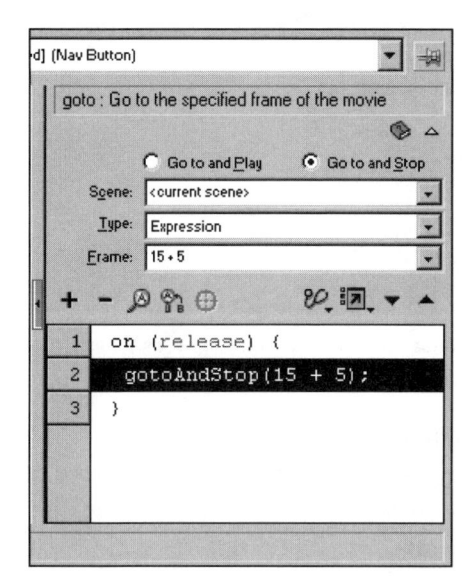

Figure 12.23
Expressions allow you to use equations that are evaluated and return a specific value, which is then used to determine how an action will work. As shown here, an expression is evaluated to determine which frame number a gotoAndStop() action should navigate to.

Let's script our remaining buttons.

12. Using any of the previously discussed methods for scripting goto actions, select the Music, External, and Projector buttons, and script them to go to and stop at the Music, External, and Projector frame labels.

13. Choose Control > Test movie to test the project to this point.

When the movie begins to play, it will pause at Frame 1 because of the stop() action on that frame. In addition, you can now navigate the movie using the buttons that we scripted—a capability enabled by the goto action.

14. Close the test movie and save your work.

Keep this file open; we'll continue to work with it in the following sections.

Linking to URLs

Hyperlinks play a huge role in making the Web the powerful communications and information-sharing tool that it is. They make it possible for you to easily open new URLs, start new email messages, and even view or download files with just a click of your mouse. Flash is able to link to these external sources using the appropriately named getURL() action.

Although you'll most often use the getURL() action when your Flash movie exists on a Web page, you can also employ it in a Flash projector to automatically open a browser window and display a specified URL, or to open a file that may exist on your hard drive.

getURL() parameters

The getURL() action has the following parameters (**Figure 12.24**):

Figure 12.24
Parameters for the getURL() action.

- **URL.** This is where you define the URL for the getURL() action. It can be a relative path, such as mypage.html, or an absolute path, such as http://www.mydomain.com/mypage.html.

  If you are using this action to send movie variables to a CGI script or a Cold Fusion template (something other than an html page), the URL entered into this box could look like http://www.mydomain.com/cgi-bin/myscript.cgi or http://www.mydomain.com/mycftemplate.cfm, respectively.

  If your Flash movie is on an HTML page, you can use this area to define a JavaScript function to call—such as javascript:newWindow()—when an event is triggered.

  To link to an email address, you would use something similar to mailto:derek@derekfranklin.com.

  To link to an external file (like a .pdf, .doc, or other file) you would use something similar to myAcrobatFile.pdf.

  You can dynamically set the URL for the getURL() action to retrieve based on the value an expression evaluates to, by selecting the Expression option to the right of the URL text box. For more information on expressions, see the following chapter.

- **Window.** Specifies the browser window or HTML frame in which to load and display the specified URL. If you have a named HTML window or frame into which you want the specified URL to load, simply type its name into this box. Otherwise, you can choose among the following options (which assume you movie is being view using a Web browser):

  _self. Loads the specified URL into the window or frame now occupied by the Flash movie.

  _blank. Opens a new browser window and loads the specified URL into it.

  _parent. Opens the URL in the parent HTML window of the current HTML window.

_top. If the Flash movie is in an HTML frame, this removes the frame set and loads the URL into the browser window.

You can dynamically set the window or frame into which a URL is loaded based on what value an expression evaluates to. To do so, select the Expression option to the right of the Window text box.

- **Variables.** You can send variable values in a movie to a server for processing. This option lets you choose how variables are dealt with when using the getURL() action. The following options are available:

MX ALERT NOTE *The new LoadVars Object is better suited for sending and retrieving variable values from an external source. The functionality described here allows backward compatibility with Flash 5. For more information about the LoadVars object, see Chapter 14, "ActionScript Objects."*

Don't send. Doesn't send variables. This option is best suited for simply opening a URL. It is also the default option.

Send using GET. Sends variable values that are appended to the specified URL for processing by the server. For example, if your movie contains two variables—name and age—using the GET method will result in something resembling the following URL: http://www.mydomain.com/mypage.html?name=Derek+Franklin&age=unknown.

Send using POST. Sends variables separate from the URL, which makes it possible for you to send more variables. On regular HTML pages, this method is most frequently used to post information collected from a form to a CGI script on the server. In the same way, it can send variable values in your Flash movie to a CGI script for processing.

TIP *When sending variables, only those in the current timeline are sent (rather than the variables from all of the movies in the Flash movie window).*

For more information about variables, see Chapter 13, "Understanding ActionScript."

Exercise

In this exercise, we'll add scripts to three buttons that exist at the Links section of our project. One button will be scripted to open a regular URL; one will be used to open an email address; and one will be used to open a file.

1. Open funInteractivity.fla from the previous exercise (if it's not already open).

2. Move the playhead to the Links frame label.

You'll notice that the stage contains three buttons: Email, Web, and File (**Figure 12.25**). The names give you a good idea of how we'll be using each, in relation to the getURL() action. Let's script them.

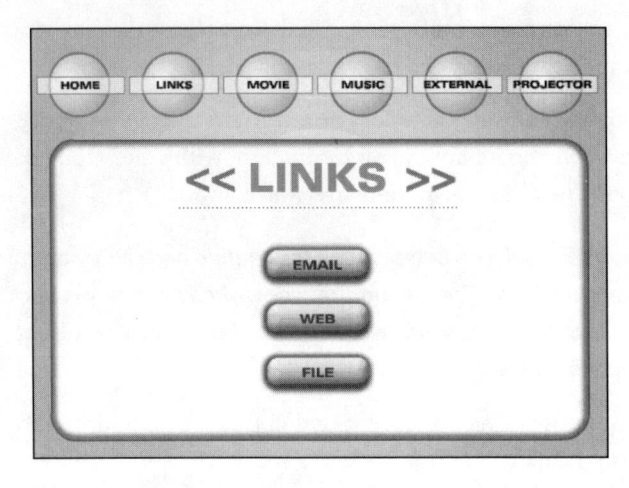

Figure 12.25
Buttons available at the Links frame label.

3. With the Actions panel open, select the Email button. Locate the getURL() action in the Toolbox List window, and double-click to add it to the script.

4. With the getURL() action selected, enter the following parameter settings (or something similar):

   URL: mailto:derek@derekfranklin.com

   Window: —leave blank—

   Variables: Don't send

   When the Email button is pressed and released, it will open up your email client so that you can send me an email (use it, if you like!).

5. With the Web button selected, add a getURL() action with the following parameter settings:

   URL: http://www.derekfranklin.com

   Window: —leave blank—

   Variables: Don't send

   When the Web button is pressed and released, it will open up my Web site in your browser (stop by and look around!).

NOTE *Instead of sending a timeline's variable values to the server via the Variables drop-down box (which will automatically append variable values to the specified URL), you can also manually specify variable values by appending them to the URL entered into the URL box. This would look something like: http://www.derekfranklin.com?name=Derek+Franklin&age=unknown (**Figure 12.26**).*

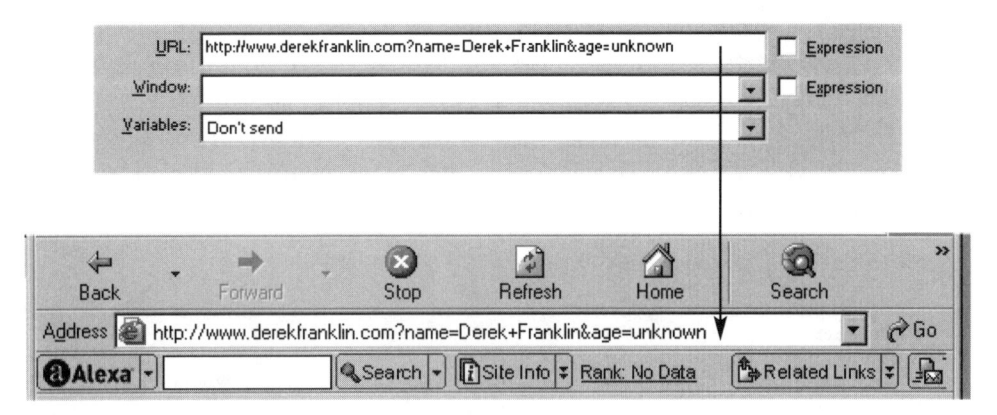

Figure 12.26
Appending variable values to the end of a URL in the URL box will cause those values to be sent to the specified URL, where they can be used or processed in some way by a server script on that page.

6. With the File button selected, add a getURL() action with the following parameter settings:

URL: sports.mp3

Window: —leave blank—

Variables: Don't send

When the File button is pressed and released, it will open up the specified file (in this case, an MP3 file).

Let's test our project.

7. Choose Control > Test Movie.

When the movie plays, press the Links button to navigate to that section. Press the Email, Web, and File buttons to see them in action.

8. Close the test movie and save your work.

Keep this file open, as we'll continue to work with it in the following sections.

Controlling a Timeline's Playback

Since a project can contain numerous timelines, you'll usually want to orchestrate the playback of those timelines in some way. Otherwise, you're likely to end up with a jumbled mess, as the timelines all play back simultaneously. Controlling a timeline's playback is a fundamental task in almost any Flash project.

You control a timeline's playback via the play() and stop() actions. The play() action causes a movie to begin playing from its current frame. If your movie has halted due to a stop() action or a gotoAndStop() action, the only way to make it resume playing is to use a play() action. The stop() action, in contrast, causes a movie to cease playing. You can use the stop() action at any point in the movie that you wish to be displayed for an extended period of time.

Neither of these actions have parameters.

Exercise

In this exercise, we'll add scripts to two buttons that exist at the Movie label of our project's timeline. These button scripts will be used to control the playback of a movie clip instance that exists on the stage.

1. Open funInteractivity.fla from the previous exercise (if it's not already open).

2. Move the playhead to the Movie frame label.

You'll notice that the stage contains two buttons, Play and Stop. In addition, you'll see a movie clip instance of what looks like a very simplified clock (**Figure 12.27**). We'll be scripting our buttons to control the playback of this movie clip instance. Before we do, it's important to see this instance in action.

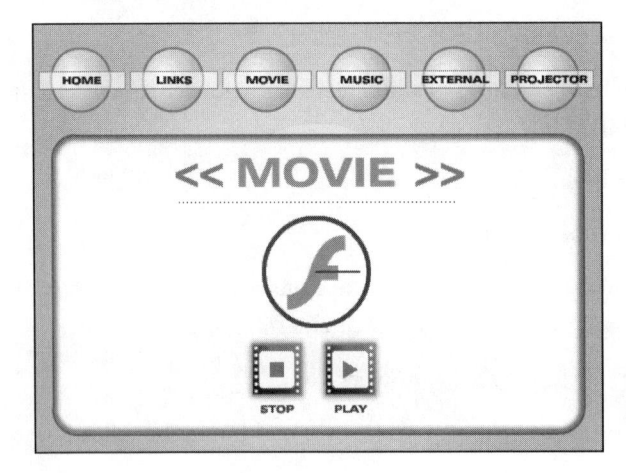

Figure 12.27 Elements on the stage at the Movie frame label.

3. Choose Control > Test Movie.

Press the Movie button to navigate to that section of our project. You'll see the thin line within our movie clip instance rotating like the second hand of a clock; we're going to script the Play and Stop buttons to play and stop this animation. In addition, we'll add a simple script to the movie clip instance itself, to specify that its playback be paused when it first loads (that is, when it appears in the scene).

4. Close the test movie to return to the authoring environment. On the stage, select the movie clip instance above the Play and Stop buttons, and with the Property inspector open, give it an instance name of **flashClock**.

You must identify the instance in this manner so that you can control it via ActionScript from another timeline (which we'll do shortly).

Next we'll attach a script to this instance.

5. With the movie clip instance still selected, open the Actions panel. In the Toolbox List window, double-click the stop() action.

The action will initially appear within a load event, which you'll remember is the default event that triggers a script attached to a movie clip instance, when the event is not specifically defined. Thus, as soon as the movie clip is loaded, its playback will be paused.

6. With the Actions panel still open, select the Stop button on the stage and attach a stop() action to it.

As this point, the stop() action will stop the main timeline, since the action is attached to a button on that timeline, and no other target for the action has been defined. However, in this case we want the action to target not the main timeline, but the movie clip instance named **flashClock**—which means we need to edit the stop() action. To do so, we need to put the Actions panel in Expert mode (in Normal mode, you can't configure the action).

7. Press the View Options button above the Actions List window, and choose Expert Mode from the menu that appears.

With the Actions panel in Expert mode, you can edit the script in the Actions List window just as if you were working within a word processor. Let's edit the stop() action so that it halts the **flashClock** movie clip instance, rather than the main timeline.

8. Edit the line containing the stop() action to read as follows:

   flashClock.stop();

   You can see that we simply placed the name of the timeline we want to control (**flashClock**) in front of the action itself (separated by a dot). Now the Stop button is scripted to stop **flashClock**'s timeline when pressed and released (**Figure 12.28**). We also need to use a similar script for the Play button; but instead of starting from scratch, let's copy and paste this script and alter it as needed.

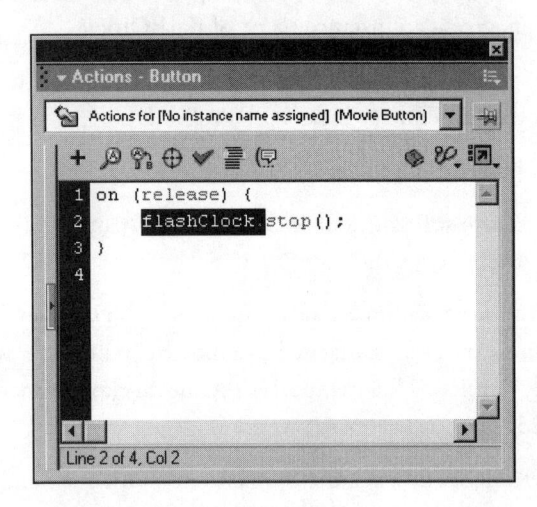

   Figure 12.28
   Placing the Actions panel in Expert mode lets you place the name of a specific timeline before the stop() action, in order to control that timeline with the action.

9. Right-click (Windows) or Control-click (Macintosh) in the Actions List window, and choose Select All from the menu that appears.

   This will select the entire script within the Actions List window.

10. Right-click (Windows) or Control-click (Macintosh) in the Actions List window and choose Copy from the menu that appears.

    This places the script on your system's clipboard.

11. Select the Play button, then within the Actions list window, right-click (Windows) or Control-click (Macintosh) and choose Paste from the menu that appears.

    At this point, the Play button is scripted to function in exactly the same manner as the Stop button (pressing it will pause **flashClock**'s timeline). However, what we really want the Play button to do is set **flashClock**'s timeline in motion, so let's alter the script a bit.

12. Edit the line with the stop() action to read as follows:

    flashClock.play();

    You can see that other than replacing the stop() action with a play() action, the script remains the same. The Play button is now scripted to play **flashClock**'s timeline when pressed and released. Let's test it.

13. Choose Control > Test Movie.

    When the movie begins to play, press the Movie button to navigate to that section. Then, press the Stop and Play buttons to see how they control **flashClock**'s timeline.

14. Close the test movie to return to the authoring environment. Put the Actions panel back into Normal mode, and save your work.

    Keep this file open, as we'll continue to work with it in the following sections.

Muting Audio

Movies usually contain audio of some sort, most commonly a soundtrack that plays in the background. Although some visitors find this enjoyable, others may prefer peace and quiet (killjoys!). By using the stopAllSounds() action, you can give your viewers a choice by allowing them to mute the audio. This action halts all currently playing audio tracks in all movies and movie clip instances within Flash Player. Once again, this action only affects any audio *currently* playing. Audio clips can be played again at any time. Consider this a quick kill-switch for audio content.

This action has no parameters.

Exercise

In this exercise we'll add scripts to a button that exists at the Music label of our project's timeline. When pressed, this button will silence any audio output.

1. Open funInteractivity.fla from the previous exercise (if it's not already open).

2. Move the playhead to the Music frame label.

You'll notice that the stage contains five buttons, four black and one white. Each of the black buttons is already set up to play a music track when clicked (**Figure 12.29**). Let's take a look at this in action.

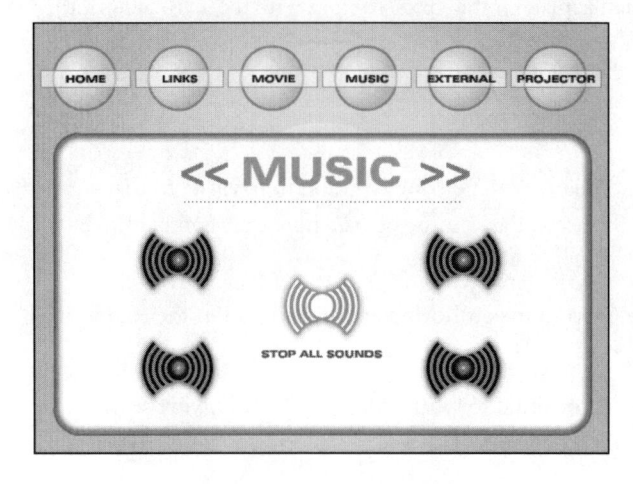

Figure 12.29
At the Music label of our project, the stage contains four black buttons that play music when pressed, and a single white button that we'll set up to silence any audio that's playing.

3. Choose Control > Test Movie.

Press the Music button to navigate to that section of the movie. Press one of the black buttons to begin playing a music track. Then click another to start playing another track simultaneously. You'll quickly notice that there's no way to stop the music! This is where the white button comes into play; we'll now add a simple script to that button to provide a solution.

4. Close the test movie to return to the authoring environment. Select the white button. In the Toolbox List window of the Actions panel, locate the stopAll-Sounds() action, and double-click to attach the action to the button.

This action, which will stop all currently playing sounds, will be executed when the button is pressed and released. Let's test it.

5. Choose Control > Test Movie.

When the movie plays, press the Music button to navigate to that section. Press one or two of the black buttons to get the music started. Then press the white button to stop any playing audio.

6. Close the test movie, and save your work.

Keep this file open, as we'll continue to work with it in the following sections.

Loading and Unloading External Movies

External movies are regular SWF files that are loaded into the Flash Player as a movie plays, allowing you to load and unload content on an as-needed basis. So instead of creating single SWF files containing hundreds of movie clips, which will cause such files to balloon past acceptable size limits, you can load those clips dynamically.

For example, think of a graphic portfolio application: There's no reason to make users download hundreds of samples at once, when they'll be viewing those samples individually, *one at a time*. It makes much more sense to place each portfolio item in a separate SWF file, which would then be loaded as needed based on user interaction—and unloaded when the user has finished viewing it or requested a new item to replace it.

Compartmentalizing a project in this manner not only improves the movie's performance, it also makes it easier to update content. Because you'll be editing smaller, individual files rather than working with one huge file, there's less chance of messing something up on a grand scale.

MX ALERT TIP *In addition to loading external SWFs, the* `loadMovie()` *action can now be used to load external JPG images.*

External movies can possess all the functionality of full-blown Flash productions. And once they're loaded, you can interact with and control them via ActionScript, in the same way you would an internal movie clip instance.

Loading and unloading external movies and JPGs is accomplished using the `loadMovie()` and `unloadMovie()` actions. Let's first look at the `loadMovie()` action, which allows you to do any of the following:

- Load a new movie into the Flash Movie window to replace an existing one (meaning you can *replace* the existing movie in the Player window without loading a different HTML page).

- Load a movie or image into the Flash Movie window, in *addition* to those already there (**Figure 12.30**).

- Load a movie or JPG into a movie clip target (thereby replacing the movie clip instance with the external movie or image).

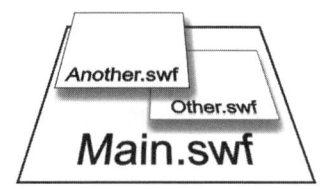

Figure 12.30
By using the `loadMovie()` action to load movies and JPGs, you can have multiple SWF and JPG files in the Flash Player window at once.

loadMovie() parameters

This action has the following parameters (**Figure 12.31**):

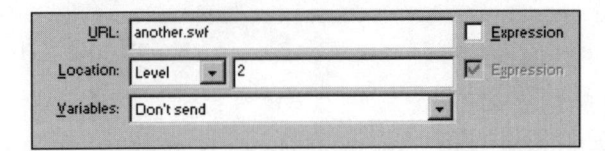

Figure 12.31 Available parameters for the loadMovie() action.

- **URL.** This is the directory path to the external SWF or JPG file you want to load. It can be a relative path, such as `mymovie.swf`, or an absolute path, such as `http://www.mydomain.com/myimage.jpg`.

  NOTE *You cannot load progressive JPGs (the kind that appear blurry initially, then gain focus as more image data is loaded) via this action.*

  You can dynamically set the URL parameter based on the value an expression evaluates to, by selecting the Expression option to the right of the URL text box.

- **Location.** This parameter defines the location within the Player window where you want the external file to be loaded. There are two options:

  Level. You can think of levels as layers within the Flash Player window. Loading a SWF or JPG into a level places it in one of these layers; the number assigned to a level determines its position relative to the other levels (**Figure 12.32**). As the bottom file in the stack, Level 0 represents the movie that appears initially. The movie in Level 0 sets the frame rate, background color, and frame size for all other movies that are loaded. SWFs and JPGs can be loaded into levels that already contain another SWF or JPG; however, remember that doing so replaces the existing file on that level. For more information, see "Working with Multiple Timelines" in Chapter 13.

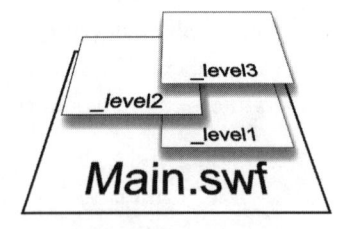

  Figure 12.32 Loading a movie into a level places all of its content on that level.

  You can dynamically set the level in which to load a file, based on the value an expression evaluates to, by entering the expression directly into the Location text box.

  Target. You can use this Location setting to load an external SWF or JPG into a location currently occupied by a movie clip instance—in essence, replacing the current movie clip instance. The newly loaded file will inherit all the current properties of the movie clip you've replaced—including its name, target path, size, and position (**Figure 12.33**). In addition, if the target movie clip instance is used in a motion tween or frame-by-frame animation, the more recently loaded SWF or JPG will be used in its place.

You can dynamically set the target name in which to load a file, based on the value an expression evaluates to, by selecting the Expression option to the right of the Target text box.

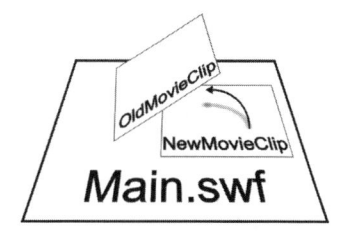

Figure 12.33
Loading a movie into a target causes an externally loaded SWF or JPG file to replace any movie clip instance that previously resided there.

- **Variables.** If you want to pass the existing variables in the current movie clip instance into the external file that's being loaded, you use this parameter to determine how those variables are sent. This means that an externally loaded movie can receive variable data before it's loaded, so that it can react to that data immediately. The following options are available:

    Don't send. No variables will be sent from the current movie to the one being loaded.

    Send using GET. Sends variables appended to the specified URL (where the external file exists).

    Send using POST. Sends variables separate from the URL (which allows you to send more variables).

    NOTE *When a JPG is loaded, it's basically treated as a single-frame timeline (with its own variables and properties), and can be controlled in the same way as a regular movie clip instance.*

The unloadMovie() action allows you to unload a movie that was previously loaded into the Player window via the loadMovie() action.

unloadMovie() parameters

This action includes the following parameter:

- ◆ **Location.** This parameter defines the level or target containing the SWF or JPG that will be unloaded. It includes the following options:

    Level. Unloads the SWF or JPG at the level specified.

    You can dynamically set the level from which to unload a file, based on the value an expression evaluates to, by entering the expression directly into the Location text box.

Target. Unloads the SWF or JPG at the specified target.

You can dynamically set the target name from which to unload a file, based on the value an expression evaluates to, by selecting the Expression option to the right of the Target text box.

Exercise

In this exercise, we'll add scripts to two buttons that exist at the External label of our project's timeline. One button will be scripted to load an external JPG into a target, while the other will load an external SWF into a level. One will be unloaded when the space bar is pressed; the other will be unloaded in response to a dragOut mouse event.

1. Open funInteractivity.fla from the previous exercise (if it's not already open).

2. Move the playhead to the External frame label.

   You'll notice that the stage contains two buttons: one to load an external file into a target, the other to load an external file into a level. You will also see a small circle just below the second *E* in *EXTERNAL*. This is a graphically empty movie clip instance that has been given an instance name of **myTarget**. We will first set up our project to load an external JPG into this instance (target) (**Figure 12.34**).

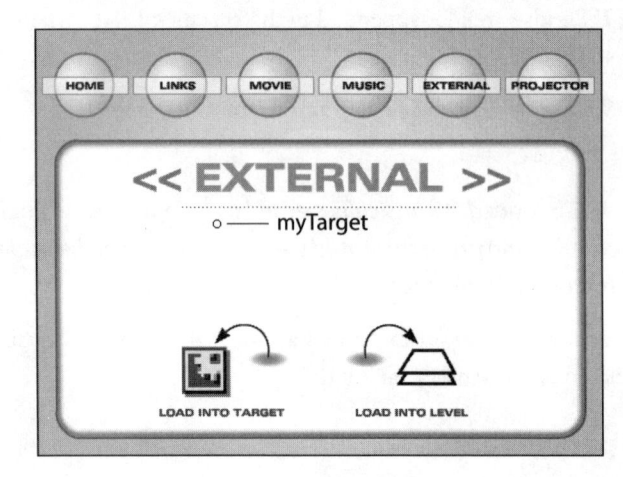

   Figure 12.34
   At the External label of our project, the stage contains two buttons and a movie clip instance named **myTarget.**

   The files you copied to your hard drive for this exercise included a SWF file named external.swf, and a JPG named flower.jpg. These are the files we will be loading.

3. Select the Load into Target button and with the Actions panel open, add a loadMovie() action with the following parameter settings.

   URL: flower.jpg

   Location: Target > myTarget

   Variables: Don't send

When the button is pressed and released, the flower.jpg file will be loaded into the **myTarget** movie clip instance, replacing any content in that instance with that of the loaded JPG (in this case our movie clip instance is empty, so there's nothing to replace). Next, we need a mechanism for unloading the JPG as well. Let's set that up.

4. Select the last line of the script in the Actions List window (it should just contain a closing bracket (})). In the Toolbox List window of the Actions panel, locate the unloadMovie() action and double-click it.

This will add three new lines of script that look like the following:

```
on (release) {
    unloadMovieNum(0);
}
```

You can see that this part of the script will execute when the button is pressed and released. We need to edit the unloadMovie() action, but first we want to edit the on() statement, so that this part of the script executes when the space bar on the keyboard is pressed—*not* when the button is pressed and released.

5. In the Actions List window, select the on() statement. In the parameters that appear at the top of the Actions panel, deselect the Release option, check the Key Press option, then press the space bar on the keyboard.

The unloadMovie() action will now execute when the space bar is pressed (**Figure 12.35**). Next we'll edit the unloadMovie() action.

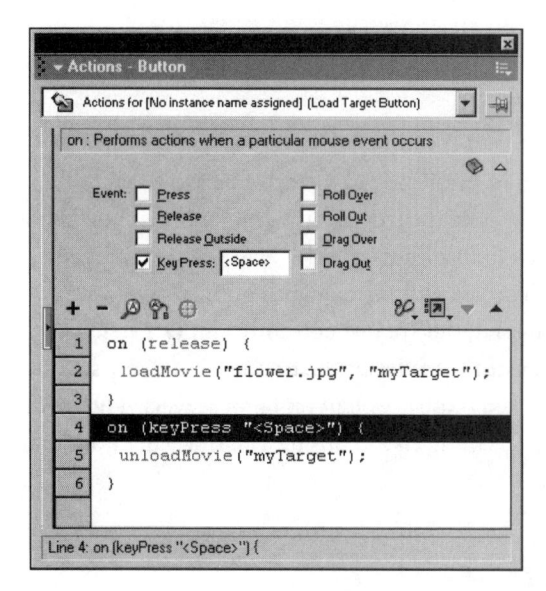

Figure 12.35
By selecting the on() statement as shown, we can edit the event that will execute the unloadMovie() action. In this case, we've set it to occur when the space bar is pressed.

6. Select the `unloadMovie()` action and adjust the Location parameter as follows:

   Location: Target > myTarget

   The action is now configured to unload any movie or JPG that has been loaded into the **myTarget** instance.

   Since the script on this button is very similar to the script we'll need for our other button, we can just copy it, then paste and edit it as needed.

7. Click the first line of the script, hold down the Shift key, and then click the last line of the script.

   This will select the entire script within the Actions List window.

8. Right-click (Windows) or Control-click (Macintosh) in the Actions List window and choose Copy from the menu that appears.

   This places the script on your system's clipboard.

9. On the stage, select the Load into Level button. With the Actions panel open, right-click (Windows) or Control-click (Macintosh) in the Actions List window, and choose Paste from the menu that appears.

   This pastes the script to the Load into Level button. We need to edit the script just a bit so that it loads our external SWF (external.swf) into Level 38. Why Level 38? We'll explain in a moment.

10. Select the `loadMovie()` action and adjust its parameters as follows:

    URL: external.swf

    Location: Level > 38

    Variables: Don't send

    This `loadMovie()` action is set up to load the external.swf file into Level 38. We chose Level 38 to demonstrate the fact that the level number you choose can be arbitrary. You don't need to load movies or JPGs in sequential levels: If you load a movie into Level 38 but haven't loaded anything into Levels 1 through 37, those levels can still be used; they're just currently empty. Later, if you wish, you can load a movie into any of those levels. Just remember that visual content on lower levels can be blocked out by content on higher levels. Thus, external.swf will display on top of everything else in our movie, since all of our other visual content exists on Level 0.

Now let's edit the rest of the script, so that it unloads the SWF on Level 38 when the mouse is rolled off of the Load into Level button. First we'll edit the unloadMovie() action.

11. Select the unloadMovie() action and adjust the Location parameter as follows:

Location: Level > 38

This action unloads the movie in Level 38. Next we'll edit the event that executes this action.

12. Select the on(KeyPress, "<Space>") statement. In the parameters that appear at the top of the Actions panel, deselect the Key Press option and select the Roll Out option.

The unloadMovie() action will now execute when the mouse is rolled off of the Load into Level button.

The scripts on both buttons are now complete (**Figure 12.36**). Let's do some testing!

```
1  on (press) {
2      loadMovieNum("external.swf", 38);
3  }
4  on (rollOut) {
5      unloadMovieNum(38);
6  }
```

Figure 12.36
The complete script attached to the Load into Level button.

13. Choose Control > Test Movie.

When the movie begins to play, press the External button to navigate to that section. Press the Load into Target level button. When you do, the external JPG image (flower.jpg) will be loaded into the **myTarget** movie clip instance. Press the space bar to unload it. Next, press the Load into Level button. When you do, our external SWF file (external.swf) will be loaded into Level 38.

NOTE *If a movie already existed at Level 38, loading the new **myTarget** clip into that level would have caused it to be replaced.*

You'll notice that the top-left corner of the externally loaded movie is in the same location as the top-left corner of our overall movie (**Figure 12.37**). By default, this is the location where a movie loaded into a level appears.

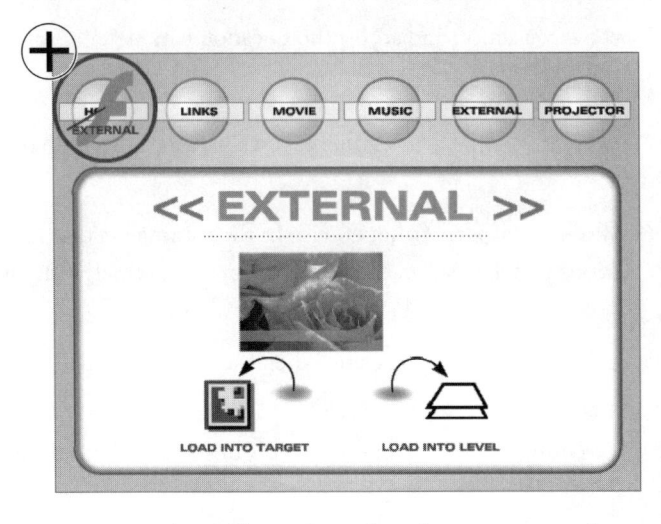

Figure 12.37
When a SWF or JPG is loaded into a level, its top-left corner is initially positioned in the same location as the top-left corner of the overall movie.

However, this will not always be where you want the externally loaded movie positioned. Fortunately, ActionScript allows you to dynamically change the X and Y (location) properties of all movies, including those loaded into a level, allowing you to reposition the loaded movie as you wish. If you roll away from the Load into Level button, the movie loaded into Level 38 will be unloaded.

NOTE *To learn more about how to load and unload a sequence of movies/JPGs, see Chapter 14, "ActionScript Objects," and Chapter 16, "Using ActionScript in Your Projects."*

14. Close the test movie, and save your work.

Keep this file open, as we'll continue to work with it in the next (last!) section.

Controlling Projectors

A projector is a stand-alone version of a Flash movie—in other words, a movie that's been created to play without requiring a browser or the Flash Player to be installed on the user's system. You can think of projectors as mini-applications containing everything needed to play your Flash movie on almost any computer. You can control your projectors via the `fscommand()` action.

You can use the `fscommand()` action in one of two ways: To control a projector, or to allow Flash to communicate with other programs—say a Web browser or any program that can host your Flash movie (that is, one in which you can embed your Flash movie).

Many people use this command to make their Flash movies interact with JavaScript on HTML pages (see the "Commanding JavaScript" sidebar later in this chapter).

fscommand() parameters

The fscommand() action has the following parameters (**Figure 12.38**):

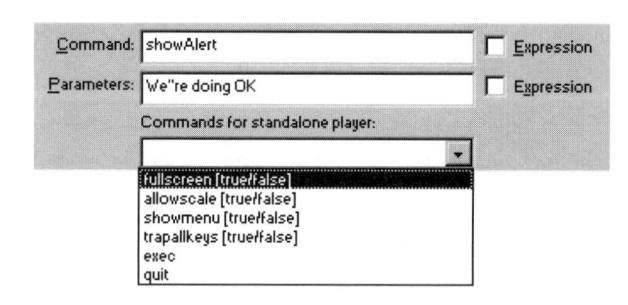

Figure 12.38
Parameters for the fscommand() action.

- **Command.** This is a unique name you assign to an fscommand() action; it can be *sausage* or *escalator*—or anything else (see the "Commanding JavaScript" sidebar).

  You can dynamically set the command to perform based on the value an expression evaluates to, by selecting the Expression option to the right of the Command text box.

- **Parameters.** If the command requires that any information be passed—for example, to a JavaScript function—you must enter it here. That information can take the form of a text string, such as "Hey Bob," or a numeric value, such as 35 (see the "Commanding JavaScript" sidebar).

  You can dynamically set the parameters that will be used, based on the value an expression evaluates to, by selecting the Expression option to the right of the Parameters text box.

- **Commands for standalone player.** When you're distributing your movie as a stand-alone application, the following settings are available for the Flash projector:

  Fullscreen. To display a projector so that it can be seen at full screen, choose "true." Choosing "false" displays the projector at the size set in the Document Properties dialog box.

  Allowscale. Choose "true" to allow users to resize the Projector window. Choosing "false" prevents the window from being resized.

  Showmenu. Choose "true" to make the projector menu available when the user right-clicks (Windows) or Control-clicks (Macintosh) the projector window. Choosing "false" prevents the menu from being displayed.

  Quit. Quits the projector and closes its window.

Exec. Use this command to start an external application from Flash. Enter the directory path to the application in the Argument box.

> ### Commanding JavaScript
>
> *The `fscommand()` action allows a Flash movie on an HTML page to communicate with (control) the Web browser via JavaScript. This allows you to do things like open alert boxes, resize the browser window, fill in HTML form elements dynamically, and much more.*
>
> **To use the `fscommand()` action to communicate with a Web browser:**
>
> 1. *Create a Flash movie with a button containing a mouse event that triggers an `fscommand()` action.*
>
> 2. *When setting up the `fscommand()` action, type* showAlert *in the Command box and* We're Doing OK *in the Parameters box. You make up the command name, which can be anything from* turtle *to* hairspray. *You'll see how it's used shortly.*
>
> 3. *For the purpose of our example, if you wish to create a second button with a different `fscommand()` action on it, simply type* htmlWrite *in the Command box, but type* Hello there! *in the Argument box.*
>
>   *You now have two buttons that make use of two different commands that we created. One command is named* showAlert, *the other* htmlWrite. *Make sure you remember these names and their associated parameters.*
>
> 4. *Place your movie on the HTML page. When setting the <object> and <embed> tags for embedding the movie, be sure to set the ID parameter (<object> tag only) and NAME parameter (<embed> tag only) to identify the movie on the page. For our demonstration, give them both a value of* myMovie *(**Figure 12.39**). It's important that the value for both the <object> and <embed> tags be the same; make sure to remember this value too. (For more information about the NAME and ID parameters, see Chapter 20, "Publishing.")*

```
1  <html>
2  <head>
3  <title>Flash MX Rocks!</title>
4  <meta http-equiv="Content-Type" content="text/html; charse
5  </head>
6
7  <body bgcolor="#FFFFFF" text="#000000">
8  <object classid="clsid:D27CDB6E-AE6D-11cf-96B8-4445535400(
9    <param name=myMovie value="funInteractivity.swf">
10   <param name=quality value=high>
11   <embed src="funInteractivity.swf" id=myMovie quality=hi
12   </embed>
13 </object>
14 </body>
15 </html>
16
```

Figure 12.39
Setting identical NAME and ID values in the <object> and <embed> tags is necessary in order for an fscommand() action to communicate properly with a Web browser.

Commanding JavaScript *continued*

5. On the HTML page that contains the movie, create a JavaScript function as follows:

```
function myMovie_DoFSCommand(command, arguments){
  if(command == "showAlert"){
    alert(arguments);
  }else if (command == "htmlWrite"){
    document.write(arguments);
  }
}
```

This JavaScript function is specifically designed to deal with `fscommand()` actions executed in the movie with the ID and NAME value of myMovie. Notice that the name of the function makes use of this value, which creates the relationship between the function and the movie (the *_DoFSCommand* part of the name is required).

Whenever one of the `fscommand()` actions (which you'll remember are named showAlert and htmlWrite) in this movie is triggered, that name and the associated parameters are sent as parameters (`command, arguments`) to this function (**Figure 12.40**).

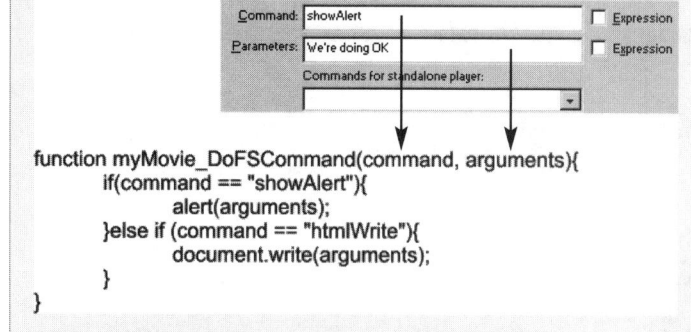

Figure 12.40 Whenever an `fscommand()` action is executed, the name of the command and its associated parameters are sent to the function on the HTML page so that that function can react accordingly.

As you can see, the function uses a conditional statement to determine whether the command that was triggered was named showAlert or htmlWrite, and then takes the appropriate action. For example, if the showAlert command is triggered, the function will create an HTML alert box that will display the text We're doing OK, which you'll remember is the associated parameter for the showAlert command. If the `fscommand()` actions had different Command names (see Steps 2 and 3), you would edit the function accordingly.

Given the power of JavaScript, and the way that the `fscommand()` allows you to communicate with it, not only can your Flash movies be interactive, but so can the HTML pages where they reside.

Exercise

In this exercise we'll add scripts to three buttons that exist at the Projector label of our project's timeline. One button will be scripted to allow the movie display to be resized proportionately within the Projector window when it is maximized; another button will turn off this functionality (so that the movie display remains the same size, regardless of the projector window's size); and the third button will be scripted to exit (or quit) the projector.

1. Open funInteractivity.fla from the previous exercise (if it's not already open).
2. Move the playhead to the Projector frame label.

   You'll notice that the stage contains the three buttons described in the paragraph above (**Figure 12.41**).

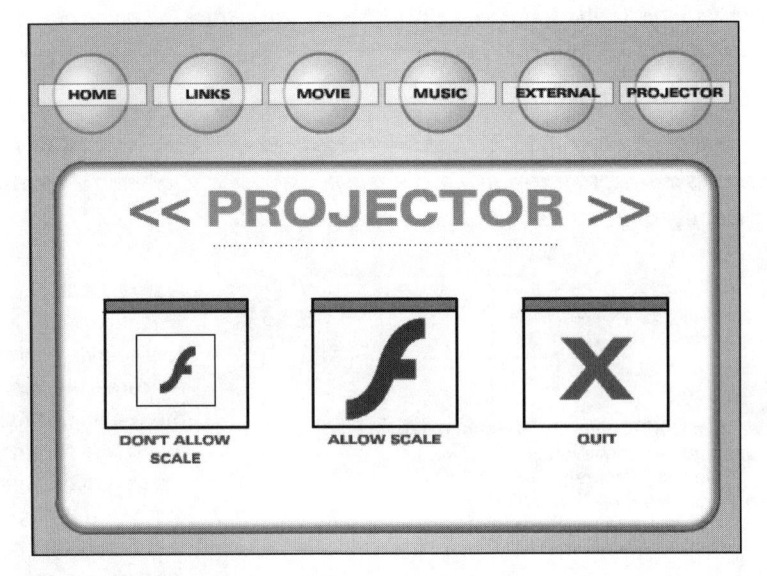

Figure 12.41
At the Projector label of our project, the stage contains three buttons, which we will script to control the projector window our movie plays within.

3. Select the Don't Allow Scale button and attach an `fscommand()` action to it.
4. With the action selected in the Actions List window, locate the "Commands for standalone player" drop-down menu and select "allowscale" from the list of choices.

As a result, the Command box will be automatically filled in with a value of *allowscale*, while the Parameters parameter will be automatically filled in with a value of *true* (**Figure 12.42**).

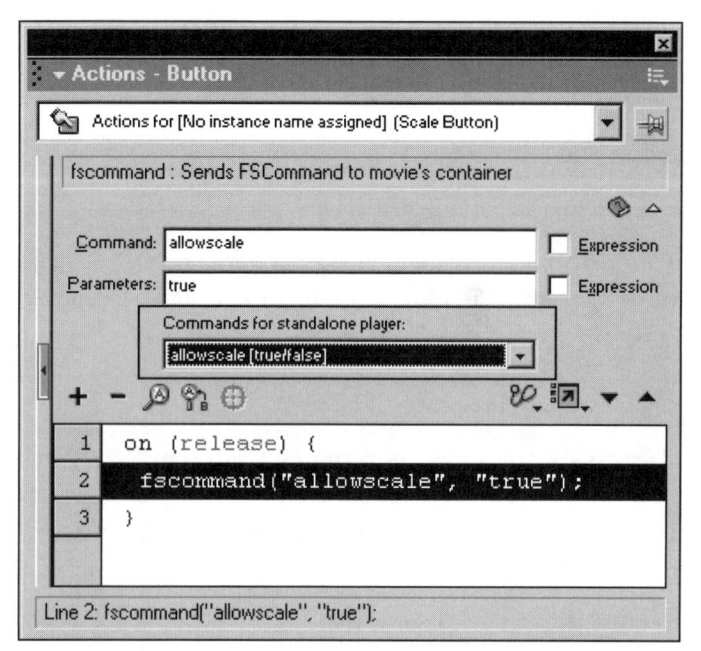

Figure 12.42
Selecting a choice from the "Commands for standalone player" drop-down menu will automatically enter appropriate values in the Command and Parameters boxes.

5. Since we want the button to which this script is attached to disable scaling, edit the Parameters box to read *false*.

When this button is pressed and released, scaling of the movie will not be possible (that is, the movie display will not be resized proportionately with the projector window). This script is now complete.

6. Next, select the Allow Scale button and repeat Steps 3 and 4, only this time leave the Parameters box with a value of *true*.

When this button is pressed and released, scaling of the movie *will* be allowed. This script is now complete.

7. Finally, select the Quit button and attach an `fscommand()` action to it.

8. With the action selected in the Actions List window, choose Quit from the "Commands for standalone player" drop-down menu.

When this button is pressed and released, the projector will close. This script is now complete. It's time to test our project, but since we need to test it in the form of a projector, choosing Control > Test Movie will not work. We need to actually generate a projector for the movie.

9. Choose File > Publish Settings.

This opens the Publish Settings dialog box.

10. On the Formats tab, select the Windows Projector option if you're using Windows, or Macintosh Projector if you're working on a Macintosh.

11. Click OK.

12. Choose File > Publish Preview > Projector.

This will export your movie as a projector for testing purposes. When the projector opens, press the Projector button to navigate to that section of our movie. Be sure to interact with the three buttons we worked with, and maximize the projector window, in order to see the effect of the scripts we set up!

13. Close the projector, and save your work.

NOTE *A completed version of this entire project can be found in the Chapter 12/Assets folder on the accompanying CD.*

Video Tutorials

- ***Working with the Actions panel.*** This tutorial demonstrates how to add and delete actions, and change their sequence, as well as helps you grasp the overall workflow in the Actions panel.

- ***Understanding Targets.*** Flash novices often find targets mysterious. This tutorial removes the mystery by showing you how to target different timelines in the movie window.

Understanding ActionScript

CHAPTER 13

What you'll learn…

About ActionScript's logic and flow

How to create and use variables in your ActionScripts

About expressions

About statements

How to use functions in your scripts

About event handler methods

About listener events

How to work with multiple timelines

About the advanced features of the Actions panel

For many Flash users, creating sophisticated animations and interactive buttons is enjoyable, but the thought of actual programming makes their toes curl. There are all kinds of reasons users might shy away from the type of programming entailed in ActionScripts; however, the bottom line is this: To take your Flash movies to the next level, you need to understand ActionScripting. Armed with even the most basic knowledge of it, you'll be able to create games, interactive forms, highly interactive interfaces, and much more.

In Chapter 12 we introduced you to some of the basic ways you can use ActionScript to create interactivity. Since you're still reading, you've obviously come to appreciate the power you have at your fingertips and are prepared to exploit it to the fullest. Great! What follows builds on the foundation you gained in the previous chapter, providing you with the knowledge you need to become a full-fledged ActionScripter.

Although you may find some of the concepts of ActionScripting new—and you may find it tough going at first—eventually things will fall into place. In this chapter we've tried to make the learning process as simple as possible by including plenty of scripts and real-world examples to demonstrate ActionScript's logic and flow. Also, since you'll be working with the Actions panel a lot more, be sure to check out the video tutorial at the end of the chapter, which explores some of that panel's more advanced features. Be patient if you have to review the information more than once—few people are able to pick up scripting languages the first time around.

Keep in mind this chapter is not intended as an exhaustive examination of all that ActionScript can do. Instead, it should provide a solid basis for continuing to explore ActionScripting on your own.

Getting Familiar with ActionScript

In the following subsections we'll deconstruct a sample strict, explaining how it's interpreted by Flash, and then provide an overview of many of the elements that make up a typical ActionScript. This should give you the foundation you need to progress through the rest of the chapter and begin to tap into the true power of ActionScript.

Deconstructing a Script

As we look at how the following sample script works and what it accomplishes, keep in mind that not all of the syntax will make sense to you immediately. However, we'll explain enough at this point for you to follow along, and you'll learn the rest as we go.

Here's the setup: On the stage is an input text field with an instance name of **savings** and a dynamic text field with an instance name of **myGreeting**. In addition to these two text fields, there are two movie clips on the stage as well as a button. One of the movie clips depicts a Porsche and has an instance name of **myPorscheMovie;** the other depicts a bicycle and has an instance name of **myBicycleMovie**. The button labeled Enter is used to trigger the following script (**Figure 13.1**).

NOTE *If this example looks familiar, that's because it is: We used a simplified version of it in the previous chapter. Here, our discussion is about more advanced ActionScript, so we've increased the script's functionality considerably.*

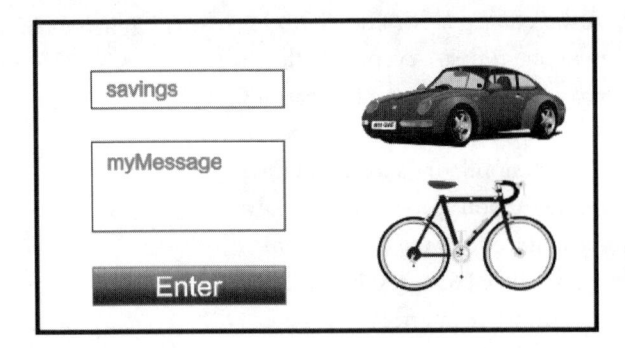

Figure 13.1
A graphical view of our fictitious project.

We ask the user if the amount in his or her savings account is closer to $50,000 or $200, and to enter that number into the input text field named **savings** and to then press the Enter button, which executes this script:

```
on(release){
  if(savings.text == 50000){
    vehicleToBuy = "Porsche";
  }else if(savings.text == 200){
    vehicleToBuy = "bicycle";
  }
  if(vehicleToBuy == "Porsche"){
    myBicycleMovie._visible = false;
    myPorscheMovie.play();
    myGreeting.text = "Hope you enjoy your new " + vehicleToBuy + ".";
  }else if(vehicleToBuy == "bicycle"){
    myPorscheMovie._visible = false;
    myBicycleMovie.play();
    myGreeting.text = "Hope you enjoy your new " + vehicleToBuy + ".";
  }
}
```

The first part of this script checks the number that the user entered. It states that if the text entered into the **savings** text field equals 50,000, set the value of vehicleToBuy to "Porsche"; if **savings** equals 200, set the value of vehicleToBuy to "Bicycle". The next part of the script performs several actions simultaneously, depending on the value of vehicleToBuy. If vehicleToBuy has a value of "Porsche", the script does three things: It makes the **myBicycleMovie** movie clip instance invisible; it starts playing the **myPorscheMovie** movie clip instance; and it displays the message "Hope you enjoy your new Porsche" in the dynamic text field named **myGreeting**. If vehicleToBuy has a value of "bicycle", the script makes the **myPorscheMovie** movie clip instance invisible; it starts playing the **myBicycleMovie** movie clip instance; and it displays the message "Hope you enjoy your new bicycle" in the dynamic text field named **myGreeting** (**Figure 13.2**).

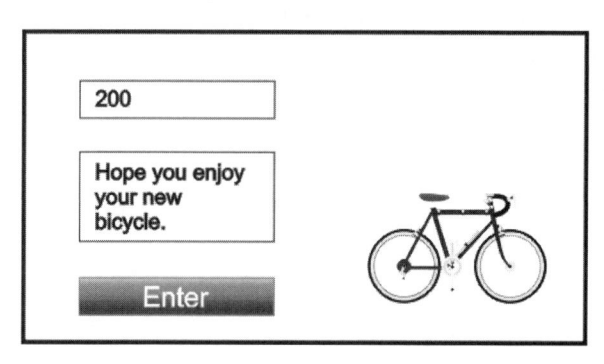

Figure 13.2
The result of entering a value of 200 in the "savings" text field and pressing the Enter button.

This example illustrates many of the syntactical elements needed in order for a script to function. An understanding of these individual elements and the role they play in a script's overall execution is essential as we begin to explore ActionScript more in depth.

Script Elements

One glance at the Toolbox List window of the Actions panel will give you an idea of how extensive ActionScript is, and the number of syntactical elements it employs. While all these details may at first seem overwhelming, don't despair: We'll take you through all of them slowly and rationally.

ActionScript uses dots, quotation marks, semicolons, parentheses, and other keyboard symbols to create interactivity. It also employs structural elements comparable to the nouns, verbs, and adjectives used in our everyday language. When combined, these elements describe what the script should do, when it should do it, and for how long. To help you start looking at these various elements from a scripting standpoint, we'll now briefly discuss many of the most important ones, and show you how they're used in ActionScript.

NOTE *We cover additional script elements, such as objects, functions, loops, properties, and methods, later in this chapter, and in subsequent chapters. We don't include them here because they're more specific in nature than the elements we're about to discuss.*

Events

These are things that occur during the playback of a movie that trigger the execution of a particular script. In other words, they define *when* a script should be executed. In our sample script above, the triggering event is on(release). This signifies that when the button to which this script is attached is released (via the user's mouse button), the script will execute. Every script is triggered by an event, and many types of events can be used to interact with your movie—everything from a button being pressed to text changing in a text field, or a sound element completing its playback. We'll look at these and other types of events later in the chapter.

Actions

In Flash, actions are those lines of your script that instruct the program to do, set, create, change, load, or delete something.

In our sample script above, each of these lines represents a different action:

```
myBicycleMovie._visible = false;
myPorscheMovie.play();
```

Actions generally include most of the lines in a script that are enclosed in curly brackets ({}); and individual actions are usually separated by semicolons (see below).

Operators

These include a number of symbols (=, <, >, +, -, *, &&, etc.) and are used to connect two elements in a script in various ways (adding them together, comparing their values, and so on). To get an idea of how they work, take a look at the following examples:

```
vehicleToBuy = "Porsche";
```

In the above line of code, the assignment operator (=) is used to assign a value of "Porshe" to the variable named vehicleToBuy.

```
amountA < amountB
```

In the above line of code, the less-than operator (<) asks if amountA is less than amountB.

```
value1 * 500
```

In the above line of code, the multiplication operator (*) is used to multiply value1 times 500.

Keywords

These are words reserved for specific purposes within ActionScript syntax. As such, they cannot be used as variable, function, or label names. For example, the word on is a keyword and can only be used in a script to denote an event that triggers a script, such as on(press), on(rollOver), on(rollOut), and so on. Attempting to use keywords in your scripts for anything other than their intended purpose will result in errors. (Other keywords include break, case, continue, delete, do, else, for, function, if, in, instanceOf, new, return, switch, this, typeOf, var, void, while, with).

Data

A dynamic script almost always creates, uses, or updates various types of data during its execution. Variables are the most common of these types: They represent pieces of data that have been assigned unique names. Once a variable has been created and assigned a value, you can access that value at any point in the script, simply by inserting its name.

In the sample script we've been looking at, the variable named vehicleToBuy is assigned a value of either "Porsche" or "Bicycle". Later in the script, the variable's name is used to refer to the value it contains.

Curly brackets

Generally speaking, any script elements that fall between opening and closing curly brackets represent a set of actions that are to be executed as a group. Think of curly brackets as being used to say, "As a result of this, {execute this group of actions}." For example:

```
if(vehicleToBuy == "Porsche"){
  myBicycleMovie._visible = false;
  myPorscheMovie.play();
  myGreeting.text = "Hope you enjoy your new " + vehicleToBuy + ".";
}
```

Semicolons

These are usually the last symbol in those lines of scripts that are enclosed within curly braces. Semicolons are used to separate multiple actions that may need to be executed as the result of a single event (similar to the way commas are used to separate different thoughts in a single sentence). The following example denotes three separate actions, separated by semicolons:

```
myBicycleMovie._visible = false;
myPorscheMovie.play();
myGreeting.text = "Hope you enjoy your new " + vehicleToBuy + ".";
```

Dot syntax

Dots, or periods, play a major role in ActionScript syntax. This is because ActionScript employs what is known as *dot syntax*. In ActionScripts, dots can be used to describe hierarchical relationships between individual movies, movies and their data, movies and their properties, and more. Dots are used in the following ways in ActionScript syntax:

- **To address movies.** The following addresses **myMovieClip2**, which is inside **myMovieClip1** (which resides on the main timeline):

  ```
  _root.myMovieClip1.myMovieClip2
  ```

- **To address variables in a specific movie.** The following sets the value of the variable myVariable, which is inside **myMovieClip**, to 27:

  ```
  _root.myMovieClip.myVariable = 27;
  ```

- **To address properties of a specific movie.** The following rotates the movie clip **myMovieClip** by a value of 45 degrees:

  ```
  _root.myMovieClip._rotation = 45;
  ```

Parentheses

ActionScript uses these in various ways. For the most part, scripts use parentheses to specify a varying value that a given action will use during its execution. For example, the following script tells the **myMovieClip** movie clip instance to go to and play, starting at Frame 50:

```
myMovieClip.gotoAndPlay(50);
```

If you change the value within the parentheses from 50 to 20, the action will still perform the same basic task (moving the timeline to a specified frame number); it simply executes it using the new value.

Quotation marks

These are used to denote textual data in the script. Because the script itself uses text, quotation marks provide the necessary means for Flash to distinguish between instructions (pieces of data) and actual text intended for display. For example, Mark (without quotes) signifies the name of a piece of data. "Mark," on the other hand, signifies the actual word *Mark*.

Comments

Comments serve as notes you can place within a script to explain what it's doing at a given point—in terms that make sense to humans, rather than the computer. When you export your movie, Flash will detect the comments you have added, and strip them from the final SWF. Thus, you're free to add as many comments as you wish without worrying about them affecting your movie's final size. Beginning programmers frequently omit this step in order to save time: However, they soon find out that changing even one aspect of a complex script—one that does not include well-placed comments—can quickly eat up an entire day if a mistake is made, and they don't have any notes to help them reconstruct the script. Comments provide a way for developers to make sense of their code whenever they (or others) need to come back to it—months or even years later.

To create comments in ActionScript, you type two forward slashes (//) followed by the text of your comment:

```
//This is a comment
```

When this script is run, Flash ignores any input that follows those two forward slashes.

You can use single lines of comments, as in the following:

```
//Create a variable and give it a value of Joe
myVariable = "Joe"
```

And if the Actions panel is in Expert mode, you can even add in-line comments like the following:

```
if(myVariable < 5){ //check the value of myVariable
  myMessage.text = "You Lose"; //display "You Lose" in the input text field
}
```

Working in Expert mode, you can also add multiline comments like these:

```
/*This is a multi-line comment.
Multi-line comments provide a means for
entering comments that are lengthy. */
if(myVariable < 5){
  myMessage.text = "You Lose";
}
```

We'll frequently use comments in the scripts contained in this chapter, to help you understand not only how and when you can use them, but also to make clear what's going on in the script. However, you shouldn't use comments to explain every line of your code; that will only make your scripts unwieldy, adding confusion rather than preventing it. Instead, use comments in places where you think a brief description would help decipher the code, if you ever need to return to it.

Indentation and white space

Although you aren't required to indent your scripts or use white (blank) space, either of these can make your scripts easier to read. For example, take a look at the following:

```
if(savings.text == 50000){
  vehicleToBuy = "Porsche";
}
```

The above script will execute in the same fashion as the following:

```
if(savings.text == 50000){
vehicleToBuy = "Porsche";
}
```

A good rule of thumb is to indent anything within curly braces to signify that it's what's known as a *code block*—that is, a chunk of code that's executed together. You can also nest code blocks inside of other code blocks—which we'll discuss more as we progress through this chapter.

For the most part, Flash ignores white space within a script. For an example of this, take a look at the following line of script:

```
myGreeting.text="Hope you enjoy your new "+vehicleToBuy+".";
```

The above line of script will execute the same way as the following line:

```
myGreeting.text = "Hope you enjoy your new " + vehicleToBuy + ".";
```

The amount of white space you use is largely a matter of preference. Some programmers find that adding white space makes their code easier to read; others feel that inserting spaces slows them down. The choice is yours; however, there are a couple of exceptions you should be aware of: Variable names cannot contain spaces, nor can there be any space between an object name and an associated property/method. While the following is acceptable:

```
myObject.propertyName
```

This is not:

```
myObject. propertyName
```

Variables

Variables are an important part of just about any programming language, and ActionScript is no exception. As you can see from the following examples, a variable is basically a container that holds a value:

```
X = 25
Name = Derek
Age = 29
Income = 500
Best Band = The Beatles
IQ = 47
```

In these examples, X, Name, Age, Income, BestBand, and IQ are all variable names, and the information that follows the equals sign is the assigned value of that variable.

In ActionScripting, the same principles apply. Using ActionScript, you might create several variables, as the following script indicates:

```
//Create three variables
name = "Derek";
age = 30;
income = 500;
```

In Flash, variables can store any of the following data (and more):

- A user's name
- Text greetings
- The number of times a button has been clicked
- A URL
- The value of a movie property (for example, width, height, location)
- The number of times an event has occurred
- A timeline's current frame number

In addition, variables can also be used for all sorts of dynamic functionality, including the following:

- To display text in a dynamic text field (see Script 1 below)
- To dynamically set various parameter values in other actions (see Script 2)
- To send the timeline to a specific frame (see Script 3)

Script 1

The following script assumes there is a dynamic text field on the stage with an instance name of **myGreeting**. This script will cause that dynamic text field to display the message "Boy, aren't you glad today is Saturday?"

```
//create a variable and assign it a value of Saturday
myFavoriteDay = "Saturday";
myGreeting.text = "Boy, aren't you glad today is " + myFavoriteDay + "?";
```

Script 2

This script shows a mouse event that sets the value of seeThrough to 45. As soon as it is set, this variable's value is applied as the transparency value of the movie clip instance **myMovieClip**:

```
on(release){
   //create a variable and assign it a value of 45
   seeThrough = 45;
   myMovieClip._alpha = seeThrough;
}
```

Script 3

This script shows a mouse event that sets the value of favoriteFrame to 34. As soon as it is set, this variable's value is used in a gotoAndPlay() action that sends the timeline to Frame 34:

```
on(release){
   //create a variable and assign it a value of 34
   favoriteFrame = 34;
   gotoAndPlay(favoriteFrame);
}
```

Types of Variables

In Flash, variable values can take the following basic forms:

- **Numbers.** A number value refers to anything from 0 to 999,999+. An age variable might have a value of 20, which in ActionScript would look like this:

   age = 20

- **Strings.** The term *string* is commonly used in programming languages to denote text values. Typical string values can include anything from "a" to "Hello, what's your name? Does your dog bite or is it a nice dog?" A string value can contain almost any number of characters (within reason), and can include text, spaces, punctuation, and even numbers. The value "345" can be thought of as a string value even though it involves numbers. In ActionScript, string values that contain numbers are distinguished from actual number values through the use of quotation marks. Thus, while 1966 is interpreted as a number value,

"1966" is interpreted as a string value. Here are some examples of variables and their assigned string values:

```
phraseThatPays = "Flash MX Rocks!";
favoriteWife = "Kathy";
favoriteWifesAge = "Amazingly, the same as in Flash 5 book, 29.";
```

- **Boolean.** This type of value defines whether or not a specific condition exists. The possible Boolean values are true and false. In Flash, false has the numerical equivalent of 0, and true can be any nonzero number. Boolean values are used for creating scripts that can analyze data and then take action accordingly (for more information, see "Statements" later in this chapter). Assigning a Boolean value to a variable in Flash would look something like this:

```
macromediaRocks = true;
macromediaRocks = 1;
```

NOTE *ActionScript Objects (Array, Date, Sound, and so on) are also considered variables; however, they are more complex than the variable types we've discussed so far. For more on these, see Chapter 14, "ActionScript Objects."*

Creating Variables

You create variables via the Actions panel in Expert mode (which is the mode we recommend you use once you develop a basic understanding of ActionScript), by simply entering a variable name (one you assign) followed by an equals sign (=), followed by a value you provide. This is known as assigning a variable to a value.

The following are some points to keep in mind when creating variables:

- **You must create a variable before its value can be accessed.** For example:

```
gotoAndPlay(myVariable);
myVariable = 35;
```

This gotoAndPlay() action won't do anything because the variable value it requires to work properly is not created until the line *following* the action. By reversing the order of the lines (as shown below), the variable is created first, which means that any action that follows can access its value:

```
myVariable = 35;
gotoAndPlay(myVariable);
```

- **Each movie or movie clip instance has a unique set of variables (Figure 13.3)**. When a script creates a variable, depending on how it's set up, that variable will be created in either the current timeline or any other present timeline (a present timeline is any movie that currently exists in the Flash Player window). To understand this, take a look at the following examples:

  ```
  on(release){
    //create a variable in the current timeline
    myVariable = 88;
    //create a variable in a timeline other than the current one
    myMovieClip.myVariable = 88
  }
  ```

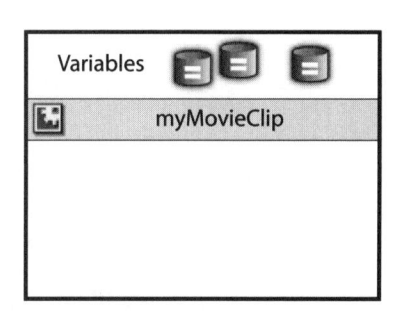

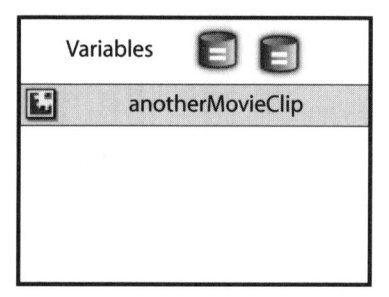

Figure 13.3
The movie clip instance on the left contains a different set of variables than the movie clip instance on the right.

- **The name of the timeline that a variable is part of acts as the variable's address when you want to use it in a script (as shown below).**

  ```
  on(release){
  //use the value of the variable named myVariable, which exists in the movie clip instance named myMovieClip, to set the transparency of the movie clip instance named myWindow
    myWindow._alpha = myMovieClip.myVariable;
  }
  ```

- **The variables in a timeline continue to exist, and their values can be set or retrieved, as long as the timeline is present—whether it's playing or not.** Thus, if a movie clip contains a variable that you've used in your scripts, and that movie clip is removed from the movie window, its variables are removed as well and are no longer available. For more information, see "Working with Multiple Timelines" later in this chapter.

Variable names

When naming variables in Flash, you need to be aware of the following:

- **All variable names must begin with a character.** The characters that follow can be letters, digits, or underscores. In addition, names are not case-sensitive, so MyVariable is the same as myvariable. Names cannot contain spaces or special characters (not letters or digits) such as @, #, $,%, and so on.

    ```
    //Examples of valid variable names
    myVariable
    my_variable
    my_variable_2
    //Examples of invalid variable names
    27myVariable
    my variable
    my@variable
    ```

- **Variable names should make sense.** If a variable holds a value for the number of times the user has clicked a mouse button, you could name that variable mouseClicks (or anything similar that will remind you of its function).

- **Even though a variable's value may change, its name will remain the same.** For example, at one point in your movie the value of x might be 25, while later on in your movie it might be 720.

Assigning values

You can assign either a literal or an expression value to a variable. A literal is a value explicitly and definitively assigned to a variable, whereas an expression is a value based on a phrase that is evaluated (see "Expressions" later in this chapter). Take a look at the following literal assignments:

```
cost = 21.00;
```

Or this one:

```
name = "John Doe";
```

Notice that the values assigned to the variables are not really dynamic. For example, if you wanted to use the value of cost elsewhere in your ActionScript, it would always have a value of 21.00. Likewise, the value of name would always be "John Doe". Not very exciting. To create more dynamically assigned values, you could use an expression instead. For example:

```
product = 20.00;
tax = 1.00;
cost = product + tax;
```

In the preceding script, the value of the cost variable is product + tax, which are themselves variables. To break cost into its most basic parts, it could be read as "cost = 20.00 + 1.00", which would total 21.00. However, if the value of product changed to 22.00 and the value of tax became 1.30, the value of cost would automatically become 23.30 because cost is based on the value of product + tax. Here's another example where the value of the variable name is based on an expression:

```
firstName = "John ";
lastName = "Doe";
name = firstName + lastName;
//name has a value of "John Doe"
```

You can assign values to variables in several other ways. For more information, see "Operators" later in this chapter.

Updating variable values

At times, you'll want to update a variable's value—for example, changing its value from "Joe" to "Fred".

Updating a variable is as simply requires assigning a new value to an existing variable name:

```
//Create a variable and give it a value of Joe
myVariable = "Joe";
//Update the value of myVariable to Fred
myVariable = "Fred";
//myVariable no longer has a value of Joe but now has a value of Fred
```

Or, using numbers:

```
//Create a variable and give it a value of 10
myVariable = 10;
//Update the value of myVariable to 20
myVariable = 20;
//myVariable no longer has a value of 10 but now has a value of 20
```

You can even change the value of a variable from a string to a number or Boolean as the following script shows:

```
//Create a variable and give it a value of 10
myVariable = 10;
//Update the value of myVariable to true
myVariable = true;
//myVariable no longer has a value of 10 but now has a value of true
```

In whichever manner you decide to do it, updating variables is an important aspect of a dynamic movie. If a number of ActionScripts rely on the value of the variable, changing it will change how all of those scripts work.

Any number of mouse, frame, or clip events can be used in updating variables. For example, if you wanted to track what button a user has clicked, you would attach the following scripts on each button, respectively:

```
//Button 1
on(release){
   whatButton = 1;
}
//Button 2
on(release){
   whatButton = 2;
}
//Button 3
on(release){
   whatButton = 3;
}
```

Depending on which button the user presses, the value of whatButton would change, and that value could be used in various ActionScripts to perform certain actions based on the current value of whatButton.

Using Variables

Once a variable has been created, any time you wish to use its value in your scripts, you simply refer to the variable's name as shown in the following script.

```
on(release){
    //create a variable and assign it a value of 27
    favoriteNumber = 27;
    //send the timeline to the frame on the value of favoriteNumber
    gotoAndPlay(favoriteNumber);
    //set the transparency and width of myMovieClip based on the value of
favoriteNumber
    myMovieClip._alpha = favoriteNumber;
    myMovieClip._width = favoriteNumber;
    //output a greeting to the dynamic text field named myGreeting based on
the value of favoriteNumber
    myGreeting.text = "The greatest number in the world is " +
favoriteNumber + ".";
}
```

This script demonstrates the power of variables just by the number of different elements that are affected by the value of `favoriteNumber`: If its value changes, so will the displayed results of all these actions.

Operators

Variables and their values are only part of the ActionScript universe. Variables simply contain data; to create truly dynamic movies, you need to manipulate that data in order to produce new data. This is where operators come into play: The most common types are arithmetic operators, such as plus (+) and minus (-) signs. Take a look at the following script:

```
10 + 5
```

In this script, the plus sign is the operator and the numbers *10* and *5* are known as *operands* (since they are the values being used by the operator to calculate a new value). You can also use variable names in conjunction with an operator to produce a similar result:

```
number1 = 10;
number2 = 5;
total = number1 + number2;
```

In this script, `total` would have a value of 15.

Flash uses many types of operators for different sorts of data manipulation. In the following section, we'll look at the most common types.

Arithmetic Operators

Arithmetic operators are commonly used for manipulating numbers by adding, subtracting, multiplying, dividing, or returning the value of a remainder (as happens when one number cannot be divided evenly by another number). Table 13.1 provides a list of arithmetic operators and a brief description of their functions.

Table 13.1
Arithmetic Operators

Operator	Function
+	Adds one value to another value
-	Subtracts one numeric value from another
*	Multiplies one numeric value by another
/	Divides one numeric value by another
%	Divides one number from another and returns the value of the remainder
++	Increments (adds 1 to) a number
--	Decrements (subtracts 1 from) a number

Let's look at some sample scripts to explain how these operators work.

Sample script

In the following script, total has a value of 11 because it simply adds the values of price and tax together.

```
on(release){
    price = 10;
    tax = 1;
    total = price + tax;
}
```

Sample script

In the following script, total still has a value of 11, but notice how the value of tax is determined: The value of price is multiplied by .10—essentially the same as saying 10 * .10, which equals 1. Thus, tax is assigned a value of 1. Then, the value of price + tax (or 10 + 1) is assigned to total.

```
on(release){
  price = 10;
  tax = price * .10;
  total = price + tax;
}
```

Sample script

The addition operator (+) can also be used with strings of text to concatenate (connect) them. It is the only arithmetic operator that can be used with text. In the following script, myLocation has a value of "Bloomington, Indiana."

```
on(release){
  city = "Bloomington, ";
  state = "Indiana";
  myLocation = city + state;
}
```

TIP *If you attempt to add a string of characters and a number, Flash will convert the number to a text string and treat it as such. Thus, 18 + "12" becomes "1812" in such cases.*

Sample script

The modulo operator (%) is used to automatically divide the first number by the second, and then return the value of the remainder. In the following script, finalNumber has a value of 1. This is because 10 divided by 3 equals 3 with a remainder of 1.

```
finalNumber = 10 % 3;
```

This operator is great for determining whether a number is odd or even, as the following script demonstrates:

```
if(inputNumber % 2 == 0){
  gotoAndStop("Even");
}else{
  gotoAndStop("Odd");
}
```

In plain English this script reads, "If the current value of inputNumber divided by 2 has no remainder, go to the frame labeled Even; otherwise, go to the frame labeled Odd." The modulo operator is commonly used to intermittently (but cyclically) perform a set of actions.

Sample script

The increment (++) and decrement (--) operators will increase or decrease by 1 the value of the variable is presented. Thus, homeRuns++ increases the value of homeRuns by 1. Take a look at the following script:

```
homeRuns = 15
score = ++homeRuns;
```

In this script, the variable score is assigned the current value of homeRuns, but first a value of 1 is added to it, thus assigning score a value of 16. Notice the position of the increment operator in relation to the variable it's incrementing: to the left. If we moved the increment operator to the right of the homeRuns variable (homeRuns++), the score variable would *first* be assigned a value of 15, *then* homeRuns would be increased by 1. In other words, one method increments homeRuns *before* score is assigned a value, the other *after*. While in both cases the value of homeRuns is incremented, the placement of the increment operator determines when.

The decrement operator works just like the increment operator, but in the opposite direction—that is, it decreases the value of the specified variable by 1.

Using these operators to increment and decrement values is an important tool for creating scripts that can handle numerous tasks at once. We'll look more closely at their use in the "Statements" section later in this chapter.

Assignment Operators

Assignment operators are used to assign values to variables. The only one of these we've used thus far is the equals sign. Table 13.2 provides a list of assignment operators, and a brief description of their functions.

Table 13.2
Assignment Operators

Assignment	Function
x = y	The value x is assigned the value of y
x += y	The value x is assigned the value of x + y or x = x + y
x -= y	The value x is assigned the value of x - y or x = x - y
x *= y	The value x is assigned the value of x * y or x = x * y
x /= y	The value x is assigned the value of x / y or x = x / y
x %= y	The value x is assigned the value of x % y or x = x % y

By now, you're familiar with the first operator listed in the table: It assigns the variable on the left side of the equals sign the value of whatever formula it finds on the right side of the equals sign. The rest of these table entries are known as *compound assignment operators*, and they represent shortcuts for writing code, as shown in the description in the right column of the table.

Sample script

```
on(release){
  x = 50; //x is assigned a value of 50
  y = 200; //y is assigned a value of 200
  x += y; // x is assigned a new value of 250, or the value of x + y
}
```

This assignment operator is commonly used to incrementally increase a particular value by a certain amount. For example:

```
onClipEvent(enterFrame){
  _x += 20;
}
```

In this script, every time the enterFrame event occurs, it will set the _x property of the movie clip instance to which this script is attached to its current _x position plus 20 (or _x = _x + 20)

The = and =+ assignment operators are also used for text, as the following script demonstrates:

Sample script

```
on(release){
  x = "Allison "; // x is assigned a value of "Allison "
  y = "Stailey"; // y is assigned a value of "Stailey"
  x += y; // x is assigned a new value of Allison Stailey, or the value of x + y
}
```

Comparison Operators

Adding and subtracting values are just a couple of ways you can manipulate values. Using comparison operators, you can compare the values of specified variables against other values, allowing your script to make decisions based on that comparison (for additional information see, "Statements" later in this chapter.)

Table 13.3 provides a list of comparison operators and a brief description of their functions.

Table 13.3
Comparison Operators

Operator	Function
==	Equal to
!=	Not equal to
<	Less than
>	Greater than
<=	Less than or equal to
>=	Greater than or equal to

Comparison operators are always used to return a value of true or false.

Sample script

The following variables have a value of true:

```
myVariable1 = 10 == 10;
myVariable2 = 50 > 20;
```

Now let's put these examples in terms you can understand: For example, 10 == 10 in English would be "Does 10 equal 10?" The answer is yes, or in ActionScript, true. In the next example, "Is 50 a greater value than 20?" the answer is yes, or true.

Sample script

Comparison operators can also be used on string values to determine the value of strings, based on their first character. In these calculations, *A* has a lower value than Z. Lowercase characters (*a* through *z*) hold greater value than capital letters (*A* through *Z*). Values of strings are case-sensitive, which means that "kathy" does not equal "Kathy". This type of functionality might be useful for verifying username/password info, or anything else where correct user input is essential. The following variables have a value of true:

```
myStringValue1 = "Jack" == "Jack";
myStringValue2 = "bcdef" > "abcde";
myStringValue3 = "Eddie" < "eddie";
```

TIP *It's easy to confuse the assignment operator (=) with the comparison operator (==). Just remember, = is used to* assign *values, whereas == is used to test* equality *between two values.*

Sample script

The following variables have a value of `false`:

```
myVariable1 = 10 == 9;
myVariable2 = "Camille"> "camille";
```

Sample script

You can also directly compare variables using any of the comparison operators:

```
myValue = myVariable1 == myVariable2;
```

If `myVariable1` has a value of 37 and `myVariable2` has a value of 15, then `myValue` is assigned a value of `false`.

Sample script

The not equal (!=) operator needs a bit of explanation. Take a look at the following scripts, which assign a value of `true` to each variable:

```
myVariable1 = 10 != 20;
myVariable2 = "Dog"!= "Cat";
```

In these scripts, we're checking for *inequality*; if it exists, the value of the variable is true.

Sample script

Let's take a look at a couple more scripts to see how a comparison operator could be used:

```
on(release){
  paycheck = 200;
  bills = 500;
  if(paycheck >= bills){
    gotoAndStop("Happiness");
  }else{
    gotoAndStop("NotSoHappy");
  }
}
```

This script creates two variables, paycheck and bills, and assigns them numeric values. The if statement (which you'll learn about shortly) checks whether the value of paycheck is greater than or equal to the value of bills. If it is, the timeline jumps to a frame labeled Happiness; if not, it jumps to a frame labeled NotSoHappy.

TIP *You can only compare numbers to numbers, or strings of text to other strings of text.*

Sample script

Imagine an input text field on the stage with an instance name of **password**. Someone has entered the text "Boom Bam" into the field. The user pushes a button, and the script below is executed:

```
on(release){
  if(password.text == "Boom Bam"){
    gotoAndStop("Accepted");
  }else{
    gotoAndStop("AccessDenied");
  }
}
```

When this script has executed (based on information entered into the password text field), the timeline will go to and stop on the frame labeled Accepted.

Logical Operators

Logical operators are used to compare Boolean values of true and false. They can also be some of the trickiest operators to understand, so don't worry if you find yourself reviewing this section more than once.

Table 13.4 provides a list of logical operators and a brief description of their functions.

Table 13.4
Logical Operators

Operator	Function
&&	Logical AND
||	Logical OR
!	Logical NOT

The AND operator (&&) compares two Boolean values to see if they're both true. The OR operator (||) compares two Boolean values to see if at least one is true. The NOT (!) operator checks whether a Boolean value is *not* true.

Like comparison operators, logical operators return a value of true or false.

Sample script

```
myValue1 = (10 == 10) && (a < b);
```

In this script, myValue1 is assigned a value of true because (10 == 10) is true and so is the code (a < b). The AND operator in this equation is used to ask, "Are the first comparison AND the second comparison true?" Compare this with the following:

```
myValue1 = (10 == 5) && (a < b);
```

In this script, myValue1 is assigned a value of false because (10 == 5) is false, even though (a < b) is true. They must both be true in order for the AND operator to return a value of true.

Sample script

Logical operators can also be used with variables, as the next example demonstrates:

```
question1 = true;
question2 = false;
hundredPercentCorrect = question1 && question2;
```

In this script, hundredPercentCorrect is assigned a value of false because only one variable contains a value of true. The AND operator in this equation is used to ask, "Do question1 and question2 both have a value of true?"

Sample script

```
myValue2 = (10 == 5) || (a < b);
```

In this script, myValue2 is assigned a value of true because although (10 == 5) is false, (a < b) is true. The OR operator only requires that one or the other be true. If *neither* is true, the OR operator returns a value of false.

Sample script

The NOT operator (!) can be a bit confusing. Let's start by looking at the following example:

```
myValue3 = !(10 == 5);
```

In this script, myValue3 is assigned a value of true. The NOT operator in this equation is used to ask, "Is the equation in parentheses—10 equals 5?—untrue?" Since the operator is trying to determine whether the equation is untrue, it returns a value of true if the numbers aren't the same. If the operator doesn't find what it's looking for, it returns a value of false—a concept you may need to review a couple of times to grasp.

Sample script

Logical operators let you enhance a script's decision-making ability, allowing it to compare multiple values at once in order to determine which course of action to take next. Take a look at the following example:

```
on(release){
    paycheck = 1000;
    decision = "Buy";
    if(paycheck >= 1000 && decision == "Buy"){
    gotoAndStop("New Computer");
    }else{
    gotoAndStop("Cry");
    }
}
```

This script first creates two variables named paycheck and decision, and assigns them the values shown. Next, it checks to determine whether the numeric value of paycheck is greater than or equal to 1000, and whether the string value of decision equals "Buy". If both are true, go get a new computer; if not, cry your brains out!

Whew! That's enough about operators for now. Although there are still more operators that you can use in ActionScripts, they're well beyond the scope of this book. The operators we've discussed here are the ones that beginning and intermediate Flash users are most likely to use.

NOTE *For real-world examples and techniques that make use of these operators, see Chapter 16, "Using ActionScript in Your Projects."*

Expressions

Expressions represent the heart of any truly dynamic and interactive Flash movie, because they can make each user's experience unique. Expressions do this by allowing you to dynamically set action parameter values, the text displayed in text fields, and other data, based on user response or other varying movie conditions, such as movie property values (rotation, position, scale, current frame) and values returned by functions or methods. (For more information about properties and methods, see Chapter 14, "ActionScript Objects." For more information about functions, see "Functions," a bit later in this chapter.)

Although many of the scripts you've seen up to this point contain expressions, we haven't yet described their function in your ActionScripts. Basically, an expression is a phrase—or collection of variables, numbers, text, and operators—that evaluates to a single value. To get an idea of what this means, take a look at the following script, which uses an expression to evaluate which frame number to go to:

```
on(release){
   gotoAndPlay(24 + 26);
}
```

The expression in the preceding script—what 24 + 26 evaluates to—would cause the timeline to jump to Frame 50. The concept is pretty simple, in fact. You could go even further and create a script that used variable values to accomplish the same thing in a different way:

```
on (release){
   favoriteNumber = 24;
   secondFavNumber = 26;
   gotoAndPlay(favoriteNumber + secondFavNumber);
}
```

Using expressions in your scripts is easy. Many parameters that you'll set for actions in the Actions panel have an Expression option. You will use expressions to set dynamic values in your scripts. Keep in mind that a single script can contain many expressions.

To use an expression in a script (with the Actions panel in Normal mode):

1. Select a button instance or a movie clip instance on the stage, or a keyframe on the timeline.

2. Open the Actions panel.

3. Click the Add (+) button, and choose Actions > Browser/Network > getURL() from the menu that appears.

   The getURL() action parameters will appear on the top of the Actions panel.

4. Check the Expression option next to the URL box, and enter an expression in the URL parameter box, such as the following:

```
"http://www." + currentDomain + ".com";
```

This expression will concatenate the text "http://www." with the current value of currentDomain, followed by the text ".com".

Depending on the value of currentDomain (which could change based on user response or other varying movie conditions), this action will open the appropriate URL. For example, if currentDomain had a value of "Macromedia", this expression would evaluate to a value of "http://www.macromedia.com" and thus cause the getURL() action to open Macromedia's Web site. However, if currentDomain had a value of "CNN" this expression would evaluate to "http://www.cnn.com", which would open CNN's site.

Parentheses and Precedence

An expression is evaluated in what's known as an *order of precedence*, which simply refers to the order in which parts of an expression are evaluated. Anything in parentheses is evaluated first, followed by anything multiplied or divided, followed by anything added or subtracted. Pay careful attention to this rule, since the order of these operations can affect the end value of an expression. Use parentheses to clarify how the expression should be evaluated. To understand this, take a look at the following example:

```
10 + 25 * 3 - 1
```

This expression evaluates to a value of 84. This is because 25 is multiplied by 3 first (since multiplication has precedence in an expression), which equals 75. Then, the 10 on the left is added to the 75, which makes it 85. Finally, 1 is subtracted from 85, resulting in a value of 84. Compare this to the following expression, which uses the same numbers and operators but uses parentheses to clarify how the expression should be evaluated.

```
(10 + 25) * (3 - 1)
```

This expression results in a value of 70. This is because 10 is added to 25, producing a value of 35. Then, 1 is subtracted from 3, which results in a value of 2. Finally, 35 is multiplied by 2, resulting in a value of 70.

Statements

Statements in ActionScript bring together all the different syntactical elements we've discussed so far. As such, a statement can be likened to a sentence describing a set of instructions to be performed (including how and in what order). Like a sentence, a statement contains words (usually variable names, operators, and expressions) to provide meaning, and punctuation to denote structure. We'll explain this structure as we go along.

Controlling the Flow

Statements control the way actions are executed in a script. Normally, lines in an ActionScript are executed one after another, from top to bottom. However, statements can alter this flow so that actions are executed based on varying conditions. Think of a flowchart as a visual representation of an ActionScript statement. The following examines some of the types of statements ActionScript allows you to use.

if statement

An if statement is also known as a conditional statement: If a condition is met, certain actions are performed. To understand this, take a look at the following conditional statement:

```
if(outside == "rain"){
   gotoAndStop("Bed");
}
//next line of code
```

In this script, if outside has a value of "rain", the action gotoAndStop("Bed"); is executed; if not, the action is ignored and the script moves to the next line of code.

if/else statement

An if/else statement is a conditional statement that adds another element to the if statement. In this case, the statement dictates that if a given condition is met, certain actions will be performed; if the condition is *not* met, a different set of actions will be performed. Take a look at the following conditional statement:

```
if(outside == "rain"){
   gotoAndStop ("Bed");
}else{
   gotoAndPlay("Park");
}
```

The above conditional statement shows that if outside has a value of "rain", go to bed; however, if outside has a value of anything else, go to the park.

if/else if statement

An if/else if statement lets you check for multiple conditions. Take a look at the following example:

```
if(outside == "rain"){
  gotoAndStop("Bed");
}else if(outside == "sun"){
  gotoAndPlay("Park");
}else if(outside == "snow"){
  gotoAndPlay("SkiResort");
}else if(outside == "tornado"){
  gotoAndStop("Basement");
}else{
  gotoAndPlay("TV");
  lifeIsGood = true;
}
```

This conditional statement also checks the value of outside; however, it does so with a twist. In our new conditional statement, different actions are possible depending on the condition that's met. This is due to the addition of else if to our conditional statement. For example, if outside has a value of "rain", it's time to go back to bed. If it has a value of "sun", it's time to go to the park and have fun. If it has a value of "snow", it's off to the ski resort. If it has a value of "tornado", you should head for the basement. Finally, if the value of outside doesn't match *any* of our conditions, it's time to go watch TV and update the value of lifeIsGood to true.

switch statement

MX ALERT

As a variation on the if/else if statement, switch statements are used to perform a set of actions depending on existing conditions (as defined by the statement). Although this type of statement offers the same functionality as an if/else if statement, many developers prefer switch statements because they're easier to read. To get a feeling for this, take a look at the following example, which includes the key ingredients of the if/else if example we just discussed, but is built around a switch statement instead:

```
switch(outside){
case "rain":
  gotoAndStop("Bed");
  break
case "sun":
  gotoAndPlay("Park");
  break
case "snow":
  gotoAndPlay("SkiResort");
  break
case "tornado":
  gotoAndStop("Basement");
  break
default:
  gotoAndPlay("TV");
  lifeIsGood = true;
}
```

The first line of the statement says to look at the value of `outside`. That value is then compared to the values of each `case` in the structure. If a match is found, the block of code associated with that `case` is executed. If no match is found, the `default` statement (at the end) is executed. In each `case` structure, `break` is used to prevent the code from running into the next `case` automatically, if a match has already been found. You can evaluate complete expressions as follows:

```
switch(year < 2004 && age > 60){
case true:
  //actions
  break
case false:
  //actions;
  break
}
```

Here, the switch statement is looking at the condition of whether *year* is less than 2004 *and* age is greater than 60. If true, one set of actions is performed; if false, the other set is performed.

while statements

You use a `while` statement to perform a series of actions for as long as a condition is true—what's known as a looping statement. The logic used in a `while` statement might look something like this: While x equals 10 (the condition), perform these actions repeatedly (loop); however, as soon as x no longer equals 10 (condition is `false`), stop performing these actions and begin performing whatever action follows the `while` statement. If you don't provide a means for the condition to eventually become `false`, you'll be creating an endless loop that prevents your movie from functioning properly.

By using `while` statements, you can provide for some sophisticated scripting within Flash (see sidebar). Take a look at the following script to understand the concept behind the way these statements work:

```
count = 1;
myPhrase = "";
while(count <= 10){
   myPhrase += "Echo ";
   count++ ;
}
//next line of code
```

Now let's break down this script into its sections. The first thing that happens is that two variables are created: The variable `count` is assigned an initial value of 1, and `myPhrase` is assigned a string value of "" (an empty text string).

```
count = 1;
myPhrase = "";
```

Next, the script sets up the `while` statement, which basically states that as long as `count` has a value less than or equal to 10, the actions defined between the curly brackets ({}) will continue to repeat or loop.

```
while(count <= 10){
```

The first action within the `while` statement sets the value of the variable `myPhrase` to be updated on each loop.

```
myPhrase += "Echo ";
```

Going into the first loop, `myPhrase` only has a value of "" (as we initially set it to have)—which means that when the action that says `myPhrase += "Echo ";` is executed, `myPhrase` is updated to its current value plus "Echo". Since `myPhrase` was empty to begin with, this results in myPhrase containing an updated value of "Echo ". On the second loop, myPhrase is updated to its current value, which is now "Echo ", plus "Echo ". This results in myPhrase having a new value of "Echo Echo ". In this script, each loop simply adds "Echo" to the value of myPhrase so that at the end of the loop, myPhrase has a value of "Echo Echo Echo Echo Echo Echo Echo Echo Echo Echo ".

The second action repeated within the while statement updates the value of count by 1, using the increment operator (++) that you learned about earlier.

```
count++ ;
```

Thus, after 10 loops, count will have a value of 11 and the loop will stop. This is an important action because without it, your while statement would be an endless loop—probably not what you want.

It only takes a split-second to loop through actions using a statement such as the previous one. Thus, unless you have a superslow computer (from the 1970s), you won't see the result of each loop iteration individually; instead, you'll just see the result of the *entire* looping statement.

When Would I Use a Looping Statement?

After looking at our example looping statement, you may be thinking, "OK, so I can repeat words—big deal." What you really want to know is how to use a looping statement in the real world. Here's a hint: They're great for repeating sets of actions. Take a look at the following ActionScript

```
on(release){
  count = 1;
  while(count <= 3){
    duplicateMovieClip("myMovieClip", "newClip" + count, count);
    count++;
  }
}
```

The while statement in this script has one purpose: to create three duplicate movie clips when a button is clicked. The operation is actually pretty simple: The duplicateMovieClip() action has three parameters, as indicated in the parentheses next to it. A comma separates the parameters. The first parameter indicates the instance name of the movie clip to duplicate. The second parameter indicates the instance name to assign to the duplicate. The third parameter indicates what depth to place the duplicate on.

continued

When Would I Use a Looping Statement? *continued*

You'll notice that the values of the second and third parameters depend on the current value of count. Since this statement is set up to loop three times, and the value of count is updated by 1 with each loop, this looping statement would result in the following:

- A duplicate movie clip instance named "newClip1" at a depth of 1
- A duplicate movie clip instance named "newClip2" at a depth of 2
- A duplicate movie clip instance named "newClip3" at a depth of 3

With one button-click you can create, name, and place three move clip instances on different levels in the movie window (**Figure 13.4**). Very powerful!

This script derives its real power, though, from being able to dynamically set the number of loops. You accomplish this by using a variable. Take a look at the next script: It's the same as the one above, except that a variable name is used to determine the number of times the statement is looped through:

```
on(release){
  count = 1;
  while(count <= myVariable){
    duplicateMovieClip("myMovieClip", "newClip" + count, count);
    count++;
  }
}
```

You'll notice that within the while statement, the 3 has been replaced by a variable named myVariable. If this were the name of a variable that a user could change in some way, it would affect the number of times the while statement looped and thus the number of duplicate movies created. For many looping statements, the number of loops is dynamically set in a similar manner.

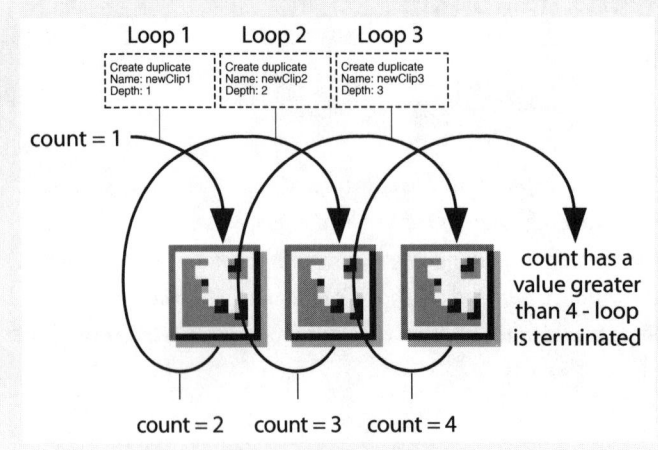

Figure 13.4
A graphic representation of the logic used by our loop in creating three duplicate movie clip instances.

for statements

The for statement also creates a loop, but in a somewhat different manner than the while statement. In most cases, either type of statement will work for the same task. If you understand the while statement, the for statement should be a breeze. Take a look at the following script, which performs the same actions as the while statement example (shown earlier), but uses the for statement's syntax:

```
myPhrase = "";
for(count = 1; count <= 10; count++){
  myPhrase += "Echo ";
}
//next line of code
```

Here's how the for statement works. The first thing that happens in this script is that the variable myPhrase is created and given an initial value of "" (nothing).

```
myPhrase = "";
```

Next, the for statement is set up.

```
for(count = 1; count <= 10; count++){
```

Here, the variable count is created and given an initial value of 1. The condition count <= 10; is set up, basically stating that as long as count has a value of less than or equal to 10, it should loop through the actions that follow between the curly brackets ({}). And finally, count++ is used to increment the value of count by 1 with each iteration of the loop. As you can see, the for statement has all the same ingredients as the while statement, only they're all in a single, convenient place.

Next, the action:

```
myPhrase += "Echo ";
```

is repeated with each loop, so that at the end of the loop myPhrase will have a value of "Echo Echo Echo Echo Echo Echo Echo Echo Echo Echo ".

continue and break statements

Both continue statements and break statements are used in conjunction with loops, to change the way they behave.

Normally, with each loop, a set of actions (as defined within the curly brackets) is executed. With a continue statement, however, you define an exception in the loop—one that means you don't want the actions to be executed. When this exception is encountered, the loop will not execute any subsequent actions, but will continue to the next iteration of the loop. Take a look at the following example:

```
myPhrase = "";
for(count = 1; count <= 30; count++){
  if(count % 3 == 0){
    continue;
  }
  myPhrase += count;
}
```

Here's how the continue statement works in this script. The first thing that happens is that the variable myPhrase is created and given an initial value of "" (nothing).

```
myPhrase = "";
```

Next, the for statement is set up:

```
for(count = 1; count <= 30; count++){
```

The variable count is created and given an initial value of 1. The condition count <= 30; is set up, basically stating that as long as count has a value of less than or equal to 30, it should repeat through the actions that follow between the curly brackets ({}). And finally, count++ is used to increment the value of count with each iteration of the loop.

Next, the continue statement is set up. Once again, this statement defines an exception in the loop where it should do nothing but continue on to the next iteration of the loop. In this case, we state that if the current value of count is divisible by 3 (see modulo operator discussed earlier in this chapter), don't do anything but continue on with the loop:

```
if(count % 3 == 0){
  continue;
}
```

Next, the action that should be performed with each iteration of the loop is defined, basically stating that the value of myPhrase is to be updated with each iteration to include the current value of count.

```
myPhrase += count;
```

At the end of the loop, myPhrase will have a value of "1 2 4 5 7 8 10 11 13 14 16 17 19 20 22 23 25 26 28 29" (note that no numbers divisible by 3 were added to the value).

break statements work in much the same way as continue statements—with one exception: Instead of skipping an iteration of a loop, a break statement will abort the looping sequence (even if the loop isn't complete), and move on to the first line of script that follows. Take a look at the following example:

```
myPhrase = ""
for(count = 1; count <= 30; count++){
  if(count == 12){
    break;
  }
  myPhrase += count;
}
//Next line of script
```

This break statement in this looping statement will cause it to abort after only 12 loops, even though it is set up to loop 30 times. This results in myPhrase having a value of "1 2 3 4 5 6 7 8 9 10 11 12".

There's no room in this book to list all of the ways break and continue statements can be used; just remember that they're both employed to deal with exceptions in looping statements. When used properly, they can free up processing power considerably. How? Imagine a looping statement that's set up to execute dozens of actions with each loop, and the loop is set to loop 1,000 times. That equates to tens of thousands of actions. By establishing exceptions to a loop (where it's not necessary or even desirable to execute actions), continue and break statements make it possible to prevent the execution of thousands of actions—which can make your project run faster and more efficiently.

Functions

Functions represent a powerful aspect of ActionScript programming, allowing you to assign a name to a section of code that has a specific purpose (or *function*). Once you've defined and named a function, you can use it in other scripts simply by referencing its name. This is known as *calling* the function. Functions save coding time by eliminating the need to create redundant code to perform the same actions, or sets of actions, across your various scripts. With functions, you script once and use many times—similar to what symbols allow you to do graphically.

Defining and Calling Functions

Functions are simply statements similar to those discussed in the previous section. To define a function, you use the `function` keyword, followed by the name you wish to give to the function, followed by a closed set of parentheses. Then, the actions this function will perform are defined.

NOTE *Function names have the same requirements and restrictions as variable names.*

For example, take a look at the following code, which defines a function:

```
function doStuffFunction(){
  gotoAndPlay("myFrameLabel");
  stopAllSounds();
  getURL("http://www.mydomain.com");
}
```

The above-defined function, named `doStuffFunction()`, does three things: It sends the timeline to the frame labeled myFrameLabel; it halts any playing sounds; and it opens a URL in a browser window. Simple, right? Now for the even easier part of using functions—calling them. Take a look at the following script, which calls the function we just defined:

```
on(release){
  doStuffFunction();
}
```

As you can see, this function is called when a button is released. Thus, when the button is released, the following happens: The timeline is sent to the frame labeled myFrameLabel; all sounds stop playing; and the URL opens in a browser window—everything the function was designed to do. This same function can be called using any event, as the next script shows with a clip event:

```
onClipEvent(keyDown){
  doStuffFunction();
}
```

The function will always execute as it was designed—regardless of where it's called from (**Figure 13.5**).

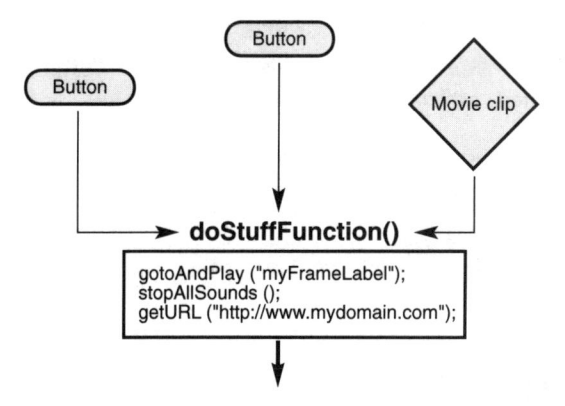

Figure 13.5
Once a function has been defined, it can be called from anywhere in your movie, and the actions within the function definition will be executed.

More Than One Way to Define a Function

As is typical with ActionScript syntax, you can structure your code for function definitions in different ways. At the beginning of this section, we showed you how a typical function definition is structured. It looked like the following:

```
function doStuffFunction(){
  gotoAndPlay("myFrameLabel");
  stopAllSounds();
  getURL("http://www.mydomain.com");
}
```

However, you could also define the same function as follows:

```
doStuffFunction = function(){
  gotoAndPlay("myFrameLabel");
  stopAllSounds();
  getURL("http://www.mydomain.com");
}
```

Here, the name of the function is defined first, and an equals sign is then used to say, "Assign this name to the following function definition." While both function definitions achieve the same results, the latter structure is used extensively when creating and defining what are known as event handler methods, which we'll discuss shortly (under "Advanced Event Handlers and Listeners"). Thus, it's important to familiarize yourself with the syntax.

TIPS *The actions that make up a function are executed only when the function is called from another script, not when it is defined.*

A function cannot be called unless it has first been defined. It's a good idea to define a function in one of the first few frames of your movie (using a frame event/action), so that you can then call it at any point thereafter.

You can use multiple function calls on a single event, as the following script shows:

```
on(release){
  doStuffFunction();
  doMoreStuffFunction();
}
```

You can even mix function calls with other ActionScript, as the next script demonstrates:

```
on(release){
  doStuffFunction();
  doMoreStuffFunction();
  play();
  flash = "fun, fun, fun!";
}
```

By now, you should understand how functions can speed project development: Define once, and use often. Anywhere and anytime you wish to execute the function, you simply call it by its name, followed by parentheses. But what about those parentheses next to the function's name: What's their purpose? That's what we'll look at next.

Passing Values to a Function

Although the doStuffFunction() that we created is a fine piece of code, it has one drawback: It always does the same thing. Let's look at that function again. In its current form, it does three things: It sends a timeline to a frame label; it stops all sounds; and it opens a URL in a browser. The frame it sends the timeline to will always be the one labeled myFrameLabel, and the URL that it opens will always be www.mydomain.com. However, by changing the way our function is defined, we can make it considerably more versatile. Take a look at the following example:

```
function doStuffFunction(whatFrame, whatURL){
  gotoAndPlay(whatFrame);
  stopAllSounds();
  getURL(whatURL);
}
```

Between the parentheses in our updated function there are now two arguments, or parameters—separated by a comma—that represent placeholders for values that can be sent to the function when it is called. To understand how this works, take a look at the following function call:

```
on(release){
    doStuffFunction("intro", "http://www.yahoo.com");
}
```

Here you can see that we added two values (separated by a comma) to our function call. These values (known as passing arguments) are sent to our function, so that it can use them to perform its duties based on those values. In our example, the values "intro" and "http://www.yahoo.com" in our function call replace the whatFrame and whatURL placeholders, respectively, in our function definition. The result looks something like this:

```
function doStuffFunction("intro", "http://www.yahoo.com"){
    gotoAndPlay("intro");
    stopAllSounds();
    getURL("http://www.yahoo.com");
}
```

As you can see, the placeholders are replaced with the values that are sent to the function when it is called. The great thing about this is that whenever we call our function again, we can send it different values. Take a look at the following function calls:

```
on(release){
    doStuffFunction("start", "http://www.cnn.com");
}
on(release){
    doStuffFunction("end", "http://www.excite.com");
}
on(release){
    doStuffFunction("learn", "http://www.derekfranklin.com");
}
```

Each of these function calls is to our single function, but because different values are sent to the function in each function call, it performs the same actions using the different values.

When sending values to a function, you can also use variables in your function call, as in the following:

```
on(release){
  doStuffFunction(myVariable1, myVariable2);
}
```

When you do this, the current value of the variable is passed to the function.

The following are some important things to remember when defining and calling functions in your scripts:

- **Although you can create a function that accepts many parameters, it's best to limit the number of parameters you use.** Functions should have a definite purpose. If you need to send lots of parameters to a single function, it's most likely a sign that you should split that single function into several. Doing this will ensure that your project will run faster and be easier to manage.

- **When defining parameters in a function, remember their order within the parentheses.** Respective values that are defined in the function definition should be listed in that same order in the function call.

- **Parameters that you define for a function only have meaning within that function.** In our example, whatFrame and whatURL have no meaning or use outside of the function itself.

Returning a Result

Not only do functions execute sets of actions, you can also use them like miniprograms within your movie, processing information sent to them and then returning values. Take a look at the following function definition:

```
function buyCD(availableFunds, currentDay){
  if(currentDay != "Sunday" && availableFunds >= 20.00){
    myVariable = true;
  }else{
    myVariable = false;
  }
  return myVariable;
}
```

In this function definition, two parameters' values—availableFunds and currentDay—are sent to the function when it is called. The function then processes those values using an if/else statement. At the end of this function, myVariable will contain a value of true or false. Using the return statement (as shown at the bottom of the function definition), the value of myVariable is returned to where the function was called. To understand this, take a look at how this function is called in the following script:

```
on(release){
  idealCircumstances = buyCD(19.00, "Friday");
  if(idealCircumstances == true){
    gotoAndPlay("Happiness");
  }else{
    gotoAndPlay("StayHome");
  }
}
```

Pay particular attention to the line that reads:

```
idealCircumstances = buyCD(19.00, "Friday");
```

To the right of the equals sign is our actual function call, which sends the values of 19.00 and "Friday" to the buyCD() function for processing. If you look back at how our function was defined, these values are used to determine a true or false value for myVariable. Sending these particular values (19.00, "Friday") to the function causes myVariable to evaluate to a value of false. Since the last line of code in our function says, return myVariable; the value of myVariable is returned to the script where the function was called. Thus,

```
idealCircumstances = false;
```

In essence, we've used a function call to assign a value to the variable idealCircumstances. This all happens in a split second. After a value has been assigned, the value of idealCircumstances can be used in the rest of the script, as our example demonstrated (**Figure 13.6**).

idealCircumstances = **buyCD(19.00, "Friday")**

buyCD(availableFunds, currentDay)

```
if (currentDay != "Sunday" && availableFunds >= 20.00) {
  myVariable = true;
} else {
  myVariable = false;
}
return myVariable;
```

idealCircumstances = **false**

Figure 13.6
Using a function call to assign the value of the variable will cause the function to execute and become a value—and that value will then be assigned to the variable that made the call.

Using Local Variables in a Function

Local variables are special variables that are created within a function definition, and only have meaning in the function definition in which they're defined. Local variables are defined by placing the keyword *var* in front of the name of a variable. Take a look at the following example:

```
function buyStuff(productCost){
  //Create a local variable with a value of 200
  var myLocalVariable = 200;
  if(productCost < myLocalVariable){
    gotoAndPlay("Purchase");
  }
}
```

In this function definition, the variable myLocalVariable only exists within the scope of this function. You cannot refer to or manipulate it outside this function. Once this function has been executed, the local variable is erased until the next time the function is called. All of the variables we've created thus far in the chapter are known as global variables, which means their values can be used or changed from any script.

So why would you want to create variables with this seemingly obvious limitation? Basically, a project can contain dozens, even hundreds, of functions, many of which use variables to do their jobs. Keeping track of the names of all these variables (so that you don't accidentally reuse a variable name, and change or erase its value) could quickly become a hair-raising experience. Local variables eliminate this worry because changing or erasing a *local* variable (named, for example, myVariable) within a function has no effect on a variable with the same name outside the function.

Calling Functions at Regular Intervals

Now that you've seen how powerful functions can be, it's time to learn how you can make them even more useful. Some functions handle tasks that are best executed on a regular basis. Say, for example, you have a slide show presentation, and you've created a function to handle the switching of pictures, which is accompanied by updated text and perhaps a new audio track: A project of this sort screams for some sort of automation, allowing the presentation to move forward on its own at a specified interval. This is exactly what the setInterval() action allows you to do. It lets you call a function repeatedly, at an interval you specify. For example, assume you've created and named the slide show function as follows:

Calling Functions at Regular Intervals continued

```
function updateSlide(){
//actions to update slide
}
```

If you wanted to call this function automatically every ten seconds, you would use the setInterval() action in the following manner:

```
setInterval(updateSlide, 10000);
```

The above script will call the updateSlide function every 10,000 milliseconds (1,000 equals 1 second).

If you wish to pass arguments to the function being called, you can simply add them to the setInterval() function as follows:

```
setInterval(updateSlide, 10000, arg1, arg2, arg3);
```

The setInterval() action can be turned on and off by assigning it a variable name, as in the following example:

```
myVariable = setInterval(updateSlide, 10000);
```

This assigns the name myVariable to the setInterval() action, as well as activating it. To remove the functionality of the setInterval() action, you would delete it, as shown by the following syntax:

```
clearInterval(myVariable);
```

Using Event Handler Methods

Mouse and Clip Event Handler Methods

In Chapter 12, you learned about the many events that can trigger the execution of scripts. These included mouse and clip events such as press, release, rollOver, load, keyDown, and so on. We also looked at how to manually select and attach scripts, which use these events, to objects such as buttons, frames, and movie clip instances. As a result, you saw how interactivity is created. However, by creating event handler methods, you can do this dynamically as well—that is, you can attach scripts to (or alter scripts on) objects such as buttons and movie clip instances as your movie plays.

To understand why you would want to do this, imagine this simple scenario: There are four buttons on the stage, all set up to execute scripts. However, say you wanted the pressing of one of these buttons to change how the other buttons functioned. Or you may have just dynamically created a movie clip instance, and want to attach a script to it (which was impossible to do in the authoring environment, since the instance was created dynamically). This is where event handler methods can help.

An event handler method is nothing more than a script that specifies a function to call, when an event occurs in relation to an object. To understand this, let's take a look at an example. Assume there is a button on the stage with an instance name of **myButton**. Initially, the button isn't scripted to do anything. If you wanted to attach an event handler method to it, so that it executes a set of actions when pressed, you would use something like the following (we'll explain where this script is placed in a moment):

```
myButton.onPress = function(){
  gotoAndPlay(25);
  stopAllSounds();
  loadMovie("mySWF.swf", "myTarget");
}
```

As you can see, using a somewhat altered function definition, we've set up **myButton** so that when pressed, it will execute the three actions shown. Notice the first line, which in essence states, "When **myButton** is pressed, execute the following unnamed function." If you wanted to call an already-defined function when **myButton** was pressed, you could use the following syntax:

```
myButton.onPress = doStuff;
```

This specifies that when **myButton** is pressed, call the doStuff function.

NOTE *As shown in the sample script above, when assigning a function to call in this manner, you do not add parentheses to the name of the function.*

If you later wanted to change the button's functionality so that it did something else when pressed, you would simply attach a different event handler method to it, such as the following:

```
myButton.onPress = function(){
  getURL("http://www.derekfranklin.com");
}
```

By using the above script, the button will only execute a single action when pressed.

You can even assign multiple event handler methods to an object (like our button) simultaneously. Take a look at the following:

```
myButton.onPress = function(){
  getURL("http://www.derekfranklin.com");
}
```

```
myButton.onRelease = function(){
   play();
}
myButton.onRollOver = function(){
   stop();
}
```

Now, **myButton** is set up to trigger the actions shown when pressed, released, or rolled over, respectively. To remove an event handler from an object, so that a specific event no longer executes a script, you can use something similar to the following:

```
myButton.onPress = null;
```

As a result, **myButton** will no longer respond to the onPress (or press) event.

For every standard event (press, release, and so on), there is an event handler method equivalent (onPress, onRelease, and so on). Table 13.5 provides a complete list of these event handler methods.

Table 13.5
Standard Events and Their Event Handler Method Equivalents

Standard Event	Event Handler Method Equivalent
press	onPress
release	onRelease
releaseOutside	onReleaseOutside
rollOver	onRollOver
rollOut	onRollOut
dragOver	onDragOver
dragOut	onDragOut
load	onLoad
unload	onUnload
enterFrame	onEnterFrame
mouseDown	onMouseDown
mouseMove	onMouseMove
mouseUp	onMouseUp
keyDown	onKeyDown
keyUp	onKeyUp
data	onData

NOTE *There are a couple of additional event handler methods available for movie clips and buttons that have no standard event equivalents. These are* onKillFocus *and* onSetFocus. *Since you can use the Tab key to select different elements on the screen, these event handler methods can be used to call functions when an element has been tabbed to (*onSetFocus*) or away from (*onKillFocus*).*

To help you understand how to implement event handler methods in your projects, we've created a sample Flash project, which you'll be able to script as we go along. This file, named eventHandlers.fla, can be found in the Chapter 13/Assets folder of the accompanying CD. Be sure to save this file to your hard drive for testing purposes.

To use event handler methods on buttons and movie clip instances:

1. Choose File > Open and navigate to the directory that contains eventHandlers.fla, and open it.

   Since we'll be using and building on this file in the exercises that follow, let's first look at its structure.

   The project contains five layers, named according to their content. We will be adding scripts to Frame 1 of the Actions layer, as well as the buttons on the stage. In this exercise, we'll only work with the elements on the top half of the stage (three buttons and a movie clip instance). We'll work with the elements on the bottom half of the stage in the next exercise.

   We've already given instance names to all of the elements. The buttons labeled Button 1, Button 2, and Button 3 have instance names of **button1**, **button2**, and **button3**, respectively. The movie clip instance is named **myMovieClip** (**Figure 13.7**). These instance names play an important role in using event handler methods, as you will soon see. Let's create our first one.

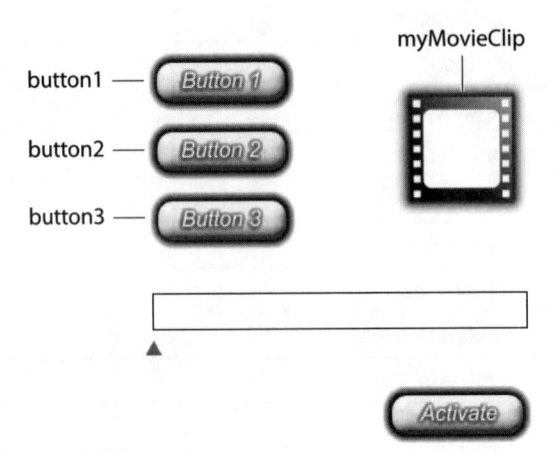

Figure 13.7
The elements of the project we will be working with in this exercise.

NOTE *Switch the Actions panel to Expert mode to add the following scripts.*

2. Select Frame 1 of the Actions layer, and with the Actions panel open, add the following script:

    ```
    button1.onRelease = function(){
      getURL("http://www.derekfranklin.com");
    }
    ```

    This event handler method will cause **button1** to execute a getURL() action when pressed and released. Thus, a script on a frame can program our button's function—which is different from selecting the button in the authoring environment and attaching a script to it directly, as you were shown in the previous chapter.

    NOTE *An object (such as a button or movie clip instance) must exist when an event handler method is assigned to it. For example, if the event handler method is assigned on Frame 1, but the object it is being assigned to doesn't appear until Frame 2, the assignment will not take.*

    Let's test our script.

3. Choose Control > Test Movie.

    Pressing **button1** will open your browser and load the URL you specified.

    Let's go back to the authoring environment, and add another event handler method to Frame 1 to make **myMovieClip** to spin.

4. Close the test movie (File > Close) to return to the authoring environment. Select Frame 1 and with the Actions panel open, add the following event handler method, just below the one you added in Step 2.

    ```
    myMovieClip.onEnterFrame = function(){
      myMovieClip._rotation += 5;
    }
    ```

    This event handler will cause **myMovieClip** to add 5 degrees to its rotation property with every enterFrame event. As a result, it will spin.

    Let's test it.

5. Choose Control > Test Movie.

    As you can see, as soon as the movie begins playing, **myMovieClip** begins rotating. Once again, the event handler we created on Frame 1 lets us attach a script to **myMovieClip** dynamically.

Next, we'll add some event handler methods to **button2** and **button3**, in order to provide you with a couple more examples of how they're implemented.

6. Close the test movie to return to the authoring environment. With the Actions panel open, select **button2** and attach the following script:

```
on(release){
  myMovieClip.onPress = function(){
    startDrag(myMovieClip, true);
  }
  myMovieClip.onRelease = function(){
    stopDrag();
  }
}
```

This script is executed when **button2** is pressed and released. It adds two new event handler methods to **myMovieClip**, in addition to the onEnterFrame event handler method assigned to it by the script discussed in Step 4 (which causes it to spin).

The first event handler method added in this script (onPress) will cause **myMovieClip** to become draggable when pressed. The second (onRelease) will cause dragging to stop. This means that after **button2** is pressed and released, **myMovieClip** will react to three different events: onEnterFrame, onPress, and onRelease (**Figure 13.8**).

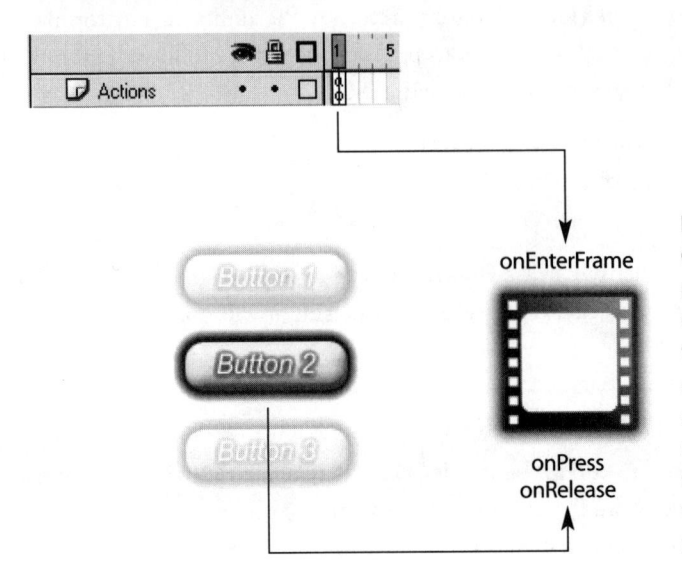

Figure 13.8
Once **button2** is pressed and released, **myMovieClip** will react to onPress and onRelease events, in addition to the onEnterFrame event that it's set up to react to as a result of the script on Frame 1.

NOTE *Button instances can only have mouse event–related event handler methods attached to them* (onPress, onRelease, *and so on); however, movie clip instances can have both mouse event– and clip event–related event handler methods attached to them. This means a movie clip instance can be set up to react to both* onRelease *and* onRollOver *events, in addition to* onEnterFrame *and* onKeyDown *events.*

Now it's time to test your movie.

7. Choose Control > Test Movie.

Before doing anything else, place your cursor over the spinning movie clip. You'll notice that a hand cursor (indicating that the element will react to mouse events) *does not* appear. The script we created in the previous step will alter the functionality of this clip, as the movie plays, so that it reacts to the events we defined. To demonstrate this, press **button2**. Now if you place your mouse over the spinning movie clip, a hand cursor will appear. Pressing the clip will cause it to become draggable; releasing will cause dragging to stop.

Last, let's look at how to remove an event handler method from a button or movie clip.

8. Close the test movie to return to the authoring environment. With the Actions panel open, select **button3** and attach the following script:

```
on(release){
    button1.onRelease = null;
    myMovieClip.onEnterFrame = null;
    myMovieClip.onPress = null;
    myMovieClip.onRelease = null;
}
```

This script is executed when **button3** is pressed and released. By using null, we prevent **button1** from reacting any longer to the onRelease event, and **myMovieClip** from reacting to the onEnterFrame, onPress, and onRelease events.

9. Choose Control > Test Movie.

Press **button1** to execute the getURL() action. Press **button2** to make **myMovieClip** draggable. Press **button3** to remove *all* of this functionality. Press **button2** in order to once again make **myMovieClip** react to the onPress and onRelease events.

This demonstrates how you can use event handler methods to affect how button and movie clip instances function, as your movie plays. However, their functionality doesn't end there: In the next section we'll look at still more (and more powerful) ways you can use event handler methods in your movies.

10. Close the test movie and save your work.

We will be using this file in the next section.

TextField, Sound, LoadVars, XML, and XMLSocket Event Handler Methods

Now that you're familiar with many of the mouse and clip events that can be used to trigger a script's execution, it's time to look at some additional events (that is, event handler methods) that you can use in conjunction with other ActionScript objects (such as text fields, sounds, and more). These allow you to call functions when a text field is clicked, when the text in a field changes, when an external sound has finished loading into your movie, when a sound has finished playing, along with many other circumstances, as listed in Table 13.6.

NOTE *Some of the event handler methods included in this table are beyond the scope of this book. For more information about any of them, see the ActionScript Dictionary that comes with Flash MX, or get a copy of* Macromedia Flash ActionScripting: Advanced Training From the Source, *published by Macromedia Press.*

Table 13.6
Additional Event Handler Methods

Event Handler Method	Description
TextField Objects	
nameOfTextField.onChanged	Calls a function every time text is changed in the field
nameOfTextField.onKillFocus	Calls a function when the text field has lost focus (that is, when it's been interacted with and then clicked away from)
nameOfTextField.onScroller	Calls a function when text in the field is scrolled
nameOfTextField.onSetFocus	Calls a function when the text field is clicked (that is, when the insertion point is placed in the field)

Table 13.6 continued
Additional Event Handler Methods

Event Handler Method	Description
Sound Objects	
nameOfSound.onLoad	Calls a function when an external MP3 file has finished loading into the Sound object.
nameOfSound.onSoundComplete	Calls a function when the Sound object has played completely.
LoadVars Objects	
nameOfLoadVars.onLoad	Calls a function when external data has finished loading into the LoadVars object
XML Objects	
nameOfXML.onData	Calls a function when XML data requested by the XML object has been received from a server
nameOfXML.onLoad	Calls a function when an XML document requested by the XML object has been downloaded completely
XMLSocket Objects	
nameOfSocket.onClose	Calls a function when an open XMLSocket connection has been closed
nameOfSocket.onConnect	Calls a function when the XMLSocket object connects to a XML Socket server
nameOfSocket.onData	Calls a function when XML data requested by the XMLSocket object has been received from a server, but has not yet been parsed (read) by the Flash Player
nameOfSocket.onXML	Calls a function when XML data requested by the XMLSocket object has been received from a server, after it has been parsed by the Flash player.

NOTE *For more information about these objects, see Chapter 14, "ActionScript Objects."*

The event handler methods shown above build on the functionality we covered in the previous section. Let's look at an example.

Assume there's a text field on the stage with an instance name of **myTextField**. Say you wanted to execute a function every time that instance was given focus (that is, each time the insertion point was placed in the field). To do so, you would create an event handler method such as the following:

```
myTextField.onSetFocus = function(){
    myMovieClip._alpha = 50;
}
```

The above event handler will cause **myMovieClip**'s transparency to be set to 50 percent whenever **myTextField** is given focus. If you wanted to return the transparency to 100 percent when **myTextField** was clicked away from (that is, when it's no longer in focus), you would use the following:

```
myTextField.onKillFocus = function(){
    myMovieClip._alpha = 100;
}
```

As discussed in the previous section, if you're using event handler methods and you want to call a function that has already been defined, you can use the following alternative syntax:

```
myTextField.onSetFocus = nameOfFunction;
```

TIP *If you define an event handler method by specifying the function it needs to call (as shown above), that function can still be called from other scripts as well.*

The following exercise will show you how to implement this type of event functionality with a text field—which will in turn provide the basis for using the other event handler methods described in this section.

To use event handler methods with a text field:

1. Open eventHandlers.fla from the previous exercise (if it's not already open).

In this exercise we will be working with the elements on the bottom half of the stage. This includes the text field (**myText**), the small arrow (a movie clip instance named **myArrow**), and the Activate button (**buttonActivate**) (**Figure 13.9**). We will add ActionScript to Frame 1 of the timeline, as well as the Activate button. In addition, we'll use a few event handler methods: one to change the border and background color of **myText** when it's given focus, another to reset those colors when the text field loses focus, and another to make the arrow (**myArrow**) move as text is typed into the field.

Chapter 13 *Understanding ActionScript*

Figure 13.9
The elements within the project that we will be working with in this exercise.

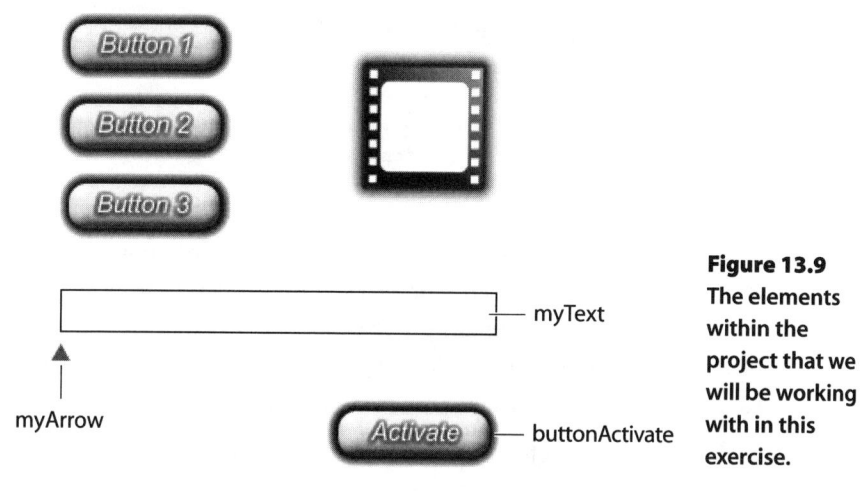

In this exercise, we'll take a slightly different approach than we did in the last exercise: Here, we'll define our event handler methods by first defining three functions, then assigning those functions to be called in response to three different events (onSetFocus, onKillFocus, and onChanged).

Let's get started!

2. With the Actions panel open, select Frame 1 of the Actions layer.

   You should see the existing script, which remains from the previous exercise. We will add to this script in the steps that follow.

3. Add the following function definition beneath the current script:

   ```
   function changeTextBackground(){
     myText.borderColor = 0x0099FF;
     myText.backgroundColor = 0xFFFFCC;
   }
   ```

   This function, named changeTextBackground(), executes two actions: The first sets the borderColor property of the **myText** text field to a hex value of 0x0099FF, which turns the field's border light blue. The next action sets the backgroundColor property of the **myText** text field to a hex value of 0xFFFFCC, making the field's background light yellow.

   Next, let's create another function that will reset these colors to their original black (border) and white (background) values.

4. Add the following function definition below the current script:

```
function resetTextField(){
  myText.borderColor = 0x000000;
  myText.backgroundColor = 0xFFFFFF;
}
```

This function, named `resetTextField()`, executes two actions, which are similar to those in the previous step: The first sets the `borderColor` property of the **myText** text field to a hex value of 0x000000, or its original color of black. The next action sets the `backgroundColor` property of the **myText** text field to a hex value of 0xFFFFFF, or its original color of white.

Now let's create one last function that will move **myArrow** when called.

5. Add the following function definition below the current script:

```
function moveArrow(){
  myArrow._x = myText._x + myText.textWidth;
}
```

This function, named `moveArrow()`, executes a single action when called: It sets the x property (horizontal position) of **myArrow** so that it equals the combined value of **myText**'s x property plus the width of any text within **myText**. This will cause the arrow to appear just below the last character typed into the field (**Figure 13.10**).

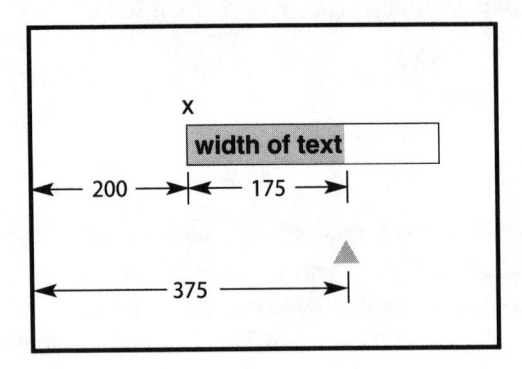

Figure 13.10
This function specifies that the x position of myArrow always matches the combined value of myText's x position and the width of the text it contains.

Now that we're finished defining our functions, it's time to put them to use.

NOTE *For more information about these text field properties, see Chapter 14, "ActionScript Objects."*

6. With the Actions panel open, select the Activate button and attach the following script:

```
on(release){
  myText.onSetFocus = changeTextBackground;
  myText.onKillFocus = resetTextField;
  myText.onChanged = moveArrow;
}
```

This script is executed when the Activate button is pressed and released. It assigns three event handler methods to the **myText** text field. The second line says that when **myText** is given focus, call the `changeTextBackground()` function. The third line says that when **myText** loses focus, call the `resetTextField()` function. The fourth line says that when text is added to or deleted from the **myText** text field, call the `moveArrow()` function. Remember, these event handler methods are not assigned *until* the button is pressed and released.

TIP *Instead of assigning these event handler methods as a result of a button being pressed and released, we could have just as easily placed the three lines of script on Frame 1 so that the event handler methods would have taken effect as soon as the movie began playing.*

It's time to do some testing.

7. Choose Control > Test Movie.

If you interact with the **myText** text field, you'll notice that not much happens. However, if you press the Activate button, now when you click on the field to enter text, its border and background colors will change. As you add or delete text, the arrow under the field will move, and if you click away from the field, its border and background colors will be reset to black and white.

8. Close the test movie and save your work.

Although we can't touch on every conceivable use of event handler methods, by now you should have a clear grasp of how you can begin putting them to use in your projects. For more examples of how to use event handler methods, see Chapter 16, "Using ActionScript in Your Projects."

Listeners

Several ActionScript objects have what are known as *listener events* (see Table 13.7). These represent a set of events that almost any object can be set to "listen for" and in response, call a function. This will make more sense in a moment.

Table 13.7
Objects with Listener Events

Event Handler Method	Description
Key Objects	
onKeyDown	Occurs when any key is pressed
onKeyUp	Occurs when any key is pressed and released
Mouse Object	
onMouseDown	Occurs when mouse has been pressed down
onMouseMove	Occurs when mouse is moved
onMouseUp	Occurs when mouse is pressed and released
Selection Object	
onSetFocus	Occurs when focus is changed from one text field to another
Stage Object	
onResize	Occurs when movie is resized
TextField Objects	
onChanged	Occurs when text in a field changes
onScroller	Occurs when text in a field is scrolled

NOTE *Although some listener events have the same name as events discussed earlier in this chapter; in this context, however, they function a bit differently (as you'll shortly see).*

As you can see from the table, the Mouse object has three listener events: onMouseDown, onMouseUp, and onMouseMove.

Each time the mouse button is pressed down, let up (released), or moved, these events occur and are "transmitted" throughout the movie. As a result, *any* object (text field, sound, color, array, and so on) can be set up to *listen* for, and react to, these listener events of the Mouse object, as demonstrated by the following:

```
myTextField.onMouseDown = function(){
  myTextField.text = "The mouse was pressed down";
  _root.play()
}
mySoundObject.onMouseDown = function(){
  mySoundObject.start();
}
myArray.onMouseUp = function(){
  myArray.push("mouseUp event");
}
```

Here we've set up two different objects that will execute functions when they hear an onMouseDown event, and a third that will execute a function when it hears an onMouseUp event. These three objects consist of a text field named myTextField, a Sound object name mySoundObject, and an array named myArray. One more step is needed to make the whole process work: All of these objects must be *registered* to listen for Mouse object listener events. In other words, although these objects are now able to listen for the events, you must activate that functionality for them to do so—which is precisely what the following lines of script do:

```
Mouse.addListener(myTextField);
Mouse.addListener(mySoundObject);
Mouse.addListener(myArray);
```

Or

```
Mouse.addListener(myTextField, mySoundObject, myArray);
```

Now, all three objects (now considered listeners) are registered to listen to all Mouse object listener events. Although they've been registered to listen to *all* Mouse object listener events, they will only react to the onMouseDown (myTextField and mySoundObject) or onMouseUp (myArray) events. Now, whenever the mouse is pressed, released, or moved, the three registered objects will be notified that a Mouse object listener event has occurred, and will execute a function related to that event (if they've been set up to do so) (**Figure 13.11**).

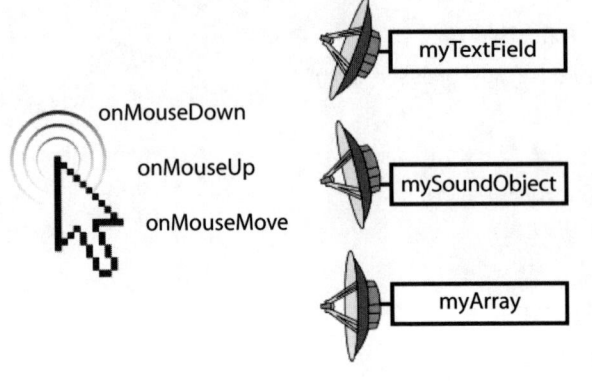

Figure 13.11
By registering objects to listen for Mouse listener events, you set them up to receive and act upon such events—sort of like receivers responding to radio signals, or waves, transmitted from a station.

If you no longer want an object to listen for events, you can unregister it using the following syntax:

```
Mouse.removeListener(myArray);
```

Now, `myArray` will no longer listen for Mouse object listener events (though `myTextField` and `mySoundObject` still will).

Listeners are great for coordinating a number of objects to react to a particular event.

Working with Multiple Timelines

A single Flash Player movie window can contain many movies, including the main movie, movie clip instances, and movies loaded into that window via the `loadMovie()` action. Each of these movies is a separate entity with its own timeline, scripts, variables, functions, and properties (**Figure 13.12**). One of Flash's most powerful features is its ability to use a set of actions that are attached to a mouse, clip, or frame event in one movie, to affect the movement, properties, and variables of any other present timeline in another movie. A timeline is considered present as long as it exists in the Player movie window. For example, if a particular movie clip instance only appears in your movie for 40 frames, it can be considered present (and thus targeted) only during those 40 frames.

Each timeline present in the Player window has an address that is used to target it to perform an action. In this section, we'll show you how to target specific movies to perform different tasks, and explain what this functionality allows you to do.

Chapter 13 **Understanding ActionScript**

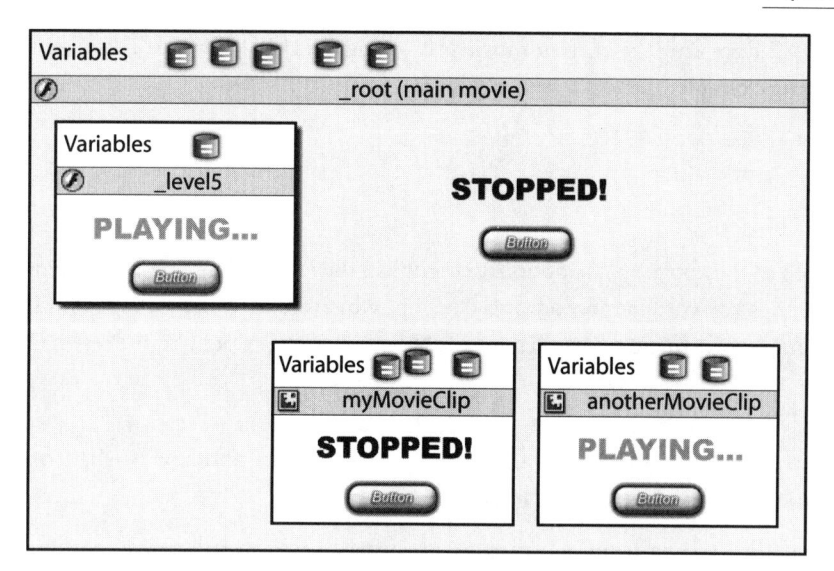

Figure 13.12
The Flash Player window can contain many movies, each of which is a separate entity, independent of the other movies in the window.

Addressing Targets in ActionScripts

To target a specific movie or timeline in a script, you need to address it in a unique way. This address is known as that movie's target path. Any of the following can be targeted: the current movie, the main movie, a movie clip instance, a parent movie, or a movie that has been loaded into a level. Let's take a look at each of these target modes in more detail.

Current movie

If a target name or level number does not preface an action, the target is understood to be the current movie or timeline. For more information on the current movie, see "Targets" in Chapter 12, "Getting Started with ActionScript."

Targeting the current movie looks something like the following:

```
on(release){
   age = 32;
}
```

This script creates the variable *age* in the timeline where the button that contains the script exists. Thus, if the button is on the main timeline, the variable will exist on the main timeline as well. If the button is in a movie clip instance, the variable will exist there instead.

Another way of addressing the current movie is by using the `this` keyword. Take a look at the following example:

```
on(release){
    this.age = 32;
}
```

Although both of the above syntax options accomplish the same thing, you would typically use the `this` keyword in more advanced scripts, which are beyond the scope of this chapter. For more information, see Chapter 16, "Using ActionScript in Your Projects."

Main movie

The main movie represents the main timeline of a .swf file. This timeline is what you see when you start a new Flash authoring file.

Targeting the main movie from any movie clip instance within it looks something like this:

```
on(release){
    _root._alpha = 45;
}
```

This script, if placed on a button in a movie clip instance, will make the main timeline 45 percent transparent.

No matter where a script exists, `_root` always signifies that you are targeting the main timeline.

TIP *When addressing movie clip instances, you may find it useful to preface their target paths with _root, indicating their relation to the main timeline. To help you get used to this concept, we've used that notation for most of the remaining scripts in this chapter.*

Movie clip instance

You assign names to instances of movie clips to identify them in ActionScripts (see "Defining an Instance" in Chapter 7). In doing so, you make it possible to control them via ActionScripts. You can give different instances of the same movie clip unique names, so that you can target them separately (**Figure 13.13**).

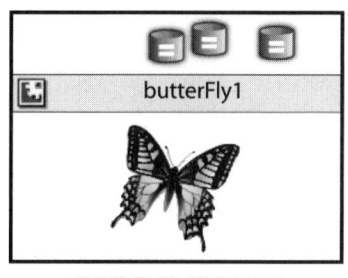

Figure 13.13
Separate instances of the same symbol can be targeted and act independently of one another, if given different instance names.

When targeting a movie clip instance in an ActionScript, you must spell its name correctly, but the letter case does not have to match (that is, **MyMovieClip** is the same as **mymovieclip**).

Targeting a movie clip instance can look like the following:

```
on(press){
    _root.myMovieClip.gotoAndPlay(20);
}
```

When executed, this script will tell the movie clip instance named **myMovieClip** (which exists on the main timeline) to go to and play from Frame 20 of its timeline.

If you were to target a movie clip instance that exists within another movie clip instance, your script would look something like the following:

```
on(press){
    _root.myMovieClip.anotherMovieClip._width = 20;
}
```

Parent movie

Just as a real family is built on a hierarchy of parents, children, and children's children, a Flash movie can contain several movies, any of which can contain several more movies, and so on. The relationship between these movies is called a parent-child relationship. A parent movie is a relative term that identifies any movie (including movie clips) that contains other movies, or children. For example, the main timeline is considered the parent movie of any movie clip instances that exist within that timeline. Thus, targeting the main timeline (parent) from a movie clip instance (child) would look something like the following:

```
on(press){
    _parent._width = 200;
}
```

If you placed this same script on a button in a movie clip instance, which itself was inside another movie clip instance (parent), the parent's width would be updated to a value of 200.

Movies on levels

Whenever you use the loadMovie() action, you are in essence loading another .swf file into an existing one (see "Loading and Unloading External Movies" in Chapter 12). This action gives you the option of loading the file onto a specific level: By identifying the level on which you want your movie to reside, you make its timeline (and the timelines of any of the movie clip instances it contains) available for targeting. If, for example, you were to load a movie into Level 5, its content would appear above content in Levels 0 through 4 (0 being the original, or main, movie).

Targeting a level's main timeline can look like the following:

```
on(release){
    _level5.gotoAndStop (25);
}
```

This script will cause the main timeline loaded into Level 5 to got to and stop at Frame 25.

If you wanted to target a movie clip instance on a particular level, your script might look like this (**Figure 13.14**):

```
on(release){
    level5.myMovieClip._rotation = 30;
}
```

This script will cause the movie clip instance **myMovieClip** (which resides within the movie loaded in Level 5) to rotate 30 degrees.

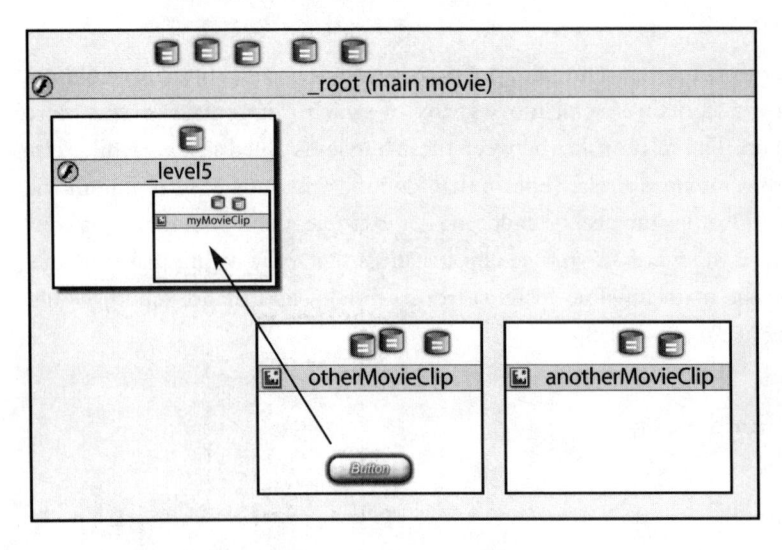

Figure 13.14
Movie clip instances on any level can be targeted from any other timeline. For example, the button in otherMovieClip can contain an ActionScript that affects myMovieClip on Level 5.

Using a with statement

In Flash, with statements are used as a special way of addressing an object (including movie timelines), so that a number of actions can be performed on it. Take a look at the following example:

```
on(release){
  with(_root.myMovieClip){
    _rotation = 30;
    _alpha = 25;
    play()
  }
}
```

In this script, we've used a with statement to address a movie once in order to rotate it, make it transparent, and start it playing. We could easily use the with statement to affect any target. Take, for example, the following:

```
on(release){
  with(_level5){
    _rotation = 30;
  }
}
```

or

```
on(release){
  with(_parent){
    _rotation = 30;
  }
}
```

NOTE *You can use* with *statements in conjunction with any ActionScript object (Array objects, Sound objects, and others) to simultaneously perform a number of actions in relation to that object.*

It's About Style

As you work with ActionScript, you'll discover that there are often many ways to accomplish a single task. To give you an idea of this, take a look at the following examples—each of which does the same thing: changes the visibility of the movie clip instance named *invisibleMan*:

Example 1

```
invisibleMan._visible = false;
```

Example 2

```
setProperty("invisibleMan", visible, false);
```

Example 3

```
with(invisibleMan){
  _visible == false;
}
```

None of these examples is right or wrong; the one you use is a matter of preference and style. In fact, just as a graphic artist can be known for his or her style, so can a programming artist. No two programmers tackle a problem exactly the same way, nor does ActionScript require them to. Work the way that's most comfortable to you.

Putting it all together

To help you understand how to target various movies, try thinking of your Flash project as a family structure, with your main movie being the mother movie. In your project, mom has some kids—Joe, Lucy, and Bob—who in Flash represent movie clip instances within the main movie. These movie clip instances are referred to as child movies.

The following shows how our family structure would look within Flash (**Figure 13.15**):

```
Mother (_level0)
Joe
Lucy
Bob
```

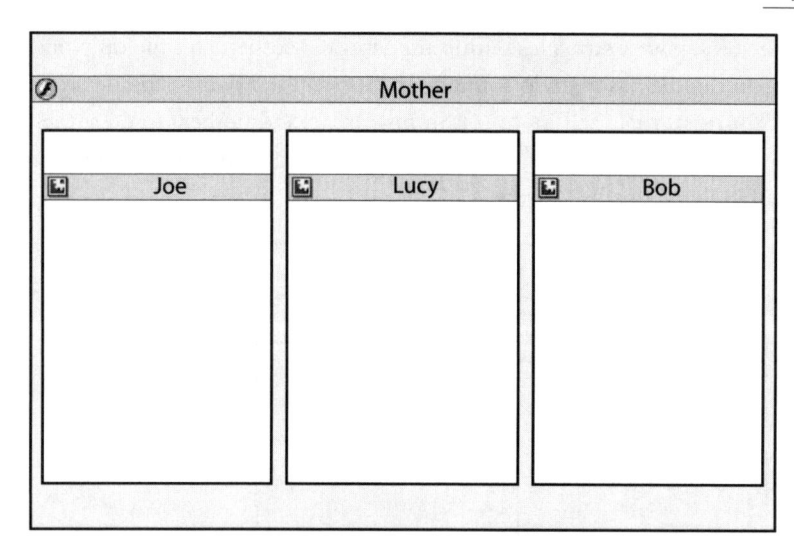

Figure 13.15
The various timelines present within the Flash Player window at any given time can be looked at as a family structure, with parent movies containing other movies, or children.

If you clicked a button in the Mother movie to make Lucy invisible, the target path in the script might look like the following:

```
on(release){
    _root.Lucy._visible = 0:
}
```

Now, let's say that **Joe** has a couple of kids himself: **Junior** and **Youngster**. If **Joe** represents a movie clip instance, his "kids" represent movie clip instances within a movie clip instance.

The overall family structure now looks like this:

```
Mother (_level0)
    Joe
       Junior
       Youngster
    Lucy
    Bob
```

With this in mind, if you were to click a button in the Mother movie that made **Joe**'s child **Junior** invisible, the target path in the script would look like the following:

```
on(release){
    _root.Joe.Junior._visible = 0
}
```

Now let's initiate some power struggles within the family: Mother isn't the only one in control here. **Joe** can tell **Lucy** to do something; **Bob** can tell **Junior** to do something; and even **Youngster** can tell mom (or, in his case, grandmother) to do something. To understand this, take a look at the following illustration and the accompanying sample target paths (**Figure 13.16**).

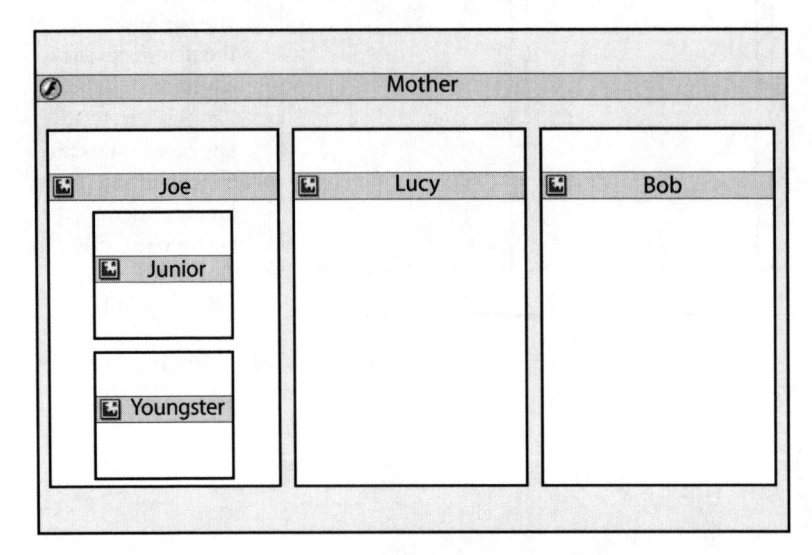

Figure 13.16
The hierarchical structure of our example.

If you wanted a mouse, clip, or frame event in **Mother** to target any of our other family members (that is, the movie clip instances within Mother), their target paths would be as follows:

- **Mother.** The target path would be blank or this.
- **Joe, Lucy, or Bob.** The target path would be Joe, Lucy, or Bob, or _root.Joe, _root.Lucy, or _root.Bob.
- **Junior or Youngster.** The target path would be Joe.Junior, or Joe.Youngster, or _root.Joe.Junior, or _root.Joe.Youngster.

If you wanted a mouse, clip, or frame event in **Bob** to target any of our other family members, their target paths would be as follows:

- **Mother.** The target would be _root or _parent.
- **Lucy or Joe.** The target path would be _root.Lucy or _root.Joe.
- **Junior or Youngster.** The target path would be _root.Joe.Junior or _root.Joe.Youngster.

If you wanted a mouse, clip, or frame event in **Lucy** to target any of our other family members, their target paths would be as follows:

- **Mother.** The target would be _root or _parent.
- **Bob or Joe.** The target path would be _root.Bob or _root.Joe.
- **Junior or Youngster.** The target path would be _root.Joe.Junior or _root.Joe.Youngster.

If you wanted a mouse, clip, or frame event in **Joe** to target any of our other family members (that is, the movie clip instances within Mother), their target paths would be as follows:

- **Mother.** The target would be _root or _parent.
- **Lucy or Bob.** The target path would be _root.Lucy or _root.Bob.
- **Junior or Youngster.** The target path would be Junior or Youngster or _root.Joe.Junior or _root.Joe.Youngster.

If you wanted a mouse, clip, or frame event in **Junior** to target any of our other family members, their target paths would be as follows:

- **Mother.** The target would be _root.
- **Lucy or Bob.** The target path would be _root.Lucy or _root.Bob.
- **Joe.** The target path would be _root.Joe or _parent.
- **Youngster.** The target path would be _root.Joe.Youngster or _parent.Youngster.

If you wanted a mouse, clip, or frame event in **Youngster** to target any of our other family members, their target paths would be as follows:

- **Mother.** The target would be _root.
- **Lucy or Bob.** The target path would be _root.Lucy or _root.Bob.
- **Joe.** The target path would be _root.Joe or _parent.
- **Junior.** The target path would be _root.Joe.Junior or _parent.Junior.

The last target paths we're going to look at are those created whenever a new .swf file is loaded into the Flash movie window, using the `loadMovie()` action.

Whenever a movie in addition to the main movie is loaded into the Flash movie window, it is given a level number. The initial movie loaded into the Flash player is automatically assigned Level 0. Any new movie loaded into a level can be thought of as another parent movie containing child movies.

For our analogy, the structure of a loaded movie placed on Level 5 would look like this:

```
Mother (_level5)
   Kathy
      Ashlie
      Carla
   Jack
   Liz
```

As you can see, in addition to our original family on Level 0, a new family exists on Level 5 (**Figure 13.17**).

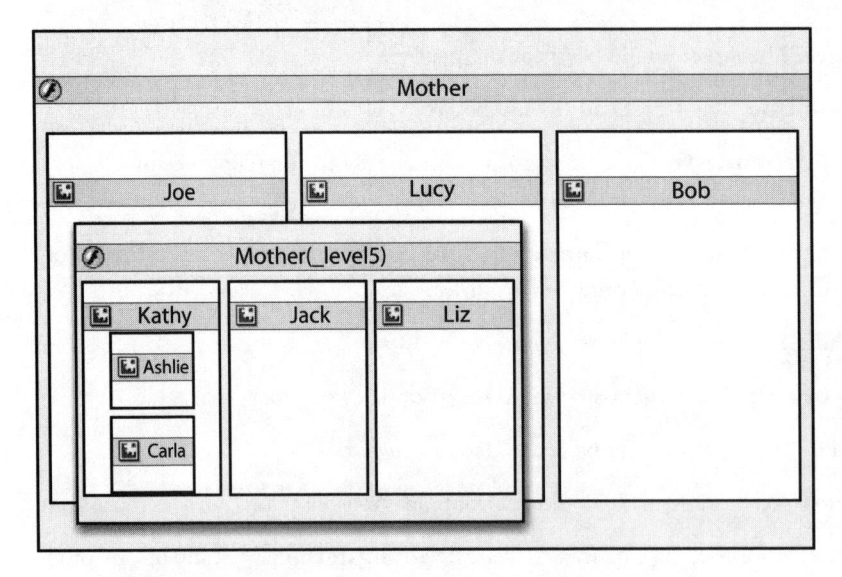

Figure 13.17
Loading another movie into the Flash Player (at Level 5) introduces a new hierarchy.

To target the main timeline of the movie on Level 5 from any other movies loaded into the Flash Player window, your script might look like this:

```
on(release){
   _level5.gotoAndStop(10);
}
```

To target the movie clip instance named **Ashlie** (which is contained in the movie on Level 5) from any other movie within the Flash Player window, your script might look like this:

```
on(release){
   _level5.Kathy.Ashlie.gotoAndStop("Bed");
}
```

TIP *If your script's syntax looks correct but is still not working, chances are that a target isn't being addressed properly.*

Chapter 13 *Understanding ActionScript*

Inserting a target's path

The Actions panel includes a useful utility called the Target Editor, to help you define target paths in your ActionScripts. The Insert Target Path dialog box shows a movie's hierarchy, or display list. From this display list, you can select a target whose path is subsequently inserted into your script.

To use the Insert Target Path dialog box:

1. Get to a point in the script where you need to define a target path.

2. Click the Insert a Target Path button above the Actions List window.

The Insert Target Path dialog box will appear with the following areas (**Figure 13.18**):

- **Display list.** This window displays a directory of available movie clip targets. If a plus sign (Windows) or a twirly (">", in Macintosh) appears next to a movie clip instance's name, that movie clip has an associated child movie clip. Clicking a name in the list displays its target path in the Target window.

- **Target.** This window displays the target path that will be inserted when the OK button on this dialog box is pressed.

- **Notation.** This option lets you choose what syntax to use in defining the target's path. Dots are the preferred notation; however, slashes can also be used.

- **Mode.** This option lets you choose how much of the target path to include. *Absolute* inserts the complete target path from the _root of the movie. *Relative* displays only instances of movie clips that exist in the current frame of the current Timeline, and their child instances.

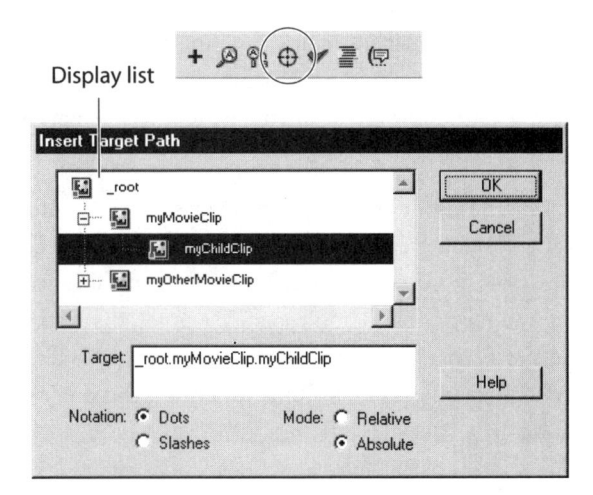

Figure 13.18
The Insert Target Path dialog box helps you define specific movies as targets for actions.

513

3. Once you have selected a target in this box, click OK to insert its target path in the script.

TIP *The path of a movie or movie clip on a level must be inserted manually into your scripts. You cannot do so from the Insert Target Path dialog box.*

> ### A Note About Targets and onClipEvent
>
> *By default, unless a target is specified, any action associated with an onClipEvent pertains to the movie clip instance to which that action is attached. For example, take a look at the following script:*
>
> ```
> onClipEvent(load){
> _rotation = 60;
> play();
> }
> ```
>
> *In this example, as soon as the movie clip instance to which this script is attached loads, the instance itself is rotated 60 degrees and begins to play. It's important to note this because when scripts attached to buttons and keyframes contain actions that don't specify a target, the target is understood to be the same timeline that the button or keyframe is part of—and this, as demonstrated, can result in different functionality in terms of scripts attached to movie clip instances.*

Using and Changing Individual Timeline Data

As mentioned, each timeline can contain its own set of variables and functions. These data elements can be accessed from scripts in any timeline as long as the timeline they are a part of is present in the Player window. For example, if a particular movie clip instance is only available for 40 frames in your movie, its variable data and functions can only be accessed during those 40 frames.

How can you tell which timeline a variable or function exists on? As with other aspects of ActionScript, any variables you create and any functions you define become part of the current movie unless you specify otherwise. Thus, if you create a variable with an action inside of a movie clip instance and don't specify a target, that variable data exists in the movie clip instance, and that instance's name acts as an address for accessing that data. A single script can draw from data in multiple timelines. But don't worry: It's not as complicated as it sounds.

Setting and using variable values on different timelines

You can create, update, or access a variable's data for any movie present in the Flash Player window (including movie clips and loaded movies). Just prefix the name of the variable with the path of the timeline with which it's associated. For example, the following script creates a variable named myVariable that will exist in the movie clip instance named **myMovieClip**, which resides on the main timeline (_root):

```
on(release){
  _root.myMovieClip.myVariable = 200;
}
```

Once the variable has been created, you can access its value from scripts on any timeline simply by addressing its location properly. Take a look at the following example, which will send the current movie's timeline to Frame 20 if the value of the variable on another timeline (the variable we created above) plus 50 equals 300:

```
if(_root.myMovieClip.myVariable + 50 == 300){
  gotoAndPlay(20);
}
```

Functions and multiple timelines

Similar to variables, a function can exist on any timeline. Simply use that timeline's address to call a function. Take a look at the following example, which defines a function in the movie clip instance named **myMovieClip** (which resides on the main timeline):

```
function _root.myMovieClip.doStuffFunction(){
  gotoAndPlay("myFrameLabel");
  stopAllSounds();
  getURL("http://www.mydomain.com");
}
```

To call this function, simply use its complete target path:

```
on(release){
  _root.myMovieClip.doStuffFunction();
}
```

Keep It Simple

Working with data and functions across timelines can get confusing if you're not careful. You may sometimes find it helpful to use the _root timeline as a central location for most of your movie's data. This way, you only need to create or use data from a single source. Take a look at the following examples:

```
//create a variable that exists on the _root timeline.
_root.myVariable = 250 ;
```

The great thing about this technique is that regardless of which timeline you use the above script on, it will always create (or update, if the variable already exists) the variable on the _root timeline.

The same thing holds true for functions:

```
//define a function that exists on the _root timeline.
function _root.doStuffFunction();
  stopAllSounds();
  getURL("http://www.mydomain.com");
}
```

Once again, using _root.doStuffFunction() will call this function no matter which timeline you call it from.

It may take a few extra keystrokes to add _root when creating variables or defining functions, but in the end you save time by not having to guess where a particular piece of data exists.

Understanding the Context of Each Line in a Script

In the scripts we've included thus far, we've demonstrated the various ways that timelines communicate with each other. In this section, you'll learn how to put it all together in a working ActionScript.

As you've already learned, just because a script is attached to a button on the main timeline doesn't mean it affects or draws data only from that timeline. A single script can communicate with multiple timelines simultaneously. Nearly every line in an ActionScript does something in the context of a particular timeline. To help you understand this concept, we'll decipher each line of the following script:

```
on(release){
  myVariable = 25;
  gotoAndPlay(myVariable);
  _root.anotherMovieClip._rotation = 120;
  _root.myMessage = "The current value of myVariable is " + myVariable + ".";
  _level3.doStuffFunction();
}
```

The actions in this script are a bit exaggerated, but they help demonstrate how context affects the way a script works. For this demonstration, assume that this script is attached to a button in a movie clip instance named **myMovieClip**. Now let's examine the script line by line.

```
myVariable = 25;
```

On this line, a variable is created and assigned a value of 25. The important thing to note here is that since no target is defined for this action, the target is considered the current movie (**myMovieClip**). Thus, the variable that's created exists on **myMovieClip**'s timeline.

```
gotoAndPlay(myVariable);
```

Once again, since no target is defined, this action sends the current movie (**myMovieClip**) to a frame number based on the value of myVariable.

```
_root.anotherMovieClip._rotation = 120;
```

This action rotates the movie clip instance named **anotherMovieClip** by 120 degrees. Since _root prefaces the target path, it is understood that this movie clip instance is a child movie of the main movie.

```
_root.myMessage.text = "The current value of myVariable is " +
myVariable + ".";
```

This action will display the text "The current value of myVariable is 25" in a dynamic text field named **myMessage**, which exists on the _root timeline.

```
_level3._alpha = _root.anotherMovieClip.anotherVariable;
```

This action will change the transparency of the movie on Level 3 based on the value of anotherVariable, which exists on **_root.anotherMovieClip**'s timeline.

```
_level3.doStuffFunction();
```

This action calls a function that was defined in a loaded .swf file that exists on Level 3.

The _global Object

MX ALERT

Now that you've learned how to address various timelines that exist in a movie (and the variables, functions, and other objects they contain), it's time to introduce you to the _global object, which lets you give functions, variables, objects, and other elements a global address. This allows you to access these elements from any timeline—without using a target path or timeline address. Take a look at the following example:

```
_global.myGlobalVariable = "Hello";
```

The above ActionScript creates a global variable named myGlobalVariable and assigns it a value of "Hello". While variables in one timeline can be accessed by another timeline (as just discussed), the name of the variable must normally be prefaced with the address of the timeline where it exists. Not so with global variables. Since we defined myGlobalVariable as a global variable, its value can be accessed from any timeline simply by using its name; you don't need to preface it with a target path. For example:

```
message.text = myGlobalVariable;
```

You can create global functions as well, such as:

```
function _global.myGlobalFunction(){
   //actions
}
```

You can call the above function from any timeline, simply by using myGlobalFunction();

You can even give a movie clip instance at a particular target path a global address:

```
_global.car = _root.myMovie.myOtherMovie.car;
```

Now, rather than use the long target path (shown to the right of the equals sign), you can refer to that movie clip instance from any timeline simply by using **car**. You can refer to it as **car** in any script (for example, car.gotoAndPlay(30);) and Flash will understand that you're actually referring to **_root.myMovieClip.myOtherMovie.car**. Pretty cool, don't you think?

All ActionScript objects (such as Array, Sound, and Color objects, which you'll learn about in the next chapter) can be given global addresses at the time they are created.

However, before you start wondering why you've spent all this time learning about timeline addresses and target paths—when you could simply use the _global object throughout your project instead—you should be aware of some potential pitfalls. First, global data/objects remain in memory as long as your movie plays. Thus, if your movie is continually creating global data/objects, you can soon run into memory problems. Second, while data/objects on different

> **The _global Object continued**
>
> timelines can have similar names, only a single global object can have a particular name at any time—meaning you have to be aware of the names of all your global data/objects, so that you don't accidentally change a value that shouldn't be changed.
>
> Bottom line: While giving data/objects a global reference can be useful in many situations, it's best to reserve this functionality for data/objects that have a "global presence" in a project—where easy access from any timeline is important.

Advanced Actions Panel Features

In Chapter 12 you were introduced to the Actions panel from the standpoint of a novice ActionScripter. Now that you're nearing the end of this chapter and your scripting skills are more finely honed, it's time to look at how some of the more advanced features of the Actions panel can help you become even more efficient at creating interactive masterpieces.

Finding and Replacing

As you grow more proficient with ActionScript and push your newfound skills to the max, your scripts will likely grow from several lines to perhaps hundreds of lines. However, you'll soon find out that a script of this length can be intimidating—even frustrating if you're attempting to find a specific piece of it. Fortunately, the Actions panel includes several features that automate the process of searching for and even replacing specific content within a script—regardless of length.

To go to a specific line number in your script:

1. With the Actions panel open, press the panel Options button and select Go To Line… from the menu.

The Go To Line dialog box will appear.

TIP Alternately, you can press Control-G (Windows) or Command-G (Macintosh) to quickly open the Go To Line dialog box.

2. Enter the line number you wish to navigate to and press OK.

That line will appear highlighted in the Actions List window.

To locate a specific word, phrase, or ActionScript code in the Actions List window:

1. With the Action panel open, press the panel Options button and select Find… from the menu.

   The Find dialog box will appear.

   TIP Alternatively you can press the Find button on the Actions panel toolbar to open the Find dialog box (**Figure 13.19**).

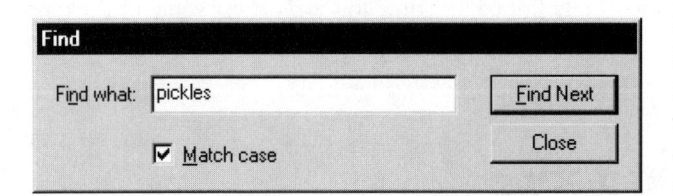

Figure 13.19 Pressing the Find button on the Actions panel toolbar provides quick access to the Find dialog box.

2. Enter the word, phrase, or ActionScript code you're looking for. Select the "Match case" option so that the search will look only for text that matches the exact text entered.

3. Press the Find Next button.

   Flash will begin searching for the text you entered. When a match is found, the matching text will be highlighted in the Actions List window.

4. If this locates the text you're looking for, press the OK button. This will allow you to edit it. If you don't wish to edit the text, continue to press the Find Next button until you find what you're looking for.

   TIPS Once you've closed the Find dialog box, you can still continue searching for the text you entered by pressing F3 on your keyboard. Doing so will automatically take you to the next found instance of the search text, highlighted and ready for editing.

When the Actions panel is in Normal mode, the Find command only searches portions of the script where Parameter fields have been used to define actions. When the Actions panel is in Expert mode, it searches the entire script.

To locate and replace a specific word, phrase, or ActionScript code in the Actions List window:

1. With the Actions panel open, press the Options button and select Replace from the menu.

   This will open the Replace dialog box.

   TIP *Alternatively, you can press the Replace button on the Actions panel toolbar to open the Replace dialog box. (**Figure 13.20**).*

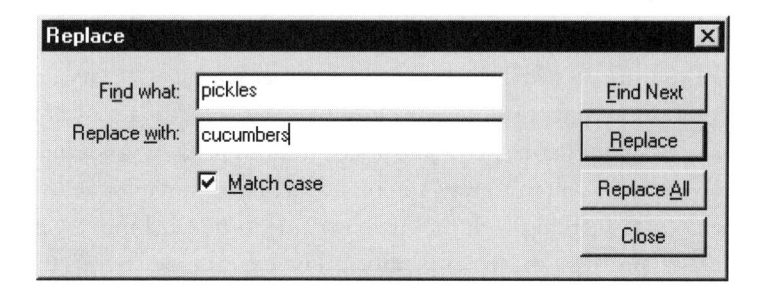

Figure 13.20 Pressing the Find button on the Actions panel toolbar provides quick access to the Find dialog box.

2. In the "Find what" text box, enter the word, phrase, or ActionScript code you're looking for. Select the "Match case" button so that the search will look only for text that matches the exact text entered.

3. In the "Replace with" text box, enter the word, phrase, or ActionScript code you want to replace with what is being searched for (as described in the previous step).

4. Press the Find Next button.

   Flash will begin searching for the text entered in the "Find what" text box. When a match is found, the matching text will be highlighted in the Actions List window.

5. Do one of the following:

- Press the Replace button to replace the highlighted text with what you entered into the Replace text box, or press the Find Next button in order to skip the currently selected match and move on to the next match found. Repeat this process until you've replaced all the instances of the searched text that you wish to replace, then press OK.

Or

- Press the Replace All button to automatically find and replace all instances of the searched text with the replacement text, then press OK.

TIP *If you feel you made an error in the process (say, for example, you replaced the wrong thing), remember the Actions panel's Undo feature, which can help you retrace your steps.*

Syntax Checking

Writing a script for Flash is a much more exacting process than writing a letter to a friend. Although your friend will likely be able to decipher your message regardless of spelling errors, misplaced punctuation, and other mistakes, Flash is not so forgiving when it comes to executing scripts. One misplaced dot can halt a script hundreds of lines long. Clearly, correct syntax is pretty important. While it's not difficult to get the code right when you're working with the Actions panel in Normal mode (since it's such a hand-holding process), the freedom afforded by Expert mode means there are greater chances for errors. Fortunately, you can use the Action panel's syntax-checking feature to have Flash check a script for errors at any time. When checking scripts in this manner, Flash not only pinpoints the error's location, it also notes the reason for it as well.

To check a script's syntax:

- With the Actions panel open, press the Options button and select Check Syntax from the menu, or press the Check Syntax button on the Actions panel toolbar.

  If no errors are found, Flash will display an alert box indicating this. If an error(s) is found, an alert box indicating that errors were found will be displayed. In addition, the Output window will open, providing information about the location of the error(s) as well as a short message indicating the reason it was detected as an error (**Figure 13.21**). Review this information and make any necessary edits to your script, then check the syntax again.

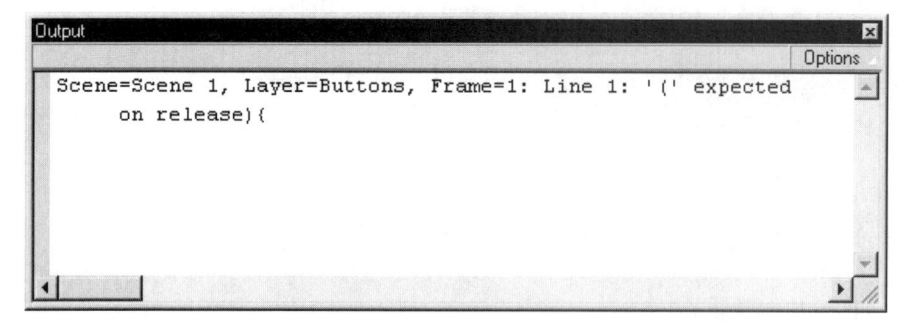

Figure 13.21
When you press the Check Syntax button, Flash will check the syntax of the script currently displayed in the Actions List window. If an error is found, an alert box will appear, indicating that errors were found, and the Output window will open, providing information about the error(s).

TIP *When the Actions panel is in Normal mode, errors in your code are identified in red. When you place your mouse over an area that contains improper syntax, a tooltip message explaining the error will appear.*

Code Hints

MX ALERT So you're feeling pretty familiar with ActionScript—but when it comes to using a specific action that requires a set of parameter values, you find you can't quite remember exactly what those parameters are, or the order in which you need to specify them. This is where code hints can help.

Code hints are used in one of three ways. The first is as tooltips: If you're typing an action with definable parameters into the Actions List window, a tooltip appears (indicating parameter names and the order in which they need to be defined) when you reach the point in your action where you need to define parameters. Usually the tooltip will contain enough information to refresh your memory about how to define the action.

To display and use tooltip-style code hints:

◆ In the Actions List window of the Actions panel, type the code for an action that has definable parameters (such as the getURL() action). Once you type the opening parenthesis, the code hint tooltip will appear. The currently definable parameter will appear bolded within the tooltip. As you enter various parameters (separated by commas), the tooltip will be updated to display the currently definable parameter in bold text. The code hint will disappear once you type the closing parenthesis for the action (**Figure 13.22**).

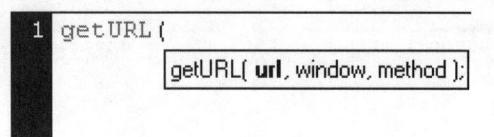

Figure 13.22
Tooltip-style code hints provide a quick reference to action parameters as you type the action.

Code hints also appear when you define an on or onClipEvent event. In this case, a drop-down menu appears, allowing you to quickly specify the particular event you wish to use.

To display and use drop down menu–style code hints:

1. In the Actions List window of the Actions panel, type the beginning code for an event (such as on or onClipEvent). Once you've typed the opening parenthesis to define the event, a drop-down menu will appear, providing a list of events to choose from (**Figure 13.23**).

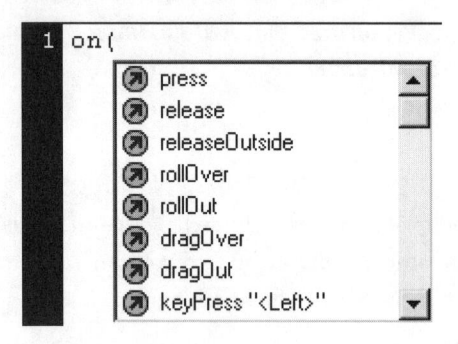

Figure 13.23
Menu-style code hints appear when you begin to define an event for a script.

2. Use the Up and Down arrow keys on your keyboard to navigate the list. When the event you wish to use is highlighted, press the Enter key.

3. Add the closing bracket to the event.

Chapter 13 **Understanding ActionScript**

You can also get code hints to appear by taking advantage of one aspect of the Action panel's built-in functionality: By naming objects (movie clip instances; Text, Sound, and Color objects; and others) via a special convention that involves the use of a suffix, you can get quick access to properties and methods available to that object via a code hint drop-down menu. For example, if we added the suffix _mc to the name of a movie clip instance and then entered that name in the Actions List window (followed by a dot, as in **myMovieClip_mc.**), a code hint drop-down menu would appear, providing quick access to actions available *only* to movie clip instances. The _mc suffix makes this possible by identifying **myMovieClip** as a movie clip instance. Naming objects in this way can save you numerous keystrokes when creating scripts (**Figure 13.24**).

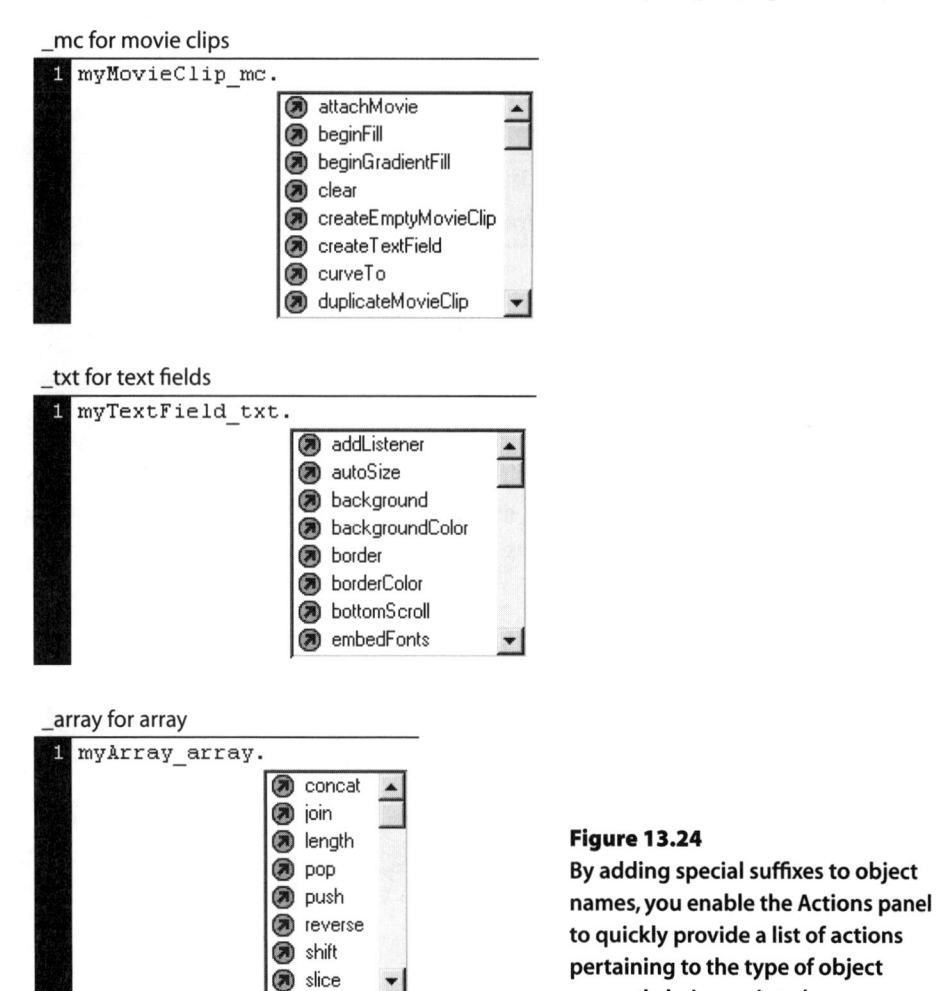

_mc for movie clips

```
1 myMovieClip_mc.
            attachMovie
            beginFill
            beginGradientFill
            clear
            createEmptyMovieClip
            createTextField
            curveTo
            duplicateMovieClip
```

_txt for text fields

```
1 myTextField_txt.
            addListener
            autoSize
            background
            backgroundColor
            border
            borderColor
            bottomScroll
            embedFonts
```

_array for array

```
1 myArray_array.
            concat
            join
            length
            pop
            push
            reverse
            shift
            slice
```

Figure 13.24
By adding special suffixes to object names, you enable the Actions panel to quickly provide a list of actions pertaining to the type of object currently being scripted.

The following table shows the available suffixes and the object types (classes) they are associated with.

Table 13.7
Object Suffixes

Object Class	Suffix
Timelines in general	_root, _level, _parent
MovieClip	_mc
Array	_array
String	_str
Button	_btn
TextField	_txt
TextFormat	_fmt
Date	_date
Sound	_sound
XML	_xml
XMLSocket	_xmlsocket
Color	_color
Video	_video

If you don't want to attach suffixes to object names but like the functionality they provide in relation to code hints, you can instead use comments in your code to associate an object with a specific object class. For example, the following line of code will cause the Actions panel to see myMovieClip as a movie clip instance—and thus display code hints pertaining to that object class:

```
//MovieClip myMovieClip;
```

Now, whenever myMovieClip (no suffix) is typed into the Actions List window, the movie clip actions will appear in a code hint drop down menu. Let's take a look at one more example.

The following identifies mySound as a Sound object:

```
//Sound mySound;
```

TIPS *You can manually display code hints at any time by placing the insertion point (cursor) at a location where code hints normally appear automatically (such as just after the opening parenthesis of an action), then pressing the Code Hint button on the Actions panel toolbar (**Figure 13.25**).*

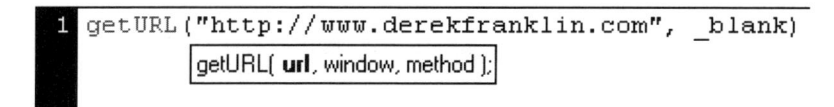

```
1  getURL ("http://www.derekfranklin.com", _blank)
    getURL( url, window, method );
```

Figure 13.25
If you place the insertion point at a location where code hints normally appear automatically, and then press the Code Hint button on the Actions panel toolbar, the appropriate code hint will be displayed.

Code hints can be turned off or otherwise configured via the Preferences dialog box. For more information, see "Setting Actions Panel Preferences" a little later in this chapter.

Auto-Formatting

MX ALERT One of the best things about using the Actions panel in Expert mode is the freedom it gives you to type code directly into the Actions List window; it's as easy as if you were typing directly into a word processor. If there is a disadvantage to this functionality, it's that it allows you to neglect formatting your script to make it easy to follow and read. Although not always necessary in order for a script to function properly, things such as line breaks and added spaces between certain operators and their operands can go a long way toward easing readability.

However, if you're simply too busy to worry about such things, don't! Let Flash take care of the formatting for you through its auto-formatting capabilities. You simply define the formatting structure you wish your scripts to follow (including line breaks, spacing, and more), and your script will be automatically formatted according to that structure as you type it into the Actions List window.

Flash comes with a default formatting structure, but you can customize it to your liking.

To customize script auto-formatting:

1. With the Actions panel open, press the Options button and choose Auto Format Options from the menu.

The Auto Format Options dialog box will appear (**Figure 13.26**). At the top of this dialog box you will find several formatting options that you can enable (check) or disable (uncheck). As you do so, the Preview window will display the effect the option will have on the scripts you create. Press the Reset to Defaults button to disable all options.

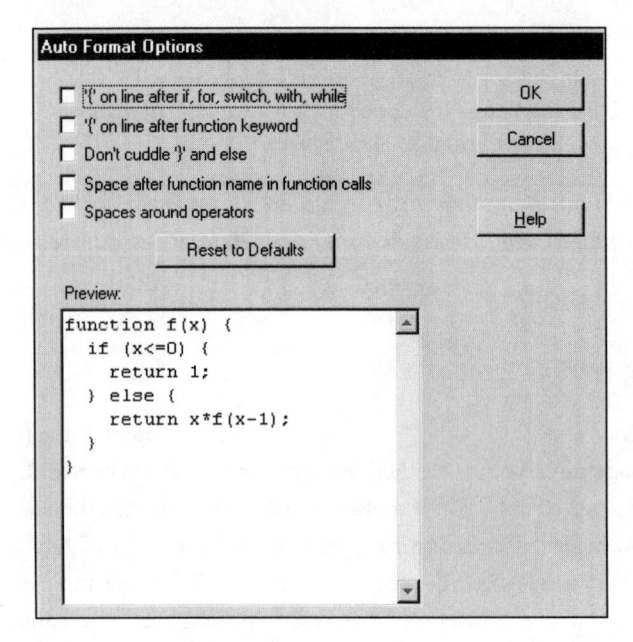

Figure 13.26
The Auto Format Options dialog box allows you to adjust how Flash formats scripts as you type them into the Actions List window.

2. When finished, press OK.

> **NOTE** Although you would think you could set indenting in the Auto Format Options dialog box, you can't. Instead, you must do so through the Preferences dialog box, which we discuss a bit later in the chapter.

> **TIP** If you've turned off auto-formatting but suddenly want to view the current script with auto-formatting, press the Auto Format button on the Actions panel toolbar.

Using and Creating External Scripts

External scripts—which exist in a text file, *outside* the actual project file (.fla)—serve several purposes within Flash development environments. Within some Flash development teams, for example, several people need to work on a project simultaneously—say with one person responsible for design and animation and another person (most likely a programmer) devoted entirely to scripting. By using external scripts, designer and programmer can work on their portions of the project separately, and then merge the files into a single Flash movie once they're finished. Flash developers can also use external files to create libraries of custom scripts, providing functionality that can be accessed simply by inserting one of these external scripts at any point in a given project. Let's take a look at how you create and use these types of external files.

External scripts can be either scripts you've created within the Actions panel and then exported as text files, or scripts that you've created in a text editor such as Notepad (Windows) or SimpleText (Macintosh). Either way, these external text files contain ActionScript code and are saved with an **.as** file extension. You can import the script within the .as file directly into the Actions List window, or you can place what is known as an #include action within a script, specifying that a specific external .as file (and the script it contains) be inserted at that point when the movie is tested, published, or exported.

To help you understand this concept, let's take a look at an example: Say you have a button with an attached 20-line script and an external .as file containing a 5-line script. On Line 10 of the script attached to the button, you've placed an #include action, which identifies the external, 5-line .as file as the file to include at that point. When your movie is exported and a SWF is created, Flash will detect that #include action and automatically insert the 5-line external script at the point of #include action, and what used to be Lines 10 through 14 will be moved down—all of which happens invisibly to the viewer. The final SWF will contain the inserted script just as if it had originally existed in the FLA. You can use #include actions throughout your projects, and Flash will import/insert the scripts as defined.

Need another example? Let's look at the development team again: The #include action allows the programmer to work on the scripts as external .as files, which he or she can later merge with the designer's work to create a complete, interactive project. In addition, if the programmer needs to edit one of the external .as files, the movie just needs to be re-exported in order for it to reflect the new functionality of the updated script.

Or take the case of that custom scripts library: If you've created a script that gives buttons double-clicking capability and saved the file as **doubleClick.as**, all you need to do to add this functionality to buttons in your projects is to place an #include action in the appropriate spot(s) to insert the script contained in the doubleClick.as file. And that's just a very basic example. External scripts can actually contain dozens, even hundreds, of lines of code.

To create an external .as file from a script in the Actions List window:

1. Create a script in the Actions panel.
2. Press the Actions panel Options button and choose Export as File from the menu.

   The Save As dialog box will appear.
3. Give the file a name and choose a directory in which to save it.
4. Press Save.

   The entire script shown in the Actions List window will be exported to the .as file.

   TIP *Remember, you can create an .as file with a text editor simply by typing your script and saving the file with an .as extension.*

To import a script from an external .as file:

1. With the Actions panel open, press the Options button and choose Import From File from the menu.
2. From the dialog box that appears, navigate to the .as file you wish to import, then press Open.

   The script in the .as file will be imported into the Actions List window, replacing any text that existed there previously. Once imported, the script becomes part of the authoring file, and you work with it just as you would any other script.

To include a script when you export your movie:

1. Create an .as file with the script you wish to include.
2. Within the script displayed in the Actions List window, place an #include action on the line where the external script should be inserted. Within the action, specify the directory path to the .as file.

For example:

```
play();
#include myASFile.as;
stopAllSounds();
```

3. When the movie is exported, the script within the external .as file will be inserted where the #include action is located (**Figure 13.27**).

myASFile.as

```
1 play();                    getURL("http://www.derekfranklin.com");    1 play();
2 #include myASFile.as;      Mouse.hide();                              2 getURL("http://www.derekfranklin.com");
3 stopAllSounds();           myVariable = getTimer();                   3 Mouse.hide();
                                                                        4 myVariable = getTimer();
                                                                        5 stopAllSounds();
```

Figure 13.27
The #include action lets you insert an external script during the exporting process.

Printing Scripts

A hard copy of a script offers several advantages. First and foremost, it allows you to view and study a script while you're away from your computer. You can also hand off hard copies to others for their review, and you can use them as backup copies if your computer melts down and you lose all your files.

To print the current script displayed in the Actions List window:

◆ From the Actions panel Options menu, choose Print.

This will open the Print dialog box, where you can set various print settings.

Setting Actions Panel Preferences

MX ALERT While code hints, automatic indentation, and color-coded scripts are all helpful, you may want to turn off these options or configure them more to your liking. You can access these settings and tweak them as you see fit via the ActionScript Editor tab of Flash's general Preferences dialog box.

To set Actions panel preferences:

1. With the Actions panel open, press the Options button and choose Preferences from the menu.

This will open the Preferences dialog box with the ActionScript Editor tab selected (**Figure 13.28**). This tab contains the following settings:

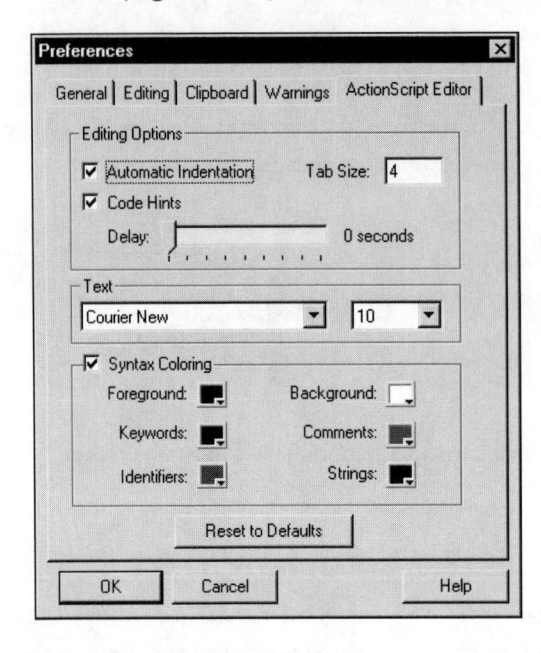

Figure 13.28
The ActionScript Editor tab on the Preferences dialog box contains settings that adjust various editing features of the Actions panel.

Editing Options

- **Automatic Indentation.** Enabling this feature will cause nested actions and scripts to be automatically indented in the Actions List window (to indicate that they're nested).

- **Tab Size.** Lets you specify the amount of indentation.

- **Code Hints.** Enables (checked) or disables (unchecked) the code hinting feature.

- **Delay.** When code hinting is enabled, this slider determines the delay (in seconds) between when a circumstance dictates that a code hint *can* appear and the time it actually does. A longer delay allows you to pause briefly when entering code; code hints won't appear unless there's a significant pause (indicating that you're stuck, and thus in need of a code hint).

Text

- **Font style and font size.** These two drop-down boxes allow you to choose the font style and size of code appearing in the Actions List window.

- **Syntax Coloring.** A checkbox is provided for enabling (checked) or disabling (unchecked) this feature. In addition, color boxes are provided so that you can set the color used for different script elements.

- **Foreground.** This is the color of general text in the script window, such as object names, operators, semicolons, and parentheses.

- **Background.** This is the background color of the Actions List window.

- **Keywords.** This is the color of ActionScript keywords, such as on, onClipEvent, if, while, with, and so on.

- **Comments.** This represents the color of script comments.

- **Identifiers.** This represents the names of properties and methods.

- **Strings.** This is the color of strings of text that are used in a script.

2. When you have finished adjusting the various settings, press OK.

   Any existing scripts will be updated to reflect your new color-coding settings.

Video Tutorials

Using the Advanced Features of the Actions Panel. This tutorial shows you how the advanced features of the Actions panel, such as code hints, auto-formatting and color syntax, can help you become a more proficient scripter.

ActionScript Objects

CHAPTER **14**

What you'll learn...

How objects are used in Flash Projects

The difference between global objects and classes of objects

About Flash object types and their uses

Just as various objects—for example, computers, cars, stoves, and vacuum cleaners—have unique functions in the physical world, each ActionScript object performs a unique role within Flash. These objects provide a means for working with text, sound, color, dates, and more—in short, allowing you to perform all sorts of interactive tasks in some very dynamic ways.

As you'll soon learn, ActionScript objects resemble their physical-world counterparts in that they have characteristics (or *properties*), which you can change via a script, and abilities (or *methods*), which allow them to perform various tasks. The primary advantage of using objects in ActionScript is that they allow you to program and manipulate data, colors, sound, dates, and so on, in a context that makes sense to humans. As you learn more about objects, you'll find that ActionScript's underlying logic becomes clearer as well.

In the text that follows, we'll examine the general structure of objects (that is, how they work), and then take a closer look at some of the specific ActionScript objects you can use to create interactivity in your own projects.

Object Primer

ActionScript objects provide a means of moving graphic elements dynamically, building applications, organizing data, and more. You accomplish these tasks by using or setting object property values and invoking object methods. In this section, we'll show you how properties and methods are used to create interactivity and explain how objects are organized within ActionScript—all of which should provide a strong foundation for the discussion of various objects that follows.

NOTE *This chapter is not meant to be an exhaustive examination of every ActionScript object. There are far too many (and their capabilities are far too diverse) to cover in a single chapter. Instead, we'll focus here on those objects that are likely to be most useful in your projects. For a more complete survey of objects, pick up a copy of* Macromedia Flash MX ActionScripting: Advanced Training from the Source, *published by Macromedia Press.*

Properties

When you look at or touch a physical object, you're naturally aware of the various properties that define its overall form: size, weight, color, age, location, power requirements, and so on. The range of properties objects can possess is as diverse as the objects themselves, and the values assigned to these properties are what make them unique.

For example, a person can be defined by properties such as name, age, height, weight, hair color, and so on. If a person were to be described as an ActionScript object, these property definitions would look like the following:

```
person.name = "Matt";
person.age = 17;
person.heightInFeet = 6.2;
person.weightInPounds = 180;
person.hairColor = "blond";
```

Although Matt is a pretty well-rounded guy, changing any of these properties will affect either his appearance or the way he interacts with his environment. For example, if we were to change his name to Jill, not only would we likely upset him, we'd also need to change the way we addressed him; the name *Matt* would no longer elicit a response. Likewise, if we were to change Matt's height, he would no longer be able to reach things that he was able to before, and if we were to alter his hair color, his appearance would change considerably (take my word on this).

In ActionScript, many (though not all) objects have properties. For example, movie clip instances (which are MovieClip objects) have properties such as _rotation, _visible, _x, _y, and so on. The values of these properties define how the movie clip instance appears, and is interacted with, in your project.

Most property values can be *set* and *read* (used) by a script; however, others are read-only—which means that scripts can see and use their values, but not *set* these values. For example, all movie clip instances have a _totalframes property, which represents the total number of frames on that instance's timeline. While a script can use the value of this property (as in myVariable = _totalframes), it cannot set that value during playback, since the number of frames a movie contains is a hard-wired value (that is, it's locked in by Flash during the export process).

In Flash, property values are identified in relation to an object by a dot that separates the object's name from its property. Although you're probably already aware of this functionality, let's briefly review it. If you have a movie clip instance named **bigDog**, and you want to change its _rotation property, you would use the following syntax:

```
bigDog._rotation = 45;
```

The above line of script will rotate **bigDog** 45 degrees. Notice that a dot (.) separates the object's name (**bigDog**) from the property you want to work with ((_rotation). You would employ a similar syntax when using an object's property value. For example:

```
if (bigDog._x = your._x){
    gotoAndPlay("scream");
}else{
    gotoAndStop("relax");
}
```

In this script, an if statement compares **bigDog**'s _x property value (horizontal location) with the value of **your**'s _x property, and then reacts accordingly.

You'll notice from the script above that an underscore (_) is used in addressing some movie clip instance properties (specifically, those from the Properties book of the Toolbox List window) (**Figure 14.1**). This is a holdover from earlier versions of Flash, where properties were identified in this manner. However, in Flash MX, many object properties are identified without an underscore. For example:

```
myArray.length
myTextField.borderColor
mySound.duration
```

As we progress through this chapter, we'll show you how you can use different objects' properties to create interactivity.

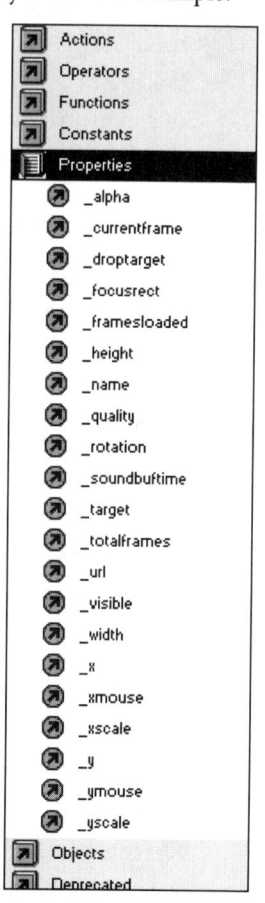

Figure 14.1
Properties listed in the Properties book of the Toolbox List window of the Actions panel are the only ActionScript properties identified with underscores.

Methods

Methods represent tasks that an object can perform. For example, if you were to look at a dog as an object, its methods would include the abilities to eat, bark, run, play, and sleep. If a dog were an ActionScript object, the syntax for these methods would look like this:

```
eat();
bark();
run();
play();
sleep();
```

The parentheses that are included in a method are sometimes used to pass it a parameter or set of parameter values, allowing it to act in a unique way, based on those values. For example, if we wanted our dog to eat a particular type of food, we could indicate this in the parentheses, as in the following:

```
eat("steak");
```

If at a later time we wanted our dog to eat again, but something other than steak, we would once again invoke the eat() method, but pass it a different value, such as:

```
eat("chicken");
```

The method still does the same thing (eats), but *what* is eaten is different. Herein lies the power of methods: They perform specific tasks, but you can often configure them to perform those tasks using unique values. To give you a better idea of how this works, let's look at a couple of real examples using a movie clip instance. One of the methods available to movie clips gives them the ability to duplicate themselves: This is the duplicateMovieClip() method, which is invoked as follows:

```
myBankAccount.duplicateMovieClip("playMoney", 1);
```

In the above example, we're duplicating the movie clip instance named **myBankAccount**, naming the duplicate **playMoney**, and giving it a depth of 1. Notice in the example how a comma separates multiple parameter values used by the method. Also note that (similar to working with properties), the name of the object (**myBankAccount**) and the method invoked are separated by a dot. You can invoke the duplicateMovieClip() method in any number of ways. Take a look at one other example:

```
chocolateCake.duplicateMovieClip("goodStuff", 15);
```

In this example, we've duplicated the movie clip instance named **chocolateCake**, given the duplicate an instance name of **goodStuff**, and a depth of 15. One method, many uses.

Not all methods take parameter values. For example, the stop() action/method doesn't, because its sole purpose is to stop a timeline.

Each type of object has its own unique set of methods—which makes sense given that each object type has a specific purpose and use in your project (**Figure 14.2**).

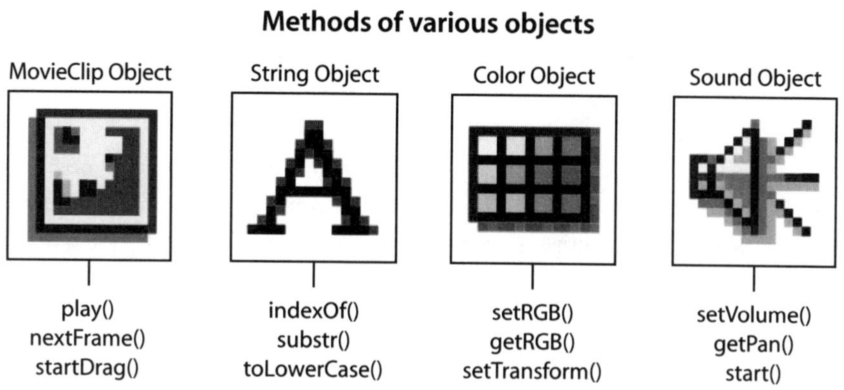

Methods of various objects

MovieClip Object	String Object	Color Object	Sound Object
play() nextFrame() startDrag()	indexOf() substr() toLowerCase()	setRGB() getRGB() setTransform()	setVolume() getPan() start()

Figure 14.2
Each type of object used in ActionScript has its own unique set of methods.

How Methods Function

If methods seem familiar, it's because they're based on functions (see Chapter 13). In fact, methods are really nothing more than functions that only have meaning in the context of the object type they're associated with. For example, the setVolume() *method only has meaning within the context of a Sound object. This bond between function and object is what makes methods different. Note also that while functions are called, methods are invoked, which is really just geek-speak for the same thing.*

Flash hides the code that defines methods for built-in ActionScript objects; however, if you were able to view their structure, you'd see that method definitions resemble function definitions. And once you understand how functions work, you can create your own methods or customize existing ones. Although these techniques are beyond the scope of this book, you can learn more about them in Macromedia Flash MX ActionScripting: Advanced Training from the Source, *published by Macromedia Press.*

Types of Objects

Not all objects are created equal. Some have a global bearing on your project (that is, on your project as a whole), while others let you create *instances* of them, which you can work with and control individually. In this section, we'll look at both types of objects, exploring their differences and explaining how you can work with each.

Global objects

Within the context of a Flash movie, some objects are global, or unique to the movie as a whole. The mouse, for example, is defined as a global object (Mouse object) because a Flash movie can only contain one mouse (cursor). You can't have more than one mouse, as you can movie clips, text fields, and sounds. Global objects are predefined within Flash, and as such are ready for use at any time. In contrast, objects such as movie clips, text fields, and sounds don't exist in your projects until you create *instances* of them (see "Objects with Instances" a little later in this chapter).

Flash contains the following global objects:

- Math
- Accessibility
- Key
- Mouse
- Selection
- Stage
- System

You address these objects *directly* within ActionScripts, as shown below:

```
Math.round();
Mouse.hide();
Key.isDown();
```

Note the lack of instance names. Because all global objects are unique—that is, only one of each exists in a given Flash movie—instance names have no meaning in the context of global objects.

Object classes

A class of objects represents a group of object instances within your project that share the same basic structure and functionality. For example, all movie clip instances belong to the MovieClip class of objects; all text field instances belong to the TextField class of objects; and so on (**Figure 14.3**). When an instance of an object is part of a class, it shares the same properties and methods as all other instances of that class.

For example, all movie clip instances have _rotation and _visible properties, as well as play() and stop() methods, which enable you to control them in various ways. These properties and methods are different than those that exist for instances of the TextField class of objects.

ActionScript contains dozens of object classes, including (but not limited to) the following:

- Arrays
- Numbers
- Strings
- Dates
- Sounds
- MovieClips
- TextFields
- XML

Classes of objects

MovieClip Object · String Object · Color Object · Sound Object

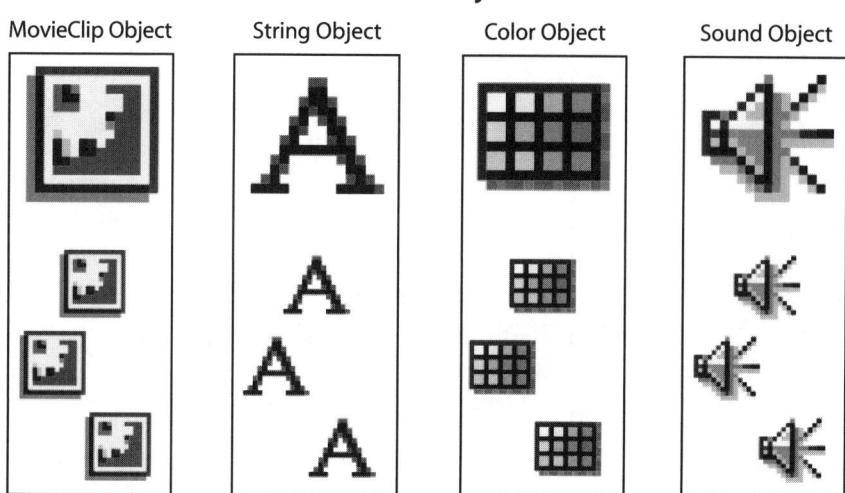

Figure 14.3
An object class represents a group of object instances within your project that share the same basic structure and functionality.

With the exception of MovieClip, Button, and TextField instances (which we'll discuss in a moment), all object-class instances are created via what's known as a *constructor*—a simple piece of ActionScript code that creates an instance of the object class you specify. For an example of this, take a look at the following:

```
mySound = new Sound();
```

The above line of code creates an instance of the Sound object class named mySound. To give you an idea of the common constructor syntax used to create all such object-class instances, let's take a look at another example:

```
//create an instance of the Color object
myColor = new Color();
//create an instance of the Date object
myDate = new Date();
//create an instance of the XML object
myXML = new XML();
```

Once an object instance has been created, you can target it for actions in scripts, attach event handler methods to it, or script other interactions with it. Take a look at the following example:

```
mySound = new Sound()
mySound.loadSound("heyJude.mp3", true);
mySound.onSoundComplete = function(){
   myMovieClip._visible = true;
}
```

The first line of the above script creates an instance of the Sound object named mySound. The next line dynamically loads an external MP3 file into this object. The last three lines attach an event handler method to it, so that it will call the unnamed function shown when the sound loaded into it completes its playback. The instance must be created first, in order for either of the other functionalities to work. It's important to maintain this flow as you work with object instances.

You can use one script to create an object instance (such as on a frame) and another (such as on a button) to script its functionality—as long as the instance is created first.

As mentioned above, MovieClip, Button, and TextField object instances are created differently than other object-class instances—that is, without a constructor. This is because these are the only object instances that you create and place directly on the stage. Thus, when you create a text field on the stage, you're actually creating (by default) an instance of the TextField object. Likewise when you place a movie clip on the stage—you're actually creating an instance of the MovieClip object. When creating these instances, you assign them instance names, which allow you to work with and communicate with them via ActionScript.

NOTE *Object instances are often simply referred to as* **objects.**

Objects are organized in the Toolbox List window in the following groups (**Figure 14.4**):

- **Core**. These objects deal with internal data storage and manipulation.
- **Movie**. These objects deal with visual content and system-related information such as movie clips, text fields, the stage, and accessibility.
- **Client/Server**. These objects are used for moving data in and out of Flash.
- **Authoring**. These objects allow you to create custom actions and components.

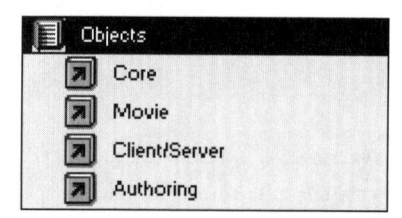

Figure 14.4
Objects are organized into four groups in the Toolbox List window of the Actions panel: Core, Movie, Client/Server, and Authoring.

Object Sampler

In the following pages, we'll look at many of the objects found in ActionScript, and provide examples of their use. Some objects (such as MovieClip, TextField, and Sound objects) are given more extensive coverage because they're likely to be the ones you'll use most often in your projects. Advanced objects, such as the XMLSocket object (which requires that you set up an XML socket server), are beyond the scope of this book (and thus are not discussed). Global objects are indicated as such in the subheads below. For all objects that don't include this indication, you must create instances.

NOTE *For additional information about any of the ActionScript objects discussed here, refer to the ActionScript Dictionary in Flash (Help > ActionScript Dictionary). Or pick up a copy of* **Macromedia Flash MX ActionScripting: Advanced Training from the Source***, published by Macromedia Press.*

Accessibility Object (Global)

MX ALERT This simple object has a single method, (isActive()), which returns a value of true (if a screen reader is active on the user's computer) or false (if no screen reader is active). Take a look at the following script:

```
if(Accessibility.isActive()){
   gotoAndStop("Accessible Version");
}else{
   gotoAndStop("Standard Version");
}
```

You can place this if statement on Frame 1 of your movie, so that as soon as the movie begins playing, the statement will check to see whether the user's system has an active screen reader. If an active screen reader is detected, the user will be taken to a scene that has been set up so that its content is accessible. If no active screen reader is detected, the script will take the user to a scene that contains a standard version of your site.

Array Object

You can think of an Array object as a supervariable: Whereas a regular variable can only contain a single value, an Array object can contain multiple values. You create an instance of the Array object in the following manner:

```
directions = new Array ("North", "East", "South", "West");
```

The above script creates an array named directions, which contains four values. Each value in an array is identified by an index number (0, 1, 2, and so on) that denotes its position in the array. In the array we just created, "North" has an index number of 0, "East" an index number of 1, and so on. To access a value that exists in an array, you would use the following syntax:

```
myVariable = directions[2];
```

In this script, myVariable is assigned a value of "South" because this is the value that exists at index position 2 in our directions array. There are numerous methods available to the Array object that let you manipulate the data within the array. For example, the directions array we created currently contains data in the following order:

```
directions[0] = "North";
directions[1] = "East";
directions[2] = "South";
directions[3] = "West";
```

Using the `reverse()` method as follows:

```
directions.reverse();
```

We can reverse the order of values to the following:

```
directions[0] = "West";
directions[1] = "South";
directions[2] = "East";
directions[3] = "North";
```

Or using the `sort()` method as follows:

```
directions.sort();
```

We can change the order of values so they exist alphabetically, as in the following:

```
directions[0] = "East";
directions[1] = "North";
directions[2] = "South";
directions[3] = "West";
```

Arrays help you logically store data in groups, making it easier to work with. For example, you could use an array to store user information, by creating four input text fields on the stage with the instance names of **name**, **age**, **phoneNumber**, and **email**, respectively, and then entering the following values:

name: Derek

age: 20;

phoneNumber: 555-1234

email: derek@derekfranklin.com

You could then create a user array, perhaps when the user presses and releases a button, as in the following:

```
on(release){
user = new Array(name.text, age.text, phoneNumber.text, email.text);
}
```

Then, whenever you needed to access a particular piece of data about your user, you could easily do so by using the array's name, followed by the index number of the particular piece of data you wished to use. Take a look at the following:

```
myMessage.text = "Hello " + user[0] + ". You seem to be " + user[1] + " years old.";
```

Assuming that **myMessage** is a dynamic text field, the preceding script will display "Hello Derek. You seem to be 20 years old" in that field.

Boolean Object

An instance of the Boolean object holds a value of `true` or `false`. You can create instances of the Boolean object in one of two ways:

```
answer = new Boolean(true);
```

Or

```
answer = true;
```

The latter is the more common method since it requires fewer keystrokes. Boolean values are frequently used in conditional statements (see Chapter 13, "Understanding ActionScript").

Button Object

MX ALERT Instances of Button objects are created when you place buttons on the stage. By assigning an instance name to a button, you can control it dynamically via ActionScript. For example, if you have a button instance named **myButton** on the stage, you can disable it at any time (so that users can no longer interact with it) by setting its `enabled` property to `false`, as in the following:

```
myButton.enabled = false;
```

To enable that button again, you would use the following syntax:

```
myButton.enabled = true;
```

You can also set several other Button object properties—determining, for example, whether it should be Tab enabled (that is, selectable by pressing the Tab key) or whether the hand cursor should appear when the user interacts with the instance (**Figure 14.5**).

In addition to the properties and methods shown for Button objects in the Toolbox List window, they also have several properties and methods that are similar to those of the MovieClip object, as shown in Table 14.1.

myButton.useHandCursor = true

myButton.useHandCursor = false

Figure 14.5
By setting the useHandCursor property for button instances to a value of true or false, you can control how the cursor appears when the user interacts with the button instance.

Table 14.1
Properties and Methods Common to Movie Clips and Buttons

Properties
_alpha
_height
_name
_rotation
_width
_x
_xmouse
_xscale
_y
_ymouse
_yscale

Methods
startDrag()
stopDrag()
swapDepths()

NOTE *For more information about Button object properties, see "MovieClip Object" later in this chapter.*

Capabilities Object (Global)

MX ALERT The Capabilities object includes properties that provide information about the user's computer, including its current screen resolution, whether it can play sounds, its ability to play video, and more. In the following example, usersScreen would have a value of 1280 (my current horizontal screen resolution) if I viewed the movie:

```
usersScreen = System.capabilities.screenResolution.x;
```

The information this object provides allows your movie to react accordingly. For example, if your site has a button (named **videoButton**) that plays a video, you can determine whether the user's computer is able to play video, and if it can't, disable the button, as in the following:

```
if(System.capabilities.hasVideoEncoder == false){
   videoButton.enabled = false;
}
```

All of this object's properties are read only.

NOTE *For additional properties for this object, see Flash's ActionScript Dictionary.*

Color Object

To manipulate a movie's color, you must create a Color object, then associate that Color object with a movie. Once you've done this, the color of the associated movie can be manipulated using the methods available to the Color object class. Take a look at the following script, which is executed when the button it's attached to is pressed and released:

```
on(release){
    //create a new Color object when this button is released.
    myColor = new Color(_root.myMovieClip);
    myColor.setRGB(0x33F366);
}
```

Now let's examine what's happening in each line of script:

```
myColor = new Color(_root.myMovieClip);
```

The line above creates an instance of the Color object—in essence, telling Flash to create a new color object named myColor, and associate it with the movie clip instance with the target path of _root.myMovieClip (**Figure 14.6**).

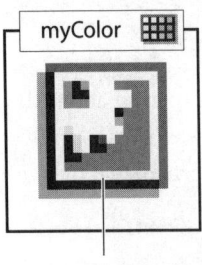

Figure 14.6
When an instance of the Color object is created, you associate it with a particular timeline, which allows you to manipulate the color of that timeline using methods of the Color object class.

Once this object has been created and associated with a movie, we can manipulate that movie's color by addressing the name of the Color object (not the name of the movie clip instance), followed by a Color object method, which is what the next line of our script does:

```
myColor.setRGB (0x33F366);
```

The above line of the script says, "Set the RGB value of `myColor` to a hex value of 33F366." This will make all graphical content within `_root.myMovieClip` turn green. For example, if the movie clip instance contains a graphic of the letter *A*, that *A* will turn green.

Manipulating a movie's color via a Color object is similar to selecting an instance of a movie clip in the authoring environment, and applying a tinting effect to it from the Property inspector. The difference is that the Color object lets you do it dynamically—that is, while the movie is playing.

A movie can contain as many Color object instances as you wish, each associated with a different movie.

Date Object

Date objects allow you to work with data that pertains to time, including years, months, days, hours, minutes, seconds, and even milliseconds. This feature lets you display the current time, as well as build clocks, counters, calendars, and more. Before you can use date data in your project, however, you must create an instance of the Date object. The following script creates a Date object, then uses that object to display a custom message (with an instance name of **myMessage**) in the dynamic text field:

```
on(release){
  //create a new Date object when this button is released.
  myDateObject = new Date();
  myMessage.text = "Can you believe it's already the year " + myDateObject.getFullYear() + "?";
}
```

Now let's take a closer look at each line of this script.

```
myDateObject = new Date();
```

The line above creates a new Date object instance named `myDateObject`. You'll notice that we didn't enter any parameters within the parentheses; this means that our Date object instance will be based on the current date and time (as defined by the computer on which Flash Player is running). We'll look more at this shortly.

```
myMessage.text = "Can you believe it's already the year" + myDateObject.getFullYear() + "?";
```

The above line determines the message that will be displayed in our dynamic text field. Using the `getFullYear()` method (which returns the four-digit year of the associated

Date object instance), this will display the message "Can you believe it's already the year 2002?"

A Date object instance doesn't have to contain the current date and time. The following creates a Date object based on February 21, 1993:

```
myWeddingDay = new Date(1993, 1, 21);
```

The three parameters in the parentheses represent the year, month, and day of the Date object instance you're creating. You'll notice that the number *1* identifies February; this is because ActionScript recognizes the first month of the year (January) as 0, and then counts upward from there (thus, February is 1, and so on).

Creating Date object instances that relate to specific dates allows you to display information about those particular dates. For example, if you wanted to let your user enter his or her birthday, so that you could display a custom message indicating what day of the week he or she was born, you could create three input text fields on the stage with instance names of **year**, **month**, and **day**, respectively. If the following values were entered:

year: 1966;

month: 7;

day: 27;

The following script would be used to display the message:

```
on(release){
  convertMonth = month.text - 1;
  userBirthDate = new Date(year.text, convertMonth, day.text);
  if(userBirthDate.getDay() == 0){
    dayOfWeek = "Sunday";
  }else if(userBirthDate.getDay() == 1){
    dayOfWeek = "Monday";
  }else if(userBirthDate.getDay() == 2){
    dayOfWeek = "Tuesday";
  }else if(userBirthDate.getDay() == 3){
    dayOfWeek = "Wednesday";
  }else if(userBirthDate.getDay() == 4){
    dayOfWeek = "Thursday";
  }else if(userBirthDate.getDay() == 5){
    dayOfWeek = "Friday";
  }else if(userBirthDate.getDay() == 6){
```

```
        dayOfWeek = "Saturday";
    }
    myMessage.text = "You were born on a " + dayOfWeek + ".";
}
```

Let's examine this script:

```
convertMonth = month.text - 1;
```

If our user was born in July and entered 7 as the month in which she was born, we would need to convert that 7 to a 6 to represent July correctly in a Date object. That's what the above line accomplishes.

```
userBirthDate = new Date(year.text, convertMonth, day.text);
```

This line creates a new Date object instance and names it `userBirthDate`. The current values entered into the **year** and **day** text fields, and the value of the `convertMonth` variable, are used to define it. Thus, `userBirthDate` is an object based on the date July 27, 1966.

```
if (userBirthDate.getDay() == 0) {
    dayOfWeek = "Sunday";
```

In this statement, the `getDay()` method is used to determine a numerical value (between 0 and 6) that denotes the day of the week for the specified Date object instance. Sunday is represented by 0, Monday by 1, Tuesday by 2, and so on. Thus, the `if` statement states, "If July 27, 1966, occurred on a Sunday (or 0), then the `dayOfWeek` variable is assigned a value of 'Sunday.'" The remaining `else if` statements in this script are used in a similar fashion to the `if` statement. In the end, `dayOfWeek` will have a string value representing the name of a particular day in the week.

```
myMessage.text = "You were born on a " + dayOfWeek + ".";
```

The last line displays a custom message in the dynamic text field named **myMessage**, based on the value of `dayOfWeek`. In our example, since July 27, 1966, occurred on a Wednesday, **myMessage** displays "You were born on a Wednesday."

Key Object (Global)

The Key object allows your movie to capture and react to the user's interaction with his or her keyboard—functionality that makes it possible for the user to perform certain tasks within the movie (such as navigating to different scenes), in response to specific key presses or even combinations of key presses (similar to keyboard shortcuts).

Scripts that involve the Key object are usually (though not always) executed as the result of onClipEvent(keyDown) or onClipEvent(keyUp) events. For example, if you want your project to navigate to the next frame in response to the spacebar being pressed, you would place the following script on a movie clip instance in the scene:

```
onClipEvent(keyDown){
  if(Key.isDown(Key.SPACE)){
    _root.nextFrame();
  }
}
```

Notice that the isDown() method is looking for the spacebar being pressed by using the syntax Key.SPACE. You can use similar syntax—for example, Key.TAB, Key.SHIFT, Key.PGUP, and so on—to determine whether other "editing" keys, (Backspace, Tab, Shift, Page Up, Page Down, and so on) have been pressed. Although a limited number of keys are identified in this manner (located in the Object > Movie > Key > Constants book in the Toolbox List window), the Key object lets you get around this limitation by using ASCII key codes to identify specific keys.

For example, the spacebar has an ASCII equivalent value of 32; thus, our previous script could be rewritten as follows:

```
onClipEvent(keyDown){
  if(Key.isDown(32)){
    _root.nextFrame();
  }
}
```

Every key on the keyboard has an ASCII equivalent, which gives you far greater flexibility in designating particular keys than the syntax approach shown in the first example.

NOTE *A complete list of ASCII key codes can be found in the Flash manual, which you can access from the authoring environment by pressing F1.*

LoadVars Object

MX ALERT The LoadVars object is used to work with variables loaded from an external source, such as a text file or Web server. For example, let's say you've created a text file containing the following text/variables:

```
&name=Dennis&age=28&maritalStatus=Single
```

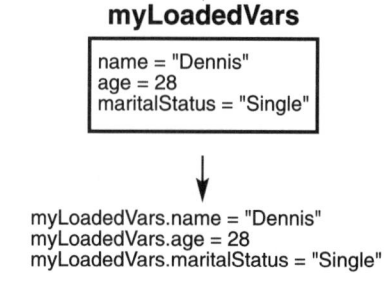

You can see that this text file contains three variables named `name`, `age`, and `maritalStatus`. Next we'll assume that this file is saved as dennisText.txt. To load this data into the main timeline of a Flash movie when it begins playing, you would use the following syntax:

```
myLoadedVars = new LoadVars();
myLoadedVars.load("dennisText.txt");
```

The first line creates an instance of the LoadVars object named `myLoadedVars`. The second line uses the `load()` method to load the variables in the dennisText.txt file into the object instance. When loaded, variable values can be accessed by addressing the name of the LoadVars object instance, followed by the name of the particular variable you wish to access (**Figure 14.7**). For example, the following script:

```
message.text = "Hello " + myLoadedVars.name;
```

Will display "Hello Dennis" in a text field named **message**.

Figure 14.7 Once external variables have been loaded into a LoadVars object, their values can be accessed by addressing the name of the LoadVars object instance they were loaded into, followed by the name of the particular variable value you wish to use.

To access data output from a CGI script or Web server, point to the URL containing the dynamic page when using the `load()` method, for instance:

```
myLoadedVars.load("http://www.myDomain.com/data.asp");
```

Math Object (Global)

The Math object is the means by which you manipulate numbers with ActionScript. Let's look at some examples.

The round() method will round a number to the nearest integer. Thus, in the following example myVariable is assigned a value of 34.

```
myMathVariable = 34.365;
myVariable = Math.round(myMathVariable);
```

The ceil() method will round a number *up* to the nearest integer. Thus, in the following example myVariable is assigned a value of 35.

```
myVariable = Math.ceil(34.365);
```

The floor() method will round a number *down* to the nearest integer. Thus, in the following example myVariable is assigned a value of 34.

```
myVariable = Math.floor(34.945);
```

The max() method determines which of two values is higher and returns that value. Thus, in the following example myVariable is assigned a value of 45.

```
mathVariable1 = 45;
mathVariable2 = 19;
myVariable = Math.max(mathVariable1, mathVariable2);
```

The min() method determines which of two values is smaller and returns that value. Thus, in the following example myVariable is assigned a value of 19.

```
mathVariable1 = 45;
mathVariable2 = 19;
myVariable = Math.min(mathVariable1, mathVariable2);
```

The Math object has additional methods, for performing trigonometry functions and more.

Mouse Object (Global)

The Mouse object's main purpose in ActionScript is to provide methods for making the mouse cursor invisible or visible. Take a look at the following script:

```
on(press){
  Mouse.hide();
  startDrag(_root.customCursor, true);
}
```

Let's now examine each line:

```
on(press) {
```

The above line shows that the script is attached to a button, and will be executed when the button is pressed.

```
Mouse.hide();
```

This line hides the mouse cursor.

```
startDrag(_root.customCursor, true);
```

This last line essentially states, "Start dragging the movie clip instance named **customCursor** on the main timeline," and, "Yes (true), I want to lock the center of the movie clip instance to the position of the cursor." This gives your project a custom cursor when the button is pressed.

When you hide the mouse cursor from view, it is still active, just not visible onscreen.

MovieClip Object

The MovieClip object is the most important type of object in a Flash movie: Not only do movie clip instances serve as the foundation for most Flash projects, you're also able to control them in more ways than any other type of object. Since movie clip instances play such a vital role, it's important to have a thorough understanding of their properties and methods, and how you can use them to create interactivity.

We'll be looking at all movie clip instance properties in this section, but will save a thorough discussion of methods for Chapter 16, "Using ActionScript in Your Projects"(see "Methods" a bit later in the chapter for more information).

Properties

Each movie/timeline has its own group of properties that can be changed dynamically while the movie is playing, and whose current values can be evaluated and used in conditional or looping statements, as well as in other areas of your scripts. As you'll see from the sample scripts, you simply use a movie's target path to access any of its properties. In this section we'll describe the various movie properties, and show you how you can manipulate them to create interactive movies. As we go along, we'll indicate (in parentheses) whether a property's value is settable and/or readable.

NOTES *As you've already learned, Flash movies can contain other movies, creating a parent/child relationship. When you change a parent timeline's properties, its children inherit those same properties. For example, if you made a parent movie transparent, the child movies it contains would become transparent as well. Keep in mind, however, that the reverse is not true: Changing the properties of a child does not affect its parent movie (**Figure 14.8**).*

Many movie properties (except those pertaining to a timeline, such as _currentframe, _framesloaded, and _totalframes) function in the context of button instances as well. To use any of the following scripts in the context of a button instance (except those pertaining to the properties just mentioned), replace the movie clip instance's name with a button instance's name.

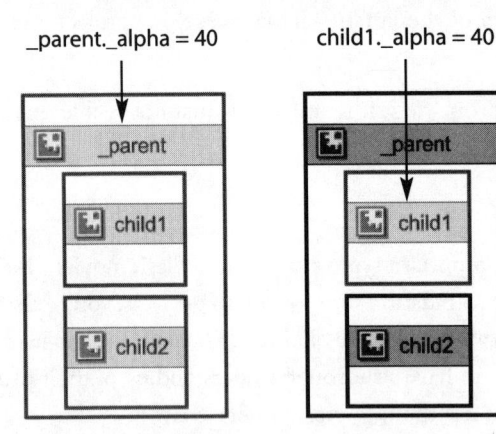

_parent._alpha = 40   child1._alpha = 40

Figure 14.8
Setting a parent timeline's properties affects all of its child timelines (left); however, the opposite is not true (right).

_alpha (can be set and read)

The _alpha property represents a movie or movie clip's transparency (expressed as a percentage).

The following script evaluates the transparency of the movie clip instance **dress**. If the clip is more than 50 percent transparent, the variable wearSlip is set to true before going to "DanceParty." Otherwise, you go straight to "DanceParty."

```
if(_root.dress._alpha > 50){
  wearSlip = true;
  gotoAndPlay("DanceParty");
}else{
  gotoAndPlay("DanceParty");
}
```

_currentframe (read-only)

The _currentframe property provides the current frame-number position of a timeline for a movie or movie clip.

In this script, when the on(release) mouse event occurs, the following script will send the main movie's timeline forward 20 frames from its current position:

```
on(release){
  _root.gotoAndStop (_root._currentframe + 20);
}
```

_droptarget (read-only)

The _droptarget property represents the target path that a dragged movie is currently on top of when dragging stops (**Figure 14.9**); this allows you to emulate drag-and-drop behavior.

The following script lets you emulate drag-and-drop behavior. When the clip event mouseDown occurs, **myMovieClip** on the root timeline is dragged, with its position centered underneath the moving mouse. When the mouseUp event occurs, dragging halts and an expression is used to evaluate the movie clip's position. The movie clip directly beneath the one being dragged is always considered the droptarget. In this script, when the drag operation stops, the droptarget is identified. If it equals _root.myTarget, then **myMovieClip** becomes invisible; otherwise, nothing happens.

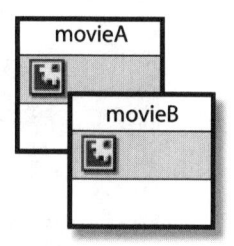

Figure 14.9
In this illustration, the droptarget for movieB is movieA.

```
onClipEvent(mouseDown){
  startDrag(_root.myMovieClip, true);
}
onClipEvent(mouseUp){
  stopDrag();
  if(eval(_root.myMovieClip._dropTarget) == _root.myTarget) {
    _root.myMovieClip._visible = false;
  }
}
```

TIP *The hitTest() method (described a little later in the chapter) offers similar functionality, but is easier to use and more flexible than the droptarget property.*

_focusrect (can be set and read)

The _focusrect property value determines whether a yellow box appears around a movie clip instance, when it has been tabbed to using the Tab key (**Figure 14.10**). The following script turns on this functionality for the movie clip instance named **myMovieClip**:

```
myMovieClip._focusrect == true;
```

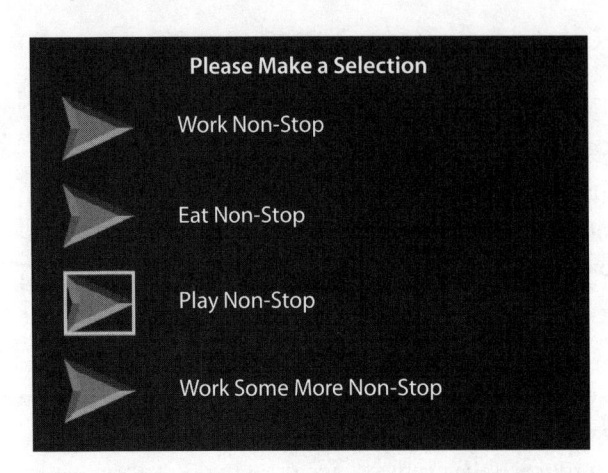

Figure 14.10
The focus rectangle outlines elements when the Tab key has been used to navigate between them.

NOTE By default, this property is set to false for all movie clip instances.

_framesloaded (read-only)

The _framesloaded property represents the number of frames of a movie that have loaded. This property can be evaluated in order to prevent a timeline's playback from moving forward until a specific number of frames has been downloaded. For example, assume the following script is placed on Frame 2 of the main timeline: If more than 200 frames have been loaded when this script is executed, the timeline would jump to and begin playing Scene 2, Frame 1. Otherwise, the timeline would go to and begin playing from Frame 1 of the current scene. This causes a loop that is not broken until more than 200 frames have been loaded.

```
if(_framesloaded > 200){
   gotoAndPlay("Scene 2", 1);
}else{
   gotoAndPlay(1);
}
```

TIP This is the logic typically employed when creating preloading animations, which appear as the movie loads.

_height (can be set and read)

The _height property provides and sets the current height of a movie; its value is based in pixels. For an example of this type of script, see the sample script for the _width property.

_name (can be set and read)

The _name property denotes the name of a movie clip instance in the form of a string value such as "myMovieClip"—similar to the _target property (see later in this chapter) but without the full path.

This property can be useful for centralizing your code. For example, assume there are three movie clip buttons on the stage with instance names of **home**, **products**, and **services**, and that there are three frame labels on the timeline with similar names. Each of the movie clip buttons has an attached script, which looks like the following:

```
on(release){
   _root.buttonFunction(_name);
}
```

Here you can see that when the button is pressed and released, it will call a function named buttonFunction() on the main timeline ,and will send that function a single parameter representing its instance name.

NOTE *We're using movie clip buttons as opposed to normal buttons here, because while button instances can be given names, the _name property in relation to regular button instances represents the name of the timeline the button instance is part of, not the instance itself. For movie clips, the _name property represents the movie clip instance's name, even if it is being used as a button, as shown in this example.*

The buttonFunction() function definition can then use that value to determine how it should work:

```
function buttonFunction(instanceName){
   gotoAndPlay(instanceName);
   message.text = "You have navigated to the" + instanceName + " section.";
++navButtonsClicked;
}
```

Here you can see that the function uses the name of the instance that is passed to it to navigate the timeline, display a message, and track the number of times a navigation button has been clicked. All buttons call this single function, but the function can react differently depending on the name of the instance that calls it, enabling you to centralize the functionality of a group of buttons.

_quality (can be set and read)

The _quality property—which can have a string value of "LOW", "MEDIUM", "HIGH", or "BEST"—specifies the playback quality of your movie. As a global property, it pertains to all movies currently playing in the Flash Player window. The following script sets the value of the movie's quality to "MEDIUM":

```
_quality = "MEDIUM";
```

_rotation (can be set and read)

The _rotation property represents a movie's rotation, in degrees, relative to the movie's parent (**Figure 14.11**).

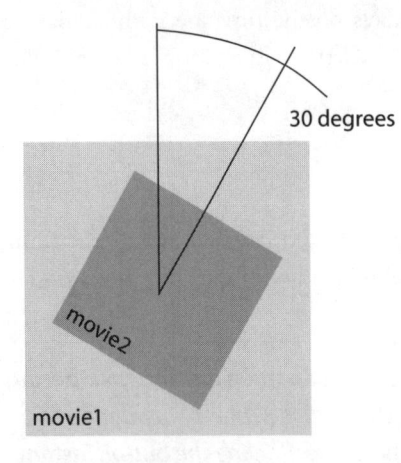

Figure 14.11
In this graphic, movie2 is rotated 30 degrees relative to its parent (movie1); thus, the value of its rotation property is 30. If movie1 were rotated by 60 degrees, movie2 would rotate that much as well (for a total of a 90-degree rotation); however, its rotation value would still be 30 because this value is based on its rotation relative to its parent, not its absolute rotation setting.

The following script is triggered by the release mouse event. When triggered, a random numeric value between 0 and 359 is generated and assigned to the variable spin. This value is used to set the rotation value for the movie clip named **myMovieClip**. In addition, using a conditional statement the value of spin is evaluated: If that value is between 0 and 45 degrees, "You spun a 1, you win!" is displayed in a dynamic text field named **message**. Otherwise, "Try again" is displayed.

```
on(release) {
    spin = random(360);
    _root.myMovieClip._rotation = spin;
    if(spin >= 0 && spin < 45){
        message.text = "You spun a 1, you win!";
    }else{
        message.text = "Try again.";
    }
}
```

_soundbuftime (can be set and read)

The _soundbuftime property is a numeric value that denotes the number of seconds of streaming sound that need to be downloaded by the user, before your movie can begin to play. The default setting is 5 (for 5 seconds). Because this is a global property, it pertains to all movies currently playing in the Flash Player window. This would normally be set on the first frame of your movie. The following script sets this property so that streamed audio will not begin playing until the user has downloaded 15 seconds of it.

```
_soundbuftime = 15;
```

_target (read-only)

The _target property provides the target name and full path (in slash syntax) of a movie clip instance in the form of a string value such as "/myMovieClip".

The following script gets the target path and name of the current movie clip when the release event occurs. The script then outputs it to a dynamic text field on the main timeline named **currentMovie**:

```
on(release){
   _root.currentMovie.text = this._target;
}
```

_totalframes (read-only)

The _totalframes property represents the number of frames in a movie or movie clip.

In the following script, when the release mouse event occurs, the following script will create the variable timeToPlay. This variable's value is based on the number of frames in the main movie, divided by the frame-per-second rate. Math.round() is used to remove any decimal places in the calculation. Next, the dynamic text element on the main timeline named **message** will display a message based on the value of timeToPlay:

```
on(release){
   timeToPlay = Math.round(_root._totalframes / 12);
   _root.message.text = "This movie will take " + timeToPlay + " seconds to play.";
}
```

If the movie has 240 frames, a text field will display the following:

"This movie will take 20 seconds to play."

_url (read-only)

This property represents the complete URL for a SWF that's been loaded into a Flash project. For example, if a SWF were loaded into the Flash Player window from the URL http://www.mydomain.com/secondmovie.swf, checking this property of the movie would return a string value of `"http://www.mydomain.com/secondmovie.swf"`.

You can use this property to ensure that others don't "borrow" your work. Here's how: If you place on Frame 1 of a movie a script that checks its URL property and instructs it to take one action if it was loaded from the "correct" URL, and another if it was loaded from the "wrong" URL, you can prevent others from stealing a SWF file from their cache and using it as their own.

The following script—which is placed on Frame 1 of your movie—evaluates the URL property of the main movie. The movie will continue playing if the script detects the correct URL; however, if the script detects an incorrect URL, the movie will cease playing, and jump to (and stop at) the frame labeled Denied.

```
if(_root._url == "http://www.properdomain.com"){
  play();
}else{
  gotoAndStop("Denied");
}
```

_visible (can be set and read)

The _visible property—which denotes a movie's visibility—represents a Boolean value of true or false: true if visible and false if not.

The following script checks the visibility of the movie clip **teacher**. If it's not visible, the movie clip **kids** is sent to a frame labeled Recess; if it is visible, **kids** is sent to Desk:

```
if(_root.teacher._visible == false){
  _root.kids.gotoAndPlay("Recess");
} else {
  _root.kids.gotoAndStop("Desk");
}
```

_width (can be set and read)

The _width property represents the current width of a movie; its value is defined in pixels. The following script evaluates the width of the current movie, and reacts accordingly:

```
on(release){
  nextMeal = 50;
  if(_width + nextMeal >= 400){
    message.text = "I'm too fat.";
  }else if(_width + nextMeal <= 100){
    message.text = "I'm too skinny.";
  }else{
    message.text = "I'm just right.";
  }
}
```

When executed, this script creates a variable named nextMeal, and gives it a value of 50. Using an if statement, the width of the current movie is determined, and the value of nextMeal is added to it. The combined total is then evaluated to determine whether it's greater than or equal to 400, less than or equal to 100, or somewhere in between. For our demonstration, the width of the movie was determined to be 230, which when combined with 50 equals 280. Thus, a dynamic text field named **message** will display the string "I'm just right."

_x (can be set and read)

The _x property of a movie represents the horizontal distance between its registration point and the registration point of its parent movie (**Figure 14.12**).

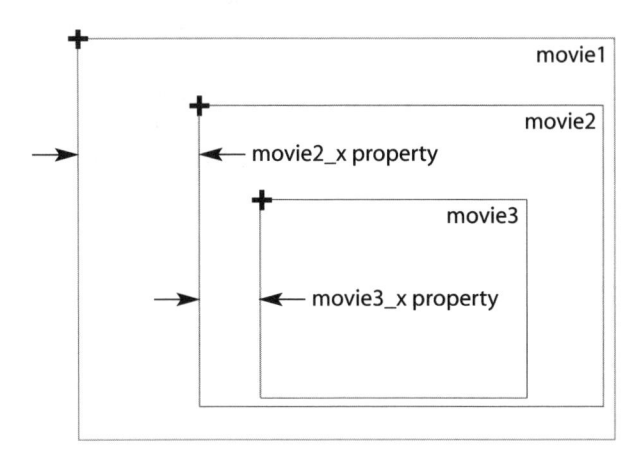

Figure 14.12
The _x property is a relative value based on the horizontal distance between its registration point (marked by a plus sign [+] here) in relation to the registration point of its parent.

The following script evaluates the horizontal position of the current movie, and reacts accordingly:

```
on(release){
  if(_x < 200){
    message.text = "I'm on the left.";
  }else if(_x > 200) {
    message.text = "I'm on the right.";
  }else{
    message.text = "I'm stuck in the middle somewhere.";
  }
}
```

For our demonstration, when this script is executed, the horizontal position of the current movie is evaluated to be exactly 200; thus, a dynamic text field named **message** will display the string "I'm stuck in the middle somewhere."

_xmouse (read-only)

The _xmouse property represents the current horizontal position of the mouse in relation to the registration point of a particular movie (**Figure 14.13**).

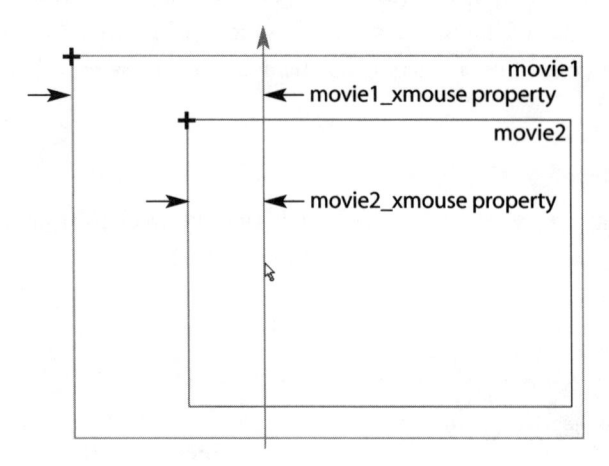

Figure 14.13
Each movie's _xmouse value is based on the horizontal distance from the mouse to that movie's registration point (indicated by a plus sign [+] in this graphic).

The following script evaluates the current horizontal position of the mouse, in relation to the registration point of the movie clip **myMovieClip**, each time the mouse is moved. That value is then displayed in a dynamic text field (named **message**) on the main timeline:

```
onClipEvent(mouseMove){
  _root.message.text = _root.myMovieClip._xmouse;
}
```

_xscale (can be set and read)

This property represents the percentage a movie or movie clip has been scaled horizontally from its original size, as the result of previous actions in which its _xscale property was changed. Thus, if a movie has been scaled to 50 percent of its original size, the value of its _xscale property is 50.

The following script evaluates, when the `release` mouse event occurs, the amount that **myMovieClip** has been scaled from its original size. If it's more than 100 percent, it will be reset to 100 percent; otherwise, its size is not changed:

```
on(release){
  if(_root.myMovieClip._xscale > 100){
    _root.myMovieClip._xscale = 100;
  }
}
```

_y (can be set and read)

The _y property of a movie represents the vertical distance between its registration point and the registration point of its parent movie.

See the _x property script for an example of how this property works.

_ymouse (read-only)

The _ymouse property represents the current vertical position of the mouse in relation to the registration point of a particular movie.

See the _xmouse property script for an example of how this property works.

_yscale (can be set and read)

This property represents the percentage a movie or movie clip has been scaled vertically from its original size, as the result of previous actions in which its _yscale property was changed (**Figure 14.14**).

For an example of this type of script, see the _xscale script sample above.

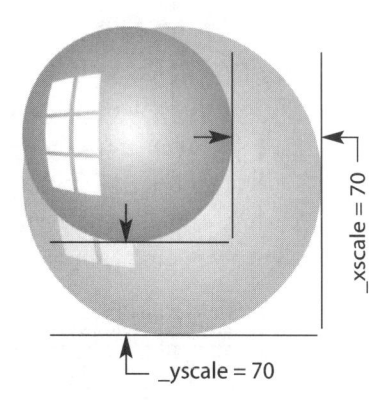

Figure 14.14
The _xscale and _yscale properties let you scale a movie's size based on percentage amounts.

NOTE *In addition to the properties discussed here, when movie clip instances are treated as buttons (see Chapter 7, "Symbols") they have several additional properties pertaining to button functionality. These allow you to enable/disable them, display the hand cursor when the mouse passes over them, and more. You can access these properties via the Toolbox List window at Objects > Movie > Movie Clip > Properties.*

Methods

MovieClip object methods allow you to perform all sorts of dynamic functions while your movie plays. These include duplicating movie clip instances, making them draggable, masking them, and more. Since methods are much more dynamic than properties, we'll cover them in the next chapter, "Using ActionScript in Your Projects," where we'll use them in a series of mini-projects.

Number Object

An instance of the Number object holds a numerical value (for example, *3* or *94234* or *54*). You can create instances of the Number object in one of two ways:

```
money = new Number(27);
```

Or

```
money = 27;
```

The latter is the more common way due to its simplicity.

Selection Object (Global)

MX ALERT The Selection object allows you to retrieve information or to set characteristics relating to selected items in your movies, most notably text fields that have focus. When the cursor is in an area of a text field, that field is said to be "in focus." You can use the Selection object to set the focus to a specific text field, to find out which text field is currently in focus, or even to programmatically select specific chunks of text in a field so that you can manipulate them in some way.

A text field must be given focus before any methods of the Selection object can be used with the field. The user can give a field focus by clicking within it, or you can manually set it using the following syntax:

```
Selection.setFocus(myTextField);
```

Here we've set the focus as the text field named **myTextField**. Using the `setFocus()` method can be helpful if you wish to place the cursor in a particular form field, when a user enters a scene containing a form. Once a field is in focus, we can highlight a portion of it using the setSelection() method.

The following script, for example, will highlight Characters 11 through 19 in the field that currently has focus (by highlighting, we mean that black text against a white background will appear as white text against a black background) (**Figure14.15**):

```
Selection.setSelection(11, 19);
```

Macromedia Flash MX!

Figure 14.15
When a text field has focus, you can use the setSelection() method to select a section of text within it (causing it to appear highlighted). Once it's selected, you can change or otherwise manipulate the text.

Sound Object

Sound objects let you manipulate aspects of sound, such as volume and panning, in your movies. In addition, the Sound object provides a means of dynamically attaching sounds that exist in the library, or loading external MP3s into you movie as it plays. As with the Color object, you create a Sound object instance, associate it with a movie, and then use Sound object methods to control the sound of that movie (**Figure 14.16**). Take a look at the following script:

```
on (release) {
  //create a new Sound object when this button is released.
  mySound = new Sound (_root.myMovieClip);
  mySound.setVolume (75);
  mySound.setPan (-50);
}
```

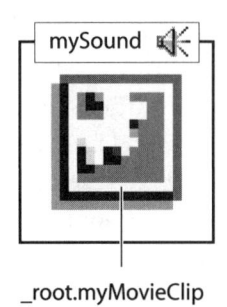

_root.myMovieClip

Figure 14.16
As with the Color object, when you create a Sound object instance, it's associated with a particular movie, whose sound you can control using the methods available to the Sound object.

Let's take a closer look at each line of the script.

```
mySound = new Sound (_root.myMovieClip);
```

The line above creates a new Sound object instance (named mySound), and attaches it to a movie clip instance named **myMovieClip**.

NOTE *If you don't define a specific movie when creating a Sound object, it will affect all existing sounds on all timelines in the Flash Player window.*

```
mySound.setVolume(75);
```

This line lowers the overall volume of any sounds on **myMovieClip**'s timeline to 75 percent of their originally set volume. This means that if there are several sounds playing at different volumes on the timeline, the volume of each will decrease by 25 percent, but their relative volumes will remain the same.

```
mySound.setPan(-100);
```

The line above sets the pan (speaker balance) of the sounds on **myMovieClip**'s timeline. A value of -100 means that the sound will only play in the left speaker; a value of 100 means that it will only play in the right speaker. A value of 0 means the sound will output equally from both speakers.

MX ALERT To load an external MP3 file into an instance of the Sound object, you employ the loadSound() method. The parameters for this method allow you to specify the location of the external file, and whether or not it should be treated as an event or streamed sound (see Chapter 5, "Sound," for more information). Take a look at the following example:

```
myLoadedSound = new Sound();
myLoadedSound.loadSound("myMP3File.mp3", true);
```

The first line of this script creates a Sound object instance named myLoadedSound. The second line uses the loadSound() method to load the external MP3 file named myMP3File.mp3 into the myLoadedSound Sound object instance. The second parameter, true, will cause the loaded sound to be treated as a streamed sound, meaning it will begin playing as soon as enough data has been downloaded.

If this setting were changed to false, the loaded sound would be treated as an event sound, meaning the entire file would be downloaded before the start() method could be employed, to initiate playback of the loaded sound. Invoking the start() method before the sound has completely loaded will have no effect. To automatically initiate a loaded (event) sound's playback as soon as it has finished loading, we can incorporate an onLoad event handler in the following manner:

Chapter 14 **ActionScript Objects**

```
myLoadedSound = new Sound();
myLoadedSound.loadSound("myMP3File.mp3", false);
myLoadedSound.onLoad = function(){
  myLoadedSound.start();
}
```

Here you can see that we've implemented an event handler method (in the last three lines of script), so that when the external file has finished loading into the `myLoaded-Sound` Sound object instance, it triggers an unnamed function whose sole function is to initiate the playback of `myLoadedSound`.

NOTE *For detailed information on event handler methods, see Chapter 13, "Understanding ActionScript."*

String Objects (Instances)

An instance of the String object—which holds a string value such as "Hello" or "What did you eat for lunch today"—can be created in one of two ways:

```
favoriteFood = new String("Pizza");
```

Or

```
favoriteFood = "Pizza";
```

The latter is the more commonly used, just because it's simpler.

Using the methods available to the String object, you can manipulate string values such as those that exist in input and dynamic text fields. The following demonstrates some of the things you can do with strings.

MX ALERT **TIP** *Both variables and text field instances can contain string values. When a variable contains a string value, String object methods are invoked in the following manner: myVariable.toLowercase(), which will convert the string value of the variable to all lowercase characters. When a text field contains text, the value of its text property (such as myTextField.text) can be considered an instance of the String object. As such, you can use String object methods to directly manipulate the text within the field; for example, myTextField.text.toLowerCase() will convert the text in the field to all lowercase characters. The sample code below can be changed as described for use in either circumstance.*

569

Let's assume there's a dynamic text field on the stage named **myText**, which contains the text "Creative Web Animation." Take a look at the following script:

```
myVariable = myText.text.charAt(4);
```

Using the charAt() method, the expression to the right of the equals sign is used to locate the fifth character in the **myText** text field, which is then assigned as the value of myVariable. As a result, the value assigned to myVariable is "t". This is because counting from the left (with *C* being 0), *t* is the fifth character in the text string "Creative Web Animation" (**Figure 14.17**).

Creative Web Animation
0   4   9   13   16

Figure 14.17
The first character in a string value is always assigned an index value of 0, the next character a value of 1, and so on.

NOTE *Within strings, spaces are counted as characters.*

The following example demonstrates how you could use this method to check the validity of a phone number entered by the user. Assume there are two text fields on the stage, one named **phone** (into which the user enters a phone number, including area code) and another named **myMessage** (which will display a message, depending on the validity of the phone number entered). The user is asked to enter his or her phone number, then press the button that has the following script attached to it:

```
on(release){
   if(phone.text.charAt(3) != "-" || phone.text.charAt(7) != "-") {
     myMessage.text = "That is an invalid phone number!";
   }else{
     myMessage.text = "That is a valid phone number!";
   }
}
```

The if statement in this script states that "if the fourth or eighth characters in the **phone** text field are not dashes, display 'That is an invalid phone number!' in the **myMessage** text field. Otherwise, display 'That is a valid phone number!' "

Next we'll look at the substring() method, which allows you to extract a portion of a string. The syntax for this method is as follows:

```
nameOfField.text.substring (from, to);
```

In the above line of script, **nameOfField** is the instance name of the text field whose text property (string) you wish to evaluate. The from parameter value is the character number (counted from the left of the string, beginning with 0) at which you wish the extraction to begin; and the to parameter value specifies the character number (again, from the left) that should serve as the ending point for the extraction.

Take a look at the following example, which assumes there is a dynamic text field on the stage named **myText**, which contains a text property (string) value of "Macromedia".

```
myVariable = myText.substring(3, 7);
```

As you can see from the script, the section of the string to be extracted begins with the character at Position 3 (or *r*), and extends to the character at Position 7 (or *e*). Thus, myVariable is assigned a value of "rome".

You would use the substring() method to isolate parts of strings, so that they could be evaluated separately from the overall string itself. Consider the following example.

Imagine a dynamic text field on the stage with an instance name of **title**. If a user were to enter the text "Dr. Frankenstein" in the field and push a button, the script below would be executed:

```
on(release){
  if(title.text.substring(0, 2) == "Ms."){
    myMessage.text = "Hello Madam.";
  }else if(title.text.substring(0, 2) == "Dr."){
    myMessage.text = "Hello Doctor.";
  }
}
```

Based on the information entered into the text field **title**, when this script has executed, another text field named **myMessage** will display the string "Hello Doctor."

You can use the toUpperCase() and toLowerCase() methods to convert a string to all uppercase or all lowercase characters. Take a look at the following example:

```
myText.text.toUpperCase();
```

If **myText** contains a string value of "Creative Web Animation!" this will change it to read "CREATIVE WEB ANIMATION!"

String object instances have a single property, length, which is a numeric value based on the number of characters in a string. For example, if you had a text element that contained the string "Flash," its length would have a numeric value of 5 because the word *Flash* has five characters.

You can use this property to easily check the length of strings—for example, to verify data that must contain a specific number of characters, such as Zip codes and phone numbers.

Say you have a text field on the stage named **zipCode**, in which a user has entered the text 46293. The user pushes a button, and the script below is executed:

```
on(release){
  if(zipCode.text.length == 5) {
    myMessage.text = "That is a valid Zip code.";
  }else{
    myMessage.text = "Please enter a valid Zip code.";
  }
}
```

Based on the information entered into the **zipCode** text field, when this script has executed, another text field named **myMessage** will display the string "That is a valid Zip code."

Stage Object (Global)

MX ALERT The Stage object allows you to control and get information about stage characteristics, such as alignment, width, height, and so on. Take a look at the following script:

```
Stage.align = "TL";
Stage.scaleMode = "noBorder";
```

You could use these two lines of script to dynamically set (that is, override) the alignment and scaling settings that are set with the <OBJECT> and <EMBED> tags when your movie is embedded on an HTML page—giving you control over how your movie is presented on an HTML page, even as it plays.

NOTE *For information about movie settings available within the <OBJECT> and <EMBED> tags, see Chapter 20, "Publishing."*

TextField Object

MX ALERT You create instances of TextField objects whenever you place an input or dynamic text field on the stage. However, you can also create them dynamically using the createTextField() method of the MovieClip object (more on this in a moment). Whichever way you create a text field, you must assign an instance name to it in order to control it dynamically via ActionScript.

Since text field instances always belong to a particular timeline, the `createTextField()` method—which dynamically creates a text field instance on a particular timeline—is actually a method of the MovieClip object (rather than the TextField object, as you might think). Using this method, you can create a text field on any present timeline by using syntax that resembles the following:

```
targetPath.createTextField(instanceName, depth, x, y, width, height);
```

The following sample script will create a text field in the movie at the target path of _root.myFormClip, and assign it a depth of 1, an x position of 50, a y position of 100, a width of 150, and a height of 20 (**Figure 14.18**):

```
_root.myFormClip.createTextField("age", 1, 50, 100, 150, 20);
```

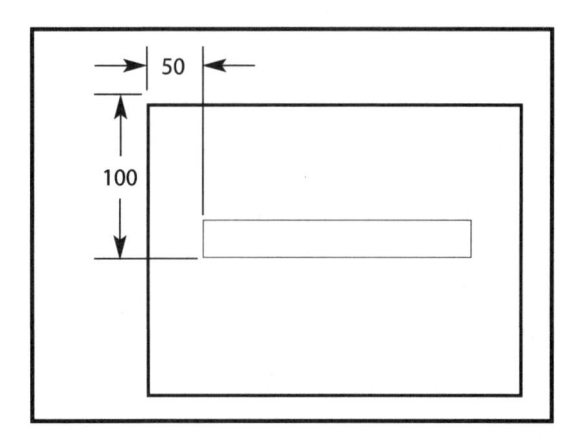

Figure 14.18
The x and y coordinates defined using the createTextField() method are calculated relative to the registration point of the movie in which the text field instance is being created (usually its top-left corner).

TIP *Although you wouldn't know it by looking at the properties available to text field instances in the Toolbox List window of the Actions panel, they share several properties with movie clip instances. These include _alpha, _height, _name, _rotation, _width, _x, _xmouse, _xscale, _y, _ymouse, and _yscale. Properties for individual instances can be set or read at any time using the following syntax: nameOfField._property*

Once a dynamic text field has been created, users can interact with it (and you can control it via ActionScript) just as you would a text field that had been manually placed on stage.

The TextField object contains several methods that allow you to format text in the field using instances of the TextFormat object, which we'll look at in the next section.

By using properties of the TextField object, you can dynamically set (and read) details such as the following:

- Whether a text field will resize automatically as text is typed into it:
  ```
  myTextField.autoSize = "left";
  ```

- Whether a text field has a border:
  ```
  myTextField.border = true;
  ```
- Whether the field can interpret HTML text:
  ```
  myTextField.html = true;
  ```
- HTML-formatted text displayed in the field:
  ```
  myTextField.htmlText = "<b>Bold text</b><i>Italicized text</i>";
  ```
- The maximum number of characters the user can enter into a field:
  ```
  myTextField.maxChars = 25;
  ```
- Whether text in the field is selectable or not:
  ```
  myTextField.selectable = false;
  ```
- Regular text (non-HTML-formatted) displayed in the field:
  ```
  myTextField.text = "I want a new iMac!";
  ```

Scrolling Text Vertically

MX ALERT

Scrolling is one of the most common tasks associated with viewing text in a field. Although Flash MX provides a Scrollbar component to quickly add this type of functionality (see "Scrollbar Component" in Chapter 15), it's worth understanding the basic functionality so that you can incorporate special scrolling features, such as text bookmarks, into your own projects.

Two properties of the Text Field object make vertical scrolling possible:

scroll *Property*

- Syntax: *myTextField.scroll*

The scroll property is a numeric value that represents the line number of the topmost visible line currently displayed in an input or dynamic text field. Thus, if the text field has ten lines of text and the user has scrolled to the point where Line 4 is the topmost visible line, the scroll value for this text element would be 4. This value is constantly updated as your movie plays. It can be evaluated in expressions, or you can create buttons that reset the topmost line to wherever you want (see script that follows).

*The following script uses an expression to evaluate the current scroll property of the text field named **myTextField**. If the value is greater than 3, the movie will stop playing:*

```
if (myTextField.scroll > 3) {
   stop();
}
```

Scrolling Text Vertically *continued*

*The following script shows a mouse event that will cause the text field named **myTextField** to make Line 6 its topmost visible line (text bookmark functionality):*

```
on (release) {
  myTextField.scroll = 6;
}
```

maxscroll **Property**

- Syntax: myTextField.maxscroll

*The maxscroll property is a numeric value that represents the line number of the topmost scrollable line in an input or dynamic text field. If you have a text field that is high enough only to show two lines of text even though it actually contains five, the maxscroll value is 4. This is because at its highest scroll point, Line 4 is the topmost visible line. If a text field contains ten lines of text but can only display four lines at a time, the maxscroll value for this text field would be 7. This is because at its highest scroll point, Line 7 is the topmost visible line (**Figure 14.19**).*

You can use the value in an expression attached to a button instance in order to create a looping scroll—that is, one in which a text element's text scrolls continuously (see the script below).

*The following script causes the text field named **myTextField** to go to a line number based on the value of count, which is updated with each click of the button. Also, with each button-click the value of count is compared to the value of myTextField.maxscroll. When the value of count equals the value of myTextField.maxscroll, this means the end of the scroll has been reached, and the count is reset so that with the next button-click, the text field will display Line 1 and start the process over again:*

```
on (release) {
  ++count
  myTextField.scroll = count;
  if (count == myTextField.maxscroll) {
    count = 0;
  }
}
```

Figure 14.19
In a ten-line text field that can only display four lines at a time, Line 7 would be the maxscroll value.

TextFormat Object (Instances)

MX ALERT TextFormat objects are used to change the format of text displayed in text fields. Once created, you *apply* the TextFormat object to a text field using the `setTextFormat()` or `setNewTextFormat()` method of the TextField object.

You create and style (set the formatting characteristics for) instances of the TextFormat object in the following manner:

```
format1 = new TextFormat();
with (format1){
   align = "left";
   bold = true;
   color = 0x003366;
   italic = true;
}
```

The first line in this script creates a new instance of the TextFormat object, named `format1`. A `with` statement is then used to define several formatting characteristics for this instance. Once you've created a TextFormat object, you can apply it to a text field in several ways: to all of the text in a field, to a portion of text in a field, or to any new text entered into the field. Take a look at the following examples:

```
myTextField.setTextFormat(format1);
```

The above script will apply the formatting of the `format1` TextFormat object instance to all text in the **myTextField** instance (and in the process will replace any existing formatting).

```
myTextField.setTextFormat(5, 25, format1);
```

The above line of script will only apply `format1`'s formatting to the characters in **myTextField** between Positions 5 and 25 (**Figure 14.20**).

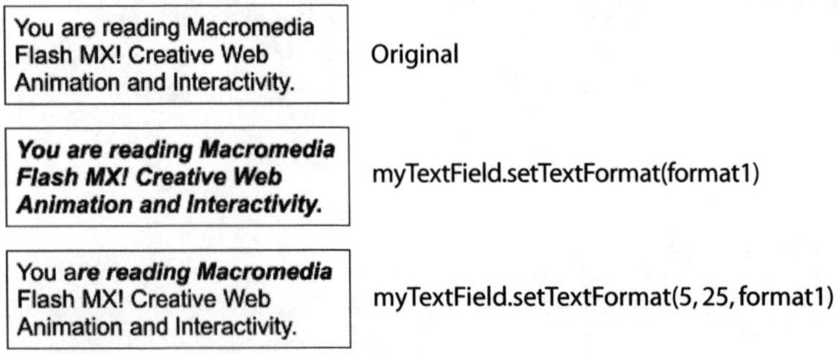

Figure 14.20
The setTextFormat() method allows you to format all the text in a field, or just portions of it.

If you want the *current* text in a field to maintain its formatting, while styling any *new* text entered into the field, you would use the `setNewTextFormat()` method as shown:

```
myTextField.setNewTextFormat(format1);
```

Any new text entered into the field will adopt the formatting described by the `format1` TextFormat object instance.

A project can contain multiple instances of the TextFormat object, any of which can be applied to text fields or portions of text fields, as just discussed.

Properties of the TextFormat object allow you to define margins, tab stops, and even a URL that will be opened when text styled in that format is clicked.

XML Object

Instances of the XML object are used to work with chunks of data that have been formatted in XML. However, to really understand this object's use, you need a basic grasp of XML-formatted data.

XML is a language for structuring data; it resembles HTML code in that it uses tags, attributes, and values. However, the similarity ends there: While HTML uses predefined tags (for example, <body>, <head>, and <html>), an XML document contains tags that *you* define. Take a look at the following XML-structured document:

```
<FlashUsers>
  <Person>
    <Firstname>Derek</Firstname>
    <FavShow Network="CBS">JAG</FavShow>
  </Person>
  <Person>
    <Firstname>Jack</Firstname>
    <FavShow Network="HGTV">Surprise Gardener</FavShow>
  </Person>
</FlashUsers>
```

This document represents a list of Flash users, and includes their names and information about their favorite TV shows. There are two users listed. As you can see, the structure of the document is similar to that of an HTML page. There are opening tags (<Person>), with accompanying closing tags (</Person>). The difference with these tags is that we made them up (their names), in order to identify the data between them. In fact, the tags have no purpose other than to describe this data. They can't create anything (as an HTML <table> tag does) or format anything (as the HTML <b> does, to make text bold). As you can see, just as HTML tags are nested (one tag is actually contained within another), some XML tags are nested in order to give the data within the document a hierarchical structure, something we'll explore shortly.

Let's proceed through the steps you would employ to load it into Flash, so that you know how to access its data. We'll assume that the XML document is named flashUsers.xml (an XML document can be created with any simple text editor by saving a text document with an .xml extension).

The first step in getting this data into Flash is creating an XML object instance, which would look like the following:

```
myXML = new XML();
```

The above script creates a new XML object instance named myXML. Next, we need to load our external XML document into this object instance. Before we do so, however, we'll add a line below the one above that reads:

```
myXML.ignoreWhite = true;
```

This line of script will cause any XML data loaded into the myXML XML object instance to be stripped of carriage returns, spaces, and so on—all of which can cause the XML data to be read incorrectly by Flash. Next, we add the action for loading the document, as shown below:

```
myXML.load("flashUsers.xml");
```

The above line of script will load the XML data in the flashUsers.xml file into the myXML XML object instance.

NOTE *It's typical to define an event handler method for the XML object instance (such as myXML.onLoad = nameOfFunction;), prior to loading an external document. This enables you to call a function (once the external data has finished loading) to extract data from the loaded-in XML. The focus of our discussion here is how Flash interprets XML, not the mechanics of its extraction. For more information on this, see Chapter 21, "Projects."*

Chapter 14 ActionScript Objects

Each beginning and ending tag group in the loaded XML document is called a *node*. The above document has a *root node* of <FlashUsers> (**Figure 14.21**). The value of everything between the <FlashUsers> and </FlashUsers> tags can be accessed using the following code:

    myVariable = myXML.firstChild;

```
              <FlashUsers>
                <Person>
          Node    <Firstname>Derek</Firstname>      Node
                  <FavShow Network="CBS">JAG</FavShow>  Node
                </Person>
Node            <Person>
          Node    <Firstname>Jack</Firstname>   Node
                  <FavShow Network="HTVG">Surprise Gardener</FavShow>   Node
                </Person>
              </FlashUsers>
```

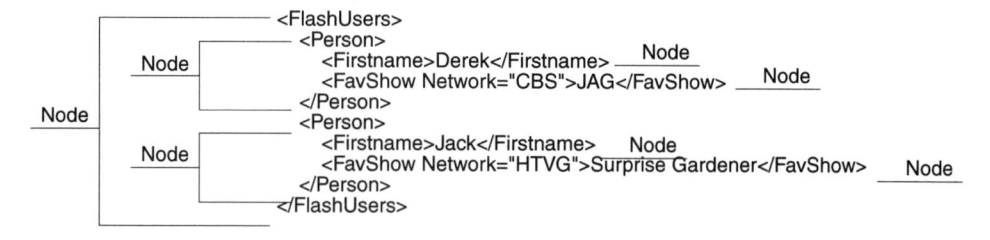

Figure 14.21
Each beginning and ending tag group in a loaded XML document is called a node. The node structure determines the code required to navigate the document's data.

As you can see, even though <FlashUsers> is the root node, it's also the first *child node* of the overall document. To move deeper into the node hierarchy, the next line of script allows us to access the value of everything between the first opening <Person> and </Person> tags:

    myVariable = myXML.firstChild.firstChild;

Here, myVariable has a value of:

    <Person>
      <Firstname>Derek</Firstname>
      <FavShow Network="CBS">JAG</FavShow>
    </Person>

To go deeper still, the following line:

    myVariable = myXML.firstChild.firstChild.firstChild;

will assign myVariable a value of:

    <Firstname>Derek</Firstname>

And finally, the following:

    myVariable = myXML.firstChild.firstChild.firstChild.firstChild;

will assign myVariable a value of:

    Derek

Whew! It takes some time to get there, but that's how it's done. As you can see, the firstChild property is used to stair-step your way down the XML object's node hierarchy. This property denotes the first node in the next level within the document.

But how do you get the value of Jack, which is in the second <Person> node of our document? This is where the concept of sibling nodes comes into play. A sibling node is simply the next node in the same level of the XML document's structure. For example, the first <Person> node is a sibling of the second <Person> node, while the <Firstname> node is a sibling of the <FavShow> node (**Figure 14.22**). Thus, to get to the value of Jack, you would use the following syntax:

    myVariable = myXML.firstChild.firstChild.nextSibling.firstChild.firstChild;

Notice the addition of the nextSibling property. This basically tells the program to look in <FlashUsers>, then <Person>, then *skip* to the next <Person>, then <Firstname>, then the value of <Firstname>, which is Jack. This can be a tricky concept, so you should review it a few times if necessary.

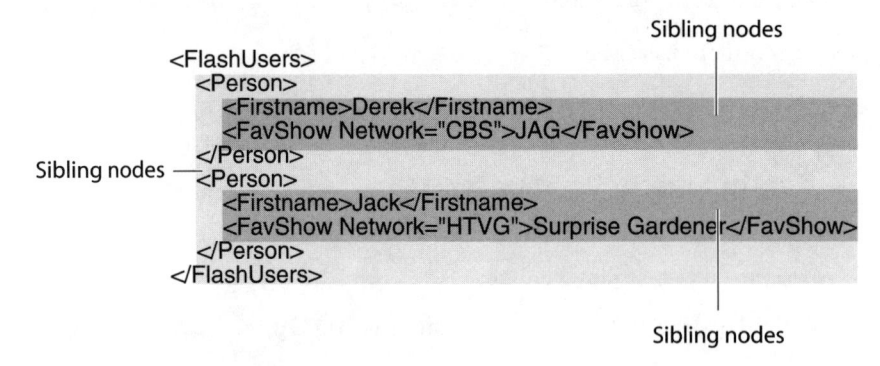

```
                                                  Sibling nodes
                                                        |
                <FlashUsers>
                    <Person>
                        <Firstname>Derek</Firstname>
                        <FavShow Network="CBS">JAG</FavShow>
                    </Person>
Sibling nodes ──    <Person>
                        <Firstname>Jack</Firstname>
                        <FavShow Network="HTVG">Surprise Gardener</FavShow>
                    </Person>
                </FlashUsers>
                                                        |
                                                  Sibling nodes
```

Figure 14.22
Sibling nodes are nodes that exist in the same level of an XML document's structure.

TIP *There are techniques that make navigating between nodes easier. For more information, see Chapter 21, "Projects."*

Let's look at one more aspect of our XML document. You'll notice that the `<FavShow>` tag has an attribute named `Network`. To access this value (for the first `<Person>` node), you would use the following syntax:

```
myVariable =
myXML.firstChild.firstChild.firstChild.nextSibling.attributes.Network
```

In essence, this states, "Look in `<FlashUsers>`, then `<Person>`, then `<Firstname>`, then *skip* to the next sibling of `<Firstname>` (which is `<FavShow>`), then the value of the attribute at this node with the name `Network`." In this case, `myVariable` is assigned a value of `"CBS"`.

These are just a few samples of how XML can be used in a Flash project. If you're ready to push Flash to its limits, XML is a language worth learning—and if you know how HTML works, XML should be a breeze.

TIP *For more information on XML, visit the XML home page at www.xml.com.*

Video Tutorial

Working with Properties. In this tutorial we'll show you how to set and work with a movie's properties, in order to make your presentation interactive.

Components

CHAPTER 15

MX ALERT

Both beginning and advanced Flash developers face challenges—albeit slightly different ones—when it comes to adding complex interactivity to their projects. More experienced users want to easily reuse the advanced functionality they've spent so much time developing and implementing, while beginning users want to implement all of the cool interactivity they know the program is capable of—*before* they've spent the requisite hours honing their Flash and ActionScripting skills. Components—reusable project elements such as scroll bars and checkboxes—provide an easy solution for both groups.

Take game development: It's not unusual for developers to spend days, nights, even weeks scripting an *engine*—a fancy name for a chunk of ActionScript—to perform a number of tasks. Say you wanted to keep track of players' scoring in a game you were creating: Wouldn't it be great if you could just pull that scoring engine functionality out of another project (for which you had created a similar scoring engine), and use it in the new one? This is precisely what components allow. And for beginners, they make adding things like draggable windows a breeze: You simply drag and drop a component into your project, adjust a few settings, and you're good to go.

Components are really nothing more than enhanced movie clips—that is, they *behave* like movie clips, but the scripting that makes them work in a specific way is easily accessible and configurable as parameter settings. Flash uses components to package different types of ActionScript-based functionality and interactivity—such as that required for menus, form elements, and behaviors—for easy distribution and customization. You can distribute components (and their functionality) to other users, drag and drop them into projects, and easily customize them by adjusting just a few parameters.

What you'll learn...

How to work with and configure components

About Flash MX's various built-in components

How to customize Flash MX's built-in components

How to download and install components

Say, for example, you wanted to create a scroll bar for a text field. With Flash 5 this required a lot of time and a firm grasp of ActionScript. But in Flash MX you can simply drag the ScrollBar component onto a text field, adjust a few parameter settings, and you're finished! For the advanced developer, this means not having to script that scroll bar functionality from scratch for each project. For beginners, it opens up a world of sophisticated interactivity without an in-depth knowledge of ActionScript.

Although an in-depth knowledge of ActionScript is not necessary to implement the basic functionality of most components, those who want total control over them have many options. Many components have their own properties and methods, which means you can configure, change and retrieve data from them, and otherwise work with them while your movie is playing. You can also change a component's appearance to suit your particular layout.

Flash MX ships with the following components installed; you'll find them on the Components panel (Window > Components) (**Figure 15.1**):

- CheckBox
- ComboBox
- ListBox
- PushButton
- RadioButton
- ScrollBar
- ScrollPane

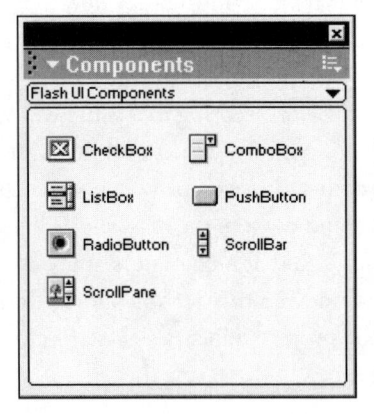

Figure 15.1
The Components panel displays all the components that have been installed on your computer. What you see here are the default Flash UI Components that ship with Flash MX.

Keep in mind, too, that you're not limited to the components that come installed with Flash MX. Additional components are being made available for download by Macromedia as well as several third-party developers (see "Downloading and Installing Additional Components," later in this chapter). And if you're feeling brave, you can even create your own—just be forewarned that this requires a general understanding of ActionScript.

NOTE *Components replace Smart Clips, which were introduced in Flash 5. Although components retain the basic functionality of Smart Clips (which were also just enhanced movie clips with configurable parameters), they are much more powerful, versatile, and easy to use because they have stronger ties to ActionScripts.*

Working with and Configuring Components

Later in this chapter we'll provide an in-depth discussion of the above components, as well as show you how to install and download additional ones. First, however, let's go over some basic principles that govern how you work with and configure components.

Adding Components

Because components function like enhanced movie clips, when you place a component in your project, you're actually placing an *instance* of that component—a concept that will become clearer as we continue.

To add a component to your project:

- With the Components panel open, *double-click* a component icon to place an instance of it in the **middle of the stage**.

- With the Components panel open, click a component icon and *drag it* to place an instance of it **anywhere on the stage**.

TIP *If the current scene contains a dynamic text field, dragging an instance of the ScrollBar component on top of that field will cause it to "snap" onto the field. When a ScrollBar component is attached to a text field in this manner, it automatically is set to scroll text in that field. Just because the ScrollBar component is attached to a particular field does not mean it is there permanently. It can be clicked and dragged onto a different field at any time.*

When you add a component to a project, a copy of it is automatically placed in that project's library: This copy becomes the master version of the component for the *current* project. At the same time that this copy is placed in the library, a folder structure containing the component's many supporting assets is placed there as well (**Figure 15.2**). We'll take a closer look at those supporting assets a bit later in this chapter.

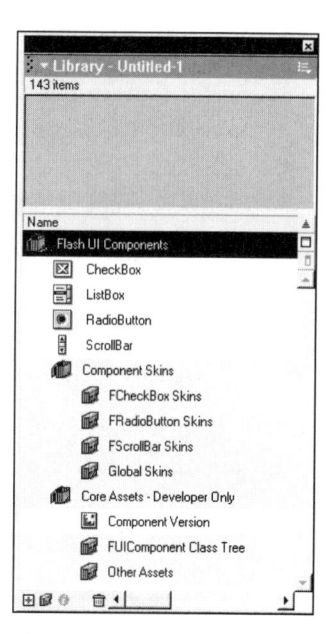

Figure 15.2
Placing instances of components in your projects automatically adds a number of supporting assets to the library.

When you want to place *additional* instances of a component that you've already used in your project, it's usually best to drag and drop an instance of it from the Library panel, rather than from the Components panel. Here's why: If you've customized that component in any way, your changes are recorded in the library versions. However, the components that are available in the Components panel are the *default* versions—that is, the ones that came installed with Flash MX.

If you attempt to drag the *default* version of a component you've already customized from the Components panel, Flash will display an alert box that gives you the option of replacing the existing component (your customized version) with the default version. You may occasionally choose to do this, but it's far more likely that you will want to use the customized version instead. You can avoid this alert by dragging and dropping additional instances of a particular component from the library, as discussed.

{ **ActionScript** } Since components are movie clips, you can place instances of them in your movie dynamically by using the `attachMovie()` method. For that to work, however, the component type must already exist in your project's library. To accomplish that, simply drag an instance of the component type from the Components panel onto the stage, then delete it from the stage.

Next, it's important to realize that when a component is added to the library, it is given an identifier name, which is used when invoking the `attachMovie()` method. For example, The ScrollPane component is given an identifier name of FscrollPaneSymbol. Thus, to attach a ScrollPane component instance dynamically, you would use syntax resembling the following:

```
_root.attachMovie("FScrollPaneSymbol", "myScrollPane", 10);
_root.myScrollPane._x = 50;
_root.myScrollPane._y = 100;
_root.myScrollPane.setScrollContent("sunrisePicture")
```

The first line of this script dynamically attaches a ScrollPane component instance to the main timeline, and assigns it an instance name of myScrollPane. The next three lines position the component instance on the stage and set the content it is to display. Additional methods will allow you to further customize it for use via ActionScript.

See Chapter 16, "Using ActionScript in Your Projects," for more information on placing component instances dynamically.

Removing Components

Because of the way components work, removing one *completely* from your project involves more than just selecting it and pressing the Delete key.

NOTE *If you only want to move a component to a different location in your project, you can just delete it and place a new instance at the desired location. The following discussion concerns deleting a component from your project altogether.*

Normally, the content of a particular symbol in the library is not exported when a SWF file is created—unless an instance of that symbol has been included somewhere in your project. Thus, the library can contain a number of assets that are saved in the FLA file, but omitted from the exported SWF. Flash normally determines which assets are included in a project (and thus belong in the SWF) and which aren't. Without this feature, your final SWF could contain all kinds of unnecessary data, making the file much larger than it need be.

With components, however, this functionality works a bit differently. When you add a component to your project but then later remove it, the content defining the component (graphics, ActionScript, and so on) is *still* exported when you create the SWF. This is because when you place a component in your project, the assets added to the library include special ActionScript code that will be included in the exported SWF—even if you subsequently removed all instances of the component from your project. (There's a reason for this, but it's too technical to interest us here.) To *completely* remove a component from a project, you must delete all of its *assets* from the library as well.

To see how to do this, let's look at the steps required to delete the RadioButton component from a project; these same principles apply to removing any type of component.

To add and then remove a RadioButton component from your project:

1. Select File > New to start a new project.

2. Open the Components panel and drag a CheckBox component onto the stage.

Although this exercise is intended to demonstrate how to remove a RadioButton component from a project, we need to first add a CheckBox component here (which will add CheckBox component assets to the project/library) to later demonstrate how you can identify assets in the library that are unique to the RadioButton component. This makes the exercise as realistic as possible, since a typical project will contain more than one type of component.

3. Choose Control > Test Movie.

   If you open the Bandwidth Profiler, you'll see that just by including the CheckBox component instance, you've caused your otherwise empty project to acquire an export file size of 16K.

4. Close the test movie and return to the authoring environment. Drag a RadioButton component onto the stage.

5. Choose Control > Test Movie.

   If you open the Bandwidth Profiler now, you'll see that adding the RadioButton component instance has caused your project to export with a file size of 30K—14K more than when it just contained the CheckBox component (**Figure 15.3**). Remember this file size.

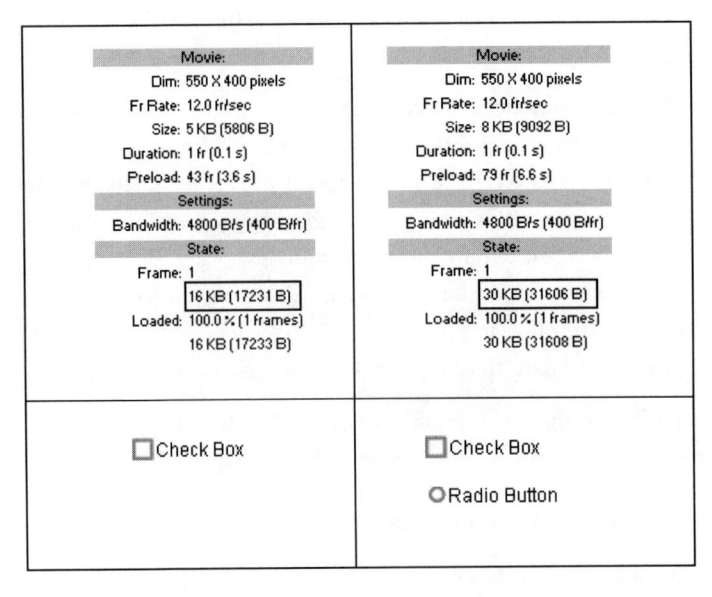

Figure 15.3
The addition of a radio button to the project increases its exported file size to 30K.

6. Close the test movie and return to the authoring environment. Open the Library panel and note the assets that have been placed there as a result of adding components to your project.

   The main folder in the library is named Flash UI Components; its contents are shown in **Figure 15.4**

7. Remove from the stage the single RadioButton component instance that you added in Step 4.

Chapter 15 **Components**

8. Choose Control > Test Movie.

   With the Bandwidth Profiler open, you can see that removing the only instance of the RadioButton component from your project did not affect your movie's overall file size—it's still 30K. This is because the assets that make up the RadioButton component still exist in the library. As a result, the component's assets are being exported even though no instances of the component exist in your project. Now we'll remove these assets and see how it affects your file's size.

9. Select the assets in the library indicated in **Figure 15.5**, and delete them by pressing the Delete button at the bottom of the Library panel.

10. Choose Control > Test Movie.

    With the Bandwidth Profiler open, you can now see that removing the RadioButton component's supporting assets from the library has dramatically decreased your movie's file size: It's now back to what it was before you added the RadioButton component.

Once an instance of a component is placed in your project, you can configure it in several ways. We'll look first at how instances of all types of components can be configured, then examine configuration options for specific component types.

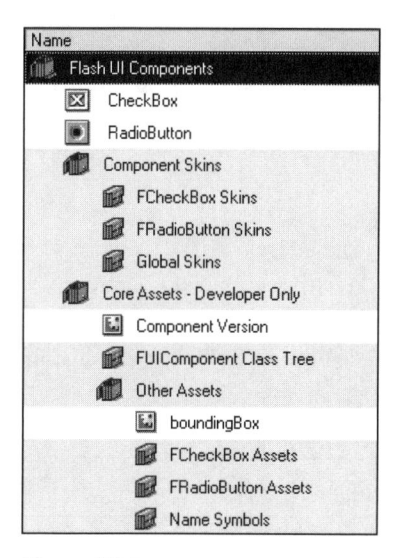

Figure 15.4
The contents of the Flash UI Components folder after placing a CheckBox and a RadioButton component in your project.

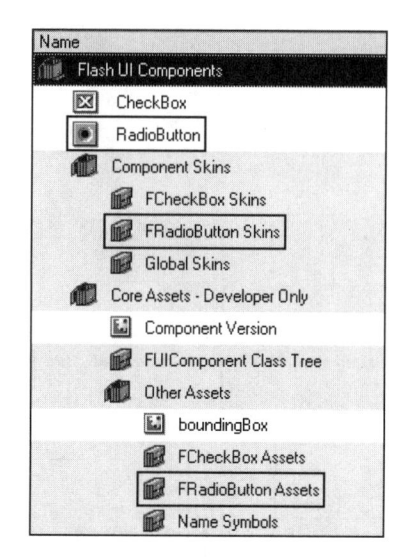

Figure 15.5
By selecting and deleting the assets indicated in this graphic, you can completely remove the RadioButton component from your project.

Configuring Instance Names

Once you've placed a component in your project, you can work with it in much the same manner as a normal movie clip instance.

When you open the Property inspector and select a component instance, you'll see that you can give it an instance name just as you would any other movie clip instance (**Figure 15.6**). This enables you to communicate with that particular instance via ActionScript. For example, if you've placed a CheckBox component instance on the stage, giving it an instance name of **myCheckbox** will allow you to determine its current state (checked or unchecked) using the getValue() method, as shown by the following:

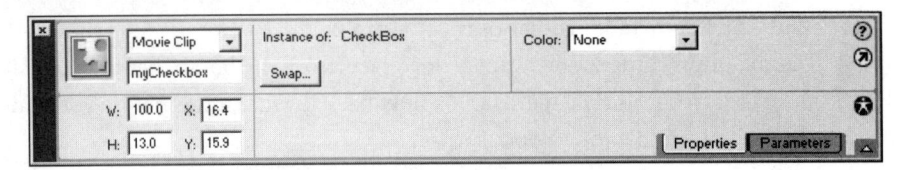

Figure 15.6
Because component instances are merely enhanced movie clip instances, they can be given instance names and be communicated with via ActionScript, just like a regular movie clip instance.

    currentValue = myCheckbox.getValue();

If **myCheckbox** is currently checked, then currentValue will be assigned a value of true.

Setting Initial Parameter Values

The Property inspector also contains a section for adjusting a component's initial parameter values, which you can view by pressing the Parameters tab on the Property inspector when a component instance is selected (**Figure 15.7**). You can customize the component in various ways by adjusting these parameter values.

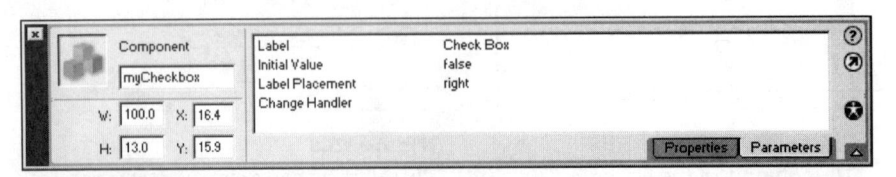

Figure 15.7
Pressing the Parameters tab on the Property inspector, while a component instance is selected, reveals a list of parameter settings that are used to set the initial state of the component instance.

TIP *As you will learn shortly, many of these values can be changed as the movie plays, via ActionScript.*

The section for setting parameter values is made up of two columns: The left column contains parameter names; the right column contains parameter values. The parameter values you can set for components range from numbers to colors, text strings, Boolean values (true or false), and so on, depending on the type of component currently selected.

To set parameter values, you must select either the parameter name or its current value; this activates the text box into which you'll enter the new value. You can set some values by entering a number or string directly into the value box; for others you'll be presented with a menu of acceptable values, a color palette, or another dialog box (**Figure 15.8**). Later in this chapter, under "Using Flash MX's Built-In Components," we'll provide an in-depth look at setting parameter values for each component type.

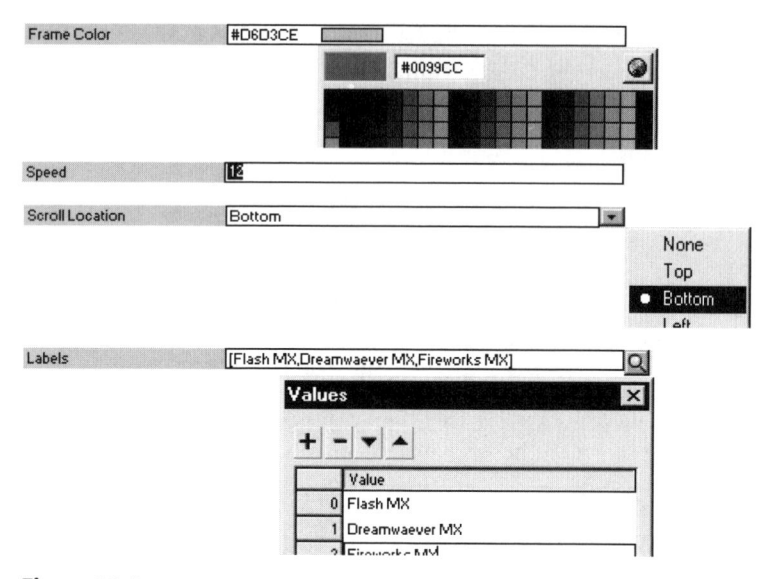

Figure 15.8
Setting parameter values for component instances is handled in various ways, depending on the parameter value type. Some parameter value settings use a dialog box or menu.

When you change the value of a parameter that affects a component's appearance, that change will be reflected in the component instance on stage.

NOTE *If a component instance on stage doesn't reflect your parameter changes, make sure that Live Preview is turned on: Choose Control > Enable Live Preview. A check mark will appear next to this menu item when it is enabled.*

Because component instances work essentially like movie clip instances, you can attach a script containing a load clip event to set the initial parameter values in a more dynamic fashion. For example, if you drag an instance of the CheckBox component onto the stage, you can dynamically set its initial parameter values by selecting that instance and attaching the following script:

```
onClipEvent(load){
   this.setLabel("Music On/Off");
   this.setValue(true);
}
```

The above script will set the label of the CheckBox component instance (that is, the text that appears next to it) as well as its initial value (to true, causing a check to appear in the box).

Understanding the Change Handler Function

Most components include an optional Change Handler setting, which is one of the most useful parameter settings for component instances. You use the Change Handler setting to specify what function is called when the value of the component instance changes (for example, when the user selects from a list, checks or unchecks a box, moves a scrollbar, and so on). To call a function named myFunction, you would enter *myFunction* (omitting the parentheses that are normally used to identify a function) as the Change Handler parameter value (**Figure 15.9**).

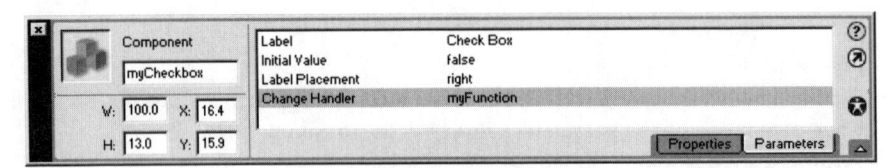

Figure 15.9
In setting the name of a function to use as a component's Change Handler setting, use the name of the function only, *without including parentheses.*

Keep in mind that whatever function you call must exist on the same timeline as the component instance. For example, if the component instance exists on the main timeline, then the function being used as the Change Handler must be defined on the main timeline as well.

Here's an example of how a Change Handler function is defined:

```
function myFunction(callingComponent){
  message.text = callingComponent.getValue();
}
```

You can see that the function definition uses a single parameter: callingComponent. When a Change Handler function is called (because a component instance value has been changed), a reference to the calling component is automatically sent to the function (as a parameter value). The function uses this reference as shown in the example above.

For example, assume that there's a CheckBox component instance on the stage with an instance name of **myCheckBox**. This instance's Change Handler has been defined as myFunction (the name of our example function, shown above). If this instance's value is changed (from, say, true/checked to false/unchecked), myFunction() will be called and evaluated in the following manner:

```
function myFunction(myCheckBox){
  message.text = myCheckBox.getValue();
}
```

Notice how the name of the component, **myCheckBox**, replaces the parameter name (callingComponent) within the function definition. In this example, the function would cause the value of **myCheckBox** to appear in the **message** text field.

To better understand this concept, let's assume there's a second component instance on the stage, named **myListBox**. This component instance is *also* set to use myFunction() as its Change Handler function. If the value of this component instance were to change, myFunction() would be evaluated in the following manner:

```
function myFunction(myListBox){
  message.text = myListBox.getValue();
}
```

The same function is used, but in this scenario it is sent a reference to the **myListBox** component instance. In this case, the value of **myListBox** would appear in the **message** text field.

Since a reference to the component instance calling the function is sent to the function as a parameter value, a single Change Handler function can be defined for several component instances—a good practice for centralizing your code (see "Creative Uses of the Change Handler Function," on the next page).

{ **ActionScript** } You can set a component instance's Change Handler function dynamically using the setChangeHandler() method—useful if you want value changes to different instances of a component to call different functions. For example, if you wanted to dynamically set the Change Handler function for the myCheckBox component instance so that it calls myOtherFunction() whenever its value changes, you would use the following syntax:

```
myCheckBox.setChangeHandler("myOtherFunction");
```

Setting the Change Handler function for a component instance in this manner overrides any Change Handler function defined for that instance in the Property inspector.

Creative uses of the Change Handler function

Generally, Change Handler functions are useful when you want a change made in a component instance's value to produce an immediate effect on your movie—either visually or on the data it contains. For example, when a user selects a value from a ListBox component instance (such as the user's age), this action might cause other component instances be enabled or disabled, depending on the user's selection. To do this, you could set the ListBox's Change Handler setting to call a function named listBoxFunction(), which might go as follows:

```
function listBoxFunction(currentComponent){
  if (currentComponent.getValue() == "Under 18"){
    marriedCheckBox.setEnabled(false);
    childrenCheckBox.setEnabled(false);
    schoolNameListBox.setEnabled(true);
  }else{
    marriedCheckBox.setEnabled(true);
    childrenCheckBox.setEnabled(true);
    schoolNameListBox.setEnabled(false);
  }
}
```

When called, this function uses an `if` statement to evaluate the current value (getValue()) of the calling component (the ListBox component, in this example). If the user chooses the "Under 18" selection, the first part of the statement is executed, disabling or enabling other component instances that pertain to people *under* the age of 18. Otherwise, the second (`else`) part of the statement is executed, enabling or disabling other component instances that pertain to people *over* the age of 18 (**Figure 15.10**).

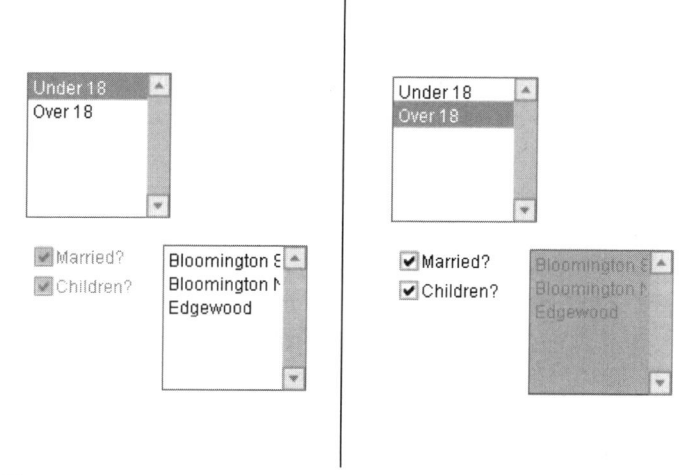

Figure 15.10
Enabling and disabling component instances on-the-fly, based on user input (such as age) is one creative way to utilize the Change Handler function.

Alternatively, say your movie is a shopping cart application that displays a running total as the user selects or deselects items to add to his or her cart. In this example, you could create a Change Handler function that would recalculate and display this total as items are added and removed.

You can use a single function as a Change Handler for multiple component instances. To do so, you must determine which component instance is currently invoking the function (using the _name property), then use if statements to execute a specific set of actions, based on that value. To illustrate this, let's look at the following example:

```
function generalChangeHandler (currentComponent)
  if (currentComponent._name == "myCheckBox"){
    //actions
  }else if (currentComponent._name == "myScrollBar"){
    //actions
  }else if (currentComponent._name == "myListBox"){
    //actions
  }
}
```

In this example, different sets of actions will be executed, depending on the name of the component that calls this Change Handler function.

Controlling Components via ActionScript

{ *ActionScript* } Since component instances are actually movie clip instances, it's important to realize that from a scripting standpoint, you can treat them as such. They can use typical movie clip instance properties such as _x, _y, _xmouse, _ymouse, _visible, and so on, as well as movie clip instance methods such as startDrag(), hitTest(), and others. By employing these properties and methods, you can make the components you use in your projects highly interactive. For example, you might use a Change Handler function to set up your project so that selecting an option on the screen (like a radio button or checkbox) would reconfigure the position of form elements (by setting X and Y property values). You could even use a Change Handler function to hide/show certain elements (by setting their visible property to true or false). Suppose you had a form set up to gather information about different family members (mother, father, sister, or brother). You could use these techniques to configure the form dynamically, tailoring it specifically to ask for different information from a father than it does from a daughter. Try doing that easily with HTML! For more information on using components dynamically, as described here, see Chapter 16, "Using ActionScript in Your Projects," and Chapter 21, "Building Projects."

Using Flash MX's Built-In Components

Up to this point, we've focused on the general ways you can work with components. Now it's time to look at them individually. In this section we'll describe in detail each of Flash MX's pre-installed components: how to use them, how to set them up, and some basic ways to control and communicate with them via ActionScript.

Keep in mind that each of Flash MX's built-in components has a set of methods that allows you to use ActionScript along with the component to accomplish various tasks—dynamically setting their appearance, the way they interact with the user, the content they contain, and more. We'll examine some of these methods here; for a more detailed discussion, see Chapter 16, "Using ActionScript in Your Projects."

You can view the component methods in the Toolbox List window of the Actions panel, under the Flash UI Components book (**Figure 15.11**).

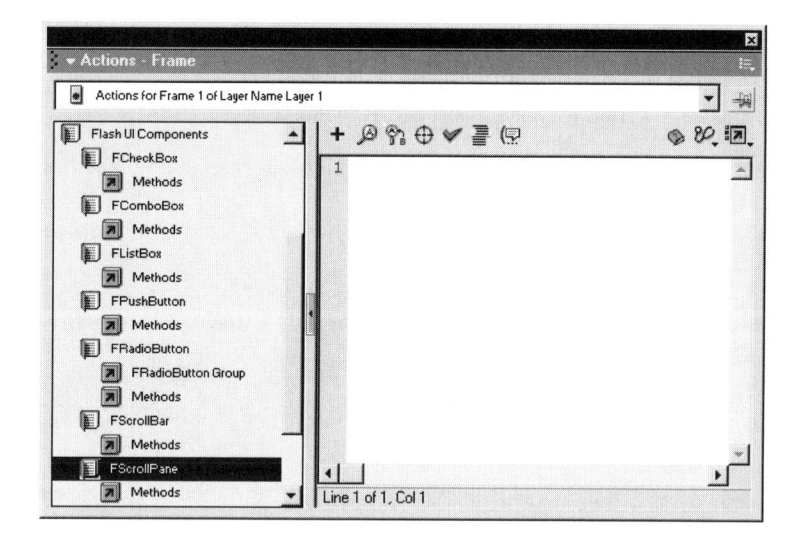

Figure 15.11
Component methods can be found in the Toolbox List window of the Actions panel.

NOTE *Be sure to check out this chapter's video tutorial on the accompanying CD: It demonstrates how to place and configure components in your projects. In addition, Chapter 21, "Building Projects," demonstrates the use of components in the context of an actual project.*

CheckBox Component

CheckBox component instances are used to toggle between true and false values. You can use them not only for Flash-based forms that require checkboxes for selecting or deselecting options, but for any type of interaction that requires a toggle switch—for example, turning music on or off or for any other setting that requires an on or off value.

A CheckBox component instance has the following Property inspector–based parameter settings:

- **Label.** This identifies the text that should appear next to the component instance. A string value should be entered.

- **Initial Value.** This determines the component instance's initial state. You can select a value of True or False from the menu provided. If you select True, the component instance will initially appear with a check mark; if you select False, it will appear unchecked.

- **Label Placement.** This determines the location of the text label that appears next to the component instance. In the menu provided, you can select a value of Left or Right.

- **ChangeHandler.** This optional setting represents the name of the function that's called when the value of this component instance changes. This function must exist on the same timeline as the component instance.

The following simple exercise demonstrates the use of a CheckBox component instance.

To use a CheckBox Component instance to make a movie clip instance visible and invisible:

1. Draw a shape (of any kind) on the stage; select it; and then convert it to a movie clip symbol.

2. With the Property inspector open, select this movie clip instance and give it a name of **myShape**.

   This is the instance we will be making visible and invisible.

3. With the Components panel open, click and drag a CheckBox component instance onto the stage.

4. With the Property inspector open, select this instance and give it a name of **myCheckBox**.

5. Assign the following initial parameter values to **myCheckBox**:

   Label: Shape Visible?

   Initial Value: True

   Label Placement: Right

   Change Handler: showHideShape

   As defined by the last parameter setting, when the value of this component instance changes, the `showHideShape()` function will be called. We'll define that function next.

6. With the Actions panel open, select Frame 1 on the timeline and add the following script:

   ```
   function showHideShape(){
     myShape._visible = myCheckBox.getValue();
   }
   ```

   This function—which you defined as the Change Handler function for the **myCheckBox** instance added in the previous step—is called any time that instance's value changes. Its only purpose is to retrieve the current value of **myCheckBox** (using the `getValue()` method) so that it can set the visible property of the **myShape** movie clip instance—causing it to appear or disappear. This method returns a value of true or false, depending on the current value of the **myCheckBox** instance.

7. Choose Control > Test Movie.

Pressing the CheckBox component instance continuously will cause the **myShape** movie clip instance to appear and disappear.

TIP *A completed version of this exercise (named checkbox.fla) can be found in the Chapter 15/Assets folder on the accompanying CD.*

ComboBox Component

A ComboBox component instance is a combination entry box and drop-down list of predefined values. You can use this type of component not only for Flash-based forms that require combo boxes for selecting or entering choices, but also for any type of interaction where a menu of selectable choices might be useful—for example, a site navigation menu.

ComboBox component instances have the following Property inspector–based parameter settings (**Figure 15.12**):

Editable	true
Labels	[Flash MX,Dreamweaver MX,Fireworks MX,ColdFusion MX]
Data	[1,2,3,4]
Row Count	3
Change Handler	

my MX
Flash MX
Dreamweaver
Fireworks MX

Figure 15.12
Making a ComboBox component instance editable enables users to type in their own values rather than select from among the predefined values. The Row Count parameter determines how many menu choices are visible on screen at one time.

- **Editable.** This determines whether the combo box is editable (true) or static (false). Making the box editable allows the user to type text directly into the component instance, which automatically scrolls to the item with the same text as the user types. If you choose the static mode, the user can only select from a list of predefined items.

- **Labels.** This represents the list of items you want to appear. Each item will appear as a separate choice in the combo box. You can enter items via the Values dialog box (see "The Values Dialog Box" sidebar later in this section).

- **Data.** This is a list of values associated with the items (labels) in the combo box. For example, if the first item on the Labels list is "Derek's Email" the first *data* value might be derek@derekfranklin.com. As a result, if the user selected "Derek's Email," the component would return a value of derek@derekfranklin.com. You enter data values via the Values dialog box. Entering data values is optional. When data values are not used, label values are returned when an item is selected. Using our previous example, selecting "Derek's Email" would return a value of "Derek's Email" since an associated data value was not defined. Data values are useful when you want the choices that appear on the list to be different from the actual selected values.

- **Row Count.** This represents the number of items that can be displayed on the list (when it is dropped down) before a scrollbar appears. A numeric value should be entered; the minimum acceptable value is 3.

- **ChangeHandler.** This optional setting represents the name of the function that is called when the value of this component instance changes (that is, when a different item is selected from the list). This function must exist on the same timeline as the component instance.

The Values Dialog Box

This simple dialog box is where you list values for components that use them (such as ComboBox and ListBox instances). You access it by pressing the Magnifying Glass icon that appears when you attempt to enter lists of values in the Property inspector.

*At the top of this dialog box you will see four buttons. To add a new item to the list, press the Plus button ("+"). You can edit the value of this item by selecting the current value, then replacing it with a new value. To delete a value, select it and then press the Minus button ("-"). You can move values up and down in the list by pressing the Up and Down Arrow buttons. Pressing OK saves the values as shown (**Figure 15.13**).*

Each value setting has an associated number that appears to the left of the value—something you need to remember when working with the component instance via ActionScript.

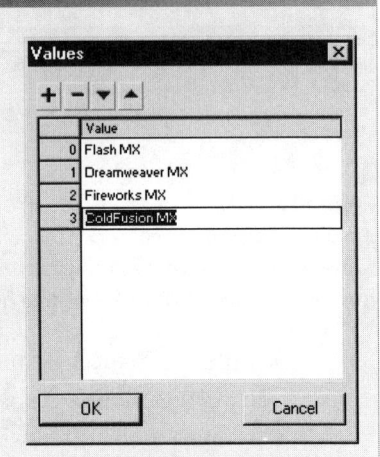

Figure 15.13
The Values dialog box lets you enter and work with lists of parameter values. You can add and delete values, or move them up or down in the list.

The following simple exercise demonstrates how to use ComboBox component instances.

To use two ComboBox instances to control the rotation and transparency of a movie clip instance:

1. Draw a square (any size and color) on the stage.

2. With the square selected, choose Insert > Convert to Symbol to turn this square into a movie clip instance.

3. In the Convert to Symbol dialog box, give the symbol a name, select the Movie Clip Behavior option, and select the center box on the Registration graphic. Then click OK (**Figure 15.14**).

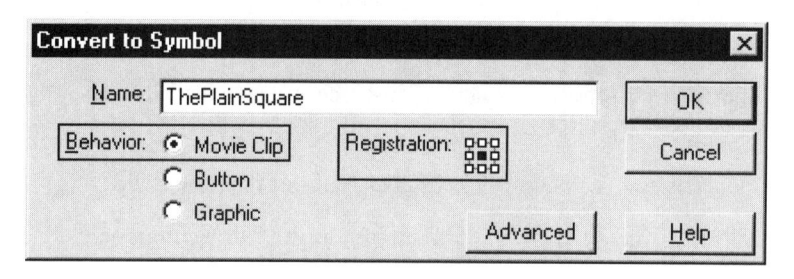

Figure 15.14
Make sure the Movie Clip Behavior option is selected and that the center box (indicating registration) is selected.

4. With the Property inspector open, select this movie clip instance and give it a name of **mySquare**.

    This is the instance we will be controlling with our two ComboBox instances.

5. With the Components panel open, click and drag a ComboBox instance onto the stage.

6. With the Property inspector open, select this instance and give it the name **rotationValue**.

    This component instance will control the movie clip's rotation.

7. Assign the following initial parameter values to the **rotationValue** component instance:

    Editable: False

    Labels: 0 degrees, 30 degrees, 150 degrees, 260 degrees

    Data: 0, 30, 150, 260

    Row Count: 3

    Change Handler: generalHandler

You'll notice that the labels we've used are a bit more descriptive than the actual associated data values. Since we've assigned associated data values to the labels, selecting an item on the list will set this component instance's value to that data value rather than the label value of the selected item. If we had not assigned data values, the label values would be used instead, which in some cases would be OK, but not for this project. The reason for this is that the value returned by this component instance will be used to set the rotation of the **mySquare** instance. This value can only be set using a numeric value of 0, 30, or 150. Values of "0 degrees," 30 degrees," and so on (label values) would not work.

When the value of this component changes, the `generalHandler()` function is called. (We'll define that function shortly.)

8. With the Components panel open, click and drag another ComboBox component instance onto the stage.

9. With the Property inspector open, select this instance and give it a name of **alphaValue**.

   This component instance will control the transparency of the movie clip.

10. Assign the following initial parameter values to the **alphaValue** component instance:

    Editable: False

    Labels: 100 percent, 75 percent, 50 percent, 25 percent, 0 percent

    Data: 100, 75, 50, 25, 0

    Row Count: 3

    Change Handler: generalHandler

    Notice that the Change Handler function for this component instance is the same as the one defined for the other **rotationValue** instance, as shown in Step 5. (We'll explain this shortly.)

11. With the Actions Panel open, select Frame 1 on the timeline and add the following script:

    ```
    function generalHandler(currentComponent){
      if(currentComponent._name == "rotationValue"){
        mySquare._rotation = currentComponent.getValue();
      }else if(currentComponent._name == "alphaValue"){
        mySquare._alpha = currentComponent.getValue();
      }
    }
    ```

This function—which we defined as the Change Handler function for *both* the **rotationValue** and the **alphaValue** instances—is called whenever an item is selected from either instance.

As mentioned earlier, any time a Change Handler function is called by a component instance, a reference to that instance is passed to the function as a parameter. This parameter value is really only useful when a single function is identified as the Change Handler function for multiple components (so that the function knows which component is calling it, and thus which set of actions to execute).

In this example, we've given the passed reference a function parameter name of currentComponent. Use of that parameter name within the function definition is actually a reference to the calling component. Thus, if the component instance named **rotationValue** calls this function (as the result of its value changing), the function parameter, currentComponent, is replaced with rotationValue. In such a case, currentComponent._name would be evaluated as rotationValue._name.

This function uses an if statement to determine the name of the calling component: **mySquare's** rotation is then set based on the currently selected value of the **rotationValue** component instance, *or* its alpha is set based on the currently selected value of the **alphaValue** component instance.

12. Choose Control > Test Movie.

    Selecting a value from either Combo Box instance results in an immediate change to the **mySquare** instance (**Figure 15.15**).

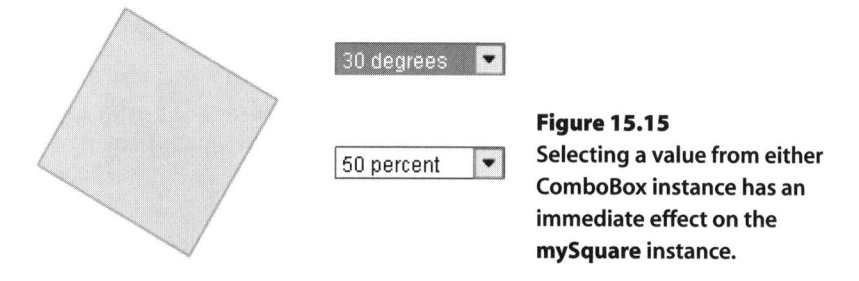

Figure 15.15
Selecting a value from either ComboBox instance has an immediate effect on the **mySquare** instance.

NOTE *A completed version of this exercise (named combobox.fla) can be found in the Chapter 15/Assets folder on the accompanying CD.*

ListBox Component

ListBox component instances display a list of items from which the user can select one or more choices. If the number of items exceeds the number that can be displayed (due to the vertical size of the ListBox instance), a scroll bar is automatically added to the ListBox instance. You can use this type of component not only to create Flash-based forms that use list boxes for selecting or entering choices, but for any type of interaction where a menu of multiple selectable choices might be useful.

ListBox component instances have the following Property inspector–based parameter settings:

- **Labels.** This is where you define the list of items that you want to appear. Each item will appear as a separate choice on the list box. You enter items via the Values dialog box.

- **Data.** This is a list of values associated with the items (labels) in the list box. It works just like the Data setting for ComboBox instances.

- **Select Multiple.** This setting determines whether multiple items can be selected from the list (true) or only single items can be selected (false). When this parameter is set to true, multiple items in the instance can be selected just as they are in an HTML list box.

- **ChangeHandler.** This optional setting lets you define the name of the function that's called when the value of this component instance changes (that is, a different item is selected from the list). This function must exist on the same timeline as the component instance.

In the following simple exercise, we'll show you how to use an instance of the ListBox component to display a list of Macromedia products. The user will be able to select the Macromedia products they own, and the selected items will immediately be output to a text field.

To use an instance of the ListBox component to display a list of Macromedia products:

1. With the Components panel open, click and drag a ListBox component instance onto the stage.

2. With the Property inspector open, select this instance and give it the name **myProducts**.

3. Assign the following initial parameter values to **myProducts**:

   Labels: Flash MX, Dreamweaver MX, Fireworks MX, ColdFusion MX, Director, FreeHand, Sitespring

   Data: Leave blank

   Select Multiple: True

   Change Handler: updateText

   You'll notice we've left the Data setting blank; thus, when an item is selected, the label value itself will be used.

   When the value of this component is changed (that is, a selection is made), the updateText() function will be called. (We'll define this function shortly.)

4. Select the Text tool on the Drawing toolbar. In the Property inspector, configure the text block that you are about to create using the following settings:

   Type: Dynamic Text

   Font: _sans

   Font Color: Black

   Font Size: 14

   Line Type: Multiline

   Show Border: Selected

5. Click and drag on the stage to create a square text field just to the right of the ListBox component instance you added in Step 1 (**Figure 15.16**).

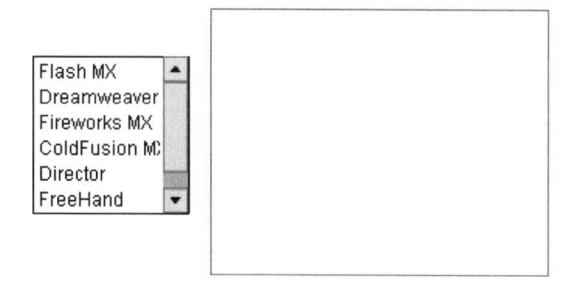

   Figure 15.16
   Place a text field on the stage, just to the right of the ListBox instance. Make sure the text box is long enough to display several lines of text.

6. With the Property inspector open, select the text field and give it an instance name of **myOutput**.

7. With the Actions panel open, select Frame 1 on the timeline and add the following script:

```
function updateText(){
  myOutput.text = "You have the following Macromedia products:" + newline;
  productsArray = myProducts.getSelectedItems();
  for(i = 0; i <= productsArray.length; ++i){
    myOutput.text += productsArray[i].label + newline;
  }
}
```

This function is called any time an item is selected from the **myProducts** list box instance.

The first thing this function does is output the first line that should appear in the **myOutput** text field. This line of text—"You have the following Macromedia products:"— simply acts as a header. The newline action is used to create a line break.

Next, using the getSelectItems() method, the function creates an array named productsArray and populates it with the label and data values of any items selected in the **myProducts** list box. For example, if Flash MX and Dreamweaver MX are currently selected, this array would contain two elements, and its structure would look like the following (**Figure 15.17**):

[label: "Flash MX", data: undefined][label: "Dreamweaver MX", data: undefined]

Thus:

productsArray[0].label; //returns "Flash MX"

productsArray[0].data; // returns undefined

productsArray[1].label; //returns "Dreamweaver MX"

productsArray[1].data; //returns undefined

productsArray

[0] [1]

[**label**: "Flash MX", **data**: undefined][**label**: "Dreamweaver MX", **data**: undefined]

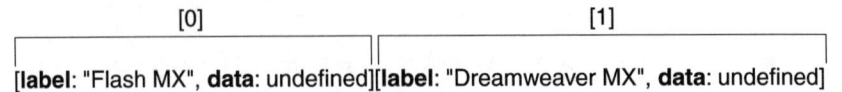

Figure 15.17
This graphic represents the structure of the productsArray array, if Flash MX and Dreamweaver MX were selected from the **myProducts** list box instance, and those selected values were retrieved using the getSelectedItems() method.

You will need to understand this structure to comprehend how the for loop (which appears next in the script) works. This loop is set up to loop through all the elements currently in the productsArray array. It does this by checking the length property of that array. Thus, if productsArray contains two elements (that is, the user has selected two items in the list box), this loop will execute twice. Using the current value of i (which increases by one with each iteration of the loop), the label value of the currently referenced array element is added to the **myOutput** text field. For example, on the first loop, the expression inside the loop will be evaluated as follows:

```
myOutput.text = productsArray[0].label + newline;
```

In our example, this will add the text "Flash MX," followed by a line break, to the text that already appears in the **myOutput** text field (which at this point is only the header). With the next loop, the expression inside the loop will be evaluated as follows:

```
myOutput.text = productsArray[1].label + newline;
```

In our example, this will add the text "Dreamweaver MX," followed by a line break, to that which already appears in the **myOutput** text field (which at this point includes the header and the text "Flash MX."

Since this function is called every time the value of the list box changes, the **myOutput** text field will be updated each time items are selected or deselected.

8. Choose Control > Test Movie.

   Selecting items on the list will update the output that appears in the **myOutput** text field (**Figure 15.18**).

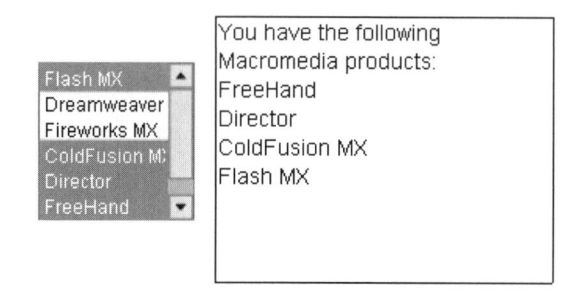

Figure 15.18
Selecting items on the list automatically updates the text displayed in the **myOutput** text field.

NOTE *A completed version of this exercise (named listbox.fla) can be found in the Chapter 15/Assets folder on the accompanying CD.*

PushButton Component

PushButton component instances are nothing more than enhanced buttons that you can control via methods in many of the same ways as you can other types of components. Why would you want to use a PushButton instance when it's so easy to create custom buttons? The advantage is that you can apply global styles to component instances via some simple ActionScript—say, for, example, making all of your component instances red.

All of your application's interface elements can benefit from this streamlined styling if you use PushButton component instances rather than custom-created buttons. For some people, this is a big selling point; for others it's not. You'll need to decide which makes the most sense for your projects.

PushButton component instances have the following Property inspector–based parameter settings:

- **Label.** This represents the text that should appear above the button.

- **ChangeHandler.** This setting defines the function that's called when the button is pressed. Keep in mind that this function must exist on the same timeline as the component instance. While you can decide whether or not you want to use Change Handler functions for other component instances, Push-Button instances are pretty much useless without them because their sole purpose is to execute actions when pressed.

PushButton component instances are simple enough that we won't include an exercise to demonstrate their use. Instead, here's what a simple Change Handler function that's called by a PushButton instance might look like:

```
function pushHandler(){
    getUrl("http://www.derekfranklin.com");
}
```

RadioButton Component

Used in groups, RadioButton Component instances allow users to make a single choice from an finite group of choices—similar to the buttons on your radio that let you choose from a number of preset stations. While you can use this functionality to create a rockin' MP3 player, you can also use RadioButton instances as a straightforward way of collecting data from users, setting site preferences, and more.

RadioButton component instances have the following Property inspector–based parameter settings:

- **Label.** This represents the text that should appear next to the component instance. A string value should be entered.

- **Initial State.** This represents the component instance's initial state. From the provided menu, you can select a value of `true` or `false`. If set to `true`, the component instance will initially appear selected. If set to `false`, it will appear deselected.

- **Group Name.** This represents the name of the group that a particular instance belongs to. When several instances have the same Group Name setting, Flash treats them as a group. This means you can only select one instance in the group at a time. (Selecting a particular instance in a group automatically causes all of the other instances in that group to be deselected.) When a particular instance in a group is selected, the *group* value is that instance's value. Selecting a different instance will update the group's value (**Figure 15.19**). This will become clearer in the exercise that follows.

- **Data.** This is the data value associated with the instance.

- **Label Placement.** This represents the location of the text label that appears next to the component instance. You can select a value of Left or Right from the menu provided.

- **ChangeHandler.** This optional setting represents the name of the function that's called when the component instance's value changes. This function must exist on the same timeline as the component instance.

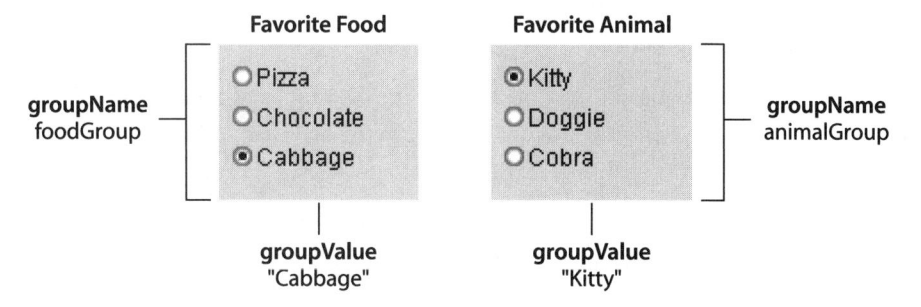

Figure 15.19
The RadioButton instances on the left have their Group Name parameter values set to *foodGroup*, making them all part of a group. When the *Cabbage* radio button is pressed, the group's value becomes "Cabbage."

The following simple exercise demonstrates how to use two groups of radio buttons to control a movie clip instance. You will use one group to navigate the instance's timeline and the other group to control its size.

To use two groups of radio buttons to control a movie clip instance:

1. Select the Text tool on the Drawing toolbar. In the Property inspector, configure the text block you are about to create using the following settings:

    Type: Static Text

    Font: _sans

    Font Color: Black

    Font Size: 96

2. Click on the stage to create a text label, then press the *1* key on the keyboard.

3. Choose Insert > Convert to Symbol to convert this text label into a movie clip.

4. On the Convert to Symbol dialog box, give the clip a name (any name), and be sure to assign it a Movie Clip Behavior. Then click OK.

5. Double-click the instance that's on the stage to edit it in place.

    This takes you to this movie clip's timeline. That timeline currently has one layer—Layer 1—which contains the text label you created in Step 2.

6. Double-click this layer's name and rename it Text.

7. On the timeline, click and drag from Frame 2 to Frame 4.

    This will select Frames 2, 3, and 4.

8. Choose Modify > Frames > Convert to Keyframes to convert the selected frames to keyframes.

9. Move the playhead to Frame 2. Select the Text tool and replace the "1" that appears in the text label with a "2." Move the playhead to Frames 3 and 4 and replace the text in those labels the same way, using "3" and "4," respectively.

    The timeline should now have four frames, each with a text label containing the number of the current frame (**Figure 15.20**).

Chapter 15 **Components**

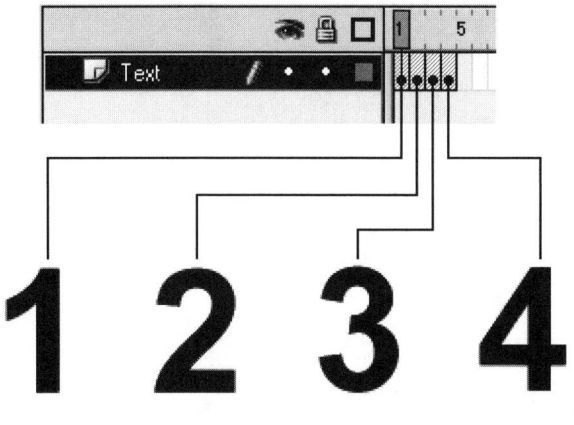

Figure 15.20
Frames 1 through 4 should have corresponding numbers appearing on the stage.

10. Add a new layer above the Text layer and name it Actions.

    This layer will contain some ActionScript.

11. With the Actions panel open, select Frame 1 of the Actions layer and place a stop() action there.

    This will prevent the timeline from moving until we instruct it to.

12. Return to the main timeline. Select the instance we've been working on and assign it an instance name of **numbersClip** in the Property inspector.

13. With the Components panel open, click and drag four RadioButton component instances onto the stage and place them in a vertical column.

    These will comprise a radio button group.

14. Drag another two instances of the RadioButton component onto the stage. Place these in a vertical column as well, just below the group of four added in the previous step.

    These will comprise a separate radio button group.

15. With the Property inspector open, select the top RadioButton instance from the group of four added in Step 13, and assign it the following settings:

    Label: Go to 1
    Initial State: True
    Group Name: gotoGroup
    Data: 1
    Label Placement: Right
    Change Handler: gotoFunction

611

This instance will be part of the radio button group named gotoGroup (see the Group Name parameter value). In a moment, we'll make the other three instances we initially dragged onto the stage part of this group. We've given this instance an initial state of True; it will be the initially selected button in the group. Its Data value is simply 1. Lastly, note that the Change Handler function defined is named gotoFunction. We will define this function shortly.

16. Assign the same parameter settings (as shown in the previous step) to the three remaining instances in this group—with the following exceptions:

Label: Go to 2, Go to 3, and Go to 4, respectively

Initial State: False

Data: 2, 3, and 4, respectively

17. Select the top RadioButton instance in the group of two that you added in Step 14, and give it the following settings:

Label: 100 percent

Initial State: true

Group Name: resizeGroup

Data: 100

Label Placement: Right

Change Handler: resizeFunction

This instance will be part of the radio button group named resizeGroup (see the Group Name parameter value). We've given this instance an initial state of True; its Data value is 100. Lastly, note that the Change Handler function defined is named resizeFunction. We will define this function shortly.

18. Give the remaining instance in this group the same parameter settings as those we just configured—with the following exceptions:

Label: 50 percent

Label: 50 percent

Initial State: False

Data: 50

Now that we've set up our project elements (**Figure 15.21**), it's time to script our Change Handler functions.

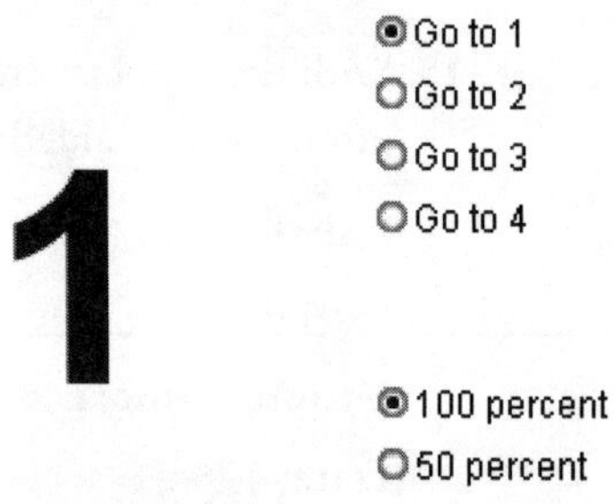

⦿ Go to 1
○ Go to 2
○ Go to 3
○ Go to 4

⦿ 100 percent
○ 50 percent

Figure 15.21
This is how the elements in this exercise should appear.

19. Add a layer to the main timeline and name it Actions. With the Actions panel open, select Frame 1 of this layer and add the following script:

```
function gotoFunction(){
  numbersClip.gotoAndStop(gotoGroup.getValue());
}
```

This function—which is called each time a user presses one of the radio buttons in the gotoGroup—simply moves the **numbersClip**'s timeline to a frame number based on the current value of the gotoGroup. The group value is based on whichever button in the group is currently selected. Since our four radio buttons have Data values of 1, 2, 3, and 4, respectively, pressing a button in the group will move the **numbersClip** instance to Frame 1, 2, 3, or 4.

20. Add the following script to the end of the script you added in the previous step:

```
function resizeFunction(){
  scaleValue = resizeGroup.getValue();
  numbersClip._xscale = scaleValue;
  numbersClip._yscale = scaleValue;
}
```

This function—which is called each time a user presses one of the radio buttons from the resizeGroup—simply scales the **numbersClip** based on the current value of the resizeGroup. The group value is based on whichever button in the group is currently selected. Since our two radio buttons have data values of 100 and 50, pressing a button in the group will scale the **numbersClip** instance to 100 percent or 50 percent.

21. Choose Control > Test Movie.

Pressing various RadioButton instances will affect the **numbersClip** as described.

NOTE *A completed version of this exercise (named radiobuttons.fla) can be found in the Chapter 15/Assets folder on the accompanying CD.*

ScrollBar Component

You can attach ScrollBar component instances to text fields and use them to scroll the text they contain, or you can use them as value sliders (where scrolling up and down changes an associated value). We'll look at both uses in this section.

NOTE *ScrollBar instances can only be used with dynamic or input text fields, not with static text fields.*

ScrollBar component instances have the following Property inspector–based parameter settings:

- **Target TextField.** This represents the text field instance that the ScrollBar component instance is associated with—that is, the field that contains the text that will be scrolled.

TIP *Dragging a ScrollBar instance from the Components panel and dropping it on top of a dynamic or input text field automatically attaches the instance to that field; it also sets the Target TextField parameter accordingly. Depending on where it's dropped, the instance will attach to the top, right, bottom, or left side of the field (**Figure 15.22**). Once a ScrollBar instance has been attached to a particular text field, you can still drag and drop it elsewhere—either onto a different side of the text field or to a different field entirely.*

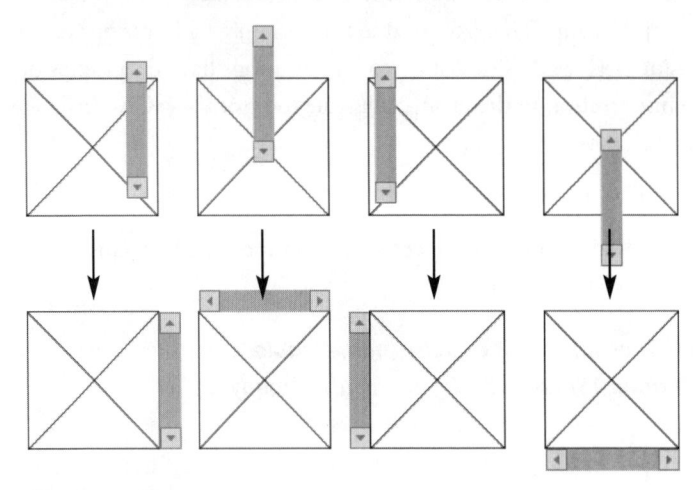

Figure 15.22
A ScrollBar component instance will "snap" to one side of a text field instance, depending on where it is dropped on screen. Here, the box represents a text field instance, and the X inside the box represents the four invisible quadrants of the field, which determine where a ScrollBar instance attaches to when dropped.

- **Horizontal.** This represents the instance's orientation. When set to True, the instance will appear horizontal and it will scroll text from left to right (rather than from top to bottom).

To use a ScrollBar Component instance to scroll text in a text field:

1. Select the Text tool on the Drawing toolbar. In the Property inspector, configure the text block you are about to create using the following settings:

   Type: Dynamic Text
   Font: _sans
   Font Color: Black
   Font Size: 14
   Line Type: Multiline
   Show Border: Selected

2. Click and drag on the stage to create a rectangular field (be careful not to make it too wide or too tall).

3. Hold down the Shift key and double-click the small, white square that appears on the bottom right corner of the field.

   This should change the square's color from white to black. You can now enter text into the field, which will not expand vertically to accommodate the text entered (that is, the field will remain the same size regardless of how much text you enter) (**Figure 15.23**). This is important for our exercise because scroll bars are used to scroll text in a field that's not large enough to display all of the entered text.

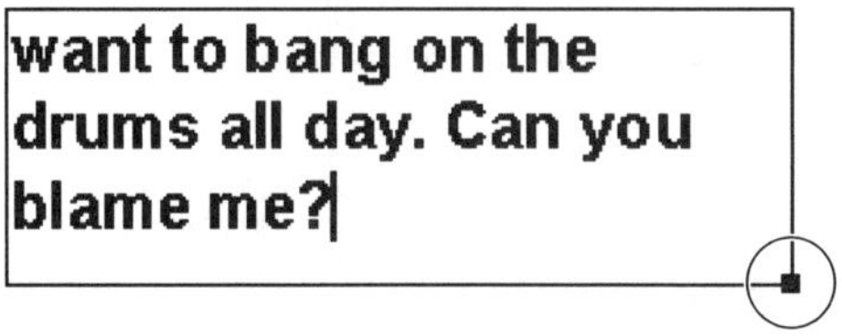

Figure 15.23
Double-clicking the small square on the bottom-right corner of a field will turn the square black, indicating that text can be entered into the field and it will not expand vertically.

4. With the Property inspector open, give the selected text field an instance name of **myText**.

5. Type 15 or 20 lines of text into this field.

   To quickly fill the field with lines of text, you can type a single letter and then hit Enter/Return, another letter and Enter/Return, and so on.

6. With the Components panel open, click and drag a ScrollBar component instance onto the stage. Drop it over the right side of the text field.

   The instance should attach itself to the right side of the text field. If not, click, drag, and drop again until it does. If the Property inspector is open and the ScrollBar instance is selected, you'll notice that the Target TextField parameter setting has been automatically set for the **myText** instance.

7. Choose Control > Test Movie.

   Try interacting with the ScrollBar instance as you would with a typical scroll bar in order to scroll the text in the **myText** text field.

   NOTE *A completed version of this exercise (named scrollbar1.fla) can be found in the Chapter 15/Assets folder on the accompanying CD.*

To use a ScrollBar component as a slider:

1. Select the Rectangle tool and draw a square (any color and size) in the middle of the stage.

2. With the square selected, choose Insert > Convert to Symbol to turn this square into a movie clip instance.

3. On the Convert to Symbol dialog box, give this symbol a name (any name), then select the Movie Clip Behavior option. Also, select the center box on the Registration graphic, then click OK.

   Using a ScrollBar component instance (which we'll add shortly), we'll control the rotation of the square that appears on the stage.

4. With the Property inspector open, select the square instance and name it **mySquare**.

5. With the Components panel open, select a ScrollBar component instance and drag it onto the stage, below the **mySquare** instance.

6. With the component instance selected, leave its Target TextField parameter setting blank, but set its Horizontal parameter to True.

   This will change the ScrollBar instance's orientation to horizontal.

7. With the component instance still selected, give it an instance name of **slider**.

8. With the Actions panel open, select Frame 1 on the timeline and add the following script:

```
slider.setScrollProperties(100, 0, 360);
function sliderFunction(){
   mySquare._rotation = slider.getScrollPosition();
}
slider.setChangeHandler("sliderFunction");
```

The first line in this script is used to set the properties of the **slider** ScrollBar instance. Normally, when a ScrollBar instance is attached to a text field, these settings are adjusted automatically. However, because here our ScrollBar instance is not attached to a text field, we'll need to set these manually, as shown. Notice that the setScrollProperties() method has three parameters: For this exercise, the first parameter value will set the size of the scroll handle that appears on the instance (the larger the value, the larger the handle); the second and third parameter values set the minimum and maximum values the instance will return as it is scrolled (**Figure 15.24**).

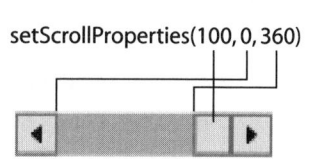

Figure 15.24
This graphic demonstrates how the three parameters for the setScrollProperties() method are set in relation to a ScrollBar instance.

The next three lines in the script are used to define a Change Handler function that we'll shortly set for the ScrollBar instance. Each time this function is called, it will set the rotation value of the **mySquare** instance based on the current position of the **slider** scroll bar instance. Since scrolling the **slider** ScrollBar instance is set up to return a value between 0 and 360, the **mySquare** instance can be rotated between 0 and 360 degrees.

The last line of the script sets the sliderFunction() as the Change Handler function for the **slider** ScrollBar instance. Each time the scroll bar is moved, that function is called—thus rotating **mySquare**.

9. Choose Control > Test Movie.

Using the slider instance in this way automatically rotates the **mySquare** instance. Is that cool, or what!? This is one of the easiest ways to create volume and value-setting controls—as well as any other setting where a slider would come in handy.

NOTE *A completed version of this exercise (named scrollbar2.fla) can be found in the Chapter 15 folder on the accompanying CD.*

{ **ActionScript** } The ScrollBar component comes with a number of methods that allow you to control text scrolling via ActionScript—useful if you want to create a set of buttons at the top of a text field to act as bookmarks. By pressing a Bookmark button, you would cause the text field to automatically scroll to a specific point in the text. For more information on ActionScript, see Chapter 16, "Using ActionScript in Your Projects."

ScrollPane Component

ScrollPane component instances are used to display content whose dimensions exceed those of the window containing it. To view content within a scroll pane, the user either employs the attached scroll bars to move the content back and forth vertically and horizontally, or he or she click-drags the content within the window. You can put just about any type of Flash content within a scroll pane—anything from a movie clip in the library (which has been given an identifier name) to a movie clip instance on the stage or even an externally loaded movie or JPG. This component is particularly useful for displaying large maps, schematics, charts, and more (**Figure 15.25**).

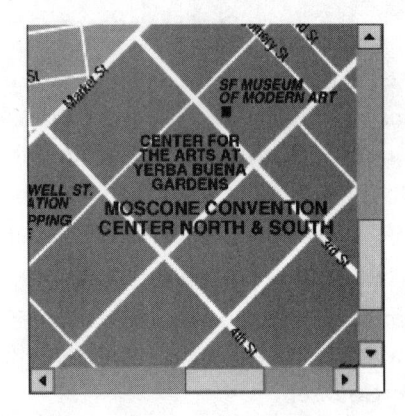

Figure 15.25
Scroll panes are ideal for displaying large graphics (such as a map) within a defined area.

ScrollPane component instances have the following Property inspector–based parameter settings:

- **Scroll Content.** This is the identifier name of the movie clip in the library that will comprise the content for this ScrollPane instance.

{ **ActionScript** } Unfortunately, if you set this parameter via the Property inspector, it will only accept the identifier name of a clip in the library. To place a movie clip instance on the stage, or an externally loaded movie within this instance, you must use the `setScrollContent()` method. For more information, see Chapter 16, "Using ActionScript in Your Projects."

- **Horizontal Scroll.** This setting determines whether a horizontal scroll bar appears on the ScrollPane instance. You can use the menu provided to select a value of True, False, or Auto. If you set the parameter to True, a horizontal scroll bar will appear. If set to False, it will not appear. If set to Auto, a scroll bar will only appear when necessary (if the content loaded into the scroll pane is larger than the actual pane, which it may not always be).

- **Vertical Scroll.** This setting determines whether a vertical scroll bar appears on the ScrollPane instance. The menu options are the same as for the Horizontal Scroll setting.

- **Drag Content.** This setting determines whether you can click and drag the pane's content without interacting with scroll bars. From the menu provided, you can select a value of True or False. If the parameter is set to True, users will be able to click and drag the content within the pane. If set to False, this type of interaction isn't enabled.

TIP *When you set the Drag Content value to True, you may want to turn off/remove the vertical and horizontal scroll bars to create a sleeker design. If you choose this approach, however, be sure to let users know that they can drag and click the content—otherwise they may not realize this is the case.*

The following simple exercise demonstrates how to use an instance of the ScrollPane component.

To use a ScrollPane Component instance to display a large movie clip (loaded from the library):

1. Choose Insert > New Symbol to create a new symbol.

2. In the Insert New Symbol dialog box, give the symbol a name and select the Movie Clip Behavior option, then click OK.

    The authoring environment changes to symbol-editing mode, with the new symbol's timeline as the active timeline.

3. Select the Oval tool and draw a large circle (the size of the entire stage perhaps) with a radial gradient fill.

   There's no technical reason for using a radial gradient fill—it's just that flat-filled graphics were beginning to get boring!

   If you want, you can add additional content to this graphic (for example, text).

4. Return to the main timeline. Choose Window > Library to open the Library panel.

5. Locate the symbol you created: Right-click (Control-click on a Mac) its name and choose Linkage from the menu that appears.

6. In the Linkage Properties dialog box that appears, choose the Export for Action-Script option and give the symbol an identifier name of bigMovie, then click OK (**Figure 15.26**).

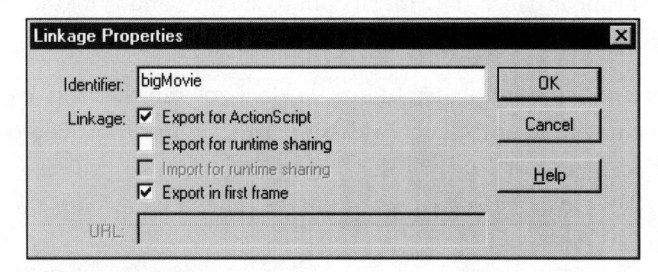

Figure 15.26
By assigning an identifier to the movie clip you created (such as *bigMovie*), you "identify" it in the library so that instances of it can be placed in a movie via ActionScript.

   Remember this name.

   In this context, setting up linkage is just a way of identifying our symbol in the library so that instances of it can be pulled from the library dynamically—that is, while the movie plays.

7. With the Components panel open, click and drag a ScrollPane instance onto the middle of the stage.

8. With the instance selected, select the Free Transform tool on the Drawing toolbar and resize the instance so that it's approximately 25 percent larger than its default size.

9. With the Property inspector open, assign the following parameter settings to the ScrollPane instance:

   Scroll Content: bigMovie

   Horizontal Scroll: Auto

   Vertical Scroll: Auto

   Drag Content: True

   If the parameters are set as shown above, the symbol in the library named bigMovie will be placed in the ScrollPane instance when it loads. Scroll bars will automatically appear if the content within the pane is larger than the pane itself. In addition, with the Drag Content parameter set to True, users can move the pane by clicking and dragging it.

10. Choose Control > Test Movie.

    When the ScrollPane instance appears, you can see that an instance of the bigMovie clip appears within it. By moving the scroll bars or click-dragging the content, you can move it around the pane.

NOTE *A completed version of this exercise (named scrollpane.fla) can be found in the Chapter 15/Assets folder on the CD that accompanies this book.*

Customizing Flash's Built-In Components

As you've no doubt noticed, Flash's built-in screen components have been styled to resemble their battleship-gray Windows-interface counterparts—for most of us, the visual equivalent of nails screeching over a chalkboard. Luckily the engineers at Macromedia have provided a way to customize them.

Actually, they've provided *two* ways to customize the look of components: via style sheets (to alter colors or basic text properties), or via component skins (graphic elements that can be used to create more elaborate effects). Think of them this way: To give a car a new paint job, you would use style sheets; however, if you needed to turn that car into a NASCAR vehicle, component skins would be the way to go. We'll discuss style-based options first, then look at how to use component skins.

Component Style Properties

Although most components *look* like they're made up of just a few parts, they actually incorporate all kinds of separate elements—everything from arrows to lines, boxes, circles, fonts, and more. Flash MX allows you to customize all of these parts by changing their color, size, and (in the case of fonts) style. The settings that determine a component's appearance are known as *style properties*. You'll find a complete list of the style properties available for Flash's built-in components in the Action panel's Toolbox List window, under Flash UI Components/FStyleFormat/Properties (**Figure 15.27**).

In many cases, the name given to a style property makes it obvious which element of the component it affects. For example, the *arrow* property represents the arrow graphic found on scroll bars and combo boxes. Changing its value will change the color of the arrow "part" of a component.

The functions of other style properties are less obvious, meaning you may have to experiment a bit to determine their function.

Keep in mind that these different component parts are nothing more than movie clip instances—and that a single component contains a number of smaller movie clip instances. We'll tinker with these individual clips later in this section.

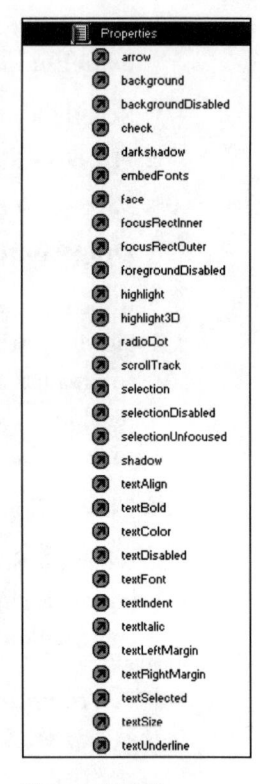

Figure 15.27
This graphic displays the list of component properties that can be styled via ActionScript.

Making Global Style Changes to Component Instances

Customizing all of a project's component instances is one way to give it a consistent look and feel. You can accomplish this by setting style property values for the globalStyleFormat object—the object you use to perform global changes to color and text styles for all component instances in a movie. For example, if you want all of your movie's component instance to have red "faces" (not due to embarrassment—*face* is actually the name of a style property of component instances), you would use the following syntax:

```
globalStyleFormat.face = 0xFF3300;
globalStyleFormat.applyChanges();
```

The first line in this script is used to define the property and its new value; the second line is used to update all component instances accordingly. Changes will only take effect after the applyChanges() method has been invoked.

Most styling done with this object simply involves changing the colors of component properties.

NOTE *When setting color values for style properties, always use the format 0xRRGGBB.*

Styling Groups of Component Instances

In some cases, global changes may not be appropriate for your component instances. If, for example, as the result of some user interaction, such as selecting an item from a menu, you wanted to highlight a group of component instances by changing their colors, you would use the FStyleFormat object—a special object used to style several component instances simultaneously.

To use the FStyleFormat object:

1. Create a new instance of the FStyleFormat object.

For example, to create a new FStyleFormat object named myCustomStyle, you would use the following:

```
myCustomStyle = new FStyleFormat();
```

2. Specify the style properties of that object (for example, face, arrow, and so on).

For example:

```
myCustomStyle.face = 0xFF3300;
myCustomStyle.arrow = 0xFF3300;
```

3. Link the component instances you wish to style with this object using the addListener() method.

For example, assume there are a couple of component instances on the stage named **myList** and **myButton**. To tie these component instances to the myCustomStyle object you would use the following syntax:

```
myCustomStyle.addListener(mylist, myButton);
```

4. Use the applyChanges() method to make myCustomStyle object affect the component instances tied to it.

For example, myCustomStyle.applyChanges();.

To help demonstrate how this works, in the following exercise we'll style some component instances to be red, and some to be blue.

To style groups of component instances using the FStyleFormat object:

1. With the Components panel open, drag a CheckBox, RadioButton, and PushButton component instance onto the stage. Place them in a column on the left side of the stage.

2. Name the component instances as follows:

CheckBox: **redCheck**

RadioButton: **redRadio**

PushButton: **redPush**

3. With the **redPush** PushButton instance selected, assign it a label of Red and a Click Handler (also known as a Change Handler) function of styleHandler (**Figure 15.28**).

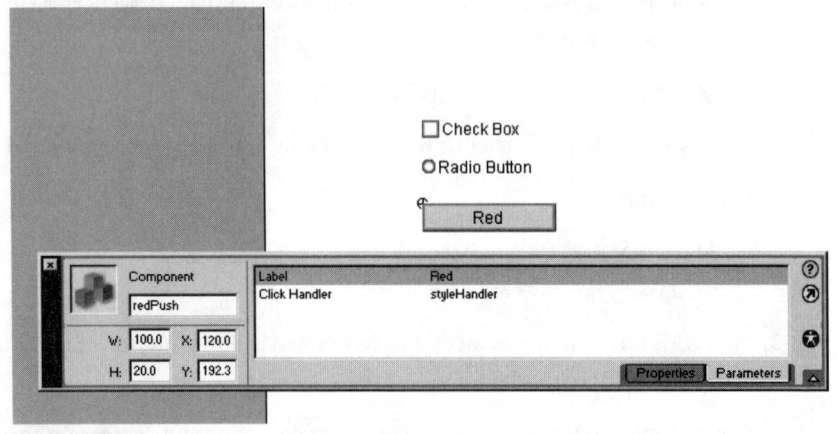

Figure 15.28
Select the **redPush** push button instance, and assign it the parameter settings shown in this graphic.

4. Select all three component instances (by holding down the Shift key and selecting them), then choose Edit > Duplicate to create duplicates of each. Move these duplicates to the right side of the stage.

5. Name these duplicate instances as follows:

CheckBox: **blueCheck**

RadioButton: **blueRadio**

PushButton: **bluePush**

6. With the **bluePush** push button instance selected, assign it a label of Blue and a Click Handler function of styleHandler.

Note that the two PushButton component instances use the same Change Handler function. We will define that function next.

7. With the Actions panel open, select Frame 1 and add the following script:

```
function styleHandler(currentComponent){
  if(currentComponent._name == "redPush"){
    redComponentStyle = new FStyleFormat();
    redComponentStyle.face = 0xFF3300;
    redComponentStyle.check = 0xFF3300;
    redComponentStyle.radioDot = 0xFF3300;
    redComponentStyle.addListener(redCheck, redRadio, redPush);
    redComponentStyle.applyChanges();
  }else if(currentComponent._name == "bluePush"){
    blueComponentStyle = new FStyleFormat();
    blueComponentStyle.face = 0x0066CC;
    blueComponentStyle.check = 0x0066CC;
    blueComponentStyle.radioDot = 0x0066CC;
    blueComponentStyle.addListener(blueCheck, blueRadio, bluePush);
    blueComponentStyle.applyChanges();
  }
}
```

This function is called each time the **redPush** or **bluePush** PushButton instance is pressed. An if statement is used to determine which instance calls it. For example, the first part of the if statement says that if the **redPush** instance is the calling instance, then a new FStyleFormat object is created and named redComponentStyle. The next three lines in the script are used to define the color (red) of the face, check, and radioDot properties for that Style object. The next line ties the **redCheck**, **redRadio**, and **redPush** component instances to that Style object. As a result, the next line, which uses the applyChanges() method, will cause those instances to reflect the color values for various properties as defined by the redComponentStyle object. The else if part of this if statement determines what happens when the **bluePush** component instance is pressed—basically the same process as described above but using the blueComponentStyle and a different color value (blue), and affecting the component instances on the right of the stage.

8. Choose Control > Test Movie.

   Press the CheckBox and RadioButton on the left side of the stage, then press the PushButton instance labeled Red. This will cause the component instances on that side of the stage to turn red. Do the same thing with the component instances on the right side of the stage, and they'll turn blue (**Figure 15.29**). Being able to easily customize movie elements like this can be extremely useful in putting together your movie.

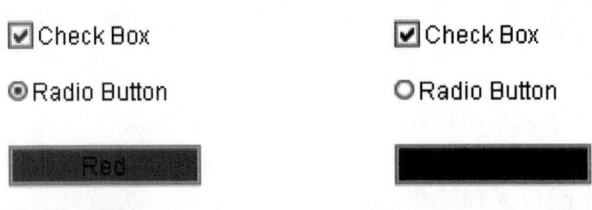

Figure 15.29
The component instances on the right have red properties, while the component instances on the right have blue properties.

TIPS *A single component instance can be tied to multiple Style objects. Whenever changes are applied to any of these Style objects, the component instance will be updated accordingly.*

If you want to disassociate a component instance from a style object, use the removeListener() *method. For example,* blueComponentStyle.removeListener(blueCheck); *will unlink the **blueCheck** instance from the* blueComponentStyle *object. Thus, any subsequent changes to that style object will not be reflected in the **blueCheck** instance.*

NOTE *A completed version of this exercise (named FStyleFormat.fla) can be found in the Chapter 15/Assets folder on the CD that accompanies this book.*

Styling Individual Component Instances

Once you know how to globally style components, as well as how to style groups of components, styling individual component instances should be a breeze. All components have a setStyleProperty() method, which allows you to target specific component instances for styling. For example, to set the color of the radioDot property of a RadioButton instance named **fmRadio**, you would use the following syntax:

    fmRadio.setStyleProperty("radioDot", 0x0066CC);

Simple indeed!

NOTE *While styling components via the globalStyleFormat and FStyleFormat objects requires that you use the* applyChanges() *method for the associated styling changes to take effect, use of the* setStyleProperty() *method does not. Changes to the specified component instance occur as soon as the method is invoked.*

Customizing Skins

Although the methods we've described thus far work fine for color changes and text formatting, if you want more detailed effects—for instance, gradient or animated fills for your components—you'll need to lift the hood and tinker with components at their most basic level: the various movie clip instances that comprise them.

To get started, we'll customize the most basic component type: the PushButton component. (Keep in mind that customizing the skin of any type of component is very similar.)

To customize the skin of the PushButton component:

1. With the Components panel open, click and drag a PushButton component instance onto the stage.

2. Open the Library panel by choosing Window > Library. Expand the folders in this path: Flash UI Components/Component Skins/FPushButtonSkins.

    When a component instance is placed within a project, the various "skins" that make up that component are placed in a folder within the Flash UI Components/Component Skins folder. In this case you'll see that by placing the PushButton component instance in your project, you've caused the FPushButton Skins folder to be placed inside this folder.

The FPushButton Skins folder contains all of the skins unique to PushButton instances (**Figure 15.30**). Note that the FPushButton Skins folder contains the following four skins (movie clips):

fpb_disabled
fpb_down
fpb_over
fpb_up

By editing these clips, we can significantly change the look of PushButton component instances in our project. Let's do that now.

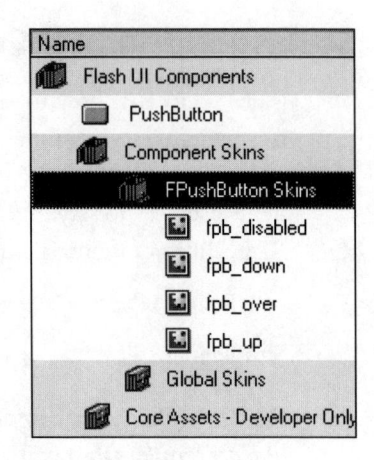

Figure 15.30
The FpushButton Skins folder contains all of the skins that make up the PushButton component.

3. From the Library panel, double-click the clip named **fpb_up**.

   This will put the authoring environment in symbol-editing mode and make the **fpb_up** movie clip's timeline the active timeline. You will now be able to see the skin elements that dictate the appearance of PushButton instances in their Up state. Although it may not be obvious initially, five individual movie clips make up this state (**Figure 15.31**). We will edit several of these to improve the appearance of component instances in our project.

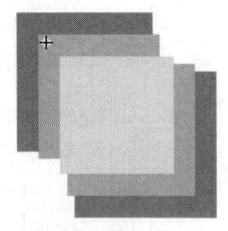

Figure 15.31
This graphic shows the five skin elements that define the appearance of the *up* state of PushButton components.

4. With the Arrow tool, double-click the movie clip instance in the center (the one that resembles a light-gray square) named **frame5**.

   This will make that clip's timeline the active timeline in the authoring environment. This clip contains nothing but a vector shape, colored gray. We'll now animate this timeline to make the clip appear to pulsate.

5. Add keyframes at Frames 7 and 15 of this timeline.

6. At Frame 7, select the gray square on the stage and color it white.

7. Create shape tweens from Frame 1 to Frame 7 and from Frame 7 to Frame 15, then navigate back to the **fpb_up** timeline.

8. On the stage, double-click the instance named **frame3** so that you can edit its content.

9. Select the shape in the middle of the stage and give it a white-to-black gradient fill.

10. Navigate back to the **fpb_up** timeline, select the instance named **frame4**, and repeat the instructions in Step 9.

11. Choose Control > Test Movie.

    The instance that you originally dragged onto the stage should appear—pulsating and with a portion of its outline appearing to have a gradient fill. Any additional PushButton instances you place in your project will share these characteristics because we've edited the component in its most basic form.

    So it's not Picasso—but at least it gives you an idea of what's possible as far as customizing a component's skin! Remember that for simple color transformations, you should stick with the Style objects and methods discussed earlier in this chapter. But if you want to add gradients and animations, customizing skins is the way to go.

NOTE *A completed version of this exercise (named custom skin.fla) can be found in the Chapter 15/Assets folder on the CD that accompanies this book.*

TIP *If you're unhappy with the changes you've made to a component skin, you can return it to its default appearance by dragging an instance of that component from the Components panel onto the stage.*

Registering Skins

Just as there's more than one way to skin a cat, there's more than one way to skin a component. In the last section, we looked at how to change the appearance of components by customizing their skins. In this section we'll go even further, by registering entirely new skins. When you *register* a skin, you create a new clip that represents a skin element of a component, then tell Flash to recognize that clip as such. In essence, you're creating a new skin from scratch (**Figure 15.32**).

Figure 15.32
Registering new skins allows you to dramatically change the look of components. Here we've registered new skins to change the look of the drop-down menu.

As discussed in the previous section, components are made up of parts, each of which comprises numerous skins. For example, a ScrollBar component *appears* to comprise four main pieces: the top and bottom scroll buttons, the scroll track (the bar that connects the top and bottom arrow buttons), and the thumb handle (the small handle that glides on the scroll track). However, in reality, that component comprises *ten* main parts—used to define its appearance when disabled, when arrow buttons are pressed, and so on (**Figure 15.33**). As you know, each of these skins is nothing more than a very basic movie clip instance. The movie clip instances that comprise a component have been intentionally "registered" to play a role in way the component looks. This means that someone—usually the component's developer—has created a graphic (such as an arrow), turned it into a movie clip instance, and then told Flash to *register*, or recognize, that instance as the arrow for the scroll-down or scroll-up button. Thus, for a single component (say, a scroll bar), many movie clip instances have been registered as the skins that comprise it. You register your skins via ActionScript, which you can easily access and change (as we'll do in the following exercise).

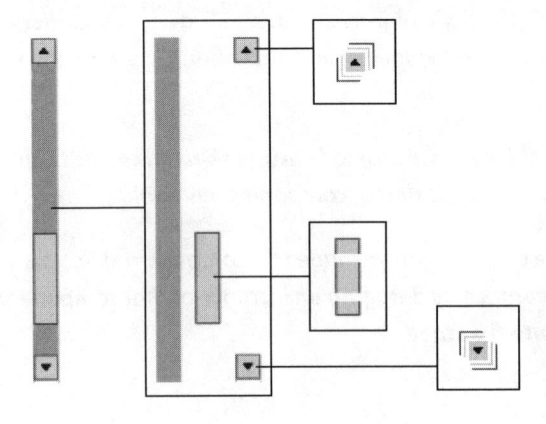

Figure 15.33
The ScrollBar Component broken down to its most basic elements.

So when we talk about registering a skin, we're describing a process in which you create a custom movie clip instance as a skin, then tell a component to recognize that movie clip instance as the new skin for the arrow or scroll track or whatever other component part you've defined. The following simple exercise shows how all of this is accomplished.

To register custom skins with a component:

1. With the Components panel open, drag an instance of the ComboBox component onto the stage.

We will register new skins for the arrow button that appears to the right of a ComboBox instance.

Chapter 15 **Components**

2. Open the Library panel. Navigate to the **fsb_downArrow** movie clip, located at: Flash UI Components/Component Skins/FScrollBar Skins.

   This movie clip is used not only as the down arrow for scroll bars, but also as the down arrow for combo boxes.

3. Double-click the **fsb_downArrow** name in the library to edit the clip. You may wish to zoom in by 800 percent to make it easier to work with the elements on the stage.

   You'll notice that this timeline contains two layers: Skin Elements and README. The Skins Elements layer contains all of the graphics that appear on the stage: six movie clip instances named **arrow_mc**, **face_mc**, **highlight_mc**, **shadow_mc**, **highlight3D_mc**, and **darkshadow_mc** (**Figure 15.34**). Remember these names, as they will be used in the next step.

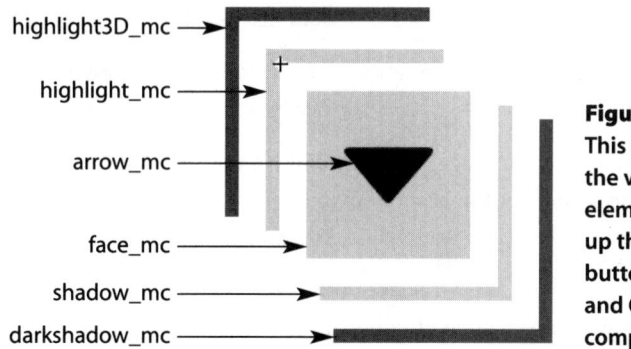

   Figure 15.34 This graphic identifies the various skin elements that make up the down arrow button on ScrollBar and ComboBox component instances.

4. With the Actions panel open, select Frame 1 of the README layer.

   This frame contains several lines of ActionScript (mostly comments). The ones we're most interested in are Lines 13 through 18, which read as follows:

   ```
   component.registerSkinElement(arrow_mc, "arrow");
   component.registerSkinElement(face_mc, "face");
   component.registerSkinElement(shadow_mc, "shadow");
   component.registerSkinElement(darkshadow_mc, "darkshadow");
   component.registerSkinElement(highlight_mc, "highlight");
   component.registerSkinElement(highlight3D_mc, "highlight3D");
   ```

These lines of script are used to register the movie clip instances on the stage to various properties of the component. For example, note that the first line registers the **arrow_mc** movie clip instance with the *arrow* property. The interesting thing is, we could remove all six lines of script and the component would still work just fine.

So what's the real reason for doing all this registering? By registering these instances with the various component properties, you allow them to be colored dynamically (using the style objects discussed earlier). For example, since the **arrow_mc** movie clip instance is registered as the *arrow* property, any time that property is colored using a style object, Flash knows to actually color the **arrow_mc** movie clip instance (because it's registered with that property).

Thus, if you don't plan to style component properties dynamically, you could simply erase those six lines of script, delete the six movie clip instance skins on the stage, and plop your own graphic or movie clip instance on the stage (with the same overall dimensions as the skins that were there—16 × 16 pixels in this case).

For this exercise, however, we **do** want to create and register movie clip instances as skins that can be styled dynamically, so let's continue.

5. Delete the six skins on the stage. Within a 16 × 16 area (with a top-left registration), create (or drag from the library) six new movie clip instances that represent the six custom skins you want to use to replace the default skins.

You don't really need to create *six* new skins if the custom look you're creating only requires two. For example, if you wanted to create something simple, like an arrow and a face, you would simply drag two movie clip instances from the library (representing an arrow and a face). Remember: The only reason you're registering skins is to enable dynamic styling. If you have only two movie clip instances you want to register, that's fine. Nothing bad will happen if you don't have skins for the other four properties.

Conversely, you can use more than six skins if you're looking for something a bit more complex. Adding skins in this manner will give you additional properties that you can style using the style objects discussed earlier.

6. Register your new movie clip instances in one of the following ways:

- **Give them the same instance names as the movie clip instances you deleted in the previous step.** In this case, you wouldn't need to edit the six lines of script in Step 4 in any way.

Chapter 15 **Components**

component.registerSkinElement(myHighlight,"highlight")

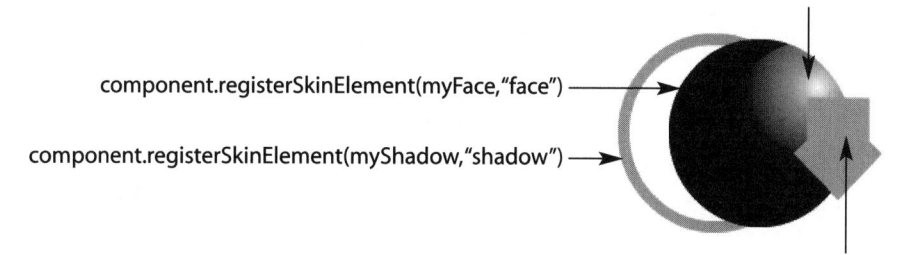

component.registerSkinElement(myFace,"face")

component.registerSkinElement(myShadow,"shadow")

component.registerSkinElement(myArrow,"arrow")

Figure 15.35
This graphic demonstrates the code you would use to register the four custom skin elements shown.

- **Give your new movie clip instances new names, then edit the lines of script in Step 4 accordingly.** For example, if you've named the movie clip instance used for the arrow something like **myArrow**, you would edit the first line to read: component.registerSkinElement(myArrow, "arrow"); (**Figure 15.35**).

- **Write entirely new lines of script.** For example, if you've added a skin (in addition to the default six), you will need to write a new line registering that skin. Something like: component.registerSkinElement(myMovieClip, "myNewProperty");.

7. In the library, the FScrollBar Skins folder has nine other movies you will need to edit as described in Steps 3 through 7 if you want to enable complete customization of the component.

8. When finished, choose Control > Test Movie.

   The component instance you dragged onto the stage in Step 1 should appear with your custom skins.

NOTE *A completed version of this exercise (named registerskin.fla) can be found in the Chapter 15/Assets folder on the CD that accompanies this book.*

Downloading and Installing Additional Components

Macromedia has made all of its products extensible, including Flash MX—which means that the components that come with Flash MX are just the beginning. As developers begin to exploit this powerful functionality, we can expect all sorts of new and useful components to begin appearing on the Web, ready for downloading. These new components should open the door for more sophisticated Flash applications. To use them, of course, you'll have to download and install them—and that operation involves a simple application known as the Extension Manager, which we'll look at next.

Using the Extension Manager to Install Components

When a user extends a Macromedia program, he or she usually does so via an *extension*. Like software plug-ins, extensions provide customized functionality that can be easily downloaded and installed—usually via single files carrying an .mpx extension. Because Macromedia products have attracted legions of devoted users (many of whom create extensions for their own purposes, then make them available to the public as well), a plethora of extensions are available for Macromedia applications (including Flash MX)—most of which you can download from the Web.

TIP *An entire section of Macromedia's Web site is devoted to extensions for its products: It's called The Exchange, http://dynamic.macromedia.com/bin/MM/exchange/flash/main.jsp (**Figure 15.36**). You can find even more third-party components at www.flashcomponents.net.*

Once you download an extension (also known as a component in Flash), you must then install it before the program it extends can actually use it. You do this via the Macromedia Extension Manager, an application designed for this purpose and available from Macromedia's Web site.

NOTE *You can download the most recent release of the Extension Manager (version 1.4 at the time of this writing) at: http://dynamic.macromedia.com/bin/MM/exchange/em_download.jsp. You will need to install this version for the exercise that follows.*

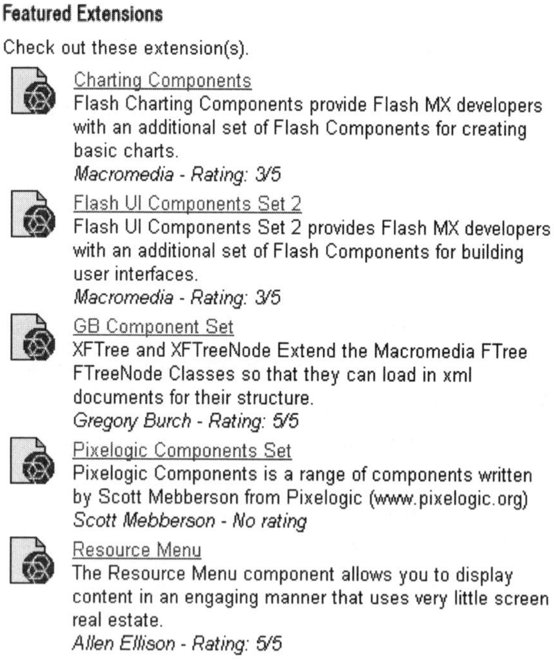

Featured Extensions

Check out these extension(s).

Charting Components
Flash Charting Components provide Flash MX developers with an additional set of Flash Components for creating basic charts.
Macromedia - Rating: 3/5

Flash UI Components Set 2
Flash UI Components Set 2 provides Flash MX developers with an additional set of Flash Components for building user interfaces.
Macromedia - Rating: 3/5

GB Component Set
XFTree and XFTreeNode Extend the Macromedia FTree FTreeNode Classes so that they can load in xml documents for their structure.
Gregory Burch - Rating: 5/5

Pixelogic Components Set
Pixelogic Components is a range of components written by Scott Mebberson from Pixelogic (www.pixelogic.org)
Scott Mebberson - No rating

Resource Menu
The Resource Menu component allows you to display content in an engaging manner that uses very little screen real estate.
Allen Ellison - Rating: 5/5

Figure 15.36
A list of featured extensions currently available at the Flash Exchange.

To help demonstrate how to download and install components, we'll go through the steps required to download and install a new set of UI components made available by Macromedia since the release of Flash MX (see "About Flash UI Components Set 2," a little later in this chapter). Besides learning something from the exercise, you'll also have some new toys to play with!

To download and install components using the Extension Manager:

1. Close Flash MX if it's currently running.

Flash MX is only able to recognize and load components during its launch process. We'll restart the program once we've installed our components.

2. On your hard drive, create a folder for downloading extensions.

For example, on my own computer the path for downloading Flash extensions is:

Macromedia\Extensions\Flash MX\

3. Open your browser and navigate to: http://dynamic.macromedia.com/bin/MM/exchange/flash/main.jsp. Locate the Flash UI Components Set 2 download link, and click it to begin downloading this set of components.

NOTE *A single extension file (.mpx) can actually contain several components/extensions, which are downloaded and installed as a set.*

4. When asked where you want to save the components, navigate to the directory you created in Step 1, them press the Save button.

5. When the downloading process is complete, launch the Extension Manager.

   Luckily for us, the Extension Manager's interface is simple and easy to understand (**Figure 15.37**). At the top you'll see four buttons and a drop-down box. Since the Extension Manager is used for managing extensions for several programs, the drop-down menu provides a list of available programs that allows you to select which extensions you would like to manage. For example, to install or remove extensions from Flash MX, you would select Flash MX from the drop-down menu. To the left of this drop-down menu, you will see two buttons used to install and remove extensions. To the right of the menu, two more buttons provide links to the Flash Exchange and the Extension Manager's help system. In addition, the interface contains two horizontal windows, whose function we will explain shortly.

6. From the drop-down menu, choose Flash MX, then press the Install button (to the left of the drop-down menu). The Select Extension to Install dialog box will

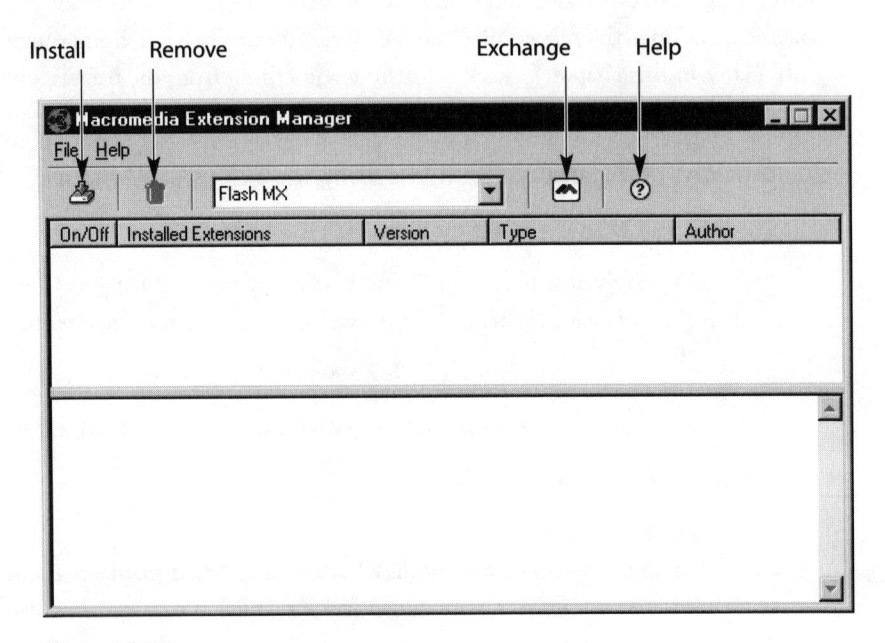

Figure 15.37
The Extension Manager interface.

appear. Navigate to the directory where you downloaded the Flash UI Components Set 2 file. Locate it, select it, and press the Install button on the dialog box.

The Extension Manager will begin the installation process, which shouldn't take more than a few seconds. After the installation is complete, basic information about the component set (version, author, and so on) will appear in the top window pane of the Extension Manager. Clicking the name of the component set will reveal more detailed information about it in the lower windowpane.

7. Check the box to the left of the component set's name to turn it on.

When it's turned on, the components set will be loaded into Flash MX when the program is launched. When turned off, the component set will still be installed, but it won't be loaded when Flash MX is launched. Because loading extensions lengthens the time it takes Flash MX to launch, if a number of component/extensions are installed and turned on, Flash's launch process takes that much longer. By turning off any extensions you're not using in your current project, you can significantly cut down on the launching time.

8. Launch Flash MX.

9. After loading, choose Window > Components in order to open the Components panel. From the category menu on the Components panel, select Flash UI Components Set 2.

The components that make up Set 2 will appear on the Components panel (**Figure 15.38**). You can drag them onto the stage and work with them in the same way as the default set of components. (For more information about this new set of components, see "About Flash UI Components Set 2").

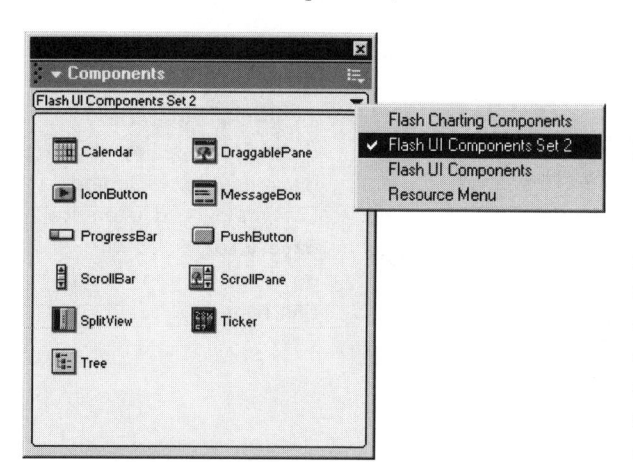

Figure 15.38
The Components panel now displays Flash UI Components Set 2. (Note: For some reason, the ScrollBar, ScrollPane, and PushButton components appear as well. You should disregard these if they appear when you're selecting the Set 2 Components because they're already included in the default component set.)

About Flash UI Components Set 2

With Flash UI Components Set 2, Macromedia has provided Flash users with a set of components that are not only useful but extremely powerful as well.

Many components (especially those developed by Macromedia, including Set 2) come with accompanying methods that allow you to manipulate the component via ActionScript. These new methods will automatically appear in the Toolbox window of the Actions panel (**Figure 15.39**). In addition, the Reference panel (Window > Reference) is updated, providing documentation pertaining to these methods and their use.

Let's take a brief look at the components that come with Set 2.

- **Calendar.** The calendar component is useful for displaying an interactive calendar in a project. This component allows the user to select dates, and includes methods that enable you to retrieve the user's choice, display a specific date, and more.

- **Draggable Pane.** This component acts as a draggable window, used to display content you choose. The component includes a title bar and scroll bars, and is expandable, collapsible, and resizable. Content within this window can be a movie clip in the library, or a movie or JPG loaded from an external source.

- **Icon Button.** This component is an enhanced version of the PushButton component that comes installed with Flash MX. The enhancement enables you to easily add a graphic to the top of the button, which you can then change dynamically by using methods of the component.

- **Message Box.** This component allows you to create your own message (dialog) boxes. You can set the text displayed and its size, include a graphic, enable/disable buttons, and more.

- **Progress Bar.** Lets you quickly implement one of the most requested functionalities in Flash movies: a bar that displays the progress of a movie download. The many methods you can use with it make it one of the most sophisticated progress bars available.

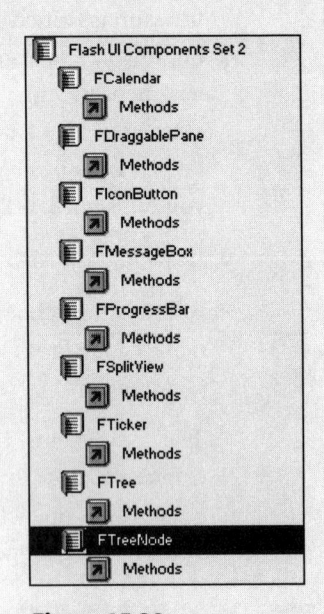

Figure 15.39
When some components are installed (especially those developed by Macromedia), the Toolbox List window and Reference panel are updated with new methods and information, respectively.

About Flash UI Components Set 2 *continued*

- **Split View.** This component allows you to display two separate pieces of content (movie clip instances) next to each other, separated by a draggable bar. Orientation of the split view can be either vertical or horizontal. Content and orientation can be set via methods available to the component.
- **Ticker.** This component allows you to display data so that it scrolls continuously without any interaction by the user. This versatile component includes 70 methods that give you all kinds of options—like setting the scrolling speed and formatting the display of data.
- **Tree.** This component allows you to display related data in a hierarchical structure, similar to the directory-exploring feature of your computer's operating system. This is an advanced component that is mostly configured via methods.

10. Close the Extension Manager, unless you have additional extensions you would like to install.

NOTE The Extension Manager does not have to be running in order for extensions that are turned on to be loaded into the corresponding program. Once they are installed and turned on, they remain in that state until you launch the Extension Manager and either uninstall the extension, or turn it off.

TIP While creating your own custom components is beyond the scope of this book, in-depth information on this subject is available from Macromedia's own online instruction guide at: www.macromedia.com/support/flash/applications/creating_comps/

Video Tutorial

Using Components. This tutorial will step you through the process of adding and configuring the different component types to your project.

Using ActionScript in Your Projects

CHAPTER 16

What you'll learn...

How to chain the loading and playback of sounds

How to integrate Flash and HTML in creative ways

How to extend the functionality of ActionScript objects

How to draw within a Flash movie dynamically

If you've made it this far, you already know a great deal about ActionScript—how to use variables and expressions; the purpose of objects, functions, and methods; and so on. Now it's time to put that knowledge to use. In this chapter, we've assembled a number of mini-tutorials to help you get started. We hope these tutorials will inspire you to look at Flash in new ways, and that you'll soon be using ActionScript to create dynamic, useful, and enjoyable projects of your own!

Chaining the Loading and Playback of External Movies

Chaining refers to setting up your project so that it loads and plays external movies in sequence: that is, loading and playing back one before moving on to the next—a process that's repeated as long as there are movies to load. In this way, you can implement self-running presentations that you can easily configure to play a sequence of external movies in any order you choose.

Creating a Sequential Playback Chain

The first aspect of chaining that we're going to look at is the *sequential* chaining of several movies, where Movie 1 loads and plays through, then Movie 2 loads and plays through, and so on.

1. Create an *empty* movie clip instance into which you will load the external SWFs. Drag an instance of this clip onto the stage and give it an instance name such as **myMovieClip**.

2. With the Actions panel open, select Frame 1 of the main timeline and attach the following script:

```
movies = new Array("intro.swf", "body.swf", "conclusion.swf");
beginAt = 0;
```

This script will create an array named `movies` that will store the file names/paths of the external SWFs you want to include in the playback chain. The next line creates a variable named `beginAt` and gives it an initial value of 0. (We'll use this variable's value in a moment.)

3. Select the **myMovieClip** movie clip instance (this is the instance into which the external SWF will be loaded), and attach the following script:

```
onClipEvent (enterFrame) {
    if(_currentframe ==_totalframes && _root.beginAt <
_root.movies.length) {
        loadMovie(_root.movies[_root.beginAt], this);
        ++_root.beginAt;
    }
}
```

This script uses a conditional statement triggered by an `enterFrame` event to constantly check whether the movie loaded into it has completed its playback (current frame is the same as the total number of frames), *and* whether the value of `beginAt` (on the root timeline) is less than the `length` of the `movies` array (also on the root timeline). When both conditions are `true`, the `loadMovie()` action is executed, and the next movie in the `movies` array is loaded. When that loaded movie has completed its playback, the `loadMovie()` action is executed again, loading the next movie in the `movies` array. Let's follow the flow of this script through a couple of loading sequences to help you solidify your understanding of this.

Since **myMovieClip** is empty when the movie begins to play, this script will determine that its current frame equals its total frames (that is, they're both 0), *and* that beginAt has a value (0) less than the length of the movies array (3, since the array contains three elements)—and thus the first loading sequence occurs. The loadMovie() action references one of the elements in the movies array as the movie to load, based on the current value of beginAt, both of which exist on the main timeline.

Since beginAt is given an initial value of 0, the loadMovie() parameter of:

_root.movies[_root.beginAt]

Is evaluated to:

_root.movies[0]

Thus, the movie located at index position 0 in the movies array ("intro.swf") is loaded into this movie clip instance. The next line within the conditional statement then increments the value of beginAt by 1, which sets its updated value to 1 (0 + 1). The movie that is loaded begins playing.

Since the conditional statement in our script cannot evaluate to true as long as _currentframe and _totalframes are not equal (which is the case when the movie is playing), the script remains dormant until the loaded movie completes its playback. When this occurs, the statement evaluates that _currentframe and _totalframe properties are equal (that condition is true), but it also checks to make sure the value of beginAt (which was incremented by 1) is still less than the length of the movies array. Since *both* conditions are true, the loadMovie() action is executed again. However, this time—since beginAt was incremented to have a value of 1—the line:

_root.movies[_root.beginAt]

Is evaluated to:

_root.movies[1]

Thus, the movie located at index position 1 in the movies array ("body.swf") is loaded, and the process begins again. This process will continue as long as beginAt (which is incremented by 1 with each loading sequence) has a value less than the length of the movies array. Why are we checking the value of beginAt against the length of the movies array? This is because our movies array only contains a limited number of movies to load. By comparing the value of beginAt against the length of the movies array, we create a mechanism for turning off the chain-loading process once all the movies in the array have been loaded (**Figure 16.1**). The movies that are loaded can have varying numbers of frames, since the script knows how to automatically check for the number of total frames and adjust accordingly.

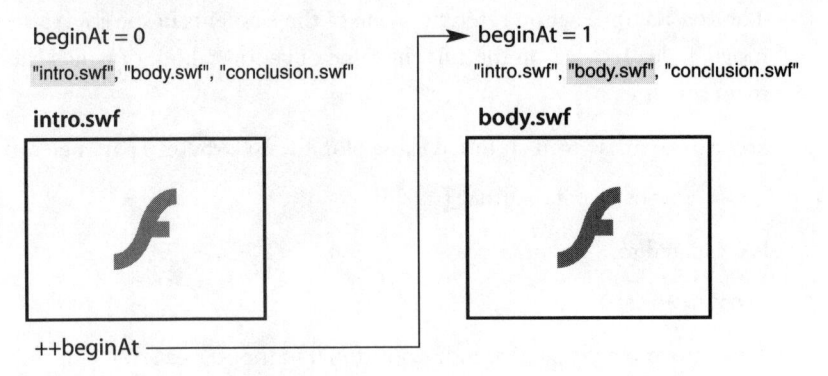

Figure 16.1
The current value of beginAt (which is incremented with each loading sequence) dictates which movie in the movies array is loaded next.

Variation 1 – Looping Playback

The previous script would quit loading movies once all of the movies in the movies array had been loaded and played through once. But what if, after the last movie in the array, you wanted to begin loading movies again, starting with the first element in the array? The following script, which would replace the one discussed in Step 3 above, creates this functionality:

```
onClipEvent(enterFrame) {
  if(_currentframe == _totalframes){
    loadMovie(_root.movies[_root.beginAt], this);
    ++_root.beginAt;
    if(_root.beginAt == _root.movies.length){
      _root.beginAt = 0;
    }
  }
}
```

This script is very similar to the one discussed in Step 3 above, except for the removal of the second condition in the main if statement, and the addition of the following nested if statement:

```
if(_root.beginAt == _root.movies.length){
  _root.beginAt = 0;
}
```

This statement is executed any time a new movie is loaded and beginAt is incremented. Its purpose is to check to see if the incremented value of beginAt is equal to the number of elements within the movies array. If it is, the value of beginAt is reset to 0. This will cause the next loading sequence to load the first element in the array, which creates a looping loading sequence.

Variation 2 – Random Playback

Now let's assume that you have an array of SWF files in the movies array and you want to play one, randomly load another, have that movie play through, randomly play another, and so on. The following script, which would replace the script in Step 3 above, creates this functionality:

```
onClipEvent (enterFrame) {
  if (_currentframe == _totalframes) {
    randomNumber = random(_root.movies.length);
    loadMovie(_root.movies[randomNumber], this);
  }
}
```

Here, whenever the movie loaded into the instance has finished its playback, a random number is generated, based on the number of elements in the movies array. Since our example script (shown in Step 1 above) creates this array with three elements, the randomNumber variable will have a value of 0, 1, or 2 when the script is run. The next line uses this value to load one of the SWF files within the movies array. Since the random number generated depends on the number of elements in the movies array, a mechanism is created where only a movie that exists within the movies array can be randomly loaded.

Things to note/uses

- You could use a ListBox component to list a number of movies from which the user could select several choices. Their selections could then be placed into an array using the getSelectedItems() method of the ListBox component, at which point you could then begin the execution of any of the aforementioned playback schemes. This allows users to sequentially view content of their choosing.

Chaining the Loading and Playback of External MP3s

Chaining the loading and playback of external MP3s can be useful if you want to create an MP3 player that plays a song, loads the next, plays that song, loads the next, and so on. This is similar to chaining the loading of external movies; however, its implementation is a bit different. Take a look at the following script, which would be placed on Frame 1 of the timeline:

```
songs = new Array("song1.mp3", "song2.mp3", "song3.mp3");
mp3Player = new Sound();
beginAt = 0;
mp3Player.loadSound(songs[beginAt++], true);
mp3Player.onSoundComplete = function(){
   mp3Player.loadSound(songs[beginAt++], true);
}
```

The first line in the above script creates an array named songs, used for storing the names/paths of the external MP3 files. The next line creates a Sound object instance named mp3Player, where we will load our external MP3s. The next line initializes the beginAt variable with a value of 0. And the following line invokes the loadSound() method in order to load one of our MP3 files into the mp3Player Sound object. Notice the part of the line that reads:

```
songs[beginAt++]
```

Here, the current value of beginAt is used to determine which song in the songs array to load, after which the value of beginAt is incremented by 1. This is just a shortcut way of writing:

```
mp3Player.loadSound(songs[beginAt], true);
++beginAt;
```

Once this part of the script is executed, the MP3 file at index position 0 of the songs array is loaded and begins playing. The last three lines of the script use the onSoundComplete event handler method to determine what should happen when an MP3 file loaded into mp3Player completes its playback. As you can see, we've set it up to load the next file in the songs array, while at the same time incrementing the value of beginAt by 1, for use during the next loading sequence. This sequence will continue for as long as there are files in the songs array.

Things to note/uses

- You would create a looping or random loading sequence in the same way we described in the previous section.

Creating Keyboard Shortcuts

Flash MX's ability to detect and react to keyboard activity makes it easy to create keyboard shortcuts for actions normally accomplished via button-presses. This is a good feature to offer since many computer users are accustomed to and like using keyboard shortcuts to accomplish various tasks in different applications.

Creating keyboard shortcuts via ActionScript is simple. Take a look at the following script, which would be placed on Frame 1 of the main timeline:

```
_root.onKeyDown = function(){
  if(Key.isDown(Key.SPACE) && Key.isDown(Key.PGDN)){
    _root.nextFrame();
  }
}
Key.addListener(_root);
```

The first several lines of the above script are used to assign an event handler method to the root timeline, telling it to execute the unnamed function when the onKeyDown event occurs. Before we look at the functionality of this event handler method, however, notice the last line of the script, which reads: `Key.addListener(_root);`. This line registers the root timeline to listen to all Key events, and thus execute any functions that the root timeline has scripted to execute in response to a particular event (such as our onKeyDown event handler method).

There are two reasons for taking this approach. First, the root timeline cannot have clip events (such as KeyDown) attached directly to it (as movie clip instances can). Thus, this is a way around that limitation. Second, since this functionality is attached to the root timeline, and the root timeline always exists as your movie plays (that is, it's not loaded and unloaded as are other timelines), the keyboard shortcut functionality will exist as long as the movie plays, regardless of what frame or scene is navigated to, or other movies are loaded or unloaded.

TIP *Attaching event handler methods to the root timeline is a great way to script a functionality that you want to use throughout your project.*

Next, let's look at how the onKeyDown event handler method we've created is used to enable keyboard shortcut functionality. It's actually quite simple: Whenever a key or keys are pressed, the conditional statement checks to determine whether the spacebar and Page Down key have been pressed simultaneously. If they have, the action within the statement (which the keyboard shortcut should perform) is executed. In this case, the main timeline moves to the next frame.

Variation 1 – Mutiple Keyboard Shortcuts

Most applications include multiple keyboard shortcuts—functionality you can add to your Flash applications simply by updating our onKeyDown event handler method as follows:

```
_root.onKeyDown = function(){
  if(Key.isDown(Key.SPACE) && Key.isDown(Key.PGDN)){
    _root.nextFrame();
  }
  if(Key.isDown(Key.SPACE) && Key.isDown(Key.PGUP)){
    _root.prevFrame();
  }
  if(Key.isDown(Key.SPACE) && Key.isDown(Key.HOME)){
    _root.gotoAndStop(1);
  }
}
Key.addListener(_root);
```

All we've done to update this script is added a couple more if statements, which handle what occurs when other key combinations are detected. Thus, when a set of keys is pressed, if the first combination is not detected, then the next one is looked for, and so on. You can add as many combinations as you wish.

Disabling Keyboard Shortcuts

If at any time you wish to disable keyboard shortcut functionality, as set up in the previous sections, you would use the following script:

```
Key.removeListener(_root);
```

To re-establish this functionality, you would use the following:

```
Key.addListener(_root);
```

Things to note/uses

- Keyboard shortcuts are not suited for every movie. Although they can come in handy for movies that cater to those with visual disabilities or applications that are used on a *regular* basis by an individual, it's impractical to think that a person who *occasionally* visits a particular Web site would want to take the time to learn and memorize keyboard shortcuts.

- If you've included keyboard shortcuts in your application, be sure to let your users know it. You might even want to provide a separate page that lists them. And if you're using shortcuts in a project that's been made accessible to the visually impaired, provide an accessible text field that lists the shortcuts so that a screen reader can read them aloud to the user.

- Keyboard shortcuts can be extremely helpful (and sometimes absolutely necessary) in creating Flash games

Dynamically Disabling Flash Movies

Disabling a movie can prove helpful in circumstances where you want the movie to stop functioning after a specified period of time, or you want to be able to enable or disable it from a remote location.

Time-Expiring a Movie

The following exercise will show you how to disable a movie if the user attempts to play it beyond a specific date.

1. Create a movie with three scenes—Initialize, Denied, and Proceed—and make sure they're listed in that order in the Scene panel.

2. On the Proceed scene, place the content you wish the user to see if your movie hasn't expired. On the Denied scene, place the content you want users to see if

your movie *has* been expired. With the Actions panel open, select Frame 1 of the Initialize scene and attach the following script:

```
currentDate = new Date();
expirationDate = new Date(2002, 8, 1);
if(currentDate.getTime() > expirationDate.getTime()){
  gotoAndStop("Denied", 1);
}else{
  gotoAndStop("Proceed", 1);
}
```

The first line creates a Date object based on the current date, as reported by the user's machine. The next line creates another Date object representing the date we want the movie to expire—in this case, September 1, 2002.

NOTE *You'll remember from our discussion of the Date object in Chapter 14, that although we've indicated 8 as the month in the above script, this actually represents the ninth month of the year (or September). Review that chapter for more information.*

The next several lines of our script use a conditional statement to compare the two dates, and act accordingly. You'll notice that the getTime() method is used in relation to both Date objects within the conditional statement: to return the number of milliseconds that have passed between January 1, 1970, and the Date object being referenced.

Thus, the conditional statement checks to see if the *current* date is further from January 1, 1970, than the *expiration* date. If it is, that indicates that the movie is being played *beyond* the expiration date, in which case the movie is sent to the Denied frame label. Otherwise the movie is sent to the Proceed label, where the user can proceed with viewing the content of the file (**Figure 16.2**).

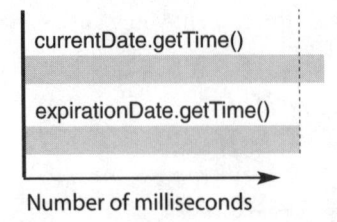

Figure 16.2
The getTime() method allows us to compare two or more dates to determine which one is further into the future. In this graphic, currentDate has passed expirationDate, which will cause our script to move the timeline to the Denied frame label.

Things to note/uses

- Smart users can always set their computers' clocks back to get around an expiration date and view expired files on *their* machines. However, if a project is being posted on the Web, it's unlikely that users would reset their clocks just to view it.

- You can take advantage of this functionality to display (or hide) time-sensitive content—for example, contests, special promotions, upcoming events, and more.

Remotely Disabling a Movie

The ability to disable a movie from a remote location gives you ultimate control over who can view your movie. The idea is simple: You simply set up your movie to load a variable from an external source (for example, a text file on a server) and then have it check the value of the loaded variable to enable or disable the movie.

1. Using Notepad (Windows) or SimpleText (Macintosh), create a text file with the following text:

    `&enableMovie=0`

    Or

    `&enableMovie=1`

    The script we're about to create will use a value of 0 to disable the movie, and a value of 1 to enable it.

2. Save the text file as project47.txt and upload it to your server.

    You can actually name the text file anything you wish. Just make sure to remember its name and the URL where it's uploaded.

3. In Flash, create a movie with four scenes—Initialize, Denied, Error, and Proceed—and list them in the Scene panel in the order shown here.

4. On the Proceed scene, place the content you wish the user to view if the movie has not been disabled. On the Denied scene, place the content you want them to see if it *has* been disabled. And on the Error scene, place the content you want the user to see if an error occurs while attempting to load the external variable.

With the Actions panel open, select Frame 1 of the Initialize scene and attach the following script:

```
stop();
status = new LoadVars();
status.onLoad = function(success){
  if(success == true){
    if(status.enableMovie == 0){
      gotoAndStop("Denied", 1);
    }else{
      gotoAndStop("Proceed", 1);
    }
  }else{
    gotoAndStop("Error", 1);
  }
}
status.load("http://www.remoteserver.com/project47.txt");
```

The first line of this script stops the timeline from moving forward until the script that follows moves it to one of the frame labels. The next line creates a LoadVars object named status, where the enableMovie variable (in the text file created in Step 1) will be loaded. Before the script begins the loading process (as shown in the last line of the above script), an onLoad event handler method is defined to specify what needs to occur when the external text file has finished loading.

Here, you'll notice that the event handler method is passed a parameter named success. But where does that parameter get its value? Well, the onLoad event handler has a built-in mechanism that determines whether the loading process was successful. This means that if you were to attempt to load external data, the onLoad event handler would be able to determine whether the external server containing the data was down, or whether the user was simply not connected to the Web. If either were the case, the success parameter would be assigned a value of false and data would not be downloaded. If, on the other hand, loading did succeed, this parameter would
be given a value of true (**Figure 16.3**).

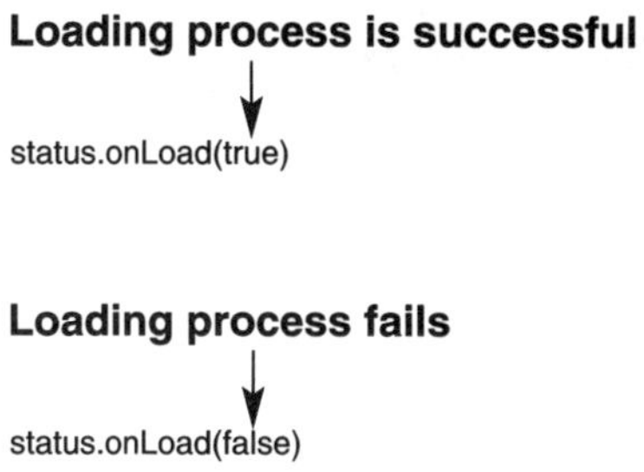

Loading process is successful
↓
status.onLoad(true)

Loading process fails
↓
status.onLoad(false)

Figure 16.3
The onLoad event handler can return a value of true or false, depending on whether the loading process succeeded or failed.

The main conditional statement within the onLoad event handler looks at the value of success to see if the loading process was successful. If it wasn't, the else part of the statement is executed and the timeline is moved to the Error frame label, indicating an error has occurred in the loading process. If loading was successful, a nested if statement evaluates the value of enableMovie (which is loaded from the external text file into the status LoadVars object). Depending on the current value of enableMovie, the movie will move either to the frame labeled Denied or the frame labeled Proceed.

As mentioned earlier, the last line of this script begins the process of loading data into the status LoadVars object.

When this movie is uploaded to any server, the above script will execute, either enabling or disabling the movie, depending on the current value of enableMovie in the remote text file. Updating this value will cause the movie to react accordingly the next time it is opened and played.

Things to note/uses

- If you're daring enough, you could use this functionality to disable a project for a client who refuses to pay!

- This functionality comes in handy when you want to be able to enable or disable a movie at any time—without opening the actual SWF.

- If you set up several movies to load the same text file, you could enable or disable them all by updating the value within that single file.

- Although you can see from the above that there are times when it's helpful to have the ability to remotely disable a movie, you risk upsetting people by doing so. For some, this raises privacy issues, and for others it raises issues of control. Be sensitive to these concerns, and use your power wisely!

Variation 1 – Checking for Online/Offline Status

This variation of the last exercise will allow a projector file (an outside-of-the-browser Flash application, see Chapter 21, "Publishing") to determine whether a user is online or offline, and move the timeline to the appropriate frame label in response.

1. Using Notepad (Windows) or SimpleText (Macintosh), create an empty text file.
2. Save the text file as online.txt and upload it to your server.

   You can actually name this file anything you wish. Just make sure you remember its name and the URL where it's uploaded.

3. In Flash, create a movie with three scenes—Initialize, Offline, and Proceed—and make sure they're listed in that order in the Scene panel.
4. On the Online scene, place the content you wish the user to see if he or she is connected to the Web. On the Offline scene, place the content you want users to see if they're offline. With the Actions panel open, select Frame 1 of the Initialize scene, and attach the following script:

```
stop();
status = new LoadVars();
status.onLoad = function(success){
  if(success == true){
    gotoAndStop("Online", 1);
  }else{
    gotoAndStop("Offline", 1);
  }
}
status.load("http://www.yourserver.com/online.txt");
```

This script functions similarly to the one discussed in Step 4 of the previous section. Pay particular attention to the `onLoad` event handler method. If the online.txt text file loads, this indicates that the user is online, and thus the `success` parameter is given a value of `true` and the timeline is moved to the Online frame label. If the user is offline, the external text file will not be loaded, and thus `success` is given a value of `false` and the timeline is moved to the frame labeled Offline.

Things to note/uses

- You can set up your projector file to load updated content from the server (news, specials, events calendar, and so on) if it determines that the user is online. Conversely, you could place default content within the movie that would appear if the user was offline.

Integrating Flash with HTML

Not all designers or clients are hip to the idea of creating Flash-only Web sites. Instead, they're more comfortable *integrating* Flash content within an existing HTML-based site. Fortunately there are several creative ways to do just this.

Dynamic Images

If you want to add some flair to those spots on an HTML page where you would normally place JPGs or GIFs, why not use Flash movies in their place? By doing this, you can *randomly* load images into your movie so that the page looks different nearly every time it's viewed.

1. Choose an area on an HTML page that is currently occupied by a GIF or JPG, and determine the current image's width and height.

2. Create a number of JPG images of the same width and height, which could, from a design perspective, replace that static image.

3. Create a Flash movie the same width and height as your images. Place the following script on Frame 1 of that movie:

   ```
   images = new Array ("image1.jpg", "image2.jpg", "image3.jpg");
   randomNumber = random(images.length);
   loadMovieNum(images[randomNumber], 0);
   ```

   The first line of the above script creates an array for holding the names/paths to all the possible replacement JPG images. The next line generates a random number based on the number of images in the array. That random number is then used to determine which image within the array to load.

4. Export this movie.

5. Place the JPG images and the exported SWF in the same directory.

6. Embed the SWF file in your HTML page in the spot formally occupied by the static image.

Now, whenever the HTML page is viewed, the spot on the page occupied by the SWF file will randomly load one of the JPG images created in Step 2 in a process that's transparent to the visitor (**Figure 16.4**).

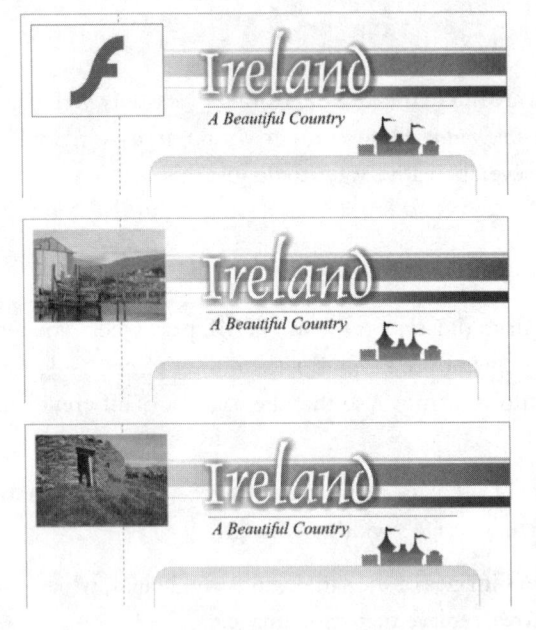

Figure 16.4
Using small SWF movies in place of static JPGs or GIFs gives you the ability to randomly load images each time the page is loaded—an easy way to make your site more dynamic and appealing.

Things to note/uses

- An HTML page can take advantage of this functionality to contain several SWF files—each of which loads random images into various spots on the page.

Variation 1 – Implementing a Random Banner System

Think you need a server-side script in order to display a random banner each time an HTML page is viewed? Think again! You can easily implement this functionality using a variation of the script employed in the previous section.

1. Determine the width and height of an area on your HTML page where you want the banner to appear.

2. Create (or have advertisers provide) several banner SWFs, at the predetermined size.

   At this point it's important to determine the total number of banners you want to rotate. For our demonstration, let's say ten.

3. Name the banner SWFs sequentially—for example, banner0.swf, banner1.swf, banner2.swf, and so on.

4. Create a Flash movie that's the same size as your banners. Place the following script on Frame 1 of that movie:

   ```
   randomNumber = random(10);
   bannerToLoad = "banner" + randomNumber + ".swf";
   loadMovieNum(bannerToLoad , 0);
   ```

   The first line of the above script creates a variable named `randomNumber` and assigns it a random value from 0 to 9. The next line uses this value to create a string value, which is assigned as the value of `bannerToLoad`. Finally, the value of `bannerToLoad` is used to determine which banner SWF to load. For example, if the number *4* is assigned to the value of `randomBanner`, `bannerToLoad` will be assigned a string value of `"banner4.swf"`. This is the banner that the `loadMovie()` action that follows will load.

5. Export this movie.

6. Place the banner SWFs and the exported SWF file in the same directory.

7. Embed the SWF file in your HTML page in the space allocated for the banner.

   Now, whenever the HTML page is viewed, a random banner SWF will load.

Things to note/uses

- When accepting banner SWFs from advertisers, make sure they understand what frame rates they should use, as well as the fact that they must include the functionality for making the banner open a URL when clicked.
- Use banner SWFs to randomly promote different products or services you offer.
- If your movie is set up to load one of ten possible banner SWFs, yet you only have three or four unique ones, simply use duplicates to create ten total banners.

Variation 2 – Adding Audio to an HTML Page

Audio (especially music) on a Web page can greatly enhance a visitor's experience of your site. Using a slight variation of the functionality discussed in the previous section, you can play an audio track when the user views an HTML page.

1. Create an MP3 file to load.

For demonstration purposes, we'll assume its name is htmlMP3.mp3.

Within Flash, you can make your movie so small (1 pixel by 1 pixel) that the user has no idea where the music is coming from, or you can make it large enough to include an icon or small graphic indicating the source of the audio. For usability sake, the latter method is preferred (**Figure 16.5**).

Figure 16.5
When using Flash to play an MP3 file on an HTML page, it's usually a good idea to provide some sort of visual indication (graphic) of where the audio is originating.

2. With Flash open, start a new document. On Frame 1 of this movie, place the following script:

```
audioTrack = new Sound();
audioTrack.load Sound ("htmlMP3.mp3", true);
```

The first line creates a Sound object named audioTrack; the second line loads the htmlMP3.mp3 file into it.

3. Export your movie.

4. Place the MP3 file and the exported SWF file in the same directory.

5. Embed the SWF file somewhere on your HTML page.

Whenever the HTML page is viewed, the MP3 file will play.

Things to note/uses

- Although not required, it's usually a good idea to provide the user with a means to halt the audio's playback. A button (perhaps the icon graphic mentioned in Step 1) containing something similar to the following script should work fine:

```
on(release){
   audioTrack.stop();
}
```

- There's more to MP3s than just music. Use this functionality to load audio advertisements, promotional information pertaining to a page's content, or any other type of audio-based information you think the user would find helpful.

- You can use the `System.accessibility.isActive()` to detect whether the user has a screen reader running on his or her machine. If a screen reader is detected, you could have the script load a narrative MP3 that describes the page and its contents for those who are visually impaired.

Class-Wide Functionality via the Prototype Object

Every class of objects in ActionScript (MovieClip, TextField, and so on) has an associated *prototype object* that lets you script functionality that's inherited by every instance of that class. While the functionality of most such prototype objects is beyond the scope of this book, they do provide access to some pretty powerful capabilities—which is why they're worth looking at briefly here.

NOTE *For more information about prototype objects, pick up a copy of Macromedia Flash MX ActionScripting: Advanced Training from the Source, published by Macromedia Press.*

Hiding the Hand Cursor for All Button Instances

Most applications (such as the Flash authoring application) don't show a hand cursor when a button is moused over on its interface. Typically, the arrow cursor remains. While ActionScript provides the `useHandCursor` property, enabling you to display or hide the hand cursor for individual button instances, if your application contains dozens of buttons, you could waste a lot of time writing dozens of lines of script in order to disable them all. By setting this value on the Button object's prototype object, you can take care of it with a single line placed on Frame 1 of the main timeline:

```
Button.prototype.useHandCursor = false;
```

That's it! Now, none of the button instances used in your application will have a hand cursor when they are moused over. Changing this value back to `true` will cause all button instances to immediately display the hand cursor again.

Adding a New Method to the MovieClip Class

To add a new method to a class of objects, you simply define a function and attach it to the class' prototype object. To demonstrate this, we're going to add a new method to the MovieClip class that will allow us to proportionately scale any movie clip instance with a single line of code. Of course, you can scale a movie clip instance proportionately without this enhancement, but it requires two lines of code, as in the following:

```
myMovieClip._xscale = 50;
myMovieClip._yscale = 50;
```

Our new method will save you some keystrokes when scripting this functionality. To create this new method, select Frame 1 of the main timeline and add the following script:

```
MovieClip.prototype.scale = function(amount){
   this._xscale = amount;
   this._yscale = amount;
}
```

As you can see, we've created a function named scale() and placed it on the MovieClip object's prototype object. Because you've placed it on the prototype object, this function is now a *method* of the MovieClip class, which means you can invoke it in relation to any movie clip instance in your project. You'll notice that this new method accepts a single parameter, amount, which is used to set the amount of scaling. The use of this in the script is a reference to the movie clip instance invoking the method. Let's take a look at an example:

```
myStomach.scale(50);
```

The above line of code will scale **myStomach** by 50 percent (how I wish it were that easy). Looking back at how our method is defined, in this circumstance, the following code:

```
this._xscale = amount;
this._yscale = amount;
```

Is evaluated as follows:

```
myStomach._xscale = amount;
myStomach._yscale = amount;
```

Thus, once again, the use of this in a method definition is a reference to the movie clip instance that's currently invoking the method.

Variation 1 – Enhancing the scale() Method

It's important to realize that our scale() method can do anything we want it to—that is, it's not limited to the movie clip instance that invokes it. For example, if you wanted to play a sound whenever the scale() method was invoked, you would update the method definition as follows:

```
MovieClip.prototype.scale = function(amount){
  this._xscale = amount;
  this._yscale = amount;
  scaleSound = new Sound();
  scaleSound.attachSound("swoosh")
  scaleSound.start();
}
```

Our scale() method is now set up so that whenever it's invoked, not only will it scale the specified movie clip instance, it will also create a Sound object, attach the sound in the library with the identifier of "swoosh" to that Sound object, and then start playing that sound. With a little imagination, you can create similar interactivity using any custom methods you define.

Changing the Background of Text Fields When Given Focus

The last aspect of the prototype object we're going to look at involves getting a class of objects to react to a single event in the same way. You already know how to use an event handler method to script a specific object to react to an event, as in the following:

```
myTextField.onSetFocus = function(){
  myTextField.backgroundColor = 0xFFCC00;
}
```

The above script will cause **myTextField**'s background to change color when it's given focus. However, if we wanted the background color of *every* instance of the text field to change when given focus, we would attach the event handler method to the TextField object's prototype object, as shown in this script, which is placed on Frame 1 of the main timeline:

```
TextField.prototype.onSetFocus = function(){
  this.backgroundColor = 0xFFCC00;
}
```

```
TextField.prototype.onKillFocus = function(){
  this.backgroundColor = 0xFFFFFF;
}
```

Now, the background of every instance of the TextField object within your movie will turn orange when given focus, and white when it no longer has focus.

Things to note/uses

- Its usually best to place scripts that involve the prototype object on Frame 1 of the main timeline. This will enable any class-wide settings or methods to take affect as soon as the movie begins playing.

Preloaders

The loading of external movies, graphics, and sounds is a large part of any Web-based Flash application's functionality. Unfortunately, due to varying connection speeds and Internet traffic jams, the download process is rarely instantaneous. As a result, it has become common practice to provide a loading-status indicator, usually in the form of an animated movie clip, or *preloader* (**Figure 16.6**). In this section, we'll show you how to create and use preloaders in your own projects.

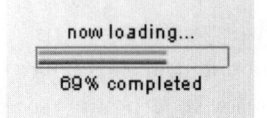

Figure 16.6
A preloader is useful for displaying a movie element's download progress.

The Basic Preloader Movie Clip

Since movie clips are commonly used to create preloader animations, we'll first examine how to create such a clip, then show you how to use it when loading various external movie elements.

1. Within Flash (either an existing project, or a new one), choose Insert > New Symbol.

The Create New Symbol dialog box will appear.

2. Choose the Movie Clip Behavior, enter a name of Preloader, and then click OK.

This takes you to the movie clip's timeline.

3. On the Drawing toolbar, select the Rectangle tool. Create a rectangle anywhere on the stage with no outline and a fill color of your choosing.

4. With the Property inspector open, select the rectangle you just created and enter the following size and position settings:

   W: 1
   H: 10
   X: 0
   Y: 0

5. Select Frame 100 on the timeline, and press F6 to insert a keyframe.

   There is now a copy of the rectangle you created on both Frame 1 and Frame 100.

6. With the Property inspector open and the timeline on Frame 100, select the rectangle on the stage and enter the following size and position settings:

   W: 100
   H: 10
   X: 0
   Y: 0

   This makes the rectangle 99 pixels wider on Frame 100 than on Frame 1. Next, let's create a tween between these frames in order to animate this size increase.

7. With the Property inspector open, select Frame 1 and select the Shape tweening option. Leave the default tweening settings as they are.

   If you move the playhead back and forth, you will see the effects of this tween, and how, as the playhead moves from Frame 1 to Frame 100, the rectangle assumes the visual characteristics of a progress bar.

8. Insert a layer on the timeline. With the new layer as the current layer, select the Text tool and create a dynamic text field below the progress bar with the following settings:

   Name: status
   W: 150
   H: 16
   X: 0
   Y: 15
   Font: _sans
   Font size: 10

This text field, named **status**, will be used to provide a text-based update of the loading process (**Figure 16.7**).

9. Insert another layer on the timeline. Select Frame 1 of this new layer, and attach a stop() action.

   This will prevent this timeline from playing when it first loads.

   Our preloader is now complete.

10. Return to the main timeline.

In the next several sections we'll explain how to use this preloader clip in various loading situations. In the process, you'll begin to see the logic behind the way we constructed it.

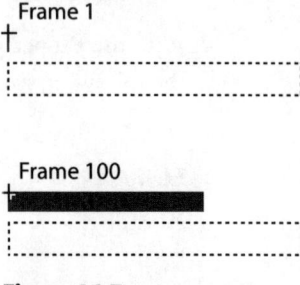

Figure 16.7
The appearance of our preloader clip at Frames 1 and 100.

Using a Preloader for the Main Movie

The following explains how to use our preloader clip in relation to the main timeline (in order to track the progress of the main movie as it loads).

1. Create a Flash movie with two scenes, Preloader and Main. Make sure the scenes are listed in the Scene panel in the order shown here.

2. On the Preloader scene, place an instance of the preloader clip we made earlier. On the Main scene, place the content you want the user to see when the movie has finished loading.

3. With the Actions panel open, select Frame 1 of the Preloader scene and place a stop() action.

   This will prevent the timeline from moving to the Main scene until the preloading script we are about to create instructs it to.

4. With the Actions panel open, select the preloader clip and attach the following script:

   ```
   onClipEvent(enterFrame){
     loaded = _root.getBytesLoaded();
     total = _root.getBytesTotal();
     framesLoaded = Math.ceil((loaded / total) * 100);
     gotoAndStop(framesLoaded);
   ```

```
status.text = framesLoaded + " % completed";
if(framesLoaded >= 90){
   _root.gotoAndPlay("Main", 1);
 }
}
```

This script uses an `enterFrame` event, which means it's constantly executed. The first line of the script assigns the variable named `loaded` a value based on the current number of bytes of the main movie that have loaded. The next line assigns the variable named `total` a value based on the *total* number of bytes representative of the entire file size of the main movie. The next line sets the value of the `framesLoaded` variable. The expression that sets this value divides the value of `loaded` by the value of `total`, which is then multiplied by 100, then rounded up using the `Math.ceil()` method. For example, if the value of `loaded` is 34567 and the value of `total` is 76543, `framesLoaded` is given a value of 46, indicating that 46 percent of the movie has been downloaded (**Figure 16.8**).

Because this script is constantly executed, these values are continually updated to represent the progress of the download. The value of `framesLoaded`, which for demonstration purposes we'll assume is 46, is used in the next several lines.

First, a `gotoAndStop()` action uses this value to move the preloader clip to Frame 46. Since this timeline contains a tween from Frame 1 to Frame 100, moving it to Frame 46 will cause the progress bar within the clip to appear at a point that represents 46 percent loaded. The next line is used to set the text displayed in the **status** text field. Since `framesLoaded` has a value of 46, it will display "46 % completed".

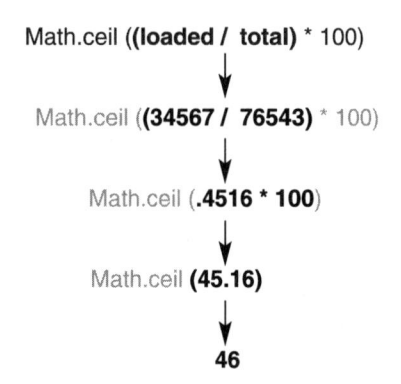

Figure 16.8
This graphic demonstrates how the expression used to set the value of framesLoaded is evaluated.

Math.ceil (**(loaded / total) * 100**)
↓
Math.ceil (**(34567 / 76543)** * 100)
↓
Math.ceil (**.4516 * 100**)
↓
Math.ceil (**45.16**)
↓
46

The last three lines contain a conditional statement, which is used to tell the preloader to quit the preloading process when `framesLoaded` has a value of more than or equal to 90, at which point the timeline is moved to and begins playing at Frame 1 of the Main scene. The value of 90 can be set to any value you choose. The value set will determine the percentage of the movie that must be loaded before it begins playing.

Variation 1 – Using a Preloader for External SWFs

Adapting our preloader/script to various loading scenarios is pretty easy. For example, to track the loading progress of an externally loaded SWF (loaded using the loadMovie() action), you would place the preloader clip at the frame where the external SWF is loaded, and edit the script attached to it in the following way:

```
onClipEvent(enterFrame){
  loaded = _root.myMovieClip.getBytesLoaded();
  total = _root.myMovieClip.getBytesTotal();
  framesLoaded = Math.ceil((loaded / total) * 100);
  gotoAndStop(framesLoaded);
  status.text = framesLoaded + " % completed";
  if(framesLoaded >= 90){
    _root.myMovieClip.play();
  }
}
```

This preloader script assumes that the external movie is being loaded into a movie clip instance named **myMovieClip**. The first two lines of the script are edited accordingly. As a result, the preloader will track the loading of movies into the **myMovieClip** instance. The only other change within the script is the action that the conditional performs when loading is 90 percent complete. At that point, the clip loaded into **myMovieClip** is instructed to play.

Variation 2 – Using a Preloader for Sounds

The Sound object also has getBytesLoaded() and getBytesTotal() methods, which enable you to use our preloader clip to track the loading of external MP3 files into a Sound object. Look at the slightly modified preloader script that allows us to accomplish this:

```
onClipEvent(enterFrame){
  loaded = _root.myFavMP3.getBytesLoaded();
  total = _root.myFavMP3.getBytesTotal();
  bytesLoaded = Math.ceil((loaded / total) * 100);
  gotoAndStop(bytesLoaded);
  status.text = bytesLoaded + " % completed";
  if (bytesLoaded == 100 || total == undefined) {
```

```
    _visible = false;
  } else {
    _visible = true;
  }
}
```

This preloader script assumes that the external MP3 files are being loaded into a Sound object instance named myFavMp3. The first two lines of the script are edited accordingly. As a result, the preloader will track the loading of MP3s into that Sound object instance. The only other change is the conditional statement at the end of the script, which is used to make the preloader clip visible when an external MP3 is being loaded but invisible when it has loaded completely. Here's how it works.

The statement looks to see if bytesLoaded has a value of 100 (indicating that the loading process is complete) or if total is undefined (which it will be initially, before an MP3 has been loaded). Thus, the preloader is initially invisible when the movie plays. As soon as an MP3 file begins loading into myFavMp3, the preloader clip will become visible and begin displaying the progress of that download. When the downloading process is complete, the preloader clip will become invisible. It will become visible again when you begin loading another MP3 file in the myFavMP3 Sound object. The reason for this is that the conditional statement that determines the clip's visibility is continually being evaluated.

Things to note/uses

- Both the LoadVars and XML objects have getBytesLoaded() and getBytesTotal() methods. By now you should understand how to use our preloader clip as well as edit the script attached to it in order to track the loading of external data into an instance of either one of the object types.

- Although our preloader clip does an adequate job of displaying the status of the loading process, you may want to use something a bit more creative than an expanding loading bar as your preloader animation. For example, if you own a landscaping business, you might create a simple animation of a tree growing leaves as content loads. There's no reason why your preloaders can't be as interesting as any other part of your movie. Just keep in mind that any preloader clip you create shouldn't be so elaborate that it needs its *own* preloader clip.

Detecting Collisions

Flash can detect when one movie clip instance is touching another, allowing you to create games where actions occur as objects collide. This functionality is made possible via the hitTest() method of the MovieClip object. To help you understand how this works, we'll create three movie clip instances. One of these movie clip instances will be scripted so that it becomes draggable when pressed. As it's being dragged, it will progressively scale up in size if, and as long as, it is in contact with one of the other two movie clip instances. Its size will be reset to 100 percent when it comes in contact with the third, remaining movie clip instance.

1. Select the Rectangle tool, and draw a rectangle on the stage.

2. Select the rectangle you just drew, and press F8.

   The Convert to Symbol dialog box will appear.

3. Choose the Movie Clip Behavior, click the central box on the Registration graphic, enter a name of Rectangle Clip, and then click OK.

   This converts the rectangle on the stage into a movie clip instance.

4. Create two more copies of this instance by holding down the Control key (Windows) or Command key (Macintosh), then clicking on it, dragging away, and then releasing.

   The stage should now contain three instances of the Rectangle Clip.

5. Select one of the instances and give it an instance name of **scaleUp**. Select another and give it an instance name of **scaleReset**. Select the third instance and give it a name of **mainClip**.

6. With the Actions panel open, select Frame 1 of the main timeline and attach this script:

```
mainClip.onPress = function(){
  mainClip.startDrag(true);
}
mainClip.onEnterFrame = function(){
  if(mainClip.hitTest(scaleUp) == true){
    mainClip._xscale += 5;
    mainClip._yscale += 5;
  }else if(mainClip.hitTest(scaleReset) == true){
    mainClip._xscale = 100;
```

```
        mainClip._yscale = 100;
    }
}
```

The first part of this script uses an onPress event handler method in order to make the **mainClip** instance draggable when it's pressed. The second part of the script contains a conditional statement that, by means of the onEnterFrame event handler method, constantly checks to see if the **mainClip** instance comes in contact with the **scaleUp** instance (mainClip.hitTest(scaleUp) == true) or the **scaleReset** instance (mainClip.hitTest(scaleReset) == true), as it's being dragged around. If it comes in contact with the **scaleUp** instance, its size is progressively scaled up by 5 percent. If it comes in contact with the **scaleReset** instance, its size is reset to 100 percent. Since this part of the script is being executed by means of an onEnterFrame event handler, **mainClip** will *continue* to progressively scale upwards as long as it is in contact with the **scaleUp** instance (**Figure 16.9**).

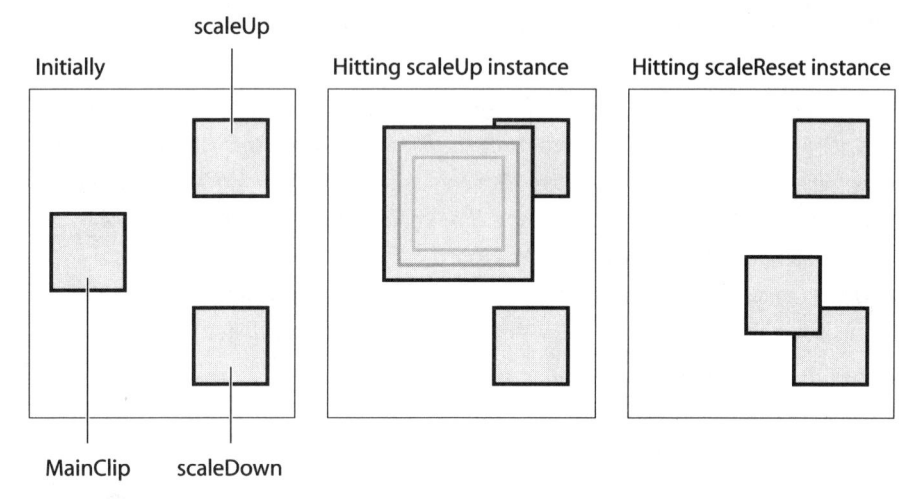

Figure 16.9
Initially, all of our movie clip instances are the same size. When the **mainClip** instance collides with the **scaleUp** instance, **mainClip** will get progressively larger. When the **mainClip** instance collides with the **scaleReset** instance, **mainClip**'s size will be reset.

Things to note/uses

- You can replace the onEnterFrame event handler in the script above with an onMouseMove event hander. This will cause scaling of the **mainClip** instance to occur only when it's in contact with one of the other movie clip instances *and* the mouse is in motion.

- Drag-and-drop functionality, where an action or set of actions is executed when one movie is dragged and dropped on top of another, is also made possible via the hitTest() method. We'll show you how to implement it in one of the projects you'll put together in Chapter 21, "Projects."

Printing Movies

Despite all the interactive and exciting ways you can use Flash to create powerful multimedia presentations, sometimes there's still nothing like the printed page to get your point across. In this section, we'll show you some of the many ways you can use the printed page to make your content more compelling.

ActionScript Printing vs. Browser Printing

Printing content using ActionScript rather than through a browser's Print command offers several advantages:

- **Content does not need to be visible to be printed.** *For content to be printed from the browser, it must be visible from within the browser window. In contrast, from Flash, you can hide printable content from the user so that it's only available for printing (its purpose). For example, a small 100-by-200-pixel Flash banner ad could contain a hidden movie (see "Printing Hidden Movies" later in this section) that is 640 by 800 pixels and contains numerous graphics that cannot be seen until printed. Thus, the physical size of the actual Flash movie has no bearing on the size of any printable material contained within it.*

- **You select what's printed.** *When you print an HTML page from a browser, everything you see is printed. This includes banner ads, navigation buttons, and more. When printing from Flash, this is not the case. You can select which content you wish to print, and which you don't.*

- **Multipage printing.** *Printing multiple HTML documents from a browser entails going to the first page and printing it, then the next page, and so on. You can avoid this tedium by printing from Flash: Since individual frames in a movie represent pages, you can easily tell Flash to print any number of these pages with a single action.*

- **High-quality output.** *Content printed from the browser sometimes suffers from being based on bitmap graphics. Although such graphics may look fine on screen, they often appear pixelated on page. Printed Flash content, in contrast, can be rendered as vector graphics to produce sharp, clear graphics.*

Preparing Movies for Printing

When using ActionScript to print content, think of every movie (including the main timeline, movie clips, and loaded movies) as a document and each frame of a movie as a printable page. By default, when you initiate a print action, all frames of the specified movie will print. For example, the following script will print frames in the movie clip instance **myMovieClip**:

```
print("myMovieClip");
```

However, by using special frame labels on the printed movie's timeline, you can specify print content from selected frames only.

1. In the authoring environment, activate the timeline whose frames you want to make printable.

2. With the Property inspector open, select a keyframe on the timeline that you wish to designate as printable.

3. In the Property inspector, enter #p in the Label text box.

4. Repeat Steps 2 and 3 to specify additional keyframes as printable (**Figure 16.10**).

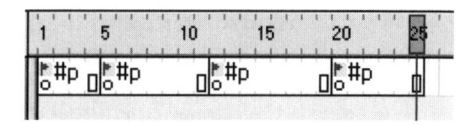

   Figure 16.10
   Giving a keyframe a label of #p will designate the graphical content on that frame as printable. Content on other frames will not print.

   When a print action targeting this timeline is initiated, only the frames you designated with a #p frame label will print.

Printing the Content in a Movie Clip Instance's Timeline

In this section, we will place a script on a button, which will be used to initiate the printing of a movie clip instance named **myPrintClip** (which we'll assume is a multi-frame movie clip instance containing content you want to make available for printing).

1. Open **myPrintClip**'s timeline and specify any frames that you wish to be printable, as described in the previous section. Or, if you wish to print all frames, do nothing.

2. Return to the main timeline. With the Actions panel open, select a button instance that exists at the same frame as the **myPrintClip** instance, and attach this script:

```
on(release){
   print("myPrintClip");
}
```

This will print all of the frames, or designated frames, in **myPrintClip**'s timeline when the button is pressed and released.

There are actually several ways of configuring the print action, depending on the content you're attempting to print and how you want it to appear when printed. Let's examine these options.

The `print` action `print("myPrintClip");` will print content within that instance at a high resolution, as vector shapes. The trade-off is that any object with a transparency will be printed opaque, and color effects (tint, brightness, and so on) applied to symbol instances within that timeline will not appear—all of which may interfere with the look you want for your printed material. By changing the action a bit, as in the following

```
printAsBitmap("myPrintClip");
```

All content within the timeline will be printed as bitmaps. While the quality of the printed material will not be as high as when printing it as vectors shapes (mentioned above), transparency and color effects applied to symbols and shapes will print.

Although we haven't done so yet, the `print` action allows use to specify the size at which content is printed. This is accomplished by adding a second parameter to the action as shown in the following examples:

```
print("myPrintClip", "bmovie");
printAsBitmap("myPrintClip", "bmovie");
```

The `bmovie` option sets the movie's bounding box as the total area of printed content. Content is printed at actual size.

```
print("myPrintClip", "bframe");
printAsBitmap("myPrintClip", "bframe");
```

The `bframe` option sets the composite bounding box of the content on all printable frames as the print area. Thus, the frame that contains content with the largest

Chapter 16 *Using ActionScript in Your Projects*

bounding box will be scaled to print as large as possible on the printed page, and the content on all other printable frames will be scaled a relative amount.

```
print("myPrintClip", "bmax");
printAsBitmap("myPrintClip", "bmax");
```

The bmax option will scale the content on each printable frame so that they all print the same size. Thus, the content on each frame will be scaled to fill the printed page (**Figure 16.11**).

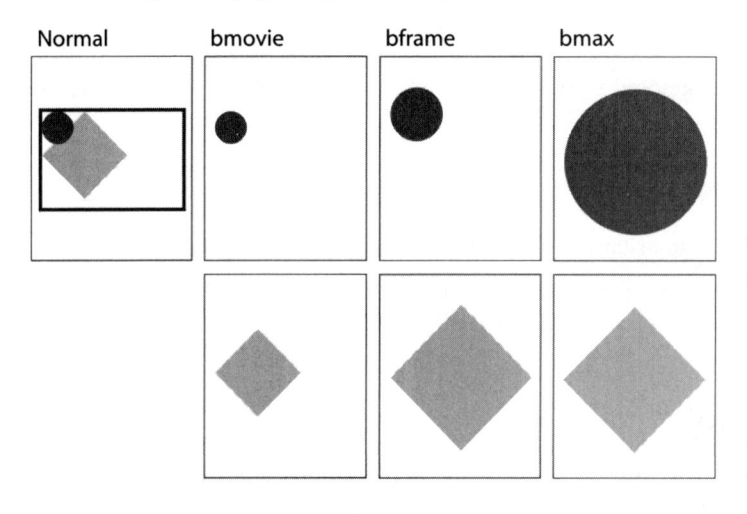

Figure 16.11
This graphic demonstrates the results of the three bounding options. Normal represents how the movie would appear against an actual sheet of paper.

Things to note/uses

- Your Flash movie can contain any number of printable movies in the form of movie clips or loaded movies.

- A movie must be fully loaded to be printed. A print action will not work on a movie that hasn't been fully loaded. Use the _framesloaded property to check whether the movie has fully loaded. Take a look at the following example:

```
if (myClip._framesloaded == myClip._totalframes) {
  print ("myClip", "bmovie");
}
```

- A movie clip instance must be given an instance name to be designated as printable.
- Only the first frame of any symbol *within* a printed movie's timeline will print.

Variation 1 – Printing the Content of a Movie on a Level

A movie loaded into a level can be printed, as described above, with a slight modification to the print action syntax. Take a look at the following examples:

```
printNum(2, "bmovie");
printAsBitmapNum(2, "bmovie");
```

There are two small changes in the syntax: First, you'll notice the addition of the word Num to the print action. This is used to indicate that the print action should print a timeline loaded into a level number. The second change is that a level number is specified in the action, as opposed to the name of a movie clip instance. Otherwise, the actions work in the same way as previously described.

Things to note/uses

- Similar to movie clip instances, all frames of a movie loaded into a level will print when using this action, unless you specify only certain frames to print using the #p frame label, as described earlier.

Disabling Printing

Even though your movie may not contain any print actions, the user can still print content via the Print command by right-clicking (Windows) or Control-clicking (Macintosh) the Flash Player. To make this feature unavailable (dimming it on the menu), select the keyframe on Frame 1 of the main timeline and give it a label of !#p. This will prevent users from printing from within Flash, though they can still print from their browsers.

Printing Hidden Movies

In some cases, you may not want printable content to be visible within Flash—say, if you wanted to hide one or more large printable movies within a small banner ad. Fortunately, a movie does not need to be visible in Flash to be targeted for the print action. Even though invisible, when printed, its content appears normal. The first step in using this technique is to attach an onClipEvent(load) event to any movie clip instance that contains printable content, along with an action that makes that movie clip instance invisible upon loading. The following script, if attached to **myMovieClip**, will make it invisible upon loading.

```
onClipEvent(load){
  _visible = 0;
}
```

While invisible, the clip can *still* be targeted for the print action (**Figure 16.12**):

```
on(release){
  print("myMovieClip", "bmovie");
}
```

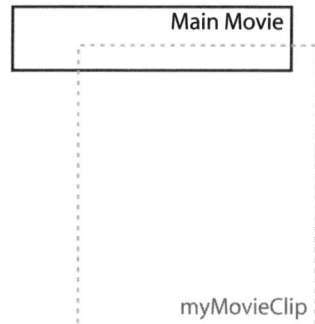

Figure 16.12
Invisible movie clip instances (in this instance, myMovieClip) can be targeted for printing, allowing you to print content that is much larger than the visible movie that contains it (Main Movie).

Things to note/uses

- Use this technique to hide coupons, simple product info, fact sheets, promotional material, and more.

Printing on Demand

Let's say you have five different product catalogs (movies) of 10 pages (frames) each that you would like to make available to your customers via Flash's printing feature—a total of 50 pages of content. If you made these movies part of your main movie, however, it would take most of the day to download. A better solution would be to make each catalog a separate SWF, then use a `loadMovie()` action in your main movie to load and print the appropriate catalog movie as needed—which we'll show you how to do next.

1. Create a new Flash authoring file (of any size that can accommodate your material), and place each page of printable content on separate keyframes on this movie's timeline. For our demonstration, you would need ten keyframes, each of which contains a page of content from one of your catalogs.

With content in place, we need to add two actions to this movie: one to make it invisible when loaded, and one to make it print when it has fully loaded.

2. Add a new layer to your movie, and name it Actions.

This layer will contain our two actions.

3. On the first frame of this new layer, add the following ActionScript:

```
this._visible = 0;
```

Because this action exists on Frame 1, this movie will be invisible when first loaded.

4. To ensure that our movie is fully loaded before we print it, add a keyframe (F6) to Frame 11 on the Actions layer, and place the following script there:

```
printNum(1, "bmovie");
stop();
```

The reason for placing this action on Frame 11 is simple: Our movie contains ten frames of content. By placing the action on Frame 11, we ensure that the movie will have completely loaded before the `print` action is triggered. The `stop()` action prevents the movie from looping.

5. Export this movie with a name such as catalog1.swf and save it in the directory that contains your main movie.

6. Repeat these steps to create any number of SWFs (named catalog2.swf, catalog3.swf, and so on), each of which contains a different catalog (or whatever content you want to make printable).

7. Open the authoring file that represents your main movie.

8. If you have created five separate SWFs that are printable documents, place five buttons in your main movie.

9. Attach the following script to each button.

```
on (release) {
   loadMovieNum ("catalog1.swf", 1);
}
```

When the button is released, catalog1.swf is loaded into Level 1. Once that movie has been completely loaded, it performs the function we set up earlier, meaning that the content within it begins printing.

For each button, you would need to change the name of the SWF file to load (as it appears in the script above) from catalog1.swf to catalog2.swf, catalog3.swf, and so on.

Things to note/uses

- This technique can be used for any printable content that you want to make available on an as-needed basis so that its file size doesn't weigh down your main movie—for example, multipage documents, portfolio images, and so forth.

Dynamic Drawing

ActionScript gives you the ability to dynamically draw lines and filled shapes, as your movie plays. In fact, only 12 lines of script are required to create a simple dynamic drawing application in which you can draw noncontiguous lines as well as clear the drawing area. In this section, we'll take a look at how you can build such an application.

Drawing Method Primer

To understand how dynamic drawing is accomplished, you must first realize that drawing is always performed in relation to a timeline, which for the purpose of this discussion we'll assume is a movie clip instance named **myDrawingClip**. This will make more sense as we progress.

The first step in dynamic drawing is setting the line style using the `lineStyle()` method. This method sets the size, color, and transparency of lines drawn dynamically in a particular timeline. Take a look at the following example:

```
myDrawingClip.lineStyle(2, 0x336699, 100);
```

This sets the line style for any dynamically drawn lines in the **myDrawingClip** instance. The parameter settings indicate that the lines will be 2 points thick, have a hex color of 0x336699 (gray-blue), and an alpha value of 100 (completely opaque).

The next step is to set the starting position, indicating the x and y locations of where the drawing process should begin. This is accomplished via the `moveTo()` method. Take a look at the following example:

```
myDrawingClip.moveTo(100, 100);
```

The above line of script moves the beginning drawing position to an x position of 100 and a y position of 100. These values are in relation to the x and y coordinates of **myDrawingClip**'s registration point (**Figure 16.13**).

The last step in the drawing process is actually drawing the line. You accomplish this by using the `lineTo()` method, as shown by the following example:

    myDrawingClip.lineTo(200, 150);

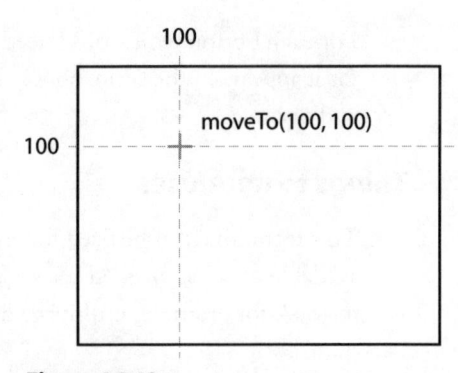

Figure 16.13
The moveTo() method sets the beginning drawing position in relation to the registration point of the specified movie clip instance.

The above script draws a line from x, y coordinates 100, 100 (as set by the `moveTo()` method above) to x, y coordinates of 200, 150 (as set by the `lineTo()` method shown here) (**Figure 16.14**). If the next line in the script used another `lineTo()` method, then another line would be drawn, connected to this line. If, however, you wanted to *move* the drawing position (that is, begin drawing from another position), you would use the `moveTo()` method, followed by another `lineTo()` method invocation.

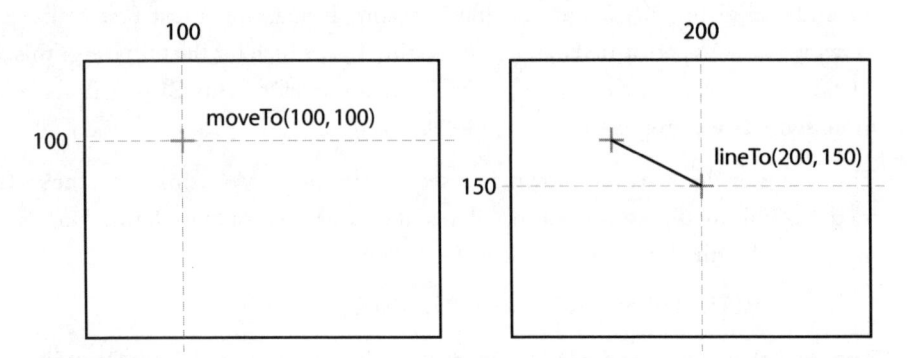

Figure 16.14
The lineTo() method is used to draw a line from the position defined by the previous moveTo() method to the position defined by the lineTo() method.

NOTE *When a line is drawn, the moveTo() position is automatically reset to the end of the drawn line.*

You can clear any dynamically drawn lines using the `clear()` method:

    myDrawingClip.clear();

Creating a Dynamic Drawing Application

In this section, we'll show you how to create a drawing application using just 12 lines of code. This application will draw lines (of random size and transparency) as you hold down the spacebar and move the mouse around. Pressing the mouse button will clear any drawing you have completed.

1. Start a new Flash document.

2. With the Actions panel open, select Frame 1 of the default layer and add the following script:

   ```
   _root.createEmptyMovieClip("canvas", 1);
   ```

   This will dynamically create an empty movie clip instance on the main timeline and assign it a depth of 1 and an instance name of **canvas**. We will be drawing lines within this timeline. We could have used an existing instance, but when doing so, any dynamically drawn lines appear behind any graphical content within that timeline. Thus, depending on the amount of content it contains, it may be difficult, or even impossible, to see any dynamically drawn lines. Hence, the reason for creating an empty movie clip instance and using it for dynamic drawing purposes.

3. Add the following script at the end of the script added in the previous step:

   ```
   canvas.onMouseMove = function(){
      if(Key.isDown(Key.SPACE)){
         canvas.lineStyle(random(21), 0x336699, random(101));
         canvas.lineTo(_root._xmouse, _root._ymouse);
      }else{
         canvas.moveTo(_root._xmouse, _root._ymouse);
      }
   }
   ```

   This script attaches an onMouseMove event handler method to the **canvas** instance just created, causing the script to execute each time the mouse is moved. As you can see, a conditional statement is used to determine whether the spacebar is being pressed down when the script is executed. If it is, the lineStyle() method is used to specify the style for lines drawn in the **canvas** movie clip instance. The size parameter for this method is set using a random value between 0 and 20; the color parameter is set to a hex value of 0x336699 (gray-blue); and the transparency parameter is set to a random value between 0 and 100. The random numbers are regenerated with each movement of the mouse, which will cause lines to appear in various sizes and transparencies (not really necessary, but fun nonetheless).

The next line within the first part of the conditional statement uses the `lineTo()` method to dynamically draw lines. Thus, each time the mouse is moved while the spacebar is pressed, a new line will be drawn from the previous mouse position to the current mouse position.

When the mouse is moved, but the spacebar is *not* pressed, then the `else` part of the statement is executed. The `lineTo()` method is not used in this part of the statement; thus, drawing will cease. Instead, the `moveTo()` method is used to reset the beginning point for when drawing resumes (that is, when the spacebar is pressed). Each time the mouse is moved and the spacebar is not pressed, this part of the statement is executed—which means the `moveTo()` position may be set numerous times before drawing resumes (**Figure 16.15**).

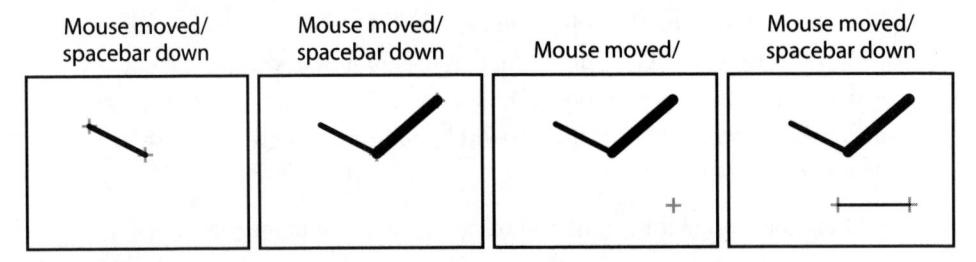

Figure 16.15
The progression of steps that will cause drawing to occur within our application.

4. Add this script at the end of the current script:

   ```
   canvas.onMouseDown = function(){
       canvas.clear();
   }
   ```

   This part of the script creates functionality so that when the mouse is pressed down, any dynamically drawn lines within the **canvas** instance will be cleared.

5. Have fun (**Figure 16.16**)!

Figure 16.16
The effect of having too much time on your hands (or not enough)!

Things to note/uses

- Dynamically drawn lines are printable in the same manner as any other content within your movie.

- Using additional drawing methods, you can create curved lines as well as shapes with solid or gradient fills. Although we don't have room to cover all of these methods here, with a little experimentation, you'll soon begin to discover what's possible.

- Coordinates used in the drawing process can come from sources other than the current position of the mouse, as shown above. For example, you can fill an array with these coordinates in order to have Flash dynamically draw a line graph based on those values.

- Although beyond the scope of this book, you can use looping statements to create some interesting, and fun, dynamically drawn graphics.

Dynamic Masking

Mask layers (where the shape of an object on the mask layer is used to mask the content on the layer below it) have always been a great feature in Flash, enabling you to create visual effects that would be otherwise impossible (for more information, see Chapter 10, "Using Animation to Build Movement"). However, the functionality of mask layers is somewhat limited by the fact that the object that acts as the mask cannot be changed while the movie plays. You can get around this problem by creating masks using ActionScript: This way, you can not only turn masking on and off dynamically, you can also set or change, at any time, the movie clip instance that acts as the mask, which we'll explore in the following exercise.

1. Start a new Flash document. Import an image onto Layer 1, Frame 1.

   This image can be any size, but something approaching the size of the stage (W: 550 × H: 400) will work best.

2. Convert the image to a movie clip instance.

3. Select the new movie clip instance, and from the Edit menu choose Copy.

4. From the Edit menu choose Paste in Place.

   This pastes the copy directly above the original.

5. With the Property inspector open, select the copy and give it an instance name of **picture**.

   This is the instance whose content we will be masking using ActionScript (and thus the reason for giving it an instance name).

6. With the copy still selected, open the Transform panel and scale this instance to 130 percent.

   There are now two instances of the same clip on the stage, with the one on top (named **picture**) 30 percent larger than, and totally concealing, the one below it. We want the larger clip to be invisible initially so that when the movie first plays, the instance below it (which is 100 percent of the actual size) will be seen instead.

7. With the Actions panel open, select the **picture** movie clip instance, and attach this script:

   ```
   onClipEvent(load){
      _visible = false;
   }
   ```

   Now when this instance loads, it will initially be invisible. The reason for doing this will become evident shortly.

8. Insert a layer on the timeline, above the only other layer that currently exists.

   This layer will soon contain two movie clip instances, one in the shape of a circle, the other in the shape of a square. We will be creating a script that allows either of these two clips (depending on which one is currently being pressed) to act as a mask for the **picture** movie clip instance created earlier.

9. With the newly inserted layer as the current layer, select the Oval tool and create a medium-size circle anywhere on the stage. Convert this circle to a movie clip, and give the instance on the stage a name of **circle**.

10. With the newly inserted layer as the current layer, select the Rectangle tool, and create a medium-sized square anywhere on the stage. Convert this square to a movie clip, and give the instance on the stage a name of **square**.

    All necessary elements are in place. Now it's time to create the script that brings it all together.

11. Insert another layer at the top of the layer stack. With the Actions panel open, select Frame 1 of this new layer and attach the following script:

    ```
    circle.onPress = function(){
       picture._visible = true;
       picture.setMask(circle);
       circle.startDrag(true);
    }
    ```

```
  circle.onRelease = function(){
    picture._visible = false;
    picture.setMask(null);
    stopDrag();
  }
  square.onPress = function(){
    picture._visible = true;
    picture.setMask(square);
    square.startDrag(true);
  }
  square.onRelease = function(){
    picture._visible = false;
    picture.setMask(null);
    stopDrag();
  }
```

The first part of this script uses an onPress event handler method to define what happens when the **circle** instance is pressed. The first action makes the **picture** instance visible. Immediately after this occurs, the setMask() method is used to cause the **circle** instance to mask the **picture** instance. The third action makes the **circle** instance draggable, creating a dynamically assigned, draggable mask.

The next part of the script uses an onRelease event handler method to define what should occur when the **circle** instance is released. When this occurs, the effects of all the actions that were executed when the instance was pressed are reversed: The **picture** instance is made invisible again; the mask is removed from the **picture** instance; and dragging of the **circle** instance ceases.

The remainder of the script enables similar functionality in relation to the **square** movie clip instance (**Figure 16.17**).

Figure 16.17
Our script allows either the circle or square movie clip instance to act as a mask when pressed. This graphic shows the effects of both being pressed (not possible within Flash, for demonstration purposes only).

Things to note/uses

- Although the movie clips used as masks in this exercise consisted of simple graphics, by using movie clip instances with animated content as masks, you can facilitate an almost endless array of visual effects.

Fast-Forwarding/Rewinding

ActionScript provides built-in functionality for stopping and playing a movie's timeline, but not for fast-forwarding and rewinding. In this section, we'll show you how to create this functionality to control the playback of any timeline, including movie clip instances and even video clips that have been encapsulated within a movie clip.

1. Open one of your own projects that contains a movie clip instance with animated content at least several hundred frames long. (Alternatively, you could import a video clip and convert it to a movie clip instance.)

2. Name this movie clip instance **myMovieClip**, and place it on the main timeline.

    This movie clip instance should be designed so that it plays immediately upon loading.

3. Create two buttons and place them on the main timeline, below the movie clip instance.

    One of these buttons will be used for rewinding, the other for fast-forwarding.

4. With the Actions panel open, select the button that will act as the Rewind button and attach this script:

```
on(press){
    activate = setInterval(ffRew, 5, "Rew");
}
on(release){
    clearInterval(activate);
    ffRew(null);
}
```

This button is set up to react to two events: press and release. When pressed, a setInterval() action is initiated and given a name of activate. You'll remember from Chapter 13 that a setInterval() action is used to call a function at a regular interval, which you specify. This setInterval() action is set up to call the ffRew() function every 5 milliseconds, as well as pass that function a string value of "Rew" each time it's called. We haven't created this function yet, but remember this parameter value for when we do. The calling of the ffRew() function will continue every 5 milliseconds until this button is released, at which point a clearInterval() action is used to clear the activate interval set into motion when the button is pressed. Thus, when the button is released, the ffRew() is no longer called at 5-millisecond intervals. Immediately following the `clearInterval()` action, the `ffRew()` function is called once, and passed a parameter value of `null` (nothing). Remember this parameter value for when we create the `ffRew()` function in a moment. Now let's script the FF button.

5. With the Actions panel open, select the button that will act as the Fast-Forwarding button and attach this script:

```
on(press){
   activate = setInterval(ffRew, 5, "FF");
}
on(release){
   clearInterval(activate);
   ffRew(null);
}
```

This script is exactly the same as the one attached to the Rewind button except for the fact that the `setInterval()` action passes a value of `"FF"` to the `ffRew()`. Let's next create that function.

6. With the Actions panel open, select Frame 1 of the main timeline and add this function definition:

```
function ffRew(direction){
   myMovieClip.stop();
   if(direction == "Rew"){
      myMovieClip.prevFrame();
   }else if(direction == "FF"){
      myMovieClip.nextFrame();
   }else{
      myMovieClip.play();
   }
}
```

This function, named `ffRew()`, accepts a single parameter named `direction`. You'll remember that our buttons are set up to send this function a parameter value of `"Rew"`, `"FF"`, or `null`. A conditional statement evaluates which value is passed to the function, so that it can react accordingly. Let's review how this function works.

The first thing that occurs within this function is that **myMovieClip**'s timeline is stopped. This is done because if it were allowed to continue to play, its playback would interfere with the rewind and fast-forward functionality that follows. The next part of the function uses a conditional statement to determine whether direction has a value of "Rew", "FF", or null when the function is called. If it has a value of "Rew", this means that the rewind button has been pressed and the setInterval() action has been initiated, as discussed earlier. This causes the action within the first part of the conditional statement to be executed every 5 milliseconds. As you can see, this action will move **myMovieClip**'s timeline to the previous frame. Executing this action every 5 milliseconds causes that timeline to appear to play in reverse. Conversely, if direction has a value of "FF", this means the FF button is being pressed, and the second part of the statement is executed every 5 milliseconds. This will move **myMovieClip**'s timeline forward at a very fast pace.

You'll remember that whenever either the rewind or fast-forward buttons are released, the setInterval() actions are cleared and this function is sent a value of null—at which point the last part of the conditional statement is executed. The action within this part of the statement simply reinitiates playback of **myMovieClip**'s timeline.

Things to note/uses

- Remember that you can use this functionality to control the playback of a video clip if it has been converted to a movie clip instance.
- By changing the number of milliseconds within the setInterval() actions, you can change the speed of the rewind and fast-forward functionalities.

Dynamic Names

As you're well aware of at this point, when defining an action to do something, you're required to specify the name of a variable, object, timeline, etc., such as in the following:

    myMovieClip._visible = 50;

The above action will always target **myMovieClip**—fine in most cases, but you may sometimes want to use a single piece of code in the context of any number of variables, objects, timelines, and so on. Let's take a look at how you would do that.

The array access operator ([]) can be used to evaluate the value of a variable or expression in order to set the name in an action. For example, take a look at the following variable assignment:

```
myVariable = "car";
```

This variable has a string value of "car". That means that the following line of script:

```
_root[myVariable]._x = 250;
```

Would be evaluated to actually read as follows (since myVariable currently has a value of "car"):

```
_root.car._x = 250;
```

Thus, the **car** movie clip instance on the main timeline would be moved to an x position of 250. Now comes the really cool part: If the value of myVariable is updated to a value of "truck", then the previously mentioned action, when executed again, will be evaluated as follows:

```
_root.truck._x = 250;
```

This will move the **truck** movie clip instance to an x position of 250.

You can extend this functionality to evaluate expressions in the following way:

```
_root["sandwich" + count]._xscale = 200;
```

If count currently has a value of 17, then this line of script would be evaluated as:

```
_root.sandwich17._xscale = 200;
```

Thus, the movie clip instance named **sandwich17** would be horizontally scaled by 200 percent. If count had a value of 5, then **sandwich5** would be scaled instead.

NOTE *When using the array access operator as shown in the examples above, you'll notice that you don't place a dot between the _root object and the opening square bracket. Doing so will cause an error.*

It's common practice to use this functionality in functions or looping statements, which is what we'll look at next.

Dynamic Naming Within a Function

The rewind/fast-forward function we created in the previous section had one fairly severe limitation: It only worked in relation to a single movie clip instance named **myMovieClip**. However, by using the principle of dynamic naming, we can make the function work in relation to *any* timeline. Doing so requires a few minor changes to that code. First, take a look at how the setInterval() action that makes a call to the function would be updated on the Fast-Forward button:

```
activate = setInterval(ffRew, 5, "FF", "car");
```

Notice the addition of the "car" parameter value. Let's look at how this value is used in the updated function, which would look like the following:

```
function ffRew(direction, movieName){
  _root[movieName].stop();
  if(direction == "Rew"){
    _root[movieName].prevFrame();
  }else if(direction == "FF"){
    _root[movieName].nextFrame();
  }else{
    _root[movieName].play();
  }
}
```

The function has been updated so that it now accepts two parameters: direction and movieName. You'll also note that references to myMovieClip have been changed to _root[movieName]. This will allow the function to work in context of the timeline whose name is passed to the function when it's called (or, in the case of our discussion, the movie clip instance named **car**).

Dynamic Naming Within a Looping Statement

Dynamic naming of variables, objects, and timelines plays an important role in looping statements as well, allowing you to create a loop that will target a different timeline with each iteration. In the following exercise, we'll use a loop to dynamically create, position, and rotate a number of duplicate movie clip instances to demonstrate how dynamic names are used to handle this kind of functionality.

1. Start a new Flash document.

2. Draw a small square (any color) on the stage, convert it to a movie clip instance, and give it an instance name of **clip**.

   Make sure that when you convert the square to a movie clip, you give it a center registration point (**Figure 16.18**).

   Figure 16.18
   When converting the square to a movie clip instance, make sure to give it a center registration point.

3. Select Frame 1 of the main timeline, and attach the following script:

   ```
   numberOfDuplicates = 60;
   for(i = 1; i <= numberOfDuplicates; ++i){
      clip.duplicateMovieClip("newClip" + i, i);
      _root["newClip" + i]._x = i * 10;
      _root["newClip" + i]._rotation = i * 5;
   }
   clip._visible = false;
   ```

   Since this script exists on Frame 1 of the timeline, it will be executed as soon as the movie begins to play. First, a variable named `numberOfDuplicates` is created and assigned a value of 60. Obviously, this variable will be used to determine the number of duplicate movie clip instances our loop will create.

   The next five lines contain our looping statement, which is set to loop as long as `i` has a value less than or equal to `numberOfDuplicates`. Since `i` is given an initial value of 1, this loop will have 60 iterations. With each iteration, three actions are executed: The first action is used to duplicate the **clip** movie clip instance. The `duplicateMovieClip()` action has two parameters used to give the duplicate a name and a depth. As you can see, each duplicate created is given a name based on the string value of "newClip" concatenated with the current value of `i`, as well as a depth based on the current value of `i`. Since `i` is incremented by a value of 1 with each loop, the first duplicate will be named **newClip1**, placed at a depth of 1. The second duplicate will be named **newClip2**, placed at a depth of 2, and so on.

Using dynamic naming, the next two actions are used to set the x position and rotation values of the duplicate instance just created. Thus, if the loop is on iteration 23, these actions are evaluated as follows:

```
_root.newClip23._x = i * 10;
_root.newclip23._rotation = i * 5;
```

These actions use the current value of i to set the x position and rotation of successive duplicates to progressive amounts. For example, during the first iteration of this loop, i has a value of 1; thus, the first duplicate's x position and rotation values will be set to 10 and 5, respectively. On the next iteration of the loop, i will have a value of 2; thus, the second duplicate's x position and rotation values will be set to 20 and 10, respectively. These values continue to increase until the completion of the loop.

The last line of the script makes the **clip** instance invisible, since its only use was to provide the script with a movie clip instance to duplicate. Playing this movie using different values within the loop will create some interesting effects (**Figure 16.19**).

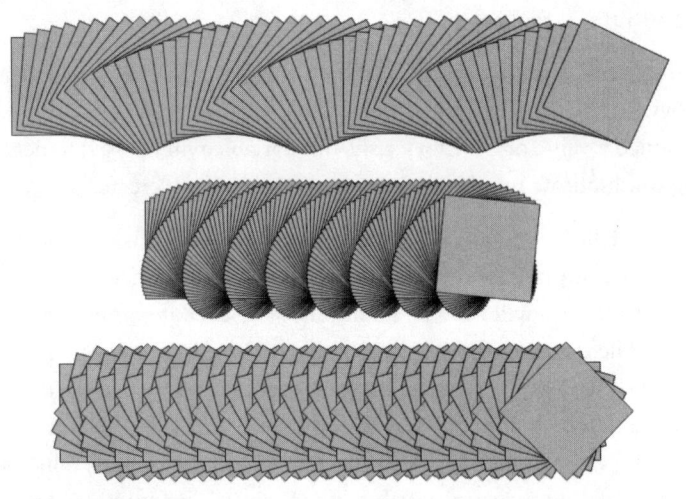

Figure 16.19
Some of the effects that can be achieved by altering the number of duplicates created, x position, and rotation settings in our loop.

Although we've touched on a number of ways you can use ActionScript in your Flash projects, we've only scratched the surface of what's possible. The possibilities are virtually limitless, and—as you've seen—you don't need a PhD in physics or computer science to put ActionScript to use. All it takes is bit of creativity and an intermediate understanding of ActionScripting syntax and principles.

5

Movie Management

> Using the Library to Manage Your Assets 693
> Using Movie Explorer to Manage Structure ... 717

A SINGLE FLASH PROJECT can contain hundreds of movie elements, including symbols, sounds, bitmaps, video, text, and scripts. Not surprisingly, organizing and managing these elements is key to working efficiently within the authoring environment. In this section, we'll examine the library, where you organize, preview, and configure your movie's visual elements, as well as Movie Explorer, which provides an overall view of your project's structure and helps you easily navigate its many elements.

Using the Library to Manage Your Assets

CHAPTER 17

What you'll learn...

About the library interface

How to manage library assets

How to work with elements from the Library panel

How to work with common and shared libraries

How to update symbols from external libraries

Think how difficult it would be to accomplish anything with your computer, if it didn't have a built-in filing system to help you keep track of your data. You could spend dozens of hours trying to locate a single file among the thousands on your hard drive—and still not find it. Fortunately, computer operating systems make file management a fairly painless process.

Most operating systems allow you to organize your files in "folders" that work the same way file folders do in the physical world. You can open and close them, name and rename them, reorder them, or discard all or part of them. In short, you can organize them in any fashion that makes sense to you.

A Flash project can contain hundreds of items, or *assets*, including symbols, sounds, bitmaps, and video. Keeping track of all of these items would be a daunting task without the library, which provides everything you need to keep your movie elements organized. You can work with items in Macromedia Flash's library much as you do with files on your hard drive—each asset in your project is identified by an icon representing its type, and all assets are organized into folders.

Introducing the Library Panel

Whenever you create a symbol or import an external asset (for example, a sound, bitmap, or video) into your authoring file, that asset is added to the library. You organize and access the various assets in the library via the Library panel.

The Interface

To begin our look at the Library panel, let's focus on its interface, which provides all kinds of information about the items in your movie. Note that because the library can contain both folders and movie assets, we use the term *item* to denote both. Where it's necessary to distinguish between the two content types, we'll point it out.

To open the Library panel:

- From the Window menu, choose Library.

   The library will remain open onscreen until you manually close it.

The Library panel display includes the following elements (**Figure 17.1**):

- **Item count.** This field shows you the number of items in your library, including folders as well as individual items such as symbols, sounds, and bitmaps.

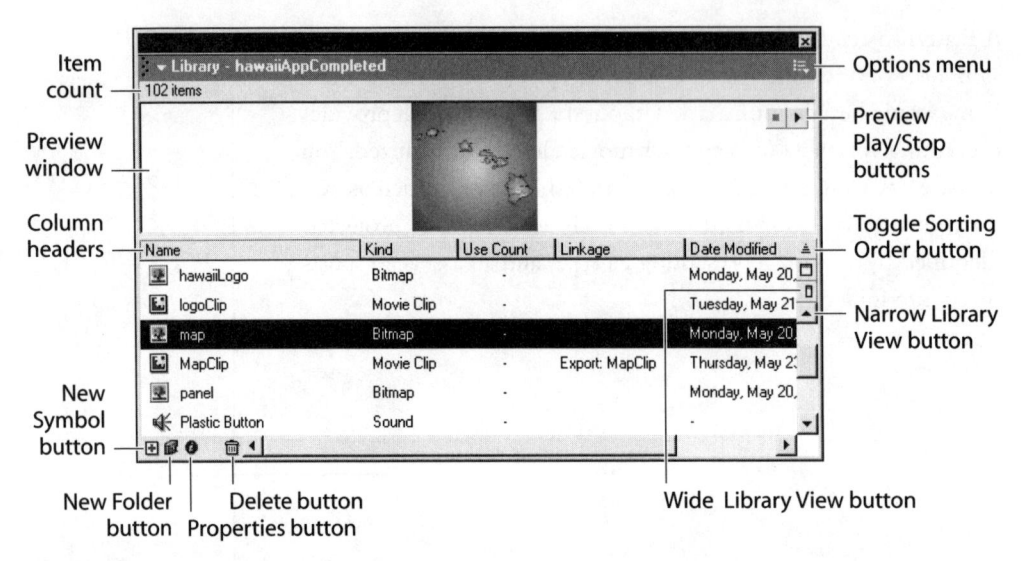

Figure 17.1
The Library panel interface.

- **Options menu.** Clicking here opens the Library panel Options menu, which provides the commands you need to work with library items. (We'll discuss these commands later in the chapter.)
- **Preview window.** This window lets you preview an asset's appearance and function.
- **Preview Play/Stop buttons.** Use these buttons to control the preview of any animated assets in your library.
- **Column headers.** These headers describe the information about each library asset displayed beneath them:

    Name. This hierarchical list includes the names of all of the items in the library. In the case of sounds, bitmaps, and videos, it includes the name of the symbol, folder, or imported file from which the asset was derived.

    Kind. This describes the kind of item (graphic, button, movie clip, bitmap, sound, video, or folder).

    Use Count. This tells you how many times your project uses an asset in the library.

    Linkage. Indicates whether the asset is part of a shared library, or has been imported from or exported to a shared library. (We'll discuss this in greater depth later in the chapter.)

    Date Modified. This indicates the date and time an item was last edited or updated.

- **Toggle Sorting Order button.** Use this button to sort your items in ascending or descending order.
- **Wide Library View button.** This button maximizes the Library panel so that all column headers are visible.
- **Narrow Library View button.** This button minimizes the Library panel so that it displays only the names and icons of the symbols it contains. You can use the horizontal scroll bar to scroll through the columns.
- **New Symbol button.** Use this button to create a new symbol from the Library panel. (It functions the same way as the New Symbol command in the Insert menu on the Flash main menu bar.)
- **New Folder button.** Use this button to create a new folder in the library directory.
- **Properties button.** Use this button to bring up the Properties dialog box, so that you can adjust the selected asset's settings.

- **Delete button.** If you select an item in the library and then press this button, the item will be deleted from your project. But be careful: You cannot undo this action.

Additional Menus

There are a couple of additional menus you'll find useful when working with the library:

- If you right-click (Windows) or Control-click (Macintosh) an item in the Library panel, a menu pops up offering several tasks that can be performed on that item (**Figure 17.2**).

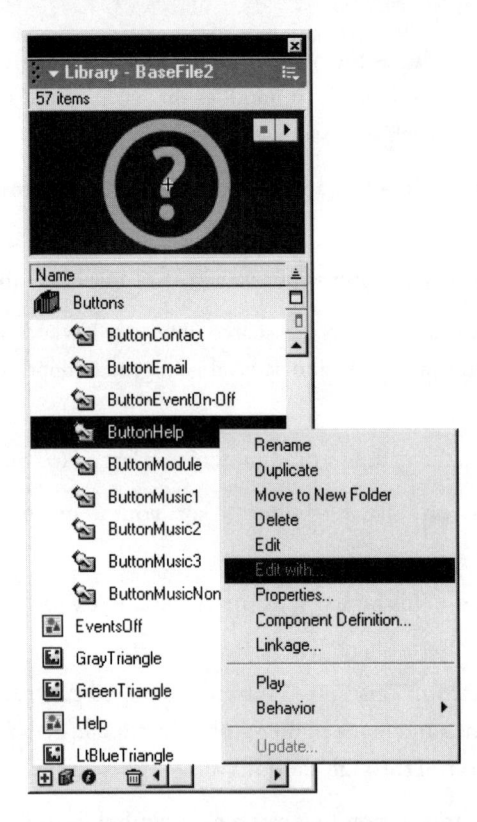

Figure 17.2
An item's contextual pop-up menu.

- If you right-click (Windows) or Control-click (Macintosh) the Preview window in the library, another menu pops up, allowing you to specify how you want the background in the Preview window to appear.

Managing Library Assets

A library asset is any element that can be used more than once in your Flash movie. Library assets can include symbols you've created, as well as sounds, bitmaps, and video that have been imported. Each asset in the library is identified by an icon that represents the asset type (**Figure 17.3**), as well as a name that differentiates it from the other assets.

TIP *There's another type of library asset, known as a Component, which we discuss in Chapter 15, "Components."*

You can perform all sorts of tasks from within the Library panel: Some of these are unique to the library, and some (such as creating new symbols or updating imported files) are the same functions you can perform elsewhere in Flash. Being able to execute such tasks from within this panel is simply a matter of convenience.

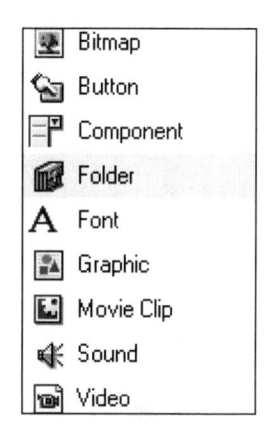

Figure 17.3 Library items and their identifying icons.

Let's take a look at some of the things you can do from within the Library panel.

Selecting Items

Selecting an item in the library allows you to move, rename, or delete it, as well as drag it onto the stage in order to work with it there. In most cases, selecting items in the library is no different than selecting items elsewhere in Flash. (You select folders and assets the same way.)

To select an item:

♦ Click it once; it will appear highlighted.

To select multiple items:

• Click an item once, hold down the Control (Windows) or Command (Macintosh) key, then click another item.

   Keep doing this to select additional items.

Once you've selected an item, you can drag it to the stage and add it to your movie (though you can't do this with folders). You can also drag items to a folder within the library.

The commands on the Options menu will always pertain to the selected item(s) (**Figure 17.4**).

Previewing Assets

When you select a graphic or sound asset, the Preview window will show you how it will appear in your movie. (For sounds, the Preview window will display a graphic of the sound waveform.) If the asset is one that plays over a span of frames (for example, a sound, movie clip, or button), you can click the Play button in the Preview window to see or hear it played live in that window. Click the Stop button to halt it.

To resize the preview window:

- Place your cursor between the Preview window and column headers. When it turns into a double-sided arrow, click and drag (**Figure 17.5**).

Figure 17.4
When you select an item in the Library panel, the commands available on the Library panel's Options menu will pertain to that item.

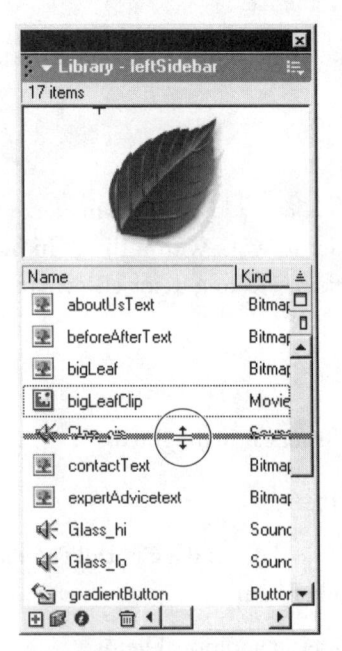

Figure 17.5
Resizing the Preview window provides a more detailed view.

Renaming Items

If you're no longer happy with an item's name, you can simply rename it.

To rename an item in the library, do one of the following:

- Double-click its name.

- Right-click (Windows) or Control-click (Macintosh), and from the pop-up menu that appears, choose Rename.

- Select the item in the library, then press the Properties button at the bottom of the Library panel.

- Select the item in the library, and from the Options menu in the Library panel choose Rename.

Deleting Items

Typically, not all of the symbols you create or the files you import will make it into your final product. However, Flash stores every one of those files and symbols in the library unless you specifically delete them. Although these unused items won't affect the file size of your final exported movie, they remain part of your Flash authoring file, making that file unnecessarily large. It's a good idea to do periodic housecleaning, in order to rid the library of all those unused files.

To delete an item from the library:

1. Select the items you wish to delete.

The item—a symbol, sound, bitmap, video, or folder—will be highlighted.

2. From the Options menu in the Library panel, choose Delete.

A delete confirmation box will appear, asking if you're sure you want to delete the item.

3. Click the Delete button to complete the action.

Flash also provides a command that allows you to search and select all of the items that aren't actually used in your project. Once selected, they can be deleted simultaneously.

To select and delete unused items:

1. From the Options menu in the Library panel, choose Select Unused Items.

   All unused items appear highlighted.

2. Click the Delete button at the bottom of the Library panel (**Figure 17.6**).

   A delete confirmation box will appear, asking whether you're sure you want to delete.

3. Click the Delete button to complete the action.

   TIP *Remember, when you delete an object from the library, it's really gone—that is, you can't undo the deletion—so be certain of your choice before completing the action.*

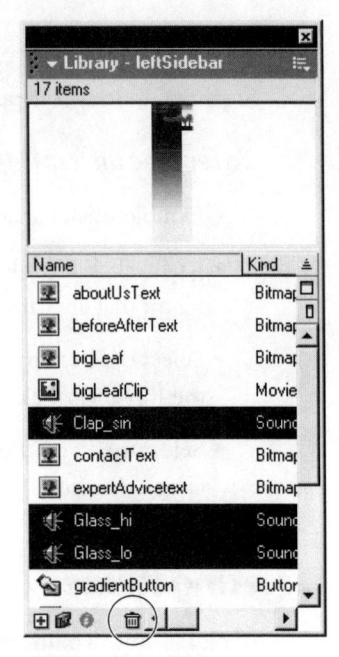

Figure 17.6
Delete unused items to keep your authoring file from becoming unnecessarily large.

Working with Symbols in the Library Panel

You can create and duplicate symbols, alter a symbol's properties, change its behavior, and even execute commands to edit its content and timeline from within the Library panel. These functions are all similar to those discussed in the chapter on symbols. Performing these tasks from a central location can save you considerable mouse clicks, since you don't have to hop around among various menus, panels, and dialog boxes to accomplish the same thing. For more information about any of the tasks that follow, see Chapter 7, "Symbols."

To create a new symbol from the Library panel:

1. From the Options menu in the Library panel, choose New Symbol, or click the New Symbol button at the bottom of the panel.

   The Create New Symbol dialog box will appear.

2. Give your new symbol a name and assign it a behavior.

3. Click OK.

   Your new symbol will be added automatically to the library, and you will be taken to its timeline and stage so that you can begin adding content to it. For more information about symbol creation, see Chapter 7, "Symbols."

   TIP *When you create a new symbol using the Library panel, it is added to the currently active directory. Selecting a folder or an asset within a folder makes it the active directory. Thus, if you select a symbol that resides in a folder named My Buttons, all new symbols or folders will initially be placed in that folder, since it represents the active directory.*

To duplicate symbols from the Library panel:

1. From the list of symbols that appears in the Library panel, select the one you wish to duplicate.

   The asset will be highlighted.

2. From the Options menu in the Library panel, choose Duplicate to make the Duplicate Symbol dialog box appear.

3. Name your new symbol, assign a behavior to it, and click OK.

   The new symbol will be added to the library.

To view a symbol's properties from the Library panel:

1. Select the symbol in the Library panel.

2. From the Options menu in the Library panel, choose Properties, or click the Properties button at the bottom of the panel.

To change a symbol's behavior from the Library panel:

1. Right-click (Windows) or Control-click (Macintosh) the symbol whose behavior you would like to change.

2. On the menu that appears, choose Behavior and then the particular behavior you would like to apply to this symbol.

Once you've changed a symbol's behavior in this manner, any new instances of it that you drag from the library will reflect the new behavior (**Figure 17.7**).

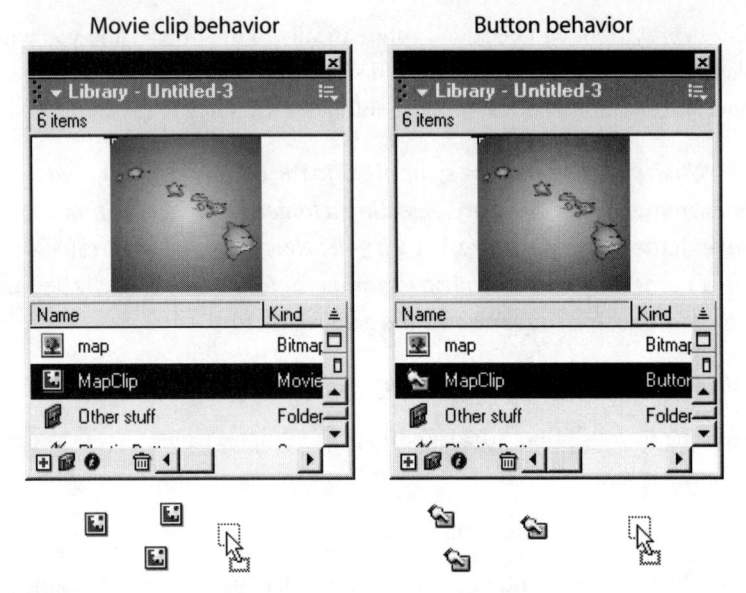

Figure 17.7
If you change a movie clip's behavior to a button behavior in the Library panel, any new instances dragged onto the stage will reflect the new behavior you applied.

To enter symbol-editing mode from the Library panel:

1. Select a symbol from the Library panel.
2. From the Options menu in the Library panel, choose Edit to open the symbol's stage and timeline for editing.

Working with Sounds, Bitmaps, and Videos in the Library Panel

Working with sounds, bitmaps, and videos in the Library panel varies only slightly from working with symbols. There are basically two tasks you can perform on these library assets: You can view or change their properties (name, compression setting, and so on), and you can import a more current version of a file to replace the version you previously imported into Flash. Both of these tasks are discussed more fully in Chapter 5, "Sound," and Chapter 6, "Bitmaps."

To view or change the properties of a sound, bitmap, or video from within the Library window:

1. Select a sound, bitmap, or video asset from the Library window; it will be highlighted.

2. From the Options menu in the Library panel, choose Properties, or click the Properties button at the bottom of the Library panel.

To update a sound, bitmap, or video file:

1. Select a sound, bitmap, or video asset from the Library panel.

2. From the Options menu on the Library panel, choose Update to update the file used in Flash, to reflect any changes you made to it using an external program.

Viewing and Organizing Library Items

Although you can perform all sorts of tasks from within the library, it's primarily an organizational tool that you can use to quickly locate, use, and adjust properties, as well as to view information about your project's various elements.

Creating and Working with Folders

Flash uses folders in much the same way your operating system does: to help you locate and work with files. Using folders effectively can save you a great deal of time and aggravation.

Any item in the library can be put into a folder; you can also place folders within folders.

To create a folder:

1. From the Options menu in the Library panel, select New Folder, or click the New Folder button at the bottom of the Library panel.

   A folder, initially called "untitled folder," will appear on the list of library items.

2. Assign a name to the folder that clearly identifies its content, such as Backgrounds (**Figure 17.8**).

3. To complete the action, click outside the text box for the name. Your new folder will be added to the library directory structure.

To expand or collapse a folder, do one of the following:

- Double-click the folder's icon.

    Or

- Select the folder in the Library panel, and from the Options menu choose Expand Folder or Collapse Folder.

    TIP *Use the Expand All or Collapse All commands on the Options menu to open or close all folders simultaneously.*

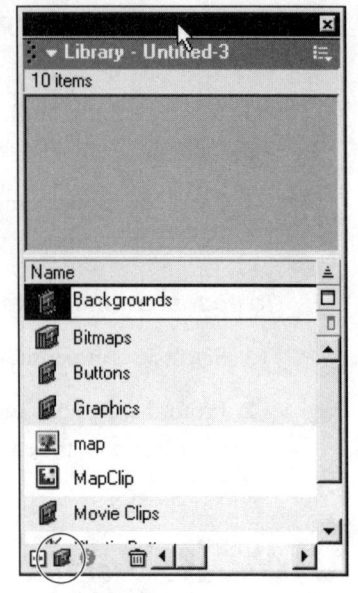

Figure 17.8
Click the New Folder button at the bottom of the Library panel to add folders to the library's directory structure.

Moving Items into Folders

As the scope of your project grows, you may need to move items into different folders to make your library's directory structure more logical.

To move an item into an existing folder:

1. Select the item(s) in the library, and begin dragging it.

    As you drag the item, the cursor display will turn into a circle with a line through it (indicating an area that you can't drag to), or an arrow with a small box in its lower right corner (indicating an area you can drag to) (**Figure 17.9**). You cannot drag an item to a folder where it already exists (hence the cursor indicates this).

2. Drag the item to the folder you wish to drop it into, and then release the mouse.

    TIP *You cannot drag and drop items into the folder in which they already reside. You can, however, drag and drop them into parent or child folders.*

To move an item into a new folder:

1. Select the item(s) in the Library panel; it will appear highlighted.

2. From the Options menu in the Library panel, choose Move to New Folder.

   A dialog box appears, asking you to name your new folder.

3. Give your folder a name, then click OK.

   A new folder is created in the Library panel, and the item you originally selected is automatically placed inside it.

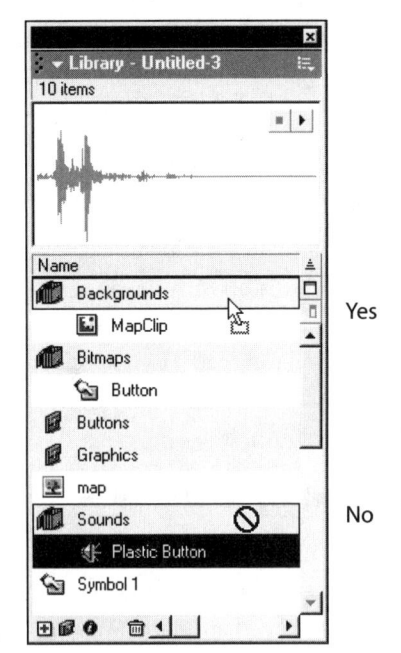

Sorting Items

Folders are great for organizing items, but how do you locate items within folders? Say, for example, you have a folder that contains every element used in Scene 1—all 50 of them. Flash makes it easy for you to find the element you want, by allowing you to change their display order in the library based on criteria you've defined.

Figure 17.9
When dragging an item to a folder, the cursor will indicate where the item can and cannot be placed.

To sort items in the library:

1. Click either the Name or Kind column header to select how you want to sort the list of library items.

   If you click the Name header, library items will be sorted in alphabetical order based on their names (**Figure 17.10**). Clicking the Kind header causes items to be grouped according to asset type. Each folder's content is sorted separately.

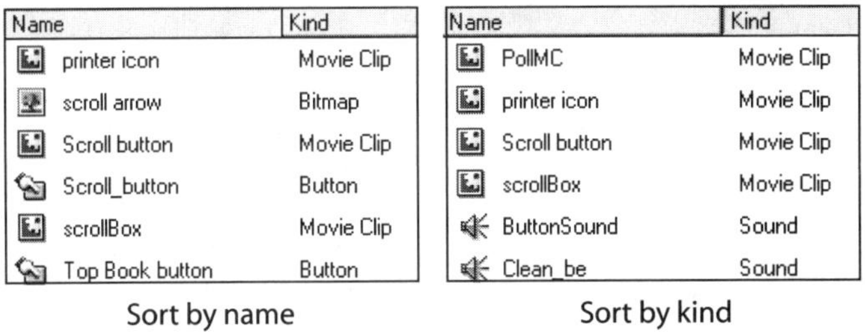

Name	Kind
printer icon	Movie Clip
scroll arrow	Bitmap
Scroll button	Movie Clip
Scroll_button	Button
scrollBox	Movie Clip
Top Book button	Button

Sort by name

Name	Kind
PollMC	Movie Clip
printer icon	Movie Clip
Scroll button	Movie Clip
scrollBox	Movie Clip
ButtonSound	Sound
Clean_be	Sound

Sort by kind

Figure 17.10
Sorting by name causes assets in the Library to be listed alphabetically. Sorting by kind groups types of assets together.

2. Click the Toggle Sorting Order button to select whether to sort your items in ascending or descending order—that is, *A-Z* or *Z-A*.

Special Libraries

Normally, the assets that appear in the Library panel are only available to the movie you're currently working on—which could be frustrating if you'd spent a great deal of time creating and fine-tuning an asset that would work perfectly in another project. Don't despair: Two special types of Flash libraries make it possible to use the same assets in more than one movie.

Common Libraries

Common libraries are nothing more than Flash authoring files (FLAs containing library assets such as symbols, sounds, and bitmaps) that you place in a special folder on your hard drive. When you place a FLA in this folder, the contents of its library become available through the Flash menu bar (**Figure 17.11**).

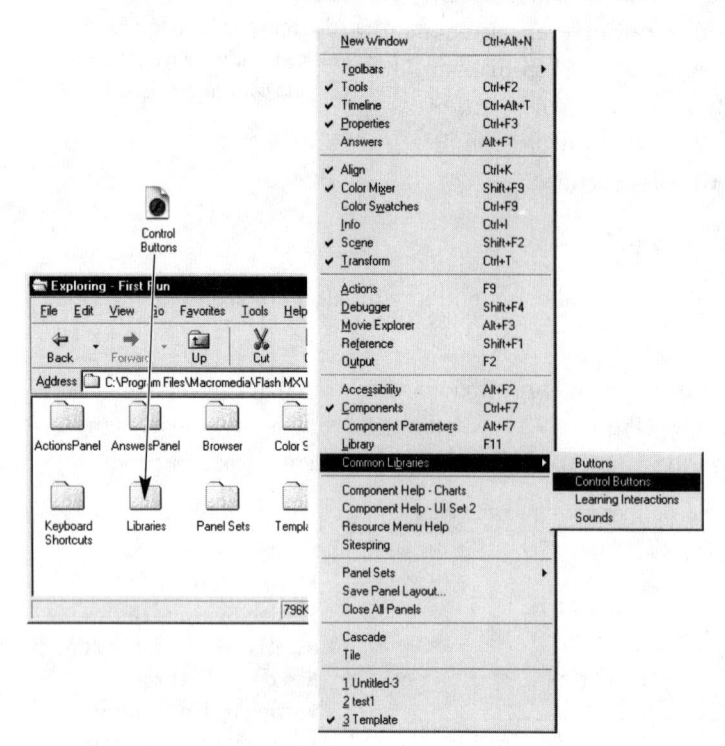

Figure 17.11
By placing an authoring file inside the Libraries folder within the Flash program folder, you make the library assets of that authoring file available on the Window > Common Libraries submenu.

To create a common library:

1. Open a new Flash authoring file.

2. Create, place, or import assets into its library.

3. Save the authoring file in the Flash MX\First Run\Libraries directory on your hard drive.

   TIP *Since the name you assign the saved authoring file will appear as a menu choice inside Flash, make sure that name reflects the contents of the authoring file's library, such as Control Buttons.fla or Text Animations.fla.*

To open a common library and use its assets:

1. Choose Window > Common Libraries > and then the name of the library from the submenu.

   A Library panel will appear containing all of the assets of the common library you just selected.

2. Click and drag an asset from that library onto the stage or into the Library panel of your current project.

   That asset and any supporting assets will be added to your current project and become part of its authoring file. Any changes you make to that asset once you've added it to your current project will affect only that version of it, not the one in the common library.

   TIP *Flash contains several built-in common libraries that contain buttons, animations, and sounds you can use immediately.*

Shared Libraries

Although shared and common libraries are based on the same principle—that is, one object, many uses—shared libraries are more dynamic. A common library asset, when added to a movie, is stored permanently in your movie's authoring file. A shared library asset, in contrast, is merely linked to your movie—which means it remains external from the movie in which it is used and is not placed in that movie until after it begins to play. While common libraries (see previous section) represent a simple solution for centralizing groups of assets (so that you can easily find and add them to projects), shared libraries (which are a bit more complex) come in handy when you want to keep assets in a centralized location and have all edits to those assets automatically reflected in any movies linked to them.

Shared library assets can include any asset that is part of a normal library:

- Graphic, button, and movie clip symbols
- Sounds
- Bitmaps
- Font symbols

There are a couple of benefits to using shared library assets in your movies:

◆ Users only need to download them once—regardless of how many movies they're used in. Say your site contained multiple SWFs that used a common movie clip: If you make that movie clip a shared library asset, users would only need to download it once to see it in all of your SWFs (**Figure 17.12**).

◆ When you edit or update a shared library asset, any linked movies will automatically reflect those edits (**Figure 17.13**).

◆ You can use shared library assets the same way you would normal library assets, employing them as animations and button states, as well as placing instances of them throughout your movie.

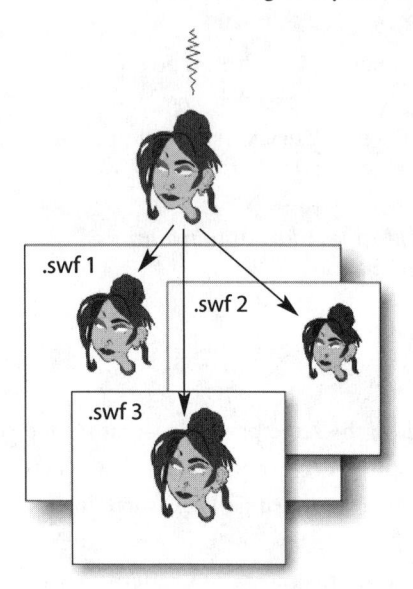

Figure 17.12
A shared library asset only needs to be downloaded once to be used across multiple SWFs.

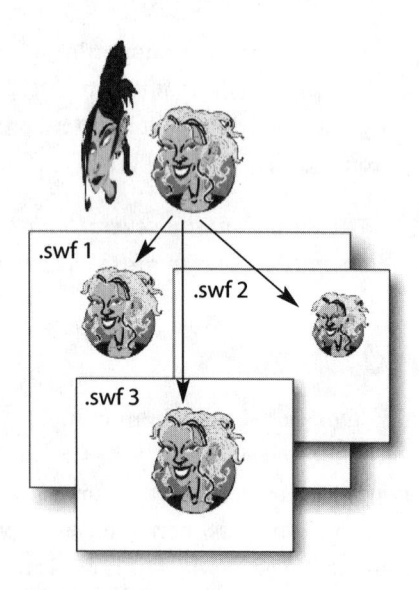

Figure 17.13
Any time you update a shared library asset, all linked SWFs are updated as well.

Understanding shared libraries

A shared library asset is nothing more than a regular library asset within a SWF file that has been set up so that it can be used by (linked to) other SWF files.

When another movie links to a shared asset, the link includes the URL for the .swf file that contains the shared asset, as well as the shared asset's identifier—a unique name (different than the asset's library name) that identifies it as a shared asset. This is how the linked movie knows where to look for the shared asset (**Figure 17.14**).

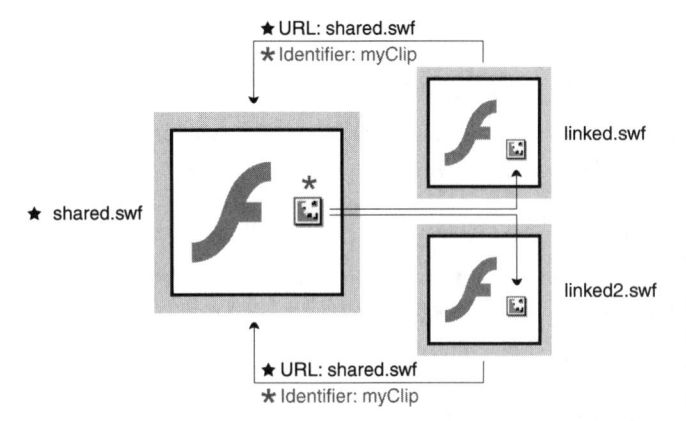

Figure 17.14
A linked movie can locate linked assets, using the URL where the shared library resides and the identifier, which identifies a particular asset in a shared library.

To create a shared asset and use it in another movie:

1. Open the Flash authoring file that contains the library asset you wish to turn into a shared library asset.

   TIP *Although a shared library asset can be stored in any FLA (including full-blown Flash productions), you may find it easier to create special FLAs to contain only shared library assets.*

2. With the Library panel open, select an asset, and from the Options menu choose Linkage.

   The Linkage Properties dialog box will appear.

3. Because you're defining a library asset that you want to designate as sharable, choose the "Export for runtime sharing" option.

   NOTE *Selecting this option will make available the "Export in first frame option" on the Linkage Properties dialog box. For more on this option, see "The Export in First Frame Option" sidebar a little later in this chapter.*

4. In the Identifier field, enter a name, or *identifier*, for this symbol (be aware that the name cannot contain spaces).

   The name you assign will be used to identify the asset within the library. But why—you may ask—do we need to come up with an identifier name when library assets already have names? The reason for this is that library asset names typically contain spaces; however, if their linking functionality is to work, *shared* library assets *cannot* include spaces in their names. Thus, such assets are given *identifier* names. This facilitates linking while allowing the asset names in the library to contain spaces.

   NOTE *Although you may choose to make the identifier name the same as the asset's normal name in the library (except without spaces), you are not required to do so. The identifier name can be anything you choose.*

5. In the URL text box, define the URL where the shared library SWF will reside.

   This can be an absolute URL (www.mydomain.com/sharedlibrary.swf) or a relative URL (sharedlibrary.swf), depending on where the shared library will exist in relation to the SWF files that will link to it.

   NOTES *The URL you enter here will automatically be used by all other assets within the library that you define as shared (because all of a shared library's assets exist in a single SWF whose eventual location is defined in the URL box).*

   The URL you define at this point is used by Flash to automatically create links to shared assets. Once you export the SWF containing the shared library, you will have to manually place it at this URL. If you defined an absolute URL, place the SWF at that location. If you defined a relative URL, make sure any linked movies are placed in the proper relative position based on the relative URL used.

6. Click OK.

7. Continue performing these steps to designate other shared assets.

   TIP *A movie's library can contain numerous assets, any of which can be designated as sharable. A shared asset can be used for animation and interactivity, in the same way any other assets in your movie can be used.*

   Now you need to create the SWF that will become the shared library, and store it at the appropriate URL.

8. Save the authoring file containing the shared library assets; export it as a Flash movie (giving it the same name you specified in Step 5; and then close the authoring file.

9. Now place the exported SWF at the URL you chose in Step 5.

10. Open a different authoring file to contain the links to shared assets.

    Now it's time to open the shared library you created earlier, which contains the assets you want to link to.

11. From the File menu, choose Open as Library and navigate to the authoring file where you earlier defined shared assets.

    The library for that file will appear.

12. Drag any asset that you defined as shared from the Library panel onto the stage of the current authoring file.

    This automatically creates a link to the asset in the shared library (**Figure 17.15**).

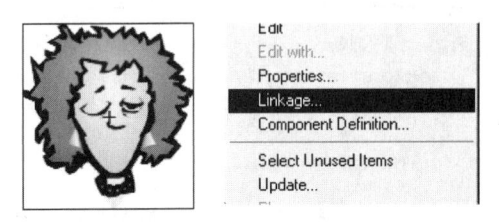

Figure 17.15
After dragging a shared library asset into your current movie, select it in the Library panel and choose Linkage from the Library Option menu. The Linkage Properties box will appear, displaying the linked asset's properties, including its identifier and the URL for the shared library SWF that contains the shared asset.

TIP *If you want to convert a linked asset into a permanent, internal part of the authoring file, select the linked asset in the Library panel, choose Linkage from the Library Option menu, and on the Linkage Properties dialog box that appears, deselect the "Import for runtime sharing" option.*

13. Close the Shared Library panel.

    Although the current authoring file contains only a link to the shared asset, that asset appears in the current movie's library like any other asset—and can be used in the same way as any other asset.

> **MX ALERT**
>
> ### The Export in First Frame Option
>
> The "Export in first frame" option in the Symbol Properties dialog box (**Figure 17.16**) is used to determine at what point a shared asset is downloaded when the movie that links to it is viewed over the Web. If you leave this box checked (the default state), the asset will be downloaded before Frame 1 of its linked movie is downloaded. This is because movie clip instances (even linked clips) can be inserted into movies dynamically using the attachMovie() method. However, for this method to work properly, the content of the dynamically inserted clip must be downloaded and available before the first opportunity to use it arises within the movie—which means before Frame 1. If the linked external assets are large (say they contain many other movie clips or sounds), the movie may appear to "hang" when in fact it's simply loading the contents of all those linked assets.
>
> **Figure 17.16**
> The "Export on first frame" option is found in the Symbol Properties dialog box.
>
> If you uncheck the "Export in first frame" option, the linked asset will not be preloaded before the first frame. Instead, you must physically place an instance of that linked asset on the stage at some point on the timeline before it is loaded. After the linked clip is loaded, you can attach it at any point on the timeline that follows. For example, if you deselect the "Export in first frame" option and place an instance of the linked clip on Frame 45 of your movie, using the attachMovie() method in relation to the clip will work properly from Frame 45 onward, but not before.
>
> As a general rule, you should choose the "Export in first frame option" if you think that a linked asset may need to be dynamically attached while the movie is playing. Deselect this option if you plan to manually place instances of the linked asset on the stage while authoring the movie.

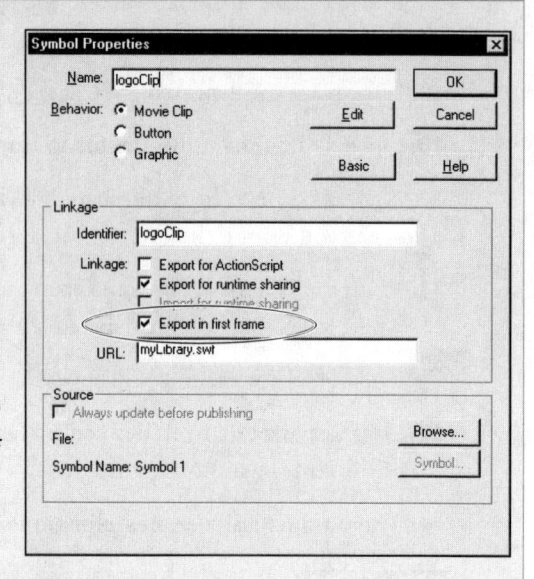

14. Finally, you need to save the current authoring file that contains the linked assets, and export it as a Flash movie. If you defined a relative URL in Step 5 above, place this exported SWF in the appropriate location relative to the SWF that contains the shared assets.

During playback, when this SWF reaches a point where it needs an asset from a shared library, it will look for it at the URL you defined in Step 5.

If you want to update or change an asset in a shared library, reopen the authoring file in which it was defined (Steps 1 through 5 above), change or edit the asset, then re-export the authoring file as a SWF and place it back at the URL you defined in Step 5. The next time a linked movie plays, it will reflect your edits.

NOTE *If a shared library asset is not available for one reason or another (for example, due to network problems), movies linked to that asset will not play properly, if at all. Splitting assets into several shared libraries may help resolve these issues.*

Updating Symbols from External Libraries

MX ALERT Any time you drag a symbol from one authoring file and drop it into another (as occurs whenever you use the Open as Library command on the File menu to open an authoring file's library, so that you can use its assets), Flash remembers the directory path to the FLA where the symbol originated. The program is able to do this because that directory path is included in the symbol's properties.

NOTE *Symbols created within the current authoring file do not have this property.*

By recording directory paths in this way, Flash is able to help facilitate version control—a capability Flash development teams will be extremely grateful for! Say your team created an authoring file—called buttons.fla—that contained nothing but button symbols for use in another (main) authoring file. If you wanted to use some of the button instances from buttons.fla in your main authoring file, you would use the Open as Library command on the File menu to open buttons.fla's library and then drag button instances from it into your main authoring file (for more information, see Chapter 7, "Symbols").

The button symbols you dragged become part of your main authoring file's library (in this case they are not linked, *unless* you specifically defined them to be as described in the previous section). What happens to the button symbols you've dragged into the main authoring when the corresponding symbols in buttons.fla get updated? By default, nothing! The main authoring file's version of the buttons will remain unchanged.

Although you could address this problem by opening the buttons.fla library again and then dragging the edited button symbols into your main authoring file (in essence, overwriting the original versions, as was required in earlier versions of Flash), Flash offers a more dynamic solution: It can look back into the buttons.fla file (via its location as defined by that directory path), determine whether any of that file's assets have been edited, and then update the main file's version of them—all with the greatest of ease.

To automatically update symbols from external libraries:

1. Drag a symbol into a movie from another movie's library, using the Open as Library command on the File menu.

   This will add that external symbol to the currently open authoring file.

2. Open the Library panel by choosing Window > Library.

3. Locate the symbol that was added from the external file. Right-click (Windows) or Control-click (Macintosh) its name, and choose Properties from the menu that appears.

   The Symbol Properties dialog box will appear.

4. In the bottom portion of the dialog box (in the Source section), check the "Always update before publishing" option, then click OK (**Figure 17.17**).

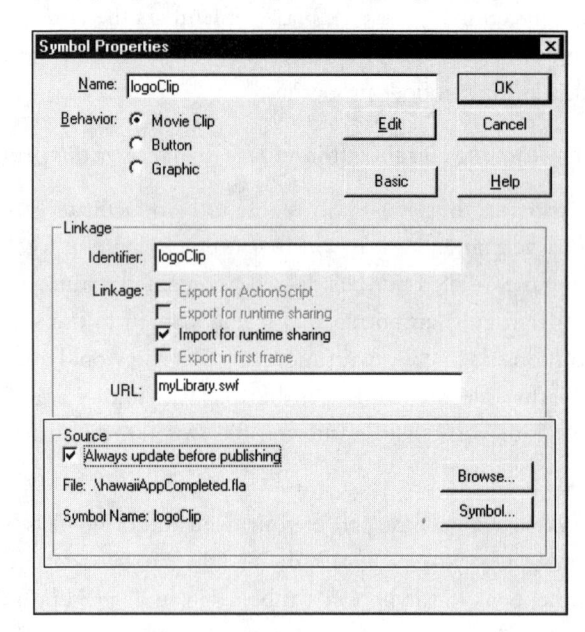

Figure 17.17
By selecting the "Always update before publishing" option, Flash will (prior to publishing the movie) update the content of the selected symbol, thus reflecting any edits made to the original version of the symbol.

If you check this option, Flash will check in the external library that provided the original version of the symbol, and determine whether the symbol's been edited. If it has, the current authoring file will automatically reflect those edits when it's exported as a SWF.

NOTE *This functionality is not to be confused with that of shared libraries (which we discussed in the previous section). Shared libraries allow for run-time sharing of assets—meaning that linked, external assets are brought into a movie as that movie plays. In contrast, the functionality described above—known as* author-time sharing—*allows external assets to be updated (at your option) before the movie is exported, not while it plays. Author-time sharing is best suited for single-machine work environments (that is, those in which project development occurs, and all files exist, on a single machine). Run-time sharing provides the flexibility needed by work groups, allowing SWFs from various team members to be uploaded to a server.*

TIP *The Source section of the Symbol Properties dialog box contains information about the original, external asset, including the directory to the FLA where it is stored and its symbol name within that file. There are also two buttons—Browse and Symbol—that allow you to change the external file/symbol on which the currently selected symbol is based (if it was brought in from an external FLA). The Browse button lets you manually point to a different external FLA, while the Symbol button allows you to choose a symbol from within that FLA.*

You may not always want symbols to be automatically updated at the time your authoring file is published. With this alternative, Flash lets you update particular symbols whenever you feel like it—particularly useful when you've dragged a symbol from an external library and changed it considerably but then want to revert back to the original version in the external library.

To selectively update symbols from external libraries:

1. Drag a symbol into a movie from another movie's library, using the Open as Library command on the File menu.

This will add that external symbol to the currently open authoring file.

2. Open the Library panel by choosing Window > Library.

3. Locate the symbol that was added from the external file. Right-click (Windows) or Control-click (Macintosh) its name, and choose Update from the menu that appears.

The Update Library Items dialog box will appear.

4. Check the symbol you wish to update, then press the Update button (**Figure 17.18**).

Any edits made to the symbol in the original source file will be reflected in your movie's library file as well.

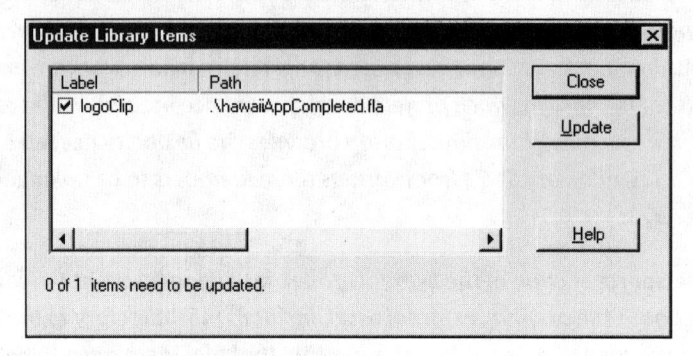

Figure 17.18
The Update Library Items dialog box.

Video Tutorials

Working with the Library. This tutorial provides a basic tour of the library, and shows you how to manage library items as well as how to organize them using folders.

Understanding and Using Shared Libraries. This tutorial steps you through the process of creating a shared library and linking to its assets.

Using Movie Explorer to Manage Structure

CHAPTER 18

What you'll learn…

How to work within the Display List window

How to view and edit assets from Movie Explorer

If you've ever worked on a large or complicated project, you've probably come to appreciate project management tools. They can help you keep track of your project's many elements, and automate the process of locating, changing, and updating items—tasks you could spend hours on without such a tool.

In the last chapter, we looked at how to use Flash's library to organize the many reusable elements of your project. In this chapter, we'll focus on a tool with a much broader scope—one that lets you work with, organize, and manage almost every aspect of your movie. Movie Explorer is a project management tool within Macromedia Flash MX, designed to help you work with information about timelines, frames, layers, symbols, text blocks, ActionScripts, and more.

Understanding the Display List

Understanding Movie Explorer's interface is the key to making effective use of this tool. It's organized so that just a quick glance provides detailed information about the overall makeup of your movie and its many parts.

To open Movie Explorer, do one of the following:

- Right-click (Windows) or Control-click (Macintosh) on an empty area of the stage, and choose Movie Explorer from the menu that appears.

Or

- Choose Window > Movie Explorer.

The Movie Explorer panel will appear.

The Display List window in Movie Explorer (**Figure 18.1**) provides a hierarchical tree diagram of your movie's content. The tree display locates individual elements within the context of the whole movie, and provides specific information about each.

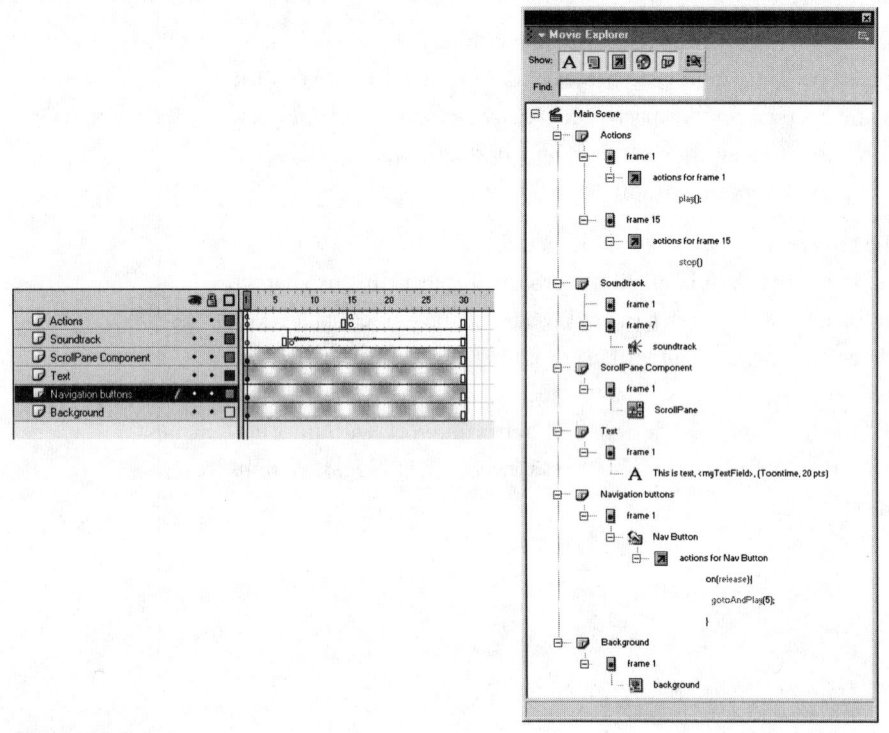

Figure 18.1
Items in the Display List window correspond to items on the timeline, identifying the hierarchical structure of your movie.

To understand this display, you need to familiarize yourself with the terms used to describe its components: The term *branch*, for example, denotes a hierarchical level in the tree. Thus, if your tree was a model of the universe, galaxies would represent a branch of that tree; solar systems would represent a branch of the galaxies; and planets would represent a branch of each solar system. Since a galaxy is a subset of the universe, in Flash's vocabulary it is considered a *child branch* of the universe. At the same time, it is considered the *parent branch* of an individual solar system.

A Flash movie's hierarchical tree contains the following parent and child branches (**Figure 18.2**):

- **Scene.** As a section of your movie's overall timeline, a scene is a child branch of the overall movie (SWF file), but a parent branch of layers.

- **Layers.** Each scene is made up of layers—which makes those layers child branches of a scene, but parent branches of frames.

- **Frames.** These are keyframes that exist on the individual scene layers. A frame is a child branch of a layer, but the parent branch of frame actions and movie elements.

- **Frame actions.** These are actions attached to keyframes. A frame action is a child branch of a keyframe.

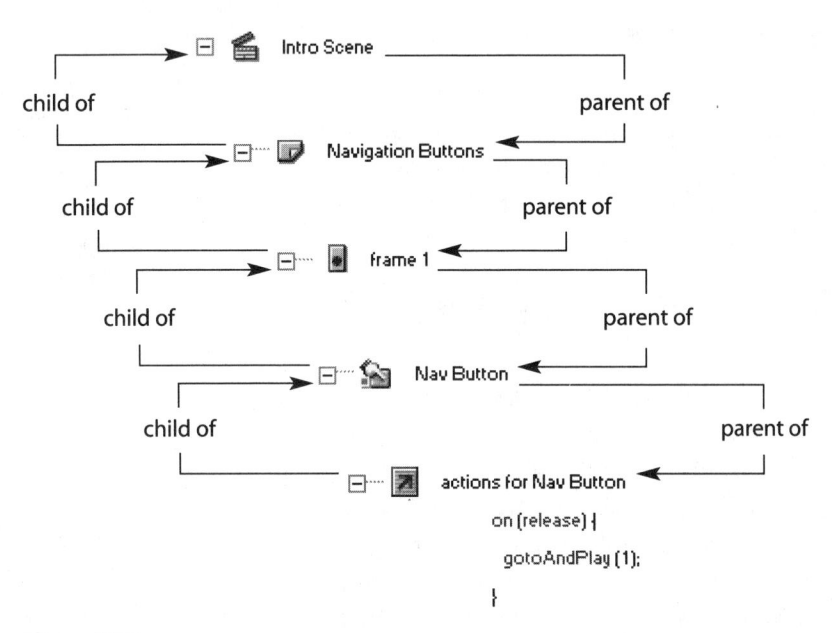

```
                    Intro Scene
child of                                    parent of

                    Navigation Buttons
child of                                    parent of

                    frame 1
child of                                    parent of

                    Nav Button
child of                                    parent of

                    actions for Nav Button
                    on (release) {
                      gotoAndPlay (1);
                    }
```

Figure 18.2
Each branch of the hierarchical tree shown here is a child of the branch above it and a parent of the branch or branches below it. (Intro Scene is a child branch of the overall movie.)

- **Graphics, button, and movie clip instances.** These elements exist at a particular keyframe on a particular layer, and include instances of graphic, button, and movie clip symbols. A graphic, button, or movie clip instance is a child branch of a frame, and the parent branch of object actions.

  NOTE *Because Component instances are really no more than enhanced movie clips, they belong to the preceding branch as well.*

- **Object actions.** These actions are attached to instances of buttons or movie clips. An object action is a child branch of a button or movie clip instance.

- **Video, sounds, and bitmaps.** These imported elements exist at a particular keyframe on a particular layer, and include instances of videos, sounds, and bitmaps. A video, sound, or bitmap instance is a child branch of a frame.

- **Text.** These elements exist at a particular keyframe on a particular layer. A text element is a child branch of a frame.

Filtering the View

A Flash project can contain hundreds of elements, which means that attempting to view them simultaneously in the Display List window can be a dizzying experience. Fortunately, Movie Explorer lets you choose which content you wish to view.

Setting the context of the Display List window

By setting the context of the Display List window, you can choose the level of detail you want to view within Movie Explorer. Normally, the Display List window shows the hierarchical tree of your entire movie, as well as the symbol definitions, which represent hierarchical trees for each symbol in your movie (**Figure 18.3**). However, if you only want to view the hierarchical tree of the movie, *or* just the symbol definitions, you can do that as well.

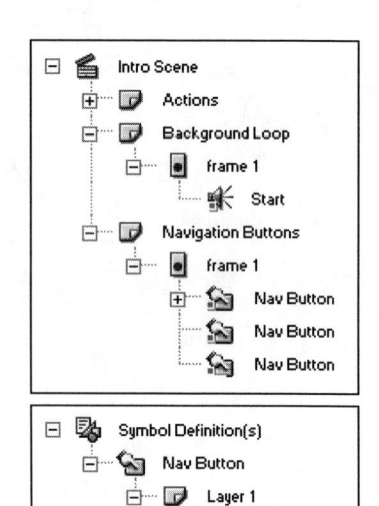

Figure 18.3
You can view the Display List window in the context of your overall movie, or its symbol definitions.

Chapter 18 Using Movie Explorer to Manage Structure

To set the context of the Display List window:

1. Press the Customize button.

The Movie Explorer Settings dialog box will appear (**Figure 18.4**).

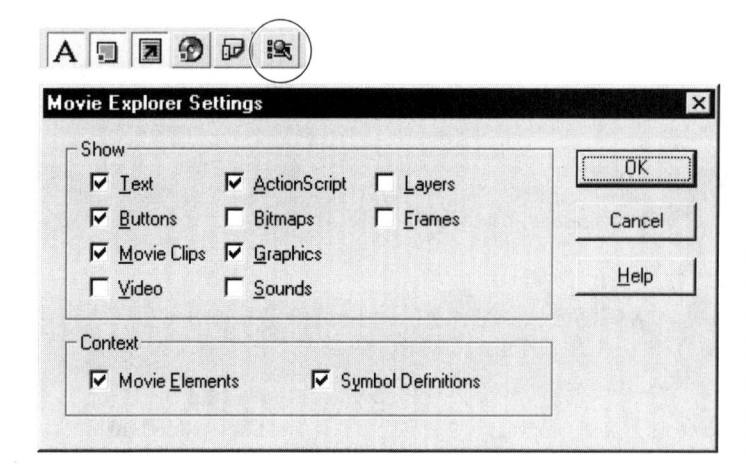

Figure 18.4
Pressing the Customize button lets you set the context of the Display List window.

2. Check the appropriate boxes in the Context section of this dialog box, then click OK.

A quicker method is to press the Options button on the top-right corner of the Movie Explorer panel (**Figure 18.5**); from the menu that appears, select Show Movie Elements, Show Symbol Definitions, or both.

Figure 18.5
The Options button.

Showing and hiding filters

Movie Explorer's Show and Hide filters let you choose which elements you want to see in the Display List window. For example, if you're only interested in viewing the ActionScripts in your movie, you can hide all the buttons, layers, frames, and so forth, so that they won't distract you.

To show or hide particular elements in the Display List window:

1. Click the Customize button.

   The Movie Explorer Settings dialog box will appear.

2. Check or uncheck the appropriate boxes in the Show section of this dialog box.

   A quicker method is to click one of the Show/Hide buttons at the top of the Movie Explorer interface (**Figure 18.6**).

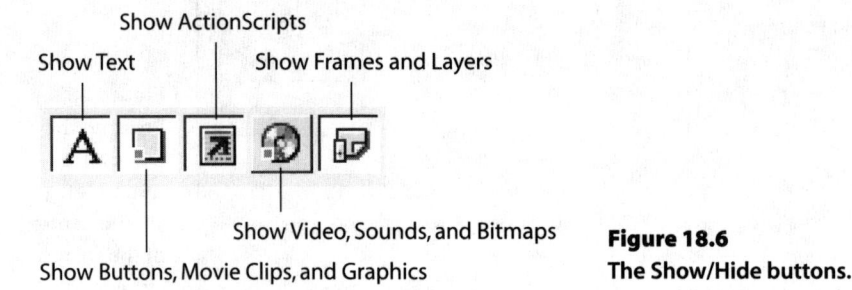

Figure 18.6
The Show/Hide buttons.

Choosing the scene mode

Because Flash uses scenes to break timelines into logical chunks, you may sometimes only want to view content pertaining to the current scene. At other times you may want to view all the content of every scene simultaneously.

To choose a scene mode:

- Press the Options button on the top-right corner of Movie Explorer. From the menu that appears, choose Show All Scenes.

   Since this is a toggle command, choosing it from the menu again will cause it to revert to the previous mode.

Collapsing branches

By expanding and collapsing branches on the tree, you can focus on particular sections of your movie without being distracted by multiple open branches.

To expand or collapse a branch, do one of the following:

- Click the plus (+) and minus (–) icons (Windows) or the small twirly arrow (Macintosh) where a branch stems, in order to open or close that branch and its child branches.

Or

- Press the Options button on the top-right corner of the Movie Explorer. From the menu that appears, choose from the following options:

  Expand Branch. Expands the tree at the selected branch, making all of its child branches visible.

  Collapse Branch. Collapses the tree at the selected branch, thus hiding its child branches.

  Collapse Others. Collapses all branches of the tree that do not contain the selected element.

Getting Information from the Display List

Each branch of the hierarchical tree has an associated icon that helps you identify its function in your movie. (For example, a button instance is identified in the Display List window by a button icon.) To the right of the icon there is text describing that branch. The following information is included for each type of branch (**Figure 18.7**):

- **Scene.** The name of the scene.
- **Layers.** The name of the layer.
- **Frames.** The frame number where the keyframe exists. Any label or comments assigned to the keyframe will appear in parentheses.
- **Frame actions.** The code for the ActionScript assigned to the keyframe.
- **Graphics, button, and movie clip instances.** The name of the symbol from which the instance is derived. If the instance is a movie clip that has been assigned an instance name, that name will also appear between greater-than/less-than signs (< >).

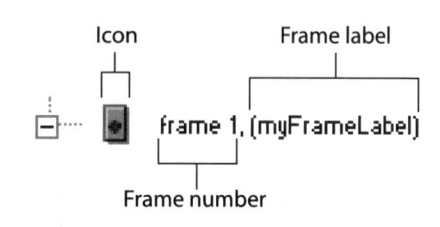

Figure 18.7
The type of information shown for items in the Display List window.

- **Object actions.** Indicates the name of the object that has the action attached to it. For example, if the action is attached to a button named "myButton," this area will read "actions for myButton." Also shown is the code for the ActionScript that has been assigned to the object.

- **Video, sounds, and bitmaps.** The name of the element as it appears in the library.

- **Text.** The text contained in the element, followed by its associated variable name (if it has one), its instance name (if it's been given one), and the font face and size (shown in parentheses).

Viewing and Editing Assets from Movie Explorer

When you select a branch in the hierarchical tree, Flash's overall interface adjusts, making it possible for you to immediately view and edit selected items.

The following describes how Flash's main interface responds when a branch of Movie Explorer's hierarchical tree is highlighted (if the display-list context is set to Movie Elements):

- **Scene.** The interface goes to the selected scene. If the Scene panel is open, the scene will be highlighted.

- **Layers.** The interface goes to that layer's scene and the layer is selected.

- **Frames.** The interface goes to the selected scene/keyframe. The keyframe sequence is highlighted on the timeline, as are all graphical elements on the stage that are included in the sequence.

- **Frame actions.** The interface goes to the scene/keyframe on which the action is based. The keyframe sequence is highlighted on the timeline, as are all graphical elements on the stage that are part of that sequence.

- **Graphics, button, and movie clip instances.** The interface goes to the scene/keyframe that contains the selected instance, and the instance is automatically selected on the stage, ready for editing.

- **Object actions.** Once again, the interface goes to the scene/keyframe that contains the selected instance, and the instance is automatically selected on the stage, ready for editing.

- **Video, sounds, and bitmaps.** If you select a sound, the interface takes you to the scene/keyframe where the sound resides. When you select a bitmap or video, the interface goes to the scene/keyframe that contains the selected item, and the item is automatically selected on the stage.

- **Text.** When you select a text element, the interface goes to the scene/keyframe that contains the selected text element, and the element is automatically selected on the stage.

TIP *When a movie element is selected, its complete hierarchical path in the movie is displayed at the bottom of the Movie Explorer window (**Figure 18.8**).*

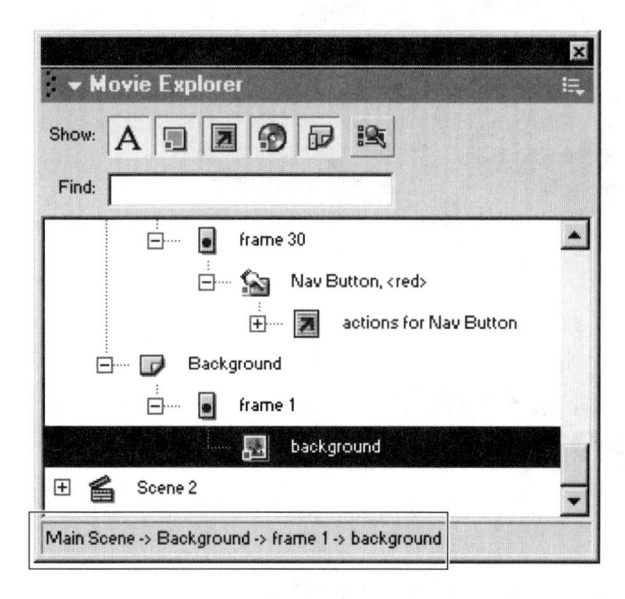

Figure 18.8
When you select a movie element, its hierarchical path is displayed at the bottom of the Movie Explorer window.

In addition, when you select any of these items, the Property inspector immediately updates so that you can edit settings pertaining to that item.

Double-Clicking

The following describes what happens when you double-click any of these branch types:

- **Scene.** Allows you to change the name of the scene.

- **Layers.** Allows you to change the name of the layer.

- **Frames.** Double-clicking frames has the same effect as selecting them (as described in the previous section).

- **Frame actions.** Opens the Actions panel, where you can edit the ActionScript attached to the frame.

- **Graphics, button, and movie clip instances.** Opens the master symbol of the instance in symbol-editing mode, so that it can be edited (**Figure 18.9**).

- **Object actions.** Opens the Actions panel, where you can edit the action attached to the object.

- **Video, sounds, and bitmaps.** Double-clicking these elements has the same effect as selecting them (as described in the previous section).

- **Text.** Allows you to edit the text in the element.

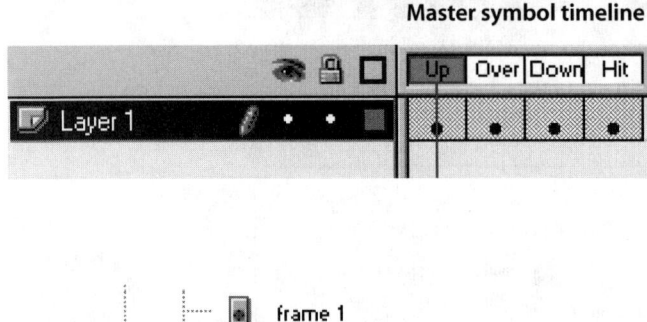

Figure 18.9
Double-clicking an instance of a symbol in the Display List window opens the timeline of the master symbol it is based on.

Movie Explorer Tasks

In addition to the wealth of information Movie Explorer provides in the Display List window, it also automates several tasks that can help you locate and edit movie elements, spell-check your movie's text, and more.

Go to Symbol Definition

When you select a symbol instance in the Display List window, you may want to look at the definition of the symbol on which the instance is based, so that you can understand its structure.

To go to a symbol definition:

1. Select a symbol instance in the Display List window.

2. Press the Movie Explorer Options button, and choose Go to Symbol Definition from the menu that appears.

> **NOTE** *For this feature to work, you must make sure the Symbol Definitions display is enabled. See "Setting the Context of the Display List Window" earlier in this chapter.*

Editing

When you select a symbol instance or definition in the Display List window, you can immediately open its timeline for editing.

To edit a symbol:

1. Select a symbol instance or definition on the hierarchical tree in the Display List window.

2. Press the Movie Explorer Options button, and choose Edit in Place or Edit in New Window from the menu that appears.

Searching by Keyword

As your project grows to contain hundreds of symbols, sounds, and other movie elements, finding any particular one of these elements can become a time-consuming task. Fortunately, Movie Explorer allows you to locate specific items using a keyword search.

If you type a string of characters, numbers, or both in the Find box, the Display List window will display only those branches that contain that string. The more text you enter into the Find box, the more specific your search will be. Any text associated with an element in the Display List window is searched, including branches of the hierarchical tree that are currently closed (**Figure 18.10**). To narrow your search further, filter the view in the Display List window as described earlier in this chapter.

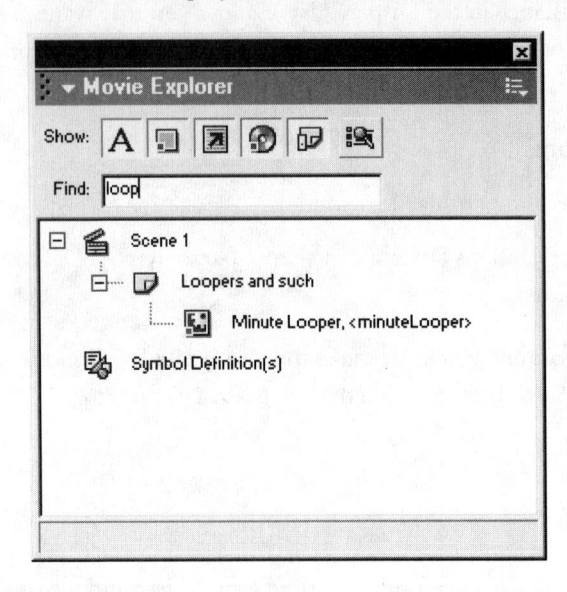

Figure 18.10
When you enter a string of text in the Find box, Movie Explorer searches all open and closed branches in the Display List window for that text.

Find in Library

Because you can work with elements in the library in ways that are not available in the Movie Explorer window, Flash offers a command that will let you select an instance of a symbol, sound, bitmap, or video in the Movie Explorer window then open the master symbol on which it is based in the Library panel.

To find a symbol in the library:

1. Select a symbol definition or instance of a symbol, sound, bitmap, or video on the hierarchical tree in the Display List window.

2. Press the Movie Explorer Options button in the upper right corner, and choose Find in Library from the menu that appears.

   This opens the Library panel (if it's not already open), where the appropriate master symbol is selected and appears in the Preview window of the library (**Figure 18.11**).

Figure 18.11
When you use the Find in Library command, the library is automatically opened, and the selected symbol is highlighted and appears in the Preview window.

Selecting Symbol Instances

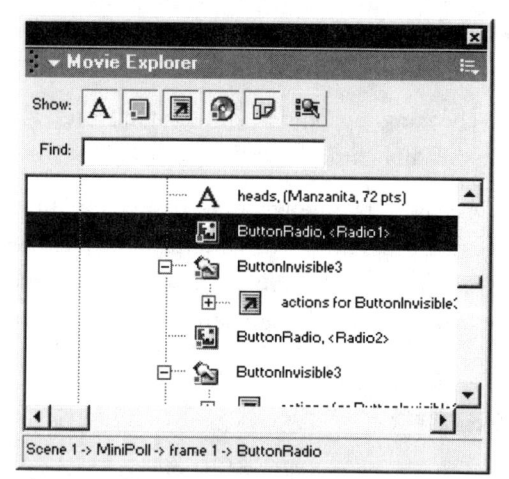

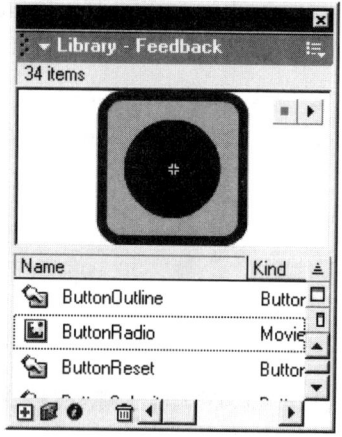

Identifying where instances of a symbol are used in your movie can help you understand the movie's overall structure. If you select a symbol on the Symbol Definition hierarchical tree and then choose Select Symbol Instances from the Movie Explorer options menu, any instances of the selected symbol that are used in your movie will be highlighted in the Display List window.

NOTE The Show Movie Elements option must be selected (on the Movie Explorer options menu) for this action to work.

Spell-Checking

Although Flash doesn't include a built-in spell-checker, it allows you to copy all of the text in your movie to the system clipboard, so that you can then paste it into another application for spell-checking. But be forewarned: Flash offers no automated process for selecting all spell-checked text from the external application and pasting it back into the appropriate text elements. You must instead select each section of spell-checked text, and individually paste it back into the appropriate text element in Flash.

To spell-check text:

1. Filter the Display List window view so that only text elements are visible.

2. Press the Movie Explorer Options button, and choose Copy Text to Clipboard from the menu that appears.

3. Open an application with spell-checking capabilities, and use the Paste command to paste the text onto the clipboard.

   All text that was visible in the Display List window will be pasted into the application window of the spell-checking program (by default, the pasted text will also include scene names, font face names, and so forth). Locate any misspelled words, then return to Flash and make any needed adjustments.

Cutting, Copying, and Clearing

You can cut, copy, or delete graphical elements that appear on the stage directly from Movie Explorer, just as you would by clicking the item on the stage and selecting the respective command from the Edit menu.

To cut, copy, or clear a graphical element:

1. Select a graphical element in the Display List window.

2. Press the Movie Explorer Options button, then choose Cut, Copy, or Clear from the menu that appears.

Printing

You may sometimes need a hard copy of the hierarchical structure of your movie: to study when you're away from your computer, or to hand out at team project meetings. To print only the currently configured hierarchical list in the Display List window, select Print from the Movie Explorer options menu.

TIP *Most of the Options menu commands discussed in this section are also available by right-clicking (Windows) or Control-clicking (Macintosh) an item on the hierarchical tree in the Display List window.*

Video Tutorial

Using the Movie Explorer. This tutorial provides a basic overview of Movie Explorer, reviewing many of the concepts covered in this chapter.

6

Movie Distribution

Testing	733
Publishing	769

ONCE YOU'VE CREATED your masterpiece, it's time to move it into the final stages of production: testing (both its visual and interactive features) and publishing (to your format of choice). In this section, you'll work within Flash's testing environment, using its many testing tools (including the Bandwidth Profiler and Debugger) to help optimize your movie and locate problems in your scripts. In addition, we'll take you through the final process of publishing your movie for distribution to the world.

Testing

CHAPTER 19

What you'll learn...

About testing within the authoring environment

About testing within the testing environment

How to test your movie's functionality

How to find bugs in your ActionScript

How to test download performance

Although it's natural for us to dread tests, they can actually be a good thing. We can burn the midnight oil, sweat blood studying, or even write the answers on our cuffs, but the point of it all is to help us get things right. Testing works the same way in Flash.

In computer-driven interactive content, mistakes are referred to as *bugs*—and they can be as ugly and bothersome as their name implies. Although your projects are probably less complex than a major piece of software, you're still likely to encounter some glitches. If you don't want to scare off your audience, you'll need to exterminate those bugs.

One of the keys to becoming a Flash master is recognizing the value of testing. It doesn't matter how good your project could be: If you fail to test it, you're needlessly putting your reputation (not to mention your neck) on the line. Nor is testing just about eliminating mistakes; it's also the key to optimizing your movie, so that it plays back in the most efficient manner. Thanks to Macromedia Flash MX's powerful testing tools, this process is relatively quick and easy.

The following are some tips to get you started:

- **Plan.** Don't even approach a project until you've created a basic outline.

- **Test everything.** Never assume something works—even if it seems like a trivial part of your project. It only takes one mistake to bring your movie to a screeching halt.

- **Test often.** Don't wait until your project is nearly complete—test it at every opportunity. It's much easier to isolate problems if you know your movie was still working five minutes ago.

- **Fix bugs in an orderly fashion.** Don't attempt to fix a bunch of bugs at the same time. It's best to tackle one or two problems at a time, and then test after each. After all, you don't want to create any new bugs in the debugging process.

- **Get a second opinion.** Sometimes you can get too close to a project to spot problems in it. One of the best things you can do is have someone else test your project. Because this person doesn't know what to expect, he or she may stumble upon problems you might have otherwise overlooked. Encourage your testers to be brutal and diligent—and don't get upset if they also provide some unsolicited opinions about design and functionality. Instead, swallow your pride and listen: Their reactions may mirror those of your target audience.

Testing Within the Flash Authoring Environment

Although it shouldn't be your first choice for heavy-duty project testing, the Flash authoring environment does accommodate some minor testing procedures. Within the authoring environment you can test the following:

- **Button states.** You can test the way buttons look in their up, down, over, and hit states.

- **Sounds on the main timeline.** You can listen to sounds placed along the main timeline (including those that are synchronized with on-stage animations) when the timeline is played.

- **Frame actions along the main timeline.** You can test any gotoAndStop(), gotoAndPlay(), play(), and stop() actions attached to frames or buttons on the main timeline, while that timeline is being played (see below for actions that won't work within the authoring environment).

- **Animation along the main timeline.** Although you can test animation along the main timeline (including shape and motion tweens), this does not include animation within movie clips or buttons (see below for more information).

To preview the current scene, do one of the following:

- Choose Control > Play.

- Press Enter/Return on your keyboard.

- Choose Window > Toolbars > Controller (Windows) or Window > Controller (Macintosh); then click the Play button when the Controller appears.

> **TIP** *To preview all of the scenes in your movie in succession, choose Control > Preview All Scenes, then play your movie.*

To test a button's visual functionality:

- Choose Control > Enable Simple Buttons.

  With buttons enabled, they'll react the same way (visually) as they will in your final movie when a user puts the cursor over them. Disable this feature to edit instances of buttons.

To test frame actions such as gotoAndStop(), gotoAndPlay(), stop(), and play():

- Choose Control > Enable Simple Frame Actions.

  With frame actions enabled, gotoAndStop(), gotoAndPlay(), play(), and stop() actions will respond accordingly when the timeline is played within the authoring environment (as long as they don't rely on ActionScript expressions or point to URLs).

Within the authoring environment you *cannot* test the following:

- **Movie clips.** Sounds, animation, and actions that are part of movie clips will not be visible or function within the authoring environment. (Only the first frame of a movie clip will appear.)

- **Actions.** gotoAndStop(), gotoAndPlay(), play(), and stop() are the only actions that work in the authoring environment. This means you can't test interactivity, mouse events, or functionality that relies on any other actions.

- **Movie speed.** The playback function within the Flash authoring environment is slower than it will be in your final optimized and exported movie.

- **Download performance.** From within the authoring environment, it's not possible to gauge how well your movie will *stream*, or download, over the Web.

Remember, however, that the above-described limitations only apply within the authoring environment. You're only a couple of clicks away from commands that you can employ to fully test your movie. Let's take a closer look at these tools.

The Test Movie and Test Scene Commands

As you just learned, testing capabilities within the Flash authoring environment are limited. To evaluate movie clips, ActionScripts, and other important movie elements, you must work outside the authoring environment: The Test Scene and Test Movie commands—both located on the Control menu—can automatically create working versions of the current scene or entire movie, and open them in a window where you can test nearly every aspect of their interactivity, animation, and functionality.

Both the Test Scene and Test Movie commands generate temporary .swf files, and place them in the same directory as the authoring file.

TIP *If your test file works as it should and you wish to use it as your final file, you can simply locate the .swf on your hard drive and upload it to your server.*

When you create .swf files with the Test Scene and Test Movie commands, the file export settings used are based on the current settings on the Flash tab in the Publish Settings dialog box (for more information, see Chapter 20, "Publishing"). To change these settings from the File menu, choose Publish Settings and make the necessary adjustments on the Flash tab.

To test the current scene:

- From the Control menu, choose Test Scene.

    Flash automatically exports the current scene and opens it in a new window ready for you to test it.

To test the entire movie:

- From the Control menu, choose Test Movie.

    Flash automatically exports all of the scenes within the current project, and opens the file in a new window ready for you to test it.

The Testing Environment

When using the Test Scene or Test Movie command, you'll notice that although you're still within Flash, the display interface has changed. This is because you're now in the testing environment rather than the authoring environment. The differences are as follows (**Figure 19.1**):

Chapter 19 **Testing**

- The menu bar has changed, as have many of the menu choices.
- The timeline has been replaced with the Bandwidth Profiler, which itself includes a timeline, graph, and number of other features (see "Understanding the Bandwidth Profiler" later in this chapter.)
- The stage and work area have been replaced with a fully functional copy of the scene or movie you are testing.

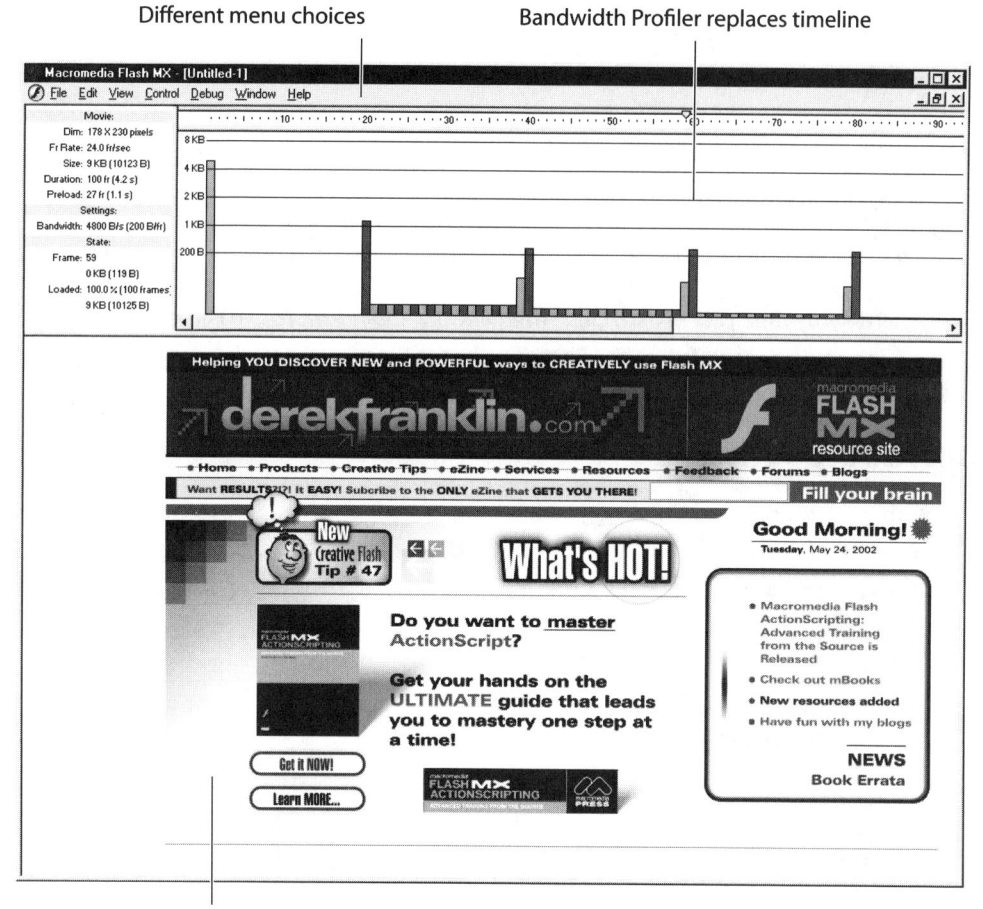

Figure 19.1
The Test Movie environment.

Unless otherwise noted, the following information and instructions assume you are working in the testing environment.

Viewing Options

You can change your movie's magnification and quality while it's playing within the testing environment. By changing the view, you can get a more detailed look at the movie; by changing the quality, you can improve playback. Both of these settings only affect the movie's appearance within the testing environment.

To set the magnification of the movie in the testing environment:

- From the View menu, choose Zoom In/Zoom Out.

    Or

- Choose View > Magnification > 100%.

To set the quality of playback:

- Choose View > Quality > then Low, Medium, or High.

    TIP *Any time you wish to close this window and return to the Flash authoring environment, from the File menu choose Close.*

Controlling Playback

Within the testing environment, you have full control over your movie's playback. You can play and test your movie from beginning to end, view certain sections or frames, rewind it, fast-forward it, and more.

To control your movie's playback:

- Open the Controller (Window > Toolbars > Controller) and use the playback control buttons it offers.

    Or

- Choose Control > and then one of the playback options.

Testing Functionality

You may find that you enjoy testing your movie's functionality, since it gives you an opportunity to see how your work is coming together, and the process itself isn't very difficult. During this phase of testing, you check animated elements for mistakes, press buttons, and run through your movie. Leave nothing unchecked—mistakes in animation and interactivity should be easy to spot at this point. And remember: If your movie doesn't work here, it won't work anywhere.

The testing environment offers the following additional commands on the menu bar to help you track down problems.

List Objects Command

The List Objects command provides a complete tally of each object in a given frame, including type, level, frame, and—if it's a target—its name and path. This will help you to determine whether all the necessary objects (graphic and/or data) are present in a particular frame.

To list objects for a particular frame:

1. Move the playhead to a frame.

2. From the Debug menu, choose List Objects.

A dialog box will appear with a list of all objects present on the current frame (**Figure 19.2**).

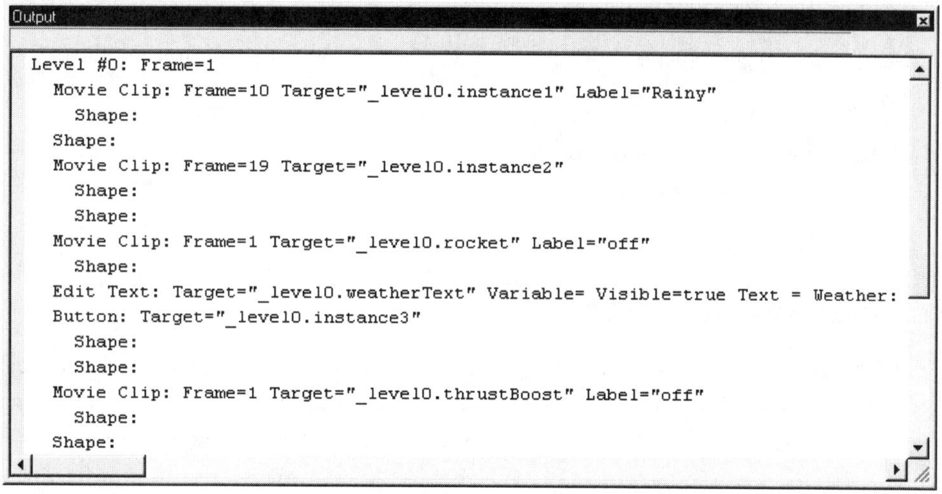

```
Output
Level #0: Frame=1
  Movie Clip: Frame=10 Target="_level0.instance1" Label="Rainy"
    Shape:
  Shape:
  Movie Clip: Frame=19 Target="_level0.instance2"
    Shape:
    Shape:
  Movie Clip: Frame=1 Target="_level0.rocket" Label="off"
    Shape:
  Edit Text: Target="_level0.weatherText" Variable= Visible=true Text = Weather:
  Button: Target="_level0.instance3"
    Shape:
    Shape:
  Movie Clip: Frame=1 Target="_level0.thrustBoost" Label="off"
    Shape:
    Shape:
```

Figure 19.2
The List Objects command provides a detailed list of objects on the current frame.

List Variables Command

The List Variables command provides a complete tally of all of the variables (and their values) in a given frame. This will help ensure that variables are created and updated properly as the timeline plays.

To list variables for a particular frame:

1. Move the playhead to a frame.
2. From the Debug menu choose List Variables.

   A dialog box will appear with a list of all variables present on the current frame, along with their current values.

Output Command

The Output command on the Window menu opens the Output window, which is always used in conjunction with the trace() action (see, Using the trace() Action" below). The trace() action makes it easy to ensure that your movie's ActionScripting logic flows in the proper manner. For more information, see Chapter 12, "Getting Started with ActionScript."

Every time a trace() action is encountered in your movie, the Output window displays a Trace message.

To display the Output window:

- From the Window menu, choose Output to bring up the Output window.

Using the trace() Action

The trace() action allows you to output a custom message to the Output window, in response to a script's execution. This is useful for getting a behind-the-scenes look at how a script is functioning—primarily to test interactivity, and to output custom messages that tell you what's happening with the data in your movie at any point in time. To get a better feel for this, take a look at the following simple example.

```
trace("The movie is currently on Frame " + _currentframe);
```

If you were to place the above script on Frame 10 of your movie, the Output window would automatically open and display the following message when your movie reaches Frame 10 when it's played in the testing environment:

"The movie is currently on Frame 10."

The trace() action is helpful for finding bugs because it allows you to trace an error by means of deduction. Let's look at a hands-on example.

To use the trace() action:

1. Choose File > New to start a new Flash project.
2. Select the Oval tool and draw a small circle anywhere on the stage.

   The appearance of your oval is not important for this exercise.
3. With the circle selected, press F8 on your keyboard.

   This opens the Convert to Symbol dialog box.
4. Give this symbol any name you choose, then select the Button behavior and click OK.

   This converts the circle to a button. Next let's create a square movie clip.
5. Select the Rectangle tool and draw a small square on the stage.

   Once again, the rectangle's appearance is not important.
6. With the square selected, Press F8.
7. Give this symbol any name you choose, then select the Movie Clip behavior and click OK.

   This converts the square to a movie clip.
8. Select the square movie clip instance and with the Property inspector open, give it an instance name of **myClip**.

   Let's next do some scripting.
9. With the circle button instance selected, open the Actions panel and enter the following script:

   ```
   on(press){
      trace("Activation button is pressed");
      myTraceTest();
   }
   ```

   This script—which is executed when the button is pressed—does two things: First it uses a trace() action to output a message to the Output window indicating that the button has been pressed. The second line in the script then calls a function we have yet to define named myTraceTest(). Now we'll define that function on Frame 1 of our timeline, so that it can be called as soon as the movie begins playing.

10. With the Actions panel still open, select Frame 1 on the main timeline and enter the following script:

```
function myTraceTest(){
  trace("myTraceTest function is executed");
  _root.myClop.onMouseDown = function(){
    trace("I now have POWER!");
  }
}
```

This function does two things when called. First, using a trace() action, it sends a message to the Output window indicating that the function has been executed. The next few lines assign an onMouseDown event handler method to the **myClip** movie clip instance, so that another custom trace message is sent to the Output window whenever the mouse is pressed down. As you can see, this event handler is not assigned to the clip until the function has been executed, which only occurs once the circle button instance has been pressed. Before continuing, note that there's an error in our script: We've intentionally misspelled **myClip** as **myClop** to help demonstrate the usefulness of trace() actions (**Figure 19.3**).

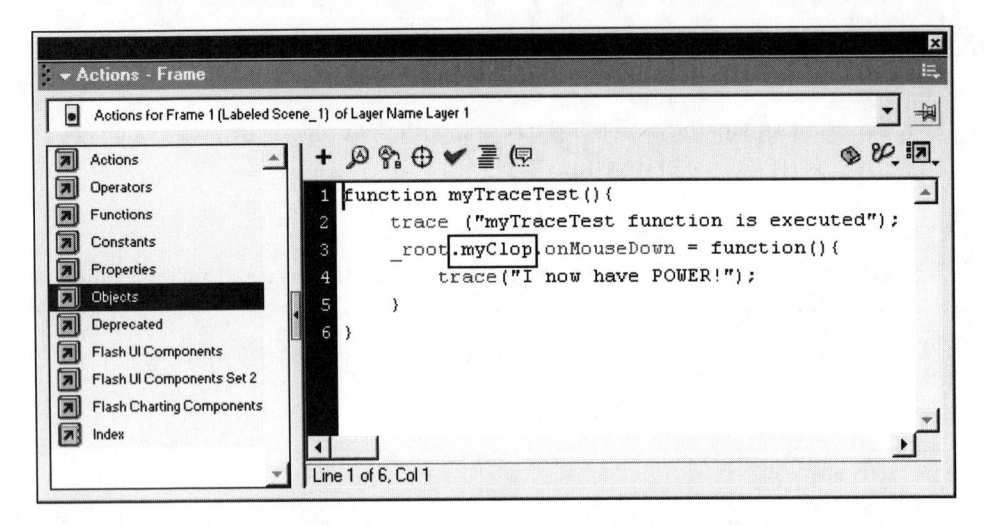

Figure 19.3
A misspelling has been intentionally placed in the script: The instance named myClip has been identified by the name myClop, to demonstrate how a trace() action could help you identify this problem if you didn't know it was there.

Let's test the project.

11. Choose Control > Test Movie.

12. In the testing environment, press the Circle button.

The Output window will open and display the following:

```
Activation button is pressed
myTraceTest function is executed
```

This indicates to us that the button worked, and that its function call to myTraceTest() was executed. So far, so good. The fact that the function executed means that **myClip** was assigned an onMouseDown event handler method, allowing us to click anywhere on the stage in order to see the trace message "I now have POWER!" in the Output window. When we click, though, nothing happens. Interesting. Using our trace() actions, we can deduce that the button was properly set up and that the function executed correctly, but that something went wrong with the event handler method assignment—which means we know where to look for a bug!

In this case, we already know the problem originated back in Step 10—where we noted that the event handler method we were assigning contained a (deliberate) spelling error. But even without help, you would still have quickly deduced that there was an error in that section of code, simply by using trace() actions.

13. Close the test movie.

14. Select Frame 1, open the Actions panel, and correct the spelling error in the function definition (that is, change **myClop** to **myClip**).

15. Choose Control > Test Movie.

16. In the testing environment, press the Circle button.

The Output window will open and display the following:

```
Activation button is pressed
myTraceTest function is executed
```

This indicates to us that the button worked, and that the function call the button made to myTraceTest() was executed.

17. Now press anywhere on the stage, and the "I now have POWER!" message will appear in the Output window, indicating that our *entire* script is now working as it should (**Figure 19.4**).

```
Activation button is pressed
myTraceTest function is executed
I now have POWER!
```

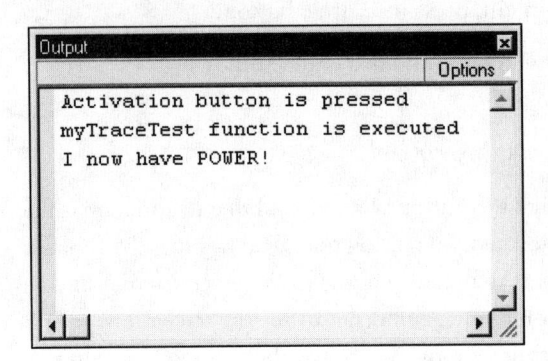

Figure 19.4
When all three of the trace() actions we placed in our project output their intended messages to the Output window, we know the script is working correctly.

18. Close the test movie, return to the authoring environment, and save this file as TraceTest.fla. In the next section, we'll build on it and use it.

> **NOTE** *A completed version of this file can be found on the accompanying CD in the Chapter 19/Assets folder.*

Debugging

MX ALERT Normally, you can't view either the data in variables, or the values associated with movie properties, while your movie is playing. However, this data is crucial in determining how your interactive movie looks and works. Visual bugs are easy to spot, but bugs in ActionScripts can be trickier to track down and correct: Not only is the data usually not displayed, it can also be constantly changing. This is where Flash's Debugger comes in: With it, you can view the real-time values of variables and properties while your movie is playing. You can also change those values, then view the effect of your changes on the flow of an individual script or your movie as a whole.

The Debugger also allows you to control the execution of a script line by line, meaning you can start and pause a script at different points in its execution. That way you can slow down to a crawl a sequence that would normally take place in milliseconds; this makes it easy to assess what effect a particular script is having on your movie's execution. By reviewing your movie's logic step by step, you can often quickly pinpoint problems in scripts.

Chapter 19 Testing

If you're creating simple presentations, chances are you'll never have to touch the Debugger—it's primarily a tool for more complex projects. If you do need to use the Debugger, however, don't be intimidated: It's very intuitive.

To debug your movie from within Flash:

- In the authoring environment, choose Control > Debug Movie.

   This opens your movie as a debug-enabled SWF in the testing environment. The Debugger appears automatically, ready to debug.

The Debugger Interface

MX ALERT The Debugger's interface includes the following areas (**Figure 19.5**):

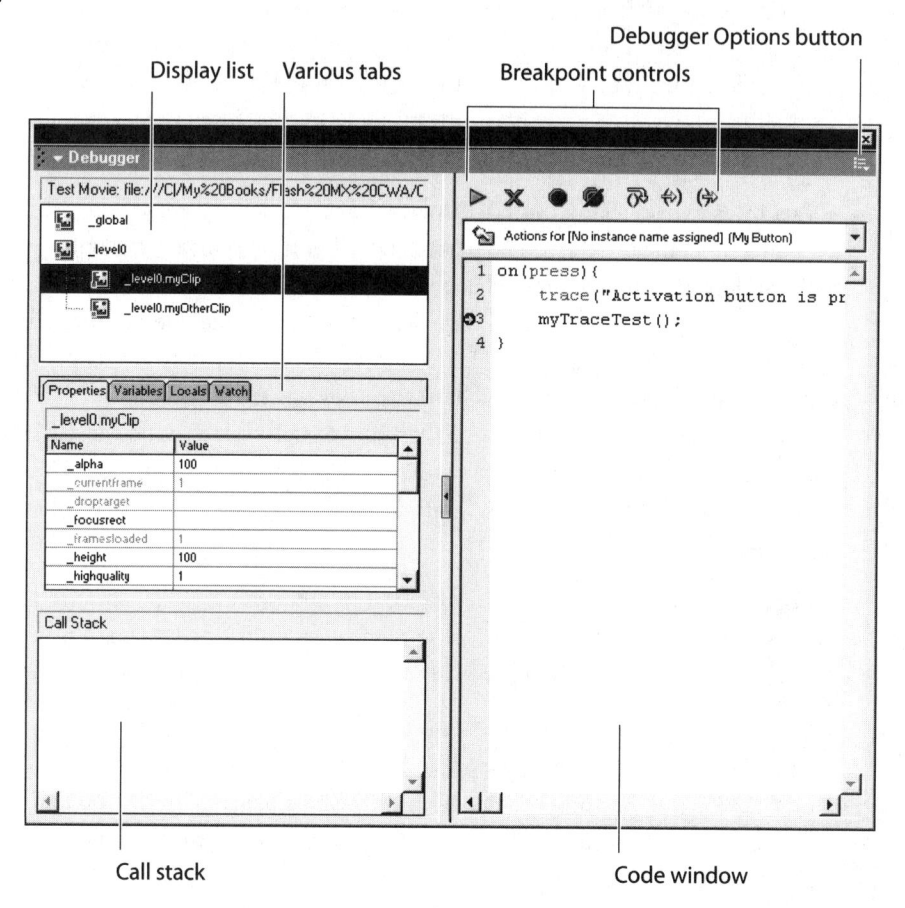

Figure 15.5
The Debugger interface.

- **Display list.** The Display list shows the hierarchical structure of the movies in the movie window, including the main movie, movie clips, and any movies that have been loaded. This list is updated in real time, as various clips and loaded movies are added and removed from the Player window while the movie plays. Selecting a movie from the Display list causes the Properties and Variable tabs to reflect that movie's current properties and variables.

- **Properties tab.** Clicking this tab displays the names and current values of the properties of the movie selected in the Display list. Some of the properties here are grayed out, meaning you can view but not change them. If you double-click a value that's not grayed out, you can change that value and immediately see the effect of those changes in your movie while it plays. Because your movie may contain scripts with conditional statements based on the current value of a specific property of a particular movie, you can make sure these conditional statements are working properly by changing a property value on this tab. Keep in mind, however, that you cannot use expressions when entering new property values from the Debugger: New values can be strings (use quotes), numbers, or a Boolean value (true or false).

- **Variables tab.** Clicking this tab displays the names and current values of the variables included in the movie that's selected in the Display list. Double-clicking a value allows you to change it, then immediately view the results of that change in your movie. Because variables provide the foundation of most Action-Scripts, using the Debugger to change individual values can help you track down the problems that might occur when your movie is fed a certain piece of data. Although you can see the values of Object and Array variables on this tab, you cannot change them, nor can you use expressions when entering new variable values from the Debugger. New values can be strings (use quotes), numbers, or a Boolean value (true or false).

- **Locals tab.** This tab displays a list of local (temporary) variables that are used within a function, when that function block is being stepped through using breakpoints (see "The Debugging Process" a little later in this chapter).

- **Watch list tab.** The "Watch list" tab contains a list of variables that you've designated to be "watched," meaning that their values are constantly monitored on this tab. You can add variables from different movies to this list, so that you can manage all of them from a single tab. To add a variable to this tab, see "The Debugging Process" later in this chapter.

- **Call stack.** When a script calls a function, and even when a function calls another function, which may in turn call another function (enough already!), this pane will display a hierarchical list of those calls. This will help you determine the path your project takes to perform a certain task, which may enable you to optimize your code, so that it performs a task in fewer steps and, ultimately, runs faster.

- **Breakpoint controls.** These buttons are used to control the execution of scripts when *breakpoints* (markers in a script indicating a pause in the script's execution) are used. We'll discuss these buttons in detail in the next section, "The Debugging Process."

- **Code window.** This window will display individual scripts within your project, similar to the code window in the Actions panel. The window is updated to display a script when a breakpoint is encountered within that script. However, you can also select a specific script to display, using the drop-down menu above the code window.

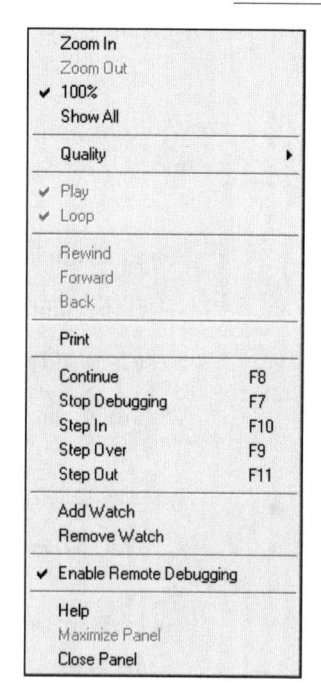

Figure 19.6
Commands available on the Debugger Options menu.

- **Debugger Options button.** Pressing this button displays a menu of commands pertaining to the Debugger (**Figure 19.6**). It also contains commands for controlling playback and view quality of the movie being debugged.

The Debugging Process

Since each project is unique, it's impossible to address every conceivable way that you might use the Debugger to track down and eliminate bugs within your project. Instead, we'll try to give you an overall feel for the process, so that you know how to insert and use breakpoints, see and work with your project's "invisible" data, and understand how to use the Debugger's various features.

We'll look first at the Display List window as well as the Properties, Variables, and Watch tabs.

To use the Display List window and the Properties, Variable, and Watch tabs on the Debugger:

1. Open TraceTest.fla, which we created in the previous exercise.

We will be adding a movie clip instance and some additional scripts to this project, in order to test the features of the Debugger panel.

2. While pressing the Control key (Windows) or Command key (Macintosh), click and drag the square movie clip instance (named **myClip**) in order to create a duplicate.

   Place this duplicate anywhere on the stage.

3. Select the duplicate and give it an instance name of **myOtherClip**.

   Now let's add some scripts to our two square movie clip instances.

4. With the Actions panel open, select the **myClip** instance and attach the following script:

   ```
   onClipEvent(load){
      myVariable = 100;
   }
   onClipEvent(enterFrame){
     if (myVariable < 100){
        _rotation += 1;
     }
   }
   ```

   This script does two things: First, when this instance is loaded, a variable named myVariable is created on this timeline and assigned a value of 100. Next, an enterFrame event is used to constantly check the value of that variable. Using an if statement, the script will make the clip begin to rotate if the variable's value drops below 100. Now let's add a similar script to our duplicate clip.

5. With the Actions panel open, select the **myOtherClip** instance and attach the following script:

   ```
   onClipEvent(load){
      myOtherVariable = 50;
   }
   onClipEvent(enterFrame){
     if (myOtherVariable < 50){
        _rotation += 1;
     }
   }
   ```

Chapter 19 *Testing*

This script does the same thing as the one in Step 4, with a couple of minor exceptions. It uses a variable named myOtherVariable that has an initial value of 50. When this variable's value drops below 50, the script will make **myOtherClip** begin to rotate.

Let's test this new functionality, and see how the Debugger can help us control these values to affect our movie as it plays.

6. Choose Control > Debug Movie.

This will open the movie in the testing environment, with the Debugger open. Initially, the movie will be paused, because Flash assumes you want absolute control over when the movie starts playing and the debugging process begins—especially when using breakpoints. Go ahead and press the Continue button on the Debugger.

The Display List window contains a hierarchical structure of timelines in the current frame, including the main timeline. Clicking one of the movie clip icons will make that movie's properties and variables the focus of the Properties and Variables tabs, respectively (**Figure 19.7**). Let's look at some of the property settings.

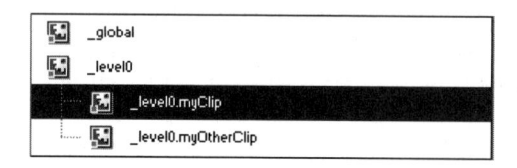

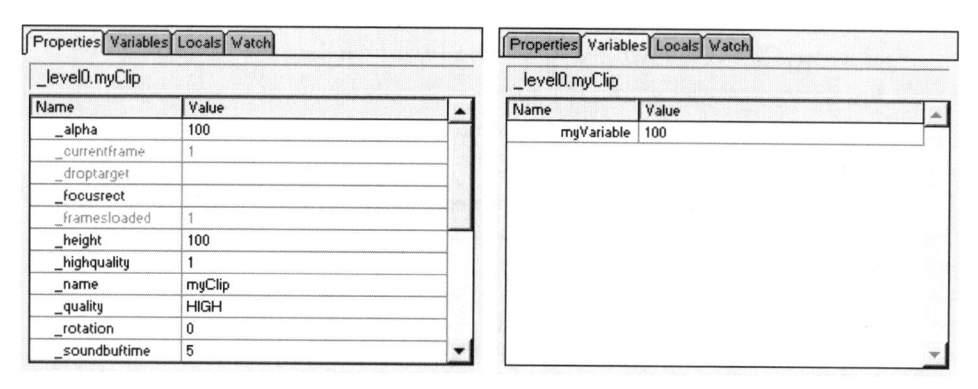

Figure 19.7
Selecting a timeline in the Display list window will make that movie's properties and variables available through the Properties and Variables tabs.

> **NOTE** *Although* `_global` *is shown as a timeline in the Display list window, it isn't one. Instead, it's a global object within the movie, which means it's available to all timelines (as you learned in Chapter 13, "Understanding ActionScript"). It's shown as a timeline because it can contain variables and properties that affect your overall movie.*

7. Click the **myClip** instance in the Display List window, then click the Properties tab to view the various properties of **myClip**.

   These are all properties we discussed in Chapter 14, "ActionScript Objects." You'll notice that some properties (and their values) are grayed out, indicating that they're *read-only:* You can view their values but not set them. However, you *can* set any of the other property values as the movie plays. Setting and viewing property values in this fashion can help you discover bugs in scripts that use these values. By targeting and setting a specific property value, you see how your project reacts to such a change (that is, if it's scripted to do something in response to a change in that value). Let's alter a property value to see how this works.

8. Scroll to the `_yscale` property at the bottom of the Properties tab. Double-click its value and enter 150, then press Enter/Return.

   Immediately you will see **myClip**'s vertical size change in the testing environment. By using the Debugger to change timeline properties, you can not only change values, but also see the visual results of the change. Next, let's look at variable values.

9. Click the Variables tab.

   Since **myClip** is still selected in the Display list window, the Variables tab will display any variables within that timeline. You'll remember that we set up that instance so that when it loaded, it would create a variable named `myVariable`. That variable, and its initial value of 100, appear on this tab. You can edit this value while the movie plays. You'll remember that we created a script that would rotate **myClip** if this variable's value dropped below 100. Let's edit its value.

10. Double-click `myVariable`'s value and enter 99, then press Enter/Return.

    Immediately, **myClip** will begin rotating (**Figure 19.8**). Setting this value back to 100 or above will stop it from rotating. Since variable values are an integral part of how most scripts work (or don't work), being able to see and set values using the Variables tab will enable you to quickly test the effect of setting different values.

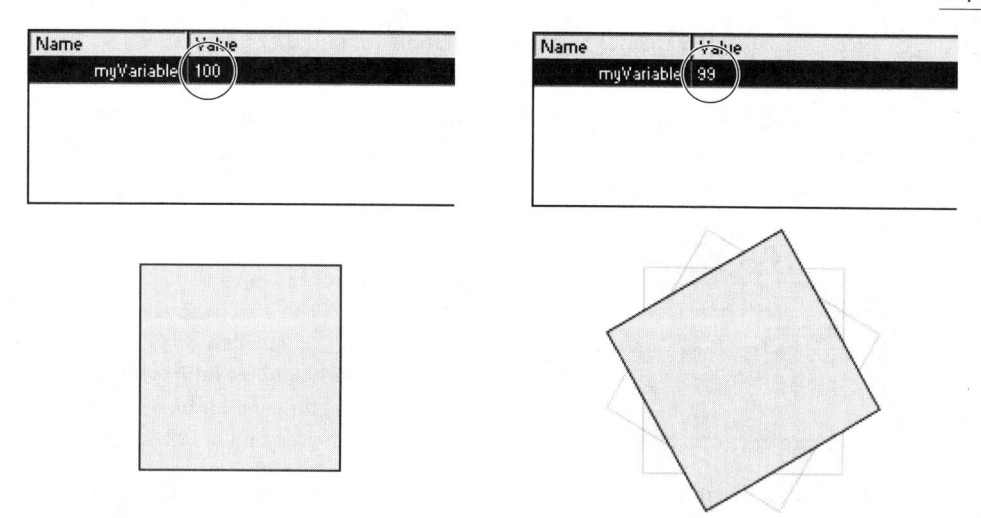

Figure 19.8
You edit values on any of the Debugger tabs by double-clicking the current value, entering a new one, and then pressing Enter/Return. The effect of the new values will be immediately reflected in the movie.

11. In the Display List window, click the **myOtherClip** icon.

    Since the Variables tab should still be open, it will display the variables within the newly selected timeline. There is only one variable in this timeline, named myOtherVariable, with an initial value of 50. If we change this value to less than 50, **myOtherClip** will begin rotating as well. You can do this if you wish.

    If you wanted to change these values repeatedly as part of the debugging process, having to constantly switch between timelines in the Display List window could quickly become a hassle. This is where "watches" can help.

12. Right-click (Windows) or Control-click (Macintosh) on the variable name on the Variables tab, and choose Watch from the menu that appears.

    This will make the variable you clicked a watched variable, and an icon will appear next to its name indicating that this is the case.

13. In the Display window, click on the **myClip** icon. On the Variables tab, right-click (Windows) or Control-click (Macintosh) the variable name, and choose Watch from the menu that appears.

14. Click the Watch tab.

The tab shows two variables from two different timelines (**Figure 19.9**), demonstrating the main function of the Watch tab: to enable you to easily work with variables from multiple timelines, without having to constantly switch between them via the Display List window. You can change variable values from the Watch tab in the same manner that we described in the preceding steps.

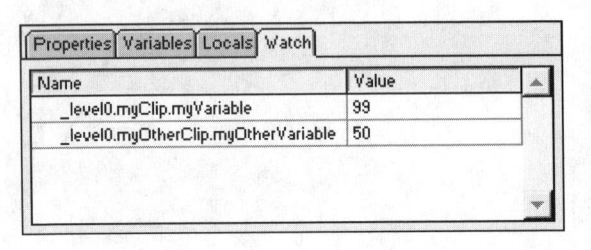

Figure 19.9
The Watch tab allows you to view and change variables from various timelines, from a single area on the Debugger.

15. To remove a variable from the Watch list, right-click (Windows) or Control-click (Macintosh) its name on the Watch tab and choose Remove from the menu that appears.

16. Close the test movie and save this file as debug1.fla. We will use it in the next exercise.

   NOTE *A completed version of this file can be found on the accompanying CD in the Chapter 19/Assets folder.*

Watching and changing property and variable values are only part of the debugging process. Next, we'll take a look at how you can pinpoint problems in your scripts by using breakpoints and stepping through your code using the Breakpoint controls on the Debugger panel (**Figure 19.10**).

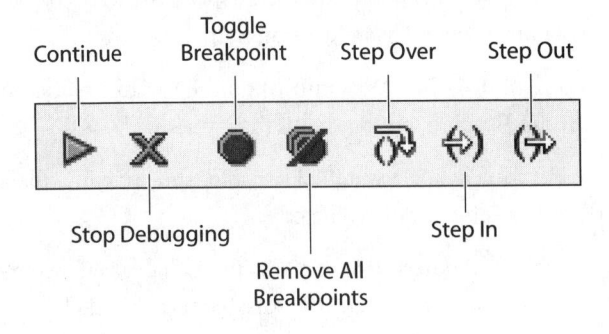

Figure 19.10
Breakpoint controls on the Debugger panel.

To add breakpoints and step through your code:

1. Open debug1.fla, which we created in the previous exercise.

2. With the Actions panel open, select the Circle button and add a breakpoint to Line 3 of the script attached to the button by doing one of the following:

    - Right-click (Windows) or Control-click (Macintosh) on Line 3 and select Set Breakpoint from the menu that appears.

    Or

    - Select Line 3, then press the Debug Options button on the Actions panel and choose Set Breakpoint from the menu that appears.

    A small, red dot will appear to the left of the line of script, indicating that a breakpoint has been placed there (**Figure 19.11**). When this script is executed (because the button has been pressed), it will pause just before Line 3, which contains a call to the myTraceTest() function. Line 2, which sends a trace message to the Output window, will still be executed.

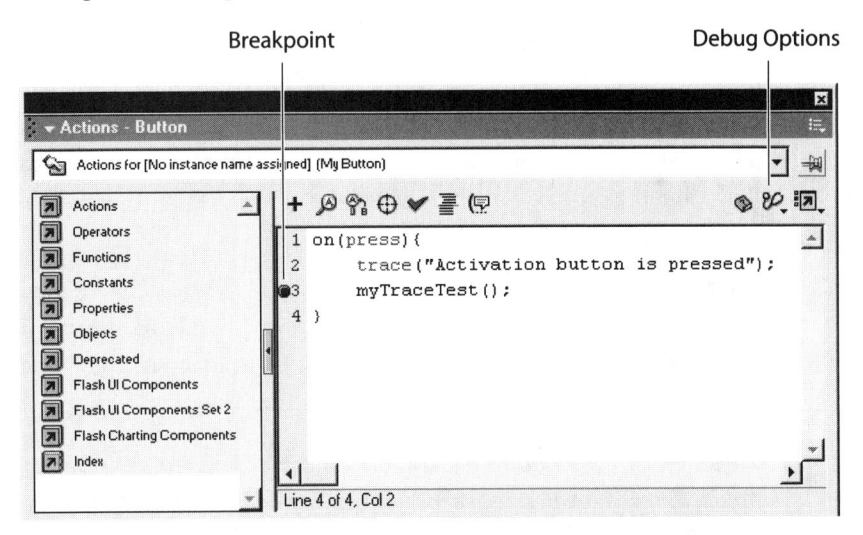

Figure 19.11
Breakpoints can be inserted by pressing the Debug Options button, and choosing Insert Breakpoint from the menu that appears. A small dot will appear next to the line where the breakpoint was inserted.

3. With the Actions panel open, select Frame 1 and insert the following line of script on Line 3:

   ```
   var myVariable = 46;
   ```

   This creates a local variable within the function named `myVariable`. The variable and its value have no real meaning within our project; we simply created them to demonstrate the functionality of the debugger (as you'll see in a moment).

4. Choose Control > Debug Movie.

   This will open the movie in the testing environment, with the Debugger open. As mentioned earlier, the movie will initially be paused.

5. Press the Continue button on the Debugger panel.

   This will make the movie start playing.

6. Press the Circle button.

   You'll remember that we placed a breakpoint on Line 3 of the script on this button. Thus, when the button is pressed, the script begins to execute but pauses at Line 3. A small arrow appears within the breakpoint dot on Line 3, to indicate that the script's execution has paused there. Line 2 contains a `trace()` action (added in the previous exercise) that sends a message to the Output window telling it to open and display the message. If we hadn't placed the breakpoint at this point, the script would have called the `myTraceTest()` function; however, now it pauses instead.

   Pausing the script's execution with breakpoints gives us a chance to examine property and variable values (to make sure everything looks the way it should), or manually enter property and variable values. In this way, you can test your program, and/or try to break it in every conceivable way.

   TIPS *You can place additional breakpoints in scripts from the Debugger panel. To set (or even remove) a breakpoint on a particular script, select the script from the drop-down list of scripts above the Code window, select the line where you would like to place the breakpoint, then press the Toggle Breakpoint button on the Debugger panel.*

   If you wish to remove all breakpoints within your movie at once, press the Remove All Breakpoints button on the Debugger panel.

Now that the script has paused (before it calls the myTraceTest() function), we need to decide how to proceed. If we press the Continue button, the script will continue executing until either another breakpoint is encountered or the script finishes executing. If we press the *Step Over* button, the script will execute the current line but pause again at the next (unless it's the end of the script).

If we press the *Step In* button, the myTraceTest() function will be called but "stepped into"—which means that the function will be displayed in the Debugger's Code window (you're *stepping* into it) (**Figure 19.12**), but its execution will be paused on the second line (since the first line simply names the function, there's no reason for the script to pause there).

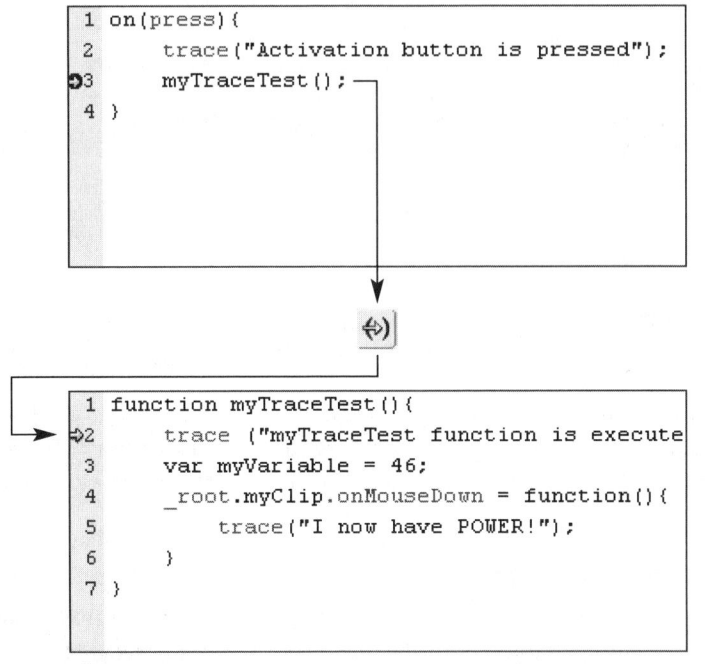

```
1  on(press){
2      trace("Activation button is pressed");
3      myTraceTest();
4  }
```

```
1  function myTraceTest(){
2      trace ("myTraceTest function is execute
3      var myVariable = 46;
4      _root.myClip.onMouseDown = function(){
5          trace("I now have POWER!");
6      }
7  }
```

Figure 19.12
When a script's execution is paused at a function call (which is usually a single line of executable code), pressing the Step In button allows you to step into the function itself, so that you can view its execution line by line.

We can use the Step In option to demonstrate a few other facets of the Debugger.

7. Press the Step In button on the Debugger panel.

Two things will occur: First, the function will appear in the Code window, paused at its second line (the first line of executable ActionScript). In addition, the name of the function (myTraceFunction()) will appear in the Call stack section of the Debugger panel (**Figure 19.13**). This indicates that the current script has made a call to this function. If this function made a call to another function at some point during its execution, that function's name would appear below the myTraceTest() function in the Call stack, indicating the overall path, or *flow*, the script takes to complete its task. As mentioned earlier, checking this flow may help you identify places where you can optimize your project's code.

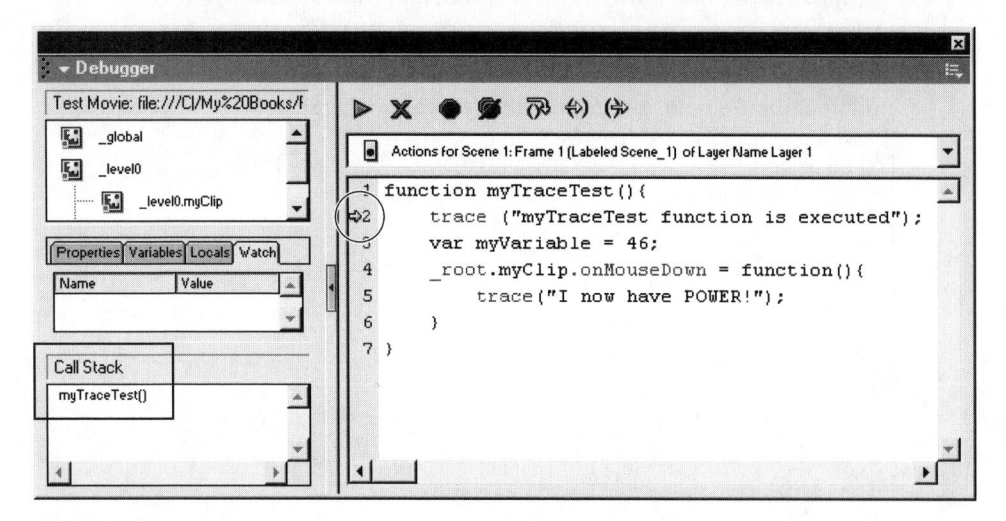

Figure 19.13
After pressing the Step In button, the myTraceTest() function will appear in the Code window, paused at Line 2 (indicated by a small arrow); the name of the function will also appear in the Call Stack window, allowing you to see the flow employed by the current script to complete its task.

Returning to the script paused in the Code window, we once again have a choice: We can press the Continue button, so that the function continues executing until another breakpoint is encountered, or the function (and the script that called it) has finished executing. We can press the Step Over button to execute the current line of the script, but pause at the one that follows. Or, we can press the Step Out button to "step out" of the function and return to executing the main script.

In this case, we're going to press the Step Over button to demonstrate one more aspect of the Debugger panel: the ability to view (and change) local variables that are created as a function executes.

8. Click the Locals tab on the Debugger panel.

9. Press the Step Over button.

   The next line in the function definition will now be executed, creating a local variable named myVariable with a value of 46 (which we set back in Step 3). This variable will appear on the Locals tab. You can change its value by double-clicking its current value and entering a new one. Being able to control the local variable values that a function uses in its execution gives you another way to test scripts—in this case, functions.

10. Press the Stop Debugging button to finish the debugging session.

11. Close the test movie and save this file as debug2.fla.

   NOTE *A completed version of this file can be found on the accompanying CD in the Chapter 19/Assets folder.*

This completes our debugging session.

Remote Debugging

Up to this point, we've focused on debugging movies as they play within the testing environment. However, Flash also allows you to debug movies over the Web—what's known as *remote* debugging.

In their default state, SWF files on the Web cannot be debugged—the assumption being that people don't necessarily want others to know how their movies have been assembled (which the debugging process reveals completely). To allow your movie to be debugged, you must do three things:

- Set up the SWF file so that debugging is allowed (which we'll discuss how to do shortly).

- Publish your movie. In addition to generating the SWF file, this produces what's knows as a SWD (for *SWF debug*) file, which exists and works in tandem with the SWF file to allow debugging. Without this file, debugging is impossible.

- Make sure that Flash is running when you view the SWF you're debugging.

Let's go through the process.

To debug a movie remotely:

1. Open the Flash document you wish to debug.

2. In the authoring environment, Choose File > Publish Settings.

3. On the Formats tab, select the Flash and HTML format types, then click the Flash tab.

4. Select the Debugging Permitted option.

   This will make the Password field editable.

5. To set a password that must be entered before debugging the movie, enter a password in the Password box (**Figure 19.14**).

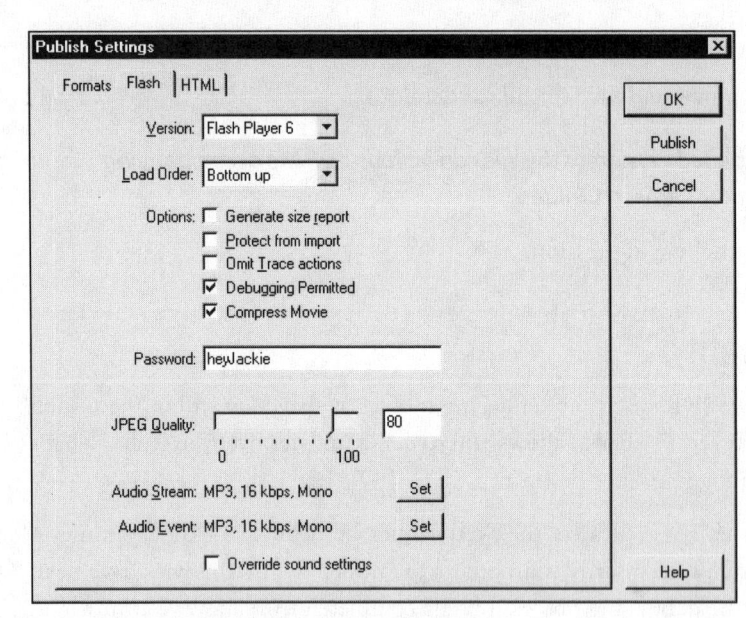

Figure 19.14 Selecting the Debugging Permitted option on the Flash tab of the Publish Settings dialog box is the first step in remotely debugging your project. This option also lets you specify a password that must be entered before remote debugging can commence.

If you leave the password field blank, you can debug the movie without first providing a password. However, you'll probably want to use a password, so that only those you authorize can view the code in your movie.

6. Publish your movie.

   Flash will create HTML, SWF, and SWD files (**Figure 19.15**).

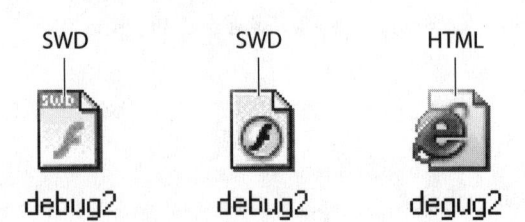

Figure 19.15 The HTML, SWF, and SWD files created when you publish your movie and debugging has been enabled. The file names generated are based on the name of the authoring file.

7. Upload all three of these files to your server, or somewhere on your hard drive.

All three files need to be stored in the same directory.

8. In Flash, choose Window > Debugger to open the Debugger panel.

9. Press the Debugger panel Options button, and select Enable Remote Debugging from the menu that appears.

10. Using your browser, navigate to your SWF file.

This will open the Remote Debug dialog box, which will ask you to indicate the location where Flash MX (the authoring tool) is running (**Figure 19.16**).

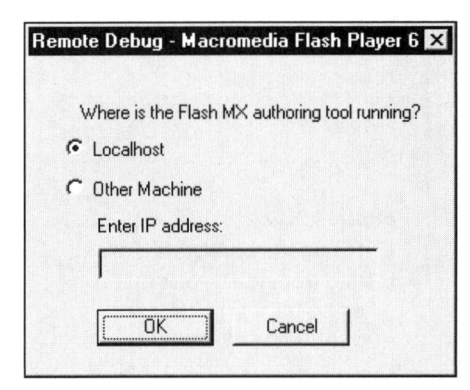

Figure 19.16
The Remote Debug dialog box.

11. Since Flash MX is most likely running on your own computer, select the Localhost option, then press OK.

If you set the file to require a password before it can be debugged (as described in Step 5), a box will appear asking you for that password.

12. Enter the password if you've specified one.

The movie will open, the Debugger will become active, and you can now debug the movie (as described in the previous section).

> **TIP** *If you want to disable debugging of the remote file, so that the SWF file simply plays when opened, either move or delete the associated SWD file that was created and uploaded to the server (as described in Steps 6 and 7). This file contains the functionality that enables debugging. Without it, debugging is not possible.*

Testing Download Performance

Testing your movie's functionality is only half the battle. Because most Flash movies are delivered over the Web, you need to plan, design, and create your movie with bandwidth limitations in mind.

To test how well your movie will stream over the Web:

1. With the testing environment open, from the Debug menu choose a bandwidth for testing the download, or *streaming*, performance, of your movie (**Figure 19.17**).

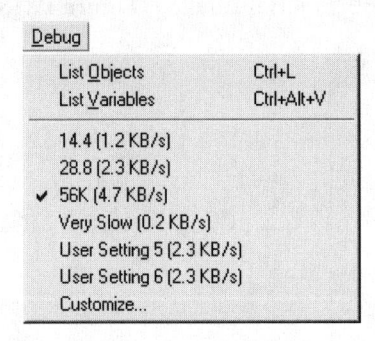

Figure 19.17
Choosing the bandwidth for testing from the Debug menu.

2. Make sure your movie has been rewound to its beginning (Control > Rewind), then from the View menu choose Show Streaming.

   Your movie will begin to play as it would over the Web, at the connection speed you chose in the previous step.

Although this method can help you identify specific problem areas in the streaming process, sometimes effective troubleshooting requires having more information. This is where the Bandwidth Profiler can help.

Understanding the Bandwidth Profiler

The Bandwidth Profiler is an invaluable source of information when testing download performance (**Figure 19.18**). At a glance, it provides you with vital data that helps pinpoint problem areas in streaming. These include information about the size of individual frames and the amount of time between when streaming begins and your movie can begin playing.

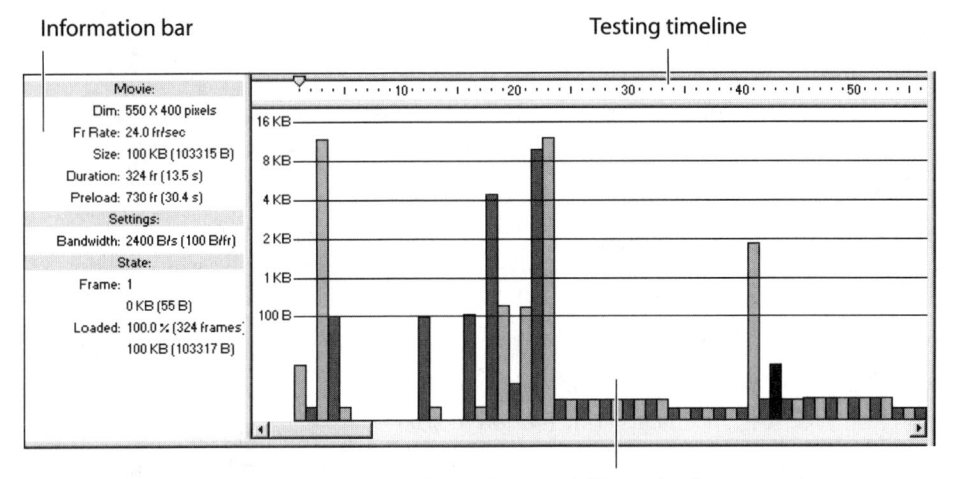

Figure 19.18
The Bandwidth Profiler.

Using the Bandwidth Profiler, you can simulate the download experience of someone using a 28.8-Kbps, 33.6-Kbps, or 56-Kbps modem. You can even use a custom setting to simulate the streaming process of an ISDN, DSL, or LAN connection. By simulating a particular modem speed, you can detect pauses in streaming caused by content-heavy frames, so that you can reedit them to achieve acceptable performance. Perhaps most important, the Profiler saves you the hassle of uploading your movie to the Web and testing it over an actual Web connection.

NOTE *Remember, these are simulated speeds; actual conditions on the Web may vary.*

To display the Bandwidth Profiler:

- From the View menu choose Bandwidth Profiler.

To resize the Bandwidth Profiler:

- Place your cursor over the horizontal bar that separates the Bandwidth Profiler from your movie. When the cursor changes to a double-sided arrow, click and drag to resize.

To help you get the most from the Bandwidth Profiler, let's take a look at its features.

The information bar

The information bar section of the Bandwidth Profiler provides a wealth of information about the movie or scene you're testing (**Figure 19.19**), including the following:

Movie:	
Dim:	550 X 400 pixels
Fr Rate:	12.0 fr/sec
Size:	23 KB (23842 B)
Duration:	15 fr (1.3 s)
Preload:	105 fr (8.8 s)
Settings:	
Bandwidth:	2400 B/s (200 B/fr)
State:	
Frame:	15
	23 KB (23788 B)
Loaded:	100.0 % (15 frames)
	23 KB (23844 B)

Figure 19.19
The Information Bar section of the Bandwidth Profiler.

- **Dim.** Your movie's dimension.
- **Fr Rate.** The speed, based on frames per second, at which your movie plays.
- **Size.** The file size of the entire movie (or if you're testing a scene, its contribution to your movie's overall file size). The number in parentheses represents the exact amount.
- **Duration.** The number of frames in the movie (or if you're testing a scene, the number of frames in the scene). The number in parentheses represents the duration of the movie or scene, measured in seconds rather than frames.
- **Preload.** The number of frames and seconds (based on the current frame rate) between the point at which the movie begins to download, and the point at which it's ready to begin playing.
- **Bandwidth.** The bandwidth speed used to simulate an actual download. This figure is only meaningful when it's used in conjunction with the Control > Show Streaming command.
- **Frame.** This area includes two numbers: The top one indicates the frame number at which the timeline playhead is currently positioned in the testing environment; the bottom one indicates the current frame's contribution to your movie's overall file size. The number in parentheses represents the exact file size. If you move the playhead on the Bandwidth Profiler's timeline, the statistics for the individual frames will appear here. This information is useful for detecting particularly large frames.

TIP ***You can also navigate to different frames along the timeline by simply clicking the gray bars that represent the frames in the Streaming/Frame-by-Frame graph area.***

- **Loaded.** The information displayed in this area relates exclusively to the Control > Show Streaming command. The display includes two numbers: The top one indicates the percentage (or number of frames) of the movie that have downloaded in the background, at any given point during playback. The bottom number indicates the total amount, in kilobytes, that has been streamed in the background.

The testing timeline

The testing timeline looks and functions like the one in the authoring environment, with one notable exception—the Streaming bar (**Figure 19.20**). When used in conjunction with the View > Show Streaming command, the Streaming bar shows how much of the of the movie has downloaded in the background, while the playhead reflects the current playback position. By observing how far the Streaming bar is ahead of actual playback, you can pinpoint areas or frames that may be causing glitches in streaming. Remember, however, that the testing environment merely simulates download and streaming; actual conditions on the Web may vary.

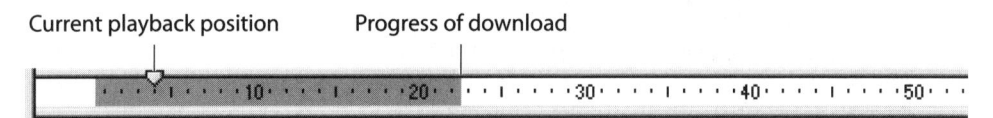

Figure 19.20
The Streaming bar.

Streaming graph and frame-by-frame graph

Depending on the option you choose (View > Streaming Graph or View > Frame by Frame Graph), you are presented with a graphical representation of your movie's frames. The gray blocks represent the different frames in your movie; the height of these blocks indicates frame size, while the alternating shades of gray are used to help you visually distinguish one frame from the next. Areas where no blocks appear indicate frames that do not add to your movie's overall file size (empty frames or frames with no movement or interactivity). Each graph has its own useful aspects:

- **Streaming graph.** This graph (**Figure 19.21**) is helpful for determining where pauses will occur when the movie is being downloaded over the Web. Each colored block represents a frame. A block above the red line indicates an area where a pause in the streaming process may occur.

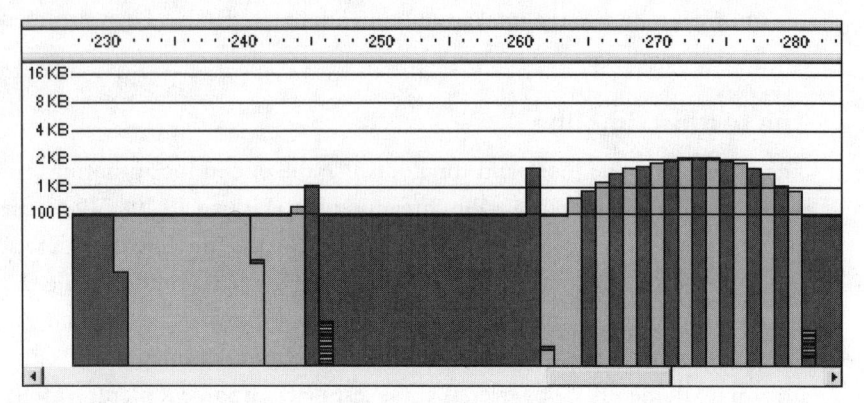

Figure 19.21
The Streaming graph provides a graphical representation of how your movie will stream. In this example, bars above the 100B line indicate areas where streaming could be interrupted during playback.

- **Frame-by-frame graph.** This graph (**Figure 19.22**) gives you a graphical representation of the size of individual frames along the timeline.

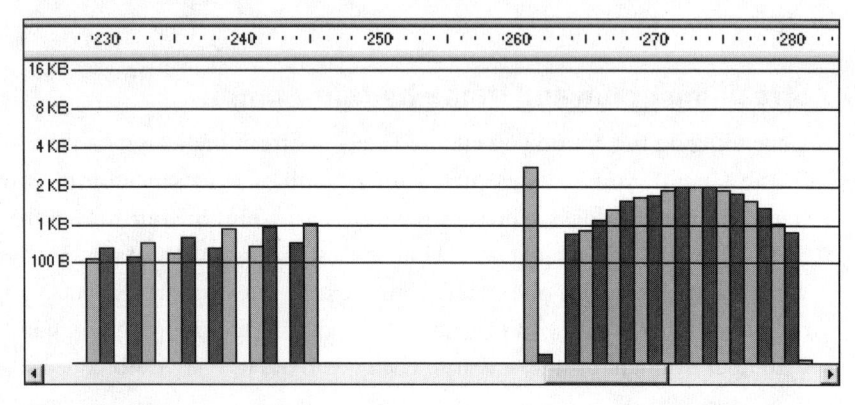

Figure 19.22
The Frame-by-Frame graph provides a graphical representation of the size of various frames in your movie. Areas where no bars appear represent frames where no changes occur.

Creating Custom Streaming Speeds

With the Web, you must always contend with varying constraints when creating content—one of which is bandwidth. When you're delivering streamed content, bandwidth issues become even more important. Fortunately, Flash allows you to test your movie's Web delivery at different modem speeds, including the most common standards of 14.4 Kbps, 28.8 Kbps, and 56 Kbps. It also allows you to test at less frequently used speeds, or whatever speed you determine, giving you complete control over the testing process.

To create custom modem speeds to test streaming:

1. From the Debug menu, choose Customize to bring up the Custom Modem Settings dialog box (**Figure 19.23**).

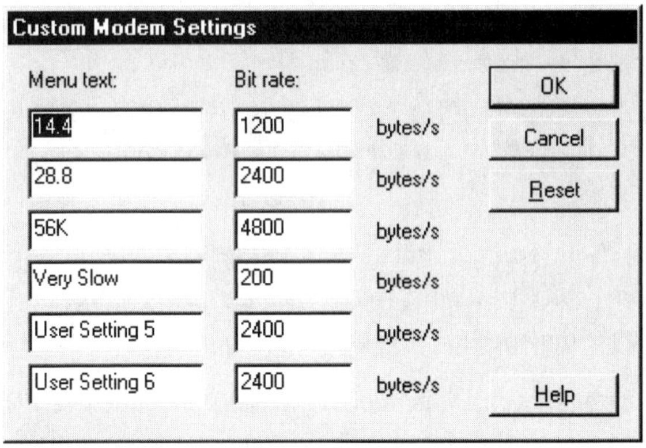

Figure 19.23
The Custom Modem Settings dialog box.

2. In one of the available "Menu text" boxes, enter the text you want to appear on the Control menu as a modem speed choice.

3. In the accompanying "Bit rate" box, enter the bit rate you want this choice to simulate.

4. Click OK.

The custom speed you created will now be available on the Debug menu.

Planning Your Project

Maximizing Streaming

Despite the benefits of streaming, many Flash developers fail to make use of it. You've probably encountered the infamous "Now Loading…" sequence that sometimes plays when a page with Flash content begins to load into your browser. Referred to as preloaders, these sequences are actually animations that are displayed before your main movie has loaded. In other words, the animation is preloaded. Such preloaders are not bad in and of themselves. However, it is a problem if viewers have to wait 5 or 10 minutes for the main movie content to begin. Where was streaming utilized? You might as well put a 1-MB video file on the page, and have your visitors download that.

To reap the benefits of streaming, you need to consider a few things in the planning process:

Imagine the parking nightmare that would occur at the Indianapolis 500 if the parking lot gates didn't open until all 250,000 spectator cars were lined up and waiting. Talk about road rage! Fortunately, the gate opens early, so some cars are being parked as others are filing in. Ideally, this continues at an even pace so that when the last car shows up, the previous 249,999 cars are already parked.

Similarly, the streaming process delivers part of your movie over the Web while the rest continues to download in the background. If you plan it right, you can usually have your preload sequence play for just a short time before the main section of your movie begins.

The difference between the car analogy and streaming is that cars are generally all about the same size, whereas frame sizes in your movie can vary wildly: Some may contain 20 KB of content while others have none; thus some frames will take longer to download than others. For your movie to stream as seamlessly as possible, you need to apply a few basic "buffering" techniques when planning your presentation's flow. If you've downloaded all of your movie's 80 frames in the background, but have only actually viewed the first 50 of them, this means that 30 frames are buffered, or already downloaded but waiting to be played. The trick to maintaining a smooth streaming presentation is to keep this buffer amount as high as possible. In the above example, the buffer amount is 30 frames. Although this may seem like a lot, if your movie is playing at 15 frames per second, that buffer amount will deplete in just 2 seconds. If zero frames are buffered, your presentation will come to a screeching halt at that point—and stay that way until the streaming process builds the buffer back up.

Elements that can quickly eat away at your buffer include sections of your movie that contain bitmaps or sounds, or a section of consecutive frames containing lots of content that changes or moves within a short interval.

Planning Your Project continued

To maintain a reasonable buffer, you need to do the following:

- **Use offsetting.** Include reasonably long stretches where your animation changes very little. Make creative use of vector graphics or text, as well as previously used symbols over a long stretch of frames, as a prelude to a section that introduces a lot of new content.

- **Use bitmaps and sounds sparingly; use symbols generously.** Symbols, symbols, symbols: Use them whenever you can.

- **Use a preloader.** This is the most common way to maintain a decent buffer. Preloaders usually contain little content and are relatively simple. This means that a good deal of your movie can download in the background, while the preloader keeps your audience occupied. The buffer amount will usually increase substantially during this process. Remember: You don't need to buffer, or download, the whole movie before it starts to play. Use a preloader just to get the streaming process going and working smoothly.

- **Give your visitor something to do**. This is a variation on using a preloader. Whereas most preloaders are simply a loading bar of some sort, you can also choose to give your users something to do while they wait. Many sites have incorporated games or even some marketing hype in their preloaders. Remember, though: Whatever you use should be short and simple—anything more defeats the purpose.

First impressions are important, and on the Web the thing people hate most is waiting. If it takes too long for action to occur on a Flash-enhanced page, viewers may get frustrated and go elsewhere. However, all Web content takes some time to download and display. With Flash, you can make this process far less tedious by making it seem like "part of the show."

You should never create preloaders that display the Now Loading message for more than 5 percent to 10 percent of the movie's duration. But pay attention: Your preloader can actually stretch as long as necessary to create a decent-sized buffer—you simply need to make it look like an interesting part of the overall presentation.

You accomplish this by starting simple: Use creatively animated vector graphics rather than bitmaps. If you must use bitmaps, use them sparingly and make sure they're small. Text, on the other hand, can be used generously, in the form of quotes or short bits of information that the viewer can read while the movie is downloading in the background. And finally, use short sounds, if any.

Publishing Your Work

CHAPTER 20

What you'll learn...

How to choose the right format to deliver your movie

How to preview your work

How to export your work

How Flash integrates with HTML

Flash Player issues

How to work with templates

As much as we may deny it, we're all vain at heart. When you've worked hard to perfect your Flash movie, there's nothing better than having others view and praise your creation. Whatever the specific purpose of our Flash movies, we all share at least one goal: to get our movies into the hands of as many people as possible.

Whether you distribute your movie via a Web page or as a stand-alone application, video, or still image, Flash offers ways to automate the process. In this chapter, we'll take a look at delivery modes and the final production process, so that you can finally begin to experience the joy of a job well done.

Delivery Methods

With Flash's Publish feature, you simply choose the formats in which you want your authoring file delivered, adjust the settings for that format, click Publish, and—voilà—Flash converts your authoring file to the selected formats, and creates files based on the settings you selected for that format.

Most of the functions we're going to look at next are available through the Publish Settings dialog box.

To open the Publish Settings dialog box:

- Choose File > Publish Settings.

Publish Settings

Flash lets you control the way your movie is delivered: You can choose a single method of delivery (such as on an HTML page), or multiple delivery modes (for example, on an HTML page, as a QuickTime movie, and as a projector). When you choose multiple delivery modes, the Publish feature creates all of the files simultaneously.

Let's take a look at the options included in the Publish Settings dialog box.

Formats

Choosing the format that you want your movie delivered in is the first task in the publishing process. The Formats tab (**Figure 20.1**) provides a list of format types; each option contains two fields:

- **Type.** Checking any format (other than Projector) generates a new tab in the Publish Settings dialog box. By clicking that tab, you make the settings for that format available for adjustment.

- **Filename.** You can name any file you create with the Publish feature. If you check "Use default names," the newly created files will have the same name as the authoring file (but with the appropriate file extensions). If you leave this option unchecked, you can specify your own file names.

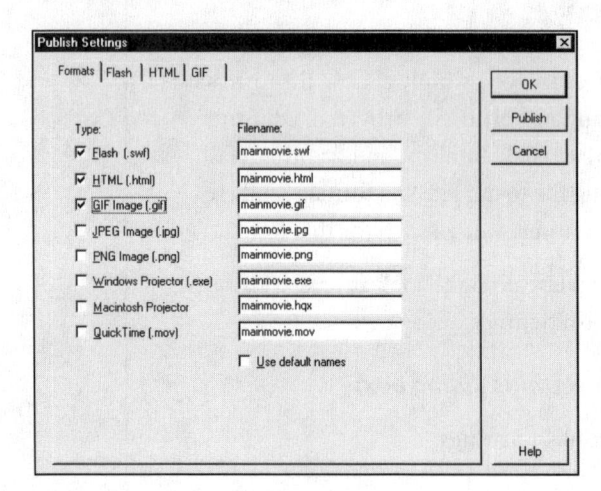

Figure 20.1
The Formats tab.

Depending on the template you choose on the HTML tab (see "HTML" later in this section), you may actually need to select more than one format from the Formats tab. For example, if you choose an HTML template that detects whether Flash Player is installed on the viewer's computer, your actual Flash movie will be displayed if the player is installed. If Flash Player is not installed, a bitmap image (GIF, JPEG, or PNG) will be displayed instead.

This type of functionality requires three elements: an HTML page, a Flash movie file, and an image file. Thus, on the Formats tab you must select Flash and HTML, and one of the bitmap file types: GIF, JPEG, or PNG (the choice of image is up to you). These settings allow the Publish feature to create all of the files (.swf, .html, .gif, .jpeg, or .png) needed for the player detection template to work (**Figure 20.2**).

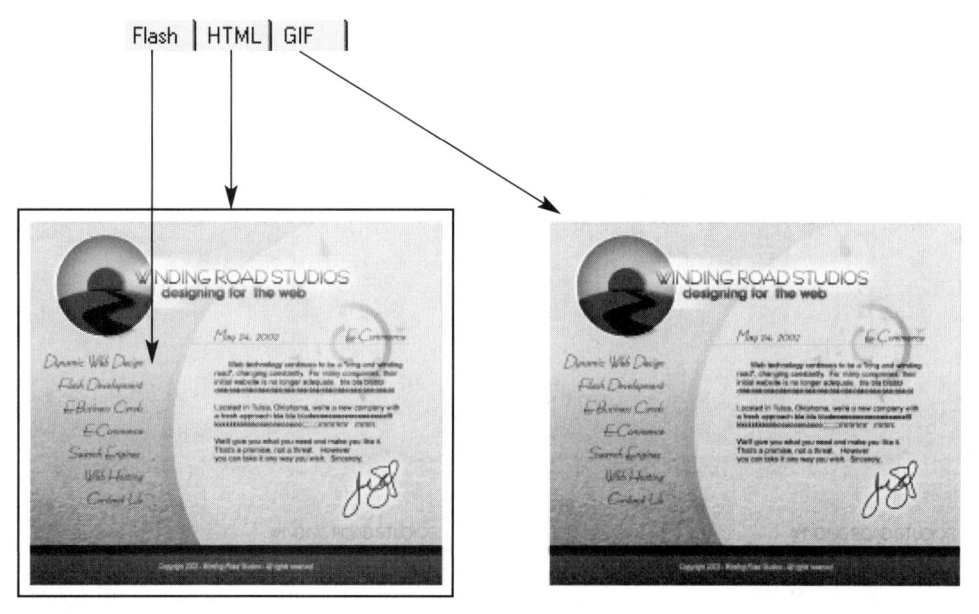

Figure 20.2
If a viewer's computer has Flash Player installed, the Flash movie plays on an HTML page (left). If Flash Player isn't installed, a .gif file will be displayed instead (right).

The files created by the Publish feature are initially placed in the same directory as your authoring file. For example, if your authoring file resides on your hard drive in a folder named Awesome Flash Project, all new files created by the Publish feature will initially be placed there as well. This set of files needs to work together, so make sure they all reside in the same folder on your server and that they retain their relative positions after uploading.

Flash (.swf)

Creating a .swf file is the most common way of delivering a Flash movie. It's also the first step toward getting your movie on the Web (see "HTML"). When you place your movie on an HTML page in this format, users can view it through a Web browser—as long as the browser has the Flash Player installed. You can also use Flash movies in this format with Macromedia Director and Authorware, or any program that can host the Flash Player ActiveX control.

When you export your project to a Flash movie, all of its interactivity and functionality remain intact.

The following settings are available when exporting in Flash format (**Figure 20.3**):

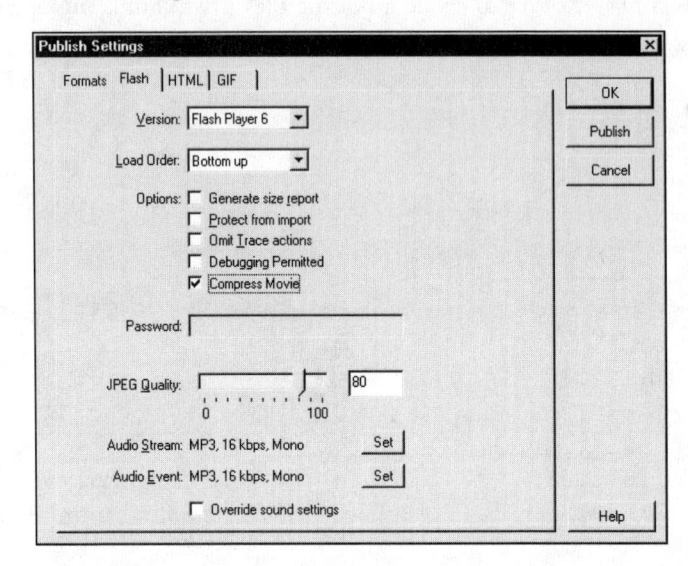

Figure 20.3
The Flash format tab.

- **Version.** Lets you export your movie in a format that is viewable using previous versions of Flash Player. Version-specific features will not work when you export to an earlier version of Flash. For example, if you've authored a movie using some of Flash MX's new features then export your movie as a Flash 5 movie, all Flash MX–specific functionality will be lost.

    TIP *Before authoring a movie, select your target player version from this drop-down menu. If you do this, Flash will then highlight various actions in the Actions panel that will not work based on the target version you selected. This takes a lot of the guesswork out of the development process.*

- **Load Order.** When your movie is downloaded over the Web, the first frame is visually "constructed" one layer at a time, as information compiles in the viewer's browser. This option allows you to set the order in which these layers are loaded:

    Bottom up. Causes the bottom layer to load first, with all subsequent layers following.

    Top down. Causes the top layer to load first, with all subsequent layers following.

- **Generate size report.** Creates a text file (with a .txt extension) containing information about individual frame sizes in your movie, as well as a list of imported files and fonts. This text file has the same name as the exported movie, and resides in the same directory. By printing and studying this text file, you can determine how you might further optimize your movie (**Figure 20.4**).

```
hawaiiApp Report - Notepad
File  Edit  Search  Help
ScrollPane Name           273              0

Bitmap                Compressed      Compression
------                ----------      -----------
hawaiiLogo                26756          180096    JPEG Quality=80
slide3                    12075          169344    =80
slide2                     8669          169344    =80
slide1                     8041          169344    =80
panel                      6064          191464    =80
background                37116          880000    =80
map                       11806          702244    =80

Event Sounds: 11KHz Mono 16 kbps MP3

Sound name            Bytes           Format
----------            -----           ------
soundtrack               196873       11KHz Mono 16 kbps MP3
Plastic Button              847       11KHz Mono 16 kbps MP3


Sound name            Bytes           Format
----------            -----           ------
Arial                      1026       .acghimnowy
Arial Bold                 1042       LMSaghiknpst
```

Figure 20.4
Flash can generate a text file with information about all the data included in your exported movie.

- **Protect from import.** Prevents your final exported movie from being reimported into Flash—in effect, preventing anyone else from claiming your work as their own creation. This option does not affect the authoring file, only the resulting Flash movie.

- **Omit Trace actions.** Removes Trace actions from the exported Flash movie, thus preventing them from appearing in the Output window when you view your movie in Flash's testing environment.

- **Debugging Permitted.** Lets you choose whether the exported movie can be debugged. If you check this box, the Password field becomes active so that you can specify a password for debugging purposes. See Chapter 19, "Testing," for more information.

- **MX ALERT** **Compress Movie (Flash 6 Player only).** If your movie contains a lot of ActionScript (which can increase its file size), selecting this option will compress the script data to further reduce your movie's file size. Only the Flash 6 player can decode a movie that has been compressed in this manner.

NOTE *To avoid confusion, it should be noted that while the newest version of the Flash authoring tool is named Flash MX, the associated player is known by its actual version number (Flash 6 Player). Thus, references to the Flash 6 player refer to the player that can play Flash MX-authored content.*

- **Password.** When debugging is permitted, this text box becomes active, allowing you to set a password that must be entered before the movie can be debugged.

- **JPEG Quality.** Allows you to set a default level of compression for all bitmaps in your movie that have not been optimized individually (see Chapter 6, "Bitmaps"). A setting of 0 will export the bitmaps at their lowest quality (producing a smaller file size for your movie), whereas a setting of 100 will export them at their highest quality (producing a larger movie file).

- **Audio Stream.** Lets you set a default level of compression for all streamed sounds in your movie that have not been optimized individually (see Chapter 5, "Sound"). The setting displayed represents the compression level that will be used for export. To change the setting, click the adjacent Set button. The available settings are the same as those in the Sound Properties dialog box.

- **Audio Event.** Allows you to set a default level of compression for all event sounds in your movie that have not been optimized individually (see "Optimizing Sounds" in Chapter 5). The setting displayed represents the compression level that will be used for export. To change the setting, click the adjacent Set button. The available settings are the same as those in the Sound Properties dialog box.

- **Override sound settings.** If you optimized sounds individually in the Sound Properties dialog box, this option allows you to override any of those settings with settings you define in the Audio Stream and Audio Event areas of this dialog box. You might choose this option if, for example, you wished to produce a version of your movie with higher-quality sound for distribution on CD.

HTML (.html or .htm)

The HTML format tab (**Figure 20.5**) allows you to choose settings that will automatically generate an HTML page containing your Flash movie. You simply upload the generated HTML page and exported movie file to your server to make it available on the Web.

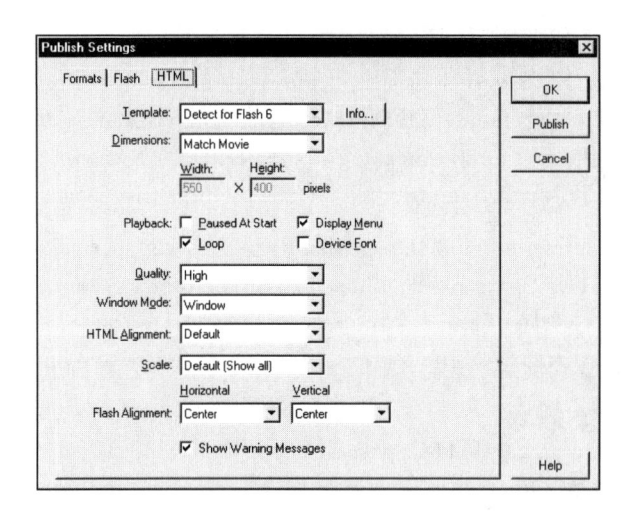

Figure 20.5
The HTML format tab.

Publishing to HTML is done in conjunction with publishing your movie to the SWF format (see "Flash" above), because the exported Flash movie is placed on the generated HTML page at the same time.

The HTML code generated by this feature includes the <object> and <embed> tags, which enable your movie to be viewed using Microsoft's Internet Explorer as well as Netscape's Navigator and Communicator Web browsers. Flash also generates the code needed to set your movie's parameters within the HTML page, including alignment, size, automatic play, and more (for more information, see "Flash and HTML" later in this chapter).

The following settings are available when exporting in this format:

- **Template.** Flash provides a choice of templates for the HTML pages that you generate using this dialog box. Each template offers specific functionality; for example, one simply places your Flash movie on the generated HTML page, enabling users to view it through a Web browser only if the Flash Player is already installed. Another template offers the same functionality, but also automatically installs the Flash Player on the user's system if it's not there already. For more on templates, see "Understanding Templates" later in this chapter.

    Detect for Flash 3. Creates an HTML page that uses JavaScript to determine whether version 3 of Flash Player is installed on the user's system. If it is, your movie will show up on the Web page. If not, Internet Explorer users will get the newest player automatically downloaded and installed; Netscape users will see an image map instead (see "Player Issues" later in this chapter).

    The image map generated for Netscape users can be created based on the content of any keyframe within your movie with buttons that have getURL()

actions attached. To specify which keyframe you wish to use for the image map, label it "#Map"; if you fail to do this, Flash will automatically create the image map using buttons on the last frame of the movie. When using this template you must select Flash 3 as the version to export to (on the Flash tab), and specify GIF, JPEG, or PNG on the Format tab in order to generate the necessary image map.

Detect for Flash 4. Generates an HTML page that uses JavaScript to detect whether version 4 of Flash Player has been installed on the user's system. This template requires you to select Flash 4 as the version to export to (on the Flash tab), but otherwise performs the same actions as the Detect for Flash 3 option described above.

Detect for Flash 5. Generates an HTML page that uses JavaScript to detect whether version 5 of Flash Player has been installed on the user's system. This template requires you to select Flash 5 as the version to export to (on the Flash tab), but otherwise performs the same actions as the Detect for Flash 3 option.

Detect for Flash 6. Generates an HTML page that uses JavaScript to detect whether version 6 of Flash Player has been installed on the user's machine. This template requires you to select Flash 6 as the version to export to (on the Flash tab), but otherwise performs the same actions as the Detect for Flash 3 option.

Flash Only (Default). Generates an HTML page with the Flash movie embedded. This template does not include Flash Player detection.

Flash Only for Pocket PC. Generates an HTML page optimally configured for viewing your movie on a Pocket PC.

Flash w/AICC Tracking. Creates an HTML page, containing your movie, which includes support for AICC tracking when using Macromedia's Learning Components.

Flash w/SCORM Tracking. Creates an HTML page, containing your movie, which includes support for SCORM tracking when using Macromedia's Learning Components.

NOTE *Macromedia Flash MX Learning Components help you create interactive online instructional courses that run in Flash. These components can send tracking information to a server-side learning management system based on AICC (Aviation Industry CBT Committee) or SCORM (Shareable Content Object Reference Model) standards. For more information, visit Macromedia at: www.macromedia.com/support/flash/applications/learning_interactions/*

Flash with FS Command. Builds an HTML page with your Flash movie embedded. This option also includes the code necessary to enable FS Commands to work on the page (see Chapter 12, "Getting Started with ActionScript"). This template does not include Flash Player detection.

Flash with Named Anchors. Creates an HTML page that includes the JavaScript required to enable named anchors (Flash's bookmarking feature).

Image Map. Creates an HTML page with an embedded image map. Any keyframe with buttons that have attached getURL() actions can be used as a basis for the generated image map. To specify which keyframe to use for the image map, label it "#Map." If you fail to do this, Flash will automatically create the image map using buttons on the last frame of the movie. This option generates only an embedded image map, not an embedded Flash movie. The image generated can be in GIF, JPEG, or PNG format, depending on which one you chose on the Format tab of the Publish Settings dialog box.

QuickTime. Creates an HTML page that displays a QuickTime 4 version of your movie. This template requires you to select Flash 4 as the version to export to (on the Flash tab), and to select QuickTime on the Format tab in order to generate the QuickTime movie.

TIP *Selecting a template and then clicking the Info button opens a small dialog box that displays information about the currently selected template, including name, function, and the formats that must be selected and adjusted for it to output properly (**Figure 20.6**). To scroll through the dialog box, press the up- or down-arrow keys on your keyboard.*

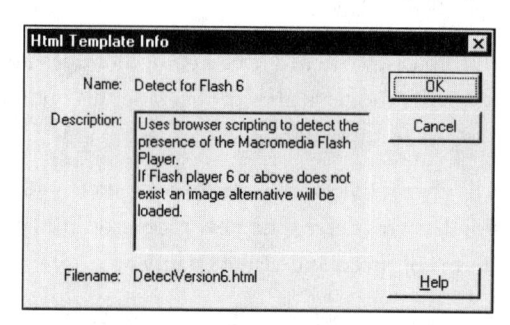

Figure 20.6
The Html Template Info box provides information about the selected template.

- **Dimensions.** Lets you set the horizontal and vertical dimensions of the window in which your movie appears within the HTML page. You can make your movie and movie window proportionately different sizes and shapes. Depending on the dimensions you specify here, your movie may not fit precisely edge to edge within the movie window (see the discussion of Scale setting later in this chapter). This setting does not affect the authoring file, only the exported movie as it will appear within the movie window on the HTML page.

Match Movie. Sets the dimensions of your movie window on the generated HTML page to match the dimensions specified in the Document Properties dialog box.

Pixels. Sets the dimensions of your movie window on the generated HTML page to a specific pixel amount.

Percent. Sets the dimensions of your movie window on the generated HTML page to a percentage amount relative to the browser window through which it is viewed.

TIP *A common practice is to enter percentage values of 100 in each of these boxes so that your Flash movie will appear full screen in the browser.*

- **Playback.** Provides options that determine what happens at the start of and during playback of your movie on the generated HTML page.

    Paused at Start. Your movie will not play back on the HTML page until the user clicks a button within your movie or selects the Play option from the Flash Player shortcut menu (see the discussion of Display Menu setting later in this chapter).

    Loop. Your movie will automatically begin playing again after the last frame.

    Display Menu. The Display menu, which provides options that let the user stop, play, and rewind your movie, will appear in the browser window when a user right-clicks (Windows) or Control-clicks (Macintosh) on your movie. If you uncheck this option, you eliminate these features, and the Display menu will only show information about Flash Player.

    Device Font (Windows only). In cases where a user's computer does not have the necessary fonts installed when the movie is played, checking this option will cause antialiased system fonts to be substituted.

- **Quality.** Because viewers of your movie will be using computers with varying processor speeds, this option lets you determine how processor limitations affect your movie's playback in terms of speed and visual quality.

    Low. This setting sacrifices visual quality for playback speed. Your movie will never be antialiased.

Autolow. This option initially turns off antialiasing, but if the user's processor is fast enough to handle it, antialiasing will be turned on to improve visual quality.

Autohigh. This option initially turns on antialiasing, but if the frame-per-second rate drops below the amount set in the Document Properties dialog box, antialiasing will be turned off to improve playback speed.

Medium. With this setting, antialiasing on bitmaps is turned off, and other elements are slightly antialiased.

High. This setting skips frames during playback to maintain visual quality on computers with slower processors. Antialiasing is always turned on with this option. If your movie is animated, bitmaps will not be smoothed; if it is not animated, they are smoothed.

Best. With this option, bitmaps are always smoothed; antialiasing is always on; and frames are never skipped due to processor limitations.

- **Window Mode (Windows only).** Allows you to take advantage of capabilities only available in a Windows version of Internet Explorer that has the Flash Player ActiveX control installed.

  Window. This selection provides the best playback performance; your movie plays within its own rectangular area on the HTML page. For more information on this and the next two options, see "Flash and HTML" later in this chapter.

  Opaque. Allows you to move elements on the HTML page behind the rectangular area of the movie, without having them show through. Use this option in conjunction with dynamic HTML layers.

  Transparent Windowless. Causes the background color of your Flash movie (as set in the Document Properties dialog box) to become transparent so that the background of the HTML page on which your movie is embedded will show through. This display setting, while visually interesting, also provides the slowest playback performance, so you should use it sparingly.

- **HTML Alignment.** Determines the alignment of your movie in relation to other elements on the page. This setting has no visible effect unless you re-edit the generated HTML page and place other elements, such as text or graphics, alongside your movie. The available options are Default, Left, Right, Top, and Bottom.

- **Scale.** If your width and height settings for the actual movie window in the Dimensions field differ from those in the Document Properties dialog box, your movie elements may not fit perfectly within the dimensions of your movie window. The Scale setting determines how the movie will look within the boundaries of the movie window you have specified (**Figure 20.7**).

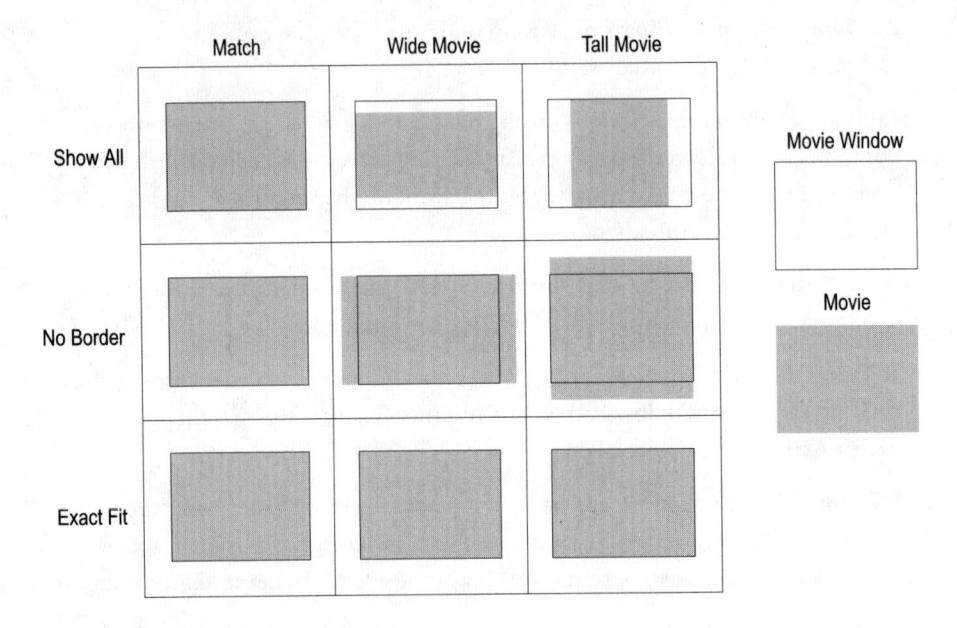

Figure 20.7
The effects of different Scale settings.

Default (Show All). Makes your entire movie visible within the movie window. All elements are scaled proportionately to fill the movie window. Borders may appear between movie elements and the movie window if the window's dimensions differ from the movie's original size.

No Border. Scales your movie proportionately so that it fills the movie window and no borders appear. As a result, elements of your movie may be cropped and not visible within the movie window.

Exact Fit. Disproportionately scales your movie to fit the dimensions of the movie window. Thus, your movie may appear squashed or bloated, depending on how the movie window's dimensions differ from the movie itself.

MX ALERT { *ActionScript* } The Scale setting can be set dynamically via the `Stage.scaleMode` property. For example, `Stage.scaleMode = "noBorder"` will have the same affect as the No Border option discussed above. If you set this property dynamically, it will override your setting in the Scale field. Other values that this property can be set to dynamically include "exactFit", "showAll", "noBorder", and "noScale".

- **Flash Alignment.** These options—which are used in conjunction with the Show All and No Border settings described above—determine your movie's alignment within the movie window (**Figure 20.8**). With the Show All setting, borders may appear between the movie and the movie window; this option affects which borders appear.

  For example, if you use vertical/horizontal alignment settings of center/center, the movie will be placed in the center of the movie window, and borders will appear on all four sides of the movie window. If, however, you use vertical/horizontal alignment settings of top/left, the movie will be placed in the top left portion of the movie window, and borders will only exist on the bottom and right sides of the movie window. Remember, these borders are displayed only if the dimensions of the movie window differ from those of the actual movie.

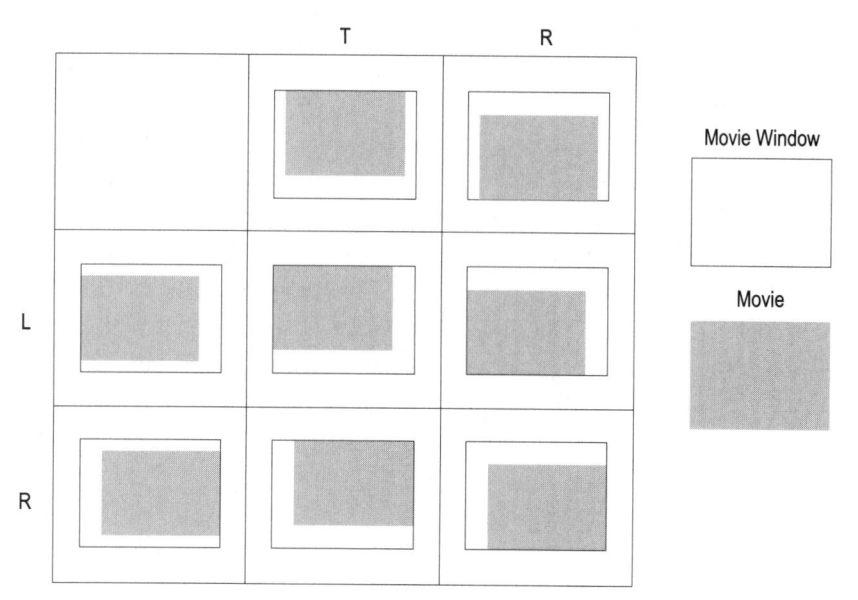

Figure 20.8
The effects produced by different Flash Alignment settings, if your movie doesn't completely fill the movie window.

With the No Border setting, your movie is scaled proportionately to completely fill the movie window; as a result, some parts of the movie image may not show within the window. The Flash Alignment settings let you determine which areas will be viewable.

For example, if you use vertical/horizontal alignment settings of bottom/right, the movie will be placed in the bottom right corner of the movie window, and sections of the top left portion of the movie will not be visible. If, however, you choose vertical/horizontal alignment settings of top/center, the movie will be placed in the top center portion of the movie window, and sections of the bottom, left, and right portions of the movie will not be visible.

> **MX ALERT** { *ActionScript* } The Flash Alignment setting can be set dynamically via the Stage.align property. For example, Stage.align = "T" will have the same affect as the T setting for the SALIGN parameter (which is the HTML parameter that handles Flash alignment on an HTML page; see "SALIGN" parameter later in this chapter). If you set this property dynamically, it will override any settings you make in the Flash Alignment fields.

- **Show Warning Messages.** When using templates, a warning message displays indicating the template in use requires you to select additional publish formats or adjust publish settings.

GIF (.gif)

GIFs are the most popular graphic format on the Web today—primarily because unlike JPEGs and PNGs, they can be compressed and animated. There are basically two scenarios where it makes sense to create a GIF from the Flash authoring file: If you simply want to use Flash as a GIF creation tool for regular HTML pages, or if you want to use a GIF file instead of a Flash movie on a Web page, because the user didn't have the proper Flash Player. Either way, Flash makes it simple to create the appropriate GIF image. The following options are available when you're creating GIFs (**Figure 20.9**).

Chapter 20 **Publishing Your Work**

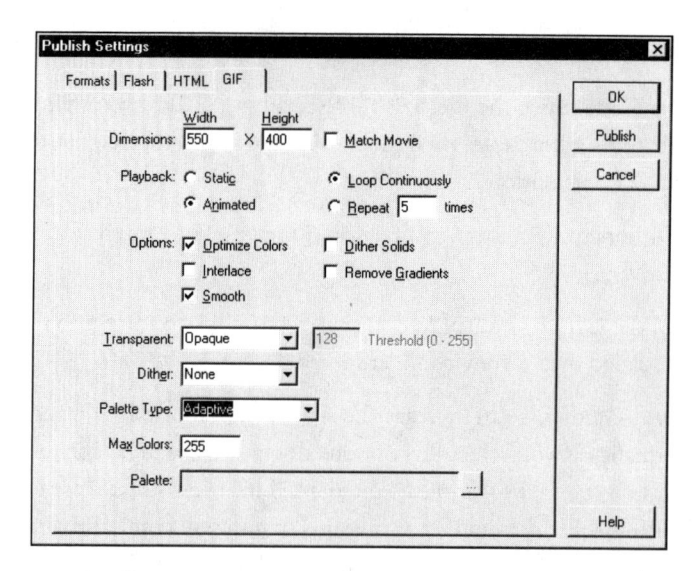

Figure 20.9
The GIF format tab.

- **Dimensions.** Lets you set the vertical and horizontal dimensions (in pixels) of the GIF that is generated. Match Movie creates a GIF with the same dimensions as those entered in the Document Properties box. If you check this option, the Width and Height boxes have no function (and thus will be grayed out). If you leave this option unchecked, you can enter a new size for the exported GIF. You only need to enter either the width or the height, because Flash will automatically generate an image that maintains the aspect ratio of the original.

- **Playback.** Lets you choose whether the exported GIF will be static or animated, and how it will play if it is animated.

    Static. Creates a nonanimated GIF based on a single keyframe in your movie. You need to label a keyframe "#Static" to make it the one that is exported. If you don't do this, Flash will use the first frame of the movie instead.

    Animated. Creates an animated GIF based on your movie or a section of it. You can specify the range of frames exported by labeling the first and last keyframes of the range "#First" and "#Last," respectively. If you do not do this, the entire movie will be exported, which could result in a huge file. Be aware that interactivity and sound are lost when you export to GIF.

    Loop Continuously. Your animated GIF will automatically, and continuously, replay after it has played its last frame.

    Repeat X times. If you check this option, your animated GIF will automatically begin to play again—as many times as you specify—when it has reached the last frame during playback.

- **Options.** The following settings determine the visual appearance of your GIF:

    Optimize Colors. Can reduce the file size of the resulting GIF by removing any unused colors from its color table. If you use an Adaptive palette (see discussion later in this chapter), this option has no effect.

    Dither Solids. Dithers solid colors, gradients, and images. For more information, see "Dither," below.

    Interlace. Causes the GIF to be displayed in stages—as if it's coming into focus—when it is downloaded over a slow connection.

    Remove Gradients. Gradients can increase the size of the exported GIF, and are usually of poor quality. If you select this option, all gradients will be converted to solid colors based on the first color of the gradient. This means that if an area is filled with a white-to-blue gradient, selecting this option will convert that filled area to white only.

    Smooth. Applies antialiasing to the exported GIF. This creates a slightly larger file, but elements of the image, especially text, appear smooth instead of jagged. If your exported GIF has a transparent background, turning this off can eliminate the halo effect that sometimes appears around the edges of the image when it is placed on a multicolored background.

- **Transparent.** When a transparent GIF is placed on a Web page, that page's background can be seen through any area of the GIF that is transparent. The following transparency settings determine which parts of the exported GIF are transparent.

    Opaque. Makes the entire rectangular area of the image opaque. The exported image will appear on the HTML page the way it does in Flash.

    Transparent. Makes the background of the exported GIF transparent. This means that any portion of the movie's background that can be seen in Flash will now become transparent.

    Alpha. This deals with colors in your movie to which an alpha value has been applied (that is, semitransparent colors). In the Threshold box, enter a number between 0 and 255. (This range corresponds to the 0–100% alpha slider in the Color window; thus, a value of 128 for this setting is equal to 50 percent in the color window.) Any colors with alpha values higher than the amount you entered will be exported as opaque; any colors with alpha values lower than the amount you entered will be exported as transparent.

- **Dither.** A GIF file, by definition, has a limited color palette (256 colors max). If the GIF you are exporting uses colors not available on the current palette, the dithering function can help approximate those colors by mixing available colors. This process tricks the eye into seeing more colors than are actually being displayed. Before you use dithering, though, be aware that it can increase the file size of your exported image, and can also, in some cases, display poorly on low-resolution monitors.

    If you do not use dithering, any colors not available on the current palette will be replaced with the closest available color. If you go with this option be sure to check the exported file, as it may include unexpected results.

    None. Exports your image without dithering.

    Ordered. Dithers the exported image at a reasonable quality, with minimal effect on file size.

    Diffused. Creates the highest-quality dithering, and also generates the biggest increase in file size.

- **Palette Type.** Because GIF files have limited color palettes, you must choose the right palette to ensure the color accuracy of your exported file. The following options provide a great deal of control in palette selection.

    Web 216. If you've mostly used Web-safe colors in your project, this selection will provide the best results. It produces a GIF file based on the 216-color palette used by Microsoft and Netscape browsers.

    Adaptive. Creates a custom palette based on the colors in the image—the result is more accurate color (than that produced by the Web 216 palette) but a larger image file. Decreasing the maximum number of colors available (see the Max Colors option) allows you to minimize file size.

    Web Snap Adaptive. Combines the best of the two previous palette options by creating a custom palette based on the image's colors, but substituting Web-safe colors (for custom ones) whenever possible.

    Custom. If you created a custom palette (with an .act file extension) in another application (such as Macromedia's Fireworks), you can use this palette when exporting your image to GIF. Choosing this option activates the Palette option beneath it. Press the button with the ellipsis (...) to locate the palette you wish to use.

- **Max Colors.** If you use either the Adaptive or Web Snap Adaptive palette option, a custom palette is created when the image is exported. This allows you to set the maximum number of colors that will be created. Including fewer colors results in a smaller image file but less accurate colors. More colors result in truer colors but a larger file.

JPEG (.jpeg or .jpg)

GIFs are great for creating simple, small images with few colors. However, if you need an image format that renders gradients well and isn't hindered by a limited color palette, JPEGs are the way to go. The JPEG format tab (**Figure 20.10**) enables you to export photographic-quality images that are compressed into a relatively small file. The main difference between JPEGs and GIFs is that JPEGs can't be exported as animated graphics. In addition, JPEGs aren't very good at exporting images with few colors; images tend to appear "blocky" rather than smooth.

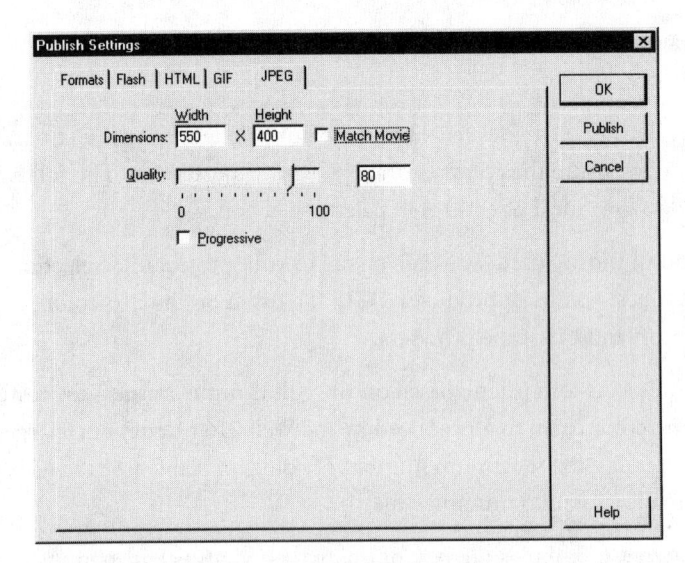

Figure 20.10
The JPEG format tab.

JPEG images can only be exported as static, or nonanimated, images. You need to label a keyframe "#Static" to make it the keyframe that is exported; if you don't do this, Flash will use the first frame of the movie.

- **Dimensions.** Lets you set the vertical and horizontal dimensions, in pixels, of the JPEG you want to create. Match Movie will create a JPEG with the same dimensions as those set for the movie in the Document Properties dialog box. If you check this option, the Width and Height boxes have no function (and thus will be grayed out). If you leave this option unchecked, you can enter new dimensions for the exported JPEG.

- **Quality.** Allows you to set the amount of compression to be applied to the exported JPEG. A setting of 0 will export the JPEG at its lowest visual quality, and result in the smallest attainable file size; a setting of 100 will export the JPEG at its highest visual quality, and produce the largest file.

- **Progressive.** This function is similar to the Interlace option for GIFs; it causes the JPEG to begin displaying in stages—as if it's coming into focus—when it is downloaded over a slow connection.

PNG (.png)

The PNG format tab (**Figure 20.11**) allows you to export an image to a format that offers numerous advantages over GIFs—especially when it comes to compression, color capabilities, and transparency. (For more information, see "Using PNGs" in Chapter 6.) However, because PNGs are not yet widely used or supported, you should use discretion in exporting to this format.

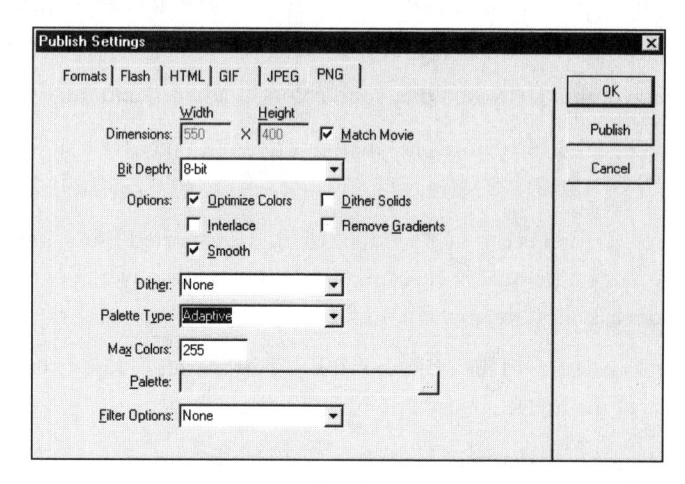

Figure 20.11
The PNG format tab.

Like JPEGs, PNG images can only be exported as static images. Label the keyframe that you wish to import as "#Static" so that Flash will use it rather than the first frame of the movie.

- **Dimensions.** Lets you set the vertical and horizontal dimensions, in pixels, of the PNG that is created. Match Movie will create a PNG with the same dimensions as those set for your movie in the Document Properties box. If you check this option, the Width and Height boxes will be grayed out. If you leave it unchecked, you can enter new dimensions for the exported PNG.

- **Bit Depth.** Bit depth determines the number of colors that will be used in the exported image. The lower you set the bit depth, the smaller the resulting file.

  8-bit. Produces an image file with a maximum palette of 256 colors. Dithering options are only available when this setting is selected (otherwise, they are grayed out).

  24-bit. Produces an image file with a maximum palette of more than 65,000 colors. This highly precise color is achieved at the cost of increased image file size.

  24-bit with Alpha. Produces an image file with a maximum palette of more than 65,000 colors as well as 256 transparency levels. These highly precise color and transparency effects are achieved at a cost of increased file size.

- **Options.** You can use the following settings to adjust your PNG's appearance:

  Optimize Colors. This option can reduce the file size of the resulting PNG by removing any unused colors from the PNG's color table. If you use an Adaptive palette (see discussion later in this chapter), this option has no effect.

  Dither Solids. This option lets you dither solid colors, gradients, and images.

  Interlace. Lets the PNG display in stages when it is downloaded over a slow connection.

  Remove Gradients. Gradients can increase the size of the exported PNG and usually produce poor image quality. Selecting this option will convert all gradients to solid colors based on the first color of the gradient.

  Smooth. Applies antialiasing to the exported PNG. This creates a slightly larger file, but elements of the image appear smooth rather than jagged.

- **Dither.** If you choose a bit depth of 8 bits (see "Bit Depth" earlier in this section), the available palette can contain a maximum of 256 colors. If the PNG you're exporting uses colors unavailable on the current palette, the dithering function can mix available colors to approximate those that aren't available. The following options are available for dithering:

  None. Exports your image without dithering.

  Ordered. Dithers the exported image to achieve reasonable color quality, but with little impact on its file size.

Diffused. This option produces the highest-quality dithering, but also generates the largest file.

- **Palette Type.** When you export an image at 8-bit depth, your color palette is limited; thus, you need too choose the right palette in order to maximize the color accuracy in your exported file. The following options give you extensive control in color palette selection.

    Web 216. If you've used mostly Web-safe colors in your project, this option will provide the best results. It produces a PNG file based on the 216-color palette used by Internet Explorer and Netscape browsers.

    Adaptive. Creates a custom palette based on the colors in the image. This option generates more accurate colors than those produced by the Web 216 palette, but also a larger image file. By decreasing the maximum number of colors available (see the Max Colors option below), you can minimize file size.

    Web Snap Adaptive. This option combines the best features of the two previous palette options by creating a custom palette based on the image's colors, but also substituting Web-safe colors (for custom ones) whenever possible.

    Custom. If you created a custom palette (with an .act file extension) in another application, you can use it when exporting your image to PNG. Press the button with the ellipse (…) to locate the palette you wish to use.

- **Max Colors.** If you use either the Adaptive or Web Snap Adaptive palette option, a custom palette is created when the image is exported. This option allows you to set the maximum number of colors that will be created. Including fewer colors results in a smaller image file, but less accurate colors. More colors result in truer colors but also a larger file size.

- **Filter Options.** A filtering function enables PNG images to be compressed in the most efficient manner. You may need to experiment to find a filter that provides the best results in terms of both image quality and file size. The available options include None, Sub, Up, Average, and Paeth.

QuickTime (.mov)

You can combine the interactive features of Flash with the multimedia and video features of QuickTime to produce a single QuickTime 5 movie that can be viewed by anyone with the QuickTime 5 plug-in.

NOTE *Only Flash 4 functionality is available when using Flash in a QuickTime movie. Thus, when you export to QuickTime, make sure to select version 4 from the Version drop-down menu on the Flash tab of the Publish Settings dialog box.*

Any Flash content you export to a QuickTime video becomes known as the Flash *track*. All of the layers that make up your Flash project are considered part of a *single* Flash track.

The following options are available in the QuickTime format tab (**Figure 20.12**):

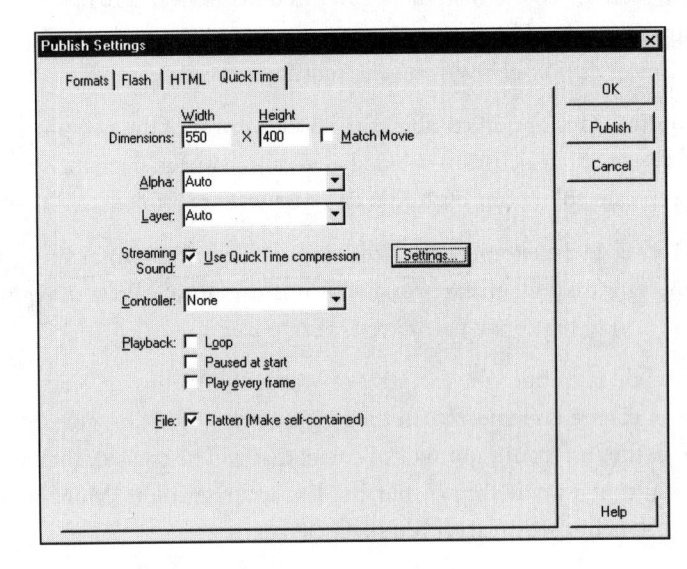

Figure 20.12
The QuickTime format tab.

- **Dimensions.** Lets you set the vertical and horizontal dimensions, in pixels, of the PNG that is created. Match Movie will create a QuickTime movie with the same dimensions as those set for your movie in the Document Properties box. If you check this option, the Width and Height boxes will be grayed out. If you leave it unchecked, you can enter a size for the QuickTime movie.

- **Alpha.** Determines the transparency mode of the Flash track in the QuickTime movie. Alpha settings used within the Flash movie are not affected by this setting.

    Auto. With this option, if the Flash track appears over other tracks, it becomes transparent. Conversely, if it's the bottom or only track in the movie, it becomes opaque.

Alpha Transparent. Makes the Flash track transparent (so that you can see content beneath).

Copy. Makes the Flash track opaque, obscuring any content beneath it.

- **Layer.** Lets you set where the Flash track will appear in relation to other tracks in the QuickTime movie.

  Top. Places the Flash track above other tracks in the QuickTime movie.

  Bottom. Places the Flash track below other tracks in the QuickTime movie.

  Auto. Detects whether Flash content has been placed in front of imported QuickTime content and, if so, places the Flash track on top. (If not, the Flash track is placed on bottom.)

- **Streaming Sound.** This allows you to convert streaming audio in the Flash movie to a QuickTime sound track, using the settings available through the Settings button. (Because these are QuickTime settings, you'll need to refer to the QuickTime documentation for more detail.)

- **Controller.** Allows you to select which QuickTime controller will be used to play back the exported QuickTime movie: The choices are None, Standard, or QuickTime VR.

- **Playback.** These options let you control the playback of your QuickTime movie.

  Loop. Allows you to specify whether the exported QuickTime movie will play from beginning to end, and then start over. Deselecting this option will cause the exported QuickTime movie to play only once.

  Paused at start. If you check this option, your QuickTime movie will not begin playing until the viewer presses a button within your movie, or the Play button on the QuickTime control panel.

  Play every frame. Slower machines sometimes skip frames of your movie to maintain the timeline's flow. By selecting this option, you cause every frame to be seen, regardless of the effect on playback. This option also disables any sound in the exported QuickTime movie.

- **File/Flatten (Make self-contained).** If you select this option, the Flash content and imported video content will be combined in a self-contained QuickTime 5 movie. Otherwise, the QuickTime movie will reference any imported video files externally.

Projectors (.exe or .hqx)

Projectors are stand-alone files (and applications in and of themselves) that can play on just about any computer, regardless of whether the Flash Player is installed. The projector file contains not only your Flash movie but everything needed to play it. This means you can create a Flash movie, turn it into a projector, and then distribute it far and wide. To view the movie, users only need to open it (like any other application), and the projector generates its own application window and begins to play (**Figure 20.13**).

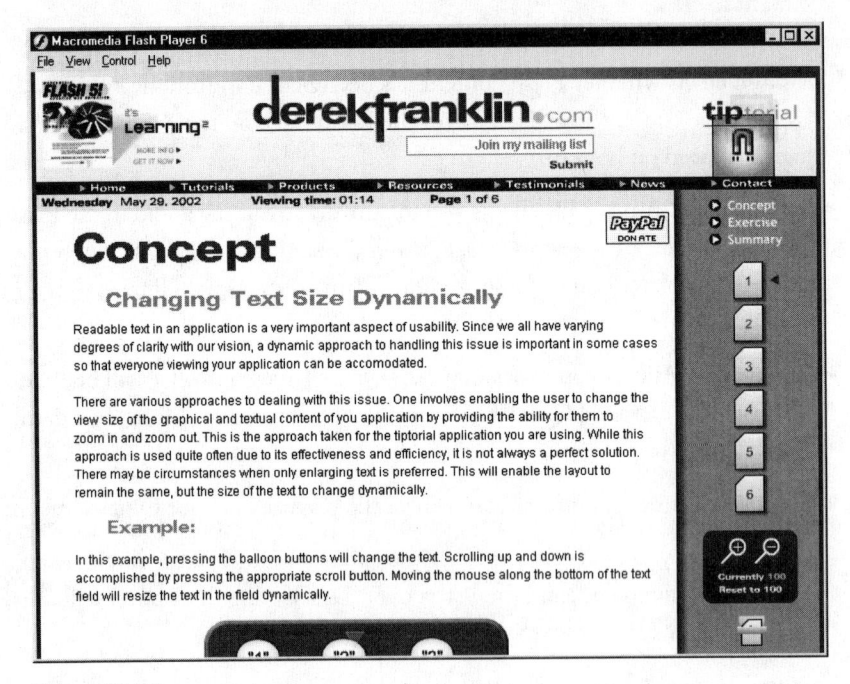

Figure 20.13
A Projector is a stand-alone application—a self-contained version of your movie that can be played and used without any other viewing software.

MX ALERT A projector can open URLs, load and unload movies, update variables, and more. And because Flash MX can now store data on the user's hard drive, you can create applications (projectors) that store and reuse data—which means the user doesn't have to go online to view any portion of your project. It doesn't take much marketing savvy to understand the potential of this: Full multimedia business presentations, Web sites on-a-disk, "Flashmercials," and more can now be presented—in their entirety—as Flash projectors.

No additional settings are available when creating projectors using the Publish Settings dialog box.

You can create both Windows and Macintosh projectors from either operating system. However, be aware that if you create a Macintosh projector from a Windows machine, you will need to convert the Mac projector file from its initial exported form into a Mac-readable application file. This is easy to do on your Macintosh using a file-encoding program (Macromedia recommends BinHex). Once converted, your projector/movie will be ready for distribution.

Previewing Your Settings

If you want to create the best Flash presentation possible, testing is a necessary evil. Fortunately, the Publish Preview command allows you to easily preview what you have exported, or created, based on the settings you selected in the Publish Settings dialog box.

The Publish Preview command creates and places temporary preview files into the same directory as your Flash authoring file. However, it does not automatically delete them when you've finished previewing; they remain on your drive until you manually remove them.

To preview your settings using Publish Preview:

1. From the Publish Settings dialog box, select the formats and adjust the settings according to your needs.

2. Click OK.

3. From the File menu, choose Publish Preview to open a submenu with the following options (**Figure 20.14**):

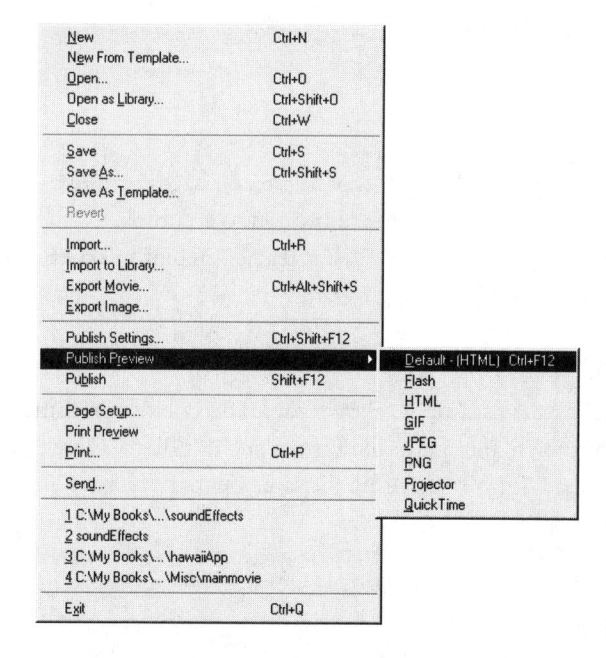

Figure 20.14
The Publish Preview menu provides options for previewing the settings you selected in the Publish Settings dialog box.

- **Default ().** This varies depending on the settings you select in the Publish Settings dialog box.

- **Flash.** Opens your movie in Flash's own testing environment (see Chapter 19, "Testing").

- **HTML.** Opens your default browser with a preview of the Web page that will be created when you publish your project. This includes all the HTML code required to make the movie look and work as it should, based on the settings and template you chose.

- **GIF.** Opens your default browser with a preview of the GIF image that will be generated, based on the settings you selected in the Publish Settings dialog box.

- **JPEG.** Opens your default browser with a preview of the JPEG image that will be generated, based on the settings you made in the Publish Settings dialog box.

- **PNG.** Opens your default browser with a preview of the PNG image that will be generated, based on the settings you made in the Publish Settings dialog box.

- **Projector.** Opens your Flash movie in its own Projector window.

- **QuickTime.** Opens a QuickTime version of your movie inside the QuickTime player.

TIP *For a QuickTime preview to work, you must have QuickTime version 4 or later installed on your machine. For more information, visit Apple's Web site at /www.apple.com/quicktime.*

Exporting

Using the Publish feature is not the only way to create images or movies from your authoring file. Flash's exporting capabilities allow you to accomplish almost the same result, though they're designed for using Flash-created content in other applications such as a photo editor or vector drawing program.

Exporting as a movie

Exporting your authoring file as a movie allows you to do one of two things: You can convert your animation to an animation file format such as Flash, QuickTime, Windows AVI, or an animated GIF. (Yes, these are the same options you have with the Publish feature—you're not confused.) Or, you can export each frame of your animation as a separate static image file. When you export in this manner, each file you create is given a name you assign, appended by a number indicating its position in the sequence. So, if you provide a file name such as "myimage" for a JPEG sequence and your movie consists of 10 frames, the resulting files would be named"myimage1.jpg through myimage10.jpg.

To export your animation as a movie or sequence:

1. From the File menu, choose Export Movie to bring up the Export Movie dialog box.

2. Name the exported movie and choose a file type to save as.

3. Click OK.

   Depending on the file type you selected, an additional Export dialog box may appear. For information on these settings, see "Export Settings" in this section.

4. Adjust any of the settings in this dialog box, and click OK.

Exporting as an image

Exporting as an image allows you to create a single image file based on the currently displayed frame. If you export the image in a vector format, you can open it in a drawing program like Macromedia Freehand or Adobe Illustrator for further editing. If you export the image as a bitmap, you can open it in a photo-editing program such as Macromedia Fireworks or Adobe Photoshop for further editing.

To export a single frame as an image:

1. From the File menu choose Export Movie to bring up the Export Image dialog box.

2. Name the exported image and choose a file type to save as.

3. Click OK.

   Depending on the file type you selected, an additional Export dialog box may appear. For information on these settings, see the "Export Settings" discussion below.

4. Adjust any of the settings in this dialog box, and click OK.

Export Settings

As you've probably figured out by now, Flash offers you different configuration options when you export your movie to most file types. The following formats are included in the Save as Type pop-up menu for the Export Movie or Export Image dialog boxes (**Figure 20.15**).

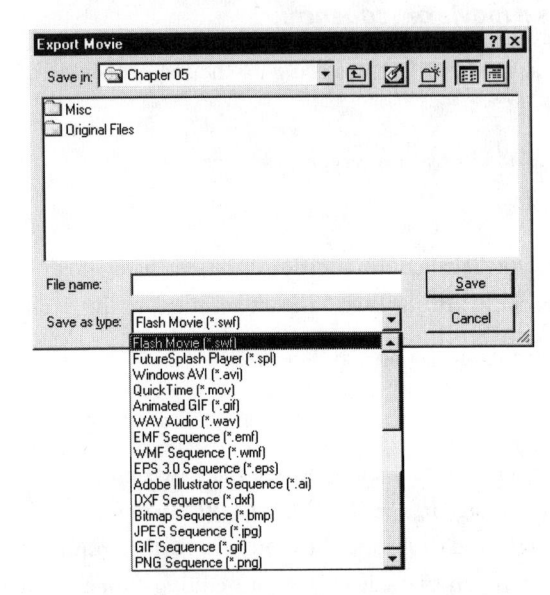

Figure 20.15
The supported export file types listed in the Export Movie dialog box.

- **Flash Movie (*.swf).** The setting options for SWF files are the same as those included on the Flash tab in the Publish Settings dialog box.

- **FutureSplash Player (*.spl).** Flash used this file format before its acquisition by Macromedia. The settings for it are the same as those included on the Flash tab on the Publish Settings dialog box.

- **Windows AVI (*.avi) (Windows only).** This format will export your movie as a Windows video; however, all interactivity will be lost, and the Mac OS doesn't support this format. The following settings are available (**Figure 20.16**):

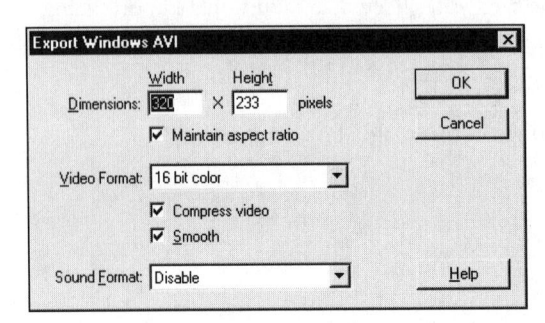

Figure 20.16
The Export Windows AVI dialog box.

Dimensions. Lets you set the vertical and horizontal dimensions, in pixels, of the AVI image. If the "Maintain aspect ratio" option is checked, you can enter either the width or the height, and Flash will export the AVI so that it maintains the aspect ratio of the original movie. If you leave this option unchecked, you can enter values that change the proportions of the exported AVI.

Video Format. Lets you set the color depth of the exported movie. A lower color depth results in a smaller exported file, but at a cost to image quality.

Compress Video. By selecting this option, you can set additional compression options for the exported file.

Smooth. Applies antialiasing to the exported AVI, creating a slightly larger file but one in which image elements—especially text—will appear smooth rather than jagged.

Sound Format. Lets you set the sample rate and size of the sound track, and choose whether to export it in mono or stereo (see "Understanding Sound" in Chapter 5). The lower the sample rate and size, the smaller the exported file—though you also sacrifice sound quality.

- **QuickTime (*.mov).** The settings here are the same as those available from the Flash tab on the Publish Settings dialog box.

- **QuickTime video (*mov) (Macintosh Only).** Allows you to export your movie in the older QuickTime 3 format. Be aware, however, that exporting to this format is not the same as exporting to QuickTime 5: All Flash interactivity will be lost, and Flash elements will be converted from vector graphics to bitmaps. The following options are available (**Figure 20.17**):

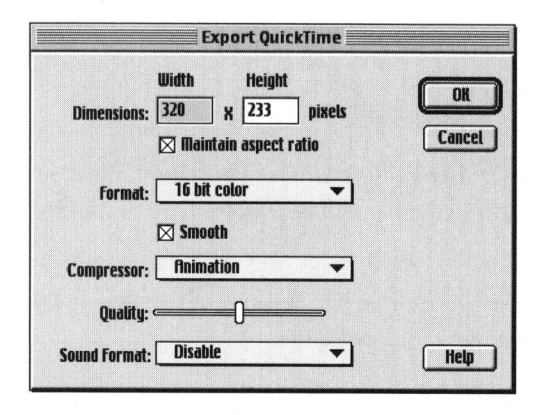

Figure 20.17
The Export QuickTime dialog box.

Dimensions. Lets you set the vertical and horizontal dimensions, in pixels, of the QuickTime movie that is created. If you check the "Maintain aspect ratio" option, you can enter either the width or height, and Flash will export the QuickTime movie so that it retains the aspect ratio of the original movie. If you leave this option unchecked, you can enter values that change the proportions of the exported QuickTime movie.

Format. Lets you set the color depth of the exported movie.

Smooth. Selecting this option applies antialiasing to the exported QuickTime movie.

Compressor. Allows you to select the standard QuickTime compressor.

Quality. Allows you to set the amount of compression that will be applied to your movie when it is exported to the QuickTime format.

Sound Format. Lets you set the sample rate and size of the sound track, and choose whether to export it in mono or stereo (see "Understanding Sound" in Chapter 5). The smaller the sample rate and size, the smaller the exported file—though you also sacrifice sound quality.

- **Animated GIF (*.gif).** The settings here are the same as those available from the GIF tab on the Publish Settings dialog box, with the following two exceptions:

  Resolution. Resolution represents the pixel density (dots per inch, or dpi) of the exported image. The higher the resolution, the larger the image will be. Thus, changing the resolution value automatically updates the width and height of the exported image. Click the Match Screen button to make the exported images match the size of the movie as it appears on your screen. A resolution of 72 dpi is usually sufficient for most graphics viewed on a computer.

  Colors. Allows you to set the number of colors that will be used to create the exported image. Although using fewer colors results in a smaller file, image quality suffers. The Standard Colors option, which uses the Web-safe 216-color palette, usually provides the best results.

- **WAV Audio (*.wav) (Windows only).** If you export your movie in this format, only the sound within the file will be exported. The extended options for this selection are:

  Sound Format. Lets you set the sample rate and size of the soundtrack, and choose whether to export it in mono or stereo.

  Ignore Sound Events. Checking this will specifically exclude Event sounds from the exported sound file.

- **EMF Sequence/Enhanced Metafile (*.emf) (Windows only).** This format allows you to export both vector and bitmap information in a single file, so that it can be imported into other applications. There are no additional settings for this selection.

- **WMF Sequence/Windows Metafile (*.wmf) (Windows only).** This is a Windows-native format for importing and exporting graphics among applications; it does not include any adjustable settings.

- **EPS 3.0 Sequence/EPS 3.0 (*.eps).** EPS is a popular format for placing image files within page-layout programs. The current frame is exported when using this option; there are no adjustable settings.

- **Adobe Illustrator Sequence/Adobe Illustrator (*.ai).** This vector format allows you to export vector elements of your movie, so that they can be brought into a vector drawing program for further editing. When you export using this format, you will be prompted to choose which version of Illustrator you want to export to.

- **DXF Sequence/DXF (*.dxf).** This 3D format allows you to export elements of your movie so that they can be brought into a DXF-compatible program for further editing. It does not include any adjustable settings.

- **PICT Sequence/PICT (*.pict) (Macintosh Only).** This format allows you to export vector or bitmap information in a file that can then be imported into other applications. The following options are available:

    Dimensions. Lets you set the dimensions, in pixels, of the PICT. Enter only the width or the height, and Flash will retain the aspect ratio of the original image in the exported image.

    Resolution. Click the Match Screen button to make the exported images match the size of the movie as it appears on your screen.

    Include. Allows you to choose which elements of your movie will be included in the exported PICT file. If you choose Minimum Image Area, the exported PICT file will be just big enough to include the graphic elements in the current frame. If you choose Full Document Size, the entire movie will be exported so that the PICT file dimensions match those entered in the Movie Properties dialog box. You can use this setting as an alternative to the Dimensions setting described above.

    Color Depth. This pop-up box serves two purposes: First, it allows you to determine whether the PICT graphic will be object based (a vector) or bitmap based. Also, if the graphic is bitmap based, you can set its color depth.

Include PostScript. If you choose to export a PICT file as object based, including PostScript information will optimize the graphic for PostScript printing.

- **Bitmap Sequence/Bitmap (*.bmp).** This format allows you to create bitmap images for use in other programs. The following options are available:

  Dimensions. Lets you set the vertical and horizontal dimensions, in pixels, of the bitmap that is created. You can enter either the width or the height, and Flash will retain the aspect ratio of the original image in the exported file.

  Resolution. Click the Match Screen button to make the exported images match the movie as it appears on your screen.

  Include. Pick which elements of your movie to include in the exported bitmap. Note that the Minimum Image Area option has no effect when you export your movie as a bitmap sequence.

  Color Depth. Lets you set the color depth of the exported bitmap. Choosing a lower color depth results in a smaller exported file, but at a cost to image quality.

  Smooth. Applies antialiasing to the exported bitmap, creating a slightly larger file but one in which image elements—especially text—will appear smooth rather than jagged.

- **JPEG Sequence/JPEG (*.jpeg).** With one exception, this option includes the same settings as those found on the JPEG tab in the Publish Settings dialog box:

  Resolution. Click the Match Screen button to make the exported images match the size of the movie as it appears on your screen.

- **GIF Sequence/GIF (*.gif).** With two exceptions, the settings here are the same as those found on the GIF tab in the Publish Settings dialog box:

  Resolution. If you click the Match Screen button, the exported image matches the size of the movie as it appears on your screen.

  Colors. Allows you to set the number of colors that can be used to create the exported image.

- **PNG Sequence/PNG (*.png).** With two exceptions, the settings here are the same as those available on the PNG tab in the Publish Settings dialog box:

  Resolution. Click the Match Screen button to make the exported images match the movie as it appears on your monitor.

  Include. Pick which elements of your movie will be included in the exported bitmap.

Flash and HTML

You can normally place a Flash movie on an HTML page automatically by using the Publish feature. However, if you wish to create your pages manually or are interested in creating custom templates, you should know how Flash integrates with HTML.

HTML Tags

As you might expect, Microsoft's Internet Explorer and Netscape's Communicator/Navigator have different tag requirements that you must follow to display your movie properly on an HTML page. To place a movie on a page so that Internet Explorer can interpret it correctly, use the <OBJECT> tag; for Communicator and Navigator, use the <EMBED> tag.

You can use these tags separately or together on the same page, and you can also use them in conjunction with other HTML content. Each of these tags has additional attributes, or parameters, that affect the look and playback of your movie. The following describes how to place your movie on an HTML page: first using each tag on separate pages, then both tags on the same page.

<OBJECT> tag

If you were to place your movie on an HTML page using the <OBJECT> tag, it would look something like this:

```
<HTML>
<HEAD>
<TITLE>Using the Object Tag</TITLE>
</HEAD>
<BODY>
<OBJECT CLASSID="clsid:D27CDB6E-AE6D-11cf-96B8-44553540000" WIDTH="400" HEIGHT="400"
CODEBASE="http://download.macromedia.com/pub/shockwave/cabs/flash/swflash.cab#version=6,0,0,0">
<PARAM NAME="MOVIE" VALUE="coolflashmovie.swf">
<PARAM NAME="PLAY" VALUE="true">
<PARAM NAME="QUALITY" VALUE="best">
<PARAM NAME="LOOP" VALUE="false">
</OBJECT>
</BODY>
</HTML>
```

Now, let's take a closer look. Within the opening <OBJECT> tag, we find four attributes in the form of ATTRIBUTE="value". These include the CLASSID, WIDTH, HEIGHT, and CODEBASE attributes. Once again, these attributes are contained within the opening <OBJECT> tag and are all required for your movie to appear on the page. After the opening <OBJECT> tag, we find a set of <PARAM> tags. Although the <OBJECT> tag actually places your movie on the page, the <PARAM> tags affect the way it looks and plays. For more information about all of these attributes as well as the <PARAM> tags, see "HTML Tag Reference" later in this chapter.

<EMBED> tag

If you were to place your movie on an HTML page using the <EMBED> tag, it would look similar to this:

```
<HTML>
<HEAD>
<TITLE>Using the Embed Tag</TITLE>
</HEAD>
<BODY>
<EMBED SRC="coolflashmovie.swf" WIDTH="400" HEIGHT="400" PLAY="true"
QUALITY="best" LOOP="false"
PLUGINSPAGE="http://www.macromedia.com/go/getflashplayer">
</EMBED>
</BODY>
</HTML>
```

You will notice two differences in the way the <OBJECT> and <EMBED> tags are used:

- The <EMBED> tag consists of only ATTRIBUTE="value" settings, which are within the opening <EMBED> tag. These are equivalent to the <OBJECT> tag's <PARAM> settings.

- There are no CLASSID or CODEBASE attributes; these are unique to the <OBJECT> tag. Instead, the <EMBED> tag includes a PLUGINSPAGE attribute, which is unique to it. For more information about all these attributes as well as <PARAM> tags, see "HTML Tag Reference" later in this chapter.

<OBJECT> and <EMBED> tags together

Chances are you'll want to enable both Microsoft and Netscape browser users to view your movie from the same page file. You can do this by using the <OBJECT> and <EMBED> tags in tandem. The following example illustrates how:

```
<HTML>
<HEAD>
<TITLE>Using the Object and Embed Tags Together</TITLE>
</HEAD>
<BODY>
<OBJECT CLASSID="clsid:D27CDB6E-AE6D-11cf-96B8-44553540000" WIDTH="400" HEIGHT="400" CODEBASE="
http://download.macromedia.com/pub/shockwave/cabs/flash/swflash.cab#version=6,0,0,0">
<PARAM NAME="MOVIE" VALUE="coolflashmovie.swf">
<PARAM NAME="PLAY" VALUE="true">
<PARAM NAME="QUALITY" VALUE="best">
<PARAM NAME="LOOP" VALUE="false">
<EMBED SRC="coolflashmovie.swf" WIDTH="400" HEIGHT="400" PLAY="true" QUALITY="best" LOOP="false"
PLUGINSPAGE="http://www.macromedia.com/go/getflashplayer">
</EMBED>
</OBJECT>
</BODY>
</HTML>
```

When you use the <OBJECT> and <EMBED> tags together on the same page, it's a good idea to enter the same values for both. This will ensure that your movie looks and plays the same using most major browsers.

HTML Tag Reference

The following key will help you understand the various tags and parameter settings that can affect the way your movie looks and acts on an HTML page.

MOVIE

Required. This value specifies the directory path to the Flash movie that is to be loaded; it can be either a relative or an absolute path. This is an <OBJECT>-only attribute.

Possible values: `YourMoviesName.swf` or `http://www.yourdomain.com/YourMoviesName.swf`

Sample: `<PARAM NAME="MOVIE" VALUE="coolflashmovie.swf">` or `<PARAM NAME="MOVIE" VALUE="http://www.derekfranklin.com/coolflashmovie.swf">`

Template variable: $MO

SRC

Required. This value specifies the directory path to the Flash movie that is to be loaded; it can be either a relative or an absolute path. This is an <EMBED>-only attribute.

Possible values: YourMoviesName.swf or http://www.yourdomain.com/YourMoviesName.swf

Sample: SRC="coolflashmovie.swf" or SRC ="http://www.derekfranklin.com/coolflashmovie.swf">

Template variables: MO

WIDTH

Required. This value determines the width of your movie window within the browser. You may enter a specific pixel amount or a percentage of the browser window.

Possible values: 18–2880 pixels or 0%–100%

Sample: WIDTH="400" or WIDTH="75%"

Template variable: $WI

HEIGHT

Required. This value indicates the height of your movie window within the browser. You may enter a specific pixel amount or a percentage of the browser window.

Possible values: 18–2880 pixels or 0%–100%

Sample: HEIGHT="400" or HEIGHT="75%"

Template variable: $HE

CLASSID

Required. The Flash Player ActiveX control identification number, which tells Internet Explorer what ActiveX control to initiate. This is an <OBJECT>-only attribute.

Possible values: D27CDB6E-AE6D-11cf-96B8-44553540000 (must be entered exactly as shown).

Sample: CLASSID="D27CDB6E-AE6D-11cf-96B8-44553540000" (must be entered exactly as shown).

Template variable: not applicable.

CODEBASE

Required. The URL from which the Flash Player ActiveX control can be downloaded, if it is not already installed on your user's Internet Explorer browser. This is an <OBJECT>-only attribute.

Possible values: http://download.macromedia.com/pub/shockwave/cabs/flash/swflash.cab#version=6,0,0,0 (must be entered exactly as shown).

Sample: CODEBASE="http://download.macromedia.com/pub/shockwave/cabs/flash/swflash.cab#"version=6,0,0,0" (must be entered exactly as shown).

Template variable: not applicable.

PLUGINSPAGE

Required. The URL from which the Flash Player can be downloaded, if it is not already installed on your user's Netscape browser. This is an <EMBED>-only attribute.

Possible values: http://www.macromedia.com/go/getflashplayer (must be entered exactly as shown).

Sample: PLUGINSPAGE="http://www.macromedia.com/go/getflashplayer" (must be entered exactly as shown).

Template variable: not applicable (value is not configurable).

ID

Optional. A name that identifies your movie on the page for use in scripting (JavaScripting, not ActionScripting). If no scripting is used in conjunction with Flash, you don't need to fill in this <OBJECT>-only attribute.

Possible values: You can choose any name you want, but it can't include spaces. When using a template variable, this value is derived from the name of the authoring file.

Sample: ID="MyMovie"

Template variable: $TI

NAME

Optional. A name that identifies your movie on the page for use in scripting (JavaScripting). If no scripting is used in conjunction with Flash, you don't need to fill in this <EMBED>-only attribute.

Possible values: You can choose any name you want, but it can't include spaces. When using a template variable, this value is derived from the name of the authoring file.

Sample: NAME="MyMovie"

Template variable: $TI

SWLIVECONNECT

Optional. If you want to use FS Commands in conjunction with JavaScripting within a Netscape browser, Java must be turned on for these FS Commands to work. This attribute either enables Java (true) or disables it (false). Java does not need to be enabled for normal JavaScripting purposes on pages that have movies that do not contain FS Commands. Enabling Java can increase the time it takes for your movie to begin playing. The default setting is "false" for this <EMBED>-only attribute.

Possible values:

- **True.** Enables Java.
- **False.** Disables Java.

Default setting: False.

Sample: SWLIVECONNECT="false"

Template variable: not applicable (must be set in the template code).

PLAY

Optional. Controls whether your movie begins playback immediately upon being loaded, or waits for user interaction.

Possible Values:

- **True.** Your movie will begin playing as soon as the first frame has loaded completely.
- **False.** Your movie will wait for user interaction to begin playing.

Default setting: True.

Sample for `<OBJECT>` **tag:** `<PARAM NAME="PLAY" VALUE="true">`

Sample for `<EMBED>` **tag:** `PLAY="true"`

Template variable: $PL

LOOP

Optional. Controls your movie's behavior once it reaches the last frame during playback.

Possible values:

- **True.** Your movie will return to the first frame and begin playing again.
- **False.** Your movie will play once and then stop at the last frame.

Default setting: True.

Sample for `<OBJECT>` **tag:** `<PARAM NAME="LOOP" VALUE="true">`

Sample for `<EMBED>` **tag:** `LOOP="true"`

Template variable: $LO

QUALITY

Optional. Lets you determine how certain processor limitations will affect your movie's playback in terms of speed and visual quality.

Possible values:

- **Low.** Sacrifices visual quality to maintain playback speed. With this option, your movie will never be antialiased.
- **Autolow.** Although initially turned off, antialiasing will be turned on to improve visual quality if the user's processor is fast enough to handle it.
- **Autohigh.** Although initially turned on, antialiasing will be turned off to improve playback speed if the frame-per-second rate drops below the amount set in the Movie Properties dialog box.
- **High.** Skips frames during playback to maintain visual quality on computers with slower processors. Antialiasing is always on when this option has been selected. If your movie is animated, bitmaps will not be smoothed; if it is not, they will be.
- **Best.** Bitmaps are always smoothed; antialiasing is always on; and frames are never skipped due to processor limitations.

Default setting: High.

Sample for `<OBJECT>` **tag:** `<PARAM NAME="QUALITY" VALUE="best">`

Sample for `<OBJECT>` **tag:** `QUALITY="best"`

Template variable: $QU

BGCOLOR

Optional. Sets the background color of the movie window, overriding the color assigned to your movie background in the Document Properties dialog box.

Possible values: any RGB hexadecimal value.

Default setting: the color of the movie background as assigned in the Movie Properties dialog box.

Sample for `<OBJECT>` **tag:** `<PARAM NAME="BGCOLOR" VALUE="#0099ff">`

Sample for `<EMBED>` **tag:** `BGCOLOR="#0099ff"`

Template variable: $BG

SCALE

Optional. If the width and height settings you selected for the actual movie window differ from those you set in the Document Properties dialog box, movie elements (which were designed for a specific size) may not fit perfectly within the new dimensions you set for the movie window. This option determines how the movie will look within the boundaries of the movie window as you specified.

Possible values:

- **Showall.** This selection makes your movie completely visible within the area you defined for the movie window. All elements are scaled to fit within the movie window. Borders may appear between movie elements and the movie window, if the movie window's dimensions differ from the movie's original size.

- **Noborder.** This scales your movie proportionately so that it fills the entire area of the movie window—no borders appear. As a result, some of your movie elements may be cropped or not even visible from within the movie window.

- **Exactfit.** This disproportionately scales your movie to exactly fit the dimensions of the movie window. Your movie may appear squashed or bloated, depending on how much the movie window's dimensions differ from the actual movie.

Default setting: Showall.

Sample for `<OBJECT>` **tag:** `<PARAM NAME="SCALE" VALUE="showall">`

Sample for `<EMBED>` **tag:** `SCALE="showall"`

Template variable: `$SC`

SALIGN

Optional. This attribute allows you to set the alignment of your movie within the movie window, if their dimensions differ.

Possible values:

- *T.* Aligns your movie vertically to the top edge of the movie window, and centers it horizontally.

- *B.* Aligns your movie vertically to the bottom edge of the movie window, and centers it horizontally.

- *L.* Aligns your movie horizontally to the left edge of the movie window, and centers it vertically.

- *R.* Aligns your movie horizontally to the right edge of the movie window, and centers it vertically.

- *TL.* Aligns your movie to the top left corner of the movie window.

- *TR.* Aligns your movie to the top right corner of the movie window.

- *BL.* Aligns your movie to the bottom left corner of the movie window.

- *BR.* Aligns your movie to the bottom right corner of the movie window.

Default setting: If this attribute is not specified, your movie will be placed in the center of the movie window.

Sample for `<OBJECT>` **tag:** `<PARAM NAME="SALIGN" VALUE="tl">`

Sample for `<EMBED>` **tag:** `SALIGN="tl"`

Template variable: `$SA`

BASE

Optional. Allows you to set the URL that serves as the basis for relative links within your movie. Thus, if your movie resides in a directory such as http://www.yourdomain.com/flash/ and you want all relative links in the movie to be referenced from http://www.adifferentdomain.com/ , you would enter the latter domain as the BASE attribute's value.

Possible values: any URL.

Default setting: same directory as the movie.

Sample for <OBJECT> **tag:** <PARAM NAME="BASE" VALUE="http://www.adifferentdomain.com/">

Sample for <EMBED> **tag:** BASE="http://www.adifferentdomain.com/"

Template variable: $SA

MENU

Optional. Allows you to determine which options are available on the Flash Player pop-up menu that appears when the user right-clicks (Windows) or Control-clicks (Macintosh) the movie in the browser window.

Possible values:

- **True.** Displays all available menu items.
- **False.** Displays only the About Flash menu item.

Default setting: True.

Sample for <OBJECT> **tag:** <PARAM NAME="MENU" VALUE="true">

Sample for <EMBED> **tag:** MENU="true"

Template variable: $ME

WMODE

Optional. Allows you to take advantage of capabilities available only on a Windows version of Internet Explorer that has the Flash Player ActiveX control installed. This attribute is not available for the <EMBED> tag.

Possible values:

- **Window.** Plays your movie within its own rectangular area on the HTML page; this selection provides the best playback quality.

- **Opaque.** Allows you to move elements on the HTML page behind the rectangular area of the movie, without having them show through. Use this option in conjunction with dynamic HTML layers.

- **Transparent.** Causes the background color of your Flash movie (as set in the Movie Properties dialog box) to become transparent instead, so that the background of the HTML page on which your movie is embedded will show through. This effect, though cool, provides the slowest playback performance; use it sparingly.

Default setting: Window.

Sample for `<OBJECT>` **tag:** `<PARAM NAME="WMODE" VALUE="opaque">`

Template variable: $WM

FlashVar

Optional. Allows you to pass data to your movie via a URL-encoded string. This data can be used by the movie immediately upon loading. Although you could pass variables from HTML to an embedded SWF file in previous versions of Flash using the `src="my.swf?var1=one&var2=two"` scenario, the new FlashVars parameter does not have the length constraints of most URL query strings (maximum of 256 characters). The Flash 5 player will ignore this tag.

Possible values: any URL-encoded string of text.

Sample for `<OBJECT>` **tag:** `<PARAM NAME="FlashVar" VALUE="var1=Hello&var2=56">`

Sample for `<EMBED>` **tag:** `FlashVar="var1=Hello&var2=56"`

Template variable: not applicable.

Setting Up the Server

When your movie is downloaded over the Web, two things are sent over the connection that enable viewers to see your movie: The first, and most obvious, is the movie file itself. The second is the movie's MIME type, which Communicator needs to determine which Player to use to show your movie. If the MIME type is not identified, your movie may not display properly—or at all—in a Netscape browser. (This is not an issue with Internet Explorer.) Leaving out this information may even cause the browser—and the user's computer—to crash, so it's a mistake you want to avoid.

You set the MIME type on the server that delivers your movie. Thus, unless you're the administrator of your own server, you'll probably never need to do this yourself. You will, however, need to call your ISP or talk to the server administrator so that they can set the MIME type for your site.

When setting up the MIME type for Flash content, you need to know the MIME type itself (application/x-shockwave-flash) and the Flash file extension (.swf). For Mac servers, the following parameters must also be set:

- **Action:** Binary
- **Type:** SWFL
- **Creator:** SWF2

Player Issues

To view Flash content, you need the Flash Player. And with each new version of Flash, comes a new version of the Player. This is not to say you can't view a Flash MX presentation using the Flash 5 Player. It just means that if you want to take advantage of all Flash MX's new features, you need the Flash 6 Player.

Currently, more than 436 million users—or more than 97 percent of those online—have the Flash Player installed. However, relatively few people have the *latest* version (Flash 6 Player) installed. The challenge is to convince users that it's worth their time to download and install the latest version—while trying to accommodate those who won't.

NOTE *Remember, while the newest authoring version of Flash is known as Flash MX, the associated player version is known as the Flash 6 Player.*

The Front-Door Approach

One of the best ways to tackle this Flash version issue is right at your site's front door—i.e., the home page. This is a logical place to notify users that they need the Flash 6 Player to truly experience the wonders of your site.

You can place the Get Macromedia Flash Player button (**Figure 20.18**) anywhere on the page and link it to Macromedia's download site at http://www.macromedia.com/shockwave/download/index.cgi?P1_Prod_Version=ShockwaveFlash. Clicking the button will take users to a well-organized page that explains the Player's benefits as well as the download procedure. There is also a link that lets users download the Player immediately. Once users have downloaded and installed the Player, they can return to your site and appreciate its full glory.

Figure 20.18
The Get Macromedia Flash Player button.

Go with What Works

If you want to provide an interesting Flash-driven site yet keep mandatory Player downloads to a minimum, the solution is simple: Design your content for Flash 5 or lower—at least until most users have made the transition to the Flash 6 Player. This, of course, means doing without the features that are unique to Flash MX.

Keep in mind, however, that you can export Flash MX–created content using the Flash 5 format. Even though the Flash MX–specific features won't work, everything else— including mouse events, load movie actions, and more—will.

Provide an Alternative

If you want to provide Flash content for those who have the Player installed, but don't want to make the Player a *requirement* for visitors to your site, you can create two versions of your site: a Flash-driven version and an HTML version. This way, if the Player is not installed on your user's computer, he or she can still view the HTML version without a hitch.

We don't really recommend this approach, because maintaining two sites can be a headache. If you think you're up to it, though, don't let us stop you.

Bold and Beautiful

If you truly don't care about annoying your users, go ahead and set up your Flash MX site so that it automatically installs the latest version of the Player. The majority of your users will thank you for it in the end! What's more, by taking this "who cares" approach, you help Flash MX proliferate.

getVersion() Script

MX ALERT { *ActionScript* } Using the getVersion() function, available in ActionScript, you can determine which Player version is attempting to access your movie and then either redirect the user to Macromedia's site (to download the latest version of Player), or have the movie go ahead and play as it normally would.

The getVersion()function returns information about the current user's OS and Player version. For example, I'm currently working on a Windows machine with the Flash 6 player; thus, in the following script, the variable named userVersion would be assigned a string value of "WIN 6,0,47,0":

```
usersVersion = getVersion();
```

This text string includes a lot of information we don't necessarily need (though you could use this info to determine the user's OS and then provide them with a different site based on that info). All we're interested in is the 6 that appears in the string, indicating the Player version installed on the user's computer. Using the charAt()string method, we can extract that character from the text string and use an if statement to take appropriate action. To understand this, take a look at the following script (which would be placed on Frame 1 of your movie's timeline):

```
if (getVersion().charAt(4) == "6"){
   gotoAndPlay("Intro");
} else{
   getURL("http://www.macromedia.com/go/getflashplayer", "_blank");
}
```

When the above script is executed, the movie will go to and play the Intro scene *if* the user has the Flash 6 Player. If not, the script detects that the correct Player is missing and opens the URL to download it in a new browser window—all of which happens immediately.

Since the getVersion() function was only introduced in Flash 5 (and remains in Flash MX), this script will not work with version 4 (or earlier) Players. However, since most Web users have at least the Flash 5 Player installed by now, this may not be a major issue.

Flash Deployment Kit

The Flash Deployment Kit is a set of files Macromedia has created to detect whether the proper version of the Flash player is installed on a user's computer. Once the program determines whether the user has the correct Player version, it redirects the user either to your Flash site (meaning he or she has the correct Player) or to the page where he or she can download the latest Player version.

Unlike the ActionScript method described above, the Deployment Kit relies on JavaScript and VBScript (browser scripting), and is probably the most complete detection method available (since it can be set up to detect versions 2 through 6 of the Player). However, it's not necessarily the easiest detection method to implement (since it requires working with several files simply to enable the detection process). The kit includes detection files, example files, an interactive demo, a Dreamweaver behavior (an installable version of the deployment kit that allows you to easily implement its functionality within Dreamweaver by setting values via a dialog box), and documentation. The kit is available for free from Macromedia's site at www.macromedia.com/software/flash/download/deployment_kit/

Understanding Templates

If you want your movie to look and function properly, you need to set numerous HTML settings and parameters. These include width and height settings, playback options, and even JavaScript in some cases. Some of us get around this problem by using custom HTML pages (sometimes with custom JavaScript) to place our Flash content. By changing just a few attributes, you can use these custom HTML pages, or *templates*, for many Flash movies. This can be very useful, since writing Player detection scripts and filling in parameters each time you place a Flash movie on a Web page can quickly become tedious.

By using templates in conjunction with the Publish feature, you can easily fill in attributes that affect not only what movie goes on the page, but also how your movie will look and play back in the Web browser. You can even eliminate the need to edit an HTML page that contains a Flash movie. This is because the template is created once, with variables placed in specific places within the template. Using the Publish feature, you then enter information (<OBJECT>and <EMBED> attributes) specifying the way you want your movie to appear and play back in the browser window.

When you publish to HTML, the variables in the template you select are replaced with the information you entered. The resulting document is an HTML page with your movie embedded. You can easily use the same template, enter different settings in the HTML tab of the Publish settings dialog box, and output a new HTML page.

The Process

There are essentially three stages in creating and using templates:

- Creating the template
- Filling in the settings on the various tabs of the Publish Settings dialog box
- Publishing from Flash (which generates an HTML page based on your template and settings)

Creating a template

A Flash template is simply a text file that contains both HTML code (which never changes) and template code, or variables (these are not the same as the variables used in ActionScripts). Flash includes prebuilt templates, which are sufficient for most users' needs; however, you can also build your own.

Creating a template is similar to creating a standard HTML page. The only difference is that you replace the values pertaining to a Flash movie with variables that begin with a dollar sign. If you need to use the dollar sign for something other than a template variable, prefix it with a backslash (\$). For a complete list of template variables, see Table 20.1 at the end of this section.

In the meantime, take a look at the following sample template code:

```
$TTCool Template
$DS
This Cool Template
is to help you understand
how to use variables.
$DF
<HTML>
<HEAD>
<TITLE>$TI</TITLE>
</HEAD>
<BODY bgcolor=$BG>
$MU
$MT
<OBJECT CLASSID="clsid:D27CDB6E-AE6D-11cf-96B8-44553540000" WIDTH="$WI" HEIGHT="$HE" CODEBASE="
download.macromedia.com/pub/shockwave/cabs/flash/swflash.cab#version=6,0,0,0
">
```

```
<PARAM NAME="MOVIE" VALUE="$MO">
<PARAM NAME="PLAY" VALUE="$PL">
<PARAM NAME="QUALITY" VALUE="$QU">
<PARAM NAME="LOOP" VALUE="$LO">
<EMBED SRC="$MO" WIDTH="$WI" HEIGHT="$HE" PLAY="$PL" QUALITY="$QU"
LOOP="$LO" PLUGINSPAGE="http://www.macromedia.com/go/getflashplayer">
<NOEMBED><IMG SRC=$IS WIDTH=$IW HEIGHT=$IH usemap=$IU BORDER=0></NOEMBED>
</EMBED>
</OBJECT>
</BODY>
</HTML>
```

Now let's take a closer look at each section of this template.

```
$TTCool Template
```

The name Cool Template will appear in the template drop-down box on the HTML tab of the Publish Settings dialog box.

```
$DS
This Cool Template
is to help you understand
how to use variables.
$DF
```

All the content between $DS and $DF will appear in the Info box that you access by clicking the Info button on the HTML tab of the Publish Settings dialog box.

```
<HTML>
<HEAD>
<TITLE>$TI</TITLE>
</HEAD>
```

This is the standard way of beginning an HTML document. The $TI variable between the <TITLE> tags represents the page title as it will appear on the Web browser. This is derived from the file name of the movie placed on the page. Thus, if your movie is named CoolFlashMovie.swf, your page will be entitled CoolFlashMovie.

```
<BODY bgcolor=$BG>
```

This will cause the generated HTML page to display the same background color as your movie.

$MU

This template variable will place a list of the URLs used in your movie on the generated HTML page.

$MT

This template variable will place a list of text used in your movie on the generated HTML page, so that search engines can index your movie's content. This text is output between HTML comment tags so that it is not viewable when the page is displayed in a browser.

```
<OBJECT CLASSID="clsid:D27CDB6E-AE6D-11cf-96B8-44553540000" WIDTH="$WI"
HEIGHT="$HE" CODEBASE="
download.macromedia.com/pub/shockwave/cabs/flash/swflash.cab#version=6,0,0,0
">
```

You will notice that the WIDTH and HEIGHT parameters of the <OBJECT> tag have been replaced with template variables.

```
<PARAM NAME="MOVIE" VALUE="$MO">
<PARAM NAME="PLAY" VALUE="$PL">
<PARAM NAME="QUALITY" VALUE="$QU">
<PARAM NAME="LOOP" VALUE="$LO">
```

Different attributes, or parameters, of the <OBJECT> tag have been substituted with template variables.

```
<EMBED SRC="$MO" WIDTH="$WI" HEIGHT="$HE" PLAY="$PL" QUALITY="$QU"
LOOP="$LO" PLUGINSPAGE="http://www.macromedia.com/go/getflashplayer">
```

The different attributes of the <EMBED> tag have been replaced with template variables.

```
<NOEMBED><IMG SRC=$IS WIDTH=$IW HEIGHT=$IH usemap=$IU BORDER=0></NOEMBED>
```

For browsers that don't support the Player, the <NOEMBED> tag provides an alternative image that Flash automatically generates when you publish. You'll notice the template variables that are used:

```
</EMBED>
</OBJECT>
</BODY>
</HTML>
```

These are the tags you need to finish creating your template. While this template does not use every possible template variable, it should still give you a pretty good idea of how template variables are used in conjunction with HTML.

You can also use template variables with other HTML content, including JavaScript, Cold Fusion, Active Server Pages, and more. Any template variables used within the syntax of these programming languages will be replaced with actual movie and image values when you publish your movie, based on the values you've entered on the HTML tab of the Publish Settings dialog box.

Save your template (as an HTML document if you wish; see "The published HTML page" later in this section for information about file extensions) and place it in the First Run\HTMLfolder of the Flash MX program directory (**Figure 20.19**). Once you have created a template and placed it in this folder, it becomes available from the Template pop-up box on the HTML tab of the Publish Settings dialog box, the next time Flash MX is loaded.

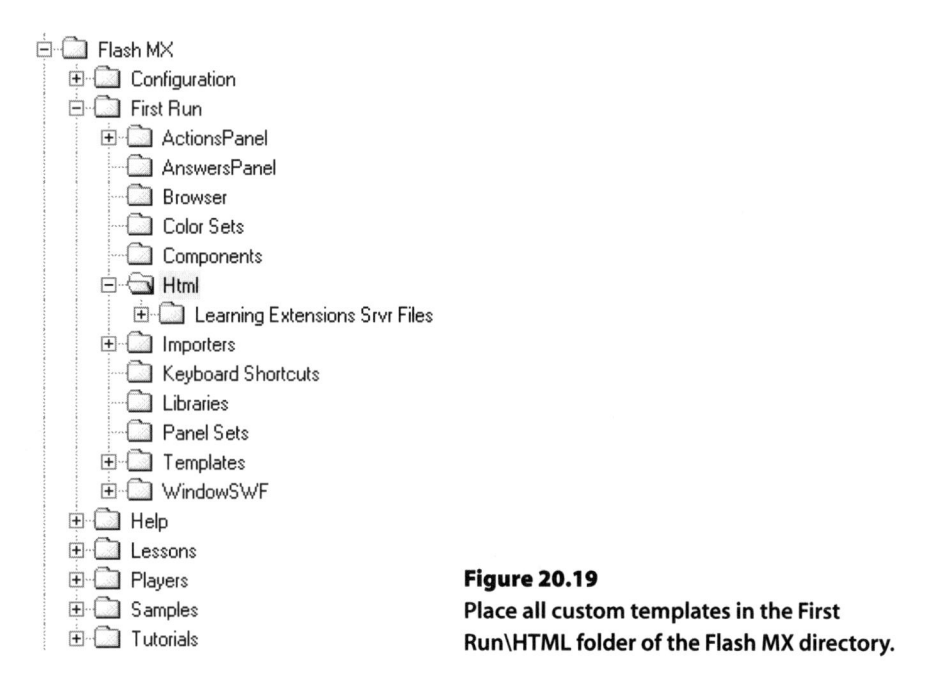

Figure 20.19
Place all custom templates in the First Run\HTML folder of the Flash MX directory.

Entering Publish settings

Now that you've created a template, you can use it for any movie in conjunction with the Publish feature.

Using an example authoring file (MapUSA.fla) that we wish to publish to HTML, we'll adjust the settings for our demonstration (**Figure 20.20**). All of these settings relate to a template variable that, when published, will be replaced with the values you set. Once you have entered all of the necessary values, click the Publish button to complete the process.

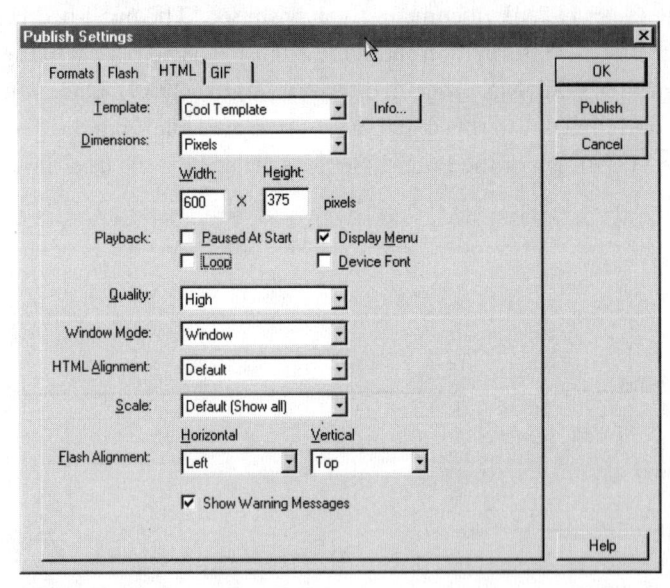

Figure 20.20
The values entered on the HTML format tab of the Publish Settings dialog box will replace corresponding template variables when you publish your movie.

The published HTML page

When you publish your movie, you need to be aware of two things: the name of the published HTML page that is created, and its location.

The name of the published HTML page will be a combination of your movie's file name and the file extension you gave the template. For example, if your movie's file name is MapUSA.swf and the file name of your template is cooltemplate.html the file name of the published HTML page will be MapUSA.html. If the template's file extension were .cfm (Cold Fusion), the resulting file name of the published HTML page would be MapUSA.cfm.

The published HTML page and all of its associated files can be found in the same directory as the authoring file used at the time of publishing.

The HTML of the published HTML page will appear similar to the following. Compare it to the HTML of the original template to help understand how the template itself, and the settings adjusted in the Publish Settings dialog box merge to become the final HTML document:

```
<HTML>
<HEAD>
<TITLE>MapUSA</TITLE>
</HEAD>
<BODY bgcolor=#FFFFFF>
<A HREF="http://www.usa.com"></A>
<A HREF="http://www.america.com"></A>
<!–This is a map of the USA -->
<OBJECT CLASSID="clsid:D27CDB6E-AE6D-11cf-96B8-44553540000" WIDTH="600" HEIGHT="375" CODEBASE="
download.macromedia.com/pub/shockwave/cabs/flash/swflash.cab#version=6,0,0,0
">
<PARAM NAME="MOVIE" VALUE="MapUSA.swf">
<PARAM NAME="PLAY" VALUE="true">
<PARAM NAME="QUALITY" VALUE="high">
<PARAM NAME="LOOP" VALUE="false">
<EMBED SRC="MapUSA.swf" WIDTH="600" HEIGHT="375" PLAY="true" QUALITY="high" LOOP="false"
PLUGINSPAGE="http://www.macromedia.com/go/getflashplayer">
<NOEMBED><IMG SRC="MapUSA.gif" WIDTH=600 HEIGHT=375 usemap="#MapUSA" BORDER=0></NOEMBED>
</EMBED>
</OBJECT>
</BODY>
</HTML>
```

Template Variables

This is a complete list of the variables you can use in creating your own templates. Keep in mind that template variables are case sensitive; thus, "$tt" will not work, but "$TT" will.

Table 20.1
Template Variables

Parameter	Variable
Template title	$TT
Template description start	$DS
Template description finish	$DF
Width	$WI
Height	$HE
Movie	$MO
Name, ID, or Title	$TI
HTML alignment	$HA
Looping	$LO
Play	$PL
Quality	$QU
Scale	$SC
Salign	$SA
Wmode	$WM
Devicefont	$DE
Bgcolor	$BG
Movie text	$MT
Movie URLs	$MU
Parameters for <OBJECT>	$PO
Parameters for <EMBED>	$PE
Image width (unspecified image type)	$IW
Image height (unspecified image type)	$IH
Image file name (unspecified image type)	$IS
Image map name	$IU

Table 20.1
Template Variables (continued)

Parameter	Variable
Image map tag location	$IM
QuickTime width	$QW
QuickTime height	$QH
QuickTime file name	$QN
GIF width	$GW
GIF height	$GH
GIF file name	$GS
JPEG width	$JW
JPEG height	$JH
JPEG file name	$JN
PNG width	$PW
PNG height	$PH
PNG file name	$PN

Video Tutorial

Publishing Your Movie. This tutorial will guide you through the steps of publishing your movie, including setting values in the Publish Settings dialog box, previewing the settings, and doing a final publish.

7
Putting It All Together

> **Projects** **827**

IF YOU'RE EAGER to put your newfound knowledge to work, this is the place. Here you'll find two separate projects that step you through the process of creating and scripting a movie from scratch. By the time you've finished, you should have a great foundation in the core Flash concepts you need to begin creating your own projects.

Projects

CHAPTER 21

Are you ready to get your hands dirty? We've covered a lot of Flash MX territory to this point; however, sometimes you need to put what you've learned to use—in the context of a real project—for it all to make sense. That's what this chapter is all about.

In the pages that follow, we'll take you step by step through the creation of two complete Flash projects. You'll see how projects of any size are best approached by breaking them up into smaller, individual tasks. In addition, you'll come to understand how you can use frame labels (or scenes, if you wish) to break up a project up into "states" (similar to HTML pages), which will make managing the overall project much easier as well. In between, you'll put to use many of the skills you've learned as well as several ones that are new in this chapter. By the time you've finished this chapter, we hope that any questions you have about how to make Flash do what you want will have been answered.

Have fun!

What you'll learn…

How to create a Flash project from the ground up

How to complete a project that contains animation, masks, hyperlinked text, and a scrollable map

How to complete a project that uses XML and contains dynamic animation, functions, event handler methods, and externally loaded JPGs and MP3s

Hawaii Travel Application (Beginner)

In this project, you'll create a travel application for the beautiful state of Hawaii. It will contain animation, sounds, buttons, a slide show, Web links, and a draggable map of the Hawaiian Islands (**Figure 21.1**). By the time you're finished, you will have:

- Set the initial settings for your project
- Imported images
- Created several tweened animations
- Added and used Frame labels
- Created and used movie clip instances
- Created and used button instances
- Used a grid and guide lines to place content on the stage
- Added sound to a button
- Attached scripts to buttons
- Created and configured text fields
- Used frame actions to create a self-running slide show
- Used a mask layer to mask off graphical content
- Created hyperlinked text
- Used the ScrollPane component to create a scrollable map

Figure 21.1
This is how the map section of our application will look.

Not only will it be fun, but if you're planning a trip to paradise anytime soon, you may even find it useful! Let's get started.

NOTES *Before starting this project be sure to copy all of the files in the Chapter 21/Assets/HawaiiApp directory, on the accompanying CD, to your hard drive.*

This tutorial assumes you are a beginning Flash user, but have gone through the other chapters of this book. Although each step will be clearly explained, it's important that you be familiar with the various terms, dialog boxes, and other interface elements that will be mentioned. If at any time you need additional information, consult the index in the back of the book.

Setting Up the Project

First let's define the size of our movie and the speed at which it will play.

1. From the File menu in Flash, choose New.

This starts a new file with a single frame and a single layer.

2. From the File menu, choose Save As… to save your project.

Navigate to the directory in which you want to save the file. Give the project a name, such as hawaiiApp.fla, and then press the Save button.

3. Choose Modify > Document.

This opens the Document Properties dialog box (**Figure 21.2**), where you set the dimensions of your project and the speed at which it plays. It's always best to set these values before doing anything else.

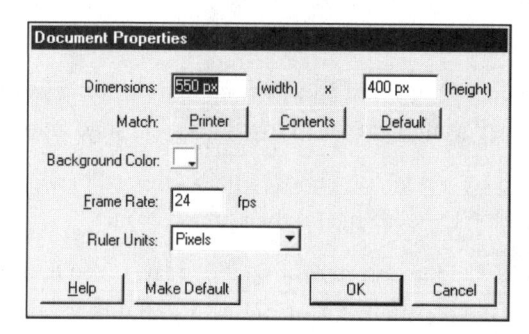

Figure 21.2
The Document Properties dialog box is where you set your movie's general settings.

4. Set the width and height values to 550 and 400, respectively.

These values represent pixel counts. By default, these dimensions should already be pixel-based. Make adjustments if necessary.

5. For the Frame Rate setting, enter 24.

This value represents the speed at which your movie will play. A value of 24 frames per second (fps) is the standard speed for most Flash movies.

6. Leave all other document settings at their default values, and Click OK.

Now that we've finished setting up our project, it's time to start importing content.

Importing Bitmap Images

In this step, we'll import the project's initial bitmap images: our project background and main logo (which we'll also animate).

1. Double-click the default layer's name, and rename it Background (**Figure 21.3**).

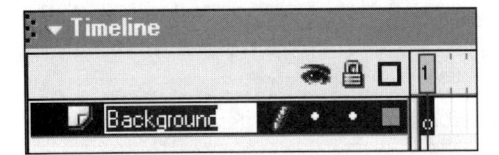

Figure 21.3
Double-clicking the default layer's name will allow you to rename it as shown.

On this layer, obviously, we'll place a graphic that represents our project's background display.

2. Choose File > Import, then navigate to the background.png file on the CD. Select it, and then press Open.

This will import the PNG file into Frame 1 of the Background layer.

3. Click the Insert Layer button (which looks like a page with a plus sign) on the timeline to insert a layer above the Background layer. Double-click this new layer's name and rename it Logo.

Since this layer is above the Background layer, any content we place on it will be superimposed over the background graphic. Now, let's add a logo graphic.

4. With Frame 1 of the Logo layer selected, choose File > Import. Navigate to the hawaiiLogo.png file on the CD, select it, and then press Open.

This will import the PNG file into Frame 1 of the Logo layer. You'll notice that this image's background is transparent (**Figure 21.4**). PNG images with transparent backgrounds can be created in nearly any image-editing application.

Figure 21.4
Our logo graphic is a PNG file with a transparent background.

5. Select the logo image, and open the Property inspector by choosing Window > Properties (by default, this should already be open). In the X box, enter a value of 30, and then press the Tab key. In the Y box, enter a value of 10 and then press the Return/Enter key.

These values set the x and y positions of the logo graphic, relative to the top-left corner of the stage, as determined by our layout requirements.

Creating Animation

Now let's animate our logo graphic so that it fades in whenever the user navigates to one of our application's three sections: Sights, Links, and Map (we'll set these up shortly). The first thing we need to do is add some frames to our project.

1. Just under the timeline ruler, at Frame 50, click and drag downward to select the empty frames on both the Background and Logo layers (**Figure 21.5**). Right-click (Windows) or Control-click (Macintosh) one of the selected frames, and from the menu that appears, choose Insert Frames.

   This will add 49 frames to both layers on the timeline (in addition to Frame 1, which already existed).

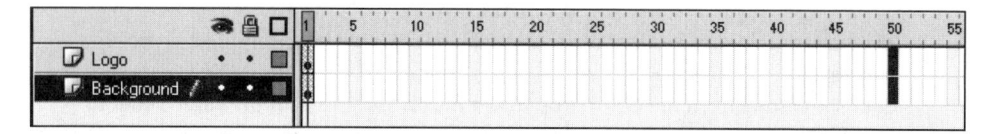

Figure 21.5
We've selected Frame 50 on both the Background and Logo layers, in preparation for inserting frames.

2. Select the logo graphic on the stage. From the Insert menu, choose Convert to Symbol. The Convert to Symbol dialog box will appear. In the Name box, enter logoClip. Make sure the Movie Clip behavior is selected, and then press OK.

    This converts the logo bitmap to a movie clip symbol. By converting the bitmap to a symbol we can then animate it to fade in.

3. Click Frame 15 of the Logo layer to select it. From the Insert menu, choose Keyframe. This inserts a keyframe at Frame 15, indicated by a small circle that appears in the frame itself.

    You'll recall that keyframes are used to indicate a change of some sort on the timeline, including points of transition in an animation. In the next few steps, we'll set the logo so that it's completely transparent at Frame 1 but completely opaque at Frame 15 (thus the need for a keyframe at Frame 15). We'll then create an animation that will cause the logo graphic to fade from transparent to opaque over that 15-frame interval.

    The Logo layer now has a keyframe at Frame 1, and another at Frame 15.

4. On the timeline, move the playhead to Frame 1. Select the logo graphic/instance on the stage. In the Property inspector, a Color drop-down menu will appear. Choose the Alpha option. A slider control will appear to the right of the menu. Click on it, and slide the value to 0 (**Figure 21.6**).

    This causes the logo to become completely transparent at Frame 1. If you move the playhead to Frame 15, you'll see that the logo is still completely opaque at that frame.

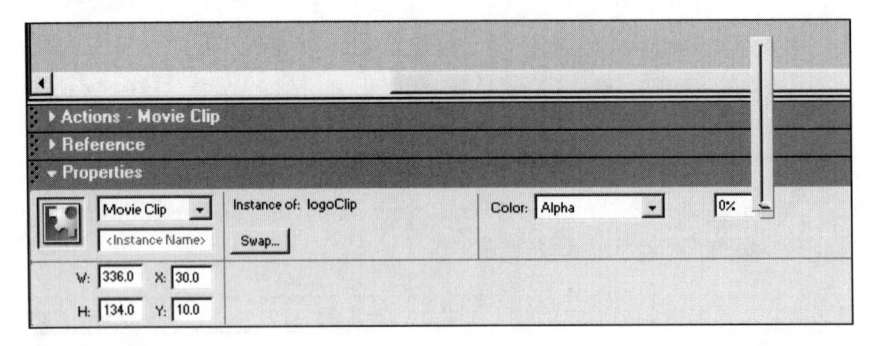

Figure 21.6
Choosing Alpha from the Color drop-down menu, then moving the value slider to 0, will cause the logo graphic on Frame 1 to become completely transparent.

Next, we need to create the transition that will cause the logo to fade in. This is accomplished by creating a tween from Frame 1 to Frame 15.

Chapter 21 **Projects**

5. On the timeline, select Frame 1 of the Logo layer. On the Property inspector, a Tween menu will appear. Choose the Motion option to create a motion tween. Leave the default settings as they are.

On the timeline, you'll notice that Frames 1 through 15 have changed colors. In addition, there is now an arrow pointing from Frame 1 to Frame 15. These are all indications that a motion tween exists between these frames.

You can move the playhead back and forth to see the effects of the motion tween on the logo.

Our project requires that our logo fade in as the result of the user navigating to different sections of the application (Sights, Links, and Map), so we actually need to insert two more copies of this tween on the timeline.

6. On the timeline, click-drag from Frame 1 to Frame 15 on the Logo layer to select the tweened frames. Click on the selected frames, and drag while pressing the Alt key (Windows) or Option key (Macintosh). This creates a draggable copy of the tween, which you'll see as an outline. Move the left edge of this copy so that it can be dropped at Frame 16 (**Figure 21.7**), and then release.

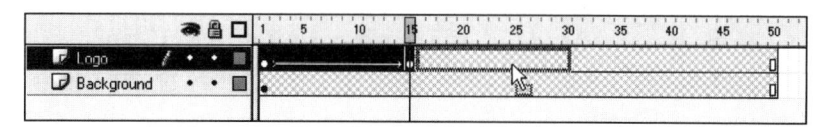

Figure 21.7
The tween that exists between Frames 1 and 15 is copied and placed on Frames 16 to 30.

This will create a copy of our original tween from Frame 16 to Frame 30.

7. The copied tweened frames should still be selected. Repeat the previous step to create another copy of this tweened animation, this one to span from Frame 31 to Frame 45.

The Logo layer should now contain three copies of the tweened animation of our logo fading in (**Figure 21.8**). You can move the playhead back and forth to see the visual effect.

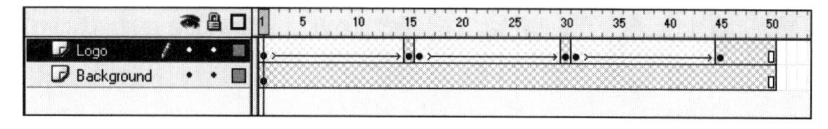

Figure 21.8
Our project's timeline now contains three motion tweens on the Logo layer.

Now let's test the project up to this point.

8. Choose Control > Test Movie.

When you play your movie, you'll notice that the logo fades in three times—the result of the three tweens we added in the last several steps. While this is pretty cool all by itself, we also want to control when these fades occur—specifically, when the user first navigates to one of the application's three sections (Sights, Links, or Map).

9. Choose File > Close.

This will return you to the authoring environment, where we can continue building on our project.

Adding Frame Labels and Controlling the Timeline's Playback

The next step is to divide our movie's timeline into sections, and use some simple ActionScript to control our movie's playback within these sections.

The first thing we need to do is add a couple of layers to the timeline: one for ActionScript, and another for several frame labels that will be used to give names to specific points on the timeline.

1. With the Logo layer selected, press the Insert Layer button twice to insert two new layers above the Logo layer. Double-click the name of the new layer closer to the Logo layer and rename it Actions, then double-click the other new layer (at the top of the layer stack) and name it Labels (**Figure 21.9**).

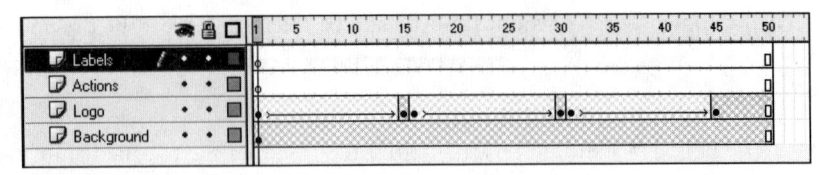

Figure 21.9
Our project's timeline up to this point.

In the next several steps, we'll add keyframes to these layers so that we can place scripts and frame labels.

2. Select Frame 16 of the Labels layer, and press F6 on the keyboard to insert a keyframe. Then select Frame 31, and press F6 to insert another keyframe on that frame.

   The keyframes on this layer will be used to define the three frame labels that identify various sections of our project.

3. Select Frame 1 of the Labels layer. On the Property inspector, look for the text box that contains the text <Frame Label>. Click on this text box and enter the word *Sights*, and then press Return/Enter.

   This places a frame label named Sights on Frame 1 of the timeline. You can look at the upper-left corner of the timeline and see it was inserted. Now we need to add frame labels at Frame 16 and Frame 31.

4. Select Frame 16 on the Labels layer, and give it a label name of Links. Then select Frame 31 and give it a label name of Map.

   We'll use these frame labels to add some simple scripting that will allow users to navigate the movie.

5. Add keyframes to frames 15, 30, and 45 on the Actions layer. (Remember that to add keyframes, you can simply select the frame and press F6.)

   Each of these keyframes will contain a simple script that prevents the timeline from playing beyond that frame. (You'll understand the reason for this in a moment.) Let's go ahead and add those scripts.

6. Select Frame 15 of the Actions layer. If the Actions panel is not already open, choose Window > Actions. Press Ctrl + Shift + E (Windows) or Command + Shift + E (Macintosh) to place the Actions panel in Expert mode.

   Placing the Actions panel in this mode enables you to type code directly into the code window.

7. Add the following script to the selected frame:

   ```
   stop();
   ```

   Because this action is attached to the keyframe on Frame 15, the movie will begin by playing the tween of our logo fading in (on Frames 1 through 15), and then stop. Now let's add a couple more stop() actions to the keyframes on Frames 30 and 45.

8. With the Actions panel still open, select the keyframe at Frame 30 of the Actions layer and add a stop()action as described in the step above. Repeat the same steps with the keyframe at Frame 45 of the Actions layer.

The Actions layer now contains three simple scripts on the keyframes at Frames 15, 30, and 45 (**Figure 21.10**). Just like the stop() action at Frame 15, which prevents the timeline from moving beyond Frame 15 once the initial logo tween finishes, these stop() actions will prevent the timeline from moving beyond the completion of the tweens on Frames 16 through 30, and Frames 31 through 45, respectively.

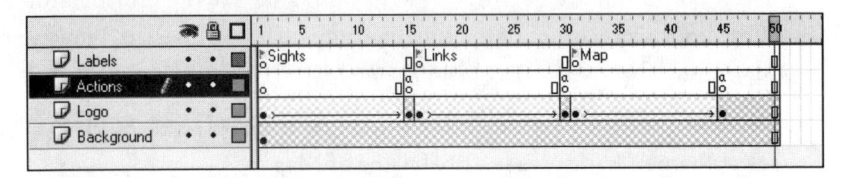

Figure 21.10
Our project's timeline now contains three frame labels (at Frames 1, 16, and 31), as well as scripts (at Frames 15, 30, and 45).

Next, we'll place some buttons in our project, which will enable the user to navigate between the three frame labels.

Creating Buttons

Our project requires three navigational buttons for moving between the frame label "sections" we created in the previous section. The buttons' displayed appearance will change as the user moves the mouse over them. We'll use guide lines and a grid to position our buttons precisely.

1. Click the Background layer's name to select that layer. Press the Insert Layer button to insert a new layer above the Background layer. Double-click the new layer's name and rename it Buttons.

    Flash lets you create buttons in a couple of ways: You can select something currently on the stage and convert it to a button, or you can create an empty button and then fill it with content. In this case we're going to take the latter approach.

2. From the Insert menu, choose Create New Symbol. The New Symbol dialog box will appear. Give this new symbol the name of Button, select the Button behavior option, and then click OK.

As soon as you click OK, the authoring environment will change to symbol-editing mode and the button's timeline will appear.

You'll recall that the four frames on the button's timeline define how the button will look in its up (no user interaction), over (mouse is moved over the button), and down (button is pressed via user's mouse) states. The hit frame is used to define the area in which the button will react to the user's mouse.

We'll design these different states in a moment, but because our button display will be made up of mostly white elements, we first need to change the color of the stage background to help us see what we're doing.

3. Click somewhere on the stage. On the Property inspector, press the small color control next to the word *Background*. This will reveal a color palette for choosing a background color (**Figure 21.11**). Click on a dark gray.

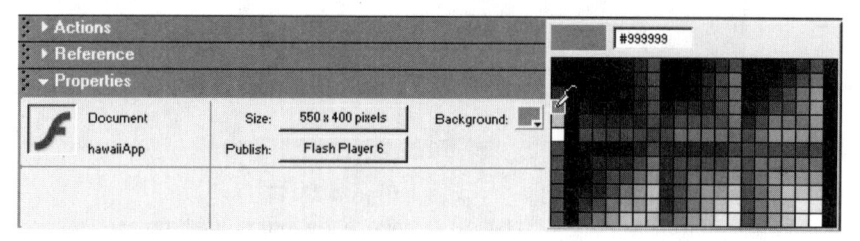

Figure 21.11
Press the Background color control on the Property inspector to change our project's background color.

The stage will immediately change to reflect the color change. In the next several steps we'll continue setting up the authoring environment, in order to draw the graphics that define how our button will appear.

4. Double-click the default layer on the button symbol's timeline to rename it Graphics.

Although this is currently the only layer on the timeline, you should get into the habit of assigning unique names to all layers.

Because we want to be fairly precise in specifying the size of our button, we'll set up a grid on the stage and add some guide lines.

5. Choose View > Grid > Edit Grid…. This will open the Grid dialog box, where you'll find various options pertaining to setting up grids. Select the Snap to Grid option; then, set the vertical and horizontal spacing of the grid by entering values of 10 in each of the two text boxes within the dialog box, and then press OK.

Although you can't see it onscreen, the grid is there—which means that any drawing operations on the stage will be snapped to the closest 10-pixel grid point.

Now we'll add some guide lines to make our button's layout even more precise.

6. From the View menu, choose Rulers. Vertical and horizontal rulers will appear on the top and left sides of the stage area. (We need to display the rulers so that we can use them to place our guide lines.)

7. Click on a ruler, then drag away from it to create a new guide line. Place four guide lines: at 10 and −10 on the vertical ruler, and at 50 and −50 on the horizontal ruler (**Figure 21.12**).

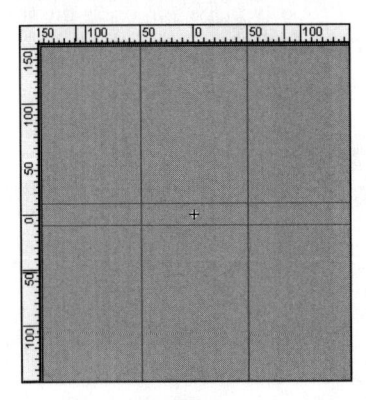

Figure 21.12
Place the four guide lines as shown in this graphic.

If you need to reposition a guide line, just move your mouse over it until a small arrow icon appears next to the cursor, then click and drag. The rectangular area in the middle of the stage, where all the guide lines intersect, is where we will create our button.

Before we start drawing, it's important to note that the playhead is currently on the Up frame. This means that what we're about to draw will define how our button will look when the user is not interacting with it in any way.

8. On the Drawing toolbar, click the Rectangle tool. On the Property inspector, click the Stroke color box and choose white from the palette that appears. Then click the Fill color box, and on the palette that appears select the "no color" option (the button with a red slash). In the Stroke Height text box, enter a value of 2.

   These represent the characteristics of the rectangle graphic we're about to draw: It will have a white outline that is 2 pixels wide, and will not include a fill.

9. Move your mouse cursor onto the stage until it becomes a crosshair. Click and drag from the top-left corner of the rectangular area created by the intersecting guide lines to the bottom-right corner of the same area. Before releasing the

mouse, press and hold the Down arrow on the keyboard. This will round the corners of the rectangle. Once they're rounded completely, release the mouse.

A rectangle with round corners will appear in the middle of the stage.

Next let's define how the button will look in its Over state (that is, when the user's mouse cursor passes over it).

10. Select the Over frame on the timeline, then press F6 to insert a keyframe.

    Remember that keyframes are used to define changes. Because the Over state of our button behaves differently than the Up state, a keyframe on the Over frame is required. Without this keyframe, the Up and Over states would look the same. You'll notice that on the stage, the content for the Over state *currently* appears the same as the content for the Up state. We'll change this by adding a transparent white fill to the shape for the Over state.

11. On the Drawing toolbar, select the Paint Bucket Tool. From the Window menu, choose Color Mixer to open the Color Mixer panel. Click the Fill color control, and choose white from the palette that appears. Then enter a value of 30 in the Alpha text box (**Figure 21.13**).

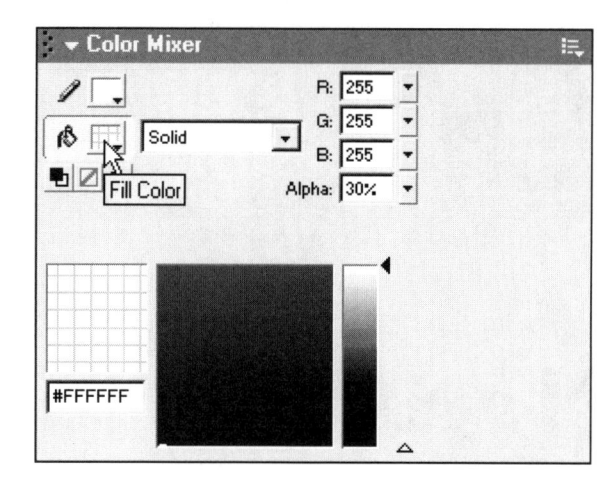

Figure 21.13
Click the Fill color control on the Color Mixer panel, choose white as the color, then set its Alpha value to 30.

This defines the characteristics of the fill we're about to add.

12. Move your mouse onto the stage until it becomes a paint bucket. Click inside the button shape on the stage to add the fill.

    The shape now has a transparent white fill in its Over state. We will not be defining the Down or Hit states of this button, though you may want to now that you know how to do it.

Adding Sound to a Button

Now let's add a simple sound to the button that will play when the mouse cursor puts the button in its Over state.

1. On the timeline, press the Insert Layer button to insert a new layer above the Graphics layer. Double-click the new layer's name and rename it Sound.

   This layer will contain a sound at the Over frame. To insert a sound at that frame, we need a keyframe.

2. Select the Over frame on the Sound layer, and press F6 to insert a keyframe.

   We can now place a sound at this keyframe. When adding sounds to a project, you usually have to import them first. However, a number of great button sounds are included in the Common Libraries installed with Flash MX: To add any of these, you simply drag and drop—which is what we're going to do to add one of the preinstalled sounds to the Over state of our button.

3. From the Window menu, choose Common Libraries > Sounds.

   This will open the Library panel and display a scrollable list of sound clips. For the purpose of this exercise, we'll use the sound clip named Plastic Button (**Figure 21.14**).

Figure 21.14
We will be using the sound clip named Plastic Button.

4. With the Over frame on the Sound layer selected, locate the sound clip named Plastic Button in the Library panel. Click its name, and drag and drop it onto the stage. Then close the Library panel.

While nothing will change graphically on the stage, you'll notice that the Over frame on the Sound layer contains a waveform, representing the sound clip that exists there. Once again, because the sound clip exists at the Over frame, it will play whenever the mouse moves over the button.

Adding Buttons to the Main Timeline

It's time to return to our project's main timeline to add some instances of the button we just created.

1. From the Edit menu, choose Edit Document. This will return the authoring environment to the main timeline. Now we'll add some instances of the button to the Buttons layer on the main timeline.

2. With the Button layer selected, open the Library panel (Window>Library), and locate the button symbol you created. Click its name and drag an instance of it onto the stage, just below and to the right of the seashell. Click and drag two additional instances of it onto the stage. Place one below the other and both below the first instance (**Figure 21.15**).

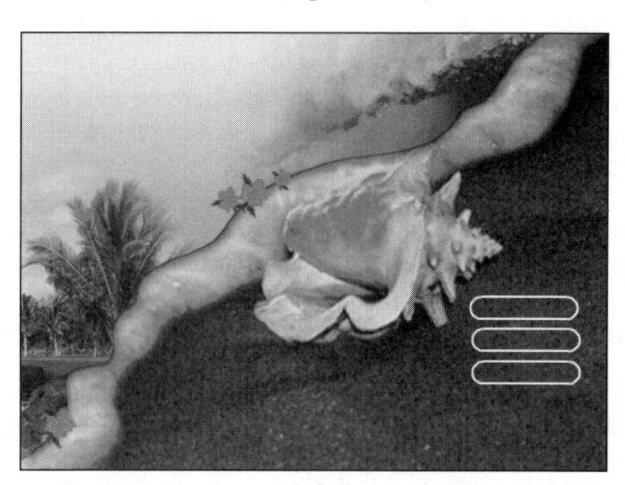

Figure 21.15
The placement of the three button instances in our project.

There are now three instances of the button we created on the stage.

3. On the stage, click the topmost button instance to select it (click the button's outline). Hold down the Shift key, then click the other button instances to select them as well. From the Window menu, choose Align. This will open the Align panel. Deselect the To Stage option, and then press the Align horizontal center and Distribute vertical center buttons to align the three selected button instances.

This fine-tunes the placement of the button instances.

Scripting Our Buttons

Next we'll add some script to each button instance, so that we can use them to navigate between the frame labels we set up earlier.

1. Click on the stage to deselect all the button instances, then select the topmost button. Open the Actions panel and attach the following script:

```
on(release){
gotoAndPlay("Sights");
}
```

When the button is pressed and released, the timeline will go to and play starting at the Sights frame label. This will cause the logo to fade in between Frames 1 and 15. It will stop playing at Frame 15 because, as you'll remember, we placed a stop() action at Frame 15.

Let's add similar scripts to our other button instances. Instead of reinventing the wheel, we'll simply copy the script we've just entered and edit it as necessary.

2. Select the script/text in the Actions List window. Right-click (Windows) or Control-click (Macintosh) on the selected text, and choose Copy from the menu that appears. On the stage, select the middle button instance. (You may need to collapse the Actions panel by clicking its title bar.) Right-click (Windows) or Control-click (Macintosh) in the Actions List window on the Actions panel, and choose Paste from the menu that appears.

This inserts the previously copied script. Because the middle button instance is currently selected, the script we just pasted is attached to it. This script is an exact copy of the script on the top button instance. We need to modify it just a bit, so that the middle button instance will go to and play the movie from the Links frame label.

3. In the gotoAndPlay() action, replace the word *Sights* with the word *Links*.

The middle button is now set up so that when it is pressed and released, it will go to and play the movie from the Links frame label. This will also cause our logo to fade in between Frames 16 and 30. It will stop playing at Frame 30 because, as you'll remember, we placed a stop() action at Frame 30.

Let's set up our last button instance.

4. Repeat Steps 2 and 3 to paste the script on the bottom button instance. Once pasted, edit the gotoAndPlay() action by replacing the word *Sights* with the word *Map*.

All three button instances should now have scripts attached to them for navigating the movie. We'll test this functionality shortly.

Using the Text Tool to Add Text to the Buttons

Next, we need to add some text to our button instances to identify their navigation points.

1. On the drawing toolbar, select the Text tool. The Property inspector will now reflect settings for creating text objects. Choose the following settings (**Figure 21.16**):

   Text Type: Static Text

   Text Color: White

   Font: Arial (or Macintosh equivalent)

   Bold: On

   Font Size: 16

   Justification: Center

   These settings define the appearance of the text objects we are about to create.

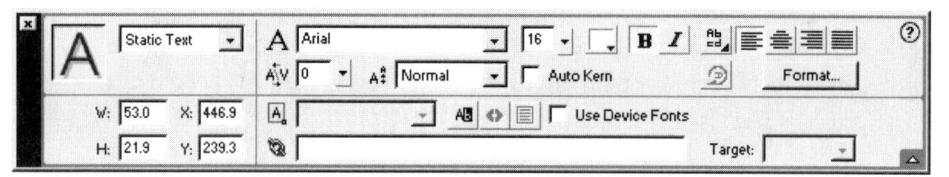

Figure 21.16
When the Text tool is selected, these are the settings available on the Property inspector.

2. On the stage, click in the middle of the top button instance to create a text label, and then type the word *Sights*. Click in the middle of the next button to create another text label, and type the word *Links*. Finally, click the bottom button instance to create a third text label, and type the word *Map*.

   If the text labels are not exactly aligned with the button instances, you can select the Arrow tool, select the text label, and then use the arrow keys on your keyboard to reposition them.

3. Choose Control > Test Movie.

Now you can interact with the button instances to see them in action. Pressing any of them will cause the logo graphic to fade in. Although it's not really apparent yet, when you're clicking the buttons you're actually navigating between the three Frame labels on the timeline. Our navigation buttons are complete!

4. Close the test movie to return to the authoring environment. Save your work.

Now let's add our content at each of these frame labels.

Creating a Self-Running Slide Show

The Sights section of our application will feature a series of pictures that change every second or so. Let's set that up.

1. On the timeline, select the Buttons layer, then press the Insert Layer button in order to insert a new layer above the Buttons layer. Double-click the new layer's name to rename it Panel.

   In this layer we're going to place a bitmap of a panel graphic, which will serve as a background for the other content we're about to add. Next we need to import that panel graphic.

2. With the Panel layer still selected, choose File > Import. Navigate to the panel.png file on your hard drive (in the directory where you copied this project's files), select it, and press Open.

   This will import the bitmap on the Panel layer. Now you'll need to reposition it a bit to fit it correctly into our design.

3. Lock the Logo layer by pressing the lock icon to the right of the layer name (to prevent your accidentally selecting anything on that layer). With the Arrow tool, select the panel graphic. On the Property inspector, set its x position to 46 and its y position to 155.

   This will position the graphic precisely where it needs to be for our design (**Figure 21.17**). We only need the panel graphic to appear in the Sights and Links section of our project, not the Map section (that section's content doesn't make use of the panel).

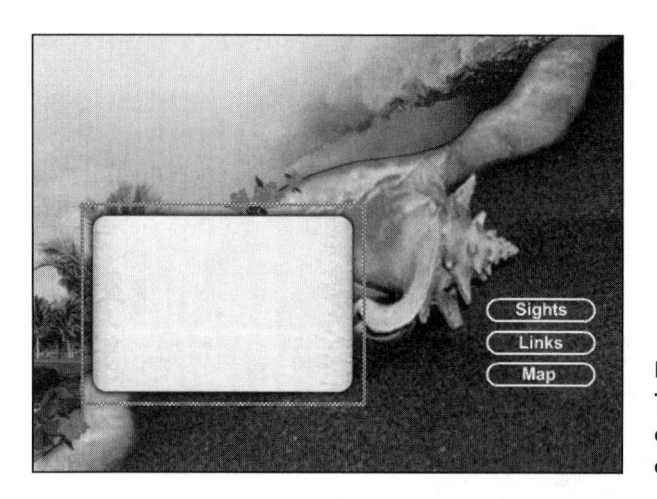

Figure 21.17
The correct position of the panel graphic on the stage.

4. Right-click (Windows) or Control-click (Macintosh) Frame 31 of the Panels layer. Choose Insert Blank Keyframe from the menu that appears. This removes the panel graphic from Frame 31 and beyond.

   Next we'll create a slide show of images that we can place on top of our panel in the Sights section of our application. We'll need to create a movie clip symbol to do this.

5. Choose Insert > New Symbol. This will open the New Symbol dialog box. Name the new symbol Slides and select the Movie Clip behavior option, then click OK.

   Now the new movie clip's timeline and stage will appear in the authoring environment. Both are blank; we still have to add content to the clip.

6. Double-click the default layer's name to rename it Images. We will be adding our slide show images to this layer.

7. Choose File > Import, then navigate to the directory on your hard drive where you've copied this project's files. Notice there are three files that include *slide* in their names: slide1.png, slide2.png, and slide3.png. These three slides/images make up our slide show. Select the slide1.png file, then click Open. Flash will display an alert box asking if you want to import this entire group. Click Yes.

   The three images will be imported and placed on the stage: slide1.png is placed on a keyframe on Frame 1; slide2.png is placed on a keyframe on Frame 2; and slide3.png is placed on a keyframe on Frame 3 (**Figure 21.18**). You can move the playhead back and forth to see this.

Chapter 21 *Projects*

845

Figure 21.18
When importing our series of images, Flash automatically places each one on its own keyframe on the timeline.

Now we need to add some space on the timeline between each of these pictures. The amount of space we add will dictate how long the picture is displayed before being replaced by the next one.

8. Select the empty frame at Frame 90, then press F5 on the keyboard. This will add 87 frames to the layer, giving us some room to maneuver the keyframes on Frames 1, 2, and 3.

9. Click the keyframe on Frame 3 to select it. Click it again and drag it to Frame 60. This moves the keyframe that was at Frame 3 to Frame 60.

10. Click the keyframe on Frame 2 to select it. Click it again and drag it to Frame 30. This moves the keyframe that was on Frame 2 to Frame 30.

Our keyframes now exist at Frames 1, 30, and 60, or approximately 30 frames apart (**Figure 21.19**). Because our movie plays at 24 frames per second, spacing the keyframes 30 frames apart will cause each image to display for 1.25 seconds (that is, 30 frames divided by 24 frames per second). Unless we place a stop() action on Frame 90 (which we're not going to do), once the timeline hits Frame 90 during its playback, it will loop back to Frame 1 and continue playing.

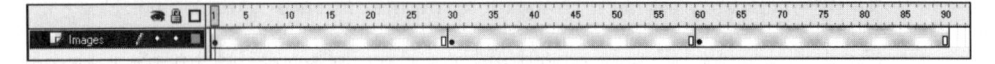

Figure 21.19
Our slide show images are spaced 30 frames apart.

Using Mask Layers

To finish creating our slide show clip, we need to do one last thing: Give our images rounded corners like the panel graphic we imported several steps ago. To do this, we need a mask layer to mask the graphical content.

1. Select the Images layer, then press the Insert Layer button to insert a new layer. Double-click the layer's name to rename it Mask.

   Right now this is just a normal layer. In the next step we'll import a graphic onto this layer, then convert it to a Mask layer. This will cause the graphic on this layer to serve as a "window" shape for the images on the Images layer. Let's import our mask graphic.

2. With Frame 1 of the Mask layer selected, choose File > Import to open the Import dialog box. Locate the panelMask.ai file in the directory where you copied the files for this project, select it, and then press Open. The Illustrator Import dialog box will appear. Retain the default settings by clicking OK.

   This will import the graphic: a simple Adobe Illustrator file of a rectangle with rounded corners. Although you could have created this graphic using Flash's own drawing tools, we're better off spending time on other tasks instead. You do, however, need to slightly resize and reposition the graphic.

3. Select the graphic you imported in the previous step, and on the Property inspector, enter the following values:

   W: 243

   H: 162

   X: 4

   Y: 3

   These values should place the graphic directly above the images on the Image layer (**Figure 21.20**).

Figure 21.20
The imported graphic should be positioned directly above the images on the Images layer.

4. Right-click (Windows) or Control-click (Macintosh) the Mask layer's name, and choose Mask from the menu that appears.

This converts the layer to a mask layer, which causes the rectangle with the rounded corners to "mask" the content of the layer below it—an effect that should be evident on the stage. By moving the playhead back and forth, you should be able to see that all the images are masked similarly, since the mask graphic exists across the entire length of the timeline.

Placing Our Slide Show Clip on the Main Timeline

Now that we've finished creating our slide show movie clip symbol, let's return to the main timeline and add an instance of this clip to it.

1. On the breadcrumb navigation bar, press either the Back button or the text that reads Scene 1. This will return you to the main timeline. Alternatively, you can choose Edit > Edit Document.

2. With the Panel layer selected on the main timeline, press the Insert Layer button to insert a new layer above the Panel layer. Double-click the new layer's name to rename it Slides.

Obviously, we'll want this layer to contain an instance of our Slides symbol. Let's add that.

3. If the Library panel isn't already open, open it by choosing Window > Library. Find the Slides symbol and drag an instance of it onto the stage, just above the panel. With the instance selected, you can position it precisely using the arrow keys on your keyboard, so that it appears directly over the panel graphic (**Figure 21.21**).

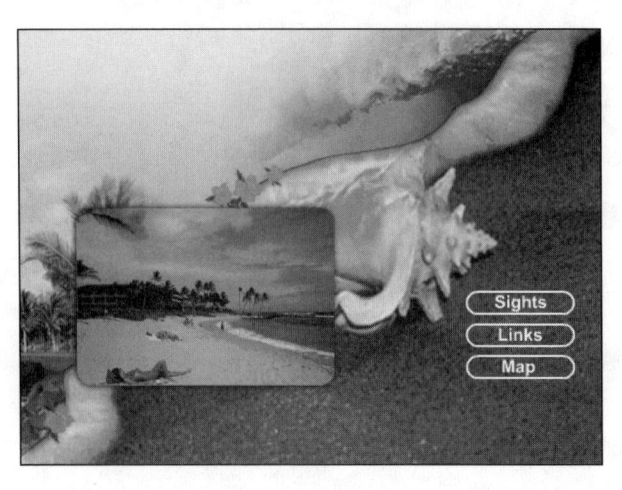

Figure 21.21
The slide show clip should be placed directly over the panel graphic, so that it completely obscures the panel graphic.

We only want our slides to be visible within the Sights section of our application, so let's take care of that next.

4. Select Frame 16 on the Slides layer, and then choose Insert > Blank Keyframe.

Doing this will remove the slide show clip from Frame 16 and beyond, where it shouldn't be visible. You can move the playhead back and forth to see the effect this action has on the content on the stage.

Now let's create the content for the Links section of our application.

Creating Hyperlinks

These days, hyperlinks to Web sites are an important component of most applications, including our project. Let's add some links to the Links section of our application.

1. With the Slides layer selected, press the Insert Layer button to insert a new layer above the Slides layer. Double-click the new layer's name to rename it Links.

This layer will hold some text links, which only need to exist only within the Links section of our application.

2. Select Frame 16 of the Links layer, and press F6 to insert a keyframe (**Figure 21.22**).

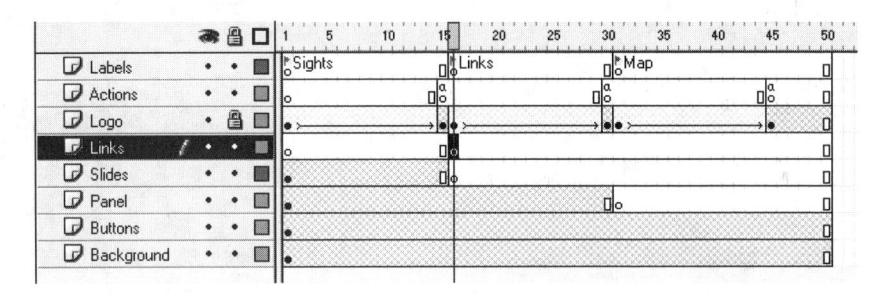

Figure 21.22
Adding a keyframe to Frame 16 of the Links layer.

Next, we'll add a text field at this keyframe in order to create some text links.

3. With the keyframe on Frame 16 of the Links layer selected, select the Text tool. On the Property inspector, choose the following settings:

Text Type: Static Text **Bold:** Off
Text Color: Blue **Font Size:** 20
Font: Arial (or Mac equivalent) **Justification:** Left

These settings will define the appearance of the text object we're about to create.

4. On the stage, click on the left side of the panel, and drag to the right side of the panel to create a text block. Click in the text box and type the following:

   www.gohawaii.com (followed by Return/Enter)

   www.hawaii.com (followed by Return/Enter)

   www.aloha.com (followed by Return/Enter)

   www.hawaiinow.com (followed by Return/Enter)

   Let's convert these to hyperlinks.

5. With the Text tool still selected, click and drag to select the text **www.gohawaii.com**. At the bottom of the Property inspector, a box will appear for entering a URL to associate with the selected text. Enter the following URL: http://www.gohawaii.com. To the right of this text box, you'll find a drop-down menu for choosing the target window in which the link should open. Select _blank from the menu to cause the link to open in a separate browser window (**Figure 21.23**).

Figure 21.23
When text is selected, entering values in the URL section of the Property inspector will link that text to the specified URL.

Now, when our movie is played and this text is clicked, it will open the www.gohawaii.com site in a new browser window.

6. Individually select the other lines of text in the text block, and associate the appropriate URL with each, as described in the previous steps.

The text block should now contain four hyperlinks, which we'll test shortly. At this point you can select the entire text block with the Arrow tool, and use the arrow keys to position it correctly above the panel.

Our links should only appear within the Links section of our application. Our timeline is already set up so that they don't appear before Frame 16, but we need to add a blank keyframe on Frame 31 to prevent them from being seen beyond that frame.

7. Select Frame 31 on the Links layer, and choose Insert > Blank Keyframe.

If you move the playhead back and forth, you'll notice that the links we added are no longer visible beyond Frame 31. Frames 31 through 45 are going to be used for our map, which is the last graphical element of our application.

Creating a Draggable Map

To help visitors get a feel for the Hawaiian Islands, we're including a draggable map of the islands—advanced interactivity that we'll facilitate by using the ScrollPane component.

1. Choose Insert > New Symbol. In the Create New Symbol dialog box, enter the name MapClip and select the Movie Clip behavior option. Then click OK.

This will open our new symbol's timeline; next we'll import our map graphic onto it.

2. From the File menu, choose Import. This will open the Import dialog box. Locate the map.png file in the directory where you copied the files for this project, select it, and then press Open.

This will import that graphic onto the stage. As you'll notice, this graphic is quite large. That's OK: Soon we'll place it inside a ScrollPane component, which is a small window in which a larger body of content can be placed and dragged around. But before we can place our graphic there, we need to identify our map symbol in the library, using an *identifier name*.

3. Locate the MapClip symbol in the library. Right-click (Windows) or Control-click (Macintosh) its name, and choose Linkage from the menu that appears. The Linkage Properties dialog box will appear. Check the Export for ActionScript option. Keep all the default settings, including the identifier name of MapClip, and then click OK (**Figure 21.24**).

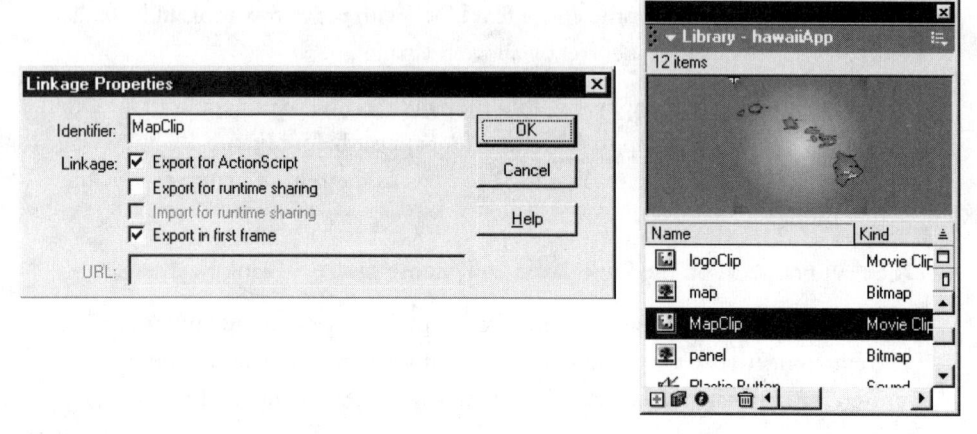

Figure 21.24
With the Linkage Properties dialog box open, use the settings shown here.

While it's true that the symbol name and the identifier name are the same, you need to give an asset in the library an identifier name in order to enable certain functionalities within Flash—including the placement of our map within a ScrollPane component. For more information about identifier names, see Chapter 17, "Using the Library to Manage Your Assets."

Let's return to the main timeline and add the ScrollPane component to our project, then add our map graphic to our ScrollPane component.

4. From the Edit menu, choose Edit Document to return to the main timeline. Insert a new layer above the Links layer and name it Map. Select Frame 31 of the Map layer and press the F6 key to insert a keyframe. Choose Window > Components to open the Components panel. Locate the ScrollPane component icon, click its name, and drag it onto the stage to place an instance of the Scroll-Pane component there.

Because we placed this component on a keyframe at Frame 31, it will only appear in our project from that frame forward. (You'll recall that Frame 31 and beyond represent the Map section of our application.)

Initially, however, the component instance we've added to our project is empty, the wrong size, and not in the correct position on the stage. Let's remedy those issues. First, we'll resize and reposition the component instance.

5. Select the component instance and enter the following values on the Property inspector:

   W: 234

   H: 162

   X: 62

   Y: 163

   Now that the component instance's size and position are correct, let's adjust how the component instance functions. We'll do this via the parameters section that appears on the Property inspector when a component instance is selected (**Figure 21.25**).

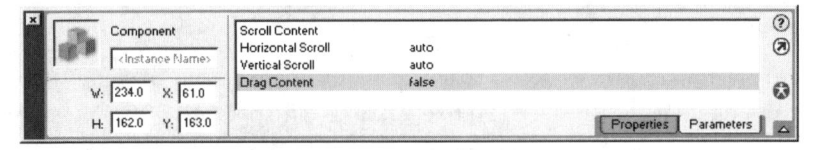

Figure 21.25
The Property inspector lets you position and resize our ScrollPane component, and also allows you to adjust its parameter settings.

6. Give the selected component instance the following values:

   Scroll Content: MapClip

   Horizontal Scroll: false

   Vertical Scroll: false

   Drag Content: true

   The Scroll Content parameter is used to specify the name of the asset in the library that you wish to place inside the component. You'll remember that MapClip is the identifier name of the MapClip symbol; thus, the content of that symbol will be placed inside the component when the movie is played.

   The next two parameter settings—Horizontal Scroll and Vertical Scroll—let you choose whether you want scrollbars to appear attached to the component. If set to true, these scrollbars would let users scroll the content within the pane. Here, we've set them to false, so they are not visible. Instead, the last parameter setting,

Drag Content, is set to true, which will enable the content within the pane to be clicked and dragged around, eliminating the need for scrollbars. We won't be able to see or interact with this window's content until we test the movie or export it as a SWF—so let's test our movie now!

7. Choose Control > Test Movie.

In the testing environment, interact with the application: Press the buttons, click the links, and click and drag the map around. You should see before you a fully functioning Flash MX project that you created from scratch!

Pat yourself on the back—and then take a deep breath: We're just getting warmed up! The next project will introduce you to some even more dynamic Flash capabilities.

Flash Folio Media Browser (Intermediate)

If you're ready to do a project that's all about ActionScript, this one is for you. The Flash Folio Media Browser (**Figure 21.26**) is an application that puts into practice many of the ActionScripting principles you've learned in other portions of the book. Once you've completed it, you will have:

- Created animation using ActionScript
- Dynamically styled components
- Set up and used a Component change handler function
- Used several event handler methods
- Validated data
- Attached a movie
- Created a LoadVars object to capture and send variable data
- Dynamically created and configured a text field
- Used arrays to store and manipulate data
- Output a dynamic message formatted with HTML
- Used an ActionScript loop

- Loaded JPGs dynamically into a target

- Implemented drag-and-drop functionality

- Used external loaded XML data to browse through a catalog of external MP3s

- Created and controlled a Sound object

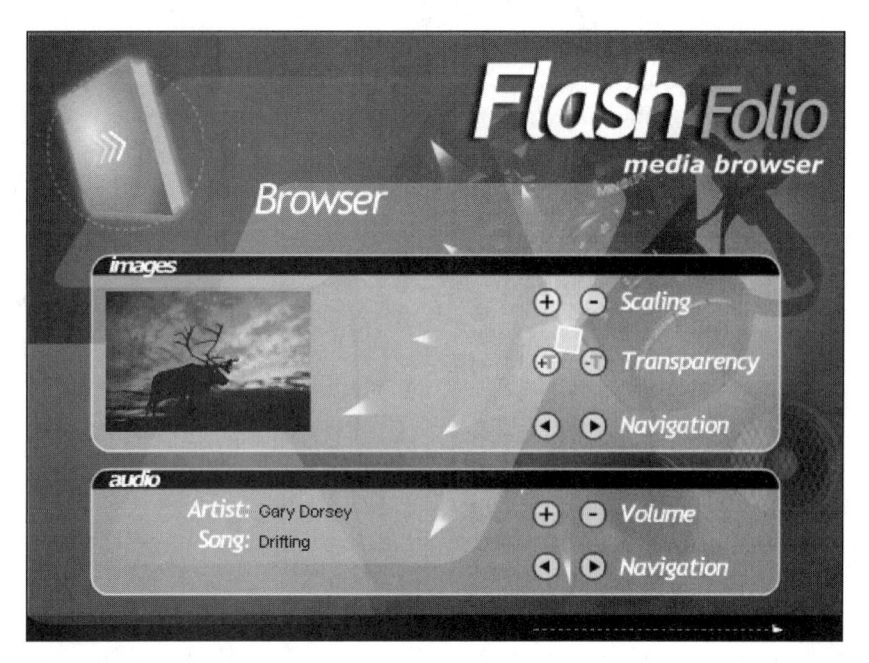

Figure 21.26
The completed version of our Flash Folio project.

The basic idea behind this project is that users fill out a registration section, which upon submission will display a custom 'Thank You' message. Users are then allowed to navigate to the main application, where they can browse and edit several images, in addition to several audio clips. There's a lot of ground to cover, so let's get started!

NOTES *Before starting this project, be sure to copy all the files in the Chapter 21/Assets/FlashFolio directory to your hard drive. This is necessary for testing purposes.*

Make sure the Actions panel is in Expert mode as you work through this tutorial. This mode more easily facilitates advanced scripting, which is what this project requires.

This project assumes a basic familiarity with Flash concepts and navigation.

Getting Started

In this section we'll look at the basic structure of the project, test its initial state, and do some minor preparation for the work that follows.

1. Chose File > Open, navigate to the directory on your hard drive where you copied flashFolio.fla, and then open it.

   Our project consists of three states, as identified by the frame labels **registration**, **thankyou**, and **browser**. At each of these labels, the content that appears on the stage is different. We will be scripting our project to move between these three states, in order to perform different tasks. All the graphical content of this project has already been imported and placed appropriately, so that you can focus on scripting.

   The project also contains eight layers, named to reflect the content they contain:

   - **Background.** This layer contains the main project background.

   - **Text.** This layer contains all static and input text objects.

   - **Nav Button.** This layer contains a navigation button that appears at the bottom of the stage.

   - **Browser Content.** This layer has several elements that can be seen by moving the playhead to the **browser** frame label.

   - **Browser Buttons.** This layer has several buttons that also appear at the **browser** label.

   - **Components.** This layer contains an instance of the ComboBox component, as well as two CheckBox component instances that appear at the **registration** frame label.

   - **Action.** This layer will contain, at the three frame labels, the majority of the ActionScript that we'll be adding to our project.

   - **Labels.** This layer contains the three frame labels already mentioned (**Figure 21.27**).

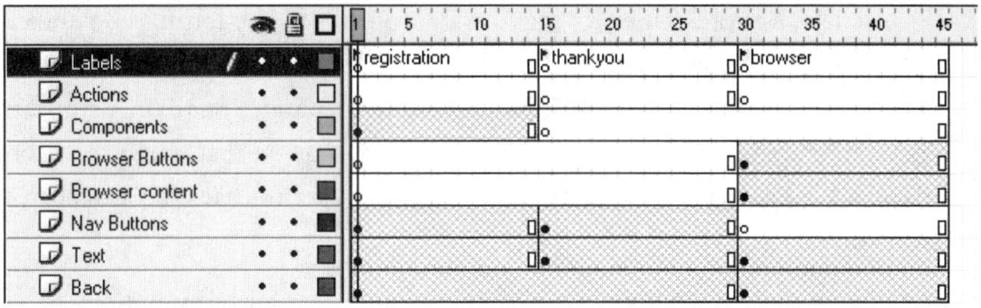

Figure 21.27
Our project's timeline.

Out project's frame rate has been set to 24 fps; we'll refer to that setting later in the tutorial.

We'll be testing our work as we go, and since it's a good idea to see what you've got initially, let's test right now.

2. Choose Control > Test Movie.

You'll immediately notice that our project in its current state does nothing more than play through the 45 frames of its main timeline, then loop back to Frame 1 to start over. By the time we're finished, you'll be amazed at the project's transformation. Our first scripting task is to add a stop() action to Frame 1 (**registration** label), so that our project's timeline remains there until the user navigates elsewhere.

3. Close the test movie to return to the authoring environment. With the Actions panel open, select Frame 1 of the Actions layer and add a stop() action.

So far, a piece of cake, right?

4. Save your work; we'll continue to build on this project in the sections that follow.

Time to take it up a notch, as we try our hand at scripted animation.

Dynamic Animation

By now you're pretty familiar with the type of animation you can achieve by using keyframes and tweens; however, that type of animation is fairly limited. Timeline-based animations like the ones described above play the same way each time a user encounters them: You can't *dynamically* move frames or alter tweening settings (though those would be cool additions for the next version of Flash MX).

Fortunately, ActionScript provides a way around this, by letting you alter a movie clip instance's properties. In this section, we'll use ActionScript (no timeline animation involved) to make the **searchlight** movie clip instance rotate on a constant basis. But we won't stop there: We'll also set the animation up so that when the user presses the spacebar, the rotation speeds up; and when the user releases the spacebar, the rotation slows down.

1. Select the **searchlight** movie clip instance, and with the Actions panel open, add the following script (**Figure 21.28**):

   ```
   onClipEvent(load){
      speed = 1;
   }
   ```

Figure 21.28 Selecting the **searchlight** movie clip instance and attaching a script to it.

The above script is executed as soon as **searchlight** loads; its sole function is to create a variable named speed (which we'll use in a moment to set the rotation speed of the clip).

2. Add the following script just below the one you added in the previous step:

   ```
   onClipEvent(enterFrame){
      _rotation += speed;
   }
   ```

This script is executed as a result of an enterFrame event, meaning it will execute 24 times a second, the frame rate of our movie. As a result, the value of speed (which is set to 1 when the movie clip loads) is being constantly added to the current _rotation property value of the **searchlight** movie clip instance. The syntax used is just shorthand for:

```
_rotation = _rotation + speed;
```

To understand how this works, imagine that **searchlight**'s _rotation property is 65 when the script is executed. This script basically says, "Set the movie clip instance's _rotation property to its current value, plus 1"—in this case, 66. The next time this same script is executed (a split-second later), the value of the _rotation property will again be raised by an increment of 1. This repetitive function will cause **searchlight** to spin onscreen. Let's test it.

3. Choose Control > Test Movie.

When the movie begins playing, you'll see that the **searchlight** movie clip instance is spinning in a leisurely manner—rotating a degree at a time, based on the value of speed. By changing that value, we can determine how fast the clip rotates.

4. Close the test movie to return to the authoring environment. With the Actions panel open, select the **searchlight** movie clip instance, and add the following script, below the last line of the current script:

```
onClipEvent(keyDown){
   if(Key.isDown(Key.SPACE)){
      speed = 10;
   }
}
```

This script is executed using a keyDown event. Every time a key is pressed, the if statement in this script checks to see if it's the spacebar that's been pressed. If it is, the value of speed is bumped up to a value of 10. Thus, instead of rotating only 1 degree with each enterFrame event (as mentioned in Step 2), **searchlight** will now rotate 10 degrees each time, causing it to spin faster. Keep in mind, however, that this only occurs once the spacebar is pressed down. In this case, we want the value of speed to be reset to 1 when the spacebar is released. We can accomplish this by adding another script to this movie clip instance.

5. Add the following script below the current one:

```
onClipEvent(keyUp){
   speed = 1;
}
```

Here, a keyUp event is used so that when the spacebar is released, the value of speed will be reset to 1, causing **searchlight**'s rotation to return to its original rate.

6. Choose Control > Test Movie.

Once the movie begins to play, press the spacebar to see **searchlight** rotate faster.

7. Close the test movie to return to the authoring environment, then save your work.

Using similar ActionScript, you can constantly update the _x, _y, _alpha, _xscale, and _yscale properties of movie clip instances to alter animation in some way. For example:

```
onClipEvent(enterFrame){
    if(myMovieCip._x > 400){
        myMovieClip._x -= 10;
    }else if (myMovieClip._x < 50){
        myMovieClip._x += 10;
    }
}
```

In this script, **myMovieClip** will move to the right if its _x property is less than 50, but it will move to the left if that property is more than 400, allowing **myMovieClip** to move back and forth across the screen. There are many other ways to animate a movie clip instance using ActionScript. Use your imagination, and you'll be surprised at what Flash lets you accomplish.

Dynamically Styling Components using the FStyleFormat Object

Although components provide a great tool for quickly and easily implementing advanced interactivity, their graphical appearance may not always mesh with the design you want to use. Fortunately, you can use the FStyleFormat object to set color and formatting attributes for the component instances in your projects.

In this section we'll create a couple of instances of this object type, in order to style the ComboBox and CheckBox component instances that appear at the **registration** label of the timeline. Our goal is to adjust their colors, so that they're more in keeping with our project's overall look. The ComboBox component instance is named **salutation**, while the CheckBox component instances are named **motherFather** and **auntUncle** (**Figure 21.29**). All three instances work in conjunction with one another (we'll discuss this more shortly). For now, just be aware of their instance names.

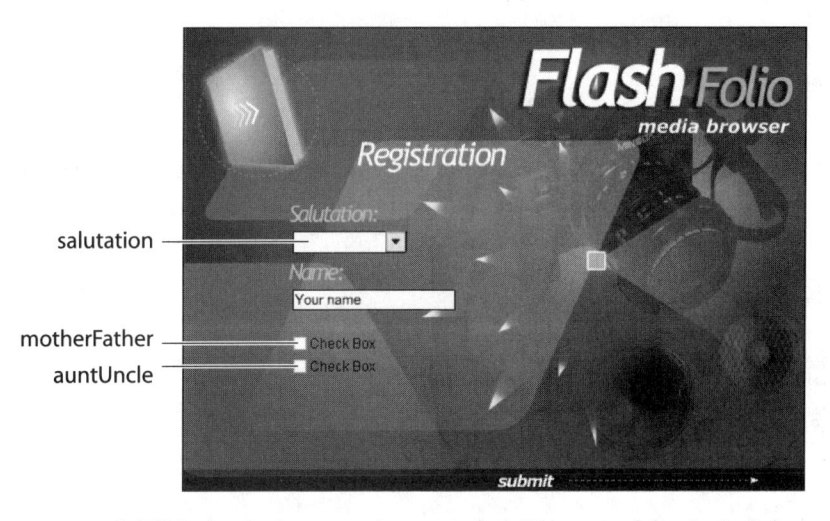

Figure 21.29
The component instances we'll be working with in this and the following section.

salutation

motherFather
auntUncle

1. With the Actions panel open, select Frame 1 of the Actions layer, and add the following script just below the existing stop() action:

   ```
   format1 = new FStyleFormat();
   format1.face = 0xFFFFFF;
   format1.textSelected = 0x000000;
   format1.selection = 0xC5E41C;
   format1.arrow = 0x2B6AB1;
   format1.darkshadow = 0x2B6AB1;
   format1.highlight3D = 0x2B6AB1;
   format1.shadow = 0xFFFFFF;
   format1.highlight = 0xFFFFFF;
   ```

   The first line creates an instance of the FStyleFormat object named format1. The next several lines are used to set the color values of various properties that can be affected by the object, when it's "applied" to a component instance. This object will be used in conjunction with the **salutation** ComboBox component instance to affect that instance's appearance. Let's put this object to use.

2. Place the following lines of script just below the ones you added in the previous step:

   ```
   format1.addListener(salutation);
   format1.applyChanges();
   ```

   The first line uses the addListener() method to make a connection between the format1 object and the **salutation** component instance. Now, whenever properties of the format1 object are updated (as in Step 1) and those changes are applied (as in the last line of script shown above), the **salutation** component instance's appearance will change to reflect the property values of the `format1` FStyleFormat object instance.

If you later want to change the color of the `arrow` property (or any other property) of the **salutation** component instance, you would actually set it for the `format1` object, then apply those changes, as in:

```
format1.arrow = 0xFFCC00;
format1.applyChanges();
```

This will cause the arrow on the **salutation** component instance to change colors.

A single FStyleFormat object instance can be used in conjunction with multiple component instances, which is what we'll look at next.

3. Place the following lines of script just below the ones added in the previous step:

```
format2 = new FStyleFormat();
format2.check = 0x2B6AB1;
format2.textColor = 0xFFFFFF;
format2.textBold = true;
format2.darkshadow = 0x2B6AB1;
format2.highlight3D = 0x2B6AB1;
format2.shadow = 0xFFFFFF;
format2.highlight = 0xFFFFFF;
format2.addListener(motherFather, auntUncle);
format2.applyChanges();
```

This script is very similar to the script discussed in the previous two steps. Here, a new FStyleFormat object is created and named `format2`. The next several lines define the various property values of this object. There are two lines that we should pay particular attention to in this script: The first is:

```
format2.textBold = true;
```

This line sets a property other than a color value: Specifically, it causes the text of any component styled with this object to be bold. The other line we should make special note of is:

```
format2.addListener(motherFather, auntUncle);
```

Here you can see that in one step, we've associated both the **motherFather** and **auntUncle** component instances with this format object. Now, whenever we invoke the `applyChanges()` method in conjunction with this object (as in the last line of the full script above), those two instances' attributes will be updated accordingly.

Since the scripts we added in this section exist on Frame 1 of the timeline, they will be executed as soon as the movie begins playing.

4. Choose Control > Test Movie.

When the movie plays, notice the appearance of the three component instances that initially appear. If you interact with them, you'll see the various ways that the FStyleFormat object has altered their appearances.

5. Close the test movie to return to the authoring environment. Save your work.

NOTE *For more information about Components and the FStyleFormat object, see Chapter 15, "Components."*

Using a Change Handler Function to Dynamically Configure Components

While our component instances may look great, they still don't do much, yet. In this section, we'll set about changing that: First, we'll manually configure them with initial values; then, we'll create a change handler function that will dynamically reconfigure the two CheckBox component instances named **motherFather** and **auntUncle**, in response to choices made using the ComboBox instance named **salutation**.

1. With the Property inspector open, select the **salutation** ComboBox component instance and configure it with the following settings:

   Editable: false
   Labels: Mr., Ms.
   Data: --blank--
   Row Count: 8
   Change Handler: updateForm

   The two label values (Mr. and Ms.) will appear as choices on the ComboBox instance. Note the Change Handler setting: updateForm is the name of a function, which we're about to create, that will be called whenever a user chooses one of these labels from the ComboBox instance. Before we create that function, however, let's manually configure our two CheckBox component instances.

2. With the Property inspector still open, select the **motherFather** CheckBox component instance and configure it with the following settings:

   Label: Father

   Initial Value: false

   Label Placement: right

   Change Handler: --blank--

   Using these settings, this instance will initially appear unchecked, with a text label of Father. This coincides with the fact that Mr. is the initial value that appears in the **salutation** instance. Father is only this instance's initial label, because the Change Handler function that we're about to define will dynamically update this label to Mother, if Ms. is selected from the **salutation** ComboBox instance. More on this in a moment. First let's configure the other CheckBox component instance.

3. With the Property inspector still open, select the **auntUncle** CheckBox component instance and configure it with the following settings:

   Label: Uncle

   Initial Value: false

   Label Placement: right

   Change Handler: --blank--

   Using these settings, this instance will initially appear unchecked, with a text label of Uncle. Once again, this coincides with the fact that *Mr.* is the initial value that appears in the **salutation** instance. As with the other CheckBox instance, Uncle is only its initial label because one of the other things our Change Handler function will do (once we define it) is dynamically update this value to Aunt, if Ms. is selected from the **salutation** ComboBox instance. So let's create the Change Handler function that will, well, *handle* this functionality.

4. With the Actions panel open, select Frame 1 of the Actions layer and add the following function definition at the end of the current script:

   ```
   function updateForm(){
     motherFather.setValue(false);
     auntUncle.setValue(false);
     if(salutation.getValue() == "Mr."){
       motherFather.setLabel("Father");
       auntUncle.setLabel("Uncle");
   ```

```
        }else if(salutation.getValue() == "Ms."){
          motherFather.setLabel("Mother");
          auntUncle.setLabel("Aunt");
        }
    }
```

The function does three things when called (which, you'll remember, occurs when a new choice is selected from the **salutation** ComboBox instance): The first two lines set the values of the **motherFather** and **auntUncle** CheckBox components to false (causing them to become unchecked if they were previously checked). Next, an if statement is used to determine whether the value selected from the **salutation** ComboBox instance was either Mr. or Ms. Then, if Mr. was selected, the text labels of the **motherFather** and **auntUncle** CheckBox component instances will be updated to read Father and Uncle, respectively.

Likewise, if Ms. is selected, those same labels will be updated with the values of Mother and Aunt, respectively (**Figure 21.30**). Let's test this functionality.

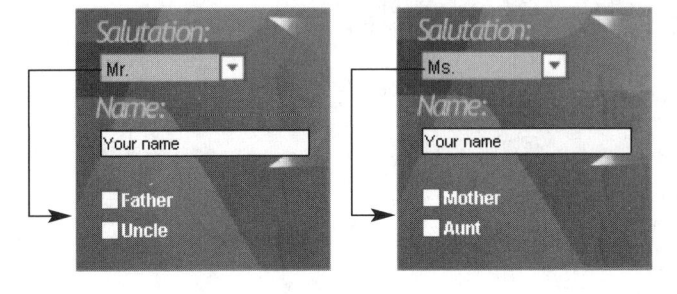

Figure 21.30
The updateForm() function will update the labels of the motherFather and auntUncle CheckBox Component instances, depending on the selection made from the salutation ComboBox.

5. Choose Control > Test Movie.

When the movie appears, interact with the ComboBox and CheckBox Component instances to see how the Change Handler function we added affects those elements.

6. Close the test movie to return to the authoring environment, then save your work.

Change Handler functions are great for dynamically reconfiguring form elements (displayed text, specifying whether elements are enabled or disabled, their position, their color, and so on) as users interact with a form (as illustrated in this section). The actions in Change Handler functions are equally handy for controlling movie clip instances, buttons, text fields, sounds, and any other movie elements. All it takes is a bit of creativity.

Using TextField Event Handler Methods

When is a text field not just a box for entering text? When it's in Flash. Although the primary function of most text fields is to capture user input or display dynamically generated text, Flash also lets you do these things with flair. Using event handler methods (see Chapter 13, "Understanding ActionScript"), we can call functions when the user interacts with a field (for example, by clicking inside a text field, adding and deleting text, and more).

In this section, we're going to set up some very simple interactions with the **name** text field, so that when the user clicks in it (that is, gives it focus), its color will change from the current white background/black border to a green background/white border. When the user clicks somewhere else (so that the text field no longer has focus), the text field's colors will be reset to black and white (**Figure 21.31**).

Has focus   Doesn't have focus

Figure 21.31
The appearance of the name text field, with and without focus.

1. With the Actions panel open, select Frame 1 of the Actions layer and add the following script below the current script:

   ```
   name.onSetFocus = function(){
      name.borderColor = 0xFFFFFF;
      name.backgroundColor = 0xC5E41C;
   }
   ```

   This script determines what happens when **name** is given focus. An unnamed function is called, which performs two actions: one that sets the border color of that field to white, and another that sets its background color to green.

2. Add the following script just below the script added in the previous step:

   ```
   name.onKillFocus = function(){
      name.borderColor = 0x000000;
      name.backgroundColor = 0xFFFFFF;
   }
   ```

   This script will reset the border and background colors of the **name** field when it loses focus (that is, when the user clicks away from it).

3. Choose Control > Test Movie.

When the movie appears, click into and away from the **name** text field to see how its appearance changes in response.

4. Close the test movie to return to the authoring environment. Save your work.

This section demonstrates how easy it is to implement event handler methods to make your movie respond to user interaction. Be sure to review Chapter 13, "Understanding ActionScript," for a list of additional event handler methods and their uses. In the next section, we'll set up another event handler method, this one a bit more sophisticated.

Attaching a Movie Clip Dynamically

One of the most common tasks performed on user-entered text is validation—that is, determining whether the text entered meets the restrictions imposed by the current application. Because valid data can take so many forms, there are lots of sophisticated ways to validate data. However, rather than focus on the validation process here, we're going to look at a creative way of indicating to the user that an error has occurred (as detected by data validation).

We will create an event handler method that checks—when text is added to or removed from the **name** text field—the number of characters within that field. If less than 2 characters, or more than 25, are entered, a small error window (a dynamically attached movie clip instance) will appear, indicating the error as defined. When the error no longer exists (once the user fixes the entry), the window will disappear. This interaction will occur in real time, as the user adds or removes text from the field.

1. Choose Window > Library to open the Library panel.

You will see two folders and a single movie clip symbol named **error panel** (**Figure 21.32**). This movie clip symbol consists of nothing more than some static graphics and a text field instance named **message** (which appears in the middle of the clip). This clip has not yet been placed on the stage anywhere within our project; it currently exists only within the library. Next we want to dynamically attach this clip to our scene whenever an error is detected, as the user enters text into the **name** text field.

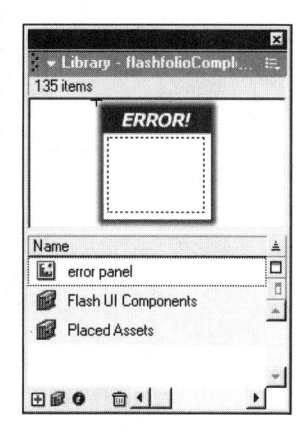

Figure 21.32
This graphic displays the contents of our project's library. In this section we will be working with the clip named **error panel**.

In order to dynamically attach a clip from the library, the clip must be given an identifier name. Let's do that.

2. Right-click (Windows) or Control-click (Macintosh) the name of the clip, and choose Linkage from the menu that appears.

The Linkage Properties dialog box will appear.

3. Choose the Export for ActionScript option.

Doing so will make the Identifier text box active. Currently, the symbol's name (**error panel**) appears in this box; however, we want to remove the space between the two words (identifier names cannot include spaces).

4. Give the symbol an Identifier name of errorPanel, then click OK.

Remember this name; it will play a role in the script we will be adding in a moment.

NOTE *For more information about giving library assets identifier names, see Chapter 17, "Using the Library to Manage Your Assets."*

In the steps that follow, we're going to use the onChanged() event handler method to call a function whenever text is added or removed from the **name** text field. However, we're going to take a slightly different approach to setting up the event handler methods than we did the previous section. First, we're going to create a named function; then we'll associate that function with the onChanged() event handler method.

5. With the Actions panel open, select Frame 1 of the Actions layer, and add this function definition to the end of the current script:

```
function validate(){
  if(name.length > 25){
    _root.attachMovie("errorPanel", "errorName",1);
    _root.errorName._y = name._y;
    _root.errorName._x = name._x + name.textWidth + 10;
    _root.errorName.message.text = "Too many characters";
    submit.enabled = false;
  }else if(name.length < 2){
    _root.attachMovie("errorPanel", "errorName",1);
    _root.errorName._y = name._y;
    _root.errorName._x = name._x + name.textWidth + 10;
    _root.errorName.message.text = "Too few characters";
    submit.enabled = false;
```

```
    }else{
      _root.errorName.removeMovieClip();
      submit.enabled = true;
    }
}
```

As you can see, this function uses a conditional statement to execute one of three sets of actions, depending on how many characters exist in the **name** text field when it's called. Let's look at each section of this statement to see how it works.

The first part of the `if` statement will execute five actions, if the number of characters in **name** exceeds 25 when the function is called. The first action attaches the errorPanel clip in the library to the root timeline, where it's given an instance name of **errorName** and placed at a depth of 1. The next two actions are used to position the attached movie, so that its y position matches that of the **name** text field, and its x position is 10 pixels past the last character in the field (**Figure 21.33**).

The next action is used to display an error message within the attached movie. You'll remember that the error panel movie clip contains a text field named **message**. When the clip is attached, as shown in this script, and given an instance name of **errorName**, then the text field in the attached instance can be referenced using the syntax: _root.errorName.message. Thus, the fourth action will display the text "Too many characters" within the **message** field of the attached instance.

The last action in the first part of the statement disables the submit button that appears at the bottom of the screen. Thus, the button cannot be pressed, and the registration process completed, until there are less than 25 characters within the **name** field.

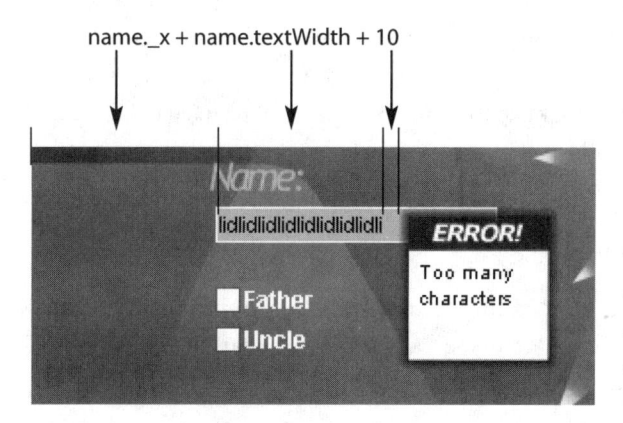

Figure 21.33
The equation used to determine the _x property of the error panel when it appears.

The second part of the if statement deals with what should occur if less than two characters exist in the **name** text field when the function is called. In this circumstance, the same five actions we just discussed will be executed, with a single adjustment: The **message** text field in the attached movie will display "Too few characters."

The final part of the if statement executes two actions if there are between 3 and 24 characters in the **name** text field when the function is called: It removes the **errorName** instance from the scene (an action that obviously only has meaning if that instance currently appears), and it enables the submit button (so that the user can press it and complete the registration process) (**Figure 21.34**).

Now let's script this function so that it's called whenever the text within the **name** field is changed.

6. Add the following line of script below the last line of the current script:

   `name.onChanged = validate;`

Less than 2 characters

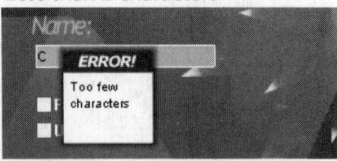

Acceptable number of characters

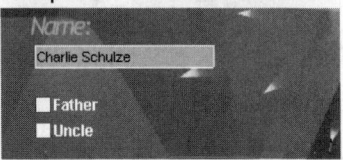

More than 25 characters

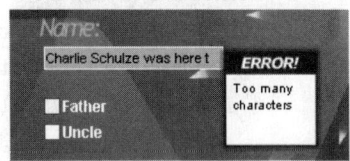

Figure 21.34
The results of typing text into the name text field.

The validate() function will now be called whenever text is entered or removed from the **name** text field.

There's just one more thing to take care of at this point. You'll remember that the Submit button is enabled and disabled, depending on the number of characters entered into the **name** field. We also want this button disabled when the movie first plays. That way, the only way to enable the button is by means of the validate() function, once the correct number of characters has been entered into the **name** field.

7. Add the following line of script at the end of the current script:

   `submit.enabled = false;`

Since this action is on Frame 1 of the movie, the Submit button (named **submit**) will be disabled as soon as the movie begins to play. Time to test everything we've added in this section.

8. Choose Control > Test Movie.

   When the movie appears, roll your mouse cursor over the Submit button to verify that it's disabled. Then place your cursor in the **name** text field, and add or remove text. Whenever the field has less than 2 or more than 25 characters, the **errorPanel** instance will appear, displaying a short message indicating the error.

   9. Close the test movie to return to the authoring environment. Save your work.

In this section we demonstrated how data entered into a field can be validated on the fly, rather than *after* the submit button has been pressed. While the traditional method works, you'll find that giving your users real-time feedback not only saves keystrokes, it's a lot more fun as well!

Creating and Using a LoadVars Object

The registration portion of our application is almost complete. We've employed components and a text field to provide a means for users to input information about themselves, as well a validation mechanism to make sure the proper amount of data is submitted. Now, our application has to do something with that user-submitted info—such as sending it to a server for processing. In this section, we'll demonstrate how to collect the data input by the user, place it into a LoadVars object, and send to a server.

We'll place most of this functionality within a function—then simply arrange to have that function called when the Submit button has been pressed.

   1. With the Actions panel open, select the Submit button and attach the following script to it:

   ```
   on(release){
      submitData();
   }
   ```

   As you can see, when the button is pressed and released, it will call a function named submitData(), which we'll create in the next step.

   2. With the Actions panel open, select Frame 1 of the Actions layer and add this function definition to the end of the current script:

   ```
   function submitData(){
      regVars = new LoadVars();
      regVars.salutation = _root.salutation.getValue();
      regVars.name = _root.name.text;
   ```

```
regVars.title1 = _root.motherFather.getLabel();
regVars.title2 = _root.auntUncle.getLabel();
regVars.value1 = _root.motherFather.getValue();
regVars.value2 = _root.auntUncle.getValue();
//regVars.send("http://www.yourDomain/registration.cfm");
gotoAndStop("thankyou");
}
```

The first line of this function creates a new instance of the LoadVars object, named regVars. The next several lines are used to fill this object with variable data collected by the user. Let's take a look at the first couple of lines (the rest should then make sense on their own):

```
regVars.salutation = _root.salutation.getValue();
```

The line above creates a variable within the regVars object named salutation. Using the getValue() method of the ComboBox component, the value of this variable will be set to the current value shown in the **salutation** ComboBox component. The next line creates a variable named name in the regVars object, and assigns it a value representing the text currently displayed in the **name** text field. The next four lines create additional variables in the regVars object, and assign them values based on the current labels (Father/Uncle, Mother/Aunt) and values (checked/true, unchecked/false) of our CheckBox component instances.

NOTE *The values created on the* regVars *object will be used in the next section, so remember their names.*

The next line uses the send() method to send the variable values in the regVars object to the specified URL. The receiving server script treats these variable values just as if they had been entered into HTML form elements, and the form had been submitted to the same script.

NOTE *We have added a comment to this line in order to demonstrate how the process works. If you have a script at a URL on your server that can process these variable values, you can enter that URL and omit the comment.*

The last line of the function will move our application to the **thankyou** frame label.

3. Choose Control > Test Movie.

   Input data using the component instances and text field, then press the Submit button. The application should move to the **thankyou** frame label. If you specified a URL as mentioned at the end of the previous step, the data you input will be sent to the server for processing.

4. Close the test movie to return to the authoring environment. Save your work.

NOTE *For more information on the LoadVars object, see Chapter 14 "ActionScript Objects."*

Dynamically Creating a Text Field and Filling it with HTML-Formatted Text

The next step in creating our application is to create and display a thank-you message to the user for registering. In this section we'll add that functionality to our application, but instead of simply placing a text field on the stage and filling it with generic text, we're going to take a more dynamic approach. We'll use ActionScript to create the text field, then fill it with HTML-formatted text. This formatted text will make use of the data the user input during the registration process, in order to display a custom message.

1. Move the playhead to the frame labeled **thankyou**.

As you can see, the middle of our project contains no content. We'll use ActionScript to place a text field here, and fill it with HTML-formatted text. In addition, the Browser button, at the bottom of the stage, will have a script attached to it via an event handler method defined at Frame 15 of the Actions layer (which is actually where all the script for this section will be placed).

2. With the Actions panel open, select Frame 15 of the Actions layer and add the following script:

```
_root.createTextField("thankyou", 1, 96, 175, 200, 180);
thankyou.border = true;
thankyou.background = true;
thankyou.html = true;
```

The first line dynamically creates a text field on the main timeline; names it **thankyou;** places it at depth of 1, an x position of 96, and a y position of 175; and sizes it to a height of 200 and a width of 180. The next three lines configure the text field to have a border and a background, and also enable it to interpret HTML-formatted text.

Initially, the text field will be empty. The next several scripts will be used to dynamically generate a custom message to be displayed within the field.

3. Add the following line of script just below the last line added in the previous step:

   ```
   messageArray = new Array();
   ```

   This creates a new array named `messageArray`. You'll remember from Chapter 14 that arrays can hold multiple values that exist in sequential index positions. For example:

   ```
   myArray[0]  //holds a value
   myArray[1]  //holds a value
   myArray[2]  //holds a value
   ```

   And so on.

   We will place sections of our custom message into sequential index positions of the `messageArray` created above, and then combine them to create a single message. We'll explain the reasoning behind this method shortly.

4. Add the following line of script at the end of the current script:

   ```
   messageArray.push("<b>Dear " + regVars.salutation + regVars.name + ",</b><br>");
   ```

   Here, the `push()` method (available to Array objects) is used to *push* a value (specified within the parentheses) into an index position at the end of the specified array. At this point in the overall script's execution, `messageArray` is empty. Therefore, the specified value is pushed into index position 0 (`messageArray[0]`). The value that's pushed into this index position is a string value, created using both HTML tags and variable values. The HTML tags format the text, while variable values are retrieved from the `regVars` object in order to customize this section of the message that will eventually be displayed.

   Although the `regVars` object was created mainly to send data to the server, when our project's timeline moves to the **thankyou** frame label, that object still exists, and the variable data it contains can continue to be used within our project (as you see demonstrated here). This section of our message uses the `salutation` and `name` variable values on the `regVars` object. Assume the user selected "Mr." from the **salutation** ComboBox component instance and entered "Bill Gates" for his or her name. As a result, the following string value will be pushed into the array:

   ```
   "<b>Dear Mr.Bill Gates,</b><br>"
   ```

   The HTML tags indicate that the text will be rendered bold, with a line break inserted at the end.

Let's *push* the next section into the array.

5. Add the following line of script below the current one:

```
messageArray.push("Registration was successful.<br>");
```

Once again, the push() method is used to push the indicated string value into an index position at the end of the messageArray array. Thus, messageArray[1] will contain the following string value (**Figure 21.35**):

```
"Registration was successful.<br>"
```

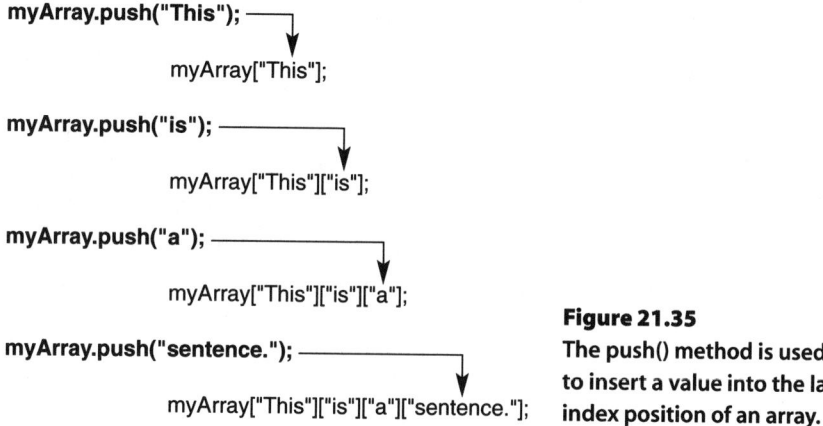

myArray.push("This");
⟶ myArray["This"];

myArray.push("is");
⟶ myArray["This"]["is"];

myArray.push("a");
⟶ myArray["This"]["is"]["a"];

myArray.push("sentence.");
⟶ myArray["This"]["is"]["a"]["sentence."];

Figure 21.35
The push() method is used to insert a value into the last index position of an array.

6. Add the following lines of script at the end of the current script:

```
messageArray.push("You entered the following information:<br>");
messageArray.push("----------------<br>");
messageArray.push("<b>Saluation: </b>" + regVars.salutation + "<br>");
messageArray.push("<b>Name: </b>" + regVars.name + "<br>");
messageArray.push("<b>You are a " + regVars.title1 + "? </b>" + regVars.value1 + "<br>");
messageArray.push("<b>You are a " + regVars.title2 + "? </b>" + regVars.value2 + "<br><br>");
messageArray.push("Thank you!");
```

Using syntax similar to that described in the previous two steps, we push several more sections of HTML-formatted strings (containing variable data from the regVars object) into messageArray. At this point, our script will have pushed eight sections of our overall custom message into the array. Next we'll we create a looping statement to combine those eight sections.

7. Add the following looping statement at the end of the current script:

```
for(i = 0; i < messageArray.length; ++i){
    thankyou.htmlText += messageArray[i];
}
```

This looping statement is used to loop through the values within `messageArray`, adding the next section of our message to the **thankyou** text field with each loop, and eventually creating the complete message. Let's examine the underlying logic.

When the `for` looping statement is initialized, `i` is given a value of 0 and the condition is set, stating that as long as `i` has a value of less than `messageArray.length`, the loop should continue. The value of `i` is then set to be incremented by 1 with each loop (++i). Since `messageArray` holds data at eight index positions, its length is 8—meaning this statement will loop eight times. You can see that with each loop, a value contained in the current index position of `messageArray` (as referenced by the current value of `i`) is concatenated to any text currently displayed in the **thankyou** text field. To help you understand this, let's go through the process for a couple of the loops.

Initially, the **thankyou** text field is empty. When the first loop occurs. `i` has a value of 0. Thus the following line:

```
thankyou.htmlText += messageArray[i];
```

Will be evaluated as:

```
thankyou.htmlText += messageArray[0];
```

Or

```
thankyou.htmlText += "<b>Dear Mr.Bill Gates,</b><br>";
```

Since the **thankyou** text field is initially empty, this will add the first part of our message to it. With the next loop, `i` is incremented by 1, and thus the following line:

```
thankyou.htmlText += messageArray[i];
```

Will be evaluated as:

```
thankyou.htmlText += messageArray[1];
```

Or

```
thankyou.htmlText += "Registration was successful.<br>";
```

Chapter 21 Projects

Using the compound operator of +=, we're adding the value to the right of the equals sign to any text that already exists in the **thankyou** text field. You'll remember that the first section of our message was added to the text field with the initial loop (as discussed above). Thus, this loop adds the *next* section to our text field.

The loop will continue six more times, with each iteration adding another section of the message to the **thankyou** text field (**Figure 21.36**). When the loop is completed, the entire message will be displayed. You'll notice the use of the htmlText property within the loop. This is used to tell the **thankyou** text field to render the text, as placed within it with each loop, with the appropriate HTML formatting.

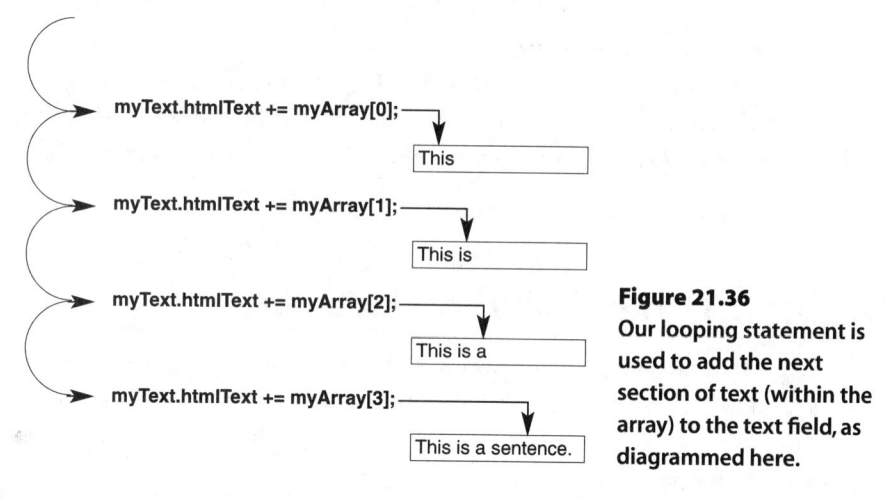

```
myText.htmlText += myArray[0];
    This
myText.htmlText += myArray[1];
    This is
myText.htmlText += myArray[2];
    This is a
myText.htmlText += myArray[3];
    This is a sentence.
```

Figure 21.36 Our looping statement is used to add the next section of text (within the array) to the text field, as diagrammed here.

NOTE *For more information on looping statements, see Chapter 13, "Understanding ActionScript."*

The reason for creating the message in sections, as we've done here, is because it's much easier to work with—and find syntactical errors in—an HTML-formatted string of text, if it's broken up into sections rather than left as single string.

The process of outputting a custom message is now complete. All we have left to do is script the Browser button that appears at the bottom of the stage, by using an event handler method.

8. Place the following script below the script added in the previous step:

```
browser.onRelease = function(){
    _root.gotoAndStop("browser");
    _root.thankyou.removeTextField();
}
```

This script instructs the **browser** button instance to execute an unnamed function when it is pressed and released. This function will move the timeline to the frame labeled **browser**, and remove the **thankyou** text field that contains our custom message. If we didn't remove the text field, it would be displayed at the browser scene—which we don't want.

All the scripts we've added in this section are placed on Frame 15, so that they are all executed as soon as the application is navigated to the **thankyou** frame label (which occurs when the Submit button is pressed on the registration screen).

9. Choose Control > Test Movie.

   Input some information in the Registration section of our application, then press the Submit button to navigate to the Thank You section. As soon as you enter that section, a thank-you message will appear in a dynamically created text field. In addition, pressing and releasing the Browser button at the bottom of the stage will take you to the Browser section, which we'll be working on next.

10. Close the test movie to return to the authoring environment. Save your work.

Browsing Dynamically Loaded JPGs

One of our application's main uses is to browse images—external JPG images, to be specific. Once you understand how to implement this functionality, you'll find it easy to create online slide shows, portfolios, or any other type of application that uses numerous images.

In this section, we'll begin to set up the image browsing aspect of our application. To do this, we'll add scripts to Frame 30 of the main timeline (the location of the **browser** frame label), as well as to several buttons on the stage. Those buttons will be used to resize and navigate the images, and to set the images' transparency.

1. Locate the directory on your hard drive that contains the files for this project.

   Among these files, you'll find three JPG images: frog.jpg, leaf.jpg, and moose.jpg. (Their visual content should be evident from their names.) Remember the names of these files: These are the images we'll load dynamically into our application.

2. Back in Flash, move the playhead to the frame labeled **browser**.

   At this frame label, the stage contains many elements. The ones we'll be working with are the large, white box (a movie clip instance named **placeholder**, into which we'll load our external JPGs) and the six buttons to the right of it: two

Chapter 21 *Projects*

scaling buttons (**scaleUp** and **scaleDown**), two buttons for setting transparency (**alphaIncrease** and **alphaDecrease**—which are actually movie clip instances that we'll script as buttons), and two arrow buttons (**prevImage** and **nextImage**), which will be used to navigate the images (**Figure 21.37**).

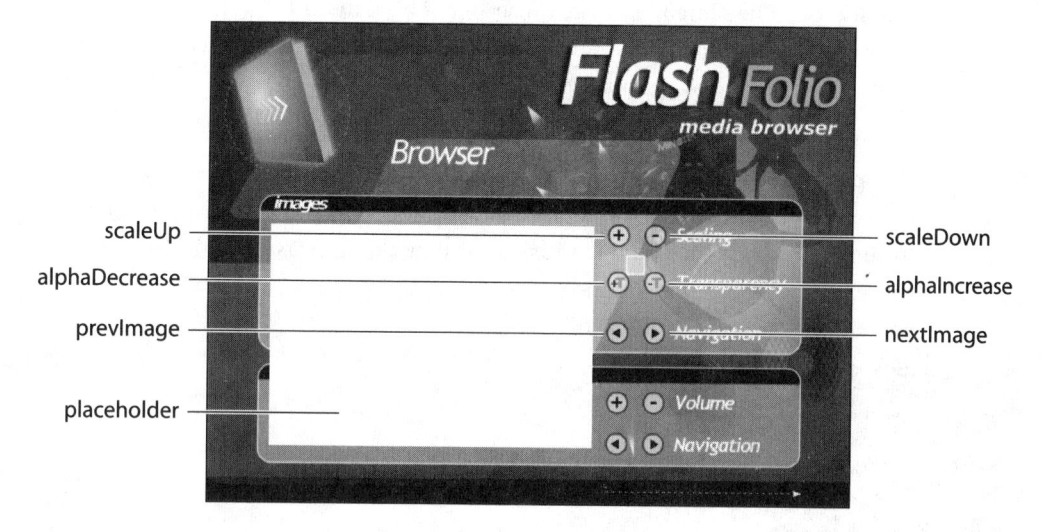

Figure 21.37
The elements on the stage that we'll be working with in the next couple of sections.

3. Choose Window > Transform to open the Transform panel.

   This panel does two things: It shows you how much the currently selected object has been scaled, skewed, and rotated from its original values. And, it allows you to specify an amount to scale, skew, or rotate the currently selected object.

4. With the Transform panel open, select the **placeholder** movie clip instance.

   Looking at the values on the Transform panel, you'll notice that this instance is currently at 100 percent of its normal size, which is a width of 275 pixels and a height of 184 pixels. These are the exact dimensions of the external images that will be loaded into it. First we need to scale this down to 50 percent, so that it doesn't initially appear so big.

5. On the Transform panel, enter 50 for both the width and height values, then press Enter/Return.

This will shrink the clip to a more manageable size. But why not just *create* the image with those dimensions rather than scale it down? Here's why: By reducing this clip to 50 percent of its original size, we make the externally loaded images 50 percent of their original size as well, once they are loaded into the application. The same holds true for scaling it back up to 100 percent (as we'll script it to do in a moment). When you scale an image to 100 percent of its actual size, image integrity is maintained.

However, if we had instead made the **placeholder** instance smaller (so that at 100 percent, it would have appeared the same size that it does now at 50 percent), we would have had to make the loaded images smaller as well—and scaling them back up would have meant scaling them to *more than* 100 percent of their original value, which causes image quality to degrade (**Figure 21.38**).

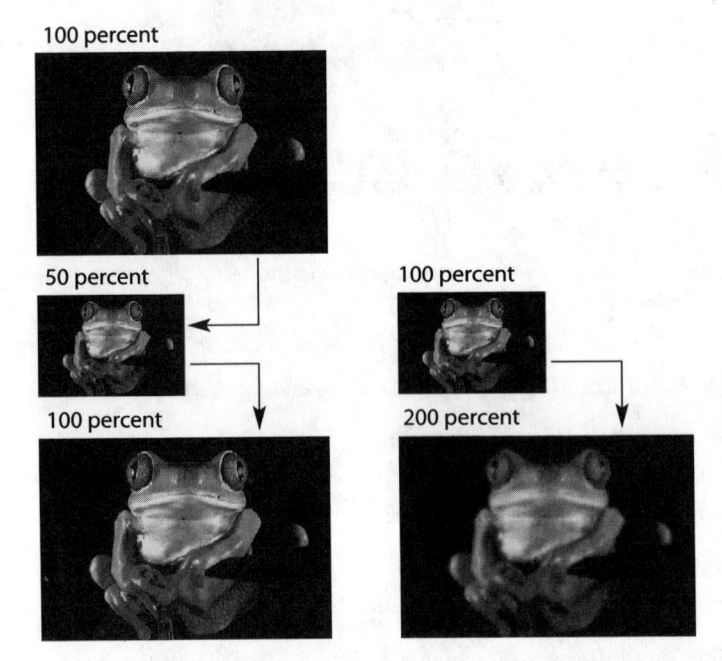

Figure 21.38
Scaling an image down to 50 percent, then scaling it back up to 100 percent (left) will provide better image quality than if you start with a smaller image and attempt to scale it by 200 percent (right).

Next we'll create the ActionScript that will load our external images into this instance.

6. With the Actions panel open, select Frame 30 of the Actions layer and add this line of script:

   `imagesArray = new Array("moose.jpg", "frog.jpg", "leaf.jpg");`

   This creates an array named `imagesArray`. As you can see, the names of our external JPG images are placed into indexes 0, 1, and 2 of this array.

NOTE *We're using only the names of the files themselves, because we're assuming that the Flash movie and the images all reside in the same directory. If the images are stored in a different directory than the exported SWF, you would need to change these values accordingly.*

Next we'll create a function to handle the process of loading and navigating our external images.

7. Add the following function definition below the script added in the previous step:

```
function updateImage(number){
  if(number >= 0 && number < imagesArray.length){
    currentImage = number;
    loadMovie(imagesArray[number], "placeholder");
  }
}
```

When called, this function, named `updateImage()`, accepts a single parameter (`number`). It then uses the value of that parameter to determine which image to load (as you'll see shortly). The `if` statement at the beginning of the function definition dictates that the actions within the function will only execute when a number within a certain range is passed to it. The lower end of the range is 0, and the upper end depends on the number of elements in `imagesArray`.

Thus, the `if` statement basically states that if `number` is greater than or equal to 0 and less than the `length` of `imagesArray` (which is 3, because the array contains three elements, see Step 6), the actions in the function should be executed. Under these circumstances, the function will only execute if `number` is 0, 1, or 2. (You'll shortly see why we've set up the function to operate this way.)

The first action in the function sets the value of `currentImage` to the value of the `number` parameter passed to the function. This variable's value will be used a bit later, when executing actions on our image-navigating buttons.

The next line in the function uses a `loadMovie()` action to load one of our external JPG images into the **placeholder** movie clip. To see how this function works, let's look at a couple of scenarios:

If a value of 1 were passed to the function when called, the `if` statement would deem that value acceptable, and thus the actions in the function would be executed—in which case they would be evaluated as follows:

```
currentImage = 1;
loadMovie(imagesArray[1], "placeholder");
```

Because the `loadMovie()` action references an element in `imagesArray` at index position 1, that line of script can be broken down even further, as shown in the following:

```
currentImage = 1;
loadMovie("frog.jpg", "placeholder");
```

The end result is that frog.jpg is loaded into **placeholder**.

Now let's look at one more scenario. If, when this function is called, a value of 3 were passed to it, the `if` statement would prevent it from executing—and thus prevent our project from loading content that doesn't exist (as defined in imagesArray). In other words, because that array doesn't contain an element at index number 3, the function would not work properly if it were allowed to execute. If, however, we were to increase the number of elements in the array, the upper limit accepted by the `if` statement would dynamically increase as well.

8. Place the following function call below the script you added in the previous step:

   ```
   updateImage(0);
   ```

   This calls the `updateImage()` function we defined in the previous step, passes it a value of 0, and as a result, displays the initial image when the movie is played and navigated to the **browser** frame label. Note that this initial function call will set the value of `currentImage` (within the function definition) to 0. This is important to keep in mind as we go through the next couple of steps.

9. With the Actions panel open, select the image navigation button that points *left* and attach the following script:

   ```
   on(release){
      updateImage(currentImage - 1);
   }
   ```

   This script calls the `updateImage()` function that we defined in Step 7. The parameter value passed to the function depends what `currentImage` - 1 evaluates to. Since that function is initially passed a value of 0 (see Step 8), `currentImage` is set to 0. Thus, pressing this button first, just after the movie begins to play, will call the function and pass it a value of –1 (0 minus 1). This value is evaluated by the `if` statement in the function, which in turn prevents the function from executing because the value is less than 0 (see Step 7).

   As a result, this button won't do anything until `currentImage` has a value greater than 0 (because there's no image available before the initial one). The other button used to navigate images—the right-pointing arrow—increases the value of `currentImage` (as shown in the next step), thus calling up the next image.

10. With the Actions panel open, select the image navigation button that points to the *right* and attach the following script:

```
on(release){
   updateImage(currentImage + 1);
}
```

This script is identical to the one in the previous step, with one exception: The parameter value passed to the function depends on the evaluation of currentImage + 1. Thus, if currentImage has a value of 0 when this button is pressed after the movie begins to play, the updateImage() function is sent a value of 1 (0 plus 1). This value is evaluated by the if statement in the function, which in turn lets the function continue to execute, in order to load the appropriate JPG. As the image loads, the value of currentImage is updated (in this case, to a value of 1) so that the navigation buttons can react accordingly on subsequent button presses (**Figure 21.39**).

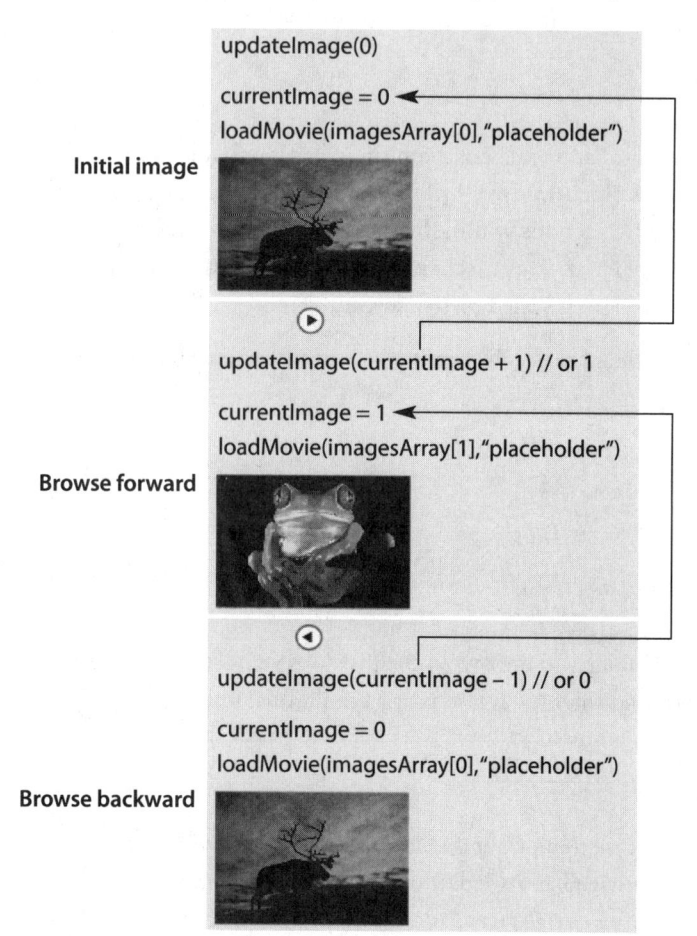

Figure 21.39
A graphical representation of the logic used for our project's image-browsing functionality.

This button cannot navigate the slide show beyond the last image in imagesArray. This is because once currentImage has a value of 2, pressing this button again would send the updateImage() function a value of 3, which the if statement in the function would analyze, and then prevent the function from executing.

In tandem, these two buttons advance and rewind the slide show, though only within the limits described above.

Next, let's script our scaling buttons.

11. With the Actions panel open, select the Scaling '+' button and attach the following script:

```
on(release){
   if(placeholder._xscale <= 90){
      placeholder._xscale += 10;
      placeholder._yscale += 10;
   }
}
```

When the button is pressed and released, a conditional statement looks at the current _xscale value of **placeholder**. If **placeholder** hasn't been scaled beyond 90 percent, the two actions within the statement will scale it vertically and horizontally by 10 percent. This mechanism prevents scaling once the **placeholder** instance has been scaled to 100 percent.

12. With the Actions panel open, select the Scaling '-' button and attach this script:

```
on(release){
   if(placeholder._xscale >= 10){
      placeholder._xscale -= 10;
      placeholder._yscale -= 10;
   }
}
```

This script functions similarly to the one in the previous step—only it scales the **placeholder** down rather than up. It also uses a conditional statement to restrict scaling beyond a certain point.

13. Choose Control > Test Movie.

Navigate to the Browser section of our application, where you will immediately see that our moose.jpg image has loaded into the **placeholder** movie clip instance. Pressing the left and right navigation buttons will load a new image.

Pressing the scaling buttons will scale the image up or down—though only to the extent defined in the previous two steps

14. Close the test movie to return to the authoring environment. Save your work.

Using the functionality we've described here, you could easily add additional image-file names to `imagesArray`, and our application would be able to display and navigate all of them automatically.

Creating Drag-and-Drop Functionality

Pressing buttons may be the most common way of interacting with a movie, but fortunately it's not the *only* way. Another common means of interacting with a Flash movie is dragging and dropping—which you probably do plenty of when working with files within your computer's operating system. Within Flash, you facilitate drag-and-drop interaction by using the `hitTest()` method, which you can use to execute actions, call functions, and more.

In this section, we'll script the **alphaIncrease** and **alphaDecrease** movie clip instances on the stage at the **browser** frame label, so that when they're dragged and dropped onto the **placeholder** movie clip instance (where our images are loaded) its transparency will be increased or decreased, depending on which instance you drag and drop. After these buttons have been dropped, they will snap back to their original positions, ready for dragging and dropping again.

NOTE *The reason we've used movie clip instances rather than buttons is that only movie clip instances can invoke the* `hitTest()` *method—which, as you'll see, is an integral part of the functionality we want to achieve.*

1. With the Actions panel open, select the movie clip instance named **alphaIncrease** and attach the following script:

```
on(press){
   thisX = _x;
   thisY = _y;
   this.startDrag(true);
}
```

This script is executed when the **alphaIncrease** movie clip instance is pressed. The first two actions capture the current horizontal and vertical positions of the instance, and save them as `thisX` and `thisY`, respectively. Next, a `startDrag()` action is executed, causing the instance to become draggable.

2. Add the following script to the end of the current script:

   ```
   on(release){
     stopDrag();
     if(hitTest(_root.placeholder)&& _root.placeholder._alpha <= 90){
       _root.placeholder._alpha += 10;
     }
     _x = thisX;
     _y = thisY;
   }
   ```

   The above script is executed when the movie clip instance is released. When this occurs, the first action will cause dragging of the instance to cease. Next, an `if` statement is used to determine whether a couple of conditions are true, in order to increase **placeholder**'s _alpha property value (and thus decrease transparency—see Note below). The `if` statement basically says that if, when dragging stops, this instance is hitting (touching) the **placeholder** instance, and the **placeholder** instance's _alpha property value is less than or equal to 90 percent, then that value is to be increased by 10 percent.

   NOTE *It may seem strange that adding 10 to the _alpha property would decrease transparency, but in Flash an _alpha value of 100 means completely opaque, while a value of 0 means completely transparent.*

   The last two actions will snap the dragged instance back to its original position, based on the `thisX` and `thisY` variable values, which were created when the movie clip was first pressed (as described in the previous step). Since these two actions are not part of the `if` statement, they're executed whenever the instance is released—whether the conditional statement is `true` or not.

3. With the Actions panel open, select the movie clip instance named **alphaDecrease** and attach the following script:

   ```
   on(press){
     thisX = _x;
     thisY = _y;
     this.startDrag(true);
   }
   on(release){
   ```

```
    stopDrag();
    if(hitTest(_root.placeholder)&& _root.placeholder._alpha >= 10){
       _root.placeholder._alpha -= 10;
    }
    _x = thisX;
    _y = thisY;
}
```

Other than a few minor adjustments to the conditional statement, this script is identical to those in Steps 1 and 2. Here, the conditional statement says that if this instance is hitting the **placeholder** instance when dragging is stopped, and the **placeholder** instance's _alpha property value is not less than or equal to 10, then that value is to be *decreased* by 10 percent (thus increasing transparency).

4. Choose Control > Test Movie.

   Navigate to the Browser section of our application. Click to drag one of the transparency movie clip instances on top of the image, then drop it in order to see how that instance changes **placeholder**'s transparency.

5. Close the test movie to return to the authoring environment. Save your work.

Using External XML to Dynamically Load External MP3s into a Sound Object

In Flash movies, XML—which we looked at in Chapter 14—can be used for much more than just displaying data. In fact, you can use the data in an XML document to set the parameter values of methods, functions, properties, and all other types of actions.

In this section, we'll set up our project to load an external XML document that contains information about several MP3 files, including the name of the file (for example, mySong.mp3), artist, and song. Once loaded, the artist and song names will be displayed in a couple of text fields, while the file name will be used to load that external MP3 file into Flash. We'll create a mechanism for navigating the nodes within the XML document, so that pressing Forward and Back buttons will load the next (or previous) song, and will also display the song's accompanying info in the text fields.

1. Locate the directory on your hard drive that contains the files for this project.

   Among these files you will find three MP3 files named song1.mp3, song2.mp3, and song3.mp3. In addition, locate the XML file named audio.xml. Let's open this XML document and take a look at its contents.

2. Using Notepad (Windows) or SimpleText (Macintosh), locate the audio.xml document on your hard drive and open it.

The contents of the document look like the following:

```
<collection>
    <song artist="Gary Dorsey" url="song1.mp3">Drifting</song>
    <song artist="Big Gary D." url="song2.mp3">Pick Me Up</song>
    <song artist="Dorsey G." url="song3.mp3">Relax</song>
</collection>
```

You can see that the root node in this document is named `<collection>` and that this node has three child nodes named `<song>`. Each of these child nodes has two attributes, `artist` and `url`, in addition to its own child node, which is the name of the song (Drifting, Pick Me Up, and Relax). It's important to understand this structure as we go along.

NOTE *For more information about nodes, see "XML Objects" in Chapter 14.*

3. Back in Flash, move the playhead to the frame labeled **browser**.

In this section, we'll work with the elements in the bottom half of the stage: two text fields (**artist**, for displaying the artist's name, and **song**, for displaying the song's name), and four buttons (two to control the song's volume, and two to navigate between songs) (**Figure 21.40**). Most of the ActionScript we'll be adding to this section will be placed on Frame 30 of the Actions layer. Let's get started.

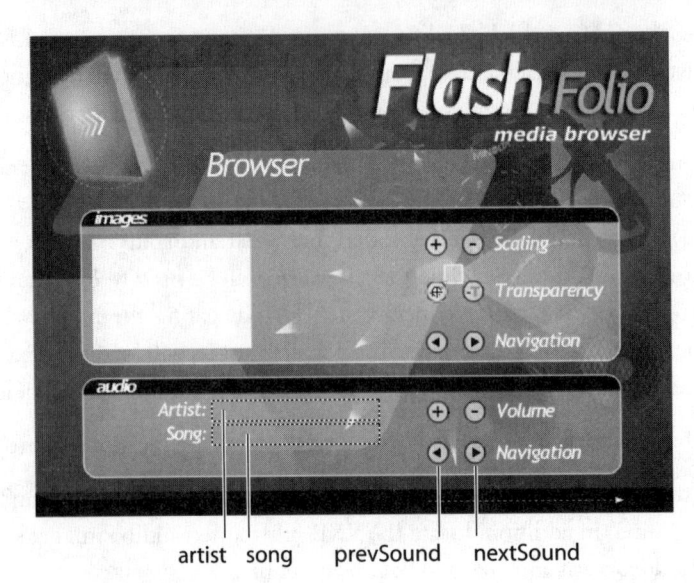

Figure 21.40 These are the project elements we will be working with in the next couple of sections.

4. With the Actions panel open, select Frame 30 of the Actions layer and add this script, at the end of the current script:

```
audioXML = new XML();
```

This creates a new XML object instance named audioXML. In a moment we'll load our external XML document into this object instance; but before we do that, we need to script a couple of other details.

5. Place the following line of script at the end of the current script:

```
audioXML.ignoreWhite = true;
```

This will cause Flash to ignore returns and spaces in the external XML document (which, in our case, could cause the XML document to be read improperly).

6. Add the following event handler method just below the end of the current script:

```
audioXML.onLoad = function(){
   currentAudio = audioXML.firstChild.firstChild;
   song.text = currentAudio.firstChild;
   artist.text = currentAudio.attributes.artist;
   audio = new Sound();
   audio.loadSound(currentAudio.attributes.url, true);
}
```

This script uses the onLoad event handler method to specify what should happen when the external XML document has finished loading into the audioXML object. Since this event handler method controls what happens after the external XML document has finished loading, the method must be defined *prior* to the script that initiates loading. This way, once the file has loaded, the actions within this unnamed function will be executed. Let's look at what they do.

First, the function creates a reference variable. This means that the name currentAudio is set up to reference audioXML.firstChild.firstChild. In other words, currentAudio now means the same thing as audioXML.firstChild.firstChild, just in shorter form. This common practice makes it much easier to work with nodes. Within our loaded XML document, we know that audioXML.firstChild.firstChild points to:

```
<song artist="Gary Dorsey" url="song1.mp3">Drifting</song>
```

This means that `currentAudio` points there as well (**Figure 21.41**). This is another important concept to grasp as we move forward.

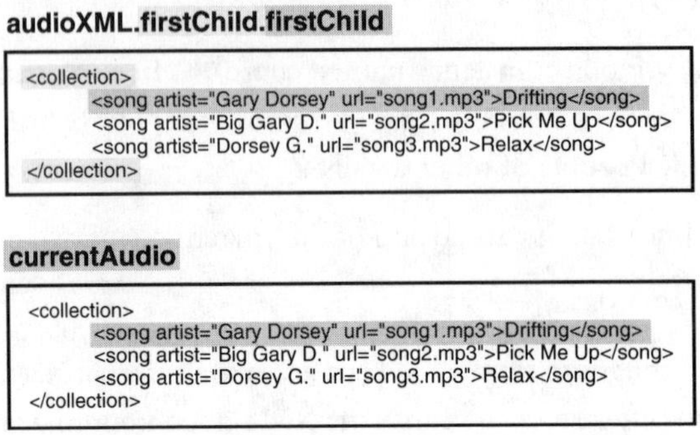

audioXML.firstChild.firstChild

```
<collection>
    <song artist="Gary Dorsey" url="song1.mp3">Drifting</song>
    <song artist="Big Gary D." url="song2.mp3">Pick Me Up</song>
    <song artist="Dorsey G." url="song3.mp3">Relax</song>
</collection>
```

currentAudio

```
<collection>
    <song artist="Gary Dorsey" url="song1.mp3">Drifting</song>
    <song artist="Big Gary D." url="song2.mp3">Pick Me Up</song>
    <song artist="Dorsey G." url="song3.mp3">Relax</song>
</collection>
```

Figure 21.41
We've created a reference so that currentAudio points to the same node as audioXML.firstChild.firstChild

TIP *Sometimes it's tricky to determine a node's value. However, you can use the trace() action to help figure it out. For example, trace(audio.firstChild.firstChild), when executed in Flash's testing environment, would open the Output window, where the value of the specified node would be displayed.*

The next line of the function sets the text displayed in the **song** text field to the firstChild node within `currentAudio`. Since `currentAudio` references the following:

```
<song artist="Gary Dorsey" url="song1.mp3">Drifting</song>
```

The song's title (Drifting) would be referenced by `currentAudio.firstChild` and displayed in the **song** text field.

The next action sets the text displayed in the **artist** text field:

```
currentAudio.attributes.artist;
```

The above references the `artist` attribute, which has a value of Gary Dorsey, which is displayed in the **artist** text field.

The last two actions within the function are used to load the external MP3 file. The line `audio = new Sound()` creates a new Sound object instance named `audio`. The following line invokes the `loadSound()` method to load an external MP3 file. This method takes two parameters: the path to/name of the external MP3 file, and a conditional statement that determines whether the loaded MP3 is treated as an event (`false`) or streamed (`true`) sound.

We've set up the method so that `currentAudio.attributes.url` determines the file loaded, and the sound is set to stream. Since the url attribute of `currentAudio` has a value of "song1.mp3", that's the file that's loaded (**Figure 21.42**). You can begin to see how data extracted from an XML document can be used in a variety of ways within Flash—once you understand how to access it.

```
currentAudio
  <collection>
    <song artist="Gary Dorsey" url="song1.mp3">Drifting</song>      → song.text = currentAudio.firstChild;
    <song artist="Big Gary D." url="song2.mp3">Pick Me Up</song>    → artist.text = currentAudio.attributes.artist;
    <song artist="Dorsey G." url="song3.mp3">Relax</song>              audio = new Sound();
  </collection>                                                   → audio.loadSound(currentAudio.attributes.url, true);
```

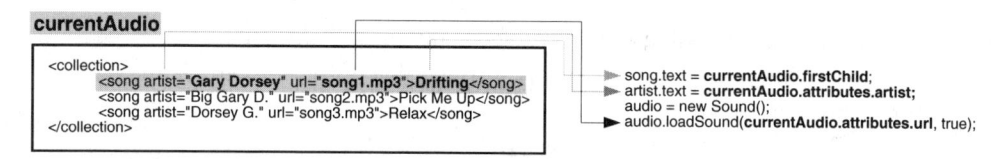

Figure 21.42
The locations from which our script extracts data from the XML document.

Now that the `onLoad` event handler method has been defined, it's time to script the project to actually load the external XML document.

7. Place the following line of script at the end of the current script:

`audioXML.load("audioXML.xml");`

This action will load the audioXML.xml document into the `audioXML` XML object instance. Since these scripts are all on Frame 30 of the timeline, they will be executed as soon as the timeline is navigated to the **browser** frame label. Let's test!

8. Choose Control > Test Movie.

Navigate to the Browser section of the application. As soon as that section appears, the song1.mp3 file will begin playing, and the artist and song names will appear.

Next, we'll set up the functionality required to browse through the songs in the XML document.

9. Close the test movie to return to the authoring environment. With the Actions panel open, select the audio navigation button that points left (**prevSound**), and attach the following script to it:

```
on(release){
   updateAudio("previous");
}
```

When pressed and released, this button will call a function named `updateAudio()` and pass that function a string value of `"previous"`. We'll define this function in a moment.

10. With the Actions panel open, select the audio navigation button that points right (**nextSound**), and attach the following script to it:

    ```
    on(release){
      updateAudio("next");
    }
    ```

    As you can see, pressing and releasing this button will also call the updateAudio() function, but in this case will pass it a string value of "next". Let's define the function.

11. With the Actions panel open, select Frame 30 of the Actions layer, and add the following function definition beneath the last line of the current script:

    ```
    function updateAudio(direction){
      if (direction == "next" && currentAudio.nextSibling != null){
        currentAudio = currentAudio.nextSibling;
        song.text = currentAudio.firstChild;
        artist.text = currentAudio.attributes.artist;
        audio.stop();
        audio.loadSound(currentAudio.attributes.url, true);
      }else if(direction == "previous" && currentAudio.previousSibling != null){
        currentAudio = currentAudio.previousSibling;
        song.text = currentAudio.firstChild;
        artist.text = currentAudio.attributes.artist;
        audio.stop();
        audio.loadSound(currentAudio.attributes.url, true);
      }
    }
    ```

    This function accepts a single parameter named direction. When either of our audio navigation buttons call the function, direction has a value of either "next" or "previous". A conditional statement analyzes this value to determine whether it should execute actions for browsing the audio forward or backward.

    The first part of the if statement says that if direction has a value of "next" and currentAudio.nextSibling is not empty, execute the actions that follow. Before we look at those actions, we need to explain the second part of the conditional statement—the part that determines whether currentAudio.nextSibling is empty (!= null). You'll recall that currentAudio initially references the node located at audioXML.firstChild.firstChild. This is the first <song> node, which you'll remember has a value of:

<song artist="Gary Dorsey" url="song1.mp3">Drifting</song>

Thus, currentAudio.nextSibling references the next <song> node, which has a value of:

<song artist="Big Gary D." url="song2.mp3">Pick Me Up</song>

Since this is not a null (empty) value, the rest of the actions in the first part of the conditional statement would be executed (**Figure 21.43**).

currentAudio

```
<collection>
    <song artist="Gary Dorsey" url="song1.mp3">Drifting</song>
    <song artist="Big Gary D." url="song2.mp3">Pick Me Up</song>
    <song artist="Dorsey G." url="song3.mp3">Relax</song>
</collection>
```

currentAudio.nextSibling

```
<collection>
    <song artist="Gary Dorsey" url="song1.mp3">Drifting</song>
    <song artist="Big Gary D." url="song2.mp3">Pick Me Up</song>
    <song artist="Dorsey G." url="song3.mp3">Relax</song>
</collection>
```

Figure 21.43 currentAudio.nextSibling makes reference to the next <song> node in the XML document.

Before we explain when and how this value could be null, let's take a look at what happens next, when the conditional statement proves true:

currentAudio = currentAudio.nextSibling;

The first thing that happens is that the above line updates currentAudio's reference to the *second* <song> node (which is the first <song> node's nextSibling). The next several actions in the conditional statement—which set the text in our text fields, and load a sound—use values from the newly referenced <song> node, as described in Step 6.

This concept of jumping from node to node, using the nextSibling (and previousSibling) properties as shown, forms the basis of this function. If the user navigates to the next sound using the **nextSound** button again, currentAudio will again be updated, this time to reference the *third* <song> node. If the user presses the **nextSound** button again, nothing will happen. Why? Well, our external XML document currently only has three <song> nodes. Thus, once it reaches the third <song> node, currentAudio.nextSibling will return a value of null because there is no nextSibling.

With this in mind, you can now see that the first part of the conditional statement will only be executed if `direction` has a value of "next", *and* there is another node to navigate to in the XML document (**Figure 21.44**).

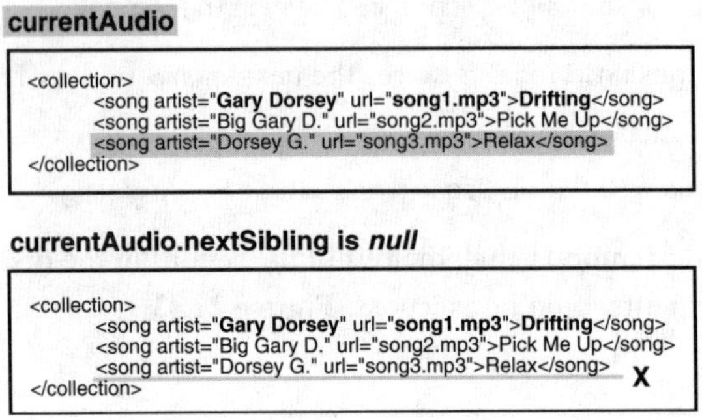

currentAudio

```
<collection>
    <song artist="Gary Dorsey" url="song1.mp3">Drifting</song>
    <song artist="Big Gary D." url="song2.mp3">Pick Me Up</song>
    <song artist="Dorsey G." url="song3.mp3">Relax</song>
</collection>
```

currentAudio.nextSibling is *null*

```
<collection>
    <song artist="Gary Dorsey" url="song1.mp3">Drifting</song>
    <song artist="Big Gary D." url="song2.mp3">Pick Me Up</song>
    <song artist="Dorsey G." url="song3.mp3">Relax</song>     X
</collection>
```

Figure 21.44
When `currentAudio` references the third `<song>` node in our document, attempting to access `currentAudio.nextSibling` will return `null`, since no node exists beyond the third one.

The `else` part of the conditional statement handles navigating audio clips in the opposite direction, moving *backward* through the `<song>` nodes each time the **previousSound** button is pressed, requesting the previous song.

You'll notice the addition of `audio.stop();` to both parts of the conditional statement. This is used to halt the currently playing sound in the `audio` Sound object, before loading a new MP3 file into it. The last detail we need to attend to is scripting our volume buttons.

12. With the Actions panel open, select the Volume '+' button and attach the following script:

```
on(release){
    currentVolume = audio.getVolume();
    if(currentVolume <= 90){
        audio.setVolume(currentVolume + 10);
    }
}
```

This script is executed when the button it's attached to is pressed and released. The first action creates a variable named `currentVolume`. The `getVolume()` method is used to return the current volume of the `audio` Sound object instance (into which our external MP3s are loaded into); that value is then assigned to the `currentVolume` variable. Next, a conditional statement looks at the value of `currentVolume` and says that if it doesn't have a value greater than or equal to 90, use the `setVolume()` method to set the volume of the `audio` Sound object to the value of `currentVolume` (which actually represents its current volume), plus 10.

For example, assume the volume of the `audio` Sound object is 60 when this script is executed. In this case, `currentVolume` is assigned a value of 60. The conditional statement then determines that 60 is less than or equal to 90. Thus, the action within the statement executes, setting the volume of the `audio` Sound object to 60 + 10, or 70. If this script is immediately executed again, `currentAudio` is given a value of 70 and the process is repeated. Once the volume has been set to 100, the conditional statement will prevent it from being increased any further.

13. With the Actions panel open, select the Volume '-' button and attach the following script:

```
on(release){
   currentVolume = audio.getVolume();
   if(currentVolume >= 10){
      audio.setVolume(currentVolume - 10);
   }
}
```

This script functions in the same manner as the one discussed in the previous step, only it decreases the volume of the `audio` Sound object by 10. Once the volume has been set to 0, the conditional statement will prevent it from being decreased any further.

14. Choose Control > Test Movie.

    Navigate to the Browser section of the application. As soon as that section appears, the song1.mp3 file will begin playing, and the artist and song names will appear. Use the audio navigation buttons to navigate forward and backward through the songs. Use the volume buttons to control the volume of the audio.

15. Close the test movie to return to the authoring environment. Save your work.

Our project is now complete!

Even though we've covered a lot of ground here, we've really only scratched the surface of the ways you can use ActionScript in your projects. Each new project, idea, or inspiration brings its own challenges, which will require you to build on what you've learned. The important thing to remember is to look at each project requirement separately. Don't start off worrying about the dozens, perhaps hundreds, of lines of scripts your project will potentially require. Tackle each functionality separately: Script it, test it, then move on to the next.

If you're interested in furthering your ActionScript knowledge, be sure to check out my other book, *Macromedia Flash MX ActionScripting: Advanced Training from the Source* (Macromedia Press), co-authored by Jobe Makar of www.electrotank.com. It has dozens of projects—similar to those you worked on in this section—that will enable you to take your scripting to the next level.

Although we've reached the end of this book, it shouldn't be the end of your Flash journey. The Flash universe is constantly expanding, and Macromedia continues to support the Flash community with new tools, links, showcase sites, and ideas and avenues for Flash implementations. Bookmark that company's home page—www.macromedia.com—and visit it regularly.

Although the next edition of this book is still a ways off, I'm always interested in your feedback: comments, complaints (got to take the bad with the good!), and of course praise. If you have anything to say, please email me at derek@derekfranklin.com. Also, be sure to check out my site at www.derekfranklin.com. While it's not as extensive as Macromedia's site, there's a good chance you'll find something there that may help in your endeavors to become a Flash master.

Actions Panel Enhancements

In Flash MX, the Actions panel includes new features that make it easier to not only create and work with scripts, but to check, format, and read them as well—welcome additions since most Flash developers use ActionScript on a daily basis.

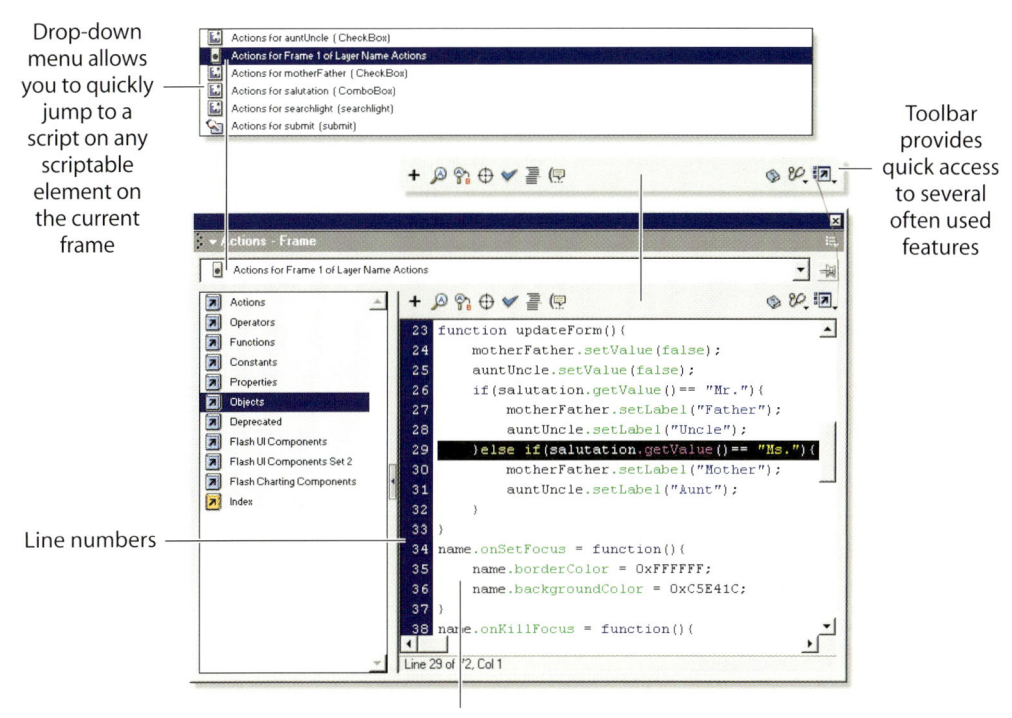

Drop-down menu allows you to quickly jump to a script on any scriptable element on the current frame

Toolbar provides quick access to several often used features

Line numbers

Auto-formatting (formats scripts as you type) and color syntax for various script elements

Dynamic Drawing

Using ActionScript, you now have the ability to draw lines and curves dynamically. By using the new drawing methods of the MovieClip object, as shown in the lines of script highlighted here, you can set line size, color, and alpha. And if you're creating an enclosed shape, you can give it a solid or gradient fill. You can draw contiguous lines, or you can draw a line and then pick up a drawing beginning at a new point.

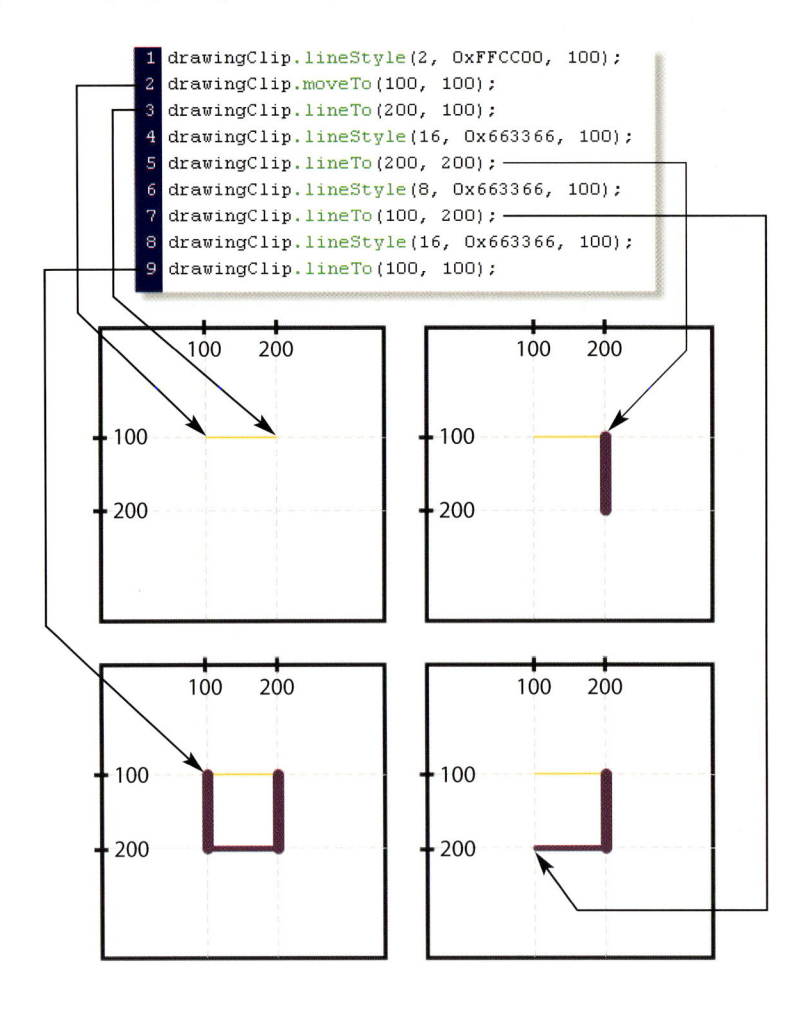

```
1  drawingClip.lineStyle(2, 0xFFCC00, 100);
2  drawingClip.moveTo(100, 100);
3  drawingClip.lineTo(200, 100);
4  drawingClip.lineStyle(16, 0x663366, 100);
5  drawingClip.lineTo(200, 200);
6  drawingClip.lineStyle(8, 0x663366, 100);
7  drawingClip.lineTo(100, 200);
8  drawingClip.lineStyle(16, 0x663366, 100);
9  drawingClip.lineTo(100, 100);
```

Code Hints

Code hints—a Flash MX addition to the Actions panel—appear automatically as you type into the Actions List window of the Actions panel, providing you with "hints" about how to configure an action, or a drop down list of choices to chose from when writing specific portions of a script.

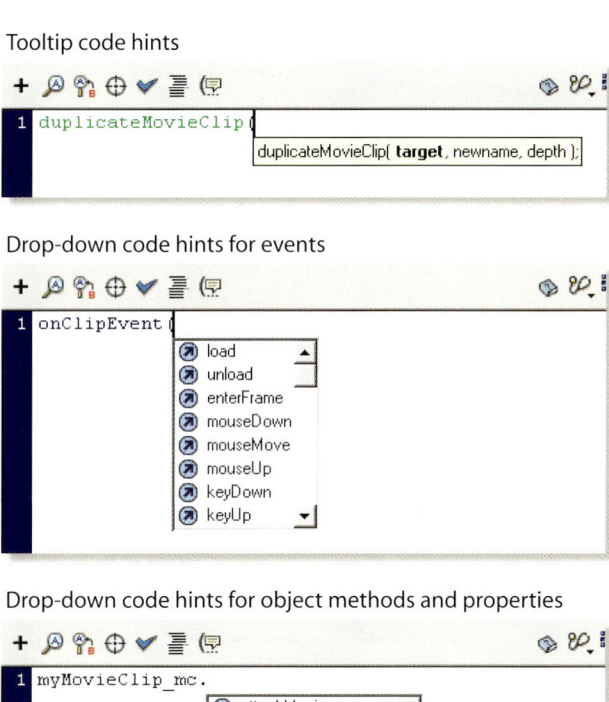

Tooltip code hints

Drop-down code hints for events

Drop-down code hints for object methods and properties

Components

Components represent one of Flash MX's more exciting new features. You use them to drag and drop highly interactive movie elements and behaviors into your projects. Flash comes with several components pre-installed for creating scroll bars, list boxes, radio buttons, and the like. You can also download and install third-party components, giving you plenty of ways of creating powerful applications even if you aren't an ActionScript genius.

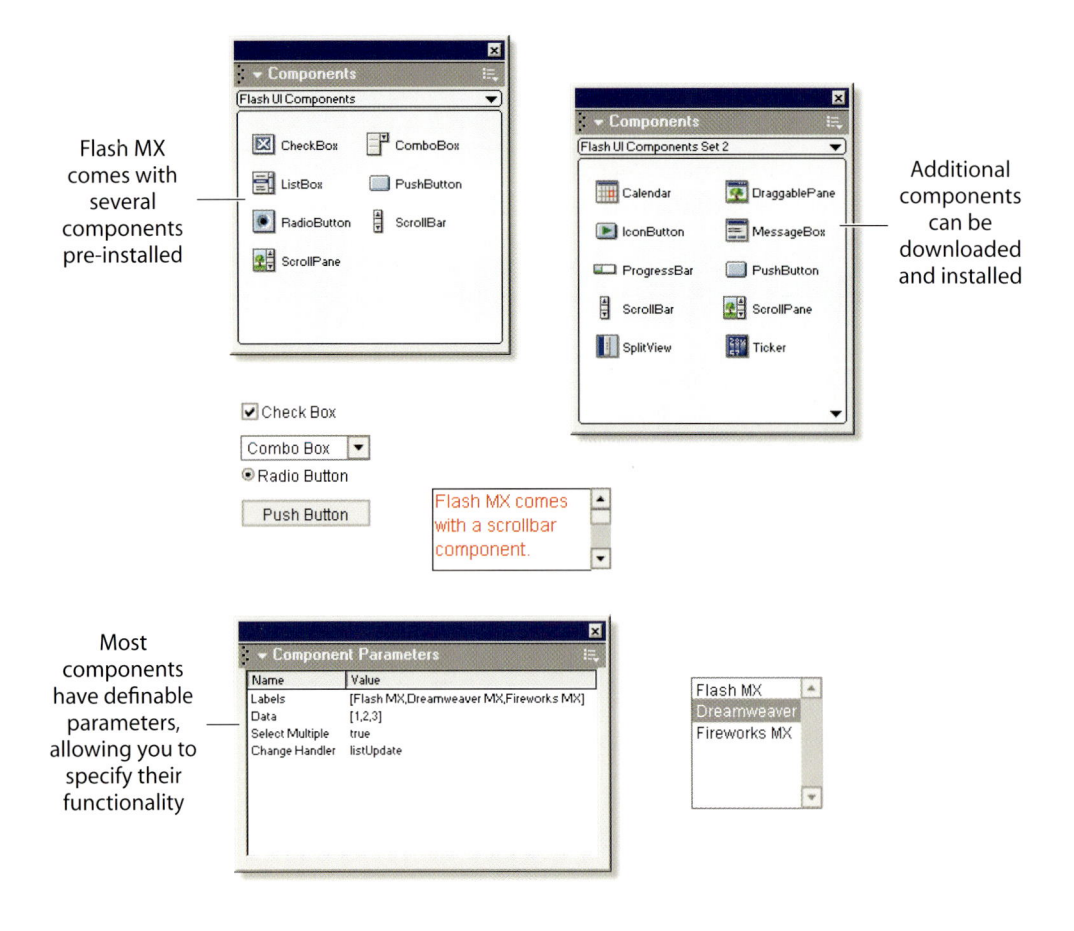

Flash MX comes with several components pre-installed

Additional components can be downloaded and installed

Flash MX comes with a scrollbar component.

Most components have definable parameters, allowing you to specify their functionality

Enhanced Debugger

As Flash applications have become more sophisticated, the need for a sophisticated debugging tool has increased as well. Flash MX meets that need with its enhanced Debugger. The tool's new features and capabilities will have you finding and stomping out bugs in no time!

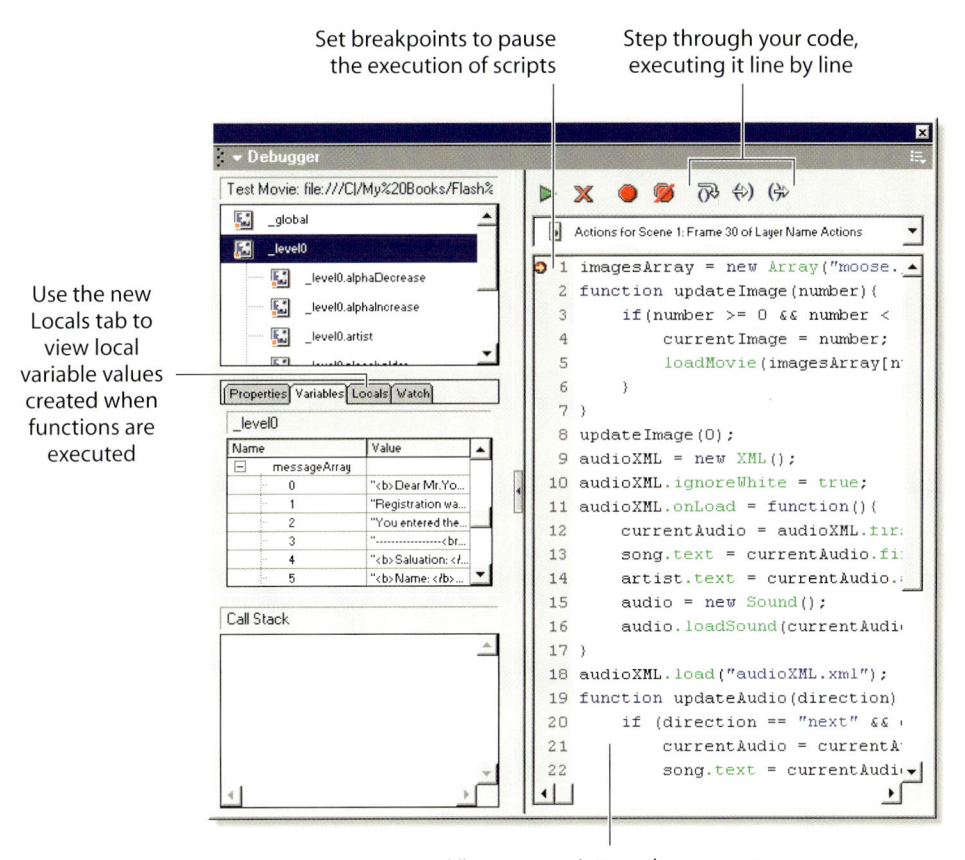

Set breakpoints to pause the execution of scripts

Step through your code, executing it line by line

Use the new Locals tab to view local variable values created when functions are executed

View your scripts as they execute

Flash MX: Highlights in Color

E

New Drawing Tools

New to the Drawing toolbar, the Free Transform tool handles some of the functionality previously achieved via the Arrow tool (such as scaling and rotation). The Free Transform tool also provides two new options: one for distorting a shape (that is, altering its perspective), and one for reshaping a vector graphic (via an envelope).

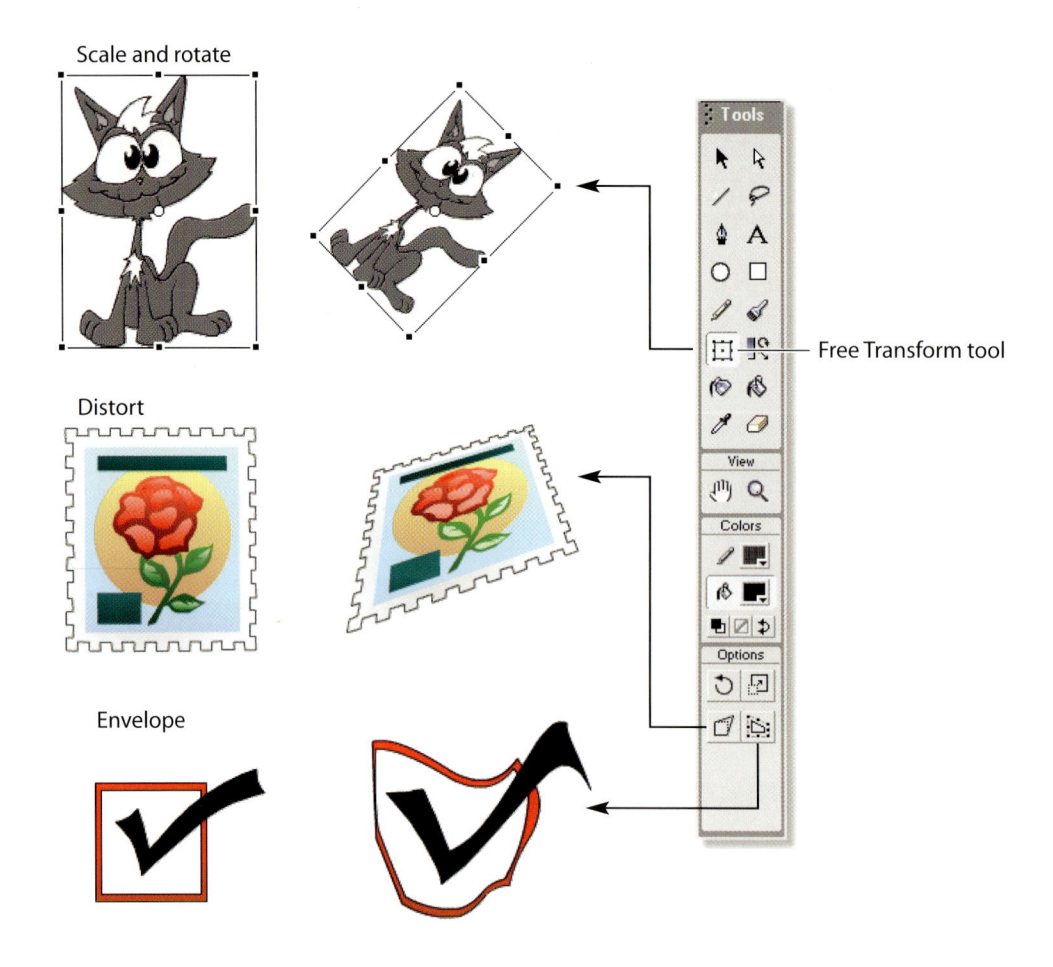

Scale and rotate

Distort

Envelope

Free Transform tool

Enhanced Masking

Masking was a great addition to Flash 4, but its usefulness has always been limited by the fact that you couldn't use animated movie clip instances as mask shapes. This has changed with Flash MX, and you can now use movie clips with multiple layers of animation as sophisticated masking effects. In addition, you can now create masks dynamically via ActionScript—which means you can assign the shape of one movie clip to be the mask of another.

Movie clip mask

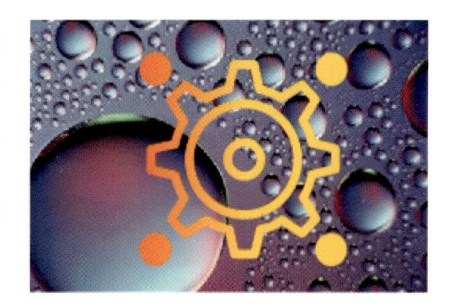

Scriptable mask

```
autumnClip.setMask(leafClip);
```

Dynamically Loaded External JPGs

Bitmap images are an important part of most Flash applications. However, if your application requires dozens, maybe even hundreds, of images, your final SWF can easily swell to an unacceptable size. Fortunately, Flash MX now allows you to load JPG images into your project via ActionScript—which means you can load and unload them from your movies on an as-needed basis, keeping file sizes to a minimum.

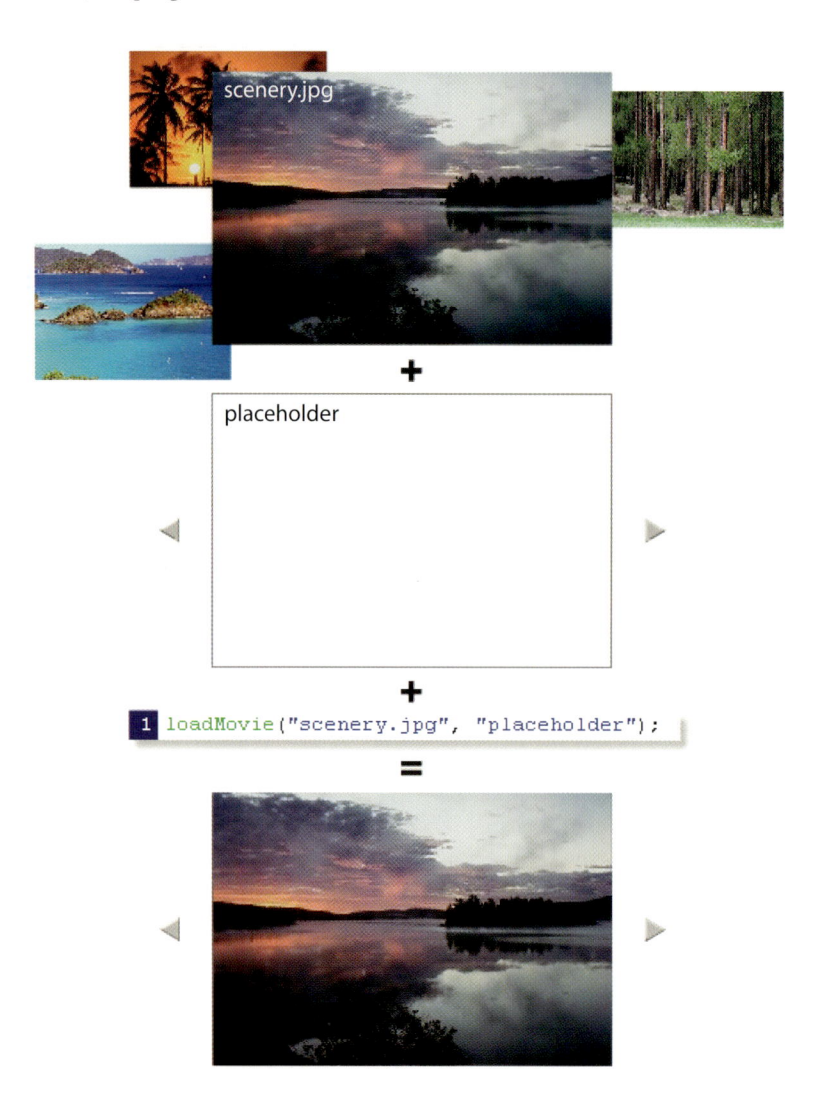

```
1  loadMovie("scenery.jpg", "placeholder");
```

Layer Folders

Layer folders allow you to group layers with similar or related content so that you can view or hide them simultaneously, depending on the task at hand. Layer folders can contain any type of layer (normal, masked, guide, and so on), as well as other layer folders—which means you can create a hierarchical structure for layers on the timeline.

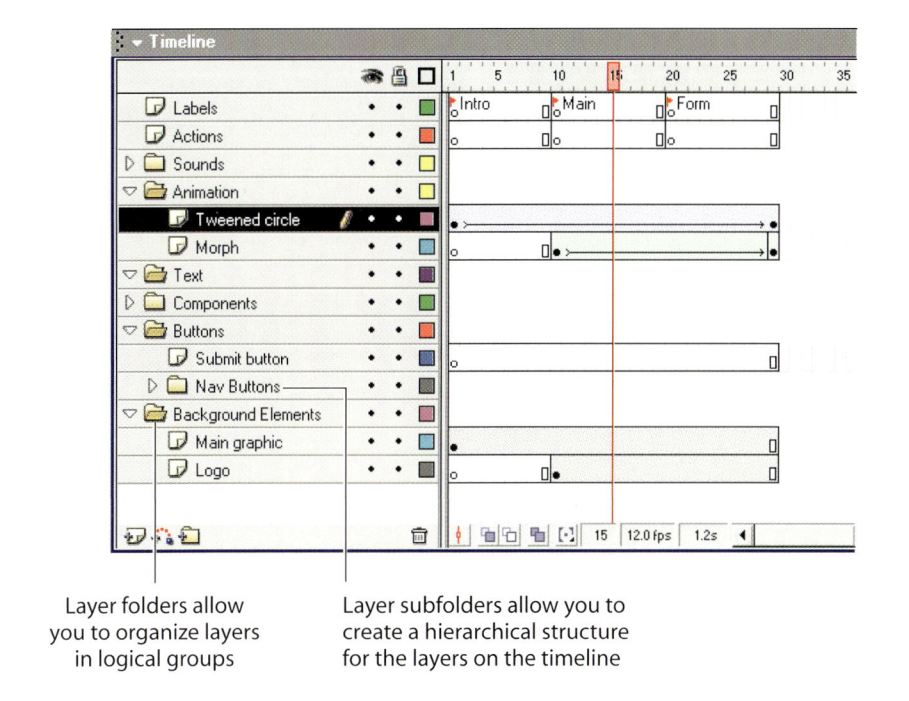

Layer folders allow you to organize layers in logical groups

Layer subfolders allow you to create a hierarchical structure for the layers on the timeline

Enhanced Panels

Although Flash 5 employed panels for making adjustments to selected movie elements, those panels are nothing compared with the panels in Flash MX—which are far easier to organize and use. You can dock Flash MX panels to any side of the screen, or group, separate, collapse, or expand them to suit your needs.

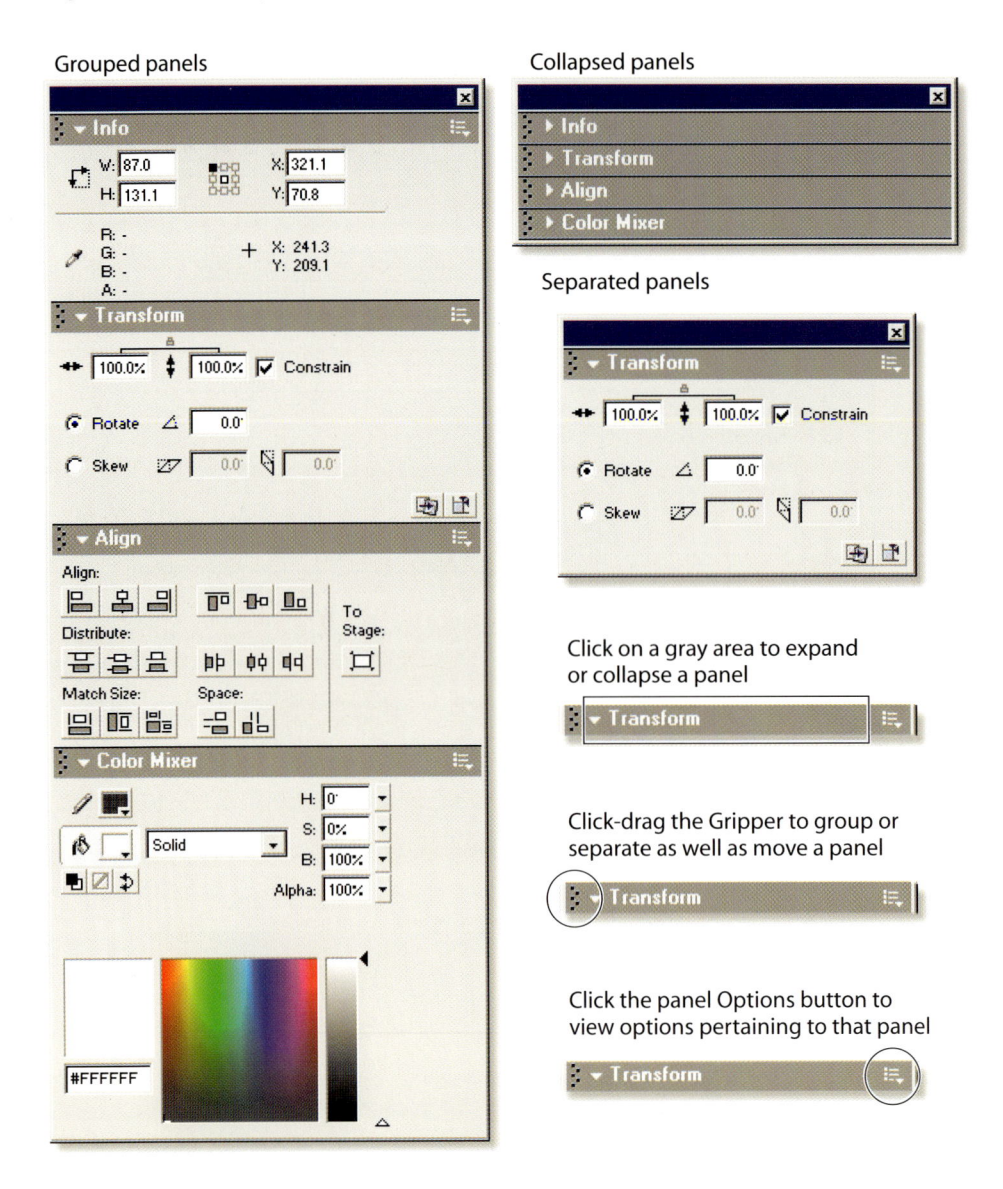

Grouped panels

Collapsed panels

Separated panels

Click on a gray area to expand or collapse a panel

Click-drag the Gripper to group or separate as well as move a panel

Click the panel Options button to view options pertaining to that panel

Property Inspector

The Property inspector is a new context-sensitive panel whose interface is automatically updated as you select various project elements, instantly providing configurable options specific to that element. The Property inspector replaces many panels that existed in Flash 5, including the Frame, Sound, Instance, Character, Paragraph, and Text Options panels (to name just a few).

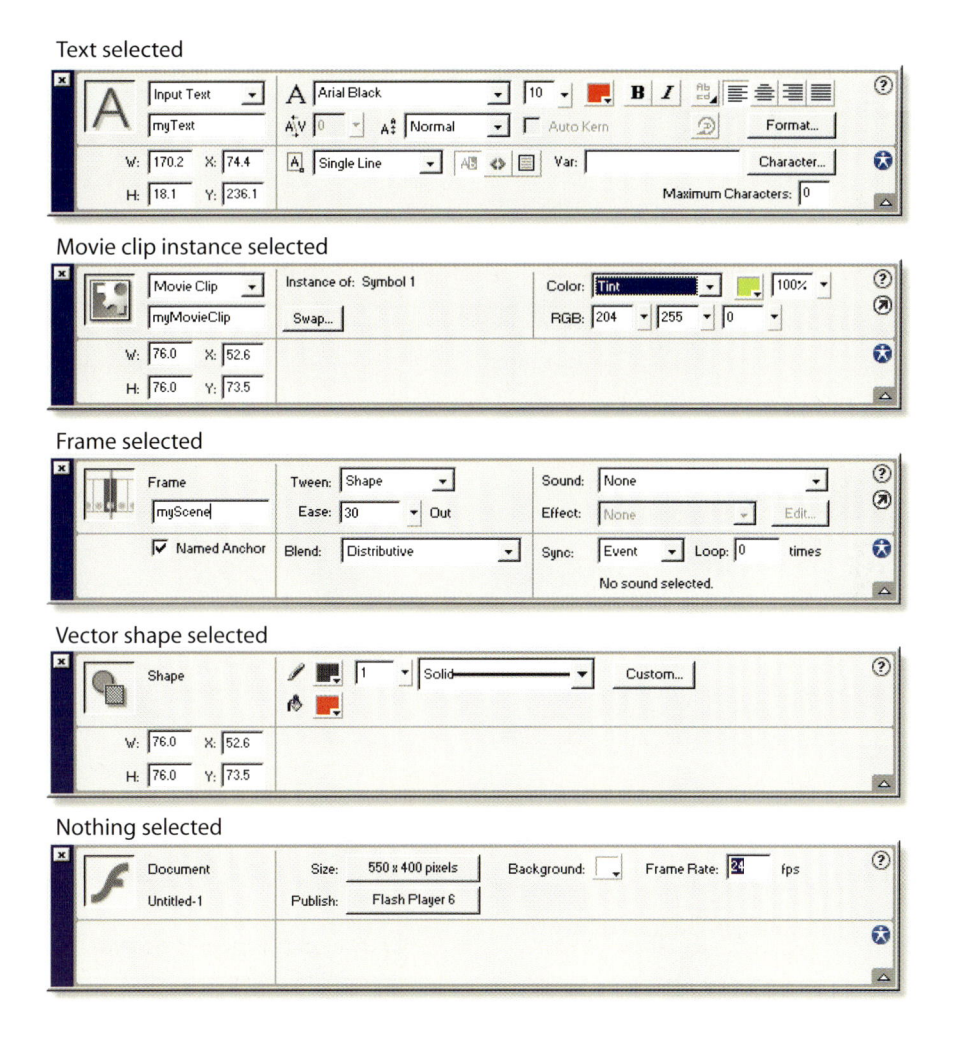

Text selected

Movie clip instance selected

Frame selected

Vector shape selected

Nothing selected

Enhanced Sound Object

In Flash MX, the Sound object has been enhanced in several ways. First and foremost, it now provides you with a means of loading external MP3 files into a movie as it plays. Two new event handlers allow you to call functions when a sound has finished loading or completed its playback. Two new properties allow you to track the length and current playback position of a sound.

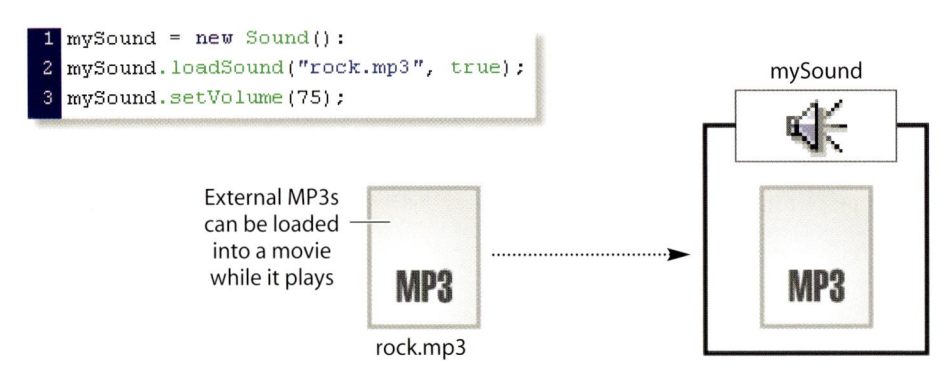

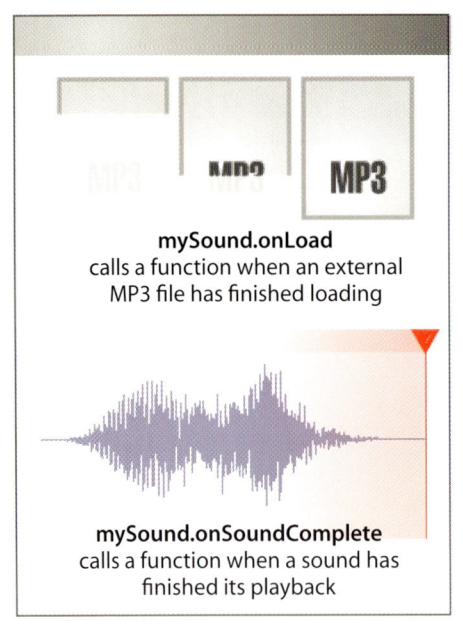

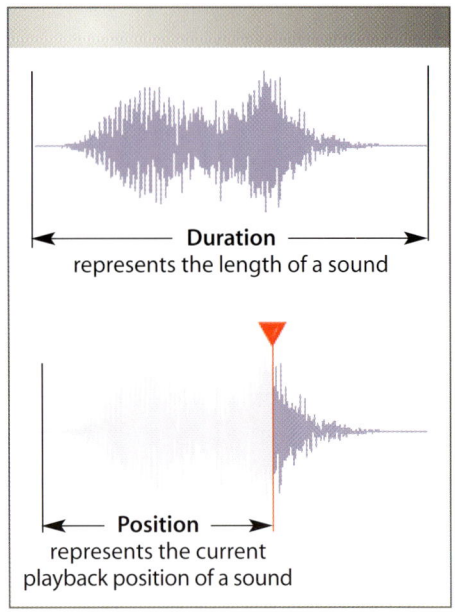

```
1  mySound = new Sound();
2  mySound.loadSound("rock.mp3", true);
3  mySound.setVolume(75);
```

External MP3s can be loaded into a movie while it plays

rock.mp3

mySound

mySound.onLoad
calls a function when an external MP3 file has finished loading

mySound.onSoundComplete
calls a function when a sound has finished its playback

Duration
represents the length of a sound

Position
represents the current playback position of a sound

Templates

Templates are partially developed Flash authoring files that provide a quick way to begin a new project. Flash MX comes with a number of templates pre-installed, ready to tweak and configure for your own use. There are templates for creating banners, presentations, PocketPC content, and more. Most of Flash's pre-installed templates contain instructions on how to use and configure them.

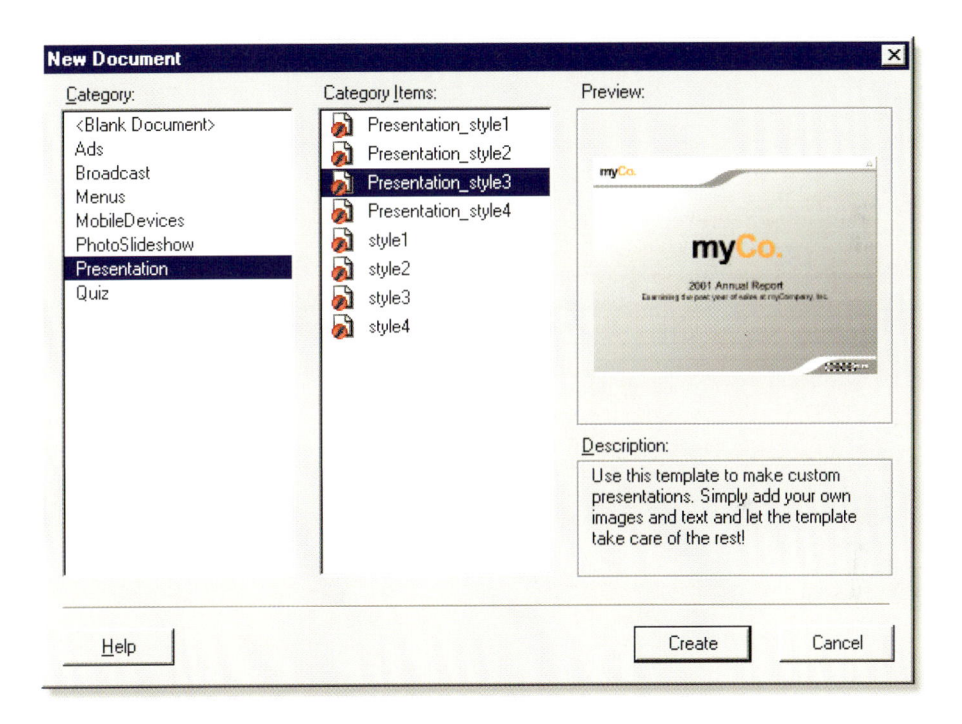

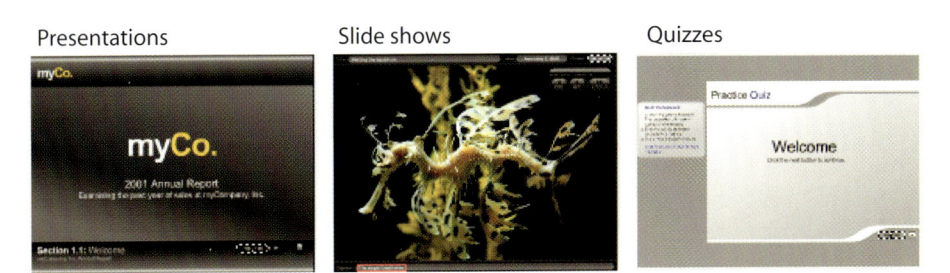

Presentations

Slide shows

Quizzes

Enhanced Text Fields

Text fields are now considered instances of the new TextField object. As such, they have dynamically configurable properties as well as the ability to respond to user interaction, such as when they're clicked into or away from, or text within them is changed (added or removed).

Text fields are now considered instances of the TextField object and, as such, are given instance names

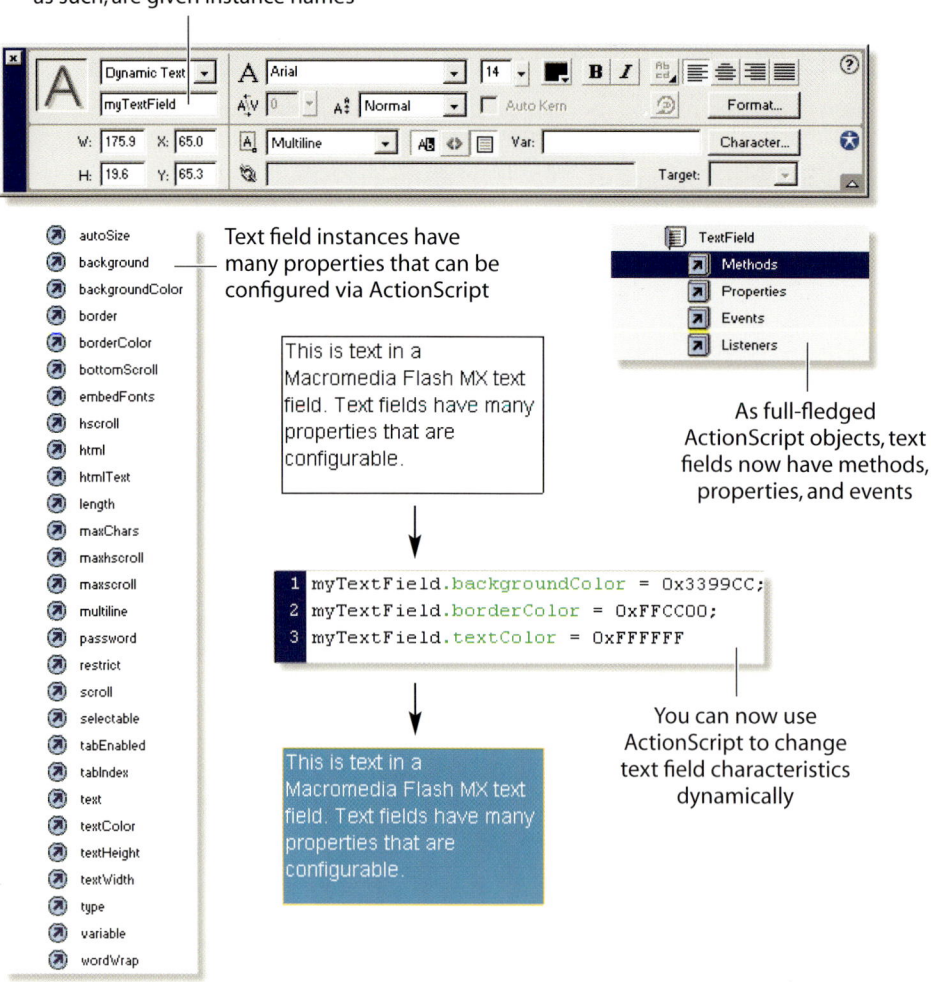

Text field instances have many properties that can be configured via ActionScript

This is text in a Macromedia Flash MX text field. Text fields have many properties that are configurable.

As full-fledged ActionScript objects, text fields now have methods, properties, and events

```
1  myTextField.backgroundColor = 0x3399CC;
2  myTextField.borderColor = 0xFFCC00;
3  myTextField.textColor = 0xFFFFFF
```

You can now use ActionScript to change text field characteristics dynamically

This is text in a Macromedia Flash MX text field. Text fields have many properties that are configurable.

Vertical Text

In an effort to appeal to Asian markets, where text is usually read from top to bottom (rather than from left to right), Flash MX can now display text within a field vertically.

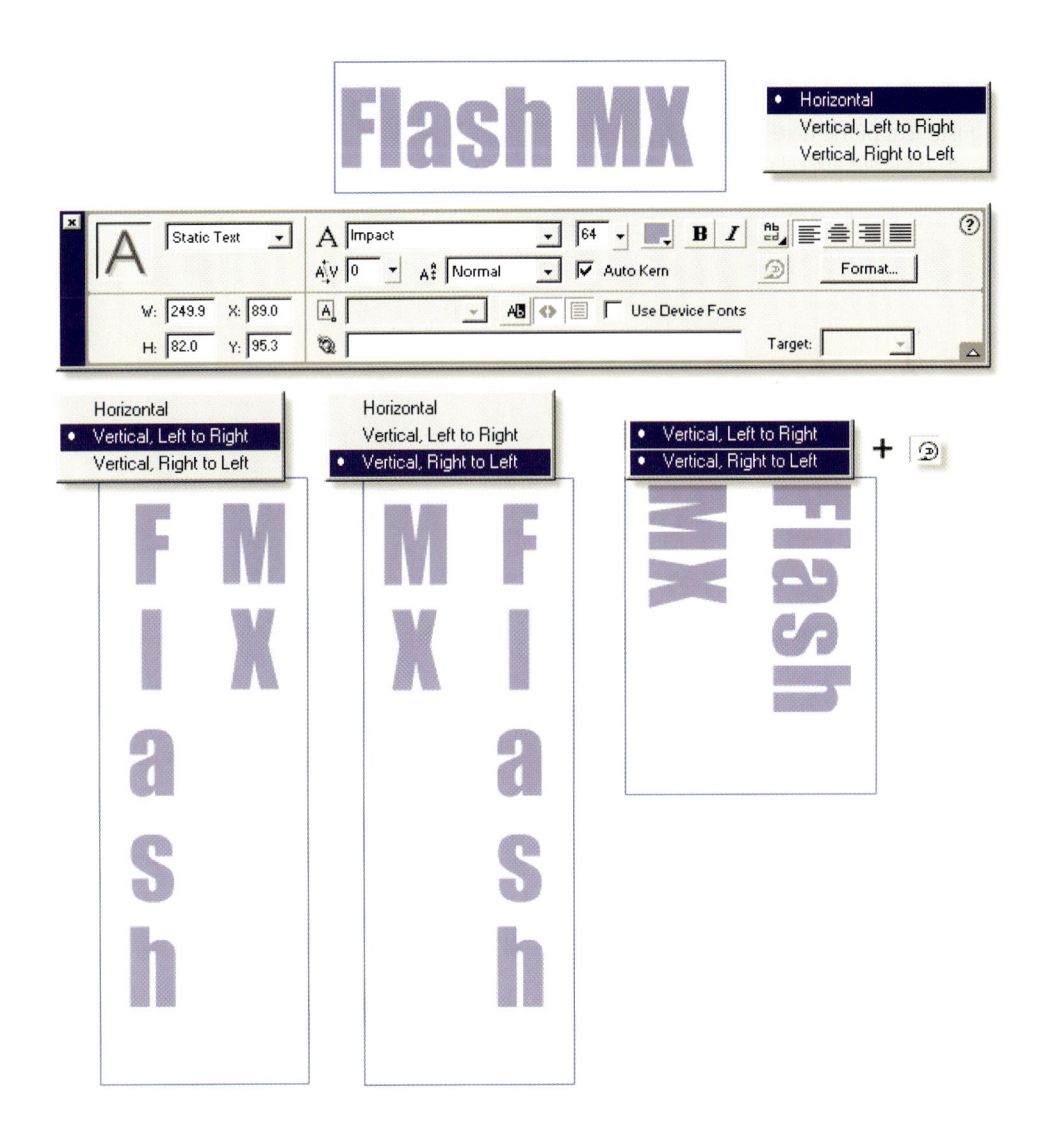

Video

The Flash Player can now play video clips embedded in Flash movies. You can convert video clips into movie clips to control their playback, size, transparency, rotation, and so on via ActionScript.

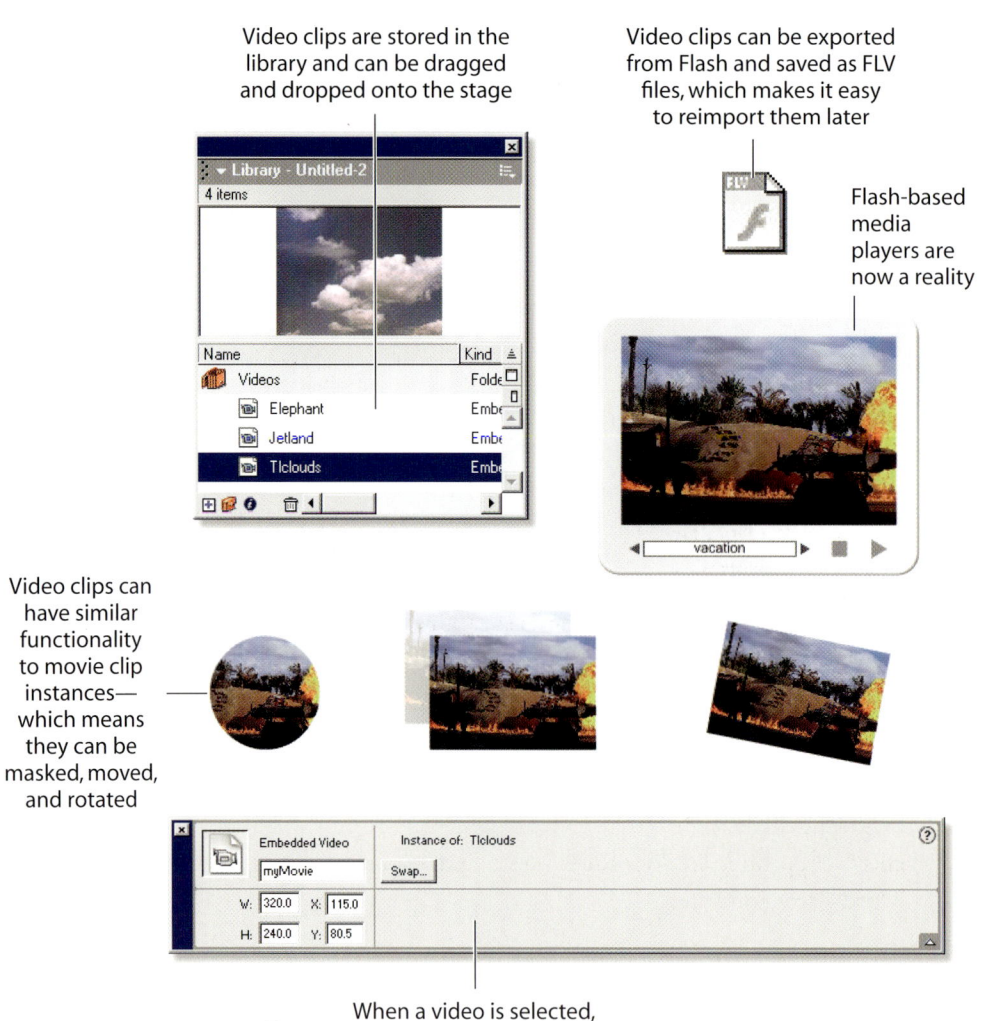

Video clips are stored in the library and can be dragged and dropped onto the stage

Video clips can be exported from Flash and saved as FLV files, which makes it easy to reimport them later

Flash-based media players are now a reality

Video clips can have similar functionality to movie clip instances—which means they can be masked, moved, and rotated

When a video is selected, the Property inspector allows you to configure it

On the CD

APPENDIX A

Using the Tutorials and Source Files

The video tutorials on the accompanying CD-ROM are in QuickTime format. To view them, you must have QuickTime 4 (or later) installed on your computer. (Since this is a common piece of software, you may have it on your machine already.) For your convenience, we've included the QuickTime 5 installer on this CD-ROM.

Most of the tutorials consist of a QuickTime video tutorial and a source file. To view a video tutorial, simply double-click its name. The QuickTime Player will start up, and the tutorial will begin to play. Use the QuickTime Player controls to play, stop, rewind, fast-forward, and skip to specific parts of the tutorial.

To open a Flash source file in the Flash authoring environment, simply double-click it. The source files are compatible only with Flash MX and will not open properly in older versions of the program.

In addition to the video tutorials, the CD contains the rest of this book's appendixes: "Appendix B: Keyboard Shortcuts," "Appendix C: Resource Sites," and "Appendix D: Third-Party Software."

The CD-ROM includes 30-day trial versions of Flash MX and Sorenson Squeeze.

Enjoy!

★★★★★★★★★★★★

Copyright 2002 Macromedia Press Inc., Derek Franklin. Individual items on this CD-ROM may be copyrighted by their licensors. All rights reserved worldwide.

Trademarks of all products provided on the CD-ROM are registered by their respective owners.

Limited Warranty and Disclaimer: This product is provided "as is," without warranty of any kind, express or implied, including but not limited to the implied warranties of merchantability and fitness for a particular purpose.

Limitation of Liability: Macromedia Press and Peachpit Press are not responsible for any damage or loss to your data or your equipment that results from the use of products, information, or instructions contained on this CD-ROM. Neither Macromedia Press, Peachpit Press, nor their providers will be liable to you or another party for any loss of profits or use, interruption of business, or indirect, special, incidental, or consequential damages of any kind.

Index

; (semicolon), 448
// (forward slashes), 449–450
{ } (curly brackets), 447, 448
( ) (parentheses), 449
" " (quotation marks), 449
[ ] (square brackets), 687
&& (AND operator), 467
= (assignment operator), 447, 462–463
\" (escape character), 159
< (less-than operator), 447
* (multiplication operator), 447
! (NOT operator), 467–468
|| (OR operator), 467
3D objects, 119
8-bit color, 215, 788
24-bit color, 215, 788
48-bit color, 215
256-color palette, 215
360-degree views, 222

A

accessibility features, 24, 42, 63–65, 252–253
Accessibility object, 544
Accessibility panel, 42, 64, 252–253
Acid/Acid Pro, 170
ACT files, 133, 134
actions
   adding multiple, 406–408
   attaching
      to buttons, 246–247, 388
      to movie clips, 247–250
   copying/cutting and pasting, 411
   deleting, 409
   descriptions of specific, 401
   frame, 333–334
   nesting, 408–409
   purpose of, 401, 446–447
   reordering sequence of, 409–410
   specifying targets for, 397–401
   using events to trigger, 387–397
Actions command, 323
Actions panel, 402–413
   advanced features, 519–533
      auto-formatting, 527–528

      code hints, 523–527
      creating/using external scripts, 529–531
      finding/replacing, 519–522
      printing scripts, 531
      setting preferences, 531–533
      syntax checking, 522–523
   attaching actions to objects with, 246–250, 405–406
   context-sensitivity of, 405
   new features, 24
   Normal/Expert modes, 402–405
   purpose of, 44, 402
   Target Editor, 513–514
   tutorials, 442, 533
   Undo/Redo commands, 411, 522
   working with scripts in, 406–413
ActionScript. *See also* scripts
   dictionary, 69, 543
   event handler methods, 487–499
   exercises/tutorials
      chaining loading/playback, 641–647
      controlling projector, 436–442
      controlling rotation/transparency, 601–603
      controlling timeline playback, 424–427
      creating keyboard shortcuts, 647–649
      creating media browser application, 854–896
      creating/using preloader, 662–667
      customizing component skin, 627–629
      detecting collisions, 668–670
      disabling Flash movie, 649–655
      displaying large movie clip, 619–621
      displaying product list, 604–607
      dynamic drawing, 677–681

      dynamic masking, 681–683
      dynamic naming, 686–690
      fast-forwarding/rewinding, 684–686
      integrating Flash with HTML, 655–659
      linking to URL, 419–423
      loading/unloading external movie, 429–436
      muting audio, 427–428
      navigating timeline, 414–419
      printing movie, 670–677
      registering component skin, 630–633
      scrolling text in text field, 615–616
      showing/hiding movie clip, 598–599
      styling component, 623–626
      using prototype objects, 659–662
      using Scrollbar component as slider, 616–618
   expressions, 468–470
   functions, 479–487
   listeners, 500–502
   objects, 535–581 (*See also* objects)
      descriptions of specific, 543–581
      how they work, 535–543
      purpose of, 535
   operators, 459–468
   performing specific tasks with
      adding components, 586
      adding movie clip to movie, 243
      addressing targets, 503–514
      adjusting movie-clip transparency, 244
      changing x/y values, 264
      controlling components, 596
      controlling sounds, 183
      creating empty movie clips, 231
      creating interactivity, 385, 386–401
      creating strokes/fills, 91

ActionScript, performing specific tasks with *(continued)*
  defining hit area of button, 250
  duplicating movie clips, 237, 280
  enabling/disabling buttons, 247
  filling text fields, 140, 152
  flipping instances, 279
  inserting images, 198
  inserting sounds, 173
  installing latest Player version, 814
  loading JPG files, 197
  producing motion tweens, 350
  setting Flash alignment on HTML page, 782
  setting height/width of text fields, 141
  setting masks, 304, 308
  setting text-field properties, 154
  setting/using variable values, 515
  setting `xscale`/`yscale` properties, 275
  using/changing timeline data, 514–516
  purpose of, 386
  recommended book on, 536, 896
  statements, 471–479
  syntax reference, 412–413
  variables, 451–459
ActionScript alerts, xii
ActionScript Editor tab, Preferences dialog box, 531–533
Active Server Pages, 819
ActiveX controls, 771
Add an Action button, 246, 247
Add Colors option, 134
Add Layer button, 172
Add Scene button, 325
Add Shape Hint command, 347
Adobe
  Illustrator, 119, 120, 799
  LiveMotion, 15
ADPCM compression, 187–188
.ai file extension, 799

AICC, 776
AIFF files, 169
Align panel, 40, 265–268
alignment
  of elements on stage, 264–268
  of graphics, 264
  of movies on HTML page, 782
  of text in text fields, 29
  tools, 48–49, 264–273
`_alpha` property, 556
alpha transparency, 215–216, 244
Alpha value, 128, 129, 244
analog sounds, 168
anchor points, 78, 93, 97–98, 103–104
anchors. *See* named anchors
AND operator, 467
animated GIFs, 212–215, 798
animation, 313–362
  creating, 341–357, 831–834, 857–860
  example, 358–362
  exporting, 795
  how it works, 314–316
  looping, 343
  methods, 314–316
  processor issues, 165–166, 341–342
  role of timeline in, 316
  of specific items
    bitmaps, 212–215
    frame sequences, 215
    symbol instances, 225
    text, 165–166, 381
  testing, 734
  tools, 166
  transitional, 214–215
  tutorials, 362
  working with frames in, 326–340
  working with scenes in, 324–326
Answers panel, 71
antialiasing, 53, 55, 138
`applyChanges()` method, 623
arithmetic operators, 460–462
array access operator, 687
Array object, 544–546, 874–876
arrow keys, 263
Arrow tool

editing lines/shapes with, 100–102
  options for, 77
  purpose of, 77
  reshaping path segment with, 96
  selecting elements with, 255–258
artwork, 75, 119. *See also* graphics
.as file extension, 529
ASCII key codes, 552
assignment operators, 447, 462–463
`attachMovie()` method, 198, 243, 586
`attachSound()` method, 173
attributes, HTML, 803–811
audience, defining your, 124–125
audio. *See also* sounds
  adding to HTML page, 658–659
  download-intensive nature of, 167
  muting, 427–428
  stopping playback of, 658
  tools for creating, 170
author-time sharing, 715
authoring environment, testing within, 734–735
authoring files
  and common libraries, 706–707
  exporting, 794–795
  file extension for, 21
  purpose of, 21
  saving as Flash 5 files, 54
  updating sounds in, 189–192
  and version control, 713
Authoring objects, 543
Authorware, Macromedia, 771
Auto Format Options dialog box, 528
auto-formatting, script, 527–528
Auto Kern option, 146
Auto Label option, 64
AutoCAD DXF, 120
Automatic Indentation option, 532
AVI files, 796
Aviation Industry CBT Committee, 776

Index

B

backgrounds
  for movies, 61–62
  for projects, 837
  for stage, 35–36
Bandwidth Profiler, 760–764
  displaying, 761
  information bar, 762–763
  purpose of, 760–761
  and RadioButton components, 588–589
  resizing, 761
banner ads, 17, 656–657
BASE attribute, 810
behaviors, 226, 231, 244–246, 701–702
BGCOLOR attribute, 808
bit depth, 788
bit rate, 189, 765
Bitmap Properties dialog box, 206–207
bitmaps, 193–222
  adding to movies, 197–198
  animated, 212–215
  breaking apart, 200–201
  compressing, 208–210
  contrasted with vector graphics, 11–12, 193
  converting to vector graphics, 202
  creating special effects with, 217–222
    360-degree views, 222
    motion blurs, 217–218
    panoramic views, 218–222
  exporting, 800
  file-size considerations, 208
  Flash support for, 12
  importing, 194–197, 207–208, 830–831
  Macintosh/Windows settings for, 53
  minimizing colors in, 208
  naming, 206
  optimizing, 207–210
  resolution of, 53, 207–208
  selecting colors in, 78, 201–202
  setting/viewing properties for, 206–207, 703
  supported file types, 195
  tracing, 202–205
  tutorial, 222
  updating, 211–212, 703
  using as fills, 111, 198–200
  using in shared libraries, 212
Black-and-White button, 127
Blend Type option, 345
blur effects, 217–218
Bold button, 145
Boolean object, 546
Boolean values, 454, 466–467
borders, text box, 153
bounding box, 256, 265–267
branches
  child/parent, 719
  double-clicking, 725–726
  expanding/collapsing, 722–723
  getting information about, 723–724
  viewing, 718–719
breadcrumb navigator bar, 241–242
Break Apart command, 86, 164–165, 201, 252
`break` statement, 477–479
Breakpoint controls, Debugger panel, 25, 745, 747, 752–757
brightness, color, 130
Brightness control, 128
browser scripting, 815
browsers. *See* Web browsers
Brush tool, 81–82, 92–93
buffering, 766–767
bugs, 44, 733, 744. *See also* Debugger panel; debugging
button actions, 388
Button object, 546–547
button symbols, 226, 232–234
buttons
  adding actions to, 246–247
  adding sound to, 840–841
  adding text to, 843–844
  adding to timeline, 841
  changing *x/y* values for, 264
  creating, 836–839
  defining hot spots for, 233
  defining states for, 233–234
  enabling/disabling, 247
  flipping, 279
  making into targets, 245
  naming, 25, 245
  scripting, 842–843
  setting accessibility options for, 252–253
  testing, 234, 734, 735
  tutorial, 254
  using movie clips as, 27, 234, 249–250

C

Calendar component, 638
Call stack, Debugger panel, 745, 747
calligraphy effect, 92
Canvas, Deneba, 119
Capabilities object, 547–548
cartoons, 313
CD-ROM, book's
  accompanying, xv, 72, 897–898
Center Frame button, 316, 320
chaining, 641–647
Change Direction of Text button, 150
Change Handler function, 592–596, 863–865
Character button, 153, 155
character-level formatting, 145–146
Character Options dialog box, 153
"Character position" setting, 146
"Character spacing" setting, 146, 155
Check Syntax button/command, 522–523
CheckBox component, 597–599, 860, 863–865
child branches, 719
child objects, 64, 508
chopping effect, 181
circles, 80, 90
classes. *See* object classes
CLASSID attribute, 804
Clear Colors option, 134
Clear command, 260, 730
Clear Frames command, 323
Clear Keyframe command, 323
`clearInterval()` action, 684–685
"Click accuracy" option, 100
click-and-wait, 7–8
Client/Server objects, 543
client/server relationship, 3

901

client software, 3–4. *See also* rich client
clip art, 119
clip events, 248, 250, 394–397, 514
clipboard, setting preferences for, 52–53
clock, computer, 651
Close All Panels command, 46
Close Panel command, 46
closed paths, 94
CLR files, 133, 134
code blocks, 451
code hints, 523–527, 532
Code window, Debugger panel, 745, 747
CODEBASE attribute, 805
codecs, video, 365
ColdFusion, 19, 819
Collapse Branch command, 723
Collapse Folder command, 704
collision detection, 668–670
color, 126–134
 creating, 128–129
 hex values for, 128, 130–131
 selecting, 126, 201–202
 for specific elements/objects
  bitmaps, 201–202
  fonts, 145, 160
  strokes/fills, 106, 107, 127
 tips for effective use of, 125
color boxes, 126
color controls
 Color Mixer panel, 127
 drawing toolbar, 106
color depth, 53
Color Mixer panel, 126–129
 bitmap settings, 202
 fill settings, 111–113, 127, 839
 purpose of, 40
 stroke settings, 107, 127
color modes, 129–131
Color object, 548–549
color palettes. *See* palettes
color space, 128
Color Swatches Options menu, 133
Color Swatches panel, 41, 132–133
color values, 128, 129

ComboBox component, 599–603, 860–863
Commands list, Keyboard Shortcuts dialog box, 58, 59
comments
 frame, 334–335
 script, 449–450
commercials, TV, 124
common libraries, 706–707
comparison operators, 464–466
Component Parameters panel, 42
components, 583–639
 adding/removing, 585–589
 Change Handler setting for, 592–596
 creating your own, 639
 customizing, 621–633
 downloading/installing, 634–639
 dynamically configuring, 863–865
 dynamically styling, 860–863
 Flash MX's built-in, 584 (*See also* specific components)
 methods/properties for, 584, 596–597
 naming, 590
 new features, 25
 providing interactivity with, 227, 583
 purpose of, 18, 583–584
 setting initial values for, 590–592
 tutorial, 639
 using specific, 596–621
Components panel, 41, 584
compression
 ADPCM, 187–188
 image, 208–210
 lossless, 210, 215
 lossy, 188, 209
 MP3, 188
 Photo (JPEG), 209–210
 Raw, 189
 sound, 185–189
 Speech, 189
 SWF, 29
 video, 365
conditional statements, 471–473
conflict resolution, library, 27
"Connect lines" option, 99
connecting shapes, 104, 105

constructors, 542
content
 creating, 23
 distributing, 15, 23–24
 streaming, 13, 23
context menus, 33
context-sensitive interfaces, 37, 76
continue statement, 477–479
contouring, 117
controller toolbar, 31, 32
Convert Lines to Fills command, 78, 117
Convert to Blank Keyframes command, 323, 333
Convert to Keyframes command, 233–234, 323, 333
Convert to Symbol command/dialog box, 228–229, 230
copier effect, 210
Copy command, 281, 411, 730
Copy Frames command, 295, 323
copying and pasting
 actions, 411
 elements, 281–282
Core objects, 543
CorelDraw, 119
corner points, 97, 102
courses, online, 776
Create Motion command, 322
Create Motion Tween command, 349
createEmptyMovieClip() method, 231
createTextField() method, 140
cross-fading effect, 183
curly brackets ({ }), 447, 448
Current Layer mode, 290
current movie, 398–399, 503–504
_currentframe property, 557
curve points, 97
curved paths, 95–96
curves, smoothing, 100
Custom Modem Settings dialog box, 765
Cut command, 281, 411, 730
Cut Frames command, 323
cutout effect, 307
cutting and pasting
 actions, 411
 elements, 281–282

Index

D

data
  changing on specific timelines, 514–515
  using in scripts, 447
  validating, 8, 16, 867
data event, 395
date, displaying current, 17
Date object, 549–551
Debug Movie command, 745, 749, 754
Debug Options button, 753
Debugger Options button, 745, 747
Debugger panel, 745–757
  debugging projects with, 747–757
  interface, 745–747
  new features, 25
  placing breakpoints in scripts from, 754
  purpose of, 44–45
debugging, 744–759. *See also* testing
  exercise, 747–757
  and guide layers, 301
  new features, 25
  and passwords, 758, 759
  remote, 757–759
  stopping, 757
decimal values, converting hex to, 131
Default Text Orientation option, 151
Delay slider, 532
Delete Layer button, 293, 309
Delete Scene button, 325
Delete Set button, 61
delivery methods, movie, 770–793
  Flash, 771–774
  GIF, 782–786
  HTML, 774–782
  JPEG, 786–787
  PNG, 787–789
  projectors, 792–793
  QuickTime, 790–791
demos, product, 204, 222
Deneba Canvas, 119
Deployment Kit, Flash, 814–815
Derek Franklin Web site, 896
design tools, Web, 5

Designer Development Center, Macromedia MX, 20
developers, and Flash rich-client environment, 11–20
Developers Center, Flash MX, 71
device fonts, 148–149, 159
Dictionary, ActionScript, 69, 543
digital sampling, 168
dimensions, movie, 61, 62
Director, Macromedia, 771
DirectX, 364
Disney cartoons, 313
Display List window
  Debugger panel, 745, 746, 749–751
  Movie Explorer, 718–730
    double-clicking items in, 725–726
    editing symbols in, 727
    getting information from, 723–724
    hiding/showing elements in, 722
    looking up symbol definitions in, 727
    purpose of, 718
    searching by keyword in, 727–728
    setting context of, 720–721
    spell-checking text in, 729–730
display options, 55
Distort button, 102
Distort feature, 26
Distort option, Free Transform tool, 83
Distribute options, Align panel, 266–267
Distribute to Layers command, 26, 164, 297–298
dithering, 785, 788–789
docking/undocking
  panels, 46–47, 51
  timeline, 51
  toolbars, 31–32
Document Properties dialog box, 61, 268, 780, 829
dot syntax, 448
Down state, 233
download performance, testing, 760–767
downloading

audio, 167
  components, 634–639
  screen reader, 63
drag-and-drop interactions, 885–887
Drag Content value, 619
drag-selecting, 258
draggable maps, 851–854
DraggablePane component, 638
dragOut event, 389
dragOver event, 389
drawing
  dynamic, 26, 677–681
  setting preferences for, 99–100
  simple shapes, 87–93
drawing toolbar, 31, 32, 76, 106
drawing tools. *See also* specific tools
  descriptions of specific, 76–85
  keyboard shortcuts for, 77
  purpose of, 75
  terminology associated with, 76
Dreamweaver, 19, 815
drop-shadow effect, 118
Dropper tool, 84, 108, 109, 113, 114
_droptarget property, 557
Duplicate command, 280
Duplicate Scene button, 326
Duplicate Symbol command, 236–237
duplicateMovieClip() method, 237, 280
DXF files, 120, 799
dynamic animation, 857–860
dynamic drawing, 26, 677–681
dynamic images, 655–656
dynamic masks, 26, 681–683
dynamic movie layout, 26
dynamic naming, 686–690
dynamic text, 136, 139–142, 151–154, 156–160

E

Easing option, 345
echoing effect, 182
Edit Document command, 848
Edit Envelope dialog box, 178–179
Edit Grid command, 269–270, 837
Edit Guides command, 270

Edit in New Window command, 240, 241
Edit in Place feature, 240–241
Edit Multiple Frames feature, 258, 339–340
editing
  and breadcrumb navigator bar, 241–242
  frames, 339–340
  setting preferences for, 99–100, 151
  specific elements/items
    fills, 113
    groups, 262
    lines, 100–102
    shapes, 100–106
    sounds, 178–179, 192
    symbols, 239–242, 727
    text, 86, 143–144
Editing tab, Preferences dialog box, 99–100, 151
Effect pop-up menu, 175, 179
effects
  360-degree view, 222
  blur, 217–218
  calligraphy, 92
  chopping, 181
  copier, 210
  cross-fading, 183
  cutout, 307
  drop-shadow, 118
  echoing, 182
  focus, 306, 661
  hole, 307
  magnifying-glass, 306
  morphing, 218, 316, 343
  motion blur, 217–218
  panning, 180, 183
  panoramic view, 218–222
  pulsing, 182
  scattered-light, 308
  shattered-mirror, 308
  sound, 167, 180–183
  spotlight, 307
  swooshing, 181
  text, 166
  transition, 360–362
  wave, 308
  window, 307
  X-ray, 307
elements, 255–282

copying/cutting and pasting, 281–282
creating/editing groups of, 261–262
defined, 76
deleting, 260, 281
distributing to layers, 296–298
duplicating, 280
grouping/ungrouping, 86
hiding bounding box for, 256
hiding/showing, 36
locking/unlocking, 260–261
positioning on stage, 262–273
selecting/deselecting, 100, 255–261
transforming, 273–279
tutorial, 282
email, contacting author via, xvi, 896
<EMBED> tag, 28, 802–803
embedded fonts, 148, 153, 159
Embedded Video Properties dialog box, 373–375
EMF files, 120, 799
Enable Live Preview command, 592
Enable Simple Buttons option, 234, 735
engines, 583
Enhanced Metafile format, 120. *See also* EMF files
enterFrame event, 395
Envelope option, Free Transform tool, 83
envelopes, 26, 103–104
EPS files, 799
Eraser tool, 84–85, 105–106
escape character, 159
event handler methods, 487–499
  contrasted with clip/mouse events, 250
  lists of, 489, 494–495
  projects/exercises
    using on buttons/movie clips, 490–494
    using with text fields, 496–499, 866–867
  purpose of, 487–488
events
  executing scripts in response to, 26
  purpose of, 446

types of, 387–397 (*See also* specific types)
Exchange, Macromedia, 634
.exe file extension, 792
Expand Branch command, 723
Expand Fill dialog box, 118
Expand Folder command, 704
Expand Shape command, 117–118
Expert mode
  contrasted with Normal mode, 54
  purpose of, 404
  setting as default, 405
  warning message, 54
Export Movie command/dialog box, 795–796
"Export on first frame" option, 712
Export QuickTime dialog box, 797
Export Windows AVI dialog box, 796
exporting
  as alternative to Publish feature, 794–795
  color palettes, 133–134, 785
  images, 795
  movies/video, 21–22, 374–375, 794–795
expressions
  order of precedence for, 470
  purpose of, 468–469
Extension Manager, 634–639
extensions
  file (*See* specific file extensions)
  Flash MX, 69–70
Extensions Manager, 70
external movies
  chaining loading/playback of, 641–645
  loading/unloading, 429–436
external scripts, 529–531
external targets, 400–401
Eyedropper tool, 36, 126

F

Fast display option, 55
fast-forwarding, 684–686
Faucet option, Eraser tool, 84, 106
FCLR files, 133
ffRew() function, 684–685

Index

.fhx file extension, 120
file compression. *See* compression
file formats
  bitmap, 195
  color palette, 133
  sound, 169
  vector graphics, 120
  video, 364–365
files
  controlling size of, 12, 22, 62, 208, 224
  exporting (*See* exporting)
  finding in folders, 705
  importing (*See* importing)
  managing, 693, 697–700, 717
Fill Color control, 106, 127
Fill Transform tool, 83, 114–116, 200
fills, 109–118
  choosing color for, 106, 127
  copying, 114
  creating, 112
  editing, 113
  reshaping lines/shapes with, 101–102
  setting default, 110, 111
  straightening/smoothing with, 100–101
  transforming, 114–116
  types of, 111
  using bitmaps as, 198–200
Find and Replace feature, 519–522
Find button, 520
Find dialog, 520
Find in Library command, 728–729
Find Next button, 520
Fireworks
  and flattened images, 195
  importing from, 195–197
  purpose of, 19
  updating images imported from, 211–212
Fireworks PNG Import Settings dialog box, 196
First Frame behavior, 245
FLA files, 21, 706. *See also* authoring files
Flash Alignment settings, HTML, 781–782
Flash Deployment Kit, 814–815
Flash Exchange, 69

Flash Folio Media Browser project, 854–896
  knowledge required for, 855
  purpose of, 855
  structure of, 856–857
  tasks covered in, 854–855
    attaching movie clips, 867–871
    browsing JPGs, 878–887
    configuring components, 863–865
    creating animation, 857–860
    creating/filling text fields, 873–878
    creating/using LoadVars object, 871–873
    loading external MP3s, 887–896
    styling components, 860–863
    using event handler methods, 866–867
Flash format. *See* SWF files
Flash Format tab, Publish Settings dialog box, 772
Flash movies. *See also* movies
  accessing sample, 70
  contrasted with regular movies, 285, 314
  controlling size of, 22
  converting authoring files to, 21–22
  disabling, 649–655
  distributing, 23–24
Flash MX
  components, 584, 596–621 (*See also* components)
  debugging tool, 744–745
  Developers Center, 71
  as drawing tool, 75
  extending capabilities of, 69
  features/benefits, 5–20
    for developers, 11–20
    for users, 5–10
  help features, 68–71
  how it works, 21–24
  identifying creators of, 71
  integrating
    with HTML, 17–18, 655–659
    with other MX applications, 19–20
  interface, 30–49

Learning Components, 776
lessons/tutorials, 69, 70, 72, 898
  (*See also* tutorials)
  as media player, 10
  as multiplatform standard, 14–15
  new features, 24–29, 68
  options/settings, 50–61
    display options, 55
    keyboard shortcuts, 57–61
    Preferences dialog box, 50–55
    viewing options, 56–57
  project management tools, 693, 717
  Publish feature, 769, 794, 801, 815 (*See also* publishing movies)
  registering, 71
  and rich-client experience, 3–11, 16
  testing tools, 733 (*See also* testing)
  trial version, 897
  user manual/documentation, 69
  video features, 363 (*See also* video)
  as Web design tool, 5, 14
  as word processor, 135, 145
Flash Player
  automatically installing latest version of, 813–814
  button, 812–813
  detecting installed version of, 814–815
  popularity of, 15, 812
  providing alternative to, 23–24, 771, 813
  and vector graphics, 120
  version considerations, 812
Flash projects. *See* projects
Flash Support Center, 70
Flash tab, Publish Settings dialog box, 185–186, 758
Flash UI Components Set 2, 638–639
Flash Video files. *See* FLV files
FlashVar attribute, 811
flattened images, 195
Flip commands, 278–279
FLV files, 364, 365, 366, 374–375
focus effect, 306, 661

_focusrect property, 558
folders
　creating, 703–704
　expanding/collapsing, 310, 704
　finding items in, 705
　moving items into, 704–705
　organizing/placing layers in, 309–310
Foley artists, 285
<font face> tag, 159
font mapping, 26, 52, 149
<font size> tag, 160
font symbols
　creating, 161–162
　formatting text with, 162
　purpose of, 161, 227
　updating style associated with, 162–163
　using shared libraries, 163
<font> tag, 159
fonts
　and antialiasing, 138
　choosing color for, 145, 160
　device, 148–149, 159
　embedding, 148, 153, 159
　warning message for missing, 54
for statement, 477
Formats tab, Publish Settings dialog box, 770–771
formatting
　character-level, 145–146
　with font symbol, 162
　paragraph-level, 147–148
　rich-text, 156–160
　script, 527–528
forms, HTML *vs.* Flash, 9
forward slashes (//), 449–450
fps, 61. *See also* frame rate
frame actions
　adding, 334
　purpose of, 333
　testing, 734, 735
frame-by-frame animation, 314–315, 327, 342–343, 362
Frame-by-Frame graph, 763–764
frame comments, 334–335
frame events, 393–394
frame labels, 295, 334–335, 378, 834–836
frame rate, 61, 318, 319
frame-sequence animation, 215
Frame View button, 316, 320

Frame Width options, 320–321
frames, 326–340. *See also* keyframes
　adding/deleting, 322, 332, 333
　and animated GIFs, 212
　contrasted with keyframes, 328–329
　converting to keyframes, 233–234
　duplicating, 331
　editing multiple, 339–340
　extending/shortening sequence of, 331
　listing objects for, 739
　listing variables for, 740
　moving, 331
　purpose of, 326
　relationship between layers and, 288
　reversing order of, 333
　selecting, 51, 330–331
　types of, 327–330
　viewing multiple, 338
　warning message on insertion of, 54
_framesloaded property, 558
Franklin Web site, Derek, 896
Free Transform tool, 27, 82–83, 102, 276, 372
FreeHand, 119, 120–122
FreeHand Import dialog box, 121–122
FreeHand Text option, 53
Fruityloops, 170
fscommand() action, 436–442, 806
FStyleFormat object, 623–626, 627, 860–863
full-motion video, 363. *See also* video
functions, 479–487
　calling, 479, 482, 484, 486–487, 515
　defining, 480–481, 484
　dynamic naming in, 688
　and multiple timelines, 515
　passing values to, 482–484
　purpose of, 479
　returning results from, 484–485
　using local variables in, 486
FutureSplash Player, 796

G

Gap Size option, Paint Bucket tool, 84, 114
General tab, Preferences dialog box, 50–52
Generator, 54
Get Macromedia Flash Player button, 812–813
getBytesLoaded() method, 666, 667
getBytesTotal() method, 666, 667
getTime() method, 650
getURL() action, 420–423
getVersion() function, 814
GIF files
　animated, 212–215, 798
　and color palettes, 133, 134, 785
　contrasted with JPEG/PNG, 215–216, 782, 786, 787
　and Publish Settings dialog box, 782–786
　and transparency settings, 194, 784
　when to use, 782
global objects, 518–519, 540
globalStyleFormat object, 622–623, 627
Go To action, 343
Go To Line dialog box, 519–520
Go to Symbol Definition command, 727
gotoAndPlay() action, 414–415, 734, 735
gotoAndStop() action, 414–415, 734, 735
gradient fills
　creating, 112–113
　and FreeHand, 121
　setting options for, 53
　transforming, 115–116
graphic objects. *See also* graphics
　breaking apart, 86, 102
　contrasted with simple shapes, 85–86
　distorting, 102
　examples of, 76
　types of, 86
graphic symbols
　behavior options for, 245
　creating, 231–232

Index

defined, 226
when to use, 226
working with timeline for, 228, 231–232
graphics, 75–134. *See also* bitmaps; images; vector graphics
  aligning, 264
  bitmap *vs.* vector, 11–13
  creating/changing, 13–14, 75, 120
  displaying random, 18
  file-size considerations, 12
  importing, 86, 119–122
  optimizing, 122–125, 207–210
  tools/options, 76–85
  tutorial, 134
graphs
  Frame-by-Frame, 763–764
  Streaming, 763–764
grids, 48–49, 269–270
gripper, panel, 45, 46
Group command, 261
groups, 86, 261–262
guide layers, 66–67, 295, 300–301
guides, 48–49, 270–271. *See also* motion guides

H

hand cursor, 659
Hand tool, 56
Hawaii Travel Application project, 828–854
  knowledge required for, 829
  setting up, 829–830
  tasks covered in
    adding buttons to timeline, 841
    adding frame labels, 834–836
    adding sound to buttons, 840–841
    adding text to buttons, 843–844
    controlling timeline playback, 834–836
    creating animation, 831–834
    creating buttons, 836–840
    creating draggable map, 851–854
    creating hyperlinks, 849–851
    creating self-running slide show, 844–846

masking graphical content, 847–848
placing slide show on timeline, 848–849
scripting buttons, 842–843
`HEIGHT` attribute, 804
`_height` property, 559
Help menu, 68–71
hex-to-decimal conversion table, 131
hex values, 128, 130–131, 160
Hidden mode, 291
Hide Edges command, 256
Hide Others command, 292
Hide Panel command, 46
hiding/showing
  bounding boxes, 256
  elements, 36, 721–722
  hand cursor, 659
  layers, 291, 292
  movie clip instances, 598–599
  panels, 46
  rulers, 268
  shape hints, 348
  toolbars, 32
  tooltips, 51
hierarchical movie structure
  expanding/collapsing branches in, 722–723
  getting information about items in, 724–726
  viewing, 718–720
Highlight Color option, 51–52
hints
  code, 523–527, 532
  shape, 343, 346–348
Hit state, 233, 234
`hitArea()` property, 250
`hitTest()` method, 668–670, 885
hole effect, 307
hot spots, 233
.hqx file extension, 792
HSB mode, 130
HTML
  forms, 9
  integrating Flash with, 17–18, 655–659, 801
  limitations of, 313
  and Publish Settings dialog box, 774–782
  publishing to, 774–775, 815
  tags, 156–157, 801–811

HTML-based text files, 157–158, 873–878
HTML tab, Publish Settings dialog box, 774–782, 815, 820
Html Template Info box, 777
hue, 130
hyperlinks, 849–851. *See also* URLs

I

IconButton component, 638
`ID` attribute, 805
`if/else if` statement, 472
`if/else` statement, 471–472
`if` statement, 471
illustration programs, 13
Illustrator, Adobe, 119, 120, 799
image editors, 198
images. *See also* graphics
  browsing, 878–885
  compressing, 208–210
  dynamic, 655–656
  exporting, 795
  flattened, 195
  importing, 830–831
  optimizing, 122–125, 207–210
  scaling, 880
Import Video Settings dialog box, 366–377
importing
  bitmaps, 194–197, 207–208, 830–831
  color palettes, 133–134
  from Fireworks, 195–197
  FreeHand files, 120–122
  graphics, 86
  sounds, 169–170
  symbols, 237–238
  vector graphics, 119–122
  video, 364–370
`#include` action, 529–531
indentation, script, 450–451, 528, 532
Info panel, 39, 263–264, 274
Ink Bottle tool, 83, 108–109
Ink option, Pencil tool, 81
input text blocks
  changing height/width of, 141
  creating, 139–141
  purpose of, 136, 154
  and rich-text formatting, 156–160
  settings for, 154–155

907

Insert Blank Keyframe command, 322, 333
Insert Frame command, 322
Insert Keyframe command, 322, 333
Insert Layer Folder button, 309
Insert Target Path dialog box, 513–514
insetting shapes, 117
instances
    adding to movies, 242–243
    animating, 225
    breaking apart, 251–252
    changing tint/transparency of, 243–244
    defined, 223
    defining, 244–246
    how they work, 223–225
    naming, 152, 245
    placing on timeline, 370–371
    setting accessibility options for, 252–253
    swapping, 373
interactivity. *See also* rich client
    adding to video clips, 375–380
    components' built-in, 227, 583
    HTML/JavaScript *vs.* Flash, 5–6
    primary ingredients for creating, 386–387
    project/exercises, 414–442
    purpose of, 385
interfaces
    capturing screen shots of, 204–205
    context-sensitive, 37, 76
    Debugger panel, 745–747
    Flash MX, 30–49
    Library panel, 694–696
    Movie Explorer, 717–726
    real-time, 8–9
    using metaphors for designing, 89
Internet
    and client/server relationship, 3
    devices for connecting to, 14–15
Internet Explorer, 811. *See also* Web browsers
Italic button, 145

J
Java, 806
JavaScript, 815, 819
JPEG compression, 209, 787
.jpeg file extension, 786. *See also* JPEG files
JPEG files
    contrasted with GIF/PNG, 215–216, 782, 786, 787
    export settings for, 800
    and Publish Settings dialog box, 786–787
JPEG tab, Publish Settings dialog box, 786–787
.jpg file extension, 786. *See also* JPG files
JPG files
    browsing dynamically loaded, 878–885
    dynamically loading, 197
    loading external, 27
    progressive, 197
justification, text, 155

K
kerning, 146, 155
key codes, ASCII, 552
Key object, 552
keyboard events, 392–393
keyboard shortcuts, 57–61
    creating, 60, 647–649
    disabling, 648
    for drawing tools, 77
    exercise/tutorial, 72, 647–649
    naming, 58, 61
    purpose of, 57
    removing, 60, 61
Keyboard Shortcuts dialog box, 58–61
keyDown event, 395
keyframe sequence, 328–329
keyframes
    adding, 322, 332–333
    assigning labels/comments to, 334–335
    bookmarking, 336
    contrasted with regular frames, 328–329
    converting frames to, 233–234
    identifying as named anchors, 335–337

purpose of, 314, 327–328
selecting, 330
setting intervals between, 367–368
keyUp event, 395
keyword-search feature, 727–728
keywords, 447

L
labels
    frame, 295, 334–335, 378, 834–836
    text, 136, 137–138
Lasso tool, 78–79, 259
layer folders, 309–310
layer modes, 290–292
layer outlines, 298–299
Layer Properties dialog box, 299, 304, 311–312
layers, 285–312
    changing stacking order for, 33, 287, 294–295
    copying, 296
    creating, 172, 288–289
    deleting, 292–293
    distributing elements to, 296–298
    elements that can be placed on, 286
    hiding/showing, 291, 292
    identifying graphical elements on, 298–299
    keeping track of elements on, 298–299
    linking/unlinking, 304–305
    locking, 291, 292
    mapping, 121
    modes for working with, 290–292
    naming, 725
    naming/renaming, 293
    organizing/placing in folders, 309–310
    purpose of, 286, 317
    relationship between frames and, 288, 317
    setting properties for, 311–312
    special-purpose, 302–308
        guide, 66–67, 295, 300–301, 311
        mask, 302–308, 847–848

motion guide, 308, 311
standardizing structure for, 294–295
tutorial, 312
using multiple, 34, 291–292, 317
Learning Components, Flash MX, 776
learning management system, 776
less-than operator (<), 447
lessons, Flash MX, 69, 70
levels
   loading movies on, 506
   undo/redo, 50–51
libraries. *See also* Library panel
   common, 706–707
   creating, 707
   deleting items from, 699–700
   dragging symbols between, 238, 713
   managing assets in, 697–700
   naming/renaming items in, 699
   opening, 707
   previewing assets in, 698
   selecting items in, 697–698
   shared (*See* shared libraries)
   special, 706–713
   tutorials, 716
   updating symbols from external, 713–716
   and version control, 713
Libraries folder, 706–707
library assets
   defined, 697
   deleting, 699–700
   icons for, 697
   managing, 697–700
   naming/renaming, 699
   previewing, 698
   selecting, 697–698
   in shared libraries, 708, 709–713
   viewing/organizing, 703–706
library conflict resolution, 27
Library panel, 693–706
   interface, 694–696
   opening, 694
   Options menu, 191, 698
   performing specific tasks in
      deleting items, 699–700
      dragging and dropping items, 27

      managing library assets, 697–700
      naming/renaming items, 699
      previewing items, 698
      selecting items, 697–698
      sorting items, 705–706
   purpose of, 42–43
   tutorial, 716
   working with specific items in
      bitmaps, 702–703
      folders, 703–706
      sounds, 190–192, 702–703
      symbols, 700–702
      videos, 702–703
Line tool, 78, 87
linear gradient fills, 111, 115
lines. *See also* strokes
   automatic connection of, 99
   changing length/angle of, 100
   configuring attributes for, 78
   constraining to angle, 87
   converting to fills, 78, 117
   drawing, 78, 79, 81, 87–88
   erasing portions of, 105–106
   recognizing, 100
   reshaping with fills, 101–102
   snapping to grid, 87
   straightening/smoothing, 100–101
`lineStyle()` method, 677
`lineTo()` method, 678, 680
Linkage Properties dialog box, 852
links, 849–851. *See also* URLs
List Objects command, 739
List Variables command, 740
ListBox component, 604–607
listeners, 500–502
Live music-composition tool, 170
Live Preview option, 592
LiveMotion, 15
Load Default Colors option, 134
`load` event, 248, 395
`loadMovie()` action, 197, 364, 379, 429–431, 506, 666
`loadSound()` method, 173
LoadVars object
   contrasted with `getURL()` action, 421
   creating/using, 553, 871–873
   event handler methods, 495
   purpose of, 553

LocalConnection object, 400
Locals tab, Debugger panel, 25, 746
Lock command, 260
Lock Fill option
   Brush tool, 82, 92
   Paint Bucket tool, 84, 114
Lock Others command, 292
Locked mode, 291
locking/unlocking
   elements, 260–261
   guides, 271
   layers, 291, 292
logical operators, 466–468
LOOP attribute, 807
Loop behavior, 245
looping
   animation, 343
   playback, 644–645
   sound, 170, 176
   statements, 474–476, 688–690, 876–877
lossless compression, 210, 215
lossy compression, 188, 209

M

Macintosh systems
   and bitmaps, 53
   and Flash toolbars, 31
   music-composition tools, 170
   and named anchors, 336
   vector formats, 120
Macromedia
   Authorware, 771
   ColdFusion, 19, 819
   Director, 771
   Dreamweaver, 19, 815
   Exchange, 634
   Extensions Manager, 70
   Fireworks (*See* Fireworks)
   Flash Exchange, 69
   Flash MX (*See* Flash MX)
   Flash MX Developers Center, 71
   Flash Support Center, 70
   FreeHand (*See* FreeHand)
   MX family of products, 19–20, 24 (*See also* specific products)
   Software Registration Center, 71
   Web site, 634, 896

Macromedia Flash MX ActionScripting, 536, 539, 543, 896
Magic Wand options, Lasso tool, 79, 259
magnification percentages, 56, 738
Magnifier tool, 57
magnifying-glass effect, 306
Makar, Jobe, 896
Make Child Objects Accessible option, 64
Make Movie Accessible option, 64
mapping
  color, 129
  font, 26, 52, 149
Mapping options, FreeHand, 121
maps, draggable, 851–854
markers, onion-skinning, 340
marquee-selecting, 258
mask layers, 302–308
  creating, 304, 847–848
  editing content on, 306
  how they work, 302–303
  linking layers to, 304
  purpose of, 302, 311
  unlinking layers from, 305
  ways of using, 306–308
masks
  dynamic, 26, 681–683
  video, 380–381
master elements, 223. *See also* symbols
master sounds, 183–192
  compressing, 185–189
  contrasted with sound instances, 183
  naming, 184
  setting properties for, 183–185
  updating, 189–192
  viewing digital representation of, 184
Match Size options, Align panel, 267, 268
Math object, 554
Maximum Chars option, 155
`maxscroll` property, 575
Media Browser project, 854–896
  knowledge required for, 855
  purpose of, 855

  structure of, 856–857
  tasks covered in, 854–855
    attaching movie clips, 867–871
    browsing JPGs, 878–887
    configuring components, 863–865
    creating animation, 857–860
    creating/filling text fields, 873–878
    creating/using LoadVars object, 871–873
    loading external MP3s, 887–896
    styling components, 860–863
    using event handler methods, 866–867
media players, 10, 812. *See also* Flash Player
`MENU` attribute, 810
menu bar, 32, 254
menus, 32–33. *See also specific* menus
MessageBox component, 638
metaphors, interface-design, 89
methods
  animation, 314–316
  event handler, 487–499, 866–867
  how they work, 539
  purpose of, 538–539
  recommended book on, 539
MIDI files, 169
MIME type, 811–812
mixing
  color (*See* Color Mixer panel)
  sound, 183
modem speeds, 765
Modify Onion Markers button, 340
morphing effect, 218, 316, 343
motion blurs, 217–218
motion guides, 308, 311, 356–357
motion-tweened animation, 322, 329–330, 348–356, 362
mouse events, 234, 249, 250, 388–391
Mouse object, 554–555
`mouseDown` event, 395
`mouseMove` event, 395

`mouseUp` event, 395
.mov file extension, 370, 790. *See also* QuickTime
`moveTo()` method, 677–678, 680
`MOVIE` attribute, 803
movie clip instances. *See also* MovieClip object
  adding actions to, 247–250
  behavior options for, 246
  changing *x/y* values for, 264
  controlling rotation/transparency of, 601–603
  controlling with radio buttons, 610–613
  flipping, 279
  hiding/showing, 598–599
  naming, 246
  setting accessibility options for, 252–253
  targeting, 504–505
  using as buttons, 27, 234, 249–250
movie clip symbols
  creating
    from animation on timeline, 235–236
    using animated GIFs, 213–214
  timeline for, 228, 235
  tutorial, 254
  ways of using, 226–227
movie elements, 76. *See also* elements
Movie Explorer, 717–730
  interface, 717–726
  opening, 718
  Options menu, 729, 730
  performing specific tasks in
    choosing scene mode, 722
    cutting/copying/clearing elements, 730
    editing symbols, 727
    finding symbols in library, 728–729
    looking up symbol definitions, 727
    printing, 730
    searching by keyword, 727–728

Index

selecting symbol instances, 729
setting view options, 720–723
spell-checking text, 729–730
viewing/editing assets, 724–725
purpose of, 43, 717
tutorial, 730
Movie Explorer panel, 43. *See also* Movie Explorer
Movie Explorer Settings dialog box, 721
Movie objects, 543
MovieClip object. *See also* movie clip instances
  importance of, 555
  methods, 555–566
  properties, 555–566
movies
  accessing sample, 70
  adding bitmaps to, 197–198
  adding symbol instances to, 242–243
  changing magnification of, 738
  choosing colors for, 125
  controlling playback of, 738 (*See also* playback)
  creating from templates, 815–819
  creating preloaders for, 662–665
  debugging, 44–45, 744–759
  disabling, 649–655
  exporting, 794–795
  file-size considerations, 22, 62, 224
  making accessible to visually impaired users, 64–65
  modifying layout dynamically, 26
  printing, 670–677
  publishing (*See* publishing movies)
  setting playback quality for, 738
  setting properties for, 61–62
  standardizing layer structure for, 294–295
  targeting, 503–504
  testing functionality of, 738–744 (*See also* testing)

using rich-text formatting in, 156–160
using sounds in, 167 (*See also* sounds)
MP3 compression, 188
MP3 files, 10, 169
  chaining loading/playback of, 646–647
  loading external, 27, 887–896
  ways of using, 659
MPEG-1 Layer 3, 188. *See also* MP3
multimedia, 10, 12–13. *See also* media players
multiplication operator (*), 447
music. *See also* sounds
  creating, 170
  playing, 17
  triggering emotions with, 167
MX Alert icon, xii, 29
MX applications, 19–20, 24. *See also* specific applications

N

NAME attribute, 806
_name property, 559
Named Anchor on Scene option, 51
named anchors, 27–28, 51, 335–337
naming
  bitmaps, 206
  buttons, 25, 245
  components, 590
  dynamic, 686–690
  instances, 152, 245
  keyboard shortcuts, 58, 61
  layers, 293, 725
  library assets, 699
  movie clip instances, 246
  objects, 525–526
  published HTML page, 820–821
  scenes, 325, 725
  sounds, 184
  variables, 456
navigation controls, timeline, 414–415
navigator bar, breadcrumb, 241–242
nested actions, 408–409

Netscape browser, 811. *See also* Web browsers
New Document dialog box, 66
New Folder button/command, 703–704
New From Template command, 66
New Symbol command, 213, 230
No Color button, 127
Normal mode, Actions panel, 402–404
NOT operator, 467–468
Number object, 566
number values, 453

O

object classes
  adding new methods to, 660–661
  creating, 542–543
  examples of, 541
  suffixes for, 526
object suffixes, 525–526
<OBJECT> tag, 28, 801–802
objects, 535–581. *See also* specific objects
  addressing/targeting, 503–514
  breaking apart, 85, 86
  classes of (*See* object classes)
  descriptions of specific, 543–581
  how they work, 535–543
  methods for, 538–539
  naming, 525–526
  organization into groups, 543
  properties for, 536–537
  prototype, 659–662
  purpose of, 535
  recommended book on, 536
  selecting, 77
  types of, 540–543 (*See also* specific types)
offsetting, 767
Onion Skin button, 338
Onion Skin Outlines button, 339
onion-skinning, 337–340
online courses, 776
online/offline status, checking for, 654–655
online resources, MX products, 20

911

online shopping, 8–9
on(press) event, 234, 249, 389
on(release) event, 234, 249, 389
on(rollOver) event, 249
Open as Library command, 237, 713
open paths, 94
operators, 459–468
   arithmetic, 460–462
   assignment, 462–463
   comparison, 464–466
   logical, 466–468
   purpose of, 447, 459
Optimize command, 123
Optimize Curves dialog box, 123
optimizing
   bitmaps, 207–210
   vector graphics, 122–125
Options button, panel, 45
Options menu
   Color Swatches, 133
   Library panel, 191, 698
   Movie Explorer, 729, 730
OR operator, 467
orientation, text, 151
Outline mode, 291
Outline options, Layer Properties dialog box, 299
outlines
   converting to fills, 117
   settings for, 107
   synonyms for, 76
   working with anchor points on, 78
Outlines display option, 55
Output command, 740
Oval tool, 80, 90
Over state, 232
overlays, 381

P

Paint Bucket tool, 83–84, 113–114
paint programs, 13
palettes
   defined, 132
   deleting swatches from, 132
   importing/exporting, 133–134, 785–786
panel sets, 48
panels, 38–48. *See also* specific panels
   common interface elements, 45

descriptions of specific, 39–45
docking/undocking, 46–47, 51
hiding/showing, 46
purpose of, 38
saving sets of, 48
panning effect, 180, 183
panoramic views, 218–222
paragraph-level formatting, 147–148
Parameters tab, Property inspector, 590
parent branches, 719
parent objects, 64, 505–506
parentheses, 449
Paste command, 282, 411
Paste Frames command, 323
Paste in Place command, 282
path segments, 93, 96
paths
   changing shape of, 96
   creating, 94–96
   open *vs.* closed, 94
   parts of, 93
   selecting anchor points in, 78
Pen tool, 93–100
   and anchor points, 97–98
   creating paths with, 94–96
   how it works, 93–94
   purpose of, 79
   setting preferences for, 99–100
Pencil tool, 81, 88
percentage values
   for resizing elements, 275
   for tints, 243
   for viewing content on stage, 56
periods, 448
personal information, updating, 6–8
Photo (JPEG) compression, 209–210
photographic images, 193
Phrazer, 170
PICT files, 53, 799
Pin button, 406
pixels, 11–12, 28, 193, 207–208, 273
placeholder frames, 327
placeholder movie clips, 879–880, 885
Plasma, 170

play() action, 424, 734, 735
PLAY attribute, 806–807
Play Once behavior, 245
playback
   chaining, 641–644, 646–647
   controls, 376–378, 381, 424–427, 684–686, 738
   looping, 644–645
   options
     GIF, 783
     HTML, 778
     QuickTime, 791
   quality settings, 738
   random, 645
Player
   Flash (*See* Flash Player)
   FutureSplash, 796
playhead, 316, 317–318
plug-ins, 10, 119
PLUGINSPAGE attribute, 805
PNG files
   and bitmaps, 194–195
   contrasted with GIF/JPEG, 215–216, 782, 787
   export settings for, 800
   exporting images as, 787
   importing, 195–196
   transparency settings for, 194
PNG tab, Publish Settings dialog box, 787–789
Polygon Mode option, Lasso tool, 79, 259
Portable Network Graphics. *See* PNG files
PostScript printers, 51, 53
Preferences dialog box, 50–55
   ActionScript Editor tab, 531–533
   Clipboard tab, 52–53
   Editing tab, 99–100, 151
   General tab, 50–52
   Warnings tab, 54
preloaders, 662–667
   and buffering, 767
   creating, 662–664
   purpose of, 662, 767
   using
     for external SWFs, 666
     for main movie, 664–665
     for sounds, 666–667
press event, 389

Index

Preview All Scenes command, 734
previewing
　components, 592
　library assets, 698
　publishing settings, 793–794
　scenes, 734
　video on timeline, 371–372
`print` action, 671
Print dialog box, 531
printing
　ActionScript *vs.* browser, 670
　on demand, 675–676
　disabling, 674
　hidden movies, 674–675
　from Movie Explorer, 730
　movies, 670–677
　scripts, 531
processor constraints, 55,
　341–342, 380
product demos, 204, 222
programming, 443. *See also* scripts
programming languages, 386. *See
　also* ActionScript
ProgressBar component, 638
progressive JPG, 197
project management tools, 693,
　717
projector files
　controlling, 436–442
　defined, 23, 792
　publishing movies as, 792–793
　purpose of, 23–24, 792
projects
　adding/removing components,
　　585–589
　basic steps for creating, 23
　creating from templates, 65–67
　　(*See also* templates)
　defining audience for, 124–125
　processor considerations,
　　341–342
　sample
　　Flash Folio Media Browser,
　　　854–896
　　Hawaii Travel Application,
　　　828–854
　testing, 733–734 (*See also*
　　testing)
　types of, 16–17, 23
　using animated GIFs in, 214
　using sound in, 167
　using transitions in, 360–362

working with video in,
　370–375
properties
　bitmap, 206–207
　document, 61, 268
　layer, 299, 304, 311–312
　movie, 61–62, 555–566
　object, 536–537
　purpose of, 536
　setting/reading, 536–537
　sound, 183–185
　symbol, 213, 230
　text-field, 154
　tutorial, 582
　video, 373–375, 379
　`xscale/yscale`, 275
Properties command, 323
Properties tab, Debugger panel,
　746, 750
Property inspector
　context-sensitivity of, 28
　Flash 5 panels replaced by, 37
　purpose of, 38
　settings/options
　　background color, 837
　　character-level formatting,
　　　145–146
　　components, 590–591
　　fill attributes, 110
　　font symbols, 161
　　Line tool, 78
　　motion tweens, 352
　　Oval tool, 80
　　paragraph-level formatting,
　　　147
　　Pen tool, 79
　　ScrollPane component, 853
　　sound instances, 174–176
　　static text fields, 148
　　stroke attributes, 107–108
　　symbol behaviors, 244–246
　　text editing, 143
　　Text tool, 843
　　tint/transparency, 243–244
prototype objects, 659–662
pseudo-symbols, 227
Publish feature, 769, 794, 801,
　815. *See also* publishing movies
Publish Preview command,
　793–794
Publish Settings dialog box,
　769–793

and bitmap compression, 209
and movie delivery methods,
　770–793
　Flash, 771–774
　GIF, 782–786
　HTML, 774–782
　JPEG, 786–787
　PNG, 787–789
　projectors, 792–793
　QuickTime, 790–791
and named anchors, 336–337
opening, 769
and remote debugging, 758
and sound compression, 186
publishing movies, 769–823. *See
　also* exporting
　choosing delivery method for,
　　770–793
　previewing settings prior to,
　　793–794
　purpose of, 769
　tutorial, 823
pulsing effect, 182
`push()` method, 874–875
PushButton component, 608,
　627–629

Q

QUALITY attribute, 807–808
quality options, HTML, 778–779
`_quality` property, 560
Quality settings, playback, 738
Quality slider, 366
QuickTime
　export settings, 797
　file formats, 364
　installer, 897
　integrating Flash with, 790
　movies, 22, 790–791
QuickTime tab, Publish Settings
　dialog box, 790–791
quotation marks, 449

R

radial gradient fills, 111, 116
RadioButton component,
　608–613
RAM allocation, 53
random banners, 656–657
`randomNumber` variable, 645
Raw compression, 189
"Recognize lines" option, 100

913

"Recognize shapes" option, 100
Rectangle tool, 80, 91
ReCycle, 170
Reference panel, 28, 71, 412–413, 638
registering skins, 629–633
Registration Center, Macromedia Software, 71
registration point, 229, 276, 279
registration section, Media Browser project, 855, 856
Registration Selection tool, 264, 275
`release` event, 389
`releaseOutside` event, 389
Remote Debug dialog box, 759
remote debugging, 757–759
remote location, disabling movie from, 651–653
Remove All Breakpoints button, 752, 754
Remove All Hints command, 348
Remove Frames command, 322, 333
Remove Shortcut button, 60
Remove Transform command, 279
`removeListener()` method, 626
Rename Set button, 61
"Render text as HTML" option, 153, 155, 156–157, 160
Replace All button, 522
Replace button, 522
Replace Colors option, 134
Replace dialog box, 521
resolution
 bitmap, 53, 207–208
 library conflict, 27
Reverse Frames command, 323, 333
RGB mode, 130
rich client
 defined, 3–4
 developer benefits, 11–20
 user benefits, 5–10
rich-text formatting, 156–160
`rollOut` event, 389
`rollOver` event, 389
`_root` timeline, 504, 516
Rotate option, Free Transform tool, 82

rotating
 shapes, 276–278
 video, 372
`_rotation` property, 560
Round Rectangle Radius option, 80
ruler
 for aligning objects, 48–49, 268
 timeline, 316, 318
run-time sharing, 715

S
`SALIGN` attribute, 809
sample rate, 168, 188
sample size, 168
sampling, color, 84
saturation, 130
Save as Default option, 134
Save as Flash 5 feature, 28, 54
Save As Template command/dialog box, 67–68
Save Colors option, 134
Save Panel Layout command/dialog box, 48
Scale and Rotate command, 275
`SCALE` attribute, 808–809
Scale option, Free Transform tool, 82
Scale settings, HTML, 780–781
Scale slider, 368
scaling
 defined, 274
 with Free Transform tool, 372
 and image quality, 372, 880
 with Info panel, 274
 with Scale slider, 368
 with Transform panel, 275, 879–880
scattered-light effect, 308
Scene button, 49
Scene panel, 41, 325
scenes
 adding/deleting, 325
 duplicating, 326
 naming/renaming, 325, 725
 navigating between, 326
 previewing, 734
 purpose of, 324
 reordering, 326
 testing, 736
SCORM, 776

SCR attribute, 804
screen reader
 detecting presence of, 65, 253, 659
 downloading demo version of, 63
 purpose of, 63
 and symbol instances, 252
screen shots, tracing interface, 204–205
script elements, 446–451. *See also* specific elements
scripts. *See also* ActionScript
 adding breakpoints to, 753–757
 auto-formatting, 527–528
 checking syntax in, 522–523
 creating/using external, 529–531
 debugging, 25, 301, 744–759
 deconstructing, 444–446, 516–517
 finding/replacing content in, 519–522
 going to specific line number in, 519–520
 indenting, 450–451, 528, 532
 printing, 531
 setting preferences for, 531–533
 using white space in, 450–451
`scroll` property, 574
ScrollBar component, 142, 614–618
ScrollPane component, 618–621, 851–854
scrubbing, 317
search engines, 17
search feature
 ActionScript, 519–522
 Movie Explorer, 727–728
segmenting, shape, 104–105
segments, path, 93, 96
Select All command, 258
Select All Frames command, 323
Select Symbol Instances command, 729
Selectable option, 148, 153
Selection object, 566–567
Selection Options, Preferences dialog box, 51
semicolon, 448

Index

server
  hiding interactions with, 10
  minimizing interactions with, 7–8, 16
  software, 3, 811–812
`setInterval()` action, 28, 684
`setMask()` method, 304
`setPan()` method, 183
`setScrollContent()` method, 619
`setStyleProperty()` method, 627
`setVolume()` method, 183
shape hints, 343, 346–348
shape-recognition feature, 88–89, 100
shape-tweened animation, 329–330, 343–348, 362
shapes
  applying strokes/fills to, 106–118
  choosing colors for, 106
  connecting, 104, 105
  creating, 87–93
  distorting, 102
  editing, 100–106
  erasing portions of, 105–106
  expanding, 117
  recognizing/perfecting, 100
  reshaping
    with envelopes, 103–104
    with fills, 101–102
  rotating, 276–278
  segmenting, 104–105
  softening edges of, 117, 118
  straightening/smoothing, 100–101
Shareable Content Object Reference Model, 776
shared libraries, 707–713
  benefits of using, 708
  compared with common libraries, 707
  creating/using library assets in, 709–713
  defined, 709
  library assets included in, 708
  tutorial, 716
  using bitmaps in, 212
  using sounds in, 192
  using symbols in, 163, 239

shared objects, 28
sharing, author- vs. run-time, 715
shattered-mirror effect, 308
Shift Select option, 51
Shift-selecting, 257
shopping-cart application, 8–9
shortcuts. See keyboard shortcuts
Show All command, 291
Show All option, 56
"Show border around text" option, 153, 155
Show Frame option, 56
Show/Hide buttons, 722
Show/Hide filters, 721–722
Show Pen Preview option, 99
Show Precise Cursors option, 99
Show Shape Hints command, 348
Show Solid Points option, 99
Show Streaming command, 763
Show Tooltips option, 51
showing/hiding
  bounding boxes, 256
  elements, 36, 721–722
  hand cursor, 659
  layers, 291, 292
  movie clip instances, 598–599
  panels, 46
  rulers, 268
  shape hints, 348
  toolbars, 32
  tooltips, 51
simple shapes. See also shapes
  contrasted with graphic objects, 85–86
  creating, 87–93
  defined, 76
  editing, 100–106
  types of, 85
Single Frame behavior, 245
size considerations
  for bitmaps, 208
  for graphics, 12
  for movies, 22, 62, 224
  for sound, 168
skewing, 276–278
skins
  customizing, 627–629
  registering, 629–633
slashes (//), 449–450
slide shows, 844–846, 848–849
sliders

Delay, 532
Quality, 366
Scale, 368
using Scrollbar components as, 616–618
Smart Clips, 18, 25, 584
Smooth button, 101
"Smooth curves" option, 100
Smooth option
  Arrow tool, 77
  Pencil tool, 81
snapping, 271–273
  to grids, 87, 269
  to guides, 271
  to objects, 77
  to pixels, 28, 273
  to points, 272
Soften Fill Edges dialog box, 118
Software Registration Center, Macromedia, 71
solid fills, 111
Sonar, 170
Sonic Foundry, 170
Sorenson
  Spark codec, 365
  Squeeze codec, 364, 365, 897
  Web site, 365
sorting
  in Color Swatches panel, 134
  in Library panel, 705–706
sound effects, 167, 180–183. See also sounds
Sound object, 567–569
  loading external MP3s into, 887–896
  methods, 173, 183, 495
  volume/panning controls, 378–379
Sound Properties dialog box, 183–185
sound timeline, 179
sound waves, 168
`_soundbuftime` property, 561
sounds, 167–192
  adding to buttons, 840–841
  adding to timeline, 171–173
  adjusting volume of, 179, 180, 183, 378–379
  balancing quality/file size, 168
  chopping, 181
  compressing, 185–189

915

sounds, 167–192 *continued*
  configuring, 174–176
  cross-fading, 183
  echoing, 182
  editing, 178–179
  event-driven, 175, 177
  fading, 175
  how they work, 168
  importing, 169–170
  inserting dynamically, 173
  instances of, 171, 183
  looping, 170, 176
  master (*See* master sounds)
  mixing, 183
  muting, 427–428
  naming, 184
  new features, 28
  panning, 180, 183, 378–379
  placing on separate layers, 173, 295
  pulsing, 182
  recording, 169
  sample, 183
  saving, 191
  setting/viewing properties for, 183–185, 703
  streaming, 176, 177
  swooshing, 181
  synchronizing, 175
  testing, 179, 185, 186, 734
  tutorials, 192
  updating, 189–192, 703
  using in shared libraries, 192
  using preloader for, 666–667
soundtracks, movie, 167
source files, 897
spacing, character, 146, 155
Span Based Selection option, 51
Spark codec, Sorenson, 365
special effects. *See* effects
special libraries, 706–713
Speech compression, 189
speed considerations, 55, 341–342
spell-checker, 729–730
spirals, 119
.spl file extension, 120, 796
SplitView component, 639
spotlight effect, 307
squares, 80, 91
Squeeze codec, Sorenson, 364, 365, 897

stacking order, 33, 287
stage, 255–282
  changing background color of, 35–36
  deleting contents of, 106
  positioning elements on, 262–273
  purpose of, 35, 255
  selecting elements on, 255–261
  stacking order for layers on, 287
  transforming elements on, 273–279
  tutorial, 282
  working with groups of elements on, 261–262
  zooming in/out on, 56, 57
Stage object, 572
`Stage.align` property, 782
standard toolbar, 31
`start()` method, 183
`startDrag()` action, 885
statements, 471–479
  `for`, 477
  `with`, 507
  `break`, 477–479
  `continue`, 477–479
  `if`, 471
  `if/else`, 471–472
  `if/else if`, 472
  `switch`, 29, 472–473
  `while`, 474–475
states, button
  defining, 232–234
  testing, 734
static text, 135, 136, 137–139, 148–151
status bar, timeline, 316, 318
status toolbar, 32
Step In button, 752, 755
Step Out button, 752, 756
Step Over button, 752, 756, 757
`stop()` action, 424, 734, 735, 835–836
Stop Debugging button, 752, 757
`stopAllSounds()` action, 427–428
`stopDrag()` action, 886
storyboards, 120
straight lines. *See* lines
Straighten button, 101

Straighten option
  Arrow tool, 77
  Pencil tool, 81
streaming
  creating custom speeds for, 765
  maximizing, 766–767
  sound, 176, 177
  testing, 760–767
  video, 13, 380
Streaming bar, 763
Streaming graph, 763–764
String object, 569–572
strings, 453–454
Stroke Color control, 106, 107, 127
strokes. *See also* lines
  adding/changing, 108–109
  choosing color for, 106, 107, 127
  copying attributes between images, 109
  setting attributes for, 106–108
  types of, 107
style properties, 622
styles
  component, 622–627
  font symbol, 162–163
submenus, 32
Subselect tool, 78, 96, 97–98
suffixes, object, 525–526
Swap Colors button, 128
Swap Embedded Video dialog box, 373
Swap Symbols button, 251
swatches, 41, 132, 133
SWD files, 757
.swf file extension, 22. *See also* SWF files
SWF files
  compressing, 29, 773
  dealing with large, 379
  debugging, 757–759
  delivering Flash movies as, 771–772
  export settings for, 796
  importing, 120
  and LiveMotion, 15
  popularity of, 119, 771
  public availability of, 15
  and Publish Settings dialog box, 771–774

Index

using preloader for, 666
Swish, 166
`switch` statement, 29, 472–473
`SWLIVECONNECT` attribute, 806
swooshing effect, 181
Symbol button, 49
symbol-editing mode, 239–240, 702
Symbol Properties dialog box, 213, 230, 712, 714
symbols, 223–254
   animating, 225
   breaking apart, 251–252
   changing behaviors for, 701–702
   creating, 228–236, 700–701
   defined, 86
   dragging between libraries, 238, 713
   duplicating, 236–237, 701
   editing, 239–242, 727
   guiding principle behind, 223
   how they work, 223–225
   impact on file size, 224
   importing, 237–238
   looking up definitions of, 727
   placing one within another, 227
   searching for, 728–729
   setting accessibility options for, 252–253
   setting registration point for, 229
   swapping, 251
   tutorials, 254
   types of, 226–227 (*See also* specific types)
   using in shared libraries, 239
   viewing properties for, 701
   when to use, 225
   working with instances of, 242–253
   working with timelines for, 228
Synchronize Symbols command, 323
synchronizing
   sound, 175
   symbols, 323
   video, 368
syntax checking, 522–523

T

T-square icon, 300
tags, HTML, 156–157, 801–811
tangent handles, 93, 103–104
Target Editor, 503
`_target` property, 561
targets
   addressing in ActionScript, 503–514
   defining, 146, 245, 513–514
   and `onClipEvent`, 514
   tutorial, 442
   types of, 397–401
templates, 815–823
   creating, 67–68, 816–819
   customizing, 67
   and Publish feature, 815
   purpose of, 29, 65, 815
   saving, 819
   starting new projects from, 66–67
   variables used in, 822–823
Test Movie command, 231, 241, 247, 371, 736
Test Scene command, 736
testing, 733–744. *See also* debugging
   in Flash authoring environment, 734–735
   importance of, 733
   in testing environment, 736–744
      with List Objects command, 739
      with List Variables command, 740
      with Output command, 740
      with Test Movie command, 736
      with Test Scene command, 736
      with `trace()` action, 740–744
   tips for performing, 733–734
testing timeline, 763
text, 135–166. *See also* text blocks; text elements
   adding to buttons, 843–844
   animating, 165–166, 381
   associating URL with, 146, 850
   breaking apart, 164–165
   dynamic (*See* dynamic text)
   editing, 143–144
   formatting, 145–148, 162
   HTML-formatted, 135, 156–160
   scrolling, 141–142, 574–575, 615–616
   selecting, 143–144
   spell-checking, 729–730
   static, 135, 136, 137–139, 148–151
   tutorial, 166
   vertical, 29, 150–151, 574–575
text blocks. *See also* text elements
   aligning text vertically in, 29
   animating, 165
   breaking apart, 86
   changing width of, 138–139
   defined, 136
   editing, 86, 143–144
   embedding font information in, 148
   loading HTML-based files into, 157–158
   selecting, 143–144
   types of, 136
text-edit mode, 143, 144
text effects, 166
text elements. *See also* text blocks
   changing core attributes for, 142–143
   changing height/width of, 141
   choosing font for, 138
   creating, 136–142
   editing/configuring, 142–160
   types of, 136
   ways of using, 135
text fields
   changing background of, 661–662
   and event handlers, 494, 866–867
   filling with HTML-formatted text, 873–878
   and instance names, 140
   resizing, 141–142
   scrolling text in, 142, 615–616
   validating data in, 867–871
text labels, 136, 137–138
Text menu, 146
text overlays, 381

Text tool, 137–139, 843–844, 850
TextField object
  creating, 572–575
  event handler methods, 494, 866–867
  and instance names, 140
  purpose of, 29
TextFormat object, 29, 576–577
this keyword, 660
Ticker component, 639
ticks, frame, 318
time-expired movies, 649–651
Time In/Out controls, 179, 181
Timeline menu, 322–323
Timeline Options, Preferences dialog box, 51
timelines, 316–323
  adding buttons to, 841
  adding sounds to, 171–173
  controlling playback of, 424–427, 684–686, 834–836
  docking/undocking, 51
  moving, 35
  navigation controls, 414–419
  parts of, 316–323
  placing video clips on, 370–371
  purpose of, 33, 316
  resizing, 34–35
  selecting elements using, 260
  setting preferences for, 51
  using/changing data on, 514–515
  working with frames in, 330–335
  working with multiple, 502–519
tint percentages, 243
title bar, panel, 45
To Stage button, 267
Toggle Breakpoint button, 752, 754
toolbars, 31–32. See also specific toolbars
Toolbox List window, 406, 543
tooltips, 51, 523–524
_totalframes property, 561
trace() action, 740–744
Trace Bitmap command, 204–205
tracing feature, 202–205
Track as Button behavior, 245
Track as Menu Item behavior, 245

Transform panel, 39, 275, 277, 879
transforming
  elements, 273–279
  fills, 114–116
transition effects, 360–362
transitional animations, 214–215
transparency, 215–216, 243–244, 379, 784
Travel Application project, 828–854
  knowledge required for, 829
  setting up, 829–830
  tasks covered in
    adding buttons to timeline, 841
    adding frame labels, 834–836
    adding sound to buttons, 840–841
    adding text to buttons, 843–844
    controlling timeline playback, 834–836
    creating animation, 831–834
    creating buttons, 836–840
    creating draggable map, 851–854
    creating hyperlinks, 849–851
    creating self-running slide show, 844–846
    masking graphical content, 847–848
    placing slide show on timeline, 848–849
    scripting buttons, 842–843
Tree component, 639
tree diagram, viewing movie's content as, 718–720
true/false values. See Boolean values
tutorials, 69, 70, 72, 897
  adding sound to button, 192
  chaining loading/playback, 641–647
  creating buttons, 254
  creating frame-by-frame animation, 362
  creating graphic elements, 134
  creating keyboard shortcuts, 72, 647–649

creating media browser application, 854–896
creating menu bars, 254
creating motion-tweened animation, 362
creating movie clips, 254
creating shape-tweened animation, 362
creating travel application, 828–854
creating/using preloaders, 662–667
creating/working with text, 166
detecting collisions, 668–670
disabling movies, 649–655
dynamic drawing, 677–681
dynamic masking, 681–683
dynamic naming, 686–690
editing sound, 192
fast-forwarding/rewinding, 684–686
importing/working with bitmaps, 222
importing/working with sound, 192
importing/working with video, 382
integrating Flash with HTML, 655–659
introducing Flash, 72
printing movies, 670–677
publishing movies, 823
syncing sound to animation, 192
understanding targets, 442
understanding/using shared libraries, 716
updating sounds, 192
using components, 639
using Movie Explorer, 730
using prototype objects, 659–662
working with Actions panel, 442, 533
working with elements on stage, 282
working with layers, 312
working with Library panel, 716
working with properties, 582
TV commercials, 124

Tween drop-down menu, 345
tweened animation, 314–316, 327, 329–330, 341, 343–356
tweened frames, 329–330

U

<u> tag, 160
underline tag, 160
Undo command, 293, 522
undo/redo levels, 50–51
Ungroup command, 261
unload event, 395
unloadMovie() action, 431–436
Unlock All command, 261
Up state, 232
Update Library Items dialog box, 190, 716
_url property, 562
URLs, 146, 420–423, 850
Use Device Fonts option, 148
Use Pressure option, 82, 92
useHandCursor property, 659
users manual, 69

V

validation, data, 8, 16, 867
values
    assigning to variables, 456–457
    passing to functions, 482–484
    updating, 457–458, 515
Values dialog box, 600
variables
    ActionScript, 451–459
        assigning values to, 456–457
        creating, 454–455
        naming, 153, 456
        purpose of, 451
        types of, 453–454
        updating values for, 457–458, 515
        ways of using, 452–453
    template, 822–823
Variables tab, Debugger panel, 746, 750–751
Vars parameter, 28
VBScript, 815
vector graphics
    contrasted with bitmaps, 11–12
    converting bitmaps to, 202
    defined, 11
    importing, 119–122

    mathematical equations for, 75
    optimizing, 122–125
    programs for working with, 119
    supported file formats, 120
vector illustration program, 120
version control, 713
vertical text, 29, 150–151, 574–575
video
    adding interactivity to, 375–380
    changing transparency of, 379
    controlling audio panning/volume in, 378–379
    controlling playback of, 376–378
    embedding, 18, 370
    exporting, 374–375
    external loading of, 379
    file formats, 364–365
    importing, 364–370
    linking, 370
    masking, 380–381
    mixing other elements with, 381
    performing transitions on, 382
    placing on timeline, 370–371
    positioning, 372, 379
    previewing on timeline, 371–372
    quality settings, 366
    replacing/swapping content of, 373, 374
    rotating, 372
    scaling, 368, 372
    setting/viewing properties for, 373–375, 379, 703
    streaming, 380
    synchronizing, 368
    tutorial, 382
    updating, 374, 703
    using in projects, 370–375
video codecs, 365
Video objects, 29
video tutorials. *See* tutorials
View pop-up menu, 56
_visible property, 562
visually impaired users, 24, 42, 63, 252. *See also* accessibility features

volume, sound, 179, 180, 183, 378–379

W

warning messages, enabling/disabling, 54
Warnings tab, Preferences dialog box, 54
Watch tab, Debugger panel, 746, 752
WAV files, 169, 188, 798
wave effect, 308
waves, sound, 168
Web 216 option, 134
Web browsers
    and Flash Player, 771
    and MIME type, 811–812
    and named anchors, 335–336
    printing via, 670
Web design tools, 5
Web servers, 811–812
Web sites
    Derek Franklin, 896
    Macromedia, 634, 896
    Sorenson, 365
    XML, 581
What's New option, 68–69
while statement, 474–475
white space, 450–451
WIDTH attribute, 804
_width property, 563
Wildswfx, 166
window effect, 307
Window Eyes, 63, 252
Windows Metafile format, 120
Windows systems
    and bitmaps, 53
    and Flash toolbars, 31
    music-composition tools, 170
    vector formats, 120
with statement, 507
WMF files, 120, 799
WMODE attribute, 810–811
word-processing features, 135, 145. *See also* text
work area, 36, 56

X

_x property, 563–564
X-ray effect, 307
x/y values, 263–264

XML
- event handler methods, 495
- objects, 577–581, 887
- Web site, 581

XMLSocket object, 495
_xmouse property, 564
_xscale property, 275, 279, 565

Y
_y property, 565
y values, 263–264
_ymouse property, 565
_yscale property, 275, 279, 565

Z
Zoom In/Out commands, 738
Zoom tool, 57